Official Guide of the PGA Championships

TRIUMPH BOOKS
CHICAGO

CONTENTS

CONTENTS

James M. Barnes drives, while Jock Hutchison (right) watches the flight of the ball during the inaugural PGA Championship, Oct. 14, 1916, at Siwanoy Country Club in Bronxville, N.Y. Barnes captured the first of two Championships, 1-up. Hutchison triumphed in 1920.

As America entered the 20th Century, golf was evolving into a popular sport, and professionals from England and Scotland were being imported to build courses and make custom golf clubs for the members of emerging clubs. Growing public interest in the tournaments that were being staged and publicized brought golf to the sports pages of a highly competitive American press, and professional golf and golfers were big news by the end of 1915.

On Jan. 17, 1916, a group of 35 New York area golf professionals, accompanied by several prominent amateur golfers, attended a lunch hosted by department store magnate Rodman Wanamaker at the Taplow Club in New York City. The purpose of the gathering was to discuss forming a national organization which would promote interest in the game of golf and help elevate the vocation of golf professional.

Many of the golf professionals who attended Wanamaker's luncheon were emigrant members of the British PGA. In their opinion, the formation of a national association was long overdue.

Wanamaker, who viewed the public's growing enthusiasm for golf as a national trend, promoted the association idea to help accelerate the growth of the game. At the lunch, he offered prizes and purse money for a professional tournament "to be run along the lines similar to the *News Of The World* tournament in England."

Little did Wanamaker or his guests realize that they were laying the groundwork for what would become the largest working sports organization in the world. Today, the Professional Golfers' Association of America has more than 23,000 members and apprentices.

When that first meeting ended, James Hepburn, a former secretary of the British PGA, had been named to chair an organizing committee of seven. Meetings were held over the next two months, and on April 10, 1916, with constitution and by-laws firmly in hand, 82 charter members created The Professional Golfers' Association of America in New York City. The Association's first order of business was to establish the organization's objectives. The members agreed to the following:

- ■ Promote interest in the game of golf.

- ■ Elevate the standards of the golf professional's vocation.

- ■ Protect the mutual interests of its members.

- ■ Hold meetings and tournaments for the benefit of members.

- ■ Assist deserving unemployed members to obtain positions.

- ■ Establish a benevolent relief fund for deserving members.

- ■ Accomplish any other objective which may be determined by the Association from time to time.

Word of the Association quickly spread, and on June 5, 1916, 139 additional golf professionals were admitted to membership. The PGA of America held its first annual meeting on June 26 at the Hotel Raddison in Minneapolis,

Minn., and Robert White, a native of St. Andrews, Scotland, was appointed the Association's first president.

White, a former schoolteacher and one of the most respected golf professionals of his day, was the first of five consecutive PGA presidents originally from the British Isles.

The first PGA Championship was held at Siwanoy Country Club in Bronxville, N.Y., on Oct. 9-14, 1916. Jim Barnes defeated Jock Hutchison, 1-up, in the finals. Wanamaker honored his pledge and donated a purse of $2,580 and the trophy which still bears his name.

World War I canceled the PGA Championship for the next two years. The Association concentrated on administrative duties and establishing a permanent office and staff in New York City. The Executive Committee, in session on Aug. 13, 1917, authorized the annual expenditure of $1,800 for "rent and salary of person in charge."

In 1919, Jim Barnes won the second PGA Championship at the Engineers Country Club in Roslyn, L.I., N.Y., defeating Fred McLeod, 6 & 5.

The next year, Jack Mackie, a Scotsman, succeeded to the presidency and in May 1920, the first issue of *The Professional Golfer of America* was published. Percy C. Pulver, a golf writer for the New York *Evening Sun*, who had attended the first meeting at the Taplow Club, was named editor. The magazine was renamed *PGA Magazine* in 1977, and today is the oldest golf publication in the U.S.

George Sargent, a British professional who had been legendary golfer Harry Vardon's assistant, was elected president of the PGA in 1921. The Association grew stronger financially under his leadership and by 1926, his last term and the PGA's 10th anniversary, membership stood at 1,548. Expansion was just beginning for the PGA of America.

The Ryder Cup Matches, pitting PGA of America professionals against their British counterparts, were inaugurated in 1927 with a U.S. victory at Worcester (Mass.) Country Club, 9½ to 2½. Since then, the U.S. has dominated this biennial competition, 23-5-2. Although the gold trophy resided on European soil for six years from 1985-1991, the United States team won an exciting 14½ - 13½ victory in 1991 at Kiawah Island, S.C., and a 15-13 comeback victory in 1993 at The Belfry in Sutton Coldfield, England, to keep the Ryder Cup on this side of the Atlantic.

Albert Gates, the PGA's first business administrator and legal advisor, was hired in 1930, just prior to the national office moving to Chicago.

In 1933, George Jacobus of the New Jersey Section became the first American-born president of the PGA of America. A New York City satellite office was maintained for Jacobus during the next six years until Tom Walsh of Illinois succeeded him as president. A dynamic and innovative leader, Jacobus was the first PGA officer to rise from the caddie ranks and the first president to use the pages of

The Professional Golfer to communicate directly with PGA members through a column in every issue.

The onset of World War II in Europe cancelled the Ryder Cup Matches in 1939. By 1941, when the PGA of America celebrated its 25th anniversary, membership had grown to 2,041.

At the 1944 Annual Meeting, PGA Vice President Joe Novak submitted a report on the attractive features of Dunedin Isles Golf Course on the Gulf Coast of Florida. The appeal of warm weather led PGA officials into an agreement which created a winter haven for members at the first

---

The Association grew stronger financially and by 1926, the PGA's 10th anniversary, membership stood at 1,548. Expansion was just beginning for the PGA of America.

PGA National Golf Course in Dunedin. The PGA home office remained in Chicago, although twice it was moved to larger offices.

The PGA Seniors' Championship, which was begun in 1937 at Augusta National at the invitation of course founder Bobby Jones, was moved to Dunedin in 1945 and remained there through 1962. In 1954, Dunedin also became the home of the PGA Winter Tournament Program and the site of the first PGA Merchandise Show.

Relocating the national office to Dunedin was discussed at the 1946 Annual Meeting, but the move didn't take place for another 10 years. In 1955, during the presidency of Harry Moffitt, the decision was made to move all PGA operations to Dunedin. The following year, the 2,500-square-foot second floor of the Dunedin First National Bank Building became the PGA of America headquarters. The Association celebrated its 40th anniversary with 3,798 members and 31 sections.

PGA members flocked to Dunedin in the winter, and the Association continued to grow. By 1961, the PGA had moved the national office to larger quarters in Baywood, Fla., six miles north of the PGA National Golf Club. The Winter Tournament Program had grown to four events, and the PGA Merchandise Show —- started in the parking lot of PGA National Golf Club by salesmen working out of their cars —- now was being staged in large tents. The need for more office space and additional playing facilities for even more PGA events created the need for another move.

PGA officials turned their eyes to the dynamic Florida east coast and began talking with Palm Beach County developer John D. MacArthur. At the time, MacArthur wanted the impact of the PGA name to help sell his Palm Beach Gardens development. It took several sessions for both parties to finally reach the agreement that was finalized on Oct. 30, 1964. In March 1965, the Association moved into 10,000 square feet of office space in the east wing of the clubhouse in MacArthur's new country club, which for the next eight years would be known as PGA National Golf Club.

In 1968, PGA tournament players, who comprised a small percentage of the membership, broke away from the Association to form a Tournament Players Division and acquire more control of the tournament schedule. In the beginning, when the PGA of America was first formed,

---

In 10 years, from 1980 to 1990, total membership in the PGA of America grew from more than 12,000 members and apprentices to more than 18,000.

---

there was no distinction between club and touring professionals. As the PGA began to develop and promote tournaments, it became easier for touring professionals to devote their efforts to just playing tournaments and exhibitions. In 1975, the Tournament Players Division was renamed the PGA Tour. Today, the PGA Tour is headquartered in Ponte Vedra, Fla. The PGA of America and PGA Tour today maintain a close working relationship, and most professional golfers maintain dual membership in the organizations.

In 1971, the 53rd PGA Championship, the first major golf championship ever held in Florida, was played at PGA National Golf Club. Two years later, the PGA's relationship with MacArthur ended and the national office was moved to a two-story office building in Lake Park, Fla.

For the next eight years, the PGA of America researched a permanent home, one which offered enough space for a rapidly expanding staff and the golf facilities to accommodate a growing tournament program.

An agreement eventually was reached with developer E. Llwyd Ecclestone Jr. Ecclestone built a multi-course development on which the national office of the PGA of America is located, a 2,300-acre complex also known today as PGA National.

The 63 members of the PGA of America staff moved into the 30,000 square-foot administration center in February 1981.

At that time, the popularity of golf and membership in the Association again was beginning to grow rapidly. In 10 years, from 1980 to 1990, total membership in the PGA of America grew from more than 12,000 members and apprentices to more than 18,000. This was a remarkable increase of over 47 percent.

This created a need for additional staff members to handle the needs of more members and apprentices. As a result, in May 1990, renovations and a new addition to the PGA national office were completed, adding 10,000 square feet to the PGA of America building.

The site of the PGA of America home office, PGA National, features a major hotel and convention center, five golf courses and homes for more than 10,000 persons. It is one of the most distinguished addresses in Palm Beach County.

Since its first course — the "Haig" — was opened in 1980, PGA National Golf Club has played host to the 1983 Ryder Cup Matches, the 1987 PGA Championship and all but two PGA Junior Championships. The PGA Seniors' Championship has been held at PGA National Golf Club since 1982. Four PGA Club Professional Championships also are among the PGA tournaments that have been played at the complex. In addition, the PGA Winter Tournament Program and several events in the PGA Tournament Series are held every year at PGA National Golf Club.

The PGA of America conducts more than 30 tournaments for its members and apprentices. However, the Association and its members maintain a total commitment to golf and the more than 25 million amateurs who play golf. The PGA of America provides golfers with instruction and leadership through a grass-roots network of 41 section offices. It is the local PGA professional who introduces new players to golf, and always is available to help players develop the skills that make golf the game for a lifetime.

Today's PGA professional is several generations removed —- in skills, knowledge, training and business acumen —— from the golf professional of the early 20th century. The PGA professional has evolved with the growth of the game into a golfer who is a well-educated, highly-skilled business executive.

Since 1916, the PGA of America has established new standards of excellence by expanding educational opportunities, programs and services for its members. However, the Association stands firm and continues to flourish on the principles that were set down by its founders.

The PGA of America conducts several major tournament events throughout the year. In 1993, in accordance with the Association's strategic direction, the PGA of America contracted to purchase Valhalla Golf Club in Louisville, Ky., the site of the 1996 PGA Championship, as an effort to control potential future venues for major championship events. Also, in an effort to offer additional playing and tournament opportunities for PGA members and apprentices, the PGA of America is moving forward with the development of a golf facility in the Treasure Coast region of South Florida, which will include up to 54 holes of golf and a learning and practice center. The first 18-hole course is anticipated to open for play in early 1995.

PGA President
Gary L. Schaal
Deer Track Golf & Country Club, Myrtle Beach, S.C.

Gary Schaal, named the 28th President of the PGA of America in November 1992, has played an active role in the growth and expansion of the Association since 1983. The first PGA President from the Carolinas Section, Schaal is serving his sixth year as a national officer. He brings a keen business sense to his leadership role in the PGA, born from his expertise as a golf course owner/operator, daily exposure to the changing nature of the golf business throughout the U.S., and a love of the game.

A 1963 graduate of Ohio Wesleyan University, Schaal received his master's degree from East Carolina University in 1970. He served in the U.S. Air Force as a captain through 1973, and was awarded the Meritorious Service Medal after serving in Vietnam.

He served the Carolinas PGA Section as its secretary/treasurer from 1981-85 and as president from 1985-86. He was named the Carolinas PGA Professional of the Year in 1985 and was awarded the section's Horton Smith Trophy in 1978 and 1980.

Schaal, a native of Akron, Ohio, was named to the national Education Committee in 1983 and has played a leading role in the development of PGA Business Schools, workshops and clinics. He was elected to the PGA of America Board of Directors in 1987 and was elected Secretary of the Association in 1988. He was elected PGA Vice President in 1990. He has also served as chairman of the Apprentice (1987-88) and Growth of Golf (1987-88) committees, and is past chairman of the Constitutional Review Committee (1988).

Schaal's first head professional position was at Pine Lakes Country Club in Myrtle Beach, S.C., in 1975. Five years later, Schaal became principal owner and operator of Deer Track Golf Resort, a 36-hole complex in Surfside Beach, S.C. He also is the owner and operator of Indigo Creek Country Club in Murrells Inlet, S.C.; co-owner of the Cotton Creek Club in Spartanburg, S.C.; and co-owner of the Country Club of Beaufort in Beaufort, S.C. Schaal also is building a golf course in Myrtle Beach, S.C., which is scheduled to be completed in the fall of 1995.

A community leader as well, Schaal served as a director of the Myrtle Beach Area Chamber of Commerce (1977-80), helped establish the Myrtle Beach Junior Golf Program, was president of the Myrtle Beach Area Convention Bureau (1979-85), and was chairman (1979-80) of the city planning and zoning board.

As a mark of Schaal's concern for collegiate golfers, he originated the Gordin Collegiate Classic, an NCAA Division III tournament at Deer Track honoring legendary Ohio Wesleyan University Coach Dr. Richard D. Gordin.

Schaal lives in Surfside Beach, S.C., with his wife, Judie. The couple have a son, Aaron, who is in graduate school at the University of South Carolina; and a daughter, Rendi, who is married and living in Murrells Inlet, S.C.

PGA Vice President
Tom Addis III

Singing Hills Country Club, El Cajon, Calif.

Tom Addis III, one of the Association's most active and dedicated members, was named to the Southern California PGA Section's Board of Directors in 1974 and served in that capacity until 1990, when he was elected Secretary of the PGA of America.

Addis, head professional at Singing Hills Country Club in El Cajon, Calif., was elected to the PGA of America in 1972. From 1973 to 1990, he also served on the San Diego Chapter Board of Directors.

The chairman of the national Committee for the Physically-Challenged from 1984-1987, and the head of the Member Services Committee from 1986-1987, Addis also was the 1987 chairman of the Association Development Program's Review Committee. In addition to serving as a member of the PGA Board of Directors from 1986-1988, Addis has served on the PGA Board of Control, National Golf Day, Constitution Review, Teaching and Growth of the Game, and Education committees.

A native of San Diego, Calif., Addis has received some of the PGA of America's most prestigious awards, at both the section and national levels. He was the Southern California PGA Golf Professional of the Year twice (1979, '89), the Southern California PGA Horton Smith Award winner three times (1981-82,'89), the national PGA Horton Smith Award winner (1981), and the national PGA Golf Professional of the Year (1989). In addition, he received the National Golf Foundation's Joe Graffis Award in 1988 for outstanding service and dedication to the advancement of golf.

Addis lives in El Cajon, Calif., with his wife, Susan, and two sons, Tom IV and Bryan.

PGA Secretary
Ken Lindsay

Colonial Country Club, Jackson, Miss.

Ken Lindsay, a PGA Master Professional since 1983, is an energetic PGA educator and one of the most decorated PGA members to hold a national office. A native of Gadsen, Ala., Lindsay joins PGA Vice President Tom Addis III and Bill Strausbaugh Jr., as one of only three individuals to have been honored as both national Horton Smith Trophy winner (1987) and national PGA Golf Professional of the Year (1983). Lindsay has served on the faculty of the PGA Business School since 1977 and has been an educational seminar instructor for 18 different sections. He has co-authored two manuals currently used in PGA workshops and has written numerous magazine articles for *Golf Digest* and *PGA Magazine*.

Lindsay was named assistant professional at Colonial Country Club in Jackson, Miss., in 1970, and was elected a member of the PGA in 1973. He became head professional at Colonial in 1975 and was appointed general manager and head professional in 1989.

Lindsay earned his degree in business administration from Memphis State University in 1966. He served in the U.S. Air Force (1966-70), and was an all-Air Force golf champion in 1968. He was inducted into the Memphis State Sports Hall of Fame in 1982 and the Gadsen, Ala., Sports Hall of Fame in 1992.

Lindsay has served in all chapter and Gulf States Section PGA offices from 1974-82. He was a member of the PGA Board of Directors (1988-91), and has served on numerous national committees.

Lindsay lives in Jackson, Miss., with his wife, Janet, and son, David Michael.

PGA Honorary President
Dick Smith

Galloway National Golf Club, Galloway, N.J.

Dick Smith concluded his term as the 27th President of The Professional Golfers' Association of America in November 1992. An accomplished professional on and off the course, Smith has more than 25 years of experience as a PGA member, section officer, national board member, committee chairman and national officer.

An active member of the Association since he was elected to membership in 1964, Smith's record of accomplishments at the local, section and national levels is impressive.

An outstanding golfer in the Philadelphia area for more than two decades, Smith is a six-time Philadelphia Section PGA Player of the Year, and has won more than 25 championships during his career.

The Akron, Ohio, native was elected vice president of the Philadelphia PGA Section in 1975, and went on to serve the section as its president from 1978-1980.

In 1984, he was elected to a three-year term on the PGA Board of Directors. He was elected Secretary of the PGA of America in 1986, and in 1988, was elected Vice President of the Association. Smith began his professional career as an assistant at Green Valley Country Club in Lafayette Hill, Pa., in 1962. He became an assistant at Laurel Oak Country Club in Gibbsboro, N.J., in 1963, and moved to Indian Spring Golf Club in Marlton, N.J., as an assistant professional in 1966. Smith was appointed head professional and general manager of High Point Golf Club in Ivyland, Pa., in 1970. Six years later, he was named lessee and head professional at Wedgwood Country Club in Turnersville, N.J. From 1981-92, Smith was head professional at Woodcrest Country Club in Cherry Hill, N.J. He accepted the head professional position at Galloway National Golf Club in November 1992.

Smith lives in Williamstown, N.J., with his wife, Adrienne. The couple have two children, Dick Jr. and Stephanie.

PGA Chief Executive Officer
Jim L. Awtrey

PGA National Office, Palm Beach Gardens, Fla.

Jim Awtrey directs the planning, development and activities of the PGA of America, and over the past seven years has orchestrated the Association's growth into the world's largest working sports organization. As Chief Executive Officer he oversees a professional staff of more than 125 people, who daily service the needs of more than 23,000 members and apprentices.

A 1966 graduate of the University of Oklahoma, Awtrey was elected to PGA membership while an assistant professional at Siwanoy Country Club in Bronxville, N.Y. He played on the PGA Tour from 1970-71, then returned to Oklahoma where he established himself as a head professional for 13 years.

Awtrey played an active role, as a member, in working for the Association on the local, section, and national levels. In 1975, he served as secretary/treasurer of the South Central PGA Section and the following year was elected president. He served as co-vice chairman of the national Rules Committee in 1984, co-vice chairman of the national Rules and Junior Golf committees in 1985, and was named to the national PGA Board of Directors in 1985.

In 1986, Awtrey moved to Palm Beach Gardens, Fla., with his wife, Jeanne, and three children, Jena, Julie and Justin, after being appointed PGA Manager of Tournament Operations. He was appointed Acting Executive Director in 1987. Later that year, he was named Executive Director and in 1988 was named Chief Executive Officer.

PAST PRESIDENTS

The first officers were elected at the PGA Annual Meeting at the Radisson Hotel in Minneapolis, June 26, 1916. They were Robert White, President; James Maiden, Vice President; George Fotheringham, Vice President; and Herbert Strong, Secretary-Treasurer.

Years	President	Section
1917 - 1919	*Robert White	Metropolitan
1920	*Jack Mackie	Metropolitan
1921 - 1926	*George Sargent	Southeastern
1927 - 1930	*Alex Pirie	Metropolitan
1931 - 1932	*Charles Hall	Central New York
1933 - 1939	*George Jacobus	New Jersey
1940 - 1941	*Tom Walsh	Illinois
1942 - 1948	*Ed Dudley	Colorado
1949 - 1951	*Joe Novak	Southern California
1952 - 1954	*Horton Smith	Michigan
1955 - 1957	*Harry Moffitt	Northern Ohio
1958 - 1960	*Harold Sargent	Southeastern
1961 - 1963	*Lou Strong	Illinois
1964 - 1965	*Warren Cantrell	Texas
1966 - 1968	Max Elbin	Middle Atlantic
1969 - 1970	*Leo Fraser	Philadelphia
1971 - 1972	Warren Orlick	Michigan
1973 - 1974	William Clarke	Middle Atlantic
1975 - 1976	Henry Poe	Dixie
1977 - 1978	Don Padgett	Indiana
1979 - 1980	*Frank Cardi	Metropolitan
1981 - 1982	Joe Black	Northern Texas
1983 - 1984	Mark Kizziar	South Central
1985 - 1986	Mickey Powell	Indiana
1987 - 1988	James Ray Carpenter	Gulf States
1989 - 1990	Patrick J. Rielly	Southern California
1991 - 1992	Dick Smith	Philadelphia

*Deceased

BOARD OF DIRECTORS/ADVISORY COMMITTEE

The PGA of America Board of Directors is composed of the President, Vice President, Treasurer, Honorary President and 16 Directors who establish Association policy. Two of the Directors are independent businessmen who are not PGA members but who advise the Association in fiscal and budgetary matters. The independent businessmen were added to the board in February 1984, following a restructuring of the policy-making group at the PGA's Annual Meeting in November 1983.

District #1
Terry Crawford
Huntington, Conn.

District #2
Jack Connelly
Huntingdon Valley, Pa.

District #3
Harry "Cotton" Berrier
Pigeon Forge, Tenn.

District #4
Frank Sluciak
Morgantown, W. Va.

District #5
Martin T. Kavanaugh II
Harrison, Ohio

District #6
William P. Heald
N. Riverside, Ill.

District #7
Jerry W. Ray
Valley Park, Mo.

District #8
Jeff Porter
Hastings, Neb.

District #9
V. Scott Whittaker
Bountiful, Utah

District #10
Hank Majewski
Westminster, Md.

District #11
Ty Caplin
Stockton, Calif.

District #12
Randy Smith
Dallas, Texas

District #13
Roger B. Kennedy
Pompano Beach, Fla.

Independent Director
Fenwick J. Crane
Indian Wells, Calif.

Independent Director
Thomas V. King
Chicago, Ill.

Player Director
Brad Faxon
PGA Tour

ADVISORY COMMITTEE

John J. Jachym (Chairman)
Thomas V. King (Vice Chairman)
Richard E. Becker
Victor G. Bloede
Fred Brand Jr.
Harry Cavanagh
George W. Chane
Judge Walter N. Colbath Jr.
John L. Cox
Fenwick Crane
Robert Dedman
Verde Dickey
Ernest Fuller
Marie Gray
Wendell W. Gunn
James S. Kemper Jr.
George R. Lewis
Larry O'Brien
Curtis Person Sr.
James C. Tappan
Jack A. Vickers
H. Franklin "Bud" Waltz
William C. Westmoreland

Honorary Member

Honorable Dan Rostenkowski

STAFF DIRECTORS

Jim Awtrey
Chief Executive
Officer

Paul Bogin
Chief Operating
Officer

Jesse Holshouser
Chief Financial
Officer

Kerry Haigh
Senior Director,
Tournaments

Chris Hunkler
Senior Director,
Membership Programs

Joe Steranka
Senior Director,
Communications
and Broadcasting

Scott Cain
Director,
Member Tournaments

Bruce Florine
Director,
Golf Promotions

Christine Garrity
Director,
Contract Administration

Mike Gilligan
Director,
1995 Ryder Cup

Jan Gilpin
Director,
Education

Larry Green
Director, Information
Systems Development

Rick Joyce
Director,
Information Systems

Steve Jubb
Director,
PGA Foundation

Paul Lamey
Director,
Marketing

Marlene Livaudais
Director,
1994 PGA Championship

Jim Magnusson
Director,
1995 PGA Championship

Julius Mason
Director, Public Relations
and Media Relations

Terry McSweeney
Director,
Communications

Kirk Pottinger
Director,
Finance

Jorge Quintero
Director, Golf Course
Development

Peter Stilwell
Director, PGA Seniors'
Championship, PGA Grand
Slam of Golf, Ryder Cup Matches

Henry Thrower
Director,
Special Programs

Rich Williams
Director,
Membership Services

John Zurek
Director,
Golf Expositions

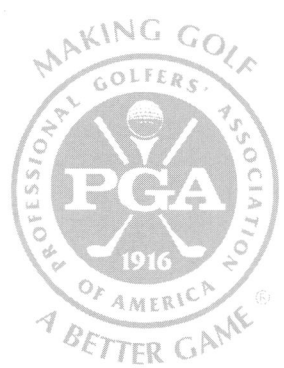

THE PGA CHAMPIONSHIP

THE PGA CHAMPIONSHIP — A MEMORABLE PAST

The PGA Championship, the annual culmination of golf's four major championships, celebrates its 76th anniversary at Southern Hills Country Club in Tulsa, Okla., in 1994. Since its inception in 1916, the Championship has developed into one of the world's premier sport events. Each summer, more than 100,000 spectators fill the galleries of the nation's best golf facilities to watch golf's best professionals compete for the Rodman Wanamaker Trophy. Winning that trophy is a thrilling experience that has been savored by only 52 individuals.

Each year, one of the nation's best courses hosts the professionals' Championship. This year the PGA returns to Tulsa, Okla., the site of Dave Stockton's 1970 PGA Championship victory, and Raymond Floyd's triumph in 1982.

Sarazen, "The Squire," owns one of the most remarkable PGA records. He qualified for match play 28 times, participated in 82 matches, with 57 victories and 25 defeats.

The Championship travels to Riviera Country Club near Los Angeles in 1995, and in 1996, the PGA will take the Championship to Valhalla Golf Club in Louisville, Ky., an area of the country that hasn't hosted a major since the 1952 PGA Championship. The 79th PGA Championship returns to the Northeast in 1997 at Winged Foot Golf Club in Mamaroneck, N.Y., and in 1998, the 80th PGA Championship will be played at Sahalee Country Club in Redmond, Wash.

In total, 64 courses in 25 states were the sites for the first 75 PGA Championships. Some of the facilities have hosted both the PGA Championship and the U.S. Open, including: Bellerive Country Club in St. Louis, Mo.; Cherry Hills Country Club in Denver, Colo.; Congressional Country Club in Bethesda, Md.; Oak Hill Country Club in Rochester, N.Y.; Oakland Hills Country Club in Birmingham, Mich.; Oakmont Country Club in Oakmont, Pa.; Pebble Beach Golf Links in Pebble Beach, Calif.; Riviera Country Club in Pacific Palisades, Calif.; Southern Hills Country Club in Tulsa, Okla.; Scioto Country Club in Columbus, Ohio; and the Inverness Club in Toledo, Ohio.

The PGA Championship got its start when department store magnate Rodman Wanamaker saw the merchandising possibilities in a professional golfers' organization. Wanamaker invited some prominent golfers to a lunch at the Taplow Club in New York City. On Jan. 16, 1916, 35 individuals, including Walter Hagen, convened for an exploratory meeting, which resulted in the formation of the PGA of America.

During the meeting, Wanamaker hinted the newly-formed organization needed an annual all-professional tournament, and offered to put up $2,500 and various trophies and medals to hold one. Wanamaker felt that the Championship should be conducted just like the British *News of the World* Tournament. That championship, a 36-hole elimination match-play tournament, was the PGA Championship of Great Britain. Both the

Gene Sarazen

British Open and the U.S. Open were played at medal play over 72 holes. Wanamaker's offer was informally accepted, and seven months later, the first PGA Championship was played at Siwanoy Country Club in Bronxville, N.Y.

British-born professional Jim Barnes and St. Andrews, Scotland, native Jock Hutchison played in the finals of the first PGA Championship. Barnes emerged from the contest a 1-up victor and the first PGA Champion.

The Championship was put on hold for two years because of World War I. When it was resumed in 1919 at the Engineers Country Club in Roslyn, N.Y., Barnes again came out the winner, turning back Fred McLeod, 6 and 5. The following year, Hutchison took revenge for his defeat, becoming the last foreign-born winner for a decade. He defeated Douglas Edgar, 1-up.

With the "Roaring '20s" in full stride, the next nine Championships were won by three different players: Walter Hagen, Gene Sarazen and Leo Diegel. In 1921, Hagen, one of the PGA's original founders, captured his first PGA Championship to begin an era of domination in which many thought he owned the event. Hagen went on to win five PGA Championships, making the finals six times, and winning four Championships in a row between 1924 and 1927. During the streak, the "Haig" won 22 consecutive matches before Leo Diegel won the title in 1928.

FROM HAGEN TO SARAZEN

In 1922, Sarazen, at the age of 20, became the youngest PGA Champion, beating Emmett French, 4 and 3, in the fi-

Rodman Wanamaker

nals. The following year evolved into one of the most exciting finals in the history of the PGA, as Sarazen successfully defended his title by defeating Hagen on the 38th hole in the Championship's first extra-hole final. Sarazen won the match by hitting a miraculous approach shot from the rough to within two feet of the hole.

Nicknamed "The Squire," Sarazen owns one of the most remarkable records in PGA Championship history. He qualified for match play 28 times, participated in 82 matches and had 57 victories and 25 defeats. When the Championship switched from match play, he competed in four more Championships before retiring after a 1972 appearance. Not only was he the youngest champion, he became the oldest participant (70) when he played in the '72 PGA Championship. In 1933, Sarazen won his third and last PGA, beating Willie Goggin, 5 and 4.

The 1920s ended with Leo Diegel, who had one of the most unorthodox putting techniques in golf, winning in 1928 and 1929. Sarazen was beaten in the 1930 finale by Tommy Armour, who won with a 12-footer on the final hole. A longshot burst on the scene in 1931, as 20-year-old Tom Creavy defeated Denny Shute, 2 and 1. Olin Dutra, who would win the 1934 U.S. Open, won the 1932 PGA Championship, defeating Frank Walsh, 4 and 3.

After Sarazen's win in 1933, Paul Runyan, who was known for his short game and putting, bested Craig Wood in 1934 in a 38-hole finale. Runyan made an eight-foot par putt to cap the drama. In 1935, another short game specialist, Johnny Revolta, was the winner, beating Tommy Armour, 5 and 4.

In 1936 and '37, Shute avenged his 1931 disappointment, and became the last golfer to win consecutive PGA Championships. In 1936, he beat Jimmy Thomson, 3 and 2, and returned the following year to edge Harold "Jug" McSpaden on the 37th hole.

In 1938, Runyan won a second title in the most one-sided victory in PGA match play history, beating a young Sam Snead, 8 and 7. Runyan completely overpowered Snead and the other five competitors with a 24-under-par for the 196 holes he played. Henry Picard won in 1939, beating superstar Byron Nelson with a birdie on the 37th hole.

LORD BYRON AND HOGAN DOMINATE

Nelson's disappointment lasted only a year. He bounced back to start one of the most amazing periods in golf history.

He won the 1940 Championship with a 1-up victory over Sam Snead. In 1941, Nelson made it to the finals for a third straight time, falling to Vic Ghezzi in an overtime match. Nelson was three holes up with nine to play, but Ghezzi won three holes in succession and then, on the second extra hole, sank a three-foot putt to win, 1-up. It was the fifth extra-hole match in PGA Championship history, and the last in match play.

With the outbreak of World War II, the match-play field was reduced to 32 players. Even with the change, Snead called the 1942 PGA Championship, his first of seven majors, his biggest thrill in golf. He defeated Jim Turnesa, 2 and 1, in

Lionel Hebert

the finale. It was Snead's third appearance in the finals and he finished the match by holing a 60-foot chip shot for birdie on the 35th hole.

Golf took a back seat to the war in 1943 and the PGA Championship was canceled. Resumed in 1944, underdog Bob Hamilton, 28, upset Byron Nelson, 1-up. Nelson had appeared in four finals and won only once. The following year, he was redeemed. Nelson handled Sam Byrd in the finals, 4 and 3, in a season where he posted 11 consecutive victories. The Championship was No. 8 on his memorable list. Though Hogan and Snead were not in the Championship field, it probably wouldn't have mattered.

Nelson was 37-under-par for his 204 holes in the 1945 Championship, and would play in one more before retiring. He lost his quarter-final match to Ed Oliver in 1946, his ninth appearance in the finals. Of the 45 matches he played, he won 37, for a PGA-record .822 winning percentage. Nelson reached the quarter-finals nine times, the semi-finals seven consecutive years, and the finals five times.

Oliver's upset of Nelson eliminated a possible dream final of Nelson against Ben Hogan. Against Oliver, Hogan fired a 30 on the front nine in the afternoon round to cruise to a 6-and-4 victory. Just like Snead, the PGA Championship was Hogan's first major.

The 1947 PGA Championship final round in Detroit pitted Jim Ferrier against Chick Harbert, the only PGA final between 1938 and 1949 that didn't include Hogan, Nelson or Snead. Just before the match, Ferrier worried that hometown hero Harbert would get special "assistance" from some overzealous fans, by either kicking Ferrier's ball into trouble or kicking Harbert's ball clear of a hazard. Harbert paid two policemen $100 to prevent such an occurrence. Ferrier's preventative measures were well worth the cost, as he downed Harbert, 2 and 1. Hogan added the 1948 Championship to his list, rolling past Mike Turnesa, 7 and 6, and would become the first player since Sarazen in 1922 to win the U.S. Open and the PGA Championship in the same year. For the week, Hogan went 35-under-par for the 213 holes he played. However, a weary Hogan said he didn't think he would play in the

The match-play format was doomed, not because of the grind of nine rounds in five days, but by the emerging power of television.

PGA Championship again. The grind of 10 rounds in five days was too much, even though he won the U.S. Open the following month and reconsidered his decision. The 1949 automobile accident that left Hogan's legs battered and unable to go 36 holes forced him to skip the PGA Championship until it switched to a stroke-play format in 1958.

Hogan also had an impressive PGA record, qualifying seven times for the match play portion, and winning 81 percent of his matches (22 of 27). He also played in three stroke-play Championships, tying for ninth in 1964 and tying for 15th in 1965.

A SMORGASBORD OF CHAMPIONS

In 1949, the PGA Championship was played in "Snead Country" in Richmond, Va. Snead didn't disappoint his fans, beating Johnny Palmer, 3 and 2, for the Championship. Snead also won the 1951 Championship, cruising past Walter Burkemo, 7 and 6, the second-most decisive victory in PGA Championship match-play history. Snead was the only PGA Champion in the 1950s to win other major championships.

The 1950s was a challenging decade, with the passing of the Hagen, Sarazen, Snead and Hogan eras. After Snead's '51 triumph, the PGA Championship began an era which saw 19 different Champions crowned between 1952 and 1970.

Chandler Harper won the 1950 Championship, defeating Henry Williams, 4 and 3. In 1952, Jim Turnesa settled a 26-year-old family jinx by beating Harbert, 1-up, to win the PGA Championship. Turnesa was a member of a family with seven golfing brothers, four having been bridesmaids in major championships.

The opening round of the 1953 Championship was dubbed "Black Friday," when the majority of "name" players were eliminated. The final matched lesser-knowns Walter Burkemo and Felice Torza. Burkemo triumphed, 2 and 1. In 1954, Burkemo returned to the finals for the third time in four years, only to have two-time runner-up Harbert beat him, 4 and 3.

The '55 PGA Championship was "Cinderella week" for Doug Ford, who became the first player since Tom Creavy in 1931 to win the Championship in his first attempt. Ford outdueled Cary Middlecoff, 4 and 3, in the finals. Ford also was the fourth player in PGA match-play history to win after earning medalist honors. Other players who matched this feat were Hagen (a co-medalist in 1926), Olin Dutra (1932) and Nelson (1945). The following year the PGA of America eliminated the 36-hole qualifier, and doubled the field (128 players) for match play. Jack Burke Jr. won the '56 Championship, defeating Ted Kroll, 3 and 2. In 1957, Lionel Hebert, as skilled with a trumpet as with a golf club, captured the last match-play PGA Championship with a 2-and-1 victory over Dow Finsterwald.

FROM MATCH PLAY TO STROKE PLAY

With Hebert's match, another chapter of PGA Championship history was closed. Discussion to change the format began in 1952 when PGA President Horton Smith released a plan that called for a combination of medal play and match play. In that plan, the original field would compete in a 72-hole stroke-play tournament, and the low seven qualifiers plus the defending champion would qualify for match play. This plan seemed to die from lack of interest, but in 1953, when "Black Friday" took its toll of favorites, new formats again became a hot topic.

The emerging power of television finally forced the issue, and in 1958, the PGA of America Board of Directors made what was viewed as the only possible decision.

Dow Finsterwald won the inaugural stroke-play Championship, firing a 3-under-par 67 the first day and sharing the 36-hole lead with Jay Hebert at 139. Snead grabbed the 54-hole lead with 207, but with a final round front nine of 31, Finsterwald finished with a 67 and 276 total, and a two-stroke victory over Billy Casper.

The following year, Bob Rosburg shot a final-round 66 at windswept Minneapolis Golf Club to finish a stroke ahead of Jerry Barber and Doug Sanders. In 1960, there were only 13 sub-par rounds in the entire Championship at the rebuilt Firestone Country Club. Jay Hebert was able to sneak in with a final round 70 for a one-stroke victory, marking the first

Nicklaus' 1973 Championship victory gave him 14 major championships, surpassing Bobby Jones' mark set 43 years earlier.

time that American brothers had scored victories in the same major championship. Club professional Jim Ferrier finished a stroke behind, making him the highest finisher of any club professional in stroke-play history.

Jerry Barber, then 45, mounted a comeback to win the 1961 PGA Championship. Four strokes behind Don January with three holes to play, Barber sank putts of 20 feet for a birdie at 16, a 40-footer for par at 17 and a 60-foot birdie at the 18th hole to tie January. In an 18-hole playoff the next day, Barber fell behind by two strokes on two different occasions but came home in 67 for a one-stroke victory.

ARNIE'S MISSING CHAMPIONSHIP

South African Gary Player became the fifth foreign-born player to win the PGA Championship, totaling a 278 in 1962 at Aronimink Golf Club in Newtown Square, Pa., and edging Bob Goalby by one stroke. Jack Nicklaus won his first of five titles in 1963 at the Dallas Athletic Club, overcoming 100-degree heat and Bruce Crampton, who had a three-stroke lead going into the final round. Crampton faded to a final-round 74 and Nicklaus charged to victory with a 68. In 1964, Nicklaus and Arnold Palmer took a back seat to Bobby Nichols, who opened with a 64 and became the first wire-to-wire winner in the Championship's medal-play history. Nichols needed only

119 putts in 72 holes for a 271 total that is still a Championship record. Palmer also set a record with rounds of 68-68-69-69, making him the first player to post four rounds in the 60s in a major championship.

This seemed to set a disappointing pattern for Palmer in the Championship. Just like Snead's U.S. Open "jinx," Palmer is considered by most golf historians as one of the best players never to have won a PGA Championship. Along with his runner-up finish in 1964, he finished second in 1968 and 1970.

1984 was the year of the rejuventated warriors, as former champions Trevino, Player and Wadkins staged one of the most exciting championships in PGA history.

In 1965, Dave Marr outplayed two titans, Nicklaus and Billy Casper, to win his only major championship by two strokes. Al Geiberger won the '66 Championship at Firestone Country Club with a four-stroke victory over Dudley Wysong. Geiberger's celebration was short-lived, however, when fellow professional Tony Lema was killed in a plane crash Sunday evening following the final round.

The 1967 PGA Championship was settled in a playoff for the second time in medal-play history. Ironically, January, who was involved in the first playoff, earned a berth and defeated Don Massengale by two strokes. Julius Boros, then 48, won the 1968 PGA Championship by surviving sweltering Texas heat and a last-hole charge by Palmer to become the oldest champion. Trailing by a stroke, Palmer hit a brilliant 3-wood recovery shot 230 yards over a creek to within 12 feet of the cup on the 18th hole. But he missed the birdie putt, and Boros pitched within two feet for victory. In the post-tournament excitement, Boros wasn't caught smiling by the camera. He later revealed he had chipped a tooth and didn't want to be photographed with a gap in his smile.

In 1969, Raymond Floyd survived a final-round 74 to defeat Gary Player by one stroke. Dave Stockton won in 1970, withstanding another Palmer rally. With his third runner-up finish, Palmer marked his last Championship as a serious contender.

NICKLAUS MAKES HIS MARK

The next PGA Championship was held only six months later, in February of 1971. Nicklaus scored a wire-to-wire victory with a 7-under-par 281 to beat Casper by two strokes. The victory made Nicklaus the first professional to win the modern Grand Slam of golf for a second time. It also was the start of a 13-year run in which Nicklaus would win four PGA Championships, finish runner-up twice and place nine times in the top four. Nicklaus' 1973 Championship victory gave him 14 major championships, surpassing Bobby Jones' mark set 43 years earlier. Nicklaus' final-round 69 in the '73 PGA Championship gave him a four-stroke win over runner-up Bruce Crampton, the victim of another Nicklaus triumph in 1975.

Nicklaus tied Hagen for most Championships in 1980,

Bob Tway

winning his fifth crown by a record seven-stroke margin. Nicklaus made one more serious challenge in 1983 when he lost to Hal Sutton by one stroke. Since then, he has finished no higher than a share of 16th place in 1986. Nicklaus has competed in 31 PGA Championships, finishing a record 14 times in the top five and has the best record in the stroke-play portion of the PGA Championship.

Wedged in the middle of Nicklaus' torrid streak was Player's second PGA title in 1972. His victory was highlighted by a "miracle" nine-iron from the right-hand rough on the 16th hole at Oakland Hills. Barely able to see the flag, Player hit the shot over trees and water to within four feet of the hole. From there it was a relatively easy birdie as Player went on to score a two-stroke victory. In 1974, Lee Trevino slogged his way to victory in a week of steady rain to beat Nicklaus by one shot. Despite an opening round of 73, Trevino found an old putter in the attic of the house he was renting and fired rounds of 66-68-69 for the victory.

During a three-year stretch (1972-74), an ageless Sam Snead was in contention. In 1972, at age 60, Snead finished tied for fourth, three strokes behind Player. The following year Snead tied for ninth, and thanks to a final-round 68, he tied for third in 1974. Snead capped his PGA career in 1981, 44 years after his first PGA Championship match in 1937. Even though he never won the Championship in stroke play, Snead finished third three times in 21 appearances. He made the cut 17 times and, in his 74 rounds, boasted a stroke average of 72.26.

Stockton won his second PGA Championship in 1976, making a 10-footer for par on the final hole to avert a playoff with January and Floyd. The weather was poor all week and rain forced a Monday finish at Congressional. After the Championship, PGA officials abandoned the 18-hole playoff format to become the first major championship to implement a sudden-death playoff. It was quickly put to the test, with the next three Championships decided in extra holes.

In 1977, the PGA went to California for the first time in nearly 50 years, and Lanny Wadkins won at Pebble Beach. Wadkins, who was six strokes behind Gene Littler with nine holes to play, caught him on the back nine with a birdie on the

18th hole. Wadkins won the Championship on the third play-off hole, sinking a six-foot par putt. In 1978, the PGA went to Oakmont Country Club for a third time, and John Mahaffey scored the greatest come-from-behind victory in PGA stroke-play history. Mahaffey's opening-round 75 put him in 47th place, eight behind the leader and even though he had 67 and 68 in the second and third rounds, he was still seven back of Tom Watson going into the final round. A par round for Watson on the last day would have won the tournament, but Watson came home in 73, while Mahaffey holed a series of putts for a 66. Mahaffey won with a 12-foot birdie putt on the second playoff hole.

David Graham captured the 1979 Championship in the event's third consecutive playoff. He had a final-round 65 marred by a final-hole double-bogey, tying Ben Crenshaw. Graham had to make a 25-footer on the first extra hole for par and a 10-footer at the second hole just to stay alive. He birdied the third extra hole to win.

In 1981, Larry Nelson became a hometown hero as he won the Championship at the Atlanta Athletic Club, a half-hour drive from his home. The following year, Floyd dominated the field with an opening 63, tying the lowest 18-hole score in PGA Championship history. After that he put it on cruise control with rounds of 69-68-72 for a three-stroke victory over Wadkins. Hal Sutton sweated out a late Nicklaus charge in 1983 to win at Riviera Country Club. Sutton opened with a 65, added a 66 for a 36-hole record 131 total, then slipped to a 72. Yet Sutton still maintained his lead. Nicklaus came home with a final-round 66, and Sutton responded by parring the final hole with a superb 1-iron to within 15 feet of the flagstick. Sutton became the fourth and final wire-to-wire champion.

1984 was the year of the rejuvenated warriors, as former champions Trevino, Player and Wadkins staged one of the most exciting Championships in PGA history. Trevino came out on top, thanks to some advice from his wife, who told him, "Even though you are 44, your clubs don't know your age." That, along with a new putter that he purchased on a trip to Holland, was enough to carry Trevino to his second PGA Championship victory. For the 48-year-old Player, the Championship marked the last regular event in which he would be in contention. As for Trevino, it was his sixth major championship victory.

In 1985, another rejuvenated warrior was on top. Hubert Green returned from oblivion to beat Trevino, who was trying to be the PGA's first repeat champion in almost 50 years. Despite leading at the halfway mark, Trevino sputtered with closing rounds of 75 and 71 to finish second, two strokes behind Green. The PGA Championship was Green's second major, along with his 1977 U.S. Open victory. It also was his 19th career victory.

A NEW GENERATION OF CHAMPIONS

The 1986 PGA Championship will be remembered most for the "shot heard 'round the world," as Bob Tway holed his greenside bunker shot on the 18th hole to edge Australian Greg Norman. The momentous shot overshadowed the fact that Norman was the only player in history to have the third-round lead in each of the four major championships in the same year. Tway became the first player in PGA stroke-play history to win the Championship on his first try; the first to post a sub-par 72-hole total in a major championship at Inverness Club in Toledo, Ohio; and the first in stroke-play history to win the Championship with a birdie on the final hole.

The 1987 PGA Championship, played on the Champion Course of PGA National Golf Club in Palm Beach Gardens, Fla., produced the Championship's highest winning score. Larry Nelson, with a 287 total, had to go overtime to beat Wadkins, who bogeyed the first playoff hole. With his victory, Nelson became the 15th and most recent multiple winner of the PGA Championship.

The following year, four holes-in-one were registered during the '88 Championship, and Jeff Sluman's 272 total at Oak Tree Golf Club in Edmond, Okla., tied the second-lowest winning score in Championship history. Floyd's third-round ace was captured on videotape, and 30 minutes later Paul Azinger, the tournament leader at the time, scored an ace on live television. During the Championship, club professional Jay Overton remained only a stroke behind Azinger until a third-round 76. Azinger was runner-up and Overton finished tied for 17th place.

In 1989, Payne Stewart won his first major championship, rallying from a six-stroke deficit in the final nine holes to overtake Mike Reid, who double-bogeyed the 71st hole. The Championship got off to a rousing start as Palmer, a month shy of his 60th birthday, started his front side with a 31, thanks to a string of five straight birdies. With a birdie at the 15th hole, Palmer momentarily held the lead, but bogeyed 17 and 18 for an opening 68 and eventually finished tied for 63rd.

In 1990, Australian Wayne Grady captured the Championship under difficult conditions of heat and high rough. Thanks to a second-round 67, and a conservative approach of just hitting fairways and greens, Grady was able to hold on for the victory. Rookie John Daly, the longest hitter on the PGA Tour, won a storybook 1991 Championship without the benefit of playing a practice round. Daly, the ninth alternate, didn't get into the Championship until Nick Price withdrew the night before the tournament. An opening-round 69 put Daly two strokes out of the lead and a second-round 67 gave him the lead for good. He overpowered the field, averaging 304 yards on his tee shots for the week, and with a 276 total went down in golf history as one of the biggest surprise winners ever.

In 1992, Price was back in the field. He overcame the memories of two runner-up finishes in the British Open and achieved a "major" breakthrough to become the 51st player to have his name engraved on the Rodman Wanamaker Trophy.

The diamond edition of the PGA Championship was conducted at Inverness Club in Toledo, Ohio, in 1993. Paul Azinger, catching fire on the final nine holes, caught Greg Norman and forced a sudden-death playoff. Norman missed a birdie putt on the first extra hole and his three-putt bogey on the par-4 10th hole allowed Azinger to earn his first major championship.

1923 Hagen vs. Sarazen — Golf's Greatest Match? *Pelham Golf Club — Pelham Manor, N.Y.*

Gene Sarazen and Walter Hagen — believed by many to be the two finest golfers of their era — squared off in the finals of the PGA Championship. The match lived up to pre-Championship hype, with Sarazen defeating Hagen in the first extra-hole finale in Championship history. The match was even after 18 holes before Sarazen grabbed a three-hole lead in the afternoon.

Hagen birdied the 29th hole to trim the deficit to two holes, and won the 34th and 35th to square the match. The two players halved the 36th hole with pars. Sarazen almost succumbed on the 37th hole, driving into deep rough, just a couple of feet from the

out-of-bounds barrier. With a small crowd gathered around him, Sarazen was heard telling the audience, "I'll put this one up so close to the hole that it will break Walter's heart." Sarazen followed with a brilliant recovery shot, with his ball coming to rest two feet from the flagstick.

Hagen dumped his approach into a greenside bunker, but almost holed his bunker approach. Sarazen closed the drama by sinking his birdie putt. Sarazen and Hagen landed in the PGA record book, ranking 1-2 for most holes played in one Championship. Sarazen went 194 holes to Hagen's 188.

1937 The Last Repeat Champion *Pittsburgh Field Club — Aspinwall, Pa.*

Defending PGA Champion Denny Shute, having outlasted U.S. Open Champion Tony Manero, 1-up, in the semifinals, faced Harold "Jug" McSpaden in the finals. The duo battled 37 holes, the third extra-hole final match in PGA Championship history. Heading into the 36th hole, McSpaden got a break when his tee shot struck a spectator and bounced into the fairway instead of heavy rough. McSpaden took the cue and hit an approach four feet from the flagstick. Shute was 50 feet away with his

second shot and putted about three feet short of the hole. As McSpaden took his stance, cameras grinded away. McSpaden stepped back and yelled, "Please give me the chance I've been fighting for all week." Once quiet was restored, McSpaden missed his putt. On the first extra hole, which had been Shute's nemesis all week, McSpaden missed a 10-footer for par. Shute knocked home his winning four-footer, and became the fifth and last PGA Champion to win back-to-back Championships.

1961 Wee Jerry Was Simply Marvelous *Olympia Fields (Ill.) Country Club*

The final three holes diminutive (5-foot-3) Jerry Barber played in the 43rd PGA Championship may go down in history as the greatest exhibition of clutch putting in a major championship. At least, they are the longest known clutch putts in succession — and they earned the 45-year-old from Los Angeles a berth in an 18-hole playoff with Don January. The duo had tied at 3-under-par 277 for 72 holes, and Barber edged January by a stroke a day later, firing a 67. In the press tent following his fourth round, Barber prefaced his description by adding, "Gentlemen, the next three holes you will not believe."

His improbable journey began on the par-4, 458-yard 16th.

Barber hit a 4-wood approach 20 feet from the cup and knocked it in for a birdie. He followed that by topping a drive barely 100 yards on the par-4, 428-yard 17th. He hit a 4-wood 90 yards short of the green and his approach was 40 feet from the cup. He sank the putt for a par. Playing the par-4, 436-yard 18th in near darkness, he hit a 3-iron 60 feet to the left of the flagstick, but rapped that putt home for a birdie. Barber, who had nine one-putt greens during the memorable round, said he had learned to putt as a youngster while practicing under a street light. Barber's victory made him the oldest PGA Champion until Julius Boros won in 1968 at age 48.

1964 From Near-Tragedy to Triumph *Columbus (Ohio) Country Club*

Twelve years before he would make history at Columbus (Ohio) Country Club, Bobby Nichols was a 16-year-old in a car loaded with four other teenagers on a joy ride. Their car went out of control at 100 miles per hour. Nichols was flung through the windshield and lay unconscious for 13 days with a broken pelvis, twisted back, collapsed lung and injured kidney. But he recovered; his spirits boosted by a letter from a player who had suffered a similar accident — Ben Hogan.

Nichols watched Hogan during the 46th PGA Championship, and was inspired. Nichols said a bargain-basement $5 putter he picked up a week earlier in a friend's golf shop was his key to victory. The putter proved warmer than the 93-degree temperatures.

Nichols set a blistering pace, opening with a 6-under-par 64 that featured 30- and 40-foot putts over elephant mounds. He never looked back while capturing the Championship with a 9-under-par 271, which remains a Championship record today. The first wire-to-wire winner in the Championship's brief medal-play history, Nichols defeated Arnold Palmer and Jack Nicklaus by three strokes. It was a record-breaking Championship for Palmer, too. He recorded rounds of 68-68-69-69, becoming the first player to have four rounds in the 60s in a major championship. Nichols' opening round remained a record until Raymond Floyd posted a 63 in 1982. Nichols took only 119 putts in 72 holes (a 29.7 average).

1970 Playing Like Arnie *Southern Hills Country Club — Tulsa, Okla.*

Dave Stockton's ability to overcome intense pressure in the final round of a major championship — and fend off playing partner Arnold Palmer — stemmed from reading a book on cybernetics that his father, Gail, a former professional and his son's only instructor, had given him. Cybernetics is the comparative study of the automatic control system formed by the nervous system and the brain. Simplified by Stockton, cybernetics "means your mind corrects your faults."

Stockton compensated for a lot of miscues during a wild final-round 73 that assured him a two-stroke victory over Palmer and Bob Murphy. Stockton played like the Palmer of old, making an

eagle on the seventh hole for a seven-stroke lead, a double-bogey on the next hole and recording a miraculous bogey at the 13th after dumping a shot into a pond and lofting a wedge approach within inches of the cup. Stockton canned a 10-foot par putt at the 17th after fighting sand and fringe rough, and played the 18th conservatively.

"I know Arnie's Army expected him to make a hole-in-one there," said Stockton. "But I just played it for a five. I felt sorry for Arnold about one-millionth of a second (big grin), because this is the only one he hasn't won." It was Palmer's third runner-up finish in the PGA Championship.

1994 FACTS AND FORMAT

DATE: August 11-14, 1994

SITE: Southern Hills Country Club, Tulsa, Okla.

DEFENDING CHAMPION: Paul Azinger

PURSE AND HONORS

A minimum purse of $1,700,000 will be shared among players who compete. The 1994 PGA Champion will receive a minimum of $300,000 and have his name engraved on the Rodman Wanamaker Trophy, which is permanently enshrined at the PGA of America national office in Palm Beach Gardens, Fla. The PGA Champion also will receive a replica of the Rodman Wanamaker Trophy.

TELEVISION (All times Eastern)

First Round, Thursday, Aug. 11: TBS, 12:00 p.m. - 6:00 p.m.; CBS, 11:30 p.m. - 11:45 p.m.

Second Round, Friday, Aug. 12: TBS, 12:00 p.m. - 6:00 p.m.; CBS, 11:30 p.m. - 11:45 p.m.

Third Round, Saturday, Aug. 13: TBS, 11:00 a.m. - 1:00 p.m.; CBS, 1:30 p.m. - 6:00 p.m.

Final Round, Sunday, Aug. 14: TBS, 11:00 a.m. - 1:00 p.m.; CBS, 1:30 p.m. - 6:00 p.m.

METHOD OF PLAY

Stroke play, four rounds of 18 holes. Following the first 36 holes of play, the field will be reduced to the 70 players having the lowest scores and those tied for 70th place. Those players will advance to complete the final two rounds. In the event of a tie for first place after 72 holes, there will be a sudden-death playoff.

RULES AND REGULATIONS

The Rules of Golf which govern play are determined by the United States Golf Association and applied by the PGA of America Board of Directors. The Championship is subject to the overall supervision of the Board.

ELIGIBILITY

The PGA of America has approved the following list of players eligible to compete in the 76th PGA Championship:

- All Former PGA Champions
- Winners of the last five U.S. Opens (1990-1994)
- Winners of the last five Masters (1990-1994)
- Winners of the last five British Opens (1990-1994)
- The current (1994) PGA Seniors' Champion
- The 15 low scorers and ties in the 1993 PGA Championship
- The 40 low scorers in the 1993 PGA Club Professional Championship
- The 70 leaders in official money standings from the 1993 Buick Open through the 1994 Federal Express St. Jude Classic
- Members of the 1993 United States Ryder Cup Team
- Winners of tournaments co-sponsored or approved by the PGA Tour from the 1993 PGA Championship to the 1994 PGA Championship (does not include pro-am and team competitions)
- In addition, the PGA of America reserves the right to invite additional players not included in the categories listed above. The total field will be a maximum of 151 players. Vacancies will be filled by the first available player from the list of alternates (those below 70th place in official money standings from the 1993 Buick Open through the 1994 Federal Express St. Jude Classic).

PROPOSED PAR AND YARDAGE OF SOUTHERN HILLS COUNTRY CLUB

Hole	1	2	3	4	5	6	7	8	9	10	11	12	13	14	15	16	17	18
Par	4	4	4	4	5	3	4	3	4	4	3	4	5	3	4	4	4	4
Yards	456	458	405	368	614	175	382	215	374	376	164	448	537	207	405	468	352	430

Front 9 Par: 35 Yardage: 3,447	Back 9 Par: 35 Yardage: 3,387	Course Par: 70 Yardage: 6,834

■ SOUTHERN HILLS COUNTRY CLUB

The only private golf club in Tulsa in the 1930s was Tulsa Country Club in the northern part of the city. The land on which the club stood was leased from the S.G. Kennedy family, who announced in 1934 that it would sell the land to the general public when the lease expired in two years. Members of the Downtown Tulsa Club, who had reciprocal rights at the Country Club, were upset and appointed W.K. Warren to attempt to negotiate the sale of the land for the then-enormous sum of $258,000, but the deal fell through.

Frustrated, Warren wrote to Waite Phillips asking that he not only donate 300 acres of land he owned in South Tulsa, but that he also advance the money to construct a lavish country club.

Phillips summoned Warren to his office on Dec. 26, 1934, and offered a counterproposal. If Warren's group pledged to spend $150,000 in two years — half to be spent the first year — to construct the family-style country club, Phillips would donate the 300 acres. But Phillips wouldn't spend a cent to build the facilities.

Phillips placed a further limitation. Pledges had to be on his desk by Jan. 15, 1935, which was less than three weeks away. A total of 140 pledges, 10 short of the goal, were presented to Phillips on Jan. 14. Phillips was convinced of the sincerity of the group and agreed to donate the land.

Golf course architect Perry Maxwell, a native Oklahoman from Ardmore and close friend of legendary amateur Bobby Jones, was contracted to design the new course. Augusta National and Southern Hills Country Club were the only courses of prominence in the nation to be built during the midst of the Great Depression. Maxwell's simple philosophy carried through to another gem of a design. He believed in adorning nature, not disturbing it. He is responsible for designing 75 golf courses and redesigning 50 more, including remedial work on Augusta National and Pine Valley (N.J.) Golf Club, currently ranked No. 1 in the nation by most golf publications. Maxwell's architectural fee was a humble $7,500.

Southern Hills Country Club, built for a remarkable $100,000, has played host to seven significant golf championships, including two PGA Championships (1970, '82), won by Dave Stockton and Raymond Floyd, respectively; two U.S. Open Championships (1958, '77); a U.S. Women's Amateur (1946); U.S. Men's Amateur (1965) and U.S. Senior Championship (1961).

CHAMPIONSHIP PREPARATION

Since the 1982 PGA Championship, Southern Hills Country Club has modified several holes, including transforming two back-nine holes. The former par-4 No. 13 hole is now a par 5, measuring 537 yards, with its original contours restored after PGA Championship contestants — except the longer hitters — played a blind approach shot to the green. The 16th has been shortened from a par-5, 569 yards to a par-4, 468 yards. Among other changes were lengthening the No. 6 back tee, eliminating the No. 10 back tee, and modifying the No. 11 tee. Rock bridges replaced wood throughout the course and the creek on the 18th hole was stabilized by a rock bed. In addition, new sand occupies the course's 85 bunkers. Southern Hills maintains crisp Penlinks bent grass greens, Bermuda and rye rough, and Bermuda fairways and tees.

SIGNIFICANT CHAMPIONSHIPS AT SOUTHERN HILLS COUNTRY CLUB

Year	Event	Winner
1946	U.S. Women's Amateur	Babe Didrikson Zaharias
1958	U.S. Open	Tommy Bolt
1961	U.S. Seniors	Dexter H. Daniels
1965	U.S. Amateur	Bob Murphy
1970	PGA Championship	Dave Stockton
1977	U.S. Open	Hubert Green
1982	PGA Championship	Raymond Floyd

AROUND THE WORLD

In 1993, the following 63 countries broadcast live or delayed coverage of the 75th PGA Championship:

Afghanistan	Argentina	Australia
Bahrain	Bangladesh	Belgium
Bhutan	Brazil	Brunei
Cambodia	Canada	China
CIS	Colombia	Cyprus
Denmark	Dominican Republic	England
Finland	France	Germany
Hong Kong	India	Indonesia
Iran	Iraq	Ireland
Israel	Italy	Japan
Jordan	Kuwait	Laos
Lebanon	Malaysia	Macau
Mongolia	Myanmar (Burma)	Nepal
New Zealand	North Korea	Northern Ireland
Norway	Oman	Pakistan
Philippines	Portugal	Qatar
Saudi Arabia	Scotland	Singapore
South Korea	Spain	Sri Lanka
Sweden	Syria	Taiwan
Thailand	Turkey	United Arab Emirates
Venezuela	Vietnam	Wales

PGA CHAMPIONSHIP

TOP OF THE LIST

There are only 36 clubs that have been included each year in *Golf Digest's* list of America's 100 Greatest Golf Courses since its inception in 1966. Future PGA Championships among the 36 clubs:

1994 - Southern Hills Country Club, Tulsa, Okla.

1995 - Riviera Country Club, Pacific Palisades, Calif.

1997 - Winged Foot Golf Club, Mamaroneck, N.Y.

Oak Hill Country Club in Rochester, N.Y., site of the 1995 Ryder Cup Matches, also is among that prestigious group of 36 clubs.

AZINGER ATTEMPTING A HISTORICAL FIRST

Paul Azinger will attempt a historic feat. No player has captured back-to-back PGA Championship titles under the stroke-play format, which began in 1958. Back-to-back winners under the match-play format: Jim Barnes (1916, 1919, no matches played in 1917-18), Gene Sarazen (1922-23), Walter Hagen (1924-27), Leo Diegel (1928-29) and Denny Shute (1936-37).

NICKLAUS STREAK

One of the most remarkable stretches of play by any one individual during stroke-play competition in the PGA Championship is Jack Nicklaus' 13-year assault from 1971-83. He won four of his record-tying five PGA Championships (1971, '73, '75, '80), finished in the top four on nine occasions, and finished runner-up twice (1974, '83).

STRONGEST FIELD

According to the Sony World Rankings, the 1993 PGA Championship featured 76 of the top 100 players in the 151-man field, the most of any PGA Championship, the second highest of any previous major championship. The Championship included 43 of the top 50 ranked players.

RECORD MEDIA COVERAGE

The 1993 PGA Championship at Inverness in Toledo, Ohio, received record international media coverage. Excluding the nearly 400 network representatives from CBS and TBS, more than 600 media representatives from 13 different countries covered the 75th PGA Championship.

RECORD TV COVERAGE

The PGA Championship is the most extensively broadcast golf event, with more than 26 hours of coverage by the CBS and TBS networks. The 1991 PGA Championship was CBS' first golf event featuring coverage of all 18 holes, and the network has since continued the format for the Championship.

■ RECORD-SETTING 75TH PGA CHAMPIONSHIP

- Inverness Club (par 71) yielded the **lowest course stroke average over 72 holes:** 71.796 (previous mark, 73.01, 1982 at Southern Hills Country Club)

- **The 36-hole cut of 143** is a PGA Championship record (previous mark, 144, in 1988 at Oak Tree Golf Club, Edmond, Okla.)

- **The 1-over-par barrier** matches the 1-over-par cut in 1989 at par-72 Kemper Lakes Golf Course in Hawthorn Woods, Ill. The 36-hole cut that year was 145.

- **Lowest second-round scoring average:** 71.8 (previous mark, 72.58 in 1988)

- **Lowest first-round scoring average by field:** 71.99

- **Most sub-par scores over 72 holes:** 166 (old mark, 153 in 1989 at Kemper Lakes)

- **Most sub-par scores in a third round:** 33 (old mark, 29 in 1989 at Kemper Lakes)

- **Most sub-par scores in a second round:** 56 (old mark, 54 in 1989 at Kemper Lakes)

- **Most sub-par scores in a first round:** 57 (old mark, 49 in 1989 at Kemper Lakes)

- **Lowest 36-hole score:** (tied)
  131 Vijay Singh, 1993 (11-under-par, 68-63)
  Hal Sutton, 1983 (11-under-par, 65-66)

- **Best 18-hole score:** (tied)
  63 Vijay Singh, 1993 (Inverness Club, 2nd round)
  Gary Player, 1984 (Shoal Creek, 2nd round)
  Ray Floyd, 1982 (Southern Hills, 1st round)
  Bruce Crampton, 1975 (Firestone CC, 2nd round)

- Vijay Singh's 63 is an **Inverness Club competitive course record,** breaking the old standard (64) shared by Bob Tway (1986, 3rd round) and Scott Simpson (1993, 1st round).

- Paul Azinger's 30 on the back nine during Friday's second round was an **Inverness Club competitive course record.**

- **Most top-100 rated players (76),** according to Sony World Rankings.

- **Most foreign-born players competing:** 32

- One statistic that may be a record: **75 different players chipped in, putted from the fringe, holed from a bunker or a fairway during the 75th PGA Championship.**

■ PGA CHAMPIONSHIP PLAYOFF HISTORY

Date	Site	Results
1923	Pelham Golf Club, Pelham Manor, N.Y.	Gene Sarazen defeated Walter Hagen, 1-up, in 38 holes
1934	Park Club of Buffalo, Williamsville, N.Y.	Paul Runyan defeated Craig Wood, 1-up, 38 holes
1937	Pittsburgh Field Club, Aspinwall, Pa.	Denny Shute defeated Harold "Jug" McSpaden, 1-up, 37 holes
1939	Pomonok Country Club, Flushing, N.Y.	Henry Picard defeated Byron Nelson, 1-up, 37 holes
1941	Cherry Hills Country Club, Denver, Colo.	Vic Ghezzi defeated Byron Nelson, 1-up, 38 holes
1961	Olympia Fields (Ill.) Country Club	Jerry Barber defeated Don January, 67 to 68, in an 18-hole playoff
1967	Columbine Country Club, Denver, Colo.	Don January defeated Don Massengale, 69 to 71, in an 18-hole playoff
1977	Pebble Beach Golf Links, Pebble Beach, Calif.	Lanny Wadkins defeated Gene Littler, making a six-foot par putt on the third extra hole in a sudden-death playoff
1978	Oakmont (Pa.) Country Club	John Mahaffey defeated Jerry Pate and Tom Watson by making a 12-foot birdie putt on the second extra hole of a sudden-death playoff
1979	Oakland Hills Country Club, Birmingham, Mich.	David Graham defeated Ben Crenshaw with a birdie on the third extra hole of a sudden-death playoff
1987	PGA National Golf Club, Palm Beach Gardens, Fla.	Larry Nelson defeated Lanny Wadkins with a par on the first extra hole of a sudden-death playoff
1993	Inverness Club, Toledo, Ohio	Paul Azinger defeated Greg Norman with a par on the second extra hole of a sudden-death playoff

PGA CHAMPIONSHIP

■ HISTORY THROUGH THE YEARS

Year	Winner	Score	Runners-up	Site
1916	James M. Barnes	1-up	Jock Hutchison	Siwanoy CC, Bronxville, N.Y.
1917-18	No Championships Played Due to World War I			
1919	James M. Barnes	6 and 5	Fred McLeod	Engineers CC, Roslyn, L.I., N.Y.
1920	Jock Hutchison	1-up	J. Douglas Edgar	Flossmoor CC, Flossmoor, Ill.
1921	Walter Hagen	3 and 2	James M. Barnes	Inwood CC, Far Rockaway, N.Y.
1922	Gene Sarazen	4 and 3	Emmet French	Oakmont CC, Oakmont, Pa.
1923	Gene Sarazen	38 holes	Walter Hagen	Pelham CC, Pelham Manor, N.Y.
1924	Walter Hagen	2-up	James M. Barnes	French Lick CC, French Lick, Ind.
1925	Walter Hagen	6 and 5	William Mehlhorn	Olympia Fields CC, Olympia Fields, Ill.
1926	Walter Hagen	5 and 3	Leo Diegel	Salisbury GC, Westbury, L.I., N.Y.
1927	Walter Hagen	1-up	Joe Turnesa	Cedar Crest CC, Dallas, Texas
1928	Leo Diegel	6 and 5	Al Espinosa	Five Farms CC, Baltimore, Md.
1929	Leo Diegel	6 and 4	Johnny Farrell	Hillcrest CC, Los Angeles, Calif.
1930	Tommy Armour	1-up	Gene Sarazen	Fresh Meadow CC, Flushing, N.Y.
1931	Tom Creavy	2 and 1	Denny Shute	Wannamoisett CC, Rumford, R.I.
1932	Olin Dutra	4 and 3	Frank Walsh	Keller GC, St. Paul, Minn.
1933	Gene Sarazen	5 and 4	Willie Goggin	Blue Mound CC, Milwaukee, Wis.
1934	Paul Runyan	38 holes	Craig Wood	Park CC, Williamsville, N.Y.
1935	Johnny Revolta	5 and 4	Tommy Armour	Twin Hills CC, Oklahoma City, Okla.
1936	Denny Shute	3 and 2	Jimmy Thomson	Pinehurst CC, Pinehurst, N.C.
1937	Denny Shute	37 holes	Harold McSpaden	Pittsburgh FC, Aspinwall, Pa.
1938	Paul Runyan	8 and 7	Sam Snead	Shawnee CC, Shawnee-On-Delaware, Pa.
1939	Henry Picard	37 holes	Byron Nelson	Pomonok CC, Flushing, L.I., N.Y.
1940	Byron Nelson	1-up	Sam Snead	Hershey CC, Hershey, Pa.
1941	Vic Ghezzi	38 holes	Byron Nelson	Cherry Hills CC, Denver, Colo.
1942	Sam Snead	2 and 1	Jim Turnesa	Seaview CC, Atlantic City, N.J.
1943	**No Championship Played Due to World War II**			
1944	Bob Hamilton	1-up	Byron Nelson	Manito G and CC, Spokane, Wash.
1945	Byron Nelson	4 and 3	Sam Byrd	Moraine CC, Dayton, Ohio
1946	Ben Hogan	6 and 4	Ed Oliver	Portland GC, Portland, Ore.
1947	Jim Ferrier	2 and 1	Chick Harbert	Plum Hollow CC, Detroit, Mich.
1948	Ben Hogan	7 and 6	Mike Turnesa	Norwood Hills CC, St. Louis, Mo.
1949	Sam Snead	3 and 2	Johnny Palmer	Hermitage CC, Richmond, Va.
1950	Chandler Harper	4 and 3	Henry Williams Jr.	Scioto CC, Columbus, Ohio
1951	Sam Snead	7 and 6	Walter Burkemo	Oakmont CC, Oakmont, Pa.
1952	Jim Turnesa	1-up	Chick Harbert	Big Spring CC, Louisville, Ky.
1953	Walter Burkemo	2 and 1	Felice Torza	Birmingham CC, Birmingham, Mich.
1954	Chick Harbert	4 and 3	Walter Burkemo	Keller GC, St. Paul, Minn.
1955	Doug Ford	4 and 3	Cary Middlecoff	Meadowbrook CC, Detroit, Mich.
1956	Jack Burke	3 and 2	Ted Kroll	Blue Hill CC, Boston, Mass.
1957	Lionel Hebert	2 and 1	Dow Finsterwald	Miami Valley CC, Dayton, Ohio
1958	Dow Finsterwald	276	Billy Casper	Llanerch CC, Havertown, Pa.
1959	Bob Rosburg	277	Jerry Barber, Doug Sanders	Minneapolis GC, St. Louis Park, Minn.
1960	Jay Hebert	281	Jim Ferrier	Firestone CC, Akron, Ohio
1961	Jerry Barber*	277	Don January	Olympia Fields CC, Olympia Fields, Ill.
1962	Gary Player	278	Bob Goalby	Aronimink GC, Newtown Square, Pa.
1963	Jack Nicklaus	279	Dave Ragan Jr.	Dallas Athletic Club, Dallas, Texas
1964	Bobby Nichols	271	Jack Nicklaus, Arnold Palmer	Columbus CC, Columbus, Ohio
1965	Dave Marr	280	Billy Casper, Jack Nicklaus	Laurel Valley CC, Ligonier, Pa.
1966	Al Geiberger	280	Dudley Wysong	Firestone CC, Akron, Ohio
1967	Don January*	281	Don Massengale	Columbine CC, Littleton, Colo.
1968	Julius Boros	281	Bob Charles, Arnold Palmer	Pecan Valley CC, San Antonio, Texas

PGA CHAMPIONSHIP

Year	Winner	Score	Runners-up	Site
1969	Ray Floyd	276	Gary Player	NCR CC, Dayton, Ohio
1970	Dave Stockton	279	Arnold Palmer, Bob Murphy	Southern Hills CC, Tulsa, Okla.
1971	Jack Nicklaus	281	Billy Casper	PGA National GC, Palm Beach Gardens, Fla.
1972	Gary Player	281	Tommy Aaron	Oakland Hills CC, Birmingham, Mich.
1973	Jack Nicklaus	277	Bruce Crampton	Canterbury GC, Cleveland, Ohio
1974	Lee Trevino	276	Jack Nicklaus	Tanglewood GC, Winston-Salem, N.C.
1975	Jack Nicklaus	276	Bruce Crampton	Firestone CC, Akron, Ohio
1976	Dave Stockton	281	Ray Floyd, Don January	Congressional CC, Bethesda, Md.
1977	Lanny Wadkins*	282	Gene Littler	Pebble Beach GL, Pebble Beach, Calif.
1978	John Mahaffey*	276	Jerry Pate, Tom Watson	Oakmont CC, Oakmont, Pa.
1979	David Graham*	272	Ben Crenshaw	Oakland Hills CC, Birmingham, Mich.
1980	Jack Nicklaus	274	Andy Bean	Oak Hill CC, Rochester, N.Y.
1981	Larry Nelson	273	Fuzzy Zoeller	Atlanta Athletic Club, Duluth, Ga.
1982	Ray Floyd	272	Lanny Wadkins	Southern Hills CC, Tulsa, Okla.
1983	Hal Sutton	274	Jack Nicklaus	Riviera CC, Pacific Palisades, Calif.
1984	Lee Trevino	273	Lanny Wadkins, Gary Player	Shoal Creek CC, Birmingham, Ala.
1985	Hubert Green	278	Lee Trevino	Cherry Hills CC, Denver, Colo.
1986	Bob Tway	276	Greg Norman	Inverness Club, Toledo, Ohio
1987	Larry Nelson*	287	Lanny Wadkins	PGA National GC, Palm Beach Gardens, Fla.
1988	Jeff Sluman	272	Paul Azinger	Oak Tree GC, Edmond, Okla.
1989	Payne Stewart	276	Andy Bean, Mike Reid Curtis Strange	Kemper Lakes GC, Hawthorn Woods, Ill.
1990	Wayne Grady	282	Fred Couples	Shoal Creek, Birmingham, Ala.
1991	John Daly	276	Bruce Lietzke	Crooked Stick GC, Carmel, Ind.
1992	Nick Price	278	John Cook, Nick Faldo Jim Gallagher Jr., Gene Sauers	Bellerive CC, St. Louis, Mo.
1993	Paul Azinger*	272	Greg Norman	Inverness Club, Toledo, Ohio

* Winner in Playoff

■ PLAYER STATS FROM THE 1993 PGA CHAMPIONSHIP

Finish	Player	Avg. Drive	Rank	Fairways Hit	Rank	GIR*	Rank	# Putts	Rank
1	Paul Azinger	291.1	2	48	T-2	54	1	114	T-44
2	Greg Norman	286.3	5	40	T-19	49	T-8	109	T-12
3	Nick Faldo	277.0	17	40	T-19	47	T-19	105	T-5
4	Vijay Singh	285.4	6	39	T-25	52	3	115	T-53
5	Tom Watson	284.1	7	38	T-32	49	T-8	114	T-44
6	Hale Irwin	263.5	T-57	50	1	42	T-46	107	T-7
	Bob Estes	268.9	40	38	T-32	47	T-19	112	T-33
	Dudley Hart	279.5	12	31	T-69	45	T-31	109	T-12
	Scott Simpson	271.3	34	42	T-14	50	T-6	116	T-55
	John Cook	271.9	33	46	T-4	49	T-8	112	T-33
	Phil Mickelson	277.6	16	45	T-6	45	T-31	111	T-29
	Nolan Henke	279.3	14	37	T-45	50	T-6	114	T-44
	Scott Hoch	263.1	T-60	44	9	51	T-4	117	T-60
14	Lanny Wadkins	261.9	66	39	T-25	43	T-40	108	T-9
	Brad Faxon	274.4	T-25	42	T-14	46	T-24	111	T-29
	Steve Elkington	273.8	28	41	T-17	44	T-37	109	T-12
	Gary Hallberg	267.4	45	37	T-45	36	T-71	99	1
	Richard Zokol	266.3	48	38	T-32	44	T-37	109	T-12
	Bruce Fleisher	261.6	T-67	45	T-6	48	T-15	110	T-21
20	Jay Haas	267.5	44	40	T 19	49	T-8	116	T-55

GIR - Greens in regulation

PGA CHAMPIONSHIP

Finish	Player	Avg. Drive	Rank	Fairways Hit	Rank	GIR*	Rank	# Putts	Rank
	Eduardo Romero	290.5	3	38	T-32	40	T-57	104	T-3
22	Jim McGovern	273.6	29	43	T-10	47	T-19	115	T-53
	Lee Janzen	263.6	56	38	T-32	46	T-24	110	T-21
	Ian Woosnam	272.4	32	37	T-45	48	T-15	118	T-63
	Gene Sauers	275.6	24	36	T-54	39	T-63	102	2
	Frank Nobilo	268.8	41	38	T-32	43	T-40	110	T-21
	Greg Twiggs	273.1	31	40	T-19	48	T-15	117	T-60
28	Loren Roberts	261.6	T-67	32	T-66	42	T-46	112	T-33
	Billy Mayfair	262.0	65	42	T-14	42	T-46	110	T-21
	Peter Jacobsen	263.3	59	37	T-45	46	T-24	113	T-36
31	Wayne Levi	270.6	36	38	T-32	45	T-31	113	T-36
	Fred Couples	283.5	9	37	T-45	43	T-40	114	T-44
	Stu Ingraham	276.9	18	28	T-73	42	T-46	110	T-21
	Mark McCumber	276.3	T-21	45	T-6	53	2	123	T-71
	Davis Love III	283.8	8	39	T-25	40	T-57	109	T-12
	Mike Hulbert	259.5	70	37	T-45	51	T-4	116	T-55
	Mark Calcavecchia	275.8	23	31	T-69	44	T-37	114	T-44
	Fulton Allem	273.3	30	41	T-17	47	T-19	119	T-66
	Nick Price	281.4	10	43	T-10	46	T-24	114	T-44
	Craig Parry	263.5	T-57	39	T-25	41	T-55	109	T-12
	Tom Wargo	266.6	47	32	T-66	43	T-40	113	T-36
	Fuzzy Zoeller	280.5	11	40	T-19	49	T-8	118	T-63
	Hal Sutton	264.3	53	31	T-69	42	T-46	113	T-36
44	Joe Ozaki	270.5	37	38	T-32	45	T-31	113	T-36
	Payne Stewart	276.6	19	32	T-66	42	T-46	110	T-21
	D.A. Weibring	256.6	72	46	T-4	40	T-57	109	T-12
	Russ Cochran	265.9	50	35	T-60	39	T-63	107	T-7
	Fred Funk	263.0	62	40	T-19	48	T-15	117	T-60
	Dan Forsman	258.0	71	38	T-32	40	T-57	108	T-9
	John Huston	292.5	1	37	T-45	40	T-57	108	T-9
51	Jeff Maggert	271.1	35	43	T-10	42	T-46	113	T-36
	Andrew Magee	268.5	42	38	T-32	46	T-24	114	T-44
	Hubert Green	251.3	73	31	T-69	38	T-67	109	T-12
	John Daly	286.8	4	34	T-62	43	T-40	114	T-44
	Peter Senior	269.9	38	37	T-45	37	70	105	T-5
56	Jose Maria Olazabal	266.0	49	28	T-73	42	T-46	110	T-21
	Larry Nelson	265.5	51	43	T-10	47	T-19	122	70
	Rick Fehr	262.3	64	34	T-62	40	T-57	110	T-21
	Sandy Lyle	267.3	46	38	T-32	45	T-31	116	T-55
	Tom Kite	268.0	43	36	T-54	41	T-55	113	T-36
61	Donnie Hammond	274.1	27	39	T-25	46	T-24	118	T-63
	Ben Crenshaw	264.1	T-54	34	T-62	34	74	104	T-3
	Michael Allen	260.1	69	37	T-45	38	T-67	109	T-12
	Jeff Sluman	262.6	63	33	65	39	T-63	111	T-29
	Mike Standly	276.4	20	39	T-25	45	T-31	119	T-66
66	Ian Baker-Finch	264.8	52	39	T-25	46	T-24	121	T-68
67	Mark Wiebe	269.3	39	36	T-54	38	T-67	113	T-36
68	Bob Ford	249.3	74	36	T-54	36	T-71	111	T-29
	Rocco Mediate	274.4	T-25	48	T-2	49	T-8	124	73
70	Steve Pate	279.1	15	36	T-54	49	T-8	126	74
71	Barry Lane	276.3	T-21	38	T-32	43	T-40	121	T-68
	Kevin Burton	263.1	T-60	38	T-32	35	73	114	T-44
73	Bob Borowicz	264.1	T-54	36	T-54	39	T-63	116	T-55
74	John Adams	279.4	13	35	T-60	42	T-46	123	T-71

*GIR - Greens in regulation

1993

Few who attended or watched the drama on television will ever forget the 75th PGA Championship at Inverness Club in Toledo, Ohio.

This PGA Championship contained about every ingredient to spice the hearts of golf fans everywhere.

Consider first 33-year-old champion Paul Azinger, who shed an unofficial media label as the "best player never to have won a major championship." Azinger emerged on top of a leader board that included players with a com-

Champion: Paul Azinger, Bradenton, Fla.
Site: Inverness Club, Toledo, Ohio
Date: Aug. 12-15, 1994   **Purse:** $1,700,000
Par: 35-36—71 (7,024 Yards)
Entries: 151   Cut at 143   74 players advanced

Note: All residences at time of victory

> *"You're looking at a guy who 12 years ago couldn't break 80 two times in a row, and here I am sitting here today having won a major. It's amazing."*

bined 23 major championships and kept alive the longest active winning streak on the PGA Tour, winning a championship in each of the past seven years.

The lanky 6' 2" Bradenton, Fla., resident birdied four of the last seven holes to post a 12-under-par 272 for a back-nine Inverness record 30. His 72-hole score forced a playoff with Greg Norman, whose game once again was at odds with Inverness Club's diminutive and treacherous greens.

Norman appeared poised to erase a seven-year-old nightmare -- he lost the 1986 PGA Championship to Bob Tway's miracle bunker shot. But Norman's birdie putt attempt on the 18th green grazed the cup and spun away. The 12th playoff in PGA Championship history ensued, beginning on the 18th

tee. Again, Norman had a chance to win, but his birdie attempt — this time much more precise — spun in and out of the hole. Both players approached the par-4, 365-yard 10th hole, where Norman's drive caught the edge of the left-hand rough. His approach shot landed 20 feet above the hole. From the fairway, Azinger laced a pitching wedge approach within eight feet of the flagstick.

"Wasn't it pure?" Azinger later said. "It's one of those shots you know you have to have to win."

Norman lagged his birdie putt attempt four feet short of the hole, while Azinger barely missed his birdie attempt. Norman stepped up and for the third time in the "Longest Day at Inverness," his par attempt rimmed the hole.

"What can I say? I'm in a daze," said Norman, who has the current longest streak (8) of rounds in the 60s in major championships. "I lost to a great player. I said to myself at the turn, 12-under will win. I said that to myself at the start of the week. I got there, but I didn't win." Norman joined Craig Wood as the only men in history to lose all four major championships in a playoff.

Azinger said his heart was pounding with every stroke.

"I was gasping for air at the end," he said. "I was sucking air. I'm not afraid

to admit it. It was hot. I was nervous. It was a very, very difficult day for me."

Azinger, who started playing golf at age five, admitted he was in a special position in time.

"You're looking at a guy who 12 years ago couldn't break 80 two times in a row," he said. "And here I am sitting here today having won a major. It's amazing, and I thank God for what He has allowed me to do."

Few major championships could boast of the spectacular shotmaking of the 75th PGA Championship. Seventy-five players either chipped in or holed out from bunkers, from the fairway, or off the green. In addition, 21 eagles and one double eagle — a Championship record stroke by PGA professional Darrell Kestner of Manhasset, N.Y. — were recorded. Among the records were 57 players breaking par in Thursday's opening round; and Fiji native Vijay Singh became the 15th player to shoot 63 in a major championship, carving up the Inverness Club layout in the second round.

HOW PAUL AZINGER PLAYED DURING THE 1993 PGA CHAMPIONSHIP

Hole	1	2	3	4	5	6	7	8	9	10	11	12	13	14	15	16	17	18
Par	4	4	3	4	4	3	4	5	4	4	4	3	5	4	4	4	4	4
Round 1	3	3	3	3	5	3	4	5	4	3	4	3	5	4	4	4	4	4
Round 2	4	3	3	5	4	4	4	5	4	3	3	2	4	3	4	5	3	3
Round 3	4	4	3	4	3	4	3	5	4	4	4	3	5	3	4	4	4	4
Round 4	4	4	3	4	5	3	4	5	4	4	4	2	4	3	4	4	3	4
Fairways Hit: 48 of 60						**Average Drive:** 291.1						**Greens Hit:** 54 of 72				**Putts:** 114	

PGA CHAMPIONSHIP SUMMARIES

	Course Avg	Under Par	At Par	Over Par	Round Leader	Low Round	Paul Azinger
Round 1:	71.99	57	16	78	Scott Simpson (64)	Scott Simpson (64)	T-23rd (69)
Round 2:	71.80	56	16	76	Vijay Singh (131)	Vijay Singh (63)	T-9th (135)
Round 3:	71.27	33	11	30	Greg Norman (203)	Brad Faxon (65)	T-2nd (204)
Round 4:	71.93	20	10	44	Azinger and Norman	Scott Hoch (67)	T-1st (272)

TOURNAMENT SUMMARY

Place	Name	Score	Winnings
1	Paul Azinger	69-66-69-68—272	$300,000.00
2	Greg Norman	68-68-67-69—272	$155,000.00
3	Nick Faldo	68-68-69-68—273	$105,000.00
4	Vijay Singh	68-63-73-70—274	$90,000.00
5	Tom Watson	69-65-70-72—276	$75,000.00
T-6	John Cook	72-66-68-71—277	$47,812.50
T-6	Bob Estes	69-66-69-73—277	$47,812.50
T-6	Dudley Hart	66-68-71-72—277	$47,812.50
T-6	Nolan Henke	72-70-67-68—277	$47,812.50
T-6	Scott Hoch	74-68-68-67—277	$47,812.50
T-6	Hale Irwin	68-69-67-73—277	$47,812.50
T-6	Phil Mickelson	67-71-69-70—277	$47,812.50
T-6	Scott Simpson	64-70-71-72—277	$47,812.50
T-14	Steve Elkington	67-66-74-71—278	$25,000.00
T-14	Brad Faxon	70-70-65-73—278	$25,000.00
T-14	Bruce Fleisher	69-74-67-68—278	$25,000.00
T-14	Gary Hallberg	70-69-68-71—278	$25,000.00
T-14	Lanny Wadkins	65-68-71-74—278	$25,000.00
T-14	Richard Zokol	66-71-71-70—278	$25,000.00
T-20	Jay Haas	69-68-70-72—279	$18,500.00
T-20	Eduardo Romero	67-67-74-71—279	$18,500.00
T-22	Lee Janzen	70-68-71-72—281	$14,500.00
T-22	Jim McGovern	71-67-69-74—281	$14,500.00
T-22	Frank Nobilo	69-66-74-72—281	$14,500.00
T-22	Gene Sauers	68-74-70-69—281	$14,500.00
T-22	Greg Twiggs	70-69-70-72—281	$14,500.00
T-22	Ian Woosnam	70-71-68-72—281	$14,500.00
T-28	Peter Jacobsen	71-67-74-70—282	$10,166.67
T-28	Billy Mayfair	68-73-70-71—282	$10,166.67
T-28	Loren Roberts	67-67-76-72—282	$10,166.66
T-31	Fulton Allem	70-71-70-72—283	$7,057.69
T-31	Mark Calcavecchia	68-70-77-68—283	$7,057.70
T-31	Fred Couples	70-68-71-74—283	$7,057.69
T-31	Mike Hulbert	67-72-72-72—283	$7,057.69
T-31	Stu Ingraham	74-69-71-69—283	$7,057.69
T-31	Wayne Levi	69-73-66-75—283	$7,057.69
T-31	Davis Love III	70-72-72-69—283	$7,057.70
T-31	Mark Mccumber	67-72-75-69—283	$7,057.70
T-31	Craig Parry	70-73-68-72—283	$7,057.69
T-31	Nick Price	74-66-72-71—283	$7,057.69
T-31	Hal Sutton	69-72-70-72—283	$7,057.69
T-31	Tom Wargo	71-70-71-71—283	$7,057.69
T-31	Fuzzy Zoeller	72-70-71-70—283	$7,057.69
T-44	Russ Cochran	69-74-70-71—284	$4,607.14
T-44	Dan Forsman	67-75-70-72—284	$4,607.14
T-44	Fred Funk	72-66-76-70—284	$4,607.15
T-44	John Huston	68-69-75-72—284	$4,607.14
T-44	Joe Ozaki	73-68-66-77—284	$4,607.14
T-44	Payne Stewart	71-70-70-73—284	$4,607.14
T-44	D.A. Weibring	68-74-72-70—284	$4,607.15
T-51	John Daly	71-68-73-73—285	$3,600.00

Place	Name	Score	Winnings
T-51	Hubert Green	70-71-69-75—285	$3,600.00
T-51	Andrew Magee	71-72-74-68—285	$3,600.00
T-51	Jeff Maggert	72-69-71-73—285	$3,600.00
T-51	Peter Senior	69-70-70-76—285	$3,600.00
T-56	Rick Fehr	70-71-72-73—286	$3,110.00
T-56	Tom Kite	73-69-71-73—286	$3,110.00
T-56	Sandy Lyle	69-73-70-74—286	$3,110.00
T-56	Larry Nelson	73-67-74-72—286	$3,110.00
T-56	Jose Maria Olazabal	73-69-73-71—286	$3,110.00
T-61	Michael Allen	73-70-75-69—287	$2,800.00
T-61	Ben Crenshaw	70-70-73-74—287	$2,800.00
T-61	Donnie Hammond	73-70-68-76—287	$2,800.00
T-61	Jeff Sluman	74-69-72-72—287	$2,800.00
T-61	Mike Standly	72-71-68-76—287	$2,800.00
66	Ian Baker-Finch	73-69-70-76—288	$2,650.00
67	Mark Wiebe	74-69-73-73—289	$2,625.00
T-68	Bob Ford	70-71-78-71—290	$2,587.50
T-68	Rocco Mediate	70-73-74-73—290	$2,587.50
70	Steve Pate	73-70-72-77—292	$2,550.00
T-71	Kevin Burton	69-73-76-76—294	$2,512.50
T-71	Barry Lane	67-74-77-76—294	$2,512.50
73	Bob Borowicz	72-71-80-72—295	$2,475.00
74	John Adams	72-70-76-78—296	$2,450.00
Cut	Joel Edwards	73-71—144	$1,200.00
Cut	Ray Floyd	71-73—144	$1,200.00
Cut	Anders Forsbrand	71-73—144	$1,200.00
Cut	Will Frantz	71-73—144	$1,200.00
Cut	Robert Gamez	67-77—144	$1,200.00
Cut	Gregg Jones	70-74—144	$1,200.00
Cut	Bernhard Langer	75-69—144	$1,200.00
Cut	Mark McNulty	74-70—144	$1,200.00
Cut	Colin Montgomerie	74-70—144	$1,200.00
Cut	Jack Nicklaus	71-73—144	$1,200.00
Cut	Jay Overton	69-75—144	$1,200.00
Cut	Todd Smith	70-74—144	$1,200.00
Cut	Bob Tway	70-74—144	$1,200.00
Cut	Grant Waite	71-73—144	$1,200.00
Cut	Robert Allenby	71-74—145	$1,200.00
Cut	David Edwards	73-72—145	$1,200.00
Cut	Wayne Grady	75-70—145	$1,200.00
Cut	Darrell Kestner	70-75—145	$1,200.00
Cut	Ken Krieger	71-74—145	$1,200.00
Cut	Dick Mast	72-73—145	$1,200.00
Cut	Mark Mielke	75-70—145	$1,200.00
Cut	Corey Pavin	73-72—145	$1,200.00
Cut	Sammy Rachels	71-74—145	$1,200.00
Cut	Chris Starkjohann	74-71—145	$1,200.00
Cut	Curtis Strange	72-73—145	$1,200.00
Cut	Billy Andrade	74-72—146	$1,200.00
Cut	Mark Brooks	75-71—146	$1,200.00
Cut	David Frost	76-70—146	$1,200.00

Place	Name	Score	Winnings
Cut	Mark James	75-71—146	$1,200.00
Cut	Bob Lohr	74-72—146	$1,200.00
Cut	Larry Mize	75-71—146	$1,200.00
Cut	Dana Quigley	73-73—146	$1,200.00
Cut	Mike Springer	74-72—146	$1,200.00
Cut	Bob Bailey	72-75—147	$1,200.00
Cut	Bob Boyd	70-77—147	$1,200.00
Cut	Brian Claar	71-76—147	$1,200.00
Cut	Jay Delsing	74-73—147	$1,200.00
Cut	Jim Gallagher Jr.	75-72—147	$1,200.00
Cut	Robert Hoyt	72-75—147	$1,200.00
Cut	Bruce Lietzke	77-70—147	$1,200.00
Cut	Gil Morgan	75-72—147	$1,200.00
Cut	Craig Stadler	73-74—147	$1,200.00
Cut	Howard Twitty	71-76—147	$1,200.00
Cut	Ken Allard	76-72—148	$1,200.00
Cut	Rodger Davis	70-78—148	$1,200.00
Cut	Tom Lehman	74-74—148	$1,200.00
Cut	Ron McDougal	74-74—148	$1,200.00
Cut	Duffy Waldorf	77-71—148	$1,200.00
Cut	Gary Groh	78-71—149	$1,200.00
Cut	John Mahaffey	73-76—149	$1,200.00
Cut	Tommy Nakajima	74-75—149	$1,200.00
Cut	Brett Ogle	77-72—149	$1,200.00
Cut	Dave Rummells	73-76—149	$1,200.00
Cut	Tony Johnstone	70-80—150	$1,200.00
Cut	J.L. Lewis	74-76—150	$1,200.00
Cut	Mark O'Meara	78-72—150	$1,200.00
Cut	Chris Peddicord	73-77—150	$1,200.00
Cut	Gary Trivisonno	75-75—150	$1,200.00
Cut	Tim Angis	81-70—151	$1,200.00
Cut	Chip Beck	73-78—151	$1,200.00
Cut	Gary Robison	76-75—151	$1,200.00
Cut	Ernie Els	74-78—152	$1,200.00
Cut	Gene George	76-76—152	$1,200.00
Cut	John Godwin	79-73—152	$1,200.00
Cut	John Nelson	79-73—152	$1,200.00
Cut	Tim Stafford	75-77—152	$1,200.00
Cut	Cleve Coldwater	78-75—153	$1,200.00
Cut	Arnold Palmer	77-76—153	$1,200.00
Cut	Brad Sherfy	76-78—154	$1,200.00
Cut	Scott Walter	78-77—155	$1,200.00
Cut	David Graham	76-81—157	$1,200.00
Cut	Jeff Fairfield	81-77—158	$1,200.00
Cut	Tom Joyce	79-79—158	$1,200.00
Cut	Jon Hoecker	81-79—160	$1,200.00
WD	Joey Sindelar	70—70	$1,200.00
WD	Ken Green	74—74	$1,200.00
WD	Keith Clearwater	78—78	$1,200.00

1992

Nick Price, who came within three strokes of winning two major championships in his 15-year career, put the pieces together in a memorable finale to the 74th PGA Championship at Bellerive Country Club. The 35-year-old native of Durban, South Africa, now an Orlando, Fla., resident, made nine straight pars on the front nine of the final round. He seized the title by sinking birdie putts of 25 feet on the par-3, 222-yard 16th and 12 feet on the par-5, 536-yard 17th. Price held off by three strokes the challenges of John Cook, Nick Faldo, Jim Gallagher Jr., and Gene Sauers, who had led the Championship for 59 holes.

Champion: Nick Price, Orlando, Fla.
Site: Bellerive CC, St. Louis, Mo.
Date: Aug. 13-16   **Purse:** $1,400,000
Par: 36-35 - 71 (7,148 Yards)
Entries: 151   Cut at 148   85 players advanced

	Course Avg	Under Par	At Par	Over Par	Round Leader	Low Round		Nick Price
Round 1:	73.88	19	12	120	G. Sauers, C. Stadler	67 -	G. Sauers, C. Stadler	70 T-12
Round 2:	74.68	17	12	122	G. Sauers	66 -	J. Gallagher Jr., S. Richardson	140 (70) T-7
Round 3:	73.29	19	6	60	G. Sauers	65 -	Maggert	208 (68) T-2
Round 4:	73.35	17	7	61	N. Price	67 -	Joe Ozaki, N. Faldo	278 (70) 1st
Totals:	73.94	72	37	363				

TOURNAMENT SUMMARY

Place	Name	Score	Winnings
1	Nick Price	70-70-68-70—278	$280,000.00
T-2	John Cook	71-72-67-71—281	$101,250.00
T-2	Nick Faldo	68-70-76-67—281	$101,250.00
T-2	Jim Gallagher Jr.	72-66-72-71—281	$101,250.00
T-2	Gene Sauers	67-69-70-75—281	$101,250.00
6	Jeff Maggert	71-72-65-74—282	$60,000.00
T-7	Russ Cochran	69-69-76-69—283	$52,500.00
T-7	Dan Forsman	70-73-70-70—283	$52,500.00
T-9	Brian Claar	68-73-73-70—284	$40,000.00
T-9	Anders Forsbrand	73-71-70-70—284	$40,000.00
T-9	Duffy Waldorf	74-73-68-69—284	$40,000.00
T-12	Billy Andrade	72-71-70-72—285	$30,166.66
T-12	Corey Pavin	71-73-70-71—285	$30,166.67
T-12	Jeff Sluman	73-71-72-69—285	$30,166.67
T-15	Mark Brooks	71-72-68-75—286	$24,000.00
T-15	Brad Faxon	72-69-75-70—286	$24,000.00
T-15	Greg Norman	71-74-71-70—286	$24,000.00
T-18	Steve Elkington	74-70-71-72—287	$19,000.00
T-18	Rick Fehr	74-73-71-69—287	$19,000.00
T-18	John Huston	73-75-71-68—287	$19,000.00
T-21	Bill Britton	70-77-70-71—288	$14,000.00
T-21	Fred Couples	69-73-73-73—288	$14,000.00
T-21	Lee Janzen	74-71-72-71—288	$14,000.00
T-21	Tom Kite	73-73-69-73—288	$14,000.00
T-21	Gil Morgan	71-69-73-75—288	$14,000.00
T-21	Tommy Nakajima	71-75-69-73—288	$14,000.00
T-21	Tom Purtzer	72-72-74-70—288	$14,000.00
T-28	Mike Hulbert	74-74-70-71—289	$9,000.00
T-28	Peter Jacobsen	73-71-72-73—289	$9,000.00
T-28	Larry Nelson	72-68-75-74—289	$9,000.00
T-28	Joe Ozaki	76-72-74-67—289	$9,000.00
T-28	Tom Wargo	72-72-73-72—289	$9,000.00
T-33	Paul Azinger	72-73-68-77—290	$7,000.00
T-33	Brad Fabel	72-76-74-68—290	$7,000.00
T-33	Bruce Fleisher	70-72-75-73—290	$7,000.00
T-33	Davis Love III	77-71-70-72—290	$7,000.00
T-33	Colin Montgomerie	72-76-69-73—290	$7,000.00
T-33	Frank Nobilo	69-74-74-73—290	$7,000.00
T-33	Dillard Pruitt	73-70-73-74—290	$7,000.00
T-40	Fulton Allem	74-72-72-73—291	$5,162.50
T-40	Billy Ray Brown	72-75-72-72—291	$5,162.50
T-40	David Edwards	74-70-77-70—291	$5,162.50
T-40	Mark James	75-72-72-72—291	$5,162.50
T-40	Bernhard Langer	72-74-72-73—291	$5,162.50
T-40	Rocco Mediate	72-68-74-77—291	$5,162.50
T-40	Larry Mize	74-74-71-72—291	$5,162.50
T-40	Lanny Wadkins	72-71-73-75—291	$5,162.50
T-48	Brad Bryant	75-71-73-73—292	$3,687.50
T-48	Mark Calcavecchia	74-69-74-75—292	$3,687.50
T-48	Ray Floyd	69-75-69-79—292	$3,687.50
T-48	Steve Pate	70-78-70-74—292	$3,687.50

Place	Name	Score	Winnings
T-48	Steven Richardson	73-66-75-78—292	$3,687.50
T-48	Peter Senior	71-76-73-72—292	$3,687.50
T-48	Vijay Singh	70-73-73-76—292	$3,687.50
T-48	Craig Stadler	67-72-75-78—292	$3,687.50
T-56	Keith Clearwater	73-72-74-74—293	$3,000.00
T-56	Gary Hallberg	71-72-72-78—293	$3,000.00
T-56	Andrew Magee	74-71-74-74—293	$3,000.00
T-56	Lee Rinker	72-75-73-73—293	$3,000.00
T-56	Joey Sindelar	72-75-75-71—293	$3,000.00
T-56	Bob Tway	74-73-72-74—293	$3,000.00
T-62	Jay Haas	75-73-74-72—294	$2,725.00
T-62	Blaine McCallister	73-75-76-70—294	$2,725.00
T-62	Jay Overton	73-73-76-72—294	$2,725.00
T-62	Tom Watson	72-71-73-78—294	$2,725.00
T-66	Hale Irwin	71-77-72-75—295	$2,575.00
T-66	Jim Kane	72-73-76-74—295	$2,575.00
T-66	Roger Mackay	76-72-71-76—295	$2,575.00
T-69	Ian Baker-Finch	71-75-78-72—296	$2,487.50
T-69	David Peoples	75-73-74-74—296	$2,487.50
T-69	Ted Schulz	75-71-74-76—296	$2,487.50
T-69	Payne Stewart	76-69-79-72—296	$2,487.50
T-73	Ben Crenshaw	71-75-78-74—298	$2,400.00
T-73	David Frost	72-76-77-73—298	$2,400.00
T-73	Bruce Lietzke	75-70-80-73—298	$2,400.00
T-76	Jay Don Blake	68-77-79-76—300	$2,325.00
T-76	Bob Estes	69-78-77-76—300	$2,325.00
T-76	Steve Veriato	70-73-77-80—300	$2,325.00
T-79	Robert Gamez	69-75-82-77—303	$2,250.00
T-79	Scott Gump	71-72-78-82—303	$2,250.00
T-79	Todd Smith	75-73-79-76—303	$2,250.00
82	John Daly	76-72-79-77—304	$2,200.00
83	Harold Perry	74-74-78-79—305	$2,175.00
T-84	Neal Lancaster	75-72-79-81—307	$2,137.50
T-84	Ken McDonald	78-69-78-82—307	$2,137.50
Cut	Chip Beck	74-75—149	$1,200.00
Cut	Bob Gilder	76-73—149	$1,200.00
Cut	David Gilford	75-74—149	$1,200.00
Cut	Scott Hoch	74-75—149	$1,200.00
Cut	Billy Mayfair	74-75—149	$1,200.00
Cut	Mike Schuchart	74-75—149	$1,200.00
Cut	Bob Borowicz	73-77—150	$1,200.00
Cut	Ed Dougherty	76-74—150	$1,200.00
Cut	David Feherty	75-75—150	$1,200.00
Cut	Denny Hepler	78-72—150	$1,200.00
Cut	Mark McCumber	73-77—150	$1,200.00
Cut	Jack Nicklaus	72-78—150	$1,200.00
Cut	Mark O'Meara	75-75—150	$1,200.00
Cut	Jose Maria Olazabal	73-77—150	$1,200.00
Cut	Eduardo Romero	73-77—150	$1,200.00
Cut	Dan Wood	76-74—150	$1,200.00
Cut	Phil Blackmar	77-74—151	$1,200.00

Place	Name	Score	Winnings
Cut	Nolan Henke	77-74—151	$1,200.00
Cut	Wayne Levi	77-74—151	$1,200.00
Cut	Jerry Tucker	76-75—151	$1,200.00
Cut	Howard Twitty	76-75—151	$1,200.00
Cut	D.A. Weibring	74-77—151	$1,200.00
Cut	Mike West	75-76—151	$1,200.00
Cut	Louis Bartoletti	74-78—152	$1,200.00
Cut	Fred Funk	70-82—152	$1,200.00
Cut	David Glenz	76-76—152	$1,200.00
Cut	Wayne Grady	75-77—152	$1,200.00
Cut	Dudley Hart	77-75—152	$1,200.00
Cut	Sandy Lyle	74-78—152	$1,200.00
Cut	Curtis Strange	74-78—152	$1,200.00
Cut	Ken Allard	75-78—153	$1,200.00
Cut	Ernie Els	73-80—153	$1,200.00
Cut	Larry Gilbert	74-79—153	$1,200.00
Cut	Tony Johnstone	74-79—153	$1,200.00
Cut	John Mahaffey	74-79—153	$1,200.00
Cut	Scott Mahlberg	76-77—153	$1,200.00
Cut	Ron McDougal	79-74—153	$1,200.00
Cut	Ian Woosnam	73-80—153	$1,200.00
Cut	Gene Fieger	77-77—154	$1,200.00
Cut	Hubert Green	72-82—154	$1,200.00
Cut	Mike Harwood	76-78—154	$1,200.00
Cut	Gordon Johnson	79-75—154	$1,200.00
Cut	Gary Ostrega	75-79—154	$1,200.00
Cut	Kirk Triplett	73-81—154	$1,200.00
Cut	Michael Burke Jr.	76-79—155	$1,200.00
Cut	Lowell Dencer	73-82—155	$1,200.00
Cut	Ed Sabo	77-78—155	$1,200.00
Cut	Hal Sutton	77-78—155	$1,200.00
Cut	Kenny Knox	76-80—156	$1,200.00
Cut	Bruce Lehnhard	77-79—156	$1,200.00
Cut	Gary Robison	77-79—156	$1,200.00
Cut	Mark Carnevale	79-78—157	$1,200.00
Cut	Tom Joyce	77-80—157	$1,200.00
Cut	Mike San Filippo	80-77—157	$1,200.00
Cut	Doug Hixon	80-78—158	$1,200.00
Cut	Bob Lohr	76-82—158	$1,200.00
Cut	Ed Whitman	75-83—158	$1,200.00
Cut	Steve Groves	83-76—159	$1,200.00
Cut	Darrell Kestner	79-80—159	$1,200.00
Cut	Randy Peterson	80-79—159	$1,200.00
Cut	Baker Maddera	83-77—160	$1,200.00
Cut	Mel Baum	81-81—162	$1,200.00
Cut	Bob Groff	79-83—162	$1,200.00
Cut	Mike Moyers	82-80—162	$1,200.00
Cut	Arnold Palmer	79-83—162	$1,200.00
WD	Ken Green	75—NC	

1991

Every sport has that one magical moment when an unknown or longshot emerges to inspire people everywhere by winning an event few believed possible. For golf, the 1991 PGA Championship produced long-driving John Daly of Dardanelle, Ark. Daly, the ninth alternate, got his chance to compete when Nick Price withdrew to be present at the birth of his child and three alternates ahead of Daly declined. Without the benefit of a practice round, Daly posted an opening-round 69 to share eighth place. He seized the lead for good, closing the Championship with rounds of 67, 69 and 71 for a 276 total, and a three-stroke victory over Bruce Lietzke.

Champion: John Daly, Dardanelle, Ark.			
Site: Crooked Stick Golf Club, Carmel, Ind.			
Date: Aug. 8-11		**Purse:** $1,400,000	
Par: 36-36 - 72 (7,295 Yards)			
Entries: 151	Cut at 147	77 players advanced	

PING

	Course Avg	Under Par	At Par	Over Par	Round Leader	Low Round	John Daly
Round 1:	73.7	38	19	94	Knox, Woosnam	67- Knox, Woosnam	69- (T-8)
Round 2:	74.85	29	17	102	John Daly	67- Daly, Sutton, Couples	136 (67)-1st
Round 3:	72.86	26	13	37	John Daly	67- Bob Gilder	205 (69)-1st
Round 4:	72.88	26	12	39	John Daly	67- Jim Gallagher Jr.	276 (71)-1st
Totals:	73.81	119	61	272			

TOURNAMENT SUMMARY

Place	Name	Score	Winnings
1	John Daly	69-67-69-71—276	$230,000.00
2	Bruce Lietzke	68-69-72-70—279	$140,000.00
3	Jim Gallagher Jr.	70-72-72-67—281	$95,000.00
4	Kenny Knox	67-71-70-74—282	$75,000.00
T-5	Bob Gilder	73-70-67-73—283	$60,000.00
T-5	Steven Richardson	70-72-72-69—283	$60,000.00
T-7	David Feherty	71-74-71-68—284	$38,000.00
T-7	Ray Floyd	69-74-72-69—284	$38,000.00
T-7	John Huston	70-72-70-72—284	$38,000.00
T-7	Steve Pate	70-75-70-69—284	$38,000.00
T-7	Craig Stadler	68-71-69-76—284	$38,000.00
T-7	Hal Sutton	74-67-72-71—284	$38,000.00
T-13	Jay Don Blake	75-72-68-68—285	$24,000.00
T-13	Andrew Magee	69-73-68-75—285	$24,000.00
T-13	Payne Stewart	74-70-71-70—285	$24,000.00
T-16	Nick Faldo	70-69-71-76—286	$17,000.00
T-16	Ken Green	68-73-71-74—286	$17,000.00
T-16	Wayne Levi	73-71-72-70—286	$17,000.00
T-16	Sandy Lyle	68-75-71-72—286	$17,000.00
T-16	Rocco Mediate	71-73-71-71—286	$17,000.00
T-16	Gil Morgan	70-71-74-71—286	$17,000.00
T-16	Howard Twitty	70-71-75-70—286	$17,000.00
T-23	Seve Ballesteros	71-72-71-73—287	$11,500.00
T-23	Chip Beck	73-73-70-71—287	$11,500.00
T-23	Mike Hulbert	72-72-73-70—287	$11,500.00
T-23	Jack Nicklaus	71-72-73-71—287	$11,500.00
T-27	Fred Couples	74-67-76-71—288	$8,150.00
T-27	Rick Fehr	70-73-71-74—288	$8,150.00
T-27	Jim Hallet	69-74-73-72—288	$8,150.00
T-27	Mark McNulty	75-71-69-73—288	$8,150.00
T-27	Loren Roberts	72-74-72-70—288	$8,150.00
T-32	Billy Andrade	73-74-68-74—289	$6,000.00
T-32	Mark Calcavecchia	70-74-73-72—289	$6,000.00
T-32	David Edwards	71-75-71-72—289	$6,000.00
T-32	Steve Elkington	74-68-74-73—289	$6,000.00
T-32	Dan Forsman	73-74-68-74—289	$6,000.00
T-32	Davis Love III	72-72-72-73—289	$6,000.00
T-32	Jodie Mudd	74-71-74-70—289	$6,000.00
T-32	Greg Norman	70-74-72-73—289	$6,000.00
T-32	Corey Pavin	72-73-71-73—289	$6,000.00
T-32	Tom Purtzer	69-76-71-73—289	$6,000.00
T-32	Doug Tewell	75-72-74-68—289	$6,000.00
T-43	Ed Dougherty	75-70-69-76—290	$4,030.00
T-43	Wayne Grady	72-70-71-77—290	$4,030.00
T-43	Scott Hoch	71-75-72-72—290	$4,030.00
T-43	Craig Parry	73-70-76-71—290	$4,030.00
T-43	Lanny Wadkins	71-74-72-73—290	$4,030.00
T-48	Keith Clearwater	72-72-76-71—291	$3,175.00
T-48	Brad Faxon	72-71-76-72—291	$3,175.00
T-48	David Frost	74-70-75-72—291	$3,175.00
T-48	Ian Woosnam	67-72-76-76—291	$3,175.00
T-52	David Graham	72-73-73-74—292	$2,725.00
T-52	Tom Kite	73-72-75-72—292	$2,725.00
T-52	Mark McCumber	74-72-71-75—292	$2,725.00
T-52	Eduardo Romero	72-75-73-72—292	$2,725.00
T-52	Tom Sieckmann	68-76-74-74—292	$2,725.00
T-57	Fred Funk	71-69-72-81—293	$2,537.50
T-57	Nolan Henke	74-70-75-74—293	$2,537.50
T-57	Blaine McCallister	71-76-77-69—293	$2,537.50
T-57	Lindy Miller	72-72-77-72—293	$2,537.50
T-61	Dave Barr	75-72-76-71—294	$2,462.50
T-61	Jeff Sluman	73-73-74-74—294	$2,462.50
T-63	Gene Sauers	75-71-70-79—295	$2,400.00
T-63	Joey Sindelar	74-73-71-77—295	$2,400.00
T-63	Bob Wolcott	73-71-79-72—295	$2,400.00
T-66	Dillard Pruitt	72-75-73-76—296	$2,312.50
T-66	Bob Tway	73-71-78-74—296	$2,312.50
T-66	Mark Wiebe	72-73-73-78—296	$2,312.50
T-66	Scott Williams	70-77-76-73—296	$2,312.50
T-70	Denny Hepler	71-75-75-76—297	$2,225.00
T-70	Lonnie Nielsen	74-71-74-78—297	$2,225.00
T-70	David Peoples	74-73-75-75—297	$2,225.00
T-73	Phil Blackmar	73-72-82-71—298	$2,137.50
T-73	Billy Ray Brown	69-75-75-79—298	$2,137.50
T-73	Hale Irwin	70-76-74-78—298	$2,137.50
T-73	Don Pooley	72-74-72-80—298	$2,137.50
77	Kenny Perry	72-73-79-76—300	$2,075.00
Cut	Bill Britton	71-77—148	$1,000.00
Cut	Mark Brooks	73-75—148	$1,000.00
Cut	Brian Claar	76-72—148	$1,000.00
Cut	Russ Cochran	73-75—148	$1,000.00
Cut	John Cook	74-74—148	$1,000.00
Cut	Bob Lohr	78-70—148	$1,000.00
Cut	Tommy Nakajima	72-76—148	$1,000.00
Cut	Peter Persons	73-75—148	$1,000.00
Cut	Peter Senior	74-74—148	$1,000.00
Cut	Dave Stockton	71-77—148	$1,000.00
Cut	Fuzzy Zoeller	72-76—148	$1,000.00
Cut	Scott Bentley	75-74—149	$1,000.00
Cut	Jay Delsing	70-79—149	$1,000.00
Cut	Terry Florence	75-74—149	$1,000.00
Cut	Rick Kawagishi	75-74—149	$1,000.00
Cut	Bernhard Langer	75-74—149	$1,000.00
Cut	Larry Mize	72-77—149	$1,000.00
Cut	Lee Rinker	73-76—149	$1,000.00
Cut	Ken Schall	74-75—149	$1,000.00
Cut	Bobby Wadkins	77-72—149	$1,000.00
Cut	Tom Watson	74-75—149	$1,000.00
Cut	Ian Baker-Finch	74-76—150	$1,000.00
Cut	Billy Mayfair	73-77—150	$1,000.00
Cut	Jose Maria Olazabal	77-73—150	$1,000.00
Cut	Ted Schulz	75-75—150	$1,000.00
Cut	Tim Simpson	74-76—150	$1,000.00
Cut	Hubert Green	73-78—151	$1,000.00
Cut	Morris Hatalsky	74-77—151	$1,000.00
Cut	Stu Ingraham	73-78—151	$1,000.00
Cut	John Mahaffey	77-74—151	$1,000.00
Cut	Scott Simpson	72-79—151	$1,000.00
Cut	Greg Farrow	74-78—152	$1,000.00
Cut	Larry Gilbert	79-73—152	$1,000.00
Cut	Mike Kallam	74-78—152	$1,000.00
Cut	Darrell Kestner	74-78—152	$1,000.00
Cut	Larry Nelson	75-77—152	$1,000.00
Cut	Sam Torrance	74-78—152	$1,000.00
Cut	Gary Trivisonno	77-75—152	$1,000.00
Cut	Jim Masserio	74-79—153	$1,000.00
Cut	Brett Upper	74-79—153	$1,000.00
Cut	Bruce Fleisher	76-78—154	$1,000.00
Cut	Buddy Gardner	74-80—154	$1,000.00
Cut	Gary Hallberg	72-82—154	$1,000.00
Cut	Mark O'Meara	75-79—154	$1,000.00
Cut	Stan Utley	77-77—154	$1,000.00
Cut	Tom Wargo	76-78—154	$1,000.00
Cut	Mel Baum	78-77—155	$1,000.00
Cut	Fran Marrello	75-80—155	$1,000.00
Cut	Arnold Palmer	77-78—155	$1,000.00
Cut	Kim Thompson	79-76—155	$1,000.00
Cut	Milan Wilor	77-78—155	$1,000.00
Cut	Bob Borowicz	80-76—156	$1,000.00
Cut	Dave Rummells	77-79—156	$1,000.00
Cut	Andy Bean	80-77—157	$1,000.00
Cut	Brent Buckman	79-78—157	$1,000.00
Cut	Terry Dear	74-83—157	$1,000.00
Cut	Mike Harwood	73-85—158	$1,000.00
Cut	Jeff Roth	80-78—158	$1,000.00
Cut	Brad Sherfy	76-82—158	$1,000.00
Cut	Bob Lendzion	76-83—159	$1,000.00
Cut	Brian Tennyson	76-83—159	$1,000.00
Cut	Brent Veenstra	77-82—159	$1,000.00
Cut	Robert Wilkin	76-84—160	$1,000.00
Cut	Tom Woodard	84-76—160	$1,000.00
Cut	Mike Lawrence	82-79—161	$1,000.00
Cut	Benny Passons	85-77—162	$1,000.00
Cut	Steve Veriato	82-80—162	$1,000.00
Cut	Gregg Wolff	81-81—162	$1,000.00
Cut	John Hendricks	83-80—163	$1,000.00
Cut	Shawn McEntee	81-82—163	$1,000.00
Cut	Jim White	76-87—163	$1,000.00
Cut	Jim Dickson	83-85—168	$1,000.00
WD	Ben Crenshaw	81—81	$1,000.00
WD	Curtis Strange	81—81	$1,000.00

1990

Native Australian Wayne Grady, who now calls Orlando, Fla., home, quietly opened with a par 72, then added rounds of 67, 72 and 71 to capture his first major golf championship. Fred Couples was one shot ahead of Grady thru 66 holes, but proceeded to bogey the next four holes while Grady was making pars to finish second, three strokes behind. Only three players, Grady, Couples and third-place finisher Gil Morgan (286), managed to break par (288) for the tournament.

Champion: Wayne Grady, Orlando, Fla.	
Site: Shoal Creek CC, Birmingham, Ala.	
Date: Aug. 9-12	**Purse:** $1,350,000
Par: 36-36 - 72 (7,145 Yards)	
Entries: 152 Cut at 151 74 players advanced	

	Course Avg	Under Par	At Par	Over Par	Round Leader	Low Round		Wayne Grady	
Round 1:	75.9	15	13	123	Bobby Wadkins	68 -	Bobby Wadkins	72 - Tied 16th	
Round 2:	76.1	17	11	121	Wayne Grady	67 -	Wayne Grady	139	(67) - 1st
Round 3:	74.8	12	8	54	Wayne Grady	65 -	Gil Morgan	211	(72) - 1st
Round 4:	75.6	6	7	61	Wayne Grady	69 -	Nick Faldo	282	(71) - 1st
Totals:	75.76	50	39	359					

TOURNAMENT SUMMARY

Place	Name	Score	Winnings	Place	Name	Score	Winnings	Place	Name	Score	Winnings
1	Wayne Grady	72-67-72-71—282	$225,000.00	T-49	Mike Hulbert	71-75-79-75—300	$2,865.62	Cut	Ken Schall	77-78—155	$1,000.00
2	Fred Couples	69-71-73-72—285	$135,000.00	T-49	Mark McCumber	73-76-74-77—300	$2,865.63	Cut	Curtis Strange	79-76—155	$1,000.00
3	Gil Morgan	77-72-65-72—286	$90,000.00	T-49	Kenny Perry	73-76-78-73—300	$2,865.63	Cut	Lanny Wadkins	74-81—155	$1,000.00
4	Bill Britton	72-74-72-71—289	$73,500.00	T-49	Hal Sutton	72-74-78-76—300	$2,865.63	Cut	Larry Emery	79-77—156	$1,000.00
T-5	Chip Beck	71-70-78-71—290	$51,666.67	T-49	Stan Utley	71-72-80-77—300	$2,865.62	Cut	Dan Forsman	76-80—156	$1,000.00
T-5	Billy Mayfair	70-71-75-74—290	$51,666.67	T-57	Ian Baker-Finch	74-71-78-78—301	$2,525.00	Cut	Stu Ingraham	75-81—156	$1,000.00
T-5	Loren Roberts	73-71-70-76—290	$51,666.66	T-57	Bob Gilder	73-78-73-77—301	$2,525.00	Cut	Jay Overton	77-79—156	$1,000.00
T-8	Mark McNulty	74-72-75-71—292	$34,375.00	T-57	John Huston	72-72-77-80—301	$2,525.00	Cut	Benny Passons	74-82—156	$1,000.00
T-8	Don Pooley	75-74-71-72—292	$34,375.00	T-57	David Peoples	77-71-77-76—301	$2,525.00	Cut	Ronan Rafferty	81-75—156	$1,000.00
T-8	Tim Simpson	71-73-75-73—292	$34,375.00	T-57	Craig Stadler	75-73-74-79—301	$2,525.00	Cut	Gene Sauers	75-81—156	$1,000.00
T-8	Payne Stewart	71-72-70-79—292	$34,375.00	62	Peter Senior	74-75-72-81—302	$2,450.00	Cut	Kim Thompson	80-76—156	$1,000.00
T-12	Hale Irwin	77-72-70-74—293	$27,000.00	T-63	Jay Delsing	75-73-73-82—303	$2,400.00	Cut	Kirk Triplett	74-82—156	$1,000.00
T-12	Larry Mize	72-68-76-77—293	$27,000.00	T-63	Donnie Hammond	77-70-80-76—303	$2,400.00	Cut	Tommy Armour	78-79—157	$1,000.00
T-14	Billy Andrade	75-72-73-74—294	$20,600.00	T-63	Nick Price	75-71-81-76—303	$2,400.00	Cut	Pat Fitzsimons	78-79—157	$1,000.00
T-14	Morris Hatalsky	73-78-71-72—294	$20,600.00	T-66	David Graham	75-75-75-79—304	$2,325.00	Cut	Phil Hancock	82-75—157	$1,000.00
T-14	Jose Maria Olazabal	73-77-72-72—294	$20,600.00	T-66	Scott Simpson	76-75-72-81—304	$2,325.00	Cut	Dana Quigley	77-80—157	$1,000.00
T-14	Corey Pavin	73-75-72-74—294	$20,600.00	T-66	Bobby Wadkins	68-75-80-81—304	$2,325.00	Cut	Dave Stockton	80-77—157	$1,000.00
T-14	Fuzzy Zoeller	72-71-76-75—294	$20,600.00	T-69	James Blair	73-76-76-80—305	$2,225.00	Cut	Ray Freeman	79-79—158	$1,000.00
T-19	Bob Boyd	74-74-71-76—295	$14,000.00	T-69	Ed Fiori	75-76-77-77—305	$2,225.00	Cut	Bob Makoski	82-76—158	$1,000.00
T-19	Nick Faldo	71-75-80-69—295	$14,000.00	T-69	Cary Hungate	72-77-79-77—305	$2,225.00	Cut	Joe Ozaki	77-81—158	$1,000.00
T-19	Blaine McCallister	75-73-74-73—295	$14,000.00	T-69	Rocco Mediate	75-72-81-77—305	$2,225.00	Cut	Mike San Filippo	81-77—158	$1,000.00
T-19	Greg Norman	77-69-76-73—295	$14,000.00	T-69	Jumbo Ozaki	75-74-79-77—305	$2,225.00	Cut	Chris Tucker	76-82—158	$1,000.00
T-19	Mark O'Meara	69-76-79-71—295	$14,000.00	74	Bob Ford	75-75-79-77—306	$2,150.00	Cut	Brad Bryant	80-79—159	$1,000.00
T-19	Tom Watson	74-71-77-73—295	$14,000.00	Cut	Billy Ray Brown	75-77—152	$1,000.00	Cut	Greg Cerulli	75-84—159	$1,000.00
T-19	Mark Wiebe	74-73-75-73—295	$14,000.00	Cut	Steve Elkington	75-77—152	$1,000.00	Cut	Rodger Davis	81-78—159	$1,000.00
T-26	Mark Brooks	78-69-76-73—296	$8,650.00	Cut	Rick Fehr	77-75—152	$1,000.00	Cut	Eduardo Romero	84-75—159	$1,000.00
T-26	Peter Jacobsen	74-75-71-76—296	$8,650.00	Cut	Steve Jones	74-78—152	$1,000.00	Cut	Jim Sobb	76-83—159	$1,000.00
T-26	Chris Perry	75-74-72-75—296	$8,650.00	Cut	Bruce Lietzke	78-74—152	$1,000.00	Cut	Seve Ballesteros	77-83—160	$1,000.00
T-26	Ray Stewart	73-73-75-75—296	$8,650.00	Cut	Bob Lohr	78-74—152	$1,000.00	Cut	Jay Haas	82-78—160	$1,000.00
T-26	Brian Tennyson	71-77-71-77—296	$8,650.00	Cut	Larry Nelson	77-75—152	$1,000.00	Cut	Jim Thorpe	77-83—160	$1,000.00
T-31	Paul Azinger	76-70-74-77—297	$6,500.00	Cut	Jack Nicklaus	78-74—152	$1,000.00	Cut	Ed Whitman	84-76—160	$1,000.00
T-31	Ben Crenshaw	74-70-78-75—297	$6,500.00	Cut	Rick Osberg	73-79—152	$1,000.00	Cut	Steve Bowen	81-80—161	$1,000.00
T-31	David Frost	76-74-69-78—297	$6,500.00	Cut	Jerry Pate	73-79—152	$1,000.00	Cut	Larry Gilbert	83-79—162	$1,000.00
T-31	Steve Pate	71-75-71-80—297	$6,500.00	Cut	Ted Schulz	78-74—152	$1,000.00	Cut	Mike Gove	86-76—162	$1,000.00
T-31	Tom Purtzer	74-74-77-72—297	$6,500.00	Cut	Mike Sullivan	75-77—152	$1,000.00	Cut	David Ishii	82-80—162	$1,000.00
T-31	Dave Rummells	73-73-77-74—297	$6,500.00	Cut	Lee Trevino	77-75—152	$1,000.00	Cut	Arnold Palmer	81-81—162	$1,000.00
T-31	Jeff Sluman	74-74-73-76—297	$6,500.00	Cut	Hubert Green	74-79—153	$1,000.00	Cut	Jim Gallagher Jr.	82-81—163	$1,000.00
T-31	Scott Verplank	70-76-73-78—297	$6,500.00	Cut	Kirk Hanefeld	76-77—153	$1,000.00	Cut	Drue Johnson	79-84—163	$1,000.00
T-31	Ian Woosnam	74-75-70-78—297	$6,500.00	Cut	Robert Hoyt	74-79—153	$1,000.00	Cut	Bob Borowicz	81-84—165	$1,000.00
T-40	Isao Aoki	72-74-78-74—298	$4,750.00	Cut	Mark James	77-76—153	$1,000.00	Cut	Chris Dachisen	84-81—165	$1,000.00
T-40	Tom Kite	79-71-74-74—298	$4,750.00	Cut	Bernhard Langer	75-78—153	$1,000.00	Cut	Hunt Gilliland	82-83—165	$1,000.00
T-40	Davis Love III	72-72-77-77—298	$4,750.00	Cut	Lonnie Nielsen	72-81—153	$1,000.00	Cut	Curt Schnell	82-84—166	$1,000.00
T-40	John Mahaffey	75-72-76-75—298	$4,750.00	Cut	Jeff Thomsen	77-76—153	$1,000.00	Cut	Ken Allard	81-86—167	$1,000.00
T-40	Craig Parry	74-72-75-77—298	$4,750.00	Cut	Mark Calcavecchia	77-77—154	$1,000.00	Cut	Noel Caruso	84-83—167	$1,000.00
T-45	Andrew Magee	75-74-73-77—299	$3,700.00	Cut	Russ Cochran	74-80—154	$1,000.00	Cut	Dale Fuller	82-87—169	$1,000.00
T-45	Sammy Rachels	75-73-76-75—299	$3,700.00	Cut	Bob Estes	77-77—154	$1,000.00	Cut	Ted Goin	87-83—170	$1,000.00
T-45	Mike Reid	71-78-78-72—299	$3,700.00	Cut	Bruce Fleisher	78-76—154	$1,000.00	WD	Mark Lye	72—72	$1,000.00
T-45	Bob Tway	72-76-73-78—299	$3,700.00	Cut	Kent Stauffer	78-76—154	$1,000.00	WD	Jay Don Blake	77—77	$1,000.00
T-49	Ray Floyd	72-77-74-77—300	$2,865.62	Cut	Mike Donald	76-79—155	$1,000.00	WD	Bill Glasson	82—82	$1,000.00
T-49	Robert Gamez	71-78-75-76—300	$2,865.62	Cut	Brad Faxon	80-75—155	$1,000.00				
T-49	Scott Hoch	78-73-72-77—300	$2,865.63	Cut	Bill Sander	80-75—155	$1,000.00				

1989

Payne Stewart birdied four of the last five holes, shooting a 31 over the final nine, to edge runners-up Mike Reid, Curtis Strange and Andy Bean, and win his first major title. Reid, who led the 71st PGA Championship until the finishing holes, bogeyed 16, double-bogeyed 17 and missed an 8-foot birdie putt on 18. Windless playing conditions at Kemper Lakes, a public golf facility, helped produce holes-in-one by Mark O'Meara, Lanny Wadkins, Scott Hoch and Davis Love III. The four aces tied a PGA Championship record established in 1988.

Champion: Payne Stewart, Orlando, Fla.
Site: Kemper Lakes GC, Hawthorn Woods, Ill.
Date: Aug. 10-13   **Purse:** $1,200,000
Par: 36-36 - 72 (7,217 Yards)
Entries: 150   Cut at 145   70 players advanced

	Course Avg	Under Par	At Par	Over Par	Round Leader	Low Round	Payne Stewart
Round 1:	73.7	49	7	94		66 - Mike Reid, Leonard Thompson	74 - Tied 77th
Round 2:	73.3	54	13	82	Mike Reid	64 - Craig Stadler	140 (66) - Tied 14th
Round 3:	71.9	29	14	27	Mike Reid	65 - Isao Aoki	209 (69) - Tied 11th
Round 4:	72.9	21	13	36	Payne Stewart	66 - Andy Bean	276 (67) - 1st
Totals:	73.11	153	47	239			

TOURNAMENT SUMMARY

Place	Name	Score	Winnings
1	Payne Stewart	74-66-69-67—276	$200,000.00
T-2	Andy Bean	70-67-74-66—277	$83,333.34
T-2	Mike Reid	66-67-70-74—277	$83,333.33
T-2	Curtis Strange	70-68-70-69—277	$83,333.33
5	Dave Rummells	68-69-69-72—278	$45,000.00
6	Ian Woosnam	68-70-70-71—279	$40,000.00
T-7	Scott Hoch	69-69-69-73—280	$36,250.00
T-7	Craig Stadler	71-64-72-73—280	$36,250.00
T-9	Nick Faldo	70-73-69-69—281	$30,000.00
T-9	Ed Fiori	70-67-75-69—281	$30,000.00
T-9	Tom Watson	67-69-74-71—281	$30,000.00
T-12	Seve Ballesteros	72-70-66-74—282	$21,900.00
T-12	Jim Gallagher Jr.	73-69-68-72—282	$21,900.00
T-12	Greg Norman	74-71-67-70—282	$21,900.00
T-12	Mike Sullivan	76-66-67-73—282	$21,900.00
T-12	Mark Wiebe	71-70-69-72—282	$21,900.00
T-17	Isao Aoki	72-71-65-75—283	$15,000.00
T-17	Ben Crenshaw	68-72-72-71—283	$15,000.00
T-17	Buddy Gardner	72-71-70-70—283	$15,000.00
T-17	Davis Love III	73-69-72-69—283	$15,000.00
T-17	Blaine McCallister	71-72-70-70—283	$15,000.00
T-17	Larry Mize	73-71-68-71—283	$15,000.00
T-17	Chris Perry	67-70-70-76—283	$15,000.00
T-24	Tommy Armour	70-69-73-72—284	$10,000.00
T-24	Dan Pohl	71-69-74-70—284	$10,000.00
T-24	Jeff Sluman	75-70-69-70—284	$10,000.00
T-27	David Frost	70-74-69-72—285	$7,535.71
T-27	Mike Hulbert	70-71-72-72—285	$7,535.72
T-27	Peter Jacobsen	70-70-73-72—285	$7,535.71
T-27	Jack Nicklaus	68-72-73-72—285	$7,535.72
T-27	Tim Simpson	69-70-73-73—285	$7,535.71
T-27	Brian Tennyson	71-69-72-73—285	$7,535.71
T-27	Howard Twitty	72-71-68-74—285	$7,535.72
T-34	Ian Baker-Finch	74-68-70-74—286	$5,750.00
T-34	Chip Beck	73-71-69-73—286	$5,750.00
T-34	Bob Gilder	72-72-74-68—286	$5,750.00
T-34	Tom Kite	67-73-72-74—286	$5,750.00
T-34	Don Pooley	70-71-72-73—286	$5,750.00
T-34	Loren Roberts	69-71-72-74—286	$5,750.00
T-34	Leonard Thompson	66-69-73-78—286	$5,750.00
T-41	Bill Britton	75-67-71-74—287	$4,260.00
T-41	David Edwards	69-72-72-74—287	$4,260.00
T-41	Steve Elkington	69-75-71-72—287	$4,260.00
T-41	Bob Lohr	75-69-69-74—287	$4,260.00
T-41	Steve Pate	70-72-74-71—287	$4,260.00
T-46	Ray Floyd	73-71-70-74—288	$3,220.00
T-46	Wayne Grady	70-75-72-71—288	$3,220.00
T-46	Bruce Lietzke	70-72-73-73—288	$3,220.00
T-46	Larry Nelson	71-74-68-75—288	$3,220.00
T-46	Nick Price	70-72-72-74—288	$3,220.00
T-51	Steve Jones	71-74-71-73—289	$2,750.00

Place	Name	Score	Winnings
T-51	Kenny Perry	71-74-70-74—289	$2,750.00
T-53	Phil Blackmar	68-75-75-72—290	$2,490.00
T-53	Tom Purtzer	69-73-74-74—290	$2,490.00
T-53	Clarence Rose	74-71-72-73—290	$2,490.00
T-53	Scott Simpson	70-74-75-71—290	$2,490.00
T-53	Doug Tewell	73-69-72-76—290	$2,490.00
T-58	Brad Bryant	70-70-72-79—291	$2,380.00
T-58	Andy North	69-75-77-70—291	$2,380.00
T-58	Gene Sauers	76-68-75-72—291	$2,380.00
T-61	Gary Koch	71-72-77-72—292	$2,330.00
T-61	Bernhard Langer	74-71-75-72—292	$2,330.00
T-63	Arnold Palmer	68-74-81-70—293	$2,290.00
T-63	Greg Twiggs	71-73-74-75—293	$2,290.00
65	Mark McCumber	70-73-74-77—294	$2,260.00
66	Hubert Green	69-73-76-77—295	$2,240.00
67	Jodie Mudd	71-70-80-75—296	$2,220.00
68	Dave Stockton	71-76-75-77—297	$2,200.00
69	Ronnie Black	73-70-74-82—299	$2,180.00
70	Curt Byrum	73-71-76-87—307	$2,170.00
Cut	Billy Andrade	73-73—146	$1,000.00
Cut	Dave Barr	76-70—146	$1,000.00
Cut	Fred Couples	73-73—146	$1,000.00
Cut	Jim Hallet	72-74—146	$1,000.00
Cut	Stu Ingraham	70-76—146	$1,000.00
Cut	Gil Morgan	73-73—146	$1,000.00
Cut	Ted Schulz	72-74—146	$1,000.00
Cut	Hal Sutton	76-70—146	$1,000.00
Cut	Scott Verplank	73-73—146	$1,000.00
Cut	Ken Allard	76-71—147	$1,000.00
Cut	John Huston	74-73—147	$1,000.00
Cut	Andrew Magee	74-73—147	$1,000.00
Cut	Chris Mitchell	74-73—147	$1,000.00
Cut	Mark O'Meara	68-79—147	$1,000.00
Cut	Jose Maria Olazabal	73-74—147	$1,000.00
Cut	Robert Wrenn	73-74—147	$1,000.00
Cut	Fuzzy Zoeller	75-72—147	$1,000.00
Cut	Bob Betley	73-75—148	$1,000.00
Cut	Jay Don Blake	74-74—148	$1,000.00
Cut	Mike Donald	76-72—148	$1,000.00
Cut	Gregg Jones	77-71—148	$1,000.00
Cut	Kenny Knox	79-69—148	$1,000.00
Cut	Roger Maltbie	74-74—148	$1,000.00
Cut	Joe Ozaki	75-73—148	$1,000.00
Cut	Joey Sindelar	71-77—148	$1,000.00
Cut	Steve Spray	74-74—148	$1,000.00
Cut	Lanny Wadkins	74-74—148	$1,000.00
Cut	Bob Boyd	77-72—149	$1,000.00
Cut	Billy Ray Brown	74-75—149	$1,000.00
Cut	Bobby Heins	75-74—149	$1,000.00
Cut	Jack Lewis	73-76—149	$1,000.00
Cut	Rick Morton	74-75—149	$1,000.00

Place	Name	Score	Winnings
Cut	Corey Pavin	75-74—149	$1,000.00
Cut	Lee Trevino	74-75—149	$1,000.00
Cut	Bob Tway	78-71—149	$1,000.00
Cut	Tom Byrum	73-77—150	$1,000.00
Cut	Russ Cochran	77-73—150	$1,000.00
Cut	Scott Davis	76-74—150	$1,000.00
Cut	Dan Forsman	75-75—150	$1,000.00
Cut	Jay Haas	80-70—150	$1,000.00
Cut	Donnie Hammond	75-75—150	$1,000.00
Cut	John Mahaffey	73-77—150	$1,000.00
Cut	Shawn McEntee	74-76—150	$1,000.00
Cut	Lindy Miller	73-77—150	$1,000.00
Cut	Sammy Rachels	76-74—150	$1,000.00
Cut	Jim Carter	80-71—151	$1,000.00
Cut	Bob Ford	79-72—151	$1,000.00
Cut	Ray Freeman	74-77—151	$1,000.00
Cut	John Jackson	75-76—151	$1,000.00
Cut	Gary Robinson	80-71—151	$1,000.00
Cut	Ron Vlosich	77-74—151	$1,000.00
Cut	Bobby Wadkins	75-76—151	$1,000.00
Cut	Brad Faxon	75-77—152	$1,000.00
Cut	Jeff Jackson	73-79—152	$1,000.00
Cut	Bob Mann	77-75—152	$1,000.00
Cut	Fulton Allem	79-74—153	$1,000.00
Cut	Paul Azinger	74-79—153	$1,000.00
Cut	Jim Cichra	75-78—153	$1,000.00
Cut	David Graham	79-74—153	$1,000.00
Cut	Mark Brooks	75-80—155	$1,000.00
Cut	Robert Gibbons	77-78—155	$1,000.00
Cut	Jerry Tucker	77-78—155	$1,000.00
Cut	Bruce Lehnhard	82-74—156	$1,000.00
Cut	Ed Terasa	77-79—156	$1,000.00
Cut	Ed Whitman	79-77—156	$1,000.00
Cut	Don Brigham	77-80—157	$1,000.00
Cut	Gene Fieger	76-81—157	$1,000.00
Cut	Bill King	83-74—157	$1,000.00
Cut	David Ogrin	77-80—157	$1,000.00
Cut	Bob Groff	78-80—158	$1,000.00
Cut	Wally Kuchar	81-77—158	$1,000.00
Cut	Bob Klein	78-82—160	$1,000.00
Cut	Lonnie Nielsen	80-80—160	$1,000.00
Cut	Mark Gardner	80-81—161	$1,000.00
Cut	Ralph Landrum	79-82—161	$1,000.00
Cut	Rick Meskell	81-82—163	$1,000.00
Cut	Greg Frederick	82-83—165	$1,000.00
Cut	John Traub	92-79—171	$1,000.00
Cut	Emil Esposito	87-87—174	$1,000.00
WD	Ken Green	75—75	$1,000.00

1988

Played at difficult Oak Tree Golf Club in Edmond, Okla., rated as one of the hardest courses in the country, players were concerned that scores would be high. Instead, the 1988 PGA Championship turned out to be the second easiest in Championship history. This made for some exciting golf, as second-round leader Paul Azinger made a hole-in-one, which was witnessed live by millions on TV during the third round. Even with Azinger having a hot hand the entire week, Jeff Sluman proved to be hotter when he fired a final-round 65. The round included an eagle-3 on the par-5 fifth hole, where Sluman holed a 100-yard wedge.

Champion: Jeff Sluman, Naples, Fla.		
Site: Oak Tree GC, Edmond, Okla.		
Date: Aug. 11-14		**Purse:** $1,000,000
Par: 36-35 - 71 (7,015 Yards)		
Entries: 150	Cut at 144	72 players advanced

	Course Avg	Under Par	At Par	Over Par	Round Leader	Low Round	Jeff Sluman
Round 1:	73.6	31	12	107	Bob Gilder	66 - Bob Gilder	69 - Tied 13th
Round 2:	73.1	44	19	86	Paul Azinger	64 - Dave Rummells	139 (70) - Tied 12th
Round 3:	73.1	18	4	50	Paul Azinger	67 - McNulty, Price	207 (68) - 3rd
Round 4:	72.7	17	8	46	Jeff Sluman	65 - Jeff Sluman	272 (65) - 1st
Totals:	73.02	110	43	289			

TOURNAMENT SUMMARY

Place	Name	Score	Winnings	Place	Name	Score	Winnings	Place	Name	Score	Winnings
1	Jeff Sluman	69-70-68-65—272	$160,000.00	T-52	Scott Bess	74-69-73-74—290	$2,092.50	Cut	Ralph Landrum	75-74—149	$1,000.00
2	Paul Azinger	67-66-71-71—275	$100,000.00	T-52	Rodger Davis	73-69-76-72—290	$2,092.50	Cut	Tom Purtzer	75-74—149	$1,000.00
3	Tommy Nakajima	69-68-74-67—278	$70,000.00	T-52	Ed Fiori	71-69-76-74—290	$2,092.50	Cut	Scott Verplank	77-72—149	$1,000.00
T-4	Tom Kite	72-69-71-67—279	$45,800.00	T-52	Jodie Mudd	70-73-77-70—290	$2,092.50	Cut	Wayne Grady	76-74—150	$1,000.00
T-4	Nick Faldo	67-71-70-71—279	$45,800.00	T-52	D.A. Weibring	72-72-73-73—290	$2,092.50	Cut	Mike Hulbert	73-77—150	$1,000.00
T-6	Bob Gilder	66-75-71-68—280	$32,500.00	T-52	Robert Wrenn	72-68-73-77—290	$2,092.50	Cut	Larry Mize	73-77—150	$1,000.00
T-6	Dave Rummells	73-64-68-75—280	$32,500.00	T-58	John Inman	73-69-75-74—291	$1,990.00	Cut	Arnold Palmer	74-76—150	$1,000.00
8	Dan Pohl	69-71-70-71—281	$28,000.00	T-58	Bob Makoski	69-72-72-78—291	$1,990.00	Cut	Tom Wargo	78-72—150	$1,000.00
T-9	Ray Floyd	68-68-74-72—282	$21,500.00	T-58	Don Pooley	72-69-73-77—291	$1,990.00	Cut	Keith Clearwater	77-74—151	$1,000.00
T-9	Steve Jones	69-68-72-73—282	$21,500.00	T-58	Peter Senior	73-69-74-76—291	$1,990.00	Cut	Mike Donald	75-76—151	$1,000.00
T-9	Kenny Knox	72-69-68-73—282	$21,500.00	T-62	Bruce Lietzke	70-72-76-74—292	$1,930.00	Cut	Bernhard Langer	74-77—151	$1,000.00
T-9	Greg Norman	68-71-72-71—282	$21,500.00	T-62	Steve Pate	71-72-72-77—292	$1,930.00	Cut	Bob Mann	78-73—151	$1,000.00
T-9	Mark O'Meara	70-71-70-71—282	$21,500.00	64	Mike Reid	68-71-79-75—293	$1,900.00	Cut	Mark McCumber	76-75—151	$1,000.00
T-9	Payne Stewart	70-69-70-73—282	$21,500.00	65	Gibby Gilbert	72-72-74-76—294	$1,880.00	Cut	Jack Nicklaus	72-79—151	$1,000.00
T-15	John Mahaffey	71-71-70-71—283	$16,500.00	T-66	Jim Carter	73-68-76-78—295	$1,840.00	Cut	Jim Weeden	75-76—151	$1,000.00
T-15	Craig Stadler	68-73-75-67—283	$16,500.00	T-66	Hal Sutton	69-74-74-78—295	$1,840.00	Cut	Jim Albus	80-72—152	$1,000.00
T-17	Mark Calcavecchia	73-69-70-72—284	$11,500.00	T-66	Bobby Wadkins	75-69-76-75—295	$1,840.00	Cut	Russ Cochran	76-76—152	$1,000.00
T-17	Ben Crenshaw	70-71-69-74—284	$11,500.00	69	Andrew Magee	71-73-74-79—297	$1,800.00	Cut	Jim Dickson	74-78—152	$1,000.00
T-17	David Graham	70-67-73-74—284	$11,500.00	70	Doug Tewell	70-68-81-79—298	$1,800.00	Cut	Gregg Jones	76-76—152	$1,000.00
T-17	Mark McNulty	73-70-67-74—284	$11,500.00	71	Dick Mast	71-72-72-85—300	$1,800.00	Cut	Mike Malaska	77-75—152	$1,000.00
T-17	Jay Overton	68-66-76-74—284	$11,500.00	Cut	Dave Barr	74-71—145	$1,000.00	Cut	Lonnie Nielsen	78-74—152	$1,000.00
T-17	Corey Pavin	71-70-75-68—284	$11,500.00	Cut	Jim Benepe	71-74—145	$1,000.00	Cut	Michael Burke Jr.	78-75—153	$1,000.00
T-17	Nick Price	74-70-67-73—284	$11,500.00	Cut	Curt Byrum	79-66—145	$1,000.00	Cut	Gene Fieger	75-78—153	$1,000.00
T-17	Richard Zokol	70-70-74-70—284	$11,500.00	Cut	Tom Byrum	73-72—145	$1,000.00	Cut	Bob Lendzion	78-75—153	$1,000.00
T-25	Ronnie Black	71-71-70-73—285	$6,666.66	Cut	Fred Couples	74-71—145	$1,000.00	Cut	Benny Passons	78-75—153	$1,000.00
T-25	Jay Don Blake	71-73-72-69—285	$6,666.67	Cut	Seve Ballesteros	71-75—146	$1,000.00	Cut	Dana Quigley	79-74—153	$1,000.00
T-25	David Edwards	71-69-77-68—285	$6,666.67	Cut	Brad Faxon	78-68—146	$1,000.00	Cut	Bill Brodell	79-75—154	$1,000.00
T-25	Scott Hoch	74-69-68-74—285	$6,666.67	Cut	Gary Hallberg	73-73—146	$1,000.00	Cut	Mark Brooks	80-74—154	$1,000.00
T-25	Blaine McCallister	73-67-75-70—285	$6,666.66	Cut	Bob Lohr	75-71—146	$1,000.00	Cut	Darrell Kestner	78-76—154	$1,000.00
T-25	Lanny Wadkins	74-69-70-72—285	$6,666.67	Cut	Mac O'Grady	70-76—146	$1,000.00	Cut	Mike Lawrence	79-75—154	$1,000.00
T-31	Chip Beck	67-72-73-74—286	$4,842.85	Cut	Scott Simpson	74-72—146	$1,000.00	Cut	Bob Menne	77-77—154	$1,000.00
T-31	Steve Elkington	73-70-74-69—286	$4,842.86	Cut	Tim Simpson	72-74—146	$1,000.00	Cut	Ray Freeman	75-81—156	$1,000.00
T-31	Donnie Hammond	72-72-73-69—286	$4,842.86	Cut	Fulton Allem	73-74—147	$1,000.00	Cut	Mark Gurnow	78-78—156	$1,000.00
T-31	Gary Koch	72-65-78-71—286	$4,842.86	Cut	Ken Brown	74-73—147	$1,000.00	Cut	Jay Lumpkin	74-82—156	$1,000.00
T-31	Rocco Mediate	68-74-70-74—286	$4,842.86	Cut	Bob Eastwood	75-72—147	$1,000.00	Cut	David Glenz	79-78—157	$1,000.00
T-31	Curtis Strange	72-72-73-69—286	$4,842.86	Cut	Ken Green	74-73—147	$1,000.00	Cut	Lynn Janson	77-80—157	$1,000.00
T-31	Tom Watson	72-68-74-72—286	$4,842.85	Cut	Bob Groff	72-75—147	$1,000.00	Cut	John Paesani	79-78—157	$1,000.00
T-38	Isao Aoki	73-71-70-73—287	$3,211.11	Cut	Clarence Rose	73-74—147	$1,000.00	Cut	Mike San Filippo	80-77—157	$1,000.00
T-38	Tom Brannen	70-71-74-72—287	$3,211.11	Cut	Gene Sauers	74-73—147	$1,000.00	Cut	Bob Klein	81-77—158	$1,000.00
T-38	Jay Haas	73-71-71-72—287	$3,211.11	Cut	Tom Sieckmann	73-74—147	$1,000.00	Cut	Jim Sobb	78-80—158	$1,000.00
T-38	Jim Hallet	72-68-74-73—287	$3,211.12	Cut	Joey Sindelar	74-73—147	$1,000.00	Cut	Carl Poche	80-79—159	$1,000.00
T-38	Hale Irwin	74-70-72-71—287	$3,211.11	Cut	Fuzzy Zoeller	74-73—147	$1,000.00	Cut	Jeff Roth	77-82—159	$1,000.00
T-38	David Ishii	73-71-74-69—287	$3,211.11	Cut	David Frost	75-73—148	$1,000.00	Cut	Rick Vershure	78-81—159	$1,000.00
T-38	Larry Nelson	70-71-76-70—287	$3,211.11	Cut	Gil Morgan	76-72—148	$1,000.00	Cut	Don Brigham	79-83—162	$1,000.00
T-38	Calvin Peete	74-66-74-73—287	$3,211.11	Cut	Andy North	74-74—148	$1,000.00	Cut	Dwight Nevil	81-84—165	$1,000.00
T-38	Mark Wiebe	74-68-73-72—287	$3,211.11	Cut	Sam Randolph	73-75—148	$1,000.00	WD	Bill Glasson	83—83	$1,000.00
47	Peter Jacobsen	73-68-75-72—288	$2,400.00	Cut	David Thore	78-70—148	$1,000.00	WD	Ian Woosnam	78-79—157	$1,000.00
T-48	John Cook	67-69-76-77—289	$2,231.25	Cut	Lee Trevino	77-71—148	$1,000.00	WD	Hubert Green	74-69-83—226	$1,000.00
T-48	Dave Stockton	70-69-75-75—289	$2,231.25	Cut	Andy Bean	78-71—149	$1,000.00				
T-48	Bob Tway	71-71-70-77—289	$2,231.25	Cut	Woody Fitzhugh	74-75—149	$1,000.00				
T-48	Denis Watson	70-70-79-70—289	$2,231.25	Cut	Morris Hatalsky	76-73—149	$1,000.00				

1987

The 1987 PGA Championship, played at the home of the PGA of America on the difficult Champion Course at PGA National Golf Club, produced the highest winning score in PGA Championship history. A final-round of even-par 72 brought 1981 PGA Champion Larry Nelson from three strokes off the pace to tie another former champion, Lanny Wadkins, at 287. Nelson won with a par 4 on the first extra hole (No. 10) to become the 15th multiple winner of the PGA Championship.

Champion: Larry Nelson, Marietta, Ga.	
Site: PGA National GC, Palm Beach Gardens, Fla.	
Date: Aug. 6-9	**Purse:** $900,000
Par: 36-36 - 72 (7,002 Yards)	
Entries: 150 Cut at 151 74 players advanced	

	Course Avg	Under Par	At Par	Over Par	Round Leader	Low Round	Larry Nelson
Round 1:	76.6	15	7	126	Bobby Wadkins	68- Bobby Wadkins	70 - Tied 4th
Round 2:	76.6	16	11	120	L. Wadkins, Floyd	69 - Jeff Sluman	142 (72) - Tied 5th
Round 3:	74.7	14	4	56	Weibring, McCumber	67 - D.A.Weibring	215 (73) - Tied 7th
Round 4:	75.6	8	7	58	Larry Nelson	69 - Dan Pohl	287 (72) - Tied 1st
Totals:	76.15	53	29	360			

TOURNAMENT SUMMARY

Place	Name	Score	Winnings
T-1	Larry Nelson	70-72-73-72—287	$150,000.00
T-1	Lanny Wadkins	70-70-74-73—287	$90,000.00
T-3	Scott Hoch	74-74-71-69—288	$58,750.00
T-3	D.A. Weibring	73-72-67-76—288	$58,750.00
T-5	Mark McCumber	74-69-69-77—289	$37,500.00
T-5	Don Pooley	73-71-73-72—289	$37,500.00
T-7	Ben Crenshaw	72-70-74-74—290	$27,500.00
T-7	Bobby Wadkins	68-74-71-77—290	$27,500.00
9	Curtis Strange	70-76-71-74—291	$22,500.00
T-10	Seve Ballesteros	72-70-72-78—292	$17,000.00
T-10	David Frost	75-70-71-76—292	$17,000.00
T-10	Tom Kite	72-77-71-72—292	$17,000.00
T-10	Nick Price	76-71-70-75—292	$17,000.00
T-14	Curt Byrum	74-75-68-76—293	$10,750.00
T-14	David Edwards	69-75-77-72—293	$10,750.00
T-14	Ray Floyd	70-70-73-80—293	$10,750.00
T-14	Dan Pohl	71-78-75-69—293	$10,750.00
T-14	Jeff Sluman	72-69-78-74—293	$10,750.00
T-14	Tom Watson	70-79-73-71—293	$10,750.00
20	Peter Jacobsen	73-75-73-73—294	$8,500.00
T-21	Jim Hallet	73-78-73-71—295	$7,500.00
T-21	Bernhard Langer	70-78-77-70—295	$7,500.00
T-21	Gil Morgan	75-74-70-76—295	$7,500.00
T-24	Ken Brown	73-74-73-76—296	$5,975.00
T-24	Jack Nicklaus	76-73-74-73—296	$5,975.00
T-24	Gene Sauers	76-74-68-78—296	$5,975.00
T-24	Payne Stewart	72-75-75-74—296	$5,975.00
T-28	Ronnie Black	76-70-76-75—297	$4,383.34
T-28	Bobby Clampett	71-72-77-77—297	$4,383.33
T-28	Russ Cochran	73-76-69-79—297	$4,383.34
T-28	John Cook	76-70-72-79—297	$4,383.33
T-28	Brad Fabel	73-73-77-74—297	$4,383.33
T-28	Nick Faldo	73-73-77-74—297	$4,383.34
T-28	Jay Haas	74-70-76-77—297	$4,383.33
T-28	Bruce Lietzke	75-76-74-72—297	$4,383.33
T-28	Roger Maltbie	74-72-75-76—297	$4,383.33
T-28	Chris Perry	75-75-74-73—297	$4,383.34
T-28	Craig Stadler	75-72-75-75—297	$4,383.33
T-28	Hal Sutton	73-74-74-76—297	$4,383.33
T-40	Phil Blackmar	74-72-80-72—298	$3,400.00
T-40	Denis Watson	76-75-72-75—298	$3,400.00
T-40	Robert Wrenn	75-72-76-75—298	$3,400.00
T-43	Bobby Cole	71-74-75-79—299	$3,050.00
T-43	Buddy Gardner	75-74-79-71—299	$3,050.00
T-43	Mac O'Grady	78-70-71-80—299	$3,050.00
T-43	Tim Simpson	71-70-81-77—299	$3,050.00
T-47	Bob Betley	72-79-77-72—300	$2,400.00
T-47	Tom Byrum	79-72-76-73—300	$2,400.00
T-47	T.C. Chen	76-75-76-73—300	$2,400.00
T-47	Fred Funk	69-79-79-73—300	$2,400.00
T-47	Donnie Hammond	76-74-79-71—300	$2,400.00

Place	Name	Score	Winnings
T-47	Tom Purtzer	75-73-81-71—300	$2,400.00
T-47	Mike Reid	71-79-74-76—300	$2,400.00
T-47	Scott Simpson	78-73-76-73—300	$2,400.00
T-47	Bob Tway	78-71-76-75—300	$2,400.00
T-56	Chip Beck	75-74-72-80—301	$1,856.00
T-56	Hubert Green	74-73-80-74—301	$1,856.00
T-56	Morris Hatalsky	76-75-75-75—301	$1,856.00
T-56	Lonnie Nielsen	78-73-74-76—301	$1,856.00
T-56	Mike Sullivan	73-72-74-82—301	$1,856.00
T-61	Steve Jones	72-75-74-81—302	$1,740.00
T-61	Steve Pate	76-73-76-77—302	$1,740.00
T-61	Jim Woodward	79-72-69-82—302	$1,740.00
64	Fuzzy Zoeller	76-71-76-80—303	$1,700.00
T-65	Andy Bean	73-78-76-79—306	$1,650.00
T-65	John Mahaffey	77-72-77-80—306	$1,650.00
T-65	Arnold Palmer	76-75-79-76—306	$1,650.00
T-65	Mark Wiebe	78-73-75-80—306	$1,650.00
69	Ray Freeman	71-77-74-85—307	$1,600.04
70	Greg Norman	73-78-79-79—309	$1,600.03
71	Lindy Miller	73-78-82-78—311	$1,600.02
72	John Jackson	77-74-84-78—313	$1,600.01
73	Lon Hinkle	74-76-79-89—318	$1,600.00
Cut	Tommy Nakajima	78-74—152	$1,000.00
Cut	J.C. Snead	73-79—152	$1,000.00
Cut	Danny Edwards	77-76—153	$1,000.00
Cut	Brad Faxon	77-76—153	$1,000.00
Cut	Ernie Gonzalez	77-76—153	$1,000.00
Cut	Andy North	75-78—153	$1,000.00
Cut	Jack Seltzer	78-75—153	$1,000.00
Cut	Tom Brannen	76-78—154	$1,000.00
Cut	Fred Couples	80-74—154	$1,000.00
Cut	Gibby Gilbert	75-79—154	$1,000.00
Cut	David Graham	79-75—154	$1,000.00
Cut	Blaine McCallister	74-80—154	$1,000.00
Cut	Jim Thorpe	75-79—154	$1,000.00
Cut	Fred Wadsworth	78-76—154	$1,000.00
Cut	Larry Gilbert	74-81—155	$1,000.00
Cut	Ken Green	75-80—155	$1,000.00
Cut	Steve Heckel	76-79—155	$1,000.00
Cut	Jim Kallam	79-76—155	$1,000.00
Cut	Mark O'Meara	77-78—155	$1,000.00
Cut	George Burns	73-83—156	$1,000.00
Cut	Rodger Davis	79-77—156	$1,000.00
Cut	Mark Hayes	75-81—156	$1,000.00
Cut	Larry Mize	75-81—156	$1,000.00
Cut	Jose Maria Olazabal	79-77—156	$1,000.00
Cut	Tony Sills	81-75—156	$1,000.00
Cut	Howard Twitty	79-77—156	$1,000.00
Cut	Steve Veriato	76-80—156	$1,000.00
Cut	David Glenz	77-80—157	$1,000.00
Cut	Mike Hulbert	73-84—157	$1,000.00

Place	Name	Score	Winnings
Cut	Davis Love III	74-83—157	$1,000.00
Cut	Corey Pavin	78-79—157	$1,000.00
Cut	Wheeler Stewart	80-77—157	$1,000.00
Cut	Doug Tewell	77-80—157	$1,000.00
Cut	Dan Forsman	78-80—158	$1,000.00
Cut	Kenny Knox	80-78—158	$1,000.00
Cut	Wayne Levi	76-82—158	$1,000.00
Cut	Pat McGowan	78-80—158	$1,000.00
Cut	Peter Oakley	83-75—158	$1,000.00
Cut	Dana Quigley	79-79—158	$1,000.00
Cut	Tom Wargo	84-74—158	$1,000.00
Cut	Paul Azinger	82-77—159	$1,000.00
Cut	Mark Calcavecchia	79-80—159	$1,000.00
Cut	Joey Sindelar	80-79—159	$1,000.00
Cut	Dave Stockton	79-80—159	$1,000.00
Cut	Isao Aoki	82-78—160	$1,000.00
Cut	Keith Clearwater	85-75—160	$1,000.00
Cut	Rick Fehr	82-78—160	$1,000.00
Cut	Gary Hallberg	74-86—160	$1,000.00
Cut	Jodie Mudd	85-76—161	$1,000.00
Cut	Don Padgett	81-80—161	$1,000.00
Cut	Clarence Rose	81-80—161	$1,000.00
Cut	Mike San Filippo	80-81—161	$1,000.00
Cut	Ian Woosnam	86-75—161	$1,000.00
Cut	Lennie Clements	86-76—162	$1,000.00
Cut	Ted Goin	82-80—162	$1,000.00
Cut	Bob Lendzion	78-84—162	$1,000.00
Cut	Dwight Nevil	85-77—162	$1,000.00
Cut	Rick Acton	79-85—164	$1,000.00
Cut	Bob Groff	83-81—164	$1,000.00
Cut	Bob Lohr	75-89—164	$1,000.00
Cut	Scott Oulds	79-85—164	$1,000.00
Cut	Jay Overton	81-83—164	$1,000.00
Cut	Tom Tatum	83-81—164	$1,000.00
Cut	David Gosiewski	88-77—165	$1,000.00
Cut	Bruce Lehnhard	84-82—166	$1,000.00
Cut	Mike Schuchart	82-84—166	$1,000.00
Cut	Jeff Bailey	84-84—168	$1,000.00
Cut	Paul Ryiz	84-84—168	$1,000.00
Cut	Tony Milam	83-87—170	$1,000.00
Cut	Jim Petralia	91-80—171	$1,000.00
Cut	Jack Kiefer	84-88—172	$1,000.00
Cut	Dick Goetz	86-87—173	$1,000.00
Cut	Jack Mckelvey	83-90—173	$1,000.00
DQ	James Blair		$1,000.00
WD	Calvin Peete	75—75	$1,000.00
WD	Johnny Miller	76—76	$1,000.00
WD	Mark McNulty	73-73-75—221	$1,000.00

1986

Bob Tway became the first player in modern history to win the PGA Championship with a birdie on the 72nd hole when he holed a shot from a greenside bunker. The Tour sophomore began the final round four strokes behind Greg Norman, who led the first three rounds. Tway, who shot a third-round Championship record-tying 64, caught Norman on the back nine, shooting a closing 1-under-par 70 to the Australian's 76. Club professional Lonnie Nielsen of East Aurora, N.Y., tied for 11th at 284.

Champion: Bob Tway, Edmond, Okla.		
Site: Inverness Club, Toledo, Ohio		
Date: Aug. 7-10		**Purse:** $801,100
Par: 35-36 - 71 (6,982 Yards)		
Entries: 150	Cut at 146	73 players advanced

	Course Avg	Under Par	At Par	Over Par	Round Leader	Low Round	Bob Tway
Round 1:	73.2	24	19	105	Greg Norman	65 - Greg Norman	72 - Tied 44th
Round 2:	73.9	23	12	115	Greg Norman	67 - P. Stewart, J. Thorpe, M. Wiebe	142 (70) - Tied 17th
Round 3:	71.9	20	9	44	Greg Norman	64 - Bob Tway	206 (64) - 2nd
Round 4:	73.4	9	12	51	Bob Tway	67 - David Graham	276 (70) - 1st
Totals:	73.32	76	52	315			

TOURNAMENT SUMMARY

Place	Name	Score	Winnings	Place	Name	Score	Winnings	Place	Name	Score	Winnings
1	Bob Tway	72-70-64-70—276	$140,000.00	T-47	Mark Wiebe	75-67-72-77—291	$2,250.00	Cut	John Mahaffey	71-78—149	$1,000.00
2	Greg Norman	65-68-69-76—278	$80,000.00	T-53	Andy Bean	74-70-72-76—292	$1,740.42	Cut	Gil Morgan	77-72—149	$1,000.00
3	Peter Jacobsen	68-70-70-71—279	$60,000.00	T-53	Phil Blackmar	67-73-79-73—292	$1,740.41	Cut	Peter Oakley	72-77—149	$1,000.00
4	D.A. Weibring	71-72-68-69—280	$42,865.00	T-53	John Cook	71-72-75-74—292	$1,740.42	Cut	Manuelo Pinero	76-73—149	$1,000.00
T-5	Bruce Lietzke	69-71-70-71—281	$32,500.00	T-53	Bob Gilder	69-75-75-73—292	$1,740.42	Cut	Curtis Strange	74-75—149	$1,000.00
T-5	Payne Stewart	70-67-72-72—281	$32,500.00	T-53	Jay Haas	69-77-74-72—292	$1,740.42	Cut	Seve Ballesteros	74-76—150	$1,000.00
T-7	David Graham	75-69-71-67—282	$20,833.33	T-53	Mark McCumber	71-74-68-79—292	$1,740.42	Cut	Gary Hardin	77-73—150	$1,000.00
T-7	Mike Hulbert	69-68-74-71—282	$20,833.34	T-53	Larry Mize	69-76-75-72—292	$1,740.41	Cut	Lynn Janson	74-76—150	$1,000.00
T-7	Jim Thorpe	71-67-73-71—282	$20,833.33	T-53	Steve Pate	76-69-71-76—292	$1,740.42	Cut	Kenny Knox	74-76—150	$1,000.00
10	Doug Tewell	73-71-68-71—283	$15,000.00	T-53	Clarence Rose	73-71-72-76—292	$1,740.41	Cut	Bob Lohr	74-76—150	$1,000.00
T-11	Ben Crenshaw	72-73-72-67—284	$12,000.00	T-53	Joey Sindelar	74-72-73-73—292	$1,740.42	Cut	Pat McGowan	76-74—150	$1,000.00
T-11	Donnie Hammond	70-71-68-75—284	$12,000.00	T-53	Dave Stockton	70-75-74-73—292	$1,740.42	Cut	Tim Simpson	73-77—150	$1,000.00
T-11	Lonnie Nielsen	73-69-72-70—284	$12,000.00	T-53	Mike Sullivan	72-73-74-73—292	$1,740.41	Cut	Larry Webb	76-74—150	$1,000.00
T-11	Lee Trevino	71-74-69-70—284	$12,000.00	65	James Blair	72-74-72-75—293	$1,600.00	Cut	Jim White	75-75—150	$1,000.00
T-11	Lanny Wadkins	71-75-70-68—284	$12,000.00	66	Gary Koch	68-77-74-75—294	$1,590.00	Cut	Ken Allard	75-76—151	$1,000.00
T-16	Chip Beck	71-73-71-70—285	$8,500.00	67	Lennie Clements	71-75-72-77—295	$1,580.00	Cut	Paul Azinger	72-79—151	$1,000.00
T-16	Jack Nicklaus	70-68-72-75—285	$8,500.00	68	David Edwards	72-69-76-79—296	$1,570.00	Cut	Bill Schumaker	74-77—151	$1,000.00
T-16	Don Pooley	71-74-69-71—285	$8,500.00	69	Bob Murphy	73-73-74-77—297	$1,560.00	Cut	Rick Vershure	75-76—151	$1,000.00
T-16	Tony Sills	71-72-69-73—285	$8,500.00	70	Ken Brown	73-73-72-80—298	$1,550.00	Cut	Ed Dougherty	74-78—152	$1,000.00
T-16	Tom Watson	72-69-72-72—285	$8,500.00	71	Denis Watson	71-74-77-77—299	$1,550.00	Cut	Danny Edwards	72-80—152	$1,000.00
T-21	Ronnie Black	68-71-74-73—286	$6,120.00	72	J.C. Snead	70-76-75-79—300	$1,550.00	Cut	Bill Glasson	79-73—152	$1,000.00
T-21	David Frost	70-73-68-75—286	$6,120.00	Cut	Jim Colbert	74-73—147	$1,000.00	Cut	Ossie Moore	76-76—152	$1,000.00
T-21	Wayne Grady	68-76-71-71—286	$6,120.00	Cut	Nick Faldo	76-71—147	$1,000.00	Cut	Jay Overton	72-80—152	$1,000.00
T-21	Corey Pavin	71-72-70-73—286	$6,120.00	Cut	Pat Fitzsimons	73-74—147	$1,000.00	Cut	Arnold Palmer	75-77—152	$1,000.00
T-21	Hal Sutton	73-71-70-72—286	$6,120.00	Cut	Ray Floyd	76-71—147	$1,000.00	Cut	Wheeler Stewart	76-76—152	$1,000.00
T-26	Ken Green	71-72-71-73—287	$4,900.00	Cut	Mark Hayes	73-74—147	$1,000.00	Cut	Leonard Thompson	79-73—152	$1,000.00
T-26	Hale Irwin	76-70-73-68—287	$4,900.00	Cut	Barry Jaeckel	73-74—147	$1,000.00	Cut	Jose Marie Canizares	72-81—153	$1,000.00
T-26	Tom Kite	72-73-71-71—287	$4,900.00	Cut	Bernhard Langer	73-74—147	$1,000.00	Cut	Jeff Foxx	78-75—153	$1,000.00
T-26	Dan Pohl	71-71-74-71—287	$4,900.00	Cut	Andrew Magee	74-73—147	$1,000.00	Cut	Nick Price	75-78—153	$1,000.00
T-30	Wayne Levi	68-73-76-71—288	$4,000.00	Cut	Mark McNulty	75-72—147	$1,000.00	Cut	Steve Veriato	72-81—153	$1,000.00
T-30	Calvin Peete	72-73-69-74—288	$4,000.00	Cut	Kevin Morris	74-73—147	$1,000.00	Cut	Robert Hoyt	77-77—154	$1,000.00
T-30	Gene Sauers	69-73-70-76—288	$4,000.00	Cut	Andy North	72-75—147	$1,000.00	Cut	Willie Wood	76-78—154	$1,000.00
T-30	Jeff Sluman	70-71-76-71—288	$4,000.00	Cut	Mark O'Meara	73-74—147	$1,000.00	Cut	Charlie Epps	77-78—155	$1,000.00
T-30	Craig Stadler	67-74-73-74—288	$4,000.00	Cut	Larry Rinker	78-69—147	$1,000.00	Cut	Dan Forsman	79-76—155	$1,000.00
T-30	Ian Woosnam	72-70-75-71—288	$4,000.00	Cut	Bob Ackerman	76-72—148	$1,000.00	Cut	Rives McBee	77-78—155	$1,000.00
T-36	Isao Aoki	73-69-74-73—289	$3,400.00	Cut	Ray Freeman	75-73—148	$1,000.00	Cut	Dwight Nevil	79-77—156	$1,000.00
T-36	Fred Couples	69-73-72-75—289	$3,400.00	Cut	Dan Halldorson	75-73—148	$1,000.00	Cut	Mike San Filippo	71-85—156	$1,000.00
T-36	Buddy Gardner	72-73-71-73—289	$3,400.00	Cut	Masahiro Kuramoto	73-75—148	$1,000.00	Cut	Roy Vucinich	76-80—156	$1,000.00
T-36	Mark Lye	72-71-70-76—289	$3,400.00	Cut	Larry Nelson	74-74—148	$1,000.00	Cut	Paul Wise	84-72—156	$1,000.00
T-36	Brett Upper	71-73-72-73—289	$3,400.00	Cut	Mac O'Grady	72-76—148	$1,000.00	Cut	Rick Acton	80-78—158	$1,000.00
T-41	Hubert Green	75-70-74-71—290	$2,850.00	Cut	Tom Purtzer	73-75—148	$1,000.00	Cut	Gary Robinson	83-75—158	$1,000.00
T-41	Scott Hoch	72-70-75-73—290	$2,850.00	Cut	Mike Schlueter	74-74—148	$1,000.00	Cut	Larry Babica	79-82—161	$1,000.00
T-41	Jodie Mudd	72-73-73-72—290	$2,850.00	Cut	Howard Twitty	72-76—148	$1,000.00	Cut	Bob Leaver	78-83—161	$1,000.00
T-41	Mike Reid	71-73-70-76—290	$2,850.00	Cut	Fuzzy Zoeller	73-75—148	$1,000.00	Cut	Gary Ostrega	77-84—161	$1,000.00
T-41	Scott Simpson	70-70-75-75—290	$2,850.00	Cut	Scott Bess	74-75—149	$1,000.00	Cut	Gregg Jones	79-83—162	$1,000.00
T-41	Bobby Wadkins	69-74-70-77—290	$2,850.00	Cut	George Burns	73-76—149	$1,000.00	Cut	Ron Wells	84-79—163	$1,000.00
T-47	Dave Barr	71-73-73-74—291	$2,250.00	Cut	T.M. Chen	75-74—149	$1,000.00	Cut	Paul Way	82-84—166	$1,000.00
T-47	Mike Donald	74-69-73-75—291	$2,250.00	Cut	Howard Clark	72-77—149	$1,000.00	WD	Johnny Miller	72-71-73—216	$1,000.00
T-47	Davis Love III	70-72-72-77—291	$2,250.00	Cut	David Duschane	75-74—149	$1,000.00				
T-47	Roger Maltbie	73-70-74-74—291	$2,250.00	Cut	Brad Faxon	77-72—149	$1,000.00				
T-47	Tommy Nakajima	71-73-71-76—291	$2,250.00	Cut	Larry Gilbert	73-76—149	$1,000.00				

PGA CHAMPIONSHIP SUMMARIES

1985

Former U.S. Open Champion Hubert Green returned from virtual oblivion to out-duel defending champion Lee Trevino at Cherry Hills Country Club in Englewood, Colo. With rounds of 66 and 68, Trevino led at the midway point, but with closing rounds of 70 and 72, Green overtook Trevino for a two-stroke victory.

Champion: Hubert Green, Birmingham, Ala.
Site: Cherry Hills CC, Englewood, Colo.
Date: Aug. 8-11 **Purse:** $702,000
Par: 35-36 - 71 (7,089 Yards)
Entries: 149 Cut at 147 76 players advanced

	Course Avg	Under Par	At Par	Over Par	Round Leader	Low Round	Hubert Green
Round 1:	73.0	31	20	98	Doug Tewell	64 - Doug Tewell	67 - Tied 6th
Round 2:	74.9	14	9	123	Lee Trevino	65 - Fred Couples	136 (69) - Tied 3rd
Round 3:	74.1	6	6	64	Hubert Green	65 - Nick Price	206 (70) - 1st
Round 4:	72.5	24	6	46	Hubert Green	65 - Tze-Ming Chen	278 (72) - 1st
Totals:	73.75	75	41	331			

TOURNAMENT SUMMARY

Place	Name	Score	Winnings	Place	Name	Score	Winnings	Place	Name	Score	Winnings
1	Hubert Green	67-69-70-72—278	$125,000.00	T-51	Ed Fiori	70-76-76-71—293	$1,905.00	Cut	Gary Ostrega	72-78—150	$1,000.00
2	Lee Trevino	66-68-75-71—280	$75,000.00	T-51	Lon Hinkle	70-75-76-72—293	$1,905.00	Cut	Larry Rinker	75-75—150	$1,000.00
T-3	Andy Bean	71-70-72-68—281	$42,500.00	T-51	Howard Twitty	70-77-74-72—293	$1,905.00	Cut	Loren Roberts	75-75—150	$1,000.00
T-3	T. M. Chen	69-76-71-65—281	$42,500.00	T-54	Nick Faldo	70-77-73-74—294	$1,764.00	Cut	Clarence Rose	72-78—150	$1,000.00
5	Nick Price	73-73-65-71—282	$25,000.00	T-54	Bill Glasson	71-76-74-73—294	$1,764.00	Cut	Mark Wiebe	71-79—150	$1,000.00
T-6	Fred Couples	70-65-76-72—283	$17,125.00	T-54	Morris Hatalsky	68-74-72-80—294	$1,764.00	Cut	Ken Allard	74-77—151	$1,000.00
T-6	Buddy Gardner	73-73-70-67—283	$17,125.00	T-54	Brett Upper	72-74-73-75—294	$1,764.00	Cut	Steve Benson	71-80—151	$1,000.00
T-6	Corey Pavin	66-75-73-69—283	$17,125.00	T-54	Fuzzy Zoeller	71-73-75-75—294	$1,764.00	Cut	Scott Bess	77-74—151	$1,000.00
T-6	Tom Watson	67-70-74-72—283	$17,125.00	T-59	Ben Crenshaw	73-72-75-75—295	$1,661.66	Cut	John Godwin	74-77—151	$1,000.00
T-10	Peter Jacobsen	66-71-75-72—284	$12,625.00	T-59	Gary Hallberg	73-74-74-74—295	$1,661.67	Cut	Bob Lohr	69-82—151	$1,000.00
T-10	Lanny Wadkins	70-69-73-72—284	$12,625.00	T-59	Dave Stockton	72-72-77-74—295	$1,661.67	Cut	Pat McGowan	73-78—151	$1,000.00
T-12	Scott Hoch	70-73-73-69—285	$9,016.67	T-62	Mike Donald	73-72-80-71—296	$1,600.00	Cut	Mac O'Grady	76-75—151	$1,000.00
T-12	Tom Kite	69-75-71-70—285	$9,016.66	T-62	Bob Murphy	73-71-80-72—296	$1,600.00	Cut	Tim Simpson	78-73—151	$1,000.00
T-12	Dan Pohl	72-74-69-70—285	$9,016.67	T-62	Don Pooley	70-71-76-79—296	$1,600.00	Cut	Russ Cochran	75-77—152	$1,000.00
T-12	Scott Simpson	72-68-72-73—285	$9,016.67	T-65	Phil Blackmar	71-74-83-70—298	$1,536.00	Cut	Dan Halldorson	75-77—152	$1,000.00
T-12	Payne Stewart	72-72-73-68—285	$9,016.66	T-65	Arnold Palmer	75-72-75-76—298	$1,536.00	Cut	Drue Johnson	74-78—152	$1,000.00
T-12	Doug Tewell	64-72-77-72—285	$9,016.67	T-65	Ron Streck	70-76-77-75—298	$1,536.00	Cut	Bob Leaver	78-74—152	$1,000.00
T-18	Bob Gilder	73-70-74-69—286	$6,600.00	T-65	Hal Sutton	69-75-76-78—298	$1,536.00	Cut	Rick Osberg	73-79—152	$1,000.00
T-18	Wayne Levi	72-69-74-71—286	$6,600.00	T-65	D.A. Weibring	72-71-77-78—298	$1,536.00	Cut	Tony Sills	73-79—152	$1,000.00
T-18	Bruce Lietzke	70-74-72-70—286	$6,600.00	T-70	Mark McNulty	74-73-77-75—299	$1,500.00	Cut	John Jackson	76-77—153	$1,000.00
T-18	Calvin Peete	69-72-75-70—286	$6,600.00	T-70	Mike Reid	72-75-75-77—299	$1,500.00	Cut	Lynn Janson	76-77—153	$1,000.00
T-18	Craig Stadler	72-73-74-67—286	$6,600.00	72	Robert Hoyt	73-74-76-77—300	$1,500.00	Cut	Jack Lewis	80-73—153	$1,000.00
T-23	T.C. Chen	73-74-74-66—287	$5,260.00	T-73	Kevin Morris	72-74-78-77—301	$1,500.00	Cut	Tommy Nakajima	73-80—153	$1,000.00
T-23	John Mahaffey	74-73-71-69—287	$5,260.00	T-73	Al Geiberger	74-73-80-75—302	$1,500.00	Cut	Jack Seltzer	71-82—153	$1,000.00
T-23	Larry Mize	71-70-73-73—287	$5,260.00	T-73	David Glenz	75-72-76-79—302	$1,500.00	Cut	Curtis Strange	77-76—153	$1,000.00
T-23	Larry Nelson	70-74-71-72—287	$5,260.00	76	Mike Smith	71-76-83-75—305	$1,500.00	Cut	Brien Charter	73-81—154	$1,000.00
T-23	Willie Wood	71-73-74-69—287	$5,260.00	Cut	George Burns	72-76—148	$1,000.00	Cut	Laurie Hammer	74-80—154	$1,000.00
T-28	Roger Maltbie	69-73-72-74—288	$4,300.00	Cut	Ed Dougherty	73-75—148	$1,000.00	Cut	Vance Heafner	80-74—154	$1,000.00
T-28	Gil Morgan	69-77-72-70—288	$4,300.00	Cut	Bob Eastwood	72-76—148	$1,000.00	Cut	Bob Lendzion	75-79—154	$1,000.00
T-28	Mark O'Meara	71-76-71-70—288	$4,300.00	Cut	Greg Norman	75-73—148	$1,000.00	Cut	Chip Beck	75-80—155	$1,000.00
T-28	Joey Sindelar	71-75-71-71—288	$4,300.00	Cut	Andy North	72-76—148	$1,000.00	Cut	Ralph Landrum	76-79—155	$1,000.00
T-32	Seve Ballesteros	73-72-68-76—289	$3,408.33	Cut	Gary Player	72-76—148	$1,000.00	Cut	Bob L. Smith	82-73—155	$1,000.00
T-32	David Graham	75-70-69-75—289	$3,408.33	Cut	Victor Regalado	75-73—148	$1,000.00	Cut	Bobby Heins	78-78—156	$1,000.00
T-32	Donnie Hammond	71-76-73-69—289	$3,408.34	Cut	Jack Renner	72-76—148	$1,000.00	Cut	Benny Passons	75-81—156	$1,000.00
T-32	Hale Irwin	71-73-72-73—289	$3,408.33	Cut	Bob Ackerman	77-72—149	$1,000.00	Cut	Jim Albus	76-81—157	$1,000.00
T-32	Bernhard Langer	69-72-76-72—289	$3,408.33	Cut	Jim Colbert	72-77—149	$1,000.00	Cut	Tommy Aycock	77-80—157	$1,000.00
T-32	Jack Nicklaus	66-75-74-74—289	$3,408.34	Cut	Keith Fergus	72-77—149	$1,000.00	Cut	Bill Schumaker	75-82—157	$1,000.00
T-38	Dave Barr	71-74-72-73—290	$2,950.00	Cut	Ray Floyd	74-75—149	$1,000.00	Cut	Gary Koch	83-75—158	$1,000.00
T-38	Jay Haas	71-75-74-70—290	$2,950.00	Cut	Dan Forsman	74-75—149	$1,000.00	Cut	Jim O'Hern	79-79—158	$1,000.00
T-40	Woody Blackburn	72-71-74-74—291	$2,500.00	Cut	David Frost	78-71—149	$1,000.00	Cut	Craig Watson	77-81—158	$1,000.00
T-40	Frank Conner	71-73-72-75—291	$2,500.00	Cut	Larry Gilbert	71-78—149	$1,000.00	Cut	Brad Faxon	78-82—160	$1,000.00
T-40	Bill Kratzert	72-71-78-70—291	$2,500.00	Cut	Mark Gurnow	75-74—149	$1,000.00	Cut	Geoff Hensley	78-82—160	$1,000.00
T-40	Bobby Nichols	75-71-75-70—291	$2,500.00	Cut	Gregg Jones	73-76—149	$1,000.00	Cut	Ron Wells	81-79—160	$1,000.00
T-40	Tim Norris	71-70-74-76—291	$2,500.00	Cut	Steve Veriato	72-77—149	$1,000.00	Cut	Gary Head	81-80—161	$1,000.00
T-40	Mark Pfeil	70-70-74-77—291	$2,500.00	Cut	Jim White	73-76—149	$1,000.00	Cut	Michael Harrigan	78-85—163	$1,000.00
T-40	Denis Watson	74-73-74-70—291	$2,500.00	Cut	Paul Azinger	74-76—150	$1,000.00	Cut	Ross Randall	83-83—166	$1,000.00
T-47	George Archer	72-71-73-76—292	$2,075.00	Cut	Ronnie Black	76-74—150	$1,000.00	WD	Mark McCumber	70—70	$1,000.00
T-47	Danny Edwards	67-76-73-76—292	$2,075.00	Cut	Rex Caldwell	71-79—150	$1,000.00	WD	Bobby Wadkins	72—72	$1,000.00
T-47	Mark Lye	70-72-77-73—292	$2,075.00	Cut	Tim Collins	75-75—150	$1,000.00	WD	Rick Werner	87—87	$1,000.00
T-47	David Ogrin	76-70-76-70—292	$2,075.00	Cut	Johnny Miller	77-73—150	$1,000.00				

1984

Three former PGA Champions, Lee Trevino (age 44), Gary Player (48), and Lanny Wadkins (35), staged one of the most exciting Championships in PGA Championship history. Wadkins tied for the first-day lead with 1982 winner Raymond Floyd and Mike Reid with a 4-under-par 68, and tied for the second-round lead at 137 with Trevino and Player. Player leaped into contention with a 63, the lowest (9-under-par) single round in PGA Championship history.

Trevino, wielding a hot putter he purchased a few weeks earlier in Holland, took the lead on Saturday with a 67 and on Sunday turned back every bid Wadkins and Player could offer until he walked off the 72nd green with a four-shot victory at 273.

Champion:	Lee Trevino, Jupiter Island, Fla.
Site:	Shoal Creek CC, Birmingham, Ala.
Date: Aug. 16-19	**Purse:** $700,300
Par:	35-36 - 71 (7,089 Yards)
Entries: 149	Cut at 148 70 players advanced

	Course Avg	Under Par	At Par	Over Par	Round Leader	Low Round	Lee Trevino
Round 1:	74.9	29	12	107		68 - L. Wadkins, R. Floyd, M. Reid	69 - Tied 4th
Round 2:	74.3	31	18	98	L. Trevino, L. Wadkins	63 - Gary Player	137 (68) - Tied 1st
Round 3:	72.7	24	9	37	Lee Trevino	64 - Hal Sutton	204 (67) - 1st
Round 4:	72.2	31	8	31	Lee Trevino	67 - R. Cochran, C. Pavin, F. Couples	273 (69) - 1st
Totals:	73.91	115	47	273			

TOURNAMENT SUMMARY

Place	Name	Score	Winnings	Place	Name	Score	Winnings	Place	Name	Score	Winnings
1	Lee Trevino	69-68-67-69—273	$125,000.00	T-48	Mark McCumber	73-74-73-72—292	$1,977.50	Cut	Paul Wise	76-76—152	$1,000.00
T-2	Gary Player	74-63-69-71—277	$62,500.00	T-48	Jack Renner	73-69-78-72—292	$1,977.50	Cut	Ben Crenshaw	80-73—153	$1,000.00
T-2	Lanny Wadkins	68-69-68-72—277	$62,500.00	T-48	Leonard Thompson	70-71-71-80—292	$1,977.50	Cut	Ed Fiori	78-75—153	$1,000.00
4	Calvin Peete	71-70-69-68—278	$35,000.00	T-54	Gary Koch	74-73-70-76—293	$1,777.50	Cut	Terry Florence	76-77—153	$1,000.00
5	Seve Ballesteros	70-69-70-70—279	$25,000.00	T-54	Mark Lye	74-74-73-72—293	$1,777.50	Cut	John Fought	75-78—153	$1,000.00
T-6	Gary Hallberg	69-71-68-72—280	$17,250.00	T-54	Gary McCord	73-73-76-71—293	$1,777.50	Cut	Al Geiberger	77-76—153	$1,000.00
T-6	Larry Mize	71-69-67-73—280	$17,250.00	T-54	Nick Price	73-74-71-75—293	$1,777.50	Cut	Bobby Nichols	77-76—153	$1,000.00
T-6	Scott Simpson	69-69-72-70—280	$17,250.00	58	Dave Barr	69-79-73-73—294	$1,710.00	Cut	Rick Osberg	76-77—153	$1,000.00
T-6	Hal Sutton	74-73-64-69—280	$17,250.00	T-59	Joe Inman Jr.	73-73-73-76—295	$1,661.67	Cut	Tom Purtzer	78-75—153	$1,000.00
T-10	Russ Cochran	73-68-73-67—281	$12,083.34	T-59	Larry Rinker	75-73-74-73—295	$1,661.67	Cut	Gary Robinson	78-75—153	$1,000.00
T-10	Tommy Nakajima	72-68-67-74—281	$12,083.33	T-59	Jim Thorpe	74-73-75-73—295	$1,661.66	Cut	Payne Stewart	80-73—153	$1,000.00
T-10	Victor Regalado	69-69-73-70—281	$12,083.33	T-62	Scott Bess	69-76-76-75—296	$1,600.00	Cut	Roger Ginsberg	79-75—154	$1,000.00
13	Ray Floyd	68-71-69-74—282	$10,000.00	T-62	Tony Sills	74-74-73-75—296	$1,600.00	Cut	Bob Murphy	76-78—154	$1,000.00
T-14	Hubert Green	70-74-66-73—283	$8,750.00	T-62	Joey Sindelar	72-76-73-75—296	$1,600.00	Cut	Peter Oosterhuis	76-78—154	$1,000.00
T-14	Mike Reid	68-72-72-71—283	$8,750.00	T-65	Jim Albus	75-71-74-77—297	$1,542.50	Cut	John Adams	77-78—155	$1,000.00
T-16	Andy Bean	69-75-70-70—284	$7,800.00	T-65	Bruce Lietzke	73-75-73-76—297	$1,542.50	Cut	Brien Charter	75-80—155	$1,000.00
T-16	Donnie Hammond	70-69-71-74—284	$7,800.00	T-65	Roger Maltbie	72-75-76-74—297	$1,542.50	Cut	Jim Dent	78-77—155	$1,000.00
T-18	Peter Jacobsen	70-72-72-71—285	$7,050.00	T-65	Mike Sullivan	76-72-79-70—297	$1,542.50	Cut	Jim King	75-80—155	$1,000.00
T-18	Craig Stadler	71-73-73-68—285	$7,050.00	69	D.A. Weibring	76-72-74-76—298	$1,510.00	Cut	Jerry Pate	77-78—155	$1,000.00
T-20	Fred Couples	72-72-75-67—286	$6,030.00	70	Lon Hinkle	74-72-72-81—299	$1,500.00	Cut	Mike San Filippo	75-80—155	$1,000.00
T-20	Nick Faldo	69-73-74-70—286	$6,030.00	Cut	Lee Elder	75-74—149	$1,000.00	Cut	Wheeler Stewart	78-77—155	$1,000.00
T-20	Keith Fergus	72-72-72-70—286	$6,030.00	Cut	John Elliott	77-72—149	$1,000.00	Cut	Ron Streck	79-76—155	$1,000.00
T-20	John Mahaffey	72-72-72-70—286	$6,030.00	Cut	Laurie Hammer	75-74—149	$1,000.00	Cut	John Dahl	79-77—156	$1,000.00
T-20	Corey Pavin	73-72-74-67—286	$6,030.00	Cut	Lynn Janson	72-77—149	$1,000.00	Cut	Charlie Epps	78-78—156	$1,000.00
T-25	Chip Beck	69-77-70-71—287	$4,506.25	Cut	Gavin Levenson	78-71—149	$1,000.00	Cut	Bob Ford	77-79—156	$1,000.00
T-25	Rex Caldwell	71-71-74-71—287	$4,506.25	Cut	Gil Morgan	70-79—149	$1,000.00	Cut	David Glenz	81-75—156	$1,000.00
T-25	Jim Colbert	71-72-74-70—287	$4,506.25	Cut	Jim Nelford	73-76—149	$1,000.00	Cut	Robert Hoyt	80-76—156	$1,000.00
T-25	Hale Irwin	71-70-74-72—287	$4,506.25	Cut	Larry Nelson	72-77—149	$1,000.00	Cut	Jimmy Wright	79-77—156	$1,000.00
T-25	Jack Nicklaus	77-70-71-69—287	$4,506.25	Cut	Clarence Rose	76-73—149	$1,000.00	Cut	Bobby Mitchell	79-78—157	$1,000.00
T-25	Mark O'Meara	75-69-71-72—287	$4,506.25	Cut	Jim Simons	74-75—149	$1,000.00	Cut	Marty Bohen	81-77—158	$1,000.00
T-25	Tim Simpson	73-70-72-72—287	$4,506.25	Cut	Isao Aoki	77-73—150	$1,000.00	Cut	Phil Hancock	81-77—158	$1,000.00
T-25	Doug Tewell	72-71-71-73—287	$4,506.25	Cut	Brad Bryant	76-74—150	$1,000.00	Cut	J.C. Snead	81-77—158	$1,000.00
33	Denis Watson	73-68-74-73—288	$3,600.00	Cut	Tom Jenkins	75-75—150	$1,000.00	Cut	Curtis Strange	79-79—158	$1,000.00
T-34	Ronnie Black	74-70-74-71—289	$3,316.67	Cut	Richard Karbowski	74-76—150	$1,000.00	Cut	Larry Webb	76-82—158	$1,000.00
T-34	Tom Kite	74-72-74-69—289	$3,316.66	Cut	Pat McGowan	76-74—150	$1,000.00	Cut	Gary Wilkins	79-79—158	$1,000.00
T-34	Don Pooley	70-73-75-71—289	$3,316.67	Cut	Tim Norris	76-74—150	$1,000.00	Cut	Gary Balleitt	79-80—159	$1,000.00
T-37	David Edwards	72-71-72-75—290	$3,050.00	Cut	Tom Weiskopf	74-76—150	$1,000.00	Cut	Doug Steffen	81-78—159	$1,000.00
T-37	Bob Gilder	70-74-73-73—290	$3,050.00	Cut	T.C. Chen	83-68—151	$1,000.00	Cut	Gary Gant	79-81—160	$1,000.00
T-39	George Cadle	74-71-73-73—291	$2,505.56	Cut	Morris Hatalsky	77-74—151	$1,000.00	Cut	Barry Holt	83-78—161	$1,000.00
T-39	Danny Edwards	72-76-72-71—291	$2,505.55	Cut	David Ogrin	78-73—151	$1,000.00	Cut	Barry Jaeckel	81-81—162	$1,000.00
T-39	Jay Haas	70-69-75-77—291	$2,505.56	Cut	Don Padgett	80-71—151	$1,000.00	Cut	Dan Murphy	79-83—162	$1,000.00
T-39	Allen Miller	72-72-71-76—291	$2,505.55	Cut	Bobby Wadkins	74-77—151	$1,000.00	Cut	Jack Slocum	83-79—162	$1,000.00
T-39	Greg Norman	75-72-73-71—291	$2,505.55	Cut	George Burns	78-74—152	$1,000.00	Cut	Mac O'Grady	79-84—163	$1,000.00
T-39	Dan Pohl	71-70-73-77—291	$2,505.56	Cut	John Cook	75-77—152	$1,000.00	Cut	Tim Collins	86-78—164	$1,000.00
T-39	Dave Stockton	73-74-71-73—291	$2,505.55	Cut	Bob Eastwood	78-74—152	$1,000.00	Cut	John Calabria	82-83—165	$1,000.00
T-39	Tom Watson	74-72-74-71—291	$2,505.56	Cut	Buddy Gardner	74-78—152	$1,000.00	Cut	Dow Finsterwald	82-84—166	$1,000.00
T-39	Richard Zokol	74-74-70-73—291	$2,505.55	Cut	Wayne Levi	76-76—152	$1,000.00	Cut	Joe Carr	85-84—169	$1,000.00
T-48	Mike Donald	74-72-75-71—292	$1,977.50	Cut	Pat Lindsey	80-72—152	$1,000.00	WD	Johnny Miller	75—75	$1,000.00
T-48	David Graham	71-72-80-69—292	$1,977.50	Cut	Arnold Palmer	79-73—152	$1,000.00				
T-48	Scott Hoch	75-73-70-74—292	$1,977.50	Cut	Jack Seltzer	74-78—152	$1,000.00				

1983

A brilliant 6-under-par 65 provided Hal Sutton the opening-round lead. The 1982 Rookie of the Year followed up with rounds of 66, 72 and 71 for a "wire-to-wire" victory in spite of a last-day charge by Jack Nicklaus, who added his fourth second-place PGA Championship finish to his record-tying five PGA victories. The one-stroke win led to Sutton's No. 1 money-winning year and his first PGA Player of the Year Award.

Champion: Hal Sutton, Shreveport, La.
Site: Riviera CC, Pacific Palisades, Calif.
Date: Aug. 4-7   **Purse:** $600,000
Par: 35-36 - 71 (6,946 Yards)
Entries: 150   Cut at 147   87 players advanced

	Course Avg	Under Par	At Par	Over Par	Round Leader	Low Round	Hal Sutton
Round 1:	73.3	26	12	112	Hal Sutton	65 - Hal Sutton	65 - 1st
Round 2:	73.5	30	15	105	Hal Sutton	65 - Jack Nicklaus	131 (66) - 1st
Round 3:	73.2	18	9	60	Hal Sutton	67 - Zoeller, B. Jaeckel	203 (72) - 1st
Round 4:	72.7	20	11	56	Hal Sutton	65 - Peter Jacobsen	274 (71) - 1st
Totals:	73.29	94	47	333			

TOURNAMENT SUMMARY

Place	Name	Score	Winnings
1	Hal Sutton	65-66-72-71—274	$100,000.00
2	Jack Nicklaus	73-65-71-66—275	$60,000.00
3	Peter Jacobsen	73-70-68-65—276	$40,000.00
4	Pat McGowan	68-67-73-69—277	$30,000.00
5	John Fought	67-69-71-71—278	$25,000.00
T-6	Bruce Lietzke	67-71-70-71—279	$19,000.00
T-6	Fuzzy Zoeller	72-71-67-69—279	$19,000.00
8	Dan Pohl	72-70-69-69—280	$16,000.00
T-9	Ben Crenshaw	68-66-71-77—282	$10,800.00
T-9	Jay Haas	68-72-69-73—282	$10,800.00
T-9	Mike Reid	69-71-72-70—282	$10,800.00
T-9	Scott Simpson	66-73-70-73—282	$10,800.00
T-9	Doug Tewell	74-72-69-67—282	$10,800.00
T-14	Keith Fergus	68-70-72-73—283	$6,750.00
T-14	David Graham	70-69-74-70—283	$6,750.00
T-14	Hale Irwin	72-70-73-68—283	$6,750.00
T-14	Roger Maltbie	71-71-71-70—283	$6,750.00
T-14	Jim Thorpe	68-72-74-69—283	$6,750.00
T-14	Lee Trevino	70-68-74-71—283	$6,750.00
T-20	John Cook	74-71-68-71—284	$4,750.00
T-20	Danny Edwards	67-76-71-70—284	$4,750.00
T-20	Ray Floyd	69-75-71-69—284	$4,750.00
T-23	Chip Beck	72-71-70-72—285	$3,912.50
T-23	Fred Couples	71-70-73-71—285	$3,912.50
T-23	Jerry Pate	69-72-70-74—285	$3,912.50
T-23	Don Pooley	72-68-74-71—285	$3,912.50
T-27	Seve Ballesteros	71-76-72-67—286	$3,200.00
T-27	Bobby Wadkins	73-72-74-67—286	$3,200.00
T-27	Buddy Whitten	66-70-73-77—286	$3,200.00
T-30	Andy Bean	71-73-71-72—287	$2,650.00
T-30	Bob Boyd	70-77-72-68—287	$2,650.00
T-30	Johnny Miller	72-75-73-67—287	$2,650.00
T-30	Mark Pfeil	73-71-70-73—287	$2,650.00
T-30	Jim Simons	69-75-72-71—287	$2,650.00
T-30	Tom Weiskopf	76-70-69-72—287	$2,650.00
T-36	Jim Colbert	73-66-76-73—288	$2,087.50
T-36	Larry Nelson	72-68-68-80—288	$2,087.50
T-36	Bobby Nichols	75-69-74-70—288	$2,087.50
T-36	Calvin Peete	69-71-76-72—288	$2,087.50
T-36	Bob Shearer	73-67-76-72—288	$2,087.50
T-36	Tim Simpson	76-70-70-72—288	$2,087.50
T-42	Lou Graham	73-74-70-72—289	$1,875.00
T-42	Gary Hallberg	71-75-71-72—289	$1,875.00
T-42	Barry Jaeckel	73-74-67-75—289	$1,875.00
T-42	Greg Norman	72-72-70-75—289	$1,875.00
T-42	Gary Player	74-68-73-74—289	$1,875.00
T-47	Gibby Gilbert	70-66-80-74—290	$1,730.00
T-47	Morris Hatalsky	69-75-73-73—290	$1,730.00
T-47	Vance Heafner	73-74-72-71—290	$1,730.00
T-47	Lon Hinkle	70-75-74-71—290	$1,730.00
T-47	Larry Mize	70-70-75-75—290	$1,730.00

Place	Name	Score	Winnings
T-47	Mike Nicolette	72-71-73-74—290	$1,730.00
T-47	Peter Oosterhuis	75-71-71-73—290	$1,730.00
T-47	Tom Watson	75-67-78-70—290	$1,730.00
T-55	John Adams	75-71-72-73—291	$1,610.00
T-55	George Burns	78-68-72-73—291	$1,610.00
T-55	Charles Coody	73-72-70-76—291	$1,610.00
T-55	Ed Fiori	75-69-73-74—291	$1,610.00
T-55	Gil Morgan	72-73-74-72—291	$1,610.00
T-55	Jack Renner	74-71-73-73—291	$1,610.00
T-61	Jim Nelford	72-72-76-72—292	$1,565.00
T-61	Scott Hoch	73-72-74-73—292	$1,565.00
T-63	Bruce Fleisher	74-73-74-72—293	$1,535.00
T-63	Bob Gilder	71-69-76-77—293	$1,535.00
T-63	Mark Lye	75-67-75-76—293	$1,535.00
T-63	Craig Stadler	72-73-76-72—293	$1,535.00
T-67	George Archer	70-77-74-73—294	$1,505.80
T-67	Mike Donald	71-71-76-76—294	$1,505.80
T-67	Tom Kite	72-75-73-74—294	$1,505.80
T-67	Arnold Palmer	74-73-74-73—294	$1,505.80
T-67	Nick Price	72-74-74-74—294	$1,505.80
72	T.C. Chen	72-75-79-69—295	$1,500.00
73	Larry Gilbert	71-74-76-75—296	$1,500.00
T-74	Rex Caldwell	74-73-75-75—297	$1,500.00
T-74	Pat Lindsey	74-72-80-71—297	$1,500.00
76	Ron Streck	72-73-77-76—298	$1,500.00
T-77	Bill Britton	74-73-77-76—300	$1,500.00
T-77	Bobby Heins	73-74-75-78—300	$1,500.00
T-77	Jim Logue	73-74-77-76—300	$1,500.00
T-80	Lee Elder	76-71-77-77—301	$1,500.00
T-80	Ed Sneed	74-73-75-79—301	$1,500.00
T-82	Bob Eastwood	76-70-77-79—302	$1,500.00
T-82	Allen Miller	69-78-77-78—302	$1,500.00
T-84	Robert Hoyt	71-72-80-80—303	$1,500.00
T-84	Leonard Thompson	73-74-75-81—303	$1,500.00
86	Curtis Strange	71-74-85-74—304	$1,500.00
87	Jim King	73-73-78-84—308	$1,500.00
Cut	Hubert Green	73-75—148	$1,000.00
Cut	Mark Hayes	72-76—148	$1,000.00
Cut	Bob Lendzion	74-74—148	$1,000.00
Cut	Mark O'Meara	72-76—148	$1,000.00
Cut	Jim Albus	74-75—149	$1,000.00
Cut	Gene Borek	71-78—149	$1,000.00
Cut	Brad Bryant	72-77—149	$1,000.00
Cut	Billy Casper	74-75—149	$1,000.00
Cut	Al Geiberger	74-75—149	$1,000.00
Cut	John Jackson	72-77—149	$1,000.00
Cut	John Mahaffey	77-72—149	$1,000.00
Cut	Jim Masserio	76-73—149	$1,000.00
Cut	Mark McCumber	79-70—149	$1,000.00
Cut	Andy North	75-74—149	$1,000.00
Cut	Peter Oakley	72-77—149	$1,000.00

Place	Name	Score	Winnings
Cut	Don Padgett	73-76—149	$1,000.00
Cut	Tom Purtzer	74-75—149	$1,000.00
Cut	Payne Stewart	78-71—149	$1,000.00
Cut	Paul Wise	77-72—149	$1,000.00
Cut	Mike Wynn	73-76—149	$1,000.00
Cut	Bruce Ashworth	72-78—150	$1,000.00
Cut	David Edwards	72-78—150	$1,000.00
Cut	Dan Halldorson	73-77—150	$1,000.00
Cut	Gary Koch	72-78—150	$1,000.00
Cut	Mike McCullough	72-78—150	$1,000.00
Cut	Tommy Nakajima	76-74—150	$1,000.00
Cut	Tim Norris	74-76—150	$1,000.00
Cut	Victor Regalado	71-79—150	$1,000.00
Cut	Lanny Wadkins	70-80—150	$1,000.00
Cut	D.A. Weibring	73-77—150	$1,000.00
Cut	Ed Whitman	76-74—150	$1,000.00
Cut	Isao Aoki	75-76—151	$1,000.00
Cut	Dave Barber	76-75—151	$1,000.00
Cut	Nick Faldo	74-77—151	$1,000.00
Cut	Kevin Morris	75-76—151	$1,000.00
Cut	Tom Robertson	74-77—151	$1,000.00
Cut	Jack Seltzer	77-74—151	$1,000.00
Cut	Mike Sullivan	76-75—151	$1,000.00
Cut	Tim Collins	76-76—152	$1,000.00
Cut	Bob Elliott	78-74—152	$1,000.00
Cut	John Elliott	77-75—152	$1,000.00
Cut	Richard Karbowski	78-74—152	$1,000.00
Cut	Vic Lipscomb	78-74—152	$1,000.00
Cut	Gary McCord	72-80—152	$1,000.00
Cut	Jack Sommers	75-77—152	$1,000.00
Cut	Dave Stockton	78-74—152	$1,000.00
Cut	Rick Werner	78-74—152	$1,000.00
Cut	Jim White	80-72—152	$1,000.00
Cut	Steve Benson	79-74—153	$1,000.00
Cut	Bobby Clampett	76-77—153	$1,000.00
Cut	Gene Littler	75-78—153	$1,000.00
Cut	Bill Rogers	81-72—153	$1,000.00
Cut	J.C. Snead	77-77—154	$1,000.00
Cut	John Gentile	79-76—155	$1,000.00
Cut	Don Maddox	79-76—155	$1,000.00
Cut	Clarence Rose	75-80—155	$1,000.00
Cut	Phil Hancock	73-83—156	$1,000.00
Cut	Thomas Gray	78-79—157	$1,000.00
Cut	Robbie Gilmore	81-79—160	$1,000.00
Cut	Jerry Barber	80-83—163	$1,000.00
Cut	Denis Husse	81-83—164	$1,000.00
Cut	Jack McConachie	82-84—166	$1,000.00
Cut	John Kirchner	87-83—170	$1,000.00

1982

Raymond Floyd opened the tournament on a broiling day with a blistering 7-under-par 63 and led for the remainder of the Championship, winning by three strokes over Lanny Wadkins. It was Floyd's second PGA Championship. The 39-year-old set the PGA Championship record of 132 for 36 holes, 200 for 54 holes and tied the 18-hole record of 63.

Champion: Raymond Floyd, Miami, Fla.
Site: Southern Hills CC, Tulsa, Okla.
Date: Aug. 5-8   **Purse:** $451,800
Par: 35-35 - 70 (6,862 Yards)
Entries: 150   Cut at 145   74 players advanced

	Course Avg	Under Par	At Par	Over Par	Round Leader	Low Round	Ray Floyd
Round 1:	73.5	17	3	130	Ray Floyd	63 - Ray Floyd	63 - 1st
Round 2:	73.2	20	14	114	Ray Floyd	66 - J. Haas, G. Morgan	132 (69) - 1st
Round 3:	71.7	12	15	47	Ray Floyd	67 - Gene Littler	200 (68) - 1st
Round 4:	72.5	17	3	54	Ray Floyd	66 - F. Couples, P. Oosterhuis	272 (72) - 1st
Totals:	73.01	66	35	345			

TOURNAMENT SUMMARY

Place	Name	Score	Winnings	Place	Name	Score	Winnings	Place	Name	Score	Winnings
1	Ray Floyd	63-69-68-72—272	$65,000.00	T-49	Tommy Valentine	73-68-70-78—289	$1,315.00	Cut	Wayne Levi	76-73—149	$650.00
2	Lanny Wadkins	71-68-69-67—275	$45,000.00	T-49	Bobby Wadkins	71-71-75-72—289	$1,315.00	Cut	Bob Menne	75-74—149	$650.00
T-3	Fred Couples	67-71-72-66—276	$27,500.00	T-54	Ed Fiori	72-71-76-71—290	$1,182.15	Cut	Larry Nelson	74-75—149	$650.00
T-3	Calvin Peete	69-70-68-69—276	$27,500.00	T-54	Gibby Gilbert	72-73-69-76—290	$1,182.14	Cut	Greg Powers	75-74—149	$650.00
T-5	Jay Haas	71-66-68-72—277	$16,000.00	T-54	Morris Hatalsky	72-73-69-76—290	$1,182.14	Cut	Tom Weiskopf	76-73—149	$650.00
T-5	Greg Norman	66-69-70-72—277	$16,000.00	T-54	Vance Heafner	68-71-76-75—290	$1,182.14	Cut	Mike Wynn	74-75—149	$650.00
T-5	Jim Simons	68-67-73-69—277	$16,000.00	T-54	Lyn Lott	70-73-72-75—290	$1,182.14	Cut	Al Geiberger	75-75—150	$650.00
8	Bob Gilder	66-68-72-72—278	$11,000.00	T-54	Roger Maltbie	71-73-72-74—290	$1,182.14	Cut	Jim King	74-76—150	$650.00
T-9	Lon Hinkle	70-68-71-71—280	$7,918.75	T-54	Mark McNulty	76-69-76-69—290	$1,182.15	Cut	Bill Kratzert	74-76—150	$650.00
T-9	Tom Kite	73-70-70-67—280	$7,918.75	T-61	Brad Bryant	74-70-71-76—291	$1,137.50	Cut	Rodney Loesch	75-75—150	$650.00
T-9	Jerry Pate	72-69-70-69—280	$7,918.75	T-61	Rex Caldwell	67-76-70-78—291	$1,137.50	Cut	Mark McCumber	74-76—150	$650.00
T-9	Tom Watson	72-69-71-68—280	$7,918.75	T-61	Jim Nelford	73-71-73-74—291	$1,137.50	Cut	Arnold Palmer	74-76—150	$650.00
13	Seve Ballesteros	71-68-69-73—281	$6,500.00	T-61	Ed Sneed	72-72-70-77—291	$1,137.50	Cut	Jack Renner	73-77—150	$650.00
T-14	Nick Faldo	67-70-73-72—282	$5,750.00	T-65	Tom Jenkins	69-71-75-77—292	$1,122.50	Cut	Gary Robinson	77-73—150	$650.00
T-14	Curtis Strange	72-70-71-69—282	$5,750.00	T-65	Jeff Mitchell	73-72-73-74—292	$1,122.50	Cut	J.C. Snead	77-73—150	$650.00
T-16	Jim Colbert	70-72-72-69—283	$4,625.00	T-67	Billy Casper	72-73-75-73—293	$1,110.00	Cut	Don Massengale	76-75—151	$650.00
T-16	Dan Halldorson	69-71-72-71—283	$4,625.00	T-67	Mark Lye	72-73-70-78—293	$1,110.00	Cut	Andy Bean	71-81—152	$650.00
T-16	Bruce Lietzke	73-71-70-69—283	$4,625.00	T-67	Don Pooley	73-71-72-77—293	$1,110.00	Cut	Bill Britton	74-78—152	$650.00
T-16	Jack Nicklaus	74-70-72-67—283	$4,625.00	T-70	Andy North	72-72-77-73—294	$1,100.00	Cut	Bobby Clampett	76-76—152	$650.00
T-16	Tom Purtzer	73-69-73-68—283	$4,625.00	T-70	Dan Pohl	71-71-73-79—294	$1,100.00	Cut	Frank Conner	73-79—152	$650.00
T-16	Craig Stadler	71-70-70-72—283	$4,625.00	72	Don Padgett	72-72-74-77—295	$1,100.00	Cut	John Calabria	79-74—153	$650.00
T-22	Danny Edwards	71-71-68-74—284	$3,600.00	73	Woody Blackburn	74-71-78-77—300	$1,100.00	Cut	Larry Gilbert	78-75—153	$650.00
T-22	Gil Morgan	76-66-68-74—284	$3,600.00	74	Lennie Clements	75-69-82-78—304	$1,100.00	Cut	Jim Marshall	77-76—153	$650.00
T-22	Peter Oosterhuis	72-72-74-66—284	$3,600.00	Cut	Chip Beck	73-73—146	$650.00	Cut	Benny Passons	79-74—153	$650.00
T-22	Mark Pfeil	68-73-76-67—284	$3,600.00	Cut	Joe Inman Jr.	73-73—146	$650.00	Cut	Bob Eastwood	77-77—154	$650.00
T-22	Ron Streck	71-72-71-70—284	$3,600.00	Cut	John Jackson	68-78—146	$650.00	Cut	Ross Randall	77-77—154	$650.00
T-22	Doug Tewell	72-70-72-70—284	$3,600.00	Cut	Don January	73-73—146	$650.00	Cut	Bruce Ashworth	74-81—155	$650.00
T-22	Leonard Thompson	72-72-71-69—284	$3,600.00	Cut	Gary Player	76-70—146	$650.00	Cut	Dick Hendrickson	76-79—155	$650.00
T-29	Mike Holland	71-73-70-71—285	$3,100.00	Cut	Tim Simpson	72-74—146	$650.00	Cut	Roger Kennedy	80-75—155	$650.00
T-29	Bill Rogers	73-71-70-71—285	$3,100.00	Cut	Dave Stockton	73-73—146	$650.00	Cut	Jack Sommers	76-79—155	$650.00
T-29	Hal Sutton	72-68-70-75—285	$3,100.00	Cut	Dick Crawford	75-72—147	$650.00	Cut	Howard Twitty	76-79—155	$650.00
T-32	Johnny Miller	76-67-73-70—286	$2,850.00	Cut	Jim Kiely	72-75—147	$650.00	Cut	Gene Ferrell	80-76—156	$650.00
T-32	Scott Simpson	71-71-75-69—286	$2,850.00	Cut	Jim Logue	77-70—147	$650.00	Cut	Robbie Gilmore	79-77—156	$650.00
T-34	George Archer	71-70-71-75—287	$2,350.00	Cut	Denis Watson	72-75—147	$650.00	Cut	Russell Helwig	77-79—156	$650.00
T-34	Miller Barber	71-74-70-72—287	$2,350.00	Cut	D.A. Weibring	75-72—147	$650.00	Cut	Vince Bizik	81-76—157	$650.00
T-34	John Cook	71-72-71-73—287	$2,350.00	Cut	Buddy Whitten	73-74—147	$650.00	Cut	Bob Moreland	80-77—157	$650.00
T-34	Mark Hayes	69-72-70-76—287	$2,350.00	Cut	Jim Booros	69-79—148	$650.00	Cut	Dave Philo	82-75—157	$650.00
T-34	Peter Jacobsen	73-70-69-75—287	$2,350.00	Cut	Dave Eichelberger	75-73—148	$650.00	Cut	Dick Smith	77-80—157	$650.00
T-34	Bob Murphy	71-74-68-74—287	$2,350.00	Cut	Steve Melnyk	72-76—148	$650.00	Cut	Dwight Nevil	80-78—158	$650.00
T-34	Bobby Nichols	73-69-74-71—287	$2,350.00	Cut	Payne Stewart	76-72—148	$650.00	Cut	Dave Ragan	80-78—158	$650.00
T-34	Jim Thorpe	72-71-73-71—287	$2,350.00	Cut	Mike Sullivan	71-77—148	$650.00	Cut	Jim Lucius	78-82—160	$650.00
T-42	Dave Barr	71-72-71-74—288	$1,642.85	Cut	Fuzzy Zoeller	74-74—148	$650.00	Cut	Joe McDermott	77-84—161	$650.00
T-42	George Burns	72-72-71-73—288	$1,642.86	Cut	Jim Albus	77-72—149	$650.00	Cut	Kevin Morris	84-77—161	$650.00
T-42	Hale Irwin	73-69-73-73—288	$1,642.86	Cut	Dave Barber	76-73—149	$650.00	Cut	James Dolan	82-82—164	$650.00
T-42	Barry Jaeckel	72-69-74-73—288	$1,642.86	Cut	Richard Bassett	73-76—149	$650.00	Cut	Gary Gant	82-83—165	$650.00
T-42	Masahiro Kuramoto	71-70-70-77—288	$1,642.85	Cut	Ben Crenshaw	73-76—149	$650.00	Cut	Jimmy Wright	81-85—166	$650.00
T-42	John Mahaffey	74-70-72-72—288	$1,642.86	Cut	Jim Dent	73-76—149	$650.00	WD	Tony Wallin	78—78	$650.00
T-42	Mike Reid	71-72-73-72—288	$1,642.86	Cut	Keith Fergus	76-73—149	$650.00	WD	Bob Shearer	79—79	$650.00
T-49	Isao Aoki	69-75-71-74—289	$1,315.00	Cut	Hubert Green	77-72—149	$650.00				
T-49	David Graham	68-71-74-76—289	$1,315.00	Cut	Gary Hallberg	77-72—149	$650.00				
T-49	Gene Littler	73-72-67-77—289	$1,315.00	Cut	Lee Harper	72-77—149	$650.00				

1981

Residing less than a half-hour from Atlanta Athletic Club, Larry Nelson leaped into the lead with his second straight 66 in the third round and cruised on to a four-stroke triumph over Fuzzy Zoeller. The 33-year-old one-time aircraft plant draftsman and Vietnam veteran began the final round with a four-stroke lead and was never challenged with his closing 1-over-par 71.

Champion: Larry Nelson, Marietta, Ga.	
Site: Atlanta Athletic Club, Duluth, Ga.	
Date: Aug. 6-9	**Purse:** $401,600
Par: 35-35 - 70 (7,070 Yards)	
Entries: 150 Cut at 147 78 players advanced	

	Course Avg	Under Par	At Par	Over Par	Round Leader	Low Round	L. Nelson
Round 1:	73.7	11	14	120	Bob Murphy	66 - B. Murphy	70 - Tied 12th
Round 2:	73.7	17	10	116	Bob Murphy	66 - L. Nelson	136 (66) - Tied 2nd
Round 3:	71.7	16	11	51	Larry Nelson	66 - L. Nelson, I. Aoki, B. Rogers	202 (66) - 1st
Round 4:	72.1	20	7	51	Larry Nelson	66 - T. Valentine, C. Strange,	273 (71) - 1st
Totals:	73.12	64	42	338		B. Gilder	

TOURNAMENT SUMMARY

Place	Name	Score	Winnings	Place	Name	Score	Winnings	Place	Name	Score	Winnings
1	Larry Nelson	70-66-66-71—273	$60,000.00	T-49	Wayne Levi	70-71-73-75—289	$912.50	Cut	Lionel Hebert	73-77—150	$550.00
2	Fuzzy Zoeller	70-68-68-71—277	$40,000.00	T-49	Gary Player	75-72-71-71—289	$912.50	Cut	Bill Kratzert	77-73—150	$550.00
3	Dan Pohl	69-67-73-69—278	$25,000.00	T-49	Jack Renner	74-70-73-72—289	$912.50	Cut	Johnny Miller	77-73—150	$550.00
T-4	Isao Aoki	75-68-66-70—279	$13,146.43	T-49	Ron Streck	69-77-75-68—289	$912.50	Cut	Scott Simpson	71-79—150	$550.00
T-4	Keith Fergus	71-71-69-68—279	$13,146.43	55	Doug Tewell	71-73-76-70—290	$825.00	Cut	Larry Gilbert	77-74—151	$550.00
T-4	Bob Gilder	74-69-70-66—279	$13,146.43	T-56	Jim Colbert	72-75-71-73—291	$810.00	Cut	Lynn Janson	75-76—151	$550.00
T-4	Tom Kite	71-67-69-72—279	$13,146.42	T-56	Tom Jenkins	73-73-73-72—291	$810.00	Cut	Gene Littler	79-72—151	$550.00
T-4	Bruce Lietzke	70-70-71-68—279	$13,146.43	T-56	Mark Lye	67-76-74-74—291	$810.00	Cut	Bruce Macdonald	75-76—151	$550.00
T-4	Jack Nicklaus	71-68-71-69—279	$13,146.43	T-56	Mark McCumber	70-74-73-74—291	$810.00	Cut	John Mahaffey	76-75—151	$550.00
T-4	Greg Norman	73-67-68-71—279	$13,146.43	T-56	Mike Sullivan	70-72-74-75—291	$810.00	Cut	Steve Benson	77-75—152	$550.00
T-11	Vance Heafner	68-70-70-72—280	$6,750.00	T-61	Danny Edwards	73-71-70-78—292	$782.50	Cut	Bruce Devlin	76-76—152	$550.00
T-11	Andy North	68-69-70-73—280	$6,750.00	T-61	John Fought	74-71-78-69—292	$782.50	Cut	Lu Hsi-Chuen	77-75—152	$550.00
T-11	Jerry Pate	71-68-70-71—280	$6,750.00	T-61	Roger Maltbie	69-78-76-69—292	$782.50	Cut	Kevin Morris	78-74—152	$550.00
T-11	Tommy Valentine	73-70-71-66—280	$6,750.00	T-61	Mike Morley	72-71-71-78—292	$782.50	Cut	Barney Thompson	78-74—152	$550.00
15	J.C. Snead	70-71-70-70—281	$5,500.00	T-61	Don Padgett	74-71-75-72—292	$782.50	Cut	Gary Wintz	76-76—152	$550.00
T-16	David Edwards	71-69-70-72—282	$4,875.00	T-61	Leonard Thompson	75-72-71-74—292	$782.50	Cut	Gene Borek	75-78—153	$550.00
T-16	Hale Irwin	71-74-68-69—282	$4,875.00	T-67	Al Geiberger	73-74-77-69—293	$760.00	Cut	Gene Ferrell	80-73—153	$550.00
18	Bob Murphy	66-69-73-75—283	$4,500.00	T-67	Barry Jaeckel	72-74-69-78—293	$760.00	Cut	Howell Fraser	76-77—153	$550.00
T-19	John Cook	72-69-70-73—284	$3,631.25	T-67	Bobby Wadkins	73-74-72-74—293	$760.00	Cut	Scott Hoch	72-81—153	$550.00
T-19	Ray Floyd	71-70-71-72—284	$3,631.25	T-70	George Burns	74-71-74-75—294	$750.00	Cut	Jumbo Ozaki	73-80—153	$550.00
T-19	Jay Haas	73-68-74-69—284	$3,631.25	T-70	Mark O'Meara	72-71-74-77—294	$750.00	Cut	John Schroeder	74-79—153	$550.00
T-19	Joe Inman Jr.	73-71-67-73—284	$3,631.25	T-70	Ed Sneed	71-75-72-76—294	$750.00	Cut	Art Silvestrome	77-76—153	$550.00
T-19	Don January	70-72-70-72—284	$3,631.25	73	George Cadle	74-72-74-75—295	$750.00	Cut	Buddy Whitten	76-77—153	$550.00
T-19	Gil Morgan	70-69-74-71—284	$3,631.25	74	Charles Coody	69-74-78-75—296	$750.00	Cut	Larry Ziegler	77-76—153	$550.00
T-19	Don Pooley	74-70-69-71—284	$3,631.25	75	John Jackson	75-70-76-77—297	$750.00	Cut	Gary Groh	76-78—154	$550.00
T-19	Tom Purtzer	70-70-73-71—284	$3,631.25	76	Arnold Palmer	74-73-74-77—298	$750.00	Cut	Jack Lewis	79-75—154	$550.00
T-27	Bobby Clampett	75-71-70-69—285	$2,850.00	77	Bruce Summerhays	73-74-75-80—302	$750.00	Cut	Jim Albus	78-77—155	$550.00
T-27	Hubert Green	71-74-71-69—285	$2,850.00	78	David Glenz	72-73-77-84—306	$750.00	Cut	Bob Ford	80-75—155	$550.00
T-27	Peter Jacobsen	74-71-71-69—285	$2,850.00	Cut	George Archer	73-75—148	$550.00	Cut	Tom Ulozas	75-80—155	$550.00
T-27	Bill Rogers	72-75-66-72—285	$2,850.00	Cut	Brad Bryant	72-76—148	$550.00	Cut	Bob Moreland	77-79—156	$550.00
T-27	Curtis Strange	73-72-74-66—285	$2,850.00	Cut	Dave Eichelberger	76-72—148	$550.00	Cut	Bobby Nichols	77-79—156	$550.00
T-27	Tom Weiskopf	71-72-72-70—285	$2,850.00	Cut	Lou Graham	71-77—148	$550.00	Cut	Jim Logue	78-79—157	$550.00
T-33	Seve Ballesteros	71-73-72-70—286	$2,250.00	Cut	Vic Lipscomb	75-73—148	$550.00	Cut	John Nichols Jr.	76-81—157	$550.00
T-33	Bob Eastwood	67-69-72-78—286	$2,250.00	Cut	Peter Oosterhuis	75-73—148	$550.00	Cut	Joe Moresco	79-79—158	$550.00
T-33	Ed Fiori	73-73-67-73—286	$2,250.00	Cut	Jim Simons	73-75—148	$550.00	Cut	Bob Nieberding	80-78—158	$550.00
T-33	Mark Hayes	74-74-68-74—286	$2,250.00	Cut	Tom Watson	75-73—148	$550.00	Cut	John Traub	77-81—158	$550.00
T-33	Greg Powers	70-70-74-72—286	$2,250.00	Cut	Al Chandler	77-72—149	$550.00	Cut	David Jimenez	74-85—159	$550.00
T-33	Lanny Wadkins	70-71-74-71—286	$2,250.00	Cut	Tim Collins	74-75—149	$550.00	Cut	Roger Kennedy	78-81—159	$550.00
T-39	Terry Diehl	72-74-71-70—287	$1,750.00	Cut	Mike Donald	79-70—149	$550.00	Cut	Gary Robinson	78-81—159	$550.00
T-39	Lon Hinkle	69-76-69-73—287	$1,750.00	Cut	Dave Haberle	76-73—149	$550.00	Cut	Dave Barber	80-80—160	$550.00
T-39	Jim Thorpe	71-72-72-72—287	$1,750.00	Cut	Gary Hallberg	75-74—149	$550.00	Cut	Gary Baker	83-79—162	$550.00
T-39	D.A. Weibring	71-74-74-68—287	$1,750.00	Cut	Laurie Hammer	75-74—149	$550.00	Cut	Terry Florence	82-80—162	$550.00
T-43	Rod Curl	75-72-69-72—288	$1,250.00	Cut	Sandy Lyle	76-73—149	$550.00	Cut	Jim Ferriell	80-84—164	$550.00
T-43	Bruce Fleisher	73-72-68-75—288	$1,250.00	Cut	Craig Stadler	72-77—149	$550.00	DQ	Cotton Dunn		$550.00
T-43	David Graham	75-69-74-70—288	$1,250.00	Cut	Bobby Walzel	74-75—149	$550.00	DQ	Lee Trevino		$550.00
T-43	Calvin Peete	74-71-74-69—288	$1,250.00	Cut	Miller Barber	71-79—150	$550.00	WD	Doug Ford	79—79	$550.00
T-43	Dave Stockton	70-75-70-73—288	$1,250.00	Cut	Dave Barr	74-76—150	$550.00	WD	Sam Snead	79—79	$550.00
T-43	Howard Twitty	74-71-74-69—288	$1,250.00	Cut	Ben Crenshaw	75-75—150	$550.00				
T-49	Rex Caldwell	68-72-71-78—289	$912.50	Cut	Gibby Gilbert	75-75—150	$550.00				
T-49	Lee Elder	75-71-74-69—289	$912.50	Cut	Phil Hancock	72-78—150	$550.00				

1980

Jack Nicklaus made PGA history by tying Walter Hagen for most PGA crowns (5) and winning by the biggest margin since the Championship switched to stroke play in 1958. With a 1-under-par 69 in the final round, Nicklaus posted a 6-under-par score of 274 for a seven-shot victory over runner-up Andy Bean.

Champion: Jack Nicklaus, North Palm Beach, Fla.
Site: Oak Hill CC, Rochester, N.Y.
Date: Aug. 7-10   **Purse:** $376,400
Par: 35-35 - 70 (6,964 Yards)
Entries: 150   Cut at 149   77 players advanced

	Course Avg	Under Par	At Par	Over Par	Round Leader	Low Round		Jack Nicklaus	
Round 1:	75.0	9	10	129	Craig Stadler	67 -	Craig Stadler	70 -	Tied 10th
Round 2:	75.4	3	6	135	Gil Morgan	66 -	Ed Sneed	139 (69) -	Tied 2nd
Round 3:	74.1	6	2	69	Jack Nicklaus	66 -	Jack Nicklaus	205 (66) -	1st
Round 4:	73.9	4	3	70	Jack Nicklaus	67 -	Tom Watson	274 (69) -	1st
Totals:	74.82	22	21	403					

TOURNAMENT SUMMARY

Place	Name	Score	Winnings
1	Jack Nicklaus	70-69-66-69—274	$60,000.00
2	Andy Bean	72-71-68-70—281	$40,000.00
T-3	Lon Hinkle	70-69-69-75—283	$22,500.00
T-3	Gil Morgan	68-70-73-72—283	$22,500.00
T-5	Curtis Strange	68-72-72-72—284	$14,500.00
T-5	Howard Twitty	68-74-71-71—284	$14,500.00
7	Lee Trevino	74-71-71-69—285	$11,000.00
T-8	Bill Rogers	71-71-72-72—286	$8,500.00
T-8	Bobby Walzel	68-76-71-71—286	$8,500.00
T-10	Terry Diehl	72-72-68-76—288	$6,000.00
T-10	Peter Jacobsen	71-73-74-70—288	$6,000.00
T-10	Jerry Pate	72-73-70-73—288	$6,000.00
T-10	Tom Watson	75-74-72-67—288	$6,000.00
T-10	Tom Weiskopf	71-73-72-72—288	$6,000.00
T-15	John Mahaffey	71-77-69-72—289	$4,375.00
T-15	Andy North	72-70-73-74—289	$4,375.00
T-17	George Archer	70-73-75-72—290	$3,900.00
T-17	Ray Floyd	70-76-71-73—290	$3,900.00
T-17	Joe Inman Jr.	72-71-75-72—290	$3,900.00
T-20	Rex Caldwell	73-70-73-75—291	$3,450.00
T-20	Rod Curl	74-71-75-71—291	$3,450.00
T-20	Tom Kite	73-70-76-72—291	$3,450.00
T-20	Bob Murphy	68-80-72-71—291	$3,450.00
T-20	Jack Newton	72-73-73-73—291	$3,450.00
T-20	Alan Tapie	74-75-69-73—291	$3,450.00
T-26	Lee Elder	70-75-74-73—292	$2,950.00
T-26	David Graham	69-75-73-75—292	$2,950.00
T-26	Gary Player	72-74-71-75—292	$2,950.00
T-26	Leonard Thompson	71-75-73-73—292	$2,950.00
T-30	Jim Colbert	73-75-77-68—293	$2,200.00
T-30	Bruce Devlin	76-73-71-73—293	$2,200.00
T-30	Bob Eastwood	72-73-73-75—293	$2,200.00
T-30	David Edwards	73-76-73-71—293	$2,200.00
T-30	Hale Irwin	69-76-74-74—293	$2,200.00
T-30	Bruce Lietzke	71-75-74-73—293	$2,200.00
T-30	Artie McNickle	71-71-76-75—293	$2,200.00
T-30	Scott Simpson	74-74-74-71—293	$2,200.00
T-30	Mike Sullivan	71-74-76-72—293	$2,200.00
T-30	Doug Tewell	73-71-75-74—293	$2,200.00
T-30	Lanny Wadkins	76-72-72-73—293	$2,200.00
T-41	Charles Coody	73-71-79-71—294	$1,300.00
T-41	Ben Crenshaw	69-74-78-73—294	$1,300.00
T-41	John Fought	72-72-76-74—294	$1,300.00
T-41	Dana Quigley	73-76-73-72—294	$1,300.00
T-41	Fuzzy Zoeller	76-73-71-74—294	$1,300.00
T-46	Gary Koch	71-71-78-75—295	$892.50
T-46	Mike Morley	71-73-76-75—295	$892.50
T-46	Don Pooley	74-75-75-71—295	$892.50
T-46	D.A. Weibring	76-73-71-75—295	$892.50
T-50	Keith Fergus	74-73-75-74—296	$796.00

Place	Name	Score	Winnings
T-50	Jay Haas	72-74-75-75—296	$796.00
T-50	Bill Kratzert	74-73-75-74—296	$796.00
T-50	Mark Pfeil	75-72-78-71—296	$796.00
T-50	J.C. Snead	74-74-78-70—296	$796.00
T-55	Bob Gilder	70-77-77-73—297	$767.50
T-55	Mike Reid	74-73-78-72—297	$767.50
T-55	Ed Sneed	80-68-72-77—297	$767.50
T-55	Craig Stadler	67-75-74-81—297	$767.50
T-59	Danny Edwards	73-73-75-77—298	$742.50
T-59	Morris Hatalsky	70-73-74-81—298	$742.50
T-59	Mark Hayes	73-75-75-75—298	$742.50
T-59	Tohru Nakamura	70-76-78-74—298	$742.50
T-59	Ron Streck	75-71-70-82—298	$742.50
T-59	Bobby Wadkins	75-74-71-78—298	$742.50
T-65	Miller Barber	74-75-73-77—299	$720.00
T-65	Dave Eichelberger	72-70-79-78—299	$720.00
T-65	Buddy Gardner	74-75-75-75—299	$720.00
T-68	Gibby Gilbert	71-73-79-77—300	$705.00
T-68	Hubert Green	74-75-76-75—300	$705.00
T-68	Johnny Miller	70-71-80-79—300	$705.00
71	Brad Bryant	78-70-74-79—301	$700.00
T-72	George Cadle	73-75-78-76—302	$700.00
T-72	Arnold Palmer	74-74-78-76—302	$700.00
74	Dewitt Weaver	75-73-77-78—303	$700.00
75	Tommy Valentine	73-71-82-79—305	$700.00
76	Victor Regalado	75-74-79-78—306	$700.00
77	Bob Byman	74-72-79-82—307	$700.00
Cut	Buddy Allin	73-77—150	$500.00
Cut	Frank Conner	72-78—150	$500.00
Cut	Doug Ford	74-76—150	$500.00
Cut	Lou Graham	77-73—150	$500.00
Cut	Dan Halldorson	78-72—150	$500.00
Cut	Jerry McGee	75-75—150	$500.00
Cut	Lonnie Nielsen	76-74—150	$500.00
Cut	Jack Renner	70-80—150	$500.00
Cut	Mike Schlueter	71-80—151	$500.00
Cut	Jim Simons	76-75—151	$500.00
Cut	Tim Simpson	79-72—151	$500.00
Cut	Mike Brannan	75-77—152	$500.00
Cut	John Calabria	77-75—152	$500.00
Cut	Lynn Janson	76-76—152	$500.00
Cut	Denny Lyons	76-76—152	$500.00
Cut	Allen Miller	77-75—152	$500.00
Cut	Tom Purtzer	74-78—152	$500.00
Cut	George Shortridge	74-78—152	$500.00
Cut	Tommy Aycock	77-76—153	$500.00
Cut	Randy Glover	76-77—153	$500.00
Cut	Wayne Levi	74-79—153	$500.00
Cut	Jeff Mitchell	77-76—153	$500.00
Cut	Larry Nelson	79-74—153	$500.00

Place	Name	Score	Winnings
Cut	Peter Oosterhuis	75-78—153	$500.00
Cut	Charles Sifford	74-79—153	$500.00
Cut	Dave Barber	79-75—154	$500.00
Cut	Julius Boros	79-75—154	$500.00
Cut	George Burns	77-77—154	$500.00
Cut	Doug Campbell	76-78—154	$500.00
Cut	Don January	82-72—154	$500.00
Cut	Gene Littler	77-77—154	$500.00
Cut	Dave Stockton	73-81—154	$500.00
Cut	Kermit Zarley	82-72—154	$500.00
Cut	Dow Finsterwald	76-79—155	$500.00
Cut	Howell Fraser	72-83—155	$500.00
Cut	Terry Mauney	76-79—155	$500.00
Cut	Bobby Nichols	78-77—155	$500.00
Cut	Jack Seltzer	77-78—155	$500.00
Cut	Ed Fiori	77-79—156	$500.00
Cut	Jack Lewis	76-80—156	$500.00
Cut	Gary McCord	79-77—156	$500.00
Cut	Roy Abrameit	79-78—157	$500.00
Cut	Woody Fitzhugh	80-77—157	$500.00
Cut	Dick Goetz	79-78—157	$500.00
Cut	Rives McBee	86-71—157	$500.00
Cut	Dean Refram	78-79—157	$500.00
Cut	Doug Dalziel	77-81—158	$500.00
Cut	Mike Hill	78-80—158	$500.00
Cut	Scott Hoch	80-78—158	$500.00
Cut	John Jackson	76-82—158	$500.00
Cut	Steve Spray	76-82—158	$500.00
Cut	Charles Volpone	74-84—158	$500.00
Cut	Mark Lye	86-73—159	$500.00
Cut	Dan Murphy	81-78—159	$500.00
Cut	Bill Pelham	81-78—159	$500.00
Cut	Buddy Whitten	81-78—159	$500.00
Cut	Joe Jimenez	81-79—160	$500.00
Cut	Perry Leslie	79-81—160	$500.00
Cut	Rex Baxter	80-81—161	$500.00
Cut	Jay Overton	84-77—161	$500.00
Cut	Chris Cole	80-83—163	$500.00
Cut	Jack McConachie	83-80—163	$500.00
Cut	Terry Florence	78-87—165	$500.00
Cut	Roger Kennedy	80-88—168	$500.00
Cut	Craig Harmon	89-80—169	$500.00
Cut	Billy Casper	82-88—170	$500.00
Cut	Robert Nichols	80-90—170	$500.00
WD	Jerry Barber	80—80	$500.00
WD	Rik Massengale	82—82	$500.00
WD	Sam Snead	82—82	$500.00
WD	Chi Chi Rodriguez	83—83	$500.00

1979

Native Australian David Graham fired a 5-under-par 65 over the final round, despite a 72nd hole double-bogey, to tie Ben Crenshaw at 8-under-par 272, the second lowest 72-hole total since the Championship switched to stroke play. Graham tied Crenshaw on the first two playoff holes with one putt of 18 feet for par on the first hole and 10 feet for birdie on the second hole. Graham won the Championship with a birdie on the third playoff hole.

Champion: David Graham, Dallas, Texas
Site: Oakland Hills CC, Birmingham, Mich.
Date: Aug. 2-5   **Purse:** $350,600
Par: 35-35 - 70 (7,014 Yards)
Entries: 150   Cut at 146   74 players advanced

	Course Avg	Under Par	At Par	Over Par	Round Leader	Low Round		David Graham	
Round 1:	74.0	15	11	124	Tom Watson	66 -	Tom Watson	69 -	Tied 5th
Round 2:	73.1	18	12	119	Ben Crenshaw	65 -	Alan Tapie	137 (68) -	Tied 2nd
Round 3:	71.5	19	8	47	Rex Caldwell	66 -	Caldwell, Renner	207 (70) -	Tied 3rd
Round 4:	72.2	14	7	53	Graham, Crenshaw	65 -	David Graham	272 (65) -	Tied 1st
Totals:	73.02	66	38	343					

TOURNAMENT SUMMARY

Place	Name	Score	Winnings
T-1	David Graham	69-68-70-65—272	$60,000.00
T-1	Ben Crenshaw	69-67-69-67—272	$40,000.00
3	Rex Caldwell	67-70-66-71—274	$25,000.00
4	Ron Streck	68-71-69-68—276	$20,000.00
T-5	Gibby Gilbert	69-72-68-69—278	$14,500.00
T-5	Jerry Pate	69-69-69-71—278	$14,500.00
T-7	Jay Haas	68-69-73-69—279	$9,200.00
T-7	Don January	69-70-71-69—279	$9,200.00
T-7	Howard Twitty	70-73-69-67—279	$9,200.00
T-10	Lou Graham	69-74-68-69—280	$6,750.00
T-10	Gary Koch	71-71-71-67—280	$6,750.00
T-12	Andy Bean	76-69-68-68—281	$5,250.00
T-12	Jerry McGee	73-69-71-68—281	$5,250.00
T-12	Jack Renner	71-74-66-70—281	$5,250.00
T-12	Tom Watson	66-72-69-74—281	$5,250.00
T-16	Bob Gilder	73-71-68-70—282	$3,780.00
T-16	Hubert Green	69-70-72-71—282	$3,780.00
T-16	Bruce Lietzke	69-69-71-73—282	$3,780.00
T-16	Gene Littler	71-71-67-73—282	$3,780.00
T-16	Graham Marsh	69-70-71-72—282	$3,780.00
T-21	Bob Byman	73-72-69-69—283	$3,250.00
T-21	John Schroeder	72-72-70-69—283	$3,250.00
T-23	Frank Conner	70-73-69-72—284	$2,900.00
T-23	Rod Funseth	70-69-76-69—284	$2,900.00
T-23	Peter Jacobsen	70-74-67-73—284	$2,900.00
T-23	Gary Player	73-70-71-70—284	$2,900.00
T-23	Alan Tapie	73-65-76-70—284	$2,900.00
T-28	Miller Barber	73-72-69-71—285	$2,300.00
T-28	George Burns	71-74-67-73—285	$2,300.00
T-28	Mark McCumber	75-68-70-72—285	$2,300.00
T-28	Artie McNickle	69-70-72-74—285	$2,300.00
T-28	Gil Morgan	72-73-70-70—285	$2,300.00
T-28	Larry Nelson	70-75-70-70—285	$2,300.00
T-28	Ed Sneed	77-67-70-71—285	$2,300.00
T-35	Lee Elder	70-71-73-73—287	$1,600.00
T-35	Lynn Janson	73-71-72-71—287	$1,600.00
T-35	Tom Kite	72-72-69-74—287	$1,600.00
T-35	Jim Masserio	69-73-71-74—287	$1,600.00
T-35	Bill Rogers	70-72-73-72—287	$1,600.00
T-35	Dave Stockton	70-75-72-70—287	$1,600.00
T-35	Lee Trevino	70-73-72-72—287	$1,600.00
T-42	Calvin Peete	75-71-70-72—288	$1,050.00
T-42	Sam Snead	73-71-71-73—288	$1,050.00
T-42	Jimmy Wright	72-69-72-75—288	$1,050.00
T-42	Kermit Zarley	73-69-71-75—288	$1,050.00
T-46	Tommy Aaron	73-73-69-74—289	$704.00
T-46	Jim Colbert	73-73-72-71—289	$704.00
T-46	Don Padgett	71-75-73-70—289	$704.00
T-46	Chi Chi Rodriguez	71-72-72-74—289	$704.00
T-46	Jim Simons	76-68-73-72—289	$704.00
T-51	Rod Curl	72-72-73-73—290	$600.00
T-51	John Mahaffey	72-74-71-73—290	$600.00
T-51	Bob Mann	71-73-71-75—290	$600.00
T-54	Wally Armstrong	74-71-73-73—291	$567.50
T-54	Dave Barber	74-69-71-77—291	$567.50
T-54	Jim Dent	70-72-76-73—291	$567.50
T-54	Leonard Thompson	72-67-78-74—291	$567.50
T-54	Dewitt Weaver	73-73-71-74—291	$567.50
T-54	Fuzzy Zoeller	70-75-75-71—291	$567.50
T-60	Keith Fergus	73-70-73-76—292	$547.50
T-60	Barry Jaeckel	71-73-75-73—292	$547.50
T-62	Ray Floyd	74-70-77-72—293	$535.00
T-62	Mark Hayes	71-73-77-72—293	$535.00
T-62	Rocky Thompson	72-72-73-76—293	$535.00
T-65	Scott Bess	73-72-75-74—294	$515.00
T-65	Al Geiberger	76-70-73-75—294	$515.00
T-65	Lon Hinkle	73-72-71-78—294	$515.00
T-65	Jack Nicklaus	73-72-78-71—294	$515.00
T-65	Austin Straub	73-70-72-79—294	$515.00
70	Lanny Wadkins	71-75-73-76—295	$500.00
71	Bobby Wadkins	77-68-75-76—296	$500.00
72	Dean Refram	75-69-75-79—298	$500.00
T-73	Dennis Coscina	76-70-74-83—303	$500.00
T-73	Ronald Smoak	72-74-78-79—303	$500.00
Cut	Tommy Aycock	75-72—147	$350.00
Cut	Mike Brannan	73-74—147	$350.00
Cut	Billy Casper	75-72—147	$350.00
Cut	Randy Erskine	72-75—147	$350.00
Cut	Al Mengert	76-71—147	$350.00
Cut	Lindy Miller	76-71—147	$350.00
Cut	Orville Moody	72-75—147	$350.00
Cut	Jim Nelford	74-73—147	$350.00
Cut	Jim Thorpe	71-76—147	$350.00
Cut	Tim Collins	74-74—148	$350.00
Cut	Woody Dame	75-73—148	$350.00
Cut	Buddy Gardner	76-72—148	$350.00
Cut	Hale Irwin	73-75—148	$350.00
Cut	Grier Jones	73-75—148	$350.00
Cut	Tom Purtzer	73-75—148	$350.00
Cut	Victor Regalado	72-76—148	$350.00
Cut	J.C. Snead	72-76—148	$350.00
Cut	Craig Stadler	73-75—148	$350.00
Cut	Ron Terry	74-74—148	$350.00
Cut	Doug Tewell	75-73—148	$350.00
Cut	Bobby Walzel	75-73—148	$350.00
Cut	Jim White	78-70—148	$350.00
Cut	John Gentile	75-74—149	$350.00
Cut	Michael Milon	75-74—149	$350.00
Cut	Bob Murphy	71-78—149	$350.00
Cut	Andy North	76-73—149	$350.00
Cut	Paul Purtzer	76-73—149	$350.00
Cut	Mike Reid	75-74—149	$350.00
Cut	Waddy Stokes	78-71—149	$350.00
Cut	D.A. Weibring	76-73—149	$350.00
Cut	Isao Aoki	78-72—150	$350.00
Cut	Julius Boros	77-73—150	$350.00
Cut	Jim Ferree	75-75—150	$350.00
Cut	Howell Fraser	73-77—150	$350.00
Cut	Phil Hancock	79-71—150	$350.00
Cut	Bill Kratzert	74-76—150	$350.00
Cut	Lloyd Monroe	74-76—150	$350.00
Cut	Ralph Montoya	76-74—150	$350.00
Cut	Jay Overton	74-76—150	$350.00
Cut	George Shortridge	76-74—150	$350.00
Cut	Curtis Strange	74-76—150	$350.00
Cut	Tom Weiskopf	79-71—150	$350.00
Cut	Charles Coody	79-72—151	$350.00
Cut	Dow Finsterwald	77-74—151	$350.00
Cut	Jimmy Paschal	76-75—151	$350.00
Cut	David Jimenez	77-75—152	$350.00
Cut	Mac McLendon	78-74—152	$350.00
Cut	Larry Ringer	78-74—152	$350.00
Cut	Larry Startzel	77-75—152	$350.00
Cut	Bruce Summerhays	78-74—152	$350.00
Cut	Guy Cullins	74-79—153	$350.00
Cut	Tom Joyce	74-79—153	$350.00
Cut	Tony Kaloustian	74-79—153	$350.00
Cut	Mike McCullough	82-71—153	$350.00
Cut	Bobby Phillips	78-75—153	$350.00
Cut	Jack Sommers	74-79—153	$350.00
Cut	Mark Alwin	77-77—154	$350.00
Cut	Roger Ginsberg	76-78—154	$350.00
Cut	Joe Inman Jr.	80-74—154	$350.00
Cut	Babe Lichardus	78-76—154	$350.00
Cut	Jim Logue	78-76—154	$350.00
Cut	Steve Spray	77-77—154	$350.00
Cut	Arnold Palmer	81-74—155	$350.00
Cut	Roy Abrameit	80-76—156	$350.00
Cut	Gary Clark	78-78—156	$350.00
Cut	Mike Davis	81-75—156	$350.00
Cut	Bobby Nichols	74-82—156	$350.00
Cut	Mike Felker	77-80—157	$350.00
Cut	Bob Galloway	82-75—157	$350.00
Cut	Jerry Barber	83-75—158	$350.00
Cut	Craig Bunker	79-80—159	$350.00
Cut	Alan White	80-79—159	$350.00
Cut	Emil Esposito	81-79—160	$350.00
Cut	Rob Bragg	81-81—162	$350.00
Cut	Doug Ford	81-82—163	$350.00
WD	Richard Martinez	81—81	$350.00

1978

John Mahaffey, trailing third-round leader Tom Watson by seven strokes, staged a PGA Championship record rally to tie Watson and Jerry Pate after 72 holes. Mahaffey won his first major championship with a dramatic 12-foot birdie putt on the par-4, second extra hole. Mahaffey's final-round 66 put him at 276, 8-under-par.

Champion: John Mahaffey, Houston, Texas	
Site: Oakmont CC, Oakmont, Pa.	
Date: Aug. 3-6	**Purse:** $300,240
Par: 36-35 - 71 (6,989 Yards)	
Entries: 150 Cut at 148 70 players advanced	

	Course Avg	Under Par	At Par	Over Par	Round Leader	Low Round	John Mahaffey
Round 1:	75.6	16	6	127	Tom Watson	67 - Tom Watson	75 - Tied 47th
Round 2:	74.8	14	17	118	Tom Watson	67 - J. Mahaffey, G. Archer, B. Nichols, T. Weiskopf	142 (67) - Tied 6th
Round 3:	72.2	20	7	44	Tom Watson	66 - Jerry Pate	210 (68) - 5th
Round 4:	73.7	14	4	52	Mahaffey, Pate, Watson	66 - J. Mahaffey, G. Morgan	276 (66) - Tied 1st
Totals:	74.51	64	34	341			

TOURNAMENT SUMMARY

Place	Name	Score	Winnings	Place	Name	Score	Winnings	Place	Name	Score	Winnings
T-1	John Mahaffey	75-67-68-66—276	$50,000.00	T-50	Ray Floyd	76-72-73-73—294	$512.50	Cut	Steve Spray	73-79—152	$303.00
T-1	Jerry Pate	72-70-66-68—276	$25,000.00	T-50	Dave Hill	69-76-75-74—294	$512.50	Cut	Buddy Whitten	76-76—152	$303.00
T-1	Tom Watson	67-69-67-73—276	$25,000.00	T-50	Jack Newton	73-71-71-79—294	$512.50	Cut	Gene Borek	79-74—153	$303.00
T-4	Gil Morgan	76-71-66-67—280	$14,500.00	T-54	Bobby Cole	75-73-73-74—295	$500.00	Cut	Billy Casper	79-74—153	$303.00
T-4	Tom Weiskopf	73-67-69-71—280	$14,500.00	T-54	Bob Murphy	71-75-71-78—295	$500.00	Cut	Rives McBee	76-77—153	$303.00
6	Craig Stadler	70-74-67-71—282	$10,000.00	T-54	Tom Purtzer	72-70-78-75—295	$500.00	Cut	Jack Nicklaus	79-74—153	$303.00
T-7	Andy Bean	72-72-70-70—284	$8,000.00	T-54	Bobby Wadkins	74-74-71-76—295	$500.00	Cut	Bob Payne	79-74—153	$303.00
T-7	Graham Marsh	72-74-68-70—284	$8,000.00	T-58	Jay Haas	73-71-77-75—296	$500.00	Cut	Art Proctor	77-76—153	$303.00
T-7	Lee Trevino	69-73-70-72—284	$8,000.00	T-58	Mike McCullough	76-71-75-74—296	$500.00	Cut	Bruce Summerhays	74-79—153	$303.00
10	Fuzzy Zoeller	75-69-73-68—285	$6,500.00	T-58	Curtis Strange	72-74-71-79—296	$500.00	Cut	Alan Tapie	77-76—153	$303.00
11	Joe Inman Jr.	72-68-69-77—286	$6,000.00	61	George Archer	76-67-77-77—297	$500.00	Cut	Russell Glover	73-81—154	$303.00
T-12	Hale Irwin	73-71-73-70—287	$4,812.50	62	Bruce Lietzke	75-72-73-78—298	$500.00	Cut	Dave Barber	80-75—155	$303.00
T-12	Bill Kratzert	70-77-73-67—287	$4,812.50	63	Lon Hinkle	73-73-74-79—299	$500.00	Cut	Bobby Brue	82-73—155	$303.00
T-12	Larry Nelson	76-71-70-70—287	$4,812.50	T-64	Laurie Hammer	74-72-77-77—300	$500.00	Cut	Doug Dalziel	82-73—155	$303.00
T-12	John Schroeder	76-69-70-72—287	$4,812.50	T-64	Jerry Heard	76-71-72-81—300	$500.00	Cut	Geoff Hensley	76-79—155	$303.00
T-16	Ben Crenshaw	69-71-75-73—288	$3,766.67	T-64	Gary Koch	74-72-77-77—300	$500.00	Cut	Rik Massengale	81-74—155	$303.00
T-16	Phil Hancock	70-73-70-75—288	$3,766.66	T-64	Ed Sneed	76-72-73-79—300	$500.00	Cut	Steve Satterstrom	79-76—155	$303.00
T-16	Grier Jones	70-73-71-74—288	$3,766.67	T-64	Howard Twitty	75-72-77-76—300	$500.00	Cut	Gene Torres	77-78—155	$303.00
T-19	Wally Armstrong	71-73-75-70—289	$3,100.00	69	Jim Colbert	74-74-73-80—301	$500.00	Cut	Jim Ahern	80-76—156	$303.00
T-19	George Burns	79-68-70-72—289	$3,100.00	70	Bill Hall	76-72-77-78—303	$500.00	Cut	Woody Dame	78-78—156	$303.00
T-19	Bob Gilder	74-71-70-74—289	$3,100.00	Cut	Julius Boros	78-71—149	$303.00	Cut	Forrest Fezler	77-79—156	$303.00
T-19	Don January	73-72-75-69—289	$3,100.00	Cut	Doug Ford	74-75—149	$303.00	Cut	Dave Marad	75-81—156	$303.00
T-19	Bobby Nichols	75-67-73-74—289	$3,100.00	Cut	Bob Galloway	71-78—149	$303.00	Cut	Rick Acton	78-79—157	$303.00
T-19	Dave Stockton	68-75-74-72—289	$3,100.00	Cut	Mark Hayes	76-73—149	$303.00	Cut	Jerry Breaux	79-78—157	$303.00
T-19	Kermit Zarley	75-71-67-76—289	$3,100.00	Cut	Tom Kite	74-75—149	$303.00	Cut	Joe Jimenez	78-79—157	$303.00
T-26	George Cadle	74-74-74-68—290	$2,350.00	Cut	Gene Littler	76-73—149	$303.00	Cut	Jeff Mitchell	82-75—157	$303.00
T-26	Rod Curl	76-71-73-70—290	$2,350.00	Cut	Pat McGowan	74-75—149	$303.00	Cut	Jim O'Hern	76-82—158	$303.00
T-26	Hubert Green	71-71-74-74—290	$2,350.00	Cut	Don Pooley	74-75—149	$303.00	Cut	Denny Lyons	76-83—159	$303.00
T-26	Peter Oosterhuis	73-72-72-73—290	$2,350.00	Cut	Jim Simons	76-73—149	$303.00	Cut	Roy Vucinich	82-77—159	$303.00
T-26	Gary Player	76-72-71-71—290	$2,350.00	Cut	Howell Fraser	78-72—150	$303.00	Cut	Bob Boldt	77-83—160	$303.00
T-26	Greg Powers	75-70-75-70—290	$2,350.00	Cut	Mike Hill	78-72—150	$303.00	Cut	Walker Inman	82-78—160	$303.00
T-26	Bob Shearer	73-73-71-73—290	$2,350.00	Cut	Allen Miller	75-75—150	$303.00	Cut	Max Anderson	81-80—161	$303.00
T-26	Bob Zender	73-69-74-74—290	$2,350.00	Cut	Larry Rinker	75-75—150	$303.00	Cut	Dick Smith	82-79—161	$303.00
T-34	Jim Dent	74-74-70-73—291	$1,750.00	Cut	David Eger	77-74—151	$303.00	Cut	Steve Benson	81-81—162	$303.00
T-34	Victor Regalado	76-71-70-74—291	$1,750.00	Cut	Dow Finsterwald	77-74—151	$303.00	Cut	Jim King	81-82—163	$303.00
T-34	Mike Sullivan	70-75-73-73—291	$1,750.00	Cut	Al Geiberger	76-75—151	$303.00	Cut	Steve Smith	79-84—163	$303.00
T-34	Lanny Wadkins	70-73-72-76—291	$1,750.00	Cut	David Graham	74-77—151	$303.00	Cut	Stan Thirsk	81-82—163	$303.00
T-38	Danny Edwards	74-73-70-75—292	$1,350.00	Cut	Lou Graham	80-71—151	$303.00	Cut	Bob Leaver	85-79—164	$303.00
T-38	Keith Fergus	71-74-72-75—292	$1,350.00	Cut	Barry Jaeckel	76-75—151	$303.00	Cut	Babe Lichardus	83-81—164	$303.00
T-38	Morris Hatalsky	77-71-69-75—292	$1,350.00	Cut	John Lister	73-78—151	$303.00	Cut	Rocky Nelson	83-81—164	$303.00
T-38	Johnny Miller	69-72-72-79—292	$1,350.00	Cut	Jim Picard	76-75—151	$303.00	Cut	Joe Lanza	83-82—165	$303.00
T-42	Dave Eichelberger	74-73-74-72—293	$812.50	Cut	Jack Renner	77-74—151	$303.00	Cut	Mac Main	86-81—167	$303.00
T-42	Lee Elder	71-76-73-73—293	$812.50	Cut	Bryan Abbott	75-77—152	$303.00	Cut	Lou Merkle	82-85—167	$303.00
T-42	Rod Funseth	70-73-72-78—293	$812.50	Cut	Paul Barkhouse	77-75—152	$303.00	Cut	Larry Wheeler	88-79—167	$303.00
T-42	Mike Morley	70-73-73-77—293	$812.50	Cut	George Bellino	76-76—152	$303.00	Cut	John Bonella	83-87—170	$303.00
T-42	Andy North	76-71-73-73—293	$812.50	Cut	Charles Coody	76-76—152	$303.00	Cut	Bob Kay	83-88—171	$303.00
T-42	Bill Rogers	72-74-73-74—293	$812.50	Cut	Bob Duden	74-78—152	$303.00	Cut	Jerry Jones	88-90—178	$303.00
T-42	Leonard Thompson	72-76-74-71—293	$812.50	Cut	Gibby Gilbert	75-77—152	$303.00	DQ	Rex Caldwell	70-75—145	$303.00
T-42	Dewitt Weaver	75-69-72-77—293	$812.50	Cut	Steve Melnyk	73-79—152	$303.00	DQ	Jerry McGee	70-74-76—220	$303.00
T-50	Tommy Aycock	74-72-75-73—294	$512.50	Cut	Arnold Palmer	78-74—152	$303.00				

1977

For the first time, a major championship was decided in a sudden-death playoff, as Lanny Wadkins made a six-foot par putt on the third extra hole to beat Gene Littler, who led from the first round. Wadkins began the final round six shots behind Littler and was still five behind with nine holes to play, despite two front-nine eagles. Littler bogeyed five of the first six holes on the back nine, allowing Jack Nicklaus to tie him at the 15th hole, with the 28-year-old Wadkins just one shot back. Nicklaus bogeyed the par-3 17th and Wadkins pulled into a tie with Littler with his only birdie of the day at the 18th.

Champion:	Lanny Wadkins, Dallas, Texas
Site:	Pebble Beach Golf Links, Pebble Beach, Calif.
Date: Aug. 11-14	**Purse:** $250,750
Par: 36-36 - 72 (6,804 Yards)	
Entries: 149 Cut at 151	71 players advanced

	Course Avg	Under Par	At Par	Over Par	Round Leader	Low Round	Lanny Wadkins
Round 1:	76.0	20	8	120	Gene Littler	67 - Gene Littler	69 - Tied 5th
Round 2:	75.6	20	8	107	Gene Littler	68 - Gil Morgan, M. Barber	140 (71) - Tied 3rd
Round 3:	73.3	25	6	40	Gene Littler	67 - L. Lott, D. Edwards	212 (72) - Tied 12th
Round 4:	75.3	6	8	57	L. Wadkins, G. Littler	70 - L. Wadkins, B. Kratzert, J. Miller	282 (70) - Tied 1st
Totals:	75.36	71	30	324			

TOURNAMENT SUMMARY

Place	Name	Score	Winnings
T-1	Lanny Wadkins	69-71-72-70—282	$45,000.00
T-1	Gene Littler	67-69-70-76—282	$25,000.00
3	Jack Nicklaus	69-71-70-73—283	$15,000.00
4	Charles Coody	70-71-70-73—284	$12,000.00
5	Jerry Pate	73-70-69-73—285	$10,000.00
T-6	Al Geiberger	71-70-73-72—286	$7,300.00
T-6	Lou Graham	71-73-71-71—286	$7,300.00
T-6	Don January	75-69-70-72—286	$7,300.00
T-6	Jerry McGee	68-70-77-71—286	$7,300.00
T-6	Tom Watson	68-73-71-74—286	$7,300.00
T-11	Joe Inman Jr.	72-69-73-73—287	$5,250.00
T-11	Johnny Miller	70-74-73-70—287	$5,250.00
T-13	Tom Kite	73-73-70-72—288	$4,350.00
T-13	Lee Trevino	71-73-71-73—288	$4,350.00
T-15	George Cadle	69-73-70-77—289	$3,700.00
T-15	Bruce Lietzke	74-70-74-71—289	$3,700.00
T-15	Gil Morgan	74-68-70-77—289	$3,700.00
T-15	Leonard Thompson	72-73-69-75—289	$3,700.00
T-19	George Archer	70-73-76-72—291	$2,700.00
T-19	George Burns	71-76-70-74—291	$2,700.00
T-19	Mark Hayes	68-75-74-74—291	$2,700.00
T-19	Arnold Palmer	72-73-73-73—291	$2,700.00
T-19	John Schroeder	73-76-68-74—291	$2,700.00
T-19	J.C. Snead	76-71-72-72—291	$2,700.00
T-25	Miller Barber	77-68-69-78—292	$1,716.66
T-25	Grier Jones	72-74-72-74—292	$1,716.67
T-25	Bill Kratzert	71-76-75-70—292	$1,716.67
T-25	Lyn Lott	76-75-67-74—292	$1,716.67
T-25	Bob Murphy	72-72-72-76—292	$1,716.66
T-25	Jim Simons	74-74-69-75—292	$1,716.67
T-31	Billy Casper	73-71-70-79—293	$1,350.00
T-31	Lon Hinkle	72-72-74-75—293	$1,350.00
T-31	Roger Maltbie	70-79-70-74—293	$1,350.00
T-31	Gary Player	74-77-68-74—293	$1,350.00
T-31	Dave Stockton	75-75-69-74—293	$1,350.00
T-36	Danny Edwards	76-74-67-77—294	$1,125.00
T-36	Rik Massengale	77-73-70-74—294	$1,125.00
T-36	John Schlee	73-73-73-75—294	$1,125.00
T-36	Ed Sneed	74-73-72-75—294	$1,125.00
T-40	Ray Floyd	74-72-73-76—295	$975.00
T-40	Mike McCullough	77-69-72-77—295	$975.00
T-42	Buddy Allin	77-72-75-72—296	$875.00
T-42	Butch Baird	75-74-73-74—296	$875.00
T-44	Hale Irwin	74-75-73-75—297	$750.00
T-44	Steve Melnyk	71-75-74-77—297	$750.00
T-44	Mike Morley	71-74-80-72—297	$750.00
47	Bob E. Smith	76-70-77-75—298	$650.00

Place	Name	Score	Winnings
T-48	Wally Armstrong	73-74-77-75—299	$550.00
T-48	Dave Hill	73-77-74-75—299	$550.00
T-48	Mac McLendon	75-73-76-75—299	$550.00
T-51	Bruce Devlin	75-73-74-78—300	$488.10
T-51	Bobby Nichols	72-75-78-75—300	$488.10
T-51	Kermit Zarley	76-75-75-74—300	$488.10
T-54	Bob Duden	74-76-79-72—301	$488.10
T-54	Larry Nelson	77-69-79-76—301	$488.10
T-54	Sam Snead	80-71-71-79—301	$488.10
T-54	Fuzzy Zoeller	70-72-79-80—301	$488.10
T-58	Julius Boros	73-75-77-77—302	$488.10
T-58	Bob Gilder	76-74-68-84—302	$488.10
T-58	Graham Marsh	74-74-77-77—302	$488.10
T-58	Tom Weiskopf	77-72-74-79—302	$488.10
T-62	Hubert Green	74-77-76-76—303	$488.09
T-62	John Lister	70-75-80-78—303	$488.09
T-62	Bob Payne	73-76-75-79—303	$488.09
65	Rusty Guernsey	78-72-77-80—307	$488.09
T-66	Phil Ferranti	75-73-79-81—308	$488.09
T-66	Jim Ferriell	78-71-79-80—308	$488.09
T-66	Tom Jenkins	78-73-77-80—308	$488.09
69	Bob Benson	74-75-75-85—309	$488.09
70	Dow Finsterwald	76-75-84-75—310	$488.09
71	Larry Ringer	77-74-79-85—315	$488.09
Cut	Tommy Aaron	74-78—152	$250.00
Cut	Tim Collins	72-80—152	$250.00
Cut	Jim Dent	76-76—152	$250.00
Cut	Dave Eichelberger	81-71—152	$250.00
Cut	Ken Folkes	76-76—152	$250.00
Cut	Larry Gilbert	74-78—152	$250.00
Cut	Larry Mowry	76-76—152	$250.00
Cut	Bill Rogers	77-75—152	$250.00
Cut	Mike Schlueter	73-79—152	$250.00
Cut	Bill Schumaker	75-77—152	$250.00
Cut	Dennis Bradley	78-75—153	$250.00
Cut	Lee Elder	75-78—153	$250.00
Cut	George Lanning	73-80—153	$250.00
Cut	Tom Purtzer	79-74—153	$250.00
Cut	Steve Taylor	77-76—153	$250.00
Cut	Bobby Walzel	79-74—153	$250.00
Cut	Bryan Abbott	78-76—154	$250.00
Cut	Laurie Hammer	76-78—154	$250.00
Cut	Jay Horton	78-76—154	$250.00
Cut	Chuck Keating	82-72—154	$250.00
Cut	David G. Smith	77-77—154	$250.00
Cut	Bob Zender	76-78—154	$250.00
Cut	Jim Albus	80-75—155	$250.00

Place	Name	Score	Winnings
Cut	Tommy Aycock	82-73—155	$250.00
Cut	Dave Barber	76-79—155	$250.00
Cut	Andy Bean	75-80—155	$250.00
Cut	Babe Lichardus	79-76—155	$250.00
Cut	Bob Moreland	75-80—155	$250.00
Cut	Gene Samborsky	79-76—155	$250.00
Cut	Dennis Coscina	76-80—156	$250.00
Cut	Woody Dame	78-78—156	$250.00
Cut	David Graham	77-79—156	$250.00
Cut	Tom Nieporte	79-77—156	$250.00
Cut	Jim Picard	78-78—156	$250.00
Cut	John Cook	81-76—157	$250.00
Cut	Lionel Hebert	79-78—157	$250.00
Cut	Al Mengert	80-77—157	$250.00
Cut	Andy North	78-79—157	$250.00
Cut	Chuck Scally	80-77—157	$250.00
Cut	Pat Fitzsimons	77-81—158	$250.00
Cut	Gary Koch	77-81—158	$250.00
Cut	Chi Chi Rodriguez	80-78—158	$250.00
Cut	Jimmy Wright	81-77—158	$250.00
Cut	Bobby Afton	77-82—159	$250.00
Cut	Vince Bizik	77-82—159	$250.00
Cut	Jay Hebert	80-79—159	$250.00
Cut	Alan White	81-78—159	$250.00
Cut	Jerry Barber	79-81—160	$250.00
Cut	George Bellino	76-84—160	$250.00
Cut	Doug Ford	81-79—160	$250.00
Cut	Bob Galloway	82-78—160	$250.00
Cut	Larry Startzel	81-79—160	$250.00
Cut	Bert Weaver	79-81—160	$250.00
Cut	Woody Blackburn	74-87—161	$250.00
Cut	Bob Wynn	81-80—161	$250.00
Cut	Charles Sifford	79-85—164	$250.00
Cut	Ed Francese	80-85—165	$250.00
Cut	Jay Morelli	86-79—165	$250.00
Cut	Eldridge Miles	88-79—167	$250.00
Cut	Bruce Summerhays	83-84—167	$250.00
Cut	Kelly Childs	86-82—168	$250.00
Cut	Tom McGuirk	83-85—168	$250.00
Cut	Dave Oliphant	87-83—170	$250.00
Cut	Gary Campbell	94-87—181	$250.00
DQ	Pat Rea	80—80	$250.00
WD	Jim Ferrier	84—84	$250.00
WD	Tony Laporte	87—87	$250.00

1976

For the first time in history, rain pushed the final round of a PGA Championship over to Monday. A record 115,450 spectators attended the four-day event. Needing a par on the treacherous 18th hole at Congressional

Champion: Dave Stockton, Mentone, Calif.		
Site: Congressional CC, Bethesda, Md.		
Date: Aug. 12-16		Purse: $250,950
Par: 35-35 - 70 (7,054 Yards)		
Entries:139	Cut at 149	73 players advanced

to win his second PGA Championship and avert a playoff with Don January and Ray Floyd, Dave Stockton made his 10-foot putt for par. His rounds of 70-72-69-70—281 matched the highest winning total in this classic at the time.

	Course Avg	Under Par	At Par	Over Par	Round Leader	Low Round	Dave Stockton
Round 1:	74.8	11	9	118	Tom Weiskopf	65 - Tom Weiskopf	70 - Tied 12th
Round 2:	74.7	11	8	119	Gil Morgan	66 - Dave Hill	142 (72) - Tied 20th
Round 3:	73.4	7	7	62	Charles Coody	67 - Charles Coody	211 (69) - Tied 5th
Round 4:	74.1	1	5	67	Dave Stockton	69 - Jerry Pate	281 (70) - 1st
Totals:	74.44	30	29	366			

TOURNAMENT SUMMARY

Place	Name	Score	Winnings
1	Dave Stockton	70-72-69-70—281	$45,000.00
T-2	Ray Floyd	72-68-71-71—282	$20,000.00
T-2	Don January	70-69-71-72—282	$20,000.00
T-4	David Graham	70-71-70-72—283	$9,750.00
T-4	Jack Nicklaus	71-69-69-74—283	$9,750.00
T-4	Jerry Pate	69-73-72-69—283	$9,750.00
T-4	John Schlee	72-71-70-70—283	$9,750.00
T-8	Charles Coody	68-72-67-77—284	$6,000.00
T-8	Ben Crenshaw	71-69-74-70—284	$6,000.00
T-8	Jerry McGee	68-72-72-72—284	$6,000.00
T-8	Gil Morgan	66-68-75-75—284	$6,000.00
T-8	Tom Weiskopf	65-74-73-72—284	$6,000.00
T-13	Tom Kite	66-72-73-75—286	$4,350.00
T-13	Gary Player	70-69-72-75—286	$4,350.00
T-15	Lee Elder	68-74-70-75—287	$3,400.00
T-15	Mark Hayes	69-72-73-73—287	$3,400.00
T-15	Mike Hill	72-70-73-72—287	$3,400.00
T-15	Mike Morley	69-72-72-74—287	$3,400.00
T-15	Arnold Palmer	71-76-68-72—287	$3,400.00
T-15	J.C. Snead	74-71-70-72—287	$3,400.00
T-15	Tom Watson	70-74-70-73—287	$3,400.00
T-22	Lou Graham	74-70-70-74—288	$2,064.28
T-22	Jerry Heard	72-74-69-73—288	$2,064.29
T-22	Dave Hill	76-66-75-71—288	$2,064.29
T-22	Joe Inman Jr.	72-69-74-73—288	$2,064.29
T-22	Gene Littler	71-69-73-75—288	$2,064.28
T-22	Don Massengale	71-74-73-70—288	$2,064.29
T-22	Leonard Thompson	73-69-72-74—288	$2,064.28
29	Joe Porter	72-71-70-76—289	$1,550.00
T-30	Hubert Green	73-70-73-74—290	$1,425.00
T-30	Grier Jones	71-70-75-74—290	$1,425.00
T-30	Rik Massengale	71-72-73-74—290	$1,425.00
T-30	Bob Zender	69-71-73-77—290	$1,425.00
T-34	Bill Collins	70-70-76-75—291	$1,225.00
T-34	Gibby Gilbert	70-78-72-71—291	$1,225.00
T-34	Hale Irwin	69-73-77-72—291	$1,225.00
T-34	Larry Nelson	75-71-74-71—291	$1,225.00
T-38	Tommy Aaron	72-72-72-76—292	$1,000.00
T-38	Bruce Crampton	74-71-75-72—292	$1,000.00
T-38	Bruce Lietzke	75-73-68-76—292	$1,000.00
T-38	Peter Oosterhuis	75-73-73-71—292	$1,000.00
T-38	Howard Twitty	73-71-74-74—292	$1,000.00
T-43	Pat Fitzsimons	77-71-73-72—293	$725.00
T-43	Rod Funseth	71-75-73-74—293	$725.00
T-43	John Lister	74-72-73-74—293	$725.00
T-43	Roger Maltbie	76-72-73-72—293	$725.00
T-43	Don Padgett	71-71-72-79—293	$725.00

Place	Name	Score	Winnings
T-43	Kermit Zarley	71-73-74-75—293	$725.00
T-49	Wally Armstrong	74-75-69-76—294	$525.00
T-49	Andy North	72-73-79-70—294	$525.00
T-51	Miller Barber	79-70-73-73—295	$450.00
T-51	Don Bies	76-71-72-76—295	$450.00
T-51	George Cadle	71-70-77-77—295	$450.00
T-51	Billy Casper	75-74-72-74—295	$450.00
T-51	Dennis Tiziani	77-68-75-75—295	$450.00
T-51	Bert Weaver	73-70-78-74—295	$450.00
T-57	Jim Colbert	72-72-75-77—296	$450.00
T-57	Ed Sneed	71-76-76-73—296	$450.00
T-57	Tom Ulozas	73-76-74-73—296	$450.00
T-60	Gene Borek	73-76-72-76—297	$450.00
T-60	Jack Kiefer	72-71-75-79—297	$450.00
T-60	Jim Simons	75-73-72-77—297	$450.00
T-60	Jimmy Wright	77-72-72-76—297	$450.00
64	Lyn Lott	70-72-76-80—298	$450.00
T-65	Bob Dickson	74-73-77-75—299	$450.00
T-65	Forrest Fezler	72-75-73-79—299	$450.00
T-65	Mac McLendon	77-72-76-74—299	$450.00
68	Labron Harris Jr.	73-73-80-75—301	$450.00
T-69	Clayton Cole	75-74-78-76—303	$450.00
T-69	Bob Gilder	75-74-79-75—303	$450.00
T-71	Don Iverson	73-76-81-75—305	$450.00
T-71	Stan Thirsk	76-71-76-82—305	$450.00
73	Mal Galletta	74-74-78-81—307	$450.00
Cut	Rick Acton	75-75—150	$250.00
Cut	Butch Baird	71-79—150	$250.00
Cut	Rex Baxter	74-76—150	$250.00
Cut	George Burns	78-72—150	$250.00
Cut	Terry Diehl	78-72—150	$250.00
Cut	Doug Ford	77-73—150	$250.00
Cut	Al Geiberger	78-72—150	$250.00
Cut	Lionel Hebert	77-73—150	$250.00
Cut	Bob Murphy	74-76—150	$250.00
Cut	Lee Trevino	70-80—150	$250.00
Cut	Julius Boros	72-79—151	$250.00
Cut	Al Chandler	79-72—151	$250.00
Cut	Randy Glover	78-73—151	$250.00
Cut	Paul Moran	75-76—151	$250.00
Cut	Dean Refram	72-79—151	$250.00
Cut	Sam Snead	75-76—151	$250.00
Cut	Lanny Wadkins	73-78—151	$250.00
Cut	Rod Curl	75-77—152	$250.00
Cut	Denny Lyons	76-76—152	$250.00
Cut	Jim Marshall	77-75—152	$250.00
Cut	Rives McBee	77-75—152	$250.00

Place	Name	Score	Winnings
Cut	Bob Post	76-76—152	$250.00
Cut	Larry Gilbert	79-74—153	$250.00
Cut	Gary Koch	74-79—153	$250.00
Cut	Bobby Nichols	74-79—153	$250.00
Cut	Art Wall	75-78—153	$250.00
Cut	Terry Wilcox	79-74—153	$250.00
Cut	Dennis Coscina	78-76—154	$250.00
Cut	Tom Joyce	80-74—154	$250.00
Cut	Gary McCord	74-80—154	$250.00
Cut	Victor Regalado	80-74—154	$250.00
Cut	Steve Taylor	76-78—154	$250.00
Cut	George Bellino	81-74—155	$250.00
Cut	Dick Goetz	79-76—155	$250.00
Cut	Tommy Jacobs	81-74—155	$250.00
Cut	Roger Watson	77-78—155	$250.00
Cut	Larry Ziegler	78-77—155	$250.00
Cut	Maurice Ver Brugge	81-75—156	$250.00
Cut	Billy Ziobro	77-79—156	$250.00
Cut	Ed Dougherty	79-78—157	$250.00
Cut	Quinton Gray	75-82—157	$250.00
Cut	Ken Mast	80-77—157	$250.00
Cut	David Jimenez	81-77—158	$250.00
Cut	Pat Schwab	77-81—158	$250.00
Cut	Jack Baldwin	83-76—159	$250.00
Cut	Jay Hebert	83-76—159	$250.00
Cut	Tony Morosco	75-86—161	$250.00
Cut	Ron Philo	78-83—161	$250.00
Cut	Bobby Brue	82-80—162	$250.00
Cut	Jerry Barber	80-83—163	$250.00
Cut	Hank Stukart	81-82—163	$250.00
Cut	Gordon Waldespuhl	80-83—163	$250.00
Cut	Bob Benning	80-84—164	$250.00
Cut	John Frillman	81-83—164	$250.00
Cut	Dick Hart	85-79—164	$250.00
Cut	Jim Barber	77-88—165	$250.00
Cut	David G. Smith	80-85—165	$250.00
Cut	Rich Bland	81-85—166	$250.00
Cut	Gene Bone	85-82—167	$250.00
Cut	Robert Atkins	82-87—169	$250.00
Cut	Jeff Mays	86-86—172	$250.00
Cut	Ron Castillo	88-87—175	$250.00
WD	John Mahaffey	76-72-71—219	$250.00
WD	Buddy Allin	71-71-78—220	$250.00
WD	Chuck Scally	74-73-84—231	$250.00

1975

Played on one of Jack Nicklaus' favorite courses, Firestone South, Nicklaus ran his string of PGA titles to four, one shy of Walter Hagen's record. With opening rounds of 70 and 68, Nicklaus found himself three shots behind Bruce Crampton, whose second-round 63 was the lowest round ever in the Championship. But on Saturday, Nicklaus had a 67 while Crampton soared to 75 for an eight-shot swing, giving Nicklaus a 4-shot lead going into the final round. In the final round, Nicklaus cruised to a 71 for a two-shot victory over runner-up Crampton.

Champion: Jack Nicklaus, North Palm Beach, Fla.	
Site: Firestone CC, Akron, Ohio	
Date: Aug. 7-10	**Purse:** $225,000
Par: 35-35 - 70 (7,180 Yards)	
Entries: 139 Cut at 148 71 players advanced	

	Course Avg	Under Par	At Par	Over Par	Round Leader	Low Round	Jack Nicklaus
Round 1:	75.1	7	9	120	Mark Hayes	67 - Mark Hayes	70 - Tied 8th
Round 2:	73.6	15	8	110	Bruce Crampton	63 - Bruce Crampton	138 (68) - Tied 3rd
Round 3:	73.9	3	7	61	Jack Nicklaus	66 - Gene Littler	205 (67) - 1st
Round 4:	73.3	7	5	59	Jack Nicklaus	65 - Andy North	276 (71) - 1st
Totals:	74.16	32	29	350			

TOURNAMENT SUMMARY

Place	Name	Score	Winnings
1	Jack Nicklaus	70-68-67-71—276	$45,000.00
2	Bruce Crampton	71-63-75-69—278	$25,700.00
3	Tom Weiskopf	70-71-70-68—279	$16,000.00
4	Andy North	72-74-70-65—281	$10,500.00
T-5	Billy Casper	69-72-72-70—283	$8,662.50
T-5	Hale Irwin	72-65-73-73—283	$8,662.50
T-7	Dave Hill	71-71-74-68—284	$6,917.50
T-7	Gene Littler	76-71-66-71—284	$6,917.50
9	Tom Watson	70-71-71-73—285	$6,075.00
T-10	Buddy Allin	73-72-70-71—286	$4,467.86
T-10	Ben Crenshaw	73-72-71-70—286	$4,467.86
T-10	Ray Floyd	70-73-72-71—286	$4,467.86
T-10	David Graham	72-70-70-74—286	$4,467.85
T-10	Don January	72-70-71-73—286	$4,467.85
T-10	John Schlee	71-68-75-72—286	$4,467.86
T-10	Leonard Thompson	74-69-72-71—286	$4,467.86
T-17	Dale Douglass	74-72-74-67—287	$2,925.00
T-17	Gibby Gilbert	73-70-77-67—287	$2,925.00
T-17	Mike Hill	72-71-70-74—287	$2,925.00
T-17	Steve Melnyk	71-72-74-70—287	$2,925.00
T-17	Gil Morgan	73-71-71-72—287	$2,925.00
T-22	Ed Dougherty	69-70-72-77—288	$2,115.00
T-22	Mark Hayes	67-71-75-75—288	$2,115.00
T-22	Chi Chi Rodriguez	73-72-74-69—288	$2,115.00
T-25	Jerry Heard	75-70-70-74—289	$1,800.00
T-25	Mac McLendon	73-71-70-75—289	$1,800.00
T-25	Bob Murphy	75-68-69-77—289	$1,800.00
T-28	Jim Colbert	79-66-72-73—290	$1,531.00
T-28	Larry Hinson	68-73-72-77—290	$1,531.00
T-28	John Mahaffey	71-70-75-74—290	$1,531.00
T-28	J.C. Snead	73-67-75-75—290	$1,531.00
T-28	Bob Wynn	69-69-80-72—290	$1,531.00
T-33	Gay Brewer	74-74-71-72—291	$1,215.00
T-33	Al Geiberger	70-70-80-71—291	$1,215.00
T-33	Tom Kite	77-71-72-71—291	$1,215.00
T-33	Bobby Nichols	72-75-72-72—291	$1,215.00
T-33	Arnold Palmer	73-72-73-73—291	$1,215.00
T-33	Gary Player	72-70-73-76—291	$1,215.00
T-33	Jimmy Powell	73-68-76-74—291	$1,215.00
T-40	Butch Baird	72-69-74-77—292	$812.85
T-40	Julius Boros	71-73-78-70—292	$812.86
T-40	Bobby Cole	71-74-71-76—292	$812.85
T-40	Jerry McGee	73-74-73-72—292	$812.86
T-40	Peter Oosterhuis	74-72-72-74—292	$812.86
T-40	Tom Shaw	75-72-71-74—292	$812.86
T-40	Bob Stanton	71-73-74-74—292	$812.86

Place	Name	Score	Winnings
47	Mike Morley	70-72-75-76—293	$585.00
T-48	Tom Jenkins	72-75-73-74—294	$517.50
T-48	Charles Sifford	74-72-75-73—294	$517.50
T-50	Jim Dent	70-71-77-77—295	$433.94
T-50	Bruce Devlin	70-73-75-77—295	$433.93
T-50	Forrest Fezler	75-72-71-77—295	$433.93
T-50	Art Wall	70-74-74-77—295	$433.94
T-54	Lou Graham	73-71-74-78—296	$428.57
T-54	George Johnson	73-74-74-75—296	$428.57
T-54	Eddie Pearce	74-73-77-72—296	$428.57
T-54	Ed Sneed	72-75-74-75—296	$428.57
T-54	Fred Wampler	69-74-80-73—296	$428.57
T-54	Jimmy Wright	73-74-76-73—296	$428.57
T-60	Bob Benson	68-77-80-72—297	$428.57
T-60	Victor Regalado	74-69-74-80—297	$428.57
T-60	Lee Trevino	74-72-78-73—297	$428.57
T-60	Maurice Ver Brugge	72-68-84-73—297	$428.57
T-60	Roger Watson	73-73-76-75—297	$428.57
T-65	Homero Blancas	72-76-78-72—298	$428.57
T-65	Ron Letellier	76-72-75-75—298	$428.57
T-67	Rolf Deming	74-73-83-70—300	$428.57
T-67	Dennis Meyer	72-74-74-80—300	$428.57
69	Paul Moran	79-69-78-76—302	$428.57
T-70	Al Chandler	71-75-78-81—305	$428.57
T-70	Dow Finsterwald	75-73-76-81—305	$428.57
Cut	Charles Coody	74-75—149	
Cut	Doug Ford	78-71—149	
Cut	Bill Garrett	74-75—149	
Cut	Dick Goetz	76-73—149	
Cut	Lionel Hebert	76-73—149	
Cut	Joe Inman Jr.	73-76—149	
Cut	Grier Jones	78-71—149	
Cut	Denny Lyons	80-69—149	
Cut	Don Massengale	75-74—149	
Cut	Lloyd Monroe	77-72—149	
Cut	Tom Nieporte	74-75—149	
Cut	Dick Smith	77-72—149	
Cut	Sam Snead	75-74—149	
Cut	Tommy Aaron	77-73—150	
Cut	Bob Bratzler	77-73—150	
Cut	Clayton Cole	73-77—150	
Cut	Rik Massengale	76-74—150	
Cut	Jerry Barber	79-72—151	
Cut	Frank Beard	75-76—151	
Cut	Pat Fitzsimons	76-75—151	
Cut	Rod Funseth	78-73—151	

Place	Name	Score
Cut	Babe Lichardus	77-74—151
Cut	Dave Stockton	77-74—151
Cut	Ken Towns	75-76—151
Cut	Don Bies	76-76—152
Cut	Gary Groh	79-73—152
Cut	Gary Head	78-74—152
Cut	Mac Main	77-75—152
Cut	Johnny Miller	78-74—152
Cut	Larry Ziegler	78-74—152
Cut	Wally Armstrong	81-72—153
Cut	Joe Carr	73-80—153
Cut	Howell Fraser	76-77—153
Cut	Terry Diehl	77-77—154
Cut	Phil Ferranti	80-74—154
Cut	Gene Ferrell	80-74—154
Cut	Roger Maltbie	76-78—154
Cut	James Riggins	74-80—154
Cut	Ed Famula	76-79—155
Cut	John Lively Jr.	77-78—155
Cut	Robert Fry	76-80—156
Cut	Gary Hopkins	80-76—156
Cut	Randy Glover	79-78—157
Cut	Larry Mancour	82-75—157
Cut	Tom Smack	80-77—157
Cut	Jon Gustin	80-78—158
Cut	Odell Massey	79-79—158
Cut	Max Anderson	82-77—159
Cut	Larry Gilbert	75-84—159
Cut	Rudy Goff	77-82—159
Cut	Ed Kroll	83-76—159
Cut	Jerry Mowlds	77-82—159
Cut	Mike Schlueter	77-82—159
Cut	Shelby Futch	78-82—160
Cut	David G. Smith	84-76—160
Cut	Dick Plummer	84-77—161
Cut	James Davis	84-79—163
Cut	John Frillman	87-77—164
Cut	Frank Freer	83-83—166
Cut	Bob Placido	81-85—166
Cut	Norman Rack	87-79—166
Cut	Ron Aleks	89-82—171
WD	Bob E. Smith	79—79
WD	Richie Karl	81—81
WD	Darrell Hickok	85—85

1974

Lee Trevino, brandishing an old putter he found in the attic of his rented home, slogged his way to victory in a week of steady rain. During the third round, Trevino moved in front with a 68 to establish a one-stroke lead over Jack Nicklaus. In the final round, Nicklaus fired a flawless 69, but couldn't overtake Trevino who matched Nicklaus' performance for a one-stroke victory.

Champion: Lee Trevino, Jupiter Island, Fla.
Site: Tanglewood GC, Clemmons, N.C.
Date: Aug. 8-11   **Purse:** $225,000
Par: 35-35 - 70 (7,050 Yards)
Entries: 143   Cut at 149   78 players advanced

	Course Avg	Under Par	At Par	Over Par	Round Leader	Low Round	Lee Trevino
Round 1:	74.8	9	10	122		68 - H. Green, R. Floyd, J. Schlee	73 - Tied 43rd
Round 2:	74.5	13	3	119	John Schlee	64 - Gary Player	139 (66) - 6th
Round 3:	73.1	6	7	63	Lee Trevino	67 - Dave Hill	207 (68) - 1st
Round 4:	72.7	13	11	54	Lee Trevino	66 - Al Geiberger	276 (69) - 1st
Totals:	74.06	41	31	358			

TOURNAMENT SUMMARY

Place	Name	Score	Winnings
1	Lee Trevino	73-66-68-69—276	$45,000.00
2	Jack Nicklaus	69-69-70-69—277	$25,700.00
T-3	Bobby Cole	69-68-71-71—279	$10,956.25
T-3	Hubert Green	68-68-73-70—279	$10,956.25
T-3	Dave Hill	74-69-67-69—279	$10,956.25
T-3	Sam Snead	69-71-71-68—279	$10,956.25
7	Gary Player	73-64-73-70—280	$7,200.00
8	Al Geiberger	70-70-75-66—281	$6,635.00
T-9	Don Bies	73-71-68-70—282	$5,850.00
T-9	John Mahaffey	72-72-71-67—282	$5,850.00
T-11	Tommy Aycock	73-68-73-70—284	$4,275.00
T-11	Frank Beard	73-67-69-75—284	$4,275.00
T-11	Lee Elder	74-69-72-69—284	$4,275.00
T-11	Ray Floyd	68-72-74-70—284	$4,275.00
T-11	Mike Hill	76-72-68-68—284	$4,275.00
T-11	Tom Watson	69-72-73-70—284	$4,275.00
T-17	Gay Brewer	72-72-72-69—285	$2,925.00
T-17	Tom Jenkins	70-73-71-71—285	$2,925.00
T-17	John Schlee	68-67-75-75—285	$2,925.00
T-17	Dan Sikes	71-75-71-68—285	$2,925.00
T-17	Leonard Thompson	69-71-70-75—285	$2,925.00
T-22	Stan Brion	71-71-74-70—286	$2,182.50
T-22	Bruce Devlin	70-74-70-72—286	$2,182.50
T-24	Don Massengale	74-71-70-72—287	$1,925.00
T-24	J.C. Snead	72-72-75-68—287	$1,925.00
T-26	Larry Hinson	74-73-69-72—288	$1,765.00
T-26	Dave Stockton	71-73-70-74—288	$1,765.00
T-28	Jim Colbert	70-76-70-73—289	$1,565.00
T-28	Gene Littler	76-72-70-71—289	$1,565.00
T-28	Arnold Palmer	72-75-70-72—289	$1,565.00
T-28	Victor Regalado	70-72-77-70—289	$1,565.00
T-32	Gene Borek	72-76-72-70—290	$1,260.00
T-32	Forrest Fezler	77-68-74-71—290	$1,260.00
T-32	Grier Jones	70-74-71-75—290	$1,260.00
T-32	Bob Murphy	74-73-71-72—290	$1,260.00
T-32	Eddie Pearce	69-72-79-70—290	$1,260.00
T-32	Bert Yancey	75-74-73-68—290	$1,260.00
T-32	Larry Ziegler	75-72-71-72—290	$1,260.00
T-39	Jim Dent	73-76-73-69—291	$817.23
T-39	Gibby Gilbert	73-73-72-73—291	$817.23
T-39	Tom Kite	71-74-73-73—291	$817.22
T-39	Johnny Miller	71-75-72-73—291	$817.22
T-39	Bobby Nichols	72-74-72-73—291	$817.22
T-39	Andy North	73-74-73-71—291	$817.23
T-39	Chi Chi Rodriguez	71-74-74-72—291	$817.22
T-39	Bob E. Smith	72-75-72-72—291	$817.22
T-39	Charles Volpone	72-75-71-73—291	$817.22
T-48	Bruce Crampton	75-71-73-73—292	$495.00

Place	Name	Score	Winnings
T-48	Lou Graham	77-72-71-72—292	$495.00
T-48	Jerry Heard	73-76-73-70—292	$495.00
T-51	Mason Rudolph	70-72-70-81—293	$321.43
T-51	Kermit Zarley	70-73-73-77—293	$321.43
T-53	Chuck Courtney	76-73-74-71—294	$321.43
T-53	Dwight Nevil	75-72-75-72—294	$321.43
T-55	Tommy Aaron	73-67-78-77—295	$321.43
T-55	Tony Jacklin	73-72-76-74—295	$321.43
T-55	Richie Karl	72-77-75-71—295	$321.43
T-55	Jerry McGee	75-73-71-76—295	$321.43
T-55	Dewitt Weaver	70-73-76-76—295	$321.43
T-60	Miller Barber	71-70-77-78—296	$321.43
T-60	Tom Nieporte	70-73-76-77—296	$321.43
T-60	Joe Porter	76-72-75-73—296	$321.43
T-63	Billy Casper	75-73-75-74—297	$321.43
T-63	Ben Crenshaw	75-74-74-74—297	$321.43
T-63	Bob Galloway	72-77-75-73—297	$321.43
T-63	Roy Pace	75-71-76-75—297	$321.43
T-67	Homero Blancas	72-75-80-71—299	$321.43
T-67	Howell Fraser	71-76-74-78—299	$321.43
T-67	Gary Hopkins	72-77-76-74—299	$321.43
T-67	Frank Mize	76-72-79-72—299	$321.43
T-71	Clayton Cole	79-69-76-77—301	$321.43
T-71	Dave Eichelberger	74-74-75-78—301	$321.43
T-73	Bob Charles	72-75-77-78—302	$321.43
T-73	Bert Greene	73-71-80-78—302	$321.43
T-73	Larry Mancour	75-73-76-78—302	$321.43
76	Bob Rosburg	75-72-74-82—303	$321.42
77	Allen Miller	71-78-74-83—306	$321.42
78	Clare Emery	74-72-80-81—307	$321.42
Cut	Ras Allen	77-73—150	
Cut	Bobby Brue	77-73—150	
Cut	Randy Glover	75-75—150	
Cut	Terry Wilcox	74-76—150	
Cut	Jimmy Wright	74-76—150	
Cut	Sam Adams	78-73—151	
Cut	Jim Logue	74-77—151	
Cut	Bob Menne	73-78—151	
Cut	Bill Robinson	76-75—151	
Cut	Ralph Baker	78-74—152	
Cut	Al Chandler	77-75—152	
Cut	John Frillman	75-77—152	
Cut	Ken Lindsay	74-78—152	
Cut	Rives McBee	78-74—152	
Cut	Ray Montgomery	76-76—152	
Cut	John Schroeder	73-79—152	
Cut	Jim Seeley	82-70—152	
Cut	Ed Sneed	72-80—152	

Place	Name	Score
Cut	Lanny Wadkins	78-74—152
Cut	Jim Wiechers	72-80—152
Cut	Rex Baxter	77-76—153
Cut	Bobby Mitchell	76-77—153
Cut	Dick Nelson	81-72—153
Cut	Dick Smith	77-76—153
Cut	Alan White	75-78—153
Cut	Joe Data	77-77—154
Cut	Doug Ford	77-77—154
Cut	Denny Lyons	78-76—154
Cut	Robert Wolfe	73-81—154
Cut	Harvey Hixon	78-77—155
Cut	Gary Howlett	79-76—155
Cut	Chuck Huckaby	78-77—155
Cut	Dean Lind	76-79—155
Cut	Robert Smith	79-76—155
Cut	Fred Wampler	80-75—155
Cut	Joe Carr	77-79—156
Cut	Dow Finsterwald	76-80—156
Cut	Jay Hebert	76-80—156
Cut	Lionel Hebert	78-78—156
Cut	Davis Love Jr.	82-74—156
Cut	George Thomas	82-74—156
Cut	Sam Harvey	77-80—157
Cut	Gene Thompson	81-76—157
Cut	Rich Bland	81-77—158
Cut	Chuck Hart	78-81—159
Cut	Darrel Knicely	77-82—159
Cut	Tom Liljeholm	76-83—159
Cut	Jerry Barber	80-80—160
Cut	Glenn Stuart	82-78—160
Cut	Carroll Armstrong	77-84—161
Cut	Paul Maguire	79-82—161
Cut	Lenny Stroup	79-82—161
Cut	Bob Haggerty	85-77—162
Cut	Roland Stafford	79-83—162
Cut	Brien Boggess	85-80—165
Cut	Tim Sweborg	81-85—166
Cut	Harold Firstman	85-82—167
WD	Tom Weiskopf	75—75
DQ	Art Proctor	77—77
WD	Bert Weaver	78—78
WD	Jerry Steelsmith	79—79
WD	Jim Jamieson	81—81
WD	Paul Runyan	84—84

1973

Jack Nicklaus made the 56th PGA Championship a memorable one by making it his 14th major championship, erasing Bobby Jones' record which had stood for 43 years. Nicklaus opened with a 72, which left him tied for 22nd, but a pair of 68s made him the third-round leader. A closing 69 gave Nicklaus a 277 and a four-shot victory over runner-up Bruce Crampton.

Champion: Jack Nicklaus, North Palm Beach, Fla.
Site: Canterbury GC, Cleveland, Ohio
Date: Aug. 9-12   **Purse:** $225,000
Par: 36-35 - 71 (6,852 Yards)
Entries: 148   Cut at 149   76 players advanced

	Course Avg	Under Par	At Par	Over Par	Round Leader	Low Round	Jack Nicklaus
Round 1:	75.5	11	10	127		67 - D. Iverson, A. Geiberger	72 - Tied 22th
Round 2:	74.3	20	13	112	Don Iverson	68 - J. Nicklaus, D. Sikes, C. Coody	140 (68) - 3rd
Round 3:	72.7	17	12	46	Jack Nicklaus	67 - D. Lyons, B. Allin	208 (68) - 1st
Round 4:	72.5	21	10	44	Jack Nicklaus	68 - Hale Irwin	277 (69) - 1st
Totals:	74.17	45	45	329			

TOURNAMENT SUMMARY

Place	Name	Score	Winnings
1	Jack Nicklaus	72-68-68-69—277	$45,000.00
2	Bruce Crampton	71-73-67-70—281	$25,700.00
T-3	Mason Rudolph	69-70-70-73—282	$11,908.33
T-3	J.C. Snead	71-74-68-69—282	$11,908.34
T-3	Lanny Wadkins	73-69-71-69—282	$11,908.33
T-6	Don Iverson	67-72-70-74—283	$7,311.66
T-6	Dan Sikes	72-68-72-71—283	$7,311.67
T-6	Tom Weiskopf	70-71-71-71—283	$7,311.67
T-9	Hale Irwin	76-72-68-68—284	$5,625.00
T-9	Sam Snead	71-71-71-71—284	$5,625.00
T-9	Kermit Zarley	76-71-68-69—284	$5,625.00
T-12	Bobby Brue	70-72-73-70—285	$3,975.00
T-12	Jim Colbert	72-70-69-74—285	$3,975.00
T-12	Larry Hinson	73-70-71-71—285	$3,975.00
T-12	Denny Lyons	73-70-67-75—285	$3,975.00
T-12	Dave Stockton	72-69-75-69—285	$3,975.00
T-12	Tom Watson	75-70-71-69—285	$3,975.00
T-18	Al Geiberger	67-76-74-69—286	$2,602.50
T-18	Gibby Gilbert	70-70-73-73—286	$2,602.50
T-18	Bob Goalby	75-70-71-70—286	$2,602.50
T-18	Jim Jamieson	71-73-71-71—286	$2,602.50
T-18	Johnny Miller	72-71-74-69—286	$2,602.50
T-18	Lee Trevino	76-70-73-67—286	$2,602.50
T-24	Miller Barber	73-73-70-71—287	$1,774.16
T-24	Bruce Devlin	73-70-74-70—287	$1,774.17
T-24	Lee Elder	71-76-70-70—287	$1,774.17
T-24	Mike Hill	69-73-75-70—287	$1,774.17
T-24	Chi Chi Rodriguez	72-71-74-70—287	$1,774.17
T-24	Bert Yancey	74-72-69-72—287	$1,774.16
T-30	Don Bies	70-72-71-75—288	$1,435.00
T-30	Lou Graham	74-71-73-70—288	$1,435.00
T-30	John Mahaffey	75-71-72-70—288	$1,435.00
T-30	Orville Moody	73-74-70-71—288	$1,435.00
34	Buddy Allin	71-78-67-73—289	$1,305.00
T-35	Billy Casper	74-72-72-72—290	$1,054.45
T-35	Charles Coody	75-68-77-70—290	$1,054.45
T-35	Ray Floyd	70-73-73-74—290	$1,054.44
T-35	Rod Funseth	73-73-75-69—290	$1,054.45
T-35	Dick Hendrickson	73-72-72-73—290	$1,054.44
T-35	Bob Murphy	74-73-71-72—290	$1,054.44
T-35	Jerry Pottman	73-70-76-71—290	$1,054.45
T-35	Ed Sneed	73-70-73-74—290	$1,054.44
T-35	Leonard Thompson	72-75-70-73—290	$1,054.44
T-44	Tommy Aaron	73-73-70-75—291	$710.00
T-44	Jim Wiechers	75-70-71-75—291	$710.00
T-46	Frank Beard	73-74-70-75—292	$540.00
T-46	Chuck Courtney	73-71-74-74—292	$540.00
T-46	Babe Hiskey	74-73-71-74—292	$540.00
T-46	Tony Jacklin	70-71-76-75—292	$540.00
T-46	Dave Marr	76-72-73-71—292	$540.00

Place	Name	Score	Winnings
T-51	George Archer	72-71-74-77—294	$360.00
T-51	Deane Beman	72-77-73-72—294	$360.00
T-51	Grier Jones	75-72-72-75—294	$360.00
T-51	Bobby Nichols	73-76-72-73—294	$360.00
T-51	Gary Player	73-72-71-78—294	$360.00
T-56	Jack Burke Jr.	73-73-76-73—295	$360.00
T-56	Doug Ford	73-76-73-73—295	$360.00
T-56	George Knudson	71-77-76-71—295	$360.00
T-56	Ken Still	77-72-73-73—295	$360.00
T-60	Gene Bone	71-74-76-75—296	$360.00
T-60	Jerry Breaux	77-72-73-74—296	$360.00
T-60	Dwight Nevil	76-70-76-74—296	$360.00
T-60	John Schlee	74-71-77-74—296	$360.00
T-64	Gay Brewer	77-70-73-77—297	$360.00
T-64	Allen Miller	74-73-77-73—297	$360.00
T-66	Bob Bruno	76-71-77-74—298	$360.00
T-66	Jerry Heard	72-75-78-73—298	$360.00
T-66	Jerry McGee	74-73-72-79—298	$360.00
T-66	Bob Rosburg	71-76-73-78—298	$360.00
T-66	Jerry Steelsmith	76-73-76-73—298	$360.00
T-71	Bob Dickson	69-78-75-78—300	$360.00
T-71	Phil Rodgers	79-69-76-76—300	$360.00
T-73	Michael Joyce	76-73-79-75—303	$360.00
T-73	Babe Lichardus	73-72-76-82—303	$360.00
75	Mal Galletta	72-77-84-73—306	$360.00
Cut	Al Chandler	73-77—150	
Cut	Gardner Dickinson	74-76—150	
Cut	Labron Harris Jr.	76-74—150	
Cut	Tommy Jacobs	78-72—150	
Cut	Bob Keller	79-71—150	
Cut	Gene Littler	77-73—150	
Cut	Larry Mancour	74-76—150	
Cut	Odell Massey	75-75—150	
Cut	Bill Ogden	77-73—150	
Cut	Arnold Palmer	76-74—150	
Cut	Roland Stafford	76-74—150	
Cut	Charles Volpone	77-73—150	
Cut	Bert Weaver	74-76—150	
Cut	Rex Baxter	75-76—151	
Cut	Julius Boros	77-74—151	
Cut	Lionel Hebert	74-77—151	
Cut	Dave Hill	74-77—151	
Cut	David Jimenez	76-75—151	
Cut	Steve Melnyk	77-74—151	
Cut	Jimmy Powell	76-75—151	
Cut	Maurice Ver Brugge	78-73—151	
Cut	Dwaine Knight	79-73—152	
Cut	Wayne Morris	76-76—152	
Cut	Pat Schwab	76-76—152	
Cut	Larry Ziegler	78-74—152	

Place	Name	Score
Cut	Homero Blancas	78-75—153
Cut	Gene Borek	76-77—153
Cut	David Graham	75-78—153
Cut	Bill Johnston	76-77—153
Cut	Dave Philo	78-75—153
Cut	Bob Reith	80-73—153
Cut	Dewitt Weaver	75-78—153
Cut	Jimmy Wright	74-79—153
Cut	Ras Allen	80-74—154
Cut	Forrest Fezler	79-75—154
Cut	Dow Finsterwald	79-75—154
Cut	Freddie Haas Jr.	75-79—154
Cut	Chuck Scally	75-79—154
Cut	Rafe Botts	82-73—155
Cut	Joe Campbell	78-77—155
Cut	Sam Carmichael	78-77—155
Cut	Bob Galloway	78-77—155
Cut	Rives McBee	81-74—155
Cut	Jerry Fisher	80-76—156
Cut	Chuck Hart	78-78—156
Cut	Charles Houts	79-77—156
Cut	Davis Love Jr.	80-77—157
Cut	Don Massengale	79-78—157
Cut	Lou Merkle	78-79—157
Cut	Craig Shankland	78-79—157
Cut	Ken Towns	83-74—157
Cut	Everett Vinzant	77-80—157
Cut	Jerry Barber	82-76—158
Cut	Ross Coon	81-77—158
Cut	John Frillman	78-80—158
Cut	Walker Inman	81-77—158
Cut	David Lee	79-79—158
Cut	Bill Kennedy	79-80—159
Cut	Ernie George	81-79—160
Cut	Duff Lawrence	79-81—160
Cut	Drew Pierson	80-80—160
Cut	Bob Ellsworth	81-80—161
Cut	Gordon Leishman	81-81—162
Cut	Jim Ferrier	79-84—163
Cut	Al Mengert	83-80—163
Cut	Bill Miller	81-82—163
Cut	Dick Pearce	78-86—164
Cut	Hank Stukart	83-81—164
Cut	Paul Runyan	88-83—171
WD	Chick Harbert	82—82
WD	Vic Ghezzi	84—84
WD	Ed Rubis	88—88
DQ	Hubert Green	71-72—143

1972

It was a "miracle" 9-iron shot from an almost impossible position that brought the Championship to Gary Player for a second time. Player bogeyed the 14th and 15th holes in the final round and seemingly ended his chances when he pushed his tee shot far to the right on the 16th hole. Unable to see the flag, Player lofted the ball over a menacing willow tree and pond to within four feet of the hole. Player birdied the hole, and went on to score a two-stroke victory over Tommy Aaron and Jim Jamieson.

Champion: Gary Player, Alaqua, Fla.
Site: Oakland Hills CC, Birmingham, Mich.
Date: Aug. 3-6   **Purse:** $224,087
Par: 35-35 - 70 (7,054 Yards)
Entries: 140   Cut at 150   74 players advanced

	Course Avg	Under Par	At Par	Over Par	Round Leader	Low Round	Gary Player
Round 1:	75.1	7	6	125	Johnny Miller	68 - S. Thirsk, B. Allin	71- Tied 14th
Round 2:	75.5	4	6	123	Jerry Heard	68 - Lanny Wadkins	142 (71) - Tied 7th
Round 3:	72.8	9	8	60	Gary Player	67 - Gary Player	209 (67) - 1st
Round 4:	75.1	2	4	71	Gary Player	69 - Sam Snead	281 (72) - 1st
Totals:	74.83	22	24	379			

TOURNAMENT SUMMARY

Place	Name	Score	Winnings	Place	Name	Score	Winnings	Place	Name	Score
1	Gary Player	71-71-67-72—281	$45,000.00	T-48	Dick Crawford	70-78-73-75—296	$471.00	Cut	Fred Marti	77-76—153
T-2	Tommy Aaron	71-71-70-71—283	$20,850.00	T-48	Babe Hiskey	73-75-72-76—296	$471.00	Cut	Mac McLendon	75-78—153
T-2	Jim Jamieson	69-72-72-70—283	$20,850.00	T-48	Jimmy Wright	74-72-75-75—296	$471.00	Cut	Tom Nieporte	76-77—153
T-4	Billy Casper	73-70-67-74—284	$9,275.00	T-51	Rod Funseth	70-74-75-78—297	$333.00	Cut	Gene Borek	78-76—154
T-4	Ray Floyd	69-71-74-70—284	$9,275.00	T-51	Freddie Haas Jr.	74-74-73-76—297	$333.00	Cut	John Cook	78-76—154
T-4	Sam Snead	70-74-71-69—284	$9,275.00	T-53	Buddy Allin	68-77-75-78—298	$333.00	Cut	Dave Eichelberger	77-77—154
T-7	Gay Brewer	71-70-70-74—285	$6,383.00	T-53	Frank Beard	80-70-72-76—298	$333.00	Cut	Doug Ford	78-76—154
T-7	Jerry Heard	69-70-72-74—285	$6,383.00	T-53	Grier Jones	72-76-74-76—298	$333.00	Cut	John Frillman	85-69—154
T-7	Phil Rodgers	71-72-68-74—285	$6,383.00	T-53	Jimmy Powell	72-74-74-78—298	$333.00	Cut	Joe Jimenez	75-79—154
T-7	Doug Sanders	72-72-68-73—285	$6,383.00	T-53	Bob Rosburg	71-79-72-76—298	$333.00	Cut	George Johnson	76-78—154
T-11	Hale Irwin	71-69-75-71—286	$4,950.00	T-58	Bob Charles	76-74-77-72—299	$333.00	Cut	Ross Coon	78-77—155
T-11	Lee Trevino	73-71-71-71—286	$4,950.00	T-58	Dow Finsterwald	75-75-72-77—299	$333.00	Cut	Tommy Jacobs	78-77—155
T-13	Jack Nicklaus	72-75-68-72—287	$4,167.00	T-58	Ron Letellier	75-75-70-79—299	$333.00	Cut	Claude King	75-80—155
T-13	Dan Sikes	70-72-72-73—287	$4,167.00	T-58	Pat Schwab	73-73-77-76—299	$333.00	Cut	Chick Evans	77-79—156
15	Charles Coody	71-73-70-74—288	$3,825.00	T-62	Bob Goalby	72-78-79-71—300	$333.00	Cut	John Weaver	79-77—156
T-16	Miller Barber	73-74-72-70—289	$3,262.00	T-62	Bobby Nichols	76-74-70-80—300	$333.00	Cut	Ken Folkes	79-78—157
T-16	Hubert Green	75-71-73-70—289	$3,262.00	T-62	Jerry Steelsmith	73-77-75-75—300	$333.00	Cut	Bob Galloway	77-81—158
T-16	Arnold Palmer	69-75-72-73—289	$3,262.00	T-62	Tom Weiskopf	73-72-75-80—300	$333.00	Cut	Babe Lichardus	76-82—158
T-16	Lanny Wadkins	74-68-72-75—289	$3,262.00	T-62	Wayne Yates	75-74-76-75—300	$333.00	Cut	Dick Stranahan	79-79—158
T-20	Johnny Miller	70-76-70-74—290	$2,385.00	67	Jack Burke Jr.	74-72-76-79—301	$333.00	Cut	Dave Marr	74-85—159
T-20	Bob Shaw	72-72-74-72—290	$2,385.00	T-68	Rex Baxter	77-73-76-76—302	$333.00	Cut	Ken Towns	81-78—159
T-20	J.C. Snead	72-72-71-75—290	$2,385.00	T-68	Jim O'Hern	74-76-76-76—302	$333.00	Cut	George Demling	82-78—160
T-20	Larry Wise	74-71-67-78—290	$2,385.00	T-68	Kermit Zarley	75-75-73-79—302	$333.00	Cut	Jim Ferrier	81-79—160
T-24	Bruce Crampton	73-74-68-76—291	$1,800.00	71	Chuck Scally	74-76-73-80—303	$333.00	Cut	George Shortridge	79-81—160
T-24	Lee Elder	73-71-71-76—291	$1,800.00	T-72	Stan Thirsk	68-82-76-80—306	$333.00	Cut	Steve Gragg	79-82—161
T-24	Chi Chi Rodriguez	71-74-73-73—291	$1,800.00	T-72	Gene Torres	79-70-77-80—306	$333.00	Cut	Walker Inman	80-81—161
T-24	Bob E. Smith	72-69-76-74—291	$1,800.00	T-74	Steve Friebert	74-76-78-79—307	$333.00	Cut	Steve Lyles	78-84—162
T-24	Art Wall	72-71-75-73—291	$1,800.00	T-74	Larry Gilbert	69-81-80-77—307	$333.00	Cut	Larry Mancour	81-81—162
T-29	Jerry McGee	73-74-72-73—292	$1,497.00	T-74	Lionel Hebert	72-76-80-79—307	$333.00	Cut	Bill Robinson	83-79—162
T-29	Mike Souchak	73-73-71-75—292	$1,497.00	77	Ralph Johnston	75-74-75-89—313	$333.00	Cut	Merle Backlund	84-79—163
T-29	Jim Wiechers	70-73-69-80—292	$1,497.00	Cut	Jerry Barber	75—151		Cut	Jim McCoy	79-84—163
T-29	Bert Yancey	72-74-71-75—292	$1,497.00	Cut	Al Geiberger	77-74—151		Cut	John Molinda	80-83—163
T-33	Lou Graham	75-75-70-73—293	$1,305.00	Cut	Labron Harris Jr.	78-73—151		Cut	Ten Denham	83-82—165
T-33	Larry Hinson	75-74-73-71—293	$1,305.00	Cut	Bill Ogden	73-78—151		Cut	John Kinsey	84-81—165
T-33	Dewitt Weaver	74-74-72-73—293	$1,305.00	Cut	Brad Anderson	78-74—152		Cut	Edward Bosse	84-82—166
T-36	George Archer	73-73-79-69—294	$1,147.00	Cut	Bruce Devlin	75-77—152		Cut	Don Essig	87-79—166
T-36	Deane Beman	75-72-72-75—294	$1,147.00	Cut	Jim Ferree	78-74—152		Cut	Denny Shute	91-85—176
T-36	Sam Carmichael	76-73-71-74—294	$1,147.00	Cut	Gibby Gilbert	76-76—152		WD	Bob Wynn	76—76
T-36	Mason Rudolph	74-75-71-74—294	$1,147.00	Cut	David Graham	76-76—152		WD	Bobby Mitchell	79—79
T-40	Dale Douglass	74-71-73-77—295	$784.00	Cut	Don January	75-77—152		WD	Orville Moody	79—79
T-40	Paul Harney	74-71-77-73—295	$784.00	Cut	Bob Lunn	73-79—152		WD	Gene Sarazen	79—79
T-40	Mike Hill	73-72-74-76—295	$784.00	Cut	George Smith	73-79—152		WD	Tommy Bolt	80—80
T-40	Denny Lyons	73-73-74-75—295	$784.00	Cut	Charles Volpone	73-79—152		WD	Julius Boros	74-75—149
T-40	Bob Murphy	75-70-70-80—295	$784.00	Cut	Fred Wampler	76-76—152		DQ	Dave Hill	72-77—149
T-40	John Schlee	75-75-69-76—295	$784.00	Cut	Homero Blancas	72-81—153				
T-40	Ken Still	72-75-72-76—295	$784.00	Cut	Jim Colbert	75-78—153				
T-40	Dave Stockton	74-73-74-74—295	$784.00	Cut	George Knudson	79-74—153				

1971

Jack Nicklaus scored a wire-to-wire victory with a 7-under-par 281 to beat Billy Casper, who birdied the last two holes to slip in front of Tommy Bolt. The victory made Nicklaus the first professional to twice conquer the Grand Slam of PGA, U.S. Open, British Open and Masters titles.

Champion: Jack Nicklaus, North Palm Beach, Fla.
Site: PGA National GC (presently known as BallenIsles CC of JDM), Palm Beach Gardens, Fla.
Date: February 25-28   **Purse:** $202,440
Par: 36-36 - 72 (7,096 Yards)
Entries: 146   Cut at 149   82 players advanced

	Course Avg	Under Par	At Par	Over Par	Round Leader	Low Round		Jack Nicklaus
Round 1:	75.3	16	16	112	Jack Nicklaus	69 -	Jack Nicklaus	69 - 1st
Round 2:	74.5	31	13	99	Jack Nicklaus	67 -	Gibby Gilbert	138 (69) - 1st
Round 3:	74.1	11	9	61	Jack Nicklaus	68 -	Gary Player	208 (70) - 1st
Round 4:	73.6	19	13	48	Jack Nicklaus	68 -	Billy Casper	281 (73) - 1st
Totals:	74.57	77	75	320				

TOURNAMENT SUMMARY

Place	Name	Score	Winnings
1	Jack Nicklaus	69-69-70-73—281	$40,000.00
2	Billy Casper	71-73-71-68—283	$22,800.00
3	Tommy Bolt	72-74-69-69—284	$14,200.00
T-4	Miller Barber	72-68-75-70—285	$8,800.00
T-4	Gary Player	71-73-68-73—285	$8,800.00
T-6	Gibby Gilbert	74-67-72-73—286	$6,500.00
T-6	Dave Hill	74-71-71-70—286	$6,500.00
T-6	Jim Jamieson	72-72-72-70—286	$6,500.00
T-9	Jerry Heard	73-71-72-71—287	$4,800.00
T-9	Bob Lunn	72-70-73-72—287	$4,800.00
T-9	Fred Marti	72-71-74-70—287	$4,800.00
T-9	Bob Rosburg	74-72-70-71—287	$4,800.00
T-13	Frank Beard	74-71-73-70—288	$3,400.00
T-13	Bob Charles	70-75-70-73—288	$3,400.00
T-13	Bruce Devlin	71-71-74-72—288	$3,400.00
T-13	Larry Hinson	71-73-73-71—288	$3,400.00
T-13	Lee Trevino	71-73-75-69—288	$3,400.00
T-18	Herb Hooper	74-71-73-71—289	$2,700.00
T-18	Arnold Palmer	75-71-70-73—289	$2,700.00
T-20	Johnny Miller	71-76-72-71—290	$2,300.00
T-20	Bob E. Smith	73-70-75-72—290	$2,300.00
T-22	Brad Anderson	71-75-75-70—291	$2,088.00
T-22	Chuck Courtney	74-71-74-72—291	$2,088.00
T-22	Hale Irwin	73-72-72-74—291	$2,088.00
T-22	Jerry McGee	73-74-71-73—291	$2,088.00
T-22	John Schroeder	72-74-74-71—291	$2,088.00
T-22	Tom Weiskopf	72-70-77-72—291	$2,088.00
T-22	Larry Wood	74-71-72-74—291	$2,088.00
T-22	Bert Yancey	71-74-70-76—291	$2,088.00
T-22	Terry Dill	75-68-75-74—292	$1,304.00
T-30	Gene Borek	72-70-73-77—292	$1,304.00
T-30	Rod Funseth	72-74-75-71—292	$1,304.00
T-30	Al Geiberger	74-69-77-72—292	$1,304.00
T-34	George Archer	74-73-74-72—293	$1,037.00
T-34	Homero Blancas	72-73-74-74—293	$1,037.00
T-34	Julius Boros	71-74-72-76—293	$1,037.00
T-34	Dave Eichelberger	74-74-72-73—293	$1,037.00
T-34	Bobby Mitchell	70-73-75-75—293	$1,037.00
T-34	Sam Snead	71-74-74-74—293	$1,037.00
T-40	Babe Hiskey	75-72-69-78—294	$693.00
T-40	Howie Johnson	77-71-75-71—294	$693.00
T-40	Grier Jones	74-75-73-72—294	$693.00
T-40	Billy Maxwell	75-71-76-72—294	$693.00
T-40	John Schlee	72-76-75-71—294	$693.00
T-40	Dave Stockton	73-73-75-73—294	$693.00
T-46	Deane Beman	71-74-75-75—295	$348.00
T-46	Jim Colbert	72-73-76-74—295	$348.00
T-46	Bob Goalby	70-74-73-78—295	$348.00
T-46	Mike Hill	72-72-74-77—295	$348.00

Place	Name	Score	Winnings
T-46	Bob Murphy	68-78-75-74—295	$348.00
T-46	Bobby Nichols	74-72-74-75—295	$348.00
T-46	Cesar Sanudo	77-72-73-73—295	$348.00
T-46	Dan Sikes	73-73-75-74—295	$348.00
T-46	Larry Ziegler	74-68-76-77—295	$348.00
T-55	Bill Garrett	74-75-75-72—296	$258.00
T-55	Al Kelley	73-74-74-75—296	$258.00
T-57	Bill Bisdorf	76-73-76-72—297	$258.00
T-57	Bruce Crampton	72-77-73-75—297	$258.00
T-57	Jacky Cupit	76-71-73-77—297	$258.00
T-57	Dick Lotz	76-73-77-71—297	$258.00
T-57	Hugh Royer	78-71-73-75—297	$258.00
T-57	Mason Rudolph	76-72-75-74—297	$258.00
T-63	Joe Campbell	73-76-74-75—298	$258.00
T-63	Labron Harris Jr.	76-72-74-76—298	$258.00
T-63	Dewitt Weaver	73-76-77-72—298	$258.00
T-66	Corky Dahl	75-69-79-76—299	$258.00
T-66	Bob Duden	72-75-79-73—299	$258.00
T-66	Chick Evans	74-74-73-78—299	$258.00
T-66	Chi Chi Rodriguez	73-76-73-77—299	$258.00
T-66	Robert Stone	73-75-72-79—299	$258.00
T-71	Pete Brown	76-70-78-76—300	$258.00
T-71	Bert Greene	76-69-73-82—300	$258.00
T-71	Larry Mancour	74-71-78-77—300	$258.00
T-71	R.H. Sikes	76-73-79-72—300	$258.00
T-75	Manuel de la Torre	74-70-79-79—302	$258.00
T-75	Gene Littler	73-71-82-76—302	$258.00
T-75	Ken Towns	75-74-76-77—302	$258.00
T-78	Steve Spray	75-73-79-76—303	$258.00
T-78	Ken Still	76-72-77-78—303	$258.00
80	John Molinda	75-72-79-78—304	$258.00
Cut	Jack Burke Jr.	75-75—150	
Cut	Don January	76-74—150	
Cut	Orville Moody	76-74—150	
Cut	Phil Rodgers	73-77—150	
Cut	Tom Shaw	75-75—150	
Cut	Art Silvestrome	76-74—150	
Cut	Bob Stanton	78-72—150	
Cut	Bob Bruno	73-78—151	
Cut	Pete Cooper	78-73—151	
Cut	Ray Floyd	77-74—151	
Cut	Chris Gers	79-72—151	
Cut	Lou Graham	78-73—151	
Cut	Ray Howell	80-71—151	
Cut	George Knudson	74-77—151	
Cut	Jimmy Powell	75-76—151	
Cut	Al Chandler	79-73—152	
Cut	Charles Coody	77-75—152	
Cut	John Cook	75-77—152	

Place	Name	Score
Cut	Dale Douglass	78-74—152
Cut	Eddie Merrins	74-78—152
Cut	Stan Thirsk	76-76—152
Cut	Kermit Zarley	76-76—152
Cut	Tommy Aaron	74-79—153
Cut	Dow Finsterwald	79-74—153
Cut	Marty Furgol	76-77—153
Cut	Jay Hebert	74-79—153
Cut	Bill Johnston	79-74—153
Cut	Johnny Pott	74-79—153
Cut	Dick Crawford	76-78—154
Cut	John Frillman	78-76—154
Cut	Doug Sanders	79-75—154
Cut	J.C. Snead	76-78—154
Cut	Sam Carmichael	74-81—155
Cut	Wright Garrett	76-79—155
Cut	Ernie George	80-75—155
Cut	Dick Smith	78-77—155
Cut	Jerry Abbott	76-80—156
Cut	Don Bies	77-79—156
Cut	Mickey Powell	78-78—156
Cut	Brad Schiefelbein	77-79—156
Cut	Pat Schwab	78-78—156
Cut	Billy Capps	78-79—157
Cut	Doug Ford	77-80—157
Cut	Jack Ortman	76-81—157
Cut	Jim Awtrey	79-79—158
Cut	Jerry Barber	78-80—158
Cut	Rex Baxter	82-76—158
Cut	Jim O'Hern	82-76—158
Cut	Gene Ferrell	78-81—159
Cut	Jim Ferriell	83-76—159
Cut	Bill Kozak	80-79—159
Cut	Jimmy Wright	82-77—159
Cut	Gene Sarazen	81-79—160
Cut	Walter Burkemo	83-79—162
Cut	Mike Fetchick	81-81—162
Cut	John Maurycy	86-78—164
Cut	Jack Webb	81-83—164
Cut	Al Morley	85-81—166
Cut	Richard Payne	87-80—167
Cut	Denny Shute	81-87—168
Cut	Juan Elizondo	83-87—170
WD	Bill Ogden	85—85
WD	Lionel Hebert	72-70—142
WD	Chandler Harper	73-76-80—229

1970

Dave Stockton, a 28-year-old California native, came out of the pack in the third round to fire a 66 and take a three-stroke lead. In the final round he held off late charges by Arnold Palmer and Bob Murphy despite a near disaster at the 13th hole where he put his second shot in a pond and then lofted a wedge shot to within inches of the hole to pull out a bogey. He finished two in front of Murphy and Palmer. For Palmer, it became the third time he finished in a second-place tie in this, the only major championship he has never won.

Champion: Dave Stockton, Mentone, Calif.
Site: Southern Hills CC, Tulsa, Okla.
Date: Aug. 13-16 **Purse:** $200,000
Par: 35-35 - 70 (6,962 Yards)
Entries: 142 Cut at 150 70 players advanced

	Course Avg	Under Par	At Par	Over Par	Round Leader	Low Round	Dave Stockton
Round 1:	75.4	4	6	126		69 - J. Nicklaus, J. Miller	70 - Tied 5th
Round 2:	75.0	5	9	119	L. Hinson, D. Stockton	68 - G. Player, L. Graham	140 (70) - Tied 1st
Round 3:	73.9	6	3	61	Dave Stockton	65 - Ray Floyd	206 (66) - 1st
Round 4:	72.9	5	5	56	Dave Stockton	65 - Lee Trevino	279 (73) - 1st
Totals:	74.62	20	23	362			

TOURNAMENT SUMMARY

Place	Name	Score	Winnings	Place	Name	Score	Winnings	Place	Name	Score
1	Dave Stockton	70-70-66-73—279	$40,000.00	T-45	Larry Ziegler	71-73-79-72—295	$560.00	Cut	Don Bies	78-76—154
T-2	Bob Murphy	71-73-71-66—281	$18,500.00	T-48	Bill Collins	72-71-77-76—296	$420.00	Cut	Jim Colbert	75-79—154
T-2	Arnold Palmer	70-72-69-70—281	$18,500.00	T-48	Bert Greene	73-73-74-76—296	$420.00	Cut	Manuel de la Torre	75-79—154
T-4	Larry Hinson	69-71-74-68—282	$8,800.00	T-48	Phil Rodgers	74-74-76-72—296	$420.00	Cut	Dow Finsterwald	73-81—154
T-4	Gene Littler	72-71-69-70—282	$8,800.00	T-48	Hugh Royer	76-74-73-73—296	$420.00	Cut	Doug Ford	78-76—154
T-6	Bruce Crampton	73-75-68-67—283	$6,800.00	T-48	Jerry Steelsmith	73-72-78-73—296	$420.00	Cut	Robert Fry	75-79—154
T-6	Jack Nicklaus	68-76-73-66—283	$6,800.00	T-48	Robert Stone	73-77-75-71—296	$420.00	Cut	Grier Jones	80-74—154
T-8	Ray Floyd	71-73-65-75—284	$5,650.00	54	Ross Coon	74-73-74-76—297	$400.00	Cut	Monty Kaser	76-78—154
T-8	Dick Lotz	72-70-75-67—284	$5,650.00	T-55	Frank Beard	73-73-77-75—298	$400.00	Cut	Claude King	80-74—154
T-10	Billy Maxwell	72-71-73-69—285	$4,800.00	T-55	Deane Beman	76-72-74-76—298	$400.00	Cut	Ken Still	76-78—154
T-10	Mason Rudolph	71-70-73-71—285	$4,800.00	T-55	Gibby Gilbert	73-74-77-74—298	$400.00	Cut	Ken Towns	79-75—154
T-12	Don January	73-71-73-69—286	$3,750.00	T-55	George Knudson	77-73-74-74—298	$400.00	Cut	Maurice Ver Brugge	82-72—154
T-12	Johnny Miller	68-77-70-71—286	$3,750.00	T-55	Jim O'Hern	75-74-73-76—298	$400.00	Cut	Willard Wood	79-75—154
T-12	Gary Player	74-68-74-70—286	$3,750.00	T-55	Jimmy Wright	74-74-76-74—298	$400.00	Cut	Dick Hendrickson	70-85—155
T-12	Sam Snead	70-75-68-73—286	$3,750.00	T-61	George Archer	77-71-75-76—299	$400.00	Cut	Jim Lucius	76-79—155
T-16	Al Geiberger	72-74-71-71—288	$3,100.00	T-61	Tommy Jacobs	77-70-75-77—299	$400.00	Cut	John Molinda	75-80—155
T-16	Mike Hill	71-70-74-73—288	$3,100.00	63	Bob Rosburg	72-75-74-81—302	$400.00	Cut	Chuck Scally	73-82—155
T-18	Billy Casper	72-70-74-73—289	$2,500.00	64	Dick Bury	75-74-77-78—304	$400.00	Cut	George Bellino	80-76—156
T-18	Bruce Devlin	75-70-71-73—289	$2,500.00	T-65	Tommy Aycock	75-73-82-75—305	$400.00	Cut	Jon Gustin	76-80—156
T-18	Al Mengert	76-72-70-71—289	$2,500.00	T-65	Joe Jimenez	75-73-80-77—305	$400.00	Cut	Billy Parker	78-78—156
T-18	Dan Sikes	74-70-75-70—289	$2,500.00	T-65	Gordon Jones	75-75-78-77—305	$400.00	Cut	Bob Reith	83-73—156
T-22	Lou Graham	75-68-74-73—290	$1,825.00	T-68	Dave Hill	76-74-79-77—306	$400.00	Cut	Al Besselink	74-83—157
T-22	Bob Stanton	71-74-72-73—290	$1,825.00	T-68	Bob Hold	76-74-81-75—306	$400.00	Cut	Don Headings	78-79—157
T-22	Bert Yancey	74-69-75-72—290	$1,825.00	70	Dick Crawford	74-76-80-79—309	$400.00	Cut	Cass Jawor	79-78—157
T-22	Kermit Zarley	73-74-73-70—290	$1,825.00	Cut	Walter Burkemo	76-75—151		Cut	Joel Taylor	76-81—157
T-26	Julius Boros	72-71-72-76—291	$1,480.00	Cut	Dale Douglass	74-77—151		Cut	Jerry Barrier	81-77—158
T-26	Bob Charles	74-73-72-72—291	$1,480.00	Cut	Lee Elder	74-77—151		Cut	Tom Shaw	82-76—158
T-26	Terry Dill	72-71-75-73—291	$1,480.00	Cut	Lionel Hebert	76-75—151		Cut	Buck Adams	83-76—159
T-26	Bobby Nichols	71-76-72-72—291	$1,480.00	Cut	Fred Marti	75-76—151		Cut	Jerry Barber	80-79—159
T-26	Lee Trevino	72-77-77-65—291	$1,480.00	Cut	Jimmy Powell	75-76—151		Cut	Bob Ford	83-76—159
T-30	Homero Blancas	70-74-72-76—292	$1,225.00	Cut	Chi Chi Rodriguez	77-74—151		Cut	Jim McCoy	80-79—159
T-30	Hale Irwin	72-69-76-75—292	$1,225.00	Cut	Pat Schwab	75-76—151		Cut	Ernie Schneiter	80-79—159
T-30	Bob Menne	73-72-75-72—292	$1,225.00	Cut	R.H. Sikes	74-77—151		Cut	Tom Sanderson	82-79—161
T-30	Jim Wiechers	72-75-73-72—292	$1,225.00	Cut	Steve Spray	78-73—151		Cut	Denny Shute	85-76—161
T-35	Charles Coody	69-79-73-72—293	$1,016.67	Cut	Wayne Yates	76-75—151		Cut	Jack Webb	80-81—161
T-35	Rod Funseth	76-70-74-73—293	$1,016.66	Cut	Gay Brewer	77-75—152		Cut	Arnold Koehler	86-76—162
T-35	Howie Johnson	71-72-76-74—293	$1,016.66	Cut	Bob Goalby	79-73—152		Cut	Art Silvestrome	83-79—162
T-35	Dave Marr	76-71-74-72—293	$1,016.67	Cut	Tom Weiskopf	72-80—152		Cut	Dean Adkisson	80-84—164
T-35	Bobby Mitchell	72-76-76-69—293	$1,016.67	Cut	Chris Blocker	77-76—153		Cut	Gaylord Currie	79-85—164
T-35	Bob E. Smith	77-73-72-71—293	$1,016.67	Cut	Tony Jacklin	74-79—153		Cut	Chuck Hart	85-79—164
T-41	Jacky Cupit	70-77-75-72—294	$750.00	Cut	Eldridge Miles	76-77—153		Cut	Merle Backlund	84-81—165
T-41	Bob Lunn	74-69-70-81—294	$750.00	Cut	Bill Ogden	77-76—153		WD	Vic Ghezzi	79—79
T-41	Orville Moody	75-72-75-72—294	$750.00	Cut	Craig Shankland	75-78—153		WD	Pete Brown	82—82
T-41	Doug Sanders	75-74-71-74—294	$750.00	Cut	Gene Thompson	74-79—153		WD	Tony Holguin	82—82
T-45	Tommy Aaron	71-74-75-75—295	$560.00	Cut	Larry Wise	76-77—153				
T-45	Jack Burke Jr.	74-74-74-73—295	$560.00	Cut	Miller Barber	81-73—154				

1969

Raymond Floyd survived an outburst of social turbulence focused on Gary Player, and a gritty stretch drive by the South African, to win the 51st PGA Championship by one stroke. Floyd took a one-stroke lead in the second round and extended it to five strokes on Saturday, the same day a group of militant protesters erupted onto the golf course while Player was preparing to putt on the 10th green. Player, however, staged a rally in the final round, carrying him within a stroke of Floyd after Floyd bogeyed the 13th and 15th holes.

Player bogeyed the 16th while Floyd ran in a 35-foot birdie putt. Player's birdie at the 17th fell short of catching Floyd, who posted a winning 276.

Champion:	Raymond Floyd, Miami, Fla.
Site: NCR CC (South Course),	Dayton, Ohio
Date: Aug. 14-17	**Purse:** $175,000
Par: 36-35 - 71 (6,915 Yards)	
Entries: 140 Cut at 149 80 players advanced	

	Course Avg	Under Par	At Par	Over Par	Round Leader	Low Round	Ray Floyd
Round 1:	74.7	19	5	114	69 - R. Floyd, B. Lunn, T. Shaw, L. Ziegler, L. Mowry, C. Coody, J. Pott, B. Henry, A. Geiberger		69 - Tied 1st
Round 2:	73.8	22	12	103	Ray Floyd	64 - Don Bies	135 (66) - 1st
Round 3:	72.0	23	14	42	Ray Floyd	64 - Miller Barber	202 (67) - 1st
Round 4:	72.8	16	14	49	Ray Floyd	66 - Gay Brewer	276 (74) - 1st
Totals:	73.62	80	45	308			

TOURNAMENT SUMMARY

Place	Name	Score	Winnings	Place	Name	Score	Winnings	Place	Name	Score
1	Ray Floyd	69-66-67-74—276	$35,000.00	T-48	Bobby Brue	73-71-74-74—292	$289.25	Cut	Chuck Courtney	73-78—151
2	Gary Player	71-65-71-70—277	$20,000.00	T-48	Dale Douglass	73-76-72-71—292	$289.26	Cut	Joe Jimenez	76-75—151
3	Bert Greene	71-68-68-71—278	$12,400.00	T-48	Gene Littler	73-76-71-72—292	$289.26	Cut	Eddie Langert	75-76—151
4	Jimmy Wright	71-68-69-71—279	$8,300.00	T-48	Dick Lotz	75-73-69-75—292	$289.25	Cut	Dick Rhyan	74-77—151
T-5	Miller Barber	73-75-64-68—280	$6,725.00	T-48	Dave Marr	78-68-71-75—292	$289.25	Cut	Doug Sanders	72-79—151
T-5	Larry Ziegler	69-71-70-70—280	$6,725.00	T-48	Bobby Mitchell	73-71-75-73—292	$289.25	Cut	George Bellino	79-73—152
T-7	Charles Coody	69-71-72-69—281	$5,143.33	T-48	Phil Rodgers	70-72-75-75—292	$289.25	Cut	Gene Borek	75-77—152
T-7	Orville Moody	70-68-71-72—281	$5,143.33	T-48	Lee Trevino	73-71-72-76—292	$289.25	Cut	Jerry Mowlds	75-77—152
T-7	Terry Wilcox	72-71-72-66—281	$5,143.34	T-48	Dudley Wysong	72-76-73-71—292	$289.26	Cut	Earl Stewart	76-76—152
10	Frank Beard	70-75-68-69—282	$4,375.00	T-57	Tommy Aaron	70-72-79-72—293	$241.38	Cut	Rocky Thompson	77-75—152
T-11	Don Bies	74-64-71-74—283	$3,543.75	T-57	Jacky Cupit	70-73-75-75—293	$241.38	Cut	Bert Yancey	76-76—152
T-11	Bunky Henry	69-68-70-76—283	$3,543.75	T-59	Howell Fraser	72-76-71-75—294	$241.38	Cut	Jim Ferrier	74-79—153
T-11	Larry Mowry	69-71-69-74—283	$3,543.75	T-59	Pat Schwab	75-72-73-74—294	$241.38	Cut	Marty Fleckman	75-78—153
T-11	Jack Nicklaus	70-68-74-71—283	$3,543.75	T-59	Mike Souchak	75-73-74-72—294	$241.38	Cut	Doug Ford	79-74—153
T-15	Bruce Crampton	70-70-72-72—284	$2,712.50	T-59	Kermit Zarley	75-74-69-76—294	$241.38	Cut	Jimmy Powell	77-76—153
T-15	Dave Hill	74-75-67-68—284	$2,712.50	T-63	Dick Crawford	73-72-75-76—296	$241.38	Cut	Ken Still	78-75—153
T-15	Don January	75-70-70-69—284	$2,712.50	T-63	Jay Hebert	75-74-73-74—296	$241.38	Cut	Carroll Armstrong	79-75—154
T-15	Chi Chi Rodriguez	72-72-71-69—284	$2,712.50	T-63	Davis Love Jr.	73-71-76-76—296	$241.38	Cut	Bob Goalby	76-78—154
T-19	Howie Johnson	73-68-72-72—285	$2,137.50	T-63	Billy Maxwell	76-73-75-72—296	$241.38	Cut	George McKeown	77-77—154
T-19	Johnny Pott	69-75-71-70—285	$2,137.50	T-63	Bob Murphy	74-71-75-76—296	$241.38	Cut	Mason Rudolph	74-80—154
T-21	Ron Cerrudo	74-66-70-76—286	$1,718.75	T-63	Sam Snead	75-72-71-78—296	$241.38	Cut	Glenn Stuart	78-76—154
T-21	Bobby Cole	72-74-71-69—286	$1,718.75	T-69	George Archer	75-74-71-77—297	$241.38	Cut	Joe Cardenas	76-79—155
T-21	Bob Lunn	69-74-73-70—286	$1,718.75	T-69	Jack Burke Jr.	74-75-74-74—297	$241.38	Cut	Jim O'Hern	81-74—155
T-21	Tom Shaw	69-75-73-69—286	$1,718.75	T-69	Stan Dudas	76-70-76-75—297	$241.38	Cut	Hampton Auld	78-78—156
T-25	Julius Boros	72-74-70-71—287	$1,300.00	T-69	Jack McGowan	76-73-72-76—297	$241.38	Cut	Bill Flynn	77-79—156
T-25	Gay Brewer	74-71-76-66—287	$1,300.00	T-73	Ed Kroll	72-70-79-77—298	$241.38	Cut	Robert Fry	74-82—156
T-25	Bob Dickson	74-72-70-71—287	$1,300.00	T-73	Bob Stanton	77-72-73-76—298	$241.38	Cut	Herman Scharlau	78-78—156
T-25	Tony Jacklin	73-70-73-71—287	$1,300.00	T-73	Stan Thirsk	73-75-75-75—298	$241.38	Cut	Ernie Vossler	79-77—156
T-25	George Knudson	70-75-67-75—287	$1,300.00	T-76	John Cook	77-69-73-80—299	$241.38	Cut	Charles Malchaski	78-79—157
T-25	Fred Marti	73-70-71-73—287	$1,300.00	T-76	Dow Finsterwald	75-73-75-76—299	$241.37	Cut	Paul Scodeller	83-74—157
T-25	Dan Sikes	71-74-69-73—287	$1,300.00	T-76	Jim Turnesa	74-74-77-74—299	$241.38	Cut	George Shortridge	79-78—157
T-32	Butch Baird	71-71-75-71—288	$1,055.00	79	Eddie Merrins	75-70-77-80—302	$241.37	Cut	Gary Lockie	82-76—158
T-32	Bruce Devlin	70-78-69-71—288	$1,055.00	Cut	Tommy Bolt	74-76—150		Cut	Dan Murphy	79-79—158
T-32	Al Mengert	74-72-72-70—288	$1,055.00	Cut	Frank Boynton	75-75—150		Cut	Jimmy Bellizzi	79-80—159
T-35	Billy Casper	72-74-70-73—289	$890.00	Cut	Manuel de la Torre	77-73—150		Cut	Mike Podolski	80-79—159
T-35	Bob Charles	75-73-72-69—289	$890.00	Cut	Lee Elder	77-73—150		Cut	Doug MacDonald	84-76—160
T-35	Al Geiberger	69-72-77-71—289	$890.00	Cut	Lou Graham	76-74—150		Cut	Charles Sifford	82-78—160
T-35	Mac McLendon	73-68-75-73—289	$890.00	Cut	Lionel Hebert	76-74—150		Cut	Stan Staszowski	86-74—160
T-35	Steve Reid	72-75-71-71—289	$890.00	Cut	Mike Krak	74-76—150		Cut	Merle Backlund	83-78—161
T-35	Dave Stockton	75-67-71-76—289	$890.00	Cut	Dean Refram	72-78—150		Cut	Alan White	86-76—162
T-41	Pete Brown	77-72-70-71—290	$686.67	Cut	Bob Rosburg	72-78—150		Cut	Denny Shute	85-80—165
T-41	Gardner Dickinson	72-70-72-76—290	$686.66	Cut	Bob E. Smith	76-74—150		Cut	Rick Jetter	80-87—167
T-41	Dick Hart	73-73-72-72—290	$686.67	Cut	Roland Stafford	76-74—150		DQ	Jim Rudolph	
T-44	Harold Henning	74-73-70-74—291	$512.50	Cut	Art Wall	78-72—150		WD	Arnold Palmer	82—82
T-44	Larry Hinson	75-74-70-72—291	$512.50	Cut	Fred Wampler	77-73—150		WD	Jim Colbert	74-73—147
T-44	Bobby Nichols	74-71-75-71—291	$512.50	Cut	Jerry Barber	75-76—151				
T-44	Tom Weiskopf	70-76-70-75—291	$512.50	Cut	Johnny Bulla	73-78—151				

1968

Julius Boros survived the wilting midsummer Texas heat and the treacherous 18th hole at Pecan Valley Country Club to snatch the 50th PGA Championship from Arnold Palmer and Bob Charles. Palmer, frustrated again in his quest for a PGA title, made a magnificent par at the final hole for a 282 after watching several good birdie putts slide past the cup in the closing round. But Boros pitched a long chip within two feet of the pin for a par, becoming, at the age of 48, the oldest winner in PGA Championship history.

Champion:	Julius Boros, Fort Lauderdale, Fla.
Site:	Pecan Valley CC, San Antonio, Texas
Date: July 18-21	**Purse:** $150,000
Par: 35-35 - 70 (7,096 Yards)	
Entries: 167 Cut at 149 74 players advanced	

	Course Avg	Under Par	At Par	Over Par	Round Leader	Low Round	Julius Boros
Round 1:	75.7	5	7	153	Marty Fleckman	66 - Marty Fleckman	71 - Tied 13th
Round 2:	75.3	4	10	146	Marty Fleckman	67 - Doug Sanders	142 (71) - Tied 9th
Round 3:	73.6	4	11	59	Marty Fleckman	68- D. Stockton, K. Zarley, D. Rhyan	212 (70) - Tied 3rd
Round 4:	73.2	5	10	59	Julius Boros	68 - Charles Coody	281 (69) - 1st
Totals:	74.88	18	38	417			

TOURNAMENT SUMMARY

Place	Name	Score	Winnings	Place	Name	Score	Winnings	Place	Name	Score
1	Julius Boros	71-71-70-69—281	$25,000.00	T-54	Don Whitt	75-71-74-77—297	$415.00	Cut	Larry Fryer	80-74—154
T-2	Bob Charles	72-70-70-70—282	$12,500.00	T-57	Laurie Hammer	70-78-78-72—298	$395.00	Cut	Jay Hebert	74-80—154
T-2	Arnold Palmer	71-69-72-70—282	$12,500.00	T-57	Bobby Nichols	75-72-76-75—298	$395.00	Cut	Paul Kelly	73-81—154
T-4	George Archer	71-69-74-69—283	$7,500.00	T-59	Ross Coon	72-76-76-75—299	$369.00	Cut	Babe Lichardus	73-81—154
T-4	Marty Fleckman	66-72-72-73—283	$7,500.00	T-59	Bob Hamilton	78-71-74-76—299	$369.00	Cut	Hugh Royer	75-79—154
T-6	Frank Beard	68-75-72-74—284	$5,750.00	T-59	Bobby Mitchell	74-75-72-78—299	$369.00	Cut	George Shortridge	76-78—154
T-6	Billy Casper	74-70-70-70—284	$5,750.00	T-59	Horace Moore	72-76-77-74—299	$369.00	Cut	Tal Smith	78-76—154
T-8	Miller Barber	70-70-72-73—285	$3,405.55	T-59	Charles Sifford	73-74-77-75—299	$369.00	Cut	Lou Warobick	74-80—154
T-8	Frank Boynton	70-73-72-70—285	$3,405.56	T-64	Bob Benning	76-71-79-74—300	$365.00	Cut	Rex Baxter	76-79—155
T-8	Charles Coody	70-77-70-68—285	$3,405.56	T-64	Bill Collins	76-73-74-77—300	$365.00	Cut	Johnny Bulla	75-80—155
T-8	Al Geiberger	70-73-71-71—285	$3,405.56	T-64	Pat Rea	76-73-74-77—300	$365.00	Cut	Joe Conrad	80-75—155
T-8	Bob Goalby	73-72-70-70—285	$3,405.56	T-67	Joe Cardenas	73-74-80-75—302	$365.00	Cut	Ronald Mattson	79-76—155
T-8	Lou Graham	73-70-70-72—285	$3,405.55	T-67	Bob Crowley	77-71-77-77—302	$365.00	Cut	Charles Volpone	79-76—155
T-8	Doug Sanders	72-67-73-73—285	$3,405.55	69	Jim Picard	77-70-77-79—303	$365.00	Cut	Jay White	79-76—155
T-8	Dan Sikes	70-72-73-70—285	$3,405.56	T-70	Gene Mitchell	75-70-82-79—306	$365.00	Cut	George Bayer	79-77—156
T-8	Kermit Zarley	72-75-68-70—285	$3,405.55	T-70	Robert Schoener	79-70-79-78—306	$365.00	Cut	Jim Ferrier	80-76—156
T-17	Dave Hill	72-74-69-71—286	$2,050.00	T-70	Gene Webb	76-73-79-78—306	$365.00	Cut	Bill Giese	82-74—156
T-17	Mason Rudolph	69-75-70-72—286	$2,050.00	T-73	Manuel de la Torre	73-76-80-78—307	$365.00	Cut	Scotty McBeath	76-80—156
T-17	Dave Stockton	75-71-68-72—286	$2,050.00	T-73	Larry Ziegler	75-73-76-83—307	$365.00	Cut	Eddie Merrins	75-81—156
T-20	Gay Brewer	71-72-72-72—287	$1,700.00	Cut	Bob Below	74-76—150		Cut	Dick Plummer	76-80—156
T-20	Al Mengert	71-73-70-73—287	$1,700.00	Cut	Robert Keith	75-75—150		Cut	Jim Turnesa	78-78—156
T-20	Dick Rhyan	72-72-68-75—287	$1,700.00	Cut	Jack Nicklaus	71-79—150		Cut	Sam Urzetta	77-79—156
T-23	Bruce Crampton	71-75-70-72—288	$1,400.00	Cut	Bob Rosburg	75-75—150		Cut	Frank Wharton	77-79—156
T-23	Lee Trevino	69-71-72-76—288	$1,400.00	Cut	Ernie Schneiter	75-75—150		Cut	Jerry Belt	82-75—157
T-23	Bert Yancey	75-71-70-72—288	$1,400.00	Cut	Mike Souchak	76-74—150		Cut	Don Headings	81-76—157
T-26	Tommy Aaron	73-73-70-73—289	$1,062.50	Cut	Stan Thirsk	77-73—150		Cut	Dan Murphy	79-78—157
T-26	Don Bies	69-73-74-73—289	$1,062.50	Cut	Fred Wampler	74-76—150		Cut	Craig Shankland	78-79—157
T-26	Dick Crawford	71-75-73-70—289	$1,062.50	Cut	Jerry Abbott	76-75—151		Cut	Bob Clark	76-82—158
T-26	Steve Reid	73-73-71-72—289	$1,062.50	Cut	Herry Barber	77-74—151		Cut	John Dalrymple	79-79—158
T-30	Gardner Dickinson	74-69-76-71—290	$862.50	Cut	James Barber	76-75—151		Cut	Wes Ellis Jr.	81-77—158
T-30	Lionel Hebert	75-71-70-74—290	$862.50	Cut	John Felus	74-77—151		Cut	Emil Scodeller	81-77—158
T-30	Gene Littler	73-74-74-69—290	$862.50	Cut	Don Massengale	75-76—151		Cut	Tom Weiskopf	77-82—159
T-30	Bob Lunn	72-75-72-71—290	$862.50	Cut	Ed Moehling	75-76—151		Cut	Don Collett	78-82—160
T-34	Johnny Pott	70-70-75-76—291	$775.00	Cut	Jimmy Powell	76-75—151		Cut	Ed Lockie	77-83—160
T-34	Sam Snead	75-71-72-73—291	$775.00	Cut	Art Proctor	76-75—151		Cut	Dick Merritt	81-79—160
T-34	Terry Wilcox	74-73-71-73—291	$775.00	Cut	R.H. Sikes	76-75—151		Cut	Werner Teichmann	80-80—160
T-37	Mac Hunter	71-72-73-76—292	$686.25	Cut	Glenn Stuart	72-79—151		Cut	Bill Grygiel	78-83—161
T-37	John Lively	74-74-72-72—292	$686.25	Cut	Walter Burkemo	74-78—152		Cut	Dennis O'Leary	86-75—161
T-37	Jerry Pittman	74-71-74-73—292	$686.25	Cut	Jerry Edwards	72-80—152		Cut	Bob Kruse	79-83—162
T-37	Bill Sporre	73-73-76-70—292	$686.25	Cut	Bob Hill	80-72—152		Cut	Gary Loustalot	82-80—162
T-41	Tim Debaufre	72-75-73-73—293	$586.25	Cut	Tom Liljeholm	76-76—152		Cut	Robert Nichols	84-78—162
T-41	Ray Floyd	79-70-73-71—293	$586.25	Cut	Sonny Ridenhour	78-74—152		Cut	Fred Nonnenberg	77-85—162
T-41	Earl Jacobson	73-74-74-72—293	$586.25	Cut	Bob Ross	77-75—152		Cut	Merle Backlund	81-82—163
T-41	Tom Shaw	76-71-77-69—293	$586.25	Cut	Dick Stranahan	80-72—152		Cut	Bill Majure	81-83—164
T-45	Harold Henning	73-74-76-71—294	$535.00	Cut	Bill Bisdorf	73-80—153		Cut	Ray Ziats	86-78—164
T-45	Robert Stone	74-72-72-76—294	$535.00	Cut	Ken Burnette	77-76—153		Cut	Warren MacCarty	86-79—165
T-45	Larry Wise	75-71-74-74—294	$535.00	Cut	Billy Farrell	76-77—153		Cut	Tom Deaton	83-85—168
T-48	Al Chandler	72-74-77-72—295	$483.33	Cut	J.C. Goosie	76-77—153		Cut	Al Stein	82-86—168
T-48	Dow Finsterwald	71-75-75-74—295	$483.34	Cut	Dave Marr	77-76—153		Cut	John Frillman	85-85—170
T-48	Ken Venturi	74-71-75-75—295	$483.34	Cut	Jim O'Hern	79-74—153		Cut	Paul Kern	86-84—170
T-51	Tommy Aycock	73-74-71-78—296	$445.00	Cut	Paul Runyan	79-74—153		WD	Freddie Haas Jr.	77—77
T-51	Sam Carmichael	73-73-79-71—296	$445.00	Cut	Dick Turner	77-76—153		WD	Jouett Brown	79—79
T-51	Don January	78-71-75-72—296	$445.00	Cut	Dudley Wysong	77-76—153		WD	Bob Galloway	80—80
T-54	Jim Mooney	75-74-73-75—297	$415.00	Cut	Paul Bondeson	79-75—154		WD	George Keyes	82—82
T-54	Stan Mosel	76-73-77-71—297	$415.00	Cut	Doug Ford	77-77—154		WD	Claude King	83—83

1967

For the second time in the 10-year history of the PGA Championship as a stroke play tournament, the winner was decided in a playoff. Played in the thin, mile-high Colorado atmosphere, two lowland neighbors from Texas, Don January and Don Massengale, adapted nicely to the rarefied air to come down to the wire deadlocked at 281. Even though January had lost the 1961 PGA Championship in a playoff, he proved the steadier of the two in an 18-hole playoff with a 3-under-par 69 to Massengale's 71.

Champion: Don January, Dallas, Texas		
Site: Columbine CC, Denver, Colo.		
Date: July 20-24	**Purse:** $148,200	
Par: 36-36 - 72 (7,436 Yards)		
Entries: 145	Cut at 151	73 players advanced

	Course Avg	Under Par	At Par	Over Par	Round Leader	Low Round	Don January
Round 1:	75.3	18	11	113	Dave Hill	66 - Dave Hill	71 - Tied 13th
Round 2:	75.9	18	7	115	Tommy Aaron	65 - Tommy Aaron	143 (72) - Tied 7th
Round 3:	73.4	25	6	42	Dan Sikes	68 - Bob Goalby	213 (70) - Tied 5th
Round 4:	72.9	22	9	42	D. Massengale, D. January	66 - Don Massengale	281 (68) - Tied 1st
Totals:	74.81	83	33	312			

TOURNAMENT SUMMARY

Place	Name	Score	Winnings	Place	Name	Score	Winnings	Place	Name	Score
1	Don January	71-72-70-68—281	$25,000.00	T-44	D.M. McBeath	74-72-75-75—296	$501.43	Cut	Monte Bradley	79-75—154
2	Don Massengale	70-75-70-66—281	$15,000.00	T-44	Robert Stone	74-74-75-73—296	$501.43	Cut	Rudy Goff	78-76—154
T-3	Jack Nicklaus	67-75-69-71—282	$9,000.00	T-51	Freddie Haas Jr.	74-72-79-72—297	$430.00	Cut	Herman Keiser	81-73—154
T-3	Dan Sikes	69-70-70-73—282	$9,000.00	T-51	Skee Riegel	76-75-74-72—297	$430.00	Cut	Frank Keller	78-76—154
T-5	Julius Boros	69-76-70-68—283	$6,500.00	T-51	Bob Toski	72-76-71-78—297	$430.00	Cut	Odell Trueblood	76-78—154
T-5	Al Geiberger	73-71-69-70—283	$6,500.00	T-51	Jimmy Wright	73-74-77-73—297	$430.00	Cut	Ken Yount	76-78—154
T-7	Frank Beard	71-74-70-70—285	$4,750.00	T-55	George Archer	74-76-75-73—298	$389.00	Cut	Jerry Barber	75-80—155
T-7	Don Bies	69-70-76-70—285	$4,750.00	T-55	Paul Harney	75-75-74-74—298	$389.00	Cut	Bob Ford	75-80—155
T-7	Bob Goalby	70-74-68-73—285	$4,750.00	T-55	Davis Love Jr.	69-79-76-74—298	$389.00	Cut	Ed Kroll	78-77—155
T-7	Gene Littler	73-72-71-69—285	$4,750.00	T-55	Bobby Mitchell	76-74-70-78—298	$389.00	Cut	Stan Mosel	77-78—155
T-11	Billy Farrell	75-72-69-70—286	$3,200.00	T-55	James Stamps	74-73-73-74—298	$389.00	Cut	Bob Wynn	77-78—155
T-11	Dave Hill	66-73-74-73—286	$3,200.00	T-60	Dow Finsterwald	74-75-74-76—299	$300.00	Cut	Andy Borkovich	73-83—156
T-11	Ken Venturi	73-74-71-68—286	$3,200.00	T-60	Dick Hart	73-75-75-76—299	$300.00	Cut	Walter Burkemo	81-75—156
T-14	Sam Carmichael	75-71-69-72—287	$2,360.00	T-60	Mac Hunter	72-75-71-81—299	$300.00	Cut	George Keyes	79-77—156
T-14	Lionel Hebert	75-71-70-71—287	$2,360.00	63	Johnny Bulla	78-73-76-73—300	$300.00	Cut	Edward Bosse	78-79—157
T-14	Bobby Nichols	75-75-67-70—287	$2,360.00	T-64	Clare Emery	73-76-79-73—301	$300.00	Cut	Ernie George	81-76—157
T-14	Arnold Palmer	70-71-72-74—287	$2,360.00	T-64	Jim Ferrier	74-75-75-77—301	$300.00	Cut	Clayton Johnson	78-79—157
T-14	R.H. Sikes	72-71-71-73—287	$2,360.00	T-64	Pat Schwab	75-76-75-75—301	$300.00	Cut	Gifford Nutbrown	81-76—157
19	Billy Casper	75-70-75-68—288	$1,900.00	T-67	Gene Bone	72-74-78-78—302	$300.00	Cut	Bob Popp	82-75—157
T-20	Tommy Aaron	70-65-76-78—289	$1,600.00	T-67	Chick Harbert	73-76-77-76—302	$300.00	Cut	Glenn Stuart	77-80—157
T-20	Bill Bisdorf	72-71-77-69—289	$1,600.00	T-67	Tommy Jacobs	74-74-76-78—302	$300.00	Cut	J.D. Taylor	77-80—157
T-20	Dick Crawford	76-73-73-67—289	$1,600.00	70	Robert Erickson	76-75-80-72—303	$300.00	Cut	George Bellino	77-81—158
T-20	Ray Floyd	74-69-74-72—289	$1,600.00	71	Roland Stafford	74-76-78-76—304	$300.00	Cut	Bobby Brue	79-79—158
T-20	Mike Souchak	70-73-70-76—289	$1,600.00	72	Richard Bassett	70-80-86-69—305	$300.00	Cut	Craig Shankland	78-80—158
25	Wes Ellis Jr.	76-71-72-71—290	$1,300.00	73	Glenn Teal	77-74-77-80—308	$300.00	Cut	Joe Cardenas	80-79—159
T-26	Bruce Crampton	71-77-74-69—291	$1,150.00	Cut	Michael Ballo	76-76—152		Cut	Don Klein	78-81—159
T-26	Earl Stewart	77-70-72-72—291	$1,150.00	Cut	Elhannon Collins	74-78—152		Cut	Ron Reitz	71-88—159
T-28	Gay Brewer	75-74-71-72—292	$900.00	Cut	Doug Ford	78-74—152		Cut	Bill Sporre	81-78—159
T-28	Gardner Dickinson	75-72-69-76—292	$900.00	Cut	Jay Hebert	77-75—152		Cut	Pat Rielly	78-82—160
T-28	Phil Rodgers	71-76-72-73—292	$900.00	Cut	Darrell Hickok	72-80—152		Cut	James Riggins	78-82—160
T-28	Mason Rudolph	72-73-73-74—292	$900.00	Cut	Joe Moresco	75-77—152		Cut	Dick Bull	77-84—161
T-28	Doug Sanders	72-71-76-73—292	$900.00	Cut	Johnny Pott	77-75—152		Cut	Jimmie Gauntt	78-83—161
T-33	Dave Marr	75-72-71-75—293	$750.00	Cut	Alex Redmond	77-75—152		Cut	Bob Hill	82-79—161
T-33	Tom Nieporte	73-73-73-74—293	$750.00	Cut	Bob Ross	73-79—152		Cut	George Schneiter	80-81—161
T-33	Jerry Pittman	72-78-69-74—293	$750.00	Cut	Al Besselink	74-79—153		Cut	Larry Crawford	81-81—162
T-33	Ernie Vossler	72-74-73-74—293	$750.00	Cut	Steve Bull	74-79—153		Cut	Tony Novitsky	79-83—162
T-33	Dudley Wysong	73-70-76-74—293	$750.00	Cut	Bob Duden	77-76—153		Cut	Ed Whalley	85-78—163
T-38	Bill Martindale	73-76-74-71—294	$632.50	Cut	John Felus	72-81—153		Cut	Dick Stranahan	81-83—164
T-38	Ken Still	73-74-76-71—294	$632.50	Cut	Bob Goetz	75-78—153		Cut	Ernest Fortner	83-82—165
T-38	Fred Wampler	73-75-74-72—294	$632.50	Cut	Don Kubiak	73-80—153		Cut	Hap Malia	81-84—165
T-38	Bob Zimmerman	76-74-76-68—294	$632.50	Cut	Duke Matthews	75-78—153		Cut	Terry Lally	86-84—170
T-42	Frank Boynton	71-76-73-75—295	$572.50	Cut	Eddie Merrins	76-77—153		Cut	Stan Mack	86-85—171
T-42	Jack Burke Jr.	73-78-71-73—295	$572.50	Cut	Horace Moore	80-73—153		DQ	Chandler Harper	
T-44	John Berry	76-70-78-72—296	$501.43	Cut	Jim Petersen	76-77—153		WD	Jacky Cupit	74—74
T-44	Pete Cooper	77-70-78-71—296	$501.43	Cut	Dick Rhyan	76-77—153		WD	Dick Marshall	77—77
T-44	Dale Douglass	74-73-72-77—296	$501.42	Cut	Walter Romans	76-77—153		WD	Bert Yancey	74-76—150
T-44	Babe Lichardus	75-75-71-75—296	$501.43	Cut	Bob Rosburg	79-74—153		WD	Bruce Devlin	80-71—151
T-44	Larry Mancour	75-76-72-73—296	$501.43	Cut	John Ruedi	75-78—153				

1966

The 1966 Championship was a triumph for 28-year-old Al Geiberger. Munching peanut butter sandwiches for stamina, the California native shared the first-round lead with Sam Snead. The lead bounced back and forth, but when Snead fired final rounds of 75 and 73, Geiberger won with four strokes to spare over Dudley Wysong, whose third-round 66 was the best of the Championship.

Champion: Al Geiberger, Solvang, Calif.
Site: Firestone CC, Akron, Ohio
Date: July 21-24   **Purse:** $149,360
Par: 35-35 - 70 (7,180 Yards)
Entries: 163   Cut at 151   76 players advanced

	Course Avg	Under Par	At Par	Over Par	Round Leader	Low Round		Al Geiberger
Round 1:	76.4	5	1	156	68 - A. Geiberger, Sam Snead			68 - Tied 1st
Round 2:	75.7	0	5	148	139 - Sam Snead	70 -	G. Player, J. Riggins, D. Finsterwald, E. Vossler, B. Farrell	140 (72) - Tied 2nd
Round 3:	74.0	6	5	65	208 - Al Geiberger	66 -	D. Wysong	208 (68) - 1st
Round 4:	73.6	5	4	66	280- Al Geiberger	68 -	R. Floyd, A. Palmer	280 (72) - 1st
Totals:	75.36	16	15	435				

TOURNAMENT SUMMARY

Place	Name	Score	Winnings	Place	Name	Score	Winnings	Place	Name	Score
1	Al Geiberger	68-72-68-72—280	$25,000.00	T-49	Al Mengert	72-77-76-73—298	$436.11	Cut	Charles Leider	80-75—155
2	Dudley Wysong	74-72-66-72—284	$15,000.00	T-49	Bob Shave	78-72-77-71—298	$436.12	Cut	Jim Lucius	79-76—155
T-3	Billy Casper	73-73-70-70—286	$8,333.34	T-49	Bert Yancey	74-75-77-72—298	$436.11	Cut	Sam Reynolds	83-72—155
T-3	Gene Littler	75-71-71-69—286	$8,333.33	T-58	Al Chandler	76-73-71-79—299	$340.00	Cut	Warner Tyree	79-76—155
T-3	Gary Player	73-70-70-73—286	$8,333.33	T-58	Robert Erickson	79-71-74-75—299	$340.00	Cut	Dick Cline	79-77—156
T-6	Julius Boros	69-72-75-71—287	$5,000.00	T-58	Ed Griffiths	73-72-73-81—299	$340.00	Cut	Bob Harrison	81-75—156
T-6	Jacky Cupit	70-73-73-71—287	$5,000.00	T-58	Bob McCallister	74-76-76-73—299	$340.00	Cut	Dan Keefe	79-77—156
T-6	Arnold Palmer	75-73-71-68—287	$5,000.00	T-58	Bo Wininger	76-75-75-73—299	$340.00	Cut	Monte Norcross	80-76—156
T-6	Doug Sanders	69-74-73-71—287	$5,000.00	63	Joe Conrad	77-74-76-73—300	$300.00	Cut	Bill Ogden	79-77—156
T-6	Sam Snead	68-71-75-73—287	$5,000.00	T-64	Errie Ball	77-74-78-72—301	$300.00	Cut	Billy Parker	78-78—156
11	Frank Beard	73-72-69-74—288	$3,500.00	T-64	Lionel Hebert	75-74-75-77—301	$300.00	Cut	George Bellino	81-76—157
T-12	Dow Finsterwald	74-70-73-72—289	$2,933.33	T-66	Jack Burke Jr.	75-76-79-72—302	$300.00	Cut	Stan Dudas	77-80—157
T-12	Jay Hebert	75-73-70-71—289	$2,933.34	T-66	Ed Kroll	75-75-74-78—302	$300.00	Cut	Rudy Goff	79-78—157
T-12	Don January	69-71-73-76—289	$2,933.33	T-66	Horace Moore	74-74-76-78—302	$300.00	Cut	Paul Haviland	78-79—157
T-15	Paul Harney	74-73-71-72—290	$2,350.00	T-66	Ed Rubis	76-72-77-77—302	$300.00	Cut	Clayton Johnson	81-76—157
T-15	Bill Martindale	73-75-70-72—290	$2,350.00	T-70	Bob Verwey	76-75-78-74—303	$300.00	Cut	Charles Rotar	84-73—157
T-15	Ken Venturi	74-72-72-72—290	$2,350.00	T-70	Wayne Yates	73-76-79-75—303	$300.00	Cut	Denny Shute	77-80—157
T-18	Gardner Dickinson	74-72-73-72—291	$1,862.50	T-72	Larry Beck	71-79-78-76—304	$300.00	Cut	Bob Kay	81-77—158
T-18	Ray Floyd	74-75-74-68—291	$1,862.50	T-72	Tom Weiskopf	75-73-80-76—304	$300.00	Cut	Harold Kneece	82-76—158
T-18	Dave Marr	75-75-68-73—291	$1,862.50	74	Bill Blanton	78-72-80-76—306	$300.00	Cut	Bud Williamson	78-80—158
T-18	Ernie Vossler	77-70-75-69—291	$1,862.50	75	James Riggins	76-70-82-79—307	$300.00	Cut	Bob Ford	79-80—159
T-22	Tommy Aaron	71-72-75-74—292	$1,400.00	Cut	Gene Bone	74-78—152		Cut	Ed Kynch	83-76—159
T-22	Frank Boynton	73-74-73-72—292	$1,400.00	Cut	Jouett Brown	79-73—152		Cut	Al Morley	78-81—159
T-22	Billy Farrell	73-70-71-78—292	$1,400.00	Cut	Johnny Bulla	73-79—152		Cut	Bobby Nichols	81-78—159
T-22	Jack Nicklaus	75-71-75-71—292	$1,400.00	Cut	J.C. Goosie	76-76—152		Cut	Skee Riegel	80-79—159
T-22	Mason Rudolph	74-73-76-69—292	$1,400.00	Cut	Chick Harbert	75-77—152		Cut	Chuck Scally	79-80—159
27	Gay Brewer	73-73-76-71—293	$1,100.00	Cut	Dick Hart	75-77—152		Cut	Glenn Stuart	80-79—159
T-28	Butch Baird	73-74-73-74—294	$900.00	Cut	Bob Hill	74-78—152		Cut	Alphonso Atkins	77-83—160
T-28	Bruce Devlin	76-71-71-76—294	$900.00	Cut	Babe Hiskey	74-78—152		Cut	George Bruno	82-78—160
T-28	Ron Howell	76-71-75-72—294	$900.00	Cut	Tommy Jacobs	75-77—152		Cut	Joe Cardenas	81-79—160
T-28	Don Massengale	74-72-75-73—294	$900.00	Cut	Tom Malone	78-74—152		Cut	Tony Novitsky	80-80—160
T-28	Dan Sikes	72-76-74-72—294	$900.00	Cut	Kel Nagle	75-77—152		Cut	Joe Zakarian	80-81—161
T-28	R.H. Sikes	75-72-73-74—294	$900.00	Cut	Dean Refram	76-76—152		Cut	Brien Charter	77-85—162
T-34	Miller Barber	76-71-72-76—295	$775.00	Cut	Phil Rodgers	76-76—152		Cut	Ernest Fortner	85-77—162
T-34	Buster Cupit	75-76-74-70—295	$775.00	Cut	Jack Rule	74-78—152		Cut	Bob Hold	82-80—162
T-34	Tony Lema	78-71-72-74—295	$775.00	Cut	Bob Spence	74-78—152		Cut	John Dalrymple	82-81—163
T-37	Bill Bisdorf	76-72-76-72—296	$659.17	Cut	Dick Whetzle	75-77—152		Cut	William Staskewicz	82-82—164
T-37	Gene Borek	75-76-75-70—296	$659.17	Cut	Walter Burkemo	74-79—153		Cut	Bob Watson	87-77—164
T-37	Chick Evans	73-75-74-74—296	$659.17	Cut	Corky Dahl	74-79—153		Cut	Arthur Harris	84-81—165
T-37	Freddie Haas Jr.	78-73-75-70—296	$659.17	Cut	Tont Evans	78-75—153		Cut	Sam Urzetta	81-84—165
T-37	Babe Lichardus	72-75-73-76—296	$659.16	Cut	Doug Ford	76-77—153		Cut	Ron Demao	82-84—166
T-37	Stan Thirsk	74-77-70-75—296	$659.16	Cut	Robert Fry	78-75—153		Cut	Harold Paddock	84-84—168
T-37	Manuel de la Torre	75-72-77-73—297	$542.50	Cut	Jerry Pittman	77-76—153		Cut	Merle Backlund	85-84—169
T-43	Bruce Crampton	74-73-74-76—297	$542.50	Cut	Mike Souchak	79-74—153		Cut	Arnold Haneke	82-89—171
T-43	Rod Funseth	73-74-74-76—297	$542.50	Cut	Jim Turnesa	80-73—153		WD	Vic Ghezzi	74—74
T-43	Walker Inman	71-76-76-74—297	$542.50	Cut	Bernie Haas	78-76—154		WD	Johnny Pott	74—74
T-43	George Knudson	72-74-77-74—297	$542.50	Cut	Gordon Jones	81-73—154		WD	James Clark	76—76
T-43	Bob Rosburg	73-76-69-79—297	$542.50	Cut	Mac Main	75-79—154		WD	Billy Capps	77—77
T-49	Jim Ferrier	71-79-76-72—298	$436.11	Cut	Ronnie Reif	77-77—154		WD	Dale Andreason	78—78
T-49	Jack Fleck	71-74-78-75—298	$436.11	Cut	Melvin Roe	79-75—154		WD	Randy Glover	78—78
T-49	Ed Furgol	74-77-71-76—298	$436.11	Cut	Joe Brown	74-81—155		WD	Bob Duden	80—80
T-49	Bob Goalby	76-73-73-76—298	$436.11	Cut	Steve Bull	79-76—155		WD	Bob Hamilton	80—80
T-49	Bob Keller	72-76-72-78—298	$436.11	Cut	Fred Gronauer	78-77—155		WD	David G. Smith	80—80
T-49	Larry Laoretti	73-77-72-76—298	$436.11	Cut	Bud Holscher	78-77—155		WD	Jerry Barber	73-78-84—235

PGA CHAMPIONSHIP SUMMARIES

1965

Dave Marr, 31, started the final round in a first place tie with Tommy Aaron. With Aaron fading with a 40 on the front nine, Billy Casper and Jack Nicklaus were threatening. Going into the last hole, Marr hooked his drive into a trap. He played his second shot short of a lake that lies in front of the green and hit an 9-iron three feet from the cup. He made the putt for a two-stroke win over Casper and Nicklaus.

Champion: Dave Marr, Houston, Texas	
Site: Laurel Valley GC, Ligonier, Pa.	
Date: Aug. 12-15	Purse: $149,700
Par: 36-35 - 71 (7,090 Yards)	
Entries: 167 Cut at 147 95 players advanced	

	Course Avg	Under Par	At Par	Over Par	Round Leader	Low Round	Dave Marr
Round 1:	75.8	12	6	147	Tommy Aaron	66 - Tommy Aaron	70 - Tied 8th
Round 2:	76.3	9	9	145	Tommy Aaron	68 - Bob McCallister	139 (69) - Tied 2nd
Round 3:	74.0	10	6	61	T. Aaron, D. Marr	69 - R. Funseth, G. Dickinson	209 (70) - Tied 1st
Round 4:	74.2	10	7	59	Dave Marr	66 - Bo Wininger	280 (71) - 1st
Totals:	75.46	41	28	412			

TOURNAMENT SUMMARY

Place	Name	Score	Winnings
1	Dave Marr	70-69-70-71—280	$25,000.00
T-2	Billy Casper	70-70-71-71—282	$12,500.00
T-2	Jack Nicklaus	69-70-72-71—282	$12,500.00
4	Bo Wininger	73-72-72-66—283	$8,000.00
5	Gardner Dickinson	67-74-69-74—284	$7,000.00
T-6	Bruce Devlin	68-75-72-70—285	$5,750.00
T-6	Sam Snead	68-75-70-72—285	$5,750.00
T-8	Tommy Aaron	66-71-72-78—287	$4,040.00
T-8	Jack Burke Jr.	75-71-72-69—287	$4,040.00
T-8	Jacky Cupit	72-76-70-69—287	$4,040.00
T-8	Rod Funseth	75-72-69-71—287	$4,040.00
T-8	Bob McCallister	76-68-70-73—287	$4,040.00
T-13	Wes Ellis Jr.	73-76-70-69—288	$2,800.00
T-13	R.H. Sikes	71-71-71-75—288	$2,800.00
T-15	Ben Hogan	72-75-70-72—289	$2,425.00
T-15	Mike Souchak	70-72-77-70—289	$2,425.00
T-17	Julius Boros	75-72-73-70—290	$2,125.00
T-17	Ray Floyd	68-73-72-77—290	$2,125.00
19	Al Geiberger	74-71-71-75—291	$1,900.00
T-20	Bruce Crampton	77-74-70-71—292	$1,450.00
T-20	Jack Fleck	76-71-72-73—292	$1,450.00
T-20	Doug Ford	73-70-77-72—292	$1,450.00
T-20	Gordon Jones	72-76-71-73—292	$1,450.00
T-20	George Knudson	75-69-73-75—292	$1,450.00
T-20	Kel Nagle	74-75-71-72—292	$1,450.00
T-20	Mason Rudolph	67-76-75-74—292	$1,450.00
T-20	Doug Sanders	71-73-74-74—292	$1,450.00
T-28	Don Bies	71-71-75-76—293	$915.00
T-28	Gay Brewer	75-70-73-75—293	$915.00
T-28	Paul Kelly	76-71-75-71—293	$915.00
T-28	Gene Littler	78-70-75-70—293	$915.00
T-28	Johnny Pott	76-70-74-73—293	$915.00
T-33	Manuel de la Torre	72-73-74-75—294	$737.50
T-33	Ed Furgol	73-74-72-75—294	$737.50
T-33	Paul Harney	74-74-72-74—294	$737.50
T-33	Al Mengert	75-76-75-68—294	$737.50
T-33	Arnold Palmer	72-75-74-73—294	$737.50
T-33	Gary Player	74-72-74-74—294	$737.50
T-33	Dave Ragan	73-73-78-70—294	$737.50
T-33	Charles Sifford	73-75-71-75—294	$737.50
T-41	Walter Burkemo	72-77-73-73—295	$602.50
T-41	Bob Charles	75-75-73-72—295	$602.50
T-43	Dale Douglass	72-76-74-74—296	$572.50
T-43	Billy Maxwell	71-75-74-76—296	$572.50
T-45	Frank Beard	74-74-72-77—297	$527.50
T-45	Billy Farrell	76-75-75-71—297	$527.50
T-45	Dick Hart	72-77-72-76—297	$527.50
T-45	Dan Sikes	74-75-73-75—297	$527.50
T-49	Vic Ghezzi	73-77-74-74—298	$466.67
T-49	Lionel Hebert	73-73-76-76—298	$466.66
T-49	Vince Sullivan	72-73-79-74—298	$466.67
T-52	Chuck Courtney	70-76-76-77—299	$440.00
T-52	Steve Reid	76-75-73-75—299	$440.00
T-54	Billy Capps	77-74-75-74—300	$402.50
T-54	Bob Crowley	78-72-74-76—300	$402.50
T-54	Jay Hebert	72-73-78-77—300	$402.50
T-54	Bobby Nichols	74-75-77-74—300	$402.50
T-54	Tom Nieporte	75-74-83-68—300	$402.50
T-54	Fred Wampler	74-74-76-76—300	$402.50
60	Jim Ferree	75-75-77-74—301	$370.00
T-61	George Archer	74-74-78-76—302	$300.00
T-61	Tony Lema	71-76-75-80—302	$300.00
T-63	Dow Finsterwald	73-78-77-75—303	$300.00
T-63	Ed Griffiths	73-75-75-80—303	$300.00
T-63	Ted Kroll	73-75-77-78—303	$300.00
T-63	Dick Marshall	74-73-84-72—303	$300.00
T-63	T.R. Sleichter	77-71-78-77—303	$300.00
T-68	Mike Fetchick	76-74-75-79—304	$300.00
T-68	Bob Goalby	75-74-77-78—304	$300.00
T-68	Jon Gustin	73-77-78-76—304	$300.00
T-71	Huston Leclair	77-74-75-79—305	$300.00
T-71	Chi Chi Rodriguez	72-77-77-79—305	$300.00
T-73	Mike Krak	71-80-76-79—306	$300.00
T-73	Roland Stafford	76-74-74-82—306	$300.00
75	Hubby Habjan	78-71-75-83—307	$300.00
76	Larry Bartosek	75-75-80-80—310	$300.00
Cut	Bill Bisdorf	75-77—152	
Cut	Tom Blaskovich	79-73—152	
Cut	Frank Boynton	76-76—152	
Cut	Charles Coody	75-77—152	
Cut	Jim Ferrier	79-73—152	
Cut	Chick Harbert	76-76—152	
Cut	Bud Holscher	77-75—152	
Cut	Tommy Jacobs	76-76—152	
Cut	Arnold Koehler	76-76—152	
Cut	Bob Reith	80-72—152	
Cut	Jim Turnesa	74-78—152	
Cut	Dick Whetzle	73-79—152	
Cut	Jerry Barber	76-77—153	
Cut	Joe Campbell	77-76—153	
Cut	Pete Cooper	75-78—153	
Cut	Chris Gers	78-75—153	
Cut	Bob Hill	77-76—153	
Cut	Jack Isaacs	79-74—153	
Cut	Sam Penecale	74-79—153	
Cut	Sam Reynolds	76-77—153	
Cut	Robert Schoener	77-76—153	
Cut	Wynsol Spencer	70-83—153	
Cut	James Stamps	78-75—153	
Cut	Stan Thirsk	74-79—153	
Cut	Stan Baluik	78-76—154	
Cut	Leo Biagetti	77-77—154	
Cut	Bill Deck	76-78—154	
Cut	Walker Inman	75-79—154	
Cut	Howie Johnson	76-78—154	
Cut	Jack McGowan	75-79—154	
Cut	Ed Rubis	74-80—154	
Cut	Bob Spence	76-78—154	
Cut	Ron Bakich	80-75—155	
Cut	Buster Cupit	75-80—155	
Cut	Edward Kuna	79-76—155	
Cut	Jerry Pittman	76-79—155	
Cut	Robert Shields	77-78—155	
Cut	Bert Weaver	77-78—155	
Cut	Johnny Allen	80-76—156	
Cut	Merle Backlund	74-82—156	
Cut	Andy Borkovich	76-80—156	
Cut	Steve Bull	79-77—156	
Cut	Ted Gwin	79-77—156	
Cut	Rick Jetter	78-78—156	
Cut	Ed Kroll	77-79—156	
Cut	Tom Malone	77-79—156	
Cut	Dick Mayer	78-78—156	
Cut	Henry Picard	75-81—156	
Cut	Dick Plummer	78-78—156	
Cut	Dick Rhyan	79-77—156	
Cut	Bob Watson	83-73—156	
Cut	John Dalrymple	76-81—157	
Cut	Gifford Nutbrown	79-78—157	
Cut	Mike Pavella	76-81—157	
Cut	Bob Rosburg	78-79—157	
Cut	Charles Rotar	76-81—157	
Cut	Glenn Stuart	75-82—157	
Cut	Frank Kiraly	76-82—158	
Cut	Charles Lepre	81-77—158	
Cut	Scotty McBeath	77-81—158	
Cut	Bob Popp	78-80—158	
Cut	John Barnum	84-75—159	
Cut	Bob Gry	80-79—159	
Cut	Dennis Bradley	78-82—160	
Cut	Frank Harned	83-77—160	
Cut	Darrell Hickok	78-82—160	
Cut	Ed Knych	78-82—160	
Cut	Ernest Fortner	81-80—161	
Cut	Buzz Garvin	79-82—161	
Cut	Jim Mooney	81-80—161	
Cut	Al Morley	76-85—161	
Cut	Alex Sinclair	83-78—161	
Cut	Pat Abbott	78-84—162	
Cut	Bob Hamrich	84-78—162	
Cut	Frank Keller	86-76—162	
Cut	Art Doering	76-87—163	
Cut	Denny Shute	82-81—163	
Cut	Walter All	80-84—164	
Cut	Edward Bosse	81-83—164	
Cut	Ray Graboski	77-87—164	
Cut	Jim O'Hern	83-81—164	
Cut	Eddie Tyree	84-80—164	
Cut	Darwin Whit	76-88—164	
Cut	Corky Dahl	87-80—167	
Cut	Roy Faber	84-83—167	
Cut	Russell Tuveson	84-83—167	
WD	Paul Runyan	84 — 84	
WD	Mike Baker	85 — 85	
DQ	Miller Barber	73-73-73—219	

1964

With an opening round of 64, Bobby Nichols, a 28-year-old Kentuckian, never looked back as he held the lead every round to win the PGA Championship. His 271 is the lowest 72-hole total in PGA Championship history.

Champion: Bobby Nichols, Fort Pierce, Fla.	
Site: Columbus CC, Columbus, Ohio	
Date: July 16-19	Purse: $100,000
Par: 34-36 - 70 (6,851 Yards)	Entries:166
36 Hole cut at 150	91 players advanced
54 Hole cut at 221	65 players advanced

	Course Avg	Under Par	At Par	Over Par	Round Leader	Low Round	Bobby Nichols
Round 1:	74.6	13	8	141	Bobby Nichols	64 - Bobby Nichols	64 - 1st
Round 2:	75.2	8	2	150	Bobby Nichols	65 - Ken Venturi	135 (71) - 1st
Round 3:	73.3	7	5	79	Bobby Nichols	68 - M. Rudolph, B. Hogan, T. Nieporte, G. Dickinson, C. Harbert	204 (69) - 1st
Round 4:	71.5	13	8	44	Bobby Nichols	64 - Jack Nicklaus	271 (67) - 1st
Totals:	74.15	41	23	414			

TOURNAMENT SUMMARY

Place	Name	Score	Winnings	Place	Name	Score	Winnings	Place	Name	Score
1	Bobby Nichols	64-71-69-67—271	$18,000.00	T-56	Bruce Crampton	72-74-74-73—293	$270.00	Cut	Joe Cheves	78-76—154
T-2	Jack Nicklaus	67-73-70-64—274	$9,000.00	T-56	Jim Ferrier	73-72-76-72—293	$270.00	Cut	Harold Paddock	77-77—154
T-2	Arnold Palmer	68-68-69-69—274	$9,000.00	T-56	Furman Hayes	74-72-74-73—293	$270.00	Cut	Mike Pavella	76-78—154
4	Mason Rudolph	73-66-68-69—276	$5,000.00	T-56	Huston Laclair	73-74-72-74—293	$270.00	Cut	Bob Popp	73-81—154
T-5	Tom Nieporte	68-71-68-72—279	$3,850.00	T-56	Bob Rosburg	72-75-71-75—293	$270.00	Cut	Tom Fonseca Jr.	75-80—155
T-5	Ken Venturi	72-65-73-69—279	$3,850.00	61	Bill Ogden	73-76-71-74—294	$240.00	Cut	Jim Hart	75-80—155
7	Bo Wininger	69-68-73-70—280	$3,200.00	T-62	Jim Browning	71-72-77-75—295	$220.00	Cut	Tom Marlowe	80-75—155
8	Gay Brewer	72-71-71-67—281	$2,900.00	T-62	Jimmy Johnson	71-74-72-78—295	$220.00	Cut	Jimmy Scott	79-76—155
T-9	Billy Casper	68-72-70-72—282	$2,300.00	T-62	Jim Turnesa	76-72-73-74—295	$220.00	Cut	Harry Umbinetti	74-81—155
T-9	Jon Gustin	69-76-71-66—282	$2,300.00	65	Dave Marr	72-73-74-77—296	$200.00	Cut	Larry Wise	79-76—155
T-9	Ben Hogan	70-72-68-72—282	$2,300.00	Cut	John Berry	73-76-73—222		Cut	John Zontek	71-84—155
T-9	Tony Lema	71-68-72-71—282	$2,300.00	Cut	Manuel de la Torre	74-76-72—222		Cut	Doug Ford	76-80—156
T-13	Ed Furgol	71-69-72-71—283	$1,650.00	Cut	Jay Hebert	74-76-72—222		Cut	Bob Kay	76-80—156
T-13	Billy Maxwell	72-71-70-70—283	$1,650.00	Cut	Dave Hill	77-71-74—222		Cut	Edward Kuna	80-76—156
T-13	Gary Player	70-71-71-71—283	$1,650.00	Cut	Johnny Pott	74-74-74—222		Cut	Terry Malan	77-79—156
T-13	Mike Souchak	67-73-71-72—283	$1,650.00	Cut	Alphonso Atkins	75-74-74—223		Cut	Jim O'Hern	78-78—156
T-17	Walter Burkemo	70-71-72-71—284	$1,350.00	Cut	Steve Bull	72-75-76—223		Cut	Donald Palmer	81-75—156
T-17	Jacky Cupit	72-71-72-69—284	$1,350.00	Cut	James Clark	73-74-76—223		Cut	Ronnie Reif	77-79—156
T-19	Bob Charles	68-71-73-73—285	$1,175.00	Cut	Bob Crowley	74-74-75—223		Cut	T.R. Sleichter	78-78—156
T-19	Al Geiberger	73-72-72-68—285	$1,175.00	Cut	Tommy Jacobs	76-71-76—223		Cut	Harold Williams	79-77—156
T-21	Tommy Aaron	72-74-70-70—286	$1,075.00	Cut	Jack Lumpkin	75-74-74—223		Cut	Louis Barbaro	78-79—157
T-21	Julius Boros	70-73-71-72—286	$1,075.00	Cut	Scotty McBeath	70-79-74—223		Cut	Dennis Bradley	78-79—157
T-23	Gardner Dickinson	74-74-68-71—287	$930.00	Cut	Al Mengert	75-72-76—223		Cut	Al Morley	80-77—157
T-23	Mike Fetchick	74-73-74-66—287	$930.00	Cut	Glenn Stuart	71-77-75—223		Cut	Jack Sellman	76-81—157
T-23	Ed Kroll	75-72-72-68—287	$930.00	Cut	Don January	68-78-78—224		Cut	Robert Swift	78-79—157
T-23	Ted Kroll	72-73-72-70—287	$930.00	Cut	Sam Reynolds	70-77-77—224		Cut	Joseph Thacker	79-78—157
T-23	Dick Rhyan	71-72-71-73—287	$930.00	Cut	Joe Kotlarczyk	77-70-78—225		Cut	Brad Anderson	77-81—158
T-28	Bill Bisdorf	73-72-73-70—288	$800.00	Cut	Joe Zakarian	73-74-78—225		Cut	Bob Bodington	79-79—158
T-28	Jim Ferree	70-72-75-71—288	$800.00	Cut	Rex Baxter	74-74-78—226		Cut	Buddy Sullivan	82-76—158
T-28	Dick Hart	73-73-72-70—288	$800.00	Cut	Robert Erickson	77-73-76—226		Cut	Bud Williamson	78-80—158
T-28	George Knudson	76-69-72-71—288	$800.00	Cut	Charles Bassler	75-73-79—227		Cut	Bill Collins	76-83—159
T-28	Doug Sanders	71-73-76-68—288	$800.00	Cut	Clayton Johnson	75-73-79—227		Cut	Ray Hill	80-79—159
T-33	Frank Beard	72-72-71-74—289	$662.50	Cut	Charles Lepre	76-73-78—227		Cut	Gene Lesch	80-79—159
T-33	Al Besselink	71-73-72-73—289	$662.50	Cut	Moon Mullins	72-76-79—227		Cut	Don Shock	78-81—159
T-33	Pete Brown	71-75-73-70—289	$662.50	Cut	Bob Hold	77-71-80—228		Cut	Denny Shute	77-82—159
T-33	Paul Haviland	68-73-73-75—289	$662.50	Cut	Charles Smith	75-74-81—230		Cut	Lou Warobick	80-79—159
T-33	Gene Littler	75-72-74-68—289	$662.50	Cut	Butch Baird	77-74—151		Cut	Mack Briggs	78-82—160
T-33	Dave Ragan	73-71-74-71—289	$662.50	Cut	Dick Bury	75-76—151		Cut	Frank Nastri	79-81—160
T-39	Don Bies	76-66-76-72—290	$526.50	Cut	Robert Fry	74-77—151		Cut	Dick Demane	78-83—161
T-39	Joe Campbell	73-72-71-74—290	$526.50	Cut	Eli Marovich	74-77—151		Cut	Everett Vinzant	81-80—161
T-39	Bruce Devlin	70-73-76-71—290	$526.50	Cut	Ernie Vossler	76-75—151		Cut	Ed Knych	82-80—162
T-39	Bob Keller	69-75-72-74—290	$526.50	Cut	Leon Butler	76-76—152		Cut	Don Kubiak	80-82—162
T-39	Jack Rule	74-71-72-73—290	$526.50	Cut	Wes Ellis Jr.	75-77—152		Cut	Roy Beattie	82-82—164
T-44	George Bayer	71-74-76-70—291	$402.50	Cut	Dow Finsterwald	74-78—152		Cut	Jack Merz	82-82—164
T-44	Jack Burke Jr.	74-72-73-72—291	$402.50	Cut	Ray Goodell	77-75—152		Cut	Aubrey Apple	80-86—166
T-44	Joe Conrad	69-72-74-76—291	$402.50	Cut	Fred Gronauer	78-74—152		Cut	Donald Williams Jr.	87-79—166
T-44	John Cook	75-72-70-74—291	$402.50	Cut	Lionel Hebert	78-74—152		Cut	Rick Jetter	85-84—169
T-44	Chick Harbert	74-75-68-74—291	$402.50	Cut	Bill Johnston	76-76—152		Cut	Gerald Levergne	83-87—170
T-44	Babe Lichardus	72-74-73-72—291	$402.50	Cut	Tom Murphy	74-78—152		DQ	Odell Trueblood	76—76
T-44	Chi Chi Rodriguez	71-74-71-75—291	$402.50	Cut	Joe Taylor	76-76—152		WD	Jerry Barber	80—80
T-44	Fred Wampler	74-73-71-73—291	$402.50	Cut	Johnny Bulla	75-78—153		WD	Vic Ghezzi	71-73—144
T-52	Pete Cooper	77-71-73-71—292	$318.75	Cut	Bob Goalby	73-80—153		WD	Tommy Bolt	74-76—150
T-52	J.C. Goosie	72-74-74-72—292	$318.75	Cut	Walker Inman	75-78—153				
T-52	Bob Hill	72-70-75-75—292	$318.75	Cut	Joe Lopez Jr.	76-77—153				
T-52	Don Spears	73-71-76-72—292	$318.75	Cut	Frank Stranahan	78-75—153				

PGA CHAMPIONSHIP SUMMARIES

1963

In 100-degree heat, Jack Nicklaus won the 45th PGA Championship. At 23 years of age, Nicklaus joined Ben Hogan, Byron Nelson and Gene Sarazen as the only men in golfing history to win the PGA, the U.S. Open, and the Masters. To win the PGA Championship, Nicklaus overcame Bruce Crampton, who had a three-stroke lead going into the final round. However, Crampton faded in the last few holes as Nicklaus posted a 68 for a 279 total to win his first of five PGA Championships.

Champion: Jack Nicklaus, North Palm Beach, Fla.
Site: Dallas Athletic Club, Dallas, Texas
Date: July 18-21   **Purse:** $80,900
Par: 36-35 - 71 (7,046 Yards)
Entries: 167   Cut at 151   81 players advanced

	Course Avg	Under Par	At Par	Over Par	Round Leader	Low Round	Jack Nicklaus
Round 1:	76.2	12	7	145	Dick Hart	66 - Dick Hart	69 - Tied 2nd
Round 2:	75.6	10	10	141	Dick Hart	69 - Doug Sanders	142 (73) - Tied 5th
Round 3:	73.2	17	8	57	Bruce Crampton	65 - Bruce Crampton	211 (69) - 3rd
Round 4:	73.4	17	7	57	Jack Nicklaus	66 - G. Dickinson	279 (68) - 1st
Totals:	75.08	56	32	400			

TOURNAMENT SUMMARY

Place	Name	Score	Winnings
1	Jack Nicklaus	69-73-69-68—279	$13,000.00
2	Dave Ragan	75-70-67-69—281	$7,000.00
T-3	Bruce Crampton	70-73-65-74—282	$3,750.00
T-3	Dow Finsterwald	72-72-66-72—282	$3,750.00
T-5	Al Geiberger	72-73-69-70—284	$3,125.00
T-5	Billy Maxwell	73-71-69-71—284	$3,125.00
7	Jim Ferrier	73-73-70-69—285	$2,750.00
T-8	Gardner Dickinson	72-74-74-66—286	$2,090.00
T-8	Tommy Jacobs	74-72-70-70—286	$2,090.00
T-8	Bill Johnston	71-72-72-71—286	$2,090.00
T-8	Gary Player	74-75-67-70—286	$2,090.00
T-8	Art Wall	73-76-66-71—286	$2,090.00
T-13	Julius Boros	69-72-73-73—287	$1,550.00
T-13	Bob Charles	69-76-72-70—287	$1,550.00
T-13	Tony Lema	70-71-77-69—287	$1,550.00
T-13	Jack Sellman	75-70-74-68—287	$1,550.00
T-17	Manuel de la Torre	71-71-74-72—288	$1,075.00
T-17	Wes Ellis Jr.	71-74-71-72—288	$1,075.00
T-17	Bob Goalby	74-70-74-70—288	$1,075.00
T-17	Dick Hart	66-72-76-74—288	$1,075.00
T-17	Dave Hill	73-72-69-74—288	$1,075.00
T-17	Doug Sanders	74-69-70-75—288	$1,075.00
T-23	Paul Harney	72-74-71-72—289	$775.00
T-23	Bobby Nichols	74-73-71-71—289	$775.00
T-23	Mason Rudolph	69-75-71-74—289	$775.00
T-23	Mike Souchak	72-72-73-72—289	$775.00
T-27	Doug Ford	70-72-71-77—290	$558.58
T-27	J.C. Goosie	74-74-74-68—290	$558.58
T-27	Freddie Haas Jr.	80-70-70-70—290	$558.57
T-27	Sam Snead	71-73-70-76—290	$558.57
T-27	Earl Stewart	70-77-70-73—290	$558.57
T-27	Bert Weaver	76-73-71-70—290	$558.57
T-27	Bo Wininger	75-71-71-73—290	$558.57
T-34	Jack Burke Jr.	75-72-73-71—291	$480.00
T-34	Billy Farrell	72-74-72-73—291	$480.00
T-34	Mike Krak	73-73-72-73—291	$480.00
T-34	Gene Littler	71-72-75-73—291	$480.00
T-34	Eddie Merrins	74-70-73-74—291	$480.00
39	Stan Mosel	71-77-74-70—292	$450.00
T-40	Jerry Barber	74-73-72-74—293	$410.00
T-40	Jay Hebert	75-76-73-69—293	$410.00
T-40	Doug Higgins	74-74-75-70—293	$410.00
T-40	Don January	76-75-69-73—293	$410.00
T-40	Arnold Palmer	74-73-73-73—293	$410.00
T-40	Jerry Pisano	72-76-69-76—293	$410.00
T-40	Bob Rosburg	72-75-74-72—293	$410.00
T-47	Tony Holguin	77-71-75-71—294	$365.00
T-47	Dan Sikes	74-70-73-77—294	$365.00
T-49	Gay Brewer	74-75-72-74—295	$335.00
T-49	Dutch Harrison	73-73-75-74—295	$335.00
T-49	Bob McCallister	71-76-73-75—295	$335.00
T-49	Joe Zakarian	75-73-76-71—295	$335.00
T-53	Don Bies	74-71-73-78—296	$318.75
T-53	Hubby Habjan	76-75-71-74—296	$318.75
T-53	Mac Hunter	76-70-75-75—296	$318.75

Place	Name	Score	Winnings
T-53	Shelley Mayfield	69-72-76-79—296	$318.75
T-57	Ray Floyd	75-73-74-75—297	$300.00
T-57	Ernie Vossler	74-77-73-73—297	$300.00
T-59	George Bayer	75-73-74-76—298	$275.00
T-59	Charles Congdon	70-79-73-76—298	$275.00
T-59	Ted Kroll	81-70-74-73—298	$275.00
T-59	Frank Stranahan	74-73-77-74—298	$275.00
T-63	Gene Borek	74-76-75-74—299	$230.00
T-63	Furman Hayes	76-71-74-78—299	$230.00
T-63	Skee Riegel	78-73-76-72—299	$230.00
T-63	Herman Scharlau	75-76-76-72—299	$230.00
T-63	Stan Thirsk	73-74-73-79—299	$230.00
68	John Cleary	75-76-75-74—300	$200.00
T-69	Bob Gajda	72-72-76-81—301	$200.00
T-69	Dick Turner	75-76-78-72—301	$200.00
T-71	Edward Kuna	73-71-79-79—302	$175.00
T-71	Jim Lucius	77-74-77-74—302	$175.00
T-73	John Barnum	74-74-74-82—304	$175.00
T-73	Tom Watrous	78-70-75-81—304	$175.00
T-75	Ron Bakich	73-77-78-77—305	$158.33
T-75	Frank Beley	75-74-79-77—305	$158.33
T-75	Ira Gwin	76-75-81-73—305	$158.34
78	Bill Ezinicki	74-71-83-78—306	$150.00
79	John Cook	75-73-79-80—307	$150.00
80	Bernie Haas	70-80-79-79—308	$150.00
81	Lou Warobick	74-77-78-80—309	$150.00
Cut	Walter Burkemo	79-73—152	
Cut	Bob Crowley	79-73—152	
Cut	Robert Fry	76-76—152	
Cut	Mickey Homa	78-74—152	
Cut	Ed Knych	73-79—152	
Cut	John Paul Jones	77-75—152	
Cut	Johnny Pott	74-78—152	
Cut	Charles Prentice	78-74—152	
Cut	Ed Whalley	77-75—152	
Cut	Lew Worsham	77-75—152	
Cut	Thomas Burke	74-79—153	
Cut	Don Clarkson	75-78—153	
Cut	Mike Fetchick	77-76—153	
Cut	George Schneiter	74-79—153	
Cut	John Zontek	74-79—153	
Cut	Ed Famula	78-76—154	
Cut	Ed Furgol	81-73—154	
Cut	Lionel Hebert	78-76—154	
Cut	Eddie Langert	82-72—154	
Cut	Charles Lepre	75-79—154	
Cut	Gene Lesch	76-78—154	
Cut	Ben Lula	77-77—154	
Cut	Dave Marr	83-71—154	
Cut	Sam Penecale	78-76—154	
Cut	Gene Shields	74-80—154	
Cut	Henry Trepsas	80-74—154	
Cut	Don Whitt	72-82—154	
Cut	Bud Williamson	77-77—154	
Cut	Bill Bisdorf	78-77—155	

Place	Name	Score
Cut	Gene Bone	81-74—155
Cut	Clare Emery	75-80—155
Cut	Chick Harbert	77-78—155
Cut	Phil Rodgers	78-77—155
Cut	T.R. Sleichter	79-76—155
Cut	John Suveges	75-80—155
Cut	Ross Carley	79-77—156
Cut	Vic Ghezzi	79-77—156
Cut	Gordon Leishman	81-75—156
Cut	Melvin Rowe	76-80—156
Cut	Jouett Brown	79-78—157
Cut	Steve Bull	80-77—157
Cut	Gene Coghill	78-79—157
Cut	Bob Hill	77-80—157
Cut	Bob Keller	77-80—157
Cut	Dick Lundahl	77-80—157
Cut	James Riggins	78-79—157
Cut	Emil Scodeller	83-74—157
Cut	Jim Turnesa	81-76—157
Cut	Frank Harned	80-78—158
Cut	Frank Keller	81-77—158
Cut	Joe Lopez Jr.	79-79—158
Cut	Dan Whalen	83-75—158
Cut	Buck Adams	78-81—159
Cut	Paul Biggy	78-81—159
Cut	Charlie Harter	81-78—159
Cut	J.D. Taylor	81-78—159
Cut	George Tiddy	80-79—159
Cut	Ernie Boros	78-82—160
Cut	Bill Grygiel	81-79—160
Cut	Corky Dahl	83-78—161
Cut	Bob Lavacek	81-80—161
Cut	Tod Menefee	84-77—161
Cut	Eric Monti	81-80—161
Cut	Horace Moore	77-84—161
Cut	Bill Blanton	78-84—162
Cut	Roger Horton	82-80—162
Cut	Eugene Johnson	80-82—162
Cut	Clyde Thomsen	82-80—162
Cut	Oran Whittington	82-80—162
Cut	Rudy Goff	84-79—163
Cut	George Preisinger	84-79—163
Cut	Don Klein	82-83—165
Cut	Beal Consolver	84-82—166
Cut	Al Starr	86-80—166
Cut	Willie Beljan	87-80—167
Cut	Don White	90-79—169
Cut	Jim Rudolph	82-88—170
Cut	James Speer	87-88—175
DQ	Gene Rolfe	
WD	Jim Ferree	74—74
WD	Jack Fleck	76—76
WD	Don Fairfield	78—78
WD	Buddy Sullivan	75-74—149
WD	Bill Collins	77-74-78—229

1962

Gary Player, posting a 2-under 278, became the second foreign citizen to win the PGA Championship, beating hard-charging Bob Goalby by one stroke. Goalby brought the Championship to a thrilling climax by making birdies at 14 and 16 during the final round, but the 26-year-old South African staved off the rally as both parred the final two holes.

Champion: Gary Player, Alaqua, Fla.	
Site: Aronimink GC, Newtown Square, Pa.	
Date: July 19-22	Purse: $69,400
Par: 35-35 - 70 (7,045 Yards)	Entries: 170
36 Hole cut at 151	89 players advanced
54 Hole cut at 222	60 players advanced

	Course Avg	Under Par	At Par	Over Par	Round Leader	Low Round	Gary Player
Round 1:	75.5	6	5	158	John Barnum	66 - John Barnum	72 - Tied 18th
Round 2:	75.2	9	9	148	Doug Ford	66 - B. McCallister, C. Middlecoff	139 (67) - Tied 2nd
Round 3:	74.0	5	7	77	Gary Player	67 - Bruce Crampton	208 (69) - 1st
Round 4:	73.0	7	6	47	Gary Player	67 - J. Nicklaus, B. Goalby	278 (70) - 1st
Totals:	74.85	27	27	430			

TOURNAMENT SUMMARY

Place	Name	Score	Winnings
1	Gary Player	72-67-69-70—278	$13,000.00
2	Bob Goalby	69-72-71-67—279	$6,700.00
T-3	George Bayer	69-70-71-71—281	$3,450.00
T-3	Jack Nicklaus	71-74-69-67—281	$3,450.00
5	Doug Ford	69-69-73-71—282	$2,900.00
6	Bobby Nichols	72-70-71-70—283	$2,500.00
T-7	Jack Fleck	74-69-70-71—284	$2,066.66
T-7	Paul Harney	70-73-72-69—284	$2,066.67
T-7	Dave Ragan	72-74-70-68—284	$2,066.67
10	Jay Hebert	73-72-70-70—285	$1,750.00
T-11	Julius Boros	73-69-74-70—286	$1,450.00
T-11	Dow Finsterwald	73-70-70-73—286	$1,450.00
T-11	Chick Harbert	68-76-69-73—286	$1,450.00
T-11	Bob McCallister	74-66-70-76—286	$1,450.00
T-15	Cary Middlecoff	73-66-74-74—287	$1,225.00
T-15	Doug Sanders	76-69-73-69—287	$1,225.00
T-17	Jack Burke Jr.	73-69-71-75—288	$966.66
T-17	Bruce Crampton	76-73-67-72—288	$966.67
T-17	Billy Farrell	73-71-73-71—288	$966.67
T-17	Arnold Palmer	71-72-73-72—288	$966.67
T-17	Sam Snead	75-70-71-72—288	$966.67
T-17	Frank Stranahan	69-73-72-74—288	$966.66
T-23	Freddie Haas Jr.	75-71-74-69—289	$665.00
T-23	Tommy Jacobs	73-73-73-70—289	$665.00
T-23	Gene Littler	73-75-72-69—289	$665.00
T-23	Art Wall	72-75-71-71—289	$665.00
T-27	Joe Campbell	70-74-74-73—291	$530.00
T-27	Don January	70-74-72-75—291	$530.00
T-27	Johnny Pott	71-77-71-72—291	$530.00
T-30	Tommy Bolt	72-74-72-74—292	$470.00
T-30	Pete Cooper	73-71-74-74—292	$470.00
T-30	Buster Cupit	76-70-76-70—292	$470.00
T-30	Wes Ellis Jr.	75-72-73-72—292	$470.00
T-30	Dick Hart	70-73-76-73—292	$470.00
T-30	Ted Kroll	73-70-76-73—292	$470.00
T-30	Shelley Mayfield	74-70-74-74—292	$470.00
T-30	Tom Nieporte	75-75-69-73—292	$470.00
T-30	Don Whitt	74-73-70-75—292	$470.00
T-39	Walter Burkemo	72-75-72-74—293	$400.00
T-39	Jim Ferrier	72-71-73-77—293	$400.00
T-39	Eric Monti	76-74-71-72—293	$400.00
T-39	Al Nelson	79-70-72-72—293	$400.00
T-39	Mike Souchak	75-73-72-73—293	$400.00
T-44	Claude Harmon	73-73-75-73—294	$360.00
T-44	Howie Johnson	75-75-72-72—294	$360.00
T-44	Bob Kay	76-73-72-73—294	$360.00
T-47	Marty Furgol	71-71-74-79—295	$325.00
T-47	Bob Gajda	71-74-77-73—295	$325.00
T-47	Bill Johnston	74-72-72-77—295	$325.00
T-47	Pat Schwab	76-75-71-73—295	$325.00
T-51	Billy Casper	74-76-70-76—296	$280.00
T-51	Gardner Dickinson	73-74-75-74—296	$280.00
T-51	George Knudson	72-75-74-75—296	$280.00
T-51	Dave Marr	71-72-77-76—296	$280.00
T-51	Ken Venturi	73-72-77-74—296	$280.00
56	Bill Collins	73-71-74-79—297	$250.00
T-57	John Barnum	66-74-77-81—298	$222.50

Place	Name	Score	Winnings
T-57	Vic Ghezzi	76-69-74-79—298	$222.50
T-57	Bob Ross	72-74-75-77—298	$222.50
T-57	James Stamps	72-72-75-79—298	$222.50
Cut	Bob Keller	74-75-74—223	
Cut	Ed Rubis	73-75-75—223	
Cut	Ernie Vossler	74-74-75—223	
Cut	Leo Biagetti	70-75-79—224	
Cut	Dick Bury	77-74-73—224	
Cut	Don Fairfield	74-74-76—224	
Cut	Jon Gustin	72-76-76—224	
Cut	Pete Fleming	73-71-81—225	
Cut	Skee Riegel	76-75-74—225	
Cut	Charles Bassler	78-73-75—226	
Cut	Jacky Cupit	75-76-75—226	
Cut	Bill Ezinicki	77-74-75—226	
Cut	Charles Farlow	75-73-78—226	
Cut	Milon Marusic	74-75-77—226	
Cut	Phil Rodgers	75-73-78—226	
Cut	Eddie Burke	75-74-78—227	
Cut	Joe Cheves	74-74-79—227	
Cut	Fred Hawkins	75-73-79—227	
Cut	Bob Hill	76-74-77—227	
Cut	Walter Romans	77-74-76—227	
Cut	Joe Taylor	76-75-76—227	
Cut	Alphonso Atkins	74-77-77—228	
Cut	Jim Ferree	76-75-77—228	
Cut	Alex Sinclair	76-74-78—228	
Cut	Jimmy Thompson	77-73-78—228	
Cut	Tony Bovitsky	77-73-79—229	
Cut	Jouett Brown	77-72-80—229	
Cut	Al Johnston	76-75-78—229	
Cut	Buck White	74-70-86—230	
Cut	Jerry Barber	79-73—152	
Cut	John Cook	78-74—152	
Cut	Bernie Haas	74-78—152	
Cut	Lionel Hebert	77-75—152	
Cut	Dave Hill	76-76—152	
Cut	Bud Holscher	76-76—152	
Cut	Arnold Koehler	76-76—152	
Cut	Stan Thirsk	77-75—152	
Cut	Emery Thomas	78-74—152	
Cut	Felice Torza	77-75—152	
Cut	Sam Urzetta	76-76—152	
Cut	Lew Worsham	74-78—152	
Cut	Joe Zakarian	73-79—152	
Cut	Dale Andreason	76-77—153	
Cut	Al Besselink	77-76—153	
Cut	Bill Bisdorf	74-79—153	
Cut	Ernie Catropa	76-77—153	
Cut	Dick Demane	75-78—153	
Cut	Joe Kotlarczyk	78-75—153	
Cut	Toby Lyons	78-75—153	
Cut	Jack Ortman	79-74—153	
Cut	Mike Pavella	76-77—153	
Cut	Billy Phillips	78-75—153	
Cut	Randy Quick	75-78—153	
Cut	Larry Tomasino	76-77—153	

Place	Name	Score
Cut	Lester Ward	79-74—153
Cut	Paul Biggy	76-78—154
Cut	Johnny Bulla	75-79—154
Cut	Bob Crowley	79-75—154
Cut	Bill Kratzert	77-77—154
Cut	Davis Love Jr.	73-81—154
Cut	Eddie Merrins	81-73—154
Cut	Moon Mullins	77-77—154
Cut	Robert Shields	74-80—154
Cut	Wa Stackhouse	77-77—154
Cut	Dick Stranahan	79-75—154
Cut	J.D. Taylor	73-81—154
Cut	Jim Turnesa	77-77—154
Cut	Eldon Briggs	77-78—155
Cut	Al Brosch	77-78—155
Cut	Ralph Hutchison	78-77—155
Cut	Charles Lepre	76-79—155
Cut	Henry McQuiston	76-79—155
Cut	George Schneiter	76-79—155
Cut	Gay Brewer	80-76—156
Cut	Lawrence Cook	79-77—156
Cut	Joe Jimenez	80-76—156
Cut	Gordon Leishman	75-82—157
Cut	Tod Menefee	79-78—157
Cut	Richard Mullen	76-81—157
Cut	Ed Whalley	77-80—157
Cut	Dave Douglas	80-78—158
Cut	Mac Hunter	77-81—158
Cut	Bob Lavacek	80-78—158
Cut	Herb Magnusson	77-81—158
Cut	Sam Penecale	77-81—158
Cut	Jim Browning	80-79—159
Cut	Hardy Loudermilk	81-78—159
Cut	Bill Moran	82-77—159
Cut	Willie Polumbo	79-80—159
Cut	Jimmy Scott	81-78—159
Cut	Russell Tuveson	77-82—159
Cut	Mike Bencriscutto	84-76—160
Cut	Jerry Pisano	78-82—160
Cut	Dick Howell	77-84—161
Cut	Joseph Capello	83-79—162
Cut	Clare Emery	82-80—162
Cut	Emory Lee	82-80—162
Cut	Frank Witt	77-85—162
Cut	Bonny Graham	79-84—163
Cut	John Ruedi	82-82—164
Cut	Jim Petersen	82-83—165
Cut	Steve Savel	84-83—167
Cut	Andy Pataky	83-86—169
Cut	Bill Grygiel	90-84—174
WD	Bob Crow	77—77
WD	Billy Maxwell	81—81
WD	Jerry Lambo	82—82
WD	Tony Lema	74-73—147
WD	Tony Holguin	74-74—148

1961

In the final round, 31-year-old Don January led 45-year-old Jerry Barber by four shots with three holes remaining. However, Barber sank putts of 20 feet for a birdie, 40 feet for a par, and 60 feet for a birdie on the last three holes to match January's 277. In the 18-hole playoff, Barber again trailed January by two strokes on two different occasions but rallied to finish with a 67, a one-stroke edge over January.

Champion: Jerry Barber, Los Angeles, Calif.
Site: Olympia Fields CC, Olympia Fields, Ill.
Date: July 27-31   **Purse:** $64,800
Par: 35-35 - 70 (6,722 Yards)
Entries: 162   Cut at 148   64 players advanced

	Course Avg	Under Par	At Par	Over Par	Round Leader	Low Round	Jerry Barber
Round 1:	75.3	6	7	148	Art Wall	67 - Art Wall	69 - Tied 4th
Round 2:	75.1	6	2	148	Jerry Barber	66 - Don January	136 (67) - 1st
Round 3:	73.2	7	2	55	Don January	67 - D. January, J. Pott	207 (71) - 2nd
Round 4:	72.9	9	4	51	J. Barber, D. January	66 - Doug Ford	277 (70) - Tied 1st
Totals:	74.62	28	15	402			

TOURNAMENT SUMMARY

Place	Name	Score	Winnings	Place	Name	Score	Winnings	Place	Name	Score
T-1	Jerry Barber	69-67-71-70—277	$11,000.00	T-55	Sam Bernardi	75-72-75-76—298	$225.00	Cut	John Alexander	78-76—154
T-1	Don January	72-66-67-72—277	$5,500.00	T-55	Pete Cooper	74-74-75-75—298	$225.00	Cut	Frank Beley	76-78—154
3	Doug Sanders	70-68-74-68—280	$3,600.00	T-57	Johnny Bulla	74-73-77-76—300	$225.00	Cut	George Buck	74-80—154
4	Ted Kroll	72-68-70-71—281	$3,100.00	T-57	Mike Krak	71-76-77-76—300	$225.00	Cut	Labron Harris Jr.	75-79—154
T-5	Wes Ellis Jr.	71-71-68-72—282	$2,208.34	T-57	Sam Penecale	72-73-79-76—300	$225.00	Cut	Charles Harter	78-76—154
T-5	Doug Ford	69-73-74-66—282	$2,208.33	60	Bill Heinlein	69-77-79-76—301	$225.00	Cut	Tony Holguin	79-75—154
T-5	Gene Littler	71-70-72-69—282	$2,208.33	61	Marshall Springer	74-71-77-80—302	$225.00	Cut	Alex Leiper	75-79—154
T-5	Arnold Palmer	73-72-69-68—282	$2,208.34	62	J.L. McReynolds	73-74-79-78—304	$225.00	Cut	Mac McElmurry	75-79—154
T-5	Johnny Pott	71-73-67-71—282	$2,208.33	63	Al Besselink	74-73-83-75—305	$225.00	Cut	Bob Moore	80-74—154
T-5	Art Wall	67-72-73-70—282	$2,208.33	64	Leon Butler	75-72-77-84—308	$225.00	Cut	Al Nelson	76-78—154
T-11	Paul Harney	70-73-69-71—283	$1,650.00	Cut	Julius Boros	74-75—149		Cut	Bill Ogden	79-75—154
T-11	Cary Middlecoff	74-69-71-69—283	$1,650.00	Cut	Joe Brown	74-75—149		Cut	Jim Turnesa	79-75—154
13	Jay Hebert	68-72-72-72—284	$1,500.00	Cut	Gene Coghill	75-74—149		Cut	Billy Booe	77-78—155
14	Walter Burkemo	71-71-73-70—285	$1,400.00	Cut	Frank Harned	77-72—149		Cut	Tom Cherok	77-78—155
T-15	Billy Casper	74-72-69-71—286	$1,225.00	Cut	Lionel Hebert	75-74—149		Cut	Mike Dietz	76-79—155
T-15	Bob Goalby	73-72-68-73—286	$1,225.00	Cut	Bob Kay	75-74—149		Cut	Bob Harris	79-76—155
T-15	Ernie Vossler	68-72-71-75—286	$1,225.00	Cut	Joe Moore Jr.	75-74—149		Cut	Johnny Revolta	77-78—155
T-15	Don Whitt	76-72-70-68—286	$1,225.00	Cut	Walter Romans	73-76—149		Cut	Herman Scharlau	79-76—155
T-19	Gardner Dickinson	71-71-71-74—287	$1,016.67	Cut	Alphonso Atkins	75-75—150		Cut	Felice Torza	78-77—155
T-19	Jack Fleck	70-74-73-70—287	$1,016.66	Cut	Mike Austin	77-73—150		Cut	John Zontek	77-78—155
T-19	Bob Rosburg	70-71-73-73—287	$1,016.66	Cut	Avery Beck	77-73—150		Cut	George Keyes	81-75—156
T-22	George Bayer	73-71-72-72—288	$780.00	Cut	Claude Harmon	72-78—150		Cut	John Rouse	75-81—156
T-22	Don Fairfield	70-71-74-73—288	$780.00	Cut	Dick Hart	73-77—150		Cut	Fred Baker	79-78—157
T-22	Fred Hawkins	75-73-71-69—288	$780.00	Cut	Bob Mix	74-76—150		Cut	Herman Barron	74-83—157
T-22	Dave Marr	72-74-73-69—288	$780.00	Cut	George Schneiter	77-73—150		Cut	Jerome Krueger	74-83—157
T-22	Shelley Mayfield	70-74-72-72—288	$780.00	Cut	Ansel Snow	74-76—150		Cut	Van-Oran Love	79-78—157
T-27	Billy Maxwell	71-72-73-73—289	$575.00	Cut	Bob Toski	76-74—150		Cut	Ken Campbell	82-76—158
T-27	Sam Snead	72-71-71-75—289	$575.00	Cut	Gene Bone	76-75—151		Cut	Bob Crow	81-77—158
T-29	Charles Bassler	73-73-72-72—290	$425.00	Cut	Jackson Bradley	76-75—151		Cut	Paul Kern	77-81—158
T-29	Bob Keller	72-73-72-73—290	$425.00	Cut	Eldon Briggs	77-74—151		Cut	Hardy Loudermilk	80-78—158
T-29	Al Mengert	72-74-72-72—290	$425.00	Cut	Al Feminelli	73-78—151		Cut	Peter Marich	79-79—158
T-29	Gary Player	72-74-71-73—290	$425.00	Cut	Donald Palmer	74-77—151		Cut	Andy Borkovich	80-79—159
T-33	Billy Farrell	75-72-72-72—291	$262.50	Cut	Jerry Pisano	78-73—151		Cut	Gene Counter	79-80—159
T-33	Jon Gustin	75-72-75-69—291	$262.50	Cut	Gerald Schultheis	73-78—151		Cut	Reggie Myles	75-84—159
T-33	Mac Hunter	74-71-73-73—291	$262.50	Cut	Don Sechrest	75-76—151		Cut	Don Street	82-77—159
T-33	Dave Ragan	73-72-73-73—291	$262.50	Cut	Frank Stranahan	75-76—151		Cut	Henry Geraldi	81-79—160
T-37	Clarence Doser	71-75-73-73—292	$250.00	Cut	Lester Ward	73-78—151		Cut	Leo Biagetti	82-79—161
T-37	Mason Rudolph	71-71-73-77—292	$250.00	Cut	Bill Bisdorf	76-76—152		Cut	Ralph Bond	80-81—161
T-37	Ken Venturi	72-72-77-71—292	$250.00	Cut	Bill Collins	72-80—152		Cut	Don Shock	84-77—161
T-37	Lew Worsham	75-73-73-71—292	$250.00	Cut	Paul Donahue	75-77—152		Cut	Joe Zelazny	81-80—161
T-41	Manuel de la Torre	72-72-76-73—293	$225.00	Cut	Bill Johnston	77-75—152		Cut	Buddy Demling	85-77—162
T-41	Dow Finsterwald	74-74-71-74—293	$225.00	Cut	Sam Reynolds	77-75—152		Cut	Robert Hendricks	81-82—163
T-43	Bud Holscher	77-68-75-74—294	$225.00	Cut	Paul Thomas	74-78—152		Cut	Ronald Fox	84-81—165
T-43	Jack McGowan	76-70-77-71—294	$225.00	Cut	Dave Tinsley	72-80—152		Cut	Andy Pataky	84-82—166
T-45	Buster Cupit	70-78-72-75—295	$225.00	Cut	Fred Wampler	76-76—152		Cut	Alex Gerlak	81-86—167
T-45	Jim Ferrier	73-73-77-72—295	$225.00	Cut	Don Waryan	77-75—152		Cut	Edward Kuna	87-80—167
T-45	Marty Furgol	71-74-72-78—295	$225.00	Cut	Ralph Williamson	76-76—152		Cut	Reggie Sauger	83-85—168
T-45	Milon Marusic	75-73-74-73—295	$225.00	Cut	Jim Burke	78-75—153		WD	Steve Bull	78—78
T-45	Mike Souchak	72-72-74-77—295	$225.00	Cut	Bob Duden	79-74—153		WD	Mike Parco	79—79
T-50	Freddie Haas Jr.	72-76-75-73—296	$225.00	Cut	Vic Ghezzi	78-75—153		WD	George Vitense	80—80
T-50	Charles Malchaski	72-73-77-74—296	$225.00	Cut	Denny Shute	76-77—153		WD	Ivan Gantz	82—82
T-52	Jack Burke Jr.	76-71-72-78—297	$225.00	Cut	T.R. Sleichter	77-76—153		WD	Bob Popp	82—82
T-52	Chick Harbert	73-73-75-76—297	$225.00	Cut	Sam Urzetta	78-75—153		WD	Tommy Bolt	72-71—143
T-52	Tom Nieporte	75-72-75-75—297	$225.00	Cut	Al Watrous	78-75—153				

1960

There were only 13 sub-par rounds in the entire Championship at the rebuilt Firestone Country Club in Akron, Ohio. With those scores, a different man turned up as the leader at the end of each round. Arnold Palmer captured the first-round lead with an opening 67.

Jay Hebert fired a final-round 70, despite a double-bogey 6 on the 10th hole, for a one-stroke victory over Jim Ferrier.

Champion: Jay Hebert, Sanford, Fla.	
Site: Firestone CC, Akron, Ohio	
Date: July 21-24	**Purse:** $63,130
Par: 35-35 - 70 (7,165 Yards)	**Entries:**185
36 Hole cut at 151	93 players advanced
54 Hole cut at 224	60 players advanced

	Course Avg	Under Par	At Par	Over Par	Round Leader	Low Round	Jay Hebert
Round 1:	76.1	4	4	175	Arnold Palmer	67 - Arnold Palmer	72 - Tied 18th
Round 2:	76.2	2	3	177	Jay Hebert	67 - Jay Hebert	139 (67) - 1st
Round 3:	74.9	6	4	83	Doug Sanders	67 - Jim Ferrier	211 (72) - Tied 2nd
Round 4:	74.5	1	2	57	Jay Hebert	69 - Wes Ellis Jr.	281 (70) - 1st
Totals:	75.70	13	15	492			

TOURNAMENT SUMMARY

Place	Name	Score	Winnings
1	Jay Hebert	72-67-72-70—281	$11,000.00
2	Jim Ferrier	71-74-66-71—282	$5,500.00
T-3	Doug Sanders	70-71-69-73—283	$3,350.00
T-3	Sam Snead	68-73-70-72—283	$3,350.00
5	Don January	70-70-72-72—284	$2,800.00
6	Wes Ellis Jr.	72-72-72-69—285	$2,500.00
T-7	Doug Ford	75-70-69-72—286	$2,125.00
T-7	Arnold Palmer	67-74-75-70—286	$2,125.00
9	Ken Venturi	70-72-73-72—287	$1,900.00
T-10	Fred Hawkins	73-69-72-74—288	$1,750.00
T-10	Dave Marr	75-71-69-73—288	$1,750.00
T-12	Bill Collins	71-75-71-73—290	$1,500.00
T-12	Ted Kroll	73-71-72-74—290	$1,500.00
T-12	Mike Souchak	73-73-70-74—290	$1,500.00
T-15	Pete Cooper	73-74-70-74—291	$1,250.00
T-15	Dow Finsterwald	73-73-69-76—291	$1,250.00
T-15	Johnny Pott	75-72-72-72—291	$1,250.00
T-18	Paul Harney	69-78-73-72—292	$1,050.00
T-18	Lionel Hebert	75-72-70-75—292	$1,050.00
T-18	Gene Littler	74-70-75-73—292	$1,050.00
T-18	Tom Nieporte	72-74-74-72—292	$1,050.00
T-22	Dave Ragan	75-75-68-75—293	$875.00
T-22	Mason Rudolph	72-71-76-74—293	$875.00
T-24	Julius Boros	76-73-72-73—294	$660.00
T-24	Walter Burkemo	72-77-73-72—294	$660.00
T-24	Billy Casper	73-75-75-71—294	$660.00
T-24	Billy Maxwell	74-77-72-71—294	$660.00
T-24	Ernie Vossler	71-77-74-72—294	$660.00
T-29	Jack Burke Jr.	73-72-78-72—295	$450.00
T-29	Cary Middlecoff	73-74-73-75—295	$450.00
T-29	Bo Wininger	73-77-71-74—295	$450.00
T-32	Jerry Barber	76-72-73-75—296	$247.15
T-32	Bob Goalby	72-79-72-73—296	$247.15
T-32	Chick Harbert	78-72-71-75—296	$247.15
T-32	Bob Harris	71-76-77-72—296	$247.15
T-32	Shelley Mayfield	73-73-75-75—296	$247.15
T-32	Henry Picard	77-73-73-73—296	$247.15
T-32	Jim Turnesa	76-73-72-75—296	$247.15
T-39	Al Besselink	71-74-73-79—297	$200.00
T-39	James Clark	74-71-78-74—297	$200.00
T-39	Don Fairfield	70-75-74-78—297	$200.00
T-39	Tony Holguin	76-72-72-77—297	$200.00
T-39	Bud Holscher	77-73-74-73—297	$200.00
T-39	Dick Lundahl	76-73-75-73—297	$200.00
T-39	Art Wall	75-74-72-76—297	$200.00
T-46	Bill Bisdorf	72-74-74-78—298	$200.00
T-46	Dick Knight	74-75-73-76—298	$200.00
T-46	Milon Marusic	74-77-73-74—298	$200.00
T-49	Frank Stranahan	75-75-74-75—299	$200.00
T-49	Fred Wampler	73-72-79-75—299	$200.00
T-51	George Bayer	71-73-76-80—300	$200.00
T-51	Joe Greer	76-73-72-79—300	$200.00
T-51	Dick Stranahan	76-72-74-78—300	$200.00
T-51	Buddy Sullivan	75-73-73-79—300	$200.00
T-55	Frank Harned	75-74-74-78—301	$200.00
T-55	Herb Marcussen	77-72-74-78—301	$200.00
T-57	Tommy Bolt	72-72-78-81—303	$200.00
T-57	Dick Shoemaker	74-76-74-79—303	$200.00
59	John Odonnell	71-71-82-81—305	$200.00
60	Sonny Rouse	74-75-75-82—306	$200.00
Cut	Brien Charter	72-74-79—225	

Place	Name	Score
Cut	Ben Hogan	74-73-78—225
Cut	Bill Johnston	73-72-80—225
Cut	George Schneiter	76-74-75—225
Cut	Henry Castillo	76-75-75—226
Cut	Mike Dietz	72-78-76—226
Cut	Jack Fleck	76-72-78—226
Cut	Ed Griffiths	71-74-81—226
Cut	Bob Rosburg	74-75-77—226
Cut	Manuel de la Torre	73-77-77—227
Cut	Jim Ferree	71-75-81—227
Cut	Robert Fry	76-74-77—227
Cut	Bob Gajda	77-74-76—227
Cut	Tommy Jacobs	72-77-78—227
Cut	Mike Krak	74-72-81—227
Cut	Joe Moore Jr.	74-74-79—227
Cut	Bill Ogden	72-77-78—227
Cut	Don Whitt	71-76-80—227
Cut	John Zontek	77-74-76—227
Cut	Avery Beck	78-73-77—228
Cut	Ros Collins	75-76-77—228
Cut	John Cook	74-74-80—228
Cut	Bob Crowley	72-79-77—228
Cut	Mac Hunter	72-77-79—228
Cut	Bert Weaver	77-74-77—228
Cut	Fred Baker	72-77-80—229
Cut	Bill Keller	76-74-79—229
Cut	Willie Beljan	75-75-80—230
Cut	Gene Coghill	78-73-80—231
Cut	Jimmy Johnson	75-74-82—231
Cut	Tom Strafaci	75-76-80—231
Cut	Paul Thomas	79-72-80—231
Cut	Errie Ball	76-75-81—232
Cut	Jackson Bradley	81-71—152
Cut	Gil Cavanaugh	76-76—152
Cut	Clare Emery	78-74—152
Cut	Chandler Harper	76-76—152
Cut	Joe Kirkwood	73-79—152
Cut	Charles Lepre	76-76—152
Cut	Sam Penecale	74-78—152
Cut	Herman Scharlau	75-77—152
Cut	Jim Shelton	74-78—152
Cut	John Barnum	77-76—153
Cut	Harry Dee	77-76—153
Cut	Stan Dudas	77-76—153
Cut	Kermit Hager	81-72—153
Cut	Jimmy Hines	79-74—153
Cut	Gus Salerno	75-78—153
Cut	James Stamps	76-77—153
Cut	Eddie Burke	73-81—154
Cut	Joe Campbell	80-74—154
Cut	Buster Cupit	76-78—154
Cut	Bill Eggers	78-76—154
Cut	Bill Ezinicki	76-78—154
Cut	George Fazio	78-76—154
Cut	Don Klein	76-78—154
Cut	Felice Torza	82-72—154
Cut	Lou Warobick	80-74—154
Cut	Frank Beley	75-80—155
Cut	Bob Frainey	79-76—155
Cut	Vic Ghezzi	76-79—155
Cut	Jim Milward	77-78—155

Place	Name	Score
Cut	Alex Redl	74-81—155
Cut	Walter Romans	80-75—155
Cut	Bud Williamson	79-76—155
Cut	Jack Doss	79-77—156
Cut	Fred Gronauer	78-78—156
Cut	John Langford	81-75—156
Cut	Gordon Leishman	78-78—156
Cut	Elroy Marti	77-79—156
Cut	Mike Parco	81-75—156
Cut	Clyde Usina	81-75—156
Cut	Al Brosch	76-81—157
Cut	Jim Guinnup	77-80—157
Cut	Bob Kay	81-76—157
Cut	Babe Lichardus	78-79—157
Cut	Horace Moore	78-79—157
Cut	Stan Staszowski	81-76—157
Cut	Sam Urzetta	81-76—157
Cut	Charles Wipperman	80-77—157
Cut	John Alexander	78-80—158
Cut	John Dalrymple	79-79—158
Cut	Buddy Demling	77-81—158
Cut	Ray Goodell	82-76—158
Cut	Denny Shute	78-80—158
Cut	Carl Beljan	78-81—159
Cut	Joe Brown	81-78—159
Cut	Clarence Doser	75-84—159
Cut	Paul Gross	77-82—159
Cut	Cosimo Tiso	78-81—159
Cut	Ken Yount	81-78—159
Cut	Ben Hodson	84-76—160
Cut	Bob Morris	78-82—160
Cut	Willie Polumbo	80-80—160
Cut	Emil Schodeller	78-82—160
Cut	Alex Sinclair	82-78—160
Cut	Leonard Wagner	74-86—160
Cut	Leonard Warren	74-86—160
Cut	Dick Cline	78-83—161
Cut	Harold Paddock	83-78—161
Cut	Jay Weitzel	80-81—161
Cut	Ivan Cantz	84-78—162
Cut	Billy Dill	83-79—162
Cut	Bob Grant	82-80—162
Cut	August Nordone	81-81—162
Cut	Don Waryan	82-80—162
Cut	Ken Wright	79-83—162
Cut	John Conley	82-81—163
Cut	Les Lesser	77-86—163
Cut	Francisco Lopez	80-83—163
Cut	Bill Moran	75-88—163
Cut	Ed Bucklin	79-85—164
Cut	Bill Grygiel	80-84—164
Cut	Fred Atkins	83-82—165
Cut	Ray Hill	84-81—165
Cut	Bob Mix	81-85—166
Cut	Harold Sanderson	81-85—166
Cut	James Yates	80-87—167
Cut	Rolie Wormstead	86-82—168
Cut	Bill Barclay	88-82—170
WD	Mac Main	77—77
WD	Freddie Haas Jr.	69-77—146
WD	Les Kennedy	78-73—151

1959

A "traffic jam" developed opening day as nine players shared the lead with 69s. Jerry Barber shot a record 65 the next day to take the 36-hole lead. He stayed on top after 54 holes with a 71. However, 33-year-old Bob Rosburg fired a final-round 66 to finish with 277, one stroke in front of Barber, who tied for second with Doug Sanders.

Champion: Bob Rosburg, Rancho Mirage, Calif.	
Site: Minneapolis GC, St. Louis Park, Minn.	
Date: July 30 - Aug. 2	**Purse:** $51,175
Par: 35-35 - 70 (6,850 Yards)	**Entries:**179
36 Hole cut at 150	96 players advanced
54 Hole cut at 221	63 players advanced

	Course Avg	Under Par	At Par	Over Par	Round Leader	Low Round	Bob Rosburg
Round 1:	75.0	9	9	156		69 - B. Casper, G. Littler, J. Barber, W. Burkemo, J. Bradley, D. Hart, C. Klein, M. Krak, M. Souchak	71 - Tied 19th
Round 2:	74.7	12	7	154	J. Barber	65 - J. Barber	143 (72) - Tied 18th
Round 3:	73.5	10	6	81	J. Barber	68 - T. Bolt, P. Cooper, T. Jacobs, B. Rosburg, D. Sanders, S. Snead	211 (68) - Tied 6th
Round 4:	73.5	6	4	53	B. Rosburg	66 - B. Rosburg	277 (66) - 1st
Totals:	74.46	37	26	444			

TOURNAMENT SUMMARY

Place	Name	Score	Winnings
1	Bob Rosburg	71-72-68-66 —277	$8,250.00
T-2	Jerry Barber	69-65-71-73 —278	$3,562.50
T-2	Doug Sanders	72-66-68-72 —278	$3,562.00
4	Dow Finsterwald	71-68-71-70 —280	$2,500.00
T-5	Bob Goalby	72-69-72-68 —281	$2,000.00
T-5	Mike Souchak	69-67-71-74 —281	$2,000.00
T-5	Ken Venturi	70-72-70-69 —281	$2,000.00
T-8	Cary Middlecoff	72-68-70-72 —282	$1,600.00
T-8	Sam Snead	71-73-68-70 —282	$1,600.00
T-10	Gene Littler	69-70-72-73 —284	$1,450.00
T-11	Doug Ford	71-73-71-70 —285	$1,250.00
T-11	Billy Maxwell	70-76-70-69 —285	$1,250.00
T-11	Ed Oliver	75-70-69-71 —285	$1,250.00
T-14	Paul Harney	74-71-71-70 —286	$1,050.00
T-14	Tommy Jacobs	73-71-68-74 —286	$1,050.00
T-14	Arnold Palmer	72-72-71-71 —286	$1,050.00
T-17	Tommy Bolt	76-69-68-74 —287	$775.00
T-17	Jack Burke Jr.	70-73-72-72 —287	$775.00
T-17	Walter Burkemo	69-72-73-73 —287	$775.00
T-17	Billy Casper	69-71-73-74 —287	$775.00
T-17	Pete Cooper	78-70-68-71 —287	$775.00
T-17	Buster Cupit	70-72-72-73 —287	$775.00
T-17	Babe Lichardus	71-73-72-71 —287	$775.00
T-17	Ernie Vossler	75-71-72-69 —287	$775.00
T-25	Jay Hebert	72-70-69-77 —288	$510.00
T-25	Ted Kroll	72-74-71-71 —288	$510.00
T-25	Art Wall	70-72-73-73 —288	$510.00
T-28	Clare Emery	74-74-72-69 —289	$390.00
T-28	Chick Harbert	73-71-71-74 —289	$390.00
T-28	Fred Hawkins	72-69-72-76 —289	$390.00
T-31	Jackson Bradley	69-74-73-74 —290	$262.50
T-31	Don Fairfield	70-73-75-72 —290	$262.50
T-31	Lionel Hebert	71-69-75-75 —290	$262.50
T-31	Eric Monti	74-72-71-73 —290	$262.50
T-35	John McMullin	76-71-69-75 —291	$200.00
T-35	Dave Ragan	74-69-74-74 —291	$200.00
T-35	Dick Stranahan	74-70-72-75 —291	$200.00
T-38	Bob Crowley	73-75-71-73 —292	$200.00
T-38	Jim Ferree	74-72-71-75 —292	$200.00
T-38	Jim Ferrier	73-71-72-76 —292	$200.00
T-38	Claude Harmon	73-73-72-74 —292	$200.00
T-38	Jim Turnesa	73-72-74-73 —292	$200.00
T-38	Don Whitt	71-77-72-72 —292	$200.00
T-44	Julius Boros	72-74-73-74 —293	$200.00
T-44	Wes Ellis Jr.	76-74-70-73 —293	$200.00
T-44	Scudday Horner	74-71-76-72 —293	$200.00
T-44	Denny Shute	75-73-70-75 —293	$200.00
T-44	Henry Williams	74-73-74-72 —293	$200.00
T-49	Don January	73-74-74-73 —294	$200.00
T-49	Mac Main	75-70-73-76 —294	$200.00
T-49	Bill Ogden	73-69-76-76 —294	$200.00
T-49	Bo Wininger	77-73-71-73 —294	$200.00
T-53	Al Feminelli	70-77-73-75 —295	$200.00
T-53	Bob Gajda	74-71-74-76 —295	$200.00
T-53	Frank Stranahan	74-72-70-79 —295	$200.00
T-56	Bill Ezinicki	77-67-76-76 —296	$200.00
T-56	George Fazio	74-76-69-77 —296	$200.00
T-58	John Barnum	75-73-72-77 —297	$200.00

Place	Name	Score	Winnings
T-58	Bud Williamson	72-75-72-78 —297	$200.00
60	Mickey Homa	71-74-75-78 —298	$200.00
61	Don Waryan	72-76-72-79 —299	$200.00
62	Wayne Otis	72-76-72-80 —300	$200.00
63	Leonard Wagner	72-73-75-85 —305	$200.00
Cut	George Bayer	74-76-72 —222	
Cut	Paul Kern	77-70-75 —222	
Cut	Dick Mayer	73-76-73 —222	
Cut	Don Shock	70-75-77 —222	
Cut	Gene Bone	72-74-77 —223	
Cut	Joe Brown	74-75-74 —223	
Cut	Gene Coghill	75-74-74 —223	
Cut	Clarence Doser	74-75-74 —223	
Cut	Ed Furgol	75-75-73 —223	
Cut	Joe Kirkwood	75-75-73 —223	
Cut	Chuck Klein	69-73-81 —223	
Cut	Mike Krak	69-76-78 —223	
Cut	Joby Connor	75-73-76 —224	
Cut	John Langford	77-73-74 —224	
Cut	Herman Scharlau	70-77-77 —224	
Cut	Bill Eggers	77-73-75 —225	
Cut	John Galeski	72-78-75 —225	
Cut	Walter Romans	75-75-75 —225	
Cut	Alex Sinclair	75-75-75 —225	
Cut	Johnny Bulla	74-75-77 —226	
Cut	Otto Greiner	72-76-78 —226	
Cut	Dick Lundahl	75-73-78 —226	
Cut	J.D. Taylor	73-74-79 —226	
Cut	Thorne Wood	74-72-80 —226	
Cut	Jim Browning	75-73-79 —227	
Cut	George Schneiter	76-74-77 —227	
Cut	Bob Carmen	76-73-79 —228	
Cut	Bill Moran	76-73-79 —228	
Cut	Jim Guinnup	77-73-79 —229	
Cut	Fred Wampler	74-76-79 —229	
Cut	Herman Barron	73-76-81 —230	
Cut	Dick Hart	69-79-82 —230	
Cut	Babe Urzetta	75-75-86 —236	
Cut	Gene Sarazen	73-74 —147	
Cut	Leon Andrews	75-76 —151	
Cut	Henry Castillo	78-73 —151	
Cut	Art Doering	73-78 —151	
Cut	Stan Dudas	75-76 —151	
Cut	Joe Greer	78-73 —151	
Cut	Charles Malchaski	78-73 —151	
Cut	Bill Markham	76-75 —151	
Cut	James Williams	74-77 —151	
Cut	Sam Bernardi	75-77 —152	
Cut	Dick Cline	75-77 —152	
Cut	Bob Crow	75-77 —152	
Cut	Manuel de la Torre	76-76 —152	
Cut	Jim Farina	78-74 —152	
Cut	Mike Fetchick	77-75 —152	
Cut	Labron Harris Jr.	78-74 —152	
Cut	Lester Moe	75-77 —152	
Cut	Al Nelson	75-77 —152	
Cut	Pat Rea	77-75 —152	
Cut	Skee Riegel	75-77 —152	

Place	Name	Score
Cut	Lou Warobick	74-78 —152
Cut	Charles Wipperman	77-75 —152
Cut	Bill Collins	77-76 —153
Cut	Wayne Haley	75-78 —153
Cut	Jack Isaacs	77-76 —153
Cut	Hans Merrell	77-76 —153
Cut	Paul Porter	77-76 —153
Cut	Paul Segerlund	72-81 —153
Cut	Charles Sheppard	76-77 —153
Cut	John Spencer	79-74 —153
Cut	Tom Stafaci	76-77 —153
Cut	Ken Stear	78-75 —153
Cut	Tom Talkington	76-77 —153
Cut	Richard Beckman	77-77 —154
Cut	Billy Capps	80-74 —154
Cut	John Cook	79-75 —154
Cut	Arthur Harris	75-79 —154
Cut	Frank Keller	80-74 —154
Cut	John Lively	81-73 —154
Cut	Tony Longo	81-73 —154
Cut	Francisco Lopez	74-80 —154
Cut	Tommy Ritter	81-73 —154
Cut	Buddy Sullivan	78-76 —154
Cut	John Zontek	77-77 —154
Cut	Jimmy Thompson	76-79 —155
Cut	Burl Bolesta	76-80 —156
Cut	Ralph Bond	82-74 —156
Cut	Bob Harris	78-78 —156
Cut	Bill Wright	80-76 —156
Cut	Buddy Demling	76-81 —157
Cut	Lou Esposito	76-81 —157
Cut	John Long	77-80 —157
Cut	Sonny Rouse	78-79 —157
Cut	Stan Staszowski	82-75 —157
Cut	Mike Dietz	77-81 —158
Cut	Wally Grant	80-78 —158
Cut	Gunnard Johnson	76-82 —158
Cut	Hardy Loudermilk	80-78 —158
Cut	Leon Pounders	81-77 —158
Cut	Bob Reith	79-79 —158
Cut	Lester Ward	80-78 —158
Cut	Jake Zastko	82-76 —158
Cut	Sam Drake	80-79 —159
Cut	Merle Lint	82-77 —159
Cut	John Suveges	81-78 —159
Cut	Bob Toski	77-82 —159
Cut	Charles Brown	79-81 —160
Cut	Eddie Hamilton	82-78 —160
Cut	Ron Montressor	78-82 —160
Cut	Reggie Sauger	82-78 —160
Cut	Chuck Alexander	79-82 —161
Cut	Bob Morris	82-80 —162
Cut	Jake Clark	80-83 —163
Cut	Jack Jones	84-80 —164
Cut	Jimmy Bellizzi	80-85 —165
WD	Mike Demassey	75 —75
WD	Chandler Harper	73-77 —150
WD	Gene Webb	76-73-72 —221

1958

Llanerch Country Club was the site of the first four-day, 72-hole stroke play contest in PGA Championship history. On the first day, 28-year-old Dow Finsterwald led with a 3-under-par 67. After 36 holes, he shared the lead with Jay Hebert at 139. Sam Snead went ahead after 54 holes with 207. Going into the final round, Finsterwald was two back and shot a 31 on the front nine, on his way to posting a 67 for a two-stroke victory over Billy Casper.

Champion: Dow Finsterwald,	Colorado Springs, Colo.
Site: Llanerch CC, Havertown, Pa.	
Date: July 17-20	**Purse:** $39,388
Par: 35-35 - 70 (6,710 Yards)	**Entries:** 167
36 Hole cut at 154	93 players advanced
54 Hole cut at 228	64 players advanced

	Course Avg	Under Par	At Par	Over Par	Round Leader	Low Round	Dow Finsterwald
Round 1:	76.8	7	2	152	Dow Finsterwald	67 - Dow Finsterwald	67 - 1st
Round 2:	76.1	6	7	141	D. Finsterwald, J. Hebert	67 - B. Casper, S. Snead	139 (72) - Tied 1st
Round 3:	75.1	9	4	80	Sam Snead	66 - Walter Burkemo	209 (70) - 3rd
Round 4:	74.3	5	4	55	Dow Finsterwald	67 - Dow Finsterwald	276 (67) - 1st
Totals:	75.94	27	17	428			

TOURNAMENT SUMMARY

Place	Name	Score	Winnings
1	Dow Finsterwald	67-72-70-67—276	$5,500.00
2	Billy Casper	73-67-68-70—278	$3,500.00
3	Sam Snead	73-67-67-73—280	$2,400.00
4	Jack Burke Jr.	70-72-69-70—281	$2,000.00
T-5	Tommy Bolt	72-70-73-70—285	$1,600.00
T-5	Julius Boros	72-68-73-72—285	$1,600.00
T-5	Jay Hebert	68-71-73-73—285	$1,600.00
T-8	Buster Cupit	71-74-69-73—287	$1,300.00
T-8	Ed Oliver	74-73-71-69—287	$1,300.00
T-8	Mike Souchak	75-69-69-74—287	$1,300.00
T-11	Doug Ford	72-70-70-76—288	$1,016.00
T-11	Bob Rosburg	71-73-76-68—288	$1,016.00
T-11	Art Wall	71-78-67-72—288	$1,016.00
T-14	Fred Hawkins	72-75-70-73—290	$875.00
T-14	Dick Mayer	69-76-69-76—290	$875.00
T-16	John Barnum	75-69-74-73—291	$740.00
T-16	Walter Burkemo	76-73-66-76—291	$740.00
T-16	Lionel Hebert	69-73-74-75—291	$740.00
T-16	Bo Wininger	76-73-69-73—291	$740.00
T-20	Ted Kroll	69-74-75-74—292	$566.00
T-20	Cary Middlecoff	71-73-76-72—292	$566.00
T-20	Eric Monti	73-71-73-75—292	$566.00
T-20	Bob Toski	79-70-71-72—292	$566.00
T-20	Ken Venturi	72-73-74-73—292	$566.00
T-25	Pete Cooper	74-77-73-69—293	$425.00
T-25	George Fazio	72-74-73-74—293	$425.00
T-25	Bob Gajda	75-70-75-73—293	$425.00
T-25	Billy Maxwell	75-69-74-75—293	$425.00
T-29	Dick Shoemaker	79-72-73-70—294	$335.00
T-29	Don Whitt	71-72-73-78—294	$335.00
T-31	Mike Fetchick	74-76-71-74—295	$270.00
T-31	Frank Stranahan	76-76-74-69—295	$270.00
T-33	Errie Ball	79-72-72-73—296	$220.00
T-33	Tom Talkington	75-73-73-75—296	$220.00
T-35	Herman Barron	75-71-75-76—297	$162.00
T-35	Dick Cline	75-72-77-73—297	$162.00
T-35	Bill Collins	71-70-77-79—297	$162.00
T-35	Mike Dietz	77-70-74-76—297	$162.00
T-35	Felice Torza	69-72-75-81—297	$162.00
T-40	Henry Castillo	75-76-75-72—298	$110.00
T-40	Bill Ezinicki	76-70-80-72—298	$110.00
T-40	Arnold Palmer	76-71-77-74—298	$110.00
T-40	Skee Riegel	76-77-74-71—298	$110.00
T-44	Eddie Burke	75-75-77-72—299	$100.00
T-44	Bob Crowley	70-76-73-80—299	$100.00
T-44	Bill Johnston	75-72-77-75—299	$100.00
T-44	Dave Marr	72-79-74-74—299	$100.00
T-48	Ed Furgol	78-76-72-74—300	$100.00
T-49	Jackson Bradley	77-77-73-74—301	$100.00
T-49	Jack Isaacs	74-75-78-74—301	$100.00
T-49	Chuck Klein	78-75-74-74—301	$100.00
T-49	Henry Williams	75-74-77-75—301	$100.00
T-53	Mike Krak	74-78-74-76—302	$100.00
T-53	Toby Lyons	75-73-74-80—302	$100.00

Place	Name	Score	Winnings
T-53	Thorne Wood	77-75-70-80—302	$100.00
T-56	Brien Charter	72-75-80-76—303	$100.00
T-56	Vic Ghezzi	75-74-76-78—303	$100.00
T-56	Claude Harmon	77-75-76-75—303	$100.00
T-59	Al Brosch	75-79-74-78—306	$100.00
T-59	James Gantz	76-76-75-79—306	$100.00
T-59	Gus Salerno	79-75-74-78—306	$100.00
62	Larry Bartosek	75-79-74-79—307	$100.00
63	Ewing Pomeroy	80-74-74-82—310	$100.00
64	George Griffin	74-76-78-83—311	$100.00
Cut	Ernie Catropa	72-81-76—229	
Cut	Dick Demane	74-79-76—229	
Cut	Max Evans	75-73-81—229	
Cut	Chick Harbert	75-76-78—229	
Cut	Jack Higgins	76-78-75—229	
Cut	Jimmy Johnson	78-74-77—229	
Cut	Charles Lepre	78-74-77—229	
Cut	Bill Ogden	76-77-76—229	
Cut	Johnny Palmer	73-80-76—229	
Cut	Denny Shute	77-72-80—229	
Cut	Leo Biagetti	71-79-80—230	
Cut	Tom Case	74-78-78—230	
Cut	Charles Harter	75-77-78—230	
Cut	Eddie Joseph	77-73-80—230	
Cut	Sam Drake	73-80-78—231	
Cut	Arthur Harris	75-76-80—231	
Cut	Bill Kaiser	75-77-79—231	
Cut	Milon Marusic	80-73-78—231	
Cut	Joe Dodich	78-76-78—232	
Cut	Bob Grant	75-77-80—232	
Cut	Frank Kiraly	75-74-83—232	
Cut	Ock Willoweit	78-75-79—232	
Cut	Phil Friel	79-74-80—233	
Cut	Bill Heinlein	75-77-81—233	
Cut	Tod Menefee	77-75-81—233	
Cut	Ray Goodell	74-79-81—234	
Cut	Monte Norcross	78-74-82—234	
Cut	Clyde Usina	75-79-80—234	
Cut	Billy Capps	76-76-84—236	
Cut	Charles Bassler	78-77—155	
Cut	Jack Bell	79-76—155	
Cut	Francis Brown	77-78—155	
Cut	George Buzzini	78-77—155	
Cut	Clare Emery	76-79—155	
Cut	Otto Greiner	79-76—155	
Cut	Bob Hayes	81-74—155	
Cut	Harry McCarthy	79-76—155	
Cut	Bob Reith	79-76—155	
Cut	Ted Schleichter	77-78—155	
Cut	Charles Sheppard	77-78—155	
Cut	Bud Williamson	78-77—155	
Cut	Louis Barbaro	79-77—156	
Cut	Al Besselink	78-78—156	
Cut	Chandler Harper	78-78—156	

Place	Name	Score
Cut	Scudday Horner	81-75—156
Cut	Paul Kern	79-77—156
Cut	Donald Palmer	81-75—156
Cut	Guy Paulsen	79-77—156
Cut	Jim Rudolph	76-80—156
Cut	Gene Sarazen	78-78—156
Cut	Jimmy Thompson	76-80—156
Cut	Jim Turnesa	78-78—156
Cut	Bob Bodington	74-83—157
Cut	Dave Douglas	84-73—157
Cut	Vince Leskosky	82-75—157
Cut	Paul McGuire	80-77—157
Cut	Chet Munson	80-77—157
Cut	John Serafin	78-79—157
Cut	Bob Stupple	81-76—157
Cut	Joe Coonor	77-81—158
Cut	Bill Eggers	78-80—158
Cut	Charles Wipperman	78-80—158
Cut	Jim Browning	79-80—159
Cut	Joseph Deigo	82-77—159
Cut	Andy Gibson	81-78—159
Cut	Furman Hayes	80-79—159
Cut	George Keyes	76-83—159
Cut	Bob Marshall	79-81—160
Cut	August Nordone	83-77—160
Cut	Walter Romans	77-83—160
Cut	Al Smith	82-78—160
Cut	Buddy Sullivan	80-80—160
Cut	Ray Bennett	78-83—161
Cut	John Cook	80-81—161
Cut	Bob Kay	81-80—161
Cut	Alex Sinclair	85-76—161
Cut	Chuck Dupree	79-84—163
Cut	Frank Whibley	86-77—163
Cut	Paul Biggy	83-81—164
Cut	Jim Farina	83-82—165
Cut	Ralph Bond	85-81—166
Cut	Gene Hamm	82-84—166
Cut	Earl Martin	83-83—166
Cut	Bob Moore	87-79—166
Cut	Art Stuhler	80-87—167
Cut	Woodrow Tucker	87-80—167
Cut	Noel Epperson	83-85—168
Cut	Leonard Kennett	86-82—168
Cut	Lester Moe	87-83—170
Cut	Carl Jans	87-84—171
DQ	Jimmy Demaret	69—69
WD	Jack Fleck	74—74
WD	Elroy Marti	80—80
WD	Ken Wright	80—80
WD	Wally Ulrich	82—82
WD	Jimmy Haynes	83—83
WD	Clark Morrow	83—83

1957

Day One: Most of the matches went as predicted, with the defending champion Jack Burke beating host professional Gene Marchi, 4 and 2, despite Burke playing with an aggravated left wrist. Sam Snead drew the largest gallery of the day in his 4-and-2 triumph over Jack Serafin. After the match, Snead reminded Serafin that in the 1938 PGA Championship, Snead beat Jack's father, Felix, in the third round. Other past champions who advanced were Vic Ghezzi over Howie de Angelus, 1-up; Walter Burkemo beat Toby Lyons, 1-up; Doug Ford defeated Denny Champagne, 4 and 3; Denny Shute beat Bob Toski, 3 and 2; while Chandler Harper, Jim Turnesa and Chick Harbert went down to defeats. The only real upset of the day saw Jim Browning defeat Ed Furgol, 2 and 1. In other matches that the favorites won, Dick Mayer was a 6-and-5 victor over Art Stuhler; Lionel Hebert beat Max Evans, 2-up; Jack Fleck was a 4-and-3 winner over Terl Johnson; and Tommy Bolt beat Henry Castille on the 19th hole, 1-up. Dow Finsterwald nipped Ted Sleichter, 1-up, while Gene Littler, who got a special invitation, shot 67 to beat Don Fairfield, 1-up.

On the second day of play, defending champion Jack Burke was ousted by Milon Marusic, 2 and 1, in the morning round. Sam Snead advanced as he beat 58-year-old PGA Seniors' champion Al Watrous, 4 and 3. In the afternoon round Snead eliminated John Thoren, 3 and 2. In other matches Ellsworth Vines upset Denny Shute, 1-up, but then lost to Don Whitt, 4 and 3, in the afternoon. Dow Finsterwald swept past Bud Williamson Jr., 3 and 2, and then Joe Kirkwood Jr., 2 and 1. Dick Mayer beat Shelley Mayfield, 1-up, and Al Smith, 5 and 3. Ted Kroll got by Bill Nary, 2 and 1, and then Ewing Pomeroy, 4 and 3. Lionel Hebert beat Marty Furgol and Charles Farlow, 3 and 1, while Tommy Bolt just got by Gene Littler, 1-up, and pounded Eldon Briggs, 7 and 6. Former Champions Doug Ford and Walter Burkemo also advanced as Burkemo beat William Heinlien, 1-up, on the 19th hole and Tony Holquin, 1-up. Ford beat James Guinnup, 4 and 3, in the morning and Robert Gajda, 3 and 2, in the afternoon.

On the third day, Dow Finsterwald got the headlines, upsetting Sam Snead, 3 and 1, in the fourth round and then beating Charles Sheppard, 2-up, in the quarter-finals. Snead blamed his faulty driving. "I just drove awful," stated Snead after his loss to Finsterwald. Snead hit two drives out-of-bounds with hooks as he was out in 39, the high nine-hole score for any of the

contestants. In the fourth round, U.S. Open Champion Dick Mayer was able to defeat Ted Kroll, 1-up, but then was upset by Don Whitt, 2 and 1, in the quarter-finals. Jay Hebert also upset Doug Ford in the fourth round, 3 and 2, but then was defeated by Walter Burkemo, 2 and 1. Claude Harmon beat Tommy Bolt, 1-up, in the fourth round, but was

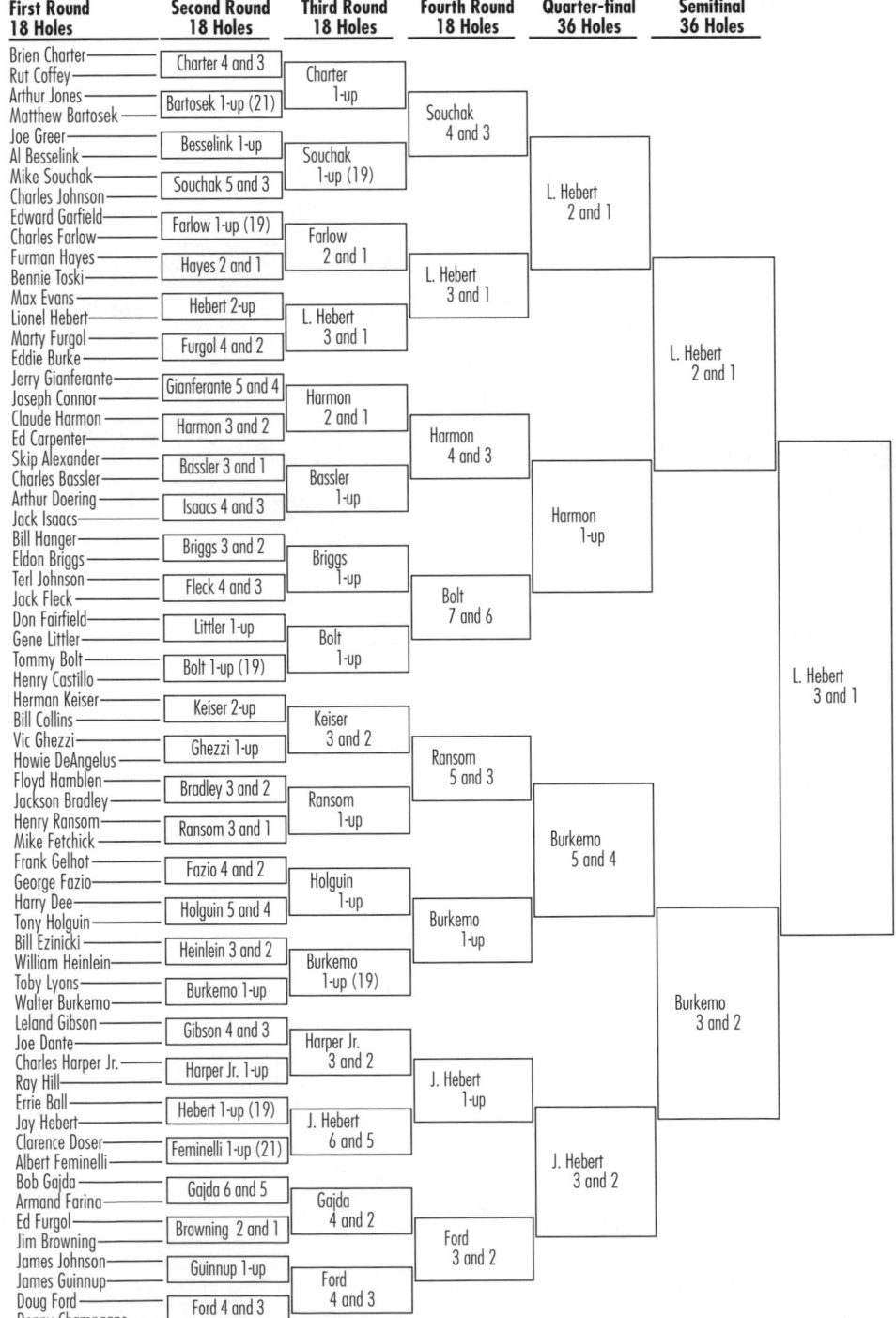

ROAD TO THE FINALS

Lionel Hebert beat	Round	Dow Finsterwald beat
Max Evans, 2-up	1st Round	Ted Sleichter, 1-up
Marty Furgol, 3 and 1	2nd Round	Bud Williamson, 3 and 2
Charles Farlow, 3 and 1	3rd Round	Joe Kirkwood Jr., 2 and 1
Mike Souchak, 2 and 1	4th Round	Sam Snead, 3 and 1
Claude Harmon, 2 and 1	Quarter-finals	Charles Sheppard, 2-up
Walter Burkemo, 3 and 1	Semifinals	Don Whitt, 2-up

First Round 18 Holes	Second Round 18 Holes	Third Round 18 Holes	Fourth Round 18 Holes	Quarter-final 36 Holes	Semifinal 36 Holes
Brien Charter / Rut Coffey	Charter 4 and 3	Charter 1-up	Souchak 4 and 3		
Arthur Jones / Matthew Bartosek	Bartosek 1-up (21)				
Joe Greer / Al Besselink	Besselink 1-up	Souchak 1-up (19)		L. Hebert 2 and 1	
Mike Souchak / Charles Johnson	Souchak 5 and 3				
Edward Garfield / Charles Farlow	Farlow 1-up (19)	Farlow 2 and 1	L. Hebert 3 and 1		
Furman Hayes / Bennie Toski	Hayes 2 and 1				
Max Evans / Lionel Hebert	Hebert 2-up	L. Hebert 3 and 1			L. Hebert 2 and 1
Marty Furgol / Eddie Burke	Furgol 4 and 2				
Jerry Gianferante / Joseph Connor	Gianferante 5 and 4	Harmon 2 and 1	Harmon 4 and 3		
Claude Harmon / Ed Carpenter	Harmon 3 and 2				
Skip Alexander / Charles Bassler	Bassler 3 and 1	Bassler 1-up		Harmon 1-up	
Arthur Doering / Jack Isaacs	Isaacs 4 and 3				
Bill Hanger / Eldon Briggs	Briggs 3 and 2	Briggs 1-up	Bolt 7 and 6		
Terl Johnson / Jack Fleck	Fleck 4 and 3				
Don Fairfield / Gene Littler	Littler 1-up	Bolt 1-up			L. Hebert 3 and 1
Tommy Bolt / Henry Castillo	Bolt 1-up (19)				
Herman Keiser / Bill Collins	Keiser 2-up	Keiser 3 and 2	Ransom 5 and 3		
Vic Ghezzi / Howie DeAngelus	Ghezzi 1-up				
Floyd Hamblen / Jackson Bradley	Bradley 3 and 2	Ransom 1-up		Burkemo 5 and 4	
Henry Ransom / Mike Fetchick	Ransom 3 and 1				
Frank Gelhot / George Fazio	Fazio 4 and 2	Holguin 1-up	Burkemo 1-up		
Harry Dee / Tony Holguin	Holguin 5 and 4				
Bill Ezinicki / William Heinlein	Heinlein 3 and 2	Burkemo 1-up (19)			Burkemo 3 and 2
Toby Lyons / Walter Burkemo	Burkemo 1-up				
Leland Gibson / Joe Dante	Gibson 4 and 3	Harper Jr. 3 and 2	J. Hebert 1-up		
Charles Harper Jr. / Ray Hill	Harper Jr. 1-up				
Errie Ball / Jay Hebert	Hebert 1-up (19)	J. Hebert 6 and 5		J. Hebert 3 and 2	
Clarence Doser / Albert Feminelli	Feminelli 1-up (21)				
Bob Gajda / Armand Farina	Gajda 6 and 5	Gajda 4 and 2	Ford 3 and 2		
Ed Furgol / Jim Browning	Browning 2 and 1				
James Johnson / James Guinnup	Guinnup 1-up	Ford 4 and 3			
Doug Ford / Denny Champagne	Ford 4 and 3				

beaten by Lionel Hebert, 2 and 1, in the quarter-finals.

In the semifinals, Lionel Hebert got some revenge for the fourth round loss to his brother Jay as he ousted Walter Burkemo, 3 and 1. Burkemo was 1-up after the morning round and was 2-up after Hebert called a penalty stroke against himself. Hebert said the ball moved on the 19th green as he was about to make his address. But in the next eight holes, Hebert out-

Champion:	Lionel Hebert, Lafayette, La.*	
Site:	Miami Valley GC, Dayton, Ohio	
Date:	July 17-21	Purse: $42,100
Par:	36-35—71	Entries: 128

putted Burkemo who had two 3-putts and took a 2-up lead at the 27th hole. Burkemo won the 28th hole, but lost the 32nd hole and Hebert ended the match with a 5-iron to within a foot for a birdie at the 35th hole.

In the other match, Dow Finsterwald defeated Don Whitt, 2-up. Finsterwald started to make it a runaway with a 33 on the front nine of the morning round, and after winning the 10th hole was 5-up. With a hole-in-one on the 13th hole with an 8-iron and a swing of momentum, Whitt finished the back side with a 31 to square the match at the halfway mark. In the afternoon Whitt went ahead at the 25th hole with a birdie, but lost the advantage with a bogey at the 27th hole. At the 30th hole Finsterwald took the lead when Whitt drove out-of-bounds, and then sealed the match with a birdie at the final hole.

In the finals, Lionel Hebert won the last match-play PGA Championship when he beat Dow Finsterwald, 3 and 1. For most of the match the biggest lead anyone had was 1-up, but the break for Hebert came at the 32nd hole when he made a 15-footer for birdie that put him 1-up. At the next two holes, both players made birdies, but another big break for Hebert came at the 34th hole when Finsterwald hit into a creek in front of the green. Even though he was allowed a free drop because a foot bridge was ruled an "artificial obstruction," he still wasn't able to make a par, which put Hebert 2-up. "That was the turning point of the match," Hebert said afterwards. With a routine par at the 35th hole, Hebert closed out the match, earning the $8,000 winning check and having the honor of being the 25th name to be engraved on the Rodman Wanamaker Trophy.

Final 36 Holes	Semifinal 36 Holes	Quarter-final 36 Holes	Fourth Round 18 Holes	Third Round 18 Holes	Second Round 18 Holes	First Round 18 Holes
					Burke 4 and 2	Jack Burke
				Marusic 2 and 1		Gene Marchi
			Marusic 2 and 1		Marusic 4 and 3	Milon Marusic
						Leonard Wagner
					Krak 3 and 2	Chandler Harper
				Krak 2 and 1		Mike Krak
		Whitt 2 and 1			Springer 3 and 2	Gil Sellers
						Marshall Springer
					Shute 3 and 2	Bob Toski
				Vines 1-up		Denny Shute
			Whitt 4 and 3		Vines 5 and 4	Clark Morrow
						Ellsworth Vines
					Lindner 3 and 2	Bob Stupple
				Whitt 1-up		Henry Lindner
	Whitt 2 and 1				Whitt 2 and 1	Donald Whitt
						Augie Nordone
					Kroll 5 and 3	Ted Kroll
				Kroll 2 and 1		Hans Merrell
			Kroll 4 and 3		Nary 2 and 1	Bill Nary
						Jim Turnesa
					Pomeroy 1-up (19)	Toney Tiso
				Pomeroy 3 and 1		Ewing Pomeroy
		Mayer 1-up			Schneiter 5 and 4	Ernest Schneiter
						Bob Kivlin
					Smith 1-up	Fred Hawkins
				Smith 1-up (19)		Al Smith
			Mayer 5 and 3		Palmer 3 and 2	Charles Wipperman
						Johnny Palmer
					Mayfield 3 and 2	Len Kennett
				Mayer 1-up		Shelley Mayfield
L. Hebert 3 and 1					Mayer 6 and 5	Dick Mayer
						Arthur Stuhler
					Riegel 1-up (19)	Chick Harbert
				Riegel 3 and 2		Skee Riegel
			Smith 3 and 2		Wall 1-up (22)	Monte Norcross
						Art Wall
					Johnston 3 and 2	William Johnston
				Smith 1-up		Palmer Lawernce
		Sheppard 4 and 3			Smith 1-up	Warren Smith
						Joseph Sodd
					Sheppard 1-up	Felice Torza
				Sheppard 2-up		Charles Sheppard
			Sheppard 1-up		Moore 3 and 2	John Dalrymple
						Robert Moore
					Keyes 1-up	George Keyes
				White 1-up (21)		Gordon Leishman
	Finsterwald 2-up				White 6 and 5	Buck White
						Robert Whitaker
					Snead 4 and 2	Sam Snead
				Snead 4 and 3		John Serafin
			Snead 3 and 2		Watrous 1-up (22)	Rod Munday
						Al Watrous
					Thoren 1-up (22)	John Thoren
				Thoren 3 and 1		James Peer
		Finsterwald 2 and 1			Bernardi 1-up (23)	Sam Bernardi
						Verl Stinchcome
					Finsterwald 1-up	Dow Finsterwald
				Finsterwald 3 and 2		Theodore Sleichter
			Finsterwald 2 and 1		Williamson 5 and 4	Bud Williamson
						Wayne Otis
					Kirkwood Jr. 3 and 2	Joe Kirkwood Jr.
				Kirkwood Jr. 1-up		John Spencer
					Watson 1-up	Earl Martin
						Robert Watson

1956

Day One: Defending champion Doug Ford led the way with a 3-and-2 win over Buddy Viar. The only upsets saw former PGA Champion Vic Ghezzi lose in overtime as Al Smith won, 1-up, and Tommy Bolt lost to Charles Prentice.

On the second day of play, Ford was involved in a controversial victory over Mike Dietz. At the 15th hole, Ford was 1-up and drove into the woods. He pitched out and hit his third shot onto the green. When the ball stopped rolling, Dietz called out to the spectators near the putting surface before hitting his second, asking them, "How far away is he?" Ford then protested the hole, calling on Rule 9, on advice. The rule states that "a player shall not give or ask for advice or take any action which may result in his receiving advice except from his caddie, his partner or his partner's caddie." While Dietz made four on the hole and Ford made 5, the match referee agreed with Ford that Dietz did break "rule 9" and the hole was awarded to Ford. Even though he was 2-up with three holes left, Ford lost the 16th and the 18th holes to square the match, then beat Dietz 1-up at the fifth extra playoff hole by holing a 40-yard wedge for a birdie 3. But in his afternoon match, Ford bowed to former PGA Champion Walter Burkemo, 5 and 3. Other than that, the only other upsets saw former champion Chick Harbert lose a third round match to Skee Riegel, 1-up. Claude Harmon lost a heartbreaker to Henry Ransom on the 23rd hole, while Jimmy Demaret also lost, 1-up, to Charles Lepre on the 21st hole. In other matches, Gene Sarazen nipped Dick Lundahl, 1-up, on the 19th hole in the morning round. Sarazen was 4-down after the 11th hole, but won the next three holes and when the match went into overtime beat Lundahl with a par on the first extra hole. In the afternoon round, Sarazen had a easier time beating Mike Krak, 3 and 2. Sam Snead also had a tough morning match against John O'Donnell, needing 20 holes to vanquish O'Donnell with a birdie at the second extra hole. In his afternoon match, Snead was a 4-and-3 victor over Bob Toski. Jim Turnesa had a tough time advancing as he beat Dean Adkisson, 2-and-1, in the morning, but took 20 holes in the afternoon to beat former U.S. Open Champion Jack Fleck, 1-up.

On the third day, some key favorites got beaten, with Sam Snead the biggest casualty. In his morning match, Snead had an easy time defeating Gene Sarazen, 5 and 4. But in the afternoon match, Snead was unable to hole short putts in his contest against

Jack Burke Jr. beat	Round	Ted Kroll beat
Leon Pounders, 2 and 1	1st Round	Roger Peacock, 2 and 1
Bill Collins, 5 and 3	2nd Round	George Keyes, 2-up
Fred Haas Jr., 1-up (20)	3rd Round	Michael Rooney, 3 and 2
Chandler Harper, 3 and 2	4th Round	Jim Turnesa, 1-up
Fred Hawkins, 4 and 2	Quarter-finals	Sam Snead, 2 and 1
Ed Furgol, 1-up (37)	Semifinals	William Johnston, 10 and 8

Ted Kroll as Kroll was a 2-and-1 winner. For Kroll, his putting was superb all day as he was a 1-up winner over former Champion Jim Turnesa in the morning. For the 35 holes that Kroll played, he one-putted eight times and avoided three-putting any greens. Walter Burkemo lost his morning match to William Johnston, 1-up,

First Round 18 Holes	Second Round 18 Holes	Third Round 18 Holes	Fourth Round 18 Holes	Quarter-final 36 Holes	Semifinal 36 Holes
Elmer Reed	Browning 1-up	Harper Jr. 2-up	Harper Jr. 1-up	Burke 3 and 2	Burke 4 and 2
Jim Browning					
Johnny Revolta	Harper Jr. by default				
Charles Harper Jr.					
Larry Bartosck	Lichardus 1-up	Lichardus 2 and 1			
Milton Lichardus					
Dick Mayer	Mayer 4 and 3				
Bob Schechter					
Joe Brown	Thoren 1-up	Haas Jr. 2 and 1	Burke 1-up (20)		
John Thoren					
Fred Haas Jr.	Haas Jr. 1-up				
Ron LaParl					
Bill Collins	Collins 4 and 3	Burke 5 and 3			
Tom Blaskovich					
Jack Burke	Burke 2 and 1				
Leon Pounders					
Fred Baker	Marti 1-up (19)	Hawkins 6 and 5	Hawkins 1-up (19)	Hawkins 4 and 3	
Elroy Marti					
Fred Hawkins	Hawkins 2 and 1				
Felice Torza					
Robert Moore	Moore 1-up	Wall 5 and 4			
Jim Rudolph					
Art Wall	Wall 5 and 4				
Warren Smith					
Howard Kluth	Moe 2-up	Hebert 2 and 1	Hebert 3 and 1		
Lester Moe					
Lionel Hebert	Hebert 6 and 4				
Fred Blanchard					
Albert Maus	Riegel 5 and 4	Riegel 1-up			
Skee Riegel					
Chick Harbert	Harbert 1-up (20)				
Henry Williams Jr.					
Furman Hayes	Lyons 3 and 2	Lyons 3 and 2	Lyons 3 and 2	Johnson 1-up (19)	Burke 1-up (37)
Toby Lyons					
Don Fairfield	Cavanaugh 2 and 1				
Gil Cavanaugh					
Emery Thomas	Lepre 2-up	Lepre 1-up (21)			
Charles Lepre					
Jimmy Demaret	Demaret 4 and 3				
Robert Hayes					
Terl Johnson	Johnson 1-up	Johnson 2 and 1	Johnson 4 and 2		
Warren Orlick					
Vic Ghezzi	Smith 1-up (22)				
Al Smith					
Charles DuPree	DuPree 1-up (19)	DuPree 3 and 2			
Babe Orff					
Tommy Bolt	Prentice 1-up				
Charles Prentice					
Tony Barkovich	Greiner 1-up (20)	Fetchick 3 and 2	Kay 1-up	Furgol 4 and 3	Furgol 1-up
Otto Greiner					
Mike Fetchick	Fetchick 3 and 2				
Jimmy Johnson					
Frank Kiraly	Kay 2 and 1	Kay 4 and 3			
Robert Kay					
Jackson Bradley	Bradley 3 and 2				
Richard Haskell					
Ralph Dillow	Isaacs 3 and 2	Furgol 5 and 4	Furgol 2 and 1		
Jack Isaacs					
Ed Furgol	Furgol 5 and 4				
Stan Dudas					
Augie Nordone	Nordone 3 and 1	Barber 4 and 3			
Earl Martin					
Jerry Barber	Barber 6 and 5				
J.L. McReynolds					

PGA CHAMPIONSHIP MATCH PLAY

as Johnston went on to defeat Henry Ransom in the afternoon, 3 and 2. In the morning match, Ransom had upset Lew Worsham, 2-up. Ed Furgol advanced to the semifinals with a 4-and-3 victory over Robert Kay and then beat Terl Johnson, 1-up, in the afternoon. Jack Burke also advanced with a 3-and-2 victory over Chandler Harper and then beat Fred Hawkins, 4 and 2.

Champion:	Jack Burke Jr., Kiamesha Lake, N.Y.*	
Site:	Blue Hill G & CC, Canton, Mass.	
Date:	July 20-24	Purse: $40,000
Par:	36-35—71	Entries: 128

In the semifinals, Jack Burke overcame a five-hole deficit to win a thrilling extra-hole match against Ed Furgol. Burke was

5-down after the 14th hole in his 36-hole match with Furgol. By winning the 15th, 16th and 18th holes he was only down by two holes going to lunch. In the afternoon, Burke fell back to 3-down, but won five holes in a row, starting at the 24th hole, to take the lead for the first time. Burke had a 2-up lead, only to see the match get squared with Furgol birdies at the 30th and 35th holes. At the final hole both players made birdie and Burke won the match with a 12-footer at the 37th hole for another birdie. In the other match, Ted Kroll demolished Bill Johnston, 10 and 8, in a contest that saw Johnston score 81 in the morning round.

In the finals, Jack Burke defeated Ted Kroll, 3 and 2, despite being 2-down after the morning round. Even though he lost the first hole in the afternoon round to go 3-down, he was able to take five of the next seven holes and shot 32 on the front side. With a 2-up lead going into the final nine, Burke was able to claim the victory on the 34th hole, as Kroll made bogey to lose the hole and the match. After it was all over, Burke claimed that, "My chipping and putting won it for me today." For Burke, it was his second major of the year, having won the Masters that year. As for Kroll, who was awarded the Purple Heart after World War II, he suffered his second disappointment in a major. He was in the hunt for the 1956 U.S. Open on the closing holes, only to see Cary Middlecoff take the title.

Bracket

Semifinal 36 Holes	Quarter-final 36 Holes	Fourth Round 18 Holes	Third Round 18 Holes	Second Round 18 Holes	First Round 18 Holes
			Ford 1-up (23)	Ford 3 and 2	Doug Ford / Buddy Viar
		Burkemo 5 and 3		Dietz 5 and 4	Mike Dietz / Richard Hendrickson
	Johnston 1-up		Burkemo 2 and 1	Burkemo 7 and 6	Walter Burkemo / "Skip" Alexander
				Zander 5 and 4	Robert Zander / Sam Speer
		Johnston 4 and 3	Johnston 2 and 1	Hebert 3 and 1	Jay Hebert / William Heinlein
Johnston 3 and 2				Johnston 2 and 1	William Johnston / Guy Paulsen
			Fortino 1-up	Kirkwood Jr. 1-up (19)	Pete Burke / Joe Kirkwood Jr.
				Fortino 3 and 2	Charles Bassler / Tony Fortino
	Ransom 2-up	Ransom 1-up (23)	Ransom 2 and 1	Furgol 3 and 1	Marty Furgol / Milon Marusic
				Ransom 1-up	Steve Doctor / Henry Ransom
			Harmon 3 and 1	Besselink 3 and 2	Al Besselink / William Doll
				Harmon 4 and 3	Clyde Usina / Claude Harmon
		Worsham 5 and 4	Worsham 3 and 2	Worsham 3 and 2	Lew Worsham / Ed Wysowski
				Kennett 5 and 4	Len Kennett / Alex Hackney
			Mayfield 1-up	Mayfield 2 and 1	Shelley Mayfield / James Scott
				Vines 3 and 2	Ellsworth Vines / James Guinnup
Burke 3 and 2	Kroll 10 and 8		Snead 1-up (20)	Snead 2 and 1	Sam Snead / Johnny Weitzel
		Snead 4 and 3		O'Donnell 2 and 1	Bob Veylupek / John O'Donnell
			Toski 3 and 1	Toski 2 and 1	Bob Toski / Steve Blatnak
				Turnesa 5 and 3	Bill Ezinicki / Mike Turnesa
	Snead 5 and 4	Sarazen 3 and 2	Sarazen 1-up (19)	Sarazen 5 and 4	Gene Sarazen / Ansel Snow
				Lundahl 3 and 2	Denny Champagne / Dick Lundahl
			Krak 2-up	Krak 3 and 2	Ed Oliver / Mike Krak
				Brandenburg 2 and 1	Buford Widener / Wilbur Brandenburg
	Kroll 2 and 1	Kroll 3 and 2	Kroll 2-up	Kroll 2 and 1	Ted Kroll / Roger Peacock
				Keyes 1-up (19)	George Keyes / Wayne Otis
			Rooney 2 and 1	Biagetti 1-up	Leo Biagetti / Tony Holguin
				Rooney 1-up (20)	Jim Milward / Michael Rooney
	Kroll 1-up	Turnesa 1-up	Fleck 6 and 5	Fleck 5 and 4	Jack Fleck / Fred Gromauer
				Malia 3 and 2	Hap Malia / Gordon Haberkorn
			Turnesa 1-up (20)	Turnesa 2 and 1	Jim Turnesa / Ted Huge
				Adkisson 2 and 1	Dean Adkisson / Edward Garfield

67

1955

Qualifying for Match Play: A 36-hole qualifying round to get into match play was conducted the Wednesday and Thursday before the Championship. Doug Ford was low qualifier with a 136. A score of 146 qualified for match play, with 11 at 147 having a playoff for seven spots. Some notables who didn't make it included Denny Shute (148), Jim Turnesa (151) and Chandler Harper (152).

Champion: Doug Ford, Lake Worth, Fla.*	
Site: Meadowbrook CC, Northville, Mich.	
Date: July 20-26	**Purse:** $20,700
Par: 35-36—71	**Entries:** 134

The first and second rounds were 18 holes each, played in one day, with the remaining matches being played at 36 holes.

Early Matches: The first day of play saw the defeat of all the past champions, including Sam Snead. Snead won his morning match, 2 and 1, over Al Feminelli, but in the afternoon was defeated by Tommy Bolt, 3 and 2. Bolt, who defeated Snead in the 1954 quarter-finals, led 1-up after a front nine of 32. Bolt ended the contest in spectacular fashion, holing out from a greenside bunker at the 16th hole to end the match. The defending champion, Chick Harbert, who beat Eric Monti, 3 and 1, in the morning match, was forced out in the afternoon, 1-up, by Johnny Palmer, who had been a finalist with Snead in 1949. Palmer had a 2-up lead with a 33 on the front side but lost the 12th hole when he made bogey. Palmer went 2-up again with a birdie on the 15th, and Harbert came back to win the 16th with a birdie. Palmer, however, halved the next two holes to win the match. Walter Burkemo was also a loser in the first round, as Cary Middlecoff shot 2-under-par in 17 holes for a 2-and-1 victory. In the afternoon, Middlecoff was 5-under in his match with Bill Nary to beat him, 3 and 2. Gene Sarazen was also eliminated, as he beat Clarence Dose, 6 and 4, in the morning but lost, 6 and 4, to Shelley Mayfield in the afternoon.

Vic Ghezzi beat Pete Cooper, 4 and 3, in the morning, only to lose 1-up in the afternoon to Don Fairfield. Ghezzi was 2-up with just three to play, but Fairfield won two holes and then took the contest to the 23rd hole before Ghezzi lost with a bogey. In other matches, 1954 U.S. Open Champion Ed Furgol captured two 20-hole matches, beating Jim Gauntt in the morning round and then sinking an 18-footer for a birdie at the second extra hole to beat Gus Salerno in the afternoon.

In the third round, two U.S. Open Champions, Furgol and Jack Fleck were eliminated, as Bolt beat Fleck, 3 and 1, and

Bracket

Qual. Score	First Round 18 Holes	Second Round 18 Holes	Third Round 36 Holes	Quarter-final 36 Holes	Semifinal 36 Holes	Final 36 Holes
144	Brien Charter	Charter 2 and 1	Charter 1-up			
147	Jimmy Johnson					
141	Jerry Barber	Hebert 2 and 1		Fairfield 2 and 1		
145	Lionel Hebert					
142	Don Fairfield	Fairfield 3 and 1	Fairfield 1-up (23)			
146	Walter Romans					
138	Pete Cooper	Ghezzi 4 and 3			Mayfield 3 and 2	
145	Vic Ghezzi					
143	Gene Sarazen	Sarazen 6 and 4	Mayfield 4 and 3			
147	Clarence Doser			Mayfield 1-up		
140	Shelley Mayfield	Mayfield 6 and 5				
145	Ted Neist					
142	Claude Harmon	Harmon 5 and 4	Harmon 2 and 1			Ford 4 and 3
146	Mike Turnesa					
137	Errie Ball	Briggs 1-up				
144	Eldon Briggs					
143	Gus Salerno	Salerno 2 and 1	Furgol 1-up (20)			
147	Gunnard Johnson			Hawkins 6 and 5		
140	Ed Furgol	Furgol 1-up (20)				
145	Jimmy Gauntt					
142	Fred Hawkins	Hawkins 3 and 2	Hawkins 2-up			
146	Eddie Joseph				Ford 5 and 4	
137	Skee Riegel	Haas Jr. 3 and 2				
145	Fred Haas Jr.					
142	Mike Dietz	Wagner 1-up	Ulrich 2-up			
147	Leonard Wagner			Ford 12 and 10		
139	Wally Ulrich	Ulrich 1-up (19)				
145	Dutch Harrison					
141	Ted Kroll	Kroll 3 and 2	Ford 2 and 1			
146	Buck White					
135	Doug Ford	Ford 2 and 1				
144	George Fazio					Ford 4 and 3
139	Chick Harbert	Harbert 3 and 1	Palmer 1-up			
144	Eric Monti			Worsham 6 and 5		
141	Johnny Palmer	Palmer 5 and 4				
146	Roy Wallin					
139	Lew Worsham	Worsham 2 and 1	Worsham 2 and 1			
145	Dick Lundahl				Bolt 8 and 7	
142	Jackson Bradley	Hill 2 and 1				
146	Ray Hill					
137	Sam Snead	Snead 2 and 1	Bolt 3 and 2			
144	Albert Feminelli			Bolt 3 and 1		
142	Tommy Bolt	Bolt by default				
146	Al Watrous					
140	Jack Fleck	Fleck 4 and 2	Fleck 2 and 1			Middlecoff 4 and 3
145	Joe Zarhardt					
143	Jay Hebert	Hebert 4 and 3				
147	Alex Redl					
137	Cary Middlecoff	Middlecoff 2 and 1	Middlecoff 3 and 2			
144	Walter Burkemo			Middlecoff 8 and 6		
142	Bill Nary	Nary 2 and 1				
146	Darwin White					
140	Ed Oliver	Browning 3 and 2	Pavella 4 and 3			
145	Jim Browning				Middlecoff 1-up (40)	
143	Mike Pavella	Pavella 3 and 2				
147	Bob Kay					
138	Marty Furgol	Furgol 3 and 2	Furgol 1-up			
145	Jack Igoe			Burke 2 and 1		
142	Tony Holguin	Holguin 1-up				
146	Joe Greer					
140	Jack Burke	Burke 4 and 2	Burke 8 and 6			
145	Guy Paulsen					
144	Dave Douglas	Douglas 4 and 3				
147	Herman Scharlau					

Fred Hawkins routed Furgol, 6 and 5. In the match between Fleck and Bolt, Fleck jumped out to an early 2-up lead after 15 holes, only to see it disappear as Bolt squared the match with three consecutive birdies. On the front side in the afternoon, both players shot 34, as Fleck played Bolt stroke for stroke between the 19th and 28th holes. On the par-3 29th hole and the par-5 30th hole, Fleck faltered and made bogeys to give Bolt a 2-up lead. They halved the next hole, but Bolt struck again at the 32nd hole with a birdie, only to lose the 34th when he made a bogey. With two holes left, Bolt held a 2-up lead, and when Fleck hooked his drive on the 35th hole and wasn't able to make par, Bolt was the win-

It was a nice touch for Ford to win after being the medalist, because the PGA eliminated the 36-hole qualifier in 1956, doubling the field to 128 participants who went straight into match play.

ner. In the match between Hawkins and Furgol, Hawkins completely dominated the match. With a 67 in the morning round, and 5-up, Furgol didn't win a single putt. The secret for Hawkins was his putting as he toured the course in just 29 putts, compared to 37 by Furgol. In the afternoon, things didn't improve for Furgol, although he did manage to win two holes before going down to defeat on the 31st hole. It was a bad day overall for the Furgols, as Marty (no relation to Ed) Furgol lost to Jack Burke Jr., 2 and 1. In another upset, Shelley Mayfield beat Claude Harmon, 1-up, in a match that was decided on the final hole when Harmon hooked his drive near some trees and went on to make bogey. Mayfield sank a five-foot par putt to win the match. In other matches, Don Fairfield defeated Brien Charter, 2 and 1, and Lew Worsham had an easy time with Johnny Palmer beating him, 6 and 5.

In the quarter-finals, the match of the day belonged to Cary Middlecoff and Jack Burke Jr., as it took nine hours and 40 holes for Middlecoff to win 1-up. Middlecoff's victory was miraculous, as he was 5-down after the morning round, 3-down after the 27th hole, and 2-down with just two holes left. But, with birdies at the 35th hole and the 36th hole, Middlecoff squared the match. The first two extra holes were

halved with pars, and Middlecoff was a bit lucky at the 39th hole as Burke's birdie winning putt almost went in the hole. However, the match came to a conclusion at the 40th hole when Burke was unable to match Middlecoff's par. Not only did Middlecoff's win eliminate Burke, but it also meant the loss of a roommate because Middlecoff and Burke were rooming together for the week. In the match between Shelley Mayfield and Don Fairfield, Mayfield scored a 3-and-2 victory, to the surprise of Fairfield, who was 4-under-par for the match. Fairfield had a 68 in the morning, but was 2-down as Mayfield scored a sensational 66. Then, Fairfield played the front side of the afternoon round in even par, only to find himself 3-down. The match ended on the 34th hole, with Mayfield 6-under-par for the day. Doug Ford had an easy 5-and-4 victory over Fred Hawkins, on the strength of a 31 on the front side of the afternoon round. Ford, who was 1-up after the morning round, won seven of the nine holes on the front side of the afternoon round to carry a 6-up lead to the back side. Hawkins made a small rally on the back side with birdies at two of the first three holes, but still it wasn't enough to overcome the big deficit. The match between Tommy Bolt and Lew Worsham was the rout of the day, as Bolt was 7-under for 29 holes in his 8-and-7 victory.

In the semifinals, both matches had 4-and-3 results, with Doug Ford beating Shelley Mayfield and Cary Middlecoff coming out on top of Tommy Bolt. Middlecoff was never behind against Bolt, even though the match was even four times in the morning. But Middlecoff broke the last standstill at the 17th hole with an eagle, and they finished the morning round with Middlecoff 1-up. On the front nine in the afternoon, Middlecoff increased the lead to 3-up with two 25-footers for birdies and closed out the match on the 33rd hole when Bolt made a bogey. Middlecoff was 4-under for the day. In the match between Ford and Mayfield, Ford was only 1-up after the morning round, but completely dominated Mayfield as Ford was 3-under par for the 15 holes in the afternoon and 5-under for the day.

In the finals, Doug Ford scored a 4-and-3 victory over Cary Middlecoff in a match that was tightly fought for the first 27 holes. Even though Ford shot 66 in the morning round, Middlecoff took a 1-up lead on the strength of a 67. But, in the af-

ROAD TO THE FINALS

Doug Ford beat	Round	Cary Middlecoff beat
George Fazio, 2 and 1	1st Round	Walter Burkemo, 2 and 1
Ted Kroll, 2 and 1	2nd Round	Bill Nary, 3 and 2
Wally Ulrich, 12 and 10	3rd Round	Mike Pavella, 8 and 6
Fred Hawkins, 5 and 4	Quarter-finals	Jack Burk Jr., 1-up (40)
Shelly Mayfield, 4 and 3	Semifinals	Tommy Bolt, 4 and 3

ternoon, Ford came back and squared the match for the fourth time in the match on the 26th hole with a birdie. He then birdied the 29th, 30th and 32nd holes to go 3-up, and sealed the contest with a par-4 at the 33rd hole. It was a Cinderella week for Ford, playing in his first PGA Championship and becoming the first player to win under that scenario since Tom Creavy in 1931. He was also the fourth player in PGA match-play history to win the Championship after winning medalist honors. Other players to achieve that feat were Walter Hagen (in 1926), Olin Dutra (in 1932), and Byron Nelson (in 1945). In 1927, Hagen shared medalist honors with Jim Turnesa.

It was a nice touch for Ford to win after being the medalist, because the PGA eliminated the 36-hole qualifier in 1956, doubling the field to 128 participants who went straight into match play.

1954

Qualifying for Match Play: A 36-hole qualifying round to get into match play was conducted the Wednesday and Thursday before the Championship. Ed Oliver was low qualifier with a 136. There were exactly 63 players with totals of 147 or under and no playoffs were necessary. Some notables who didn't make the cut included Chandler Harper (148), Lew Worsham (149), Johnny Revolta (149), Vic Ghezzi (150) and Felice Torza (151),

The first and second rounds were 18

Champion:	Chick Harbert, Northville, Mich.*	
Site:	Keller GC, St. Paul, Minn.	
Date:	July 21-27	Purse: $20,700
Par:	36-35 - 71	Entries: 134

Bracket

Columns: Qual. Score / First Round 18 Holes / Second Round 18 Holes / Third Round 36 Holes / Quarter-final 36 Holes / Semifinal 36 Holes / Final 36 Holes

Top Half:
- 144 Tommy Bolt, 147 Mike Turnesa → Bolt 2 and 1
- 142 Bob Kay, 146 Arthur Doering → Doering 1-up
  - Bolt 2 and 1
- 143 Pat Circelli, 147 Jim Browning → Browning 2 and 1
- 140 Ed Furgol, 145 Johnny Weitzel → Furgol 3 and 2
  - Browning 1-up
    - Bolt 2 and 1
- 144 Jim Milward, 147 Mike Homa → Milward 2 and 1
- 141 Tony Holguin, 146 Sam Snead → Snead 1-up
  - Snead 4 and 3
- 142 Johnny Palmer, 146 Labron Harris → Palmer 3 and 2
- 137 Jack Burke, 145 Dutch Harrison → Harrison 1-up
  - Harrison 4 and 3
    - Snead 7 and 6
      - Bolt 1-up (39)
- 144 Joe Greer, 147 Bill Trombley → Trombley 3 and 2
- 141 Toney Penna, 146 Charles Bassler → Bassler 3 and 1
  - Bassler 5 and 4
- 142 Jerry Barber, 146 Bob Gajda → Barber 2 and 1
- 139 Fred Haas Jr., 145 Lou Barbaro → Haas Jr. 1-up (19)
  - Barber 1-up (19)
    - Barber 1-up (38)
- 143 Chick Harbert, 147 Mike Krak → Harbert 5 and 3
- 141 Phil Friel, 146 John O'Donnell → O'Donnell 3 and 2
  - Harbert 3 and 1
- 142 Clarence Doser, 146 Bill Nary → Nary 3 and 1
- 136 Ed Oliver, 145 Jackson Bradley → Oliver 4 and 3
  - Oliver 1-up
    - Harbert 3 and 1
      - Harbert 1-up

Top Half Final result: **Harbert 1-up**

Bottom Half:
- 141 Walter Burkemo, 144 Dave Douglas → Burkemo 4 and 2
- 142 Claude Harmon, 146 Eric Monti → Harmon 6 and 5
  - Burkemo 2 and 1
- 140 Johnny Revolta, 146 Ellsworth Vines → Revolta 3 and 2
- 143 Jimmy Clark, 147 Toby Lyons → Lyons 1-up
  - Revolta 5 and 4
    - Burkemo 4 and 3
- 139 Roberto De Vicenzo, 145 Gene Webb → De Vicenzo 5 and 4
- 142 Henry Ransom, 146 Herman Keiser → Ransom 2 and 1
  - De Vicenzo 4 and 3
- 141 Marty Furgol, 146 Elroy Marti → Marti 4 and 3
- 144 Frank Commisso, 147 Henry Williams Jr. → Williams Jr. 3 and 2
  - Marti 2-up
    - De Vicenzo 8 and 6
      - Burkemo 5 and 4
- 137 Cary Middlecoff, 145 Joe Brown → Middlecoff 1-up
- 142 Bob Toski, 146 Jim Turnesa → Toski 5 and 4
  - Middlecoff 2 and 1
- 141 Ted Kroll, 146 Leonard Wagner → Kroll 3 and 2
- 144 Orville White, 147 Max Evans → Evans 2 and 1
  - Kroll 1-up (24)
    - Middlecoff 5 and 4
- 139 Shelley Mayfield, 145 Jimmy Hines → Mayfield 4 and 3
- 143 Wally Ulrich, 147 Pat Abbott → Ulrich 2 and 1
  - Mayfield 5 and 4
- 142 James Scott, 146 Horton Smith → Smith 5 and 4
- 144 Milon Marusic, 147 Jack Isaacs → Isaacs 3 and 2
  - Smith 3 and 2
    - Mayfield 3 and 2
      - Middlecoff 3 and 1

Bottom Half result: **Burkemo 1-up (37)**

FINAL: Harbert 4 and 3

holes each, played in one day, with the remaining matches being played at 36 holes.

Early Matches: In one of the few upsets of the day, former PGA Champion Jim Turnesa was beaten in a morning match by Bob Toski, 5 and 4. In that contest, Toski took command of things early with a 34 to go 3-up on the front side, which was too much for Turnesa to overcome. U.S. Open winner Ed Furgol succumbed to Jim Browning, 1-up, as Browning surprised everyone with a 1-under-par 70. Defending champion Walter Burkemo defeated Dave Douglas, 4 and 2, and then Claude Harmon, 2 and 1. Burkemo had beaten both men in 1953 en route to his victory. One of the best matches of the day saw Jack Burke Jr. shoot a 67, before losing 1-down to Dutch Harrison, who shot 66. Harrison cruised through the afternoon by beating Johnny Palmer, 4 and 3. Sam Snead won both of his matches, but his morning contest was a struggle to beat Tony Holquin, 1-up. Snead shot 76 in a contest that wasn't decided until Holquin bogeyed the final hole to give the win to Snead. In the afternoon match, Snead played better as he was 5-under-par in his 4-and-3 victory over Jim Milward. Cary Middlecoff also had a tough day, needing to go 18 holes to beat Joe Brown, 1-up, in the morning and then 17 holes in the afternoon for a 2-and-1 victory over Toski. In other matches: PGA President Horton Smith was a 5-and-4 winner over Jim Scott in the morning and then beat Jack Isaacs, 3 and 2, in the afternoon; Ted Kroll was a 3-and-2 winner over Len Wagner in the morning and then took 24 holes to beat Max Evans, 1-up; Roberto De Vicenzo had two easy matches beating Gene Webb, 5 and 4, and Henry Ransom, 4 and 3; Ed Oliver was a 4-and-3 winner over Jackson Bradley and then nipped Bill Nary, 1-up; Jerry Barber had two tough matches, triumphing over Bob Gajda, 2 and 1, and then taking 19 holes to beat Fred Haas; Tommy Bolt took 17 holes in beating Mike Turnesa and Art Doering, 2 and 1; and PGA past champion Johnny Revolta had easy wins over Ellsworth Vines, 3 and 2, and Toby Lyons, 5 and 4.

In the third round, all of the favorites were winners, with Snead leading the way with a 7-and-6 rout of Dutch Harrison. Snead played well in front of a huge gallery, and for the 30 holes they played, Snead was 6-under-par. Another impressive triumph belonged to Roberto De Vicenzo, who defeated Elroy Marti, 8 and 6. Marti was overmatched in the contest and won only one hole, a chip-in for birdie at the 18th hole to close the morning round.

*A*t the final hole, Bolt hit a terrific second shot to within three feet, and Harbert hit his second shot out of the rough 15 feet away. Harbert didn't give Bolt a chance, rolling his putt in for the victory.

Another rout belonged to Cary Middlecoff who beat Ted Kroll, 5 and 4. The former dentist had a new putter for the contest, and, even though he finished the morning round 1-up, the new putter performed better in the afternoon, leading to the match being closed out on the 32nd hole. Other winners were Walter Burkemo, who beat Johnny Revolta, 4 and 3; Shelley Mayfield, who won, 3 and 2, over Horton Smith; Tommy Bolt, who beat Jim Browning, 2 and 1; and Chick Harbert, who withstood a closing rally by Ed Oliver to beat him, 3 and 1. In the longest match of the day, Jerry Barber was 3-down after the 28th hole to Charles Bassler, but caught him by winning the 32nd, 33rd and 36th holes to send the match, into overtime. Barber made an 18-footer at the 38th hole for the 1-up win.

In the quarter-finals, three-time PGA champion Sam Snead was beaten by Tommy Bolt, 1-up, in the day's best match, which took 39 holes for a decision. Both players were 5-under-par for 36 holes, as Snead saw a 2-up lead after the 32nd hole disappear when he three-putted the 33rd hole for a bogey and then bogeyed the 34th hole. At the 35th hole, Bolt was lucky to escape with a half as Snead missed a seven-footer for a birdie, while Bolt made a tricky sidehill five-footer for par. With pars at the final hole, the match went into overtime.

The first two holes were halved with pars, but Snead bogeyed the par-5 39th hole to lose the match. In another match that went the distance, Chick Harbert beat Jerry Barber, 1-up. After leading by one at the 27th hole, Harbert took the 29th when Barber made bogey, but gave it back on the next hole. He won the 31st with a par to go 2-up, and, even though he bogeyed the 33rd hole, he was able to hold on for the victory. Burkemo halted the bid of De Vicenzo, the first foreign challenger ever to advance to the quarter-finals, by 5 and 4. With a morning round of 69 to De Vicenzo's 74, Burkemo went to lunch 5-up, which proved to be too big a lead for De Vicenzo to overcome. In the last match of the day, Cary Middlecoff eliminated Shelley Mayfield, 3 and 1, in a contest that was even after the 27th hole. Middlecoff made birdies at the 28th and 29th holes to go 2-up, but Mayfield got one back with a birdie at the 30th hole. They halved the next two holes, and another birdie by Middlecoff on the 33rd hole put him back to 2-up. The match ended at the 35th hole when Mayfield's drive landed in a divot and he made bogey.

In the semifinals, Burkemo moved to the finals for the third time in four years with an overtime 1-up win over Middlecoff. The match was even after the morning round when both players shot 69, but in the afternoon, Burkemo played the front nine in 31 and took a 3-up lead to the back nine. Middlecoff fought back to win the 29th hole with a par, which Burkemo took back with a Middlecoff bogey at the 30th hole. At the next three holes, Middlecoff made three successive 3s, winning two of them, and was just 1-down going into the 35th hole. Burkemo had a chance to end the match, but missed a six-footer for birdie. At the final hole, Middlecoff hit his second shot four feet away but didn't have to make the putt when Burkemo missed a 12-footer for par and conceded Middlecoff's putt, sending the contest into extra holes. At the 37th hole, Burkemo almost holed his second shot, putting it inches away for a birdie, and when Middlecoff was unable to make his six-footer for birdie, the match ended. The other contest had an exciting finish as Chick Harbert nipped Tommy Bolt, 1-up. Both competitors played well with Harbert 6-under, and Bolt 5-under. Bolt was 2-down with just two holes left when he tightened things up by making a downhill 25-footer for birdie to get one back. At the final hole, Bolt hit a terrific second shot to within three feet, and Harbert hit his second

shot out of the rough 15 feet away. Harbert didn't give Bolt a chance, rolling his putt in for the victory.

In the finals, Harbert, who lost in the finals in 1947 and 1952, got a bit of revenge as he beat Burkemo, 4 and 3. Burkemo won three of the first four holes in his attempt to become the first repeating PGA Champion since Denny Shute in 1936-37. However, Harbert played the next 29 holes in 8-under-par and let Burkemo win only one hole as he completely dominated the match. Harbert took control of the contest with wedge shots landing within inches at the 19th and 20th holes, giving him a 3-up lead. As the match progressed, Burkemo had opportunities to cut the lead but couldn't seem to make the putts, and the match came to an end at the 33rd hole.

ROAD TO THE FINALS		
Chick Harbert beat	**Round**	**Walter Burkemo beat**
Mike Krak, 5 and 3	1st Round	Dave Douglas, 4 and 2
John O'Donnell, 3 and 1	2nd Round	Claude Harmon, 2 and 1
Ed Oliver, 3 and 1	3rd Round	Johnny Revolta, 4 and 3
Jerry Barber, 1-up	Quarter-finals	Roberto De Vicenzo, 8 and 6
Tommy Bolt, 1-up	Semifinals	Cary Middlecoff, 3 and 1

1953

Qualifying for Match Play: A 36-hole qualifying round to get into match play was conducted the Wednesday and Thursday before the Championship. Jim Turnesa, the defending champion, was exempt from qualifying, and Johnny Palmer was low qualifier with a 134. A score of 148 qualified for match play, with seven at 149 having a playoff for four spots. Some notable players who didn't make the cut included Horton Smith (150), Lawson Little (151), Toney Penna (156), Henry Picard (WD) and Bob Hamilton (WD).

Champion:	Walter Burkemo, Birmingham, Mich.*
Site:	Birmingham CC, Birmingham, Mich.
Date: July 1-7	**Purse:** $20,700
Par: 36-35 - 71	**Entries:** 136

Bracket

Qual. Score / First Round 18 Holes	Second Round 18 Holes	Third Round 36 Holes	Quarter-final 36 Holes	Semifinal 36 Holes	Final 36 Holes
140 Jim Turnesa	Turnesa 6 and 4	Torza 4 and 3	Torza 1-up (38)	Torza 1-up	Torza 1-up (39)
146 Max Evans					
142 Felice Torza	Torza 2 and 1				
147 Gene Sarazen					
141 Jack Fleck	Ulrich 3 and 2	Ulrich 2 and 1			
146 Wally Ulrich					
144 Jack Shields	White 2-up				
148 Buck White					
139 Vic Ghezzi	Clark 2 and 1	Clark 5 and 4	Clark 4 and 3		
146 Jimmy Clark					
143 Jerry Barber	Middlecoff 2 and 1				
148 Cary Middlecoff					
142 Charles Bassler	Bassler 2-up	Williams Jr. 3 and 1			
147 Clarence Doser					
145 Ed Oliver	Williams Jr. 1-up (20)				
149 Henry Williams Jr.					
137 Chandler Harper	Isaacs 4 and 3	Isaacs 1-up	Isaacs 5 and 4	Isaacs 1-up	
146 Jack Isaacs					
143 Fred Haas Jr.	Haas Jr. 1-up (20)				
147 Toby Lyons					
141 Marty Furgol	Furgol 5 and 3	Harris 1-up			
146 Milon Marusic					
144 Labron Harris	Harris 1-up (19)				
148 Eddie Joseph					
140 Jimmy Hines	Smith 2 and 1	Smith 3 and 2	Ransom 1-up		
146 Al Smith					
144 Iverson Martin	Martin 6 and 5				
148 Stan Dudas					
142 Bob Toski	Toski 2 and 1	Ransom 3 and 2			
147 Fred Baker					
145 Henry Ransom	Ransom 3 and 2				
149 Milton Lichardus					
149 Tommy Bolt	Bolt 3 and 2	Bradley 1-up	Douglas 1-up (37)	Burkemo 2-up	Burkemo 1-up
145 Virgil Shreeve					
142 Ellsworth Vines	Bradley 1-up				
147 Jackson Bradley					
144 Lew Worsham	Douglas 1-up (20)	Douglas 1-up (19)			
148 Dave Douglas					
140 Sam Snead	Snead 6 and 5				
146 Bennie Adams					
144 Mike Turnesa	Turnesa 4 and 2	Burkemo 3 and 1	Burkemo 3 and 2		
148 Eric Monti					
142 Walter Burkemo	Burkemo 7 and 5				
147 Lou Barbaro					
143 Rod Munday	Dodson 3 and 1	Cooper 6 and 5			
147 Leonard Dodson					
138 Pete Cooper	Cooper 3 and 2				
146 Chick Harbert					
145 Chuck Klein	Nary 5 and 4	Nary 1-up	Nary 6 and 5	Harmon 6 and 5	
149 Bill Nary					
142 Dutch Harrison	Harrison 3 and 2				
147 Charles Harter					
143 George Fazio	Plemmons 1-up (22)	Browning 3 and 1			
148 Broyles Plemmons					
140 Jim Browning	Browning 2 and 1				
146 Elroy Marti					
144 Ed Furgol	Furgol 1-up (20)	Furgol 3 and 2	Harmon 5 and 3		
148 Johnny Weitzel					
141 Jim Ferrier	Ferrier 1-up				
146 Al Watrous					
143 Claude Harmon	Harmon 4 and 2	Harmon 4 and 2			
147 Ted Kroll					
146 Jack Grout	Grout 2 and 1				
134 Johnny Palmer					

Burkemo 2 and 1

The first and second rounds were 18 holes each, played in one day, with the remaining matches being played at 36 holes.

Early Matches: In the first day of play, *Golf World* called it "Black Friday" as "a carnage of name players" were eliminated. Some upsets: Gene Sarazen bowing to Felice Torza, 2 and 1; Jack Fleck upset by Wally Ulrich, 3-and-2; Vic Ghezzi nipped by Jimmy Clark, 2 and 1; Ed Oliver beaten in overtime by Henry Williams, 1-up, 20 holes; Jack Isaacs downing Chandler Harper, 4 and 3; Lew Worsham losing to Dave Douglas, 1-up, on the 20th hole; Pete Cooper beating 1952 runner-up Chick Harbert, 3 and 2; Broyles Plemmons going to the 22nd hole to beat George Fazio, 1-up; and medalist Johnny Palmer being beaten by Jack Grout, 2 and 1. If that wasn't bad enough, in the afternoon the only name players left found themselves eliminated: Jim Turnesa lost to Felice Torza, 4 and 3; Cary Middlecoff was trounced by Jimmy Clark, 5 and 4; Fred Haas was nipped by Jack Isaacs, 1-up; Tommy Bolt was beaten by Jackson Bradley, 1-up; Mike Turnesa won over Walter Burkemo, 3 and 1; Dutch Harrison lost a squeaker to Bill Nary, 1-up; and Jim Ferrier was a 3-and-2 loser to Ed Furgol. In the upset of the day, Sam Snead was beaten in 19 holes by Dave Douglas, who birdied the 16th hole to tie the match, halved 17 and 18, then made a six-footer for birdie at the first playoff hole to win, 1-up.

In the third round, favorite Claude Harmon rolled by Ed Furgol, 5 and 3. In other matches, Bill Nary had the rout of the day in his 6-and-5 triumph over Jim Browning, while Jack Isaacs had an easy day, beating Labron Harris, 5 and 4. Jimmy Clark defeated Henry Williams, 4 and 3, while Walter Burkemo eliminated Pete Cooper, 3 and 2. Henry Ransom nipped Al Smith, 1-up, while Felice Torza took 38 holes to beat

Wally Ulrich, 1-up. Another match decided on the 38th hole saw Dave Douglas, for the third match in a row, go into overtime to beat Jackson Bradley, 1-up.

It was an exciting match as Douglas, 1-down with just two holes left, saved the match on the 35th hole by blasting out of a greenside bunker and one-putting for the half. He sent the match into overtime with a 30-footer for birdie at the final hole and won the match with another birdie at the 38th hole.

In the quarter-finals, Claude Harmon had the easiest day with his 6-and-5 triumph over Bill Nary. After the morning round, Harmon was 1-down, but in the af-

In the finals, over 10,000 people came to watch their new hero, Walter Burkemo, and they weren't disappointed, as Burkemo defeated Felice Torza, 2 and 1.

ternoon round, Harmon won eight of the first 10 holes and closed out the match on the 31st hole. The other three matches had outcomes decided on the final green. Felice Torza beat Jimmy Clark, 1-up, when Torza made a birdie at the final hole to win the contest. In a duel of veterans, Jack Isaacs also birdied the final hole to beat Henry Ransom, 1-up. In the match between Walter Burkemo and Dave Douglas, Burkemo had a 1-up lead going into the final hole and had just about wrapped things up when he put his second shot two feet away on the par-5 hole. But Douglas didn't give up and also hit an incredible second shot to within six feet of the hole. When he missed his eagle attempt, he was forced to concede the hole to Burkemo.

In the semifinals, both matches went the distance, with the contest between Felice Torza and Jack Isaacs going three extra holes before Torza pulled out a 1-up victory. Torza was 4-up after the 26th hole and it looked like he would be the winner, but when Torza bogeyed the 27th hole, Isaacs mounted a rally. Isaacs captured the 30th hole with a birdie, then the 31st with a Torza bogey, squaring the match at the 34th with a birdie. They halved the next two holes with pars to send the match into overtime. Both made birdies at the 37th hole and pars at the 38th, but when Isaacs was unable to match Torza's par at the 39th,

Torza won the contest. In the other match, a partisan crowd saw Detroit-born Burkemo come from behind to defeat Harmon, 1-up, even though Burkemo was 3-down with just 11 holes left. The rally started with a 35-footer for a birdie at the 26th hole. Burkemo continued the charge with a 15-foot birdie at the 28th. At the next hole, another birdie with a 7-footer squared the match and Burkemo was forced to make another 7-footer at the 30th for a half. Harmon regained the lead at the 31st hole with a par, with the next hole being halved with birdies. The next two holes were halved with pars, but, at the 35th, Harmon was unable to make a 12-footer for par that would have halved the hole. So with the match square, Harmon tried to get home in two on the par-5 and was unsuccessful, hitting the ball into the creek in front of the green. Harmon took his penalty and almost holed his fourth shot, while Burkemo pitched his third shot 15 feet away. Harmon's great recovery meant that Burkemo had to sink his putt or face a play-off. That is what Burkemo did, to the approval of the large crowd that swarmed onto the green to congratulate the victor.

In the finals, over 10,000 people came to watch their new hero, Walter Burkemo, and they weren't disappointed, as Burkemo defeated Felice Torza, 2 and 1. In the morning round, Burkemo shot a 1-over-par 72 but still held a 1-up lead over Torza's 73. In the afternoon, Burkemo came out strong by starting his round with two birdies and a par to increase his lead to 2-up. Torza reduced the lead to 1-up on the back side with a bogey from Burkemo on the 29th hole, but his bogey at the 31st hole gave it back. Burkemo made bogeys at the 32nd and 34th holes to let Torza get within two holes, but with a par at the 35th hole he closed out the match.

1952

Qualifying for Match Play: A 36-hole qualifying round to get into match play was conducted the Wednesday and Thursday before the Championship. Defending champion Sam Snead was exempt from qualifying, and Dutch Harrison was low qualifier with a 136. A score of 146 qualified for match play, with 12 at 147 having a playoff for nine spots. Some

notable players who didn't make the cut included Jimmy Thomson (150) and Ed Oliver (WD).

Champion:	Jim Turnesa, Blair Cliff, N.Y.*	
Site:	Big Spring CC, Louisville, Ky.	
Date:	June 18-25	Purse: $17,700
Par:	36-36—72	Entries: 128

The first and second rounds were 18 holes each, played in one day, with the remaining matches being played at 36 holes.

Early Matches: In the first day of play, most of the favorites were eliminated, with Sam Snead making an early exit by losing 1-up to Lew Worsham. Snead had a 1-up lead after the 16th hole, but Worsham birdied the 17th to square the match, halved the final hole and then beat Snead on the 19th hole with a birdie. Snead had no excuse for his loss, but a muscle strain under his right arm had been causing him a considerable amout of pain just before the Championship, almost causing Snead to withdraw. In the afternoon, Worsham was beaten by Fred Haas, 1-up, in a match that saw Haas take a 1-up lead after the 13th hole and halve the remaining five holes. First-round matches where favorites got beaten included: Ted Kroll's 1-up victory over Lawson Little, Marty Furgol's 2-up victory over Dutch Harrison, Chick Harbert's 5-and-4 drumming of Denny Shute, Sam Bernardi's 1-up win over Mike Turnesa, Dave Douglas' 2- and-1 victory over Johnny Palmer, and Vic Ghezzi's 1-up victory in 19 holes over Claude Harmon. In the afternoon round the upsets included: Ted Kroll beating Lloyd Mangrum, 2-up, Jim Turnesa's 3-and-1 victory over Chandler Harper, Argentinian Roberto De Vicenzo's 1-up win over Jack Burke Jr. and Jack Issac's 3-and-2 triumph over Marty Furgol. Only two former champions moved on to the third round, as Bob Hamilton beat Jackson Bradley, 4 and 3, and Sam Bernardi, 3 and 1, and Vic Ghezzi beat Claude Harmon on the 19th hole and Mel Carpenter, 5 and 3.

In the third round, Cary Middlecoff was picked as the favorite for the Championship after his 4-and-2 victory over Al Smith. Middlecoff had come from behind to beat Smith, getting two eagles in the af-

Bracket

Qual. Score	First Round 18 Holes	Second Round 18 Holes	Third Round 36 Holes	Quarter-final 36 Holes	Semifinal 36 Holes	Final 36 Holes
143 Jim Ferrier		Ferrier 1-up (19)	Honsberger 1-up			
147 Leonard Dodson						
140 Ray Honsberger		Honsberger 1-up		Kroll 2 and 1		
146 Tom Blaskovich						
142 Ted Kroll		Kroll 1-up	Kroll 2-up		Kroll 1-up (38)	
147 Lawson Little						
139 Lloyd Mangrum		Mangrum 4 and 3				
145 Frank Newell						
143 Charles Harter		Harter 2 and 1	Middlecoff 3 and 2	Middlecoff 4 and 2		
147 William Heinlein						
139 Cary Middlecoff		Middlecoff 5 and 4				
145 Joe Taylor						
141 Al Smith		Smith 4 and 2	Smith 1-up (19)			
146 Frank Commisso						
138 Fred Gromauer		Harris 3 and 1				Turnesa 4 and 2
144 Labron Harris						
143 Jim Turnesa		Turnesa 4 and 2	Turnesa 3 and 1			
147 Bob Toski						
140 Chandler Harper		Harper 6 and 5		Turnesa 5 and 4		
145 Charles Lepre						
141 Jack Burke		Burke 1-up	De Vicenzo 1-up		Turnesa 2 and 1	
146 Jimmy Walkup						
138 Roberto De Vicenzo		De Vicenzo 1-up				
144 Eric Monti						
143 Clarence Doser		Doser 4 and 3	Doser 3 and 2	Doser 1-up		
147 James Alcroft						
139 Bob Gajda		Gajda 2 and 1				
145 Ed Furgol						
141 Jack Isaacs		Isaacs 3 and 2	Isaacs 3 and 2			
146 Pat Abbott						
136 Dutch Harrison		Furgol 2-up				
143 Marty Furgol						
144 Sam Snead		Worsham 1-up (19)	Haas Jr. 1-up			Turnesa 1-up
143 Lew Worsham						
141 Fred Haas Jr.		Haas Jr. 2 and 1		Haas Jr. 1-up (38)		
146 Henry Ransom						
139 Milon Marusic		Marusic 5 and 4	Marusic by default			
145 Eddie Joseph						
142 Mike Pavella		Eaton 2 and 1				
147 Zell Eaton						
138 Henry Williams Jr.		Williams Jr. 5 and 4	Williams Jr. 1-up			
144 Jim Gantz						
141 Roy Wallin		Jones 5 and 4		Harbert 6 and 5		
146 Jack Jones						
140 Chick Harbert		Harbert 5 and 4	Harbert 3 and 2		Harbert 2 and 1	
145 Denny Shute						
143 Bob Carmen		Schmutte 2-up				
147 Leonard Schmutte						
137 Harry Todd		Champ 3 and 1	Champ 2 and 1			Harbert 2 and 1
143 Frank Champ						
141 Otto Greiner		Trish 3 and 2		Champ 3 and 1		
146 John Trish						
139 Dave Douglas		Douglas 2 and 1	Burkemo 1-up			
145 Johnny Palmer						
143 Iverson Martin		Burkemo 1-up				
147 Walter Burkemo					Hamilton 2 and 1	
139 Claude Harmon		Ghezzi 1-up (19)	Ghezzi 5 and 3			
144 Vic Ghezzi						
142 Horton Smith		Carpenter 2 and 1		Hamilton 9 and 8		
146 Mel Carpenter						
140 Bob Hamilton		Hamilton 4 and 3	Hamilton 3 and 1			
145 Jackson Bradley						
143 Sam Bernardi		Bernardi 1-up				
147 Mike Turnesa						

ternoon round. Middlecoff was 6-under-par for the 34 holes of the match. The rout of the day belonged to Bob Hamilton, who defeated Vic Ghezzi, 9 and 8. Hamilton compiled a 68 in the morning round, while Ghezzi had a 76, giving Hamilton a 7-up lead going into the afternoon.

For the day, Ghezzi only won two holes. Chick Harbert also enjoyed an easy day as he was a 6-and-5 victor over Henry Williams. Mike Turnesa turned back De Vicenzo, 5 and 4, as De Vicenzo was unable to come back from a poor start where he shot 39 and was 4-down after the first nine holes. Turnesa had given De Vicenzo a ride to the course on the morning of the match, but that was the extent of Turnesa's

The semifinals were witnessed by 6,000 people who braved 100-degree heat to see Chick Harbert beat Bob Hamilton, 2 and 1, and Jim Turnesa turn back Ted Kroll, 4 and 2.

generosity as he won the contest on the 32nd hole. In the only overtime match, Fred Haas beat Milon Marusic, 1-up, on the 38th hole. Even though Haas (who putted cross-handed, a rare sight in the '50s) took a 1-up lead with a birdie at the 35th hole, a bogey at the next hole squared up the match and sent it into overtime. Haas picked up the victory when Marusic was unable to make par at the 38th hole. In other matches: Ted Kroll nipped Ray Honsberger, 2 and 1, Clarence Doser and Jack Isaacs battled to the final hole where Doser won, 1-up, and Frank Champ upset runner-up Walter Burkemo, 3 and 1.

In the quarter-finals, the highlight of the day saw Ted Kroll, who was wounded four times in World War II and awarded the purple heart, upset Cary Middlecoff, 1-up, on the 38th hole. The match was all even after 32 holes until the Memphis dentist drove the par-4 33rd hole and made the birdie to go 1-up. But Middlecoff gave the hole back when he missed a five-foot par putt at the 34th to square the match, letting Kroll off the hook again at the 36th hole by missing another five-footer that would have won the match. At the 37th hole, both players made birdies, but Kroll closed out the match with a tee shot to within two feet of the par-3, 38th hole, to make a birdie. The other three matches were won on the

35th green. Chick Harbert surprised Fred Haas, 2 and 1 in a match where Haas had a 2-up lead after the 27th hole, but, in the final eight holes, Harbert picked up four birdies, with three of them coming in succession on the 33rd, 34th and 35th holes to close out the match. In other matches, Jim Turnesa beat Clarence Doser, 2 and 1, while Bob Hamilton advanced to the semifinals with a 2-and-1 victory over Frank Champ.

The semifinals were witnessed by 6,000 people who braved 100-degree heat to see Chick Harbert beat Bob Hamilton, 2 and 1, and Jim Turnesa turn back Ted Kroll, 4 and 2. In the contest between Harbert and Hamilton, the former champion took a 2-up lead after the morning round and in the afternoon increased his lead to 3-up with a birdie at the 20th hole. Even though Harbert made three, little did anyone know that it would be the first of six 3s in a row, with birdies coming on four of the holes. By the 27th hole Harbert was 1-up, and for the first time in the Championship, Hamilton was down in a match. Hamilton squared the match with a birdie at the 29th hole and then lost the 31st. He squared the match again with a Harbert bogey at the 32nd. That, however, would be Harbert's last error in the contest, as he birdied the next hole to go 1-up. Harbert won the 34th hole when Hamilton made bogey and closed out the match by matching Hamilton's birdie at the 35th hole. In the other match, Turnesa was 10-under-par for the day but won the contest with his domination of the last seven holes, winning the 30th hole with an eagle, the 32nd with a par and closing out with a birdie at the 34th hole. For the 38-year-old, it would be his second trip to the finals.

In the finals, Jim Turnesa finally settled a 26-year-old family jinx by beating Chick Harbert on the final green for a 1-up victory. Turnesa is a member of a family with seven golfing brothers. His younger brother, Willie, the only one to remain an amateur, gained attention by winning the U.S. and British Amateurs. But, for the other brothers who turned professional, the only tournament success they gained was that of being bridesmaids but never brides. In 1926, Joe Turnesa was runner-up to Bobby Jones in the U.S. Open and in 1927 lost in the finals of the PGA Championship to Walter Hagen. Jim Turnesa lost the 1942 PGA Championship to Sam Snead in the finals, and brother Mike lost the 1940 PGA Championship to Ben Hogan.

In 1948 and 1949, Jim finished third in

the U.S. Open. But in 1952, Jim Turnesa finally settled the family score by winning the PGA Championship in dramatic fashion. At the end of the morning round he was 3-down. He shot a 34 on the front side of the afternoon round, then picked up two holes and squared the match for the first time since the 7th hole with a birdie at the 32nd hole. The contest remained square until the final hole, when Harbert hooked his drive under an evergreen tree and made bogey while Turnesa parred the hole for the victory. It was the eighth and final contest in PGA match-play history to end on the final green. Of those eight, it was only the second time that a match was actually won by the results of the final hole.

ROAD TO THE FINALS

Jim Turnesa beat	Round	Chick Harbert beat
Bob Toski, 4 and 2	1st Round	Denny Shute, 5 and 4
Chandler Harper, 4 and 2	2nd Round	Leonard Schmutte, 3 and 2
Roberto De Vicenzo, 1-up	3rd Round	Henry Williams, 6 and 5
Clarence Doser, 2 and 1	Quarter-finals	Fred Haas, 2 and 1
Ted Kroll, 4 and 2	Semifinals	Bob Hamilton, 2 and 1

1951

Qualifying for Match Play: A 36-hole qualifying round to get into match play was conducted the Wednesday and Thursday before the Championship. Chandler Harper, the defending PGA Champion, was exempt and 63 players qualified. Claude Harmon, Lloyd Mangrum and Pete Cooper were the low qualifiers with a 142. A score of 153 qualified for match play, with six players at 154 having a playoff for one spot. Notable players who didn't make it into match play in-

Champion:	Sam Snead, Hot Springs, Va.*	
Site:	Oakmont CC, Oakmont, Pa.	
Date:	June 27-July 3	Purse: $17,700
Par:	37-35—72	Entries: 140

cluded Paul Runyan (154), Roberto De Vicenzo (158) and Jimmy Thomson (WD). Oakmont Country Club, site of the 1922 PGA Championship, was the first venue to host a second Championship.

The first and second rounds were 18 holes each, played in one day, with the remaining matches being played at 36 holes.

Early Matches: In the first day of play, Sam Snead was the topic of discussion as he had two very tough matches to move into the third round. In his morning match, Snead beat Fred Haas, 1-up, making a birdie at the final hole to secure the contest. In the second round, Snead beat Marty Furgol, 1-up, but it took 21 holes. Furgol was 2-up at the 10th, but Snead birdied the 11th and holed out a bunker shot at the 13th for a birdie 2 to square the match. At the next green, Snead hovered over the ball, waving and blowing at an insect, trying to dislodge it from the ball. Furgol immediately protested Snead had cleaned his ball. The referee ruled that Snead had not broken any rules, but Furgol requested the committee make a ruling. The match continued all even to the final hole, which was halved with pars, calling for a playoff. Furgol, however, went into the clubhouse to hear the committee's decision, while Snead went to the first tee, where he had to wait a half-hour before Furgol announced that he was withdrawing the protest. Both players had pars at the 19th and 20th holes before Snead made birdie at the 21st to bring the match to a close. Another overtime match saw defending champion Chandler Harper beaten by Jim Turnesa, 1-up, in the longest match of the day, 23 holes. Turnesa was 3-down with three holes left and caught Harper with birdies at the 16th and 17th before dropping a five-footer for a par at the final hole to force the playoff. For Harper, who was ill before the Championship, the contest ended five holes later when Turnesa

Qual. Score	First Round 18 Holes	Second Round 18 Holes	Third Round 36 Holes	Quarter-final 36 Holes	Semifinal 36 Holes	Final 36 Holes
149 Jim Turnesa	Turnesa 1-up (23)					
144 Chandler Harper		Bassler 5 and 4				
148 Charles Bassler	Bassler 1-up		Bassler 1-up (37)			
151 Ed Furgol				Bassler 1-up		
144 Ed Oliver	Oliver 5 and 4	Bolesta 2 and 1				
150 Herman Keiser						
148 George Bolesta	Bolesta 2 and 1					
153 Willie Goggin						
143 Lew Worsham	Worsham 4 and 3	Brosch 5 and 4				
150 Harold Williams			Brosch 6 and 5			
148 Al Brosch	Brosch 1-up					
152 Frank Kiraly						
151 Toney Penna	Penna 4 and 2	Harden 5 and 3				
145 George Fazio						Snead 9 and 8
149 Jack Harden	Harden 3 and 2					
153 Sherman Elworthy					Snead 1-up	
142 Lloyd Mangrum	Mangrum 4 and 3	Mangrum 2 and 1				
150 Henry Ransom			Snead 3 and 2			
151 Buck White	White 2 and 1					
147 Dave Douglas						
145 Sam Snead	Snead 1-up	Snead 1-up (21)				
150 Fred Haas Jr.						
148 Marty Furgol	Furgol 2 and 1			Snead 2 and 1		
153 Harold Oatman						
150 Jack Burke	Burke 1-up (21)	Burke 5 and 3				
143 Chuck Klein			Burke 4 and 3			
148 Gene Sarazen	Sarazen 2 and 1					
152 Charles Harter						
146 Ray Gafford	Gafford 1-up (19)	Kunes 2 and 1				
151 Ted Kroll						
153 Gene Kunes	Kunes 4 and 2					
149 Henry Williams Jr.						
149 Dick Shoemaker	Shoemaker 3 and 1	Shoemaker 2 and 1				
142 Claude Harmon			Burkemo 2 and 1			
147 Lawson Little	Little 3 and 2					
151 Johnny Weitzel						
145 Chick Harbert	Harbert 1-up (22)	Burkemo 1-up (19)				
150 Clayton Heafner				Burkemo 1-up		
148 Walter Burkemo	Burkemo 1-up (20)					
153 Toby Lyons						
143 Vic Ghezzi	Ghezzi 3 and 2	Ghezzi 4 and 3				
150 Eddie Burke			Myles 1-up			
148 Rod Munday	Munday 5 and 3					
152 Bob Toski						
151 Mike Pavella	Pavella 2 and 1	Myles 1-up (20)				
146 Johnny Palmer						Burkemo 1-up (37)
153 Reggie Myles	Myles 1-up (20)					
149 Andy Gaspar					Vines 1-up	
149 Denny Shute	Shute 3 and 2	Bradley 2 and 1				
142 Pete Cooper			Vines 2 and 1			
146 Jackson Bradley	Bradley 4 and 3					
151 Bobby Cruickshank						
151 Henry Picard	Picard 4 and 2	Vines 1-up				
145 Frank Commisso				Vines 1-up		
148 Ellsworth Vines	Vines 3 and 2					
153 Phil Friel						
143 Jim Ferrier	Ferrier 3 and 2	Ferrier 3 and 2				
150 Sam Bernardi			Bulla 9 and 8			
152 Milon Marusic	Marusic 2 and 1					
148 Ray Hill						
151 Bob Hamilton	Hamilton 1-up	Bulla 5 and 3				
146 Max Evans						
149 Johnny Bulla	Bulla 5 and 4					
154 Walter Ambo						

Snead 7 and 6

rolled in a 25-footer for a birdie. For Turnesa, his match with Harper took its toll.

Noticeably tired, Turnesa had no time between matches to regroup, and he was beaten in the afternoon by Charles Bassler, 5 and 4. Gene Sarazen had an interesting day, winning his first match, 2 and 1, against Charles Harter, but losing the afternoon match to Jack Burke Jr., 5 and 3. It is interesting to note that Sarazen's last loss to a Burke was to Jack's father, who beat him, 8 and 7, in the 1925 PGA Championship. Other former Champions who were vanquished the first day were Denny Shute, losing in the afternoon to Jackson Bradley, 2 and 1; Bob Hamilton beating Max Evans,

---

Snead's victory also marked the end of an era in which nine of the 18 PGA Champions won the Championship more than once. In the course of the next 19 years, 19 different winners would be crowned PGA Champion.

1-up, then losing the second match to Johnny Bulla, 5 and 3; and Henry Picard eliminated in the morning round by Ellsworth Vines, 1-up. Jim Ferrier beat Sam Bernardi and Milon Marusic, 3 and 2, and Vic Ghezzi eliminated Eddie Burke, 3 and 2, and then Rod Munday, 4 and 3. Some upsets saw Oakmont professional Lew Worsham lose a second round match to Al Brosch, 5 and 4, while Claude Harmon was a first round loser to Dick Shoemaker, 3 and 1.

In the third round, Snead beat Jimmy Demaret, 3 and 2, on a stormy day where play was suspended once for several hours. Even though Snead had a 5-up lead after the 10th hole, Demaret whittled it down by squaring the match at the 28th hole. But with birdies at the 29th and 30th holes and a bogey by Demaret at the 31st hole, Snead took a 3-up lead, which he held for the rest of the match. In other matches, Ferrier was defeated by Johnny Bulla, 9 and 8, in the biggest margin of victory of the day, and Reggie Myles surprised Ghezzi. Ghezzi had a 2-up lead after the 27th hole but lost the next three in a row. Clinging to a 1-up lead, Myles was able to halve the remaining holes to win. Another surprise saw Jack Burke Jr. eliminate Gene Kunes, 4 and 3, in

a match in which Burke had 10 one-putt greens in the morning round. Walter Burkemo beat Dick Shoemaker, 2 and 1, in a contest which Shoemaker led most of the way, and Al Borsch defeated Jack Harden, 6 and 5, on a day where both players, who wore glasses, couldn't see much because of the rain. The day's only overtime match saw Charles Bassler beat George Bolesta, 1-up, on the 37th hole as Bolesta bogeyed the first playoff hole.

In the quarter-finals, Snead defeated Jack Burke Jr., 2 and 1, in a match that saw Burke fight back from being behind most of the day. Snead finished the morning round 4-up, and with a 37 on the front side of the afternoon round, was 3-up. Burke made a rally on the final nine, making pars on the first six holes and picking up two on Snead, who bogeyed the 29th and 33rd holes. His rally stalled at the 34th hole when he made bogey for a half. The match closed out on him when Snead birdied the 35th hole. For the day, Snead was 1-under-par and the only player to break par. The other matches went to the final hole, with two of them being decided at the final green. In one of those affairs, Vines defeated Bulla, 1-up. Squared on the final hole, Bulla three-putted for a six, while Vines was unable to get his third shot out of a greenside bunker. He pitched his fourth shot to within a yard of the hole and made the bogey putt to give him the victory. In the match between Myles and Burkemo, Myles wasn't as lucky as Vines. He bogeyed the final hole after not being able to get it up and down from the greenside bunker, which cost him the match, as Burkemo did make par for a 1-up win. In the last match, Bassler, despite being 3-over par, defeated Brosch, 1-up, in a sloppy match. Bassler led the contest 1-up after 27 holes, and he increased his lead at the 32nd when Brosch bogeyed. Brosch also bogeyed the 33rd, but this time it was a winner, because Bassler had problems off the tee and made a six. Then Brosch birdied the 34th to square the match, but Bassler got the lead back when Brosch bogeyed the 35th hole. Bassler won the contest at the final hole when both players made bogeys.

In the semifinals, Snead, for the second day in a row, was the only player below par, as the other three didn't play very well. Snead defeated Bassler, 9 and 8, in a contest in which Bassler won only one hole. The other match was decided in overtime, as Burkemo edged Vines, 1-up, winning the last three holes. With Vines 2-up with

just two holes left, Burkemo birdied the 35th hole and then won the 36th when Vines missed a seven-footer for par and Burkemo made his par putt from four feet. At the extra hole, Vines was short of the green in two, while Burkemo hit the green and was 30 feet away for eagle. Vines chipped up to within 10 feet, but wasn't able to make the birdie as Burkemo two-putted for the winning birdie. In some circles, Burkemo was considered another Cinderella story, winning a playoff just to get into match play. Four of his five matches went to the final green, with three of those going into overtime.

In the finals, Snead completely dominated Burkemo as he cruised to a 7-and-6 victory. Snead won five of the first six holes, starting with an eagle, two birdies and three pars. These proved to be too much for Burkemo to overcome, even though a brief rally cut Snead's lead to 3-up at lunch. When they started the afternoon round, Snead started fast again with birdies on the 19th and 22nd holes, giving him a 5-up lead. The match came to an end at the 30th hole. Snead's secret in winning was his play on the front side, where he was 24-under. He played the 202 holes of the Championship in 21-under-par. Snead's victory also marked the end of an era in which nine of the 18 PGA Champions won the Championship more than once. In the course of the next 19 years, until Jack Nicklaus broke the streak in 1971, 19 different winners would be crowned PGA Champion.

ROAD TO THE FINALS		
Sam Snead beat	**Round**	**Walter Burkemo beat**
Fred Haas, 1-up	1st Round	Toby Lyons, 1-up (20)
Marty Furgol, 1-up (21)	2nd Round	Chick Harbert, 1-up (19)
Lloyd Mangrum, 3 and 2	3rd Round	Dick Shoemaker, 2 and 1
Jack Burke Jr., 2 and 1	Quarter-finals	Reggie Myles, 1-up
Charles Bassler, 9 and 8	Semifinals	Ellsworth Vines, 1-up (37)

1950

Qualifying for Match Play: A 36-hole qualifying round to get into match play was conducted the Wednesday and Thursday before the Championship. Even though he didn't have to qualify, defending champion Sam Snead was the low qualifier of 64 players with a 140. A score of 152 qualified for match play, with seven players at 153 having a playoff for three spots. Some notables who didn't qualify included Lawson Little (153), Jack Grout (154), Dutch Harrison (155), Mike Turnesa (155), Ed Oliver (155), Joe Creavy (159), Tony Manero (162) and Jimmy Thomson (WD).

Champion:	Chandler Harper, Portsmouth, Va.*	
Site:	Scioto CC, Columbus, Ohio	
Date:	June 21–27	Purse: $17,700
Par:	36-36—72	Entries: 128

The first and second rounds were 18 holes each, played in one day, with the remaining matches being played at 36 holes.

Early Matches: In first day of play, Sam Snead opened his defense of his crown with a 1-up squeaker over Sam Byrd. His chance of repeating ended on the 18th green in his afternoon round when Eddie Burke, younger brother of former U.S. Open Champion Billy Burke, rolled in a 30-foot chip shot from off the green for an eagle 3 to eliminate Snead. Since the match was the last of the day, Burke's shot was witnessed by all in attendance, stunning the gallery, who thought that Snead would pull the match out. Snead wasn't the only favorite eliminated in the first day, as former PGA Champion Jim Ferrier was upset by Elmer Reed, 5 and 4. Reed, an airline pilot who had given up on tournament golf the previous year, was a 2-up winner over Gene Kunes in the morning round. Vic Ghezzi was a 2-and-1 loser to Dick Metz in the first round, while Bob Hamilton lost on the 20th hole to Henry Picard. George Fazio won his morning match, 4 and 3, over Frank Staszowski, but Bob Toski, in a come-from-behind victory, nipped George Fazio, 1-up, in the afternoon. Favorites who moved on to the third round were: Denny Shute, who beat Augie Nordone, 1-up, in the morning and then easily coasted by Ellsworth Vines, 4 and 3, in the afternoon; Jimmy Demaret had a tough time beating Charley Farlow, 1-up, in the morning while he routed Rod Munday, 5 and 3, in the afternoon; Lloyd Mangrum got by Pete Cooper, 4 and 3, in the morning and then frustrated Skip Alexander, 1-up, in a match that had Mangrum take a 1-up lead after the 13th hole and hold on with pars to win the match on the final hole.

Bracket

Qual. Score / First Round 18 Holes	Second Round 18 Holes	Third Round 36 Holes	Quarter-final 36 Holes	Semifinal 36 Holes	Final 36 Holes
140 Sam Snead	Snead 1-up	Burke 1-up	Gafford 4 and 3	Demaret 5 and 4	Harper 2 and 1
149 Sam Byrd					
147 Eddie Burke	Burke 2 and 1				
150 Pete Lamb					
145 Jack Ryan	Schmutte 1-up	Gafford 1-up			
149 Leonard Schmutte					
147 Ray Gafford	Gafford 4 and 2				
151 Dale Andreason					
145 Denny Shute	Shute 1-up	Shute 4 and 3	Demaret 4 and 3		
149 Augie Nordone					
147 Ellsworth Vines	Vines 5 and 3				
151 Bob Tucker					
146 Joe Zarhardt	Munday 1-up	Demaret 5 and 3			
150 Rod Munday					
148 Jimmy Demaret	Demaret 1-up				
153 Charley Farlow					
144 Lloyd Mangrum	Mangrum 4 and 3	Mangrum 1-up	Mangrum 6 and 5	Harper 1-up	
149 Pete Cooper					
147 Skip Alexander	Alexander 4 and 3				
151 George Buck					
145 Chick Harbert	Harbert 6 and 5	Harbert 5 and 3			
150 Herman Scharlau					
148 Toney Penna	Williams 3 and 2				
152 Harold Williams					
145 Al Smith	Toski 2 and 1	Toski 1-up	Harper 2 and 1		
152 Bob Toski					
147 George Fazio	Fazio 4 and 3				
151 Frank Staszowski					
146 Dick Metz	Metz 2 and 1	Harper 1-up			
150 Vic Ghezzi					
148 Chandler Harper	Harper 5 and 3				
153 Fred Annon					
142 Al Brosch	Brosch 2 and 1	Harmon 2 and 1	Williams Jr. 1-up (38)	Williams Jr. 1-up	Williams Jr. 1-up (38)
149 Charles Sheppard					
147 Paul Runyan	Harmon 2 and 1				
150 Claude Harmon					
145 Henry Williams Jr.	Williams Jr. 5 and 3	Williams Jr. 6 and 5			
149 William Heinlein					
148 Emery Thomas	Thomas 2 and 1				
152 Errie Ball					
145 Jim Ferrier	Ferrier 3 and 2	Reed 5 and 4	Douglas 3 and 2		
149 Frank Commisso					
147 Gene Kunes	Reed 2-up				
151 Elmer Reed					
146 Marty Furgol	Douglas 3 and 1	Douglas 5 and 4			
150 Dave Douglas					
148 Jimmy Hines	Hines 1-up				
153 Harold Whittington					
144 Charles Bassler	Shafer 1-up	Bradley 4 and 3	Picard 1-up	Picard 10 and 8	
149 George Shafer					
147 Leland Gibson	Bradley 1-up				
151 Jackson Bradley					
146 Bob Hamilton	Picard 1-up (20)	Picard 4 and 2			
150 Henry Picard					
148 Sam Bernardi	Doser 2-up				
152 Clarence Doser					
145 Lew Worsham	Worsham 2 and 1	Palmer 4 and 2	Palmer 1-up		
149 Jerry Gianferante					
147 Johnny Palmer	Palmer 4 and 3				
151 Joe Taylor					
146 Al Watrous	Watrous 1-up	Kroll 2 and 1			
150 Jock Hutchison Jr.					
149 Ted Kroll	Kroll 5 and 4				
153 Ray Hill					

Champion: Harper 4 and 3

The runner-up in 1949, Johnny Palmer rolled over Joe Taylor, 4 and 3, in the morning, then beat Lew Worsham, 4 and 2, in the afternoon.

The third round produced a match between Denny Shute and Jimmy Demaret. Even though Shute had a 2-up lead after the morning round, Demaret went on to win, 4 and 3. Demaret dominated the afternoon round as he shot 33 on the front side to get one back and then with two birdies, won five holes in a row starting at the 27th hole. Demaret closed out the match on the 32nd hole. This left 43-year-old Henry Picard as the only former PGA Champion still in the field, as he barely got by Jackson Bradley, 1-up. The match had a sensational ending

*B*efore the conclusion of the match, Williams had been in nine bunkers, but despite the problems in the morning round, he regrouped in the afternoon and was even par on the front side.

as Picard was 1-up coming to the final hole. Bradley chipped in for an eagle, which looked like it was good enough to send the contest into overtime. But Picard saved his victory by sinking a 20-foot putt for a match-winning eagle. Another match that went the distance saw Palmer beat Ted Kroll, 1-up. The morning round was a low-scoring affair that saw Palmer 2-up after shooting 66 to Kroll's 68. In the afternoon both played terribly, and despite shooting 75, Palmer was able to hold on. The widest margin of victory was Mangrum's 6-and-5 rout of Chick Harbert, which saw Mangrum shoot 66 in the morning and take a 4-up lead to lunch. Mangrum continued his sub-par spurt in the afternoon round by shooting 32 on the front side to take a 5-up lead to the final nine holes. Harbert got one back with a Mangrum bogey at the 28th hole, but Harbert lost the match with bogeys at the 30th and 31st holes. In one of the thrilling encounters of the day, it took two extra holes for Henry Williams to score a 1-up victory over Claude Harmon. Harmon was 3-down with three to play, and on the 34th hole, rammed a 35-footer into the hole for a birdie. At the next hole, the margin was cut to one when Williams made bogey. At the final hole, Harmon squared

the contest with a 20-footer for birdie, but lost the match when he was unable to make par at the 38th hole. In other matches, Ray Gafford beat Eddie Burke, 4 and 3, while Chandler Harper outlasted Bob Toski, 2 and 1, and Dave Douglas eliminated Elmer Reed, 3 and 2.

In the quarter-finals, Henry Picard defeated Johnny Palmer, 10 and 8, in a day which saw Palmer win only one hole in the match. Picard, an arthritis sufferer, wore gloves on both of his hands, but his hands didn't seem to bother him as he picked up three holes per nine. When Palmer made birdie at the 27th hole, it was only good for a half as he was 9-down, with nine holes left. The match ended at the next hole, and it was funny to think that Picard played only because of an invitation from Scioto professional Jack Grout, an old friend. Another upset saw Mangrum lose to Chandler Harper, 1-up, in a match that saw both players 4-under-par. Harper built a 4-up lead after the 22nd hole, and even though Mangrum started to whittle away at the lead and squared the match on the 30th hole, Harper parred the next four holes. On the par-3 35th hole, Mangrum hit his tee shot 12 feet away, and then Harper followed to get his six feet away. When Mangrum missed, Harper took his 10-year-old putter and made the putt to go 1-up. At the last hole, Harper's putter again came through as he made a 10-foot birdie putt, which won the match. Another match that was decided at the final hole saw Henry Williams make a birdie to win his match, 1-up, over Dave Douglas. In the match between Demaret and Ray Gafford, Demaret easily won, 5 and 4, despite being down after the first nine holes.

In the semifinals, Williams beat Picard, 1-up, on the 38th hole in one of the greatest comebacks in the history of the PGA. Williams found himself 6-down with just eight holes left in the match, and then went on a tear. He won the 29th hole when Picard made a bogey and took the 30th with a birdie. Williams halved the 31st after missing a five-footer for birdie, but made a 20-footer for birdie at the 32nd to be only 3-down. Williams won the 33rd with a par and then captured the 34th with another 20-footer for birdie. When Picard bogeyed the 35th hole, the match was square. Both players made birdies at the final hole to send the match into overtime. Both made pars at the 37th hole, with Williams having to make a five-footer. At the next hole, Picard three-putted for a bogey, missing one from 20

inches to give the match to Williams, who made par. In the other match, Harper surprised all by upsetting Demaret, 2 and 1. It was the third time that Demaret had lost a semifinal match, losing two previously to Ben Hogan in 1946 and 1948.

Harper turned back Williams, 4 and 3, in one of the sloppiest finals ever played in the PGA. Despite shooting a 75 in the morning round, Harper was 3-up as Williams shot 41-38 for a 79. In Williams' first 11 holes, he hit only one green in regulation and was in five bunkers. Before the conclusion of the match, Williams had been in nine bunkers, but despite the problems in the morning round, he regrouped in the afternoon and was even par on the front side. Going into the final nine, Williams was still 3-down, and a bogey at the 30th hole just about sealed the contest. Harper won the match on the 33rd hole, to become the second Virginian in a row to win the PGA Championship.

ROAD TO THE FINALS

Chandler Harper beat	Round	Henry Williams beat
Fred Annon, 5 and 3	1st Round	Bill Heinlein, 5 and 3
Dick Metz, 1-up	2nd Round	Emery Thomas, 6 and 5
Bob Toski, 2 and 1	3rd Round	Claude Harmon, 1-up (38)
Lloyd Mangrum, 6 and 5	Quarter-finals	Dave Douglas, 1-up
Jimmy Demaret, 2 and 1	Semifinals	Henry Picard, 1-up (38)

1949

Qualifying for Match Play: A 36-hole qualifying round to get into match play was conducted the Wednesday and Thursday before the Championship. 1948 PGA Champion Ben Hogan was unable to defend his title because of an auto accident. Ray Hill was the low qualifier of 64 players with a 136. A score of 148 earned a match play berth, with six players at 149 having a playoff for three spots. Some notables who didn't qualify included Vic Ghezzi (150), Toney Penna (150),

Champion:	Sam Snead, Hot Springs, Va.*	
Site:	Hermitage CC, Richmond, Va.	
Date:	May 25-31	Par: 36-35—71
Purse:	$17,700	

Chick Harbert (151) and Ky Laffoon (151).

The first and second rounds were 18 holes each, played in one day, with the remaining matches being played at 36 holes.

Early Matches: After the first day of play, only two former PGA Champions remained, Sam Snead and Jim Ferrier. Denny Shute was routed in the first round by Lloyd Mangrum, 6 and 5, and Mangrum chalked up another win over a former champion by beating Bob Hamilton, 3 and 2. In the afternoon Gene Sarazen had a tough time, losing to Henry Williams, 2 and 1, despite having a 1-up lead at the turn. Other upsets saw Jack Issacs making a birdie on the final hole to beat Lawson Little, 1-up, while Frank Moore was making a birdie on the final hole to send his match into overtime with Ed Oliver, who then lost the match at the 19th hole with a bogey. Another upset winner in overtime was Johnny Palmer, who beat 1948 runner-up Mike Turnesa, 1-up, on the 20th hole when Turnesa made a bogey. Other upsets saw the early elimination of Craig Wood to Jack Harden, 1-up, and Clayton Heafner's 6-and-5 defeat of Tony Manero. The second round was free of upsets as the favorites cruised into the third round. Sam Snead beat Jack Burke, 3 and 2, in the morning round. After finishing the 13th hole, Burke took his driver from his caddie, and by the time he was supposed to hit his second shot, he couldn't find the caddie. An official ran back to the 13th green where the boy was sleeping under a tree, called for a jeep and raced the boy and clubs back to Burke, where they completed the round without further incident. Snead went on to beat Henry Ransom, 3 and 1, in the afternoon. Jim Ferrier also made it to the third round with victories over Andy LaPola, 4 and 2, and Skip Alexander, 1-up. Jimmy Demaret also advanced as he beat Harold

Bracket

Qual. Score	First Round 18 Holes	Second Round 18 Holes	Third Round 36 Holes	Quarter-final 36 Holes	Semifinal 36 Holes	Final 36 Holes
136	Ray Hill	Hill 2 and 1	Hill 3 and 2	Hill 5 and 4		
144	Ted Neist					
141	Jack Isaacs	Isaacs 1-up				
147	Lawson Little					
140	Ed Oliver	Moore 1-up (19)	Romans 4 and 2		Mangrum 7 and 6	
145	Frank Moore					
143	Jack Ryan	Romans 2 and 1				
148	Walter Romans					
138	Howard Schmidt	Thomson 4 and 3	Barron 2 and 1	Mangrum 4 and 3		
145	Jimmy Thomson					
142	Herman Barron	Barron 3 and 2				
147	Milon Marusic					
141	Lloyd Mangrum	Mangrum 6 and 5	Mangrum 3 and 2			Palmer 6 and 5
146	Denny Shute					
144	Bob Hamilton	Hamilton 2 and 1				
148	Chandler Harper					
138	Johnny Palmer	Palmer 1-up (20)	Palmer 8 and 6	Palmer 2 and 1		
145	Mike Turnesa					
142	Clay Gaddie	Gaddie 1-up				
147	Andy Gaspar					
140	George Schneiter	Schneiter 2-up	Worsham 5 and 4		Palmer 7 and 6	
146	Frank Staszowski					
143	Lew Worsham	Worsham 6 and 5				
148	Stan Staszowski					
140	Henry Williams Jr.	Williams Jr. 2 and 1	Williams Jr. 1-up	Williams Jr. 7 and 6		
145	Gene Sarazen					
143	Jack Harden	Harden 1-up				
148	Craig Wood					
141	Al Brosch	Brosch 3 and 1	Brosch 5 and 4			
147	John Thoren					
144	Herman Keiser	Smith 6 and 4				
149	Horton Smith					
137	Sam Snead	Snead 3 and 2	Snead 3 and 1	Snead 1-up		
145	Jack Burke					
142	Henry Ransom	Ransom 1-up				
147	Ray Gafford					
140	Pete Cooper	Douglas 1-up	Douglas 3 and 2		Snead 4 and 3	
145	Dave Douglas					
143	Mike DeMassey	DeMassey 2 and 1				
148	Matt Kowal					
139	George Fazio	Fazio 1-up	Demaret 3 and 1	Demaret 5 and 3		
145	Errie Ball					
143	Jimmy Demaret	Demaret 1-up				
148	Harold Oatman					
141	Johnny Bulla	Bulla 1-up	Turnesa 1-up			Snead 3 and 2
146	Ellsworth Vines					
144	Jim Turnesa	Turnesa 7 and 5				
149	Al Smith					
138	Clayton Heafner	Heafner 6 and 5	Heafner 2 and 1	Heafner 5 and 4		
145	Tony Manero					
142	Claude Harmon	Harmon 1-up				
147	Clarence Doser					
140	Eric Monti	Patroni 1-up	Patroni 1-up		Ferrier 3 and 2	
146	Jack Patroni					
144	Jimmy Johnson	Johnson 3 and 2				
148	Charles Sheppard					
140	Jim Ferrier	Ferrier 4 and 2	Ferrier 1-up	Ferrier 8 and 6		
145	Andy LaPola					
143	Bill Nary	Alexander 5 and 4				
148	Skip Alexander					
141	Eddie Burke	Burke 6 and 5	Furgol 2 and 1			
147	George Stuhler					
144	Marty Furgol	Furgol 2 and 1				
149	William Heinlein					

Oatman, 1-up, and Errie Ball, 3 and 1. Johnny Palmer had the most sizable win of the day with an 8-and-6 defeat of Clay Gaddie.

In the third round, Snead had to stage a last-hole rally to nip Dave Douglas, 1-up. Snead, who was 3-down after the 27th hole, managed to square the match at the 33rd hole after making three straight 3s, only to see Douglas take the lead again with a birdie at the 34th hole. But Douglas bogeyed the last two holes, missing from four feet at the final hole to lose the match. Of the eight matches, that was the only one that went the distance. The other matches weren't close, as Lloyd Mangrum beat Herman Barron, 4 and 3; Ray Hill stopped Wal-

When Snead made an unanswered birdie at the 31st hole, nothing could stop him. The match ended three holes later, with Snead claiming his second PGA Championship and a winner's check for $3,500.

ter Romans, 5 and 4; Clayton Heafner defeated Jack Patroni, 5 and 4; Jimmy Demaret beat Jim Turnesa 5 and 3; Henry Williams defeated Al Brosch, 7 and 6; and Ferrier had an easy time in his 8-and-6 victory over Marty Furgol.

In the quarter-finals, none of the matches were close. Ferrier played the best in his 3-and-2 victory over Heafner. Ferrier was 4-up after a morning round of 66, and when he was 1-under for the first 16 holes of the afternoon round, he closed out the match on the 34th hole. In the semifinals he faced Snead, who had beat Demaret, 4 and 3. In the 33-hole match, Demaret won only four holes, while Snead won eight. The other two matches were lopsided 7-and-6 victories, with Palmer beating Williams and Mangrum victorious over medalist Ray Hill.

In the semifinals, Palmer had another easy day, routing Mangrum, 6 and 5. After a morning round of 66, Palmer went into the afternoon round 2-up and increased the lead to 7-up with birdies at four of the last five holes on the front side, for a 31. The match ended at the 31st hole. In the match of the day, Snead beat Ferrier, 3 and 2. Ferrier gained the advantage with a morning round 67 to finish 2-up, but Snead started a

rally when he holed his second shot from 30 yards for an eagle 2 at the 21st hole. He won three of the next six holes to finish the nine at 1-up. Ferrier squared the match with a birdie at the 28th hole, but gave it back with a bogey on the next hole. Snead then closed out the match with birdies at the 31st and 33rd holes. Snead advanced to the finals for the fourth time in his career, finishing the day 8-under-par, with nine one-putt greens in the afternoon.

The finals were played in front of a partisan crowd and they all got their wish when Snead, a native Virginian, beat Palmer, 3 and 2. Snead had a tough time in the morning round, as he was 2-down after the front side. He regained the two back to finish the round square. In the afternoon it was a different story for Palmer, who had won only one of the 16 holes when Snead made a seven-footer for a birdie at the 22nd hole, an eight-footer at the 24th hole and another seven-footer at the 25th hole. Despite losing the 27th hole with a bogey, Snead went to the final nine 2-up. Palmer's chance for a comeback got slimmer when both birdied the 28th hole. When Snead made an unanswered birdie at the 31st hole, nothing could stop him. The match ended three holes later, with Snead claiming his second PGA Championship and a winner's check for $3,500.

ROAD TO THE FINALS		
Sam Snead beat	**Round**	**Johnny Palmer beat**
Jack Burke, 3 and 2	1st Round	Mike Turnesa, 1-up (20)
Henry Ransom, 3 and 1	2nd Round	Clay Gaddie, 8 and 6
Dave Douglas, 1-up	3rd Round	Lew Worsham, 2 and 1
Jimmy Demaret, 4 and 3	Quarter-finals	Henry Williams, 7 and 6
Jim Ferrier, 3 and 2	Semifinals	Lloyd Mangrum, 6 and 5

1948

Qualifying for Match Play: A 36-hole qualifying round to get into match play was conducted the Wednesday and Thursday before the Championship. Defending champion Jim Ferrier was exempt and 63 players qualified for the field. Skip Alexander was low qualifier with a 134. A score of 149 qualified for match play, with six players at 150 having a play-off for four spots. Some notables who didn't qualify included: Johnny Revolta (151), Denny Shute (151) and Jimmy Thomson (152).

Champion:	Ben Hogan, Hershey, Pa.*	
Site:	Norwood Hills CC, St. Louis, Mo.	
Date:	May 19-25	Par: 35-36—71
Purse:	$17,700	

The first and second rounds were 18 holes each, played in one day, with the remaining matches being played at 36 holes.

Early Matches: In the first day of play, extra holes were the pattern of the day as seven of the 32 morning matches and two in the afternoon went into overtime. In the morning round, Ben Hogan's 23-hole match was the longest. Hogan's birdie against Jock Hutchison Jr. at the 23rd hole won the contest, 1-up. In the afternoon round, Hogan played better, shooting 68, but he had to fashion a rally to beat Johnny Palmer, 1-up. Palmer was 2-up, with just four holes left, when Hogan went on a tear to play those next four holes in eagle, par, birdie and birdie to beat Palmer on the final hole. Former PGA Champion Bob Hamilton was on the losing end of a 20-hole match as Zell Eaton won, 1-up. Hamilton had to fight hard just to go into overtime, as he made a 35-footer at the 17th for a half and then won the 18th hole with a par. He bogeyed the 19th hole, but still got a half when Eaton three-putted. His luck ran out at the 20th hole when Eaton ran in a 15-footer for birdie to win the match. Another first round extra-hole victim was Jim Turnesa, who lost to Armand Farina on the 22nd hole, despite having a 2-hole lead after the 13th. Farina squared the match at the 16th, and when they halved the remaining holes, the contest went into overtime. At the 20th hole, both players made birdies to halve the hole, but at the 22nd, Turnesa failed to get his par and lost the match. It also took Jim Ferrier 20 holes to beat Dutch Harrison, 1-up.

In the second round, Ferrier fell victim to Claude Harmon, who shot 66 and won the contest, 1-up. The match had an exciting finish as Harmon bogeyed the 17th hole to trim his lead to 1-up. When Ferrier hit a great shot to within inches of the final hole, Harmon was up against the ropes. But Har-

Bracket

Qual. Score	First Round 18 Holes	Second Round 18 Holes	Third Round 36 Holes	Quarter-final 36 Holes	Semifinal 36 Holes	Final 36 Holes
	Jim Ferrier	Ferrier 1-up (20)	Harmon 1-up	Harmon 2 and 1	Harmon 1-up (42)	Turnesa 1-up (37)
145	Dutch Harrison					
142	Claude Harmon	Harmon 1-up				
148	Elroy Marti					
140	Lloyd Mangrum	Mangrum 1-up	Ransom 3 and 2			
148	George Schneiter					
144	Henry Ransom	Ransom 1-up				
149	Andrew Gibson					
136	Sam Snead	Snead 6 and 5	Snead 4 and 3	Snead 5 and 3		
146	Clay Gaddie					
143	Frank Moore	Moore 7 and 6				
148	Vic Ghezzi					
141	Pete Cooper	Cooper 4 and 3	Gibson 1-up			
148	Frank Champ					
145	Leland Gibson	Gibson 1-up				
150	Pete Burke					
135	Toney Penna	Bulla 4 and 3	Bulla 4 and 3	Bulla 6 and 5	Turnesa 6 and 5	
146	Johnny Bulla					
143	Jim Turnesa	Farina 1-up (22)				
148	Armand Farina					
140	Ky Laffoon	Laffoon 1-up (22)	Laffoon 3 and 2			
148	Jack Ryan					
145	Chandler Harper	Harper 4 and 3				
149	Sam Schneider					
139	Bob Hamilton	Eaton 1-up (20)	Turnesa 1-up (21)	Turnesa 3 and 2		
147	Zell Eaton					
144	Mike Turnesa	Turnesa 1-up				
148	Charles Sheppard					
141	Lawson Little	Smith 2 and 1	Smith 4 and 3			
148	Al Smith					
145	Jimmy Hines	Hines 5 and 4				
150	J.S. Johnson					
134	Stewart Alexander	Alexander 4 and 3	Alexander 2-up	Harbert 11 and 10	Hogan 2 and 1	Hogan 7 and 6
146	John Stapp					
142	Al Brosch	Brosch 6 and 5				
148	Jules Platte					
140	Chick Harbert	Harbert 4 and 2	Harbert 1-up (26)			
148	Joe Zarhardt					
145	Augie Nordone	Burke 1-up (19)				
149	Eddie Burke					
138	Ben Hogan	Hogan 1-up (23)	Hogan 1-up	Hogan 1 up		
147	Jock Hutchison Jr.					
143	Johnny Palmer	Palmer 5 and 4				
148	Denny Champagne					
141	Gene Sarazen	Sarazen 4 and 3	Sarazen 2 and 1			
148	Harvey Raynor					
145	Jackson Bradley	Bradley 5 and 3				
150	Otey Crisman					
136	Jimmy Demaret	Demaret 1-up (20)	Demaret 3 and 1	Demaret 3 and 2	Demaret 5 and 4	
146	Horton Smith					
143	George Getchell	Getchell 1-up				
148	Andy Gaspar					
140	Herman Keiser	Ball 4 and 3	Worsham 7 and 6			
148	Errie Ball					
145	Lew Worsham	Worsham 1-up				
149	Al Watrous					
140	Ed Oliver	Oliver 7 and 6	Oliver 3 and 2	Fazio 1-up		
147	Walter Ambo					
144	Joe Belfore	Elworthy 1-up				
149	Sherman Elworthy					
141	George Fazio	Fazio 6 and 5	Fazio 7 and 6			
148	Edmond Onoretta					
145	Henry Williams Jr.	Williams Jr. 2 and 1				
150	Ferdy Catropa					

mon was up to the challenge as he hit his second shot 10 feet away and rolled the putt in for a birdie and the victory. Chick Harbert, who won his first match, 4 and 2, against Joe Zarhardt had a close call with Eddie Burke in the second match. Burke, who is the younger brother of 1931 U.S. Open Champion Billy Burke, had just beat Augie Nordone, 1-up, in a 19-hole match. It appeared he was going to upset Harbert in the afternoon round. Burke was 3-up with just five holes left, but Harbert birdied the 14th and 15th holes to get within one. After halving the next two holes, a par at the final hole was good enough to square the match and send it into overtime. Their match turned into the longest overtime

The finals had an unusual touch, because for the third time someone from the Turnesa family was trying to win the PGA Championship. In 1927, Mike's brother, Joe, lost to Hagen in the finals, and his brother, Jim, was beaten by Sam Snead in 1942.

match in the history of the PGA Championship. The contest dragged on for eight extra holes before Burke finally pushed his tee shot at the par-3 26th hole. He wasn't able to match Harbert's par, giving Harbert the contest, 1-up. In other matches, former Champions Gene Sarazen and Sam Snead advanced to the third round as Sarazen beat Harvey Raynor, 4 and 3, and Jackson Bradley, 2 and 1, while Snead was easily winning his matches, routing Clay Gaddie, 6 and 5, and Frank Moore, 4 and 3.

In the third round, the match of the day had Ben Hogan hanging on for a 1-up victory over Gene Sarazen. After 27 holes, it looked like Hogan was going to have an easy day as he was 4-up, which seemed too much for the 46-year-old Sarazen to overcome. But with birdies at the 28th, and then an unanswered par at the 34th hole, Sarazen rallied to just 2-down. He got another one back at the 35th hole with a 10-footer for a birdie 2, but the rally ended at the final hole when Sarazen was unable to get a birdie. The low round of the day was produced by Chick Harbert, an 11-under-par morning 61, en route to defeating medalist Skip Alexander, 11 and 10. Johnny Bulla surprised Ky Laffoon, 6 and

5, while Sam Snead vanquished Leland Gibson, 5 and 3. Claude Harmon, despite a cut left hand which bothered him, won his match against Henry Ransom, 2 and 1, while Mike Turnesa beat Al Smith, 3 and 2. In other matches, Jimmy Demaret beat Lew Worsham, 3 and 2, in a match that saw Demaret play the last seven holes in 4-under-par, and George Fazio was able to hang on to a 1-up victory over a charging Ed Oliver.

In the quarter-finals, Claude Harmon eliminated Sam Snead, 1-up, in the longest quarter-final match in the history of the PGA. Harmon dominated the contest most of the day, thanks to a morning round 64 which put him 5-up. But Snead was able to reverse the tables in the afternoon and shot his own 64. When Snead sank a five-footer at the final hole, he sent the match into overtime. On the 37th hole, Snead was within seven feet for a birdie, but when Harmon placed a dead stymie, Snead had no choice but to putt around and tie the hole with par. The next four holes were halved, with both players placing their second shots 20 feet away at the 42nd hole. The balls were measured and it was determined that Harmon would putt first. He took advantage of the situation by making the putt, and when Snead wasn't able to follow suit, the match ended. The rest of the matches were routs, even though Hogan's 2-and-1 victory over Chick Harbert didn't look like a rout. That's because Hogan had a 5-up morning advantage, and Harbert chipped away. It wasn't until Harbert made a birdie at the 34th hole that Hogan started to get concerned. However, he was still 2-up and Hogan laid Harbert a partial stymie at the next hole where Harbert could only get a par-3, which closed the match. Mike Turnesa eliminated Johnny Bulla with a 6-and-5 victory, while George Fazio got the day's award as the most unlucky golfer because he caught Jimmy Demaret on the wrong day. Demaret beat Fazio, 5 and 4, but what the score doesn't tell is that Fazio was a remarkable 11-under for the 32-hole match and still lost. Fazio was 4-under on the morning round and must have been scratching his head as he went to lunch 7-down. Demaret was spectacular, shooting 61 in the morning round. Even though Fazio was 3-under on the front nine of the afternoon round, Demaret also fired a 33 and didn't lose ground. It turned into a matter of Fazio just running out of holes. He played the remaining five holes in 4-under-par and picked up two holes, but with a par at the 32nd hole, the match went to Demaret, who was 16-under-par for the day.

Ben Hogan beat	Round	Mike Turnesa beat
Jock Hutchison Jr., 1-up (37)	1st Round	Charles Shepard, 2 and 1
Johnny Palmer, 1-up	2nd Round	Zell Eaton, 1-up (21)
Gene Sarazan, 1-up	3rd Round	Al Smith, 3 and 2
Chick Harbert, 2 and 1	Quarter-finals	Johnny Bulla, 6 and 5
Art Bell, 2 and 1	Semifinals	Claude Harmon, 1-up (37)

In the semifinals, both matches were close, with Mike Turnesa coming from behind to beat Claude Harmon in overtime, 1-up. Turnesa missed an 18-inch putt that should have won the 33rd hole and found himself in the unenviable position of being 2-down with just three holes left. However, Harmon bogeyed the 34th and 35th holes, sending the match to the final hole square. That hole was halved with pars, and Turnesa won the contest on the first extra hole when he made a 15-footer for a birdie 3. In the other contest, Ben Hogan beat Jimmy Demaret, 2 and 1, in a match where both players were 10-under-par. The match was even at the 33rd hole, but Demaret took three putts and then lost the next hole when Hogan made an 18-footer for birdie. Both made pars at the next two holes, which ended the match.

The finals had an unusual touch, because for the third time someone from the Turnesa family was trying to win the PGA Championship. In 1927, Mike's brother, Joe, lost to Hagen in the finals, and his brother, Jim, was beaten by Sam Snead in 1942. Ben Hogan was trying to win the U.S. Open and the PGA in the same year for the first time since Gene Sarazen did it in 1922, and, despite being outdriven by Turnesa on every hole, Hogan used his irons with deadly accuracy in his 7-and-6 victory. Hogan toured the morning round in 66 to go 4-up, and in spite of a short rally from Turnesa in the afternoon, won the 28th, 29th and 30th holes to close out the match. For the week, Hogan was 35-under for the 213 holes he played, and after the Championship, a weary Hogan said he didn't think he would ever play in the PGA Championship again. The grind of 10 rounds in five days was too much, even though he won the U.S. Open the following month and reconsidered his decision. His automobile accident of 1949 left his battered legs unable to go 36 holes. He didn't return to the PGA Championship until 1960, the third year after the switch to a stroke-play format.

1947

Qualifying for Match Play: A 36-hole qualifying round to get into match play was conducted the Wednesday and Thursday before the Championship. Defending champion Ben Hogan was exempt and 63 players qualified. Jimmy Demaret was low qualifier with a 137. A score of 148 qualified for match play, with 11 players at 149 having a playoff for one spot. Notable players failing to qualify for match play included Paul Runyan (149, lost in playoff), Denny Shute (151),

Champion:	Jim Ferrier, San Francisco, Calif.*
Site:	Plum Hollow CC, Detroit, Mich.
Date: June 18-24	**Par:** 36-36—72
Purse:	$17,700

Lawson Little (152) and Craig Wood (155).

The first and second rounds were 18 holes each, played in one day, with the remaining matches being played at 36 holes.

Early Matches: In the first day of play, upsets were shaping the course of the Championship. Defending PGA Champion Ben Hogan was ousted by Toney Penna, 3 and 1, in a match that saw superb golf from both players. Hogan toured the front side in 32, but was 1-down as Penna also shot 32. Penna continued his barrage of birdies on the back side, with a birdie at 13 to increase his lead to 2-up. The next hole was halved with birdies, and with pars at 15 and 16 the match stayed square. At 17, Hogan succumbed when Penna birdied to close the match. It was a disappointment for Hogan, who was 5-under for the day, while Penna was 8-under. In another upset, 45-year-old Gene Sarazen showed that despite his age he could still play golf. In his first match, he just got by former champion Johnny Revolta, 1-up, then pulled the ultimate by eliminating Sam Snead, 2 and 1. Snead missed several putts within three feet during the match, while Sarazen played error-free golf. Another former champion to fall was Bob Hamilton, who was defeated by Jack Smith, 2-and-1. Other first-round surprises saw Jimmy Demaret go down to a 2-and-1 defeat at the hands of Earl Martin, who then was routed by Vic Ghezzi, 6 and 5, in the second round. Bobby Locke also lost a close match to Henry Ransom where Locke was 1-up with just two holes left, only to lose, 17 and 18. Overall, it was one of the most exciting first days, as 22 of the 48 matches went the distance.

In the third round, U.S. Open Champion Lew Worsham became the favorite as he trounced Reggie Myles, 7 and 6, in the day's biggest margin of victory.

Another U.S. Open Champion, Lloyd

Bracket

Qual. Score / First Round 18 Holes	First Round 18 Holes	Second Round 18 Holes	Third Round 36 Holes	Quarter-final 36 Holes	Semifinal 36 Holes	Final 36 Holes
Ben Hogan	Penna 3 and 1	Laffoon 1-up	Laffoon 4 and 3	Bell 2-up	Ferrier 10 and 9	Ferrier 2 and 1
146 Toney Penna						
143 Ky Laffoon	Laffoon 3 and 1					
147 Bruce Coltart						
141 Sam Snead	Snead 2-up	Sarazen 2 and 1				
146 Jimmy Thomson						
144 Johnny Revolta	Sarazen 1-up					
147 Gene Sarazen						
139 Bobby Locke	Ransom 1-up	Metz 1-up	Bell 1-up (37)			
146 Henry Ransom						
144 Dick Metz	Metz 4 and 3					
147 Henry Kaiser						
143 Johnny Bulla	Bulla 2 and 1	Bell 4 and 3				
146 Elmer Reed						
145 Arthur Bell	Bell 4 and 2					
148 Dick Govern						
138 Claude Harmon	Harmon 1-up	Harmon 5 and 3	Ferrier 1-up (37)	Ferrier 4 and 3		
146 Sam Byrd						
143 Fred Annon	Milward 1-up					
147 Jim Milward						
142 Jim Ferrier	Ferrier 1-up (19)	Ferrier 3 and 2				
146 Willie Goggin						
144 Herman Barron	Barron 1-up					
148 Leo Fraser						
141 Chandler Harper	Harper 2 and 1	Turnesa 1-up (22)	Mangrum 1-up			
146 Chick Rutan						
144 Sherman Elworthy	Turnesa 2-up					
147 Mike Turnesa						
143 Lloyd Mangrum	Mangrum 2-up	Mangrum 4 and 3				
147 Harold McSpaden						
145 Walter Romans	Dudley 2 and 1					
148 Ed Dudley						
137 Jimmy Demaret	Martin 2 and 1	Ghezzi 6 and 5	Ghezzi 4 and 3	Ghezzi 3 and 2	Harbert 2-up	
146 Earl Martin						
143 Herman Keiser	Ghezzi 6 and 5					
147 Vic Ghezzi						
142 Jim Turnesa	Turnesa 1-up (20)	Turnesa 4 and 3				
146 Al Watrous						
144 Walter Ambo	Ambo 3 and 1					
147 Mike DeMassey						
140 Clarence Doser	Doser 1-up	Worsham 5 and 4	Worsham 7 and 6			
146 Al Smith						
144 Lew Worsham	Worsham 4 and 3					
143 John Morris						
143 George Schneiter	Schneiter 4 and 3	Myles 1-up				
147 Art Smith						
148 Reggie Myles	Myles 1-up					
148 Jack Mitchell						
138 Clayton Heafner	Heafner 1-up (19)	Harbert 1-up (20)	Harbert 3 and 2	Harbert 6 and 5		
146 Jack Isaacs						
144 Chick Harbert	Harbert 2 and 1					
147 Ted Neist						
143 Al Huske	Oliver 2 and 1	Oliver 4 and 3				
146 Ed Oliver						
144 Al Brosch	Bassler 2-up					
148 Harry Bassler						
141 Jackson Bradley	Joseph 1-up	Joseph 1-up (19)	Gibson 1-up (37)			
146 Eddie Joseph						
144 Lloyd Watkins	Watkins 1-up					
147 Gil Sellers						
143 Dick Shoemaker	Gibson 3 and 2	Gibson 3 and 2				
147 Leland Gibson						
145 Bob Hamilton	Smith 2 and 1					
149 Jack Smith						

Mangrum, also advanced with a 1-up victory over Mike Turnesa in a match that turned from a rout to near defeat. After the 19th hole, Mangrum had a 7-up lead, but one by one, Turnesa got the holes back until he came to the final hole just 1-down. Turnesa made birdie on the hole, but it wasn't good enough to send the match into overtime, as Mangrum responded to the challenge to halve the hole with his own birdie. Jim Ferrier also had a tough time keeping Claude Harmon from charging back from a 2-down deficit after the morning round. Harmon played the afternoon round in 69, squaring the match on the 35th hole and then taking the contest into overtime, where he hooked his drive on the 37th

Chick Harbert and Jim Ferrier were each wild off the tees and in the fairways, with Ferrier's drives and second shots hitting seven spectators. But in spite all of his wild shots, Ferrier's ball bounced to enough favorable spots.

hole, leading to a bogey and Ferrier winning, 1-up. In other overtime matches, Art Bell beat Dick Metz, 1-up, on the 37th hole, while Leland Gibson beat Ed Joseph, also by 1-up, on the 37th hole. Other upsets occurred, as Gene Sarazen's legs gave out on him in his 4-and-3 defeat by Ky Laffoon, and Chick Harbert defeated 1946's runner-up Ed Oliver, 3 and 2.

In the quarter-finals, the Championship favorite, Lew Worsham, was defeated by former champion Vic Ghezzi, 3 and 2. Worsham had a 2-up advantage after the morning round, but on the front side of the afternoon round Ghezzi was 3-under and picked up three holes. With pars at all of the holes on the back side, Ghezzi was able to win two more holes and close out the match with a par on the 34th hole. Another surprise saw Jim Ferrier beat Lloyd Mangrum, 4 and 3, in a match which Ferrier controlled from the second hole. In the best match, Art Bell beat Ky Laffoon, 2-up, in a seesaw affair which saw 22 of the 36 holes change hands. Laffoon staged a great comeback after being 7-down after the 19th hole, but in the course of the next seven holes, Laffoon reeled off two birdies and an eagle to win

six holes. When they made the turn, Bell was still 1-up, despite shooting 39 to Laffoon's 33. Laffoon continued his birdie barrage on the 28th hole to square the match, but Bell got it back with a birdie at the next hole. Bell took control of the match at the 31st hole with a 30-footer for birdie and then won the 33rd hole with a Laffoon bogey. Even though Laffoon was now 3-down, with just three holes left, he didn't give up, and birdied the 34th and 35th holes to go 1-down. But at the last hole, he ran out of steam, putting his second shot on the par-5 hole into a ditch that guarded the front of the green; when he tried to slash it out, he couldn't and was forced to concede the match. The last match of the day went the distance with Chick Harbert beating Leland Gibson, 2-up.

Until the semifinals, most of the matches were close affairs, but the two semis turned into big routs as Jim Ferrier beat Art Bell, 10 and 9, and Chick Harbert clobbered Vic Ghezzi, 6 and 5. Ferrier, who learned to play golf in his native Australia, completely overpowered Bell, who started the day with a birdie and two pars, but lost those holes when Ferrier started eagle, birdie, birdie. Bell was 1-over-par for the 27 holes, while Ferrier played them in 9-under-par. Harbert's game wasn't as impressive as Ferrier's, but he was still 5-under for the 31 holes, and Ghezzi was nowhere near top form as he was 3-over-par. If there was a secret weapon for Harbert, it was the nine par-3 holes that they played. Harbert won five of them, as Ghezzi played them in 7-over par.

For the first time since 1937, a final match didn't include Ben Hogan, Byron Nelson or Sam Snead. But that didn't discourage nearly 7,000 spectators from attending. That presented a problem for Jim Ferrier, who spent the night before pondering whether the crowd would be a factor in his match with Michigan hero, Harbert, by either kicking his ball into the woods or kicking Harbert's ball out of the woods. Ferrier solved the problem the morning before the contest by hiring two policemen, one on each side of the fairway, to guard against overzealous fans playing a part in the match. Afterwards, Ferrier admitted, "that it was the best $100 that I have ever spent," as he beat Harbert, 2 and 1. If there was a secret in the match, it was Ferrier's putting, as he took only 52 putts over the course of the 35-hole match, and finished 6-under par. For the Championship, Ferrier was 27-under-par for the 243 holes he

ROAD TO THE FINALS		
Jim Ferrier beat	**Round**	**Chick Harbert beat**
Willie Goggin, 1-up (19)	1st Round	Ted Neist, 2 and 1
Herman Barron, 3 and 2	2nd Round	Clayton Heafner, 1-up (20)
Claude Harmon, 1-up (37)	3rd Round	Ed Oliver, 3 and 2
Lloyd Mangrum, 4 and 3	Quarter-finals	Leland Gibson, 2-up
Art Bell, 10 and 9	Semifinals	Vic Ghezzi, 6 and 5

played. The Championship match was square after the morning round, but Ferrier's game heated up in the afternoon when he was around in 32 and went to the final nine 3-up. Even though Harbert got one back with a birdie at the 30th hole, Ferrier's birdie at the next hole put him back at 3-up. Ferrier bogeyed the 34th hole to give one back, but, when Harbert was unable to make his birdie at the 34th hole, the match came to an end. Chick Harbert and Jim Ferrier were each wild off the tees and in the fairways, with Ferrier's drives and second shots hitting seven spectators. But in spite all of his wild shots, Ferrier's ball bounced to enough favorable spots.

PGA CHAMPIONSHIP MATCH PLAY

1946

Qualifying for Match Play: A 36-hole qualifying round to get into match play was conducted the Monday and Tuesday before the Championship. Defending PGA Champion Byron Nelson was exempt and 63 players qualified. Jim Ferrier was low qualifier with a record 134, which included a 63 in the second 18. A score of 149 qualified for match play, with three players at 150 having a playoff for two spots. With World War II over, all of the best golfers on the PGA Tour participated in the Championship

Champion:	Ben Hogan, Hershey, Pa.*	
Site:	Portland GC, Portland, Ore.	
Date:	Aug. 19-25	Par: 35-37—72
Purse:	$17,700	

The first and second rounds were 18 holes each, played in one day, with the remaining matches being played at 36 holes.

Early Matches: The first day's 48 matches went as predicted, with the exception of two losses which eliminated British Open Champion Sam Snead, and Lloyd Mangrum, the U.S. Open winner. Mangrum was a first-round loser to Harry Bassler, with the match going the distance in Bassler's 1-up win. For Sam Snead, who beat Bob McKendrick, 4 and 3, in the first round, his second round upset came at the hands of George Schneiter, who played the front side in 32 and was 5-up. Schneiter continued his pace on the back side and when he made four straight pars, he closed out Snead, 6 and 5. Dick Shoemaker was another long-shot who gained entry into the third round by beating last year's runner-up Sam Byrd, 3 and 2, and then nipping past former champion Vic Ghezzi, 1-up. Bob Hamilton, who despite beating Andrew Gibson, 4 and 3, in the first round, went two extra holes before he lost to Harold McSpaden, 1-down. Defending PGA Champion Byron Nelson had an easy time in his two matches. Despite an aching back, he played 27 holes in 10-under-par to rout Frank Rodia, 8 and 7, and then beat the host professional Larry Lamberger, 3 and 2. While Nelson was having an easy time getting into the third round, his arch-rival Ben Hogan had a tougher time as he just got by Charles Wesner. He had an easier time in the second round, beating Bill Heinlein, 4 and 3. Jim Ferrier, who amazed everyone with his record-scoring qualifying rounds, continued his fine play in beating Sam Schneider, 4 and 3, and then eliminated Lawson Little in the afternoon.

In the third round, Nelson rolled on to beat Herman Barron, 3 and 2, in a day which saw Nelson 9-under-par for the 34 holes. McSpaden, who was 7-under-par for

Bracket

Qual. Score	First Round 18 Holes	Second Round 18 Holes	Third Round 36 Holes	Quarter-final 36 Holes	Semifinal 36 Holes	Final 36 Holes
	Byron Nelson	Nelson 8 and 7	Nelson 3 and 2	Nelson 3 and 2	Oliver 1-up	Oliver 6 and 5
145	Frank Rodia					
143	Larry Lamberger	Lamberger 1-up				
147	Orville White					
142	Herman Barron	Barron 6 and 5	Barron 3 and 2			
147	Ellsworth Vines					
142	Herman Keiser	Coleman 1-up (20)				
146	Fay Coleman					
141	Al Zimmerman	Metz 2-up	Oliver 3 and 1	Oliver 5 and 4		
145	Dick Metz					
143	Clay Gaddie	Oliver 2-up				
147	Ed Oliver					
141	Chandler Harper	Harper 5 and 3	Harper 2 and 1			
146	Bob Gutwein					
144	Jimmy Thomson	Thomson 3 and 2				
148	Al Jamison					
136	Dutch Harrison	Harrison 6 and 4	Harrison 1-up	McSpaden 4 and 3	McSpaden 5 and 3	
145	Joe Mozel					
144	Toney Penna	Penna 4 and 3				
148	Dick Stenard					
141	Bob Hamilton	Hamilton 4 and 3	McSpaden 4 and 3			
146	Andrew Gibson					
143	Harold McSpaden	McSpaden 4 and 3				
147	Claude Harmon					
138	Chick Harbert	Bassler 3 and 1	Congdon 1-up (19)	Congdon 2 and 1		
145	Newton Bassler					
143	Chuck Congdon	Congdon 6 and 5				
148	Ray McGuire					
141	George Schneiter	Schneiter 1-up	Schneiter 6 and 5			
146	Ray Gafford					
147	Sam Snead	Snead 4 and 3				
143	Bob McKendrick					
134	Jim Ferrier	Ferrier 4 and 3	Ferrier 3 and 2	Demaret 3 and 2	Demaret 6 and 5	Hogan 6 and 4
145	Sam Schneider					
144	Lawson Little	Little 1-up				
146	John Hoetmer					
142	Jimmy Demaret	Demaret 3 and 2	Demaret 3 and 2			
146	Joe Zarhardt					
143	Leonard Schmutte	Tinsley 2-up				
147	Dave Tinsley					
141	Harold West	Ransom 1-up	Turnesa 1-up	Turnesa 5 and 4		
146	Henry Ransom					
143	Jim Turnesa	Turnesa 5 and 4				
148	Ewing Pomeroy					
141	Vic Ghezzi	Ghezzi 1-up	Shoemaker 1-up			
146	Jim Gantz					
142	Sam Byrd	Shoemaker 3 and 2				
147	Dick Shoemaker					
137	Ben Hogan	Hogan 2 and 1	Hogan 4 and 3	Hogan 5 and 4	Hogan 5 and 4	Hogan 10 and 9
145	Charles Weisner					
148	Elroy Marti	Heinlein 2 and 1				
144	William Heinlein					
142	Arthur Bell	Bell 4 and 3	Bell 4 and 3			
146	Ralph Hutchison					
143	Clayton Heafner	Nelson 2 and 1				
147	Al Nelson					
148	George Fazio	Fazio 4 and 3	Moore 2 and 1	Moore 4 and 3		
145	Armand Farina					
143	Frank Moore	Moore 4 and 3				
148	Ted Longworth					
141	Lew Worsham	Worsham 3 and 1	Bassler 1-up			
146	Jimmy Hines					
147	Lloyd Mangrum	Bassler 1-up				
143	Harry Bassler					

86

his 33-hole match with Dutch Harrison, was 4 and 3. Hogan had a good day, shooting 6-under-par in his 5-and-4 triumph over Art Bell. Both players shot 67 in the morning round, but Bell couldn't keep up the pace on the back side. Jim Ferrier's hopes for the Championship were dashed by Jimmy Demaret, who beat him, 3 and 2, in a match that saw Ferrier 2-up after the morning round. In other matches, Ed Oliver was 8-under-par in his 5-and-4 rout of Chandler Harper, while Frank Moore was 4-under-par in his 4-and-3 victory over Harry Bassler. Chuck Congdon was a 2-and-1 winner over George Schneiter, while Jim Turnesa returned to the quarter-finals

The finals had the lightest competitor in the field, Hogan at 135 pounds, squaring off with one of the heaviest competitors, Oliver at 220 pounds. Hogan got the best of the match, defeating Oliver, 6 and 4.

with an easy 5-and-4 victory over Dick Shoemaker.

In the quarter-finals, Byron Nelson was eliminated with a bogey at the final hole as Ed Oliver nipped him 1-up. The match, which saw Nelson 2-up with just five holes left, seesawed back to Oliver's favor when he squared the match with a birdie at the 32nd hole, a par at the 33rd and went 1-up with a birdie at the 34th hole. Nelson came back, however, with a birdie 2 at the 35th hole to square the match. He lost the final hole when he hooked his second shot under some trees and was unable to make a 25-footer that would have sent the match into overtime. This was the last match that Nelson would ever play in the PGA Championship. His record would stand at 37 wins in 45 matches.

The other three matches were routs, as Ben Hogan beat Frank Moore, 5 and 4, Harold McSpaden demoralized Chuck Congdon, 5 and 3, and Jimmy Demaret demolished Jim Turnesa, 6 and 5.

In the semifinals, Ben Hogan defeated Jimmy Demaret, 10 and 8, the second biggest margin of victory in PGA history. The front side saw Demaret jump out to a 2-up lead after the third hole. Hogan birdied three of the next four holes and finished the front side 3-up, before picking up three

more holes on the back side to finish the morning round 6-up. Hogan didn't let up in the afternoon round, shooting 31 and closing out the match with a birdie at the 27th hole. Hogan was 11-under-par for the day. The other match saw Ed Oliver shoot 9-under-par to defeat Harold McSpaden, 6 and 5. Oliver was 2-up after the morning round, then won the 23rd hole with a birdie 4 and halved the next five holes. On the 28th hole, Oliver made a 45-foot chip shot for an eagle 3 to win the hole before going 5-up with a birdie 3 on the 29th hole. The match ended at the 31st hole when McSpaden put his tee shot into the woods after Oliver hit his second shot close. McSpaden conceded the match.

The finals had the lightest competitor in the field, Hogan at 135 pounds, squaring off with one of the heaviest competitors, Oliver at 220 pounds. Hogan got the best of the match, defeating Oliver, 6 and 4. In the morning round Hogan had troubles with his putting and found himself 3-down, but with a 30 on the front nine of the afternoon round he took control of the match, going into the final nine 2-up. Hogan wrapped things up when he won four of the final five holes, making birdies on three of them, concluding the match on the 32nd hole with a birdie 3. For the day, Hogan was 7-under-par, playing the afternoon 14 holes in 8-under-par.

ROAD TO THE FINALS

Ben Hogan beat	Round	Ed Oliver beat
Charles Weisner, 2 and 1	1st Round	Clay Gaddie, 2-up
Bill Heinlein, 4 and 3	2nd Round	Dick Metz, 3 and 1
Art Bell, 5 and 4	3rd Round	Chandler Harper, 5 and 4
Frank Moore, 5 and 4	Quarter-finals	Byron Nelson, 1-up
Jimmy Demaret, 10 and 9	Semifinals	Harold McSpaden, 6 and 5

1945

Qualifying for Match Play: A 36-hole qualifying round to get into match play was conducted the Monday and Tuesday before the Championship. Defending PGA Champion Bob Hamilton was exempt and 31 players qualified. Byron Nelson and Johnny Revolta were the low qualifiers with 138. A score of 147 qualified for match play, with 10 players at 148 having to play for eight spots. Some notable players who didn't make it to match play included Tony Manero (150), Craig Wood (150), Jimmy Thomson (154) and Joe Turnesa (157). All matches played were 36 holes.

Early Matches: In the first round, Byron Nelson rolled to a 4-and-3 win over Gene Sarazen in a match that saw Sarazen take a 2-up lead after the second hole. But Nelson fought back to square the match after five and was never behind again. It was an important match for Nelson, who was suffering from a pulled back muscle and was receiving osteopathic treatments the nights before he played. While Nelson rolled on, the defending PGA Champion was eliminated, as Jack Grout played 33 holes in 1-under-par to beat Bob Hamilton, 4 and 3. In other upsets, Dutch Harrison was on the short end of a 1-up defeat to Sterling Johnson in a match that should have gone to extra holes. Harrison couldn't get it up and down at the final hole to force the overtime. Harold McSpaden also was on the losing side of a 5-and-4 upset to

Champion: Byron Nelson, Toledo, Ohio*		
Site:	Moraine CC, Dayton, Ohio	
Date:	July 9-15	Purse: $14,700

ROAD TO THE FINALS

Byron Nelson beat	Round	Sam Byrd beat
Gene Sarazen, 4 and 3	1st Round	Augie Nordone, 4 and 3
Mike Turnesa, 1-up	2nd Round	Johnny Revolta, 2 and 1
Denny Shute, 3 and 2	Quarter-finals	Vic Ghezzi, 7 and 6
Claude Harmon, 5 and 4	Semifinals	Clarence Doser, 7 and 6

long-shot Clarence Doser. The most lopsided matches of the day saw Johnny Revolta beat Frank Kringle, 10 and 9, while Jim Turnesa shackled Byron Harcke, 9 and 7, and Vic Ghezzi only lost one hole as he routed Ed Dudley, 7 and 6.

In the second round, Byron Nelson had a tough time beating Mike Turnesa, 1-up, in a match that saw Nelson 2-down with just four holes left. Nelson responded to the challenge by making birdies at the 33rd and 34th holes to square the match. He made eagle at the next hole and halved the final hole. It was a heart-breaking loss for Turnesa, who was 7-under-par, but Nelson was 10-under-par with rounds of 68 and 66. After the match, Turnesa told reporters that, "I don't think anyone can beat him." The upset of the day saw former New York Yankee star Sam Byrd beat former PGA Champion Johnny Revolta, 2 and 1. In another duel, Ky Laffoon nipped by Jack Grout, 1-up. The most lopsided contests saw Claude

Harmon rout Jim Turnesa, 8 and 7, while Ralph Hutchison triumph over Sterling Johnson, 6 and 5.

In the quarter-finals, one match pitted former PGA Champions, as Byron Nelson beat Denny Shute, 3 and 2. The victory put Nelson in the semifinals for the sixth time in a row. The other three matches saw different winners than the predictors envisioned, with Clarence Doser upsetting Ky Laffoon, 2 and 1, and Claude Harmon, who was 4-under for the day, beating Ralph Hutchison, 4 and 3. In the final match, Byrd overpowered Vic Ghezzi, 7 and 6, in a contest that saw Byrd take the lead on the second hole without ever looking back.

The semifinals turned into routs, as Byrd clobbered Doser, 7 and 6, while Nelson easily beat Harmon, 5 and 4. The night after Nelson's victory, he told his wife, Louise, that the pressure of the year was starting to get to him. He was in the midst of his streak of 11 straight wins and had already won seven in a row. Louise revealed years later that Nelson was disappointed that nobody had beaten him.

The finals matched Byron Nelson, in his fifth appearance in the finals, against Sam Byrd, who was making just his third PGA appearance. After the morning 18, when Byrd finished the round with four straight birdies and a 2-up lead, Nelson was demoralized. When Byrd opened with par, par, birdie to gain another hole, it looked impossible. But Nelson didn't give up and won the 22nd, 25th and 26th holes to square the match. He went in front with a birdie at the 29th hole, which turned out to be the first of four straight holes that he won, and wrapped up the match. Nelson was 2-under for the day and a total of 37-under-par for the 204 holes, he played in the Championship. Byrd played well in the finals, as he was also 2-under-par for the day. But over the course of the 197 holes he played in the Championship, he was only 14-under-par.

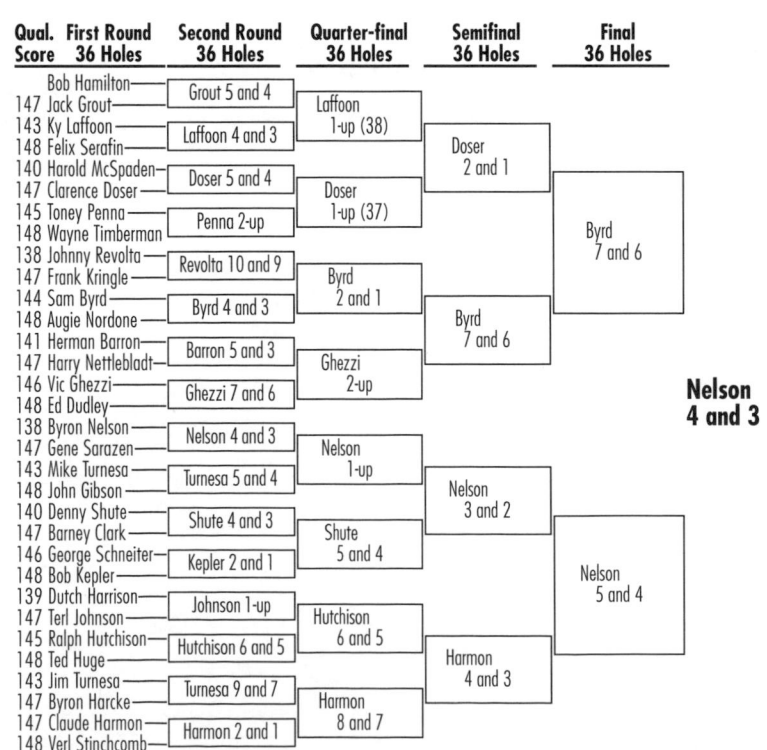

Qual. Score	First Round 36 Holes	Second Round 36 Holes	Quarter-final 36 Holes	Semifinal 36 Holes	Final 36 Holes
	Bob Hamilton				
147	Jack Grout	Grout 5 and 4			
143	Ky Laffoon		Laffoon 1-up (38)		
148	Felix Serafin	Laffoon 4 and 3			
140	Harold McSpaden			Doser 2 and 1	
147	Clarence Doser	Doser 5 and 4			
145	Toney Penna		Doser 1-up (37)		
148	Wayne Timberman	Penna 2-up			
138	Johnny Revolta				Byrd 7 and 6
147	Frank Kringle	Revolta 10 and 9			
144	Sam Byrd		Byrd 2 and 1		
148	Augie Nordone	Byrd 4 and 3			
141	Herman Barron			Byrd 7 and 6	
147	Harry Nettlebladt	Barron 5 and 3			
146	Vic Ghezzi		Ghezzi 2-up		
148	Ed Dudley	Ghezzi 7 and 6			
138	Byron Nelson				
147	Gene Sarazen	Nelson 4 and 3			
143	Mike Turnesa		Nelson 1-up		
148	John Gibson	Turnesa 5 and 4			
140	Denny Shute			Nelson 3 and 2	
147	Barney Clark	Shute 4 and 3			
146	George Schneiter		Shute 5 and 4		
148	Bob Kepler	Kepler 2 and 1			
139	Dutch Harrison				Nelson 5 and 4
147	Terl Johnson	Johnson 1-up			
145	Ralph Hutchison		Hutchison 6 and 5		
148	Ted Huge	Hutchison 6 and 5			
143	Jim Turnesa			Harmon 4 and 3	
147	Byron Harcke	Turnesa 9 and 7			
147	Claude Harmon		Harmon 8 and 7		
148	Verl Stinchcomb	Harmon 2 and 1			

Nelson 4 and 3

1944

Qualifying for Match Play: A 36-hole qualifying round to get into match play was conducted the Monday and Tuesday before the Championship. Byron Nelson was low qualifier with 138. A score of 149 qualified for match play and two players at 149 had a playoff for one spot. Some notable players who didn't make it to match play included Harry Cooper (150) and Olin Dutra (152). Sam Snead was unable to defend his title because he was in a naval hospital in San Diego, undergoing treatment for a recurrence of an old back injury. All matches played at 36 holes.

Early Matches: In the first round all of the favorites won, with only two of the 16 matches making it to the final hole. Both of those matches required extra holes, as Tony Manero took 38 holes to beat Clayton Aleridge and Arthur Bell won a 37-hole match against Joe Zarhardt.

In the second round, Byron Nelson breezed to a 7-and-6 victory over Mark Fry, and Harold McSpaden had the most impressive victory as he trashed Fred Annon, 8 and 7. The big upset of the day saw Willie Goggin beat Manero, 4 and 3, in a contest that was dominated from the very start by Goggin. In other matches, Art Bell upset Craig Wood, 2-and-1, and Sam Byrd was beaten by Charles Congdon by the same 2 and 1 margin.

In the quarter-finals, the match of the day had Bob Hamilton upsetting the leading money-winner, McSpaden, 2 and 1. In a remarkable day of golf, Hamilton played more shots from the woods than on the fairways and played the 35 holes in 5-under-par. McSpaden also played well shooting 3-under-par for a losing cause. Nelson also had a good day of golf as he shot 66 in the morning round and went on to beat Willie Goggin, 4 and 3, while Ed Dudley fell victim to Charles Congdon in a 6-and-5 rout.

In the semifinals, Nelson clobbered Charles Congdon, 8 and 7, in a match that saw Congdon only win two holes over the 29-hole contest. Nelson shot 67 in the morning round and went to lunch 7-up. For the day, Nelson was 5-under-par and 26-under for the 160 holes he played in the Championship. In the other match, Bob Hamilton beat George Schneiter, 1-up. The contest was square after the 32nd hole, with Hamilton making an eagle 3 to forge ahead. Both made pars the rest of the way, with Schneiter almost squaring the match on the final hole with a close chip shot that would have sent the match into overtime.

In the finals, the 28-year-old Hamilton was a 10-1 long-shot but still went on to

Champion:	Bob Hamilton, Evansville, Ind.*	
Site:	Manito G & CC, Spokane, Wash.	
Date:	Aug. 14-20	Purse: $14,500

ROAD TO THE FINALS

Bob Hamilton beat	Round	Byron Nelson beat
Gene Kunes, 6 and 5	1st Round	Mike Demassey, 5 and 4
Harry Bassler, 6 and 5	2nd Round	Mark Fry, 7 and 6
Harold McSpaden, 2 and 1	Quarter-finals	Willie Goggin, 4 and 3
George Schneiter, 1-up	Semifinals	Charles Congdon, 8 and 7

upset Nelson, 1-up. After the morning round the match was even as both players shot 70. In the afternoon round, Hamilton won the 19th hole with a birdie 3 and it was the first time in the Championship that Nelson had been down to an opponent. Nelson would never get the lead again. Hamilton got to 2-up when Nelson bogeyed the 29th hole, but Nelson birdied the next hole. Another birdie by Nelson at the 33rd hole squared the match, but Hamilton came back to win the next hole with a birdie. They halved the 35th hole with par and went to the final hole, which was a drive-able 300 yards. Nelson's drive landed in heavy grass short of the green, while Hamilton was just short of the green. Nelson pitched to within 10 feet of the hole, while Hamilton almost chipped it in, his ball stopping 20 inches away. Even though it was an

exciting moment for Hamilton, Nelson forced him to earn the Championship by making his birdie putt. Hamilton quickly got over his putt and stroked it in, telling reporters afterwards, "I putted the last one as quick as possible. It was less than two feet, but the longer I looked, the longer the distance seemed." Nelson was dejected afterwards, telling reporters, "four times in the Championship finals and I've won only one; maybe I should give up the game." Nelson had rightful cause to give up, as he shot 140, 4-under-par, and lost to Hamilton, who was 5-under-par. Over the course of the seven-day Championship, Nelson was 30-under-par for the 196 holes he played.

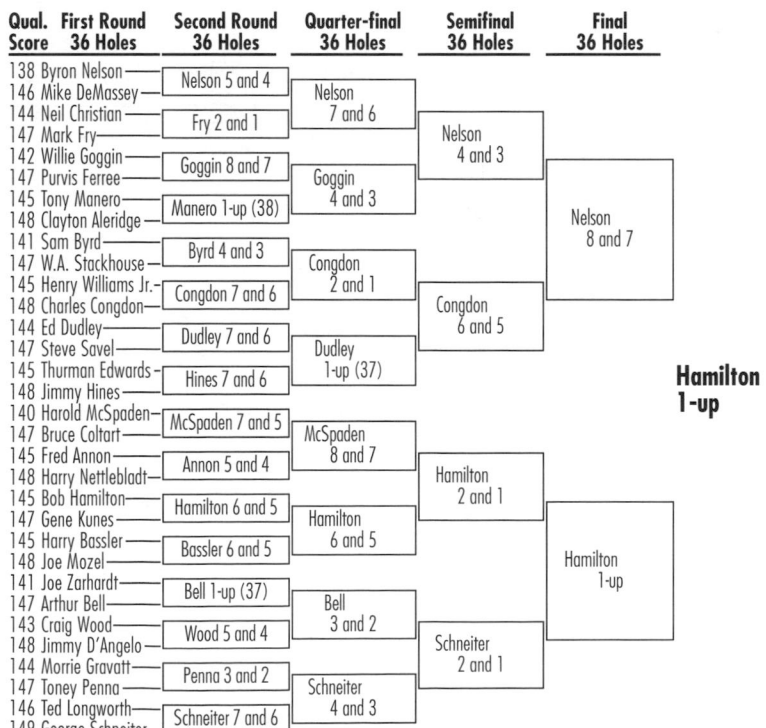

Qual. Score	First Round 36 Holes	Second Round 36 Holes	Quarter-final 36 Holes	Semifinal 36 Holes	Final 36 Holes
138 Byron Nelson	Nelson 5 and 4		Nelson 7 and 6		
146 Mike DeMassey				Nelson 4 and 3	
144 Neil Christian	Fry 2 and 1				
147 Mark Fry					
142 Willie Goggin	Goggin 8 and 7		Goggin 4 and 3		Nelson 8 and 7
147 Purvis Ferree					
145 Tony Manero	Manero 1-up (38)				
148 Clayton Aleridge					
141 Sam Byrd	Byrd 4 and 3		Congdon 2 and 1		
147 W.A. Stackhouse				Congdon 6 and 5	
145 Henry Williams Jr.	Congdon 7 and 6				
148 Charles Congdon					
144 Ed Dudley	Dudley 7 and 6		Dudley 1-up (37)		
147 Steve Savel					
145 Thurman Edwards	Hines 7 and 6				
148 Jimmy Hines					Hamilton 1-up
140 Harold McSpaden	McSpaden 7 and 5		McSpaden 8 and 7		
147 Bruce Coltart					
145 Fred Annon	Annon 5 and 4			Hamilton 2 and 1	
148 Harry Nettlebladt					
145 Bob Hamilton	Hamilton 6 and 5		Hamilton 6 and 5		
147 Gene Kunes					
145 Harry Bassler	Bassler 6 and 5				Hamilton 1-up
148 Joe Mozel					
141 Joe Zarhardt	Bell 1-up (37)		Bell 3 and 2		
147 Arthur Bell					
143 Craig Wood	Wood 5 and 4			Schneiter 2 and 1	
148 Jimmy D'Angelo					
144 Morrie Gravatt	Penna 3 and 2		Schneiter 4 and 3		
147 Toney Penna					
146 Ted Longworth	Schneiter 7 and 6				
149 George Schneiter					

1943   No Championship played due to World War II

1942

Qualifying for Match Play: A 36-hole qualifying round to get into match play was conducted the Tuesday before the Championship. Defending PGA Champion Vic Ghezzi was exempt and 31 players qualified. Harry Cooper was low qualifier with 138. A score of 146 qualified for match play, and eight players at 147 had a playoff for five spots. Notable players who lost in the playoff were Paul Runyan and Al Watrous. Others missing a berth included Gene Sarazen (149), Horton Smith (150), Johnny Revolta (150), Ralph Guldahl (150), Leo Diegel (155) and Walter Hagen (156). All matches at 36 holes.

Early Matches: The first round saw only one upset, as defending PGA Champion Vic Ghezzi was eliminated by Jimmy Demaret, 4 and 3.

In the second round, Ben Hogan and Sam Snead again had easy matches, beating Ky Laffoon and Willie Goggin by 9-and-8 margins. Craig Wood also had an easy time in defeating Leland Gibson, 7 and 6, while Jimmy Demaret beat Tommy Harmon, 3 and 2. In some tough matches, Byron Nelson had a surprising contest with Joe Kirkwood, needing 35 holes for a 2-and-1 victory. Another good match had Jim Turnesa nipping Harold McSpaden, 1-up, as Turnesa tied the match with a birdie on the 34th hole and made a four-foot par putt on the next hole just to get a half. Turnesa went on to win the match at the final hole when McSpaden hit his tee shot in the woods and couldn't match Turnesa's par.

In the quarter-finals, the match of the day was Byron Nelson beating Harry Cooper, 1-up, on the 39th hole. After 27 holes the match was even, but when Cooper birdied the 28th, 29th and 30th, and Nelson bogeyed the 31st hole, Cooper was in the driver's seat with a 3-up lead with just five holes left to play. Things looked hopeless for Nelson when they halved the 32nd hole, but, with birdies at the 33rd and 34th holes he got two back. Cooper made a great putt at the 35th hole for a par and a half, but Nelson played a great second shot on the final hole and made a birdie to complete the comeback and send the match into extra holes. They halved the first two holes, but when Cooper bogeyed the 39th hole, it spelled doom as Nelson made par and won the match. The upset of the day belonged to Jim Turnesa, who eliminated Ben Hogan, 2 and 1, in a match that saw Hogan take the lead only once.

In the semifinals, Byron Nelson was forced into overtime again, but this time he was on the losing side as he drove it out of

bounds on the 37th hole to lose to Jim Turnesa.

The finals turned into a pride match with Corporal Jim Turnesa of the Army taking on Sam Snead, who was to report to the Navy the day after his match. As the match was about to start, no one gave him much of a chance to beat Snead, even though Turnesa had beaten the best golfers in the world to get there. Turnesa needed little aid during the morning round, as he toured the course in 70 and went to lunch 3-up. In the afternoon, Turnesa maintained his lead until a bogey on the 24th cost him a hole. By

the end of the front nine, Snead had the match square, and before they teed off the 28th hole, he saw some changes in Turnesa that gave him confidence. "I saw that he took more waggles than usual on his drive, and then he hooked it. I knew he was getting tight, and then I had more confidence in myself." Snead was right in his assessment as Turnesa bogeyed the hole to go 1-down, then made another bogey at the 30th hole to go 2-down. The match ended on the 35th hole when Snead holed a spectacular 60-foot chip shot for a birdie to secure the 2-and-1 victory and his first major championship.

Champion: Sam Snead, Hot Springs, Va.*	
Site: Seaview CC, Atlantic City, N.J.	
Date: May 23-31	**Par:** 36-35—71
Purse: $7,550	

ROAD TO THE FINALS

Sam Snead beat	Round	Jim Turnesa beat
Sam Byrd, 7 and 6	1st Round	Dutch Harrison, 6 and 5
Willie Goggin, 9 and 8	2nd Round	Harold McSpaden, 1-up
Ed Dudley, 1-up	Quarter-finals	Ben Hogan, 2 and 1
Jimmy Demaret, 3 and 2	Semifinals	Byron Nelson, 1-up (37)

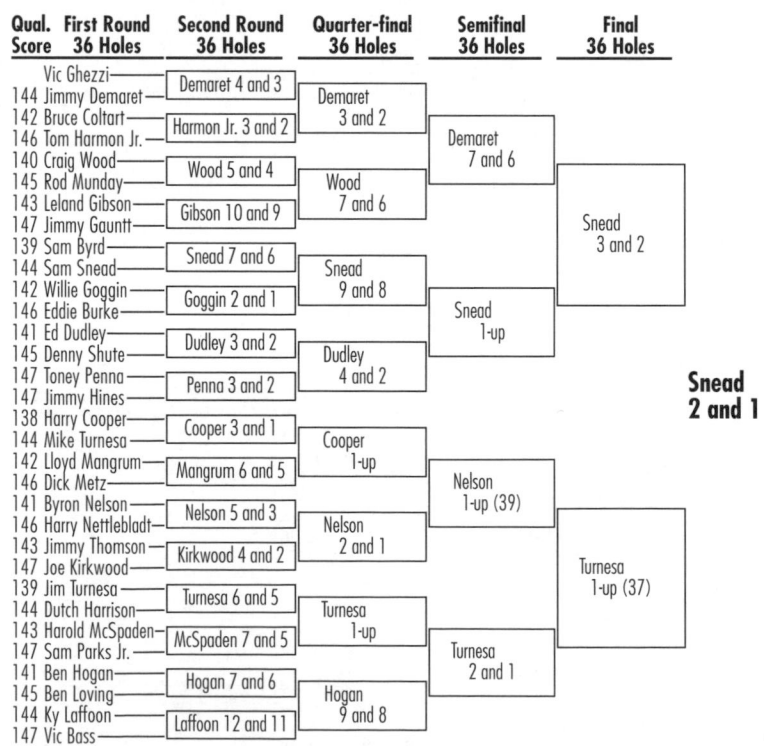

Qual. Score	First Round 36 Holes	Second Round 36 Holes	Quarter-final 36 Holes	Semifinal 36 Holes	Final 36 Holes
	Vic Ghezzi	Demaret 4 and 3	Demaret 3 and 2		
144	Jimmy Demaret				
142	Bruce Coltart	Harmon Jr. 3 and 2		Demaret 7 and 6	
146	Tom Harmon Jr.				
140	Craig Wood	Wood 5 and 4	Wood 7 and 6		
145	Rod Munday				
143	Leland Gibson	Gibson 10 and 9			Snead 3 and 2
147	Jimmy Gauntt				
139	Sam Byrd	Snead 7 and 6	Snead 9 and 8		
144	Sam Snead				
142	Willie Goggin	Goggin 2 and 1		Snead 1-up	
146	Eddie Burke				
141	Ed Dudley	Dudley 3 and 2	Dudley 4 and 2		
145	Denny Shute				
147	Toney Penna	Penna 3 and 2			Snead 2 and 1
147	Jimmy Hines				
138	Harry Cooper	Cooper 3 and 1	Cooper 1-up		
144	Mike Turnesa				
142	Lloyd Mangrum	Mangrum 6 and 5		Nelson 1-up (39)	
146	Dick Metz				
141	Byron Nelson	Nelson 5 and 3	Nelson 2 and 1		
146	Harry Nettlebladt				
143	Jimmy Thomson	Kirkwood 4 and 2			Turnesa 1-up (37)
147	Joe Kirkwood				
139	Jim Turnesa	Turnesa 6 and 5	Turnesa 1-up		
144	Dutch Harrison				
143	Harold McSpaden	McSpaden 7 and 5		Turnesa 2 and 1	
147	Sam Parks Jr.				
141	Ben Hogan	Hogan 7 and 6	Hogan 9 and 8		
145	Ben Loving				
144	Ky Laffoon	Laffoon 12 and 11			
147	Vic Bass				

1941

Qualifying for Match Play: A 36-hole qualifying round to get into match play was conducted the Monday and Tuesday before the Championship. Defending PGA Champion Byron Nelson was exempt and 63 qualified for the field. Sam Snead was low qualifier with 138. A score of 153 qualified for match play, with three players at 154 having a playoff for two spots.

Champion: Vic Ghezzi, Deal, N.J. *	
Site: Cherry Hills Club, Denver, Colo.	
Date: July 7-13	**Par:** 35-36—71
Purse: $10,600	

The first and second rounds were 18 holes each, played in one day, with the remaining matches being played at 36 holes.

Early Matches: In the first day of play,

numerous upsets saw some of the past champions getting eliminated early, with Paul Runyan losing a tough match on the last hole to Horton Smith, 1-up. Henry Picard was beaten by Phil Greenwaldt, 5 and 4. Jimmy Demaret was eliminated by Jack Nicklaus' future teacher, Jack Grout, 4 and 3, and Dutch Harrison bowed to Jim Foulis, 2 and 1. Another veteran campaigner who had an early departure was Jimmy Thomson, who took Harold McSpaden to the 21st hole before McSpaden won 1-up. Another favorite who had a tough 1-up win in overtime was Sam Snead, who beat Earl Martin on the 23rd hole. Snead needed some breaks to win. He was 2-down with just two holes left when he stymied Martin to win the 17th hole and then made a four-footer on the last hole, making a bogey and sending the match into overtime. Snead brought an end to the match with a birdie on the fifth extra hole. Favorite Ben Hogan won his two matches by routing Frank Walsh, 5 and 4, and then having a tough time beating Bud Oakley, 2-up.

The third round was absent of any real upsets as most of the favorites advanced to the quarter-finals. If there was a match that could have been classified as an upset, it was Jimmy Hines' 6-and-4 rout of McSpaden. Sarazen had the rout of the day, clobbering Bruce Coltart, 9 and 7, covering the 29 holes in 2-under-par. Byron Nelson had an easy 4-and-3 victory over Ralph Guldahl, who before the day was 7-under-par for his 63 holes. Hogan had a tough match against Horton Smith, but still won, 2 and 1. The match was square after 26 holes, then Hogan staged a rally where he won four consecutive holes and closed the match with a par at the 35th hole. The last three matches went to the final hole with the favorites needing to win the final holes to advance. Vic Ghezzi beat Jack Grout, 1-up, with the key to the match coming on the

Bracket

Qual. Score	First Round 18 Holes	Second Round 18 Holes	Third Round 18 Holes	Quarter-final 36 Holes	Semifinal 36 Holes	Final 36 Holes
	Byron Nelson	Nelson 1-up	Nelson 1-up			
147	Bunny Torpey			Nelson 4 and 3		
143	William Heinlein	Heinlein 1-up				
152	Frank Kringle					
141	Ralph Guldahl	Guldahl 7 and 6	Guldahl 2 and 1		Nelson 2 and 1	
149	Jim Fogerty					
145	Gene Kunes	Kunes 2-up				
153	Frank Commisso					
140	Ben Hogan	Hogan 5 and 3	Hogan 2-up	Hogan 2 and 1		
148	Frank Walsh					
144	Bud Oakley	Oakley 1-up				
152	Earl Fry					
142	Horton Smith	Smith 1-up	Smith 3 and 2			Nelson 2 aup
150	Paul Runyan					
146	Frank Champ	Stonehouse 3 and 2				
153	Ralph Stonehouse					
139	Dutch Harrison	Foulis 2 and 1	Shute 1-up			
148	Jim Foulis					
144	Denny Shute	Shute 1-up		Shute 5 and 3		
152	Ray Mangrum					
141	Jack Ryan	Ryan 3 and 2	Ott by default		Sarazen 7 and 6	
150	Bob Hunsick Jr.					
146	Leonard Ott	Ott 3 and 2				
153	Dave O'Connell					
140	George Fazio	Fazio 1-up	Coltart 1-up (19)			
149	Charles Malloy					
145	Bruce Coltart	Coltart 3 and 2		Sarazen 9 and 7		
153	Carl Beljan					
143	Gene Sarazen	Sarazen 5 and 4	Sarazen 1-up (19)			Ghezzi 1-up (38)
151	Joe Burch					
146	William Francis	Penna 5 and 4				
154	Toney Penna					
138	Sam Snead	Snead 1-up (23)	Snead 7 and 6			
148	Earl Martin					
144	Henry Picard	Greenwaldt 5 and 4		Snead 1-up		
152	Phil Greenwaldt					
141	Harry Bassler	Bassler 4 and 3	Turnesa 4 and 2		Mangrum 6 and 4	
149	Rut Coffey					
146	Mike Turnesa	Turnesa 2 and 1				
153	Lee Kosten					
140	Henry Ransom	Fry 2 and 1	Fry 6 and 5			
148	Mark Fry					
145	Craig Wood	Wood 3 and 2		Mangrum 1-up		
152	C. Norsworthy					
142	Lloyd Mangrum	Mangrum 5 and 4	Mangrum 3 and 1			Ghezzi 1-up
150	Floyd Farley					
146	Charles Sheppard	Sheppard 2 and 1				
153	Leo Mallory					
140	Jimmy Demaret	Grout 4 and 3	Grout 1-up		Ghezzi 8 and 7	
148	Jack Grout					
144	Fay Coleman	Coleman 1-up		Ghezzi 1-up		
152	Joe Robinson					
142	Vic Ghezzi	Ghezzi 3 and 2	Ghezzi 1-up			
150	Joe Pezzullo					
146	Dick Metz	Nordone 4 and 2				
153	Augie Nordone					
141	Herman Keiser	Schneiter 4 and 2	McSpaden 3 and 2			
149	George Schneiter					
145	Harold McSpaden	McSpaden 1-up (21)		Hines 6 and 4		
153	Jimmy Thomson					
143	Ed Dudley	Dudley 2 and 1	Hines 3 and 2			
151	Buddy Poteet					
147	Al Nelson	Hines 1-up				
154	Jimmy Hines					

35th hole when Grout hit into the lake and conceded the hole. The 35th hole also played a pivotal role in Lloyd Mangrum's 1-up win over Mark Fry, as Mangrum birdied the hole to take a 1-up lead to the final hole. Sam Snead also pulled a big turnaround in his 1-up win over Mike Turnesa, as Snead was 3-down after the morning round. He shot a 1-under-par 70 in the afternoon and the match was square going into the final hole. Turnesa was not able to match Snead's par, which made Snead the winner.

The quarter-finals saw boyhood rivals Nelson and Hogan battle it out in a match

*O*n *the next hole, both Vic Ghezzi and Byron Nelson missed the green with their second shots and chipped up to within three feet. They were so close that even the referee couldn't determine who would putt first, so they flipped a coin. Nelson won the toss but missed his putt.*

that was decided on the final holes. In the morning round, Hogan shot a 66 to gain a 1-up lead, with Nelson squaring the match on the 26th hole. Hogan won the 29th hole with a birdie to go 1-up, and Nelson squared the match with his own birdie on the 34th hole. Nelson won the next hole when Hogan hit his third shot into the water and closed out the match at the final hole when he hit his second shot to within three feet and birdied the hole for his 2-up victory. Another great match had Ray Mangrum tumble Snead in a lopsided 6-and-4 win. Mangrum was 8-under-par in the 32-hole contest that saw him square with Snead after 25 holes. Mangrum won the match at the 32nd hole when he sank a 45-footer for a birdie 3. In the other matches, Vic Ghezzi had an easy time with Jimmy Hines, blowing past him, 8 and 7, while Sarazen advanced to the semifinals for a seventh time as he handed past champion Denny Shute a crushing 7-and-6 defeat.

In the semifinals, the match of the day was between Nelson and Sarazen. Lord Byron was only 12 years old when Sarazen won the first of his three PGA crowns. Even though Sarazen had the experience, Nelson proved that he was the superior

golfer, dealing Sarazen a 2-and-1 defeat. After the morning round, Sarazen had a 1-up lead as he shot 69, but after the 28th hole, Nelson had the lead for the first time in the match. Going into the 35th hole, Nelson had a 1-up lead. Sarazen ran his birdie putt five feet past, then missed that putt to lose the hole and the match. In the other match, Vic Ghezzi was able to hang on to beat Ray Mangrum 1-up, despite shooting a 40. Ghezzi had a 3-up lead going into the last nine holes, but Mangrum scraped away at the lead and caught Ghezzi with a birdie at the 35th hole. However, Mangrum caught a bad break on the final hole, and drove the ball 275 yards to the edge of the lake. He was forced to wade in the water and chip back into the fairway, while Ghezzi was just off the green with his second shot. Mangrum went on to make bogey and Ghezzi was able to get his chip within inches of the hole to win the match.

In the finals, Vic Ghezzi dethroned Nelson in an extra-hole match that had one of the most bizarre finishes ever. Ghezzi was 3-down after the 27th hole, but squared the match by winning the first three holes on the final nine. The match was square for the fourth time when Ghezzi made bogey at the par-5 35th hole. On the final hole, both missed the green with their second shots. Nelson pitched up to within 15 feet, while Ghezzi chipped his ball four feet away. When Nelson missed his putt, Ghezzi had a shot at ending the contest, but instead lost almost everything as he missed the match-winning putt. At the 37th hole, Ghezzi had another chance to win the match with a 10-footer for birdie, but missed. On the next hole, both missed the green with their second shots and chipped up to within three feet. They were so close that even the referee couldn't determine who would putt first, so they flipped a coin. Nelson won the toss but missed his putt. Ghezzi had another chance at victory, and he almost didn't take advantage, as the ball barely slithered in the side door for a 1-up victory.

ROAD TO THE FINALS		
Vic Ghezzi beat	**Round**	**Byron Nelson beat**
Joe Pezzullo, 3 and 2	1st Round	Bunny Torpey, 1-up
August Nordone, 1-up	2nd Round	William Heinlein, 1-up
Jack Grout, 1-up	3rd Round	Ralph Guldahl, 4 and 3
Jimmy Hines, 8 and 7	Quarter-finals	Ben Hogan, 2-up
Lloyd Mangrum, 1-up	Semifinals	Gene Sarazen, 2 and 1

1940

Qualifying for Match Play: A 36-hole qualifying round to get into match play was conducted the Sunday and Monday before the Championship. Dick Metz was the low qualifier with 140, and 64 players qualified for the field. A score of 153 qualified for match play, with seven players at 154 having a playoff for three spots. Notable players who didn't make it

Champion:	Byron Nelson, Toledo, Ohio*	
Site:	Hershey CC, Hershey Pa.	
Date:	Aug. 26 - Sept. 2	Par: 36-37—73
Purse:	$11,050	

to match play were Leo Diegel (155), Jim Barnes (157), Sam Parks Jr. (158) and Tom Creavy (158).

Qual. Score	First Round 18 Holes	Second Round 18 Holes	Third Round 18 Holes	Quarter-final 36 Holes	Semifinal 36 Holes	Final 36 Holes
142 Henry Picard		Picard 6 and 4				
153 Leonard Gallett			Picard 4 and 3			
153 Jimmy Thomson		Gerlak 1-up				
153 Alex Gerlak				Sarazen 1-up		
148 George Fazio		Mangrum 3 and 2				
151 Ray Mangrum			Sarazen 2 and 1			
148 Gene Sarazen		Sarazen 4 and 3				
151 Stan Staszowski					Snead 1-up	
151 Reggie Myles		Hill 1-up (21)				
148 Ray Hill			Hines 2 and 1			
148 Jimmy Hines		Hines 1-up (19)				
150 Eddie Burke				Snead 7 and 6		
154 Nelson Giddens		Snead 2 and 1				
147 Sam Snead			Snead 3 and 2			
151 Gene Marchi		Sheppard 4 and 3				
150 Charles Sheppard						Snead 5 and 4
148 John Gibson		Gibson 4 and 3				
149 Al Espinosa			Dudley 2 and 1			
145 Ed Dudley		Dudley 5 and 4				
154 Henry Bontempo				Runyan 4 and 3		
152 Alex Follmer		Watrous 5 and 4				
147 Al Watrous			Runyan 3 and 2			
149 Paul Runyan		Runyan 1-up				
153 Al Zimmerman					McSpaden 8 and 6	
152 Walter Hagen		Hagen 1-up				
153 Gil Sellers			Hagen 2 and 1			
146 Vic Ghezzi		Ghezzi 2 and 1				
152 George Smith				McSpaden 1-up		
141 Harold McSpaden		McSpaden 3 and 2				
150 Stan Parzick			McSpaden 2 and 1			
149 Herman Keiser		Keiser 5 and 3				
153 Harry Cooper						Nelson 1-up
148 Ky Laffoon		Laffoon 1-up (20)				
154 Joe Turnesa			Metz 3 and 2			
151 John Thoren		Metz 3 and 2				
140 Dick Metz				Nelson 2 and 1		
153 Dutch Harrison		Walsh 2 and 1				
147 Frank Walsh			Nelson 1-up (20)			
152 Dick Shoemaker		Nelson 4 and 3				
151 Byron Nelson					Nelson 6 and 5	
152 Arthur Clark		Clark 1-up				
148 Johnny Revolta			Clark 1-up			
149 Tom Harmon Jr.		Burke 3 and 2				
152 Billy Burke				Kirk 5 and 4		
148 Jimmy Demaret		Demaret 3 and 2				
152 Errie Ball			Kirk 2 and 1			
149 Eddie Kirk		Kirk 1-up (19)				
152 Rod Munday						Nelson 1-up
149 Toney Penna		Francis 1-up (20)				
152 Red Francis			Brosch 5 and 4			
150 Horton Smith		Brosch 3 and 2				
152 Al Brosch				Hogan 5 and 4		
145 Ben Hogan		Hogan 3 and 2				
152 Frank Champ			Hogan 5 and 4			
153 Leland Gibson		Nettlebladt 3 and 1				
152 Harry Nettlebladt					Guldahl 3 and 2	
146 John Kinder		Kinder 2 and 1				
153 Pat Tiso			Guldahl 6 and 5			
153 George Picard		Guldahl 3 and 2				
152 Ralph Guldahl				Guldahl 5 and 3		
153 Walter Romans		Wood 5 and 4				
152 Craig Wood			Foulis 1-up (19)			
153 Henry Kaiser		Foulis 2 and 1				
149 Jim Foulis						

Nelson 1-up

The first and second rounds were 18 holes each, played in one day, with the remaining matches being played at 36 holes.

Early Matches: Walter Hagen turned back the hands of time by winning his two matches. In the first round, Hagen was forced to play the last five holes in 1-under to beat Gil Sellers, 1-up. In the afternoon, after losing the first two holes, he beat Vic Ghezzi, 2 and 1. The Haig's victory against Ghezzi would be his 40th and last in the PGA Championship. While Hagen was winning his 40th all-time match, his arch-rival Gene Sarazen was winning his 42nd and 43rd all-time matches, beating Stan Stazowski, 4-and-3, and Ray Mangrum, 2 and 1. Defending PGA Champion Henry Picard crushed Leonard Gallet, 6 and 4, before cruising to a 4-and-3 victory over Alex Gerlak, who had upset Jimmy Thomson in the first round, 1-up. Another past champion, Paul Runyan, had a tough morning match with Al Zimmerman, beating him 1-up when he holed a lengthy birdie putt at the final hole. In the afternoon, Runyan fired a sub-par round against Al Watrous, triumphing, 3 and 2. Past PGA Champion Johnny Revolta was beaten by Arthur Clark, 1-up, in a hard fought first-round match. Clark then went on to defeat former U.S. Open Champion Billy Burke by the similiar score in the afternoon. In both matches, Clark gained an early lead and hung on. Horton Smith also was beaten, losing to Al Brosch, 3 and 2, while Craig Wood lost a second round match to Jim Foulis on the 19th hole. Jimmy Demaret also had a tough match as Eddie Kirk beat him, 2 and 1. Some of the favorites who advanced into the third round were Byron Nelson, who had an easy contest against Dick Shoemaker, winning, 4 and 3, before having a tough match against Frank Walsh. Nelson was 2-down after the 11th hole but fought back to send the match into over-time before beating Walsh on the 20th hole.

Sam Snead also had a tough first-round match, nipping Nelson Giddens, 2 and 1, then beating Charles Sheppard, 3 and 2, in the second round. Ben Hogan had an easier time triumphing over Frank Champ, 3 and 2, then handling Harry Nettlebladt, 5 and 4.

In the third round, Hagen bowed out for the last time as Harold McSpaden beat him, 1-up. In the other matches, Sarazen defeated Picard, 1-up, despite the fact that Picard finished with three birdies and forced Sarazen to make an eight-footer on the final green for a birdie. Another close match had

*T*he real drama came on the last three holes, as Snead had a 1-up lead on the 34th hole with Nelson two feet away for birdie. Snead almost ran in a 20-footer that would have tied the hole.

Nelson nipping Dick Metz, 2 and 1. Past PGA Champion Paul Runyan eliminated Ed Dudley, 4 and 3, while Ralph Guldahl beat Jim Foulis, 5 and 3. In easy matches, Ben Hogan beat Al Brosch, 5 and 4, and Sam Snead defeated Jimmy Hines, 7 and 6.

In the quarter-finals, the match of the day had Sarazen pitted against Snead, with Snead winning, 1-up. Snead was 3-down after the 28th hole, but won the 29th with a birdie, the 31st with a par and the 33rd with a par. When Snead made a birdie at the 34th hole to take a 1-up lead, it was the first time in the match that he had been up. The 35th and 36th holes were halved with pars. The Snead-Sarazen match was the only close contest, as McSpaden destroyed Paul Runyan, 8 and 6, and Nelson was an easy 6-and-5 winner over Eddie Kirk. Ralph Guldahl played a sensational match against Hogan, beating him, 3 and 2, even though Hogan was 5-under-par for the 34 holes.

The semifinal matches took two days because of rain, but they ended with Nelson beating Guldahl, 1-up, and Snead routing McSpaden, 5 and 4. In the match between Guldahl and Nelson, Guldahl was 1-down after the 34th hole and squared the match with a five-foot birdie putt on the 35th hole. On the final hole, Nelson was in trouble off the tee and was off the green in two, but Guldahl hit a poor second shot 30 feet away, and when Nelson chipped up to

within inches of the cup, Guldahl missed his putt and lost the match.

In the finals, the losers of the last two PGA Championships fought it out with Nelson edging Snead, 1-up. Nelson started early, taking a 2-up lead by shooting 71 in the morning round, but Snead fought back in the afternoon round, shooting 68. The real drama came on the last three holes, as Snead had a 1-up lead on the 34th hole with Nelson two feet away for birdie. Snead almost ran in a 20-footer that would have tied the hole. At the 35th hole, Nelson hit a superb wedge to within two feet, while Snead was six feet away. Snead missed his putt, and Nelson made his to go 1-up. At the final hole, a par-3, Nelson hit another splendid shot, this time with a 3-iron to just 10 feet away. Snead hit his shot just off the green. When Snead missed his shot, Nelson cozied his up to within inches for a tap-in.

ROAD TO THE FINALS

Byron Nelson beat	Round	Sam Snead beat
Dick Shoemaker, 4 and 3	1st Round	Nelson Giddens, 2 and 1
Frank Walsh, 1-up (20)	2nd Round	Charles Sheppard, 3 and 2
Dick Metz, 2 and 1	3rd Round	Jimmy Hines, 7 and 6
Eddie Kirk, 6 and 5	Quarter-finals	Gene Sarazen, 1-up
Ralph Guldahl, 1-up	Semifinals	Harold McSpaden, 5 and 4

1939

Qualifying for Match Play: A 36-hole qualifying round to get into match play was conducted the Sunday and Monday before the Championship. Ben Hogan, Dutch Harrison, Ky Laffoon and Emerick Kocsis were low qualifiers with 138, and 64 players qualified. A score of 147 qualified for match play, with 11 players at 148 having a playoff for five spots.

Champion:	Henry Picard, Hershey, Pa.*	
Site:	Pomonok CC, Flushing, N.Y.	
Date:	July 9-15	Purse: $10,600

Some notable players who didn't qualify were Ed Dudley (148), Sam Snead (149), Joe Turnesa (151), Jimmy Hines (151) and Tom Creavy (153).

Qual. Score	First Round 18 Holes	Second Round 18 Holes	Third Round 18 Holes	Quarter-final 36 Holes	Semifinal 36 Holes	Final 36 Holes
144 Paul Runyan	Runyan 3 and 1	Runyan 3 and 2	Runyan 3 and 2	Metz 2 and 1	Picard 1-up	
144 Mortie Dutra						
142 Fay Coleman	Champ 1-up					
148 Frank Champ						
143 Tony Joy	Espinosa 1-up (19)	Hogan 5 and 4				
143 Abe Espinosa						
138 Ben Hogan	Hogan 7 and 6					
148 Steve Zappe						
144 Jimmy Thomson	Barron 2-up	Burke 2 and 1	Metz 6 and 4			
142 Herman Barron						
142 Billy Burke	Burke 1-up					
143 Jim Foulis						
140 Dick Metz	Metz 7 and 6	Metz 1-up				
144 Pat Circelli						
140 Al Brosch	Brosch 1-up					
145 Reggie Myles						
138 Ky Laffoon	Laffoon 3 and 2	O'Connor 2-up	Munday 2-up	Picard 2 and 1		
144 Dick Shoemaker						
143 Tom O'Connor	O'Connor 7 and 5					
148 Al Morley						
140 Gene Sarazen	Ryan 1-up	Munday 2-up				
146 Jack Ryan						
148 Felix Serafin	Munday 1-up (21)					
146 Rod Munday						
140 Henry Picard	Picard 6 and 4	Picard 2-up	Picard 8 and 7			
146 Earl Martin						
142 Louis Chiapetta	Zarhardt 2-up					
147 Joe Zarhardt						
144 Harold McSpaden	Tucker 1-up	Watrous 5 and 3				
144 Ken Tucker						
140 Al Watrous	Watrous 1-up					
145 Tom Lo Presti						
138 Dutch Harrison	Harrison 3 and 2	Harrison 3 and 2	Harrison 10 and 9	Harrison 4 and 3	Nelson 9 and 8	
148 John Kinder						
147 Johnny Farrell	Farrell 1-up					
140 Charles Schneider						
142 Harry Cooper	Turnesa 2 and 1	Coltart 1-up (21)				
145 Mike Turnesa						
142 Bruce Coltart	Coltart 4 and 3					
147 Buddy Peteet						
145 Clarence Doser	Doser 3 and 1	Doser 2-up	Smith 4 and 2			
144 Rut Coffey						
141 Ralph Guldahl	Guldahl 4 and 3					
145 Clarence Owens						
139 Ray Mangrum	Mangrum 6 and 5	Smith 3 and 2				
143 Sam Parks Jr.						
141 Horton Smith	Smith 5 and 4					
143 Eddie Schultz						
138 Emerick Kocsis	Kocsis 1-up	Kocsis 3 and 1	Kocsis 3 and 2	Nelson 10 and 9		
143 John Gibson						
142 Vic Ghezzi	Ghezzi 3 and 2					
143 Joe Belfore						
143 Denny Shute	Shute 1-up	Shute 3 and 1				
144 Ted Luther						
145 Willie Goggin	Diegel 2 and 1					
145 Leo Diegel						
142 Joe Turnesa	Revolta 2 and 1	Revolta 3 and 2	Nelson 6 and 4			
142 Johnny Revolta						
144 Walter Hagen	Manero 1-up					
146 Tony Manero						
143 Byron Nelson	Nelson 4 and 2	Nelson 3 and 1				
147 Chuck Garringer						
143 Guy Paulsen	Francis 2 and 1					
147 William Francis						

Picard 1-up (37)

The first and second rounds were 18 holes each, played in one day, with the remaining matches being played at 36 holes.

Early Matches: The opening day saw Walter Hagen and Gene Sarazen, who between them had won eight of the 22 Championships, lose first-round matches. Tony Manero beat Hagen 1-up, and Jack Ryan beat Sarazen 1-up, with Sarazen hitting his tee shot out of bounds on the final hole. Herman Barron beat Jimmy Thomson, 2-up; Mike Turnesa eliminated Harry Cooper, 2 and 1; Ray Mangrum trounced 1935 U.S. Open Champion Sam Parks, 6 and 5; and Harold McSpaden was beaten 1-up by Ken Tucker. In the second round, Ky Laffoon bowed to Tom O'Connor, 2-up, and Emerick Kocsis beat Vic Ghezzi, 3 and 1. Defending PGA Champion Paul Runyan advanced to the third round, beating Mortie Dutra, 3 and 1, and Frank Champ, 3 and 2. Other favorites who advanced included Ben Hogan, who had an easy day defeating Stephen Zappe, 7 and 6, and Abe Espinosa, 5 and 4. Byron Nelson also had a relatively easy time beating Chuck Garringer, 4 and 2, and William Francis, 3 and 1. Henry Picard had an easy morning match, as he beat Earl Martin, 6 and 5, but had a tough match with Joe Searhardt in the afternoon. The contest was square going to the 16th, which Picard won with a bogey, the 17th was halved, and with Searhardt within easy birdie range at the final hole, Picard closed out the match by chipping in for birdie to win 2-up.

In the third round, Dutch Harrison reeled off the day's best round, beating Bruce Coltart, 10 and 9, in a match that saw Harrison play the 27 holes in just 99 strokes. Horton Smith also played well, but he didn't have as easy a match, as he beat Clarence Doser, 4 and 2.

In the early going, Smith looked like he was in trouble when he was 5-down after eight holes, but a back side 32 produced one of the greatest about-faces ever when Smith won seven holes in a row and finished the morning round 2-up. The match ended on the 34th green, and despite Doser being 5-under for the day, he lost to Smith, who was 9-under par. Henry Picard was 10-under for the day in a 29-hole match, beating Al Watrous, 8 and 7. Runyan had the toughest match of the day, beating Hogan, 2 and 1. Not once in the morning round was either one more than 1-up, as they finished the first 18 even. Runyan jumped out to an early 2-up lead by winning the 20th and 21st holes, but Hogan got one back at the 26th hole. They halved the next eight holes, and when Hogan made bogey at the 35th

---

*T**he semifinals provided another sensational day of golf for Nelson, as he steamrolled Harrison, 10 and 9. In Nelson's 156 holes of golf, he was 28-under-par.*

---

hole, Runyan won the match. The upset of the day was the loss of past champion Denny Shute to Emerick Kocsis, 3 and 2, in a match that saw Shute miss several short putts. Another past PGA Champion, Johnny Revolta, lost to Byron Nelson, 6 and 4. Nelson took advantage of Revolta's poor play in the morning round and built up a substantial lead of 7-up that was too much for Revolta to overcome.

The quarter-finals saw the departure of the defending PGA Champion, as Dick Metz beat Runyan, 2 and 1. Metz shot 66 in the morning round to take a 4-up lead to lunch, but in the afternoon, Runyan whittled away at the lead, and, with a birdie at the 32nd hole, the match was square. All his hard work was in vain, however, as Metz birdied the next hole to go 1-up and then, on the 34th green, laid a perfect stymie which Runyan couldn't maneuver around to go 2-up. When both players parred the 35th hole, Runyan was eliminated. Another match that ended on the 35th hole saw Henry Picard beat Rod Munday, 2 and 1. Munday was up most of the day and was 1-up after 27 holes. When Munday bogeyed the 28th hole, the match was square. Picard won the 31st with a par and made a tough putt at the next hole for a half to protect his 1-up lead. Munday drew even at the 33rd with a birdie, and lost it on the next hole when he bogeyed. The match ended at

the 35th when Munday buried his tee shot on the par-3 hole and was unable to match Picard's par. In the remaining matches, Dutch Harrison had an easy time in his match with Horton Smith, winning, 4 and 3, while Nelson matched Harrison's 99 in 27 holes to demolish Emerick Kocsis, 10 and 9.

The semifinals provided another sensational day of golf for Nelson, as he steamrolled Harrison, 10 and 9. In Nelson's 156 holes of golf, he was 28-under-par. In the other match, Picard had a tough time with Dick Metz, and the match was settled on the final green, with Picard getting a 1-up victory.

The finals were decided in overtime for the fourth time, as Picard won a 1-up decision over Nelson with birdies on the 36th and 37th holes. Picard led most of the way until Nelson birdied the 29th hole to square the match. When Nelson birdied the 32nd hole, it was the first time in the match that he was in the lead. It was a dramatic birdie for Nelson, who almost drove the 330-yard green. Picard stuck his second shot just seven feet away. Nelson chipped up, hitting the flag and bouncing back just three feet away. Picard putted first and missed, but laid Nelson a perfect stymie, which he successfully jumped into the hole. They halved the 33rd hole with birdies and on the next hole, Picard saved the match by making a 25-footer for par to prevent him from going 2-down. They halved the 35th hole with pars and then, at the final hole, which was only 300 yards long, both players were just short of the green with their drives. Nelson hit a poor second shot to within 12 feet, and Picard hit his four feet away. Nelson missed his putt, and Picard made his to send the match into overtime. At the 37th hole, Picard hit his drive under a movie truck, while Nelson was down the middle. Nelson was first from the fairway and hit a great shot, just five feet away. After Picard got relief for the obstruction, he knocked his second shot seven feet away. Again, Picard found himself in a do-or-die situation, and after all the cameras stopped, Picard stepped up and made the putt. Nelson missed his attempt.

ROAD TO THE FINALS		
Henry Picard beat	**Round**	**Byron Nelson beat**
Earl Martin, 6 and 4	1st Round	Chuck Garringer, 4 and 2
Joseph Zarhardt, 2-up	2nd Round	William Francis, 3 and 1
Al Waltrous, 8 and 7	3rd Round	Johnny Revolta, 6 and 4
Rod Munday, 2 and 1	Quarter-finals	Emerick Kocsis, 10 and 9
Dick Metz, 1-up	Semifinals	Dutch Harrison, 9 and 8

1938

Qualifying for Match Play: A 36-hole qualifying round for match play was conducted the Sunday and Monday before the Championship. Defending PGA Champion Denny Shute was exempt and 63 players qualified. Frank Moore was low qualifier with 136. A score of 150 qualified for match play, with seven players at 151 having a playoff for four spots.

Champion: Paul Runyan, White Plains, N.Y.*	
Site:	Shawnee CC, Shawnee-on-Delaware, Pa.
Date: July 10-16	Par: 37-35—72
Purse: $10,000	

Notable players who didn't make it to match play were Mortie Dutra (153) and Willie Hunter (154).

Bracket

Qual. Score	First Round 18 Holes	Second Round 18 Holes	Third Round 18 Holes	Quarter-final 36 Holes	Semifinal 36 Holes	Final 36 Holes
Denny Shute	Shute 3 and 2	Shute 7 and 6	Hines 2 and 1	Hines 2 and 1	Snead 1-up	Runyan 8 and 7
151 Clyde Usina						
145 John Thoren	Thoren 4 and 2					
145 Leo Mallory						
143 Frank Walsh	Walsh 2 and 1	Hines 2 and 1				
148 Tony Butler						
143 Jimmy Hines	Hines 3 and 1					
148 Alex Watson						
140 Byron Nelson	Nelson 5 and 4	Nelson 1-up (20)	Nelson 11 and 10			
151 Clarence Yockey						
144 Alvin Krueger	Krueger 2 and 1					
146 Ian Robertson						
141 Ed Dudley	Dudley 3 and 2	Bassler 4 and 3				
150 Johnny Farrell						
144 Harry Bassler	Bassler 2-up					
146 Alex Gerlak						
138 Marvin Stahl	Stahl 4 and 3	Stahl 6 and 5	Foulis 6 and 5	Snead 8 and 7		
151 Clarence Clark						
145 Gene Marchi	Whitehead 1-up (19)					
145 George Whitehead						
141 Jimmy Thomson	Thomson 5 and 4	Foulis 1-up				
150 Guy Paulsen						
144 Jim Foulis	Foulis 1-up					
147 Willie Goggin						
139 Sam Snead	Snead 4 and 3	Snead 4 and 3	Snead 4 and 3			
150 Frank Champ						
144 Terl Johnson	Johnson 2 and 1					
146 Henry Ransom						
141 Harry Cooper	Serafin 4 and 3	Serafin 3 and 2				
150 Felix Serafin						
144 Ky Laffoon	Laffoon 1-up					
147 Alex Follmer						
136 Frank Moore	Moore 1-up (19)	Burke 1-up (19)	Smith 3 and 2	Runyan 4 and 3	Runyan 4 and 3	
151 Errie Ball						
145 Willie Klein	Burke 2 and 1					
145 Billy Burke						
143 Horton Smith	Smith 2 and 1	Smith 2 and 1				
148 Mike DeMassey						
143 Francis Gallett	Diegel 2 and 1					
147 Leo Diegel						
140 Ray Mangrum	Mangrum 3 and 2	Mangrum 1-up (20)	Runyan 1-up (37)			
150 Ted Luther						
144 Sam Parks Jr.	McSpaden 3 and 2					
146 Harold McSpaden						
141 Paul Runyan	Runyan 5 and 4	Runyan 3 and 2				
150 Levi Lynch						
144 Tony Manero	Manero 5 and 4					
147 Joe Belfore						
138 Harry Nettlebladt	Nettlebladt 4 and 3	Sarazen 6 and 5	Sarazen 1-up (38)	Picard 3 and 2		
151 John Kinder						
145 Gene Sarazen	Sarazen 4 and 3					
145 Leo Walper						
142 Jimmy Demaret	Demaret 5 and 4	Demaret 2-up				
149 Frank Rodio						
143 Johnny Revolta	Revolta 4 and 3					
147 Wiffy Cox						
140 Henry Picard	Picard 3 and 2	Picard 3 and 2	Picard 4 and 3			
150 Andrew Gibson						
144 Leo Fraser	Shave 4 and 3					
146 Bob Shave						
141 Dick Metz	Metz 4 and 3	Metz 1-up				
150 Dick Renagan						
144 Ralph Guldahl	Guldahl 4 and 2					
147 John Malutic						

The first and second rounds were 18 holes each, played in one day, with the remaining matches being played at 36 holes.

Early Matches: In the first day of play, Felix Serafin, a 32-year-old from the coal fields of nearby Scranton, Pa., grabbed the headlines as he upset both Harry Cooper in the first round, 4 and 3, and Ky Laffoon in the second round, 3 and 2. Other upsets saw the departures of past PGA Champions Johnny Revolta and Leo Diegel. Both upsets occurred in the second round, with Jimmy Demaret winning a tough match against Revolta, 2-up. Horton Smith, with a two, three 3s and only one five on his card, easily defeated Leo Diegel, 4 and 3. The 1939 runner-up, Harold McSpaden, also lost in the second round as Ray Mangrum took him 20 holes. After both players shot a 33 on the back side to send the match into overtime, both halved the 19th hole with birdies. Mangrum birdied the 20th hole to win the match, 1-up. Defending PGA Champion Denny Shute had an easy time in his two matches, defeating Clyde Usina, 3 and 2, and John Thoren, 7 and 6. Gene Sarazen also had an easy time in his two matches, beating Leo Walper, 4 and 3, then beating Harry Nettlebladt on the 13th hole, 6 and 5. Tony Manero had an easy first round match, beating Joe Belfore, 5 and 4, but lost his second round match to Paul Runyan, 3 and 2. Byron Nelson easily beat Clarence Yockey, 5 and 4, but in the second round, had to shoot 33 on the back side to square his match with Alvin Krueger. Nelson won the match on the 20th hole, when Krueger hit his tee shot out of bounds. In another overtime match, Billy Burke beat Frank Moore with a 15-foot birdie on the 19th hole.

In the third round, Shute's attempt to win his third straight PGA crown was halted when Jimmy Hines eliminated him, 2-and-1. The match was square after the morning round, but Shute shot a 38 on the front side of the afternoon round to fall 2-down to Hines. With a birdie and a par, Shute was able to square the match again. However, a dead stymie on the 30th hole that Shute tried unsuccessfully to jump was the turning point, giving Hines an edge which he maintained and finally built up to a 2-and-1 victory.

Nelson routed Harry Bassler, 11 and 10, in perhaps the most sensational day of golf in PGA history. Nelson was 8-under-par in his 26 holes. He had a 64 in the morn-

---

The semifinals featured one of the best matches in PGA history, with Snead beating Hines, 1-up. It took a finish of four consecutive 3s on Snead's part to win, and if the contest had been decided by stroke play, Hines, who was 8-under for the day, would have defeated Snead by one stroke.

---

ing round in which he won eight of the first nine holes. He went to lunch after winning 12 holes and halving the rest. In the afternoon, he made eight consecutive pars, and Bassler actually was able to win two holes with birdies. In another rout, Jim Foulis steamrolled over Marvin Stahl, 6 and 5, and Serafin, the first-day hero who upset Cooper and Laffoon, was given a dose of reality when Sam Snead was 7-under for the day to win, 4-and-3. Henry Picard advanced to the quarter-finals with his 4-and-3 victory over Dick Metz, and faced Gene Sarazen, who, despite playing poorly, still had beaten Jimmy Demaret, 1-up, in a match that went 38 holes. Another extra-hole match saw Ray Mangrum miss an 18-inch putt on the 37th green, which enabled Paul Runyan to win the match.

In the quarter-finals, Sarazen had a tough time in his match against Henry Picard. Sarazen finished the morning round 1-up, but Picard quickly squared the match at the 19th hole with a birdie. At the 20th hole, Sarazen missed a four-foot birdie that would have restored his lead, and his game became ragged. Sarazen lost the 21st hole when he couldn't get out of a bunker and was forced to pick up. Then Sarazen got a disappointing half at the par-3, 23rd hole

when he laid Picard a dead stymie, which Picard jumped over and made to halve the hole. Sarazen lost the next hole, missing a three-footer to go 2-down. When Picard drove his tee shot out of bounds at the 27th, but still won the hole, it was just a matter of time before Sarazen would fall. Sarazen gave it a valiant try on the back side, but Picard won the contest on the 34th hole. Another surprising upset had Jimmy Hines beating Nelson, 2 and 1. Hines won the last four holes of the morning round to go 4-up, but Nelson squared the match after the 29th hole. The contest stayed that way until Hines made an 18-footer on the 34th hole to go 1-up, then won the match on the 35th hole with a stymie that forced Nelson into a bogey. In other matches, Sam Snead rolled past Jim Foulis, 8 and 7, and Paul Runyan was a 4-and-3 winner over Horton Smith.

The semifinals featured one of the best matches in PGA history, with Snead beating Hines, 1-up. It took a finish of four consecutive 3s on Snead's part to win, and if the contest had been decided by stroke play, Hines, who was 8-under for the day, would have defeated Snead by one stroke. In the 147 holes of match play, Snead was 21-under-par. In the other match, Paul Runyan was 6-under in 33 holes and easily beat Henry Picard, 4 and 3.

In the finals, Paul Runyan beat Sam Snead, 8 and 7, to win the PGA crown for the second time. Up to this point, it was the most decisive victory in the finals. Runyan's masterful short game produced a 67 in the morning, good for a 5-up lead. In the afternoon, the momentum continued. He made the turn in 35, with a 7-up advantage, then won the 28th hole, closing out the match with a half on the 29th. Runyan was 24-under-par for the 196 holes he played and in his last 70 holes only made one bogey.

ROAD TO THE FINALS

Paul Runyan beat	Round	Sam Snead beat
Levi Lynch, 5 and 4	1st Round	Frank Champ, 4 and 3
Tony Manero, 3 and 2	2nd Round	Terl Johnson, 4 and 3
Ray Mangrum, 1-up (37)	3rd Round	Felix Serafin, 4 and 3
Horton Smith, 4 and 3	Quarter-finals	Jim Foulis, 8 and 7
Henry Picard, 4 and 3	Semifinals	Jimmy Hines, 1-up

1937

Qualifying for Match Play: A 36-hole qualifying round for match play was conducted the Monday and Tuesday before the Championship. Defending PGA Champion Denny Shute was exempt and 63 players qualified. Byron Nelson was low qualifier with 139. A score of 156 qualified for match play, and 10 players at 157 had a playoff for three spots. The only notable player who didn't make it to match play was 1931 PGA Champion Tom Creavy, who withdrew after a first-round 79.

Champion: Denny Shute, W. Newton, Mass.*	
Site:	Pittsburgh Field Club, Aspinwall, Pa.
Date: May 26-30	**Purse:** $9,200

The first and second rounds were 18 holes each, played in one day, with the remaining matches being played at 36 holes.

Early Matches: In the first day of play, five former PGA Champions went down in defeat, with the only survivors being the defender, Shute, and Paul Runyan. In the second round, Gene Sarazen, who won his first round match against Eddie Schultz, 3 and 2, was eliminated by Jim Foulis on the final green when he left a putt that would have sent the match into overtime. Johnny Revolta also was a loser in the second round, as Harry Cooper beat him, 1-up. Both Cooper and Revolta, who had easy first-round matches, beating Ben Richter and Sal DiBuono, 3 and 2, were tied after the 13th hole, with Revolta winning the 14th with a bogey. The next two holes were halved with pars and Cooper squared the match with a birdie at 17. On the final hole, Revolta hit his second shot over the green, and when he couldn't get it down in two, Cooper won the match, 1-up, with his par. Another great comeback occurred in the second round in the match between Sam Snead and Alvin Krueger. Snead, who was 4-down with just seven holes left, won six of the seven holes, capping it off with a six-foot birdie putt on the final hole to win 2-up. The second round also featured Denny Shute beating Olin Dutra, 3 and 2. To get there Shute defeated Joe Turnesa, 2 and 1, in the first round, even though he was 2-down at the turn, while Dutra beat Clarence Doser, 3 and 2.

In the third round, 1936 runner-up Jimmy Thomson found his long-hitting onslaught of no use as Ky Laffoon beat him, 4 and 3. Thomson was 2-up in the morning round, but a front side 42 in the afternoon turned the match around, and when Laffoon captured the 30th hole with a birdie 4, Thomson was 1-down. He lost the next three holes as Laffoon made two birdies

Bracket

Qual. Score	First Round 18 Holes	Second Round 18 Holes	Third Round 18 Holes	Quarter-final 36 Holes	Semifinal 36 Holes	Final 36 Holes
149 Denny Shute		Shute 2 and 1	Shute 3 and 2			
151 Joe Turnesa				Shute 3 and 2		
148 Olin Dutra		Dutra 3 and 2				
154 Clarence Doser					Shute 4 and 3	
145 Ed Dudley		Dudley 5 and 3	Dudley 4 and 3			
152 Herman Barron						
149 Bruce Coltart		Wilcox 2 and 1				
156 Pat Wilcox						
143 Paul Runyan		Runyan 4 and 3	Runyan 2 and 1			
151 Levi Lynch				Hines 2 and 1		
148 Willie Goggin		Goggin 6 and 4				
155 Sam Schneider						
147 Jimmy Hines		Hines 6 and 4	Hines 1-up			
153 Clarence Owens						
150 Al Espinosa		Espinosa 3 and 1				Shute 1-up
156 Clark Morse						
142 Harry Cooper		Cooper 4 and 3	Cooper 1-up			
151 Ben Richter				Cooper 5 and 4		
148 Sal DiBuono		Revolta 4 and 3				
154 Johnny Revolta					Manero 1-up	
147 Eddie Schultz		Sarazen 3 and 2	Foulis 1-up			
153 Gene Sarazen						
150 Jim Foulis		Foulis 5 and 4				
156 George Kerrigan						
145 Vic Ghezzi		Ghezzi 3 and 2	Ghezzi 1-up			
152 Mike Turnesa				Manero 3 and 1		
148 Jimmy Demaret		Parks Jr. 2 and 1				
156 Sam Parks Jr.						
147 Lloyd Gullickson		Manero 2 and 1	Manero 4 and 3			
153 Tony Manero						
151 Bud Oakley		Macfarlane 1-up				
157 Willie Macfarlane						Shute 1-up (37)
139 Byron Nelson		Nelson 2 and 1	Nelson 4 and 2			
151 Leo Diegel				Nelson 5 and 4		
148 Craig Wood		Wood 1-up				
154 Joe Belfore						
146 Neil Christian		Schneider 4 and 3	Farrell 1-up			
152 Charles Schneider						
149 George Schneiter		Farrell 2-up				
156 Johnny Farrell					Laffoon 2-up	
143 Ky Laffoon		Laffoon 5 and 4	Laffoon 2 and 1			
152 John Shimkonis				Laffoon 4 and 3		
148 Billy Burke		Burke 5 and 4				
155 Steve Zappe						
147 Jimmy Thomson		Thomson 3 and 1	Thomson 2 and 1			
153 Dan Galgano						
151 Ralph Guldahl		Guldahl 6 and 4				
157 John Kinder						McSpaden 2 and 1
143 Harold McSpaden		McSpaden 3 and 2	McSpaden 1-up (20)			
151 Clarence Clark				McSpaden 3 and 2		
148 Ted Longworth		Torpey 3 and 2				
154 Bunny Torpey						
147 Sam Snead		Snead 4 and 3	Snead 2-up			
153 Jack Sabol					McSpaden 1-up (39)	
150 Alvin Kreuger		Kreuger 3 and 2				
156 George Diffenbaugh						
157 Sam Bernardi		Bernardi 1-up	Picard 1-up			
151 Tommy Armour				Picard 4 and 3		
148 Henry Picard		Picard 5 and 4				
154 Perry Del Vecchio						
149 Horton Smith		Smith 3 and 2	Smith 1-up (19)			
156 Harry Nettleblodt						
152 Al Watrous		Watrous 1-up (23)				
145 Bill Mehlhorn						

and a par to close out the match on the 33rd hole. Another upset saw Harold McSpaden defeating Sam Snead, 3 and 2. Thanks to a morning round 69, McSpaden went to lunch with a 1-up lead. On the 21st hole in the afternoon, Snead hit his second shot out of bounds, which cost him another hole, and they finished the front side with McSpaden holding a 2-up lead. Snead managed to get one of the holes back when McSpaden bogeyed the 32nd hole, but McSpaden's putter came to the rescue on the next two holes, where he holed a 25-

> *McSpaden took his stance over the putt, and when several cameras started grinding away, was forced to back away from the putt. He yelled at the offenders: "Please give me the chance I've been fighting for all week."*

footer on the 33rd hole and then a five-footer on the 34th hole to close out the match. Of the two past champions still in the field, Paul Runyan was eliminated by Jimmy Hines, 2 and 1, in a match that saw Runyan 2-up after the morning round. The other past champion, Denny Shute, had a more favorable outcome as he beat Ed Dudley, 3 and 2, in a match with the turning point coming on the 31st hole. Shute slammed in a 30-foot downhill putt for a birdie to win the hole.

In the quarter-finals, Denny Shute rolled to a 4-and-3 victory over Jimmy Hines in a match that Shute dominated from the 9th hole on. It was the only match of the day that didn't go to the final green. Ky Laffoon outlasted Nelson in a match that saw Nelson up most of the day. Nelson's downfall occurred on the back side of the afternoon round as he lost the 28th and 29th holes to go 1-down. Nelson squared the match for the last time at the 30th hole, but at the next hole, Laffoon canned a 15-foot putt for a birdie to go 1-up. He held on from there, dropping a 15-footer for a birdie at the final hole to win 2-up. Another match decided on the final green had Tony Manero coming from behind to defeat Harry Cooper, 1-up. Cooper had the match easily within his grasp, as he was 4-up after 27 holes, but made two bogeys and a double-bogey to lose the first three holes on the

back side. On the 32nd hole, Manero squared the match with a par and took a 1-up lead on the 35th hole with a 10-footer for a birdie. Manero emerged the winner when Cooper was unable to make a birdie at the final hole. The final match of the day was the most sensational, with McSpaden beating Henry Picard, 1-up, but it took 39 holes for an outcome. McSpaden had a 3-up lead after the 28th hole, but when Picard made birdies at the 29th and 30th holes, McSpaden's lead was reduced to 1. McSpaden got one back with a birdie at the 31st hole, but gave it back with a bogey on the 33rd hole. Picard squared the match with a 20-foot birdie putt on the 34th hole, and the 35th hole was halved with pars. On the final hole, Picard had a six-footer to win the match, but missed, sending the match into overtime. The 37th hole was halved with pars, and Picard had another six-footer to win the match at the 38th hole, but missed the putt. The match ended on the 39th hole when Picard couldn't make birdie to halve the hole and the match was over.

The semifinals were billed as the "battle of champions," as Shute, the reigning PGA titleholder, faced Tony Manero, U.S. Open Champion. In the match, Manero won the first hole, but lost the next and was never up again. Manero managed to hang on, never permitting Shute to open more than a 2-up lead, until the end when Shute won the 33rd and 34th holes to win the match, 3 and 2. The other match between McSpaden and Ky Laffoon had McSpaden take a 3-up lead after the first 9 holes, but Laffoon, hanging tight after that, didn't lose any ground as they went into the final nine with McSpaden still just 2-up. Laffoon squared the match with birdies on the 28th and 30th holes, but with a bogey on the 33rd hole he fell 1-down. They halved the 34th holes with pars and with two holes left, McSpaden was 1-up. On the 35th hole, McSpaden hit his second shot to within three feet of the hole to win, 2 and 1.

In the finals, Shute's prospect of becoming the first repeater since Leo Diegel in 1929 looked gloomy, as McSpaden jumped out to a 3-up lead after the first five holes. But Shute found his putting stroke, one-putting nine of the next 13 holes, squaring the match after the front side and then turning things around to finish the morning round 3-up. In the early stages of the afternoon round, McSpaden was 2-under-par and won four holes to go to the back

ROAD TO THE FINALS		
Denny Shute beat	**Round**	**Harold McSpaden beat**
Joe Turnesa, 2 and 1	1st Round	Clarence Clark, 3 and 2
Olin Dutra, 3 and 2	2nd Round	Bunny Torpey, 1-up (20)
Ed Dudley, 3 and 2	3rd Round	Sam Snead, 3 and 2
Jimmy Hines, 4 and 3	Quarter-finals	Henry Picard, 1-up (39)
Tony Manero, 1-up	Semifinals	Ky Laffoon, 2 and 1

side with a 1-up lead. When McSpaden bogeyed the 28th hole, the match was square. When Shute made bogeys at the 31st and 32nd holes, McSpaden was 2-up again. Both made pars at the 33rd hole, but McSpaden bunkered his tee shot on the par-3 34th hole. He wasn't able to get it up and down for par and was only 1-up. Then came the hole that spelled disaster for McSpaden. Both hit perfect tee shots, but when McSpaden badly pulled his second shot under a tree, he wasn't able to extract the ball and lost the hole to Shute's bogey. Going into the last hole, the match was square again for the sixth time in the day, and McSpaden got a lucky break when his tee shot hit a spectator, bouncing into the fairway instead of going into the heavy rough. McSpaden then hit a great second shot to within four feet of the hole in what looked like a sure birdie and victory, since Shute was 50 feet away with his second shot. Shute hit his first putt about three feet short of the hole, giving McSpaden a chance to win the match. He took his stance over the putt, and when several cameras started grinding away, was forced to back away from the putt. He yelled at the offenders: "Please give me the chance I've been fighting for all week." When quiet was restored among the cameras and the 7,000 spectators who were gathering around, McSpaden went back to the business of making the putt, but missed it. Shute made his putt to send the match into overtime for only the third time in its 20-year history. The first hole had played havoc on Shute all week. But this time, the hole proved to be McSpaden's nemesis, as he missed a 10-footer for par and Shute made his four-footer to win, 1-up, and become not only the fifth repeat champion, but the last to accomplish this feat.

1936

Qualifying for Match Play: A 36-hole qualifying round to get into match play was conducted the Monday and Tuesday before the Championship. Defending PGA Champion Johnny Revolta was exempt and 63 players qualified. Fay Coleman was low qualifier with 143. A score of 155 qualified for match play, and eight players at 156 competed in a playoff for seven spots. Notable players who didn't make it to match play were Walter Hagen (157), Leo Diegel (157), Sam Parks Jr. (157), Byron Nelson (158) and Jim Turnesa (159). The first and sec-

Champion:	Denny Shute, Boston, Mass.*
Site:	Pinehurst CC, Pinehurst, N.C.
Date: Nov. 17-22	**Par:** 36-36—72
Purse: $9,200	

Bracket

Qual. Score / First Round 18 Holes	Second Round 18 Holes	Third Round 18 Holes	Quarter-final 36 Holes	Semifinal 36 Holes	Final 36 Holes
145 Johnny Revolta — Revolta 6 and 5	McSpaden 1-up (19)	McSpaden 4 and 3	Thomson 1-up	Thomson 5 and 4	Shute 3 and 2
155 Marshall Crischton					
150 Harold McSpaden — McSpaden 6 and 4					
154 Joe Belfore					
147 Leo Walper — Walper 5 and 3	Walper 2 and 1				
155 Walter Kozak					
152 Clarence Hackney — Hackney 1-up (21)					
156 Orm Beaupre					
152 Willie Klein — Klein 2 and 1	Thomson 3 and 2	Thomson 4 and 2			
153 Ralph Beach					
150 Jimmy Thomson — Thomson 5 and 4					
153 Rod Munday					
152 Alvin Krueger — Krueger 2 and 1	Picard 5 and 4				
156 Eddie Schultz					
147 Henry Picard — Picard 2-up					
155 Leo Mallory					
148 Harry Cooper — Cooper 2 and 1	Cooper 3 and 2	Wood 2 and 1	Wood 5 and 4		
154 Ted Luther					
155 Clarence Doser — Doser 2 and 1					
151 Paul Runyan					
147 Craig Wood — Wood 2 and 1	Wood 1-up				
156 John Kinder					
155 Frank Walsh — Walsh 5 and 4					
152 Ian Robertson					
149 Errie Ball — Ball 1-up (19)	Cruickshank 2 and 1	Manero 4 and 2			
153 Ralph Stonehouse					
151 Bobby Cruickshank — Cruickshank 4 and 3					
154 Matt Kowal					
152 Mortie Dutra — Dutra 4 and 3	Manero 6 and 5				
152 Tommy Armour					
145 Tony Manero — Manero 1-up (23)					
152 Jimmy Demaret					
151 Horton Smith — Smith 1-up	Smith 6 and 5	Smith 2 and 1	Shute 3 and 2	Shute 1-up	
154 Jack Forrester					
156 Jack Patroni — Patroni 1-up					
145 Gene Sarazen					
152 Willie Goggin — Goggin 3 and 2	Goggin 5 and 4				
155 Louis Chiapetta					
149 Les Madison — Madison 3 and 2					
156 Radar Jewett					
152 Al Zimmerman — Zimmerman 1-up	Shute 3 and 2	Shute 2 and 1			
154 Bill Jelliffe					
149 Alex Gerlak — Shute 5 and 4					
154 Denny Shute					
146 Billy Burke — Burke 1-up	Burke 4 and 3				
155 Francis Gallett					
154 Ky Laffoon — Laffoon 4 and 3					
151 Walter Pursey					
154 Bill Mehlhorn — Mehlhorn 6 and 5	Mehlhorn 1-up (23)	Mehlhorn 6 and 4	Mehlhorn 4 and 2		
147 Neil Christian					
151 Dick Metz — Metz 2-up					
155 Les Bolstad					
147 Ed Dudley — Dudley 3 and 2	Dudley 2 and 1				
155 Herman Barron					
152 Tom LoPresti — LoPresti 5 and 4					
155 Clarence Yockey					
150 Jimmy Hines — Hines 2-up	Hines 2 and 1	Hines 4 and 3			
153 Ted Turner					
146 Ray Mangrum — Mangrum 2 and 1					
156 Abe Espinosa					
152 Vic Ghezzi — Ghezzi 5 and 4	Ghezzi 1-up				
153 Mike Turnesa					
143 Fay Coleman — Coleman 1-up					
156 Ben Richter					

Shute 3 and 2

ond rounds were 18 holes played in one day, with the remaining matches being played at 36 holes.

Early Matches: In first day play, all former PGA Champions in the field were defeated as Gene Sarazen, Tommy Armour and Paul Runyan lost first-round matches. Defending PGA Champion Johnny Revolta was eliminated in the second round. In first round matches Jack Patroni triumphed over Sarazen on the 18th green by sinking an 8-foot par putt to halve the hole and preserve his 1-up lead. Sensational recoveries and putting were the secrets of Patroni's victory as he one-putted seven of the first nine holes in the match. In the match between Tommy Armour and Mortie Dutra, brother of the former PGA and U.S. Open Champion, Dutra had a 1-up lead after the first nine holes and took the first three holes on the back side to coast to his 4-and-3 victory. Paul Runyan fell to Clarence Doser, who fired a 1-under-par 35 on the front side to take a 3-up lead. The best match of the first round was between Tony Manero and Jimmy Demaret. A Manero bogey at 13 put him back to 1-down, and despite making bogey at the next, he won the hole when Demaret took four strokes to get down from the edge of the green for a double-bogey. Going into the final hole, Manero was still 1-down but sank a 40-footer for a birdie 3 to square the match. They halved the first three extra holes, and Manero got lucky on the 22nd hole when Demaret missed a two-foot putt which could have won the match. The match ended on the next hole when Manero made a birdie. Vic Ghezzi beat the medalist, Fay Coleman, 1-up. But Coleman made a gallant run as he was 4-down with just six holes left to play and won 13, 15 and 16 to carry the match to the final hole where his par wasn't good enough to catch Ghezzi. In another match, Jack Patroni, who had beaten Gene Sarazen earlier in the day, fell prey to Horton Smith in an embarrassing 6-and-5 loss.

In the third round, none of the eight matches made it to the final green while all of the favorites won. One near upset ultimately saw Smith beat Willie Goggin, 2 and 1, but after the morning round Goggin was 5-up. By playing the afternoon round 2-under-par, Smith was able to overtake Goggin and best him on the 35th hole. Tony Manero was a winner over Bobby Cruickshank, 4 and 3, and even though he shot 72

The semifinals were won by Thomson and Shute, but it took major turnarounds on both players' parts to achieve their victories.

in the morning round and was 5-up, Cruickshank rallied in the afternoon. He took four of the first five holes before Manero birdied the 24th and 26th holes to crush Cruickshank's rally. In the match that saw Craig Wood beat Harry Cooper, 2 and 1, the contest was all even after the morning round. In the afternoon, Wood went 2-up at the turn, but Cooper made a 28-foot birdie putt at the 28th hole to get within 1. Cooper missed a two-footer to lose the 33rd hole to go 2-down, and the 34th hole was halved with birdies. When they halved the 35th hole with pars, the match was over. Long-driver Jimmy Thomson also advanced to the quarter-finals by conquering Henry Picard, 4 and 2. In that match, Thomson shot 40 on the first nine holes, while Picard shot 37, somehow keeping the match square. When Thomson shot 35 on the back side he went to lunch with a 3-up lead. On the front side of the afternoon round, Thomson picked up another hole with a 34, and closed out the match at the 34th hole with a birdie.

In the quarter-finals, favorite Tony Manero was eliminated, 5 and 4, by Craig Wood. Wood won four of the last six holes on the front side to go into the final nine with a 3-up lead. Manero won the 30th and 31st holes and the match with a par at the 32nd hole. The match between Denny Shute and Horton Smith had been hyped as the match of the day, but it turned into the dull match of the day as Shute won, 3 and 2. The match wasn't as close as the score indicated as Shute finished the morning round 6-up. He was still 6-up going into the

final nine. In the afternoon, Smith found his game, but it was too late. He was 2-under-par on the front nine and didn't pick up any holes. On the back side he started to pick at Shute's lead by taking the 29th, 30th and 32nd holes. With four holes left, he was 3-down. When both players made par at the 33rd and birdies at the 34th the match ended, even though Smith was 5-under in the afternoon round. The only match that went the distance was the contest between Thomson and McSpaden, which Thomson won 1-up. The match was even after the morning round, and in the afternoon, Thomson ran off four birdies in a row and made the turn 4-up. When McSpaden bogeyed the 29th hole to fall to 5-down, the battle seemed finished. But a birdie 3 on the 30th hole by McSpaden put him back to 4-down. When Thomson missed a two-footer at the next hole it seemed like he had an outside chance. McSpaden managed to get a half at the 32nd hole when Thomson left a partial stymie and was running out of holes with another half at the 33rd hole. So with three holes left, McSpaden was dormie, but he didn't give up. He won the 34th hole with a birdie 4 and took the 35th when Thomson made bogey. At the final hole, both hit great shots to the green and when Thomson missed his birdie winning putt, McSpaden had a chance to send the match into overtime. But McSpaden's putt missed and Thomson, who had dodged the giant bullet, advanced to the semis. The last player to advance was Bill Mehlhorn, who despite having a tough time in the early going with Jimmy Hines, finally won, 4 and 2.

The semifinals were won by Thomson and Shute, but it took major turnarounds on both players' parts to achieve their victories. Thomson beat Craig Wood, 5 and 4, but after the first six holes a Thomson victory seemed out of the question. Wood put on a brilliant exhibition of golf as he birdied five of the six holes and had a 4-up lead over Thomson. But Wood developed a chink in his armor, hitting his second shot fat at the 7th, which led to a bogey and a lost hole. He pushed his second shot at the 8th and a bogey lost him another hole. His 4-hole lead was cut in half, and although he took the 9th hole with a par, Wood's early-hole play was in shambles and he had 27 holes left to play. On the back side of the morning round Wood was 4-over-par, and even though Thomson was 2-over-par, Wood went to lunch just 1-up. On the front side of the afternoon round Wood played the first six holes in 1-over-par, and in con-

trast to his play earlier in the day, lost four of those holes as Thomson played them in 4-under-par. Even though Wood won the 27th with a par, he went to the final nine 3-down. When Thomson played the first six holes in par figures, the match concluded on the 33rd hole. In the other match, between Shute and Mehlhorn, Shute was 3-up after the morning round, but ran into a sensational burst from Mehlhorn on the front nine of the afternoon round. Mehlhorn won the 19th hole with a par and then birdied three holes in succession to win those three holes. When they finished the front nine, Mehlhorn held a one-hole lead and added the 29th when Shute made bogey. Mehlhorn gave that back with a 3-putt bogey at the 31st hole, but got it back at the next hole when Shute missed a five-footer for par. Things looked grim for Shute, as he was 2-down with four holes left, but when Mehlhorn missed two four-footers at the 33rd and 34th, the match was square. At the 35th hole, Shute had a short putt for par to win the hole and missed it. He took advantage of another Mehlhorn bogey at the final hole with a match-winning par.

In the finals, Shute played David to Thomson's Goliath. Outdriven by as much as 60 yards on many holes, Shute used his irons and his putter to turn back Thomson, 3 and 2. In the morning round, Thomson shot 77 to Shute's 74, but Shute only had a 1-up lead. After the front side of the afternoon round, Shute still maintained his 1-up lead, and started to pull away with a 30-foot birdie putt at the 29th hole. Despite a 2-up lead, Shute struggled with every aspect of his game except his putting. On the 31st hole, Shute hit a poor drive in the waste area and scuffed his next shot short of the green. Thomson hit his second shot on the green. Shute pitched up 20 feet away and after Thomson safely secured his par, Shute made his putt for a half. The next two holes were halved with pars, and Shute closed out the match on the 34th hole when he hit a spectacular second shot, three feet away on the par-5 hole. When Thomson missed his putt for birdie, Shute knocked his putt in for eagle, a 3-and-2 victory and the Championship.

ROAD TO THE FINALS		
Denny Shute beat	Round	Jimmy Thomson beat
Alex Gerlak, 5 and 4	1st Round	Rod Munday, 5 and 4
Al Zimmerman, 3 and 2	2nd Round	Willie Klein, 3 and 2
Billy Burke, 2 and 1	3rd Round	Henry Picard, 4 and 2
Horton Smith, 3 and 2	Quarter-finals	Harold McSpaden, 1-up
Bill Mehlhorn, 1-up	Semifinals	Craig Wood, 4 and 3

1935

Qualifying for Match Play: A 36-hole qualifying round was conducted the Thursday before the Championship. Defending PGA Champion Paul Runyan was exempt and 63 players qualified. Walter Hagen was low qualifier with 139. A score of 153 qualified for match play and 10 players tied at 154 competed in a playoff for three spots. Notable players who didn't make it to match play were Johnny Farrell (154 lost in playoff), Jack Burke (156) and Leo Diegel (157).

The first and second rounds were 18 holes, with the remaining matches played at 36 holes.

Champion:	Johnny Revolta, Milwaukee, Wis.*
Site:	Twin Hills CC, Oklahoma City, Okla.
Date:	Oct. 18-23 Purse: $7,820

Early Matches: In the first round, medalist Walter Hagen was defeated by Johnny Revolta, 1-up, in a match that went to the bitter end. Hagen was 3-down after the 7th hole, only to come back and take two holes to make the turn 1-down. Revolta went 2-up on the 12th, only to see Hagen win the next hole. At the 14th, Hagen missed a four-footer that would have given him the hole, while Revolta was able to get up and down from greenside bunkers at 15 and 16. At 18, Hagen had a chance to tie the match after Revolta made bogey, but Hagen missed his par putt. In other matches, defending PGA Champion Paul Runyan had an easy time in his 5-and-3 victory over Louis Chiapetta. Gene Sarazen eliminated George Christ, 4 and 3, while Tommy Armour was taken to the 18th hole to beat Willie Klein, 1-up. Another match that went to the final hole featured the U.S. Open Champion Sam Parks Jr. and Harry Cooper, with Parks winning 1-up. Another U.S. Open Champion, Billy Burke, had a different result, as he lost 2-down to Vic Ghezzi.

In the second round, Sarazen was upset by Alvin Krueger, 2 and 1. Sarazen was 2-down on the 17th hole and laid what many thought was a perfect stymie. Krueger took out his wedge and pitched his ball over Sarazen's ball into the cup for a half and the match. Runyan had an easy match against Mortie Dutra as he won, 3 and 2, while former Champion Tommy Armour advanced with a 3-and-2 victory over Charles Schneider. Ed Dudley was 1-under-par for the 17 holes it took to beat Dick Metz, 3 and 1, while Horton Smith shot a 76, and still beat Ray Mangrum, who shot 77, 1-up. In the only extra hole match of the day, Ky Laffoon defeated Eddie Loos on the 21st hole when Loos was unable to match Laffoon's par.

In the third round, Runyan was even

Bracket

Qual. First Round	Second Round	Third Round	Quarter-final	Semifinal	Final
Score 18 Holes	18 Holes	18 Holes	36 Holes	36 Holes	36 Holes

Paul Runyan — Runyan 5 and 3 — Runyan 3 and 2 — Runyan 9 and 8
145 Louis Chiapetta
146 Mortie Dutra — Dutra 6 and 5
150 Gordon Brunton
152 Tony Manero — Manero 4 and 2 — Manero 1-up
154 Len Mattson
145 Clarence Doser — Doser 2 and 1
151 Wm. Malcolm

Runyan 9 and 8 — Zimmerman 3 and 2

152 Levi Lynch — Lynch 1-up (19) — Lynch 4 and 2
142 Herman Barron
144 Arthur Bell — Bell 3 and 2
148 Joe Turnesa
146 Vic Ghezzi — Ghezzi 2-up — Zimmerman 2 and 1
147 Billy Burke
151 Al Zimmerman — Zimmerman 2 and 1
149 Ed Williams

Zimmerman 7 and 6

151 Pat Circelli — Circelli 1-up (20) — Circelli 3 and 2
151 Jerry Gianferante
149 Orville White — White 3 and 2
151 Clarence Clark
145 Jimmy Hines — Hines 1-up — Revolta 1-up
147 Jimmy Demaret
144 Johnny Revolta — Revolta 1-up
139 Walter Hagen

Revolta 4 and 2 — Revolta 4 and 3

142 Alvin Krueger — Krueger 1-up — Krueger 2 and 1
150 Frank Walsh
148 Gene Sarazen — Sarazen 4 and 3
149 George Christ
151 G. Slingerland — Slingerland 2 and 1 — Schultz 2 and 1
151 John Golden
149 Eddie Schultz — Schultz 3 and 1
147 Jim Foulis

Schultz 1-up (37)

Revolta 5 and 4

150 Harold Sampson — Sampson 1-up — Watrous 2 and 1
150 E. Zimmerman
149 Al Watrous — Watrous 3 and 2
147 Charles Lacey
149 Sam Parks Jr. — Parks Jr. 1-up — Parks Jr. 1-up
144 Harry Cooper
151 F. Scheider — Scheider 4 and 2
152 Dave Trufelli

Watrous 4 and 3 — Watrous 1-up

143 Horton Smith — Smith 1-up — Smith 1-up
147 Henry Picard
143 Ray Mangrum — Mangrum 5 and 4
149 Harry Nettlebladt
153 Henry Bontempo — Bontempo 2 and 1 — Shute 4 and 3
148 Eric Seavall
149 Denny Shute — Shute 4 and 3
149 Gene Kunes

Smith 2 and 1

146 Jimmy Thomson — Thomson 4 and 3 — Thomson 6 and 4
154 Bill Jelliffe
148 J.G. Collins — Collins 1-up
150 Gunnar Nelson
147 Ed Dudley — Dudley 1-up — Dudley 3 and 1
152 L.G. Wilcox
147 Dick Metz — Metz 5 and 3
148 Ralph Stonehouse

Dudley 6 and 4 — Armour 1-up (39)

153 Ky Laffoon — Laffoon 1-up — Laffoon 1-up (21)
151 Paul Erath
149 Eddie Loos — Loos 2 and 1
146 Ted Turner
153 Charles Schneider — Schneider 4 and 3 — Armour 3 and 2
154 Steve Holloway
145 Tommy Armour — Armour 1-up
153 Willie Klein

Armour 3 and 2 — Armour 2 and 1

par for 28 holes and routed Tony Manero, 9 and 8. Armour had a tough time with his putter as he beat Ky Laffoon, 3 and 2. Armour was 2-up after the morning round but had trouble on the front side of the afternoon round as he shot 40, three-putting the last four holes. Things didn't look good as Armour missed a 24-inch putt at the 27th hole to square the match with Laffoon, but he was able to regroup on the final nine. A string of fours and one three beat Laffoon on the 34th hole. In other matches, Alvin Krueger had a 2-up lead on Eddie Schultz

*I*n the finals, the weather played a key role, with frigid northern blasts numbing both players' hands. In the end, 24-year-old Revolta, who was from Wisconsin, was able to handle the conditions better than Armour.

after the morning round, but in the afternoon Krueger shot a 39 as Schultz took a 37 to pick up a hole. Schultz squared the match on the 30th hole, and they halved the rest of the holes to force a playoff. At the 37th hole, Krueger missed a four-footer, and Schultz won the match with a par. Jimmy Thomson was no match to Ed Dudley's short game as Dudley beat the giant, 6 and 4, and Al Watrous defeated Sam Parks, 4 and 3. The match of the day was between Horton Smith and Denny Shute. After 31 holes Smith was 1-down, but won the 32nd hole with a birdie. He also won the 34th and 35th holes with birdies to advance with a 2-and-1 victory over Shute.

In the quarter-finals, long-shot Al Zimmerman beat Runyan, 3 and 2. The match was square after the morning round, but Runyan's short game was left at the lunch table as Zimmerman shot a 1-under-par 34 to Runyan's 37 to finish the first 27 holes 3-up on the defending PGA Champion. They halved the rest of the holes, and Zimmerman finished the day 2-under-par to advance to the semifinals. Playing Zimmerman was Johnny Revolta, who had an easy time with Eddie Schultz, beating him, 4 and 2. In the match between Horton Smith and Al Watrous, Watrous finished 1-up in face of a late rally by Smith. Watrous was 3-up after the morning round, carding a 71 to Smith's 74. But in the afternoon, Smith was out in 34 to cut Watrous' lead to

1-up. However, Watrous matched Smith's par 35 on the last nine of the afternoon round. The key to the round for Watrous was the 33rd hole, when he was 2-up and Smith made a 35-footer for birdie. He calmly stepped up to his 10-footer and stroked it in for a half. The match of the day was between Tommy Armour and Ed Dudley. After a 79 in the morning round, Armour found himself down in a struggle to redeem himself. In the afternoon, Dudley shot 74, which allowed Armour to square the match after 36 holes. Both made pars at the 37th and 38th holes, and on the 39th hole, Dudley was in the rough off the tee. He shanked his shot, and it took four to get on the green. Armour was on with two. When Dudley missed his bogey putt, Armour coaxed his birdie putt within gimmie range to win the match.

The semifinals were held on a rainy day, and a cold, chilling wind was playing havoc with the players. Johnny Revolta had an easy time with Al Zimmerman, beating him, 4 and 3. Revolta won the first hole with a par and, despite shooting a 3-over-par 73 in the morning round, went to lunch 3-up. He started the afternoon round with a par and picked up another hole on Zimmerman, who again bogeyed the starting hole. He finished the nine with a birdie to enter the final nine 5-up, a lead too big for Zimmerman to overcome. The match ended on the 33rd hole with Revolta winning, 4 and 3. In the other match between Tommy Armour and Al Watrous, Armour shot a front nine 34 to take a 4-up lead on Watrous. When the "Silver Scot" ballooned to a 41 on the back side, he finished the morning round 2-up. On the front nine of the afternoon round, Watrous was able to tie the match when Armour bogeyed the 21st and 23rd holes, but Armour won the 26th, 27th, 28th and 30th holes to go back to 4-up. At the 32nd hole, Watrous won the hole with a par-3, and again, a par was the winner on the 34th hole. Despite another bogey by Armour at the 35th hole, he was able to win the match, 2 and 1, as Watrous 3-putted from 12 feet.

In the finals, the weather played a key role, with frigid northern blasts numbing both players' hands. In the end, 24-year-old Revolta, who was from Wisconsin, was able to handle the conditions better than Armour. In spite of being 16 years older and having won every major tournament a professional could win, Armour couldn't secure his second PGA Championship. Revolta started his day on the right foot

with a birdie on the first hole, and Armour was never able to square the match again. After a front nine 33, Revolta was 3-up and even though he was 2-over-par on the back nine, was able to pick up another hole, going to lunch 4-up. Armour's game improved in the afternoon; he won the first hole with a par, but it would be the last hole he would win for 12 holes. Despite playing the first seven holes in the afternoon in even par, he lost one more hole. Armour bogeyed the eighth hole, and when they went to the back side, Revolta was 6-up. Armour matched par on the first three holes of the back nine and won the 31st hole when Revolta made bogey. When Revolta put his tee shot on the par-3, 32nd hole just 10 feet away, Armour knew the match was over. If there was a secret to Revolta's 5-and-4 win, it had to be his putting. Over the course of the 31-hole match, Revolta didn't have a 3-putt and one-putted 13 greens. For his efforts Armour won $500, while Revolta won $1,000.

ROAD TO THE FINALS		
Johnny Revolta beat	**Round**	**Tommy Armour beat**
Walter Hagen, 1-up	1st Round	Willie Klein, 1-up
Jimmy Hines, 1-up	2nd Round	Charles Schneider, 3 and 2
Pat Circelli, 4 and 2	3rd Round	Ky Laffoon, 3 and 2
Eddie Schultz, 4 and 2	Quarter-finals	Ed Dudley, 1-up (39)
Al Zimmerman, 4 and 3	Semifinals	Al Watrous, 2 and 1

1934

Qualifying for Match Play: A 36-hole qualifying round was conducted the Tuesday before the Championship. Defending PGA Champion Gene Sarazen was exempt from qualifying, and Bob Crowley was low qualifier with 138. A score of 145 qualified for match play, with 10 players at 146 having to play for eight spots. Some notables who qualified in the playoff were Walter Hagen, Denny Shute and Leo Diegel. All matches were played at 36 holes.

Early Matches: In the first round, defending PGA Champion Gene Sarazen almost went down in defeat to Herman Barron. Sarazen was 2-down after the 28th hole, but won five of the next seven holes to win, 3 and 2. Less fortunate were two former PGA champions, Hagen and Diegel. Hagen had the misfortune to play Denny Shute, who was 10-under-par in a 4-and-3 victory. Diegel lost to Fay Coleman, 4 and 2, in a match that found Diegel behind from the beginning. Other upsets in the first round saw former U.S. Open Champions Billy Burke and Johnny Farrell both eliminated. Burke went down to Vic Ghezzi in a 2-and-1 decision, and Johnny Farrell was routed, 8 and 6, by Paul Runyan. In another upset, Ky Laffoon overwhelmed Horton Smith, 12 and 10, in one of the biggest routs in PGA Championship history. Of the 16 matches, only one made it to the 36th hole, as Ted Turner beat Willie Goggin, 1-up, in a match that was decided in 37 holes.

In the second round, Sarazen was eliminated by Al Watrous, 4 and 3, in a match where Sarazen attempted to make a comeback. Although 2-down after the 29th hole, Sarazen birdied the next hole to get within one, but Watrous birdied the 31st and 32nd holes. When Sarazen bogeyed the 33rd hole the match was over. In another match, Ted Turner had Bob Crowley 2-down with three holes to play, but bogeyed the 34th and 35th holes to put things all square going into the final hole. Crowley birdied the hole to sneak by Turner, 1-up. In the morning round, Shute registered a 66 and was 6-up on Ky Laffoon, but Laffoon wouldn't give up, playing the afternoon front nine in 32 to pick up two holes. Laffoon birdied the 28th and 31st holes to get to just 2-down with five holes left, but Shute sank a 10-footer at the 32nd hole to go 3-up. He halved the next two with par-4s to win the match, 3 and 2. In disgust over his loss, Laffoon played the rest of the holes for an unofficial course-record 64.

In the quarter-finals, Shute continued his sub-par pace with a 7-under-par day to

beat Al Houghton, 6 and 5. The most unusual thing about the match was that Shute was 2-down to Houghton after the eighth hole, but a rally of four successive birdies swung the match into his favor as he finished the morning round with a 68 to be 4-up. Shute played the front nine in the afternoon in 33 to increase his lead to 5-up and he finished the match on the 31st hole, making an 80-footer for a birdie. In other matches, Gene Kunes eliminated the medalist, Bob Crowley, 4 and 3, while Craig Wood had to fight back in the afternoon match to gain a 2-and-1 victory over Watrous. Wood was 3-down after the 19th hole and then ran a streak of four 3s in a row. When he made the turn, he was 1-up. They halved the next two holes, then Watrous made birdie at the 30th hole to square the match. Wood birdied the 32nd hole and with another birdie at the 35th hole, closed the match, 2 and 1. In the closest match of the day, Runyan scored a 1-up victory over Dick Metz, who never had the lead during the day. Runyan bogeyed the 33rd hole to square the match for the fourth time, but on

Champion:	Paul Runyan, White Plains, N.Y.*
Site:	Park Club of Buffalo, Williamsville, N.Y.
Date:	July 24-29 **Purse:** $7,200

the next hole hit a pitching wedge to within a foot of the hole to gain a 1-up lead. Playing the last hole, Metz had a two-footer for par, while Runyan had some problems and was left with a 10-footer for par. Runyan made the putt.

In the semifinals, Shute continued his assault on par, as he was 6-under-par, but ran into Wood, who also was 6-under and beat him, 2 and 1. For Wood it was some retribution for losing to Shute in a playoff for the 1933 British Open. Wood had a sensational morning round of 65, which gave him a 6-up lead, but when Shute shot a 34 on the front side of the afternoon round,

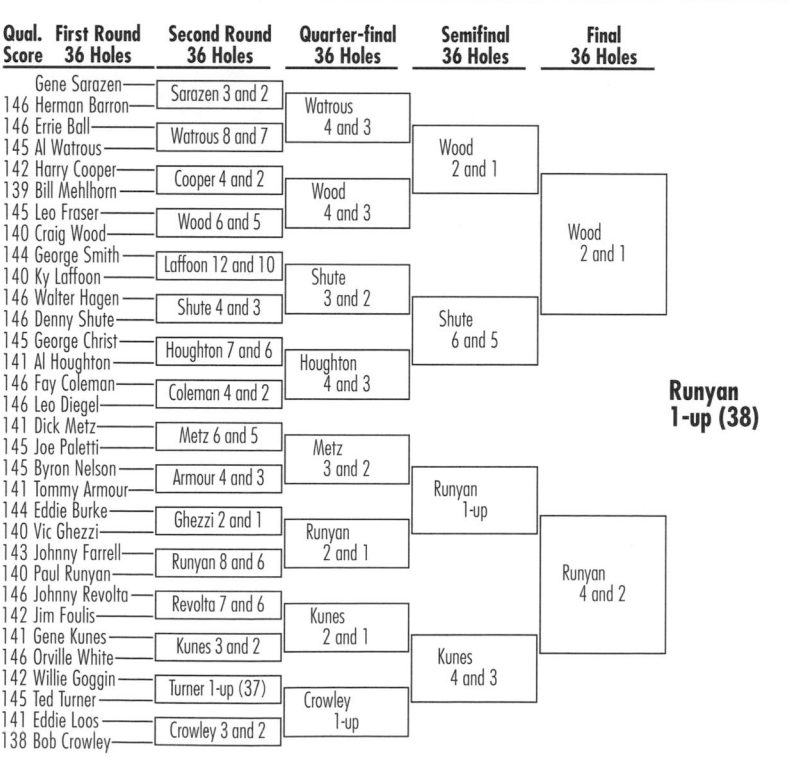

Qual. Score	First Round 36 Holes	Second Round 36 Holes	Quarter-final 36 Holes	Semifinal 36 Holes	Final 36 Holes
	Gene Sarazen				
146	Herman Barron	Sarazen 3 and 2			
146	Errie Ball		Watrous 4 and 3		
145	Al Watrous	Watrous 8 and 7			
142	Harry Cooper			Wood 2 and 1	
139	Bill Mehlhorn	Cooper 4 and 2			
145	Leo Fraser		Wood 4 and 3		
140	Craig Wood	Wood 6 and 5			
144	George Smith				Wood 2 and 1
140	Ky Laffoon	Laffoon 12 and 10			
146	Walter Hagen		Shute 3 and 2		
146	Denny Shute	Shute 4 and 3			
145	George Christ			Shute 6 and 5	
141	Al Houghton	Houghton 7 and 6			
146	Fay Coleman		Houghton 4 and 3		
146	Leo Diegel	Coleman 4 and 2			
141	Dick Metz				
145	Joe Paletti	Metz 6 and 5			
145	Byron Nelson		Metz 3 and 2		
141	Tommy Armour	Armour 4 and 3			
144	Eddie Burke			Runyan 1-up	
140	Vic Ghezzi	Ghezzi 2 and 1			
143	Johnny Farrell		Runyan 2 and 1		
140	Paul Runyan	Runyan 8 and 6			Runyan 4 and 2
146	Johnny Revolta				
142	Jim Foulis	Revolta 7 and 6			
141	Gene Kunes		Kunes 2 and 1		
146	Orville White	Kunes 3 and 2			
142	Willie Goggin			Kunes 4 and 3	
145	Ted Turner	Turner 1-up (37)			
141	Eddie Loos		Crowley 1-up		
138	Bob Crowley	Crowley 3 and 2			

Runyan
1-up (38)

Wood's lead was down to two. Shute birdied the 29th hole, but Wood birdied the 30th to keep the lead at two. Shute made another birdie at the 31st which put him 1-down again and after both players made fours at the 32nd hole, Wood made a 12-footer at the 33rd hole to go back to 2-up. When Shute couldn't make a birdie at the 34th or 35th hole, the match ended. Even though Shute was 34-under-par in the 133 holes of match play, he was eliminated, winning $200 for his efforts. Paul Runyan stopped Gene Kunes, 4 and 2, despite the fact that

*N*ot since 1923 had any PGA final been so close and gone so long as the 1934 PGA Championhip. Runyan, the pupil and putting wizard, beat his former instructor, the power-hitting Wood, 1-up.

he was 4-down after 10 holes of play. Runyan won the 11th hole and then won 17 and 18 to go to lunch just 1-down. By the 25th hole, Runyan had squared the match, and with a 20-footer for birdie at the 29th hole, was finally up in the match. Two holes later Runyan made another birdie, and with a Kunes bogey at the 32nd hole, became 3-up. Runyan halved the next hole and won the match when Kunes missed his par putt at the 33rd hole.

Not since 1923 had any PGA final been so close and gone so long as the 1934 PGA Championhip. Runyan, the pupil and putting wizard, beat his former instructor, the power-hitting Wood, 1-up. In the morning round, Wood, had a 1-up lead but lost his advantage on the front side of the afternoon round. Wood got his lead back at the 29th hole with an eagle 3, but Runyan squared the match three holes later with a birdie. Runyan picked up a hole with a Wood bogey at the 33rd hole. At the 35th hole, Wood almost holed his second shot, making birdie and bringing the match all square going into the last hole. Both players missed the final green with their second shots, and chipped within 12 feet. It took PGA President George Jacobus to decide who would putt first and, with considerable care, he determined that Runyan's ball was away. Runyan made his putt, and even though Wood had a tougher putt, he putted into the hole, forcing extra holes. At the par-5 37th hole, Runyan was short of the green in two,

while Wood was just eight feet away for an eagle. Runyan hit a great chip within two feet of the hole and was able to halve the hole when Wood missed his match-winning putt. At the next hole, Wood hooked his drive under a tree and sent his second shot into the crowd, left of the green. Runyan didn't do much better with his second shot, as he pushed it right of the green. He had a tough shot over a bunker, but he played a good shot and the ball stopped eight feet away. Wood chipped 12 feet short of the cup and almost made his par putt. Runyan then took his aluminum-headed putter and made the winning putt to the cheers of 2,500 enthusiastic fans.

ROAD TO THE FINALS

Paul Runyan beat	Round	Craig Wood beat
Johnny Farrell, 8 and 6	1st Round	Leo Fraser, 6 and 5
Vic Ghezzi, 2 and 1	2nd Round	Harry Cooper, 4 and 3
Dick Metz, 1-up	Quarter-finals	Al Watrous, 2 and 1
Gene Kunes, 4 and 2	Semifinals	Denny Shute, 2 and 1

1933

Qualifying for Match Play: A 36-hole qualifying round was conducted the Tuesday before the Championship. Defending PGA Champion Olin Dutra was exempt from qualifying, and Mortie Dutra and Jimmy Hines were the low qualifiers with 138. A score of 146 qualified for match play. Notable players who didn't qualify were Jim Foulis (148), Billy Burke (148) and Ralph Guldahl (150). Walter Hagen, Craig Wood and Denny Shute decided to not enter the event. All matches played at 36 holes

Early Matches: In the first round, all favorites advanced with the exception of two-time PGA Champion Leo Diegel, who was eliminated by Willie Goggin, 4 and 3. Goggin was 5-under-par for the 33-hole match. Horton Smith also was beaten by long-shot Clarence Clark, 6 and 5. The most lopsided match of the day belonged to Johnny Revolta, who beat Alex Gerlak, 12 and 11. In the annals of PGA Championship match-play history, it would tie as the widest margin of victory.

In the second round, Olin Dutra was beaten by Johnny Farrell, 1-up. Dutra was 5-down after 28 holes and won four of the next five holes with a dazzling comeback. Farrell stopped the rally with a five-footer for a birdie, only to have Dutra win the next hole and go to the finishing hole 1-down. Both players were on the green in regulation and Farrell putted to within three feet of the hole. Dutra then had a 15-footer to send the match into overtime, but his putt rimmed the hole and stopped in front of Farrell's ball for what looked like a perfect stymie. It would have been a dead stymie except for a slight undulation on the putting surface which Farrell maneuvered perfectly for the 1-up win. Farrell was 1-over-par for the 36 holes, shooting a 68 in the morning and a 73 in the afternoon. In other matches, Sarazen beat Harry Cooper, 4 and 3, and Goggin, who was 5-under-par, had the widest margin of victory in his match with Al Espinosa, beating him, 8 and 7. Paul Runyan was able to reverse a 1-down disadvantage after the morning round to eliminate Johnny Revolta, 2 and 1.

In the quarter-finals, Goggin defeated Paul Runyan, 6 and 5, and Hines eliminated past champion Tom Creavy, 4 and 3. Johnny Farrell beat John Golden, 5 and 4, despite having a tough time in the early parts of the round. Farrell found himself tied with Golden after the 16th hole, but drew away when he won the 17, 21st, 22nd and 23rd holes. With a Farrell birdie on the 27th hole, Golden didn't have a chance as he just ran out of holes. In the match be-

tween Gene Sarazen and Ed Dudley, Sarazen led all the way as he played the 31 holes in 4-under-par to beat Dudley, 6 and 5. Sarazen was so overpowering during the day, that if Dudley hadn't laid three dead stymies in the afternoon round, the margin would have been eight holes.

In the semifinals, the match between Sarazen and Farrell turned into a rout, as Sarazen completely outplayed Farrell on the front side of the Blue Mound Country Club. For the two times the players toured the beginning nine holes, Farrell was 9-over-par, compared to Sarazen's 1-over effort. So even though Farrell was 1-under-par for the back nine, the damage was done with a 5-and-4 defeat. The other match between Hines and Goggin was a close affair, as the pair were tied five times

before the deadlock was broken on the 35th hole with a birdie by Goggin.

In the finals, Sarazen had a lot to prove to people. Earlier in the week, Tommy Armour had said that Sarazen was "all washed up as a championship contender." The remark lit a spark in Sarazen, who spent the whole week routing his competitors. After the morning round he was only 1-up on Goggin, despite a 1-under-par 69. Sarazen went to work in the afternoon, winning three of the first five holes, shooting 34 and going into the final nine 4-up. With a birdie on the 32nd hole, Sarazen closed out the match, 5 and 4. As he was receiving his prize of $1,000 and the Wanamaker Trophy for the third time, he told the audience, "Pretty good for a washed-up golfer."

Champion:	Gene Sarazen, Miami, Fla.*	
Site:	Blue Mound CC, Milwaukee, Wis.	
Date:	Aug. 8-13	Par: 35-35—70
Purse:	$7,200	

ROAD TO THE FINALS

Gene Sarazen beat	Round	Willie Goggin beat
Vincent Eldred, 8 and 7	1st Round	Leo Diegel, 4 and 3
Harry Cooper, 4 and 3	2nd Round	Al Espinosa, 9 and 7
Ed Dudley, 6 and 5	Quarter-finals	Paul Runyan, 6 and 5
Johnny Farrell, 5 and 4	Semifinals	Jimmy Hines, 1-up

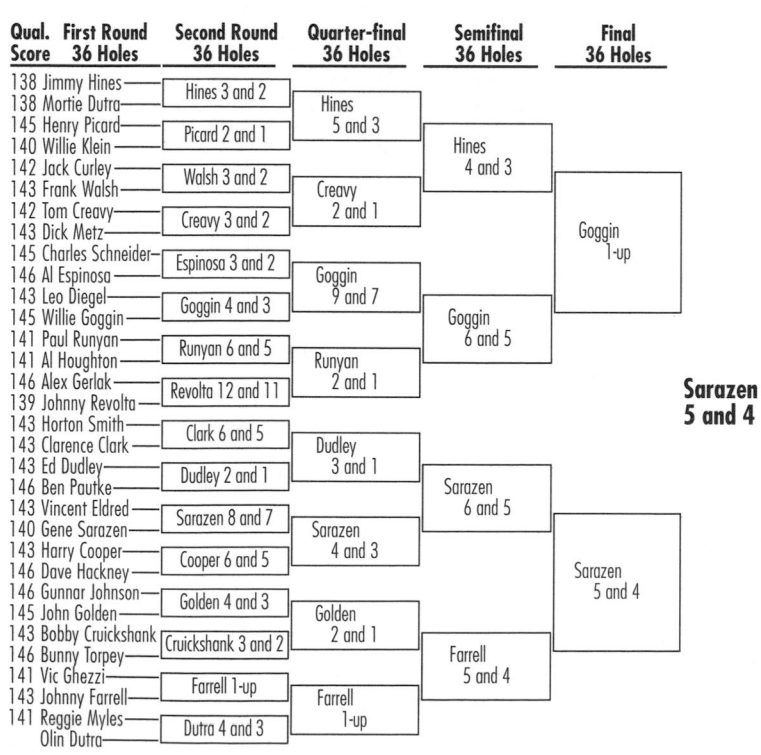

Qual. Score	First Round 36 Holes	Second Round 36 Holes	Quarter-final 36 Holes	Semifinal 36 Holes	Final 36 Holes
138 Jimmy Hines		Hines 3 and 2	Hines 5 and 3	Hines 4 and 3	Goggin 1-up
138 Mortie Dutra					
145 Henry Picard		Picard 2 and 1			
140 Willie Klein					
142 Jack Curley		Walsh 3 and 2	Creavy 2 and 1		
143 Frank Walsh					
142 Tom Creavy		Creavy 3 and 2			
143 Dick Metz					
145 Charles Schneider		Espinosa 3 and 2	Goggin 9 and 7	Goggin 6 and 5	
146 Al Espinosa					
143 Leo Diegel		Goggin 4 and 3			
145 Willie Goggin					
141 Paul Runyan		Runyan 6 and 5	Runyan 2 and 1		
141 Al Houghton					
146 Alex Gerlak		Revolta 12 and 11			
139 Johnny Revolta					
143 Horton Smith		Clark 6 and 5	Dudley 3 and 1	Sarazen 6 and 5	Sarazen 5 and 4
143 Clarence Clark					
143 Ed Dudley		Dudley 2 and 1			
146 Ben Pautke					
143 Vincent Eldred		Sarazen 8 and 7	Sarazen 4 and 3		
140 Gene Sarazen					
143 Harry Cooper		Cooper 6 and 5			
146 Dave Hackney					
146 Gunnar Johnson		Golden 4 and 3	Golden 2 and 1	Farrell 5 and 4	
145 John Golden					
143 Bobby Cruickshank		Cruickshank 3 and 2			
146 Bunny Torpey					
141 Vic Ghezzi		Farrell 1-up	Farrell 1-up		
143 Johnny Farrell					
141 Reggie Myles		Dutra 4 and 3			
Olin Dutra					

Sarazen 5 and 4

1932

Qualifying for Match Play: A 36-hole qualifying round was conducted the Tuesday before the Championship and 31 players qualified for the field. Defending PGA Champion Tom Creavy was exempt from qualifying and Olin Dutra was low qualifier with 140. A score of 153 qualified for match play, with Al Collins and Abe Espinosa having to beat six other players for the last two spots. Notable players who didn't qualify were Tommy Armour, Harry Cooper, Billy Burke and Harold McSpaden, who shot 153 and lost in the playoff. All matches played at 36 holes.

Early Matches: The first round was full of overtime surprises and upsets as several of the favorites were eliminated. In a

For Dutra, his performance is remembered as one of the most dominant victories in the history of the PGA Championship. He played 196 holes and was 19-under-par.

stunning defeat that went seven extra holes (second longest match in the PGA Championship), five-time Champion Walter Hagen lost to Johnny Golden, who rolled in a 10-footer for birdie on the 43rd hole. Other upsets that went extra holes had Reggie Myles beating Horton Smith on the 37th hole, and Vincent Eldred staggering past Paul Runyan on the 38th hole. But the most amazing match was between Bobby Cruickshank and Al Watrous. At the 22nd hole, Watrous was 9-up and when his rival had a six-foot downhill putt for a half, he conceded the putt. At the time it was a good-natured act, but in some respects, it came back to haunt Watrous when Cruickshank won nine of the next 11 holes. The match went into overtime, and on the 41st hole, Watrous missed from three feet to lose the match. Defending PGA Champion Tom Creavy had an easy time in his match against Johnny Hines with a 7-and-6 victory.

In the quarter-finals, Frank Walsh provided a minor upset as he demolished Bobby Cruickshank, 8 and 7, while Olin Dutra broke par for the fourth successive day to rout Herman Barron, 5 and 4. Tom Creavy was able to beat Ralph Stonehouse, 3 and 2, with the match of the day between Ed Dudley and Al Collins having to go to 38 holes for a decision.

Champion:	Olin Dutra, Santa Monica, Calif.*	
Site:	Keller GC, St. Paul, Minn.	
Date:	Aug. 31-Sept. 4	Purse: $7,200

ROAD TO THE FINALS

Olin Dutra beat	Round	Frank Walsh beat
George Smith, 9 and 8	1st Round	Ted Longworth, 7 and 6
Reggie Myles, 5 and 3	2nd Round	Gene Kunes, 9 and 8
Herman Barron, 5 and 4	Quarter-finals	Bobby Cruickshank, 8 and 7
Ed Dudley, 3 and 2	Semifinals	Tom Creavy, 1-up (38)

In the semifinals, Dutra continued his streak of sub-par golf in his match against Dudley. In the morning round he fired a 67 to take a 4-up advantage to lunch, and while Dudley didn't lose any ground on the front nine despite being under par, it proved to be too little, too late. Dudley ran out of holes and was beaten, 3 and 2. In the other match between Creavy and Frank Walsh, Creavy was humiliated as he finished the afternoon round 8-down. Things didn't look any better when he missed his chance to win a hole for the first time in the match and missed a three-footer on the 20th hole. But Creavy battled back with five birdies and sent the match into overtime. However,

he didn't have the same happy ending as Cruickshank. Creavy took three putts on the 38th hole, missing his second putt from three feet.

In the finals, Dutra continued his assault on par and beat Walsh, 4 and 3. For Walsh, it was a valiant try at the Championship that seven months previously would have seemed impossible. He had suffered a fractured skull and was sidelined eight weeks. For Dutra, his performance is remembered as one of the most dominant victories in the history of the PGA Championship. Over the course of the six days of the Championship, Dutra played 196 holes and was 19-under-par.

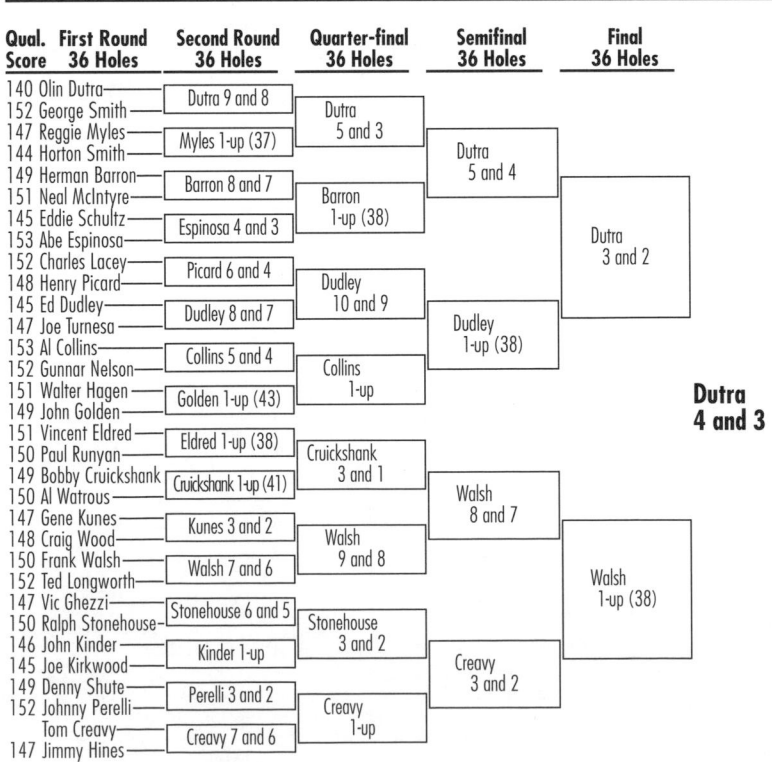

Qual. Score	First Round 36 Holes	Second Round 36 Holes	Quarter-final 36 Holes	Semifinal 36 Holes	Final 36 Holes
140 Olin Dutra	Dutra 9 and 8		Dutra 5 and 3		
152 George Smith				Dutra 5 and 4	
147 Reggie Myles	Myles 1-up (37)				
144 Horton Smith					
149 Herman Barron	Barron 8 and 7		Barron 1-up (38)		Dutra 3 and 2
151 Neal McIntyre					
145 Eddie Schultz	Espinosa 4 and 3				
153 Abe Espinosa					
152 Charles Lacey	Picard 6 and 4		Dudley 10 and 9		
148 Henry Picard				Dudley 1-up (38)	
145 Ed Dudley	Dudley 8 and 7				
147 Joe Turnesa					
153 Al Collins	Collins 5 and 4		Collins 1-up		
152 Gunnar Nelson					
151 Walter Hagen	Golden 1-up (43)				Dutra 4 and 3
149 John Golden				Walsh 8 and 7	
151 Vincent Eldred	Eldred 1-up (38)		Cruickshank 3 and 1		
150 Paul Runyan					
149 Bobby Cruickshank	Cruickshank 1-up (41)				
150 Al Watrous					Walsh 1-up (38)
147 Gene Kunes	Kunes 3 and 2		Walsh 9 and 8		
148 Craig Wood					
150 Frank Walsh	Walsh 7 and 6				
152 Ted Longworth					
147 Vic Ghezzi	Stonehouse 6 and 5		Stonehouse 3 and 2		
150 Ralph Stonehouse				Creavy 3 and 2	
146 John Kinder	Kinder 1-up				
145 Joe Kirkwood					
149 Denny Shute	Perelli 3 and 2		Creavy 1-up		
152 Johnny Perelli					
Tom Creavy	Creavy 7 and 6				
147 Jimmy Hines					

1931

Qualifying for Match Play: A 36-hole qualifying round was conducted the Monday before the Championship. Defending PGA Champion Tommy Armour was exempt from qualifying, and Gene Sarazen was low qualifier with 145. A score of 152 qualified for match play, and Johnny Farrell beat five other players for the last spot at 153. A notable player that didn't make it to match play was Al Watrous. All matches played at 36 holes.

Early Matches: The first round saw a number of upsets, with Walter Hagen, Leo Diegel, Johnny Farrell, Ed Dudley and Al

Champion:	Tom Creavy, Albany, N.Y.*	
Site:	Wannamoisett CC, Rumford, R.I.	
Date:	Sept. 7-14	Par: 34-35—69
Purse:	$7,200	

Only one second-round match got to the final hole, and only half of the eight matches went past the 34th hole. Sarazen, who started the match 4-up after the seventh hole, produced the biggest win in his 7-and-6 rout of Paul Runyan. Armour also had an easy match of Walter Murray, despite leading by only one after the morning round, and beat Murray, 5 and 3. Horton Smith was also a big winner in his 6-and-5 conquest of Willie MacFarlane, while 1924 U.S. Open Champion Cyril Walker outdistanced Johnny Golden, 5 and 4.

In the quarter-finals, the reign of Tommy Armour as PGA Champion came to an end at the hands of Denny Shute, 3 and 1, in the day's best match. With a front-nine 33, Shute was 4-up on the defender, who fought back with a 33 on the back nine to go to lunch only 2-down. Armour started the afternoon round with a bogey to lose the 19th hole, and only managed to reduce his deficit to 1-down by winning the 22nd and 26th holes. He lost the next hole and the

A t 20 years old, Creavy would go on to be the second youngest winner in PGA history, beating Sarazen, who was the youngest Champion of all time.

hole after that, and when Shute hit his pitching wedge to within inches of the 35th hole, Armour was forced to concede the putt and the match. For the day Shute was 5-under-par. Another good match saw Tom Creavy eliminate Cyril Walker, 3 and 1.

The semifinals saw the defeat of the two favorites, as Creavy beat Sarazen, 5 and 3, and Shute defeated Burke, 1-up. At 20 years old, Creavy would go on to be the second youngest winner in PGA history, beating Sarazen, who was the youngest Champion of all time. In the match between Billy Burke and Shute, Shute was 1-up af-

Espinosa becoming first-round casualties. The biggest of the upsets was in the Walter Hagen match, as veteran professional Peter O'Hara eliminated the five-time PGA Champion, 4 and 3. O'Hara started strong, building a 3-up lead in the afternoon round despite shooting a 75, but many still thought it was a fluke and that Hagen would be the victor in the end. But O'Hara kept the assault going in the afternoon round, winning three out of the first four holes and making the turn at 4-up. He went on to win the match on the 33rd hole. In another surprising upset, Johnny Farrell suffered a 2-down defeat at the hands of Jim Foulis, a young Chicago professional whose uncle won the U.S. Open in 1896. In the match between former PGA Champion Leo Diegel and Bill Mehlhorn, who shot 70 in the morning round and held a 5-up lead, Diegel whittled the lead down to two with three birdies in succession starting on the 24th hole. His momentum was stopped on the 28th hole when he missed a one-footer for the win, and with that, Foulis went on to win, 3 and 2. In the match between Gene Sarazen and Al Espinosa, Sarazen went out in 34 to be 4-up on Espinosa, and came home in 37 to be 3-up after the morning round. In the afternoon, the match got out of hand on the front side as Sarazen shot 33 to increase the lead to 8-up and with an Espinosa bogey at the 28th hole, the contest ended, 9 and 8.

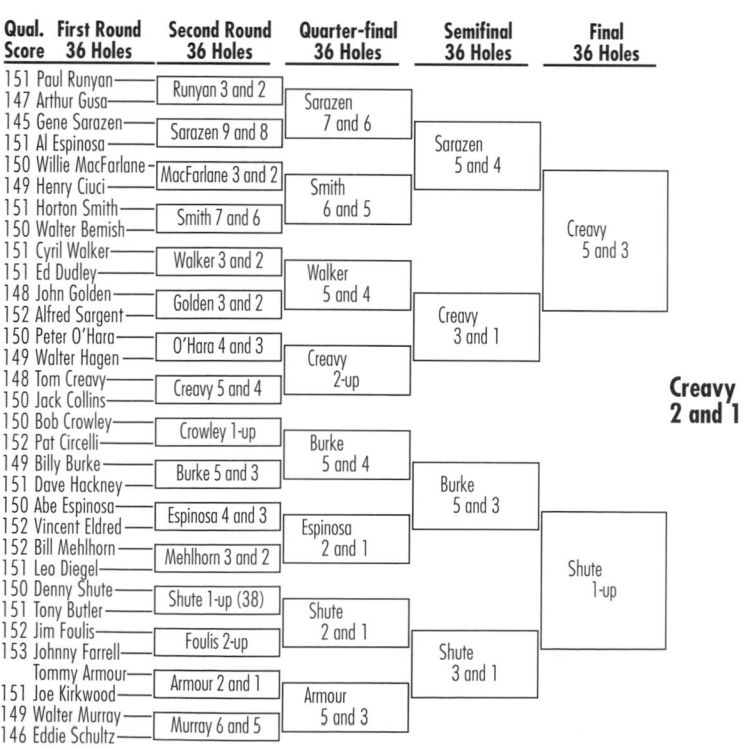

ter the 27th hole. But Burke won the next two holes with par to go 1-up until Shute squared the match with a 15-foot birdie putt at the 31st hole. Shute then won the 32nd and 33rd holes with pars, which put Shute 2-up, but Burke won the 34th hole with a par. Both players parred the 35th and 36th holes, which helped Shute hold on for a 1-up victory.

In the finals, Creavy, who was playing in his first national championship, was able to hold on to beat Denny Shute, 2 and 1. After the 30th hole, it looked like Creavy was going to be an easy winner as he was 4-up with just six holes left, but Shute fought back. On the 31st hole Creavy made bogey, while Shute made par to get one back. Despite Shute hitting his drive into a water hazard at the 32nd hole, they still halved the hole. At the 33rd hole, Shute made a birdie to get another one back. When Creavy made a double-bogey at the 34th hole, it looked like he was folding. But that was as far as Shute was able to go, as he made bogey at the 35th hole to lose, 2 and 1. Creavy got a great thrill afterwards when his golfing hero, Bobby Jones, who was refereeing the match told him, "It was one of the finest matches I think that was ever played."

ROAD TO THE FINALS

Tom Creavy beat	Round	Denny Shute beat
Jock Collins, 5 and 4	1st Round	Tony Butler, 1-up (38)
Peter O'Hara, 2-up	2nd Round	James Foulis, 2 and 1
Cyril Walker, 3 and 1	Quarter-finals	Tommy Armour, 3 and 1
Gene Sarazen, 5 and 3	Semifinals	Billy Burke, 1-up

1930

Qualifying for Match Play: A 36-hole qualifying round was conducted the Monday before the Championship and 32 players qualified. Horton Smith and Johnny Farrell were low qualifiers at 145 and a score of 157 qualified for match play,. Six players tied at 156 which forced a playoff for the last spot, won by Billy Burke. Notable players who failed to qualify in sectional qualifying were past champions Walter Hagen, Jock Hutchison and Jim Barnes. All matches were played at 36 holes.

Early Matches: In the first round, most of the favorites won, with Gene Sarazen coming the closest to losing in his match against Charles Schneider. Sarazen enjoyed a 3-up lead after the 19th hole, but his putting became erratic and Schneider squared the match on the 28th hole. Schneider chipped in for birdie at the 31st hole but gave it back to Sarazen when a bad drive put his ball up against a fence. After two unsuccesful swipes at the ball, he conceded the hole. They halved the next hole, and on the 34th hole, Sarazen hit a great second shot out of the rough, giving him a birdie and a 1-up lead. The match went to the final hole, where Sarazen was in trouble, but he hit a fine recovery shot out of the rough to win the match, 1-up. While Sarazen had a tough time, defending PGA Champion Leo Diegel had an easy time in his match against Henry Ciuci, winning 8 and 7. Tommy Armour also had an easy time against Dave Hackney. Armour was 7-up after a morning round 70 and finished the match on the 26th hole, winning 11 and 10.

The second round saw Diegel end his two-year reign as Champion, losing to Harold Sampson, 1-up. Johnny Farrell managed to stay alive with his match against Denny Shute. That match went the distance and the former U.S. Open Champion was able to win, 1-up. Sarazen, Horton Smith and Armour had easy passage into the quarter-finals. Sarazen defeated Bob Crowley, 7 and 6, Smith beat Laurie Ayton, 5 and 4, and Armour defeated Bob Shave, 7 and 5.

In the quarter-finals, the best match was between Joe Kirkwood and Horton Smith. After the 27th hole, the match was square, but Smith won the 21st and 31st holes to go 2-up. Kirkwood got one back with a birdie-3 at the 33rd hole, and they halved the next hole. Then, at a critical juncture in the match, the 35th hole, Smith hooked his drive out of bounds and lost the hole. Going into the final hole all square, Smith hit his second shot into a greenside bunker, lead-

ing to a bogey and letting Kirkwood come from behind to win, 1-up. Another exciting contest saw Tommy Armour eliminate Johnny Farrell, 2 and 1, in a match where Armour lost five of the first six holes. Gene Sarazen beat Al Espinosa, 2 and 1.

In the semifinals, Gene Sarazen beat Joe Kirkwood, 5 and 4. For the first 22 holes, it was a very close contest with the match squared. Then the Australian trick shot expert developed a streak of wildness, and Sarazen won four of the next seven holes. The match between Tommy Armour and Charles Lacey was more spectacular, especially at the finish, with Armour winning 1-up.

The final was something out of a Hollywood script, with two great golfers battling to the final putts to determine the champion. Even though Sarazen should have been the favorite because he was playing on his home course, it was one of those matches where neither player had the upper hand. The biggest lead in the match was

just two holes, which both players had at one time during the contest. After the morning round, Armour had a 1-up lead after shooting 71 to Sarazen's 72. On the front nine of the afternoon round, Sarazen got the hole back and they went to the final nine all square. On the 18th hole Sarazen hooked his tee shot while Armour hit the fairway. Sarazen put his second shot into a greenside bunker, then Armour, who had a poor lie, hit his second shot into the bunker. Sarazen put his bunker shot 10 feet past the hole, while Armour exploded 12 feet away. As Armour got over his putt, he was forced to back away as a photographer disturbed him. He got back over the putt and finally hit the ball, which had just enough momentum to topple in to win, 1-up. Sarazen, who looked surprised that Armour made it, putted hurriedly and missed.

Champion:	Tommy Armour, Detroit, Mich.*	
Site:	Fresh Meadows CC, Flushing, N.Y.	
Date:	Sept. 8-13	Purse: $10,300

ROAD TO THE FINALS

Tommy Armour beat	Round	Gene Sarazen beat
Clarence Hackney, 11 and 10	1st Round	Charles Schneider, 1-up
Bob Shave, 7 and 5	2nd Round	Bob Crowley, 7 and 6
Johnny Farrell, 2 and 1	Quarter-finals	Al Espinosa, 2 and 1
Charles Lacey, 1-up	Semifinals	Joe Kirkwood, 5 and 4

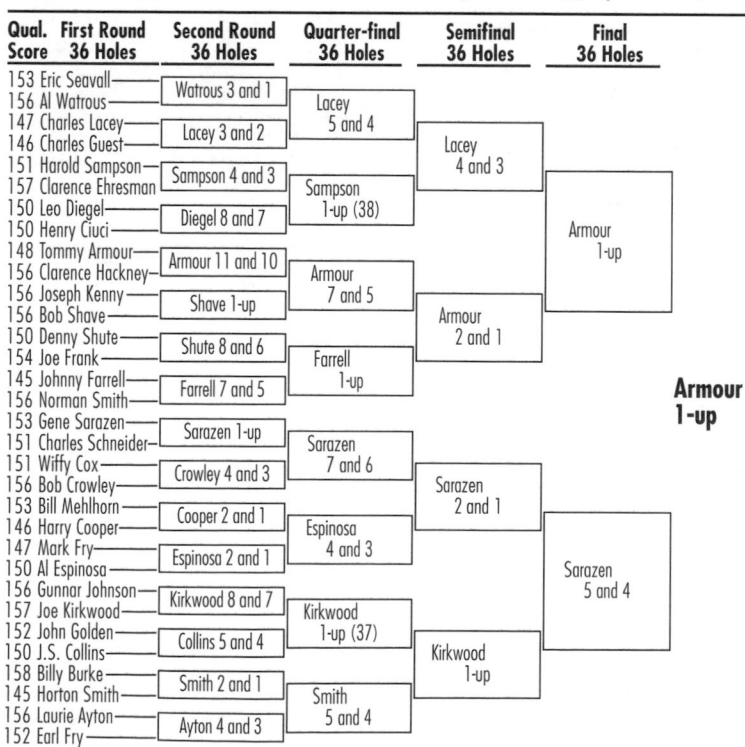

Qual. Score	First Round 36 Holes	Second Round 36 Holes	Quarter-final 36 Holes	Semifinal 36 Holes	Final 36 Holes
153 Eric Seavall	Watrous 3 and 1				
156 Al Watrous		Lacey 5 and 4			
147 Charles Lacey	Lacey 3 and 2				
146 Charles Guest			Lacey 4 and 3		
151 Harold Sampson	Sampson 4 and 3				
157 Clarence Ehresman		Sampson 1-up (38)			
150 Leo Diegel	Diegel 8 and 7				
150 Henry Ciuci				Armour 1-up	
148 Tommy Armour	Armour 11 and 10				
156 Clarence Hackney		Armour 7 and 5			
156 Joseph Kenny	Shave 1-up				
156 Bob Shave			Armour 2 and 1		
150 Denny Shute	Shute 8 and 6				
154 Joe Frank		Farrell 1-up			
145 Johnny Farrell	Farrell 7 and 5				
156 Norman Smith					Armour 1-up
153 Gene Sarazen	Sarazen 1-up				
151 Charles Schneider		Sarazen 7 and 6			
151 Wiffy Cox	Crowley 4 and 3				
156 Bob Crowley			Sarazen 2 and 1		
153 Bill Mehlhorn	Cooper 2 and 1				
146 Harry Cooper		Espinosa 4 and 3			
147 Mark Fry	Espinosa 2 and 1				
150 Al Espinosa				Sarazen 5 and 4	
156 Gunnar Johnson	Kirkwood 8 and 7				
157 Joe Kirkwood		Kirkwood 1-up (37)			
152 John Golden	Collins 5 and 4				
150 J.S. Collins			Kirkwood 1-up		
158 Billy Burke	Smith 2 and 1				
145 Horton Smith		Smith 5 and 4			
156 Laurie Ayton	Ayton 4 and 3				
152 Earl Fry					

1929

Qualifying for Match Play: A 36-hole qualifying round was conducted the Monday before the Championship. Fred Morrison was the low qualifier of 32 players with 136. A score of 149 qualified for match play, with Bill Mehlhorn, Walter Hagen and Henry Cuici having to beat Al Houghton and Waldo Crowder for the last three spots. Tommy Armour withdrew due to illness before the qualifying round. Meanwhile, Harry Cooper qualified with a score of 146, but, on the morning of the first round of match play, it came to the attention of officials that Cooper had been admitted to the Championship by committee rather than by qualifying in his district so he was disqualifed. Notable players who didn't make it to match play were James Foulis (150), Harold McSpaden (150) and Fred McLeod (154). All matches were played at 36 holes.

Early Matches: In the first round, all the favorites won with the exception of the Craig Wood - Horton Smith match, which had no favorite. It was a disappointment that the two were drawn to play each other in an early match. As it happened, it was a great match that was decided on the 37th hole, with Wood scoring a birdie to win, 1-up.

In the second round, all of the matches were blowouts with the exception of the Al Espinosa - Bill Mehlhorn and Henry Ciuci - Johnny Farrell matches. Farrell was able to win his match, 2 and 1, but it took 40 holes before Espinosa was able to beat "Wild Bill" Mehlhorn, thanks to a well-placed stymie.

In the quarter-finals, Al Watrous beat Espinosa, 2-up, and in the match between Farrell and Wood, Farrell was 3-down with five holes left to play. He holed putts for birdies on three of the last five holes, made a seven-footer on the final green to send the match into overtime, then rolled in a 15-footer for another birdie on the first extra hole to beat Wood, 1-up. In another match, Johnny Farrell won easily over Al Watrous, 6 and 5. Hagen beat Tony Manero rather handily, 6 and 5, setting up another rematch with defending PGA Champion Diegel, who beat Gene Sarazen, 3 and 2. So, for the fourth time in five years, Leo Diegel was to meet Walter Hagen. Many believed that Diegel couldn't stop Hagen twice in a row. However, Diegel was a much different golfer than the highly nervous person who had folded under pressure in previous years.

In the semifinal match between Diegel and Hagen, Diegel opened with a morning round of 68, while Hagen played the course

Champion:	Leo Diegel, Tijuana, Mexico*	
Site:	Hillcrest CC, Los Angeles, Calif.	
Date:	Dec. 2-7	Par: 36-35—71
Purse:	$5,000	

ROAD TO THE FINALS

Leo Diegel beat	Round	Johnny Farrell beat
P.O. Hart, 10 and 9	1st Round	John Golden, 1-up
Herman Barron, 10 and 9	2nd Round	Henry Ciuci, 2 and 1
Gene Sarazen, 3 and 2	Quarter-finals	Craig Wood, 1-up (37)
Walter Hagen, 3 and 2	Semifinals	Al Watrous, 6 and 5

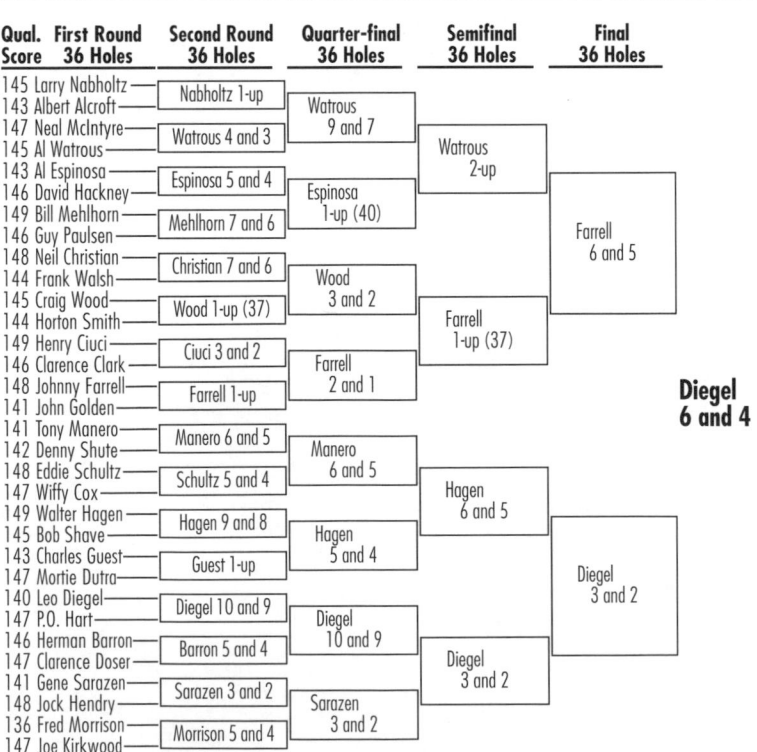

in par 71. Hagen continued to shoot par, but it wasn't enough to beat Diegel, who would not crack under the pressure. Diegel won the match on the 34th hole, 3 and 2. The loss marked the start of a losing streak for Hagen. Despite a record in the 1920s of 36 wins and just three losses, Hagen played in five matches in the 1930s and lost them all.

In the finals, neither player shot well. Diegel, at one point, took four straight holes from Farrell, only to lose the next three. Farrell won the 18th hole to finish the morning round 1-up, with both players shooting 3-over-par 74s. Diegel started the afternoon round on the right foot by winning the 19th hole to square the match and then, on several of the next eight holes,

frustated Farrell with some well-placed stymies. This came to a head at the 27th green when Diegel, who was 1-up at the time, missed a short putt. His ball stopped in a position that partly covered the cup and blocked Farrell's five-foot putt. Farrell tried to negotiate the putt around Diegel's ball, but he failed and knocked Diegel's ball into the cup and lost the hole. The same thing happened on the next green. Instead of being all square or perhaps 1-down through safer play, Farrell found himself 3-down. At the next hole, Farrell again had a three-footer for a win, and even though Diegel's ball wasn't in his way, still missed the putt. The match was all but over and Diegel parred the rest of the holes to beat Farrell, 6 and 4.

Qual. Score	First Round 36 Holes	Second Round 36 Holes	Quarter-final 36 Holes	Semifinal 36 Holes	Final 36 Holes
145 Larry Nabholtz	Nabholtz 1-up				
143 Albert Alcroft		Watrous 9 and 7			
147 Neal McIntyre	Watrous 4 and 3		Watrous 2-up		
145 Al Watrous					
143 Al Espinosa	Espinosa 5 and 4				
146 David Hackney		Espinosa 1-up (40)			
149 Bill Mehlhorn	Mehlhorn 7 and 6			Farrell 6 and 5	
146 Guy Paulsen					
148 Neil Christian	Christian 7 and 6				
144 Frank Walsh		Wood 3 and 2			
145 Craig Wood	Wood 1-up (37)		Farrell 1-up (37)		
144 Horton Smith					
149 Henry Ciuci	Ciuci 3 and 2				
146 Clarence Clark		Farrell 2 and 1			
148 Johnny Farrell	Farrell 1-up				
141 John Golden					Diegel 6 and 4
141 Tony Manero	Manero 6 and 5				
142 Denny Shute		Manero 6 and 5			
148 Eddie Schultz	Schultz 5 and 4		Hagen 6 and 5		
147 Wiffy Cox					
149 Walter Hagen	Hagen 9 and 8				
145 Bob Shave		Hagen 5 and 4			
143 Charles Guest	Guest 1-up			Diegel 3 and 2	
147 Mortie Dutra					
140 Leo Diegel	Diegel 10 and 9				
147 P.O. Hart		Diegel 10 and 9			
146 Herman Barron	Barron 5 and 4		Diegel 3 and 2		
147 Clarence Doser					
141 Gene Sarazen	Sarazen 3 and 2				
148 Jock Hendry		Sarazen 3 and 2			
136 Fred Morrison	Morrison 5 and 4				
147 Joe Kirkwood					

1928

Qualifying for Match Play: A 36-hole qualifying round was conducted the Monday before the championship. Al Espinosa was the low qualifier of 32 players with 142. A score of 160 qualified for match play. One notable player who didn't qualify in his local district was the U.S. Open Champion Johnny Farrell. All matches were played at 36 holes.

Early Matches: In the first round, all the favorites won, with the exception of the match between two past PGA Champions, Tommy Armour and Jim Barnes. Barnes advanced with a 3-and-2 win. Gene Sarazen had a tough match with Bill Mehlhorn. Sararzen was 2-down after the morning match and didn't gain any ground until the 27th hole. He also won the next hole, went ahead at the 31st hole and won the match at the 34th hole, 3 and 2. Defending PGA Champion Hagen easily won his match from Willie Ogg, 4 and 3.

In the second round, Hagen disposed of unknown Julian Blanton, 2-up. Al Espinosa turned an easy win into a hard fought victory against Bob MacDonald. Espinosa was 6-up after his first nine holes and finished the morning round 5-up. Espinosa won the 19th hole to go back to 6-up, but then MacDonald won six of the next seven holes to square the match. MacDonald won the 35th hole to take the lead for the first time, but Espinosa won the final hole to send the match into overtime. He won that match on the first extra hole when his ball caromed off MacDonald's for a match winning three. Another match that went to the 37th hole in the same manner was between Perry Del Vecchio and Glenn Spencer. Del Vecchio was 5-up after the morning round, but Spencer squared the match, only to lose to Del Vecchio at the 37th hole. In other matches, young Horton Smith, playing in his first PGA Championship, gained some attention as he beat Willie MacFarlane, 1-up, and Gene Sarazen tied the course record with a 69 in his morning match against Jim Barnes. Sarazen finally won the match, 3 and 2.

Fireworks erupted in the quarter-final round. Hagen was known as the "master of match play" after 22 straight match wins over four years. In achieving this, he had eliminated Leo Diegel in a 40-hole match, when Diegel seemed to be a certain winner, and again in the 1926 finals. Diegel was looking for revenge and he was determined not to extend his winless streak against Hagen. Diegel started fast, finishing the front nine 5-up. But Hagen was also determined and won back three holes to finish

the morning round 2-down. In the afternoon round, Hagen lost another hole in the outgoing nine and made a rally that left him only 1-down on the 35th hole. Both players hit the par-3 green, with Diegel putting first from 15 feet. Diegel made his putt and Hagen missed his from 12 feet. Thus ended the longest reign any professional has ever held in the history of the PGA Championship. Going into this match Hagen had played in 33 matches in the 1920s and had lost only once, to Sarazen, in the 1923 finals. Sarazen was an easy winner over Ed Dudley, 7 and 6, with Horton Smith beating Perry Del Vecchio, 2-up, and 1920 champion Jock Hutchison being eliminated by Al Espinosa, 5 and 4.

The two semifinal matches turned into blow-outs, as Espinosa defeated Smith, 6 and 5. Sarazen was no match for Diegel,

who was in excellent form while Sarazen missed several short putts in a 9 and 8 defeat.

In the finals, Espinosa's putting touch deserted him. He got off to a good start when he won the second hole and it looked as if he would also win the third, but a three-putt stopped that. Espinosa won the sixth hole but Diegel made up the ground with two birdies in a row. He played brilliantly on the back nine and at the end of the morning round was 4-up. Espinosa hung on during the first nine of the afternoon round but was unable to cut down Diegel's lead. The 28th hole was halved, but Espinosa three-putted the next two and the match ended on the 31st hole with Diegel winning, 6 and 5.

Champion: Leo Diegel, Tijuana, Mexico*		
Site:	Five Farms CC, Baltimore, Md.	
Date:	Oct. 1-6	**Par:** 35-35—70
Purse:	$10,400	

ROAD TO THE FINALS

Leo Diegel beat	Round	Al Espinosa beat
Tony Manero, 10 and 8	1st Round	John Golden, 8 and 7
George Christ, 6 and 4	2nd Round	Bob MacDonald, 1-up (37)
Walter Hagen, 2 and 1	Quarter-finals	Jock Hutchison, 5 and 4
Gene Sarazen, 9 and 8	Semifinals	Horton Smith, 6 and 5

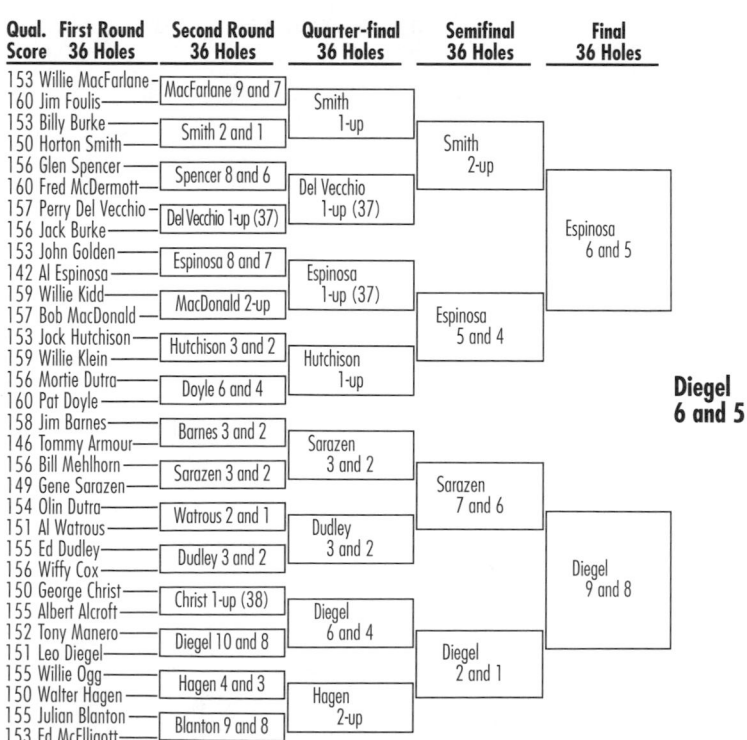

Qual. Score	First Round 36 Holes	Second Round 36 Holes	Quarter-final 36 Holes	Semifinal 36 Holes	Final 36 Holes
153 Willie MacFarlane		MacFarlane 9 and 7			
160 Jim Foulis			Smith 1-up		
153 Billy Burke		Smith 2 and 1			
150 Horton Smith				Smith 2-up	
156 Glen Spencer		Spencer 8 and 6			
160 Fred McDermott			Del Vecchio 1-up (37)		
157 Perry Del Vecchio		Del Vecchio 1-up (37)			
156 Jack Burke					Espinosa 6 and 5
153 John Golden		Espinosa 8 and 7			
142 Al Espinosa			Espinosa 1-up (37)		
159 Willie Kidd		MacDonald 2-up			
157 Bob MacDonald				Espinosa 5 and 4	
153 Jock Hutchison		Hutchison 3 and 2			
159 Willie Klein			Hutchison 1-up		
156 Mortie Dutra		Doyle 6 and 4			
160 Pat Doyle					
158 Jim Barnes		Barnes 3 and 2			
146 Tommy Armour			Sarazen 3 and 2		
156 Bill Mehlhorn		Sarazen 3 and 2			
149 Gene Sarazen				Sarazen 7 and 6	
154 Olin Dutra		Watrous 2 and 1			
151 Al Watrous			Dudley 3 and 2		
155 Ed Dudley		Dudley 3 and 2			
156 Wiffy Cox					Diegel 9 and 8
150 George Christ		Christ 1-up (38)			
155 Albert Alcroft			Diegel 6 and 4		
152 Tony Manero		Diegel 10 and 8			
151 Leo Diegel				Diegel 2 and 1	
155 Willie Ogg		Hagen 4 and 3			
150 Walter Hagen			Hagen 2-up		
155 Julian Blanton		Blanton 9 and 8			
153 Ed McElligott					

Diegel 6 and 5

PGA CHAMPIONSHIP MATCH PLAY

1927

Qualifying for Match Play: A 36-hole qualifying round was conducted the Monday before the Championship. Walter Hagen was the low qualifier of 32 players with 141. A score of 154 made it into match play, with six players tying for the last five spots, forcing a playoff which Leonard Loos lost. Notable players who didn't make it to match play were James Foulis (156) and Harold McSpaden (157). All matches played at 36 holes.

Early Matches: In the first round, the match between Tommy Armour and Johnny Farrell had the most star appeal, as the U.S. and Canadian Open Champion eliminated Farrell, 4 and 3. Former PGA Champion Gene Sarazen was given a scare, as he was forced into extra holes to beat long-shot J.G. Curley. Curley had a chance to win the match on the home green but missed the two-foot winning putt. Hagen, the defending PGA Champion and medalist, won his match against Jack Farrell, 3 and 2, but the score didn't show the reality of the match. After shooting around 80 in the morning round, "The Haig" was 4-down and some in the gallery scented an upset. But in the afternoon Hagen turned things around and played under par to beat Farrell.

In the second round, Hagen played a spotless round as he decimated Tony Manero, 11 and 10. Tommy Armour also played great golf in his 7-and-6 victory over Tom Harmon, which set up a quarter-final match between the defending U.S. Open and PGA Champions. For the second round huge crowds showed up, with most of them watching the match between local hero Harry Cooper and Al Espinosa. However, his popularity didn't help a poor putting day as the "home boy" was eliminated, 5 and 4, by Espinosa. The match of the day was played between Joe Turnesa and Willie Klein. After the first eight holes of play, Klein was 6-up and it took a furious rally by Turnesa to square the match by the 35th hole. Then with a 20-foot putt on the final green, Turnesa was able to win the match, 1-up.

In the quarter-finals, Hagen found a hot putter but still had a hard-fought match against Armour in his 4-and-3 win. Espinosa beat Mortie Dutra, 1-up, but again the score was very misleading. With three holes left to play in the morning round Espinosa was 6-up, but Dutra won the last three holes, and in the afternoon round took the first four holes. Espinosa was able to turn things around and led the match by one after the 27th hole. He was able to hold on by that margin. The match between Sarazen and Joe Turnesa matched two

Champion: Walter Hagen, Rochester, N.Y.*
Site: Cedar Crest CC, Dallas, Texas
Date: Oct. 31-Nov. 5   **Par:** 36-35—71
Purse: $15,441

ROAD TO THE FINALS

Walter Hagen beat	Round	Joe Turnesa beat
Jack Farrell, 3 and 2	1st Round	Charles McKenna, 5 and 3
Tony Manero, 11 and 10	2nd Round	Willie Klein, 1-up
Tommy Armour, 4 and 3	Quarter-finals	Gene Sarazen, 3 and 2
Al Espinosa, 1-up (37)	Semifinals	John Golden, 7 and 6

Americans of Italian descent, with Turnesa handing Sarazen a 3-and-2 defeat.

Of the two semifinal matches, Turnesa had an easy time of John Golden, who was mired in a putting slump. Turnesa had a 9-up lead after the morning round and it was just a matter of time before he won the match, 7 and 6. In the other match, between Espinosa and Hagen, it looked as if the defending PGA Champion was going to be beaten. Espinosa won the 35th hole to go 1-up. On the second shots to the final green, Espinosa was 25 feet away with Hagen over the green. It seemed certain that Hagen was going to lose because he didn't have any chance to make the birdie he needed. He hit a great chip shot and was conceded his four. Espinosa had two putts for the victory. He looked very uncomfortable over the situation and left his approach putt a yard short. He then missed the match-winning putt. The match went into extra

holes and on the first hole, Espinosa again repeated his three-putt and Hagen won the match.

In the finals, Turnesa got off to a good start when he shot a 71 in the morning round to Hagen's 77. Despite the six-shot difference, he went to lunch with only a 2-up lead. Turnesa added another hole at the 19th, but then the tide started to turn, as five-footers that were no problem in his earlier matches became a struggle for Turnesa. On the 29th hole, Hagen made a birdie to square the match, and with a Turnesa bogey at the 31st hole Hagen took a 1-up lead. On the last six holes, Turnesa nervously missed short and easy putts. At the final hole, Turnesa had a putt which would have sent the match into overtime, but he left the putt short on the lip and gave the match to Hagen, 1-up.

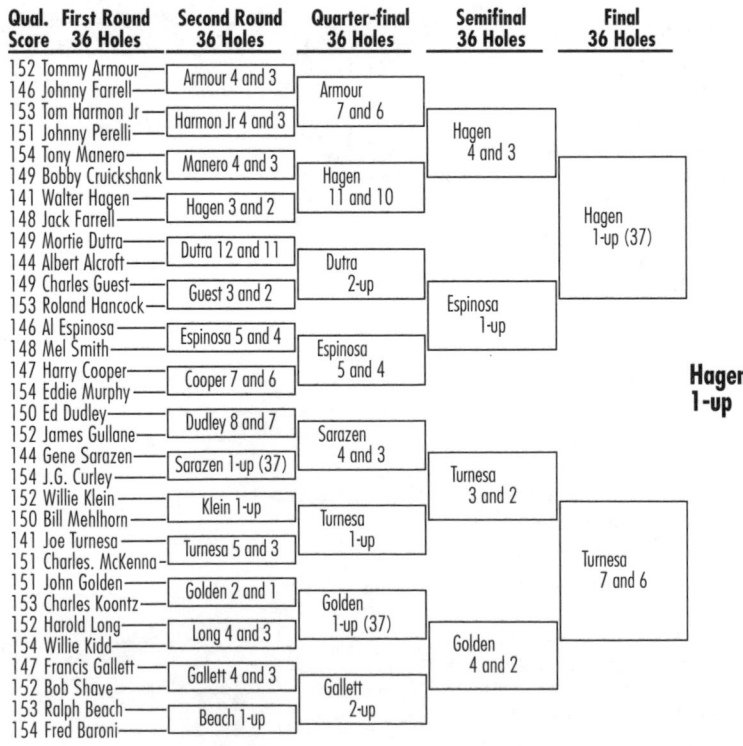

Qual. Score	First Round 36 Holes	Second Round 36 Holes	Quarter-final 36 Holes	Semifinal 36 Holes	Final 36 Holes
152 Tommy Armour		Armour 4 and 3	Armour 7 and 6	Hagen 4 and 3	Hagen 1-up (37)
146 Johnny Farrell					
153 Tom Harmon Jr		Harmon Jr 4 and 3			
151 Johnny Perelli					
154 Tony Manero		Manero 4 and 3	Hagen 11 and 10		
149 Bobby Cruickshank					
141 Walter Hagen		Hagen 3 and 2			
148 Jack Farrell					
149 Mortie Dutra		Dutra 12 and 11	Dutra 2-up	Espinosa 1-up	
144 Albert Alcroft					
149 Charles Guest		Guest 3 and 2			
153 Roland Hancock					
146 Al Espinosa		Espinosa 5 and 4	Espinosa 5 and 4		
148 Mel Smith					
147 Harry Cooper		Cooper 7 and 6			
154 Eddie Murphy					
150 Ed Dudley		Dudley 8 and 7	Sarazen 4 and 3	Turnesa 3 and 2	Turnesa 7 and 6
152 James Gullane					
144 Gene Sarazen		Sarazen 1-up (37)			
154 J.G. Curley					
152 Willie Klein		Klein 1-up	Turnesa 1-up		
150 Bill Mehlhorn					
141 Joe Turnesa		Turnesa 5 and 3			
151 Charles. McKenna					
151 John Golden		Golden 2 and 1	Golden 1-up (37)	Golden 4 and 2	
153 Charles Koontz					
152 Harold Long		Long 4 and 3			
154 Willie Kidd					
147 Francis Gallett		Gallett 4 and 3	Gallett 2-up		
152 Bob Shave					
153 Ralph Beach		Beach 1-up			
154 Fred Baroni					

Hagen 1-up

1926 Qualifying for Match Play:

A 36-hole qualifying round was conducted the Monday before the Championship. Walter Hagen was the low qualifier of 32 players with 140. A score of 154 qualified for match play, with Abe Espinosa tying five other players at 155 and beating them in a playoff. Notable players who didn't make it to match play were Emmet French (155 lost in playoff), Cyril Walker (157) and Bill Mehlhorn (157). All matches played at 36 holes.

Early Matches: In the first round, the match between Gene Sarazen and Jim Barnes gained the most attention. Both former PGA Champions, Sarazen was 1-up during the afternoon round when he breezed along to make the turn in 32 and eventually won, 5 and 4. In other matches: Joe Turnesa, who finished second to Bobby Jones in the U.S.

I n the final between Hagen and Diegel, it was obvious that Diegel was suffering from an attack of nerves when he became 2-down after 6 holes.

Open, was beaten, 3 and 2, by Walter Hagen; Al Watrous lost to Johnny Farrell, 6 and 5; and Larry Nabholtz, who defeated Sarazen in 1924, went down to Harry Hampton, 6 and 5.

In the second round, Gene Sarazen was defeated by Johnny Golden, 4 and 3. For Sarazen, it was the third year in a row that he lost a match in either the first or second round. The best match of the day was between Abe Espinosa and Mike Brady, with Espinosa winning, 1-up.

In the quarter-finals Golden crushed George Christ, 7 and 6; while Johnny Farrell defeated Harry Hampton, 3 and 1; Leo Diegel beat Abe Espinosa, 3 and 2; and Walter Hagen rolled over Pat Doyle, 6 and 5.

In the semifinal match between Hagen and Farrell, Hagen tied the course record of 68 in the morning round, while Farrell shot 70 to find himself 2-down at the mid-way point. In the afternoon, Hagen continued his fine play as he made the turn in 33 strokes to Farrell's 36 and went on to win the match, 6 and 5. Hagen was 8-under, and for the 31 holes played had required 52 putts against Farrell's 57. The other semifinal match between Diegel and Golden looked like a rout, as Diegel played the

morning round in 68, having as much as a 5-up lead. But Golden fought back and by the 34th hole was down 2. He won the 35th hole, but was only able to get a four at the last hole, despite a chip which hung on the lip, to give Diegel a 1-up win.

In the final between Hagen and Diegel, it was obvious that Diegel was suffering from an attack of nerves when he became 2-down after 6 holes. He was able to reduce it by one at the turn with a par 36 against Hagen's 35. Diegel squared the match on the 11th, but Hagen won the next hole with a birdie. The next four holes were halved, but Hagen got a birdie on the 17th. The final hole of the morning round was halved, and although

Diegel regained his composure and shot a 1-under-par 71, he was 2-down as Hagen shot 69 for the round.

Starting out in the afternoon, Diegel had problems on the first hole, as he overshot the green and his ball stopped on a road, under a car. When the owner moved the car, Diegel's ball was in a deep rut. It took him three swipes to get it on the green and he lost the hole to go 3-down. Even with the bad start, Diegel won the next hole and after 27 holes was still 2-down. But Hagen won the 28th and 31st and was 4-up. It was only a matter of time, as Diegel produced a six on the 33rd hole to give Hagen a 5-and-3 victory and his fourth PGA Championship in six years.

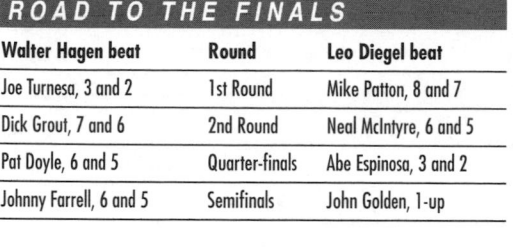

Champion: Walter Hagen, Rochester, N.Y.*	
Site: Salisbury Golf Links, Westbury, Long Island, N.Y.	
Date: Sept. 20-25	Par: 36-36—72
Purse: $11,100	

ROAD TO THE FINALS

Walter Hagen beat	Round	Leo Diegel beat
Joe Turnesa, 3 and 2	1st Round	Mike Patton, 8 and 7
Dick Grout, 7 and 6	2nd Round	Neal McIntyre, 6 and 5
Pat Doyle, 6 and 5	Quarter-finals	Abe Espinosa, 3 and 2
Johnny Farrell, 6 and 5	Semifinals	John Golden, 1-up

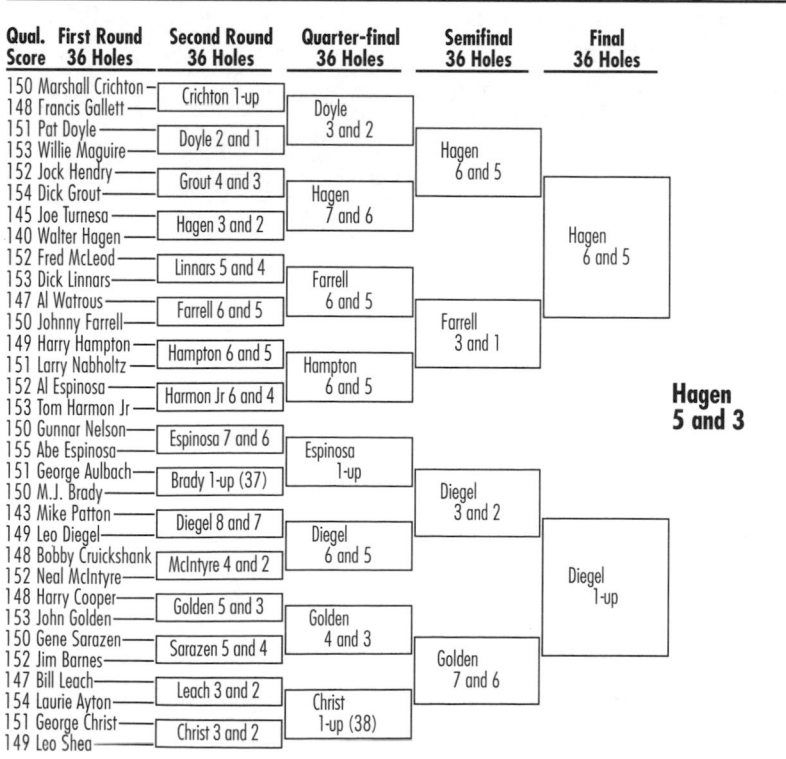

Qual. Score	First Round 36 Holes	Second Round 36 Holes	Quarter-final 36 Holes	Semifinal 36 Holes	Final 36 Holes
150 Marshall Crichton		Crichton 1-up			
148 Francis Gallett			Doyle 3 and 2		
151 Pat Doyle		Doyle 2 and 1			
153 Willie Maguire				Hagen 6 and 5	
152 Jock Hendry		Grout 4 and 3			
154 Dick Grout			Hagen 7 and 6		
145 Joe Turnesa		Hagen 3 and 2			
140 Walter Hagen					Hagen 6 and 5
152 Fred McLeod		Linnars 5 and 4			
153 Dick Linnars			Farrell 6 and 5		
147 Al Watrous		Farrell 6 and 5			
150 Johnny Farrell				Farrell 3 and 1	
149 Harry Hampton		Hampton 6 and 5			
151 Larry Nabholtz			Hampton 6 and 5		
152 Al Espinosa		Harmon Jr 6 and 4			
153 Tom Harmon Jr					
150 Gunnar Nelson		Espinosa 7 and 6			
155 Abe Espinosa			Espinosa 1-up		
151 George Aulbach		Brady 1-up (37)			
150 M.J. Brady				Diegel 3 and 2	
143 Mike Patton		Diegel 8 and 7			
149 Leo Diegel			Diegel 6 and 5		
148 Bobby Cruickshank		McIntyre 4 and 2			
152 Neal McIntyre					Diegel 1-up
148 Harry Cooper		Golden 5 and 3			
153 John Golden			Golden 4 and 3		
150 Gene Sarazen		Sarazen 5 and 4			
152 Jim Barnes				Golden 7 and 6	
147 Bill Leach		Leach 3 and 2			
154 Laurie Ayton			Christ 1-up (38)		
151 George Christ		Christ 3 and 2			
149 Leo Shea					

Hagen 5 and 3

1925

Qualifying for Match Play: A 36-hole qualifying round was conducted the Monday before the Championship. Al Watrous was the low qualifier of 32 players with 140. A score of 157 qualified for match play. All matches played at 36 holes.

Early Matches: The biggest suprise of the first round was the defeat of two-time PGA Champion Gene Sarazen, who went down in an 8-and-7 drubbing at the hands of Jack Burke. Another key match in the first round saw the defending PGA Champion Walter Hagen face low qualifier Al Watrous. Throughout the morning round Hagen trailed, but neither player was able to gather an advantage of more than one hole. Hagen came to the final hole in the

> *The biggest surprise of the first round was the defeat of two-time PGA Champion Gene Sarazen, who went down in an 8-and-7 drubbing at the hands of Jack Burke.*

afternoon dormie one, but lost the hole to send the match into overtime. Hagen won the 39th hole.

No real upsets in the second round, but Al Espinosa did take Bill Mehlhorn to the final hole before losing 1-down.

In the quarter-finals Johnny Farrell was beaten by Harry Cooper, 2 and 1, Mortie Dutra defeated Tommy Armour, 2-up, and Bill Mehlhorn crushed Tom Kerrigan, 7 and 6. In the match between Leo Diegel and Hagen, it looked like the defending PGA Champion was about to go down in defeat. In the morning round, Hagen got off to a poor start, taking five holes before he finally made a par. After the front nine, Diegel stood 4-up and finished the round 5-up. Hagen cut it to 2-down after the 27th hole, but both players halved the next five holes. Hagen got another hole back and sent the match into overtime by winning the 36th hole. On the fourth extra hole, Hagen won to advance to the semifinals.

There he met Harry Cooper, a young professional from Texas. They played even through the morning round, each having a 74, but on the first nine of the afternoon round, Hagen picked up a two-hole advantage and carried it to the 35th tee. A win on this hole gave him the match, 3 and 1. Mehlhorn had an easy match against Mor-

Champion:	Walter Hagen, Rochester, N.Y.*	
Site:	Olympia Fields CC, Olympia Fields, Ill.	
Date:	Sept. 21-26	Purse: $6,330

ROAD TO THE FINALS

Walter Hagen beat	Round	Bill Mehlhorn beat
Al Watrous, 1-up 39 holes	1st Round	Emmett French, 5 and 4
Mike Brady, 7 and 6	2nd Round	Al Espinosa, 1-up
Leo Diegel, 1-up 40 holes	Quarter-finals	Tom Kerrigan, 7 and 6
Harry Cooper, 3 and 1	Semifinals	Mortie Dutra, 8 and 6

tie Dutra, despite a close morning round where he held Mehlhorn close. In the afternoon, Dutra's game fell apart on the front nine and Mehlhorn cruised to an 8-and-6 win.

In the final, Hagen started strong with an eagle on the first hole, birdie at the second and a front nine of 33, 2-under-par. But Hagen was only 1-up as Mehlhorn also shot a 33. Hagen's hot round continued on

the back side, where he matched par on every hole except for a birdie at the 13th for a 67. Despite equalling par on the round, Mehlhorn found himself 4-down.

In the afternoon round, Hagen again shot 33 on the front nine and picked up another hole on Mehlhorn who had a 1-under-par 34. By then it was only a matter of time as Hagen won two more holes and closed out the match on the 31st hole, 6 and 5.

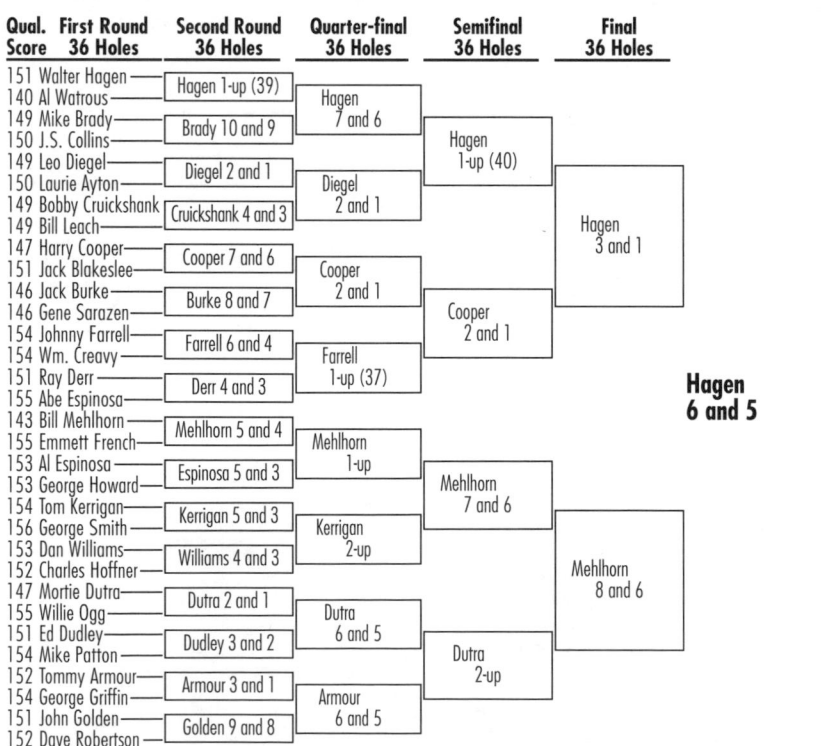

Qual. Score	First Round 36 Holes	Second Round 36 Holes	Quarter-final 36 Holes	Semifinal 36 Holes	Final 36 Holes
151 Walter Hagen	Hagen 1-up (39)				
140 Al Watrous		Hagen 7 and 6			
149 Mike Brady	Brady 10 and 9				
150 J.S. Collins			Hagen 1-up (40)		
149 Leo Diegel	Diegel 2 and 1				
150 Laurie Ayton		Diegel 2 and 1			
149 Bobby Cruickshank	Cruickshank 4 and 3				
149 Bill Leach				Hagen 3 and 1	
147 Harry Cooper	Cooper 7 and 6				
151 Jack Blakeslee		Cooper 2 and 1			
146 Jack Burke	Burke 8 and 7				
146 Gene Sarazen			Cooper 2 and 1		
154 Johnny Farrell	Farrell 6 and 4				
154 Wm. Creavy		Farrell 1-up (37)			
151 Ray Derr	Derr 4 and 3				
155 Abe Espinosa					Hagen 6 and 5
143 Bill Mehlhorn	Mehlhorn 5 and 4				
155 Emmett French		Mehlhorn 1-up			
153 Al Espinosa	Espinosa 5 and 3				
153 George Howard			Mehlhorn 7 and 6		
154 Tom Kerrigan	Kerrigan 5 and 3				
156 George Smith		Kerrigan 2-up			
153 Dan Williams	Williams 4 and 3				
152 Charles Hoffner				Mehlhorn 8 and 6	
147 Mortie Dutra	Dutra 2 and 1				
155 Willie Ogg		Dutra 6 and 5			
151 Ed Dudley	Dudley 3 and 2				
154 Mike Patton			Dutra 2-up		
152 Tommy Armour	Armour 3 and 1				
154 George Griffin		Armour 6 and 5			
151 John Golden	Golden 9 and 8				
152 Dave Robertson					

1924

Qualifying for Match Play: A 36-hole qualifying round was conducted the Monday before the Championship. Johnny Farrell was the low qualifier of 32 players with 140. A score of 150 qualified for match play. All matches played at 36 holes.

Early Matches: The opening round featured a number of close matches, as Jim Barnes defeated Mike Brady on the 39th hole, and defending PGA Champion Gene Sarazen beat the 1919 runner-up Fred McLeod, 5 and 4. Two notable upsets were recorded, as Francis Gallett defeated Bill Mehlhorn, 4 and 3, and 1920 PGA Cham-

Champion: Walter Hagen, Rochester, N.Y.*	
Site:	French Springs GC, French Lick, Ind.
Date:	Sept. 15-20 Purse: $6,830

ROAD TO THE FINALS

Walter Hagen beat	Round	Jim Barnes beat
Tom Harmon, 6 and 5	1st Round	Mike Brady, 1-up 39 holes
Al Watrous, 4 and 3	2nd Round	Eddie Towns, 10 and 9
Johnny Farrell, 3 and 2	Quarter-finals	Emmett French, 6 and 4
Ray Derr, 8 and 7	Semifinals	Larry Nabholtz, 1-up

The final was Barnes' chance to avenge his loss to Hagen in the finals of the 1921 Championship, but a balky putter failed him in crucial periods.

pion Jock Hutchison was beaten by Eddie Towns, 4 and 3.

In the second round, Sarazen, undefeated in two previous Championships, was beaten by Larry Nabholtz, a youngster from Lima, Ohio, 2 and 1. Bobby Cruickshank was also a victim as he lost to Ray Derr, 2 and 1, despite the fact that Cruickshank held a 3-up advantage after the morning round.

In the quarter-finals, the only match that was close to a struggle was the one between Ray Derr and Al Espinosa, with Derr winning, 2 and 1. Hagen defeated Johnny Farrell easily, 3 and 2, Nabholtz beat Henry Ciuci, 5 and 4, while Barnes smothered 1922 runner-up, Emmett French, 6 and 4. Barnes had a 69 during the morning round, a 34 out in the afternoon and even fours for the next five holes.

In the semifinal, Hagen had an easy time beating Derr, 8 and 7, while Barnes was having a little tougher time beating Nabholtz. He was 1-down after the morning round and didn't gain any of it back with two holes left to play. But thanks to a three at the 35th hole, he squared the match, and Nabholtz's inexperience in major competition cost him the match. The 24-year-old's second shot to the home hole was over the green. Instead of putting the ball down the slope, he used a niblick and skidded his ball way past the hole. He two-putted and,

with Barnes making a routine par, Nabholtz lost the match, 1-down.

The final was Barnes' chance to avenge his loss to Hagen in the finals of the 1921 Championship, but a balky putter failed him in crucial periods. During the morning round he had four three-putt greens and each one cost him a hole as he went to lunch 4-down. In the afternoon, Barnes fought back with a front nine of 34 and, with a

birdie on the 29th hole, cut Hagen's lead to 1-up. They traded wins at the 30th and 31st holes, but when Hagen won the 34th hole Barnes was dormie two. On the 35th hole, Hagen took three putts, his second one missing from three feet. Going to the finishing hole, Barnes needed a win to send the match into overtime, but a bad drive followed by a shanked mashie niblick gave the match to Hagen, 2-up.

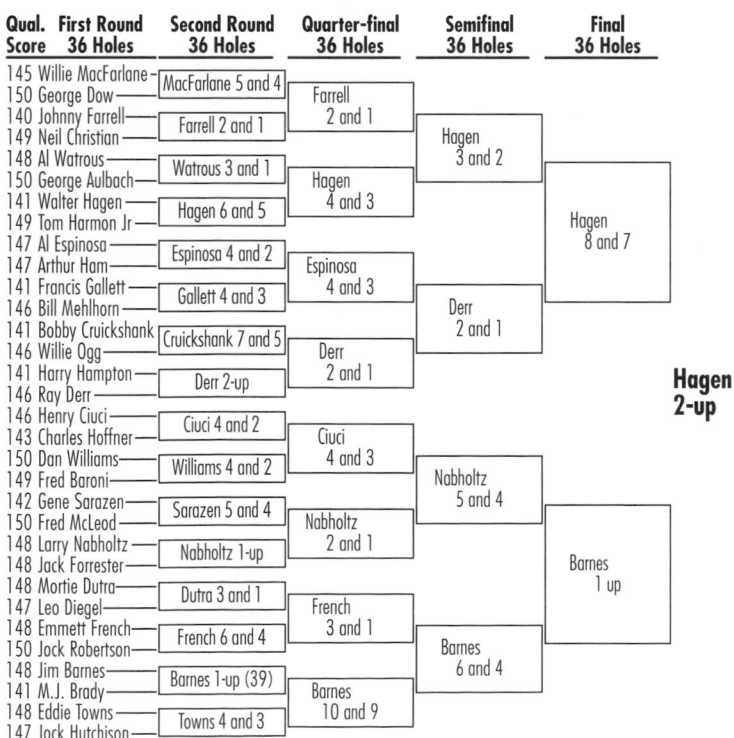

Qual. Score	First Round 36 Holes	Second Round 36 Holes	Quarter-final 36 Holes	Semifinal 36 Holes	Final 36 Holes
145 Willie MacFarlane	MacFarlane 5 and 4				
150 George Dow		Farrell 2 and 1			
140 Johnny Farrell	Farrell 2 and 1				
149 Neil Christian			Hagen 3 and 2		
148 Al Watrous	Watrous 3 and 1				
150 George Aulbach		Hagen 4 and 3			
141 Walter Hagen	Hagen 6 and 5				
149 Tom Harmon Jr				Hagen 8 and 7	
147 Al Espinosa	Espinosa 4 and 2				
147 Arthur Ham		Espinosa 4 and 3			
141 Francis Gallett	Gallett 4 and 3				
146 Bill Mehlhorn			Derr 2 and 1		
141 Bobby Cruickshank	Cruickshank 7 and 5				
146 Willie Ogg		Derr 2-up			
141 Harry Hampton	Derr 2-up				
146 Ray Derr					Hagen 2-up
146 Henry Ciuci	Ciuci 4 and 2				
143 Charles Hoffner		Ciuci 4 and 3			
150 Dan Williams	Williams 4 and 2				
149 Fred Baroni			Nabholtz 2 and 1		
142 Gene Sarazen	Sarazen 5 and 4				
150 Fred McLeod		Nabholtz 2 and 1			
148 Larry Nabholtz	Nabholtz 1-up				
148 Jack Forrester				Nabholtz 5 and 4	
148 Mortie Dutra	Dutra 3 and 1				
147 Leo Diegel		French 3 and 1			
148 Emmett French	French 6 and 4				
150 Jock Robertson			Barnes 6 and 4		
148 Jim Barnes	Barnes 1-up (39)				
141 M.J. Brady		Barnes 10 and 9			
148 Eddie Towns	Towns 4 and 3				
147 Jock Hutchison				Barnes 1 up	

1923

Qualifying for Match Play: The field for match play consisted of 64 players who qualified in local districts. All matches played at 36 holes.

Early Matches: No surprises in the first three rounds set up quarter-final matches of Bobby Cruickshank and Willie MacFarlane, Gene Sarazen and Jim Barnes, Joe Kirkwood and George McLean and Fred McLeod and Walter Hagen. In the McLean/Kirkwood match, McLean won handily, 5 and 4, with Hagen handing McLeod a 5-and-4 loss. It took Cruickshank 39 holes to beat MacFarlane, 1-up, and Sarazen won his match, 1-up. But Sarazen had to struggle to beat Barnes. Even though he had a 3-up lead after the morning round, Barnes fought back. Barnes made an eagle-3 at the 35th hole to square the match. It took a birdie at the final hole for Sarazen to claim victory.

The semifinals were rollovers for both Sarazen and Hagen. For the second year in a row, Sarazen met Cruickshank in the semis, with Sarazen outputting Cruickshank to easily beat him, 6 and 5. Hagen gained a decisive 12-and-11 victory over McLean to gain a berth in the finals, which matched two PGA Champions.

In one of the PGA Championship's most exciting finals, Sarazen successfully defended his title by defeating Hagen in the first extra-hole final in the history of the Championship. But it took one of Hagen's patented charges to get it to extra holes.

After the morning round the match was even. After the front nine in the afternoon, Sarazen had a 3-up lead. Hagen birdied the 29th hole to cut the lead to two, and won the 34th and 35th to square the match. The final hole was halved, sending the match into overtime. The first hole was halved, but the match almost ended on the tee shots at the second hole when Sarazen hit into heavy rough, just a couple of feet away from an out-of-bounds fence. With a crowd gathered around him, he was heard telling some of them, "I'll put this one up so close to the hole that it will break Walter's heart," and he did it. It was one of the most magnificent shots ever made in championship golf, dropping short of the pin and coming to rest two feet away from a certain birdie.

With the situation drastically changed and Hagen knowing he must have a birdie to halve the hole, he succumbed to the pressure and flubbed his ball into a greenside trap. Hagen was determined not to lose and came very close to holing his bunker shot, coming within inches of getting his birdie.

Champion: Gene Sarazen, New York, N.Y.*
Site: Pelham GC, Pelham Manor, N.Y.
Date: Sept. 23-29 **Par:** 36-36—72 **Purse:** $3,600

ROAD TO THE FINALS

Gene Sarazen beat	Round	Walter Hagen beat
Lloyd Gullickson, 8 and 7	1st Round	George Griffin, 4 and 3
D.K. White, 11 and 10	2nd Round	Jack Elplick, 10 and 9
Alec Campbell, 3 and 2	3rd Round	John Golden, 4 and 3
Jim Barnes, 1-up	Quarter-finals	Fred McLeod, 5 and 4
Bobby Cruickshank, 6 and 5	Semifinals	George McLean, 12 and 11

First Round 36 Holes	Second Round 36 Holes	Third Round 36 Holes	Quarter-final 36 Holes	Semifinal 36 Holes	Final 36 Holes
Herbert Obendorf / George Underwood	Obendorf 5 and 4	Cruickshank 7 and 5			
Bobby Cruickshank / Bill Leach	Cruickshank 2 and 1		Cruickshank 1-up		
Frank Coltart / John Edmundson	Coltart 1-up	Derr 5 and 4		Cruickshank 1-up (39)	
Ray Derr / Charles Hoffner	Derr 2 and 1				
Willie MacFarlane / George Stark	MacFarlane 6 and 5	MacFarlane 3 and 2			
Louis Chiapetta / Wilfred Reid	Reid 4 and 2		MacFarlane 5 and 4		
Jack Stait / Harry Ellis	Stait 7 and 6	Stait 1-up			
Jack Forrester / Herbert Nicoll	Forrester 6 and 4				Sarazen 6 and 5
George Dernback / Jim Barnes	Barnes 12 and 11	Barnes 12 and 11			
John Cowan / Herbert Meyering	Cowan 9 and 8		Barnes 8 and 7		
Alex Ellis, Jr / Harry Cooper	Cooper 7 and 6	Walker 2 and 1			
Willie Maguire / Cyril Walker	Walker 5 and 4			Sarazen 1-up	
Chas. Rowe / Willie Klein	Klein 4 and 3	Campbell 4 and 3			
Nick DeMane / Alec Campbell	Campbell 4 and 3		Sarazen 3 and 2		
Lloyd Gullickson / Gene Sarazen	Sarazen 8 and 7	Sarazen 11 and 10			
D.K. White / Carl Rocco	White 9 and 8				
Clarence Hackney / Al Hackbarth	Hackney 6 and 5	Hackney 7 and 6			
Jim Carberry / R.S. Miner	Miner 4 and 2		McLeod 1-up		
James Meehan / Austie Claeyssens	Meehan 7 and 6	McLeod 4 and 3			
Fred McLeod / Wiffy Cox	McLeod 5 and 4			Hagen 5 and 4	
Walter Hagen / George Griffin	Hagen 4 and 3	Hagen 10 and 9			
Jack Elplick / Ralph Thomas	Elplick 4 and 2		Hagen 4 and 3		
Pat Doyle / Robert Barnett	Barnett 5 and 4	Golden 1-up			
Wilbur Jack / John Golden	Golden 5 and 4				Hagen 12 and 11
Joe Kirkwood / Wm. Goebel	Kirkwood 6 and 4	Kirkwood 2-up			
James West / Alex Gerard	West 5 and 3		Kirkwood 1-up		
Al Watrous / Willie Hunter	Hunter 2 and 1	Farrell 4 and 3			
Dave McKay / Johnny Farrell	Farrell 1-up		McLean 1-up (38)		
George McLean / Dave Stevens	McLean by default	McLean 6 and 4		McLean 5 and 4	
Jimmie Donaldson / Eddie Loos	Donaldson by default				
Carl Anderson / Stuart Sanderson	Anderson 1-up (37)	Ogg 12 and 11			
Willie Ogg / Fred Baroni	Ogg 2 and 1				

Sarazen 1-up (38)

118

1922

Qualifying for Match Play: The field for match play was 64 players who qualified in local districts. All first matches were played at 18 holes with the rest of the matches played at 36 holes.

Early Matches: The early surprise of the Championship was that Walter Hagen would not defend his title due to exhibition engagements. In the first three rounds there were no upsets except for last year's runner-up, Jim Barnes, losing to Johnny Farrell by one hole in the second round. Farrell then was eliminated by his former mentor, Tom Kerrigan, 4 and 3.

Going into the quarter-finals, Jock

*G*ene Sarazan, a 20-year-old Italian youngster, had reached a new milestone in golf as he became the first player to hold the U.S. Open and PGA Championship titles at the same time.

Hutchison was given a chance to avenge his loss in the 1921 PGA Championship when he met Gene Sarazen, the U.S. Open Champion. The match went to the 35th hole, with Sarazen winning, 3 and 1, after trailing Hutchison through the morning half and the greater part of the afternoon.

In the semifinals, Sarazen met Bobby Cruickshank in what was called the battle of the midgets, but Sarazen came out on top with a 3-and-2 victory. In the other match, Emmet French handily disposed of John Golden, 8 and 7.

The first 18 was nip and tuck with the match going to lunch all square. After 26 holes the match was still even, but Sarazen won the 27th, 28th and 29th holes. They halved the 30th but Sarazen won the 31st. With halves at the 32nd and 33rd holes, Sarazen won the match, 4 and 3. The 20-year-old Italian youngster had reached a new milestone in golf as he became the first player to hold the U.S. Open and PGA Championship titles at the same time.

Champion: Gene Sarazen, Flushing, N.Y.*
Site: Oakmont CC, Oakmont, Pa.
Date: Aug. 12-18 **Par:** 36-35—71 **Purse:** $2,580

ROAD TO THE FINALS

Gene Sarazen beat	Round	Emmett French beat
Tom Mahan, 3 and 2	1st Round	George Gordon, 4 and 2
Willie Ogg, 2 and 1	2nd Round	Mike Brady, 3 and 1
Frank Sprogell, 9 and 7	3rd Round	R.S. Minor, 8 and 7
Jock Hutchison, 3 and 1	Quarter-finals	Emil Loeffler, 4 and 2
Bobby Cruickshank, 3 and 2	Semifinals	John Golden, 8 and 7

First Round 18 Holes	Second Round 18 Holes	Third Round 18 Holes	Quarter-final 36 Holes	Semifinal 36 Holes	Final 36 Holes
Fred Brand / Chas. Clarke	Brand by default	Gallett 5 and 4	Cruickshank 7 and 6	Cruickshank 3 and 2	Sarazen 3 and 2
Francis Gallett / Wilfred Reid	Gallett 6 and 4				
Al Watrous / George Sargent	Watrous 1-up	Cruickshank 3 and 2			
Bobby Cruickshank / George Underwood	Cruickshank 7 and 6				
Peter Walsh / Dave McKay	Walsh 2 and 1	Burgess 3 and 2	Rowe 6 and 5		
Jack Burgess / A.J. Chapman	Burgess 4 and 3				
Tom Boyd / John Edmundson	Boyd 5 and 4	Rowe 3 and 1			
Chas. Rowe / Wm. Robinson	Rowe 1-up				
Frank Sprogell / Willie Hunter	Sprogell 3 and 1	Sprogell 4 and 3	Sarazen 9 and 7	Sarazen 3 and 1	
Dan Kenny / Earl Rowly	Kenny 2-up				
Gene Sarazen / Tom Mahan	Sarazen 3 and 2	Sarazen 2 and 1			
Willie Ogg / Clarence Hackney	Ogg 2-up				
Dan Goss / N. Zimmerman	Goss 6 and 5	Hutchison 6 and 4	Hutchison 4 and 3		
Jock Hutchison / L. Goldbeck	Hutchison 6 and 5				
Charles Hoffner / Larry Nabholtz	Hoffner 3 and 1	Hampton 3 and 2			
Harry Hampton / Jack Gordon	Hampton 3 and 2				
Tom Kerrigan / Archie Loeffler	Kerrigan 5 and 4	Kerrigan 5 and 4	Kerrigan 4 and 3	Golden 4 and 3	French 8 and 7
Chas. Hilgendorf / George Dernback	Hilgendorf 5 and 4				
Johnny Farrell / Jack Campbell	Farrell 6 and 5	Farrell 1-up			
Jim Barnes / George McLean	Barnes 2 and 1				
John Golden / Frank Coltart	Golden 4 and 3	Golden 8 and 7	Golden 3 and 2		
P.J. Gaudin / T.K. Minley	Gaudin 3 and 2				
Al Ciuci / Carl Giehler	Ciuci 2 and-up	Ciuci 4 and 2			
George Stark / John Rogers	Stark 1-up (20)				
Emil Loeffler / Walter Leoffler	Loeffler 4 and 3	Loeffler 4 and 3	Loeffler 2 and 1	French 4 and 2	
Dave Robertson / Tom McNamara	Robertson 3 and 2				
Matt Duffy / Laurie Ayton	Duffy by default	Towns 1-up			
Eddie Towns / Tom Harmon Jr	Towns by default				
Fred Baroni / John Rowe	Baroni 4 and 3	Miner 1-up (19)	French 8 and 7		
R.S. Miner / Jim Carberry	Miner by default				
Emmett French / George Gordon	French 4 and 2	French 7-up			
Mike Brady / Gil Nichols	Brady 1-up				

Sarazen 4 and 3

1921

Qualifying for Match Play: The field for match play was selected on a basis of the best 31 finishers in the U.S. Open, with last year's champion, Jock Hutchison, becoming the 32nd person. All matches played at 36 holes.

Early Matches: The surprise in the early rounds was the defeat of defending PGA Champion and newly-crowned British Open Champion Jock Hutchison in the second round by a 19-year-old youngster named Gene Sarazen. A former caddie, Sarazen had Hutchison 8-down after the first 18 holes, thanks in part to a brilliant 69. It was only a matter of time before Sarazen won the match, 8 and 6. Hutchison, who had been hitting the ball erratically since his return from the British Open, showed signs that he wasn't going to repeat his performance of the previous year when it took three extra holes to decide his first round match with Pat O'Hara.

In the third round, Sarazen came back down to earth when he shot a morning

Champion:	Walter Hagen, Rochester, N.Y.*	
Site:	Inwood CC, Far Rockaway, N.Y.	
Date:	Sept. 26-Oct. 1	Purse: $2,580

ROAD TO THE FINALS

Walter Hagen beat	Round	Jim Barnes beat
Jack Forrester, 6 and 4	1st Round	Clarence Hackney, 3 and 2
Tim Boyd, 6 and 5	2nd Round	Bob Cruickshank, 8 and 7
Jack Golden, 8 and 7	Quarter-finals	Fred McLeod, 11 and 9
Emmett French, 5 and 3	Semifinals	Cyril Walker, 5 and 4

Walter Hagen offered to postpone their match, but Cyril Walker refused and they went on to the bitter end with Hagen winning, 5 and 4.

In the finals, it was a perfect match-up of two players at the peak of their games. Barnes, who in previous matches had four rounds under 70, was unable to hold Hagen. Hagen had a 69 to finish the morning round 1-up. In the afternoon, Hagen continued his brilliant all-around game and putted spectacularly with a front nine 4-under 33 to go 4-up. Hagen closed the match at the 34th hole, winning the match, 3 and 2.

---

*H*utchison, who had been hitting the ball erratically since his return from the British Open, showed signs that he wasn't going to repeat his performance of the previous year.

---

round 80 against Cyril Walker, and went down to defeat, 5 and 4. Emmet French defeated George McLean, 5 and 3; Walter Hagen clobbered Jack Golden, 8 and 7; and Jim Barnes, the U.S. Open Champion, rolled along to an 11-and-9 victory over 1919 runner-up Fred McLeod.

The semifinals were contested in miserable weather conditions with a terrific rainstorm putting a halt to the French-Barnes match, with Barnes leading 2-up. The next morning they finished off the remaining 12 holes of the match, with Barnes winning, 5 and 3. In the other semifinal match,

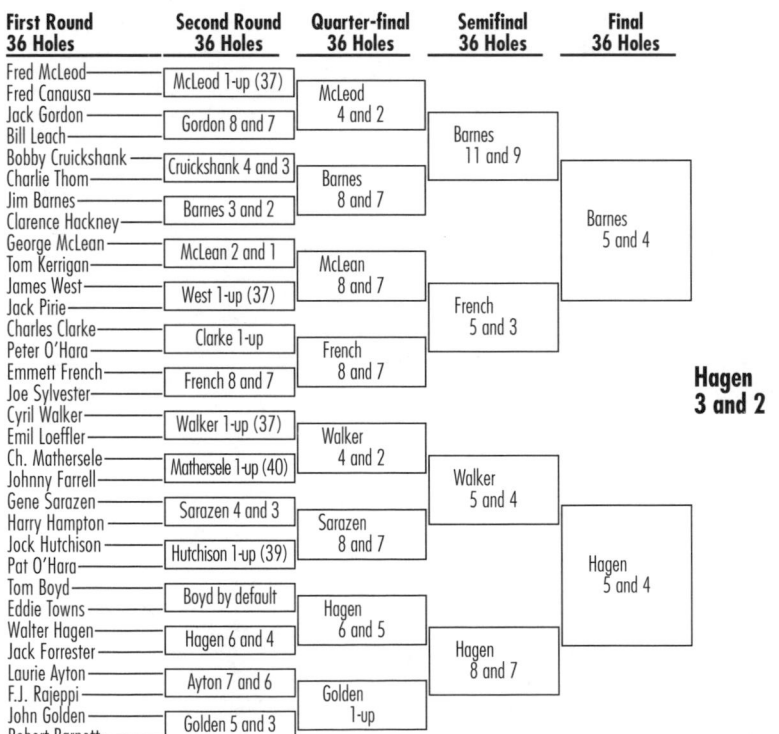

First Round 36 Holes	Second Round 36 Holes	Quarter-final 36 Holes	Semifinal 36 Holes	Final 36 Holes
Fred McLeod / Fred Canausa	McLeod 1-up (37)	McLeod 4 and 2		
Jack Gordon / Bill Leach	Gordon 8 and 7		Barnes 11 and 9	
Bobby Cruickshank / Charlie Thom	Cruickshank 4 and 3	Barnes 8 and 7		
Jim Barnes / Clarence Hackney	Barnes 3 and 2			Barnes 5 and 4
George McLean / Tom Kerrigan	McLean 2 and 1	McLean 8 and 7		
James West / Jack Pirie	West 1-up (37)		French 5 and 3	
Charles Clarke / Peter O'Hara	Clarke 1-up	French 8 and 7		
Emmett French / Joe Sylvester	French 8 and 7			
Cyril Walker / Emil Loeffler	Walker 1-up (37)	Walker 4 and 2		
Ch. Mathersele / Johnny Farrell	Mathersele 1-up (40)		Walker 5 and 4	
Gene Sarazen / Harry Hampton	Sarazen 4 and 3	Sarazen 8 and 7		
Jock Hutchison / Pat O'Hara	Hutchison 1-up (39)			Hagen 5 and 4
Tom Boyd / Eddie Towns	Boyd by default	Hagen 6 and 5		
Walter Hagen / Jack Forrester	Hagen 6 and 4		Hagen 8 and 7	
Laurie Ayton / F.J. Rajeppi	Ayton 7 and 6	Golden 1-up		
John Golden / Robert Barnett	Golden 5 and 3			

Hagen 3 and 2

1920

Qualifying for Match Play: Qualification rounds were held in different sections of the country before the Championship. All matches played at 36 holes.

Early Matches: Although Jock Hutchison failed initially to qualify for the 1920 Championship, he emerged as the Champion, thanks in part to George Fotheringhan and Arthur Clarkson being unable to attend, which allowed Hutchison into the match play.

Athough there were no major upsets in the first round, the second round brought about the elimination of two-time Cham-

In the semifinals Hutchison beat Hampton, 4 and 3, but victory was much harder than the margin indicated. Had it not been for a brilliant start and a couple of stymies the match probably would have gone to the final hole.

pion Jim Barnes, who was unbeaten in 11 previous Championship matches. He was beaten by Clarence Hackney, 5 and 4, as Hackney dominated the match from the beginning, winning the first three holes and taking a 4-up lead at the mid-way point. In the afternoon, Barnes was not able to pull off one of his record-breaking rounds as he had done in previous Championships.

In the third round, George McLean, who was 5-down at the 24th hole to Peter O'Hara, gradually trimmed the deficit. He won the home hole, squared the match and eventually won on the 38th green. McLean's incoming round was 33, 5-under-par. In other matches, Douglas Edgar beat Bob MacDonald, 5 and 4, thanks to a morning round of 71 and a stretch of holes where he scored 3, 3, 4, 3, 3 and 3. This great run gave Edgar a lead of 6-up at the 27th hole and he closed MacDonald out at the 32nd hole with a birdie 3. Harry Hampton beat Hackney, 4 and 3, with Hutchison defeating Louis Tellier, 6 and 5.

In the semifinals Hutchison beat Hampton, 4 and 3, but victory was much harder than the margin indicated. Had it not been for a brilliant start and a couple of stymies the match probably would have gone

to the final hole. In the other semifinal match, Edgar gained entrance to the final by trouncing McLean, 8 and 6.

In the finals, Edgar won the first two holes, but Hutchison was 1-up after the morning round play, due to Edgar missing a three-footer at 16 and an 18-inch putt on the 17th hole. The afternoon round was full of incidents as Hutchison was out in 35 to Edgar's 37, making Hutchison 3-up at the turn. Hutchison increased his lead with a win at the 28th hole, but Edgar got it back at the 29th. They halved the next two holes and with five holes left to play, Hutchison

was 3-up. Hutchison had driving problems the next two holes and lost both of them. He was 1-up with three holes to play and again hit a bad tee shot into the rough, but made a wonderful shot to the green, to help him get a four. Edgar was on the green in two, but three-putted, missing a five-footer. Instead of winning the hole and drawing the match even, he went to the tee 2-down. On a stymie, Hutchison lost the hole, but won the match, 1-up, when Edgar trapped his second shot on the final hole and both players halved in five.

Champion:	Jock Hutchison, Glenview, Ill.*	
Site:	Flossmoor CC, Chicago, Ill.	
Date:	Aug. 17-21	Purse: $2,580

ROAD TO THE FINALS

Jock Hutchison beat	Round	Douglas Edgar beat
Eddie Loos, 4 and 3	1st Round	Pat O'Hara, 1-up
L. Ayton, 5 and 3	2nd Round	J. Sylvester, 11 and 9
Louis Tellier, 6 and 5	Quarter-finals	Bob MacDonald, 5 and 4
Harry Hampton, 4 and 3	Semifinals	George McLean, 8 and 6

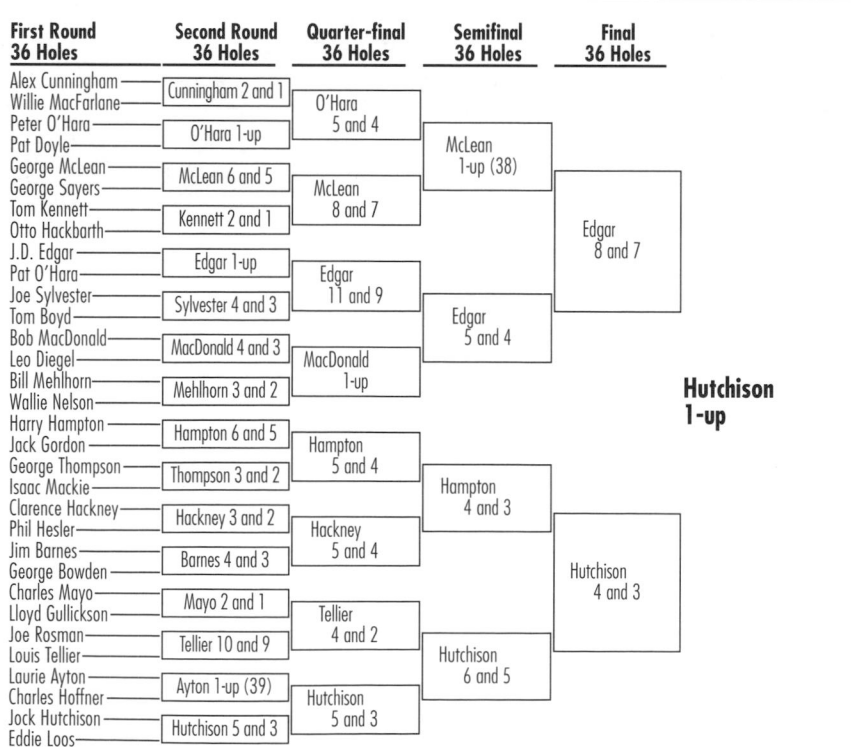

First Round 36 Holes	Second Round 36 Holes	Quarter-final 36 Holes	Semifinal 36 Holes	Final 36 Holes
Alex Cunningham / Willie MacFarlane	Cunningham 2 and 1	O'Hara 5 and 4	McLean 1-up (38)	Edgar 8 and 7
Peter O'Hara / Pat Doyle	O'Hara 1-up			
George McLean / George Sayers	McLean 6 and 5	McLean 8 and 7		
Tom Kennett / Otto Hackbarth	Kennett 2 and 1			
J.D. Edgar / Pat O'Hara	Edgar 1-up	Edgar 11 and 9	Edgar 5 and 4	
Joe Sylvester / Tom Boyd	Sylvester 4 and 3			
Bob MacDonald / Leo Diegel	MacDonald 4 and 3	MacDonald 1-up		
Bill Mehlhorn / Wallie Nelson	Mehlhorn 3 and 2			
Harry Hampton / Jack Gordon	Hampton 6 and 5	Hampton 5 and 4	Hampton 4 and 3	Hutchison 4 and 3
George Thompson / Isaac Mackie	Thompson 3 and 2			
Clarence Hackney / Phil Hesler	Hackney 3 and 2	Hackney 5 and 4		
Jim Barnes / George Bowden	Barnes 4 and 3			
Charles Mayo / Lloyd Gullickson	Mayo 2 and 1	Tellier 4 and 2	Hutchison 6 and 5	
Joe Rosman / Louis Tellier	Tellier 10 and 9			
Laurie Ayton / Charles Hoffner	Ayton 1-up (39)	Hutchison 5 and 3		
Jock Hutchison / Eddie Loos	Hutchison 5 and 3			

Hutchison 1-up

1919

Qualifying for Match Play: Qualification rounds were held in different sections of the country before the Championship. All matches played at 36 holes.

Early Matches: The first round opened with perfect golfing weather, which continued all through the week and produced no surprises.

The second round found a couple of upsets when George McLean beat Mike Brady, 6 and 5, and Jimmy West defeated Wilfred Reid, 2 and 1. It also had the battle of two giants, Otto Hackbarth and Jim Barnes, the two tallest players in the tournament. Barnes won the match on the 34th

Champion:	Jim Barnes, St. Louis, Mo.*	
Site:	Engineers CC, Roslyn, Long Island, N.Y.	
Date:	Sept. 15-20	Par: 35-35—70
Purse:	$2,580	

ROAD TO THE FINALS

Jim Barnes beat	Round	Fred McLeod beat
Carl Anderson, 8 and 6	1st Round	James Rose, 9 and 7
Otto Hackbarth, 3 and 2	2nd Round	George Gordon, 2-up
Emmett French, 3 and 2	Quarter-finals	J.D. Edgar, 8 and 6
Bob McDonald, 5 and 4	Semifinals	George McLean, 3 and 2

*J*ust like in 1916, there was an Englishman and a Scot in the final, as the smallest man in the field (McLeod at 5'3") was meeting the tallest man in the field (Barnes 6'3").

green, 3 and 2, thanks to some great putting.

The quarter-finals saw 1916 runner-up Jock Hutchison lose to Bob McDonald, 3 and 2. In the rest of the matches, Barnes defeated Emmet French, 3 and 2, McLean clobbered West, 9 and 7; and Fred McLeod, the 1908 U.S. Open Champion from Carnoustie, Scotland, gave an 8-and-6 drubbing to J.D. Edgar.

Three "Macs" gave the semifinals a Scottish atmosphere, with Fred McLeod beating McLean, 3 and 2, thanks to some great putting. In the afternoon half of the match, McLeod had five straight one-putts, which helped decide the contest. In the other match, Barnes proved that he was the player to beat from the tees through greens as he overpowered Bob McDonald, 5 and 4.

Just like in 1916, there was an Englishman and a Scot in the final, as the smallest man in the field (McLeod at 5'3") was meeting the tallest man in the field (Barnes 6'3"). It was billed as David vs. Goliath and, after a front nine 37, McLeod had a

1-up lead. He won the 10th hole but, at the 11th, McLeod's approach to the green was a bit strong; then he missed a 1 1/2 foot putt. He went on to lose six of the remaining seven holes to end the first 18 holes 5-down. In the afternoon it seemed nothing went right for the wee Scotsman as long

putts hung on the lip of the hole, and Barnes proved to be too good as he holed a 40-foot birdie putt on the 31st hole for a 6-and-5 victory. Again for his win, Barnes won $500 and a diamond medal, and McLeod won $250 and a gold medal.

First Round 36 Holes	Second Round 36 Holes	Quarter-final 36 Holes	Semifinal 36 Holes	Final 36 Holes
Jim Barnes / Carl Anderson	Barnes 8 and 6	Barnes 3 and 2	Barnes 3 and 2	Barnes 5 and 4
Joe Sylvester / Otto Hackbarth	Hackbarth 5 and 4			
Bill Mehlhorn / Tom Kerrigan	Kerrigan 3 and 2	French 2-up		
Emmett French / Clarence Hackney	French 7 and 6			
Bob MacDonald / Tom Boyd	MacDonald 1-up	MacDonald 2 and 1	MacDonald 3 and 2	
George Fotheringham / Eddie Loos	Fotheringham 8 and 6			
Tom McNamara / Louis Martucci	McNamara 7 and 6	Hutchison 8 and 6		
Jock Hutchison / John Bredemus	Hutchison 6 and 5			
Jack Hobens / Harry Hampton	Hampton 7 and 6	Edgar 5 and 4	McLeod 8 and 6	
Joe Rosman / J.D. Edgar	Edgar by default			
James Rose / Fred McLeod	McLeod 9 and 7	McLeod 2-up		McLeod 3 and 2
Dave Wilson / George Gordon	Gordon 3 and 2			
Pat Doyle / Wilfred Reid	Reid 1-up	West 2 and 1	McLean 9 and 7	
James West / Willie Kidd	West by default			
Louis Tellier / M.J. Brady	Brady 7 and 6	McLean 6 and 5		
Johnny Farrell / George McLean	McLean 7 and 6			

Barnes 6 and 5

1917-18 No Championship Played Due To World War I

1916

Qualifying for Match Play: Qualification rounds were held in different sections of the country before the Championship. All matches played at 36 holes.

Early Matches: Thomas Kerrigan has the distinction of being the first player to hit a shot in the inaugural PGA Championship, en route to a 6-and-4 victory over Charles Adams. In the first round, everything went as expected, although Wilfred Reid, after being 5-down to J.J. O'Brien, squared the match only to lose at the last hole.

In the second round, the match of the day was between Walter Hagen and Bob

Champion: Jim Barnes, Philadelphia, Pa.*	
Site:	Siwanoy CC, Bronxville, N.Y.
Date: Oct. 9-14	Purse: *$2,580

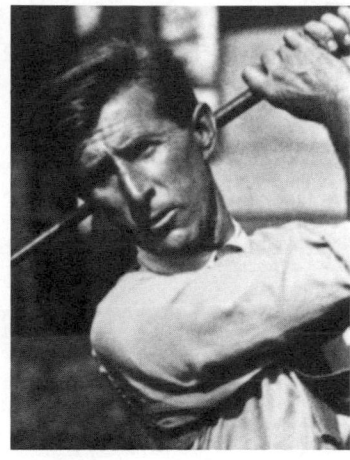

ROAD TO THE FINALS

Jim Barnes beat	Round	Jock Hutchison beat
G. Fotheringham, 8 and 7	1st Round	Joe Mitchell, 11 and 7
Alexander Smith, 8 and 7	2nd Round	William Brown, 11 and 9
Tom Kerrigan, 3 and 1	Quarter-finals	Cyril Walker, 4 and 3
Willie MacFarlane, 6 and 5	Semifinals	Walter Hagen, 2-up

On the final green, both Hutchison and Barnes had five-footers for fours and after a measurement it was decided that Hutchison was out. Hutchison missed the putt and Barnes made his, winning 1-up.

McDonald. Even though Hagen won, 3 and 2, it took nine putts on the last seven greens for Hagen to account for the win.

In the quarter-finals, Siwanoy Club's home professional Tom Kerrigan did battle with "Big Jim" Barnes. Despite playing the last 13 holes of their 36-hole match in even fours, Kerrigan lost, 3 and 1, to Barnes, who registered the lowest score by any professional in the Championship, an even par 71. In the other contests, all the favorites won, with Hagen beating O'Brien, 10 and 9; Willie MacFarlane beating Jack Dowling, 2 and 1; and Jock Hutchison beating Cyril Walker, 4 and 3.

In the semifinals, three British-born golfers and one American-born were matched. After 27 holes in the match between Hagen and Hutchison, Hagen was 1-up, but lost the 12th and 13th holes. The next four holes were halved and with Hagen hitting his second shot into a brook short of the green, Hutchison won the match, 2-up. In the other half of the semifinals, Jim Barnes had no difficulty in outplaying Willie MacFarlane, 6 and 5. Large galleries followed the matches despite the fact that rain fell during the afternoon.

In the morning round, Hutchison jumped out to a 3-up lead, shooting 37 to

Barnes' 39. On the back side, Barnes reduced the lead to one, with both players scoring 77 in the first 18 holes. After a break the match resumed with Barnes telling the crowd, before his drive on the first hole, "I always do better after lunch." Barnes squared the match at the 21st hole and took the lead for the first time at the 25th hole with an 18-foot putt. The 27th hole was halved in birdie threes with Barnes making a 35-footer putt. Barnes made another long (25 feet) curling putt on the next hole to go 2-up. Hutchison didn't give up

and made a 15-foot birdie at the next hole to go to 1-down. Hutchison squared the match with a three at the 31st hole and took a 1-up lead at the 33rd hole. The 34th hole was halved in fours but Hutchison missed a five-footer on the next hole to square the match. On the final green, both players had five-footers for fours and after a measurement it was decided that Hutchison was out. Hutchison missed the putt and Barnes made his, winning 1-up. "Big Jim" won $500 and a diamond medal. Hutchison got a gold medal and $250.

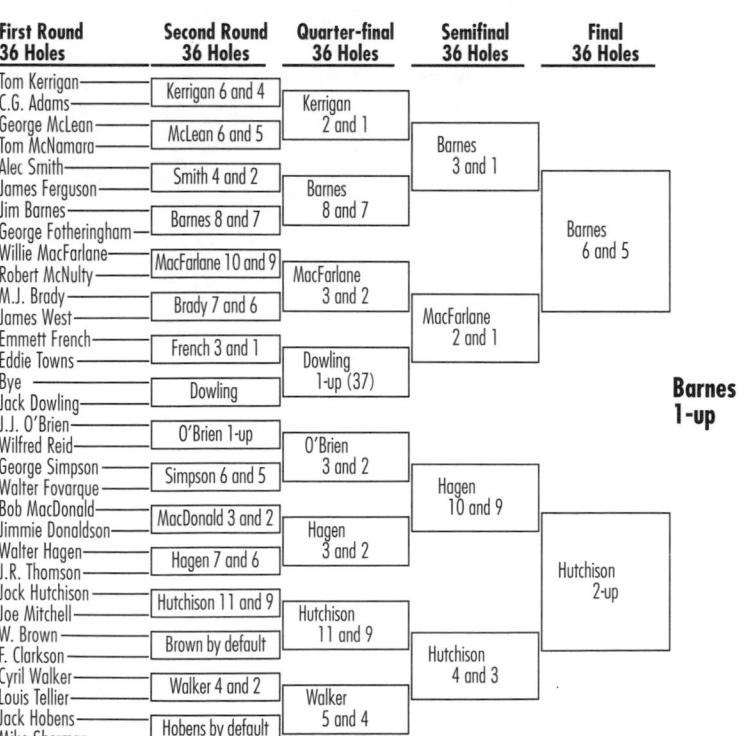

First Round 36 Holes	Second Round 36 Holes	Quarter-final 36 Holes	Semifinal 36 Holes	Final 36 Holes
Tom Kerrigan / C.G. Adams	Kerrigan 6 and 4	Kerrigan 2 and 1		
George McLean / Tom McNamara	McLean 6 and 5		Barnes 3 and 1	
Alec Smith / James Ferguson	Smith 4 and 2	Barnes 8 and 7		
Jim Barnes / George Fotheringham	Barnes 8 and 7			Barnes 6 and 5
Willie MacFarlane / Robert McNulty	MacFarlane 10 and 9	MacFarlane 3 and 2		
M.J. Brady / James West	Brady 7 and 6		MacFarlane 2 and 1	
Emmett French / Eddie Towns	French 3 and 1	Dowling 1-up (37)		
Bye / Jack Dowling	Dowling			Barnes 1-up
J.J. O'Brien / Wilfred Reid	O'Brien 1-up	O'Brien 3 and 2		
George Simpson / Walter Fovarque	Simpson 6 and 5		Hagen 10 and 9	
Bob MacDonald / Jimmie Donaldson	MacDonald 3 and 2	Hagen 3 and 2		
Walter Hagen / J.R. Thomson	Hagen 7 and 6			Hutchison 2-up
Jock Hutchison / Joe Mitchell	Hutchison 11 and 9	Hutchison 11 and 9		
W. Brown / F. Clarkson	Brown by default		Hutchison 4 and 3	
Cyril Walker / Louis Tellier	Walker 4 and 2	Walker 5 and 4		
Jack Hobens / Mike Sherman	Hobens by default			

■ SELECTED PLAYER RECORDS FOR THE PGA CHAMPIONSHIP
Stroke-Play Records (1958 to present)

Player	Best Finish	Years	Rds	Cuts Made	3	5	10	25	Low Rd	High Rd	Avg.	Rds 65 or Better	Rds in 60s	Rds Under Par	Par Rounds	Money	$ Per Stroke	$ Per Event
Tommy Aaron	T-2nd in 1972	15	54	12	1	1	2	5	65	79	72.89	1	4	7	128	$33,814.31	$8.59	$2,254.29
Bryan Abbott	Missed Cut	2	4	0	0	0	0	0	75	78	76.50	0	0	0	20	$553.00	$1.81	$276.50
Jerry Abbott	Missed Cut	2	4	0	0	0	0	0	75	80	76.75	0	0	0	23	$0.00	$0.00	$0.00
Pat Abbott	Missed Cut	1	2	0	0	0	0	0	78	84	81.00	0	0	0	20	$0.00	$0.00	$0.00
Roy Abrameit	Missed Cut	2	4	0	0	0	0	0	76	80	78.25	0	0	0	33	$850.00	$2.72	$425.00
Bob Ackerman	Missed Cut	1	2	0	0	0	0	0	72	76	74.00	0	0	0	6	$1,000.00	$6.76	$1,000.00
Rick Acton	Missed Cut	4	8	0	0	0	0	0	75	85	78.63	0	0	0	61	$2,553.00	$4.06	$638.25
Buck Adams	Missed Cut	2	4	0	0	0	0	0	76	83	79.50	0	0	0	36	$0.00	$0.00	$0.00
John Adams	T-55th in 1983	3	10	2	0	0	0	0	70	78	74.20	0	0	1	32	$5,060.00	$6.82	$1,686.67
Sam Adams	Missed Cut	1	2	0	0	0	0	0	73	78	75.50	0	0	0	11	$0.00	$0.00	$0.00
Dean Adkisson	Missed Cut	1	2	0	0	0	0	0	80	84	82.00	0	0	0	24	$0.00	$0.00	$0.00
Bobby Afton	Missed Cut	1	2	0	0	0	0	0	77	82	79.50	0	0	0	15	$250.00	$1.57	$250.00
Jim Ahern	Missed Cut	1	2	0	0	0	0	0	76	80	78.00	0	0	0	14	$303.00	$1.94	$303.00
Bob Akcerman	Missed Cut	1	2	0	0	0	0	0	72	77	74.50	0	0	0	7	$1,000.00	$6.71	$1,000.00
Jim Albus	T-65th in 1984	7	16	1	0	0	0	0	71	81	75.88	0	0	1	80	$5,992.50	$4.94	$856.07
Ron Aleks	Missed Cut	1	2	0	0	0	0	0	82	89	85.50	0	0	0	31	$0.00	$0.00	$0.00
Chuck Alexander	Missed Cut	1	2	0	0	0	0	0	79	82	80.50	0	0	0	21	$0.00	$0.00	$0.00
John Alexander	Missed Cut	2	4	0	0	0	0	0	76	80	78.00	0	0	0	32	$0.00	$0.00	$0.00
Walter All	Missed Cut	1	2	0	0	0	0	0	80	84	82.00	0	0	0	22	$0.00	$0.00	$0.00
Ken Allard	Missed Cut	6	12	0	0	0	0	0	71	86	76.42	0	0	1	61	$6,400.00	$6.98	$1,066.67
Fulton Allem	T-31st in 1993	4	12	2	0	0	0	0	70	79	72.83	0	0	2	20	$14,220.19	$16.27	$3,555.05
Johnny Allen	Missed Cut	1	2	0	0	0	0	0	76	80	78.00	0	0	0	14	$0.00	$0.00	$0.00
Michael Allen	T-61st in 1993	1	4	1	0	0	0	0	69	75	71.75	0	1	2	3	$2,800.00	$9.76	$2,800.00
Ras Allen	Missed Cut	2	4	0	0	0	0	0	73	80	76.00	0	0	0	22	$0.00	$0.00	$0.00
Robert Allenby	Missed Cut	1	2	0	0	0	0	0	71	74	72.50	0	0	0	3	$1,200.00	$8.28	$1,200.00
Buddy Allin	T-10th in 1975	6	21	4	0	0	1	1	67	78	73.29	0	2	2	57	$7,730.86	$5.02	$1,288.48
Mark Alwin	Missed Cut	1	2	0	0	0	0	0	77	77	77.00	0	0	0	14	$350.00	$2.27	$350.00
Brad Anderson	T-22nd in 1971	3	8	1	0	0	0	1	70	81	75.13	0	0	2	33	$2,088.00	$3.47	$696.00
Max Anderson	Missed Cut	2	4	0	0	0	0	0	77	82	80.00	0	0	0	38	$303.00	$0.95	$151.50
Billy Andrade	T-12th in 1992	5	16	3	0	0	0	2	68	75	72.50	0	1	2	14	$58,966.66	$50.83	$11,793.33
Dale Andreason	Missed Cut	2	3	0	0	0	0	0	76	78	77.00	0	0	0	21	$0.00	$0.00	$0.00
Leon Andrews	Missed Cut	1	2	0	0	0	0	0	75	76	75.50	0	0	0	11	$0.00	$0.00	$0.00
Tim Angis	Missed Cut	1	2	0	0	0	0	0	70	81	75.50	0	0	1	9	$1,200.00	$7.95	$1,200.00
Isao Aoki	T-4th in 1981	10	32	6	0	1	1	2	65	82	73.00	1	5	7	64	$44,172.54	$18.91	$4,417.25
Aubrey Apple	Missed Cut	1	2	0	0	0	0	0	80	86	83.00	0	0	0	26	$0.00	$0.00	$0.00
George Archer	T-4th in 1968	15	58	14	0	1	1	3	67	79	73.43	0	4	6	151	$24,955.18	$5.86	$1,663.68
Tommy Armour	T-24th in 1989	2	6	1	0	0	0	1	69	79	73.50	0	1	2	9	$11,000.00	$24.94	$5,500.00
Carroll Armstrong	Missed Cut	2	4	0	0	0	0	0	75	84	78.75	0	0	0	33	$0.00	$0.00	$0.00
Wally Armstrong	T-19th in 1978	5	18	4	0	0	0	1	69	81	73.67	0	1	2	54	$4,742.50	$3.58	$948.50
Bruce Ashworth	Missed Cut	2	4	0	0	0	0	0	72	81	76.25	0	0	0	23	$1,650.00	$5.41	$825.00
Alphonso Atkins	Missed Cut	4	10	0	0	0	0	0	74	83	76.10	0	0	0	61	$0.00	$0.00	$0.00
Fred Atkins	Missed Cut	1	2	0	0	0	0	0	82	83	82.50	0	0	0	25	$0.00	$0.00	$0.00
Robert Atkins	Missed Cut	1	2	0	0	0	0	0	82	87	84.50	0	0	0	29	$250.00	$1.48	$250.00
Hampton Auld	Missed Cut	1	2	0	0	0	0	0	78	78	78.00	0	0	0	14	$0.00	$0.00	$0.00
Mike Austin	Missed Cut	1	2	0	0	0	0	0	73	77	75.00	0	0	0	10	$0.00	$0.00	$0.00
Jim Awtrey	Missed Cut	1	2	0	0	0	0	0	79	79	79.00	0	0	0	14	$0.00	$0.00	$0.00
Tommy Aycock	T-11th in 1974	8	24	4	0	0	0	1	68	82	74.63	0	1	1	101	$7,732.50	$4.32	$966.56
Paul Azinger	Won in 1993	8	24	4	2	2	2	2	66	82	72.79	0	7	8	35	$417,500.00	$238.98	$52,187.50
Larry Babica	Missed Cut	1	2	0	0	0	0	0	79	82	80.50	0	0	0	19	$1,000.00	$6.21	$1,000.00
Merle Backlund	Missed Cut	6	12	0	0	0	0	0	74	85	81.42	0	0	0	133	$0.00	$0.00	$0.00
Bob Bailey	Missed Cut	1	2	0	0	0	0	0	72	75	73.50	0	0	0	5	$1,200.00	$8.16	$1,200.00
Jeff Bailey	Missed Cut	1	2	0	0	0	0	0	84	84	84.00	0	0	0	24	$1,000.00	$5.95	$1,000.00
Butch Baird	T-28th in 1966	6	20	4	0	0	0	0	69	79	73.55	0	1	1	59	$3,892.85	$2.65	$648.81
Fred Baker	Missed Cut	2	5	0	0	0	0	0	72	80	77.20	0	0	0	36	$0.00	$0.00	$0.00
Gary Baker	Missed Cut	1	2	0	0	0	0	0	79	83	81.00	0	0	0	22	$550.00	$3.40	$550.00
Mike Baker	Withdrew, 1965	1	1	0	0	0	0	0	85	85	85.00	0	0	0	14	$0.00	$0.00	$0.00
Ralph Baker	Missed Cut	1	2	0	0	0	0	0	74	78	76.00	0	0	0	12	$0.00	$0.00	$0.00
Ian Baker-Finch	T-34th in 1989	5	18	4	0	0	0	0	68	78	73.39	0	2	5	33	$14,412.50	$10.91	$2,882.50
Ron Bakich	T-75th in 1963	2	6	1	0	0	0	0	73	80	76.67	0	0	0	34	$158.33	$0.34	$79.17
Jack Baldwin	Missed Cut	1	2	0	0	0	0	0	76	83	79.50	0	0	0	19	$250.00	$1.57	$250.00
Errie Ball	T-33rd in 1958	3	11	2	0	0	0	0	72	81	75.36	0	0	0	59	$520.00	$0.63	$173.33
Gary Balleitt	Missed Cut	1	2	0	0	0	0	0	79	80	79.50	0	0	0	17	$1,000.00	$6.29	$1,000.00
Seve Ballesteros	5th in 1984	11	38	8	0	1	2	5	66	83	72.05	0	6	13	34	$93,758.33	$34.24	$8,523.48
Michael Ballo	Missed Cut	1	2	0	0	0	0	0	76	76	76.00	0	0	0	8	$0.00	$0.00	$0.00
Stan Baluik	Missed Cut	1	2	0	0	0	0	0	76	78	77.00	0	0	0	12	$0.00	$0.00	$0.00
Louis Barbaro	Missed Cut	2	4	0	0	0	0	0	77	79	78.25	0	0	0	33	$0.00	$0.00	$0.00
Dave Barber	T-54th in 1979	7	16	1	0	0	0	0	69	80	75.94	0	1	1	87	$3,820.50	$3.14	$545.79
James Barber	Missed Cut	1	2	0	0	0	0	0	75	76	75.50	0	0	0	11	$0.00	$0.00	$0.00
Jerry Barber	Won in 1961	22	52	4	2	2	2	2	65	84	75.94	1	5	5	288	$17,569.65	$4.45	$798.62
Jim Barber	Missed Cut	1	2	0	0	0	0	0	77	82	82.50	0	0	0	25	$250.00	$1.52	$250.00
Miller Barber	T-4th in 1971	15	55	12	0	2	3	6	64	81	72.69	1	6	8	121	$33,149.80	$8.29	$2,209.99
Bill Barclay	Missed Cut	1	2	0	0	0	0	0	82	88	85.00	0	0	0	30	$0.00	$0.00	$0.00

PGA CHAMPIONSHIP STROKE-PLAY STATISTICS

Player	Best Finish	Years	Rds	Cuts Made	3	5	10	25	Low Rd	High Rd	Avg.	Rds 65 or Better	Rds in 60s	Rds Under Par	Par Rounds	Money	$ Per Stroke	$ Per Event
Paul Barkhouse	Missed Cut	1	2	0	0	0	0	0	75	77	76.00	0	0	0	10	$303.00	$1.99	$303.00
John Barnum	T-16th in 1958	6	20	4	0	0	0	1	66	84	75.10	0	2	2	96	$1,337.50	$0.89	$222.92
Dave Barr	T-38th in 1985	8	26	5	0	0	0	0	69	79	73.00	0	1	3	52	$13,565.35	$7.15	$1,695.67
Jerry Barrier	Missed Cut	1	2	0	0	0	0	0	77	81	79.00	0	0	0	18	$0.00	$0.00	$0.00
Herman Barron	T-5 in 1958	3	9	1	0	0	0	0	71	83	76.00	0	0	0	54	$62.00	$0.24	$54.00
Louis Bartoletti	Missed Cut	1	2	0	0	0	0	0	74	78	76.00	0	0	0	10	$1,200.00	$7.89	$1,200.00
Larry Bartosek	62nd in 1958	2	8	2	0	0	0	0	74	80	77.13	0	0	0	53	$400.00	$0.65	$200.00
Richard Bassett	72nd in 1967	2	6	1	0	0	0	0	69	86	75.67	0	1	2	26	$950.00	$2.09	$475.00
Charles Bassler	T-29th in 1961	4	12	1	0	0	0	0	72	79	74.83	0	0	0	58	$425.00	$0.47	$106.25
Mel Baum	Missed Cut	2	4	0	0	0	0	0	77	81	79.25	0	0	0	31	$2,200.00	$6.94	$1,100.00
Rex Baxter	T-68th in 1972	8	19	1	0	0	0	0	73	82	76.63	0	0	0	120	$1,083.00	$0.74	$135.38
George Bayer	T-3rd in 1962	7	25	5	1	1	1	2	69	80	73.44	0	1	1	82	$5,107.50	$2.78	$729.64
Andy Bean	2nd in 1980 & '89	13	44	9	3	3	4	6	66	81	72.41	0	8	15	60	$195,823.76	$61.46	$15,063.37
Frank Beard	T-6th in 1968	12	46	11	0	0	3	6	67	80	72.52	0	6	13	88	$28,513.00	$8.55	$2,376.08
Roy Beattie	Missed Cut	1	2	0	0	0	0	0	82	82	82.00	0	0	0	24	$0.00	$0.00	$0.00
Avery Beck	Missed Cut	2	5	0	0	0	0	0	73	78	75.60	0	0	0	28	$0.00	$0.00	$0.00
Chip Beck	T-5th in 1990	12	40	8	0	1	1	5	67	80	72.70	0	3	13	54	$96,584.27	$33.21	$8,048.69
Larry Beck	T-72nd in 1966	1	4	1	0	0	0	0	71	79	76.00	0	0	0	24	$300.00	$0.99	$300.00
Richard Beckman	Missed Cut	1	2	0	0	0	0	0	77	77	77.00	0	0	0	14	$0.00	$0.00	$0.00
Frank Beley	T-75th in 1963	3	8	1	0	0	0	0	74	80	76.75	0	0	0	50	$158.33	$0.26	$52.78
Carl Beljan	Missed Cut	1	2	0	0	0	0	0	78	81	79.50	0	0	0	19	$0.00	$0.00	$0.00
Willie Beljan	Missed Cut	2	5	0	0	0	0	0	75	87	79.40	0	0	0	45	$0.00	$0.00	$0.00
Jack Bell	Missed Cut	1	2	0	0	0	0	0	76	79	77.50	0	0	0	15	$0.00	$0.00	$0.00
George Bellino	Missed Cut	7	14	0	0	0	0	0	73	84	77.86	0	0	0	98	$803.00	$0.74	$114.71
Jimmy Bellizzi	Missed Cut	2	4	0	0	0	0	0	79	85	81.00	0	0	0	42	$0.00	$0.00	$0.00
Bob Below	Missed Cut	1	2	0	0	0	0	0	74	76	75.00	0	0	0	10	$0.00	$0.00	$0.00
Jerry Belt	Missed Cut	1	2	0	0	0	0	0	75	82	78.50	0	0	0	17	$0.00	$0.00	$0.00
Deane Beman	T-36th in 1972	4	16	4	0	0	0	0	71	77	73.81	0	0	1	49	$2,255.00	$1.91	$563.75
Mike Bencriscutto	Missed Cut	1	2	0	0	0	0	0	76	84	80.00	0	0	0	20	$0.00	$0.00	$0.00
Jim Benepe	Missed Cut	1	2	0	0	0	0	0	71	74	72.50	0	0	0	3	$1,000.00	$6.90	$1,000.00
Ray Bennett	Missed Cut	1	2	0	0	0	0	0	78	83	80.50	0	0	0	21	$0.00	$0.00	$0.00
Bob Benning	T-64th in 1968	2	6	1	0	0	0	0	71	84	77.33	0	0	0	44	$615.00	$1.33	$307.50
Bob Benson	T-60th in 1975	2	8	2	0	0	0	0	68	85	75.75	0	1	1	38	$916.66	$1.51	$458.33
Steve Benson	Missed Cut	4	8	0	0	0	0	0	71	81	77.25	0	0	0	52	$2,853.00	$4.62	$713.25
Scott Bentley	Missed Cut	1	2	0	0	0	0	0	74	75	74.50	0	0	0	5	$1,000.00	$6.71	$1,000.00
Sam Bernardi	T-55th in 1961	2	6	1	0	0	0	0	72	77	75.00	0	0	0	30	$225.00	$0.50	$112.50
John Berry	T-44th in 1967	2	7	1	0	0	0	0	70	78	74.00	0	0	1	20	$501.43	$0.97	$250.72
Scott Bess	T-52nd in 1988	5	16	3	0	0	0	0	69	77	73.75	0	2	2	48	$6,207.50	$5.26	$1,241.50
Al Besselink	T-33rd in 1964	7	20	3	0	0	0	0	71	83	75.50	0	0	0	106	$1,087.50	$0.72	$155.36
Bob Betley	T-47th in 1987	2	6	1	0	0	0	0	72	79	74.67	0	0	0	16	$3,400.00	$7.59	$1,700.00
Leo Biagetti	Missed Cut	4	10	0	0	0	0	0	70	82	76.90	0	0	0	67	$0.00	$0.00	$0.00
Don Bies	T-7th in 1967	12	42	9	0	0	2	3	64	79	72.93	1	5	8	95	$18,851.50	$6.15	$1,570.96
Paul Biggy	Missed Cut	3	6	0	0	0	0	0	76	83	79.50	0	0	0	55	$0.00	$0.00	$0.00
Bill Bisdorf	T-20th in 1967	10	30	5	0	0	0	1	69	80	74.43	0	1	2	113	$3,517.17	$1.58	$351.72
Vince Bizik	Missed Cut	2	4	0	0	0	0	0	76	82	79.00	0	0	0	32	$900.00	$2.85	$450.00
Ronnie Black	T-21st in 1986	6	22	5	0	0	0	2	68	82	73.00	0	1	6	36	$23,666.67	$14.74	$3,944.45
Woody Blackburn	T-40th in 1985	3	10	2	0	0	0	0	71	87	75.20	0	0	0	44	$3,850.00	$5.12	$1,283.33
Phil Blackmar	T-40th in 1987	6	22	5	0	0	0	0	67	83	73.95	0	2	4	53	$12,503.91	$7.69	$2,083.99
James Blair	65th in 1986	3	8	2	0	0	0	0	72	80	74.75	0	0	0	26	$4,825.00	$8.07	$1,608.33
Jay Don Blake	T-13th in 1991	5	15	3	0	0	0	2	68	79	73.00	0	3	4	23	$34,991.67	$31.96	$6,998.33
Homero Blancas	T-30th in 1970	6	20	4	0	0	0	0	70	81	74.40	0	0	0	78	$3,012.00	$2.02	$502.00
Rich Bland	Missed Cut	2	4	0	0	0	0	0	77	85	81.00	0	0	0	44	$250.00	$0.77	$125.00
Bill Blanton	74th in 1966	2	6	1	0	0	0	0	72	84	78.00	0	0	0	46	$300.00	$0.64	$150.00
Tom Blaskovich	Missed Cut	1	2	0	0	0	0	0	73	79	76.00	0	0	0	10	$0.00	$0.00	$0.00
Chris Blocker	Missed Cut	1	2	0	0	0	0	0	76	77	76.50	0	0	0	13	$0.00	$0.00	$0.00
Bob Bodington	Missed Cut	2	4	0	0	0	0	0	74	83	78.75	0	0	0	35	$0.00	$0.00	$0.00
Brien Boggess	Missed Cut	1	2	0	0	0	0	0	80	85	82.50	0	0	0	25	$0.00	$0.00	$0.00
Marty Bohen	Missed Cut	1	2	0	0	0	0	0	77	81	79.00	0	0	0	16	$1,000.00	$6.33	$1,000.00
Bob Boldt	Missed Cut	1	2	0	0	0	0	0	77	83	80.00	0	0	0	18	$303.00	$1.89	$303.00
Burl Bolesta	Missed Cut	1	2	0	0	0	0	0	76	80	78.00	0	0	0	16	$0.00	$0.00	$0.00
Tommy Bolt	3rd in 1971	9	27	5	1	2	2	3	68	81	73.11	0	4	4	74	$17,245.00	$8.74	$1,916.11
Ralph Bond	Missed Cut	3	6	0	0	0	0	0	74	85	80.50	0	0	0	63	$0.00	$0.00	$0.00
Paul Bondeson	Missed Cut	1	2	0	0	0	0	0	75	79	77.00	0	0	0	14	$0.00	$0.00	$0.00
Gene Bone	T-60th in 1973	7	19	2	0	0	0	0	71	85	76.11	0	0	0	102	$910.00	$0.63	$130.00
John Bonella	Missed Cut	1	2	0	0	0	0	0	83	87	85.00	0	0	0	28	$303.00	$1.78	$303.00
Billy Booe	Missed Cut	1	2	0	0	0	0	0	77	78	77.50	0	0	0	15	$0.00	$0.00	$0.00
Jim Booros	Missed Cut	1	2	0	0	0	0	0	69	79	74.00	0	1	1	8	$650.00	$4.39	$650.00
Gene Borek	T-30th in 1971	11	32	5	0	0	0	0	70	79	74.63	0	0	1	128	$5,756.17	$2.41	$523.29
Andy Borkovich	Missed Cut	3	6	0	0	0	0	0	73	83	78.50	0	0	0	45	$0.00	$0.00	$0.00
Ernie Boros	Missed Cut	1	2	0	0	0	0	0	78	82	80.00	0	0	0	18	$0.00	$0.00	$0.00
Julius Boros	Won in 1968	22	74	15	1	3	4	10	68	79	72.84	0	7	11	170	$51,680.96	$9.59	$2,349.13
Bob Borowicz	73rd in 1993	4	10	1	0	0	0	0	71	84	76.60	0	0	0	52	$5,675.00	$7.41	$1,418.75
Edward Bosse	Missed Cut	3	6	0	0	0	0	0	78	84	81.17	0	0	0	61	$0.00	$0.00	$0.00
Rafe Botts	Missed Cut	1	2	0	0	0	0	0	73	82	77.50	0	0	0	13	$0.00	$0.00	$0.00
Tony Bovitsky	Missed Cut	1	3	0	0	0	0	0	73	79	76.33	0	0	0	19	$0.00	$0.00	$0.00

Player	Best Finish	Years	Rds	Cuts Made	3	Top 5	10	25	Low Rd	High Rd	Avg.	Rds 65 or Better	Rds in 60s	Rds Under Par	Par Rounds	Money	$ Per Stroke	$ Per Event
Steve Bowen	Missed Cut	1	2	0	0	0	0	0	80	81	80.50	0	0	0	17	$1,000.00	$6.21	$1,000.00
Bob Boyd	T-19th in 1990	4	12	2	0	0	0	1	68	77	73.17	0	1	4	20	$18,850.00	$21.47	$4,712.50
Frank Boynton	T-8th in 1968	5	16	3	0	0	1	2	70	76	73.38	0	0	1	42	$5,378.06	$4.58	$1,075.61
Dennis Bradley	Missed Cut	3	6	0	0	0	0	0	75	82	78.33	0	0	0	44	$250.00	$0.53	$83.33
Jackson Bradley	T-31st in 1959	4	12	2	0	0	0	0	69	81	74.50	0	1	1	54	$362.50	$0.41	$90.63
Monte Bradley	Missed Cut	1	2	0	0	0	0	0	75	79	77.00	0	0	0	10	$0.00	$0.00	$0.00
Rob Bragg	Missed Cut	1	2	0	0	0	0	0	81	81	81.00	0	0	0	22	$350.00	$2.16	$350.00
Mike Brannan	Missed Cut	2	4	0	0	0	0	0	73	77	74.75	0	0	0	19	$850.00	$2.84	$425.00
Tom Brannen	T-38th in 1988	2	6	1	0	0	0	0	70	78	73.50	0	0	1	13	$4,211.11	$9.55	$2,105.56
Bob Bratzler	Missed Cut	1	2	0	0	0	0	0	73	77	75.00	0	0	0	10	$0.00	$0.00	$0.00
Jerry Breaux	T-60th in 1973	2	6	1	0	0	0	0	72	79	75.50	0	0	0	27	$663.00	$1.46	$331.50
Gay Brewer	T-7th in 1972	13	48	11	0	0	2	5	66	80	72.79	0	3	6	110	$20,033.00	$5.73	$1,541.00
Eldon Briggs	Missed Cut	2	4	0	0	0	0	0	74	78	76.50	0	0	0	26	$0.00	$0.00	$0.00
Mack Briggs	Missed Cut	1	2	0	0	0	0	0	78	82	80.00	0	0	0	20	$0.00	$0.00	$0.00
Don Brigham	Missed Cut	2	4	0	0	0	0	0	77	83	79.75	0	0	0	33	$2,000.00	$6.27	$1,000.00
Stan Brion	T-22nd in 1974	1	4	1	0	0	0	1	70	74	71.50	0	0	0	6	$2,182.50	$7.63	$2,182.50
Bill Britton	4th in 1990	6	20	4	0	1	1	2	67	78	73.20	0	1	6	36	$94,910.00	$64.83	$15,818.33
Bill Brodell	Missed Cut	1	2	0	0	0	0	0	75	79	77.00	0	0	0	12	$1,000.00	$6.49	$1,000.00
Mark Brooks	T-15th in 1992	6	16	2	0	0	0	1	68	80	74.06	0	2	2	41	$36,850.00	$31.10	$6,141.67
Al Brosch	T-59th in 1958	3	8	1	0	0	0	0	74	81	77.25	0	0	0	58	$100.00	$0.16	$33.33
Billy Ray Brown	T-40th in 1992	4	12	2	0	0	0	0	69	79	74.17	0	1	1	30	$9,300.00	$10.45	$2,325.00
Charles Brown	Missed Cut	1	2	0	0	0	0	0	79	81	80.00	0	0	0	20	$0.00	$0.00	$0.00
Francis Brown	Missed Cut	1	2	0	0	0	0	0	77	78	77.50	0	0	0	15	$0.00	$0.00	$0.00
Joe Brown	Missed Cut	4	9	0	0	0	0	0	74	81	76.22	0	0	0	56	$0.00	$0.00	$0.00
Jouett Brown	Missed Cut	4	8	0	0	0	0	0	72	80	77.13	0	0	0	55	$0.00	$0.00	$0.00
Ken Brown	T-24th in 1987	3	10	2	0	0	0	1	72	80	74.10	0	0	0	27	$8,525.00	$11.50	$2,841.67
Pete Brown	T-33rd in 1964	4	13	3	0	0	0	0	70	82	73.92	0	0	2	39	$1,607.17	$1.67	$401.79
Jim Browning	T-62nd in 1964	4	11	1	0	0	0	0	71	80	76.36	0	0	0	70	$220.00	$0.26	$55.00
Bobby Brue	T-12th in 1973	6	16	2	0	0	0	1	70	82	75.13	0	0	2	68	$4,817.25	$4.01	$802.88
Bob Bruno	T-66th in 1973	2	6	1	0	0	0	0	71	78	74.83	0	0	0	21	$360.00	$0.80	$180.00
George Bruno	Missed Cut	1	2	0	0	0	0	0	78	82	80.00	0	0	0	20	$0.00	$0.00	$0.00
Brad Bryant	T-48th in 1992	8	24	4	0	0	0	0	70	80	74.21	0	0	2	81	$11,455.00	$6.43	$1,431.88
George Buck	Missed Cut	1	2	0	0	0	0	0	74	80	77.00	0	0	0	14	$0.00	$0.00	$0.00
Ed Bucklin	Missed Cut	1	2	0	0	0	0	0	79	85	82.00	0	0	0	24	$0.00	$0.00	$0.00
Brent Buckman	Missed Cut	1	2	0	0	0	0	0	78	79	78.50	0	0	0	13	$1,000.00	$6.37	$1,000.00
Dick Bull	Missed Cut	1	2	0	0	0	0	0	77	84	80.50	0	0	0	17	$0.00	$0.00	$0.00
Steve Bull	Missed Cut	6	12	0	0	0	0	0	72	80	76.83	0	0	0	74	$0.00	$0.00	$0.00
Johnny Bulla	T-57th in 1961	8	21	2	0	0	0	0	73	80	75.76	0	0	0	111	$525.00	$0.33	$65.63
Craig Bunker	Missed Cut	1	2	0	0	0	0	0	79	80	79.50	0	0	0	19	$350.00	$2.20	$350.00
Eddie Burke	T-44th in 1958	3	9	1	0	0	0	0	72	81	75.56	0	0	0	50	$100.00	$0.15	$33.33
Jim Burke	Missed Cut	1	2	0	0	0	0	0	75	78	76.50	0	0	0	13	$0.00	$0.00	$0.00
Thomas Burke	Missed Cut	1	2	0	0	0	0	0	74	79	76.50	0	0	0	11	$0.00	$0.00	$0.00
Jack Burke Jr.	4th in 1958	15	58	14	0	1	2	4	69	79	73.31	0	3	4	164	$11,706.04	$2.75	$780.40
Michael Burke Jr.	Missed Cut	2	4	0	0	0	0	0	75	79	77.00	0	0	0	24	$2,200.00	$7.14	$1,100.00
Walter Burkemo	14th in 1961	13	40	7	0	0	0	5	66	83	73.88	0	2	2	141	$5,927.50	$2.01	$455.96
Ken Burnette	Missed Cut	1	2	0	0	0	0	0	76	77	76.50	0	0	0	13	$0.00	$0.00	$0.00
George Burns	T-19th in 1977 & '78	12	36	6	0	0	0	2	67	83	73.53	0	3	6	101	$16,852.86	$6.37	$1,404.41
Kevin Burton	T-71st in 1993	1	4	1	0	0	0	0	69	76	73.50	0	1	1	10	$2,512.50	$8.55	$2,512.50
Dick Bury	64th in 1970	3	9	1	0	0	0	0	73	78	75.44	0	0	0	49	$400.00	$0.59	$133.33
Leon Butler	64th in 1961	2	6	1	0	0	0	0	72	84	76.67	0	0	0	40	$225.00	$0.49	$112.50
George Buzzini	Missed Cut	1	2	0	0	0	0	0	77	78	77.50	0	0	0	15	$0.00	$0.00	$0.00
Bob Byman	T-21st in 1979	2	8	2	0	0	0	1	69	82	73.75	0	2	2	30	$3,950.00	$6.69	$1,975.00
Curt Byrum	T-14th in 1987	3	10	2	0	0	0	1	66	87	74.50	0	2	3	27	$13,920.00	$18.68	$4,640.00
Tom Byrum	T-47th in 1987	3	8	1	0	0	0	0	72	79	74.38	0	0	0	21	$4,400.00	$7.39	$1,466.67
George Cadle	T-15th in 1977	6	24	6	0	0	0	1	68	78	73.42	0	2	4	66	$10,455.56	$5.93	$1,742.59
John Calabria	Missed Cut	3	6	0	0	0	0	0	74	83	78.33	0	0	0	48	$2,150.00	$4.57	$716.67
M. Calcavecchia	T-17th in 1988	6	20	4	0	0	0	1	68	80	73.05	0	4	7	33	$30,245.20	$20.70	$5,040.87
Rex Caldwell	3rd in 1979	8	28	6	1	1	1	3	66	79	72.29	0	4	8	52	$37,809.25	$18.68	$4,726.16
Doug Campbell	Missed Cut	1	2	0	0	0	0	0	76	78	77.00	0	0	0	14	$500.00	$3.25	$500.00
Gary Campbell	Missed Cut	1	2	0	0	0	0	0	87	94	90.50	0	0	0	37	$250.00	$1.38	$250.00
Joe Campbell	T-27th in 1962	6	18	3	0	0	0	0	70	80	74.50	0	0	0	69	$1,314.50	$0.98	$219.08
Ken Campbell	Missed Cut	1	2	0	0	0	0	0	76	82	79.00	0	0	0	18	$0.00	$0.00	$0.00
J. M. Canizares	Missed Cut	1	2	0	0	0	0	0	72	81	76.50	0	0	0	11	$1,000.00	$6.54	$1,000.00
Ivan Cantz	Missed Cut	1	2	0	0	0	0	0	78	84	81.00	0	0	0	22	$0.00	$0.00	$0.00
Joseph Capello	Missed Cut	1	2	0	0	0	0	0	79	83	81.00	0	0	0	22	$0.00	$0.00	$0.00
Billy Capps	T-54th in 1965	5	12	1	0	0	0	0	74	84	77.00	0	0	0	76	$402.50	$0.44	$80.50
Joe Cardenas	T-67th in 1968	4	10	1	0	0	0	0	73	81	77.60	0	0	0	70	$365.00	$0.47	$91.25
Ross Carley	Missed Cut	1	2	0	0	0	0	0	77	79	78.00	0	0	0	14	$0.00	$0.00	$0.00
Bob Carmen	Missed Cut	1	3	0	0	0	0	0	73	79	76.00	0	0	0	18	$0.00	$0.00	$0.00
Sam Carmichael	T-14th in 1967	5	16	3	0	0	0	1	69	81	74.19	0	1	2	53	$3,952.00	$3.33	$790.40
Mark Carnevale	Missed Cut	1	2	0	0	0	0	0	78	79	78.50	0	0	0	15	$1,200.00	$7.64	$1,200.00
Joe Carr	Missed Cut	3	6	0	0	0	0	0	73	85	79.67	0	0	0	56	$1,000.00	$2.09	$333.33
Jim Carter	T-66th in 1988	2	6	1	0	0	0	0	68	80	74.33	0	1	2	18	$2,840.00	$6.37	$1,420.00
Noel Caruso	Missed Cut	1	2	0	0	0	0	0	83	84	83.50	0	0	0	23	$1,000.00	$5.99	$1,000.00

Player	Best Finish	Years	Rds	Cuts Made	3	5	10	25	Low Rd	High Rd	Avg.	Rds 65 or Better	Rds in 60s	Rds Under Par	Par Rounds	Money	$ Per Stroke	$ Per Event
Tom Case	Missed Cut	1	3	0	0	0	0	0	74	78	76.67	0	0	0	20	$0.00	$0.00	$0.00
Billy Casper	2nd in 1958, '65 & '71	24	88	20	4	6	8	13	67	88	72.48	0	9	17	178	$87,789.72	$13.76	$3,657.91
Henry Castillo	T-40th in 1958	3	9	1	0	0	0	0	72	78	75.00	0	0	0	45	$110.00	$0.16	$36.67
Ron Castillo	Missed Cut	1	2	0	0	0	0	0	87	88	87.50	0	0	0	35	$250.00	$1.43	$250.00
Ernie Catropa	Missed Cut	2	5	0	0	0	0	0	72	81	76.40	0	0	0	32	$0.00	$0.00	$0.00
Gil Cavanaugh	Missed Cut	1	2	0	0	0	0	0	76	76	76.00	0	0	0	12	$0.00	$0.00	$0.00
Ron Cerrudo	T-21st in 1969	1	4	1	0	0	0	1	66	76	71.50	0	1	2	2	$1,718.75	$6.01	$1,718.75
Greg Cerulli	Missed Cut	1	2	0	0	0	0	0	75	84	79.50	0	0	0	15	$1,000.00	$6.29	$1,000.00
Al Chandler	T-48th in 1968	8	22	3	0	0	0	0	71	81	75.14	0	0	0	107	$2,051.90	$1.24	$256.49
Bob Charles	T-2nd in 1968	9	36	9	1	1	1	4	68	78	72.72	0	3	6	78	$22,251.93	$8.50	$2,472.44
Brien Charter	T-56th in 1958	5	13	1	0	0	0	0	72	85	76.85	0	0	0	85	$2,100.00	$2.10	$420.00
T.C. Chen	T-23rd in 1985	4	14	3	0	0	0	1	66	83	73.79	0	3	3	35	$10,160.00	$9.84	$2,540.00
T.M. Chen	T-3rd in 1985	2	6	1	1	1	1	1	65	76	71.67	1	2	2	4	$43,500.00	$101.16	$21,750.00
Tom Cherok	Missed Cut	1	2	0	0	0	0	0	77	78	77.50	0	0	0	15	$0.00	$0.00	$0.00
Joe Cheves	Missed Cut	2	5	0	0	0	0	0	74	79	76.20	0	0	0	31	$0.00	$0.00	$0.00
Kelly Childs	Missed Cut	1	2	0	0	0	0	0	82	86	84.00	0	0	0	24	$250.00	$1.49	$250.00
Jim Cichra	Missed Cut	1	2	0	0	0	0	0	75	78	76.50	0	0	0	9	$1,000.00	$6.54	$1,000.00
Brian Claar	T-9th in 1992	3	8	1	0	0	1	1	68	76	72.38	0	1	2	9	$42,200.00	$72.88	$14,066.67
Bobby Clampett	T-27th in 1981	4	12	2	0	0	0	0	69	77	73.92	0	1	2	37	$8,883.33	$10.02	$2,220.83
Bob Clark	Missed Cut	1	2	0	0	0	0	0	76	82	79.00	0	0	0	18	$0.00	$0.00	$0.00
Gary Clark	Missed Cut	1	2	0	0	0	0	0	78	78	78.00	0	0	0	16	$350.00	$2.24	$350.00
Howard Clark	Missed Cut	1	2	0	0	0	0	0	72	77	74.50	0	0	0	7	$1,000.00	$6.71	$1,000.00
Jake Clark	Missed Cut	1	2	0	0	0	0	0	80	83	81.50	0	0	0	23	$0.00	$0.00	$0.00
James Clark	T-39th in 1960	3	8	1	0	0	0	0	71	78	74.50	0	0	0	36	$200.00	$0.34	$66.67
Don Clarkson	Missed Cut	1	2	0	0	0	0	0	75	78	76.50	0	0	0	11	$0.00	$0.00	$0.00
Keith Clearwater	T-48th in 1991	5	13	2	0	0	0	0	71	85	74.85	0	0	1	44	$9,375.00	$9.64	$1,875.00
John Cleary	68th in 1963	1	4	1	0	0	0	0	74	76	75.00	0	0	0	16	$200.00	$0.67	$200.00
Lennie Clements	67th in 1986	3	10	2	0	0	0	0	69	86	76.10	0	1	1	53	$3,680.00	$4.84	$1,226.67
Dick Cline	T-35th in 1958	4	10	1	0	0	0	0	72	83	76.60	0	0	0	66	$162.00	$0.21	$40.50
Russ Cochran	T-7th in 1992	9	26	4	0	0	2	2	67	80	73.12	0	7	8	45	$78,573.82	$41.33	$8,730.42
Gene Coghill	Missed Cut	4	10	0	0	0	0	0	73	80	76.00	0	0	0	58	$0.00	$0.00	$0.00
Jim Colbert	T-12th in 1973	17	58	12	0	0	0	3	66	80	73.05	0	5	8	147	$25,301.75	$5.97	$1,488.34
Cleve Coldwater	Missed Cut	1	2	0	0	0	0	0	75	78	76.50	0	0	0	11	$1,200.00	$7.84	$1,200.00
Bobby Cole	T-3rd in 1974	5	20	5	1	1	1	2	68	79	72.55	0	3	4	35	$17,037.85	$11.74	$3,407.57
Chris Cole	Missed Cut	1	2	0	0	0	0	0	80	83	81.50	0	0	0	23	$500.00	$3.07	$500.00
Clayton Cole	T-69th in 1976	3	10	2	0	0	0	0	69	79	75.40	0	1	1	54	$771.43	$1.02	$257.14
Don Collett	Missed Cut	1	2	0	0	0	0	0	78	82	80.00	0	0	0	20	$0.00	$0.00	$0.00
Bill Collins	T-12th in 1960	10	33	6	0	0	0	1	70	83	74.67	0	0	0	151	$3,922.00	$1.59	$392.20
Elhannon Collins	Missed Cut	1	2	0	0	0	0	0	74	78	76.00	0	0	0	8	$0.00	$0.00	$0.00
Ros Collins	Missed Cut	1	3	0	0	0	0	0	75	77	76.00	0	0	0	18	$0.00	$0.00	$0.00
Tim Collins	Missed Cut	6	12	0	0	0	0	0	72	86	76.25	0	0	0	65	$4,150.00	$4.54	$691.67
Charles Congdon	T-59th in 1963	1	4	1	0	0	0	0	70	79	74.50	0	0	1	14	$275.00	$0.92	$275.00
John Conley	Missed Cut	1	2	0	0	0	0	0	81	82	81.50	0	0	0	23	$0.00	$0.00	$0.00
Frank Conner	T-23rd in 1979	4	12	2	0	0	0	0	69	79	73.08	0	1	1	33	$6,550.00	$7.47	$1,637.50
Joby Connor	Missed Cut	1	3	0	0	0	0	0	73	76	74.67	0	0	0	14	$0.00	$0.00	$0.00
Joe Conrad	T-44th in 1964	3	10	2	0	0	0	0	69	80	74.60	0	1	1	46	$702.50	$0.94	$234.17
Beal Consolver	Missed Cut	1	2	0	0	0	0	0	82	84	83.00	0	0	0	24	$0.00	$0.00	$0.00
Charles Coody	4th in 1977	15	50	10	0	1	4	5	67	79	72.84	0	8	13	114	$36,758.01	$10.09	$2,450.53
John Cook	T-2nd in 1992	10	36	8	1	1	2	4	66	79	71.97	0	7	8	37	$170,148.75	$65.67	$17,014.88
Lawrence Cook	Missed Cut	1	2	0	0	0	0	0	77	79	78.00	0	0	0	16	$0.00	$0.00	$0.00
John Cook	T-44th in 1964	10	27	3	0	0	0	0	69	81	76.11	0	1	1	149	$1,043.88	$0.51	$104.39
Ross Coon	54th in 1970	4	12	2	0	0	0	0	72	81	75.75	0	0	0	67	$769.00	$0.85	$192.25
Joe Coonor	Missed Cut	1	2	0	0	0	0	0	77	81	79.00	0	0	0	18	$0.00	$0.00	$0.00
Pete Cooper	T-15th in 1960	9	32	7	0	0	0	3	68	78	73.53	0	2	4	99	$3,965.18	$1.69	$440.58
Dennis Coscina	T-73rd in 1979	3	8	1	0	0	0	0	70	83	76.63	0	1	1	49	$1,000.00	$1.63	$333.33
Gene Counter	Missed Cut	1	2	0	0	0	0	0	79	80	79.50	0	0	0	19	$0.00	$0.00	$0.00
Fred Couples	2nd in 1990	12	42	9	2	2	3	6	65	80	71.62	1	9	14	18	$225,175.19	$74.86	$18,764.60
Chuck Courtney	T-22nd in 1971	5	18	4	0	0	0	1	70	78	73.72	0	0	2	49	$3,389.43	$2.55	$677.89
Bruce Crampton	2nd in 1973 & '75	15	60	15	3	3	4	9	63	77	72.15	2	9	15	97	$73,994.67	$17.09	$4,932.98
Dick Crawford	T-20th in 1967	7	24	5	0	0	0	1	67	80	74.17	0	1	1	84	$4,286.88	$2.41	$612.41
Larry Crawford	Missed Cut	1	2	0	0	0	0	0	81	81	81.00	0	0	0	18	$0.00	$0.00	$0.00
Ben Crenshaw	T-2nd in 1979	19	67	15	1	1	5	9	66	81	72.45	0	12	18	108	$149,217.62	$30.74	$7,853.56
Bob Crow	Missed Cut	3	5	0	0	0	0	0	75	81	77.40	0	0	0	37	$0.00	$0.00	$0.00
Bob Crowley	T-38th in 1959	8	26	4	0	0	0	0	70	80	75.00	0	0	0	124	$1,067.50	$0.55	$133.44
Guy Cullins	Missed Cut	1	2	0	0	0	0	0	74	79	76.50	0	0	0	13	$350.00	$2.29	$350.00
Buster Cupit	T-8th in 1958	7	24	5	0	0	1	2	69	80	73.54	0	1	1	83	$3,545.00	$2.01	$506.43
Jacky Cupit	T-6th in 1966	8	28	6	0	0	2	3	69	77	72.93	0	2	5	64	$11,639.38	$5.70	$1,454.92
Rod Curl	T-20th in 1980	5	18	4	0	0	0	1	69	77	72.83	0	1	2	47	$7,900.00	$6.03	$1,580.00
Gaylord Currie	Missed Cut	1	2	0	0	0	0	0	79	85	82.00	0	0	0	24	$0.00	$0.00	$0.00
Chris Dachisen	Missed Cut	1	2	0	0	0	0	0	81	84	82.50	0	0	0	21	$1,000.00	$6.06	$1,000.00
Corky Dahl	T-66th in 1971	4	10	1	0	0	0	0	69	87	78.00	0	1	1	68	$258.00	$0.33	$64.50
John Dahl	Missed Cut	1	2	0	0	0	0	0	77	79	78.00	0	0	0	14	$1,000.00	$6.41	$1,000.00
John Dalrymple	Missed Cut	4	8	0	0	0	0	0	76	82	79.50	0	0	0	74	$0.00	$0.00	$0.00
John Daly	Won in 1991	3	12	3	1	1	1	1	67	79	72.08	0	4	5	9	$235,800.00	$272.60	$78,600.00
Doug Dalziel	Missed Cut	2	4	0	0	0	0	0	73	82	78.25	0	0	0	31	$803.00	$2.57	$401.50

PGA CHAMPIONSHIP STROKE-PLAY STATISTICS

Player	Best Finish	Years	Rds	Cuts Made	Top 3	5	10	25	Low Rd	High Rd	Avg.	Rds 65 or Better	Rds in 60s	Rds Under Par	Par Rounds	Money	$ Per Stroke	$ Per Event
Woody Dame	Missed Cut	3	6	0	0	0	0	0	73	78	76.67	0	0	0	34	$903.00	$1.96	$301.00
Joe Data	Missed Cut	1	2	0	0	0	0	0	77	77	77.00	0	0	0	14	$0.00	$0.00	$0.00
James Davis	Missed Cut	1	2	0	0	0	0	0	79	84	81.50	0	0	0	23	$0.00	$0.00	$0.00
Mike Davis	Missed Cut	1	2	0	0	0	0	0	75	81	78.00	0	0	0	16	$350.00	$2.24	$350.00
Rodger Davis	T-52nd in 1988	4	10	1	0	0	0	0	69	81	75.30	0	1	2	39	$5,292.50	$7.03	$1,323.13
Scott Davis	Missed Cut	1	2	0	0	0	0	0	74	76	75.00	0	0	0	6	$1,000.00	$6.67	$1,000.00
Manuel De La Torre	T-17th in 1963	11	36	6	0	0	0	1	70	80	74.61	0	0	1	148	$3,203.00	$1.19	$291.18
Terry Dear	Missed Cut	1	2	0	0	0	0	0	74	83	78.50	0	0	0	13	$1,000.00	$6.37	$1,000.00
Tom Deaton	Missed Cut	1	2	0	0	0	0	0	83	85	84.00	0	0	0	28	$0.00	$0.00	$0.00
Tim Debaufre	T-41st in 1968	1	4	1	0	0	0	0	72	75	73.25	0	0	0	13	$586.25	$2.00	$586.25
Bill Deck	Missed Cut	1	2	0	0	0	0	0	76	78	77.00	0	0	0	12	$0.00	$0.00	$0.00
Harry Dee	Missed Cut	1	2	0	0	0	0	0	76	77	76.50	0	0	0	13	$0.00	$0.00	$0.00
Joseph Deigo	Missed Cut	1	2	0	0	0	0	0	77	82	79.50	0	0	0	19	$0.00	$0.00	$0.00
Jay Delsing	T-63rd in 1990	3	8	1	0	0	0	0	70	82	74.88	0	0	1	25	$4,600.00	$7.68	$1,533.33
Dick Demane	Missed Cut	3	7	0	0	0	0	0	74	83	77.57	0	0	0	53	$0.00	$0.00	$0.00
Ron Demao	Missed Cut	1	2	0	0	0	0	0	82	84	83.00	0	0	0	26	$0.00	$0.00	$0.00
Jimmy Demaret	Disqualified, 1958	1	1	0	0	0	0	0	69	69	69.00	0	1	1	-1	$0.00	$0.00	$0.00
Mike Demassey	Withdrew, 1959	1	1	0	0	0	0	0	75	75	75.00	0	0	0	5	$0.00	$0.00	$0.00
Rolf Deming	T-67th in 1975	1	4	1	0	0	0	0	70	83	75.00	0	0	0	20	$428.57	$1.43	$428.57
Buddy Demling	Missed Cut	3	6	0	0	0	0	0	76	85	79.50	0	0	0	57	$0.00	$0.00	$0.00
George Demling	Missed Cut	1	2	0	0	0	0	0	78	82	80.00	0	0	0	20	$0.00	$0.00	$0.00
Lowell Dencer	Missed Cut	1	2	0	0	0	0	0	73	82	77.50	0	0	0	13	$1,200.00	$7.74	$1,200.00
Ten Denham	Missed Cut	1	2	0	0	0	0	0	82	83	82.50	0	0	0	25	$0.00	$0.00	$0.00
Jim Dent	T-34th in 1978	7	22	4	0	0	0	0	69	80	73.82	0	1	2	74	$5,468.67	$3.37	$781.24
Bruce Devlin	T-6th in 1965	14	50	11	0	0	1	5	68	80	73.00	0	2	9	118	$21,760.20	$5.96	$1,554.30
Gardner Dickinson	5th in 1965	10	38	9	0	1	2	5	66	76	72.45	0	6	7	71	$15,628.33	$5.68	$1,562.83
Bob Dickson	T-25th in 1969	3	12	3	0	0	0	1	69	78	73.83	0	1	2	38	$2,110.00	$2.38	$703.33
Jim Dickson	Missed Cut	2	4	0	0	0	0	0	74	85	80.00	0	0	0	34	$2,000.00	$6.25	$1,000.00
Terry Diehl	T-10th in 1980	4	12	2	0	0	1	1	68	78	73.25	0	1	1	39	$8,000.00	$9.10	$2,000.00
Mike Dietz	T-35th in 1958	4	11	1	0	0	0	0	70	81	76.00	0	0	0	66	$162.00	$0.19	$40.50
Billy Dill	Missed Cut	1	2	0	0	0	0	0	79	83	81.00	0	0	0	22	$0.00	$0.00	$0.00
Terry Dill	T-22nd in 1971	2	8	2	0	0	0	1	68	75	72.88	0	1	1	15	$2,784.00	$4.78	$1,392.00
Joe Dodich	Missed Cut	1	3	0	0	0	0	0	76	78	77.33	0	0	0	22	$0.00	$0.00	$0.00
Art Doering	Missed Cut	2	4	0	0	0	0	0	73	87	78.50	0	0	0	32	$0.00	$0.00	$0.00
James Dolan	Missed Cut	1	2	0	0	0	0	0	82	82	82.00	0	0	0	24	$650.00	$3.96	$650.00
Paul Donahue	Missed Cut	1	2	0	0	0	0	0	75	77	76.00	0	0	0	12	$0.00	$0.00	$0.00
Mike Donald	T-47th in 1986	8	24	4	0	0	0	0	69	80	74.00	0	1	2	70	$10,883.30	$6.13	$1,360.41
Clarence Doser	T-37th in 1961	3	9	1	0	0	0	0	71	84	74.89	0	0	0	44	$250.00	$0.37	$83.33
Jack Doss	Missed Cut	1	2	0	0	0	0	0	77	79	78.00	0	0	0	16	$0.00	$0.00	$0.00
Ed Dougherty	T-22nd in 1975	6	16	2	0	0	0	1	69	79	74.06	0	2	3	51	$9,595.00	$8.10	$1,599.17
Dave Douglas	Missed Cut	2	4	0	0	0	0	0	73	84	78.75	0	0	0	35	$0.00	$0.00	$0.00
Dale Douglass	T-17th in 1975	7	24	5	0	0	0	1	67	78	73.71	0	1	1	69	$5,072.18	$2.87	$724.60
Sam Drake	Missed Cut	2	5	0	0	0	0	0	73	80	78.00	0	0	0	40	$0.00	$0.00	$0.00
Stan Dudas	T-69th in 1969	4	10	1	0	0	0	0	70	80	75.80	0	0	1	54	$241.38	$0.32	$60.35
Bob Duden	T-54th in 1977	6	15	2	0	0	0	0	72	80	75.87	0	0	0	66	$1,049.10	$0.92	$174.85
Cotton Dunn	Disqualified, 1981	1	0	0	0	0	0	0	0	0	0	0	0	0	0	$550.00	$0.00	$550.00
Chuck Dupree	Missed Cut	1	2	0	0	0	0	0	79	84	81.50	0	0	0	23	$0.00	$0.00	$0.00
David Duschane	Missed Cut	1	2	0	0	0	0	0	74	75	74.50	0	0	0	7	$1,000.00	$6.71	$1,000.00
Bob Eastwood	T-30th in 1980	7	20	3	0	0	0	0	67	79	74.10	0	2	3	72	$9,600.00	$6.48	$1,371.43
Danny Edwards	T-20th in 1983	10	36	8	0	0	0	2	67	80	73.11	0	4	7	82	$18,930.55	$7.19	$1,893.06
David Edwards	T-14th in 1987	11	40	9	0	0	0	3	68	79	72.53	0	6	11	57	$46,734.17	$16.11	$4,248.56
Jerry Edwards	Missed Cut	1	2	0	0	0	0	0	72	80	76.00	0	0	0	12	$0.00	$0.00	$0.00
Joel Edwards	Missed Cut	1	2	0	0	0	0	0	71	73	72.00	0	0	0	2	$1,200.00	$8.33	$1,200.00
David Eger	Missed Cut	1	2	0	0	0	0	0	74	77	75.50	0	0	0	9	$303.00	$2.01	$303.00
Bill Eggers	Missed Cut	3	7	0	0	0	0	0	73	80	76.71	0	0	0	47	$0.00	$0.00	$0.00
Dave Eichelberger	T-34th in 1971	8	24	4	0	0	0	0	70	81	74.50	0	0	1	92	$4,340.93	$2.43	$542.62
Lee Elder	T-11th in 1974	13	44	9	0	0	0	4	68	78	73.05	0	4	6	114	$20,274.17	$6.31	$1,559.55
Juan Elizondo	Missed Cut	1	2	0	0	0	0	0	83	87	85.00	0	0	0	26	$0.00	$0.00	$0.00
Steve Elkington	T-14th in 1993	6	22	5	0	0	0	2	66	77	71.77	0	5	8	7	$60,102.86	$38.06	$10,017.14
Bob Elliott	Missed Cut	1	2	0	0	0	0	0	74	78	76.00	0	0	0	10	$1,000.00	$6.58	$1,000.00
John Elliott	Missed Cut	2	4	0	0	0	0	0	72	77	75.25	0	0	0	17	$2,000.00	$6.64	$1,000.00
Wes Ellis Jr.	T-5th in 1961	9	32	7	0	1	2	5	68	81	72.75	0	3	6	72	$10,553.34	$4.53	$1,172.59
Bob Ellsworth	Missed Cut	1	2	0	0	0	0	0	80	81	80.50	0	0	0	19	$0.00	$0.00	$0.00
Ernie Els	Missed Cut	2	4	0	0	0	0	0	73	80	76.25	0	0	0	21	$2,400.00	$7.87	$1,200.00
Clare Emery	T-28th in 1959	7	20	3	0	0	0	0	69	82	76.05	0	1	1	111	$1,011.42	$0.66	$144.49
Larry Emery	Missed Cut	1	2	0	0	0	0	0	77	79	78.00	0	0	0	12	$1,000.00	$6.41	$1,000.00
Noel Epperson	Missed Cut	1	2	0	0	0	0	0	83	85	84.00	0	0	0	28	$0.00	$0.00	$0.00
Charlie Epps	Missed Cut	2	4	0	0	0	0	0	77	79	77.75	0	0	0	27	$2,000.00	$6.43	$1,000.00
Robert Erickson	T-58th in 1966	3	11	2	0	0	0	0	71	80	75.27	0	0	0	50	$640.00	$0.77	$213.33
Randy Erskine	Missed Cut	1	2	0	0	0	0	0	72	75	73.50	0	0	0	7	$350.00	$2.38	$350.00
Emil Esposito	Missed Cut	2	4	0	0	0	0	0	79	87	83.50	0	0	0	50	$1,350.00	$4.04	$675.00
Lou Esposito	Missed Cut	1	2	0	0	0	0	0	76	81	78.50	0	0	0	17	$0.00	$0.00	$0.00
Don Essig	Missed Cut	1	2	0	0	0	0	0	79	87	83.00	0	0	0	26	$0.00	$0.00	$0.00
Bob Estes	T-6th in 1993	3	10	2	0	0	1	1	66	78	73.10	0	4	4	19	$51,137.50	$69.96	$17,045.83
Chick Evans	T-37th in 1966	3	10	2	0	0	0	0	73	79	75.10	0	0	0	43	$917.17	$1.22	$305.72

Player	Best Finish	Years	Rds	Cuts Made	Top 3	Top 5	Top 10	Top 25	Low Rd	High Rd	Avg.	Rds 65 or Better	Rds in 60s	Rds Under Par	Par Rounds	Money	$ Per Stroke	$ Per Event
Max Evans	Missed Cut	1	3	0	0	0	0	0	73	81	76.33	0	0	0	19	$0.00	$0.00	$0.00
Tont Evans	Missed Cut	1	2	0	0	0	0	0	75	78	76.50	0	0	0	13	$0.00	$0.00	$0.00
Bill Ezinicki	T-40th in 1958	5	17	3	0	0	0	0	67	83	75.29	0	1	1	86	$460.00	$0.36	$92.00
Brad Fabel	T-28th in 1987	2	8	2	0	0	0	0	68	77	73.38	0	1	1	15	$11,383.33	$19.39	$5,691.67
Roy Faber	Missed Cut	1	2	0	0	0	0	0	83	84	83.50	0	0	0	25	$0.00	$0.00	$0.00
Don Fairfield	T-22nd in 1961	5	16	3	0	0	0	1	70	78	73.56	0	0	0	56	$1,242.50	$1.06	$248.50
Jeff Fairfield	Missed Cut	1	2	0	0	0	0	0	77	81	79.00	0	0	0	16	$1,200.00	$7.59	$1,200.00
Nick Faldo	T-2nd in 1992	12	44	10	2	3	4	8	67	80	71.64	0	13	21	16	$332,977.34	$105.64	$27,748.11
Ed Famula	Missed Cut	2	4	0	0	0	0	0	76	79	77.25	0	0	0	27	$0.00	$0.00	$0.00
Jim Farina	Missed Cut	2	4	0	0	0	0	0	74	83	79.25	0	0	0	37	$0.00	$0.00	$0.00
Charles Farlow	Missed Cut	1	3	0	0	0	0	0	73	78	75.33	0	0	0	16	$0.00	$0.00	$0.00
Billy Farrell	T-11th in 1967	7	26	6	0	0	0	3	69	78	73.00	0	1	2	62	$6,836.67	$3.60	$976.67
Greg Farrow	Missed Cut	1	2	0	0	0	0	0	74	78	76.00	0	0	0	8	$1,000.00	$6.58	$1,000.00
Brad Faxon	T-14th in 1993	9	24	3	0	0	0	2	65	82	73.75	1	3	7	56	$58,175.00	$32.87	$6,463.89
George Fazio	T-25th in 1958	3	10	2	0	0	0	1	69	78	74.30	0	1	1	43	$625.00	$0.84	$208.33
David Feherty	T-7th in 1991	2	6	1	0	0	1	1	68	75	72.33	0	1	3	4	$39,200.00	$90.32	$19,600.00
Rick Fehr	T-18th in 1992	5	16	3	0	0	0	1	69	82	73.31	0	1	4	29	$32,260.00	$27.50	$6,452.00
Mike Felker	Missed Cut	1	2	0	0	0	0	0	77	80	78.50	0	0	0	17	$350.00	$2.23	$350.00
John Felus	Missed Cut	2	4	0	0	0	0	0	72	81	76.00	0	0	0	20	$0.00	$0.00	$0.00
Al Feminelli	T-53rd in 1959	2	6	1	0	0	0	0	70	78	74.33	0	0	0	26	$200.00	$0.45	$100.00
Keith Fergus	T-4th in 1981	8	28	6	0	1	1	3	68	77	72.36	0	3	5	52	$30,269.93	$14.94	$3,783.74
Phil Ferranti	T-66th in 1977	2	6	1	0	0	0	0	73	81	77.00	0	0	0	34	$488.09	$1.06	$244.05
Jim Ferree	T-28th in 1964	8	23	3	0	0	0	0	70	81	74.43	0	0	0	97	$1,720.00	$1.00	$215.00
Gene Ferrell	Missed Cut	4	8	0	0	0	0	0	73	81	77.75	0	0	0	58	$1,200.00	$1.93	$300.00
Jim Ferriell	T-66th in 1977	3	8	1	0	0	0	0	71	84	78.88	0	0	1	59	$1,038.09	$1.65	$346.03
Jim Ferrier	2nd in 1960	14	43	8	1	1	2	2	66	84	74.58	0	2	3	177	$10,331.11	$3.22	$737.94
Mike Fetchick	T-23rd in 1964	6	18	3	0	0	0	1	66	81	75.17	0	1	1	83	$1,500.00	$1.11	$250.00
Forrest Fezler	T-32nd in 1974	5	16	3	0	0	0	0	68	79	74.63	0	1	1	70	$2,446.93	$2.05	$489.39
Gene Fieger	Missed Cut	3	6	0	0	0	0	0	75	81	77.33	0	0	0	36	$3,200.00	$6.90	$1,066.67
Dow Finsterwald	Won in 1958	23	74	14	2	3	3	6	66	84	74.31	0	5	5	281	$22,335.70	$4.06	$971.12
Ed Fiori	T-9th in 1989	9	32	7	0	0	1	1	67	79	73.28	0	5	7	75	$42,764.65	$18.24	$4,751.63
Harold Firstman	Missed Cut	1	2	0	0	0	0	0	82	85	83.50	0	0	0	27	$0.00	$0.00	$0.00
Jerry Fisher	Missed Cut	1	2	0	0	0	0	0	76	80	78.00	0	0	0	14	$0.00	$0.00	$0.00
Woody Fitzhugh	Missed Cut	2	4	0	0	0	0	0	74	80	76.50	0	0	0	24	$1,500.00	$4.90	$750.00
Pat Fitzsimons	T-43rd in 1976	5	12	1	0	0	0	0	71	81	75.50	0	0	0	56	$2,975.00	$3.28	$595.00
Jack Fleck	T-7th in 1962	7	21	4	0	0	1	3	69	84	73.19	0	1	1	62	$4,969.43	$3.23	$709.92
Marty Fleckman	T-4th in 1968	2	6	1	0	1	1	1	66	78	72.67	0	1	1	14	$7,500.00	$17.20	$3,750.00
Bruce Fleisher	T-14th in 1993	6	20	4	0	0	0	1	67	78	72.85	0	4	5	37	$36,785.00	$25.25	$6,130.83
Pete Fleming	Missed Cut	1	3	0	0	0	0	0	71	81	75.00	0	0	0	15	$0.00	$0.00	$0.00
Terry Florence	Missed Cut	4	8	0	0	0	0	0	74	87	78.63	0	0	0	63	$3,050.00	$4.85	$762.50
Raymond Floyd	Won in 1969 & '82	30	112	26	3	4	8	17	63	80	72.05	2	23	29	136	$258,722.92	$32.06	$8,624.10
Bill Flynn	Missed Cut	1	2	0	0	0	0	0	77	79	78.00	0	0	0	14		$0.00	$0.00
Ken Folkes	Missed Cut	2	4	0	0	0	0	0	76	79	77.25	0	0	0	25	$250.00	$0.81	$125.00
Tom Fonseca Jr.	Missed Cut	1	2	0	0	0	0	0	75	80	77.50	0	0	0	15	$0.00	$0.00	$0.00
Bob Ford	T-68th in 1993	8	20	2	0	0	0	0	70	83	76.55	0	0	1	109	$7,287.50	$4.76	$910.94
Doug Ford	5th in 1961 & '62	24	63	8	0	2	3	6	66	82	74.40	0	5	7	249	$14,070.91	$3.00	$586.29
Anders Forsbrand	T-9th in 1992	2	6	1	0	0	1	1	70	73	71.33	0	0	2	2	$41,200.00	$96.26	$20,600.00
Dan Forsman	T-7th in 1992	8	22	3	0	0	1	1	67	80	73.82	0	2	6	52	$68,107.14	$41.94	$8,513.39
Ernest Fortner	Missed Cut	3	6	0	0	0	0	0	77	85	81.33	0	0	0	62	$0.00	$0.00	$0.00
John Fought	5th in 1983	4	14	3	0	1	1	1	67	78	72.64	0	3	3	31	$28,082.50	$27.61	$7,020.63
Ronald Fox	Missed Cut	1	2	0	0	0	0	0	81	84	82.50	0	0	0	25	$0.00	$0.00	$0.00
Jeff Foxx	Missed Cut	1	2	0	0	0	0	0	75	78	76.50	0	0	0	11	$1,000.00	$6.54	$1,000.00
Bob Frainey	Missed Cut	1	2	0	0	0	0	0	76	79	77.50	0	0	0	15	$0.00	$0.00	$0.00
Ed Francese	Missed Cut	1	2	0	0	0	0	0	80	85	82.50	0	0	0	21	$250.00	$1.52	$250.00
Will Frantz	Missed Cut	1	2	0	0	0	0	0	71	73	72.00	0	0	0	2	$1,200.00	$8.33	$1,200.00
Howell Fraser	T-59th in 1969	7	18	2	0	0	0	0	71	83	75.22	0	0	0	88	$2,265.81	$1.67	$323.69
Greg Frederick	Missed Cut	1	2	0	0	0	0	0	82	83	82.50	0	0	0	21	$1,000.00	$6.06	$1,000.00
Ray Freeman	69th in 1987	5	12	1	0	0	0	0	71	85	76.67	0	0	1	60	$5,600.04	$6.09	$1,120.01
Frank Freer	Missed Cut	1	2	0	0	0	0	0	83	83	83.00	0	0	0	26	$0.00	$0.00	$0.00
Steve Friebert	T-74th in 1972	1	4	1	0	0	0	0	74	79	76.75	0	0	0	27	$333.00	$1.08	$333.00
Phil Friel	Missed Cut	1	3	0	0	0	0	0	74	80	77.67	0	0	0	23	$0.00	$0.00	$0.00
John Frillman	Missed Cut	7	14	0	0	0	0	0	69	81	79.71	0	1	1	130	$250.00	$0.22	$35.71
David Frost	T-10th in 1987	9	30	6	0	0	1	2	68	78	73.07	0	3	9	46	$45,930.71	$20.95	$5,103.41
Robert Fry	Missed Cut	7	15	0	0	0	0	0	74	82	76.60	0	0	0	95	$0.00	$0.00	$0.00
Larry Fryer	Missed Cut	1	2	0	0	0	0	0	74	80	77.00	0	0	0	14	$0.00	$0.00	$0.00
Dale Fuller	Missed Cut	1	2	0	0	0	0	0	82	87	84.50	0	0	0	25	$1,000.00	$5.92	$1,000.00
Fred Funk	T-44th in 1993	4	14	3	0	0	0	0	66	82	73.50	0	3	6	27	$10,744.65	$10.44	$2,686.16
Rod Funseth	T-8th in 1965	10	38	9	0	0	1	2	69	78	73.08	0	4	6	97	$12,728.11	$4.58	$1,272.81
Ed Furgol	T-13th in 1964	6	21	4	0	0	0	1	69	81	73.90	0	1	1	76	$2,923.61	$1.88	$487.27
Marty Furgol	T-45th in 1961	3	10	2	0	0	0	0	71	79	74.30	0	0	0	39	$550.00	$0.74	$183.33
Shelby Futch	Missed Cut	1	2	0	0	0	0	0	78	82	80.00	0	0	0	20	$0.00	$0.00	$0.00
Bob Gajda	T-25th in 1958	5	19	4	0	0	0	1	70	81	74.26	0	0	0	77	$1,150.00	$0.82	$230.00
John Galeski	Missed Cut	1	3	0	0	0	0	0	72	78	75.00	0	0	0	15	$0.00	$0.00	$0.00
Jim Gallagher Jr.	T-2nd in 1992	5	16	3	2	2	2	3	66	82	72.13	0	4	5	8	$220,350.00	$190.94	$44,070.00
Mal Galletta	73rd in 1976	2	8	2	0	0	0	0	72	84	76.63	0	0	0	49	$810.00	$1.32	$405.00

Player	Best Finish	Years	Rds	Cuts Made	Top 3	Top 5	Top 10	Top 25	Low Rd	High Rd	Avg.	Rds 65 or Better	Rds in 60s	Rds Under Par	Par Rounds	Money	$ Per Stroke	$ Per Event
Bob Galloway	T-63rd in 1974	7	15	1	0	0	0	0	71	82	77.07	0	0	0	98	$1,224.43	$1.06	$174.92
Robert Gamez	T-49th in 1990	3	10	2	0	0	0	0	67	82	74.70	0	2	3	33	$6,315.62	$8.45	$2,105.21
Gary Gant	Missed Cut	2	4	0	0	0	0	0	79	83	81.25	0	0	0	43	$1,650.00	$5.08	$825.00
Ivan Gantz	Withdrew, 1961	1	1	0	0	0	0	0	82	82	82.00	0	0	0	12	$0.00	$0.00	$0.00
James Gantz	T-59th in 1958	1	4	1	0	0	0	0	75	79	76.50	0	0	0	26	$100.00	$0.33	$100.00
Buddy Gardner	T-6th in 1985	8	26	5	0	0	1	2	67	80	73.35	0	1	6	57	$41,645.00	$21.84	$5,205.63
Mark Gardner	Missed Cut	1	2	0	0	0	0	0	80	81	80.50	0	0	0	17	$1,000.00	$6.21	$1,000.00
Bill Garrett	T-55th in 1971	2	6	1	0	0	0	0	72	75	74.17	0	0	0	17	$258.00	$0.58	$129.00
Wright Garrett	Missed Cut	1	2	0	0	0	0	0	76	79	77.50	0	0	0	11	$0.00	$0.00	$0.00
Buzz Garvin	Missed Cut	1	2	0	0	0	0	0	79	82	80.50	0	0	0	19	$0.00	$0.00	$0.00
Jimmie Gauntt	Missed Cut	1	2	0	0	0	0	0	78	83	80.50	0	0	0	17	$0.00	$0.00	$0.00
Al Geiberger	Won in 1966	22	76	16	1	3	6	10	66	80	72.55	0	11	16	144	$70,130.06	$12.72	$3,187.73
John Gentile	Missed Cut	2	4	0	0	0	0	0	74	79	76.00	0	0	0	22	$1,350.00	$4.44	$675.00
Ernie George	Missed Cut	3	6	0	0	0	0	0	75	81	78.67	0	0	0	42	$0.00	$0.00	$0.00
Gene George	Missed Cut	1	2	0	0	0	0	0	76	76	76.00	0	0	0	10	$1,200.00	$7.89	$1,200.00
Henry Geraldi	Missed Cut	1	2	0	0	0	0	0	79	81	80.00	0	0	0	20	$0.00	$0.00	$0.00
Alex Gerlak	Missed Cut	1	2	0	0	0	0	0	81	86	83.50	0	0	0	27	$0.00	$0.00	$0.00
Chris Gers	Missed Cut	2	4	0	0	0	0	0	72	79	76.00	0	0	0	18	$0.00	$0.00	$0.00
Vic Ghezzi	T-49th in 1965	10	23	3	0	0	0	0	69	84	75.83	0	1	1	127	$789.17	$0.45	$78.92
Robert Gibbons	Missed Cut	1	2	0	0	0	0	0	77	78	77.50	0	0	0	11	$1,000.00	$6.45	$1,000.00
Andy Gibson	Missed Cut	1	2	0	0	0	0	0	78	81	79.50	0	0	0	19	$0.00	$0.00	$0.00
Bill Giese	Missed Cut	1	2	0	0	0	0	0	74	82	78.00	0	0	0	16	$0.00	$0.00	$0.00
Gibby Gilbert	T-5th in 1979	15	52	11	0	1	2	4	66	80	73.06	0	7	10	133	$36,319.86	$9.56	$2,421.32
Larry Gilbert	73rd in 1983	13	30	2	0	0	0	0	69	84	76.37	0	1	1	165	$9,733.00	$4.25	$748.69
Bob Gilder	T-4th in 1981	16	62	15	0	2	4	7	66	84	72.42	0	13	17	92	$147,632.45	$32.88	$9,227.03
David Gilford	Missed Cut	1	2	0	0	0	0	0	74	75	74.50	0	0	0	7	$1,200.00	$8.05	$1,200.00
Hunt Gilliland	Missed Cut	1	2	0	0	0	0	0	82	83	82.50	0	0	0	21	$1,000.00	$6.06	$1,000.00
Robbie Gilmore	Missed Cut	2	4	0	0	0	0	0	77	81	79.00	0	0	0	34	$1,650.00	$5.22	$825.00
Roger Ginsberg	Missed Cut	2	4	0	0	0	0	0	75	79	77.00	0	0	0	26	$1,350.00	$4.38	$675.00
Bill Glasson	T-54th in 1985	4	8	1	0	0	0	0	71	83	76.38	0	0	0	42	$4,764.00	$7.80	$1,191.00
David Glenz	T-73rd in 1985	6	16	2	0	0	0	0	72	84	76.88	0	0	0	96	$6,450.00	$5.24	$1,075.00
Randy Glover	Missed Cut	5	9	0	0	0	0	0	73	79	76.56	0	0	0	59	$750.00	$1.09	$150.00
Russell Glover	Missed Cut	1	2	0	0	0	0	0	73	81	77.00	0	0	0	12	$303.00	$1.97	$303.00
Bob Goalby	2nd in 1962	15	54	12	1	2	4	7	67	80	73.00	0	6	12	132	$23,422.32	$5.94	$1,561.49
John Godwin	Missed Cut	2	4	0	0	0	0	0	73	79	75.75	0	0	0	19	$2,200.00	$7.26	$1,100.00
Bob Goetz	Missed Cut	1	2	0	0	0	0	0	75	78	76.50	0	0	0	9	$0.00	$0.00	$0.00
Dick Goetz	Missed Cut	4	8	0	0	0	0	0	73	87	79.25	0	0	0	70	$1,750.00	$2.76	$437.50
Rudy Goff	Missed Cut	4	8	0	0	0	0	0	76	84	79.13	0	0	0	67	$0.00	$0.00	$0.00
Ted Goin	Missed Cut	2	4	0	0	0	0	0	80	87	83.00	0	0	0	44	$2,000.00	$6.02	$1,000.00
Ernie Gonzalez	Missed Cut	1	2	0	0	0	0	0	76	77	76.50	0	0	0	9	$1,000.00	$6.54	$1,000.00
Ray Goodell	Missed Cut	3	7	0	0	0	0	0	74	82	77.71	0	0	0	54	$0.00	$0.00	$0.00
J. C. Goosie	T-27th in 1963	4	12	2	0	0	0	0	68	77	73.92	0	1	1	43	$877.33	$0.99	$219.33
David Gosiewski	Missed Cut	1	2	0	0	0	0	0	77	88	82.50	0	0	0	21	$1,000.00	$6.06	$1,000.00
Mike Gove	Missed Cut	1	2	0	0	0	0	0	76	86	81.00	0	0	0	18	$1,000.00	$6.17	$1,000.00
Ray Graboski	Missed Cut	1	2	0	0	0	0	0	77	87	82.00	0	0	0	22	$0.00	$0.00	$0.00
Wayne Grady	Won in 1990	7	22	4	1	1	1	2	67	77	72.41	0	2	8	19	$241,770.00	$151.77	$34,538.57
Steve Gragg	Missed Cut	1	2	0	0	0	0	0	79	82	80.50	0	0	0	21	$0.00	$0.00	$0.00
Bonny Graham	Missed Cut	1	2	0	0	0	0	0	79	84	81.50	0	0	0	23	$0.00	$0.00	$0.00
David Graham	T-Winner in 1979	20	66	13	1	2	4	6	65	81	72.91	1	12	17	138	$133,005.01	$27.64	$6,650.25
Lou Graham	T-6th in 1977	15	50	10	0	0	3	5	68	80	72.74	0	4	9	113	$28,236.40	$7.76	$1,882.43
Bob Grant	Missed Cut	2	5	0	0	0	0	0	75	82	78.80	0	0	0	44	$0.00	$0.00	$0.00
Wally Grant	Missed Cut	1	2	0	0	0	0	0	78	80	79.00	0	0	0	18	$0.00	$0.00	$0.00
Quinton Gray	Missed Cut	1	2	0	0	0	0	0	75	82	78.50	0	0	0	17	$250.00	$1.59	$250.00
Thomas Gray	Missed Cut	1	2	0	0	0	0	0	78	79	78.50	0	0	0	15	$1,000.00	$6.37	$1,000.00
Hubert Green	Won in 1985	21	71	14	2	2	2	5	66	83	72.87	0	10	14	143	$175,962.34	$34.01	$8,379.16
Ken Green	T-16th in 1991	7	16	2	0	0	0	1	68	82	73.81	0	1	2	38	$27,300.00	$23.12	$3,900.00
Bert Greene	3rd in 1969	4	16	4	1	1	1	1	68	82	73.50	0	3	3	44	$13,399.43	$11.39	$3,349.86
Joe Greer	T-51st in 1960	2	6	1	0	0	0	0	72	79	75.17	0	0	0	31	$200.00	$0.44	$100.00
Otto Greiner	Missed Cut	2	5	0	0	0	0	0	72	79	76.20	0	0	0	31	$0.00	$0.00	$0.00
George Griffin	64th in 1958	1	4	1	0	0	0	0	74	83	77.75	0	0	0	31	$100.00	$0.32	$100.00
Ed Griffiths	T-58th in 1966	3	11	2	0	0	0	0	71	81	75.27	0	0	0	54	$640.00	$0.77	$213.33
Bob Groff	Missed Cut	4	8	0	0	0	0	0	72	83	78.88	0	0	0	59	$4,200.00	$6.66	$1,050.00
Gary Groh	Missed Cut	3	6	0	0	0	0	0	71	79	75.83	0	0	0	33	$1,750.00	$3.85	$583.33
Fred Gronauer	Missed Cut	3	6	0	0	0	0	0	74	78	77.17	0	0	0	43	$0.00	$0.00	$0.00
Paul Gross	Missed Cut	1	2	0	0	0	0	0	77	82	79.50	0	0	0	19	$0.00	$0.00	$0.00
Steve Groves	Missed Cut	1	2	0	0	0	0	0	76	83	79.50	0	0	0	17	$1,200.00	$7.55	$1,200.00
Bob Gry	Missed Cut	1	2	0	0	0	0	0	79	80	79.50	0	0	0	17	$0.00	$0.00	$0.00
Bill Grygiel	Missed Cut	4	8	0	0	0	0	0	78	90	82.38	0	0	0	97	$0.00	$0.00	$0.00
Rusty Guernsey	65th in 1977	1	4	1	0	0	0	0	72	80	76.75	0	0	0	19	$488.09	$1.59	$488.09
Jim Guinnup	Missed Cut	2	5	0	0	0	0	0	73	80	77.20	0	0	0	36	$0.00	$0.00	$0.00
Scott Gump	T-79th in 1992	1	4	1	0	0	0	0	71	82	75.75	0	0	0	19	$2,250.00	$7.43	$2,250.00
Mark Gurnow	Missed Cut	2	4	0	0	0	0	0	74	78	76.25	0	0	0	21	$2,000.00	$6.56	$1,000.00
Jon Gustin	T-9th in 1964	6	19	3	0	0	1	1	66	80	74.47	0	3	3	81	$2,862.50	$2.02	$477.08
Ira Gwin	T-75th in 1963	1	4	1	0	0	0	0	73	81	76.25	0	0	0	21	$158.34	$0.52	$158.34
Ted Gwin	Missed Cut	1	2	0	0	0	0	0	77	79	78.00	0	0	0	14	$0.00	$0.00	$0.00

Player	Best Finish	Years	Rds	Cuts Made	Top 3	Top 5	Top 10	Top 25	Low Rd	High Rd	Avg.	Rds 65 or Better	Rds in 60s	Rds Under Par	Par Rounds	Money	$ Per Stroke	$ Per Event
Bernie Haas	80th in 1963	3	8	1	0	0	0	0	70	80	76.75	0	0	1	50	$150.00	$0.24	$50.00
Jay Haas	T-5th in 1982	15	56	13	0	1	3	5	66	82	72.39	0	13	18	86	$78,942.67	$19.47	$5,262.84
Freddie Haas Jr.	T-23rd in 1962	9	29	6	0	0	0	1	69	80	73.86	0	2	5	98	$2,870.74	$1.34	$318.97
Dave Haberle	Missed Cut	1	2	0	0	0	0	0	73	76	74.50	0	0	0	9	$550.00	$3.69	$550.00
Hubby Habjan	T-53rd in 1963	2	8	2	0	0	0	0	71	83	75.38	0	0	0	35	$618.75	$1.03	$309.38
Kermit Hager	Missed Cut	1	2	0	0	0	0	0	72	81	76.50	0	0	0	13	$0.00	$0.00	$0.00
Bob Haggerty	Missed Cut	1	2	0	0	0	0	0	77	85	81.00	0	0	0	22	$0.00	$0.00	$0.00
Wayne Haley	Missed Cut	1	2	0	0	0	0	0	75	78	76.50	0	0	0	13	$0.00	$0.00	$0.00
Bill Hall	70th in 1978	1	4	1	0	0	0	0	72	78	75.75	0	0	0	19	$500.00	$1.65	$500.00
Gary Hallberg	T-6th in 1984	10	30	5	0	0	1	2	68	86	73.10	0	4	6	63	$52,986.67	$24.16	$5,298.67
Dan Halldorson	T-16th in 1982	5	12	1	0	0	0	1	69	78	73.58	0	1	1	37	$8,125.00	$9.20	$1,625.00
Jim Hallet	T-21st in 1987	4	14	3	0	0	0	1	68	78	72.57	0	2	3	12	$18,336.12	$18.05	$4,584.03
Bob Hamilton	T-59th in 1968	2	5	1	0	0	0	0	71	80	75.80	0	0	0	29	$369.00	$0.97	$184.50
Eddie Hamilton	Missed Cut	1	2	0	0	0	0	0	78	82	80.00	0	0	0	20	$0.00	$0.00	$0.00
Gene Hamm	Missed Cut	1	2	0	0	0	0	0	82	84	83.00	0	0	0	26	$0.00	$0.00	$0.00
Laurie Hammer	T-57th in 1968	6	16	2	0	0	0	0	70	80	75.25	0	0	0	72	$3,695.00	$3.07	$615.83
Donnie Hammond	T-11th in 1986	8	30	7	0	0	0	2	68	80	72.77	0	5	11	43	$36,651.20	$16.79	$4,581.40
Bob Hamrich	Missed Cut	1	2	0	0	0	0	0	78	84	81.00	0	0	0	20	$0.00	$0.00	$0.00
Phil Hancock	T-16th in 1978	6	14	1	0	0	0	1	70	83	75.64	0	0	2	67	$7,666.66	$7.24	$1,277.78
Kirk Hanefeld	Missed Cut	1	2	0	0	0	0	0	76	77	76.50	0	0	0	9	$1,000.00	$6.54	$1,000.00
Arnold Haneke	Missed Cut	1	2	0	0	0	0	0	82	89	85.50	0	0	0	31	$0.00	$0.00	$0.00
Chick Harbert	T-11th in 1962	11	34	6	0	0	0	1	68	82	74.44	0	3	3	138	$3,014.65	$1.19	$274.06
Gary Hardin	Missed Cut	1	2	0	0	0	0	0	73	77	75.00	0	0	0	8	$1,000.00	$6.67	$1,000.00
Claude Harmon	T-38th in 1959	4	14	3	0	0	0	0	72	78	74.21	0	0	0	59	$660.00	$0.64	$165.00
Craig Harmon	Missed Cut	1	2	0	0	0	0	0	80	89	84.50	0	0	0	29	$500.00	$2.96	$500.00
Frank Harned	T-55th in 1960	4	10	1	0	0	0	0	72	83	76.80	0	0	0	64	$200.00	$0.26	$50.00
Paul Harney	T-7th in 1962	9	36	9	0	0	1	6	69	78	72.53	0	3	3	75	$10,852.17	$4.16	$1,205.80
Chandler Harper	Missed Cut	5	9	0	0	0	0	0	73	80	76.33	0	0	0	51	$0.00	$0.00	$0.00
Lee Harper	Missed Cut	1	2	0	0	0	0	0	72	77	74.50	0	0	0	9	$650.00	$4.36	$650.00
Michael Harrigan	Missed Cut	1	2	0	0	0	0	0	78	85	81.50	0	0	0	21	$1,000.00	$6.13	$1,000.00
Arthur Harris	Missed Cut	3	7	0	0	0	0	0	75	84	78.57	0	0	0	60	$0.00	$0.00	$0.00
Bob Harris	T-32nd in 1960	3	8	1	0	0	0	0	71	79	75.88	0	0	0	47	$247.15	$0.41	$82.38
Labron Harris Jr.	T-63rd in 1971	6	16	2	0	0	0	0	72	80	75.38	0	0	0	76	$708.00	$0.59	$118.00
Bob Harrison	Missed Cut	1	2	0	0	0	0	0	75	81	78.00	0	0	0	16	$0.00	$0.00	$0.00
Dutch Harrison	T-49th in 1963	1	4	1	0	0	0	0	73	75	73.75	0	0	0	11	$335.00	$1.14	$335.00
Chuck Hart	Missed Cut	3	6	0	0	0	0	0	78	85	79.83	0	0	0	57	$0.00	$0.00	$0.00
Dick Hart	T-17th in 1963	10	33	6	0	0	0	1	66	85	74.24	0	2	2	120	$4,109.17	$1.68	$410.92
Dudley Hart	T-6th in 1993	2	6	1	0	0	1	1	66	77	71.50	0	2	2	3	$49,012.50	$114.25	$24,506.25
Jim Hart	Missed Cut	1	2	0	0	0	0	0	75	80	77.50	0	0	0	15	$0.00	$0.00	$0.00
Charles Harter	Missed Cut	2	5	0	0	0	0	0	75	78	76.80	0	0	0	34	$0.00	$0.00	$0.00
Charlie Harter	Missed Cut	1	2	0	0	0	0	0	78	81	79.50	0	0	0	17	$0.00	$0.00	$0.00
Sam Harvey	Missed Cut	1	2	0	0	0	0	0	77	80	78.50	0	0	0	17	$0.00	$0.00	$0.00
Mike Harwood	Missed Cut	2	4	0	0	0	0	0	73	85	78.00	0	0	0	26	$2,200.00	$7.05	$1,100.00
Morris Hatalsky	T-14th in 1990	10	34	7	0	0	0	1	68	80	73.82	0	4	5	94	$32,224.64	$12.84	$3,222.46
Paul Haviland	T-33rd in 1964	2	6	1	0	0	0	0	68	79	74.33	0	1	1	26	$662.50	$1.49	$331.25
Fred Hawkins	T-10th in 1960	5	19	4	0	0	1	3	69	79	72.74	0	3	3	52	$3,795.00	$2.75	$759.00
Bob Hayes	Missed Cut	1	2	0	0	0	0	0	74	81	77.50	0	0	0	15	$0.00	$0.00	$0.00
Furman Hayes	T-56th in 1964	3	10	2	0	0	0	0	71	80	75.10	0	0	0	47	$500.00	$0.67	$166.67
Mark Hayes	T-15th in 1976	11	36	7	0	0	0	3	67	81	73.06	0	5	5	92	$17,395.50	$6.61	$1,581.41
Jimmy Haynes	Withdrew, 1958	1	1	0	0	0	0	0	83	83	83.00	0	0	0	13	$0.00	$0.00	$0.00
Gary Head	Missed Cut	2	4	0	0	0	0	0	74	81	78.25	0	0	0	31	$1,000.00	$3.19	$500.00
Don Headings	Missed Cut	2	4	0	0	0	0	0	76	81	78.50	0	0	0	34	$0.00	$0.00	$0.00
Vance Heafner	T-11th in 1981	4	14	3	0	0	0	1	68	80	72.43	0	2	2	28	$10,662.14	$10.51	$2,665.54
Jerry Heard	T-7th in 1972	7	28	7	0	0	2	4	69	81	72.82	0	2	4	63	$16,402.29	$8.04	$2,343.18
Jay Hebert	Won in 1960	16	51	9	1	2	3	6	67	83	73.65	0	5	5	162	$20,847.22	$5.55	$1,302.95
Lionel Hebert	T-14th in 1967	21	58	8	0	0	0	3	69	80	74.47	0	2	6	233	$7,424.66	$1.72	$353.56
Steve Heckel	Missed Cut	1	2	0	0	0	0	0	76	79	77.50	0	0	0	11	$1,000.00	$6.45	$1,000.00
Bill Heinlein	60th in 1961	2	7	1	0	0	0	0	69	81	76.29	0	1	1	44	$225.00	$0.42	$112.50
Bobby Heins	T-77th in 1983	3	8	1	0	0	0	0	73	78	75.63	0	0	0	35	$3,500.00	$5.79	$1,166.67
Russell Helwig	Missed Cut	1	2	0	0	0	0	0	77	79	78.00	0	0	0	16	$650.00	$4.17	$650.00
John Hendricks	Missed Cut	1	2	0	0	0	0	0	80	83	81.50	0	0	0	19	$1,000.00	$6.13	$1,000.00
Robert Hendricks	Missed Cut	1	2	0	0	0	0	0	81	82	81.50	0	0	0	23	$0.00	$0.00	$0.00
Dick Hendrickson	T-35th in 1973	3	8	1	0	0	0	0	70	85	75.00	0	0	0	36	$1,704.44	$2.84	$568.15
Nolan Henke	T-6th in 1993	3	10	2	0	0	1	1	67	77	72.10	0	2	4	7	$51,550.00	$71.50	$17,183.33
Harold Henning	T-44th in 1969	2	8	2	0	0	0	0	70	76	73.13	0	0	1	21	$1,047.50	$1.79	$523.75
Bunky Henry	T-11th in 1969	1	4	1	0	0	0	1	68	76	70.75	0	2	3	-1	$3,543.75	$12.52	$3,543.75
Geoff Hensley	Missed Cut	2	4	0	0	0	0	0	76	82	78.75	0	0	0	31	$1,303.00	$4.14	$651.50
Denny Hepler	T-70th in 1991	2	6	1	0	0	0	0	71	78	74.50	0	0	1	17	$3,425.00	$7.66	$1,712.50
Darrell Hickok	Missed Cut	3	5	0	0	0	0	0	72	85	79.40	0	0	0	41	$0.00	$0.00	$0.00
Doug Higgins	T-40th in 1963	1	4	1	0	0	0	0	70	75	73.25	0	0	1	9	$410.00	$1.40	$410.00
Jack Higgins	Missed Cut	1	3	0	0	0	0	0	75	78	76.33	0	0	0	19	$0.00	$0.00	$0.00
Bob Hill	T-52nd in 1964	7	17	1	0	0	0	0	70	82	76.12	0	0	0	96	$318.75	$0.25	$45.54
Dave Hill	T-3rd in 1974	15	53	11	1	1	3	8	66	79	72.72	0	11	14	106	$36,938.04	$9.58	$2,462.54
Mike Hill	T-11th in 1974	9	32	7	0	0	0	5	68	80	72.84	0	3	4	77	$17,409.17	$7.47	$1,934.35
Ray Hill	Missed Cut	2	4	0	0	0	0	0	79	84	81.00	0	0	0	44	$0.00	$0.00	$0.00

Player	Best Finish	Years	Rds	Cuts Made	Top 3	5	10	25	Low Rd	High Rd	Avg.	Rds 65 or Better	Rds in 60s	Rds Under Par	Par Rounds	Money	$ Per Stroke	$ Per Event
Jimmy Hines	Missed Cut	1	2	0	0	0	0	0	74	79	76.50	0	0	0	13	$0.00	$0.00	$0.00
Lon Hinkle	T-3rd in 1980	10	40	10	1	1	2	2	68	89	73.40	0	5	7	104	$41,268.75	$14.06	$4,126.88
Larry Hinson	T-4th in 1970	7	28	7	0	1	1	3	68	77	72.04	0	4	8	41	$21,288.50	$10.55	$3,041.21
Babe Hiskey	T-40th in 1971	4	14	3	0	0	0	0	69	78	73.86	0	1	1	42	$1,704.00	$1.65	$426.00
Doug Hixon	Missed Cut	1	2	0	0	0	0	0	78	80	79.00	0	0	0	16	$1,200.00	$7.59	$1,200.00
Harvey Hixon	Missed Cut	1	2	0	0	0	0	0	77	78	77.50	0	0	0	15	$0.00	$0.00	$0.00
Scott Hoch	T-3rd in 1987	13	46	10	1	1	3	5	67	81	72.59	0	10	15	61	$174,033.97	$52.12	$13,387.23
Ben Hodson	Missed Cut	1	2	0	0	0	0	0	76	84	80.00	0	0	0	20	$0.00	$0.00	$0.00
Jon Hoecker	Missed Cut	1	2	0	0	0	0	0	79	81	80.00	0	0	0	18	$1,200.00	$7.50	$1,200.00
Ben Hogan	T-9th in 1964	3	11	2	0	0	1	2	68	78	72.36	0	1	2	22	$4,725.00	$5.94	$1,575.00
Bob Hold	T-68th in 1970	3	9	1	0	0	0	0	71	82	77.33	0	0	0	66	$400.00	$0.57	$133.33
Tony Holguin	T-39th in 1960	5	13	2	0	0	0	0	71	82	75.00	0	0	0	61	$565.00	$0.58	$113.00
Mike Holland	T-29th in 1982	1	4	1	0	0	0	0	70	73	71.25	0	0	0	5	$3,100.00	$10.88	$3,100.00
Bud Holscher	T-39th in 1960	5	14	2	0	0	0	0	68	78	75.00	0	1	1	68	$425.00	$0.40	$85.00
Barry Holt	Missed Cut	1	2	0	0	0	0	0	78	83	80.50	0	0	0	19	$1,000.00	$6.21	$1,000.00
Mickey Homa	60th in 1959	2	6	1	0	0	0	0	71	78	75.00	0	0	0	28	$200.00	$0.44	$100.00
Herb Hooper	T-18th in 1971	1	4	1	0	0	0	1	71	74	72.25	0	0	2	1	$2,700.00	$9.34	$2,700.00
Gary Hopkins	T-67th in 1974	2	6	1	0	0	0	0	72	80	75.83	0	0	0	35	$321.43	$0.71	$160.72
Scudday Horner	T-44th in 1959	2	6	1	0	0	0	0	71	81	74.83	0	0	0	29	$200.00	$0.45	$100.00
Jay Horton	Missed Cut	1	2	0	0	0	0	0	76	78	77.00	0	0	0	10	$250.00	$1.62	$250.00
Roger Horton	Missed Cut	1	2	0	0	0	0	0	80	82	81.00	0	0	0	20	$0.00	$0.00	$0.00
Charles Houts	Missed Cut	1	2	0	0	0	0	0	77	79	78.00	0	0	0	14	$0.00	$0.00	$0.00
Dick Howell	Missed Cut	1	2	0	0	0	0	0	77	84	80.50	0	0	0	21	$0.00	$0.00	$0.00
Ray Howell	Missed Cut	1	2	0	0	0	0	0	71	80	75.50	0	0	1	7	$0.00	$0.00	$0.00
Ron Howell	T-28th in 1966	1	4	1	0	0	0	0	71	76	73.50	0	0	0	14	$900.00	$3.06	$900.00
Gary Howlett	Missed Cut	1	2	0	0	0	0	0	76	79	77.50	0	0	0	15	$0.00	$0.00	$0.00
Robert Hoyt	72nd in 1985	6	16	2	0	0	0	0	71	80	75.81	0	0	0	75	$7,200.00	$5.94	$1,200.00
Lu Hsi-Chuen	Missed Cut	1	2	0	0	0	0	0	75	77	76.00	0	0	0	12	$550.00	$3.62	$550.00
Chuck Huckaby	Missed Cut	1	2	0	0	0	0	0	77	78	77.50	0	0	0	15	$0.00	$0.00	$0.00
Mike Hulbert	T-7th in 1986	8	28	6	0	0	1	2	67	84	72.61	0	3	8	31	$60,792.37	$29.90	$7,599.05
Cary Hungate	T-69th in 1990	1	4	1	0	0	0	0	72	79	76.25	0	0	0	17	$2,225.00	$7.30	$2,225.00
Mac Hunter	T-33rd in 1961	6	21	4	0	0	0	0	70	81	74.48	0	0	2	82	$1,567.50	$1.00	$261.25
Denis Husse	Missed Cut	1	2	0	0	0	0	0	81	83	82.00	0	0	0	22	$1,000.00	$6.10	$1,000.00
John Huston	T-7th in 1991	5	18	4	0	0	1	2	68	80	72.39	0	3	5	15	$65,132.14	$49.99	$13,026.43
Ralph Hutchison	Missed Cut	1	2	0	0	0	0	0	77	78	77.50	0	0	0	15	$0.00	$0.00	$0.00
Stu Ingraham	T-31st in 1993	4	10	1	0	0	0	0	69	81	73.60	0	2	3	20	$10,057.69	$13.67	$2,514.42
John Inman	T-58th in 1988	1	4	1	0	0	0	0	69	75	72.75	0	1	1	7	$1,990.00	$6.84	$1,990.00
Walker Inman	T-43rd in 1966	6	14	1	0	0	0	0	71	82	77.36	0	0	0	97	$845.50	$0.78	$140.92
Joe Inman Jr.	11th in 1977 & '78	9	30	6	0	0	0	5	67	80	72.63	0	5	5	63	$23,507.21	$10.79	$2,611.91
Hale Irwin	T-5th in 1975	21	82	20	0	1	3	10	65	78	72.17	1	15	23	110	$140,706.55	$23.78	$6,700.31
Jack Isaacs	T-49th in 1958	3	8	1	0	0	0	0	74	79	75.88	0	0	0	45	$100.00	$0.16	$33.33
David Ishii	T-38th in 1988	2	6	1	0	0	0	0	69	82	74.83	0	1	1	21	$4,211.11	$9.38	$2,105.56
Don Iverson	T-6th in 1973	2	8	2	0	0	1	1	67	81	73.50	0	1	2	24	$7,761.66	$13.20	$3,880.83
Tony Jacklin	T-25th in 1969	4	14	3	0	0	0	1	70	79	73.36	0	0	2	39	$2,161.43	$2.10	$540.36
Jeff Jackson	Missed Cut	1	2	0	0	0	0	0	73	79	76.00	0	0	0	8	$1,000.00	$6.58	$1,000.00
John Jackson	72nd in 1987	7	18	2	0	0	0	0	68	84	75.94	0	1	1	91	$6,500.01	$4.75	$928.57
Tommy Jacobs	T-8th in 1963	12	36	5	0	0	1	3	68	81	74.33	0	1	3	140	$4,755.00	$1.78	$396.25
Peter Jacobsen	3rd in 1983 & '86	14	56	14	2	2	4	7	65	76	71.46	1	9	18	30	$180,027.38	$44.98	$12,859.10
Earl Jacobson	T-41st in 1968	1	4	1	0	0	0	0	72	74	73.25	0	0	0	13	$586.25	$2.00	$586.25
Barry Jaeckel	T-42nd in 1982 & '83	7	22	4	0	0	0	0	67	81	73.73	0	3	3	72	$7,128.36	$4.39	$1,018.34
Mark James	T-40th in 1992	3	8	1	0	0	0	0	71	77	73.75	0	0	0	20	$7,362.50	$12.48	$2,454.17
Jim Jamieson	T-2nd in 1972	4	13	3	1	1	2	3	69	81	72.00	0	1	2	14	$29,952.50	$32.00	$7,488.13
Carl Jans	Missed Cut	1	2	0	0	0	0	0	84	87	85.50	0	0	0	31	$0.00	$0.00	$0.00
Lynn Janson	T-35th in 1979	7	16	1	0	0	0	0	71	80	74.94	0	0	0	71	$6,650.00	$5.55	$950.00
Don January	Won in 1967	21	77	16	3	4	7	12	66	82	72.00	0	15	20	125	$93,129.93	$16.80	$4,434.76
Lee Janzen	T-21st in 1992	2	8	2	0	0	0	2	68	74	71.13	0	1	2	1	$28,500.00	$50.09	$14,250.00
Cass Jawor	Missed Cut	1	2	0	0	0	0	0	78	79	78.50	0	0	0	17	$0.00	$0.00	$0.00
Tom Jenkins	T-17th in 1974	6	22	5	0	0	0	1	69	80	73.64	0	1	1	70	$6,863.09	$4.24	$1,143.85
Rick Jetter	Missed Cut	3	6	0	0	0	0	0	78	87	82.00	0	0	0	68	$0.00	$0.00	$0.00
David Jimenez	Missed Cut	4	8	0	0	0	0	0	74	85	77.50	0	0	0	58	$1,150.00	$1.85	$287.50
Joe Jimenez	T-65th in 1970	6	14	1	0	0	0	0	73	81	77.36	0	0	0	99	$1,203.00	$1.11	$200.50
Clayton Johnson	Missed Cut	3	7	0	0	0	0	0	73	81	77.29	0	0	0	47	$0.00	$0.00	$0.00
Drue Johnson	Missed Cut	2	4	0	0	0	0	0	74	84	78.75	0	0	0	29	$2,000.00	$6.35	$1,000.00
Eugene Johnson	Missed Cut	1	2	0	0	0	0	0	80	82	81.00	0	0	0	20	$0.00	$0.00	$0.00
George Johnson	T-54th in 1975	2	6	1	0	0	0	0	73	78	75.00	0	0	0	30	$428.57	$0.95	$214.29
Gordon Johnson	Missed Cut	1	2	0	0	0	0	0	75	79	77.00	0	0	0	12	$1,200.00	$7.79	$1,200.00
Gunnard Johnson	Missed Cut	1	2	0	0	0	0	0	76	82	79.00	0	0	0	18	$0.00	$0.00	$0.00
Howie Johnson	T-19th in 1969	5	18	4	0	0	0	1	68	78	73.33	0	1	3	46	$4,207.16	$3.19	$841.43
Jimmy Johnson	T-62nd in 1964	3	10	1	0	0	0	0	71	82	75.50	0	0	0	55	$220.00	$0.29	$73.33
Al Johnston	Missed Cut	1	3	0	0	0	0	0	75	78	76.33	0	0	0	19	$0.00	$0.00	$0.00
Bill Johnston	T-8th in 1963	8	23	3	0	0	1	1	71	80	74.57	0	0	0	95	$2,515.00	$1.47	$314.38
Ralph Johnston	77th in 1972	1	4	1	0	0	0	0	74	89	78.25	0	0	0	33	$333.00	$1.06	$333.00
Tony Johnstone	Missed Cut	2	4	0	0	0	0	0	70	80	75.75	0	0	1	19	$2,400.00	$7.92	$1,200.00
Gordon Jones	T-20th in 1965	3	10	2	0	0	0	1	71	81	75.10	0	0	0	47	$1,850.00	$2.46	$616.67
Gregg Jones	Missed Cut	5	10	0	0	0	0	0	70	83	75.50	0	0	2	43	$5,200.00	$6.89	$1,040.00

Player	Best Finish	Years	Rds	Cuts Made	Top 3	Top 5	Top 10	Top 25	Low Rd	High Rd	Avg.	Rds 65 or Better	Rds in 60s	Rds Under Par	Par Rounds	Money	$ Per Stroke	$ Per Event
Grier Jones	T-16th in 1978	10	34	7	0	0	0	2	70	80	73.44	0	0	1	93	$9,904.34	$3.97	$990.43
Jack Jones	Missed Cut	1	2	0	0	0	0	0	80	84	82.00	0	0	0	24	$0.00	$0.00	$0.00
Jerry Jones	Missed Cut	1	2	0	0	0	0	0	88	90	89.00	0	0	0	36	$303.00	$1.70	$303.00
John Paul Jones	Missed Cut	1	2	0	0	0	0	0	75	77	76.00	0	0	0	10	$0.00	$0.00	$0.00
Steve Jones	T-9th in 1988	4	14	3	0	0	1	1	68	81	73.21	0	2	4	21	$26,990.00	$26.33	$6,747.50
Eddie Joseph	Missed Cut	1	3	0	0	0	0	0	73	80	76.67	0	0	0	20	$0.00	$0.00	$0.00
Michael Joyce	T-73rd in 1973	1	4	1	0	0	0	0	73	79	75.75	0	0	0	19	$360.00	$1.19	$360.00
Tom Joyce	Missed Cut	4	8	0	0	0	0	0	74	80	77.75	0	0	0	58	$3,000.00	$4.82	$750.00
Bill Kaiser	Missed Cut	1	3	0	0	0	0	0	75	79	77.00	0	0	0	21	$0.00	$0.00	$0.00
Jim Kallam	Missed Cut	1	2	0	0	0	0	0	76	79	77.50	0	0	0	11	$1,000.00	$6.45	$1,000.00
Mike Kallam	Missed Cut	1	2	0	0	0	0	0	74	78	76.00	0	0	0	8	$1,000.00	$6.58	$1,000.00
Tony Kaloustian	Missed Cut	1	2	0	0	0	0	0	74	79	76.50	0	0	0	13	$350.00	$2.29	$350.00
Jim Kane	T-66th in 1992	1	4	1	0	0	0	0	72	76	73.75	0	0	0	11	$2,575.00	$8.73	$2,575.00
Richard Karbowski	Missed Cut	2	4	0	0	0	0	0	74	78	75.50	0	0	0	18	$2,000.00	$6.62	$1,000.00
Richie Karl	T-55th in 1974	2	5	1	0	0	0	0	71	81	75.20	0	0	0	26	$321.43	$0.85	$160.72
Monty Kaser	Missed Cut	1	2	0	0	0	0	0	76	78	77.00	0	0	0	14	$0.00	$0.00	$0.00
Ricky Kawagishi	Missed Cut	1	2	0	0	0	0	0	74	75	74.50	0	0	0	5	$1,000.00	$6.71	$1,000.00
Bob Kay	T-44th in 1962	7	16	1	0	0	0	0	72	88	77.88	0	0	0	124	$663.00	$0.53	$94.71
Chuck Keating	Missed Cut	1	2	0	0	0	0	0	72	82	77.00	0	0	0	10	$250.00	$1.62	$250.00
Dan Keefe	Missed Cut	1	2	0	0	0	0	0	77	79	78.00	0	0	0	16	$0.00	$0.00	$0.00
Herman Keiser	Missed Cut	1	2	0	0	0	0	0	73	81	77.00	0	0	0	10	$0.00	$0.00	$0.00
Robert Keith	Missed Cut	1	2	0	0	0	0	0	75	75	75.00	0	0	0	10	$0.00	$0.00	$0.00
Bill Keller	Missed Cut	1	3	0	0	0	0	0	74	79	76.33	0	0	0	19	$0.00	$0.00	$0.00
Bob Keller	T-29th in 1961	6	19	3	0	0	0	0	69	80	74.11	0	1	1	74	$1,387.61	$0.99	$231.27
Frank Keller	Missed Cut	4	8	0	0	0	0	0	74	86	78.50	0	0	0	60	$0.00	$0.00	$0.00
Al Kelley	T-55th in 1971	1	4	1	0	0	0	0	73	75	74.00	0	0	0	8	$258.00	$0.87	$258.00
Paul Kelly	T-28th in 1965	2	6	1	0	0	0	0	71	81	74.50	0	0	0	23	$915.00	$2.05	$457.50
Bill Kennedy	Missed Cut	1	2	0	0	0	0	0	79	80	79.50	0	0	0	17	$0.00	$0.00	$0.00
Les Kennedy	Withdrew, 1960	1	2	0	0	0	0	0	73	78	75.50	0	0	0	11	$0.00	$0.00	$0.00
Roger Kennedy	Missed Cut	3	6	0	0	0	0	0	75	88	80.33	0	0	0	62	$1,700.00	$3.53	$566.67
Leonard Kennett	Missed Cut	1	2	0	0	0	0	0	82	86	84.00	0	0	0	28	$0.00	$0.00	$0.00
Paul Kern	Missed Cut	4	9	0	0	0	0	0	70	86	78.44	0	0	0	76	$0.00	$0.00	$0.00
Darrell Kestner	Missed Cut	4	8	0	0	0	0	0	70	80	76.25	0	0	1	40	$4,400.00	$7.21	$1,100.00
George Keyes	Missed Cut	4	7	0	0	0	0	0	75	83	79.00	0	0	0	59	$0.00	$0.00	$0.00
Jack Kiefer	T-60th in 1976	2	6	1	0	0	0	0	71	88	78.17	0	0	0	45	$1,450.00	$3.09	$725.00
Jim Kiely	Missed Cut	1	2	0	0	0	0	0	72	75	73.50	0	0	0	7	$650.00	$4.42	$650.00
Bill King	Missed Cut	1	2	0	0	0	0	0	74	83	78.50	0	0	0	13	$1,000.00	$6.37	$1,000.00
Claude King	Missed Cut	3	5	0	0	0	0	0	74	83	78.40	0	0	0	42	$0.00	$0.00	$0.00
Jim King	87th in 1983	4	10	1	0	0	0	0	73	84	77.60	0	0	0	68	$3,453.00	$4.45	$863.25
John Kinsey	Missed Cut	1	2	0	0	0	0	0	81	84	82.50	0	0	0	25	$0.00	$0.00	$0.00
Frank Kiraly	Missed Cut	2	5	0	0	0	0	0	74	83	78.00	0	0	0	38	$0.00	$0.00	$0.00
John Kirchner	Missed Cut	1	2	0	0	0	0	0	83	87	85.00	0	0	0	28	$1,000.00	$5.88	$1,000.00
Joe Kirkwood	Missed Cut	2	5	0	0	0	0	0	73	79	75.00	0	0	0	25	$0.00	$0.00	$0.00
Tom Kite	T-3rd in 1988	20	78	19	1	2	4	9	66	79	72.01	0	12	16	87	$149,024.51	$26.53	$7,451.23
Bob Klein	Missed Cut	2	4	0	0	0	0	0	77	82	79.50	0	0	0	32	$2,000.00	$6.29	$1,000.00
Chuck Klein	T-49th in 1958	2	7	1	0	0	0	0	69	81	74.86	0	1	1	34	$100.00	$0.19	$50.00
Don Klein	Missed Cut	3	6	0	0	0	0	0	76	83	79.67	0	0	0	52	$0.00	$0.00	$0.00
Harold Kneece	Missed Cut	1	2	0	0	0	0	0	76	82	79.00	0	0	0	18	$0.00	$0.00	$0.00
Darrel Knicely	Missed Cut	1	2	0	0	0	0	0	77	82	79.50	0	0	0	19	$0.00	$0.00	$0.00
Dick Knight	T-46th in 1960	1	4	1	0	0	0	0	73	76	74.50	0	0	0	18	$200.00	$0.67	$200.00
Dwaine Knight	Missed Cut	1	2	0	0	0	0	0	73	79	76.00	0	0	0	10	$0.00	$0.00	$0.00
Kenny Knox	4th in 1991	6	16	2	0	1	2	2	67	80	73.50	0	4	6	32	$100,700.00	$85.63	$16,783.33
George Knudson	T-20th in 1965	9	32	7	0	0	0	2	67	79	73.66	0	3	4	101	$5,132.50	$2.18	$570.28
Ed Knych	Missed Cut	3	6	0	0	0	0	0	73	82	79.00	0	0	0	50	$0.00	$0.00	$0.00
Gary Koch	T-10th in 1979	11	36	7	0	0	1	1	65	83	73.86	1	3	5	107	$21,382.86	$8.04	$1,943.90
Arnold Koehler	Missed Cut	3	6	0	0	0	0	0	76	86	77.67	0	0	0	44	$0.00	$0.00	$0.00
Joe Kotlarczyk	Missed Cut	2	5	0	0	0	0	0	70	78	75.60	0	0	0	28	$0.00	$0.00	$0.00
Bill Kozak	Missed Cut	1	2	0	0	0	0	0	79	80	79.50	0	0	0	15	$0.00	$0.00	$0.00
Mike Krak	T-34th in 1963	7	24	4	0	0	0	0	69	81	74.96	0	1	1	109	$1,105.00	$0.61	$157.86
Bill Kratzert	T-12th in 1978	8	24	4	0	0	0	2	67	78	73.75	0	1	5	74	$11,375.17	$6.43	$1,421.90
Ken Krieger	Missed Cut	1	2	0	0	0	0	0	71	74	72.50	0	0	0	3	$1,200.00	$8.28	$1,200.00
Ed Kroll	T-23rd in 1964	6	18	3	0	0	0	1	68	83	75.39	0	1	2	87	$1,471.38	$1.08	$245.23
Ted Kroll	4th in 1961	8	32	8	0	1	1	5	68	81	72.84	0	2	3	83	$7,651.00	$3.28	$956.38
Jerome Krueger	Missed Cut	1	2	0	0	0	0	0	74	83	78.50	0	0	0	17	$0.00	$0.00	$0.00
Bob Kruse	Missed Cut	1	2	0	0	0	0	0	79	83	81.00	0	0	0	22	$0.00	$0.00	$0.00
Don Kubiak	Missed Cut	2	4	0	0	0	0	0	73	82	78.75	0	0	0	31	$0.00	$0.00	$0.00
Wally Kuchar	Missed Cut	1	2	0	0	0	0	0	77	81	79.00	0	0	0	14	$1,000.00	$6.33	$1,000.00
Edward Kuna	T-71st in 1963	4	10	1	0	0	0	0	71	87	78.00	0	0	0	74	$175.00	$0.22	$43.75
Masahiro Kuramoto	T-42nd in 1982	2	6	1	0	0	0	0	70	77	72.67	0	0	0	14	$2,642.85	$6.06	$1,321.43
Ed Kynch	Missed Cut	1	2	0	0	0	0	0	76	83	79.50	0	0	0	19	$0.00	$0.00	$0.00
Huston Laclair	T-56th in 1964	1	4	1	0	0	0	0	72	74	73.25	0	0	0	13	$270.00	$0.92	$270.00
Terry Lally	Missed Cut	1	2	0	0	0	0	0	84	86	85.00	0	0	0	26	$0.00	$0.00	$0.00
Jerry Lambo	Withdrew, 1962	1	1	0	0	0	0	0	82	82	82.00	0	0	0	12	$0.00	$0.00	$0.00
Neal Lancaster	T-84th in 1992	1	4	1	0	0	0	0	72	81	76.75	0	0	0	23	$2,137.50	$6.96	$2,137.50
Ralph Landrum	Missed Cut	3	6	0	0	0	0	0	74	82	77.50	0	0	0	37	$3,000.00	$6.45	$1,000.00

Player	Best Finish	Years	Rds	Cuts Made	3	Top 5	10	25	Low Rd	High Rd	Avg.	Rds 65 or Better	Rds in 60s	Rds Under Par	Par Rounds	Money	$ Per Stroke	$ Per Event
Barry Lane	T-71st in 1993	1	4	1	0	0	0	0	67	77	73.50	0	1	1	10	$2,512.50	$8.55	$2,512.50
Bernhard Langer	T-21st in 1987	9	26	4	0	0	0	1	69	78	73.50	0	2	5	53	$23,600.83	$12.35	$2,622.31
Eddie Langert	Missed Cut	2	4	0	0	0	0	0	72	82	76.25	0	0	0	21	$0.00	$0.00	$0.00
John Langford	Missed Cut	2	5	0	0	0	0	0	73	81	76.00	0	0	0	30	$0.00	$0.00	$0.00
George Lanning	Missed Cut	1	2	0	0	0	0	0	73	80	76.50	0	0	0	9	$250.00	$1.63	$250.00
Joe Lanza	Missed Cut	1	2	0	0	0	0	0	82	83	82.50	0	0.	0	23	$303.00	$1.84	$303.00
Larry Laoretti	T-49th in 1966	1	4	1	0	0	0	0	72	77	74.50	0	0	0	18	$436.11	$1.46	$436.11
Tony Laporte	No Card, 1977	1	1	0	0	0	0	0	87	87	87.00	0	0	0	15	$250.00	$2.87	$250.00
Bob Lavacek	Missed Cut	2	4	0	0	0	0	0	78	81	79.75	0	0	0	37	$0.00	$0.00	$0.00
Duff Lawrence	Missed Cut	1	2	0	0	0	0	0	79	81	80.00	0	0	0	18	$0.00	$0.00	$0.00
Mike Lawrence	Missed Cut	2	4	0	0	0	0	0	75	82	78.75	0	0	0	29	$2,000.00	$6.35	$1,000.00
Bob Leaver	Missed Cut	3	6	0	0	0	0	0	74	85	79.50	0	0	0	51	$2,303.00	$4.83	$767.67
Huston Leclair	T-71st in 1965	1	4	1	0	0	0	0	74	79	76.25	0	0	0	21	$300.00	$0.98	$300.00
David Lee	Missed Cut	1	2	0	0	0	0	0	79	79	79.00	0	0	0	16	$0.00	$0.00	$0.00
Emory Lee	Missed Cut	1	2	0	0	0	0	0	80	82	81.00	0	0	0	22	$0.00	$0.00	$0.00
Tom Lehman	Missed Cut	1	2	0	0	0	0	0	74	74	74.00	0	0	0	6	$1,200.00	$8.11	$1,200.00
Bruce Lehnhard	Missed Cut	3	6	0	0	0	0	0	74	84	79.67	0	0	0	48	$3,200.00	$6.69	$1,066.67
Charles Leider	Missed Cut	1	2	0	0	0	0	0	75	80	77.50	0	0	0	15	$0.00	$0.00	$0.00
Alex Leiper	Missed Cut	1	2	0	0	0	0	0	75	79	77.00	0	0	0	14	$0.00	$0.00	$0.00
Gordon Leishman	Missed Cut	4	8	0	0	0	0	0	75	82	78.88	0	0	0	67	$0.00	$0.00	$0.00
Tony Lema	T-9th in 1964	5	18	4	0	0	1	2	68	80	72.94	0	2	3	45	$4,925.00	$3.75	$985.00
Bob Lendzion	Missed Cut	5	10	0	0	0	0	0	74	84	77.60	0	0	0	62	$5,000.00	$6.44	$1,000.00
Charles Lepre	Missed Cut	6	14	0	0	0	0	0	73	81	76.79	0	0	0	91	$0.00	$0.00	$0.00
Gene Lesch	Missed Cut	2	4	0	0	0	0	0	76	80	78.25	0	0	0	31	$0.00	$0.00	$0.00
Vince Leskosky	Missed Cut	1	2	0	0	0	0	0	75	82	78.50	0	0	0	17	$0.00	$0.00	$0.00
Perry Leslie	Missed Cut	1	2	0	0	0	0	0	79	81	80.00	0	0	0	20	$500.00	$3.13	$500.00
Les Lesser	Missed Cut	1	2	0	0	0	0	0	77	86	81.50	0	0	0	23	$0.00	$0.00	$0.00
Ron Letellier	T-58th in 1972	2	8	2	0	0	0	0	70	79	74.63	0	0	0	37	$761.57	$1.28	$380.79
Gavin Levenson	Missed Cut	1	2	0	0	0	0	0	71	78	74.50	0	0	1	7	$1,000.00	$6.71	$1,000.00
Gerald Levergne	Missed Cut	1	2	0	0	0	0	0	83	87	85.00	0	0	0	30	$0.00	$0.00	$0.00
Wayne Levi	T-16th in 1991	10	30	5	0	0	0	2	66	82	73.17	0	4	6	67	$39,920.19	$18.19	$3,992.02
J. L. Lewis	Missed Cut	1	2	0	0	0	0	0	74	76	75.00	0	0	0	8	$1,200.00	$8.00	$1,200.00
Jack Lewis	Missed Cut	4	8	0	0	0	0	0	73	80	76.50	0	0	0	46	$3,050.00	$4.98	$762.50
Babe Lichardus	T-17th in 1959	12	34	5	0	0	0	1	71	83	75.47	0	0	1	168	$3,601.09	$1.40	$300.09
Bruce Lietzke	2nd in 1991	18	68	16	1	3	4	8	67	80	72.24	0	9	20	86	$242,727.26	$49.42	$13,484.85
Tom Liljeholm	Missed Cut	2	4	0	0	0	0	0	76	77	77.75	0	0	0	31	$0.00	$0.00	$0.00
Dean Lind	Missed Cut	1	2	0	0	0	0	0	76	79	77.50	0	0	0	15	$0.00	$0.00	$0.00
Ken Lindsay	Missed Cut	1	2	0	0	0	0	0	74	78	76.00	0	0	0	12	$0.00	$0.00	$0.00
Pat Lindsey	T-74th in 1983	2	6	1	0	0	0	0	71	80	74.83	0	0	0	23	$2,500.00	$5.57	$1,250.00
Merle Lint	Missed Cut	1	2	0	0	0	0	0	77	82	79.50	0	0	0	19	$0.00	$0.00	$0.00
Vic Lipscomb	Missed Cut	2	4	0	0	0	0	0	73	78	75.00	0	0	0	18	$1,550.00	$5.17	$775.00
John Lister	T-43rd in 1976	3	10	2	0	0	0	0	70	80	74.70	0	0	1	37	$1,516.09	$2.03	$505.36
Gene Littler	T-2nd in 1977	24	86	19	2	4	7	11	66	82	72.42	0	14	19	166	$73,718.70	$11.84	$3,071.61
John Lively	T-37th in 1968	2	6	1	0	0	0	0	72	81	74.33	0	0	0	26	$686.25	$1.54	$343.13
John Lively Jr.	Missed Cut	1	2	0	0	0	0	0	77	78	77.50	0	0	0	15	$0.00	$0.00	$0.00
Ed Lockie	Missed Cut	1	2	0	0	0	0	0	77	83	80.00	0	0	0	20	$0.00	$0.00	$0.00
Gary Lockie	Missed Cut	1	2	0	0	0	0	0	76	82	79.00	0	0	0	16	$0.00	$0.00	$0.00
Rodney Loesch	Missed Cut	1	2	0	0	0	0	0	75	75	75.00	0	0	0	10	$650.00	$4.33	$650.00
Jim Logue	T-77th in 1983	5	12	1	0	0	0	0	70	79	75.75	0	0	0	65	$3,050.00	$3.36	$610.00
Bob Lohr	T-41st in 1989	9	20	1	0	0	0	0	69	89	75.10	0	3	4	72	$12,660.00	$8.43	$1,406.67
John Long	Missed Cut	1	2	0	0	0	0	0	77	80	78.50	0	0	0	17	$0.00	$0.00	$0.00
Tony Longo	Missed Cut	1	2	0	0	0	0	0	73	81	77.00	0	0	0	14	$0.00	$0.00	$0.00
Francisco Lopez	Missed Cut	2	4	0	0	0	0	0	74	83	79.25	0	0	0	37	$0.00	$0.00	$0.00
Joe Lopez Jr.	Missed Cut	2	4	0	0	0	0	0	76	79	77.75	0	0	0	29	$0.00	$0.00	$0.00
Lyn Lott	T-25th in 1977	3	12	3	0	0	0	1	67	80	73.33	0	1	1	32	$3,348.81	$3.81	$1,116.27
Dick Lotz	T-8th in 1970	3	12	3	0	0	1	1	67	77	72.75	0	2	3	21	$6,197.25	$7.10	$2,065.75
Hardy Loudermilk	Missed Cut	3	6	0	0	0	0	0	78	81	79.17	0	0	0	55	$0.00	$0.00	$0.00
Gary Loustalot	Missed Cut	1	2	0	0	0	0	0	80	82	81.00	0	0	0	22	$0.00	$0.00	$0.00
Van-Oran Love	Missed Cut	1	2	0	0	0	0	0	78	79	78.50	0	0	0	17	$0.00	$0.00	$0.00
Davis Love III	T-17th in 1989	7	26	6	0	0	0	1	69	83	72.73	0	3	6	31	$43,057.70	$22.77	$6,151.10
Davis Love Jr.	T-55th in 1967	5	14	2	0	0	0	0	69	82	75.79	0	1	1	67	$630.38	$0.59	$126.08
Jim Lucius	T-71st in 1963	4	10	1	0	0	0	0	74	82	77.20	0	0	0	68	$825.00	$1.07	$206.25
Ben Lula	Missed Cut	1	2	0	0	0	0	0	77	77	77.00	0	0	0	12	$0.00	$0.00	$0.00
Jack Lumpkin	Missed Cut	1	3	0	0	0	0	0	74	75	74.33	0	0	0	13	$0.00	$0.00	$0.00
Jay Lumpkin	Missed Cut	1	2	0	0	0	0	0	74	82	78.00	0	0	0	14	$1,000.00	$6.41	$1,000.00
Dick Lundahl	T-39th in 1960	3	9	1	0	0	0	0	73	80	75.56	0	0	0	48	$200.00	$0.29	$66.67
Bob Lunn	T-9th in 1971	5	18	4	0	0	1	2	69	81	72.72	0	2	4	37	$8,131.25	$6.21	$1,626.25
Mark Lye	T-36th in 1986	8	27	6	0	0	0	0	67	86	73.41	0	2	4	74	$12,407.50	$6.26	$1,550.94
Sandy Lyle	T-16th in 1991	4	12	2	0	0	0	1	68	78	72.75	0	2	4	19	$21,860.00	$25.04	$5,465.00
Steve Lyles	Missed Cut	1	2	0	0	0	0	0	78	84	81.00	0	0	0	22	$0.00	$0.00	$0.00
Denny Lyons	T-12th in 1973	7	18	2	0	0	0	1	67	83	74.78	0	2	3	80	$5,812.00	$4.32	$830.29
Toby Lyons	T-53rd in 1958	2	6	1	0	0	0	0	73	80	75.83	0	0	0	35	$100.00	$0.22	$50.00
Warren MacCarty	Missed Cut	1	2	0	0	0	0	0	79	86	82.50	0	0	0	25	$0.00	$0.00	$0.00
Bruce MacDonald	Missed Cut	1	2	0	0	0	0	0	75	76	75.50	0	0	0	11	$550.00	$3.64	$550.00
Doug MacDonald	Missed Cut	1	2	0	0	0	0	0	76	84	80.00	0	0	0	18	$0.00	$0.00	$0.00

Player	Best Finish	Years	Rds	Cuts Made	Top 3	5	10	25	Low Rd	High Rd	Avg.	Rds 65 or Better	Rds in 60s	Rds Under Par	Par Rounds	Money	$ Per Stroke	$ Per Event
Stan Mack	Missed Cut	1	2	0	0	0	0	0	85	86	85.50	0	0	0	27	$0.00	$0.00	$0.00
Roger MacKay	T-66th in 1992	1	4	1	0	0	0	0	71	76	73.75	0	0	0	11	$2,575.00	$8.73	$2,575.00
Baker Maddera	Missed Cut	1	2	0	0	0	0	0	77	83	80.00	0	0	0	18	$1,200.00	$7.50	$1,200.00
Don Maddox	Missed Cut	1	2	0	0	0	0	0	76	79	77.50	0	0	0	13	$1,000.00	$6.45	$1,000.00
Andrew Magee	T-13th in 1991	7	24	5	0	0	0	1	68	79	73.04	0	3	3	39	$38,100.00	$21.73	$5,442.86
Jeff Maggert	6th in 1992	2	8	2	0	0	1	1	65	74	70.88	1	2	2	-1	$63,600.00	$112.17	$31,800.00
Herb Magnusson	Missed Cut	1	2	0	0	0	0	0	77	81	79.00	0	0	0	18	$0.00	$0.00	$0.00
Paul Maguire	Missed Cut	1	2	0	0	0	0	0	79	82	80.50	0	0	0	21	$0.00	$0.00	$0.00
John Mahaffey	T-Winner in 1978	20	65	12	1	1	2	6	66	80	72.83	0	6	9	132	$106,823.86	$22.57	$5,341.19
Scott Mahlberg	Missed Cut	1	2	0	0	0	0	0	76	77	76.50	0	0	0	11	$1,200.00	$7.84	$1,200.00
Mac Main	T-49th in 1959	5	11	1	0	0	0	0	70	86	76.73	0	0	0	72	$503.00	$0.60	$100.60
Bill Majure	Missed Cut	1	2	0	0	0	0	0	81	83	82.00	0	0	0	24	$0.00	$0.00	$0.00
Bob Makoski	T-58th in 1988	2	6	1	0	0	0	0	69	82	74.83	0	1	1	21	$2,990.00	$6.66	$1,495.00
Terry Malan	Missed Cut	1	2	0	0	0	0	0	77	79	78.00	0	0	0	16	$0.00	$0.00	$0.00
Mike Malaska	Missed Cut	1	2	0	0	0	0	0	75	77	76.00	0	0	0	10	$1,000.00	$6.58	$1,000.00
Charles Malchaski	T-50th in 1961	3	8	1	0	0	0	0	72	79	75.50	0	0	0	42	$225.00	$0.37	$75.00
Hap Malia	Missed Cut	1	2	0	0	0	0	0	81	84	82.50	0	0	0	21	$0.00	$0.00	$0.00
Tom Malone	Missed Cut	2	4	0	0	0	0	0	74	79	77.00	0	0	0	26	$0.00	$0.00	$0.00
Roger Maltbie	T-14th in 1983	11	40	9	0	0	0	1	69	79	73.15	0	3	7	90	$24,265.47	$8.29	$2,205.95
Larry Mancour	T-44th in 1967	6	18	3	0	0	0	0	71	82	75.94	0	0	1	89	$1,080.85	$0.79	$180.14
Bob Mann	T-51st in 1979	3	8	1	0	0	0	0	71	78	74.13	0	0	0	27	$2,600.00	$4.38	$866.67
Dave Marad	Missed Cut	1	2	0	0	0	0	0	75	81	78.00	0	0	0	14	$303.00	$1.94	$303.00
Herb Marcussen	T-55th in 1960	1	4	1	0	0	0	0	72	78	75.25	0	0	0	21	$200.00	$0.66	$200.00
Peter Marich	Missed Cut	1	2	0	0	0	0	0	79	79	79.00	0	0	0	18	$0.00	$0.00	$0.00
Bill Markham	Missed Cut	1	2	0	0	0	0	0	75	76	75.50	0	0	0	11	$0.00	$0.00	$0.00
Tom Marlowe	Missed Cut	1	2	0	0	0	0	0	75	80	77.50	0	0	0	15	$0.00	$0.00	$0.00
Eli Marovich	Missed Cut	1	2	0	0	0	0	0	74	77	75.50	0	0	0	11	$0.00	$0.00	$0.00
Dave Marr	Won in 1965	14	50	11	1	1	2	4	68	85	73.48	0	5	8	152	$32,568.42	$8.86	$2,326.32
Fran Marrello	Missed Cut	1	2	0	0	0	0	0	75	80	77.50	0	0	0	11	$1,000.00	$6.45	$1,000.00
Graham Marsh	T-7th in 1978	3	12	3	0	0	1	2	68	77	72.33	0	2	3	16	$12,268.10	$14.13	$4,089.37
Bob Marshall	Missed Cut	1	2	0	0	0	0	0	79	81	80.00	0	0	0	20	$0.00	$0.00	$0.00
Dick Marshall	T-63rd in 1965	2	5	1	0	0	0	0	72	84	76.00	0	0	0	24	$300.00	$0.79	$150.00
Jim Marshall	Missed Cut	2	4	0	0	0	0	0	75	77	76.25	0	0	0	25	$900.00	$2.95	$450.00
Elroy Marti	Missed Cut	2	3	0	0	0	0	0	77	80	78.67	0	0	0	26	$0.00	$0.00	$0.00
Fred Marti	T-9th in 1971	4	12	2	0	0	1	2	70	77	73.17	0	0	3	26	$6,100.00	$6.95	$1,525.00
Earl Martin	Missed Cut	1	2	0	0	0	0	0	83	83	83.00	0	0	0	26	$0.00	$0.00	$0.00
Bill Martindale	T-15th in 1966	2	8	2	0	0	0	1	70	76	73.00	0	0	1	16	$2,982.50	$5.11	$1,491.25
Richard Martinez	Withdrew, 1979	1	1	0	0	0	0	0	81	81	81.00	0	0	0	11	$350.00	$4.32	$350.00
Milon Marusic	T-45th in 1961	4	14	2	0	0	0	0	73	80	75.00	0	0	0	70	$425.00	$0.40	$106.25
Don Massengale	2nd in 1967	8	25	4	1	1	1	3	66	79	73.16	0	1	4	68	$20,539.29	$11.23	$2,567.41
Rik Massengale	T-30th in 1976	5	13	2	0	0	0	0	70	82	74.69	0	0	1	51	$3,353.00	$3.45	$670.60
Jim Masserio	T-35th in 1979	3	8	1	0	0	0	0	69	79	73.63	0	1	1	23	$3,600.00	$6.11	$1,200.00
Odell Massey	Missed Cut	2	4	0	0	0	0	0	75	79	77.00	0	0	0	26	$0.00	$0.00	$0.00
Dick Mast	71st in 1988	2	6	1	0	0	0	0	71	85	74.17	0	0	0	19	$3,000.00	$6.74	$1,500.00
Ken Mast	Missed Cut	1	2	0	0	0	0	0	77	80	78.50	0	0	0	17	$250.00	$1.59	$250.00
Duke Matthews	Missed Cut	1	2	0	0	0	0	0	75	78	76.50	0	0	0	9	$0.00	$0.00	$0.00
Ronald Mattson	Missed Cut	1	2	0	0	0	0	0	76	79	77.50	0	0	0	15	$0.00	$0.00	$0.00
Terry Mauney	Missed Cut	1	2	0	0	0	0	0	76	79	77.50	0	0	0	15	$500.00	$3.23	$500.00
John Maurycy	Missed Cut	1	2	0	0	0	0	0	78	86	82.00	0	0	0	20	$0.00	$0.00	$0.00
Billy Maxwell	T-5th in 1963	11	41	10	0	1	2	6	69	81	72.68	0	4	5	90	$13,991.88	$4.70	$1,271.99
Dick Mayer	T-14th in 1958	3	9	1	0	0	0	1	69	78	74.22	0	2	2	36	$875.00	$1.31	$291.67
Billy Mayfair	T-5th in 1990	4	12	2	0	1	1	1	68	77	72.58	0	1	4	13	$64,033.34	$73.52	$16,008.34
Shelley Mayfield	T-22nd in 1961	4	16	4	0	0	0	1	69	79	73.25	0	1	1	48	$1,815.90	$1.55	$453.98
Jeff Mays	Missed Cut	1	2	0	0	0	0	0	86	86	86.00	0	0	0	32	$250.00	$1.45	$250.00
Dm McBeath	T-44th in 1967	1	4	1	0	0	0	0	72	75	74.00	0	0	0	8	$501.43	$1.69	$501.43
Scotty McBeath	Missed Cut	3	7	0	0	0	0	0	70	81	76.71	0	0	0	45	$0.00	$0.00	$0.00
Rives McBee	Missed Cut	6	12	0	0	0	0	0	71	86	77.00	0	0	0	78	$2,053.00	$2.22	$342.17
Blaine McCallister	T-17th in 1989	6	22	5	0	0	0	3	67	80	72.91	0	2	8	28	$41,929.16	$26.14	$6,988.19
Bob McCallister	T-8th in 1965	4	16	4	0	0	1	2	66	76	72.94	0	2	3	39	$6,165.00	$5.28	$1,541.25
Harry McCarthy	Missed Cut	1	2	0	0	0	0	0	76	79	77.50	0	0	0	15	$0.00	$0.00	$0.00
Jack McConachie	Missed Cut	2	4	0	0	0	0	0	80	84	82.25	0	0	0	47	$1,500.00	$4.56	$750.00
Gary McCord	T-54th in 1984	4	10	1	0	0	0	0	71	79	75.50	0	0	1	49	$3,727.50	$4.94	$931.88
Jim McCoy	Missed Cut	2	4	0	0	0	0	0	79	84	80.50	0	0	0	42	$0.00	$0.00	$0.00
Mike McCullough	T-40th in 1977	4	12	2	0	0	0	0	69	82	74.50	0	1	1	40	$2,825.00	$3.16	$706.25
Mark McCumber	T-5th in 1987	14	45	9	0	1	1	1	67	79	73.07	0	6	10	87	$64,086.25	$19.49	$4,577.59
Joe McDermott	Missed Cut	1	2	0	0	0	0	0	77	84	80.50	0	0	0	21	$650.00	$4.04	$650.00
Ken McDonald	T-84th in 1992	1	4	1	0	0	0	0	69	82	76.75	0	1	1	23	$2,137.50	$6.96	$2,137.50
Ron McDougal	Missed Cut	2	4	0	0	0	0	0	74	79	75.25	0	0	0	17	$2,400.00	$7.97	$1,200.00
Mac McElmurry	Missed Cut	1	2	0	0	0	0	0	75	79	77.00	0	0	0	14	$0.00	$0.00	$0.00
Shawn McEntee	Missed Cut	2	4	0	0	0	0	0	74	82	78.25	0	0	0	25	$2,000.00	$6.39	$1,000.00
Jerry McGee	T-6th in 1977	10	37	8	0	0	2	4	68	79	72.68	0	4	8	76	$24,432.29	$9.09	$2,443.23
Jim McGovern	T-22nd in 1993	1	4	1	0	0	0	1	67	74	70.25	0	2	2	-3	$14,500.00	$51.60	$14,500.00
Jack McGowan	T-43rd in 1961	3	10	2	0	0	0	0	70	79	74.50	0	0	0	39	$466.38	$0.63	$155.46
Pat McGowan	4th in 1983	6	14	1	0	1	1	1	67	80	73.93	0	3	3	39	$34,303.00	$33.14	$5,717.17
Paul McGuire	Missed Cut	1	2	0	0	0	0	0	77	80	78.50	0	0	0	17	$0.00	$0.00	$0.00

PGA CHAMPIONSHIP STROKE-PLAY STATISTICS

Player	Best Finish	Years	Rds	Cuts Made	Top 3	Top 5	Top 10	Top 25	Low Rd	High Rd	Avg.	Rds 65 or Better	Rds in 60s	Rds Under Par	Par Rounds	Money	$ Per Stroke	$ Per Event
Tom McGuirk	Missed Cut	1	2	0	0	0	0	0	83	85	84.00	0	0	0	24	$250.00	$1.49	$250.00
Jack McKelvey	Missed Cut	1	2	0	0	0	0	0	83	90	86.50	0	0	0	29	$1,000.00	$5.78	$1,000.00
George McKeown	Missed Cut	1	2	0	0	0	0	0	77	77	77.00	0	0	0	12	$0.00	$0.00	$0.00
Mac McLendon	T-25th in 1975	6	20	4	0	0	0	1	68	78	74.05	0	1	1	69	$4,040.00	$2.73	$673.33
John McMullin	T-35th in 1959	1	4	1	0	0	0	0	69	76	72.75	0	1	1	11	$200.00	$0.69	$200.00
Artie McNickle	T-28th in 1979	2	8	2	0	0	0	0	69	76	72.25	0	1	1	18	$4,500.00	$7.79	$2,250.00
Mark McNulty	T-8th in 1990	8	27	5	0	0	1	2	67	77	72.78	0	4	8	41	$59,907.15	$30.49	$7,488.39
Henry McQuiston	Missed Cut	1	2	0	0	0	0	0	76	79	77.50	0	0	0	15	$0.00	$0.00	$0.00
J. L. McReynolds	62nd in 1961	1	4	1	0	0	0	0	73	79	76.00	0	0	0	24	$225.00	$0.74	$225.00
Rocco Mediate	T-16th in 1991	5	20	5	0	0	0	1	68	81	72.90	0	2	7	30	$31,817.86	$21.82	$6,363.57
Steve Melnyk	T-17th in 1975	5	14	2	0	0	0	1	70	79	73.93	0	0	1	43	$4,628.00	$4.47	$925.60
Tod Menefee	Missed Cut	3	7	0	0	0	0	0	75	84	78.71	0	0	0	59	$0.00	$0.00	$0.00
Al Mengert	T-18th in 1970	10	33	6	0	0	0	2	68	83	73.82	0	1	2	112	$7,453.61	$3.06	$745.36
Bob Menne	T-30th in 1970	4	10	1	0	0	0	0	72	78	74.60	0	0	0	44	$2,875.00	$3.85	$718.75
Lou Merkle	Missed Cut	2	4	0	0	0	0	0	78	85	81.00	0	0	0	40	$303.00	$0.94	$151.50
Hans Merrell	Missed Cut	1	2	0	0	0	0	0	76	77	76.50	0	0	0	13	$0.00	$0.00	$0.00
Eddie Merrins	T-34th in 1963	6	16	2	0	0	0	0	70	81	75.50	0	0	2	72	$721.37	$0.60	$120.23
Dick Merritt	Missed Cut	1	2	0	0	0	0	0	79	81	80.00	0	0	0	20	$0.00	$0.00	$0.00
Jack Merz	Missed Cut	1	2	0	0	0	0	0	82	82	82.00	0	0	0	24	$0.00	$0.00	$0.00
Rick Meskell	Missed Cut	1	2	0	0	0	0	0	81	82	81.50	0	0	0	19	$1,000.00	$6.13	$1,000.00
Dennis Meyer	T-67th in 1975	1	4	1	0	0	0	0	72	80	75.00	0	0	0	20	$428.57	$1.43	$428.57
Phil Mickelson	T-6th in 1993	1	4	1	0	0	1	1	67	71	69.25	0	2	3	-7	$47,812.50	$172.61	$47,812.50
Cary Middlecoff	T-8th in 1959	5	20	5	0	0	1	4	66	76	71.95	0	4	4	39	$5,491.00	$3.82	$1,098.20
Mark Mielke	Missed Cut	1	2	0	0	0	0	0	70	75	72.50	0	0	1	3	$1,200.00	$8.28	$1,200.00
Tony Milam	Missed Cut	1	2	0	0	0	0	0	83	87	85.00	0	0	0	26	$1,000.00	$5.88	$1,000.00
Eldridge Miles	Missed Cut	2	4	0	0	0	0	0	76	88	80.00	0	0	0	36	$250.00	$0.78	$125.00
Allen Miller	T-39th in 1984	6	20	4	0	0	0	0	69	83	74.90	0	1	2	84	$5,489.97	$3.66	$915.00
Bill Miller	Missed Cut	1	2	0	0	0	0	0	81	82	81.50	0	0	0	21	$0.00	$0.00	$0.00
Johnny Miller	T-11th in 1977	16	51	10	0	0	0	5	67	80	72.82	0	5	9	108	$29,209.72	$7.86	$1,825.61
Lindy Miller	T-57th in 1991	4	12	2	0	0	0	0	71	82	75.08	0	0	0	41	$5,487.52	$6.09	$1,371.88
Michael Milon	Missed Cut	1	2	0	0	0	0	0	74	75	74.50	0	0	0	9	$350.00	$2.35	$350.00
Jim Milward	Missed Cut	1	2	0	0	0	0	0	77	78	77.50	0	0	0	15	$0.00	$0.00	$0.00
Bobby Mitchell	T-34th in 1971	8	25	5	0	0	0	0	69	79	74.56	0	1	3	92	$4,100.92	$2.20	$512.62
Chris Mitchell	Missed Cut	1	2	0	0	0	0	0	73	74	73.50	0	0	0	3	$1,000.00	$6.80	$1,000.00
Gene Mitchell	T-70th in 1968	1	4	1	0	0	0	0	70	82	76.50	0	0	0	26	$365.00	$1.19	$365.00
Jeff Mitchell	T-65th in 1982	3	8	1	0	0	0	0	72	82	75.25	0	0	0	40	$1,925.50	$3.20	$641.83
Bob Mix	Missed Cut	2	4	0	0	0	0	0	74	85	79.00	0	0	0	36	$0.00	$0.00	$0.00
Frank Mize	T-67th in 1974	1	4	1	0	0	0	0	72	79	74.75	0	0	0	19	$321.43	$1.08	$321.43
Larry Mize	T-6th in 1984	11	36	7	0	0	1	4	67	81	72.69	0	5	11	49	$77,342.91	$29.55	$7,031.17
Lester Moe	Missed Cut	2	4	0	0	0	0	0	75	87	80.50	0	0	0	42	$0.00	$0.00	$0.00
Ed Moehling	Missed Cut	1	2	0	0	0	0	0	75	76	75.50	0	0	0	11	$0.00	$0.00	$0.00
John Molinda	80th in 1971	3	8	1	0	0	0	0	72	83	77.75	0	0	0	54	$258.00	$0.41	$86.00
Lloyd Monroe	Missed Cut	2	4	0	0	0	0	0	72	77	74.75	0	0	0	19	$350.00	$1.17	$175.00
Colin Montgomerie	T-33rd in 1992	2	6	1	0	0	0	0	69	76	72.33	0	1	2	8	$8,200.00	$18.89	$4,100.00
Ray Montgomery	Missed Cut	1	2	0	0	0	0	0	76	76	76.00	0	0	0	12	$0.00	$0.00	$0.00
Eric Monti	T-20th in 1958	4	14	3	0	0	0	1	71	81	74.00	0	0	0	54	$1,228.50	$1.19	$307.13
Ralph Montoya	Missed Cut	1	2	0	0	0	0	0	74	76	75.00	0	0	0	10	$350.00	$2.33	$350.00
Ron Montressor	Missed Cut	1	2	0	0	0	0	0	78	82	80.00	0	0	0	20	$0.00	$0.00	$0.00
Orville Moody	T-7th in 1969	6	17	3	0	0	1	1	68	79	72.88	0	1	3	37	$7,678.33	$6.20	$1,279.72
Jim Mooney	T-54th in 1968	2	6	1	0	0	0	0	73	81	76.33	0	0	0	36	$415.00	$0.91	$207.50
Bob Moore	Missed Cut	2	4	0	0	0	0	0	74	87	80.00	0	0	0	40	$0.00	$0.00	$0.00
Horace Moore	T-59th in 1968	5	14	2	0	0	0	0	72	84	76.57	0	0	0	86	$669.00	$0.62	$133.80
Ossie Moore	Missed Cut	1	2	0	0	0	0	0	76	76	76.00	0	0	0	10	$1,000.00	$6.58	$1,000.00
Joe Moore Jr.	Missed Cut	2	5	0	0	0	0	0	74	79	75.20	0	0	0	26	$0.00	$0.00	$0.00
Bill Moran	Missed Cut	3	7	0	0	0	0	0	73	88	78.57	0	0	0	60	$0.00	$0.00	$0.00
Paul Moran	69th in 1975	2	6	1	0	0	0	0	69	79	75.50	0	1	1	33	$678.57	$1.50	$339.29
Bob Moreland	Missed Cut	3	6	0	0	0	0	0	75	80	78.00	0	0	0	44	$1,450.00	$3.10	$483.33
Jay Morelli	Missed Cut	1	2	0	0	0	0	0	79	86	82.50	0	0	0	21	$250.00	$1.52	$250.00
Joe Moresco	Missed Cut	2	4	0	0	0	0	0	75	79	77.50	0	0	0	26	$550.00	$1.77	$275.00
Gil Morgan	3rd in 1980 & '90	19	66	14	2	3	4	11	65	79	71.95	1	12	19	69	$198,766.25	$41.85	$10,461.38
Al Morley	Missed Cut	4	8	0	0	0	0	0	76	85	80.38	0	0	0	77	$0.00	$0.00	$0.00
Mike Morley	T-15th in 1976	6	24	6	0	0	0	1	69	80	73.21	0	1	3	65	$7,222.50	$4.11	$1,203.75
Tony Morosco	Missed Cut	1	2	0	0	0	0	0	75	86	80.50	0	0	0	21	$250.00	$1.55	$250.00
Bob Morris	Missed Cut	2	4	0	0	0	0	0	78	82	80.50	0	0	0	42	$0.00	$0.00	$0.00
Kevin Morris	T-73rd in 1985	5	12	1	0	0	0	0	72	84	76.00	0	0	0	64	$4,700.00	$5.15	$940.00
Wayne Morris	Missed Cut	1	2	0	0	0	0	0	76	76	76.00	0	0	0	10	$0.00	$0.00	$0.00
Clark Morrow	Withdrew, 1958	1	1	0	0	0	0	0	83	83	83.00	0	0	0	13	$0.00	$0.00	$0.00
Rick Morton	Missed Cut	1	2	0	0	0	0	0	74	75	74.50	0	0	0	5	$1,000.00	$6.71	$1,000.00
Stan Mosel	39th in 1963	3	10	2	0	0	0	0	70	78	74.40	0	0	1	36	$865.00	$1.16	$288.33
Jerry Mowlds	Missed Cut	2	4	0	0	0	0	0	75	82	77.75	0	0	0	29	$0.00	$0.00	$0.00
Larry Mowry	T-11th in 1969	2	6	1	0	0	0	1	69	76	72.50	0	2	2	7	$3,793.75	$8.72	$1,896.88
Mike Moyers	Missed Cut	1	2	0	0	0	0	0	80	82	81.00	0	0	0	20	$1,200.00	$7.41	$1,200.00
Jodie Mudd	T-32nd in 1991	5	18	4	0	0	0	0	70	85	73.67	0	0	6	38	$14,162.50	$10.68	$2,832.50
Richard Mullen	Missed Cut	1	2	0	0	0	0	0	76	81	78.50	0	0	0	17	$0.00	$0.00	$0.00
Moon Mullins	Missed Cut	2	5	0	0	0	0	0	72	79	76.20	0	0	0	31	$0.00	$0.00	$0.00

Player	Best Finish	Years	Rds	Cuts Made	Top 3	5	10	25	Low Rd	High Rd	Avg.	Rds 65 or Better	Rds in 60s	Rds Under Par	Par Rounds	Money	$ Per Stroke	$ Per Event
Chet Munson	Missed Cut	1	2	0	0	0	0	0	77	80	78.50	0	0	0	17	$0.00	$0.00	$0.00
Bob Murphy	T-2nd in 1970	17	62	14	1	1	1	5	66	80	73.06	0	8	8	152	$41,264.48	$9.11	$2,427.32
Dan Murphy	Missed Cut	4	8	0	0	0	0	0	78	83	79.50	0	0	0	72	$1,500.00	$2.36	$375.00
Tom Murphy	Missed Cut	1	2	0	0	0	0	0	74	78	76.00	0	0	0	12	$0.00	$0.00	$0.00
Reggie Myles	Missed Cut	1	2	0	0	0	0	0	75	84	79.50	0	0	0	19	$0.00	$0.00	$0.00
Kel Nagle	T-20th in 1965	2	6	1	0	0	0	1	71	77	74.00	0	0	0	20	$1,450.00	$3.27	$725.00
Tommy Nakajima	T-3rd in 1988	9	26	4	1	1	2	3	67	80	72.69	0	6	6	40	$103,533.33	$54.78	$11,503.70
Tohru Nakamura	T-59th in 1980	1	4	1	0	0	0	0	70	78	74.50	0	0	0	18	$742.50	$2.49	$742.50
Frank Nastri	Missed Cut	1	2	0	0	0	0	0	79	81	80.00	0	0	0	20	$0.00	$0.00	$0.00
Jim Nelford	T-55th in 1983	4	12	2	0	0	0	0	71	76	73.25	0	0	0	33	$4,052.50	$4.61	$1,013.13
Al Nelson	T-39th in 1962	3	8	1	0	0	0	0	70	79	74.88	0	0	0	39	$400.00	$0.67	$133.33
Dick Nelson	Missed Cut	1	2	0	0	0	0	0	72	81	76.50	0	0	0	13	$0.00	$0.00	$0.00
John Nelson	Missed Cut	1	2	0	0	0	0	0	73	79	76.00	0	0	0	10	$1,200.00	$7.89	$1,200.00
Larry Nelson	Won in 1981 & '87	18	60	12	2	2	2	4	66	80	72.53	0	8	15	92	$249,864.21	$57.41	$13,881.35
Rocky Nelson	Missed Cut	1	2	0	0	0	0	0	81	83	82.00	0	0	0	22	$303.00	$1.85	$303.00
Dwight Nevil	T-53rd in 1974	6	16	2	0	0	0	0	70	85	76.94	0	0	1	99	$4,331.43	$3.52	$721.91
Jack Newton	T-20th in 1980	2	8	2	0	0	0	1	71	79	73.13	0	0	0	21	$3,962.50	$6.77	$1,981.25
Bobby Nichols	Won in 1964	24	84	18	1	1	2	5	64	82	73.43	1	7	10	234	$42,673.82	$6.92	$1,778.08
Robert Nichols	Missed Cut	2	4	0	0	0	0	0	78	90	83.00	0	0	0	52	$500.00	$1.51	$250.00
John Nichols Jr.	Missed Cut	1	2	0	0	0	0	0	76	81	78.50	0	0	0	17	$550.00	$3.50	$550.00
Jack Nicklaus	Won in '63, 71, '73, '75 & '80	32	116	26	12	14	15	23	64	79	71.16	2	39	50	42	$427,725.49	$51.82	$13,366.42
Mike Nicolette	T-47th in 1983	1	4	1	0	0	0	0	71	74	72.50	0	0	0	6	$1,730.00	$5.97	$1,730.00
Bob Nieberding	Missed Cut	1	2	0	0	0	0	0	78	80	79.00	0	0	0	18	$550.00	$3.48	$550.00
Lonnie Nielsen	T-11th in 1986	7	20	3	0	0	0	0	69	81	74.85	0	1	3	67	$19,581.00	$13.08	$2,797.29
Tom Nieporte	T-5th in 1964	10	34	7	0	1	1	2	68	83	73.74	0	4	4	111	$7,318.93	$2.92	$731.89
Frank Nobilo	T-22nd in 1993	2	8	2	0	0	0	1	66	74	71.38	0	3	3	3	$21,500.00	$37.65	$10,750.00
Fred Nonnenberg	Missed Cut	1	2	0	0	0	0	0	77	85	81.00	0	0	0	22	$0.00	$0.00	$0.00
Monte Norcross	Missed Cut	2	5	0	0	0	0	0	74	82	78.00	0	0	0	40	$0.00	$0.00	$0.00
August Nordone	Missed Cut	2	4	0	0	0	0	0	77	83	80.50	0	0	0	42	$0.00	$0.00	$0.00
Greg Norman	2nd in 1986 & '93	13	50	12	2	4	5	8	65	79	71.54	1	14	20	19	$358,527.02	$100.23	$27,579.00
Tim Norris	T-40th in 1985	3	8	1	0	0	0	0	70	76	73.88	0	0	1	23	$4,500.00	$7.61	$1,500.00
Andy North	4th in 1975	15	46	8	0	1	1	3	65	79	73.13	1	4	5	116	$32,859.73	$9.77	$2,190.65
Tony Novitsky	Missed Cut	2	4	0	0	0	0	0	79	83	80.50	0	0	0	38	$0.00	$0.00	$0.00
Gifford Nutbrown	Missed Cut	2	4	0	0	0	0	0	76	81	78.50	0	0	0	28	$0.00	$0.00	$0.00
John O'Donnell	59th in 1960	1	4	1	0	0	0	0	71	82	76.25	0	0	0	25	$200.00	$0.66	$200.00
Mac O'Grady	T-43rd in 1987	5	12	1	0	0	0	0	70	84	75.58	0	0	3	51	$7,050.00	$7.77	$1,410.00
Dennis O'Leary	Missed Cut	1	2	0	0	0	0	0	75	86	80.50	0	0	0	21	$0.00	$0.00	$0.00
Mark O'Meara	T-9th in 1988	12	34	5	0	0	1	3	68	79	73.44	0	3	8	77	$52,456.25	$21.01	$4,371.35
Peter Oakley	Missed Cut	3	6	0	0	0	0	0	72	83	76.00	0	0	0	28	$3,000.00	$6.58	$1,000.00
Bill Ogden	T-49th in 1959	10	25	2	0	0	0	0	69	85	75.72	0	1	1	139	$440.00	$0.23	$44.00
Brett Ogle	Missed Cut	1	2	0	0	0	0	0	72	77	74.50	0	0	0	7	$1,200.00	$8.05	$1,200.00
David Ogrin	T-47th in 1985	3	8	1	0	0	0	0	70	80	75.00	0	0	2	30	$4,075.00	$6.79	$1,358.33
Jim O'Hern	T-55th in 1970	9	22	2	0	0	0	0	73	83	77.36	0	0	0	150	$2,036.00	$1.20	$226.22
Jose Maria Olazabal	T-14th in 1990	6	16	2	0	0	0	1	69	79	73.94	0	1	1	37	$27,910.00	$23.59	$4,651.67
Dave Oliphant	Missed Cut	1	2	0	0	0	0	0	83	87	85.00	0	0	0	26	$250.00	$1.47	$250.00
Ed Oliver	T-8th in 1958	2	8	2	0	0	1	2	69	75	71.50	0	2	2	12	$2,550.00	$4.46	$1,275.00
Peter Oosterhuis	T-22nd in 1982	8	26	5	0	0	0	1	66	78	73.19	0	1	1	73	$11,542.86	$6.07	$1,442.86
Jack Ortman	Missed Cut	2	4	0	0	0	0	0	74	81	77.50	0	0	0	26	$0.00	$0.00	$0.00
Rick Osberg	Missed Cut	3	6	0	0	0	0	0	73	79	76.17	0	0	0	29	$3,000.00	$6.56	$1,000.00
Gary Ostrega	Missed Cut	3	6	0	0	0	0	0	72	84	77.50	0	0	0	39	$3,200.00	$6.88	$1,066.67
Wayne Otis	62nd in 1959	1	4	1	0	0	0	0	73	79	75.00	0	0	0	20	$200.00	$0.67	$200.00
Scott Oulds	Missed Cut	1	2	0	0	0	0	0	79	85	82.00	0	0	0	20	$1,000.00	$6.10	$1,000.00
Jay Overton	T-17th in 1988	8	20	2	0	0	0	1	66	84	75.25	0	3	3	85	$19,275.00	$12.81	$2,409.38
Jumbo Ozaki	T-69th in 1990	2	6	1	0	0	0	0	73	80	76.33	0	0	0	30	$2,775.00	$6.06	$1,387.50
Joe Ozaki	T-28th in 1992	4	12	2	0	0	0	0	66	81	73.25	0	3	3	23	$15,607.14	$17.76	$3,901.79
Roy Pace	T-63rd in 1974	1	4	1	0	0	0	0	71	76	74.25	0	0	0	17	$321.43	$1.08	$321.43
Harold Paddock	Missed Cut	3	6	0	0	0	0	0	77	84	80.50	0	0	0	63	$0.00	$0.00	$0.00
Don Padgett	T-43rd in 1976	7	22	4	0	0	0	0	70	81	74.09	0	0	1	82	$6,311.50	$3.87	$901.64
John Paesani	Missed Cut	1	2	0	0	0	0	0	78	79	78.50	0	0	0	15	$1,000.00	$6.37	$1,000.00
Arnold Palmer	T-2nd in 1964, '68 & '70	36	119	24	3	4	6	13	67	83	73.45	0	13	18	331	$86,944.31	$9.95	$2,415.12
Donald Palmer	Missed Cut	3	6	0	0	0	0	0	74	81	77.17	0	0	0	43	$0.00	$0.00	$0.00
Johnny Palmer	Missed Cut	1	3	0	0	0	0	0	73	80	76.33	0	0	0	19	$0.00	$0.00	$0.00
Mike Parco	Missed Cut	2	3	0	0	0	0	0	75	81	78.33	0	0	0	25	$0.00	$0.00	$0.00
Billy Parker	Missed Cut	2	4	0	0	0	0	0	78	78	78.00	0	0	0	32	$0.00	$0.00	$0.00
Craig Parry	T-31st in 1993	3	12	3	0	0	0	0	68	77	72.58	0	1	4	11	$15,837.69	$18.18	$5,279.23
Jimmy Paschal	Missed Cut	1	2	0	0	0	0	0	75	76	75.50	0	0	0	11	$350.00	$2.32	$350.00
Benny Passons	Missed Cut	5	10	0	0	0	0	0	74	85	78.00	0	0	0	68	$4,650.00	$5.96	$930.00
Andy Pataky	Missed Cut	2	4	0	0	0	0	0	82	86	83.75	0	0	0	55	$0.00	$0.00	$0.00
Jerry Pate	T-2nd in 1978	10	36	8	1	4	6	8	66	79	71.17	0	12	15	20	$85,831.25	$33.50	$8,583.13
Steve Pate	T-7th in 1991	8	32	8	0	0	1	1	69	80	73.06	0	2	11	50	$60,407.92	$25.84	$7,550.99
Guy Paulsen	Missed Cut	1	2	0	0	0	0	0	77	79	78.00	0	0	0	16	$0.00	$0.00	$0.00
Mike Pavella	Missed Cut	3	6	0	0	0	0	0	76	81	77.33	0	0	0	42	$0.00	$0.00	$0.00
Corey Pavin	T-6th in 1985	10	34	7	0	0	1	6	66	79	72.29	0	4	8	32	$100,741.67	$40.99	$10,074.17

Player	Best Finish	Years	Rds	Cuts Made	Top 3	Top 5	Top 10	Top 25	Low Rd	High Rd	Avg.	Rds 65 or Better	Rds in 60s	Rds Under Par	Par Rounds	Money	$ Per Stroke	$ Per Event
Bob Payne	T-62nd in 1977	2	6	1	0	0	0	0	73	79	76.00	0	0	0	26	$791.09	$1.73	$395.55
Richard Payne	Missed Cut	1	2	0	0	0	0	0	80	87	83.50	0	0	0	23	$0.00	$0.00	$0.00
Dick Pearce	Missed Cut	1	2	0	0	0	0	0	78	86	82.00	0	0	0	22	$0.00	$0.00	$0.00
Eddie Pearce	T-32nd in 1974	2	8	2	0	0	0	0	69	79	73.25	0	1	1	26	$1,688.57	$2.88	$844.29
Chris Peddicord	Missed Cut	1	2	0	0	0	0	0	73	77	75.00	0	0	0	8	$1,200.00	$8.00	$1,200.00
Calvin Peete	T-3rd in 1982	9	33	8	1	2	2	3	66	76	71.33	0	10	13	22	$81,698.61	$34.71	$9,077.62
Bill Pelham	Missed Cut	1	2	0	0	0	0	0	78	81	79.50	0	0	0	19	$500.00	$3.14	$500.00
Sam Penecale	T-57th in 1961	5	12	1	0	0	0	0	72	81	76.42	0	0	0	73	$225.00	$0.25	$45.00
David Peoples	T-57th in 1990	3	12	3	0	0	0	0	71	77	74.50	0	0	1	34	$7,237.50	$8.10	$2,412.50
Chris Perry	T-17th in 1989	3	12	3	0	0	0	1	67	76	73.00	0	1	3	12	$28,033.34	$32.00	$9,344.45
Harold Perry	83rd in 1992	1	4	1	0	0	0	0	74	79	76.25	0	0	0	21	$2,175.00	$7.13	$2,175.00
Kenny Perry	T-49th in 1990	3	12	3	0	0	0	0	70	79	74.08	0	0	2	25	$7,690.63	$8.65	$2,563.54
Peter Persons	Missed Cut	1	2	0	0	0	0	0	73	75	74.00	0	0	0	4	$1,000.00	$6.76	$1,000.00
Jim Petersen	Missed Cut	2	4	0	0	0	0	0	76	83	79.50	0	0	0	34	$0.00	$0.00	$0.00
Randy Peterson	Missed Cut	1	2	0	0	0	0	0	79	80	79.50	0	0	0	17	$1,200.00	$7.55	$1,200.00
Jim Petralia	Missed Cut	1	2	0	0	0	0	0	80	91	85.50	0	0	0	27	$1,000.00	$5.85	$1,000.00
Mark Pfeil	T-22nd in 1982	4	16	4	0	0	0	1	67	78	72.38	0	2	5	30	$9,546.00	$8.24	$2,386.50
Billy Phillips	Missed Cut	1	2	0	0	0	0	0	75	78	76.50	0	0	0	13	$0.00	$0.00	$0.00
Bobby Phillips	Missed Cut	1	2	0	0	0	0	0	75	78	76.50	0	0	0	13	$350.00	$2.29	$350.00
Dave Philo	Missed Cut	2	4	0	0	0	0	0	75	82	77.50	0	0	0	28	$650.00	$2.10	$325.00
Ron Philo	Missed Cut	1	2	0	0	0	0	0	78	83	80.50	0	0	0	21	$250.00	$1.55	$250.00
Henry Picard	T-32nd in 1960	2	6	1	0	0	0	0	73	81	75.33	0	0	0	30	$247.15	$0.55	$123.58
Jim Picard	69th in 1968	3	8	1	0	0	0	0	70	79	76.25	0	0	0	44	$918.00	$1.50	$306.00
Drew Pierson	Missed Cut	1	2	0	0	0	0	0	80	80	80.00	0	0	0	18	$0.00	$0.00	$0.00
Manuelo Pinero	Missed Cut	1	2	0	0	0	0	0	73	76	74.50	0	0	0	7	$1,000.00	$6.71	$1,000.00
Jerry Pisano	T-40th in 1963	3	8	1	0	0	0	0	69	82	75.50	0	1	1	40	$410.00	$0.68	$136.67
Jerry Pittman	T-33rd in 1967	4	12	2	0	0	0	0	69	79	74.42	0	1	1	43	$1,436.25	$1.61	$359.06
Bob Placido	Missed Cut	1	2	0	0	0	0	0	81	85	83.00	0	0	0	26	$0.00	$0.00	$0.00
Gary Player	Won in 1962 & '72	23	88	21	5	6	8	12	63	78	71.65	3	13	17	99	$193,398.33	$30.67	$8,408.62
Dick Plummer	Missed Cut	3	6	0	0	0	0	0	76	84	78.83	0	0	0	51	$0.00	$0.00	$0.00
Carl Poche	Missed Cut	1	2	0	0	0	0	0	79	80	79.50	0	0	0	17	$1,000.00	$6.29	$1,000.00
Mike Podolski	Missed Cut	1	2	0	0	0	0	0	79	80	79.50	0	0	0	17	$0.00	$0.00	$0.00
Dan Pohl	3rd in 1981	9	36	9	1	1	3	6	67	79	71.47	0	9	17	17	$107,272.23	$41.69	$11,919.14
Willie Polumbo	Missed Cut	2	4	0	0	0	0	0	79	80	79.75	0	0	0	39	$0.00	$0.00	$0.00
Ewing Pomeroy	63rd in 1958	1	4	1	0	0	0	0	74	82	77.50	0	0	0	30	$100.00	$0.32	$100.00
Don Pooley	T-5th in 1987	13	50	12	0	1	2	5	68	80	72.64	0	4	11	78	$105,018.42	$28.91	$8,078.34
Bob Popp	Missed Cut	4	7	0	0	0	0	0	73	82	78.71	0	0	0	55	$0.00	$0.00	$0.00
Joe Porter	29th in 1976	2	8	2	0	0	0	0	70	76	73.13	0	0	0	25	$1,871.43	$3.20	$935.72
Paul Porter	Missed Cut	1	2	0	0	0	0	0	76	77	76.50	0	0	0	13	$0.00	$0.00	$0.00
Bob Post	Missed Cut	1	2	0	0	0	0	0	76	76	76.00	0	0	0	12	$250.00	$1.64	$250.00
Johnny Pott	T-5th in 1961	11	34	6	0	1	1	3	67	79	73.12	0	2	4	88	$7,815.83	$3.14	$710.53
Jerry Pottman	T-35th in 1973	1	4	1	0	0	0	0	70	76	72.50	0	0	1	6	$1,054.45	$3.64	$1,054.45
Leon Pounders	Missed Cut	1	2	0	0	0	0	0	77	81	79.00	0	0	0	18	$0.00	$0.00	$0.00
Jimmy Powell	T-33rd in 1975	7	18	2	0	0	0	0	68	78	74.78	0	1	1	78	$1,548.00	$1.15	$221.14
Mickey Powell	Missed Cut	1	2	0	0	0	0	0	78	78	78.00	0	0	0	12	$0.00	$0.00	$0.00
Greg Powers	T-26th in 1978	3	10	2	0	0	0	0	70	75	72.50	0	0	2	21	$5,250.00	$7.24	$1,750.00
George Preisinger	Missed Cut	1	2	0	0	0	0	0	79	84	81.50	0	0	0	21	$0.00	$0.00	$0.00
Charles Prentice	Missed Cut	1	2	0	0	0	0	0	74	78	76.00	0	0	0	10	$0.00	$0.00	$0.00
Nick Price	Won in 1992	10	38	9	1	2	3	4	65	81	72.37	1	4	13	40	$350,660.99	$127.51	$35,066.10
Art Proctor	Missed Cut	3	5	0	0	0	0	0	75	77	76.20	0	0	0	29	$303.00	$0.80	$101.00
Dillard Pruitt	T-33rd in 1992	2	8	2	0	0	0	0	70	76	73.25	0	0	1	14	$9,312.50	$15.89	$4,656.25
Paul Purtzer	Missed Cut	1	2	0	0	0	0	0	73	76	74.50	0	0	0	9	$350.00	$2.35	$350.00
Tom Purtzer	T-16th in 1982	15	46	8	0	0	0	3	68	81	73.43	0	4	8	106	$45,246.25	$13.39	$3,016.42
Randy Quick	Missed Cut	1	2	0	0	0	0	0	75	78	76.50	0	0	0	13	$0.00	$0.00	$0.00
Dana Quigley	T-41st in 1980	5	12	1	0	0	0	0	72	80	75.67	0	0	0	56	$5,500.00	$6.06	$1,100.00
Sammy Rachels	T-45th in 1990	3	8	1	0	0	0	0	71	76	74.25	0	0	0	20	$5,900.00	$9.93	$1,966.67
Norman Rack	Missed Cut	1	2	0	0	0	0	0	79	87	83.00	0	0	0	26	$0.00	$0.00	$0.00
Ronan Rafferty	Missed Cut	1	2	0	0	0	0	0	75	81	78.00	0	0	0	12	$1,000.00	$6.41	$1,000.00
Dave Ragan	2nd in 1963	8	30	7	1	1	2	3	67	80	72.70	0	5	7	73	$12,454.17	$5.71	$1,556.77
Ross Randall	Missed Cut	2	4	0	0	0	0	0	77	83	80.00	0	0	0	38	$1,650.00	$5.16	$825.00
Sam Randolph	Missed Cut	1	2	0	0	0	0	0	73	75	74.00	0	0	0	6	$1,000.00	$6.76	$1,000.00
Pat Rea	T-64th in 1968	3	7	1	0	0	0	0	73	80	76.00	0	0	0	40	$615.00	$1.16	$205.00
Alex Redl	Missed Cut	1	2	0	0	0	0	0	74	81	77.50	0	0	0	15	$0.00	$0.00	$0.00
Alex Redmond	Missed Cut	1	2	0	0	0	0	0	75	77	76.00	0	0	0	8	$0.00	$0.00	$0.00
Dean Refram	72nd in 1979	5	12	1	0	0	0	0	69	79	75.67	0	1	1	66	$1,250.00	$1.38	$250.00
Victor Regalado	T-10th in 1984	9	28	5	0	0	1	1	69	80	73.71	0	3	5	92	$19,126.90	$9.27	$2,125.21
Mike Reid	T-2nd in 1989	11	42	10	1	1	2	3	66	79	72.79	0	5	11	73	$117,993.69	$38.60	$10,726.70
Steve Reid	T-26th in 1968	3	12	3	0	0	0	0	71	76	73.08	0	0	0	29	$2,392.50	$2.73	$797.50
Ronnie Reif	Missed Cut	2	4	0	0	0	0	0	77	79	77.50	0	0	0	30	$0.00	$0.00	$0.00
Bob Reith	Missed Cut	5	10	0	0	0	0	0	72	83	77.40	0	0	0	70	$0.00	$0.00	$0.00
Ron Reitz	Missed Cut	1	2	0	0	0	0	0	71	88	79.50	0	0	1	15	$0.00	$0.00	$0.00
Jack Renner	T-12th in 1979	8	24	4	0	0	0	1	66	80	73.00	0	2	2	60	$12,203.00	$6.97	$1,525.38
Johnny Revolta	Missed Cut	1	2	0	0	0	0	0	77	78	77.50	0	0	0	15	$0.00	$0.00	$0.00
Sam Reynolds	Missed Cut	4	9	0	0	0	0	0	70	83	76.00	0	0	0	52	$0.00	$0.00	$0.00
Dick Rhyan	T-20th in 1968	5	14	2	0	0	0	2	68	79	73.86	0	1	1	46	$2,630.00	$2.54	$526.00

Player	Best Finish	Years	Rds	Cuts Made	3	Top 5	10	25	Low Rd	High Rd	Avg.	Rds 65 or Better	Rds in 60s	Rds Under Par	Par Rounds	Money	$ Per Stroke	$ Per Event
Steven Richardson	T-5th in 1991	2	8	2	0	1	1	1	66	78	71.88	0	2	3	3	$63,687.50	$110.76	$31,843.75
Sonny Ridenhour	Missed Cut	1	2	0	0	0	0	0	74	78	76.00	0	0	0	12	$0.00	$0.00	$0.00
Skee Riegel	T-40th in 1958	6	19	3	0	0	0	0	71	80	75.26	0	0	0	88	$770.00	$0.54	$128.33
Pat Rielly	Missed Cut	1	2	0	0	0	0	0	78	82	80.00	0	0	0	16	$0.00	$0.00	$0.00
James Riggins	75th in 1966	4	10	1	0	0	0	0	70	82	77.80	0	0	0	72	$300.00	$0.39	$75.00
Larry Ringer	71st in 1977	2	6	1	0	0	0	0	74	85	77.83	0	0	0	39	$838.09	$1.79	$419.05
Larry Rinker	T-59th in 1984	4	10	1	0	0	0	0	69	78	74.20	0	1	1	32	$3,964.67	$5.34	$991.17
Lee Rinker	T-56th in 1992	2	6	1	0	0	0	0	72	76	73.67	0	0	0	14	$4,000.00	$9.05	$2,000.00
Tommy Ritter	Missed Cut	1	2	0	0	0	0	0	73	81	77.00	0	0	0	14	$0.00	$0.00	$0.00
Loren Roberts	T-5th in 1990	5	18	4	0	1	1	1	67	76	72.00	0	3	7	6	$76,733.32	$59.21	$15,346.66
Tom Robertson	Missed Cut	1	2	0	0	0	0	0	74	77	75.50	0	0	0	9	$1,000.00	$6.62	$1,000.00
Bill Robinson	Missed Cut	2	4	0	0	0	0	0	75	83	78.25	0	0	0	33	$0.00	$0.00	$0.00
Gary Robinson	Missed Cut	5	10	0	0	0	0	0	71	83	77.10	0	0	1	63	$4,200.00	$5.45	$840.00
Gary Robison	Missed Cut	2	4	0	0	0	0	0	75	79	76.75	0	0	0	23	$2,400.00	$7.82	$1,200.00
Phil Rodgers	T-7th in 1972	9	29	5	0	0	1	1	68	79	74.07	0	2	4	96	$8,352.25	$3.89	$928.03
Chi Chi Rodriguez	T-15th in 1969	12	41	9	0	0	0	4	69	83	73.59	0	2	3	123	$11,633.39	$3.86	$969.45
Melvin Roe	Missed Cut	1	2	0	0	0	0	0	75	79	77.00	0	0	0	14	$0.00	$0.00	$0.00
Bill Rogers	T-8th in 1980	7	24	5	0	0	1	1	66	81	72.54	0	1	1	51	$18,112.50	$10.40	$2,587.50
Gene Rolfe	Disqualified, 1963	1	0	0	0	0	0	0	0	0	0	0	0	0	0	$0.00	$0.00	$0.00
Walter Romans	Missed Cut	6	14	0	0	0	0	0	73	83	76.36	0	0	0	85	$0.00	$0.00	$0.00
Eduardo Romero	T-20th in 1993	4	12	2	0	0	0	1	67	84	73.33	0	2	2	22	$23,425.00	$26.62	$5,856.25
Bob Rosburg	Won in 1959	16	55	11	1	1	2	4	66	82	73.80	0	4	6	185	$17,719.58	$4.37	$1,107.47
Clarence Rose	T-53rd in 1986 & '89	7	18	2	0	0	0	0	71	81	74.67	0	0	1	60	$9,230.41	$6.87	$1,318.63
Bob Ross	T-57th in 1962	3	8	1	0	0	0	0	72	79	75.25	0	0	0	38	$222.50	$0.37	$74.17
Charles Rotar	Missed Cut	2	4	0	0	0	0	0	73	84	78.50	0	0	0	32	$0.00	$0.00	$0.00
Jeff Roth	Missed Cut	2	4	0	0	0	0	0	77	82	79.25	0	0	0	31	$2,000.00	$6.31	$1,000.00
John Rouse	Missed Cut	1	2	0	0	0	0	0	75	81	78.00	0	0	0	16	$0.00	$0.00	$0.00
Sonny Rouse	60th in 1960	2	6	1	0	0	0	0	74	82	77.17	0	0	0	43	$200.00	$0.43	$100.00
Melvin Rowe	Missed Cut	1	2	0	0	0	0	0	76	80	78.00	0	0	0	14	$0.00	$0.00	$0.00
Hugh Royer	T-48th in 1970	3	10	2	0	0	0	0	71	79	74.70	0	0	1	39	$678.00	$0.91	$226.00
Ed Rubis	T-66th in 1966	4	10	1	0	0	0	0	72	88	76.70	0	0	0	64	$300.00	$0.39	$75.00
Jim Rudolph	Missed Cut	3	4	0	0	0	0	0	76	88	81.50	0	0	0	44	$0.00	$0.00	$0.00
Mason Rudolph	T-3rd in 1973	14	54	13	1	2	3	8	66	81	72.54	0	8	10	107	$31,134.76	$7.95	$2,223.91
John Ruedi	Missed Cut	2	4	0	0	0	0	0	75	82	79.25	0	0	0	33	$0.00	$0.00	$0.00
Jack Rule	T-39th in 1964	2	6	1	0	0	0	0	71	78	73.67	0	0	0	22	$526.50	$1.19	$263.25
Dave Rummells	5th in 1989	5	16	3	0	1	2	2	64	79	72.50	1	5	5	14	$86,200.00	$74.31	$17,240.00
Paul Runyan	Missed Cut	4	6	0	0	0	0	0	74	88	82.00	0	0	0	69	$0.00	$0.00	$0.00
Paul Ryiz	Missed Cut	1	2	0	0	0	0	0	84	84	84.00	0	0	0	24	$1,000.00	$5.95	$1,000.00
Ed Sabo	Missed Cut	1	2	0	0	0	0	0	77	78	77.50	0	0	0	13	$1,200.00	$7.74	$1,200.00
Gus Salerno	T-59th in 1958	2	6	1	0	0	0	0	74	79	76.50	0	0	0	39	$100.00	$0.22	$50.00
Gene Samborsky	Missed Cut	1	2	0	0	0	0	0	76	79	77.50	0	0	0	11	$250.00	$1.61	$250.00
Mike San Filippo	Missed Cut	6	12	0	0	0	0	0	71	85	78.67	0	0	0	88	$6,200.00	$6.57	$1,033.33
Bill Sander	Missed Cut	1	2	0	0	0	0	0	75	80	77.50	0	0	0	11	$1,000.00	$6.45	$1,000.00
Doug Sanders	T-2nd in 1959	14	52	12	3	3	6	9	66	79	72.00	0	12	14	82	$31,500.55	$8.41	$2,250.04
Harold Sanderson	Missed Cut	1	2	0	0	0	0	0	81	85	83.00	0	0	0	26	$0.00	$0.00	$0.00
Tom Sanderson	Missed Cut	1	2	0	0	0	0	0	79	82	80.50	0	0	0	21	$0.00	$0.00	$0.00
Cesar Sanudo	T-46th in 1971	1	4	1	0	0	0	0	72	77	73.75	0	0	0	7	$348.00	$1.18	$348.00
Gene Sarazen	Missed Cut	4	7	0	0	0	0	0	73	81	77.43	0	0	0	48	$0.00	$0.00	$0.00
Steve Satterstrom	Missed Cut	1	2	0	0	0	0	0	76	79	77.50	0	0	0	13	$303.00	$1.95	$303.00
Gene Sauers	T-2nd in 1992	8	28	6	1	1	1	3	67	81	72.68	0	7	12	33	$132,505.00	$65.11	$16,563.13
Reggie Sauger	Missed Cut	2	4	0	0	0	0	0	78	85	82.00	0	0	0	48	$0.00	$0.00	$0.00
Steve Savel	Missed Cut	1	2	0	0	0	0	0	83	84	83.50	0	0	0	27	$0.00	$0.00	$0.00
Chuck Scally	71st in 1972	6	15	1	0	0	0	0	73	84	77.27	0	0	0	103	$833.00	$0.72	$138.83
Ken Schall	Missed Cut	2	4	0	0	0	0	0	74	78	76.00	0	0	0	16	$2,000.00	$6.58	$1,000.00
Herman Scharlau	T-63rd in 1963	5	13	1	0	0	0	0	70	79	75.85	0	0	0	70	$230.00	$0.23	$46.00
Brad Schiefelbein	Missed Cut	1	2	0	0	0	0	0	77	79	78.00	0	0	0	12	$0.00	$0.00	$0.00
John Schlee	T-4th in 1976	7	28	7	0	1	2	3	67	77	72.61	0	4	5	53	$20,104.86	$9.89	$2,872.12
Ted Schleichter	Missed Cut	1	2	0	0	0	0	0	77	78	77.50	0	0	0	15	$0.00	$0.00	$0.00
Mike Schlueter	Missed Cut	4	8	0	0	0	0	0	71	82	76.25	0	0	0	44	$1,750.00	$2.87	$437.50
Ernie Schneiter	Missed Cut	2	4	0	0	0	0	0	75	80	77.25	0	0	0	29	$0.00	$0.00	$0.00
George Schneiter	Missed Cut	6	14	0	0	0	0	0	73	81	76.50	0	0	0	85	$0.00	$0.00	$0.00
Curt Schnell	Missed Cut	1	2	0	0	0	0	0	82	84	83.00	0	0	0	22	$1,000.00	$6.02	$1,000.00
Emil Schodeller	Missed Cut	1	2	0	0	0	0	0	78	82	80.00	0	0	0	20	$0.00	$0.00	$0.00
Robert Schoener	T-70th in 1968	2	6	1	0	0	0	0	70	79	76.50	0	0	0	37	$365.00	$0.80	$182.50
John Schroeder	T-12th in 1978	6	20	4	0	0	0	4	68	79	72.85	0	3	5	37	$13,400.50	$9.20	$2,233.42
Mike Schuchart	Missed Cut	2	4	0	0	0	0	0	74	84	78.75	0	0	0	29	$2,200.00	$6.98	$1,100.00
Gerald Schultheis	Missed Cut	1	2	0	0	0	0	0	73	78	75.50	0	0	0	11	$0.00	$0.00	$0.00
Ted Schulz	T-69th in 1992	4	10	1	0	0	0	0	71	78	74.40	0	0	0	28	$5,487.50	$7.38	$1,371.88
Bill Schumaker	Missed Cut	3	6	0	0	0	0	0	74	82	76.67	0	0	0	32	$2,250.00	$4.89	$750.00
Pat Schwab	T-47th in 1962	8	24	4	0	0	0	0	71	81	75.25	0	0	0	108	$1,449.38	$0.80	$181.17
Emil Scodeller	Missed Cut	2	4	0	0	0	0	0	74	83	78.75	0	0	0	33	$0.00	$0.00	$0.00
Paul Scodeller	Missed Cut	1	2	0	0	0	0	0	74	83	78.50	0	0	0	15	$0.00	$0.00	$0.00
Jimmy Scott	Missed Cut	2	4	0	0	0	0	0	76	81	78.50	0	0	0	34	$0.00	$0.00	$0.00
Don Sechrest	Missed Cut	1	2	0	0	0	0	0	75	76	75.50	0	0	0	11	$0.00	$0.00	$0.00
Jim Seeley	Missed Cut	1	2	0	0	0	0	0	70	82	76.00	0	0	0	12	$0.00	$0.00	$0.00

PGA CHAMPIONSHIP STROKE-PLAY STATISTICS

Player	Best Finish	Years	Rds	Cuts Made	3	Top 5	10	25	Low Rd	High Rd	Avg.	Rds 65 or Better	Rds in 60s	Rds Under Par	Par Rounds	Money	$ Per Stroke	$ Per Event
Paul Segerlund	Missed Cut	1	2	0	0	0	0	0	72	81	76.50	0	0	0	13	$0.00	$0.00	$0.00
Jack Sellman	T-13th in 1963	2	6	1	0	0	0	1	68	81	74.00	0	1	2	20	$1,550.00	$3.49	$775.00
Jack Seltzer	Missed Cut	5	10	0	0	0	0	0	71	82	76.40	0	0	0	54	$4,500.00	$5.89	$900.00
Peter Senior	T-48th in 1992	5	18	4	0	0	0	0	68	81	73.22	0	2	4	34	$12,727.50	$9.66	$2,545.50
John Serafin	Missed Cut	1	2	0	0	0	0	0	78	79	78.50	0	0	0	17	$0.00	$0.00	$0.00
Craig Shankland	Missed Cut	4	8	0	0	0	0	0	75	80	78.13	0	0	0	59	$0.00	$0.00	$0.00
Bob Shave	T-49th in 1966	1	4	1	0	0	0	0	71	78	74.50	0	0	0	18	$436.12	$1.46	$436.12
Bob Shaw	T-20th in 1972	1	4	1	0	0	0	1	72	74	72.50	0	0	0	10	$2,385.00	$8.22	$2,385.00
Tom Shaw	T-21st in 1969	5	16	3	0	0	0	1	69	82	73.69	0	3	3	51	$3,117.86	$2.64	$623.57
Bob Shearer	T-26th in 1978	3	9	2	0	0	0	0	67	79	73.00	0	1	1	19	$5,087.50	$7.74	$1,695.83
Jim Shelton	Missed Cut	1	2	0	0	0	0	0	74	78	76.00	0	0	0	12	$0.00	$0.00	$0.00
Charles Sheppard	Missed Cut	2	4	0	0	0	0	0	76	78	77.00	0	0	0	28	$0.00	$0.00	$0.00
Brad Sherfy	Missed Cut	2	4	0	0	0	0	0	76	82	78.00	0	0	0	26	$2,200.00	$7.05	$1,100.00
Gene Shields	Missed Cut	1	2	0	0	0	0	0	74	80	77.00	0	0	0	12	$0.00	$0.00	$0.00
Robert Shields	Missed Cut	2	4	0	0	0	0	0	74	80	77.25	0	0	0	27	$0.00	$0.00	$0.00
Don Shock	Missed Cut	3	7	0	0	0	0	0	70	84	77.43	0	0	0	52	$0.00	$0.00	$0.00
Dick Shoemaker	T-29th in 1958	2	8	2	0	0	0	0	70	79	74.63	0	0	0	37	$535.00	$0.90	$267.50
George Shortridge	Missed Cut	5	10	0	0	0	0	0	74	81	77.30	0	0	0	71	$850.00	$1.10	$170.00
Denny Shute	T-44th in 1959	11	25	1	0	0	0	0	70	91	79.28	0	0	0	224	$200.00	$0.10	$18.18
Tom Sieckmann	T-52nd in 1991	2	6	1	0	0	0	0	68	76	73.17	0	1	1	9	$3,725.00	$8.49	$1,862.50
Charles Sifford	T-33rd in 1965	6	18	3	0	0	0	0	71	85	75.78	0	0	0	94	$2,374.00	$1.74	$395.67
Dan Sikes	T-3rd in 1967	11	44	11	1	1	3	7	68	77	72.23	0	4	7	66	$32,749.73	$10.31	$2,977.25
R. H. Sikes	T-13th in 1965	6	20	4	0	0	0	2	71	79	73.55	0	0	2	51	$6,318.00	$4.30	$1,053.00
Tony Sills	T-16th in 1986	4	12	2	0	0	0	1	69	81	74.08	0	1	1	35	$12,100.00	$13.61	$3,025.00
Art Silvestrome	Missed Cut	3	6	0	0	0	0	0	74	83	77.50	0	0	0	41	$550.00	$1.18	$183.33
Jim Simons	T-5th in 1982	9	28	5	0	1	1	2	67	77	72.82	0	6	6	63	$23,873.67	$11.71	$2,652.63
Scott Simpson	T-6th in 1984 & '93	13	46	10	0	0	3	4	64	81	72.48	1	6	13	64	$102,544.17	$30.76	$7,888.01
Tim Simpson	T-8th in 1990	11	32	5	0	0	1	2	69	81	73.28	0	1	8	63	$56,704.46	$24.18	$5,154.95
Alex Sinclair	Missed Cut	5	12	0	0	0	0	0	74	85	77.92	0	0	0	93	$0.00	$0.00	$0.00
Joey Sindelar	T-28th in 1985	9	27	5	0	0	0	0	70	80	73.63	0	0	3	63	$17,240.42	$8.67	$1,915.60
Vijay Singh	4th in 1993	2	8	2	0	1	1	1	63	76	70.75	1	2	4	-2	$93,687.50	$165.53	$46,843.75
T. R. Sleichter	T-63rd in 1965	4	10	1	0	0	0	0	71	79	76.70	0	0	0	61	$300.00	$0.39	$75.00
Jack Slocum	Missed Cut	1	2	0	0	0	0	0	79	83	81.00	0	0	0	20	$1,000.00	$6.17	$1,000.00
Jeff Sluman	Won in 1988	8	32	8	1	1	1	4	65	78	71.88	1	7	11	12	$226,679.17	$98.56	$28,334.90
Tom Smack	Missed Cut	1	2	0	0	0	0	0	77	80	78.50	0	0	0	17	$0.00	$0.00	$0.00
Al Smith	Missed Cut	1	2	0	0	0	0	0	78	82	80.00	0	0	0	20	$0.00	$0.00	$0.00
Bob E. Smith	T-20th in 1971	7	23	5	0	0	0	2	69	79	73.57	0	1	3	64	$6,583.89	$3.89	$940.56
Bob L. Smith	Missed Cut	1	2	0	0	0	0	0	73	82	77.50	0	0	0	13	$1,000.00	$6.45	$1,000.00
Charles Smith	Missed Cut	1	3	0	0	0	0	0	74	81	76.67	0	0	0	20	$0.00	$0.00	$0.00
David G. Smith	Missed Cut	4	7	0	0	0	0	0	76	85	79.86	0	0	0	65	$500.00	$0.89	$125.00
Dick Smith	Missed Cut	5	10	0	0	0	0	0	72	82	77.50	0	0	0	69	$953.00	$1.23	$190.60
George Smith	Missed Cut	1	2	0	0	0	0	0	73	79	76.00	0	0	0	12	$0.00	$0.00	$0.00
Mike Smith	76th in 1985	1	4	1	0	0	0	0	71	83	76.25	0	0	0	21	$1,500.00	$4.92	$1,500.00
Robert Smith	Missed Cut	1	2	0	0	0	0	0	76	79	77.50	0	0	0	15	$0.00	$0.00	$0.00
Steve Smith	Missed Cut	1	2	0	0	0	0	0	79	84	81.50	0	0	0	21	$303.00	$1.86	$303.00
Tal Smith	Missed Cut	1	2	0	0	0	0	0	76	78	77.00	0	0	0	14	$0.00	$0.00	$0.00
Todd Smith	T-79th in 1992	2	6	1	0	0	0	0	70	79	74.50	0	0	1	21	$3,450.00	$7.72	$1,725.00
Ronald Smoak	T-73rd in 1979	1	4	1	0	0	0	0	72	79	75.75	0	0	0	23	$500.00	$1.65	$500.00
J.C. Snead	T-3rd in 1973	15	48	9	1	1	1	6	67	81	73.33	0	4	6	132	$35,695.34	$10.14	$2,379.69
Sam Snead	3rd in 1958, '60 & '74	21	74	17	3	4	8	10	67	82	72.26	0	10	15	135	$54,697.97	$10.23	$2,604.67
Ed Sneed	T-28th in 1979	11	42	10	0	0	0	0	67	80	73.71	0	2	3	136	$10,013.01	$3.23	$910.27
Ansel Snow	Missed Cut	1	2	0	0	0	0	0	74	76	75.00	0	0	0	10	$0.00	$0.00	$0.00
Jim Sobb	Missed Cut	2	4	0	0	0	0	0	76	83	79.25	0	0	0	31	$2,000.00	$6.31	$1,000.00
Jack Sommers	Missed Cut	3	6	0	0	0	0	0	74	79	76.67	0	0	0	38	$2,000.00	$4.35	$666.67
Mike Souchak	T-5th in 1959	13	48	11	0	1	2	7	67	79	72.60	0	5	9	105	$13,613.38	$3.91	$1,047.18
Don Spears	T-52nd in 1964	1	4	1	0	0	0	0	71	76	73.00	0	0	0	12	$318.75	$1.09	$318.75
James Speer	Missed Cut	1	2	0	0	0	0	0	87	88	87.50	0	0	0	33	$0.00	$0.00	$0.00
Bob Spence	Missed Cut	2	4	0	0	0	0	0	74	78	76.50	0	0	0	24	$0.00	$0.00	$0.00
John Spencer	Missed Cut	1	2	0	0	0	0	0	74	79	76.50	0	0	0	13	$0.00	$0.00	$0.00
Wynsol Spencer	Missed Cut	1	2	0	0	0	0	0	70	83	76.50	0	0	1	11	$0.00	$0.00	$0.00
Bill Sporre	T-37th in 1968	2	6	1	0	0	0	0	70	81	75.17	0	0	0	27	$686.25	$1.52	$343.13
Steve Spray	T-78th in 1971	6	14	1	0	0	0	0	73	82	76.14	0	0	0	72	$2,411.00	$2.26	$401.83
Marshall Springer	61st in 1961	1	4	1	0	0	0	0	71	80	75.50	0	0	0	22	$225.00	$0.75	$225.00
Mike Springer	Missed Cut	1	2	0	0	0	0	0	72	74	73.00	0	0	0	4	$1,200.00	$8.22	$1,200.00
W. A. Stackhouse	Missed Cut	1	2	0	0	0	0	0	77	77	77.00	0	0	0	14	$0.00	$0.00	$0.00
Craig Stadler	6th in 1978	16	58	13	0	0	3	7	64	81	72.33	1	11	15	73	$138,023.33	$32.90	$8,626.46
Tom Stafaci	Missed Cut	1	2	0	0	0	0	0	76	77	76.50	0	0	0	13	$0.00	$0.00	$0.00
Roland Stafford	71st in 1967	5	14	2	0	0	0	0	74	83	76.57	0	0	0	76	$600.00	$0.56	$120.00
Tim Stafford	Missed Cut	1	2	0	0	0	0	0	75	77	76.00	0	0	0	10	$1,200.00	$7.89	$1,200.00
James Stamps	T-55th in 1967	4	12	2	0	0	0	0	72	79	75.17	0	0	0	52	$611.50	$0.68	$152.88
Mike Standly	T-61st in 1993	1	4	1	0	0	0	0	68	76	71.75	0	1	1	3	$2,800.00	$9.76	$2,800.00
Bob Stanton	T-22nd in 1970	4	14	3	0	0	0	1	71	78	73.57	0	0	0	42	$2,879.24	$2.80	$719.81
Chris Starkjohann	Missed Cut	1	2	0	0	0	0	0	71	74	72.50	0	0	0	3	$1,200.00	$8.28	$1,200.00
Al Starr	Missed Cut	1	2	0	0	0	0	0	80	86	83.00	0	0	0	24	$0.00	$0.00	$0.00
Larry Startzel	Missed Cut	2	4	0	0	0	0	0	75	81	78.00	0	0	0	28	$600.00	$1.92	$300.00

Player	Best Finish	Years	Rds	Cuts Made	Top 3	Top 5	Top 10	Top 25	Low Rd	High Rd	Avg.	Rds 65 or Better	Rds in 60s	Rds Under Par	Par Rounds	Money	$ Per Stroke	$ Per Event
William Staskewicz	Missed Cut	1	2	0	0	0	0	0	82	82	82.00	0	0	0	24	$0.00	$0.00	$0.00
Stan Staszowski	Missed Cut	3	6	0	0	0	0	0	74	86	79.00	0	0	0	52	$0.00	$0.00	$0.00
Kent Stauffer	Missed Cut	1	2	0	0	0	0	0	76	78	77.00	0	0	0	10	$1,000.00	$6.49	$1,000.00
Ken Stear	Missed Cut	1	2	0	0	0	0	0	75	78	76.50	0	0	0	13	$0.00	$0.00	$0.00
Jerry Steelsmith	T-48th in 1970	4	13	3	0	0	0	0	72	79	74.85	0	0	0	59	$1,113.00	$1.14	$278.25
Doug Steffen	Missed Cut	1	2	0	0	0	0	0	78	81	79.50	0	0	0	17	$1,000.00	$6.29	$1,000.00
Al Stein	Missed Cut	1	2	0	0	0	0	0	82	86	84.00	0	0	0	28	$0.00	$0.00	$0.00
Earl Stewart	T-26th in 1967	3	10	2	0	0	0	0	70	77	73.30	0	0	3	19	$1,708.57	$2.33	$569.52
Payne Stewart	Won in 1989	12	42	9	1	2	4	7	66	80	72.07	0	7	17	31	$337,111.30	$111.37	$28,092.61
Ray Stewart	T-26th in 1990	1	4	1	0	0	0	0	73	75	74.00	0	0	0	8	$8,650.00	$29.22	$8,650.00
Wheeler Stewart	Missed Cut	3	6	0	0	0	0	0	76	80	77.33	0	0	0	36	$3,000.00	$6.47	$1,000.00
Ken Still	T-38th in 1967	6	20	4	0	0	0	0	71	78	74.70	0	0	1	72	$2,034.50	$1.36	$339.08
Dave Stockton	Won in 1970 & '76	24	82	17	2	2	2	5	66	81	72.99	0	10	14	179	$117,632.89	$19.65	$4,901.37
Waddy Stokes	Missed Cut	1	2	0	0	0	0	0	71	78	74.50	0	0	0	9	$350.00	$2.35	$350.00
Robert Stone	T-44th in 1967	4	16	4	0	0	0	0	71	79	74.06	0	0	0	49	$1,714.43	$1.45	$428.61
Tom Strafaci	Missed Cut	1	3	0	0	0	0	0	75	80	77.00	0	0	0	21	$0.00	$0.00	$0.00
Dick Stranahan	T-35th in 1959	6	16	2	0	0	0	0	70	83	76.19	0	0	0	95	$400.00	$0.33	$66.67
Frank Stranahan	T-17th in 1962	7	24	5	0	0	0	1	69	79	74.13	0	2	2	95	$1,911.66	$1.07	$273.09
Curtis Strange	T-2nd in 1989	16	47	8	1	2	3	4	66	85	73.36	0	6	10	114	$143,526.19	$41.63	$8,970.39
Austin Straub	T-65th in 1979	1	4	1	0	0	0	0	70	79	73.50	0	0	0	14	$515.00	$1.75	$515.00
Ron Streck	4th in 1979	7	26	6	0	1	1	2	68	82	73.00	0	5	6	68	$29,291.00	$15.43	$4,184.43
Don Street	Missed Cut	1	2	0	0	0	0	0	77	82	79.50	0	0	0	19	$0.00	$0.00	$0.00
Lenny Stroup	Missed Cut	1	2	0	0	0	0	0	79	82	80.50	0	0	0	21	$0.00	$0.00	$0.00
Glenn Stuart	Missed Cut	7	15	0	0	0	0	0	71	80	77.40	0	0	0	103	$0.00	$0.00	$0.00
Art Stuhler	Missed Cut	1	2	0	0	0	0	0	80	87	83.50	0	0	0	27	$0.00	$0.00	$0.00
Hank Stukart	Missed Cut	2	4	0	0	0	0	0	81	83	81.75	0	0	0	45	$250.00	$0.76	$125.00
Bob Stupple	Missed Cut	1	2	0	0	0	0	0	76	81	78.50	0	0	0	17	$0.00	$0.00	$0.00
Buddy Sullivan	T-51st in 1960	5	12	1	0	0	0	0	73	82	76.75	0	0	0	79	$200.00	$0.22	$40.00
Mike Sullivan	T-12th in 1989	10	34	7	0	0	0	1	66	82	73.47	0	2	4	84	$34,448.91	$13.79	$3,444.89
Vince Sullivan	T-49th in 1965	1	4	1	0	0	0	0	72	79	74.50	0	0	0	14	$466.67	$1.57	$466.67
Bruce Summerhays	77th in 1981	4	10	1	0	0	0	0	73	84	77.40	0	0	0	68	$1,653.00	$2.14	$413.25
Hal Sutton	Won in 1983	12	44	10	1	1	3	4	64	78	72.34	2	9	13	49	$184,352.65	$57.92	$15,362.72
John Suveges	Missed Cut	2	4	0	0	0	0	0	75	81	78.50	0	0	0	32	$0.00	$0.00	$0.00
Tim Sweborg	Missed Cut	1	2	0	0	0	0	0	81	85	83.00	0	0	0	26	$0.00	$0.00	$0.00
Robert Swift	Missed Cut	1	2	0	0	0	0	0	78	79	78.50	0	0	0	17	$0.00	$0.00	$0.00
Tom Talkington	T-33rd in 1958	2	6	1	0	0	0	0	73	77	74.83	0	0	0	29	$220.00	$0.49	$110.00
Alan Tapie	T-20th in 1980	3	10	2	0	0	0	2	65	77	72.80	1	2	2	26	$6,653.00	$9.14	$2,217.67
Tom Tatum	Missed Cut	1	2	0	0	0	0	0	81	83	82.00	0	0	0	20	$1,000.00	$6.10	$1,000.00
J. D. Taylor	Missed Cut	4	9	0	0	0	0	0	73	81	77.33	0	0	0	60	$0.00	$0.00	$0.00
Joe Taylor	Missed Cut	2	5	0	0	0	0	0	75	76	75.80	0	0	0	29	$0.00	$0.00	$0.00
Joel Taylor	Missed Cut	1	2	0	0	0	0	0	76	81	78.50	0	0	0	17	$0.00	$0.00	$0.00
Steve Taylor	Missed Cut	2	4	0	0	0	0	0	76	78	76.75	0	0	0	23	$500.00	$1.63	$250.00
Glenn Teal	73rd in 1967	1	4	1	0	0	0	0	74	80	77.00	0	0	0	20	$300.00	$0.97	$300.00
Werner Teichmann	Missed Cut	1	2	0	0	0	0	0	80	80	80.00	0	0	0	20	$0.00	$0.00	$0.00
Brian Tennyson	T-26th in 1990	3	10	2	0	0	0	0	69	83	74.00	0	1	4	20	$17,185.71	$23.22	$5,728.57
Ed Terasa	Missed Cut	1	2	0	0	0	0	0	77	79	78.00	0	0	0	12	$1,000.00	$6.41	$1,000.00
Ron Terry	Missed Cut	1	2	0	0	0	0	0	74	74	74.00	0	0	0	8	$350.00	$2.36	$350.00
Doug Tewell	T-9th in 1983	12	44	10	0	0	2	5	64	81	72.41	1	7	10	66	$57,587.92	$18.08	$4,798.99
Joseph Thacker	Missed Cut	1	2	0	0	0	0	0	78	79	78.50	0	0	0	17	$0.00	$0.00	$0.00
Stan Thirsk	T-37th in 1966	10	30	5	0	0	0	0	68	82	75.80	0	1	1	158	$2,216.54	$0.97	$221.65
Emery Thomas	Missed Cut	1	2	0	0	0	0	0	74	78	76.00	0	0	0	12	$0.00	$0.00	$0.00
George Thomas	Missed Cut	1	2	0	0	0	0	0	74	82	78.00	0	0	0	16	$0.00	$0.00	$0.00
Paul Thomas	Missed Cut	2	5	0	0	0	0	0	72	80	76.60	0	0	0	33	$0.00	$0.00	$0.00
Barney Thompson	Missed Cut	1	2	0	0	0	0	0	74	78	76.00	0	0	0	12	$550.00	$3.62	$550.00
Gene Thompson	Missed Cut	2	4	0	0	0	0	0	74	81	77.50	0	0	0	30	$0.00	$0.00	$0.00
Jimmy Thompson	Missed Cut	3	7	0	0	0	0	0	73	80	77.00	0	0	0	49	$0.00	$0.00	$0.00
Kim Thompson	Missed Cut	2	4	0	0	0	0	0	76	80	77.75	0	0	0	23	$2,000.00	$6.43	$1,000.00
Leonard Thompson	T-10th in 1975	14	54	13	0	0	1	5	66	81	72.65	0	8	12	109	$33,151.58	$8.45	$2,367.97
Rocky Thompson	T-62nd in 1979	2	6	1	0	0	0	0	72	77	74.17	0	0	0	23	$535.00	$1.20	$267.50
Clyde Thomsen	Missed Cut	1	2	0	0	0	0	0	80	82	81.00	0	0	0	20	$0.00	$0.00	$0.00
Jeff Thomsen	Missed Cut	1	2	0	0	0	0	0	76	77	76.50	0	0	0	9	$1,000.00	$6.54	$1,000.00
David Thore	Missed Cut	1	2	0	0	0	0	0	70	78	74.00	0	0	1	6	$1,000.00	$6.76	$1,000.00
Jim Thorpe	T-7th in 1986	8	26	5	0	0	1	2	67	83	72.88	0	3	3	55	$35,694.99	$18.84	$4,461.87
George Tiddy	Missed Cut	1	2	0	0	0	0	0	79	80	79.50	0	0	0	17	$0.00	$0.00	$0.00
Dave Tinsley	Missed Cut	1	2	0	0	0	0	0	72	80	76.00	0	0	0	12	$0.00	$0.00	$0.00
Cosimo Tiso	Missed Cut	1	2	0	0	0	0	0	78	81	79.50	0	0	0	19	$0.00	$0.00	$0.00
Dennis Tiziani	T-51st in 1976	1	4	1	0	0	0	0	68	77	73.75	0	1	1	15	$450.00	$1.53	$450.00
Larry Tomasino	Missed Cut	1	2	0	0	0	0	0	76	77	76.50	0	0	0	13	$0.00	$0.00	$0.00
Sam Torrance	Missed Cut	1	2	0	0	0	0	0	74	78	76.00	0	0	0	8	$1,000.00	$6.58	$1,000.00
Gene Torres	T-72nd in 1972	2	6	1	0	0	0	0	70	80	76.83	0	0	0	39	$303.00	$0.66	$151.50
Felice Torza	T-35th in 1958	4	10	1	0	0	0	0	69	82	75.80	0	1	1	58	$162.00	$0.21	$40.50
Bob Toski	T-20th in 1958	4	12	2	0	0	0	1	70	82	74.83	0	0	1	50	$996.00	$1.11	$249.00
Ken Towns	T-75th in 1971	5	12	1	0	0	0	0	74	83	76.92	0	0	0	73	$258.00	$0.28	$51.60
John Traub	Missed Cut	2	4	0	0	0	0	0	77	92	82.25	0	0	0	45	$1,550.00	$4.71	$775.00
Henry Trepsas	Missed Cut	1	2	0	0	0	0	0	74	80	77.00	0	0	0	12	$0.00	$0.00	$0.00

Player	Best Finish	Years	Rds	Cuts Made	Top 3	Top 5	Top 10	Top 25	Low Rd	High Rd	Avg.	Rds 65 or Better	Rds in 60s	Rds Under Par	Par Rounds	Money	$ Per Stroke	$ Per Event
Lee Trevino	Won in 1974 & '84	21	72	16	3	3	5	12	65	80	71.76	1	17	24	73	$307,050.32	$59.43	$14,621.44
Kirk Triplett	Missed Cut	2	4	0	0	0	0	0	73	82	77.50	0	0	0	24	$2,200.00	$7.10	$1,100.00
Gary Trivisonno	Missed Cut	2	4	0	0	0	0	0	75	77	75.50	0	0	0	16	$2,200.00	$7.28	$1,100.00
Odell Trueblood	Missed Cut	2	3	0	0	0	0	0	76	78	76.67	0	0	0	16	$0.00	$0.00	$0.00
Chris Tucker	Missed Cut	1	2	0	0	0	0	0	76	82	79.00	0	0	0	14	$1,000.00	$6.33	$1,000.00
Jerry Tucker	Missed Cut	2	4	0	0	0	0	0	75	78	76.50	0	0	0	20	$2,200.00	$7.19	$1,100.00
Woodrow Tucker	Missed Cut	1	2	0	0	0	0	0	80	87	83.50	0	0	0	27	$0.00	$0.00	$0.00
Dick Turner	T-69th in 1963	2	6	1	0	0	0	0	72	78	75.67	0	0	0	30	$200.00	$0.44	$100.00
Jim Turnesa	T-32nd in 1960	11	30	4	0	0	0	0	72	81	75.47	0	0	0	156	$908.53	$0.40	$82.59
Russell Tuveson	Missed Cut	2	4	0	0	0	0	0	77	84	81.50	0	0	0	44	$0.00	$0.00	$0.00
Bob Tway	Won in 1986	8	28	6	1	1	1	1	64	78	73.07	1	1	8	44	$155,843.75	$76.17	$19,480.47
Greg Twiggs	T-22nd in 1993	2	8	2	0	0	0	1	69	75	71.75	0	1	4	2	$16,790.00	$29.25	$8,395.00
Howard Twitty	T-5th in 1980	13	42	8	0	1	2	3	67	79	72.95	0	5	10	90	$57,940.72	$18.91	$4,456.98
Eddie Tyree	Missed Cut	1	2	0	0	0	0	0	80	84	82.00	0	0	0	22	$0.00	$0.00	$0.00
Warner Tyree	Missed Cut	1	2	0	0	0	0	0	76	79	77.50	0	0	0	15	$0.00	$0.00	$0.00
Tom Ulozas	T-57th in 1976	2	6	1	0	0	0	0	73	80	75.17	0	0	0	31	$1,000.00	$2.22	$500.00
Wally Ulrich	Withdrew, 1958	1	1	0	0	0	0	0	82	82	82.00	0	0	0	12	$0.00	$0.00	$0.00
Harry Umbinetti	Missed Cut	1	2	0	0	0	0	0	74	81	77.50	0	0	0	15	$0.00	$0.00	$0.00
Brett Upper	T-36th in 1986	3	10	2	0	0	0	0	71	79	73.60	0	0	0	24	$6,164.00	$8.38	$2,054.67
Babe Urzetta	Missed Cut	1	3	0	0	0	0	0	75	86	78.67	0	0	0	26	$0.00	$0.00	$0.00
Sam Urzetta	Missed Cut	5	10	0	0	0	0	0	75	84	78.30	0	0	0	83	$0.00	$0.00	$0.00
Clyde Usina	Missed Cut	2	5	0	0	0	0	0	75	81	78.00	0	0	0	40	$0.00	$0.00	$0.00
Stan Utley	T-49th in 1990	2	6	1	0	0	0	0	71	80	75.67	0	0	1	22	$3,865.62	$8.51	$1,932.81
Tommy Valentine	T-11th in 1981	3	12	3	0	0	0	1	66	80	72.83	0	2	2	34	$8,765.00	$10.03	$2,921.67
Brent Veenstra	Missed Cut	1	2	0	0	0	0	0	77	82	79.50	0	0	0	15	$1,000.00	$6.29	$1,000.00
Ken Venturi	T-5th in 1959 & '64	9	36	9	0	2	3	6	65	77	72.17	1	5	6	70	$14,879.34	$5.73	$1,653.26
Maurice Verbrugge	T-60th in 1975	4	10	1	0	0	0	0	68	84	75.80	0	1	1	56	$678.57	$0.90	$169.64
Steve Veriato	T-76th in 1992	5	12	1	0	0	0	0	70	82	76.67	0	0	1	64	$6,325.00	$6.88	$1,265.00
Scott Verplank	T-31st in 1990	3	8	1	0	0	0	0	70	78	74.00	0	0	1	18	$8,500.00	$14.36	$2,833.33
Rick Vershure	Missed Cut	2	4	0	0	0	0	0	75	81	77.50	0	0	0	26	$2,000.00	$6.45	$1,000.00
Bob Verwey	T-70th in 1966	1	4	1	0	0	0	0	74	78	75.75	0	0	0	23	$300.00	$0.99	$300.00
Everett Vinzant	Missed Cut	2	4	0	0	0	0	0	77	81	79.50	0	0	0	36	$0.00	$0.00	$0.00
George Vitense	Withdrew, 1961	1	1	0	0	0	0	0	80	80	80.00	0	0	0	10	$0.00	$0.00	$0.00
Ron Vlosich	Missed Cut	1	2	0	0	0	0	0	74	77	75.50	0	0	0	7	$1,000.00	$6.62	$1,000.00
Charles Volpone	T-39th in 1974	5	12	1	0	0	0	0	71	84	75.50	0	0	0	64	$1,317.22	$1.45	$263.44
Ernie Vossler	T-15th in 1961	9	31	6	0	0	0	4	68	79	73.48	0	3	3	94	$5,572.50	$2.45	$619.17
Roy Vucinich	Missed Cut	2	4	0	0	0	0	0	76	82	78.75	0	0	0	31	$1,303.00	$4.14	$651.50
Bobby Wadkins	T-7th in 1987	14	47	10	0	0	1	1	67	81	73.60	0	6	8	126	$45,532.50	$13.16	$3,252.32
Lanny Wadkins	Won in 1977	21	74	16	5	5	6	10	65	81	71.96	1	15	25	79	$333,104.50	$62.55	$15,862.12
Fred Wadsworth	Missed Cut	1	2	0	0	0	0	0	76	78	77.00	0	0	0	10	$1,000.00	$6.49	$1,000.00
Leonard Wagner	63rd in 1959	2	6	1	0	0	0	0	72	86	77.50	0	0	0	45	$200.00	$0.43	$100.00
Grant Waite	Missed Cut	1	2	0	0	0	0	0	71	73	72.00	0	0	0	2	$1,200.00	$8.33	$1,200.00
Gordon Waldespuhl	Missed Cut	1	2	0	0	0	0	0	80	83	81.50	0	0	0	23	$250.00	$1.53	$250.00
Duffy Waldorf	T-9th in 1992	2	6	1	0	0	1	1	68	77	72.00	0	2	2	6	$41,200.00	$95.37	$20,600.00
Art Wall	T-5th in 1961	10	36	8	0	1	2	6	66	78	72.75	0	3	3	93	$9,173.27	$3.50	$917.33
Tony Wallin	Withdrew, 1982	1	1	0	0	0	0	0	78	78	78.00	0	0	0	8	$650.00	$8.33	$650.00
Scott Walter	Missed Cut	1	2	0	0	0	0	0	77	78	77.50	0	0	0	13	$1,200.00	$7.74	$1,200.00
Bobby Walzel	T-8th in 1980	4	10	1	0	0	1	1	68	79	73.60	0	1	1	32	$9,650.00	$13.11	$2,412.50
Fred Wampler	T-38th in 1967	11	33	5	0	0	0	0	69	80	74.79	0	1	1	144	$2,066.07	$0.84	$187.82
Lester Ward	Missed Cut	3	6	0	0	0	0	0	73	80	77.00	0	0	0	42	$0.00	$0.00	$0.00
Tom Wargo	T-28th in 1992	5	14	2	0	0	0	0	70	84	73.86	0	0	1	36	$19,057.69	$18.43	$3,811.54
Lou Warobick	81st in 1963	5	12	1	0	0	0	0	74	80	77.33	0	0	0	84	$150.00	$0.16	$30.00
Leonard Warren	Missed Cut	1	2	0	0	0	0	0	74	86	80.00	0	0	0	20	$0.00	$0.00	$0.00
Don Waryan	61st in 1959	3	8	1	0	0	0	0	72	82	76.63	0	0	0	53	$200.00	$0.33	$66.67
Al Watrous	Missed Cut	1	2	0	0	0	0	0	75	78	76.50	0	0	0	13	$0.00	$0.00	$0.00
Tom Watrous	T-73rd in 1963	1	4	1	0	0	0	0	70	81	76.00	0	0	1	20	$175.00	$0.58	$175.00
Bob Watson	Missed Cut	2	4	0	0	0	0	0	73	87	80.00	0	0	0	38	$0.00	$0.00	$0.00
Craig Watson	Missed Cut	1	2	0	0	0	0	0	77	81	79.00	0	0	0	16	$1,000.00	$6.33	$1,000.00
Denis Watson	33rd in 1984	6	22	5	0	0	0	0	68	79	73.27	0	1	5	48	$13,931.25	$8.64	$2,321.88
Roger Watson	T-60th in 1975	2	6	1	0	0	0	0	73	78	75.33	0	0	0	32	$678.57	$1.50	$339.29
Tom Watson	T-2nd in 1978	21	80	19	1	2	8	15	65	79	71.54	1	19	29	51	$237,922.16	$41.57	$11,329.63
Paul Way	Missed Cut	1	2	0	0	0	0	0	82	84	83.00	0	0	0	24	$1,000.00	$6.02	$1,000.00
Bert Weaver	T-27th in 1963	7	18	2	0	0	0	0	70	81	75.33	0	0	1	84	$1,258.57	$0.93	$179.80
Dewitt Weaver	T-33rd in 1972	7	26	6	0	0	0	0	69	78	74.08	0	1	1	92	$3,964.43	$2.06	$566.35
John Weaver	Missed Cut	1	2	0	0	0	0	0	77	79	78.00	0	0	0	16	$0.00	$0.00	$0.00
Gene Webb	T-70th in 1968	2	7	1	0	0	0	0	72	79	75.29	0	0	0	37	$365.00	$0.69	$182.50
Jack Webb	Missed Cut	2	4	0	0	0	0	0	80	83	81.25	0	0	0	41	$0.00	$0.00	$0.00
Larry Webb	Missed Cut	2	4	0	0	0	0	0	74	82	77.00	0	0	0	24	$2,000.00	$6.49	$1,000.00
Jim Weeden	Missed Cut	1	2	0	0	0	0	0	75	76	75.50	0	0	0	9	$1,000.00	$6.62	$1,000.00
D.A. Weibring	T-3rd in 1987	12	40	8	1	2	2	2	67	78	72.93	0	5	6	85	$117,203.15	$40.18	$9,766.93
Tom Weiskopf	3rd in 1975	18	59	12	1	2	5	6	65	82	73.03	1	5	10	145	$61,033.27	$14.16	$3,390.74
Jay Weitzel	Missed Cut	1	2	0	0	0	0	0	80	81	80.50	0	0	0	21	$0.00	$0.00	$0.00
Ron Wells	Missed Cut	2	4	0	0	0	0	0	79	84	80.75	0	0	0	39	$2,000.00	$6.19	$1,000.00
Rick Werner	Missed Cut	2	3	0	0	0	0	0	74	87	79.67	0	0	0	26	$2,000.00	$8.37	$1,000.00
Mike West	Missed Cut	1	2	0	0	0	0	0	75	76	75.50	0	0	0	9	$1,200.00	$7.95	$1,200.00

Player	Best Finish	Years	Rds	Cuts Made	Top 3	Top 5	Top 10	Top 25	Low Rd	High Rd	Avg.	Rds 65 or Better	Rds in 60s	Rds Under Par	Par Rounds	Money	$ Per Stroke	$ Per Event
Dan Whalen	Missed Cut	1	2	0	0	0	0	0	75	83	79.00	0	0	0	16	$0.00	$0.00	$0.00
Ed Whalley	Missed Cut	3	6	0	0	0	0	0	75	85	78.67	0	0	0	46	$0.00	$0.00	$0.00
Frank Wharton	Missed Cut	1	2	0	0	0	0	0	77	79	78.00	0	0	0	16	$0.00	$0.00	$0.00
Larry Wheeler	Missed Cut	1	2	0	0	0	0	0	79	88	83.50	0	0	0	25	$303.00	$1.81	$303.00
Dick Whetzle	Missed Cut	2	4	0	0	0	0	0	73	79	76.00	0	0	0	22	$0.00	$0.00	$0.00
Frank Whibley	Missed Cut	1	2	0	0	0	0	0	77	86	81.50	0	0	0	23	$0.00	$0.00	$0.00
Darwin Whit	Missed Cut	1	2	0	0	0	0	0	76	88	82.00	0	0	0	22	$0.00	$0.00	$0.00
Alan White	Missed Cut	4	8	0	0	0	0	0	75	86	79.13	0	0	0	67	$600.00	$0.95	$150.00
Buck White	Missed Cut	1	3	0	0	0	0	0	70	86	76.67	0	0	0	20	$0.00	$0.00	$0.00
Don White	Missed Cut	1	2	0	0	0	0	0	79	90	84.50	0	0	0	27	$0.00	$0.00	$0.00
Jay White	Missed Cut	1	2	0	0	0	0	0	76	79	77.50	0	0	0	15	$0.00	$0.00	$0.00
Jim White	Missed Cut	5	10	0	0	0	0	0	70	87	76.20	0	0	0	52	$4,350.00	$5.71	$870.00
Ed Whitman	Missed Cut	4	8	0	0	0	0	0	74	84	78.00	0	0	0	52	$4,200.00	$6.73	$1,050.00
Don Whitt	T-15th in 1961	7	25	5	0	0	0	1	68	82	73.68	0	1	1	90	$2,645.00	$1.44	$377.86
Buddy Whitten	T-27th in 1983	5	12	1	0	0	0	0	66	81	74.75	0	1	2	51	$5,203.00	$5.80	$1,040.60
Oran Whittington	Missed Cut	1	2	0	0	0	0	0	80	82	81.00	0	0	0	20	$0.00	$0.00	$0.00
Mark Wiebe	T-12th in 1989	8	30	7	0	0	0	2	67	80	73.20	0	4	6	50	$48,948.61	$22.29	$6,118.58
Jim Wiechers	T-29th in 1972	4	14	3	0	0	0	0	69	80	73.36	0	1	2	43	$3,432.00	$3.34	$858.00
Terry Wilcox	T-7th in 1969	4	12	2	0	0	1	1	66	79	72.92	0	1	1	31	$6,168.34	$7.05	$1,542.09
Robert Wilkin	Missed Cut	1	2	0	0	0	0	0	76	84	80.00	0	0	0	16	$1,000.00	$6.25	$1,000.00
Gary Wilkins	Missed Cut	1	2	0	0	0	0	0	79	79	79.00	0	0	0	16	$1,000.00	$6.33	$1,000.00
Harold Williams	Missed Cut	1	2	0	0	0	0	0	77	79	78.00	0	0	0	16	$0.00	$0.00	$0.00
Henry Williams	T-44th in 1959	2	8	2	0	0	0	0	72	77	74.25	0	0	0	34	$300.00	$0.51	$150.00
James Williams	Missed Cut	1	2	0	0	0	0	0	74	77	75.50	0	0	0	11	$0.00	$0.00	$0.00
Scott Williams	T-66th in 1991	1	4	1	0	0	0	0	70	77	74.00	0	0	1	8	$2,312.50	$7.81	$2,312.50
Donald Williams Jr.	Missed Cut	1	2	0	0	0	0	0	79	87	83.00	0	0	0	26	$0.00	$0.00	$0.00
Bud Williamson	T-58th in 1959	6	14	1	0	0	0	0	72	80	76.93	0	0	0	95	$200.00	$0.19	$33.33
Ralph Williamson	Missed Cut	1	2	0	0	0	0	0	76	76	76.00	0	0	0	12	$0.00	$0.00	$0.00
Ock Willoweit	Missed Cut	1	3	0	0	0	0	0	75	79	77.33	0	0	0	22	$0.00	$0.00	$0.00
Milan Wilor	Missed Cut	1	2	0	0	0	0	0	77	78	77.50	0	0	0	11	$1,000.00	$6.45	$1,000.00
Bo Wininger	4th in 1965	7	28	7	0	1	2	3	66	77	72.57	0	4	4	64	$13,488.57	$6.64	$1,926.94
Gary Wintz	Missed Cut	1	2	0	0	0	0	0	76	76	76.00	0	0	0	12	$550.00	$3.62	$550.00
Charles Wipperman	Missed Cut	3	6	0	0	0	0	0	75	80	77.83	0	0	0	47	$0.00	$0.00	$0.00
Larry Wise	T-20th in 1972	4	12	2	0	0	0	1	67	79	74.33	0	1	1	52	$2,920.00	$3.27	$730.00
Paul Wise	Missed Cut	3	6	0	0	0	0	0	72	84	76.17	0	0	0	31	$3,000.00	$6.56	$1,000.00
Frank Witt	Missed Cut	1	2	0	0	0	0	0	77	85	81.00	0	0	0	22	$0.00	$0.00	$0.00
Bob Wolcott	T-63rd in 1991	1	4	1	0	0	0	0	71	79	73.75	0	0	1	7	$2,400.00	$8.14	$2,400.00
Robert Wolfe	Missed Cut	1	2	0	0	0	0	0	73	81	77.00	0	0	0	14	$0.00	$0.00	$0.00
Gregg Wolff	Missed Cut	1	2	0	0	0	0	0	81	81	81.00	0	0	0	18	$1,000.00	$6.17	$1,000.00
Dan Wood	Missed Cut	1	2	0	0	0	0	0	74	76	75.00	0	0	0	8	$1,200.00	$8.00	$1,200.00
Larry Wood	T-22nd in 1971	1	4	1	0	0	0	1	71	74	72.75	0	0	1	3	$2,088.00	$7.18	$2,088.00
Thorne Wood	T-53rd in 1958	2	7	1	0	0	0	0	70	80	75.43	0	0	0	38	$100.00	$0.19	$50.00
Willard Wood	Missed Cut	1	2	0	0	0	0	0	75	79	77.00	0	0	0	14	$0.00	$0.00	$0.00
Willie Wood	T-23rd in 1985	2	6	1	0	0	0	1	69	78	73.50	0	1	1	15	$6,260.00	$14.20	$3,130.00
Tom Woodard	Missed Cut	1	2	0	0	0	0	0	76	84	80.00	0	0	0	16	$1,000.00	$6.25	$1,000.00
Jim Woodward	T-61st in 1987	1	4	1	0	0	0	0	69	82	75.50	0	1	1	14	$1,740.00	$5.76	$1,740.00
Ian Woosnam	6th in 1989	8	26	5	0	0	1	2	67	86	73.35	0	3	9	47	$71,375.00	$37.43	$8,921.88
Rolie Wormstead	Missed Cut	1	2	0	0	0	0	0	82	86	84.00	0	0	0	28	$0.00	$0.00	$0.00
Lew Worsham	T-37th in 1961	3	8	1	0	0	0	0	71	78	74.50	0	0	0	34	$250.00	$0.42	$83.33
Robert Wrenn	T-40th in 1987	3	10	2	0	0	0	0	68	77	73.50	0	1	1	19	$6,492.50	$8.83	$2,164.17
Bill Wright	Missed Cut	1	2	0	0	0	0	0	76	80	78.00	0	0	0	16	$0.00	$0.00	$0.00
Jimmy Wright	4th in 1969	13	40	7	0	1	1	1	68	85	74.83	0	3	3	169	$13,429.57	$4.49	$1,033.04
Ken Wright	Missed Cut	2	3	0	0	0	0	0	79	83	80.67	0	0	0	32	$0.00	$0.00	$0.00
Bob Wynn	T-28th in 1975	4	9	1	0	0	0	0	69	81	75.78	0	2	2	44	$1,781.00	$2.61	$445.25
Mike Wynn	Missed Cut	2	4	0	0	0	0	0	73	76	74.50	0	0	0	16	$1,650.00	$5.54	$825.00
Dudley Wysong	T-2nd in 1966	4	14	3	1	1	1	1	66	77	73.00	0	1	2	30	$16,039.26	$15.69	$4,009.82
Bert Yancey	T-22nd in 1970 & '71	9	32	7	0	0	0	4	68	77	73.06	0	3	5	80	$10,280.27	$4.40	$1,142.25
James Yates	Missed Cut	1	2	0	0	0	0	0	80	87	83.50	0	0	0	27	$0.00	$0.00	$0.00
Wayne Yates	T-62nd in 1972	3	10	2	0	0	0	0	73	79	75.40	0	0	0	54	$633.00	$0.84	$211.00
Ken Yount	Missed Cut	2	4	0	0	0	0	0	76	81	78.25	0	0	0	29	$0.00	$0.00	$0.00
Joe Zakarian	T-49th in 1963	4	11	1	0	0	0	0	71	81	75.73	0	0	0	59	$335.00	$0.40	$83.75
Kermit Zarley	T-8th in 1968	12	44	10	0	0	2	4	67	82	73.27	0	6	6	120	$17,614.46	$5.46	$1,467.87
Jake Zastko	Missed Cut	1	2	0	0	0	0	0	76	82	79.00	0	0	0	18	$0.00	$0.00	$0.00
Joe Zelazny	Missed Cut	1	2	0	0	0	0	0	80	81	80.50	0	0	0	21	$0.00	$0.00	$0.00
Bob Zender	T-26th in 1978	3	10	2	0	0	0	0	69	78	73.40	0	2	2	26	$4,025.00	$5.48	$1,341.67
Ray Ziats	Missed Cut	1	2	0	0	0	0	0	78	86	82.00	0	0	0	24	$0.00	$0.00	$0.00
Larry Ziegler	T-5th in 1969	9	28	5	0	1	1	1	68	83	74.25	0	2	4	105	$10,058.00	$4.84	$1,117.56
Bob Zimmerman	T-38th in 1967	1	4	1	0	0	0	0	68	76	73.50	0	1	1	6	$632.50	$2.15	$632.50
Billy Ziobro	Missed Cut	1	2	0	0	0	0	0	77	79	78.00	0	0	0	16	$250.00	$1.60	$250.00
Fuzzy Zoeller	2nd in 1981	15	50	10	1	1	3	4	67	80	72.78	0	6	11	87	$103,627.29	$28.48	$6,908.49
Richard Zokol	T-14th in 1993	3	12	3	0	0	0	2	66	74	71.08	0	1	6	1	$39,005.55	$45.73	$13,001.85
John Zontek	Missed Cut	5	11	0	0	0	0	0	71	84	76.73	0	0	0	72	$0.00	$0.00	$0.00

■ PGA CHAMPIONSHIP RECORDS
Stroke-Play Records (1958 to Present)

▒ Best 72-Hole Score
271 (9 under) by Bobby Nichols (64-71-69-67) in 1964
272 (8 under) by David Graham (69-68-70-65) in 1979
272 (8 under) by Ben Crenshaw (69-67-69-67) in 1979
272 (8 under) by Raymond Floyd (63-69-68-72) in 1982
272 (12 under) by Jeff Sluman (69-70-68-65) in 1988
272 (12 under) by Paul Azinger (69-66-69-68) in 1993
272 (12 under) by Greg Norman (68-68-67-69) in 1993
273 (7 under) by Larry Nelson (70-66-66-71) in 1981
273 (11 under) by Lee Trevino (69-68-67-69) in 1984

▒ Best 72-Hole Score By A Non-Winner
272 (8 under) by Ben Crenshaw (69-67-69-67) in 1979
272 (12 under) by Greg Norman (68-68-67-69) in 1993
274 (6 under) by Arnold Palmer (68-68-69-69) in 1964
274 (6 under) by Jack Nicklaus (67-73-70-64) in 1964
274 (6 under) by Rex Caldwell (67-70-66-71) in 1979

▒ Highest 72-Hole Score By A Winner
287 (1 under) by Larry Nelson (70-72-73-72) in 1987
282 (6 under) by Lanny Wadkins (69-71-72-70) in 1977
282 (6 under) by Wayne Grady (72-67-72-71) in 1990

▒ Best Score - First 54 Holes
200 (10 under) by Ray Floyd (63-69-68) in 1982
202 (11 under) by Ray Floyd (69-66-67) in 1969
202 (8 under) by Larry Nelson (70-66-66) in 1981
202 (11 under) by Greg Norman (65-68-69) in 1986
203 (10 under) by Tom Watson (67-69-67) in 1978
203 (7 under) by Rex Caldwell (67-70-66) in 1979
203 (10 under) by Hal Sutton (65-66-72) in 1983
203 (13 under) by Mike Reid (66-67-70) in 1989
203 (10 under) by Greg Norman (68-68-67) in 1993

▒ Best Score - Last 54 Holes
201 (12 under) by John Mahaffey (67-68-66) in 1978
202 (11 under) by Jack Nicklaus (65-71-66) in 1983
202 (14 under) by Payne Stewart (66-69-67) in 1989

▒ Largest 54-Hole Lead
5 by Ray Floyd (202) in 1969
5 by Tom Watson (203) in 1978
5 by Ray Floyd (200) in 1982

▒ Best Score - First 36 Holes
131 (11 under) by Hal Sutton (65-66) in 1983
131 (11 under) by Vijay Singh (68-63) in 1993
132 (8 under) by Ray Floyd (63-69) in 1982
133 (9 under) by Greg Norman (65-68) in 1986
133 (9 under) by Paul Azinger (67-66) in 1988
133 (11 under) by Mike Reid (66-67) in 1989
133 (9 under) by Steve Elkington (67-66) in 1993
133 (9 under) by Lanny Wadkins (65-68) in 1993

▒ Best Score - Last 36 Holes
132 (10 under) by Miller Barber (64-68) in 1969
133 (9 under) by Gil Morgan (66-67) in 1978
133 (9 under) by Peter Jacobsen (68-65) in 1983
133 (11 under) by Hal Sutton (64-69) in 1984
133 (9 under) by Jeff Sluman (68-65) in 1988

▒ Largest 36-Hole Lead
4 by Tommy Aaron (135) in 1967
4 by Gil Morgan (134) in 1976
4 by Tom Watson (136) in 1978
4 by Greg Norman (133) in 1986

▒ Best 18-Hole Score
63 (7 under) by Bruce Crampton (31-32), Second round, 1975
63 (7 under) by Ray Floyd (33-30), First round, 1982
63 (9 under) by Gary Player (30-33), Second round, 1984
63 (8 under) by Vijay Singh (32-31), Second round, 1993
64 has been shot 11 times

▒ Largest 18-Hole Lead
3 by Bobby Nichols (64) in 1964
3 by Ray Floyd (63) in 1982

▒ Best 9-Hole Score
29 by Fred Couples on back nine, first round, 1982
29 by Gibby Gilbert on front nine, second round, 1983

▒ Best First-Round Score
63 (7 under) by Ray Floyd in 1982
64 (7 under) by Scott Simpson in 1993
64 (6 under) by Bobby Nichols in 1964
64 (7 under) by Doug Tewell in 1985

▒ Highest First-Round Score
94 (22 over) by Gary Campbell in 1977

▒ Best Second-Round Score
63 (7 under) by Bruce Crampton in 1975
63 (9 under) by Gary Player in 1984
63 (8 under) by Vijay Singh in 1993

▒ Highest Second-Round Score
90 (19 over) by Jerry Jones in 1978

▒ Best Third-Round Score
64 (7 under) by Miller Barber in 1969
64 (8 under) by Hal Sutton in 1984
64 (7 under) by Bob Tway in 1986

▒ Highest Third-Round Score
86 (16 over) by Babe Urzetta in 1959

▒ Best Fourth-Round Score
64 (6 under) by Jack Nicklaus in 1964
65 (5 under) by Lee Trevino in 1970
65 (5 under) by Andy North in 1975
65 (5 under) by David Graham in 1979
65 (6 under) by Peter Jacobsen in 1983
65 (6 under) by T.M. Chen in 1985
65 (6 under) by Jeff Sluman in 1988

▒ Highest Fourth-Round Score
89 (19 over) by Ralph Johnston in 1972

▒ Largest Winning Margin
Seven shots, by Jack Nicklaus in 1980

▒ Best Comeback By Winner
Seven shots by John Mahaffey in 1978
Six shots by Bob Rosburg in 1959
Six shots by Lanny Wadkins in 1977
Six shots by Payne Stewart in 1989

PGA CHAMPIONSHIP STROKE-PLAY RECORDS

Highest First-Round Score By Winner
75 (4 over) by John Mahaffey in 1978
74 (2 over) by Payne Stewart in 1989

Lowest First-Round Score By Winner
63 (7 under) by Ray Floyd in 1982
64 (6 under) by Bobby Nichols in 1964

Highest Second-Round Score By Winner
73 (2 over) by Jack Nicklaus in 1963

Lowest Second-Round Score By Winner
66 (5 under) by Ray Floyd in 1969
66 (4 under) by Lee Trevino in 1974
66 (4 under) by Larry Nelson in 1981
66 (5 under) by Hal Sutton in 1983
66 (6 under) by Payne Stewart in 1989
66 (5 under) by Paul Azinger in 1993

Highest Third-Round Score By Winner
73 (1 over) by Larry Nelson in 1987
72 (2 over) by Jay Hebert in 1960
72 (Even) by Lanny Wadkins in 1977
72 (1 over) by Hal Sutton in 1983
72 (Even) by Larry Nelson in 1987
72 (Even) by Wayne Grady in 1990

Lowest Third-Round Score By Winner
64 (7 under) by Bob Tway in 1986
66 (4 under) by Dave Stockton in 1970
66 (4 under) by Jack Nicklaus in 1980
66 (4 under) by Larry Nelson in 1981

Highest Final-Round Score By Winner
74 (3 over) by Ray Floyd in 1969
73 (3 over) by Dave Stockton in 1970
73 (1 over) by Jack Nicklaus in 1971

Lowest Final-Round Score By Winner
65 (5 under) by David Graham in 1979
65 (6 under) by Jeff Sluman in 1988
66 (4 under) by Bob Rosburg in 1959
66 (5 under) by John Mahaffey in 1978

Hardest Course Average Over 72 Holes
76.15 - 1987 PGA at PGA National Golf Club

Lowest Course Average Over 72 Holes
71.90 - 1993 PGA at Inverness Golf Club
73.01 - 1982 PGA at Southern Hills Country Club

Most Under Par Rounds, 1st Round
57 - 1993 PGA at Inverness Golf Club

Most Under Par Rounds, 2nd Round
56 - 1993 PGA at Inverness Golf Club

Most Under Par Rounds, 3rd Round
33 - 1993 PGA at Inverness Golf Club

Most Under Par Rounds, 4th Round
31 - 1984 PGA at Shoal Creek Country Club

Most Under Par Rounds Over 72 Holes
166 - 1993 PGA at Inverness Golf Club
153 - 1989 PGA at Kemper Lakes Golf Course

Least Under Par Rounds, 1st Round
4 - 1960 PGA at Firestone Country Club
4 - 1970 PGA at Southern Hills Country Club

Least Under Par Rounds, 2nd Round
0 - 1966 PGA at Firestone Country Club

Least Under Par Rounds, 3rd Round
3 - 1975 PGA at Firestone Country Club

Least Under Par Rounds, 4th Round
1 - 1960 PGA at Firestone Country Club
1 - 1976 PGA at Congressional Country Club

Least Under Par Rounds Over 72 Holes
13 - 1960 PGA at Firestone Country Club

Most Over Par Rounds Over 72 Holes
492 - 1960 PGA at Firestone Country Club

Least Over Par Rounds Over 72 Holes
228 - 1993 PGA at Inverness Golf Club
239 - 1989 PGA at Kemper Lakes Golf Course

Most Money Won
$427,725 by Jack Nicklaus, spanning 32 Championships
$417,500 by Paul Azinger, spanning 8 Championships
$358,527 by Greg Norman, spanning 13 Championships
$350,661 by Nick Price, spanning 10 Championships
$337,111 by Payne Stewart, spanning 12 Championships
$333,105 by Lanny Wadkins, spanning 21 Championships
$332,977 by Nick Faldo, spanning 12 Championships
$307,050 by Lee Trevino, spanning 21 Championships
$258,723 by Ray Floyd, spanning 30 Championships
$249,864 by Larry Nelson, spanning 18 Championships
$242,727 by Bruce Lietzke, spanning 18 Championships
$241,770 by Wayne Grady, spanning 7 Championships
$237,922 by Tom Watson, spanning 21 Championships
$235,800 by John Daly, spanning 3 Championships

Money Won Per Tournament
$78,600 by John Daly, spanning 3 championships
$52,188 by Paul Azinger, spanning 8 championships
$47,813 by Phil Mickelson, spanning 1 championship
$46,844 by Vijay Singh, spanning 2 championships
$44,070 by Jim Gallagher Jr., spanning 5 championships
$35,066 by Nick Price, spanning 10 championships
$34,539 by Wayne Grady, spanning 7 championships
$31,844 by Steven Richardson, spanning 2 championships
$31,800 by Jeff Maggert, spanning 2 championships
$28,335 by Jeff Sluman, spanning 8 championships
$28,093 by Payne Stewart, spanning 12 championships
$27,748 by Nick Faldo, spanning 12 championships
$27,748 by Greg Norman, spanning 13 championships

Highest Dollar Per Stroke
$272.60 by John Daly, spanning 3 championships
$238.98 by Paul Azinger, spanning 8 championships
$190.94 by Jim Gallagher Jr., spanning 5 championships
$172.61 by Phil Mickelson, spanning 1 championship
$165.53 by Vijay Singh, spanning 2 championships
$151.77 by Wayne Grady, spanning 7 championships
$127.51 by Nick Price, spanning 10 championships
$114.25 by Dudley Hart, spanning 2 championships
$112.17 by Jeff Maggert, spanning 2 championships
$111.37 by Payne Stewart, spanning 12 championships
$110.76 by Steven Richardson, spanning 2 championships
$105.64 by Nick Faldo, spanning 12 championships
$101.16 by T.M. Chen, spanning 2 championships
$100.23 by Greg Norman, spanning 13 championships

Lowest Scoring Average
69.00 with 1 round by Jimmy Demaret
69.25 with 4 rounds by Phil Mickelson
70.25 with 4 rounds by Jim McGovern
70.75 with 8 rounds by Vijay Singh
70.75 with 4 rounds by Bunky Henry
70.88 with 8 rounds by Jeff Maggert
71.08 with 12 rounds by Richard Zokol
71.13 with 8 rounds by Lee Janzen
71.16 with 116 rounds by Jack Nicklaus
71.17 with 36 rounds by Jerry Pate

Lowest Scoring Average, Minimum of 30 Rounds
71.16 with 116 rounds by Jack Nicklaus
71.17 with 36 rounds by Jerry Pate
71.33 with 33 rounds by Calvin Peete
71.46 with 56 rounds by Peter Jacobsen
71.47 with 36 rounds by Dan Pohl
71.54 with 50 rounds by Greg Norman
71.54 with 80 rounds by Tom Watson
71.62 with 42 rounds by Fred Couples
71.64 with 44 rounds by Nick Faldo
71.65 with 88 rounds by Gary Player
71.76 with 72 rounds by Lee Trevino

Lowest Scoring Average, Minimum of 50 Rounds
71.16 with 116 rounds by Jack Nicklaus
71.46 with 56 rounds by Peter Jacobsen
71.54 with 50 rounds by Greg Norman
71.54 with 80 rounds by Tom Watson
71.65 with 88 rounds by Gary Player
71.76 with 72 rounds by Lee Trevino
71.95 with 66 rounds by Gil Morgan
71.96 with 74 rounds by Lanny Wadkins
72.00 with 77 rounds by Don January
72.00 with 52 rounds by Doug Sanders
72.01 with 78 rounds by Tom Kite
72.05 with 112 rounds by Ray Floyd

Most Appearances
36 by Arnold Palmer
    (Has played in every PGA Championship in Stroke Play)
32 by Jack Nicklaus
30 by Raymond Floyd
24 by Dave Stockton
24 by Doug Ford
24 by Bobby Nichols
24 by Billy Casper
24 by Gene Littler

Most Rounds Played
119 by Arnold Palmer
116 by Jack Nicklaus
112 by Raymond Floyd
88 by Gary Player
88 by Billy Casper
86 by Gene Littler
84 by Bobby Nichols
82 by Hale Irwin
82 by Dave Stockton
80 by Tom Watson

Highest Number of Strokes Over The Years
8,740 by Arnold Palmer averaging 73.45 strokes per round
8,254 by Jack Nicklaus averaging 71.16 strokes per round
8,070 by Ray Floyd averaging 72.05 strokes per round

Most Top 3 Finishes
12 by Jack Nicklaus
5 by Lanny Wadkins
5 by Gary Player
4 by Billy Casper

Most Top 5 Finishes
14 by Jack Nicklaus
6 by Billy Casper
6 by Gary Player
5 by Lanny Wadkins

Most Top 10 Finishes
15 by Jack Nicklaus
8 by Tom Watson
8 by Raymond Floyd
8 by Gary Player
8 by Billy Casper
8 by Sam Snead

Most Top 25 Finishes
23 by Jack Nicklaus
17 by Raymond Floyd
15 by Tom Watson
13 by Arnold Palmer
13 by Billy Casper

Player With The Most Subpar Rounds
50 by Jack Nicklaus
29 by Raymond Floyd
29 by Tom Watson
25 by Lanny Wadkins
24 by Lee Trevino
23 by Hale Irwin
20 by Greg Norman
20 by Bruce Lietzke
20 by Don January

Player With The Most Rounds In The 60s
39 by Jack Nicklaus
23 by Raymond Floyd
19 by Tom Watson
17 by Lee Trevino
15 by Lanny Wadkins
15 by Hale Irwin
15 by Don January
14 by Greg Norman
14 by Gene Littler

Player With The Most Rounds At 65 Or Better
3 by Gary Player
2 by Jack Nicklaus
2 by Raymond Floyd
2 by Bruce Crampton

Player With The Most Par Rounds
16 by Gary Player
15 by Tom Kite
14 by Raymond Floyd
13 by John Mahaffey
13 by Billy Casper
12 by Jack Nicklaus
11 by Al Geiberger
11 by Sam Snead

Player That Has Made The Most Cuts
26 by Jack Nicklaus
26 by Raymond Floyd
24 by Arnold Palmer
21 by Gary Player
20 by Hale Irwin
20 by Billy Casper
19 by Tom Kite
19 by Tom Watson
19 by Gene Littler

Four Subpar Rounds In The Same PGA Championship
Arnold Palmer (68-68-69-69) in 1964
Don January (71-72-70-68-69) in 1967
(includes Playoff Round)
Don Massengale (70-75-70-66-71) in 1967
(includes Playoff Round)
Ben Crenshaw (69-67-69-67) in 1979
Lee Trevino (69-68-67-69) in 1984
Calvin Peete (71-70-69-68) in 1984
Seve Ballesteros (70-69-70-70) in 1984
Jeff Sluman (69-70-68-65) in 1988
Curtis Strange (70-68-70-69) in 1989
Ian Woosnam (68-70-70-71) in 1989
John Daly (69-67-69-71) in 1991
Nick Price (70-70-68-70) in 1992
Paul Azinger (69-66-69-68) in 1993
Greg Norman (68-68-67-69) in 1993
Nick Faldo (69-66-69-68) in 1993

Four Rounds In The 60s In The Same PGA Championship
Arnold Palmer (68-68-69-69) in 1964
Ben Crenshaw (69-67-69-67) in 1979
Lee Trevino (69-68-67-69) in 1984
Paul Azinger (69-66-69-68) in 1993
Greg Norman (68-68-67-69) in 1993
Nick Faldo (69-66-69-68) in 1993

Wire To Wire Winners
Bobby Nichols in 1964
Raymond Floyd in 1969
Jack Nicklaus in 1971
Raymond Floyd in 1982
Hal Sutton in 1983

Number Of Times A Leader Went On To Win
1st Round - 7 in 36 championships
2nd Round - 11 in 36 championhips
3rd Round - 19 in 36 championships

Winning The PGA Championships On First Try
Jim Barnes in 1916
Walter Hagen in 1921
Tom Creavy in 1931
Bob Hamilton in 1944

Doug Ford in 1955
Bob Tway in 1986
John Daly in 1991

Record Low 36-Hole Cut
145 (five over par) in 1982
145 (three over par) in 1988
145 (one over par) in 1989

Record High 36-Hole Cut
154 (fourteen over par) in 1958

Most "Heartbreaking" Rounds
1959 by 1st round co-leader Dick Hart, 69-79-82 to miss cut
1959 by 1st round co-leader Mike Krak, 69-76-78 to miss cut
1959 by 1st round co-leader Chuck Klein, 69-73-81 to miss cut
1964 by Don January, 68-78-78 to miss cut
1970 by Dick Hendrickson, 70-85 to miss cut
1972 by 1st round co-leader Stan Thirsk, 68-82-76-80 to finish tied for 72nd
1972 by Larry Gilbert, 69-81-80-77 to finish T-74th
1982 by John Jackson, 68-78 to miss cut
1983 by Gibby Gilbert, 70-66-80-74 to finish T-47th
1985 by Bob Lohr, 69-82 to miss cut
1986 by 1st, 2nd & 3rd round leader Greg Norman 65-68-69-76 to finish 2nd
1988 by Doug Tewell, 70-68-81-79 to finish 70th
1990 by 1st round leader Bobby Wadkins, 68-75-80-81 to finish T-47th
1992 by Jay Don Blake, 68-77-79-76 to finish T-76

Most Championships Won
5 by Walter Hagen (1921, 1924, 1925, 1926, and 1927)
5 by Jack Nicklaus (1963, 1971, 1973, 1975 and 1980)
3 by Gene Sarazen (1922, 1923 and 1933)
3 by Sam Snead (1942, 1949 and 1951)
2 by Jim Barnes (1916 and 1919)
2 by Leo Diegel (1928 and 1929)
2 by Paul Runyan (1934 and 1938)
2 by Denny Shute (1936 and 1937)
2 by Byron Nelson (1940 and 1945)
2 by Ben Hogan (1946 and 1948)
2 by Gary Player (1962 and 1972)
2 by Dave Stockton (1970 and 1976)
2 by Raymond Floyd (1969 and 1982)
2 by Lee Trevino (1974 and 1984)
2 by Larry Nelson (1981 and 1987)

Champion Breakdown By Native Country
66 - United States
4 - Great Britain
2 - Australia
3 - South Africa

Most Times Runnerup
4 by Jack Nicklaus (1964, 1965, 1974 and 1983)
3 by Byron Nelson (1939, 1941 and 1944)
3 by Arnold Palmer (1964, 1968 and 1970)
3 by Billy Casper (1958, 1965 and 1971)

Oldest Winner
48 years old, Julius Boros (Born March, 3 1920) in 1968

Youngest Winner
20 years old, Gene Sarazen (Born Feb. 27, 1902) in 1922
20 years old, Tom Creavy (Born Feb. 3, 1911) in 1931

■ PLAYOFFS

1961 Jerry Barber shot 67 to beat Don January, who shot 68
1967 Don January shot 69 to beat Don Massengale, who shot 71
In 1977, the PGA of America adopted the sudden-death method for playoffs.

1977 Lanny Wadkins beat Gene Littler with a par on the third playoff hole

	1st hole - Par 4	2nd hole - Par 5	3rd hole - Par 3
Wadkins	Par	Birdie	Par
Littler	Par	Birdie	Bogey

1978 John Mahaffey beat Jerry Pate and Tom Watson with a birdie on the second playoff hole

	1st hole - Par 4	2nd hole - Par 4
Mahaffey	Par	Birdie
Watson	Par	Par
Pate	TPaⁱPar	

1979 David Graham beat Ben Crenshaw with a birdie on the third playoff hole

	1st hole - Par 4	2nd hole - Par 5	3rd hole - Par 3
Graham	Par	Birdie	Birdie
Crenshaw	Par	Birdie	Bogey

1987 Larry Nelson beat Lanny Wadkins with a par on the first playoff hole

	1st hole (10th)- Par 4
Nelson	Par
Wadkins	Bogey

1993 Paul Azinger beat Greg Norman with a par on the second playoff hole

	1st hole (18th)- Par 4	2nd hole (10th) - Par 4
Azinger	Par	Par
Norman	Par	Bogey

■ A LOOK AT THE WINNERS (Stroke-Play Only)

Year	Winner	Margin of Win	# Times It Took to Win	How Did Previous Year	How Did While Defending	Year	Winner	Margin of Win	# Times It Took to Win	How Did Previous Year	How Did While Defending
1958	Dow Finsterwald	2	1	-	4th	1976	Dave Stockton	1	9	Missed Cut	T-31st
1959	Bob Rosburg	1	2	T-11th	Missed 3rd rd. cut	1977	Lanny Wadkins	Playoff	5	Missed Cut	T-34th
1960	Jay Herbert	1	3	T-25th	13th	1978	John Mahaffey	Playoff	5	Withdrew after 3rd rd.	T-51st
1961	Jerry Barber	Playoff	3	T-32nd	Missed 2nd rd. cut	1979	David Graham	Playoff	7	Missed Cut	T-26th
1962	Gary Player	1	2	T-29th	T-8th	1980	Jack Nicklaus	7	19	T-65th	T-4th
1963	Jack Nicklaus	2	2	T-3rd	2nd	1981	Larry Nelson	4	6	Missed Cut	Missed Cut
1964	Bobby Nichols	3	3	T-23rd	T-54th	1982	Ray Floyd	3	19	T-19th	T-20th
1965	Dave Marr	2	7	65th	T-18th	1983	Hal Sutton	1	2	T-29th	T-6th
1966	Al Geiberger	4	4	T-19th	T-5th	1984	Lee Trevino	4	16	T-14th	2nd
1967	Don January	Playoff	8	T-12th	T-51st	1985	Hubert Green	2	13	T-14th	T-41st
1968	Julius Boros	1	11	T-5th	T-25th	1986	Bob Tway	2	1	-	T-47th
1969	Ray Floyd	1	6	T-41st	T-8th	1987	Larry Nelson	Playoff	12	Missed Cut	T-38th
1970	Dave Stockton	2	3	T-35th	T-40th	1988	Jeff Sluman	3	3	T-14th	T-24th
1971	Jack Nicklaus	2	10	T-6th	T-13th	1989	Payne Stewart	1	8	T-9th	T-8th
1972	Gary Player	2	10	T-4th	T-51st	1990	Wayne Grady	3	4	T-46th	T-43rd
1973	Jack Nicklaus	4	12	T-13th	2nd	1991	John Daly	3	1	-	82nd
1974	Lee Trevino	1	7	T-18th	T-60th	1992	Nick Price	3	9	Withdrew before 1st rd.	T-31st
1975	Jack Nicklaus	2	14	2nd	T-4th	1993	Paul Azinger	Playoff	8	T-33rd	-

■ PGA CHAMPIONSHIP PLAYOFF STROKE-PLAY HISTORY

1961
Jerry Barber defeated Don January in an 18-hole playoff at Olympia Fields (Ill.) Country Club. Barber had a 67 to January's 68. Both players had tied at 277 after 72 holes.

1967
Don January defeated Don Massengale in an 18-hole playoff at Columbine Country Club in Denver, Colo. January had a 69 to Massengale's 71. Both players had tied at 281 after 72 holes.

1977
For the first time, a major championship was decided by a sudden-death playoff. Lanny Wadkins defeated Gene Littler, sinking a six-foot putt on the third extra hole. Both players had tied at 282 at Pebble Beach Golf Links.

1978
John Mahaffey defeated Jerry Pate and Tom Watson on the second extra hole at Oakmont (Pa.) Country Club. Mahaffey made a 12-foot birdie putt. The trio had tied at 276 after 72 holes.

1979
David Graham defeated Ben Crenshaw on the third extra hole at Oakland Hills Country Club in Birmingham, Mich. Graham sank a 10-foot birdie putt. Both players had tied at 272.

1987
Larry Nelson defeated Lanny Wadkins at PGA National Golf Club in Palm Beach Gardens, Fla., on the first extra hole (the 10th). Nelson parred the hole to become the 15th multiple winner of the PGA Championship. Wadkins became the first player in stroke-play history of the Championship to participate in more than one playoff.

1993
Paul Azinger defeated Greg Norman at Inverness Club in Toledo, Ohio, on the second extra hole (the 10th) with a par. It was Azinger's first major championship.

PGA CHAMPIONSHIP STROKE-PLAY RECORDS

■ PGA CLUB PROFESSIONAL RECORDS (Stroke-Play Only)

▦ Best First-Round Score
66 by Buddy Whitten (Belmont, Mich.) in 1983. Tied for second, one stroke behind leader
66 by Dick Hart (Hinsdale, Ill.) in 1963 - Leader
66 by John Barnum (Grand Rapids, Mich.) in 1962 - Leader

▦ Best Second-Round Score
66 by Jay Overton (Tarpon Springs, Fla.) in 1988
68 by Dennis Tiziani (Madison, Wis.) in 1976
68 by Jimmy Powell (Dallas, Texas) in 1975
68 by Tommy Aycock (Alice, Texas) in 1974
68 by Jimmy Wright (Scarsdale, N.Y.) in 1969

▦ Best Third-Round Score
66 by Pete Cooper, (Branford, Fla.) in 1959

▦ Best Fourth-Round Score
67 by Bob Zimmerman (Dayton, Ohio) in 1967

▦ Best 36-Hole Score
134 (68-66) by Jay Overton (Tarpon Springs, Fla.) in 1988

▦ Best 54-Hole Score
207 (68-71-68) by Tom Nieporte (Locust Valley, N.Y.) in 1964 - Tied for third, three strokes behind leader

▦ Best 72-Hole Score
279 (71-68-69-71) by Jimmy Wright (Scarsdale, N.Y.) in 1969-4th place

▦ Best Finish
Fourth by Jimmy Wright (Scarsdale, N.Y.) in 1969
Tied for 5th by Tom Nieporte (Locust Valley N.Y.) in 1964
Tied for 11th by Tommy Aycock (Alice, Texas) in 1974
Tied for 11th by Lonnie Nielsen (E. Aurora, N.Y.) in 1986
Tied for 17th by Jay Overton (Tarpon Springs, Fla.) in 1988
Tied for 19th by Bob Boyd (Rockville, Md.) in 1990
Tied for 27th by Buddy Whitten (Belmont, Mich.) in 1983.
Tied for 28th by Tom Wargo (Centralia, Ill.) in 1992
Tied for 31st by Stu Ingraham (Bryn Mawr, Pa.) in 1993

■ PURSE THROUGH THE YEARS

Year	First Place Money	Total Purse	Year	First Place Money	Total Purse	Year	First Place Money	Total Purse
1916	*	$ 2,580	1943	(No Championship Played)		1969	35,000	175,000
1917- 1918	(No Championship Played)		1944	3,500	14,500	1970	40,000	200,000
1919	*	2,580	1945	3,750	14,700	1971	40,000	202,440
1920	*	2,580	1946	3,500	17,700	1972	45,000	224,087
1921	*	2,580	1947	3,500	17,700	1973	45,000	225,000
1922	*	2,580	1948	3,500	17,700	1974	45,000	225,000
1923	*	3,600	1949	3,500	17,700	1975	45,000	225,000
1924	*	6,830	1950	3,500	17,700	1976	45,000	250,950
1925	*	6,830	1951	3,500	17,700	1977	45,000	250,750
1926	*	11,100	1952	3,500	17,700	1978	50,000	300,240
1927	*	15,441	1953	5,000	20,700	1979	60,000	350,600
1928	*	10,400	1954	5,000	20,700	1980	60,000	376,400
1929	*	5,000	1955	5,000	20,700	1981	60,000	401,600
1930	*	10,300	1956	5,000	40,000	1982	65,000	451,800
1931	*	7,200	1957	8,000	42,100	1983	100,000	608,099
1932	*	7,200	1958	5,500	39,388	1984	125,000	700,300
1933	*	7,200	1959	8,250	51,175	1985	125,000	702,000
1934	*	7,200	1960	11,000	63,130	1986	140,000	801,100
1935	*	7,820	1961	11,000	64,800	1987	150,000	901,275
1936	*	9,200	1962	13,000	69,400	1988	160,000	1,000,000
1937	*	9,200	1963	13,000	80,900	1989	200,000	1,120,000
1938	*	10,000	1964	18,000	100,002	1990	225,000	1,350,000
1939	*	10,600	1965	25,000	149,700	1991	230,000	1,400,000
1940	*	11,050	1966	25,000	149,360	1992	280,000	1,608,000
1941	*	10,600	1967	25,000	148,200	1993	300,000	1,702,750
1942	*	7,550	1968	25,000	150,000			

■ SELECTED PLAYER RECORDS FOR THE PGA CHAMPIONSHIP
Match-Play Records (1916 through 1957)

Name	No. of Wins	Yrs in Match Play	Highest Round Played In	Matches Played	Wins	Losses	Win %	Holes Played	Wins in Round 1	Semifinals	Finals
Tommy Armour	1	9	Finals	25	17	8	68%	773	6	2	2
Laurie Ayton	0	6	2nd Round	9	3	6	33%	272	3	0	0
Errie Ball	0	9	2nd Round	11	2	9	18%	199	2	0	0
Jerry Barber	0	4	Quarter-finals	9	5	4	56%	189	2	0	0
Jim Barnes	2	9	Finals	31	24	7	77%	962	8	4	4
Herman Barron	0	11	Quarter-finals	21	10	11	48%	511	7	0	0
Charles Bassler	0	6	Semifinals	15	9	6	60%	321	4	1	0
Harry Bassler	0	5	3rd Round	12	7	5	58%	254	5	0	0
Joe Belfore	0	5	1st Round	5	0	5	00%	80	0	0	0
Arthur Bell	0	4	Semifinals	13	9	4	69%	331	4	1	0
Sam Bernardi	0	5	2nd Round	8	3	5	38%	145	3	0	0
Al Besselink	0	2	2nd Round	4	2	2	50%	70	2	0	0
Tommy Bolt	0	5	Semifinals	17	12	5	71%	376	4	2	0
Jackson Bradley	0	10	3rd Round	19	9	10	47%	371	6	0	0
M.J. Brady	0	4	2nd Round	7	3	4	43%	237	3	0	0
Mike Brady	0	2	2nd Round	4	2	2	50%	92	2	0	0
Al Brosch	0	7	Quarter-finals	17	9	8	53%	341	6	0	0
Jim Browning	0	4	3rd Round	12	7	5	58%	235	5	0	0
Johnny Bulla	0	4	Quarter-finals	12	8	4	67%	253	4	0	0
Billy Burke	0	8	Semifinals	17	9	8	53%	424	5	1	0
Eddie Burke	0	8	3rd Round	12	4	8	33%	264	3	0	0
Jack Burke	1	2	2nd Round	3	1	2	33%	101	1	0	0
Jack Burke Jr.	0	7	Finals	21	15	6	71%	483	5	1	1
Walter Burkemo	1	7	Finals	33	27	6	82%	838	6	4	3
Sam Byrd	0	6	Finals	11	5	6	45%	311	2	1	1
Frank Champ	0	6	Quarter-finals	10	4	6	40%	200	2	0	0
Brien Charter	0	2	3rd Round	6	4	2	67%	118	2	0	0
George Christ	0	4	Quarter-finals	7	3	4	43%	217	2	0	0
Henry Ciuci	0	4	Quarter-finals	7	3	4	43%	231	2	0	0
Jimmy Clark	0	2	Quarter-finals	5	3	2	60%	118	1	0	0
Al Collins	0	1	Quarter-finals	3	2	1	67%	106	1	0	0
Bruce Coltart	0	6	3rd Round	10	4	6	40%	226	2	0	0
Frank Commisso	0	5	1st Round	5	0	5	00%	82	0	0	0
Charles Congdon	0	2	Semifinals	8	6	2	75%	225	2	1	0
Harry Cooper	0	14	Semifinals	29	15	14	52%	838	9	1	0
Pete Cooper	0	6	3rd Round	9	3	6	33%	160	2	0	0
Wiffy Cox	0	5	1st Round	5	0	5	00%	146	0	0	0
Tom Creavy	1	3	Finals	12	10	2	83%	409	3	2	1
Bob Crowley	0	3	Quarter-finals	7	4	3	57%	234	3	0	0
Bobby Cruickshank	0	11	Semifinals	27	16	11	59%	782	8	2	0
Perry Del Vecchio	0	2	Quarter-finals	4	2	2	50%	124	1	0	0
Jimmy Demaret	0	13	Semifinals	35	22	13	63%	856	8	4	0
Mike DeMassey	0	4	2nd Round	5	1	4	20%	99	1	0	0
Ray Derr	0	3	Semifinals	9	6	3	67%	308	3	1	0
Roberto De Vicenzo	0	2	Quarter-finals	7	5	2	71%	159	2	0	0
Leo Diegel	2	13	Finals	30	19	11	63%	902	7	3	3
Clarence Doser	0	14	Semifinals	26	12	14	46%	575	7	1	0
Dave Douglas	0	7	Quarter-finals	17	10	7	59%	378	5	0	0
Pat Doyle	0	5	Quarter-finals	8	3	5	38%	272	2	0	0
Ed Dudley	0	16	Semifinals	41	25	16	61%	1114	14	1	0
Mortie Dutra	1	9	Semifinals	17	8	9	47%	475	5	1	0
Olin Dutra	0	4	Finals	10	7	3	70%	296	3	1	1
J. D. Edgar	0	2	Finals	8	6	2	75%	222	2	1	1
Abe Espinosa	0	6	Quarter-finals	12	6	6	50%	355	4	0	0
Al Espinosa	0	11	Finals	27	16	11	59%	851	8	2	1
Max Evans	0	4	2nd Round	5	1	4	20%	91	1	0	0
Don Fairfield	0	3	Quarter-finals	6	3	3	50%	144	1	0	0
Johnny Farrell	0	16	Finals	39	23	16	59%	1201	10	3	1
George Fazio	0	10	Quarter-finals	18	8	10	44%	335	6	0	0
Jim Ferrier	1	8	Finals	25	18	7	72%	563	8	2	1
Mike Fetchick	0	2	3rd Round	4	2	2	50%	67	1	0	0
Dow Finsterwald	1	1	Finals	7	6	1	86%	175	1	1	1
Jack Fleck	0	4	3rd Round	9	5	4	56%	162	3	0	0
Doug Ford	1	3	Finals	13	11	2	85%	274	3	1	1
Jim Foulis	0	9	Quarter-finals	18	9	9	50%	429	5	0	0
Emmett French	0	6	Finals	19	13	6	68%	555	5	2	1
Ed Furgol	0	7	Semifinals	17	10	7	59%	359	4	1	0
Marty Furgol	0	9	3rd Round	18	9	9	50%	337	7	0	0
Ray Gafford	0	4	Quarter-finals	8	4	4	50%	171	2	0	0
Bob Gajda	0	3	3rd Round	6	3	3	50%	95	2	0	0
Francis Gallett	0	6	Quarter-finals	11	5	6	45%	298	3	0	0
Vic Ghezzi	1	21	Finals	47	27	20	57%	1104	14	2	1

PGA CHAMPIONSHIP MATCH-PLAY STATISTICS

Name	No. of Wins	Yrs in Match Play	Highest Round Played In	Matches Played	Wins	Losses	Win %	Holes Played	Wins in Round 1	Semifinals	Finals
Leland Gibson	0	6	Quarter-finals	13	7	6	54%	297	4	0	0
Willie Goggin	0	10	Finals	20	10	10	50%	523	5	1	1
John Golden	0	13	Semifinals	32	19	13	59%	974	9	3	0
Jack Grout	0	3	3rd Round	7	4	3	57%	172	3	0	0
Ralph Guldahl	0	5	Semifinals	14	9	5	64%	292	5	1	0
Fred Haas Jr.	0	6	Quarter-finals	14	8	6	57%	291	5	0	0
Clarence Hackney	0	7	Quarter-finals	12	5	7	42%	342	3	0	0
Walter Hagen	5	15	Finals	50	40	10	75%	1580	10	8	6
Bob Hamilton	1	9	Finals	20	12	8	60%	490	5	2	1
Harry Hampton	0	6	Semifinals	14	8	6	57%	422	4	1	0
Chick Harbert	1	11	Finals	34	24	10	71%	841	8	3	3
Claude Harmon	0	13	Semifinals	40	26	14	65%	912	10	3	0
Tom Harmon Jr.	0	6	2nd Round	9	3	6	33%	241	3	0	0
Chandler Harper	1	9	Finals	19	11	8	58%	407	5	1	1
Dutch Harrison	0	11	Semifinals	20	9	11	45%	440	4	1	0
Fred Hawkins	0	3	Quarter-finals	10	7	3	70%	213	2	0	0
Clayton Heafner	0	4	Quarter-finals	8	4	4	50%	174	2	0	0
Jay Hebert	0	3	Quarter-finals	11	7	4	64%	219	3	0	0
Lionel Hebert	1	3	Finals	13	11	2	85%	272	3	1	1
Ray Hill	0	6	Quarter-finals	11	5	6	45%	216	3	0	0
Jimmy Hines	0	15	Semifinals	37	22	15	59%	916	10	2	0
Ben Hogan	2	7	Finals	27	22	5	81%	700	6	2	2
Tony Holguin	0	4	3rd Round	7	3	4	43%	122	2	0	0
Al Houghton	0	2	Quarter-finals	4	2	2	50%	125	1	0	0
Willie Hunter	0	2	2nd Round	3	1	2	33%	85	1	0	0
Jock Hutchison	1	7	Finals	23	17	6	74%	718	6	2	2
Ralph Hutchison	0	2	Quarter-finals	4	2	2	50%	110	1	0	0
Jack Isaacs	0	7	Semifinals	17	10	7	59%	356	6	1	0
Terl Johnson	0	4	Quarter-finals	10	6	4	60%	220	3	0	0
William Johnston	0	2	Semifinals	8	6	2	75%	163	2	1	0
Herman Keiser	0	9	3rd Round	12	3	9	25%	190	2	0	0
Tom Kerrigan	0	5	Quarter-finals	13	8	5	62%	367	4	0	0
Eddie Kirk	0	1	Quarter-finals	4	3	1	75%	99	1	0	0
Joe Kirkwood	0	6	Semifinals	13	7	6	54%	442	3	1	0
Willie Klein	0	7	2nd Round	9	3	6	33%	242	3	0	0
Emerick Kocsis	0	1	Quarter-finals	4	3	1	75%	96	1	0	0
Mike Krak	0	3	3rd Round	7	4	3	57%	115	2	0	0
Ted Kroll	0	8	Finals	26	18	8	69%	582	6	2	1
Gene Kunes	0	7	Semifinals	13	7	6	54%	330	4	1	0
Charles Lacey	0	3	Semifinals	6	3	3	50%	183	1	1	0
Ky Laffoon	0	11	Semifinals	30	19	11	63%	735	11	1	0
Lawson Little	0	5	2nd Round	7	2	5	29%	120	2	0	0
Gene Littler	0	1	2nd Round	2	1	1	50%	36	1	0	0
Bobby Locke	0	1	1st Round	1	0	1	00%	18	0	0	0
Emil Loeffler	0	2	Quarter-finals	5	3	2	60%	136	1	0	0
Toby Lyons	0	5	4th Round	9	4	5	44%	157	2	0	0
Bob MacDonald	0	4	Semifinals	11	7	4	64%	379	4	1	0
Willie MacFarlane	0	7	Semifinals	17	10	7	59%	528	6	1	0
Tony Manero	0	10	Semifinals	25	15	10	60%	632	8	1	0
Lloyd Mangrum	0	9	Semifinals	28	19	9	68%	678	8	2	0
Ray Mangrum	0	6	3rd Round	12	6	6	50%	219	5	0	0
Elroy Marti	0	5	3rd Round	8	3	5	38%	147	2	0	0
Milon Marusic	0	7	3rd Round	10	5	5	50%	165	3	0	0
Dick Mayer	0	2	Quarter-finals	9	7	2	78%	166	2	0	0
Shelley Mayfield	0	4	Semifinals	14	10	4	71%	312	4	1	0
George McLean	0	6	Semifinals	19	13	6	68%	558	5	3	0
Fred McLeod	0	5	Finals	14	9	5	64%	455	3	1	1
Tom McNamara	0	3	2nd Round	4	1	3	25%	107	1	0	0
Harold McSpaden	0	11	Finals	33	21	12	64%	882	8	3	1
Bill Mehlhorn	0	12	Finals	23	11	12	48%	735	5	2	1
Dick Metz	0	12	Semifinals	28	16	12	57%	661	9	1	0
Cary Middlecoff	0	4	Finals	17	13	4	76%	440	4	2	1
Eric Monti	0	5	1st Round	5	0	5	00%	82	0	0	0
Frank Moore	0	4	Quarter-finals	10	6	4	60%	197	4	0	0
Rod Munday	0	8	Quarter-finals	13	5	8	38%	279	3	0	0
Reggie Myles	0	6	Quarter-finals	12	6	6	50%	320	3	0	0
Larry Nabholtz	0	3	Semifinals	7	4	3	57%	221	2	1	0
Bill Nary	0	5	Quarter-finals	11	6	5	55%	210	4	0	0
Byron Nelson	2	10	Finals	45	37	8	82%	1305	9	6	5
Harry Nettlebladt	0	7	2nd Round	9	2	7	22%	187	2	0	0
Augie Nordone	0	6	2nd Round	8	2	6	25%	153	2	0	0
J. J. O'Brien	0	1	Quarter-finals	3	2	1	67%	97	1	0	0
Pat O'Hara	0	2	1st Round	2	0	2	00%	75	0	0	0
Peter O'Hara	0	3	Quarter-finals	6	3	3	50%	211	2	0	0
Bud Oakley	0	2	2nd Round	3	1	2	33%	54	1	0	0
Willie Ogg	0	5	3rd Round	8	3	5	38%	232	2	0	0

PGA CHAMPIONSHIP MATCH-PLAY STATISTICS

Name	No. of Wins	Yrs in Match Play	Highest Round Played In	Matches Played	Wins	Losses	Win %	Holes Played	Wins in Round 1	Semifinals	Finals
Ed Oliver	0	9	Finals	21	12	9	57%	466	5	1	1
Johnny Palmer	0	9	Finals	22	13	9	59%	469	6	1	1
Sam Parks Jr.	0	5	3rd Round	8	3	5	38%	164	2	0	0
Guy Paulsen	0	5	1st Round	5	0	5	00%	94	0	0	0
Toney Penna	0	11	2nd Round	18	7	11	39%	409	7	0	0
Henry Picard	1	11	Finals	34	24	10	71%	869	9	3	1
Henry Ransom	0	12	Quarter-finals	28	16	12	57%	552	8	0	0
Wilfred Reid	0	4	2nd Round	6	2	4	33%	189	2	0	0
Johnny Revolta	1	12	Finals	27	16	11	59%	619	9	1	1
Skee Riegel	0	3	3rd Round	7	4	3	57%	116	2	0	0
Chas. Rowe	0	2	Quarter-finals	6	3	3	50%	132	1	0	0
Paul Runyan	2	12	Finals	35	25	10	71%	946	8	2	2
Harold Sampson	0	2	Quarter-finals	5	3	2	60%	139	2	0	0
Gene Sarazen	3	28	Finals	82	57	25	70%	2221	22	7	4
Eddie Schultz	0	7	Quarter-finals	11	4	7	36%	279	2	0	0
Charles Sheppard	0	6	Quarter-finals	14	6	8	43%	289	3	0	0
Denny Shute	2	18	Finals	51	35	16	69%	1374	13	4	3
Al Smith	0	8	3rd Round	17	9	8	53%	343	5	0	0
Horton Smith	0	17	Semifinals	43	26	17	60%	1126	11	1	0
Sam Snead	3	17	Finals	64	50	14	78%	1546	16	5	5
Ralph Stonehouse	0	4	Quarter-finals	7	3	4	43%	165	2	0	0
Jimmy Thomson	0	11	Finals	22	12	10	55%	469	6	1	1
Felice Torza	0	3	Finals	8	5	3	63%	215	1	1	1
Bob Toski	0	7	3rd Round	12	6	6	50%	215	4	0	0
Eddie Towns	0	4	3rd Round	7	3	4	43%	148	2	0	0
Jim Turnesa	1	12	Finals	34	23	11	68%	822	9	2	2
Joe Turnesa	0	7	Finals	11	4	7	36%	302	1	1	1
Mike Turnesa	0	14	Finals	27	13	14	48%	621	7	1	1
Wally Ulrich	0	3	3rd Round	8	5	3	63%	165	3	0	0
Ellsworth Vines	0	8	Semifinals	16	8	8	50%	321	4	1	0
Cyril Walker	0	4	Semifinals	13	9	4	69%	429	4	1	0
Art Wall	0	2	3rd Round	5	3	2	60%	85	2	0	0
Frank Walsh	0	8	Finals	15	8	7	53%	375	5	1	1
Al Watrous	0	20	Semifinals	39	19	20	49%	1009	12	2	0
James West	0	4	Quarter-finals	8	4	4	50%	229	3	0	0
Henry Williams Jr.	0	9	Finals	23	14	9	61%	530	6	1	1
Craig Wood	0	10	Finals	26	16	10	62%	720	8	2	1
Lew Worsham	0	10	Quarter-finals	27	17	10	63%	531	9	0	0
Al Zimmerman	0	4	Semifinals	9	5	4	56%	202	2	1	0

■ PGA CHAMPIONSHIP RECORDS

Match-Play Records (1916 through 1957)

■ Most Finals

6 by Walter Hagen (winner, 1921, '24, '25, '26 & '27; runner-up, 1923)

5 by Sam Snead (winner 1942, '49 & '51; runner-up, 1938 & '40)

5 by Byron Nelson (winner, 1940 & '45; runner-up, 1939, '41 & '44)

4 by Jim Barnes (winner, 1916 & '19; runner-up, 1921 & '24)

4 by Gene Sarazen (winner, 1922, '23 & '33; runner-up, 1930)

3 by Denny Shute (runner-up, 1931; winner, 1936 & '37)

3 by Leo Diegel (runner-up, 1926; winner, 1928 & '29)

3 by Chick Harbert (runner-up, 1947 & '51; winner, 1954)

3 by Walter Burkemo (runner-up, 1951 & '54; winner, 1953)

■ Most Times In Semifinals

8 by Walter Hagen (1916, '21, '23, '24, '25, '26, '27 & '29)

7 by Gene Sarazen (1922, '23, '28, '30, '31, '33 & '41)

6 by Byron Nelson (1939, '40, '41,'42, '44 & '45)

5 by Sam Snead (1938, '40, '42, '49 & '51)

4 by Denny Shute (1931, '34, '36 & '37)

4 by Jim Barnes (1916, '19, '21 & '24)

4 by Jimmy Demaret (1942, '46, '48 & '50)

4 by Walter Burkemo (1951, '53, '54 & '57)

■ Most Consecutive Times in Finals

*5 by Walter Hagen (runner-up, 1923; winner, 1924, '25, '26 & '27)

3 by Byron Nelson (runner-up, 1939; winner, 1940; runner-up 1941)

*Hagen made it into finals in 1921, but did not play in 1922 PGA Championship.

■ Most YearsQualified for Match Play

28 by Gene Sarazen

21 by Vic Ghezzi

20 by Al Watrous

18 by Denny Shute

17 by Horton Smith

17 by Sam Snead

■ Most Matches Played In

82 by Gene Sarazen

64 by Sam Snead

51 by Denny Shute

50 by Walter Hagen

47 by Vic Ghezzi

45 by Byron Nelson

■ Most Holes Played in Match Play

2,221 by Gene Sarazen

1,580 by Walter Hagen

1,546 by Sam Snead

1,374 by Denny Shute

1,305 by Bryon Nelson

■ Most Matches Won

57 by Gene Sarazen

50 by Sam Snead

40 by Walter Hagen

37 by Byron Nelson

35 by Denny Shute

■ Highest Winning Percentage (Minimum of 15 matches required)

82% by Byron Nelson   37 wins - 8 losses

82% by Walter Burkemo   27 wins - 6 losses

81% by Ben Hogan   22 wins - 5 losses

78% by Sam Snead   50 wins - 14 losses

77% by Jim Barnes   24 wins - 7 losses

■ Most Consecutive Matches Won

22 by Walter Hagen - (five in 1924, five in 1925, five in 1926, five in 1927, two in 1928); streak was broken in the quarter-finals of 1928 with Leo Diegel's 2 & 1 win

14 by Denny Shute - (six in 1936, six in 1937, two in 1938); streak was broken in the 3rd round of 1938 with Jimmy Hines' 2 & 1 win

13 by Gene Sarazen - (six in 1922, six in 1923, one in 1924); streak was broken in the 2nd round of 1924 with Larry Nabholtz's 2 & 1 win

11 by Jim Barnes - (five in 1916, five in 1919, one in 1920); streak was broken in the 2nd round of 1920 with Clarence Hackney's 5 & 4 win

11 by Walter Burkemo - (six in 1953, five in 1954); streak was broken in the finals of 1954 with Chick Harbert's 4 & 3 win

11 by Leo Diegel - (five in 1928, five in 1929, one in 1930); streak was broken in the 2nd round of 1930 with Harold Sampson's 1-up (38) win

11 by Byron Nelson - (six in 1940, five in 1941); streak was broken in the finals of 1941 with Vic Ghezzi's 1-up (38) win

*10 by Walter Hagen - (five in 1921, five in 1923); streak was broken in finals of 1923 with Gene Sarazen's 1-up (38) win

*Note: Hagen did not play in 1922 PGA Championship

■ Most Wins in First Round

22 by Gene Sarazen

16 by Sam Snead

14 by Ed Dudley

14 by Vic Ghezzi

13 by Denny Shute

■ Most Holes Played in a Year

194 by Gene Sarazen in 1923 -1st Round: 29, 2nd Round: 26, 3rd Round: 34, Quarter-finals: 36, Semifinals: 31, Finals: 38

188 by Walter Hagen in 1923 -1st Round: 33, 2nd Round: 27, 3rd Round: 34, Quarter-finals: 32, Semifinals: 25, Finals: 38

182 by Harold McSpaden in 1937 -1st Round: 16, 2nd Round: 20, 3rd Round: 34, Quarter-finals: 39, Semifinals: 36, Finals: 37

■ Winners Taking the Fewest Holes to Win

154 by Leo Diegel in 1928 - 1st Round: 28, 2nd Round: 32, Quarter-finals: 35, Semifinals: 28, Finals: 31

154 by Leo Diegel in 1929 - 1st Round: 27, 2nd Round: 27, Quarter-finals: 34, Semifinals: 34, Finals: 32

155 by Ben Hogan in 1946 - 1st Round: 17, 2nd Round: 15, 3rd Round: 32, Quarter-finals: 32, Semifinals: 27, Finals: 32

157 by Gene Sarazen in 1933 - 1st Round: 29, 2nd Round: 33, Quarter-finals: 31, Semifinals: 32, Finals: 32

Biggest Winning Margin of Victory
12 & 11
Jim Barnes beat George Denback in 1st round of the 1923 PGA Championship

Jim Barnes beat John Cowan in 2nd round of the 1923 PGA Championship

Willie Ogg beat Carl Anderson in 2nd round of the 1923 PGA Championship

Walter Hagen beat George McLean in semifinals of the 1923 PGA Championship

Mortie Dutra beat Albert Alcroft in 1st round of the 1927 PGA Championship

Johnny Revolta beat Alex Gerlak in 1st round of the 1933 PGA Championship

Ky Laffoon beat Vic Bass in 1st round of the 1942 PGA Championship

12 & 10
Ky Laffoon beat George Smith in 1st round of the 1934 PGA Championship

Doug Ford beat Wally Ulrich in the 3rd round of the 1955 PGA Championship

Biggest Winning Margin of Victory in a Final
Paul Runyan beat Sam Snead 8 & 7 in the 1938 PGA Championship Finals

Ben Hogan beat Mike Turnesa 7 & 6 in the 1948 PGA Championship Finals

Sam Snead beat Walter Burkemo 7 & 6 in the 1951 PGA Championship Finals

Playoffs in the Finals
1923 - Gene Sarazen beat Walter Hagen on the 38th hole

1934 - Paul Runyan beat Craig Wood on the 38th hole

1937 - Denny Shute beat Harold McSpaden on the 37th hole

1939 - Henry Picard beat Byron Nelson on the 37th hole

1941 - Vic Ghezzi beat Bryon Nelson on the 38th hole

Most Playoffs
7 by Claude Harmon	2 wins - 5 losses
7 by Harold McSpaden	4 wins - 3 losses
7 by Sam Snead	3 wins - 4 losses
6 by Chick Harbert	4 wins - 2 losses
6 by Byron Nelson	3 wins - 3 losses
6 by Al Watrous	2 wins - 4 losses

Most Wins in Playoffs
5 by Gene Sarazen in five playoffs

4 by Harold McSpaden in seven playoffs

4 by Chick Harbert in six playoffs

4 by Jim Turnesa in five playoffs

4 by Walter Burkemo in four playoffs

4 by Jim Ferrier in four playoffs

4 by Ky Laffoon in four playoffs

Most Extra-Hole Matches Played in One Year
3 by Harold McSpaden in 1937 - beat Bunny Torpey in the 2nd round (20 holes), beat Henry Picard in quarter-finals (39 holes), lost to Denny Shute in the finals (37 holes)

3 by Walter Burkemo in 1951 - beat Tody Lyons in the 1st round (20 holes), beat Chick Harbert in the 2nd round (19 holes), beat Ellsworth Vines in the semifinals (37 holes)

3 by Dave Douglas in 1953 - beat Lew Worsham in the 1st round (20 holes), beat Sam Snead in the 2nd round (19 holes), beat Jackson Bradley in the 3rd round (37 holes)

Longest Matches (36 Holes)
43 holes - John Golden beat Walter Hagen in the 1st round in 1932

42 holes - Claude Harmon beat Sam Snead in the quarter-finals in 1948

41 holes - Bobby Cruickshank beat Al Watrous in the 1st round in 1932

Longest Matches (18 Holes)
26 holes - Chick Harbert beat Eddie Burke in the 2nd round in 1948

24 holes - Ted Kroll beat Max Evans in the 2nd round in 1954

Lowest Qualifying Score
134 by Jim Ferrier in 1946

134 by Stewart Alexander in 1948

134 by Johnny Palmer in 1953

Highest Qualifying Score by a Winner
154 by Denny Shute in 1936, 155 made it into match play that year

151 by Walter Hagen in 1925, 157 made it into match play that year

151 by Leo Diegel in 1928, 60 made it into match play that year

151 by Byron Nelson in 1940, 53 made it into match play that year

149 by Denny Shute in 1937, Shute was exempt from qualifying, 63 made it into match play

Medalist Going On to Win The PGA Championship
140 by Walter Hagen in 1926

141 by Walter Hagen in 1927 (shared low medalist honors)

140 by Olin Dutra in 1932

138 by Byron Nelson in 1945 (shared low medalist honors)

135 by Doug Ford in 1955

PGA CLUB PROFESSIONALS IN THE 76TH PGA CHAMPIONSHIP

Top 40 finishers in the 1993 PGA Club Professional Championship received exemptions into the 1994 PGA Championship. Eligible PGA club professionals who become PGA Tour players prior to the PGA Championship are not exempt into the field.

◀BOB ACKERMAN

Birthdate: March 27, 1953
Birthplace: Benton Harbor, Mich.
Age: 41 **Ht:** 5'11" **Wt:** 200
Home: Aurora, Ill.
College: Indiana University (1975)
Turned Professional: 1975

Player Notes: Head professional at Aurora (Ill.) CC. Elected to PGA membership, Feb. 1, 1982. Played in the 1981 U.S. Open finishing T-43rd. Missed the cut in 1986 PGA Championship. Played in eight PGA Club Professional Championships, best finish T-18th in 1984.

◀RICK ACTON

Birthdate: Jan. 5, 1946
Birthplace: Portland, Ore.
Age: 48 **Ht:** 5'11" **Wt:** 210
Home: Redmond, Wash.
College: Washington
Turned Professional: 1969

Player Notes: Head professional for the last ten years at Sahalee CC... Played on the PGA Tour between 1973-1980, best finish 3rd in 1977 Buick Open... Two-time Washington Open champion, three-time Pacific Northwest Open champion, four-time Oregon Open champion, five-time Pacific Northwest PGA champion and five-time Washington PGA champion... Member, 1986 & '94 PGA Cup team... Missed the cut in 1977 U.S. Open. Missed the cut in four (1976, '78, '86 & '87) PGA Championships. Played in seven PGA Club Professional Championships, best finish 3rd in 1985.

◀MEL BAUM

Birthdate: Nov. 29, 1956
Age: 37 **Ht:** 6'1" **Wt:** 230
Home: Larchmont, N.Y.
College: Onondaga Community College
Turned Professional: 1979

Player Notes: Currently teaching professional at Bonnie Briar CC in Larchmont, N.Y... Won Met PGA Championship in 1989 and '90, Central New York PGA Championship in 1987, New York State Open in 1987, Central New York Assistant Professional Championship in 1984 and '86, Central New York Open in 1986 and Woodstock Open in 1989... Six-time Central New York PGA Player of the Year... Played in 1977 U.S. Amateur and missed the cut in the 1982 U.S. Open. Missed the cut in 1991 and '92 PGA Championships. Best finish in six PGA Club Professional Championships, T-10th in 1990 and 1993.

◀JOHN BERMEL

Birthdate: July 8, 1962
Birthplace: Iowa City, Iowa
Age: 32 **Ht:** 6'1" **Wt:** 200
Home: Cedar Falls, Iowa
College: Central College, Pella, Iowa
Turned Professional: 1986

Player Notes: Head professional for the last five years at Beaver Hills CC... Winner, 1990 and '93 Iowa PGA Section Championships. Best finish in two PGA Club Professional Championships, T-31st in 1993.

◀MIGUEL BIAMAN

Birthdate: Jan. 11, 1962
Birthplace: Chestnut Hill, Pa.
Age: 32 **Ht:** 6' **Wt:** 205
Home: White Marsh, Pa.
College: East Stroudsburg State
Turned Professional: 1984

Player Notes: Assistant professional at Waynesborough CC in Paoli, Pa... Winner 1988 and 1991 Philadelphia PGA Section Championships. Best finish in five PGA Club Professional Championships, T-31st in 1993.

Note: age has been determined as of the first day of the PGA Championship

◄GEORGE BOWMAN

Birthdate: Sept. 7, 1963
Birthplace: Flint, Mich.
Age: 30 **Ht:** 5'10" **Wt:** 175
Home: Flushing, Mich.
College: Western Michigan
Turned Professional: 1988

Player Notes: Assistant professional at Orchard Lake CC... Winner of four tournaments, 1988 Venezuela Open, 1990 West Orange Open, 1991 and '92 Schuss Classics... Was a member of the Nike Tour in 1993 and played in nine events (best finish T-27th, Panama City Open) before hurting his wrist, which has forced him off the Tour. T-3rd in his only PGA Club Professional Championship start in 1993.

◄BOB BOYD

Birthdate: July 29, 1955
Birthplace: Mt. Olive, N.C.
Age: 39 **Ht:** 6'2" **Wt:** 200
Home: Hilton Head, S.C.
College: Maryland
Turned Professional: 1977

Player Notes: Head professional at Melrose Club in Hilton Head, S.C... Played on PGA Tour 1982-85. Best finish, T-6th 1983 Houston Open... Played U.S. Open 1983, '87, '88, '90. Winner: Carolinas Open, 1982, '89 and '93; Carolinas PGA, 1984, '89; South Carolina Open, 1985, '89, '92 and '93; PGA Club Professional Championship, Carolinas PGA Match Play, 1988; RJR Classic of the Carolinas, 1989; Wilson Club Professional Championship, 1990; Maryland Open, 1990; Michael Thomas Tradition, 1993. Carolinas PGA Section Player of the Year, 1988-89. 1992 South Carolina Player of the Year. PGA Cup Team, 1990; Played in four PGA Championships (1983, '89, '90 and '93), best finish T-19th in 1990... Played in five U.S. Opens (1983, '87, '88, '90 and '91), best finish T-50th in 1983... T-10th in 1993 PGA Club Professional Championship.

◄KEVIN CASHMAN

Birthdate: May 19, 1962
Birthplace: Minneapolis, Minn.
Age: 32 **Ht:** 6'3" **Wt:** 185
Home: Plymouth, Minn.
College: Ferris State
Turned Professional: 1986

Player Notes: Head professional at the Pines at Grand View Lodge... Played on the Australasia tour 1987 and '88... Winner 1987 Minnesota State Open. Runner-up in 1993 Minnesota PGA Section Championship and was Minnesota PGA Player of the Year in 1987... In June of 1988, suffered a back injury in an automobile accident and did not play golf for a year and a half. Didn't play competitive golf for three years after accident. Best finish in four PGA Club Professional Championships, T-31st in 1993.

◄WALT CHAPMAN

Birthdate: Nov. 8, 1961
Birthplace: Avingdon, Va.
Age: 32 **Ht:** 6'3" **Wt:** 195
Home: Knoxville, Tenn.
College: Tennessee
Turned Professional: 1986

Player Notes: Head professional at River Island GC in Kodak, Tenn... 1991, '92 and '93 Knoxville Section PGA champion and 1993 Tennessee Section PGA champion... Missed the cut in 1986 U.S. Open. Best finish in two PGA Club Professional Championships, T-3rd in 1993.

◄TOM CLEAVER

Birthdate: July 9, 1958
Birthplace: New Orleans, La.
Age: 36 **Ht:** 6' **Wt:** 178
Home: Boca Raton, Fla.
College: Univ. of South Florida
Turned Professional: 1980

Player Notes: Assistant professional at Wycliffe CC in Lake Worth, Fla... Winner 1984 North Dakota and 1985 South Dakota Opens. Two-time runner-up in Florida Open and runner-up in 1991 Foot-Joy Assistant Championship. T-8th in his only PGA Club Professional Championship in 1993.

◄JOHN DEFOREST

Birthdate: Nov. 20, 1956
Birthplace: Catskill, N.Y.
Age: 37 **Ht:** 6'4" **Wt:** 220
Home: Cottehill, N.Y.
College: Florida
Turned Professional: 1980

Player Notes: Head professional at Roundout CC... Played on the PGA Tour in 1985 and the European Tour in 1988 and 1989... Missed the cut in 1984 U.S. Open. T-31st in his only PGA Club Professional Championship in 1993.

◀ TOM DOLBY

Birthdate: Dec. 27, 1961
Birthplace: St. Paul, Minn.
Age: 32 **Ht:** 6' **Wt:** 235
Home: St. Paul, Minn.
College: Saint Thomas
Turned Professional: 1986

Player Notes: Head professional at Southview CC in West St. Paul, Minn. . . . Reached final stage of 1994 PGA Tour Qualifying School in La Quinta, Calif. . . . Two-time runner-up, Minnesota PGA Match Play Championship 1992, '93; top-five finisher, Minnesota PGA State Open 1992, '93; winner, Indian Hills Pro-Am, Stillwater, Minn., 1993; two-time qualifier, PGA Club Professional Championship, 1992, '93. Best finish in PGA Club Professional Championship, T-30th, 1993.

◀ WILL FRANTZ

Birthdate: Dec. 27, 1952
Birthplace: Huntington, W.Va.
Age: 41 **Ht:** 6'3" **Wt:** 175
Home: Ocala, Fla.
College: Marshall University
Turned Professional: 1972

Player Notes: Head professional at CC of Ocala...1986, '88, '89, and '93 North Florida PGA Player of the Year... Missed the cut in 1993 PGA Championship. Best finish in five PGA Club Professional Championships, T-3rd in 1992... 1993 North Florida PGA Section Stroke Play Champion.

◀ MIKE GOVE

Birthdate: June 22, 1957
Birthplace: Seattle, Wash.
Age: 37 **Ht:** 6'2" **Wt:** 185
Home: Gearhart, Ore.
College: Weber State
Turned Professional: 1980

Player Notes: Head professional, Astoria G and CC... Three-time NCAA All-American, 1978-80. Member Walker Cup, 1979. Played on the PGA Tour 1980-86, best finish T-4th in 1980 Pensacola and Walt Disney Opens... Winner: New Hampshire Classic, 1984 (TPS); Washington State Open, Northwest Open, 1985; Southern California PGA Inland Desert Chapter Championship, 1988. Southern California PGA Inland Desert Chapter Player of the Year, 1989. Also Pacific Northwest Player of the Year in 1992... Missed the cut in the 1984 and '86 U.S. Opens. Missed the cut in 1990 PGA Championship. Best finish in four PGA Club Professional Championships, T-15th in 1989.

◀ THOMAS GRAY

Birthdate: May 7, 1957
Birthplace: Weimar, Texas
Age: 37 **Ht:** 5'10" **Wt:** 165
Home: Linn Creek, Mo.
College: Arizona State
Turned Professional: 1980

Player Notes: Director of Golf for the last four years at the Marriott's Tan-Tar-A Resort. Played on the PGA Tour between 1981 and 1984, best finish 2nd in 1982 LaJet Classic... Winner of 1978 Arizona State Amateur Championship and 1989 Southwest Assistant Championship... T-43rd in 1981 U.S. Open. Missed the cut in 1983 PGA Championship. Best finish in four PGA Club Professional Championships, T-15th in 1993.

◀ DENNY HEPLER

Birthdate: June 15, 1955
Birthplace: Warsaw, Ind.
Age: 39 **Ht:** 6'3" **Wt:** 210
Home: Warsaw, Ind.
College: Florida State
Turned Professional: 1978

Player Notes: Currently teaching professional at Stonehenge GC in Warsaw, Ind. Played golf in college on the same team as Kenny Knox and finished 2nd in the Metro Conference Championship in 1976 to Knox. Played on the PGA Tour in 1986 and '87, Asian Tour and won 1982 Malaysian Open... Has also won 1992 Indiana PGA Match Play Championship, 1985 and '90 Indiana Opens, 1989 and '92 Indiana PGA Section Assistant Championships and 1993 Indiana Stroke Play Championship... Has played in four U.S. Opens (missing the cut each time, 1983, '84, '89 and '90) and one British Open...Best finish in two PGA Championships, T-70th in 1991. Best finish in three PGA Club Professional Championships, T-17th in 1990. T-23rd in 1993.

◀ ROBERT HOYT

Birthdate: Sept. 1, 1954
Birthplace: Ft. Worth, Texas
Age: 39 **Ht:** 6'8" **Wt:** 245
Home: Irving, Texas
College: Houston
Turned Professional: 1976

Player Notes: Head professional for 12 years at Brook Hollow GC, Dallas, Texas... Winner, Texas State Amateur, 1975; Northern Texas PGA Club Professional Championships, 1985, '86 and '91. Northern Texas PGA Player of the Year, 1984... Played in six PGA Championships (1983, '84, '85, '86, '90 and '93), best finish 72nd in 1985... Best finish in 10 PGA Club Professional Championships, T-11th in 1992; in 1993 he finished T-18th.

◀GREGG JONES

Birthdate: Oct. 25, 1956
Birthplace: Eavs, Colo.
Age: 37 **Ht:** 6'1" **Wt:** 160
Home: Colorado Springs, Colo.
College: Texas Tech
Turned Professional: 1982

Player Notes: Head professional for six years at Pine Creek GC... Winner 1984 &'89 Colorado PGA Section Championships and 1992 Wyoming Open... Missed the cut in five PGA Championships (1985, '86, '88, '89 and '93)... Missed cut in 1981 U.S. Open... Best finish in nine PGA Club Professional Championships, T-9th in 1992; in 1993 finished T-18th.

◀DARRELL KESTNER

Birthdate: Aug. 15, 1953
Birthplace: Cover, Pa.
Age: 40 **Ht:** 6' **Wt:** 180
Home: Manhasset, N.Y.
College: Concord
Turned Professional: 1975

Player Notes: Currently head professional, Deepdale GC in Manhasset, N.Y... 1989 PGA Stroke Play Champion... 1982 and '83 Met Open champion... 1982 and '87 Foot-Joy PGA Assistant Professional champion... 1987 and '88 Met PGA Section Assistant Professional champion... 1988 and '89 Westchester PGA champion... Missed the cut in four PGA Professional Championships (1988, '91, '92 and '93)... Missed the cut in four U.S. Opens (1979, '87, '88 and '91)... T-23rd in 1992 PGA Club Professional Championship... Best finish in seven PGA Club Professional Championships, T-7th in 1990.

◀JOHN D. LEE

Birthdate: Feb. 6, 1962
Birthplace: Victorville, Calif.
Age: 32 **Ht:** 6'8" **Wt:** 195
Home: Naples, Fla.
College: Auburn
Turned Professional: 1985

Player Notes: Head professional at Imperial GC in Naples, Fla... 3rd in 1993 Florida State Open... 1993 South Florida Player of the Year. Best finish in two PGA Club Professional Championships, 2nd in 1993.

◀J. L. LEWIS

Birthdate: July 18, 1960
Birthplace: Emporia, Kan.
Age: 34 **Ht:** 6'3" **Wt:** 210
Home: Austin, Texas
College: Southwest Texas State
Turned Professional: 1984

Player Notes: Part owner and teaching professional at Ben White Golf Center in Austin, Texas... Also exempt on the Nike Tour and is planning on playing 11 events before the PGA Championship... Played on the PGA Tour in 1989... Winner 1992 Eastern, Western and Southern Texas Sectional Championships... Missed the cut in 1993 PGA Championship. Best finish in two PGA Club Professional Championships, T-10th in 1993.

◀SCOTT MAHLBERG

Birthdate: Oct. 7, 1955
Birthplace: Chicago, Ill.
Age: 38 **Ht:** 6'1" **Wt:** 180
Home: San Diego, Calif.
College: Florida
Turned Professional: 1979

Player Notes: Teaching professional at Stardust CC in San Diego, Calif... Winner: 1992 Southern California Section Four-ball; 1990 Southern California Championship; 1981, '83, '85 and '86 San Diego Match Play tournaments; 1986 Southern California PGA Stroke Play Championship; 1988 and '90 San Diego Stroke Play Championships; 1990 Southern California PGA Championship and 1993 Chrysler Pro-Am... Missed the cut in 1992 PGA Championship. Best finish in nine PGA Club Professional Championships, T-21st in 1991; in 1993 finished T-23rd.

◀RON MCDOUGAL

Birthdate: Oct. 23, 1962
Birthplace: Houston, Texas
Age: 31 **Ht:** 5'10" **Wt:** 170
Home: Purchase, N.Y.
College: Texas
Turned Professional: 1986

Player Notes: Assistant professional at Century CC.. Winner: 1989 Westchester Open, 1990 Woodstock Open and 1991 Bermuda Open... Runner-up in 1990 Jamaica Open. Member of 1992 PGA Cup Team... Missed the cut in the 1992 and '93 PGA Championships. In three PGA Club Professional Championships, he finished 2nd in 1991, won in 1992 and T-3rd in 1993.

◄**LONNIE NIELSEN**

Birthdate: June 29, 1953
Birthplace: Belle Plaine, Iowa
Age: 41 **Ht:** 5'11" **Wt:** 175
Home: East Aurora, N.Y.
College: Iowa
Turned Professional: 1976

Player Notes: Head professional Crag Burn GC, East Aurora, N.Y... Played on the PGA Tour 1977-83. Winner: Iowa Amateur, 1975; Western New York PGA, 1985, '86, '87, and '89; New York State Opens, 1985, and '89; Central New York Open, 1985; PGA Match Play Championships, 1987 and '88; PGA Stroke Play Championship, Wilson PGA Club Professional Classic, American West Pro-Amateur, 1987; LaMode Team Championship (with Cotton Dunn), 1988; Western New York PGA Match Play Championship, 1990. PGA Club Professional Player of the Year, 1986, '87,and '89; Western New York PGA Player of the Year, 1985, '86, '89, and '90; PGA Cup Team, 1988... Missed the cut in the 1977 and 1983 U.S. Opens. Best finish in eight PGA Club Professional Championships, T-6th in 1990; in 1993, T-23rd.

◄**ROD NUCKOLLS**

Birthdate: Jan. 25, 1957
Birthplace: Wichita, Kan.
Age: 37 **Ht:** 5'10" **Wt:** 180
Home: Wichita, Kan.
College: Wichita State
Turned Professional: 1980

Player Notes: Head professional Wichita CC... Played on the PGA Tour between 1981 and 1985, best finish T-13th in 1983 Western Open... 1989 and '93 South Central Player of the Year. T-39th in the 1982 U.S. Open and missed the cut in 1985 U.S. Open. Best finish in six PGA Club Professional Championships, T-31st in 1993.

◄**PAT O'BRIEN**

Birthdate: Oct. 30, 1942
Birthplace: San Antonio, Texas
Age: 51 **Ht:** 5'5" **Wt:** 150
Home: Indianapolis, Ind.
College: LSU
Turned Professional: 1967

Player Notes: Head professional Broadmoor CC... Winner: 1972 and '74 Indiana Stroke Play Championships, 1993 Indiana Senior Match Play Championship, Indiana Senior Open and Indiana Senior PGA... 1974 Indiana Player of the Year and 1993 Indiana Senior Player of the Year... Fourth in the PGA Senior Club Professional Championship, he missed qualifying for the 1994 Senior PGA Tour by a stroke in the Senior Tour Q-school in November 1993. Best finish in eight PGA Club Professional Championships, T-23rd in 1993.

◄**PETE OAKLEY**

Birthdate: June 28, 1949
Birthplace: Panama City, Fla.
Age: 45 **Ht:** 5'8" **Wt:** 155
Home: Lewes, Del.
College: Florida
Turned Professional: 1972

Player Notes: Head professional at the Rehoboth Beach CC... Four time Delaware Open Champion, winner of the 1989 and '90 Philadelphia Opens, 1993 Philadelphia PGA Match Play champion... Four time Philadelphia Player of the Year. Best finish in nine PGA Club Professional Championships, T-3rd in 1993.

◄**RON PHILO JR.**

Birthdate: Dec. 22, 1965
Birthplace: Tallahassee, Fla.
Age: 28 **Ht:** 6'1" **Wt:** 180
Home: Amelia Island, Fla.
College: Florida State
Turned Professional: 1986

Player Notes: Co-director of the Amelia Island Plantation Golf School... Also will play full time on the Nike Tour in 1994. Played on the Australia and Canadian tours in 1991... 1990 Assistant Professional of the Year. Winner 1993 North Florida PGA Championship. Best finish in two PGA Club Professional Championships, T-23rd in 1993.

◄**BARRY REDMOND**

Birthdate: Feb. 18, 1960
Birthplace: Detroit, Mich.
Age: 34 **Ht:** 5'10" **Wt:** 162
Home: Royal Oak, Mich.
Turned Professional: 1979

Player Notes: Teaching professional at Franklin Hills CC... Winner: 1987 Michigan Assistant Professional Championship, 1989 Michigan State Open, 1990 and '92 Michigan PGA Championships and was Michigan Player of the Year in 1992. Best finish in six PGA Club Professional Championships, T-31st in 1993.

◄JEFF ROTH

Birthdate: Sept. 8, 1957
Birthplace: Milwaukee, Wis.
Age: 36 **Ht:** 5'9" **Wt:** 190
Home: Flushing, Mich.
College: Arizona
Turned Professional: 1979

Player Notes: Head professional for the last six years at Flint GC... Went to Arizona thanks to Dan Pohl recruiting him... Played on the TPS in 1984 and the South African Tour in 1988... Won the 1993 PGA Club Professional Championship and was runner-up in 1987. Also won the 1981 Michigan Section PGA Assistant Professional Championship and the 1987 and '88 Yamaha Classics... Michigan PGA Player of the Year in 1987... Member of the PGA Cup Team in 1988 and will play on the team in 1994. Also a member of every Fuller Cup team since 1986. Missed the cut in the 1988 and '91 PGA Championships. Has played in seven PGA Club Professional Championships.

◄BRAD SHERFY

Birthdate: Jan. 9, 1956
Birthplace: Seattle, Wash.
Age: 38 **Ht:** 6' **Wt:** 185
Home: Camarillo, Calif.
College: UCLA
Turned Professional: 1979

Player Notes: Currently teaching professional at Mulligan Golf Center in Torrance, Calif. One of his pupils is Ted Oh, the 16-year-old who made an appearance in the 1993 U.S. Open... All-American in 1978... Winner, 1990 Southern California PGA Players Championship... Southern California Player of the Year in 1993... Missed the cut in 1991 and '93 PGA Championships... Played in four U.S. Opens (1979, '82, '90 and '91), missing the cut... Best finish in three PGA Club Professional Championships, T-9th in 1992; in 1993 finished T-10th.

◄TODD SMITH

Birthdate: April 12, 1963
Birthplace: Bloomington, Ind.
Age: 31 **Ht:** 6' **Wt:** 165
Home: Wabash, Ind.
College: Auburn
Turned Professional: 1985

Player Notes: Head professional at Rock Hollow GC in Peru, Ind... Winner 1991 Northern Open... Was runner-up in the 1991 Indiana PGA Championship... 1991 Indiana PGA Player of the Year... T-10th in 1991 PGA Club Professional Championship... Won 1992 Indianapolis PGA Championship and 1993 Indiana PGA Match Play Championship. T-79th in 1992 PGA Championship and missed the cut in 1993. Best finish in six PGA Club Professional Championships, T-3rd in 1993.

◄WES SMITH

Birthdate: July 31, 1945
Birthplace: Miami, Fla.
Age: 49 **Ht:** 6' **Wt:** 185
Home: Cooper City, Fla.
College: Miami J.C.
Turned Professional: 1972

Player Notes: Teaching professional at the Club at Emerald Hills in Hollywood, Fla... Teacher of the Year in the Southern Florida Chapter in 1989 and '91, and was the Southern Florida Chapter Player of the Year in 1990, '91 and '92. Best finish in five PGA Club Professional Championships, T-18th in 1993.

◄STEVE SMITHA

Birthdate: Feb. 4, 1966
Birthplace: Madison, Ind.
Age: 28 **Ht:** 6' **Wt:** 190
Home: Lexington, Ky.
College: Eastern Kentucky
Turned Professional: 1988

Player Notes: Head professional at Champions GC in Nicholasville, Ky... Winner: 1992 and '93 Kentucky PGA Match Play Championships, 1992 Kentucky PGA Stroke Play Championship and was Kentucky Player of the Year in 1992. Best finish in two PGA Club Professional Championships, T-23rd in 1993.

◄SCOTT STEGER

Birthdate: June 11, 1956
Birthplace: Madison, Ind.
Age: 38 **Ht:** 6'1" **Wt:** 225
Home: Noblesville, Ind.
College: Ball State
Turned Professional: 1979

Player Notes: Head professional at Pebble Brook GC... Played on the PGA Tour 1979, '80 and '82... Winner, 1980 Indiana State Open, 1989 and '91 Indiana PGA Section Championships. Two-time Indiana PGA Match Play Championship... Played in four U.S. Opens (1977, '79, '82 and '87), missing the cut. Best finish in six PGA Club Professional Championships, T-31st in 1993.

◄EDDIE TERASA

Birthdate: June 19, 1960
Birthplace: Madison, Wis.
Age: 34 **Ht:** 5'10" **Wt:** 175
Home: Waukesaku, Wis.
College: Sam Houston State
Turned Professional: 1984

Player Notes: Head professional for the last seven years at the Oconomowoc GC... Winner, 1985 Wisconsin State Open... Three-time Wisconsin PGA Match Play Champion and five-time Wisconsin PGA Medal Play Champion... Also, five-time Wisconsin Player of the Year. T-10th in his first PGA Club Professional Championship in 1993.

◄JIM WHITE

Birthdate: April 16, 1950
Birthplace: Hastings, Neb.
Age: 44 **Ht:** 6' **Wt:** 175
Home: Lincoln, Neb.
College: Hastings College
Turned Professional: 1972

Player Notes: Director of Golf for 10 years at Firethorn GC... Played on the PGA Tour 1977, '78 and 79... Winner of 1982, '85 and '86 Nebraska Open Championships and eight-time Nebraska PGA Section champion... 12-time Nebraska PGA Player of the Year... Missed the cut in the 1981 and '87 U.S. Opens. Missed the cut in 1979, '83, '85, '86 and '91 PGA Championships. Best finish in 15 PGA Club Professional Championships, 2nd in 1985; in 1993 finished T-15th.

◄SCOTT WILLIAMS

Birthdate: July 14, 1959
Birthplace: Seattle, Wash.
Age: 35 **Ht:** 5'8" **Wt:** 145
Home: Redmond, Wash.
College: San Diego State
Turned Professional: 1983

Player Notes: Currently teaching professional at Redmond Golf Center... NCAA Division I All-American 1980 & '82... Played junior golf with Fred Couples... Won 1980 U.S. Intercollegiate, 1990 and '91 Washington State PGA Championships, 1990 Pacific Northwest PGA Section Championship and 1991 Al Guisti Championship. Also won the 1993 Washington State and Pacific Northwest Assistant Professional Championships. Runner-up in 1993 Washington and Oregon state opens... Missed the cut in 1986 and '89 U.S. Opens. T-66th in 1991 PGA Championship. Best finish in three PGA Club Professional Championships, T-18th in 1993.

◄JERRY WISZ

Birthdate: June 7, 1953
Birthplace: Alhambra, Calif.
Age: 41 **Ht:** 6'2" **Wt:** 185
Home: Covina, Calif.
College: University of California
at Irvine
Turned Professional: 1978

Player Notes: Head professional at the Alhambra Municipal GC for the last 11 years. Played on the Asian tour in 1978... Winner of NCAA Division II Championship in 1975 for both individual and team... 1993 Southern California Stroke Play champion. Best finish in five PGA Club Professional Championships, T-23rd in 1993.

◄BRUCE ZABRISKI

Birthdate: Aug. 3, 1957
Birthplace: Southampton, N.Y.
Age: 37 **Ht:** 6'4" **Wt:** 205
Home: New York, N.Y.
Turned Professional: 1980

Player Notes: Assistant professional at Oyster Bay GC in Woodbury, N.Y.... Played on the PGA Tour in 1988 and 1992...Winner of 1984 New York Open; 1989, '90 and '93 Dodge Opens. Also winner of 1991 Panama City Beach Classic on the Hogan Tour and the 1993 Met Open. Was the Met Player of the Year in 1990, '91 and '93... Missed the cut in 1986 and '91 U.S. Opens. Best finish in three PGA Club Professional Championships, T-5th in 1991; in 1993 finished T-31st. Tied for all-time victories (10) in Avon Grips PGA Tournament Series.

THE RYDER CUP MATCHES

■ IN THE BEGINNING

The matches were first proposed in 1920 by James Harnett, a circulation representative for Golf Illustrated. Harnett had attempted to attract potential readers by raising funds to pay expenses for a professional match between the U.S. and Great Britain

The Ryder Cup Matches, one of the last great sporting events based upon prestige rather than prize money, span 66 years and 30 competitions. The origin of the idea to stage international matches between the best American professionals and those of Great Britain is a subject of debate among golf historians. Past PGA President George Sargent (1921-26) of the Southeastern Section PGA credited Sylvanus P. Jermain, president of Inverness Club in Toledo, Ohio, for first presenting the concept in 1921.

However, Bob Harlow, founder of *Golf World* and one-time manager of Walter Hagen, reported in 1951 that the matches were first proposed in 1920 by James Harnett, a circulation representative for *Golf Illustrated*. Harnett had attempted to attract potential readers by raising funds to pay expenses for a professional match between the U.S. and Great Britain, Harnett didn't get the support he needed until the PGA of America voted at its Annual Meeting, Dec. 15, 1920, to advance Harnett some funds. The rivalry Harnett so eagerly attempted to develop eventually became the Ryder Cup Matches.

Regardless of who takes credit, the first informal matches were played in 1921 in Gleneagles, Scotland. Harnett, most likely with Hagen's assistance, selected the American team. The matches were played just before the 2,000 Guineas Match Play Championship, with the British soundly defeating the U.S. Team, 9-3.

Another unofficial match occurred when the R & A decreed regional qualifying rounds before the 1926 British Open, forcing overseas competitors to make their trans-Atlantic trek earlier. With extra time on their hands, the American contingent agreed to form a team for an unofficial match against the British professionals at Wentworth.

This time, the Americans' defeat was worse — a 13 1/2 to 1 1/2 rout. A member of the appreciative gallery was English seed merchant and entrepreneur Samuel Ryder

Ryder was an English nurseryman from St. Albans in Hertfordshire, who made his fortune selling penny seed packets. Before the matches in Wentworth, Ryder had engaged the British star Abe Mitchell as his personal golf tutor. Mitchell beat the reigning British Open Champion Jim Barnes, 8 and 7, in the singles, and then partnered with George Duncan in the foursomes to beat Hagen and Barnes, 9 and 8.

After the matches, Ryder had tea with British team members George Duncan and Mitchell. Also joining them were Hagen and American teammate Emmett French. Duncan sug-gested Ryder provide a trophy and encourage the establishment of matches on a regular basis. Ryder agreed at once, and commissioned the design of the gold chalice that bears his name and Mitchell's likeness on the top.

Unfortunately, Mitchell was suffering from appendicitis and could not join his countrymen at Worcester (Mass.) Country Club in 1927 for the inaugural Matches. The United States team defeated the team from Great Britain in that historic first match, 9 1/2 - 2 1/2.

The inaugural U.S. Ryder Cup team was captained by Hagen, a charter member of the PGA of America. Only American-born players were allowed to join the team, according to a Selection Committee ruling, April 5, 1927, in Chicago. Joining Hagen on the team were Leo Diegel, Johnny Farrell, Johnny Golden, Bill Mehlhorn, Gene Sarazen, Joe Turnesa and Al Watrous. Mike Brady and Al Espinosa were named alternates.

The British PGA team was originally set with Mitchell as captain, but he remained home due to appendicitis. Ted Ray took over the duties, and was joined on the team by Aubrey Boomer, Archie Compston, George Duncan, George Gadd, Arthur Havers, Herbert Jolly, Fred Robson and C.A. (Charles) Whitcombe.

SAMUEL RYDER SOWED THE SEED

Few amateurs who took up golf after their 50th birthdays have left as many positive impressions upon the game as Samuel Ryder. Born in 1858, he was the son of a Manchester corn merchant and educated at Manchester University. His father doubted the wisdom of his son's plans to sell penny seed packets to English garden lovers. The young Ryder decided he would go into business on his own, moved south to St. Albans in Hertfordshire and formed the Heath and Heather Seed Company. His business quickly prospered, and in 1906 his social standing improved to the point where he was elected mayor of St. Albans. He became ill due to overwork, and fresh air and light exercise were prescribed as part of the cure. He was encouraged to take up golf. Reared on music and cricket, Ryder at first spurned the idea, but later relented.

Samuel Ryder

Ryder first enlisted a professional named Hill from a local 9-hole course to guide him through his golf fundamentals. Later, Ryder employed Mitchell as his exclusive instructor at an annual fee of £1,000. Ryder practiced rain or shine, six days a week (never on Sunday), for a year. He was given instruction at Marlborough House, his home, on driving and iron shots, and he hit chip shots over a hedge in the paddock.

He followed up with putting.

After his rigorous practice regimen, Ryder decided he could apply for membership at Verulam Golf Club. By age 51, he boasted a 6 handicap and joined the Verulam Golf Club in St. Albans in 1910. Within a year he was elected captain of the club, and later held the title in 1926 and '27. He sponsored a Heath and Heather Tournament in 1923, which was restricted to professionals. Among the field was Mitchell, a former gardener himself, and considered one of the finest players in Great Britain to have ever won an Open Championship.

Ryder relished the 1926 unofficial international match between the Americans and British at Wentworth, watching Mitchell and Duncan defeat Hagen and Barnes.

"Why can't they all get to know each other?" said Ryder. "I will give £5 to each of the winning players, and give a party afterwards, with champagne and chicken sandwiches."

Later that evening in a pub, Duncan turned to Ryder and said, "This is wonderful. It's too bad we don't have a match like this which is official."

"Why not?" Ryder said. Soon, the deed of gift was drafted, with Ryder agreeing to donate a solid golf cup, worth £250 (nearly $1,000 today by today's rate of inflation). The cup was designed by Mappin & Webb Company with the trophy crafted in gold. Ryder insisted that a golfing figure adorn the lid and that it resemble Mitchell. The first official Ryder Cup Matches were arranged for June 3-4, 1927, at the Worcester (Mass.) Country Club.

An appeal for £3,000 to finance the first British Ryder Cup team was met with apathy and fell £500 short of the goal, but Ryder made up the deficit. After Ryder, the biggest single contribution was £210 from the Stock Exchange Golf Society. With no Order of Merit money-winning list available, the famed British triumvirate of Harry Vardon, James Braid and James Taylor acted as team selection committee.

Samuel Ryder, who would serve two terms as mayor of St. Albans, lived to see two Ryder Cup Matches on his home soil before his death. While celebrating the holidays with his family in London, he died of a massive hemorrhage on Jan. 2, 1936. He was 77. His eldest daughter, Mrs. Marjorie Claisen, sent her father's favorite mashie (5-iron) to be placed in his coffin. Another of his daughters, Mrs. Thomas Scarfe, took over the family business. However, she never shared her father's passion for golf.

Ryder's youngest daughter, Joan, was her father's constant companion at all his golfing events. She witnessed every Ryder Cup match in Great Britain, and once in America, in 1983, when the U.S. edged the Europeans at PGA National Golf Club in Palm Beach Gardens, Fla.

In 1981, Joan met the Duke of Kent at the Matches at Walton Heath Golf Club in Surrey, England. She told the royal guest that her father had been "surprised" by the success of the Matches.

"He had the idea that when the Americans came over for a match he would give a 'small friendly lunch party' to both teams," said Joan. The Duke gazed at the spectators swarming near the 18th green, and said, "I wonder what your father would think of this little lunch party!" Joan Ryder's final appearance at the Ryder Cup Matches was at The Belfry in 1985. She called that edition of the Matches "the most exciting ever." Later that year, she died at her home in Sussex at age 81.

WAR-TORN MATCHES

From 1939 - 1945, because of World War II, the Ryder Cup Matches were not held and the United States retained the trophy from the 1937 victory. However, in 1939 and 1941, the United States continued to select a Ryder Cup team. The Ryder Cup teams of 1939 and 1941 did not compete against Europeans, but did participate in an informal competition against amateurs in the United States. Walter Hagen served as Captain on the '39 and '41 Ryder Cup teams.

1939 Ryder Cup Team	1941 Ryder Cup Team
Walter Hagen (Captain)	*Walter Hagen (Captain)*
Vic Ghezzi	*Vic Ghezzi*
Ralph Guldahl	*Ralph Guldahl*
Jimmy Hines	*Jimmy Hines*
Harold (Jug) McSpaden	*Harold (Jug) McSpaden*
Dick Metz	*Dick Metz*
Byron Nelson	*Byron Nelson*
Henry Picard	*Henry Picard*
Paul Runyan	*Paul Runyan*
Horton Smith	*Horton Smith*
Sam Snead	*Sam Snead*

EUROPEANS JOIN THE FIGHT FOR THE CUP

In 1973, the British Ryder Cup Team was expanded to include players from the Republic of Ireland. That year marked the first time the Matches were held in Scotland.

In 1978, Jack Nicklaus' counsel was sought by the PGA of Great Britain to improve the competitive level of the Matches. In fact, Nicklaus approached British PGA President Lord Derby to implore a change, adding, "It is vital to widen the selection procedures if the Ryder Cup is to continue to enjoy its past prestige."

The changes in team selection procedure were approved by descendants of the Samuel A. Ryder family along with the PGA of America. The major change was expanding selection procedures to include players from the British PGA European Tournament Division Order of Merit, and "that European members be entitled to play on the team."

This meant that professional players on the European Tournament Players Order of Merit could be natives and residents of countries other than the British Isles, as long as they were from continental Europe. The recommendation and succeeding approval of the new selection process followed another American victory at Royal Lytham & St. Annes in 1977. The first Ryder Cup Matches under the expanded European selection format were played at The Greenbrier in White Sulphur Springs, W. Va. The first two Europeans to make the overseas squad were a pair of Spaniards—Severiano

The first two Europeans to make the overseas squad were a pair of Spaniards— Severiano Ballesteros and Antonio Garrido. Ballesteros has gone on to become one of the all-time winners in the Matches.

Expanding the selection procedure to include the European Tour provided the British PGA with a much greater pool of talent from which to select their team. The European Tour Order of Merit also ensured a team comprised of golfers who were playing their best at the time of selection.

The effect of this continental tour, with its varying types of golf courses, climates, food, language and customs, was to produce players of unprecedented durability. They possessed the technique and confidence to deal with all course situations

Ballesteros and Antonio Garrido.

Ballesteros has gone on to become one of the all-time winners in the Matches. He has a 17-8-5 record and has earned 19 1/2 points in 30 Ryder Cup Matches.

The move to include the continental players was a major step in upgrading the Ryder Cup competitive level. The U.S. had won all but one outing from 1959 to 1977, being tied, 16-16, in a memorable duel in 1969 at Royal Birkdale in Southport, England.

and make the Ryder Cup Matches even more of a quality event.

RYDER CUP FORMAT CHANGES COMPLEXION

From the beginning of the series through 1959, the Ryder Cup competition was comprised of four foursome (alternate shot) matches on one day and eight singles matches on the other day, each of 36 holes.

The format was changed in 1961, to provide four 18-hole foursome matches the morning of the first day, four more foursomes that afternoon, eight 18-hole singles the morning of the second day and eight more singles that afternoon. One point was at stake in each match, so the total number of points was doubled. In 1963, four-ball (better-ball) matches were added for the first time, boosting the total number of points available to 32.

The format was altered again in 1977, this time with five foursomes on opening day, five four-ball matches on the second day, and 10 singles matches on the final day. This reduced the total points to 20.

In 1979, when the Great Britain/Ireland team was expanded to include players from European countries, the format was revised to provide for four four-ball and four foursome matches the first day, the same playing format for the second day and 12 singles matches scheduled for the third day. Total points were 28. This format will continue through the 1995 Matches.

1961 Let's Call It Even

Royal Lytham & St. Annes, St. Annes, England

Arnold Palmer and Peter Alliss were dead even in their singles match heading into the 18th hole. Palmer hit his approach 18 feet short of the pin and Alliss was 30 yards off the putting surface. With a home crowd and his father, Percy Alliss — a Ryder Cup veteran of the 1930s — watching, Peter chipped to within 20 inches of the hole. Palmer conceded the putt to Alliss. Palmer then charged his potential match-winning putt 30 inches past the cup. As Palmer regrouped and crouched to putt, Alliss said, "That's all right, Arnold, pick it up. We've had a good match; let's leave it that way."

1929 A Captain's Choice is Final

Moortown Golf Club, Leeds, England

Captain Walter Hagen endured much criticism for pairing Ed Dudley, not Horton Smith, with Gene Sarazen in their foursome match with Britain's Abe Mitchell and Fred Robson in the second Ryder Cup Matches. Dudley was playing poorly, and Smith would most likely have secured a win. But Hagen said, "It would be unthinkable to bring them all the way from the States without giving each man a chance to strike a blow for his country." Dudley and Sarazen lost the match, 2 and 1, and the U.S. dropped the Matches, 7-5.

Following his team's defeat, Hagen — himself a humbled 10-and-8 loser to Briton George Duncan — spoke to reporters:

"To lose in a game is not a national calamity. Besides, one country cannot always expect to win. If such a thing were to happen, world interest in golf would evaporate. Though naturally disappointed, I cannot help thinking that Britain's triumph is the finest thing that could have happened to the game. It will act as a tonic all round. America will prepare to win the Cup back, while Britain — stimulated by success long deferred — will go from strength to strength."

1957 A Show of Class in the Gallery

Lindrick Golf Club, Yorkshire, England

It was a case of one man looking like a hero and another a heel. British Captain Dai Rees decided Harry Weetman and Max Faulkner weren't playing well enough to be allowed in the singles matches and replaced them with Peter Mills and Harry Bradshaw. The U.S. was leading 3-1. The decision was met with bitterness by Weetman, who complained to reporters. Meanwhile, Faulkner turned cheerleader. With no leaderboards or other means of communication on the course, Faulkner ran from match to match to report the progress of his team. This inspired the British, who won six of eight singles matches in the afternoon. Many on the British team credited Faulkner for the team victory.

The British PGA suspended Weetman from tournament golf for a year, but Rees later helped shorten the suspension to several months.

1967 The Iceman Speaks

Champions Golf Club, Houston, Texas

A stone-faced Ben Hogan, making his third appearance as U.S. Captain, was the last to speak during a team dinner before the 17th renewal of the Matches. Following British Captain Dai Rees' flowery introduction of his players, Hogan politely asked the audience to hold its applause until he had introduced all his players. Hogan then paused momentarily for dramatic effect and issued his brief address: "Ladies and gentlemen, I present the American team — the 10 greatest golfers in the world." Most present at the dinner believed the Matches were decided at that point.

The U.S. went on to its most lopsided victory, 23 1/2 to 8 1/2.

1987 A Fruitful Locker Room "Chat"

Muirfield Village, Columbus, Ohio

European Captain Tony Jacklin and his team had a "locker room discussion" with officials of the PGA European Tour on the eve of Europe's defense of the Ryder Cup. The players, one by one, laid out their complaints about unsatisfactory conditions on the European circuit — everything from poor practice facilities to inconsistent greens. Official George O'Grady later said the session took the players' minds off golf and its tactics in order that they would come out refreshed the following morning. Europe held on to win its first Ryder Cup on American soil, 15-13.

■ How The U.S. Ryder Cup Team Has Been Chosen - *(A chronology of format changes)*

1927 *Only American-born players were eligible to compete, according to a PGA Selection Committee ruling, April 5, 1927, in Chicago. Eight players were chosen based "entirely on performance during the last three years." Information was compiled by Melvin Taylor of the USGA Executive Committee.*

1931 *Five players were selected during the PGA Annual Meeting. Three others were chosen from 14 players invited to compete in a 72-hole competition at Scioto Country Club in Columbus, Ohio, a week before the Ryder Cup.*

1933 *Team selected by vote of PGA Executive Committee and PGA section presidents.*

1935 *Selection based on playing records of previous two years. Automatic qualifiers: Walter Hagen, team captain; Paul Runyan, 1934 PGA Champion; Olin Dutra, 1934 U.S. Open Champion; Sam Parks, 1935 U.S. Open Champion; and six players based on scoring average: Ky Laffoon, Henry Picard, Johnny Revolta, Gene Sarazen, Horton Smith and Craig Wood.*

1937 *Six players were chosen on basis of performance during past two years. Four more players added after performance in the U.S. Open.*

1939 *Team was announced in May during previous selection process, but Matches cancelled due to outbreak of World War II.*

1947 *Points system used for the first time, devised by George Schneiter, chairman of the PGA Tournament Committee. The current U.S. Open and PGA Champions were automatic choices. The remainder of the team was selected by a PGA Executive Committee largely based on points list.*

Under this system, points were awarded to top-10 finishers in all events except the PGA Championship, where only the first eight earned points. Points accrued from Jan. 1, 1946, through Sept. 1, 1947. The winners of the PGA Championship and U.S. Open received 100 points;

the Masters champion, 95; the Western Open champion, 80; and winners of all other PGA-sanctioned events received 70 points.

1953 *The PGA Executive Committee added 1952 PGA Champion Jim Turnesa to the automatic qualifier list, along with 1953 PGA Champion Walter Burkemo. The remainder of the team was from the points list.*

1957 *Team members must have played in both the 1956 and '57 PGA Championships. The 1957 PGA Champion was an automatic choice.*

1959 *Points standings from Aug. 1, 1957, through Sept. 7, 1959. Point values assigned were the same as in 1947.*

1963 *Selection based on two-year point standings through the 1963 PGA Championship.*

1969 *Team increased by two players to 12, and selection based primarily on points accrued from 1968 PGA Championship (July 18, 1968) through 1969 PGA Championship (Aug. 17, 1969). Candidates must have competed in two PGA Championships unless excused for reasons justified by the PGA Executive Committee*

1977 *Points earned from July 1976 through July 1977. Bonus points awarded for winning the 1976 PGA Championship and World Series of Golf. Automatic berths to winners of 1977 PGA Championship and World Series of Golf.*

1979 *Selections based on the top 12 players from the points list.*

1981 *Selections based on the top 11 players from the points list and the 1981 PGA Champion.*

1985 *Selections based on points from Jan. 1, 1985, through 1985 PGA Championship (Aug. 11, 1985). Bonus points awarded for PGA Championship, U.S. Open and Tournament Players Championship. The current U.S. Open and PGA Champions were automatic choices.*

1987 *Selections based on points from Jan. 1, 1986, through 1987 PGA Championship (Aug. 9, 1987). Bonus points awarded for 1986 and 1987 PGA Championships. The current U.S. Open and PGA Champions were automatic choices.*

1989 *For the first time, the U.S. Captain was given two nominations of his own, provided the PGA Champion already qualified; otherwise one choice. Bonus points were awarded for PGA Championship, U.S. Open, British Open and Masters. The 1989 PGA Champion was an automatic choice. U.S. Captain Raymond Floyd picked Lanny Wadkins and Tom Watson.*

1991 *The PGA Champion was no longer given an automatic berth. The U.S. Captain's two nominations continue, with Captain Dave Stockton choosing Chip Beck and Raymond Floyd.*

1993 *U.S. Captain Tom Watson chose Raymond Floyd and Lanny Wadkins to complete the 12-member team.*

The points system was changed to allow added "weight" to the current year and added importance to golf's four major championships: Masters, U.S. Open, British Open and PGA Championship.

The top-10 finishers in PGA sanctioned events and major championships were awarded points in the following increments:

| | "Regular" Events | | "Majors" | |
	1992	1993(x2)	1992(x3)	1993(x4)
1st	75	150	225	300
2nd	45	90	135	180
3rd	40	80	120	160
4th	35	70	105	140
5th	30	60	90	120
6th	25	50	75	100
7th	20	40	60	80
8th	15	30	45	60
9th	10	20	30	40
10th	5	10	15	20

If a player who was ineligible finished in one of these positions, no points were awarded for that position and no points were carried to the next position.

■ How The British, Great Britain-Ireland and European Ryder Cup Teams Have Been Chosen

1927 *The initial selection committee was comprised of Harry Vardon, James Braid and J.H. Taylor.*

1929 *Five-man selection committee.*

1931 *Three trial matches were held at Royal Lytham, Frilford Heath and Fulwell. The team was then chosen by a committee drawn from British PGA regions.*

1933 - 37 *Chosen by selection committee.*

1939 *Chosen by selection committee; Matches not played due to outbreak of World War II.*

1947 *Selection committee drew up a list of 14 candidates. The Match-Play champion earned an automatic berth.*

1949 *Selection committee agreed to use "List of Merit" in compiling a list of 16 candidates.*

1951 *Selection committee picked eight players, and the newly-organized Order of Merit (money list) acted as a guide. The final two berths were determined at the conclusion of the Match-Play Championship.*

1953 *Selection committee drawn from British PGA regions was replaced by a tournament committee. A list of 17 candidates was drawn from those who played a sequence of trial matches at Wentworth.*

1955 *Following a meeting with tournament players, the tournament committee determined that the first seven places would be filled from the Order of Merit following the British Open Championship. The remaining three places were determined by a British PGA tournament subcommittee in consultation with players already chosen.*

1957 *For the first time, the team was chosen by a points system. Points were awarded to top-20 finishers in all stroke-play events, including the British Open. Further points were awarded to top-10 finishers in the Dunlop Masters and the final 16 players in the Match-Play Championship.*

1959 *The top seven players in the Order of Merit earned automatic berths. The remaining three spots were filled by Match-Play champion and Dunlop Masters champion or, if already qualified, by ballot among team members and the British PGA sub-committee.*

1961 *The British Open and Match-Play champion were added to eight players selected from the Order of Merit. Eligibility was based on players competing in seven of the nine British PGA events.*

1963 *The points system was reintroduced. Points were awarded to top 40 players. The British Open and Match-Play champions earned automatic berths. No points were awarded for limited-field events such as the Dunlop Masters.*

1965 *The points system was extended over two seasons, beginning with the 1964 British Open through the 1965 Esso tournament. The British Open champion earned an automatic berth, and the remaining places were determined by the points system.*

1969 *The team was expanded to 12 players, but the selection process remained the same as in 1965, with the British Open champion earning an automatic berth, and the remaining places determined by the points system.*

1971 *Six players were automatic selections from the Order of Merit, and the remaining six chosen by selection committee.*

1973 *The points system ran from August 1972 to August 1973. Thirty points were awarded to winners of major British PGA tournaments. Additional points were awarded in increments of 24, 23, 22, down to one point for 25th place. Eight players were selected automatically, and four by invitation.*

1975 *The leading eight players from the Order of Merit were chosen. The remaining four were by invitation from a three-member selection committee chaired by Great Britain-Ireland Captain Bernard Hunt.*

1979 *The top 10 players from the money list earned berths, and two were selected by invitation. It was the first time in Ryder Cup history that players from Continental Europe were included.*

1983 *The entire 12-player team was chosen on the basis of finish in the Order of Merit.*

1985 *The top nine players from the Order of Merit list through the Benson and Hedges Open were automatic selections. The three other team members were chosen at the discretion of the European Captain.*

1995 *For the first time, European players' performances in U.S.-based major championships — the Masters, U.S. Open and PGA Championship — are used to determine the makeup of the European Ryder Cup Team. Player earnings in the U.S. major championships will be converted from dollars to pounds to make up the points list. The currency exchange rate is determined on the first day of each championship. Captains' selections are reduced to two players, and 10 automatic qualifiers through the Order of Merit standings complete the team.*

1995 FACTS AND FORMAT

DATES: Sept. 22-24

SITE: Oak Hill Country Club, Rochester, N.Y.

HONORARY CHAIRMAN:
Gary Schaal, Honorary President, PGA of America

U.S. CAPTAIN: Lanny Wadkins

EUROPEAN CAPTAIN: Bernard Gallacher

TENTATIVE TV SCHEDULE

The tentative television schedule for the 1995 Ryder Cup Matches is:

Friday, Sept. 22   USA Network 8:00 a.m. - 6:00 p.m. (ET)
Saturday, Sept. 23 NBC Sports 8:00 p.m. -12:30 a.m. (ET)
Sunday, Sept. 24 NBC Sports 9:00 a.m. - 3:30 p.m. (ET)

OAK HILL COUNTRY CLUB

At the 1991 Ryder Cup Matches, golfers throughout the world were introduced to the Ocean Course at Kiawah Island, S.C., where lush fairways blended with nature's marshland and sand dunes along the Atlantic Ocean.

Golfers will find another masterpiece during the 31st renewal of the Ryder Cup Matches, at Oak Hill Country Club in Rochester, N.Y. There, in scenic northwestern New York State, is one of the most unusual landmarks in golf: a natural amphitheater created from oak trees.

The Hill of Fame, located on the East Course, bears the imprint of another artist: the late Dr. John R. Williams, one of the nation's most respected research physicians. A member of Oak Hill and a self-taught arborist, Williams made it his personal project in 1926 to transform the bleak property primarily with oak trees.

From a pile of dying shrubs, Oak Hill today proudly displays over 80,000 trees, 34,000 of them on the East Course. The Hill of Fame, with its towering oaks, overlooks the par-5, 594-yard 13th hole.

Today, the Hill of Fame's U-shaped ridge honors 28 men and two women (Babe Didrikson Zaharias and Kathy Whitworth) for their contributions to the game.

Scottish-born architect Donald Ross was given the task of transforming Oak Hill into lush, rolling fairways and crowned greens that were once the crests of small hills. The East Course has been the site of four major championships. Each championship played at Oak Hill had its particular imprint in golf history.

- **1956 U.S. Open** — Cary Middlecoff captured the first U.S. Open played at Oak Hill by withstanding Ben Hogan's charge.

- **1968 U.S. Open** — Lee Trevino equaled what was then the 72-hole Open record with a 275 total.

- **1980 PGA Championship** — Jack Nicklaus was honored with his own plaque by capturing the only PGA Championship played at Oak Hill. Nicklaus took his fifth PGA Championship by what remains a record seven strokes and tied Walter Hagen for most PGA Championship victories.

- **1989 U.S. Open** — Curtis Strange became the first player in 38 years to win back-to-back Open championships.

Mighty oaks have remained constant at Oak Hill Country Club since its 1926 opening, but the course has seen its share of facelifts to accommodate the demands of hosting major championships.

For a five-year period (1972-77), the architectural team of George and Tom Fazio produced the most marked changes at Oak Hill. The Fazios lengthened some holes, adjusted others to minimize spectator logjams and eliminated several blind bunkers.

Still it is the Hill of Fame, above all of Oak Hill's splendor, that continues to inspire and attract golfers and golf fans.

THE TROPHY

In 1927, Samuel Ryder presented the Ryder Cup to the British PGA as the prize for an international competition between American and British professional golfers. The Ryder Cup is nearly 19 inches tall. The golfer depicted on top of the trophy is Abe Mitchell, Ryder's friend and private instructor.

RULES AND REGULATIONS

The Rules of Golf which govern play are determined by the United States Golf Association and applied by the PGA of America Board of Directors. The Matches are subject to the overall supervision of the board of directors and the PGA Rules Committee.

METHOD OF PLAY

Match Play, including foursomes (two-man teams in alternate shot), four-ball (two-man teams in better ball) and singles (18 holes at match play).

ELIGIBILITY

The 1995 U.S. Ryder Cup Team will be chosen on the basis of points, compiled by the PGA of America, which players accumulate from Jan. 12, 1994, through the 77th PGA Championship Aug. 10-13, 1995, at Riviera Country Club in Pacific Palisades, Calif. The top 10 finishers on the points list will qualify for the 12-man team, and U.S. Captain Lanny Wadkins will select the two final players. Points are awarded for top-10 finishes at PGA Tour co-sponsored events, with added emphasis on major championships and events played during the Ryder Cup year.

Only American-born players represent the U.S. team, as the result of a ruling in Chicago, by the Selection Committee, April 5, 1927. Players must be PGA members.

REVISED U.S. POINT SYSTEM

In 1991, the PGA of America changed the point system for selecting the United States Ryder Cup Team. The following method gives added weight to the "current" year and also attaches considerable importance to golf's four major championships: Masters, U.S. Open, British Open and PGA Championship.

| | "Regular" Events | | "Majors" | |
	1994	1995 (x2)	1994 (x3)	1995 (x4)
1st	75	150	225	300
2nd	45	90	135	180
3rd	40	80	120	160
4th	35	70	105	140
5th	30	60	90	120
6th	25	50	75	100
7th	20	40	60	80
8th	15	30	45	60
9th	10	20	30	40
10th	5	10	15	20

If a player who is ineligible finishes in one of these positions, no points are awarded for that position and no points are carried to the next position.

SPAIN IN 1997

As the Ryder Cup Matches grow in popularity worldwide, the event also expands its borders.

Spain will host the 32nd Ryder Cup Matches as the United States and Europe mark the debut of the biennial event in continental Europe, Sept. 26-28, 1997. A site for the historic renewal of the Matches has yet to be announced.

Spain began attracting the attention of the golf world with the meteoric rise of its native star, Seve Ballesteros, winner of 68 championships worldwide, including three British Open and two Masters championships. In 1994, Spain will host seven championships on the PGA European Tour.

■ OAK HILL COUNTRY CLUB

Official yardages used for the most recent major championship at Oak Hill Country Club - the 1989 U.S. Open. Ryder Cup official yardages will be released in early 1995.

HOLE	1	2	3	4	5	6	7	8	9	10	11	12	13	14	15	16	17	18
PAR	4	4	3	5	4	3	4	4	4	4	3	4	5	4	3	4	4	4
YARDS	440	401	211	570	406	167	431	430	419	432	192	372	594	323	177	439	458	440
Front Nine - 35 - 3,475						**Back Nine** - 35 - 3,427						**Totals** - 70 - 6,902						

■ JERRY LANSTON "LANNY" WADKINS - 1995 U.S. Ryder Cup Captain

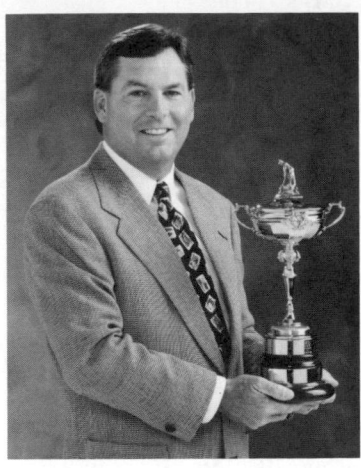

Birth Date: Dec. 5, 1949
Birthplace: Richmond, Va.
Education: Wake Forest University
Family: *Wife,* Penelope;
 Children, Jessica (10/14/73);
 Travis (8/25/87); Tucker (8/19/92)
Residence: Dallas, Texas;
 plays out of Mauna Lani, Hawaii
Turned Professional: 1971
Joined PGA Tour: Fall 1971
Elected to PGA of America: June 1, 1975
PGA Honors: PGA Player of the Year (1985)
Career Victories: 26
PGA Tour Career Earnings: $5,877,257
 (prior to 1994 season)

RYDER CUP RECORD

Years Played	Teams	Matches	Pts.	Won	Lost	Halved	Winning Pct.
1977-79-83-85-87-89-91-93	8	34	21.5	20	11	3	.632

Tournament Victories:
(26, including 21 on the PGA Tour)

1972 — Sahara Invitational

1973 — Byron Nelson Classic
 USI Classic

1977 — PGA Championship
 World Series of Golf

1978 — Canadian PGA
 Garden State PGA (Australia)

1979 — Glen Campbell Los Angeles Open
 Tournament Players Championship
 Bridgestone Open (Japan)

1982 — Phoenix Open
 MONY Tournament of Champions
 Buick Open

1983 — Greater Greensboro Open
 MONY Tournament of Champions

1984 — World Nissan Championship
 (Japan)

1985 — Bob Hope Classic
 Los Angeles Open
 Walt Disney World/Oldsmobile Classic

1987 — Doral-Ryder Open

1988 — Hawaiian Open
 Colonial National Invitation

1990 — Anheuser-Busch Golf Classic
 Fred Meyer Challenge
 (with Bobby Wadkins)

1991 — United Hawaiian Open

1992 — Canon Greater Hartford Open

Other Achievements:
- PGA Player of the Year (1985)
- Three-time World Cup Team member (1977, '84, '85)
- Two-time Walker Cup Team member (1969, '71)
- Member World Amateur Cup (1970)
- Team member, U.S. vs. Japan (1982, '83)
- Team member, 1985 Nissan Cup, 1987 Kirin Cup teams

■ BERNARD GALLACHER - 1995 European Ryder Cup Captain

Birthdate: Sept. 2, 1949
Birthplace: Bathgate, Scotland
Family: *Wife:* Lesley
 Children: Kirsty, Jamie, Laura Kate
Residence: Wentworth, England
Turned Professional: 1967
Career Earnings: £482,259

RYDER CUP RECORD

Years Played	Teams	Matches	Pts.	Won	Lost	Halved	Winning Pct.
1969-71-73-75-77-81-83	8	31	15.5	13	13	5	.500

Tournament Victories:
(21, including 14 on the European Tour)

1969 — Schweppes PGA Championship
 WD & HO Wills Open
 Kawacha Eagle Open (Zambia)
 Cock O' The North (Zambia)

1970 — Mufulira Open (Zambia)

1971 — Martini Open

1973 — Coca-Cola Young Professionals
 Championship
 Scottish Professional Championship

1974 — Carrolls Irish Open
 Dunlop Masters
 Scottish Professional Championship

1975 — Dunlop Masters

1977 — Spanish Open
 Scottish Professional Championship

1979 — French Open

1980 — Haig Whisky TPC

1981 — Cold Shield Greater Manchester Open

1982 — Martini International
 Jersey Open

1983 — Scottish Professional Championship

1984 — Jersey Open

Other Achievements:
- Five-time World Cup Team member (1969, '71, '74, '82, '83)
- Four-time Hennessey Cognac Cup Team member (1974, '78, '82, '84)
- Vardon Trophy winner (1969)
- Rookie of the Year (1968)
- Scottish Open Amateur Championship winner (1967)

1993

To erase the ghosts of frustrating past visits, the 1993 United States Ryder Cup Team — guided by Captain Tom Watson — needed something special while competing at The Belfry in Sutton Coldfield, England. The Americans had suffered a loss in 1985 and a tie in 1989 at The Belfry, a course which has much of the same characteristics as U.S. courses — narrow fairways and water hazards around most every turn.

Watson declared he wanted players with "the heart and guts" to play pressure golf.

Watson found the right combinations, including comeback singles victories by rookie Davis Love III and veteran Chip Beck to lead a 15-13 victory. "Our team had the biggest heart I've ever seen," said an emotional Watson.

The 30th Ryder Cup Matches may be remembered as some of the most outstanding golf from both U.S. and Europeans teams to have been played in the event. The Matches will equally be remembered for a grand stroke of sportsmanship by Lanny Wadkins, who made his eighth overall appearance as a wild-card Captain's selection. Wadkins sat out the final day's singles matches to allow a player who earned his way on the team to get the opportunity to compete. Wadkins asked Watson that his name be "placed in the envelope" when the news came late Saturday night that Europe's Sam Torrance could not compete due to an infected toe. Under Ryder Cup rules, if one team member can't compete, the other team must select a player to sit out the competition.

Watson had enough reserve firepower on his squad during the singles matches. Beck remained unbeaten in singles competition for his career (3-0) by rallying from a three-hole deficit to defeat England's Barry Lane, 1-up. Love, who suffered from putting woes throughout the week, edged Italy's Costantino Rocca, 1-up, making a six-foot par putt on the 18th green.

The Americans opened the final round trailing the Europeans, 8 1/2 to 7 1/2, before receiving inspiring performances by rookie Jim Gallagher Jr., who defeated Spain's Seve Ballesteros, 3 and 2; and by Tom Kite, who cruised past Germany's Bernhard Langer, 5 and 3. Raymond Floyd, the oldest Ryder Cup competitor in history at 51, defeated Spain's Jose Maria Olazabal, 2-up. Floyd roared down the finish, making three birdie putts on the back nine and nearly aced the par-3 14th hole in the process. Moments later at the 14th, England's Nick Faldo stole some of Floyd's thunder. Then the world's No. 1-ranked player, Faldo posted his fifth career hole-in-one in his match with PGA Champion Paul Azinger.

Azinger, however, rallied to halve the match by sinking a birdie putt on the 18th green. It was a rollercoaster performance by the Americans, who fell behind, 5-3, after the first day and dropped three of four Saturday morning foursome matches. The Americans bounced back with victories in the Saturday four-balls by the teams of Corey Pavin and Gallagher; Beck and John Cook; and Floyd and Payne Stewart.

Watson said Beck and Cook's victory over Faldo and Colin Montgomerie, a 2-up four-ball triumph, set the mood for a prosperous final day's competition. "It was the heart of the victory," said Watson. "We had the horse and the rider. Saturday was a night the players will always remember. We had a

night of revelry, of laughter, a night of just plain fun and it stemmed from Chip's and John's victory over Nick and Colin."

Europe's Peter Baker, at 25 the youngest player in the field, completed a remarkable three days' putting exhibition, with a 2-and-1 conquest of Pavin. Sweden's Joakim Haeggman downed Cook, 1-up. The U.S. then caught fire to close out the Matches, winning five of the remaining six matches and halving the other.

The triumph at The Belfry boosted the U.S. record in Ryder Cup Matches to 23 victories, five defeats and two ties.

1993 RYDER CUP TOTALS

UNITED STATES			EUROPE		
Player	Totals	Pts.	Player	Totals	Pts.
Tom Watson - Captain			Bernard Gallacher - Captain		
Paul Azinger	0-3-2	1	Peter Baker	3-1-0	3
Chip Beck	2-0-0	2	Seve Ballesteros	2-2-0	2
John Cook	1-1-0	1	Nick Faldo	2-1-2	3
Fred Couples	0-3-2	1	Joakim Haeggman	1-1-0	1
Raymond Floyd	3-1-0	3	Mark James	0-3-0	0
Jim Gallagher Jr.	2-1-0	2	Barry Lane	0-3-0	0
Lee Janzen	0-2-0	0	Bernhard Langer	2-2-2	2
Tom Kite	2-2-0	2	Colin Montgomerie	3-1-1	3.5
Davis Love III	2-2-0	2	Jose Maria Olazabal	2-3-0	2
Corey Pavin	3-2-0	3	Costantino Rocca	0-2-0	0
Payne Stewart	3-1-0	3	Sam Torrance	0-1-1	.5
Lanny Wadkins	2-1-1	2.5	Ian Woosnam	4-0-1	4.5

1993 U.S. Ryder Cup Team Final Point Standings

1.	Paul Azinger	1437.167
2.	Fred Couples	1030.500
3.	Tom Kite	998.333
4.	Lee Janzen	873.810
5.	Corey Pavin	842.500
6.	Payne Stewart	808.393
7.	John Cook	735.000
8.	Davis Love III	640.000
9.	Chip Beck	574.167
10.	Jim Gallagher Jr.	567.500

Captain's Selections:

	Raymond Floyd	(22nd, 377.500)
	Lanny Wadkins	(32nd, 290.000)

1993 European Ryder Cup Team Final Point Standings

1.	Bernhard Langer (Germany)	520,438.98
2.	Nick Faldo (England)	513,022.50
3.	Colin Montgomerie (Scotland)	482,003.08
4.	Costantino Rocca (Italy)	381,315.25
5.	Barry Lane (England)	379,440.75
6.	Ian Woosnam (Wales)	374,938.12
7.	Peter Baker (England)	362,659.17
8.	Mark James (England)	351,820.08
9.	Sam Torrance (Scotland)	326,929.20

Captain's Selections:

	Joakim Haeggman	(Sweden; 10th, 288,808.43)
	Jose Maria Olazabal	(Spain; 12th, 282,488.14)
	Seve Ballesteros	(Spain, 38th, 104,216.70)

1993

U.S. Captain Tom Watson declared he wanted players with "the heart and guts" to play pressure golf, and found the right combinations as the Americans mounted a memorable comeback by winning six singles matches and halving two. Led by rookie Davis Love III and veteran Chip Beck, the 15-13 victory was capped on the final day by Raymond Floyd sinking three birdie putts on the back nine to seal the triumph. Beck remained unbeaten in singles competition for his career (3-0) by rallying from a three-hole deficit to defeat England's Barry Lane, 1-up. Love, who suffered from putting woes throughout the week, edged Italy's Costantino Rocca, 1-up, making a six-foot par putt on the 18th green. The 51-year-old Floyd, the oldest Ryder Cup competitor in history, downed Spain's Jose Maria Olazabal in their singles match, 2-up.

	Site:	THE BELFRY (Brabazon Course)	
		Sutton Coldfield, England	
	Date:	Sept. 24-26	
	Results:	USA 15	Europe 13
	Captains:	United States -	Tom Watson
		Europe -	Bernard Gallacher

	Morning Foursomes	Afternoon Four-Balls	Morning Foursomes	Afternoon Four-Balls	Singles Matches
Europe	2	2 1/2	3	1	4 1/2
United States	2	1 1/2	1	3	7 1/2

United States Players
Paul Azinger   Lee Janzen
Chip Beck   Tom Kite
John Cook   Davis Love III
Fred Couples   Corey Pavin
Raymond Floyd*   Payne Stewart
Jim Gallagher Jr.   Lanny Wadkins*

European Players
Peter Baker   Bernhard Langer
Seve Ballesteros*   Colin Montgomerie
Nick Faldo   Jose Maria Olazabal*
Joakim Haeggman*   Costantino Rocca
Mark James   Sam Torrance
Barry Lane   Ian Woosnam

*Captain's picks

U.S. Team: *(Back Row, Left to Right) Chip Beck, Corey Pavin, Lanny Wadkins, Tom Kite, Payne Stewart, Jim Gallagher Jr., Raymond Floyd, Fred Couples. (Front Row, Left to Right) Lee Janzen, John Cook, Tom Watson (Captain), Paul Azinger, Davis Love III.*

UNITED STATES		EUROPE	
Morning Foursomes (Day One)			
Lanny Wadkins & Corey Pavin (4 and 3)	1	Sam Torrance & Mark James	0
Payne Stewart & Fred Couples	0	Ian Woosnam & Bernhard Langer (7 and 5)	1
Tom Kite & Davis Love III (2 and 1)	1	Seve Ballesteros & Jose Maria Olazabal	0
Raymond Floyd & Fred Couples	0	Nick Faldo & Colin Montgomerie (4 and 3)	1
Afternoon Four-Balls (Day One)			
Jim Gallagher Jr. & Corey Pavin	0	Ian Woosnam & Peter Baker (1-up)	1
Lanny Wadkins & Corey Pavin (4 and 2)	1	Bernhard Langer & Barry Lane	0
Paul Azinger & Fred Couples (halved)	1/2	Nick Faldo & Colin Montgomerie (halved)	1/2
Tom Kite & Davis Love III	0	Seve Ballesteros & Jose Maria Olazabal (4 and 3)	1
Day One Total	**3 1/2**	**Day One Total**	**4 1/2**
Morning Foursomes (Day Two)			
Lanny Wadkins & Corey Pavin	0	Nick Faldo & Colin Montgomerie (3 and 2)	1
Paul Azinger & Fred Couples	0	Ian Woosnam & Bernhard Langer (2 and 1)	1
Raymond Floyd & Payne Stewart (3 and 2)	1	Peter Baker and Barry Lane	0
Tom Kite & Davis Love III	0	Seve Ballesteros & Jose Maria Olazabal(2 and 1)	1
Afternoon Four-Balls (Day Two)			
John Cook & Chip Beck (2-up)	1	Nick Faldo & Colin Montgomerie	0
Corey Pavin & Jim Gallagher Jr.(5 and 4)	1	Mark James & Costantino Rocca	0
Paul Azinger & Fred Couples	0	Ian Woosnam & Peter Baker (6 and 5)	1
Raymond Floyd & Payne Stewart (2 and 1)	1	J. Olazabal & Joakim Haeggman	0
Day Two Total	**4**	**Day Two Total**	**4**
Two-Day Total	**7 1/2**	**Two-Day Total**	**8 1/2**
Singles (Day Three)			
Lanny Wadkins (halved, match not played)	1/2	Sam Torrance (injured; halved, match not played)	1/2
Chip Beck (1-up)	1	Barry Lane	0
Lee Janzen	0	Colin Montgomerie (1-up)	1
Corey Pavin	0	Peter Baker (2-up)	1
Fred Couples (halved)	1/2	Ian Woosnam (halved)	1/2
John Cook	0	Joakim Haeggman (1-up)	1
Payne Stewart (3 and 2)	1	Mark James	0
Davis Love III (1-up)	1	Costantino Rocca	0
Jim Gallagher Jr. (3 and 2)	1	Seve Ballesteros	0
Raymond Floyd (2-up)	1	Jose Maria Olazabal	0
Tom Kite (5 and 3)	1	Bernhard Langer	0
Paul Azinger (halved)	1/2	Nick Faldo (halved)	1/2
Day Three Total	**7 1/2**	**Day Three Total**	**4 1/2**

European Team: *(Back Row, Left to Right) Ian Woosnam, Jose Maria Olazabal, Barry Lane, Costantino Rocca, Peter Baker, Colin Montgomerie, Mark James, Sam Torrance. (Front Row, Left to Right) Joakim Haeggman, Seve Ballesteros, Bernard Gallacher (Captain), Nick Faldo, Bernhard Langer.*

UNITED STATES	15	EUROPE	13

1991

Germany's Bernhard Langer missed a six-foot par putt on the 18th hole at the Ocean Course in Kiawah Island, S.C., allowing the U.S. to escape with its first Ryder Cup victory since 1983. Langer's putt halved a match with Hale Irwin, who had chipped poorly only moments before and settled for a bogey. The U.S. won the final-day singles, 6½ to 5½. Lanny Wadkins and Fred Couples led the Americans by winning 3½ points, while Seve Ballesteros led the Europeans with 4½ out of a possible five points.

Site:	THE OCEAN COURSE,	
	Kiawah Island, S.C.	
Date:	Sept. 26-29	
Results:	USA 14½	Europe 13½
Captains:	United States -	Dave Stockton
	Europe -	Bernard Gallacher

	Morning Foursomes	Afternoon Four-balls	Morning Foursomes	Afternoon Four-balls	Singles Matches
Europe	1	2½	1	3½	5½
United States	3	1½	3	½	6½

United States Team
Paul Azinger
Chip Beck*
Mark Calcavecchia
Fred Couples
Raymond Floyd*
Hale Irwin

Wayne Levi
Mark O'Meara
Steve Pate
Corey Pavin
Payne Stewart
Lanny Wadkins

European Team
Seve Ballesteros
Paul Broadhurst
Nick Faldo*
David Feherty
David Gilford
Mark James*

Bernhard Langer
Colin Montgomerie
Jose Maria Olazabal*
Steven Richardson
Sam Torrance
Ian Woosnam

*Captain's picks

UNITED STATES | EUROPE

Morning Foursomes (Day One)

UNITED STATES		EUROPE	
Paul Azinger & Chip Beck	0	Seve Ballesteros & J.M. Olazabal (2 and 1)	1
Lanny Wadkins & Hale Irwin (4 and 2)	1	David Gilford & Colin Montgomerie	0
Fred Couples & Raymond Floyd (2 and 1)	1	Bernhard Langer & Mark James	0
Payne Stewart & Mark Calcavecchia (1 up)	1	Nick Faldo & Ian Woosnam	0

Afternoon Four-balls (Day One)

UNITED STATES		EUROPE	
Corey Pavin & Mark Calcavecchia	0	Steven Richardson & Mark James (5 and 4)	1
Lanny Wadkins & Mark O'Meara (halved)	½	Sam Torrance & David Feherty (halved)	½
Fred Couples & Raymond Floyd (5 and 3)	1	Nick Faldo & Ian Woosnam	0
Paul Azinger & Chip Beck	0	Seve Ballesteros & J.M. Olazabal (2 and 1)	1
Day One Total	**4½**	**Day One Total**	**3½**

Morning Foursomes (Day Two)

UNITED STATES		EUROPE	
Paul Azinger & Mark O'Meara (7 and 6)	1	Nick Faldo & David Gilford	0
Lanny Wadkins & Hale Irwin (4 and 2)	1	David Feherty & Sam Torrance	0
Payne Stewart & Mark Calcavecchia (1 up)	1	Mark James & Steven Richardson	0
Fred Couples & Raymond Floyd	0	Seve Ballesteros & J.M. Olazabal (3 and 2)	1

Afternoon Four-balls (Day Two)

UNITED STATES		EUROPE	
Paul Azinger & Hale Irwin	0	Ian Woosnam & Paul Broadhurst (2 and 1)	1
Corey Pavin & Steve Pate	0	Bernhard Langer & Colin Montgomerie (2 and 1)	1
Lanny Wadkins & Wayne Levi	0	Mark James & Steven Richardson (3 and 1)	1
Payne Stewart & Fred Couples (halved)	½	Seve Ballesteros & J.M. Olazabal (halved)	½
Day Two Total	**3½**	**Day Two Total**	**4½**
Two-Day Total	**8**	**Two-Day Total**	**8**

Singles (Day Three)

UNITED STATES		EUROPE	
Steve Pate (injured; halved, match not played)	½	David Gilford (halved, match not played)	½
Payne Stewart	0	David Feherty (2 and 1)	1
Raymond Floyd	0	Nick Faldo (2 up)	1
Mark Calcavecchia (halved)	½	Colin Montgomerie (halved)	½
Corey Pavin (2 and 1)	1	Steven Richardson	0
Wayne Levi	0	Seve Ballesteros (3 and 2)	1
Paul Azinger (2 up)	1	Jose Maria Olazabal	0
Chip Beck (3 and 1)	1	Ian Woosnam	0
Mark O'Meara	0	Paul Broadhurst (3 and 1)	1
Fred Couples (3 and 2)	1	Sam Torrance	0
Lanny Wadkins (3 and 2)	1	Mark James	0
Hale Irwin (halved)	½	Bernhard Langer (halved)	½
Day Three Total	**6½**	**Day Three Total**	**5½**

UNITED STATES	**14½**	**EUROPE**	**13½**

U.S. Team: (Back Row, Left to Right) Mark O'Meara, Fred Couples, Steve Pate, Corey Pavin, Wayne Levi, Mark Calcavecchia, Payne Stewart, Chip Beck. (Seated, Left to Right) Hale Irwin, Lanny Wadkins, Dave Stockton (Non-playing Captain), Paul Azinger, Raymond Floyd.

European Team: (Back Row, Left to Right) Severiano Ballesteros, Colin Montgomerie, Steven Richardson, Nick Faldo, Paul Broadhurst, David Feherty, Sam Torrance, Mark James. (Seated, Left to Right) David Gilford, Jose Maria Olazabal, Bernard Gallacher (Non-playing Captain), Bernhard Langer, Ian Woosnam.

1989

For only the second time in Ryder Cup history, the biennial matches were halved, 14-14. Because Europe won the 1987 Ryder Cup Matches at Muirfield Village in Dublin, Ohio, the Europeans retained the right of possession to the Cup. Jose Maria Olazabal led the Europeans with four victories and one half, while Paul Azinger and Chip Beck combined for a 6-1-1 record for the United States.

Site:	THE BELFRY, Brabazon Course	
	Sutton Coldfield, England	
Date:	Sept. 22-24	
Results:	Europe 14	USA 14
Captains:	United States -	Raymond Floyd
	Europe -	Tony Jacklin

	Morning Foursomes	Afternoon Four-balls	Morning Foursomes	Afternoon Four-balls	Singles Matches
Europe	1	4	2	2	5
United States	3	0	2	2	7

United States Team
Paul Azinger   Mark McCumber
Chip Beck   Mark O'Meara
Mark Calcavecchia   Payne Stewart
Fred Couples   Curtis Strange
Ken Green   Lanny Wadkins*
Tom Kite   Tom Watson*

European Team
Seve Ballesteros   Bernhard Langer*
Gordon Brand Jr.   Christy O'Connor Jr.*
Jose Maria Canizares   Jose Maria Olazabal
Howard Clark*   Ronan Rafferty
Nick Faldo   Sam Torrance
Mark James   Ian Woosnam

*Captain's picks

UNITED STATES		EUROPE	
Morning Foursomes (Day One)			
Curtis Strange & Tom Kite (halved)	½	Nick Faldo & Ian Woosnam (halved)	½
Payne Stewart & Lanny Wadkins (1 up)	1	Howard Clark & Mark James	0
Mark Calcavecchia & Ken Green (2 and 1)	1	Bernhard Langer & Ronan Rafferty	0
Tom Watson & Chip Beck (halved)	½	Seve Ballesteros & J.M. Olazabal (halved)	½
Afternoon Four-balls (Day One)			
Tom Watson & Mark O'Meara	0	Seve Ballesteros & J.M. Olazabal (6 and 5)	1
Lanny Wadkins & Fred Couples	0	Howard Clark & Mark James (3 and 2)	1
Curtis Strange & Paul Azinger	0	Sam Torrance & Gordon Brand Jr. (1 up)	1
Mark Calcavecchia & Mark McCumber	0	Nick Faldo & Ian Woosnam (2 up)	1
Day One Total	3	**Day One Total**	5
Morning Foursomes (Day Two)			
Chip Beck & Paul Azinger (4 and 3)	1	Gordon Brand Jr. & Sam Torrance	0
Lanny Wadkins & Payne Stewart	0	Ian Woosnam & Nick Faldo (3 and 2)	1
Mark Calcavecchia & Ken Green (3 and 2)	1	Ronan Rafferty & C. O'Connor Jr.	0
Curtis Strange & Tom Kite	0	Seve Ballesteros & J.M. Olazabal (1 up)	1
Afternoon Four-balls (Day Two)			
Chip Beck & Paul Azinger (2 and 1)	1	Nick Faldo & Ian Woosnam	0
Tom Kite & Mark McCumber (2 and 1)	1	Bernhard Langer & J.M. Canizares	0
Mark Calcavecchia & Ken Green	0	Seve Ballesteros & J.M. Olazabal (4 and 2)	1
Curtis Strange & Payne Stewart	0	Howard Clark & Mark James (1 up)	1
Day Two Total	4	**Day Two Total**	4
Two-Day Total	7	**Two-Day Total**	9
Singles (Day Three)			
Tom Kite (8 and 7)	1	Howard Clark	0
Chip Beck (3 and 1)	1	Bernhard Langer	0
Paul Azinger (1 up)	1	Seve Ballesteros	0
Mark O'Meara	0	Mark James (3 and 2)	1
Payne Stewart	0	Jose Maria Olazabal (1 up)	1
Mark Calcavecchia	0	Ronan Rafferty (1 up)	1
Fred Couples	0	Christy O'Connor Jr. (1 up)	1
Ken Green	0	Jose Maria Canizares (1 up)	1
Tom Watson (3 and 1)	1	Sam Torrance	0
Mark McCumber (1 up)	1	Gordon Brand Jr.	0
Lanny Wadkins (1 up)	1	Nick Faldo	0
Curtis Strange (2 up)	1	Ian Woosnam	0
Day Three Total	7	**Day Three Total**	5
UNITED STATES	**14**	**EUROPE**	**14**

U.S. Team: (Back Row, Left to Right) Chip Beck, Tom Kite, Ken Green, Tom Watson, Mark McCumber, Curtis Strange, Lanny Wadkins, Mark O'Meara. (Seated, Left to Right) Fred Couples, Paul Azinger, Raymond Floyd (Non-playing Captain), Payne Stewart, Mark Calcavecchia.

European Team: (Back Row, Left to Right) Mark James, Christy O'Connor Jr., Bernhard Langer, Tony Jacklin (Non-playing Captain) Severiano Ballesteros, Nick Faldo, Jose Maria Olazabal. (Seated, Left to Right) Gordon Brand Jr., Howard Clark, Ronan Rafferty, Ian Woosnam, Sam Torrance, Jose Maria Canizares.

1987

For the second time in a row and for the first time on American soil, the Europeans won in the 27th renewal of the Ryder Cup Matches. The Europeans took a 10½ to 5½ lead after the first two days. The U.S. Team fought back to capture 7½ points on the final day, but lost the matches. Ballesteros led the Europeans with four points.

Site:	MUIRFIELD VILLAGE GOLF CLUB, Dublin, Ohio	
Date:	Sept. 25-27	
Results:	Europe 15	USA 13
Captains:	United States -	Jack Nicklaus
	Europe -	Tony Jacklin

	Morning Foursomes	Afternoon Four-balls	Morning Foursomes	Afternoon Four-balls	Singles Matches
Europe	2	4	2½	2	4½
United States	2	0	1½	2	7½

United States Team
Andy Bean Dan Pohl
Mark Calcavecchia Scott Simpson
Ben Crenshaw Payne Stewart
Tom Kite Curtis Strange
Larry Mize Hal Sutton
Larry Nelson Lanny Wadkins

European Team
Seve Ballesteros Bernhard Langer
Gordon Brand Jr. Sandy Lyle*
Ken Brown* Jose Maria Olazabal*
Howard Clark Jose Rivero
Eamonn Darcy Sam Torrance
Nick Faldo Ian Woosnam

*Captain's picks

UNITED STATES		EUROPE	
Morning Foursomes (Day One)			
Curtis Strange & Tom Kite (4 and 2)	1	Sam Torrance & Howard Clark	0
Hal Sutton & Dan Pohl (2 and 1)	1	Ken Brown & Bernhard Langer	0
Lanny Wadkins & Larry Mize	0	Nick Faldo & Ian Woosnam (2 up)	1
Larry Nelson & Payne Stewart	0	Seve Ballesteros & J.M. Olazabal (1 up)	1
Afternoon Four-balls (Day One)			
Ben Crenshaw & Scott Simpson	0	Gordon Brand Jr. & Jose Rivero (3 and 2)	1
Andy Bean & Mark Calcavecchia	0	Sandy Lyle & Bernhard Langer (1 up)	1
Hal Sutton & Dan Pohl	0	Nick Faldo & Ian Woosnam (2 and 1)	1
Curtis Strange & Tom Kite	0	Seve Ballesteros & J.M. Olazabal (2 and 1)	1
Day One Total	**2**	**Day One Total**	**6**
Morning Foursomes (Day Two)			
Curtis Strange & Tom Kite (3 and 1)	1	Jose Rivero & Gordon Brand Jr.	0
Hal Sutton & Larry Mize (halved)	½	Nick Faldo & Ian Woosnam (halved)	½
Lanny Wadkins & Larry Nelson	0	Sandy Lyle & Bernhard Langer (2 and 1)	1
Ben Crenshaw & Payne Stewart	0	Seve Ballesteros & J.M. Olazabal (1 up)	1
Afternoon Four-balls (Day Two)			
Curtis Strange & Tom Kite	0	Nick Faldo & Ian Woosnam (5 and 4)	1
Andy Bean & Payne Stewart (3 and 2)	1	Eamonn Darcy & Gordon Brand Jr.	0
Hal Sutton & Larry Mize (2 and 1)	1	Seve Ballesteros & J.M. Olazabal	0
Lanny Wadkins & Larry Nelson	0	Sandy Lyle & Bernhard Langer (1 up)	1
Day Two Total	**3½**	**Day Two Total**	**4½**
Two-Day Total	**5½**	**Two-Day Total**	**10½**
Singles (Day Three)			
Andy Bean (1 up)	1	Ian Woosnam	0
Dan Pohl	0	Howard Clark (1 up)	1
Larry Mize (halved)	½	Sam Torrance (halved)	½
Mark Calcavecchia (1 up)	1	Nick Faldo	0
Payne Stewart (2 up)	1	Jose Maria Olazabal	0
Scott Simpson (2 and 1)	1	Jose Rivero	0
Tom Kite (3 and 2)	1	Sandy Lyle	0
Ben Crenshaw	0	Eamonn Darcy (1 up)	1
Larry Nelson (halved)	½	Bernhard Langer (halved)	½
Curtis Strange	0	Seve Ballesteros (2 and 1)	1
Lanny Wadkins (3 and 2)	1	Ken Brown	0
Hal Sutton (halved)	½	Gordon Brand Jr. (halved)	½
Day Three Total	**7½**	**Day Three Total**	**4½**
UNITED STATES	**13**	**EUROPE**	**15**

U.S. Team: (Back Row, Left to Right) Jack Nicklaus (Non-playing Captain), Larry Nelson, Ben Crenshaw, Curtis Strange, Lanny Wadkins, Hal Sutton, Tom Kite. (Seated, Left to Right) Mark Calcavecchia, Payne Stewart, Andy Bean, Scott Simpson, Dan Pohl, Larry Mize.

European Team: (Back Row, Left to Right) Tony Jacklin (Non-playing Captain), Gordon Brand Jr., Howard Clark, Sandy Lyle, Sam Torrance, Ken Brown, Bernhard Langer. (Seated, Left to Right) Eamonn Darcy, Severiano Ballesteros, Jose Rivero, Jose Maria Olazabal, Ian Woosnam, Nick Faldo.

1985

For the first time in 28 years, the United States was defeated, with Manuel Pinero leading the European charge with four points and Seve Ballesteros adding 3½ points.

	Site:	THE BELFRY, Brabazon Course
		Sutton Coldfield, England
	Date:	Sept. 13-15
	Results:	Europe 16½ USA 11½
	Captains:	United States - Lee Trevino
		Europe - Tony Jacklin

	Morning Foursomes	Afternoon Four-balls	Morning Foursomes	Afternoon Four-balls	Singles Matches
Europe	1	2½	2½	3	7½
United States	3	1½	1½	1	4½

United States Team
Ray Floyd	Mark O'Meara
Hubert Green	Craig Stadler
Peter Jacobsen	Hal Sutton
Tom Kite	Curtis Strange
Andy North	Lanny Wadkins
Calvin Peete	Fuzzy Zoeller

European Team
Seve Ballesteros	Sandy Lyle
Ken Brown*	Manuel Pinero
Jose Maria Canizares	Jose Rivero*
Howard Clark	Sam Torrance
Nick Faldo*	Paul Way
Bernhard Langer	Ian Woosnam

*Captain's picks

UNITED STATES		EUROPE	
Morning Foursomes (Day One)			
Curtis Strange & Mark O'Meara	0	Seve Ballesteros & Manuel Pinero (2 and 1)	1
Calvin Peete & Tom Kite (3 and 2)	1	Bernhard Langer & Nick Faldo	0
Lanny Wadkins & Ray Floyd (4 and 3)	1	Sandy Lyle & Ken Brown	0
Craig Stadler & Hal Sutton (3 and 2)	1	Howard Clark & Sam Torrance	0
Afternoon Four-balls (Day One)			
Fuzzy Zoeller & Hubert Green	0	Paul Way & Ian Woosnam (1 up)	1
Andy North & Peter Jacobsen	0	Seve Ballesteros & Manuel Pinero (2 and 1)	1
Craig Stadler & Hal Sutton (halved)	½	Bernhard Langer & J.M. Canizares (halved)	½
Ray Floyd & Lanny Wadkins (1 up)	1	Sam Torrance & Howard Clark	0
Day One Total	4½	**Day One Total**	3½
Morning Four-balls (Day Two)			
Tom Kite & Andy North	0	Sam Torrance & Howard Clark (2 and 1)	1
Hubert Green & Fuzzy Zoeller	0	Paul Way & Ian Woosnam (4 and 3)	1
Mark O'Meara & Lanny Wadkins (3 and 2)	1	Seve Ballesteros & Manuel Pinero	0
Craig Stadler & Curtis Strange (halved)	½	Bernhard Langer & Sandy Lyle (halved)	½
Afternoon Foursomes (Day Two)			
Tom Kite & Calvin Peete	0	J.M. Canizares & Jose Rivero (7 and 5)	1
Craig Stadler & Hal Sutton	0	Seve Ballesteros & Manuel Pinero (5 and 4)	1
Curtis Strange & Peter Jacobsen (4 and 2)	1	Paul Way & Ian Woosnam	0
Ray Floyd & Lanny Wadkins	0	Bernhard Langer & Ken Brown (3 and 2)	1
Day Two Total	2½	**Day Two Total**	5½
Two-Day Total	7	**Two-Day Total**	9
Singles (Day Three)			
Lanny Wadkins	0	Manuel Pinero (3 and 1)	1
Craig Stadler (2 and 1)	1	Ian Woosnam	0
Ray Floyd	0	Paul Way (2 up)	1
Tom Kite (halved)	½	Seve Ballesteros (halved)	½
Peter Jacobsen	0	Sandy Lyle (3 and 2)	1
Hal Sutton	0	Bernhard Langer (5 and 4)	1
Andy North	0	Sam Torrance (1 up)	1
Mark O'Meara	0	Howard Clark (1 up)	1
Calvin Peete (1 up)	1	Jose Rivero	0
Hubert Green (3 and 1)	1	Nick Faldo	0
Fuzzy Zoeller	0	Jose Maria Canizares (2 up)	1
Curtis Strange (4 and 2)	1	Ken Brown	0
Day Three Total	4½	**Day Three Total**	7½
UNITED STATES	**11½**	**EUROPE**	**16½**

U.S. Team: *(Left to Right) Lee Trevino (Non-playing Captain), Lanny Wadkins, Craig Stadler, Fuzzy Zoeller, Calvin Peete, Mark O'Meara, Hubert Green, Andy North, Peter Jacobsen, Raymond Floyd, Hal Sutton, Curtis Strange, Tom Kite.*

European Team: *(Back Row, Left to Right) Sam Torrance, Severiano Ballesteros, Ken Brown, Nick Faldo, Sandy Lyle, Howard Clark, Jose Maria Canizares, Manuel Pinero. (Seated, Left to Right) Paul Way, Ian Woosnam, Tony Jacklin (Non-playing Captain), Bernhard Langer, Jose Rivero.*

1983

With Tony Jacklin leading the Europeans and Jack Nicklaus leading the Americans, the teams were tied 8-8 after the first two days. The teams were deadlocked after the first 10 singles matches, and Lanny Wadkins was 1-down going into 18 against Jose Maria Canizares when he birdied the par-5 final hole — after hitting a 60-yard pitching wedge to within a foot — to halve the match. This put the Ryder Cup into the hands of Tom Watson who was handling Bernard Gallacher. A bogey-4 on 17 by Watson won the hole and secured America's closest victory since 1953.

Site:	PGA NATIONAL GOLF CLUB, Palm Beach Gardens, Fla.	
Date:	Oct. 14-16	
Results:	USA 14½	Europe 13½
Captains:	United States -	Jack Nicklaus
	Europe -	Tony Jacklin

	Morning Foursomes	Afternoon Four-balls	Morning Foursomes	Afternoon Four-balls	Singles Matches
Europe	2	2½	1½	2	5½
United States	2	1½	2½	2	6½

United States Team
Ben Crenshaw — Calvin Peete
Ray Floyd — Craig Stadler
Bob Gilder — Curtis Strange
Jay Haas — Lanny Wadkins
Tom Kite — Tom Watson
Gil Morgan — Fuzzy Zoeller

European Team
Seve Ballesteros — Bernhard Langer
Gordon Brand Sr. — Sandy Lyle
Ken Brown — Sam Torrance
Jose Maria Canizares — Brian Waites
Nick Faldo — Paul Way
Bernard Gallacher — Ian Woosnam

UNITED STATES / EUROPE

Morning Foursomes (Day One)
UNITED STATES		EUROPE	
Tom Watson & Ben Crenshaw (5 and 4)	1	Bernard Gallacher & Sandy Lyle	0
Lanny Wadkins & Craig Stadler	0	Nick Faldo & Bernhard Langer (4 and 2)	1
Tom Kite & Calvin Peete (2 and 1)	1	Seve Ballesteros & Paul Way	0
Ray Floyd & Bob Gilder	0	J.M. Canizares & Sam Torrance (4 and 3)	1

Afternoon Four-balls (Day One)
UNITED STATES		EUROPE	
Gil Morgan & Fuzzy Zoeller	0	Brian Waites & Ken Brown (2 and 1)	1
Tom Watson & Jay Haas (2 and 1)	1	Nick Faldo & Bernhard Langer	0
Ray Floyd & Curtis Strange	0	Seve Ballesteros & Paul Way (1 up)	1
Ben Crenshaw & Calvin Peete (halved)	½	Sam Torrance & Ian Woosnam (halved)	½
Day One Total	**3½**	**Day One Total**	**4½**

Morning Four-balls (Day Two)
UNITED STATES		EUROPE	
Lanny Wadkins & Craig Stadler (1 up)	1	Brain Waites & Ken Brown	0
Ben Crenshaw & Calvin Peete	0	Nick Faldo & Bernhard Langer (4 and 2)	1
Gil Morgan & Jay Haas (halved)	½	Seve Ballesteros & Paul Way (halved)	½
Tom Watson & Bob Gilder (5 and 4)	1	Sam Torrance & Ian Woosnam	0

Afternoon Foursomes (Day Two)
UNITED STATES		EUROPE	
Tom Kite & Ray Floyd	0	Nick Faldo & Bernhard Langer (3 and 2)	1
Jay Haas & Curtis Strange (3 and 2)	1	Brian Waites & Ken Brown	0
Gil Morgan & Lanny Wadkins (7 and 5)	1	Sam Torrance & J.M. Canizares	0
Tom Watson & Bob Gilder	0	Seve Ballesteros & Paul Way (2 and 1)	1
Day Two Total	**4½**	**Day Two Total**	**3½**
Two-Day Total	**8**	**Two-Day Total**	**8**

Singles (Day Three)
UNITED STATES		EUROPE	
Fuzzy Zoeller (halved)	½	Seve Ballesteros (halved)	½
Jay Haas	0	Nick Faldo (2 and 1)	1
Gil Morgan	0	Bernhard Langer (2 up)	1
Bob Gilder (2 up)	1	Gordon Brand Sr.	0
Ben Crenshaw (3 and 1)	1	Sandy Lyle	0
Calvin Peete (1 up)	1	Brian Waites	0
Curtis Strange	0	Paul Way (2 and 1)	1
Tom Kite (halved)	½	Sam Torrance (halved)	½
Craig Stadler (3 and 2)	1	Ian Woosnam	0
Lanny Wadkins (halved)	½	J.M. Canizares (halved)	½
Ray Floyd	0	Ken Brown (4 and 3)	1
Tom Watson (2 and 1)	1	Bernard Gallacher	0
Day Three Total	**6½**	**Day Three Total**	**5½**

UNITED STATES	14½	EUROPE	13½

U.S. Team: *(Back Row, Left to Right) Craig Stadler, Jay Haas, Gil Morgan, Bob Gilder, Jack Nicklaus (Non-playing Captain), Tom Watson, Raymond Floyd, Curtis Strange, Fuzzy Zoeller. (Front Row, Left to Right) Tom Kite, Ben Crenshaw, Calvin Peete, Lanny Wadkins.*

European Team: *(Left to Right) Nick Faldo, Sandy Lyle, Gordon Brand, Bernhard Langer, Sam Torrance, Ian Woosnam, Tony Jacklin (Non-playing Captain), Paul Way, Bernard Gallacher, Severiano Ballesteros, Jose Maria Canizares, Brian Waites, Ken Brown.*

1981

For the 16th time in 24 matches, the U. S. won by five or more points. Larry Nelson continued his unbeaten Ryder Cup play and won four matches. However, this would be the last time an American team would dominate the Ryder Cup Matches.

Site:	WALTON HEATH GOLF CLUB, Surrey, England	
Date:	Sept. 18-20	
Results:	USA 18½	Europe 9½
Captains:	United States -	Dave Marr
	Europe -	John Jacobs

	Morning Foursomes	Afternoon Four-balls	Morning Foursomes	Afternoon Four-balls	Singles Matches
Europe	2	2½	1	0	4
United States	2	1½	3	4	8

United States Team

Ben Crenshaw	Larry Nelson
Ray Floyd	Jack Nicklaus
Hale Irwin	Jerry Pate
Tom Kite	Bill Rogers
Bruce Lietzke	Lee Trevino
Johnny Miller	Tom Watson

European Team

Jose Maria Canizares	Bernhard Langer
Howard Clark	Sandy Lyle
Eamonn Darcy	Peter Oosterhuis*
Nick Faldo	Manuel Pinero
Bernard Gallacher	Des Smyth
Mark James*	Sam Torrance

*Captain's picks

UNITED STATES		EUROPE	
Morning Foursomes (Day One)			
Lee Trevino & Larry Nelson (1 up)	1	Bernhard Langer & Manuel Pinero	0
Bill Rogers & Bruce Lietzke	0	Sandy Lyle & Mark James (2 and 1)	1
Hale Irwin & Ray Floyd	0	Bernard Gallacher & Des Smyth (3 and 2)	1
Tom Watson & Jack Nicklaus (4 and 3)	1	Peter Oosterhuis & Nick Faldo	0
Afternoon Four-balls (Day One)			
Tom Kite & Johnny Miller (halved)	½	Sam Torrance & Howard Clark (halved)	½
Ben Crenshaw & Jerry Pate	0	Sandy Lyle & Mark James (3 and 2)	1
Bill Rogers & Bruce Lietzke	0	Des Smyth & Jose Maria Canizares (6 and 5)	1
Hale Irwin & Ray Floyd (2 and 1)	1	Bernard Gallacher & Eamonn Darcy	0
Day One Total	3½	**Day One**	4½
Morning Four-balls (Day Two)			
Lee Trevino & Jerry Pate (7 and 5)	1	Nick Faldo & Sam Torrance	0
Larry Nelson & Tom Kite (1 up)	1	Sandy Lyle & Mark James	0
Ray Floyd & Hale Irwin	0	Bernhard Langer & Manuel Pinero (2 and 1)	1
Jack Nicklaus & Tom Watson (3 and 2)	1	Jose Maria Canizares & Des Smyth	0
Afternoon Foursomes (Day Two)			
Lee Trevino & Jerry Pate (2 and 1)	1	Peter Oosterhuis & Sam Torrance	0
Jack Nicklaus & Tom Watson (3 and 2)	1	Bernhard Langer & Manuel Pinero	0
Bill Rogers & Ray Floyd (3 and 2)	1	Sandy Lyle & Mark James	0
Tom Kite & Larry Nelson (3 and 2)	1	Des Smyth & Bernard Gallacher	0
Day Two Total	7	**Day Two Total**	1
Two-Day Total	10½	**Two-Day Total**	5½
Singles (Day Three)			
Lee Trevino (5 and 3)	1	Sam Torrance	0
Tom Kite (3 and 2)	1	Sandy Lyle	0
Bill Rogers (halved)	½	Bernard Gallacher (halved)	½
Larry Nelson (2 up)	1	Mark James	0
Ben Crenshaw (6 and 4)	1	Des Smyth	0
Bruce Lietzke (halved)	½	Bernhard Langer (halved)	½
Jerry Pate	0	Manuel Pinero (4 and 2)	1
Hale Irwin (1 up)	1	Jose Maria Canizares	0
Johnny Miller	0	Nick Faldo (2 and 1)	1
Tom Watson	0	Howard Clark (4 and 3)	1
Ray Floyd (1 up)	1	Peter Oosterhuis	0
Jack Nicklaus (5 and 3)	1	Eamonn Darcy	0
Day Three Total	8	**Day Three Total**	4
UNITED STATES	18½	**EUROPE**	9½

U.S. Team: (Back Row, Left to Right) Ben Crenshaw, Jerry Pate, Raymond Floyd, Bruce Lietzke, Johnny Miller, Hale Irwin, Larry Nelson, Tom Kite. (Front Row, Left to Right) Lee Trevino, Tom Watson, Dave Marr (Non-playing Captain), Jack Nicklaus, Bill Rogers.

European Team: (Back Row, Left to Right) Bernard Gallacher, Jose Maria Canizares, Mark James, Sandy Lyle, Eamonn Darcy, Des Smyth, Bernhard Langer, Manuel Pinero. (Front Row, Left to Right) Nick Faldo, Peter Oosterhuis, John Jacobs (Non-playing Captain), Sam Torrance, Howard Clark.

1979

The final format change made the matches worth 28 points with eight foursomes, eight four-balls, and 12 singles. Most importantly, though, the British side expanded to become a European team. Even with the change, the U.S. took the match. Larry Nelson won five matches, four of which were against Seve Ballesteros.

Site:	THE GREENBRIER,	
	White Sulphur Springs, W. Va.	
Date:	Sept. 14-16	
Results:	USA 17	Europe 11
Captains:	United States -	Billy Casper
	Europe -	John Jacobs

	Morning Four-balls	Afternoon Foursomes	Morning Foursomes	Afternoon Four-balls	Singles Matches
Europe	1	1½	3	2	3½
United States	3	2½	1	2	8½

United States Team
Andy Bean   John Mahaffey
Lee Elder   Gil Morgan
Hubert Green   Larry Nelson
Mark Hayes   Lee Trevino
Hale Irwin   Lanny Wadkins
Tom Kite   Fuzzy Zoeller

European Team
Seve Ballesteros   Tony Jacklin
Brian Barnes   Mark James
Ken Brown   Michael King
Nick Faldo   Sandy Lyle
Bernard Gallacher   Peter Oosterhuis*
Antonio Garrido   Des Smyth*

*Captain's picks

UNITED STATES		EUROPE	
Morning Four-balls (Day One)			
Lanny Wadkins & Larry Nelson (2 and 1)	1	Antonio Garrido & S. Ballesteros	0
Lee Trevino & Fuzzy Zoeller (3 and 2)	1	Ken Brown & Mark James	0
Andy Bean & Lee Elder (2 and 1)	1	Peter Oosterhuis & Nick Faldo	0
Hale Irwin & John Mahaffey	0	Bernard Gallacher & Brian Barnes (2 and 1)	1
Afternoon Foursomes (Day One)			
Hale Irwin & Tom Kite (7 and 6)	1	Ken Brown & Des Smyth	0
Fuzzy Zoeller & Hubert Green	0	Seve Ballesteros & A. Garrido (3 and 2)	1
Lee Trevino & Gil Morgan (halved)	½	Sandy Lyle & Tony Jacklin (halved)	½
Lanny Wadkins & Larry Nelson (4 and 3)	1	Bernard Gallacher & Brian Barnes	0
Day One Total	5½	**Day One Total**	2½
Morning Foursomes (Day Two)			
Lee Elder & John Mahaffey	0	Tony Jacklin & Sandy Lyle (5 and 4)	1
Andy Bean & Tom Kite	0	Nick Faldo & Peter Oosterhuis (6 and 5)	1
Fuzzy Zoeller & Mark Hayes	0	Bernard Gallacher & Brian Barnes (2 and 1)	1
Lanny Wadkins & Larry Nelson (3 and 2)	1	Seve Ballesteros & A. Garrido	0
Afternoon Four-balls (Day Two)			
Lanny Wadkins & Larry Nelson (5 and 4)	1	Seve Ballesteros & A. Garrido	0
Hale Irwin & Tom Kite (1 up)	1	Tony Jacklin & Sandy Lyle	0
Lee Trevino & Fuzzy Zoeller	0	Bernard Gallacher & Brian Barnes (3 and 2)	1
Lee Elder & Mark Hayes	0	Nick Faldo & Peter Oosterhuis (1 up)	1
Day Two Total	3	**Day Two Total**	5
Two-Day Total	8½	**Two-Day Total**	7½
Singles (Day Three)			
Lanny Wadkins	0	Bernard Gallacher (3 and 2)	1
Larry Nelson (3 and 2)	1	Seve Ballesteros	0
Tom Kite (1 up)	1	Tony Jacklin	0
Mark Hayes (1 up)	1	Antonio Garrido	0
Andy Bean (4 and 3)	1	Michael King	0
John Mahaffey (1 up)	1	Brian Barnes	0
Lee Elder	0	Nick Faldo (3 and 2)	1
Hale Irwin (5 and 3)	1	Des Smyth	0
Hubert Green (2 up)	1	Peter Oosterhuis	0
Fuzzy Zoeller	0	Ken Brown (1 up)	1
Lee Trevino (2 and 1)	1	Sandy Lyle	0
Gil Morgan (halved, match not played)	½	Mark James (injured, halved, match not played)	½
Day Three Total	8½	**Day Three Total**	3½
UNITED STATES	**17**	**EUROPE**	**11**

U.S. Team: (Back Row, Left to Right) Mark Hayes, Larry Nelson, Lee Trevino, Fuzzy Zoeller, Lee Elder, Hubert Green, John Mahaffey, Lanny Wadkins, Gil Morgan, Hale Irwin, Tom Kite, Andy Bean. (Front Row, Left to Right) Mark Kizziar (PGA Treasurer), Joe Black (PGA Secretary), Frank Cardi (PGA President), Billy Casper (Non-playing Captain), Don Padgett (PGA Honorary President), Mark Cox (PGA Executive Director)

European Team: (Left to Right) Tony Jacklin, Sandy Lyle, Mark James, Ken Brown, Peter Oosterhuis, Nick Faldo, John Jacobs (Non-playing Captain), Michael King, Brian Barnes, Severiano Ballesteros, Anthony Garrido, Bernard Gallacher, Des Smyth.

1977

In another format change, this match consisted of five foursomes the first day, five four-balls on the second day, and 10 singles on the last day for a total of 20 points. Even this change made no difference to the outcome. The Great Britain & Ireland Team trailed 7 1/2 - 2 1/2 after the first two days. Although they went on to split the singles, it was too little too late.

Site:	ROYAL LYTHAM & ST. ANNES,
	St. Annes, England
Date:	Sept. 15-17
Results:	USA 12 1/2 GBI 7 1/2
Captains:	United States - Dow Finsterwald
	Great Britain & Ireland - Brian Huggett

Foursome Matches: USA 3 1/2 GBI 1 1/2

Four-ball Matches: USA 4 GBI 1   **Singles Matches:** USA 5 GBI 5

United States Team		Great Britain & Ireland Team	
Ray Floyd	Jerry McGee	Brian Barnes	Nick Faldo
Lou Graham	Jack Nicklaus	Ken Brown	Bernard Gallacher
Hubert Green	Ed Sneed	Howard Clark	Tommy Horton
Dave Hill	Dave Stockton	Neil Coles	Tony Jacklin
Hale Irwin	Lanny Wadkins	Eamonn Darcy	Mark James
Don January	Tom Watson	Peter Dawson	Peter Oosterhuis

UNITED STATES		GREAT BRITAIN/IRELAND	
Foursomes (Day One)			
Lanny Wadkins & Hale Irwin (3 and 1)	1	Bernard Gallacher & Brian Barnes	0
Dave Stockton & Jerry McGee (1 up)	1	Neil Coles & Peter Dawson	0
Ray Floyd & Lou Graham	0	Nick Faldo & Peter Oosterhuis (2 and 1)	1
Ed Sneed & Don January (halved)	1/2	Eamonn Darcy & Tony Jacklin (halved)	1/2
Jack Nicklaus & Tom Watson (5 and 4)	1	Tommy Horton & Mark James	0
Day One Total	**3 1/2**	**Day One Total**	**1 1/2**
Four-balls (Day Two)			
Tom Watson & Hubert Green (5 and 4)	1	Brian Barnes & Tommy Horton	0
Ed Sneed & Lanny Wadkins (5 and 3)	1	Neil Coles & Peter Dawson	0
Jack Nicklaus & Ray Floyd	0	Nick Faldo & Peter Oosterhuis (3 and 1)	1
Dave Hill & Dave Stockton (5 and 3)	1	Tony Jacklin & Eamonn Darcy	0
Hale Irwin & Lou Graham (1 up)	1	Mark James & Ken Brown	0
Day Two Total	**4**	**Day Two Total**	**1**
Two-Day Total	**7 1/2**	**Two-Day Total**	**2 1/2**
Singles (Day Three)			
Lanny Wadkins (4 and 3)	1	Howard Clark	0
Lou Graham (5 and 3)	1	Neil Coles	0
Don January	0	Peter Dawson (5 and 4)	1
Hale Irwin	0	Brian Barnes (1 up)	1
Dave Hill (5 and 4)	1	Tommy Horton	0
Jack Nicklaus	0	Bernard Gallacher (1 up)	1
Hubert Green (1 up)	1	Eamonn Darcy	0
Ray Floyd (2 and 1)	1	Mark James	0
Tom Watson	0	Nick Faldo (1 up)	1
Jerry McGee	0	Peter Oosterhuis (2 up)	1
Day Three Total	**5**	**Day Three Total**	**5**
UNITED STATES	**12 1/2**	**GREAT BRITAIN/IRELAND**	**7 1/2**

U.S. Team: (Left to Right) Raymond Floyd, Lou Graham, Hubert Green, Dave Hill, Hale Irwin, Don January, Dow Finsterwald (Non-playing Captain), Jerry McGee, Jack Nicklaus, Ed Sneed, Dave Stockton, Lanny Wadkins, Tom Watson.

Great Britain-Ireland Team: (Left to Right) Neil Coles, Brian Barnes, Peter Dawson, Peter Oosterhuis, Eamonn Darcy, Tony Jacklin, Ken Brown, Bernard Gallacher, Tommy Horton, Brian Huggett (Non-playing Captain), Nick Faldo, Mark James, Howard Clark.

1975

In another rout for the U. S., this match was memorable because of Jack Nicklaus' two losses to Brian Barnes, who smoked a pipe and wore shorts during play. Hale Irwin led the way for the Americans with 4½ points.

<table>
<tr><td></td><td>Morning Foursomes</td><td>Afternoon Foursomes</td><td>Morning Four-balls</td><td>Afternoon Four-balls</td><td>Morning Singles</td><td>Afternoon Singles</td></tr>
<tr><td>G.B. & Ireland</td><td>0</td><td>1½</td><td>1</td><td>1</td><td>3</td><td>4½</td></tr>
<tr><td>United States</td><td>4</td><td>2½</td><td>3</td><td>3</td><td>5</td><td>3½</td></tr>
</table>

United States Team	
Billy Casper	Johnny Miller
Ray Floyd	Bob Murphy
Al Geiberger	Jack Nicklaus
Lou Graham	J.C. Snead
Hale Irwin	Lee Trevino
Gene Littler	Tom Weiskopf

Great Britain & Ireland Team	
Brian Barnes	Guy Hunt
Maurice Bembridge	Tony Jacklin
Eamonn Darcy	Christy O'Connor Jr.
Bernard Gallacher	John O'Leary
Tommy Horton	Peter Oosterhuis
Brian Huggett	Norman Wood

Site:	LAUREL VALLEY GOLF CLUB, Ligonier, Pa.	
Date:	Sept. 19-21	
Results:	USA 21	GBI 11
Captains:	United States -	Arnold Palmer
	Great Britain & Ireland -	Bernard Hunt

UNITED STATES		GREAT BRITAIN/IRELAND	
Morning Foursomes (Day One)			
Jack Nicklaus & Tom Weiskopf (5 and 4)	1	Brian Barnes & Bernard Gallacher	0
Gene Littler & Hale Irwin (4 and 3)	1	Norman Wood & Maurice Bembridge	0
Al Geiberger & Johnny Miller (3 and 1)	1	Tony Jacklin & Peter Oosterhuis	0
Lee Trevino & J.C. Snead (2 and 1)	1	Tommy Horton & John O'Leary	0
Afternoon Four-balls (Day One)			
Billy Casper & Ray Floyd	0	Peter Oosterhuis & Tony Jacklin (2 and 1)	1
Tom Weiskopf & Lou Graham (3 and 2)	1	Eamonn Darcy & C. O'Connor Jr.	0
Jack Nicklaus & Bob Murphy (halved)	½	Brian Barnes & Bernard Gallacher (halved)	½
Lee Trevino & Hale Irwin (2 and 1)	1	Tommy Horton & John O'Leary	0
Day One Total	**6½**	**Day One Total**	**1½**
Morning Four-balls (Day Two)			
Billy Casper & Johnny Miller (halved)	½	Peter Oosterhuis & Tony Jacklin (halved)	½
Jack Nicklaus & J.C. Snead (4 and 2)	1	Tommy Horton & Norman Wood	0
Gene Littler & Lou Graham (5 and 3)	1	Brian Barnes & Bernard Gallacher	0
Al Geiberger & Ray Floyd (halved)	½	Eamonn Darcy & Guy Hunt (halved)	½
Afternoon Foursomes (Day Two)			
Lee Trevino & Bob Murphy	0	Tony Jacklin & Brian Huggett (3 and 2)	1
Tom Weiskopf & Johnny Miller (5 and 3)	1	C. O'Connor Jr. & John O'Leary	0
Hale Irwin & Billy Casper (3 and 2)	1	P. Oosterhuis & M. Bembridge	0
Al Geiberger & Lou Graham (3 and 2)	1	Eamonn Darcy & Guy Hunt	0
Day Two Total	**6**	**Day Two Total**	**2**
Two-Day Total	**12½**	**Two-Day Total**	**3½**
Morning Singles (Day Three)			
Bob Murphy (2 and 1)	1	Tony Jacklin	0
Johnny Miller	0	Peter Oosterhuis (2 up)	1
Lee Trevino (halved)	½	Bernard Gallacher (halved)	½
Hale Irwin (halved)	½	Tommy Horton (halved)	½
Gene Littler (4 and 2)	1	Brian Huggett	0
Billy Casper (3 and 2)	1	Eamonn Darcy	0
Tom Weiskopf (5 and 3)	1	Guy Hunt	0
Jack Nicklaus	0	Brian Barnes (4 and 2)	1
Afternoon Singles (Day Three)			
Ray Floyd (1 up)	1	Tony Jacklin	0
J.C. Snead	0	Peter Oosterhuis (3 and 2)	1
Al Geiberger (halved)	½	Bernard Gallacher (halved)	½
Lou Graham	0	Tommy Horton (2 and 1)	1
Hale Irwin (2 and 1)	1	John O'Leary	0
Bob Murphy (2 and 1)	1	Maurice Bembridge	0
Lee Trevino	0	Norman Wood (2 and 1)	1
Jack Nicklaus	0	Brian Barnes (2 and 1)	1
Day Three Total	**8½**	**Day Three Total**	**7½**
UNITED STATES	**21**	**GREAT BRITAIN/IRELAND**	**11**

U.S. Team: (Back Row, Left to Right) Jack Nicklaus, Hale Irwin, Lee Trevino, Arnold Palmer (Non-playing Captain), Bob Murphy, Lou Graham, Gene Littler. (Front Row, Left to Right) Billy Casper, Al Geiberger, Tom Weiskopf, Johnny Miller, J.C. Snead, Raymond Floyd.

Great Britain-Ireland Team: (Left to Right) Geoffrey Hunt, Brian Huggett, Maurice Bembridge, Bernard Gallacher, Tommy Horton, Tony Jacklin, Bernard Hunt (Non-playing Captain), Christy O'Connor Jr., Norman Wood, Eamonn Darcy, John O'Leary, Brian Barnes, Peter Oosterhuis.

1973

For the first time in Ryder Cup history, the matches were held in Scotland, and players from the Republic of Ireland were eligible. After the second day, it was like a replay of the '69 matches with everything square at eight points each. The U.S. won the singles 11-5 to take the Cup for the 16th time. Leading the charge for the U.S. were Jack Nicklaus with 4½ points and Lee Trevino with four points.

Site:	MUIRFIELD,
	Muirfield, Scotland
Date:	Sept. 20-22
Results:	USA 19 GBI 13
Captains:	United States - Jack Burke
	Great Britain & Ireland - Bernard Hunt

	Morning Foursomes	Afternoon Four-balls	Morning Foursomes	Afternoon Four-balls	Morning Singles	Afternoon Singles
G.B. & Ireland	2½	3	2	½	2½	2½
United States	1½	1	2	3½	5½	5½

United States Team
Tommy Aaron   Jack Nicklaus
Homero Blancas   Arnold Palmer
Gay Brewer   Chi Chi Rodriguez
Billy Casper   J.C. Snead
Lou Graham   Lee Trevino
Dave Hill   Tom Weiskopf

Great Britain & Ireland Team
Brian Barnes   John Garner
Maurice Bembridge   Brian Huggett
Peter Butler   Tony Jacklin
Clive Clark   Christy O'Connor Sr.
Neil Coles   Peter Oosterhuis
Bernard Gallacher   Eddie Polland

UNITED STATES		GREAT BRITAIN/IRELAND	
Morning Foursomes (Day One)			
Lee Trevino & Billy Casper	0	Brian Barnes & Bernard Gallacher (1 up)	1
Tom Weiskopf & J.C. Snead	0	Christy O'Connor & Neil Coles (3 and 2)	1
Chi Chi Rodriguez & Lou Graham (halved)	½	Tony Jacklin & Peter Oosterhuis (halved)	½
Jack Nicklaus & Arnold Palmer (6 and 5)	1	Maurice Bembridge & Eddie Polland	0
Afternoon Four-balls (Day One)			
Tommy Aaron & Gay Brewer	0	Brian Barnes & Bernard Gallacher (5 and 4)	1
Jack Nicklaus & Arnold Palmer	0	Maurice Bembridge & Brian Huggett (3 and 1)	1
Tom Weiskopf & Billy Casper	0	Tony Jacklin & Peter Oosterhuis (3 and 1)	1
Lee Trevino & Homero Blancas (2 and 1)	1	Neil Coles & Christy O'Connor Sr.	0
Day One Total	**2½**	**Day One Total**	**5½**
Morning Foursomes (Day Two)			
Jack Nicklaus & Tom Weiskopf (1 up)	1	Brian Barnes & Peter Butler	0
Arnold Palmer & Dave Hill	0	Peter Oosterhuis & Tony Jacklin (2 up)	1
Chi Chi Rodriguez & Lou Graham	0	Maurice Bembridge & Brian Huggett (5 and 4)	1
Lee Trevino & Billy Casper (2 and 1)	1	Neil Coles & Christy O'Connor Sr.	0
Afternoon Four-balls (Day Two)			
J.C. Snead & Arnold Palmer (2 up)	1	Brian Barnes & Peter Butler	0
Gay Brewer & Billy Casper (3 and 2)	1	Tony Jacklin & Peter Oosterhuis	0
Jack Nicklaus & Tom Weiskopf (3 and 2)	1	Clive Clark & Eddie Polland	0
Lee Trevino & Homero Blancas (halved)	½	Maurice Bembridge & B. Huggett (halved)	½
Day Two Total	**5½**	**Day Two Total**	**2½**
Two-Day Total	**8**	**Two-Day Total**	**8**
Morning Singles (Day Three)			
Billy Casper (2 and 1)	1	Brian Barnes	0
Tom Weiskopf (3 and 1)	1	Bernard Gallacher	0
Homero Blancas (5 and 4)	1	Peter Butler	0
Tommy Aaron	0	Tony Jacklin (3 and 1)	1
Gay Brewer (halved)	½	Neil Coles (halved)	½
J.C. Snead (1 up)	1	Christy O'Connor Sr.	0
Jack Nicklaus (halved)	½	Maurice Bembridge (halved)	½
Lee Trevino (halved)	½	Peter Oosterhuis (halved)	½
Afternoon Singles (Day Three)			
Homero Blancas	0	Brian Huggett (4 and 2)	1
J.C. Snead (3 and 1)	1	Brian Barnes	0
Gay Brewer (6 and 5)	1	Bernard Gallacher	0
Billy Casper (2 and 1)	1	Tony Jacklin	0
Lee Trevino (6 and 5)	1	Neil Coles	0
Tom Weiskopf (halved)	½	Christy O'Connor Sr. (halved)	½
Jack Nicklaus (2 up)	1	Maurice Bembridge	0
Arnold Palmer	0	Peter Oosterhuis (4 and 2)	1
Day Three Total	**11**	**Day Three Total**	**5**
UNITED STATES	**19**	**GREAT BRITAIN/IRELAND**	**13**

U.S. Team: (Back Row, Left to Right) Dave Hill, J.C. Snead, Tommy Aaron, Tom Weiskopf, Jackie Burke Jr. (Non-playing Captain), Lou Graham, Jack Nicklaus, Chi Chi Rodriguez. (Front Row, Left to Right) Homero Blancas, Arnold Palmer, Billy Casper, Gay Brewer, Lee Trevino.

Great Britain-Ireland Team: (Back Row Left to Right) Peter Oosterhuis, Peter Butler, Tony Jacklin, Eddie Polland, Brian Barnes, John Garner. (Front Row, Left to Right) Maurice Bembridge, Christy O'Connor Sr., Bernard Gallacher, Bernard Hunt (Non-playing Captain), C.A. Clark, Neil Coles, Brian Huggett.

1971

The second day four-ball matches broke the spirit of the young British Team when the U. S. won six and a half of the available eight points. This gave the Americans a comfortable 10-6 lead going into the final day's singles match. Jack Nicklaus scored five of America's 18½ points.

Site:	OLD WARSON COUNTRY CLUB, St. Louis, Mo.	
Date:	Sept. 16-18	
Results:	USA 18½	Great Britain 13½
Captains:	United States -	Jay Hebert
	Great Britain -	Eric Brown

	Morning Foursomes	Afternoon Foursomes	Morning Four-balls	Afternoon Four-balls	Morning Singles	Afternoon Singles
Great Britain	3	1½	0	1½	3½	4
United States	1	2½	4	2½	4½	4

United States Team		Great Britain Team	
Miller Barber	Jack Nicklaus	Harry Bannerman	John Garner
Frank Beard	Arnold Palmer	Brian Barnes	Brian Huggett
Billy Casper	Mason Rudolph	Maurice Bembridge	Tony Jacklin
Charles Coody	J.C. Snead	Peter Butler	Christy O'Connor Sr.
Gardner Dickinson	Dave Stockton	Neil Coles	Peter Oosterhuis
Gene Littler	Lee Trevino	Bernard Gallacher	Peter Townsend

UNITED STATES		GREAT BRITAIN	

Morning Foursomes (Day One)

Billy Casper & Miller Barber	0	Neil Coles & Christy O'Connor Sr. (2 and 1)	1
Arnold Palmer & Gardner Dickinson (2 up)	1	Peter Townsend & Peter Oosterhuis	0
Jack Nicklaus & Dave Stockton	0	Brian Huggett & Tony Jacklin (3 and 2)	1
Charles Coody & Frank Beard	0	Maurice Bembridge & Peter Butler (1 up)	1

Afternoon Foursomes (Day One)

Billy Casper & Miller Barber	0	Harry Bannerman & B. Gallacher (2 and 1)	1
Arnold Palmer & Gardner Dickinson (1 up)	1	Peter Townsend & P. Oosterhuis	0
Lee Trevino & Mason Rudolph (halved)	½	Brian Huggett & Tony Jacklin (halved)	½
Jack Nicklaus & J.C. Snead (5 and 3)	1	Maurice Bembridge & Peter Butler	0
Day One Total	**3½**	**Day One Total**	**4½**

Morning Four-balls (Day Two)

Lee Trevino & Mason Rudolph (2 and 1)	1	Christy O'Connor Sr. & Brian Barnes	0
Frank Beard & J.C. Snead (2 and 1)	1	Neil Coles & John Garner	0
Arnold Palmer & Gardner Dickinson (5 and 4)	1	Peter Oosterhuis & B. Gallacher	0
Jack Nicklaus & Gene Littler (2 and 1)	1	Peter Townsend & Harry Bannerman	0

Afternoon Four-balls (Day Two)

Lee Trevino & Billy Casper	0	Bernard Gallacher & P. Oosterhuis (1 up)	1
Gene Littler & J.C. Snead (2 and 1)	1	Tony Jacklin & Brian Huggett	0
Arnold Palmer & Jack Nicklaus (1 up)	1	Peter Townsend & Harry Bannerman	0
Charles Coody & Frank Beard (halved)	½	Neil Coles & Christy O'Connor Sr. (halved)	½
Day Two Total	**6½**	**Day Two Total**	**1½**
Two-Day Total	**10**	**Two-Day Total**	**6**

Morning Singles (Day Three)

Lee Trevino (1 up)	1	Tony Jacklin	0
Dave Stockton (halved)	½	Bernard Gallacher (halved)	½
Mason Rudolph	0	Brian Barnes (1 up)	1
Gene Littler	0	Peter Oosterhuis (4 and 3)	1
Jack Nicklaus (3 and 2)	1	Peter Townsend	0
Gardner Dickinson (5 and 4)	1	Christy O'Connor Sr.	0
Arnold Palmer (halved)	½	Harry Bannerman (halved)	½
Frank Beard (halved)	½	Neil Coles (halved)	½

Afternoon Singles (Day Three)

Lee Trevino (7 and 6)	1	Brian Huggett	0
J.C. Snead (1 up)	1	Tony Jacklin	0
Miller Barber	0	Brian Barnes (2 and 1)	1
Dave Stockton (1 up)	1	Peter Townsend	0
Charles Coody	0	Bernard Gallacher (2 and 1)	1
Jack Nicklaus (5 and 3)	1	Neil Coles	0
Arnold Palmer	0	Peter Oosterhuis (3 and 2)	1
Gardner Dickinson	0	Harry Bannerman (2 and 1)	1
Day Three Total	**8½**	**Day Three Total**	**7½**

UNITED STATES	18½	GREAT BRITAIN	13½

U.S. Team: (Back Row, Left to Right) Mason Rudolph, Dave Stockton, J.C. Snead, Jay Hebert (Non-playing Captain), Charles Coody, Miller Barber, Frank Beard. (Front Row, Left to Right) Gene Littler, Jack Nicklaus, Billy Casper, Arnold Palmer, Lee Trevino, Gardner Dickinson.

Great Britain Team: (Back Row, Left to Right) Brian Huggett, Peter Butler, Brian Barnes, Eric Brown (Non-playing Captain), Peter Oosterhuis, Harry Bannerman, Peter Townsend. (Front Row, Left to Right) John Garner, Christy O'Connor Sr., Neil Coles, Tony Jacklin, Bernard Gallacher, Maurice Bembridge.

1969

In the closest contest in Ryder Cup history, 17 of the 32 matches went down to the last hole. With the matches tied going into the last day, the British won five of the eight morning singles. But the U. S. roared back, winning four of the first six afternoon matches to even the score. In Brian Huggett's match against Billy Casper, Huggett made a four-foot putt to halve the match. That left the Ryder Cup to be decided by the last group of Tony Jacklin and Jack Nicklaus, who were tied going into the last hole. In one of golf's most memorable moments of sportsmanship, Nicklaus, playing in his first Ryder Cup, conceded a two-footer to Jacklin after making a four-footer for par on the last green, resulting in the first tie in the matches' history.

Site:	ROYAL BIRKDALE GOLF CLUB, Southport, England	
Date:	Sept. 18-20	
Results:	USA 16	Great Britain 16
Captains:	United States -	Sam Snead
	Great Britain -	Eric Brown

	Morning Foursomes	Afternoon Foursomes	Morning Four-balls	Afternoon Four-balls	Morning Singles	Afternoon Singles
Great Britain	3½	1	2½	1	5	3
United States	½	3	1½	3	3	5

United States Team		Great Britain Team	
Tommy Aaron	Dave Hill	Peter Alliss	Bernard Gallacher
Miller Barber	Gene Littler	Brian Barnes	Brian Huggett
Frank Beard	Jack Nicklaus	Maurice Bembridge	Bernard Hunt
Billy Casper	Dan Sikes	Peter Butler	Tony Jacklin
Dale Douglass	Ken Still	Alex Caygill	Christy O'Connor Sr.
Ray Floyd	Lee Trevino	Neil Coles	Peter Townsend

UNITED STATES		GREAT BRITAIN	
Morning Foursomes (Day One)			
Miller Barber & Ray Floyd	0	Neil Coles & Brian Huggett (3 and 2)	1
Lee Trevino & Ken Still	0	Bernard Gallacher & M. Bembridge (2 and 1)	1
Dave Hill & Tommy Aaron	0	Tony Jacklin & Peter Townsend (3 and 1)	1
Billy Casper & Frank Beard (halved)	½	Christy O'Connor Sr. & Peter Alliss (halved)	½
Afternoon Foursomes (Day One)			
Dave Hill & Tommy Aaron (1 up)	1	Neil Coles & Brian Huggett	0
Lee Trevino & Gene Littler (1 up)	1	Bernard Gallacher & M. Bembridge	0
Billy Casper & Frank Beard	0	Tony Jacklin & Peter Townsend (1 up)	1
Jack Nicklaus & Dan Sikes (1 up)	1	Peter Butler & Bernard Hunt	0
Day One Total	3½	**Day One Total**	4½
Morning Four-balls (Day Two)			
Dave Hill & Dale Douglass	0	Christy O'Connor Sr. & Peter Townsend (1 up)	1
Ray Floyd & Miller Barber (halved)	½	Brian Huggett & Alex Caygill (halved)	½
Lee Trevino & Gene Littler (1 up)	1	Brian Barnes & Peter Alliss	0
Jack Nicklaus & Dan Sikes	0	Tony Jacklin & Neil Coles (1 up)	1
Afternoon Four-balls (Day Two)			
Billy Casper & Frank Beard (2 up)	1	Peter Butler & Peter Townsend	0
Dave Hill & Ken Still (2 and 1)	1	Brian Huggett & Bernard Gallacher	0
Tommy Aaron & Ray Floyd (halved)	½	Maurice Bembridge & Bernard Hunt (halved)	½
Lee Trevino & Miller Barber (halved)	½	Tony Jacklin & Neil Coles (halved)	½
Day Two Total	4½	**Day Two Total**	3½
Two-Day Total	8	**Two-Day Total**	8
Morning Singles (Day Three)			
Lee Trevino (2 and 1)	1	Peter Alliss	0
Dave Hill (5 and 4)	1	Peter Townsend	0
Tommy Aaron	0	Neil Coles (1 up)	1
Billy Casper (1 up)	1	Brian Barnes	0
Frank Beard	0	Christy O'Connor Sr. (5 and 4)	1
Ken Still	0	Maurice Bembridge (1 up)	1
Ray Floyd	0	Peter Butler (1 up)	1
Jack Nicklaus	0	Tony Jacklin (4 and 3)	1
Afternoon Singles (Day Three)			
Dave Hill (4 and 2)	1	Brian Barnes	0
Lee Trevino	0	Bernard Gallacher (4 and 3)	1
Miller Barber (7 and 6)	1	Maurice Bembridge	0
Dale Douglass	0	Peter Butler (3 and 2)	1
Dan Sikes (4 and 3)	1	Neil Coles	0
Gene Littler (2 and 1)	1	Christy O'Connor Sr.	0
Billy Casper (halved)	½	Brian Huggett (halved)	½
Jack Nicklaus (halved)	½	Tony Jacklin (halved)	½
Day Three Total	8	**Day Three Total**	8
UNITED STATES	**16**	**GREAT BRITAIN**	**16**

U.S. Team: (Left to Right) Sam Snead (Non-playing Captain), Lee Trevino, Raymond Floyd, Gene Littler, Ken Still, Frank Beard, Dave Hill, Dan Sikes, Miller Barber, Billy Casper, Dale Douglass, Tommy Aaron, Jack Nicklaus.

Great Britain Team: (Back Row, Left to Right) Christy O'Connor Sr., Peter Alliss, Bernard Hunt, Brian Barnes, Peter Butler, Neil Coles. (Front Row, Left to right) Maurice Bembridge, Peter Townsend, Tony Jacklin, Eric Brown (Non-playing Captain), Bernard Gallacher, Brian Huggett, Alex Caygill.

1967

By the end of the four-ball matches on the second day, it was almost time for the U.S. Team to break out the champagne and celebrate one of the most one-sided wins in Ryder Cup history. Arnold Palmer and Gardner Dickinson led the way, winning all their matches and five points each.

Site:	CHAMPIONS GOLF CLUB, Houston, Texas	
Date:	Oct. 20-22	
Results:	USA 23½	Great Britain 8½
Captains:	United States -	Ben Hogan
	Great Britain -	Dai Rees

	Morning Foursomes	Afternoon Foursomes	Morning Four-balls	Afternoon Four-balls	Morning Singles	Afternoon Singles
Great Britain	1½	1	0	½	3	2½
United States	2½	3	4	3½	5	5½

United States Team
Julius Boros   Gene Littler
Gay Brewer   Bobby Nichols
Billy Casper   Arnold Palmer
Gardner Dickinson   Johnny Pott
Al Geiberger   Doug Sanders

Great Britain Team
Peter Alliss   Bernard Hunt
Hugh Boyle   Tony Jacklin
Neil Coles   Christy O'Connor Sr.
Malcolm Gregson   Dave Thomas
Brian Huggett   George Will

UNITED STATES | GREAT BRITAIN

Morning Foursomes (Day One)

UNITED STATES		GREAT BRITAIN	
Billy Casper & Julius Boros (halved)	½	Brian Huggett & George Will (halved)	½
Arnold Palmer & Gardner Dickinson (2 and 1)	1	Peter Alliss & Christy O'Connor Sr.	0
Doug Sanders & Gay Brewer	0	Tony Jacklin & Dave Thomas (4 and 3)	1
Bobby Nichols & Johnny Pott (6 and 5)	1	Bernard Hunt & Neil Coles	0

Afternoon Foursomes (Day One)

UNITED STATES		GREAT BRITAIN	
Billy Casper & Julius Boros (1 up)	1	Brian Huggett & George Will	0
Gardner Dickinson & Arnold Palmer (5 and 4)	1	Malcolm Gregson & Hugh Boyle	0
Gene Littler & Al Geiberger	0	Tony Jacklin & Dave Thomas (3 and 2)	1
Bobby Nichols & Johnny Pott (2 and 1)	1	Peter Alliss & Christy O'Connor Sr.	0
Day One Total	**5½**	**Day One Total**	**2½**

Morning Four-balls (Day Two)

UNITED STATES		GREAT BRITAIN	
Billy Casper & Gay Brewer (3 and 2)	1	Peter Alliss & Christy O'Connor Sr.	0
Bobby Nichols & Johnny Pott (1 up)	1	Bernard Hunt & Neil Coles	0
Gene Littler & Al Geiberger (1 up)	1	Tony Jacklin & Dave Thomas	0
Gardner Dickinson & Doug Sanders (3 and 2)	1	Brian Huggett & George Will	0

Afternoon Four-balls (Day Two)

UNITED STATES		GREAT BRITAIN	
Billy Casper & Gay Brewer (5 and 3)	1	Bernard Hunt & Neil Coles	0
Gardner Dickinson & Doug Sanders (3 and 2)	1	Peter Alliss & Malcom Gregson	0
Arnold Palmer & Julius Boros (1 up)	1	George Will & Hugh Boyle	0
Gene Littler & Al Geiberger (halved)	½	Tony Jacklin & Dave Thomas (halved)	½
Day Two Total	**7½**	**Day Two Total**	**½**
Two-Day Total	**13**	**Two-Day Total**	**3**

Morning Singles (Day Three)

UNITED STATES		GREAT BRITAIN	
Gay Brewer (4 and 3)	1	Hugh Boyle	0
Billy Casper (2 and 1)	1	Peter Alliss	0
Arnold Palmer (3 and 2)	1	Tony Jacklin	0
Julius Boros	0	Brian Huggett (1 up)	1
Doug Sanders	0	Neil Coles (2 and 1)	1
Al Geiberger (4 and 2)	1	Malcolm Gregson	0
Gene Littler (halved)	½	Dave Thomas (halved)	½
Bobby Nichols (halved)	½	Bernard Hunt (halved)	½

Afternoon Singles (Day Three)

UNITED STATES		GREAT BRITAIN	
Arnold Palmer (5 and 3)	1	Brian Huggett	0
Gay Brewer	0	Peter Alliss (2 and 1)	1
Gardner Dickinson (3 and 2)	1	Tony Jacklin	0
Bobby Nichols (3 and 2)	1	Christy O'Connor Sr.	0
Johnny Pott (3 and 1)	1	George Will	0
Al Geiberger (2 and 1)	1	Malcolm Gregson	0
Julius Boros (halved)	½	Bernard Hunt (halved)	½
Doug Sanders	0	Neil Coles (2 and 1)	1
Day Three Total	**10½**	**Day Three Total**	**5½**

UNITED STATES	**23½**	**GREAT BRITAIN**	**8½**

U.S. Team: (Left to Right) Al Geiberger, Julius Boros, Arnold Palmer, Gardner Dickinson, Ben Hogan (Non-playing Captain), Gene Littler, Billy Casper, Johnny Pott, Bobby Nichols, Gay Brewer, Doug Sanders.

Great Britain Team: (Back Row, Left to Right) Tony Jacklin, Peter Alliss, Dave Thomas, Bernard Hunt, George Will, Christy O'Connor Sr. (Front Row, Left to Right) Malcolm Gregson, Hugh Boyle, Dai Rees (Non-playing Captain), Brian Huggett, Neil Coles.

1965

After the first two days of foursomes and four-ball matches, the U. S. had a 9-7 lead, but won 10 of the possible 16 points in the singles matches, cruising to another easy victory. Tony Lema led the charge with five points. Julius Boros, Dave Marr and Arnold Palmer each scored four points.

Site:	ROYAL BIRKDALE GOLF CLUB, Southport, England	
Date:	Oct. 7-9	
Results:	USA 19½	Great Britain 12½
Captains:	United States -	Byron Nelson
	Great Britain -	Harry Weetman

	Morning Foursomes	Afternoon Foursomes	Morning Four-balls	Afternoon Four-balls	Morning Singles	Afternoon Singles
Great Britain	2	2	1½	1½	2½	3
United States	2	2	2½	2½	5½	5

United States Team
Julius Boros / Gene Littler
Billy Casper / Dave Marr
Tommy Jacobs / Arnold Palmer
Don January / Johnny Pott
Tony Lema / Ken Venturi

Great Britain Team
Peter Alliss / Jimmy Martin
Peter Butler / Christy O'Connor Sr.
Neil Coles / Lionel Platts
Jimmy Hitchcock / Dave Thomas
Bernard Hunt / George Will

UNITED STATES		GREAT BRITAIN	
Morning Foursomes (Day One)			
Julius Boros & Tony Lema (1 up)	1	Lionel Platts & Peter Butler	0
Arnold Palmer & Dave Marr	0	Dave Thomas & George Will (6 and 5)	1
Billy Casper & Gene Littler (2 and 1)	1	Bernard Hunt & Neil Coles	0
Ken Venturi & Don January	0	Peter Alliss & Christy O'Connor Sr. (5 and 4)	1
Afternoon Foursomes (Day One)			
Arnold Palmer & Dave Marr (6 and 5)	1	Dave Thomas & George Will	0
Billy Casper & Gene Littler	0	Peter Alliss & Christy O'Connor Sr. (2 and 1)	1
Julius Boros & Tony Lema (5 and 4)	1	Jimmy Martin & Jimmy Hitchcock	0
Ken Venturi & Don January	0	Bernard Hunt & Neil Coles (3 and 2)	1
Day One Total	**4**	**Day One Total**	**4**
Morning Four-balls (Day Two)			
Don January & Tommy Jacobs (1 up)	1	Dave Thomas & George Will	0
Billy Casper & Gene Littler (halved)	½	Lionel Platts & Peter Butler (halved)	½
Arnold Palmer & Dave Marr (6 and 4)	1	Peter Alliss & Christy O'Connor Sr.	0
Julius Boros & Tony Lema	0	Bernard Hunt & Neil Coles (1 up)	1
Afternoon Four-balls (Day Two)			
Arnold Palmer & Dave Marr	0	Peter Alliss & Christy O'Connor Sr. (2 up)	1
Don January & Tommy Jacobs (1 up)	1	Dave Thomas & George Will	0
Billy Casper & Gene Littler (halved)	½	Lionel Platts & Peter Butler (halved)	½
Ken Venturi & Tony Lema (1 up)	1	Bernard Hunt & Neil Coles	0
Day Two Total	**5**	**Day Two Total**	**3**
Two-Day Total	**9**	**Two-Day Total**	**7**
Morning Singles (Day Three)			
Arnold Palmer (3 and 2)	1	Jimmy Hitchcock	0
Julius Boros (4 and 2)	1	Lionel Platts	0
Tony Lema (1 up)	1	Peter Butler	0
Dave Marr (2 up)	1	Neil Coles	0
Gene Littler	0	Bernard Hunt (2 up)	1
Tommy Jacobs (2 and 1)	1	Dave Thomas	0
Billy Casper	0	Peter Alliss (1 up)	1
Don January (halved)	½	George Will (halved)	½
Afternoon Singles (Day Three)			
Tony Lema (6 and 4)	1	Christy O'Connor Sr.	0
Julius Boros (2 and 1)	1	Jimmy Hitchcock	0
Arnold Palmer (2 up)	1	Peter Butler	0
Ken Venturi	0	Peter Alliss (3 and 1)	1
Billy Casper	0	Neil Coles (3 and 2)	1
Gene Littler (2 and 1)	1	George Will	0
Dave Marr (1 up)	1	Bernard Hunt	0
Tommy Jacobs	0	Lionel Platts (1 up)	1
Day Three Total	**10½**	**Day Three Total**	**5½**
UNITED STATES	**19½**	**GREAT BRITAIN**	**12½**

U.S. Team: (Left to Right) Byron Nelson (Non-playing Captain), Tommy Jacobs, Billy Casper, Don January, Johnny Pott, Tony Lema, Ken Venturi, Dave Marr, Gene Littler, Julius Boros, Arnold Palmer.

Great Britain Team: (Back Row, Left to Right) Dave Thomas, Christy O'Connor, Peter Alliss, George Will, Lionel Platts, Bernard Hunt. (Front Row, Left to Right) Peter Butler, Neil Coles, Harry Weetman (Non-playing Captain), Jimmy Hitchcock, James Martin.

1963

Four-ball matches first appeared, increasing the point total to 32. Dow Finsterwald and Billy Casper each won four matches and halved one to help lead the U. S. to an easy victory. This would be the last time an American captain would compete in the matches.

Site:	EAST LAKE COUNTRY CLUB, Atlanta, Ga.	
Date:	Oct. 11-13	
Results:	USA 23	Great Britain 9
Captains:	United States -	Arnold Palmer
	Great Britain -	J. Fallon

	Morning Foursomes	Afternoon Foursomes	Morning Four-balls	Afternoon Four-balls	Morning Singles	Afternoon Singles
Great Britain	2	0	1½	½	4½	½
United States	2	4	2½	3½	3½	7½

United States Team
Julius Boros   Tony Lema
Billy Casper   Billy Maxwell
Dow Finsterwald   Arnold Palmer
Bob Goalby   Johnny Pott
Gene Littler   Dave Ragan

Great Britain Team
Peter Alliss   Geoffrey Hunt
Neil Coles   Christy O'Connor Sr.
Tom Haliburton   Dave Thomas
Brian Huggett   Harry Weetman
Bernard Hunt   George Will

UNITED STATES / GREAT BRITAIN

Morning Foursomes (Day One)
UNITED STATES		GREAT BRITAIN	
Arnold Palmer & Johnny Pott	0	Brian Huggett & George Will (3 and 2)	1
Billy Casper & Dave Ragan (1 up)	1	Peter Alliss & Christy O'Connor Sr.	0
Julius Boros & Tony Lema (halved)	½	Neil Coles & Bernard Hunt (halved)	½
Gene Littler & Dow Finsterwald (halved)	½	Dave Thomas & Harry Weetman (halved)	½

Afternoon Foursomes (Day One)
Billy Maxwell & Bob Goalby (4 and 3)	1	Dave Thomas & Harry Weetman	0
Arnold Palmer & Billy Casper (5 and 4)	1	Brian Huggett & George Will	0
Gene Littler & Dow Finsterwald (2 and 1)	1	Neil Coles & Geoffrey Hunt	0
Julius Boros & Tony Lema (1 up)	1	Tom Haliburton & Bernard Hunt	0
Day One Total	**6**	**Day One Total**	**2**

Morning Four-balls (Day Two)
Arnold Palmer & Dow Finsterwald (5 and 4)	1	Brian Huggett & Dave Thomas	0
Gene Littler & Julius Boros (halved)	½	Peter Alliss & Bernard Hunt (halved)	½
Billy Casper & Billy Maxwell (3 and 2)	1	Harry Weetman & George Will	0
Bob Goalby & Dave Ragan	0	Neil Coles & Christy O'Connor Sr. (1 up)	1

Afternoon Four-balls (Day Two)
Arnold Palmer & Dow Finsterwald (3 and 2)	1	Neil Coles & Christy O'Connor Sr.	0
Tony Lema & Johnny Pott (1 up)	1	Peter Alliss & Bernard Hunt	0
Billy Casper & Billy Maxwell (2 and 1)	1	Tom Haliburton & Geoffrey Hunt	0
Bob Goalby & Dave Ragan (halved)	½	Brian Huggett & Dave Thomas (halved)	½
Day Two Total	**6**	**Day Two Total**	**2**
Two-Day Total	**12**	**Two-Day Total**	**4**

Morning Singles (Day Three)
Tony Lema (5 and 3)	1	Geoffrey Hunt	0
Johnny Pott	0	Brian Huggett (3 and 1)	1
Arnold Palmer	0	Peter Alliss (1 up)	1
Billy Casper (halved)	½	Neil Coles (halved)	½
Bob Goalby (3 and 2)	1	Dave Thomas	0
Gene Littler (1 up)	1	Christy O'Connor Sr.	0
Julius Boros	0	Harry Weetman (1 up)	1
Dow Finsterwald	0	Bernard Hunt (2 up)	1

Afternoon Singles (Day Three)
Arnold Palmer (3 and 2)	1	George Will	0
Dave Ragan (2 and 1)	1	Neil Coles	0
Tony Lema (halved)	½	Peter Alliss (halved)	½
Gene Littler (6 and 5)	1	Tom Haliburton	0
Julius Boros (2 and 1)	1	Harry Weetman	0
Billy Maxwell (2 and 1)	1	Christy O'Connor Sr.	0
Dow Finsterwald (4 and 3)	1	Dave Thomas	0
Bob Goalby (2 and 1)	1	Bernard Hunt	0
Day Three Total	**11**	**Day Three Total**	**5**

UNITED STATES	**23**	**GREAT BRITAIN**	**9**

U.S. Team: *(Left to Right) Arnold Palmer (Captain), Tony Lema, Dave Ragan, Dow Finsterwald, Gene Littler, Billy Casper, Bob Goalby, Johnny Pott, Billy Maxwell, Julius Boros.*

Great Britain Team: *(Back Row, Left to Right) Neil Coles, Christy O'Connor Sr., Peter Alliss, Dave Thomas, Geoffrey Hunt. (Front Row, Left to Right) Thomas Haliburton, Bernard Hunt, John Fallon (Non-playing Captain), Brian Huggett, Harry Weetman.*

1961

For the first time in Ryder Cup history, the format was changed. Unlike the traditional 36-hole matches, incorporation of 18-hole matches allowed both morning and afternoon matches to be played, doubling the total point score to 24. The U. S. continued its winning streak with a five-point win, aided by Arnold Palmer's 3 1/2 points in his first Ryder Cup appearance.

Site:	ROYAL LYTHAM & ST. ANNES,
	St. Annes, England
Date:	Oct. 13-14
Results:	USA 14½ Great Britain 9½
Captains:	United States - Jerry Barber
	Great Britain - Dai Rees

Foursomes Matches: USA 6 Great Britain 2   **Singles Matches: USA 8½ Great Britain 7½**

United States Team		Great Britain Team	
Jerry Barber	Jay Hebert	Peter Alliss	Ralph Moffitt
Billy Casper	Gene Littler	Ken Bousfield	Christy O'Connor Sr.
Bill Collins	Arnold Palmer	Neil Coles	John Panton
Dow Finsterwald	Mike Souchak	Tom Haliburton	Dai Rees
Doug Ford	Art Wall	Bernard Hunt	Harry Weetman

UNITED STATES		GREAT BRITAIN	
Morning Foursomes (Day One)			
Doug Ford & Gene Littler	0	Christy O'Connor Sr. & Peter Alliss (4 and 3)	1
Art Wall & Jay Hebert (4 and 3)	1	John Panton & Bernard Hunt	0
Billy Casper & Arnold Palmer (2 and 1)	1	Dai Rees & Ken Bousfield	0
Bill Collins & Mike Souchak (1 up)	1	Tom Haliburton & Neil Coles	0
Afternoon Foursomes (Day One)			
Art Wall & Jay Hebert (1 up)	1	Christy O'Connor Sr. & Peter Alliss	0
Billy Casper & Arnold Palmer (5 and 4)	1	John Panton & Bernard Hunt	0
Bill Collins & Mike Souchak	0	Dai Rees & Ken Bousfield (4 and 2)	1
Jerry Barber & Dow Finsterwald (1 up)	1	Tom Haliburton & Neil Coles	0
Day One Total	**6**	**Day One Total**	**2**
Morning Singles (Day Two)			
Doug Ford (1 up)	1	Harry Weetman	0
Mike Souchak (5 and 4)	1	Ralph Moffitt	0
Arnold Palmer (halved)	½	Peter Alliss (halved)	½
Billy Casper (5 and 3)	1	Ken Bousfield	0
Jay Hebert	0	Dai Rees (2 and 1)	1
Gene Littler (halved)	½	Neil Coles (halved)	½
Jerry Barber	0	Bernard Hunt (5 and 4)	1
Dow Finsterwald (2 and 1)	1	Christy O'Connor Sr.	0
Afternoon Singles (Day Two)			
Art Wall (1 up)	1	Harry Weetman	0
Bill Collins	0	Peter Alliss (3 and 2)	1
Mike Souchak (2 and 1)	1	Bernard Hunt	0
Arnold Palmer (2 and 1)	1	Tom Haliburton	0
Doug Ford	0	Dai Rees (4 and 3)	1
Jerry Barber	0	Ken Bousfield (1 up)	1
Dow Finsterwald	0	Neil Coles (1 up)	1
Gene Littler (halved)	½	Christy O'Connor Sr. (halved)	½
Day Two Total	**8½**	**Day Two Total**	**7½**
UNITED STATES	**14½**	**GREAT BRITAIN**	**9½**

U.S. Team: (Back Row, Left to Right) Bill Collins, Doug Ford, Dow Finsterwald, Art Wall, Billy Casper, Gene Littler. (Front Row, Left to Right) Jerry Barber (Captain), Jay Hebert, Arnold Palmer, Mike Souchak.

Great Britain Team: (Back Row, Left to Right) John Panton, Robert Moffitt, Bernard Hunt, Harry Weetman, Christy O'Connor Sr. (Front Row, Left to Right) Ken Bousfield, Neil Coles, Dai Rees (Captain), Thomas Haliburton, Peter Alliss.

1959

The British savored their 1957 victory for two years before the Americans got their revenge. Bob Rosburg, Dow Finsterwald and Mike Souchak each contributed two points in a runaway U.S. victory.

Site:	ELDORADO COUNTRY CLUB, Palm Desert, Calif.	
Date:	Nov. 6-7	
Results:	USA 8½	Great Britain 3½
Captains:	United States -	Sam Snead
	Great Britain -	Dai Rees

Foursomes Matches: USA 2½ Great Britain 1½ **Singles Matches: USA 6 Great Britain 2**

United States Team		Great Britain Team	
Julius Boros	Cary Middlecoff	Peter Alliss	Bernard Hunt
Jack Burke Jr.	Bob Rosburg	Ken Bousfield	Christy O'Connor Sr.
Dow Finsterwald	Sam Snead	Eric Brown	Dai Rees
Doug Ford	Mike Souchak	Norman Drew	Dave Thomas
Jay Hebert	Art Wall		Harry Weetman

UNITED STATES		GREAT BRITAIN	
Foursomes (Day One)			
Bob Rosburg & Mike Souchak (5 and 4)	1	Bernard Hunt & Eric Brown	0
Julius Boros & Dow Finsterwald (2 up)	1	Dai Rees & Ken Bousfield	0
Art Wall & Doug Ford	0	Christy O'Connor Sr. & Peter Alliss (3 and 2)	1
Sam Snead & Cary Middlecoff (halved)	½	Harry Weetman & Dave Thomas (halved)	½
Day One Total	2½	**Day One Total**	1½
Singles (Day Two)			
Doug Ford (halved)	½	Norman Drew (halved)	½
Mike Souchak (3 and 2)	1	Ken Bousfield	0
Bob Rosburg (6 and 5)	1	Harry Weetman	0
Sam Snead (6 and 5)	1	Dave Thomas	0
Art Wall (7 and 6)	1	Christy O'Connor Sr.	0
Dow Finsterwald (1 up)	1	Dai Rees	0
Jay Hebert (halved)	½	Peter Alliss (halved)	½
Cary Middlecoff	0	Eric Brown (4 and 3)	1
Day Two Total	6	**Day Two Total**	2
UNITED STATES	**8½**	**GREAT BRITAIN**	**3½**

U.S. Team: *(Back Row, Left to Right) Julius Boros, Bob Rosburg, Doug Ford, Dow Finsterwald, Jay Hebert. (Front Row, Left to Right) Mike Souchak, Cary Middlecoff, Sam Snead (Captain), Art Wall, Jack Burke Jr.*

Great Britain Team: *(Left to Right) Robert Hudson Jr. (American Patron), Dai Rees (Captain), Norman Drew, Ken Bousfield, Peter Mills, Eric Brown, Christy O'Connor Sr., Harry Weetman, Peter Alliss, Dave Thomas, Bernard Hunt.*

1957

In one of the most dramatic turnarounds in Ryder Cup history, the British trailed, 3-1, after the first day foursomes but won six of the next day's singles matches and halved another for their first Ryder Cup victory since 1933.

Site:	LINDRICK GOLF CLUB,
	Yorkshire, England
Date:	Oct. 4-5
Results:	Great Britain 7½ USA 4½
Captains:	United States - Jack Burke
	Great Britain - Dai Rees

Foursomes Matches: USA 3 Great Britain 1

United States Team

Tommy Bolt	Fred Hawkins
Jack Burke Jr.	Lionel Hebert
Dow Finsterwald	Ted Kroll
Doug Ford	Dick Mayer
Ed Furgol	Art Wall

Singles Matches: USA 1½ Great Britain 6½

Great Britain Team

Peter Alliss	Bernard Hunt
Ken Bousfield	Peter Mills
Harry Bradshaw	Christy O'Connor Sr.
Eric Brown	Dai Rees
Max Faulkner	Harry Weetman

UNITED STATES

Foursomes (Day One)

Doug Ford & Dow Finsterwald (2 and 1)	1
Art Wall & Fred Hawkins.	0
Ted Kroll & Jack Burke Jr. (4 and 3)	1
Dick Mayer & Tommy Bolt (7 and 5)	1
Day One Total	**3**

Singles (Day Two)

Tommy Bolt.	0
Jack Burke Jr.	0
Fred Hawkins (2 and 1)	1
Lionel Hebert.	0
Ed Furgol.	0
Doug Ford.	0
Dow Finsterwald	0
Dick Mayer (halved)	½
Day Two Total	**1½**

GREAT BRITAIN

Foursomes (Day One)

Peter Alliss & Bernard Hunt	0
Ken Bousfield & Dai Rees (3 and 2).	1
Max Faulkner & Harry Weetman.	0
Christy O'Connor Sr. & Eric Brown	0
Day One Total	**1**

Singles (Day Two)

Eric Brown (4 and 3)	1
Peter Mills (5 and 3)	1
Peter Alliss.	0
Ken Bousfield (4 and 3)	1
Dai Rees (7 and 6)	1
Bernard Hunt (6 and 5)	1
Christy O'Connor Sr. (7 and 6)	1
Harry Bradshaw (halved)	½
Day Two Total	**6½**

UNITED STATES	4½	GREAT BRITAIN	7½

U.S. Team: *(Back Row, Left to Right) Art Wall, Tommy Bolt, Ed Furgol, Fred Hawkins, Dow Finsterwald. (Front Row, Left to Right) Jack Burke Jr., Dick Mayer, Lionel Hebert, Ted Kroll, Doug Ford.*

Great Britain Team: *(Left to Right)Harry Bradshaw, Peter Mills, Peter Alliss, Bernard Hunt, Harry Weetman. (Front Row, Left to Right) Max Faulkner, Eric Brown, Dai Rees (Captain), Ken Bousfield, Christy O'Connor Sr.*

1955

Doug Ford, Jack Burke Jr., Tommy Bolt and Sam Snead each scored two points, giving the U. S. an easy victory over the British.

Site:	THUNDERBIRD GOLF & COUNTRY CLUB,	
	Palm Springs, Calif	
Date:	Nov. 5-6	
Results:	USA 8	Great Britain 4
Captains:	United States -	Chick Harbert
	Great Britain -	Dai Rees

Foursomes Matches: USA 3 Great Britain 1

United States Team

Jerry Barber	Chick Harbert
Tommy Bolt	Chandler Harper
Jack Burke Jr.	Ted Kroll
Doug Ford	Cary Middlecoff
Marty Furgol	Sam Snead

Singles Matches: USA 5 Great Britain 3

Great Britain Team

Ken Bousfield	Arthur Lees
Harry Bradshaw	Christy O'Connor Sr.
Eric Brown	Dai Rees
John Fallon	Syd Scott
John Jacobs	Harry Weetman

UNITED STATES

GREAT BRITAIN

Foursomes (Day One)

Chandler Harper & Jerry Barber	0	John Fallon & John Jacobs (1 up)	1
Doug Ford & Ted Kroll (5 and 4)	1	Eric Brown & Syd Scott	0
Jack Burke Jr. & Tommy Bolt (1 up)	1	Arthur Lees & Harry Weetman	0
Sam Snead & Cary Middlecoff (3 and 2)	1	Harry Bradshaw & Dai Rees	0
Day One Total	**3**	**Day One Total**	**1**

Singles (Day Two)

Tommy Bolt (4 and 2)	1	Christy O'Connor Sr.	0
Chick Harbert (3 and 2)	1	Syd Scott	0
Cary Middlecoff	0	John Jacobs (1 up)	1
Sam Snead (3 and 1)	1	Dai Rees	0
Marty Furgol	0	Arthur Lees (3 and 2)	1
Jerry Barber	0	Eric Brown (3 and 2)	1
Jack Burke Jr. (3 and 2)	1	Harry Bradshaw	0
Doug Ford (3 and 2)	1	Harry Weetman	0
Total	**5**	**Total**	**3**

UNITED STATES	8	GREAT BRITAIN	4

U.S. Team: (Left to Right) Cary Middlecoff, Marty Furgol, Chandler Harper, Doug Ford, Lloyd Mangrum, Chick Harbert (Captain), Tommy Bolt, Sam Snead, Jackie Burke Jr., Ted Kroll, Jerry Barber.

Great Britain Team: (Back Row, Left to Right) Harry Weetman, Christy O'Connor Sr., John Fallon, John Jacobs, Harry Bradshaw. (Front Row, Left to Right) Eric Brown, Syd Scott, Dai Rees (Captain), Ken Bousfield, Art Lees.

1953

After falling behind 3-1 in the first-day foursomes, the British fought back in the singles, but their hopes were dashed when 22-year-old Peter Alliss fluffed a chip shot on the last hole to lose 1-down to Jim Turnesa. Bernard Hunt then missed a short putt on the last hole that would have defeated Dave Douglas and tied the match.

Site:	WENTWORTH GOLF CLUB, Wentworth, England	
Date:	Oct. 2-3	
Results:	USA 6½	Great Britain 5½
Captains:	United States -	Lloyd Mangrum
	Great Britain -	Henry Cotton

Foursomes Matches: USA 3 Great Britain 1   **Singles Matches: USA 3½ Great Britain 4½**

United States Team		Great Britain Team	
Jack Burke Jr.	Lloyd Mangrum	Jimmy Adams	Max Faulkner
Walter Burkemo	Cary Middlecoff	Peter Alliss	Bernard Hunt
Dave Douglas	Ed Oliver	Harry Bradshaw	John Panton
Fred Haas Jr.	Sam Snead	Eric Brown	Dai Rees
Ted Kroll	Jim Turnesa	Fred Daly	Harry Weetman

UNITED STATES		GREAT BRITAIN	
Foursomes (Day One)			
Dave Douglas & Ed Oliver (2 and 1)	1	Harry Weetman & Peter Alliss	0
Lloyd Mangrum & Sam Snead (8 and 7)	1	Eric Brown & John Panton	0
Ted Kroll & Jack Burke Jr. (7 and 5)	1	Jimmy Adams & Bernard Hunt	0
Walter Burkemo & Cary Middlecoff	0	Fred Daly & Harry Bradshaw (1 up)	1
Day One Total	**3**	**Day One Total**	**1**
Singles (Day Two)			
Jack Burke (2 and 1)	1	Dai Rees	0
Ted Kroll	0	Fred Daly (9 and 7)	1
Lloyd Mangrum	0	Eric Brown (2 up)	1
Sam Snead	0	Harry Weetman (1 up)	1
Cary Middlecoff (3 and 1)	1	Max Faulkner	0
Jim Turnesa (1 up)	1	Peter Alliss	0
Dave Douglas (halved)	½	Bernard Hunt (halved)	½
Fred Haas Jr.	0	Harry Bradshaw (3 and 2)	1
Day Two Total	**3½**	**Day Two Total**	**4½**

UNITED STATES	6½	GREAT BRITAIN	5½

U.S. Team: (Back Row, Left to Right) Jim Turnesa, Walter Burkemo, Fred Haas Jr., Dave Douglas, Ed (Porky) Oliver, Ted Kroll. (Front Row, Left to Right) Cary Middlecoff, Lloyd Mangrum (Captain), Sam Snead, Jack Burke Jr.

Great Britain Team: (Back Row, Left to Right) John Panton, Jimmy Adams, Bernard Hunt, Eric Brown, Harry Weetman, Peter Alliss, Harry Bradshaw. (Front Row, Left to Right) Fred Daly, Henry Cotton (Non-playing Captain), Max Faulkner, Dai Rees.

1951

In a lopsided win by the Americans, only two of the 12 matches made it to the last hole. Arthur Lees won two of Britain's 2 1/2 points.

Site:	PINEHURST COUNTRY CLUB, Pinehurst, N. C.	
Date:	Nov. 2-4	
Results:	USA 9 1/2	Great Britain 2 1/2
Captains:	United States - Sam Snead	
	Great Britain - Arthur Lacey	

Foursomes Matches: USA 3 Great Britain 1

United States Team	
Skip Alexander	Ben Hogan
Jack Burke Jr.	Lloyd Mangrum
Jimmy Demaret	Ed Oliver
Dutch Harrison	Henry Ransom
Clayton Heafner	Sam Snead

Singles Matches: USA 6 1/2 Great Britain 1 1/2

Great Britain Team	
Jimmy Adams	Arthur Lees
Ken Panton	John Panton
Fred Daly	Dai Rees
Max Faulkner	Charles Ward
Jack Hargreaves	Harry Weetman

UNITED STATES		GREAT BRITAIN	
Foursomes (Day One)			
Clayton Heafner & Jack Burke Jr. (5 and 3)	1	Max Faulkner & Dai Rees	0
Ed Oliver & Henry Ransom	0	Charles Ward & Arthur Lees (2 and 1)	1
Sam Snead & Lloyd Mangrum (5 and 4)	1	Jimmy Adams & John Panton	0
Ben Hogan & Jimmy Demaret (5 and 4)	1	Fred Daly & Ken Bousfield	0
Day One Total	**3**	**Day One Total**	**1**
Singles (Day Two)			
Jack Burke Jr. (4 and 3)	1	Jimmy Adams	0
Jimmy Demaret (2 up)	1	Dai Rees	0
Clayton Heafner (halved)	1/2	Fred Daly (halved)	1/2
Lloyd Mangrum (6 and 5)	1	Harry Weetman	0
Ed Oliver	0	Arthur Lees (2 and 1)	1
Ben Hogan (3 and 2)	1	Charles Ward	0
Skip Alexander (8 and 7)	1	John Panton	0
Sam Snead (4 and 3)	1	Max Faulkner	0
Day Two Total	**6 1/2**	**Day Two Total**	**1 1/2**
UNITED STATES	**9 1/2**	**GREAT BRITAIN**	**2 1/2**

U.S. Team: (Left to Right) Jack Burke Jr., Ben Hogan, Ed Oliver, Jimmy Demaret, Henry Ransom, Sam Snead (Captain), Lloyd Mangrum, Clayton Heafner, Skip Alexander, Dutch Harrison.

Great Britain Team: (Back Row, Left to Right) Art Lees, Ken Bousfield, Harry Weetman, Jack Hargreaves, Johnny Adams, John Panton. (Front Row, Left to Right) Charles Ward, Dai Rees, Arthur Lacey (Non-playing Captain), Max Faulkner, Fred Daly.

1949

Non-playing Captain Ben Hogan, still crippled from his February 1949 automobile accident, complained about the grooves on the clubs of some of the British players. Although the problem was solved the next day, an incensed British team established an opening day lead of 3-1 in the foursomes. However, the U. S. retaliated by winning six singles matches the next day for a 7-5 victory.

Site:	GANTON GOLF CLUB,
	Scarborough, England
Date:	Sept. 16-17
Results:	USA 7	Great Britain 5
Captains:	United States - Ben Hogan
	Great Britain - Charles Whitcombe

Foursomes Matches: USA 1 Great Britain 3

Singles Matches: USA 6 Great Britain 2

United States Team

Skip Alexander	Clayton Heafner
Jimmy Demaret	Lloyd Mangrum
Bob Hamilton	Johnny Palmer
Chick Harbert	Sam Snead
Dutch Harrison	

Great Britain Team

Jimmy Adams	Max Faulkner
Laurie Ayton	Sam King
Ken Bousfield	Arthur Lees
Richard Burton	Dai Rees
Fred Daly	Charles Ward

UNITED STATES / GREAT BRITAIN

Foursomes (Day One)

UNITED STATES		GREAT BRITAIN	
Dutch Harrison & Johnny Palmer	0	Max Faulkner & Jimmy Adams (2 and 1)	1
Bob Hamilton & Skip Alexander	0	Fred Daly & Ken Bousfield (4 and 2)	1
Jimmy Demaret & Clayton Heafner (4 and 3)	1	Charles Ward & Sam King	0
Sam Snead & Lloyd Mangrum	0	Richard Burton & Arthur Lees (1 up)	1
Day One Total	**1**	**Day One Total**	**3**

Singles (Day Two)

UNITED STATES		GREAT BRITAIN	
Dutch Harrison (8 and 7)	1	Max Faulkner	0
Johnny Palmer	0	Jimmy Adams (2 and 1)	1
Sam Snead (6 and 5)	1	Charles Ward	0
Bob Hamilton	0	Dai Rees (6 and 4)	1
Clayton Heafner (3 and 2)	1	Richard Burton	0
Chick Harbert (4 and 3)	1	Sam King	0
Jimmy Demaret (7 and 6)	1	Arthur Lees	0
Lloyd Mangrum (4 and 3)	1	Fred Daly	0
Day Two Total	**6**	**Day Two Total**	**2**

UNITED STATES	7	GREAT BRITAIN	5

U.S. Team: *(Left to Right) Dutch Harrison, Johnny Palmer, Bob Hamilton, Sam Snead, Ben Hogan (Non-playing Captain), Clayton Heafner, Jimmy Demaret, Lloyd Mangrum, Chick Harbert. Absent: Skip Alexander.*

Great Britain Team: *(Back Row, Left to Right) Alfred Padgham, Art Lees, Jimmy Adams, Max Faulkner, Fred Daly, Richard Burton, Laurie Ayton, Arthur Havers. (Front Row, Left to Right) Commander R. Roe (Manager), Sam King, Charles Ward, Charles Whitcombe (Non-playing Captain), Ken Bousfield, Dai Rees, Arthur Lacey.*

1947

The Ryder Cup might not have resumed in 1947 if Oregon fruit packer Bob Hudson hadn't bankrolled the British team. After the war years, the British were no contest for the American team, which included Hogan, Snead, Mangrum, Nelson and Demaret. Only a couple of the matches were close, with Sam King's 4-and-3 win over Herman Keiser the lone point for the British.

Site:	PORTLAND GOLF CLUB, Portland, Ore.	
Date:	Nov. 1-2	
Results:	USA 11	Great Britain 1
Captains:	United States -	Ben Hogan
	Great Britain -	Henry Cotton

Foursomes Matches: USA 4 Great Britain 0

United States Team

Herman Barron	Lloyd Mangrum
Jimmy Demaret	Byron Nelson
Dutch Harrison	Ed Oliver
Ben Hogan	Sam Snead
Herman Keiser	Lew Worsham

Singles Matches: USA 7 Great Britain 1

Great Britain Team

Jimmy Adams	Reg Horne
Henry Cotton	Sam King
Fred Daly	Arthur Lees
Max Faulkner	Dai Rees
Eric Green	Charles Ward

UNITED STATES		GREAT BRITAIN	
Foursomes (Day One)			
Ed Oliver & Lew Worsham (10 and 9)	1	Henry Cotton & Arthur Lees	0
Sam Snead & Lloyd Mangrum (6 and 5)	1	Fred Daly & Charles Ward	0
Ben Hogan & Jimmy Demaret (2 up)	1	Jimmy Adams & Max Faulkner	0
Byron Nelson & Herman Barron (2 and 1)	1	Dai Rees & Sam King	0
Day One Total	**4**	**Day One Total**	**0**
Singles (Day Two)			
Dutch Harrison (5 and 4)	1	Fred Daly	0
Lew Worsham (3 and 2)	1	Jimmy Adams	0
Lloyd Mangrum (6 and 5)	1	Max Faulkner	0
Ed Oliver (4 and 3)	1	Charles Ward	0
Byron Nelson (2 and 1)	1	Arthur Lees	0
Sam Snead (5 and 4)	1	Henry Cotton	0
Jimmy Demaret (3 and 2)	1	Dai Rees	0
Herman Keiser	0	Sam King (4 and 3)	1
Day Two Total	**7**	**Day Two Total**	**1**
UNITED STATES	**11**	**GREAT BRITAIN**	**1**

U.S. Team: (Left to Right) Sam Snead, Jimmy Demaret, Herman Barron, Lew Worsham, Ben Hogan (Captain), Lloyd Mangrum, Byron Nelson, Dutch Harrison, Herman Keiser. Absent: Ed Oliver.

Great Britain Team: (Back Row, Left to Right) Com. R. Roe (Manager), Jimmy Adams, Max Faulkner, Eric Green, Charles Ward, Reg Horne. (Front Row, Left to Right) Sam King, Fred Daly, Henry Cotton (Captain), Dai Rees, Art Lees.

■ **No matches played from 1939-1945 due to World War II.**

1937

In the last pre-World War II Ryder Cup competition, the American team earned its first victory on British soil, breaking the pattern of home turf victories. For the first time in Ryder Cup history, Walter Hagen did not participate as a player, but did serve as captain for the U.S. Team.

Site:	SOUTHPORT & AINSDALE GOLF CLUB, Southport, England	
Date:	June 29-30	
Results:	USA 8	Great Britain 4
Captains:	United States -	Walter Hagen
	Great Britain -	Charles Whitcombe

Foursomes Matches: USA 2½ Great Britain 1½   Singles Matches: USA 5½ Great Britain 2½

United States Team		Great Britain Team	
Ed Dudley	Johnny Revolta	Percy Alliss	Arthur Lacey
Ralph Guldahl	Gene Sarazen	Richard Burton	Alf Padgham
Tony Manero	Denny Shute	Henry Cotton	Alf Perry
Byron Nelson	Horton Smith	Bill Cox	Dai Rees
Henry Picard	Sam Snead	Sam King	Charles Whitcombe

UNITED STATES		GREAT BRITAIN	
Foursomes (Day One)			
Ed Dudley & Byron Nelson (4 and 2)	1	Alf Padgham & Henry Cotton	0
Ralph Guldahl & Tony Manero (2 and 1)	1	Arthur Lacey & Bill Cox	0
Gene Sarazen & Denny Shute (halved)	½	Charles Whitcombe & Dai Rees (halved)	½
Henry Picard & Johnny Revolta	0	Percy Alliss & Richard Burton (2 and 1)	1
Day One Total	**2½**	**Day One Total**	**1½**
Singles (Day Two)			
Ralph Guldahl (8 and 7)	1	Alf Padgham	0
Denny Shute (halved)	½	Sam King (halved)	½
Byron Nelson	0	Dai Rees (3 and 1)	1
Tony Manero	0	Henry Cotton (5 and 3)	1
Gene Sarazen (1 up)	1	Percy Alliss	0
Sam Snead (5 and 4)	1	Richard Burton	0
Ed Dudley (2 and 1)	1	Alf Perry	0
Henry Picard (2 and 1)	1	Arthur Lacey	0
Day Two Total	**5½**	**Day Two Total**	**2½**

UNITED STATES	8	GREAT BRITAIN	4

U.S. Team: *(Back Row, Left to Right) Walter Hagen (Captain), Ed Dudley, Henry Picard, Gene Sarazan, Sam Snead, Horton Smith, Fred Corcoran (PGA Tournament Bureau Manager). (Front Row, Left to Right) Byron Nelson, Tony Manero, Ralph Guldahl, Denny Shute, Johnny Revolta.*

Great Britain Team: *(Back Row, Left to Right) Com. R. Roe (Manager), William Cox, Alfred Padgham, Henry Cotton, Alf Perry, Richard Burton. (Front Row, Left to Right) Arthur Lacey, Sam King, Charles Whitcombe (Captain), Dai Rees, Percy Alliss.*

1935

Sending a team that included the three Whitcombe brothers, the British were defeated as the U. S. breezed to a six-point victory. Gene Sarazen, Paul Runyan, Henry Picard and Olin Dutra each won two points.

Site:	RIDGEWOOD COUNTRY CLUB, Ridgewood, N. J.	
Date:	Sept. 28-29	
Results:	USA 9	Great Britain 3
Captains:	United States -	Walter Hagen
	Great Britain -	Charles Whitcombe

Foursomes Matches: USA 3 Great Britain 1

United States Team

Olin Dutra	Johnny Revolta
Walter Hagen	Paul Runyan
Ky Laffoon	Gene Sarazen
Sam Parks	Horton Smith
Henry Picard	Craig Wood

Singles Matches: USA 6 Great Britain 2

Great Britain Team

Percy Alliss	Alf Padgham
Richard Burton	Alf Perry
Jack Busson	Charles Whitcombe
Bill Cox	Ernest Whitcombe
Edward Jarman	Reg Whitcombe

UNITED STATES / GREAT BRITAIN

Foursomes (Day One)

Gene Sarazen & Walter Hagen (7 and 6)	1	Alf Perry & Jack Busson	0
Henry Picard & Johnny Revolta (6 and 5)	1	Alf Padgham & Percy Alliss	0
Paul Runyan & Horton Smith (9 and 8)	1	Bill Cox & Edward Jarman	0
Olin Dutra & Ky Laffoon	0	C. Whitcombe & E. Whitcombe (1 up)	1
Day One Total	**3**	**Day One Total**	**1**

Singles (Day Two)

Gene Sarazen (3 and 2)	1	Jack Busson	0
Paul Runyan (5 and 3)	1	Richard Burton	0
Johnny Revolta (2 and 1)	1	Reg Whitcombe	0
Olin Dutra (4 and 2)	1	Alf Padgham	0
Craig Wood	0	Percy Alliss (1 up)	1
Horton Smith (halved)	½	Bill Cox (halved)	½
Henry Picard (3 and 2)	1	Ernest Whitcombe	0
Sam Parks (halved)	½	Alf Perry (halved)	½
Day Two Total	**6**	**Day Two Total**	**2**

UNITED STATES	9	GREAT BRITAIN	3

U.S. Team: (Back Row, Left to Right) Olin Dutra, Horton Smith, Craig Wood, Walter Hagen (Captain), Sam Parks, Henry Picard. (Front Row, Left to Right) Johnny Revolta, George Jacobus, Paul Runyan, Gene Sarazen, Ky Laffoon.

Great Britain Team: (Back Row, Left to Right) William Cox, E. Jarman, Richard Burton, Com. R. Roe (Manager), Reginald Whitcombe, Alfred Padgham. (Front Row, Left to Right) Ernest Whitcombe, Percy Alliss, Charles Whitcombe (Captain), Alf Perry, Jack Busson.

1933

With 15,000 spectators on hand, the final singles match was one of the most exciting finishes in Ryder Cup history. Britain's Syd Easterbrook and American Denny Shute stood all square on the last green with 30-foot putts. Easterbrook putted first and left his approach putt within tap-in range. Shute then hit his first putt four feet past the hole and missed the return putt. This gave the trophy back to Britain, a victory that would not be repeated for the next 24 years. This tied the series, 2-2, and was the last match that Samuel Ryder would attend. Ryder died in 1936, before the matches returned to Britain.

Site:	SOUTHPORT & AINSDALE GOLF CLUB, Southport, England
Date:	June 26-27
Results:	Great Britain 6½ USA 5½
Captains:	United States - Walter Hagen
	Great Britain - J.H. Taylor

Foursomes Matches: USA 1½ Great Britain 2½   Singles Matches: USA 4 Great Britain 4

United States Team		Great Britain Team	
Billy Burke	Paul Runyan	Percy Alliss	Arthur Lacey
Leo Diegel	Gene Sarazen	Allan Dailey	Abe Mitchell
Ed Dudley	Denny Shute	William Davies	Alf Padgham
Olin Dutra	Horton Smith	Syd Easterbrook	Alf Perry
Walter Hagen	Craig Wood	Arthur Havers	Charles Whitcombe

UNITED STATES		GREAT BRITAIN	
Foursomes (Day One)			
Gene Sarazen & Walter Hagen (halved)	½	Percy Alliss & Charles Whitcombe (halved)	½
Olin Dutra & Denny Shute	0	Abe Mitchell & Arthur Havers (3 and 2)	1
Craig Wood & Paul Runyan	0	William Davies & Syd Easterbrook (1 up)	1
Ed Dudley & Billy Burke (1 up)	1	Alf Padgham & Alf Perry	0
Day One Total	**1½**	**Day One Total**	**2½**
Singles (Day Two)			
Gene Sarazen (6 and 4)	1	Alf Padgham	0
Olin Dutra	0	Abe Mitchell (9 and 8)	1
Walter Hagen (2 and 1)	1	Arthur Lacey	0
Craig Wood (4 and 3)	1	William Davies	0
Paul Runyan	0	Percy Alliss (2 and 1)	1
Leo Diegel	0	Arthur Havers (4 and 3)	1
Denny Shute	0	Syd Easterbrook (1 up)	1
Horton Smith (2 and 1)	1	Charles Whitcombe	0
Day Two Total	**4**	**Day Two Total**	**4**
UNITED STATES	**5½**	**GREAT BRITAIN**	**6½**

U.S. Team: (Left to Right) Walter Hagen (Captain), Craig Wood, Denny Shute, Ed Dudley, Paul Runyan, Horton Smith, Gene Sarazen, Olin Dutra, Leo Diegel, Billy Burke.

Great Britain Team: *(Back Row, Left to Right) Alf Perry, Syd Easterbrook, Arthur Havers, A. Stark (Trainer), Alfred Padgham, Arthur Lacey, Percy Alliss. (Front Row, Left to Right) Charles Whitcombe, J.H. Taylor (Non-playing Captain), Abe Mitchell. (Seated on ground) A. Dailey, Bill Davies.*

1931

Playing in stifling heat, Walter Hagen, Gene Sarazen, Denny Shute, Billy Burke, Al Espinosa and Wiffy Cox all won their singles matches to help the Americans to a 9 - 3 victory.

Site:	SCIOTO COUNTRY CLUB, Columbus, Ohio	
Date:	June 26-27	
Results:	USA 9	Great Britain 3
Captains:	United States -	Walter Hagen
	Great Britain -	Charles Whitcombe

United States Team
Billy Burke	Walter Hagen
Wilfred Cox	Gene Sarazen
Leo Diegel	Denny Shute
Al Espinosa	Horton Smith
Johnny Farrell	Craig Wood

Great Britain Team
Percy Alliss	Arthur Havers
Archie Compston	Bert Hodson
William Davies	Abe Mitchell
George Duncan	Fred Robson
Syd Easterbrook	Charles Whitcombe
	Ernest Whitcombe

UNITED STATES   GREAT BRITAIN

Foursomes (Day One)

Gene Sarazen & Johnny Farrell (8 and 7)	1	Archie Compston & William Davies	0
Walter Hagen & Denny Shute (10 and 9)	1	George Duncan & Arthur Havers	0
Leo Diegel & Al Espinosa	0	Abe Mitchell & Fred Robson (3 and 1)	1
Billy Burke & Wilfred Cox (3 and 2)	1	Syd Easterbrook & E. Whitcombe	0
Day One Total	**3**	**Day One Total**	**1**

Singles (Day Two)

Billy Burke (7 and 6)	1	Archie Compston	0
Gene Sarazen (7 and 6)	1	Fred Robson	0
Johnny Farrell	0	William Davies (4 and 3)	1
Wilfred Cox (3 and 1)	1	Abe Mitchell	0
Walter Hagen (4 and 3)	1	Charles Whitcombe	0
Denny Shute (8 and 6)	1	Bert Hodson	0
Al Espinosa (2 and 1)	1	Ernest Whitcombe	0
Craig Wood	0	Arthur Havers (4 and 3)	1
Day Two Total	**6**	**Day Two Total**	**2**

UNITED STATES	9	GREAT BRITAIN	3

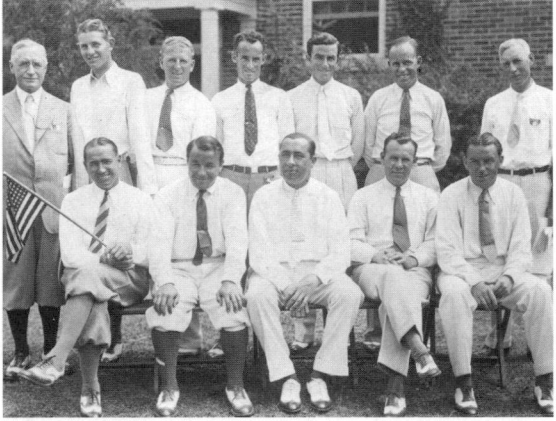

U.S. Team: (Back Row, Left to Right) Albert Gates (PGA Official), Horton Smith, Craig Wood, Denny Shute, Johnny Farrell, Wiffy Cox, George Sargent (PGA Official). (Front Row, Left to Right) Leo Diegel, Gene Sarazen, Walter Hagen (Captain), Al Espinosa, Billy Burke.

Great Britain Team: (Back Row, Left to Right) Ernest Whitcombe, Percy Alliss, Bert Hodson, F. Pignon (Manager), Abe Mitchell, Bill Davies, Syd Easterbrook. (Front Row, Left to Right) Archie Compston, George Duncan, Charles Whitcombe (Captain), Arthur Havers, Fred Robson.

1929

Britain took revenge in 1929 against Walter Hagen's team with a splendid comeback in the singles after trailing 2½-1½ in the foursomes. In a match between the two captains, George Duncan lambasted Hagen, 10 and 8, while Archie Compston beat Gene Sarazen, 6 and 4. One of the key victories was 22-year-old Henry Cotton's 4-and-3 win over Al Watrous, securing the British victory.

Site:	MOORTOWN GOLF CLUB, Leeds, England
Date:	May 26-27
Results:	Great Britain 7 USA 5
Captains:	United States - Walter Hagen
	Great Britain - George Duncan

United States Team

Leo Diegel	Walter Hagen
Ed Dudley	Gene Sarazen
Al Espinosa	Horton Smith
Johnny Farrell	Joe Turnesa
Johnny Golden	Al Watrous

Great Britain Team

Percy Alliss	George Duncan
Aubrey Boomer	Abe Mitchell
Stewart Burns	Fred Robson
Archie Compston	Charles Whitcombe
Henry Cotton	Ernest Whitcombe

UNITED STATES		GREAT BRITAIN	
Foursomes (Day One)			
Johnny Farrell & Joe Turnesa (halved)	½	Charles Whitcombe & A. Compston (halved)	½
Leo Diegel & Al Espinosa (7 and 5)	1	Aubrey Boomer & George Duncan	0
Gene Sarazen & Ed Dudley	0	Abe Mitchell & Fred Robson (2 and 1)	1
Johnny Golden & Walter Hagen (2 up)	1	Ernest Whitcombe & Henry Cotton	0
Day One Total	**2½**	**Day One Total**	**1½**
Singles (Day Two)			
Johnny Farrell	0	Charles Whitcombe (8 and 6)	1
Walter Hagen	0	George Duncan (10 and 8)	1
Leo Diegel (9 and 8)	1	Abe Mitchell	0
Gene Sarazen	0	Archie Compston (6 and 4)	1
Joe Turnesa	0	Aubrey Boomer (4 and 3)	1
Horton Smith (4 and 2)	1	Fred Robson	0
Al Watrous	0	Henry Cotton (4 and 3)	1
Al Espinosa (halved)	½	Ernest Whitcombe (halved)	½
Day Two Total	**2½**	**Day Two Total**	**5½**

UNITED STATES	5	GREAT BRITAIN	7

U.S. Team: (Back Row, Left to Right) Ed Dudley, Al Watrous, Gene Sarazen, Leo Diegel, Al Espinosa, Johnny Farrell. (Front row, Left to Right) Horton Smith, Walter Hagen (Captain), Joe Turnesa, Johnny Golden.

Great Britain Team: *(Back Row, Left to Right) Stewart Burns, Abe Mitchell, Charles Whitcombe, Fred Robson. (Front Row, Left to Right) Ernest Whitcombe, Percy Alliss, George Duncan (Captain), Henry Cotton. (Seated) Archie Compston, Aubrey Boomer.*

1927

Beginning with the first formal match, the American team was limited to native-born Americans. Thus, only Walter Hagen, Bill Mehlhorn and Al Watrous remained from the informal team of the previous year. The British team was virtually intact from 1926, with the exception of Charles Whitcombe, who replaced his brother Ernie, and Ted Ray, who took over the Captain's duties from ailing Abe Mitchell. In a competition consisting of four foursomes and eight singles matches, the American squad won nine of the matches, with only two losses and one halve.

Site:	WORCESTER COUNTRY CLUB, Worcester, Mass.	
Date:	June 3-4	
Results:	USA 9½	Great Britain 2½
Captains:	United States -	Walter Hagen
	Great Britain -	Ted Ray

Foursomes Matches: USA 3 Great Britain 1

United States Team

Leo Diegel	Walter Hagen
Al Espinosa	Bill Mehlhorn
Johnny Farrell	Gene Sarazen
Johnny Golden	Joe Turnesa
	Al Watrous

Singles Matches: USA 6½ Great Britain 1½

Great Britain Team

Aubrey Boomer	Herbert Jolly
Archie Compston	Ted Ray
George Duncan	Fred Robson
George Gadd	Charles Whitcombe
Arthur Havers	

UNITED STATES		GREAT BRITAIN	
Foursomes (Day One)			
Walter Hagen & Johnny Golden (2 and 1)	1	Ted Ray & Fred Robson	0
Johnny Farrell & Joe Turnesa (8 and 6)	1	George Duncan & Archie Compston	0
Gene Sarazen & Al Watrous (3 and 2)	1	Arthur Havers & Herbert Jolly	0
Leo Diegel & Bill Mehlhorn	0	Aubrey Boomer & Charles Whitcombe (7 and 5)	1
Day One Total	**3**	**Day One Total**	**1**
Singles (Day Two)			
Bill Mehlhorn (1 up)	1	Archie Compston	0
Johnny Farrell (5 and 4)	1	Arthur Boomer	0
Johnny Golden (8 and 7)	1	Herbert Jolly	0
Leo Diegel (7 and 5)	1	Ted Ray	0
Gene Sarazen (halved)	½	Charles Whitcombe (halved)	½
Walter Hagen (2 and 1)	1	Arthur Havers	0
Al Watrous (3 and 2)	1	Fred Robson	0
Joe Turnesa	0	George Duncan (1 up)	1
Day Two Total	**6½**	**Day Two Total**	**1½**
UNITED STATES	**9½**	**GREAT BRITAIN**	**2½**

U.S. Team: (Back Row, Left to Right) Johnny Golden, Joe Turnesa, Johnny Farrell, Al Watrous. (Front row, Left to Right) Leo Diegel, Bill Mehlhorn, Walter Hagen (Captain), Al Espinosa, Gene Sarazen.

Great Britain Team: (Left to Right) George Duncan, Archie Compston, Ted Ray (Captain), Fred Robson, Samuel Ryder (with dog); George Gadd, Charles Whitcombe, Arthur Havers, Abe Mitchell, G. Philpott (Manager), Absent: Herbert Jolly, Aubrey Boomer.

Player	Years Played	Years	No. of Matches	R.C. Records W-L-H	Singles Record W-L-H	Foursomes Record W-L-H	Four-balls Record W-L-H	Total Points Won	Point Pct*
Tommy Aaron	1969-73	2	6	1-4-1	0-2-0	1-1-0	0-1-1	1.5	.25
Skip Alexander	1949-51	2	2	1-1-0	1-0-0	0-1-0	0-0-0	1.0	.50
Paul Azinger	1989-91-93	3	14	5-7-2	2-0-1	2-3-0	1-4-1	6.0	.43
Jerry Barber	1955-61	2	5	1-4-0	0-3-0	1-1-0	0-0-0	1.0	.20
Miller Barber	1969-71	2	7	1-4-2	1-1-0	0-3-0	0-0-2	2.0	.29
Herman Barron	1947	1	1	1-0-0	0-0-0	1-0-0	0-0-0	1.0	1.00
Andy Bean	1979-87	2	6	4-2-0	2-0-0	0-1-0	2-1-0	4.0	.67
Frank Beard	1969-71	2	8	2-3-3	0-1-1	0-2-1	2-0-1	3.5	.44
Chip Beck	1989-91-93	3	9	6-2-1	3-0-0	1-1-1	2-1-0	6.5	.72
Homero Blancas	1973	1	4	2-1-1	1-1-0	0-0-0	1-0-1	2.5	.63
Tommy Bolt	1955-57	2	4	3-1-0	1-1-0	2-0-0	0-0-0	3.0	.75
Julius Boros	1959-63-65-67	4	16	9-3-4	3-2-1	5-0-2	1-1-1	11.0	.69
Gay Brewer	1967-73	2	9	5-3-1	2-1-1	0-1-0	3-1-0	5.5	.61
Billy Burke	1931-33	2	3	3-0-0	1-0-0	2-0-0	0-0-0	3.0	1.00
Jack Burke Jr.	1951-53-55-57-59	5	8	7-1-0	3-1-0	4-0-0	0-0-0	7.0	.88
Walter Burkemo	1953	1	1	0-1-0	0-0-0	0-1-0	0-0-0	0.0	.00
Mark Calcavecchia	1987-89-91	3	11	5-5-1	1-1-1	4-0-0	0-4-0	5.5	.50
Billy Casper	1961-63-65-67-69-71-73-75	8	37	20-10-7	6-2-2	8-5-2	6-3-3	23.5	.64
Chi Chi Rodriguez	1973	1	2	0-1-1	0-0-0	0-1-1	0-0-0	0.5	.25
Bill Collins	1961	1	3	1-2-0	0-1-0	1-1-0	0-0-0	1.0	.33
Charles Coody	1971	1	3	0-2-1	0-1-0	0-1-0	0-0-1	0.5	.17
John Cook	1993	1	2	1-1-0	0-1-0	0-0-0	1-0-0	1.0	.50
Fred Couples	1989-91-93	3	12	3-6-3	1-1-1	1-3-0	1-2-2	4.5	.38
Wilfred Cox	1931	1	2	2-0-0	1-0-0	1-0-0	0-0-0	2.0	1.00
Ben Crenshaw	1981-83-87	3	9	3-5-1	2-1-0	1-1-0	0-3-1	3.5	.39
Jimmy Demaret	1947-49-51	3	6	6-0-0	3-0-0	3-0-0	0-0-0	5.0	1.00
Gardner Dickinson	1967-71	2	10	9-1-0	2-1-0	4-0-0	3-0-0	9.0	.90
Leo Diegel	1927-29-31-33	4	6	3-3-0	2-1-0	1-2-0	0-0-0	3.0	.50
Dave Douglas	1953	1	2	1-0-1	0-0-1	1-0-0	0-0-0	1.5	.75
Dale Douglass	1969	1	2	0-2-0	0-1-0	0-0-0	0-1-0	0.0	.00
Ed Dudley	1929-33-37	3	4	3-1-0	1-0-0	2-1-0	0-0-0	3.0	.75
Olin Dutra	1933-35	2	4	1-3-0	1-1-0	0-2-0	0-0-0	1.0	.25
Lee Elder	1979	1	4	1-3-0	0-1-0	0-1-0	1-1-0	1.0	.25
Al Espinosa	1927-29-31	3	4	2-1-1	1-0-1	1-1-0	0-0-0	2.5	.63
Johnny Farrell	1927-29-31	3	6	3-2-1	1-2-0	2-0-1	0-0-0	3.5	.58
Dow Finsterwald	1957-59-61-63	4	13	9-3-1	3-3-0	4-0-1	2-0-0	9.5	.73
Raymond Floyd	1969-75-77-81-83-85-91-93	8	30	12-16-2	4-4-0	4-8-0	4-4-2	13.0	.43
Doug Ford	1955-57-59-61	4	9	4-4-1	2-2-1	2-2-0	0-0-0	4.5	.50
Ed Furgol	1957	1	1	0-1-0	0-1-0	0-0-0	0-0-0	0.0	.00
Marty Furgol	1955	1	1	0-1-0	0-1-0	0-0-0	0-0-0	0.0	.00
Jim Gallagher Jr.	1993	1	3	2-1-0	1-0-0	0-0-0	1-1-0	2.0	.67
Al Geiberger	1967-75	2	9	5-1-3	2-0-1	2-1-0	1-0-2	6.5	.72
Bob Gilder	1983	1	4	2-2-0	1-0-0	0-2-0	1-0-0	2.0	.50
Bob Goalby	1963	1	5	4-0-1	2-0-0	1-0-0	1-0-1	4.5	.90
Johnny Golden	1927-29	2	3	3-0-0	1-0-0	2-0-0	0-0-0	3.0	1.00
Lou Graham	1973-75-77	3	9	5-3-1	1-1-0	1-2-1	3-0-0	5.5	.61
Hubert Green	1977-79-85	3	7	4-3-0	3-0-0	0-1-0	1-2-0	4.0	.57
Ken Green	1989	1	4	2-2-0	0-1-0	2-0-0	0-1-0	2.0	.50
Ralph Guldahl	1937	1	2	2-0-0	1-0-0	1-0-0	0-0-0	2.0	1.00
Jay Haas	1983	1	4	2-1-1	0-1-0	1-0-0	1-0-1	2.5	.63
Fred Haas Jr.	1953	1	1	0-1-0	0-1-0	0-0-0	0-0-0	0.0	.00
Walter Hagen	1927-29-31-33-35	5	9	7-1-1	3-1-0	4-0-1	0-0-0	7.5	.83
Bob Hamilton	1949	1	2	0-2-0	0-1-0	0-1-0	0-0-0	0.0	.00
Chick Harbert	1949-55	2	2	2-0-0	2-0-0	0-0-0	0-0-0	2.0	1.00
Chandler Harper	1955	1	1	0-1-0	0-0-0	0-1-0	0-0-0	0.0	.00
Dutch Harrison	1947-49-51	3	3	2-1-0	2-0-0	0-1-0	0-0-0	2.0	.67
Fred Hawkins	1957	1	2	1-1-0	1-0-0	0-1-0	0-0-0	1.0	.50
Mark Hayes	1979	1	3	1-2-0	1-0-0	0-1-0	0-1-0	1.0	.33
Clayton Heafner	1949-51	2	4	3-0-1	1-0-1	2-0-0	0-0-0	3.5	.88
Jay Hebert	1959-61	2	4	2-1-1	0-1-1	2-0-0	0-0-0	2.5	.63
Lionel Hebert	1957	1	1	0-1-0	0-1-0	0-0-0	0-0-0	0.0	.00
Dave Hill	1969-73-77	3	9	6-3-0	3-0-0	1-2-0	2-1-0	6.0	.67
Ben Hogan	1947-51	2	3	3-0-0	1-0-0	2-0-0	0-0-0	3.0	1.00
Hale Irwin	1975-77-79-81-91	5	20	13-5-2	3-1-2	6-1-0	4-3-0	14.0	.70
Tommy Jacobs	1965	1	4	3-1-0	1-1-0	0-0-0	2-0-0	3.0	.75
Peter Jacobsen	1985	1	3	1-2-0	0-1-0	1-0-0	0-1-0	1.0	.33
Don January	1965-77	2	7	2-3-2	0-1-1	0-2-1	2-0-0	3.0	.43
Lee Janzen	1993	1	2	0-2-0	0-1-0	0-0-0	0-1-0	0.0	.00
Herman Keiser	1947	1	1	0-1-0	0-1-0	0-0-0	0-0-0	0.0	.00
Tom Kite	1979-81-83-85-87-89-93	7	28	15-9-4	5-0-2	7-5-1	3-4-1	17.0	.61
Ted Kroll	1953-55-57	3	4	3-1-0	0-1-0	3-0-0	0-0-0	3.0	.75

*Note: To better evaluate a player's performance in the Ryder Cup, the percentage category reflects the number of total points earned versus the number of matches (possible points) played.

Player	Years Played	Years	No. of Matches	R.C. Records W-L-H	Singles Record W-L-H	Foursomes Record W-L-H	Four-balls Record W-L-H	Total Points Won	Point Pct*
Ky Laffoon	1935	1	1	0-1-0	0-0-0	0-1-0	0-0-0	0.0	.00
Tony Lema	1963-65	2	11	8-1-2	3-0-1	3-0-1	2-1-0	9.0	.82
Wayne Levi	1991	1	2	0-2-0	0-1-0	0-0-0	0-1-0	0.0	.00
Bruce Lietzke	1981	1	3	0-2-1	0-0-1	0-1-0	0-1-0	0.5	.17
Gene Littler	1961-63-65-67-69-71-75	7	27	14-5-8	5-2-3	4-3-1	5-0-4	18.0	.67
Davis Love III	1993	1	4	2-2-0	1-0-0	1-1-0	0-1-0	2.0	.50
John Mahaffey	1979	1	3	1-2-0	1-0-0	0-1-0	0-1-0	1.0	.33
Tony Manero	1937	1	2	1-1-0	0-1-0	1-0-0	0-0-0	1.0	.50
Lloyd Mangrum	1947-49-51-53	4	8	6-2-0	3-1-0	3-1-0	0-0-0	6.0	.75
Dave Marr	1965	1	6	4-2-0	2-0-0	1-1-0	1-1-0	4.0	.67
Billy Maxwell	1963	1	4	4-0-0	1-0-0	1-0-0	2-0-0	4.0	1.00
Dick Mayer	1957	1	2	1-0-1	0-0-1	1-0-0	0-0-0	1.5	.75
Mark McCumber	1989	1	3	2-1-0	1-0-0	0-0-0	1-1-0	2.0	.67
Jerry McGee	1977	1	2	1-1-0	0-1-0	1-0-0	0-0-0	1.0	.50
Bill Mehlhorn	1927	1	2	1-1-0	1-0-0	0-1-0	0-0-0	1.0	.50
Cary Middlecoff	1953-55-59	3	6	2-3-1	1-2-0	1-1-1	0-0-0	2.5	.42
Johnny Miller	1975-81	2	6	2-2-2	0-2-0	2-0-0	0-0-2	3.0	.50
Larry Mize	1987	1	4	1-1-2	0-0-1	0-1-1	1-0-0	2.0	.50
Gil Morgan	1979-83	2	6	1-2-3	0-1-1	1-0-1	0-1-1	2.5	.42
Bob Murphy	1975	1	4	2-1-1	2-0-0	0-1-0	0-0-1	2.5	.63
Byron Nelson	1937-47	2	4	3-1-0	1-1-0	2-0-0	0-0-0	3.0	.75
Larry Nelson	1979-81-87	3	13	9-3-1	2-0-1	4-2-0	3-1-0	9.5	.73
Bobby Nichols	1967	1	5	4-0-1	1-0-1	2-0-0	1-0-0	4.5	.90
Jack Nicklaus	1969-71-73-75-77-81	6	28	17-8-3	4-4-2	8-1-0	5-3-1	18.5	.66
Andy North	1985	1	3	0-3-0	0-1-0	0-0-0	0-2-0	0.0	.00
Mark O'Meara	1985-89-91	3	8	2-5-1	0-3-0	1-1-0	1-1-1	2.5	.31
Ed Oliver	1947-51-53	3	5	3-2-0	1-1-0	2-1-0	0-0-0	3.0	.60
Arnold Palmer	1961-63-65-67-71-73	6	32	22-8-2	6-3-2	9-3-0	7-2-0	23.0	.72
Johnny Palmer	1949	1	2	0-2-0	0-1-0	0-1-0	0-0-0	0.0	.00
Sam Parks	1935	1	1	0-0-1	0-0-1	0-0-0	0-0-0	0.5	.50
Jerry Pate	1981	1	4	2-2-0	0-1-0	1-0-0	1-1-0	2.0	.50
Steve Pate	1991	1	2	0-1-1	0-0-1	0-0-0	0-1-0	0.5	.25
Corey Pavin	1991-93	2	8	4-4-0	1-1-0	1-1-0	2-2-0	4.0	.50
Calvin Peete	1983-85	2	7	4-2-1	2-0-0	2-1-0	0-1-1	4.5	.64
Henry Picard	1935-37	2	4	3-1-0	2-0-0	1-1-0	0-0-0	3.0	.75
Dan Pohl	1987	1	3	1-2-0	0-1-0	1-0-0	0-1-0	1.0	.33
Johnny Pott	1963-65-67	3	7	5-2-0	1-1-0	2-1-0	2-0-0	5.0	.71
Dave Ragan	1963	1	4	3-0-1	1-0-0	1-0-0	1-0-1	3.5	.88
Henry Ransom	1951	1	1	0-1-0	0-0-0	0-1-0	0-0-0	0.0	.00
Johnny Revolta	1935-37	2	3	2-1-0	1-0-0	1-1-0	0-0-0	2.0	.67
Bill Rogers	1981	1	4	1-2-1	0-0-1	1-1-0	0-1-0	1.5	.38
Bob Rosburg	1959	1	2	2-0-0	1-0-0	1-0-0	0-0-0	2.0	1.00
Mason Rudolph	1971	1	3	1-1-1	0-1-0	0-0-1	1-0-0	1.5	.50
Paul Runyan	1933-35	2	4	2-2-0	1-1-0	1-1-0	0-0-0	2.0	.50
Doug Sanders	1967	1	5	2-3-0	0-2-0	0-1-0	2-0-0	2.0	.40
Gene Sarazen	1927-29-31-33-35-37	6	12	7-2-3	4-1-1	3-1-2	0-0-0	8.5	.71
Denny Shute	1931-33-37	3	6	2-2-2	1-1-1	1-1-1	0-0-0	3.0	.50
Dan Sikes	1969	1	3	2-1-0	1-0-0	1-0-0	0-1-0	2.0	.67
Scott Simpson	1987	1	2	1-1-0	1-0-0	0-0-0	0-1-0	1.0	.50
Horton Smith	1929-31-33-35-37	5	4	3-0-1	2-0-1	1-0-0	0-0-0	3.5	.88
J.C. Snead	1971-73-75	3	11	9-2-0	3-1-0	2-1-0	4-0-0	9.0	.82
Sam Snead	1937-47-49-51-53-55-59	7	13	10-2-1	6-1-0	4-1-1	0-0-0	10.5	.81
Ed Sneed	1977	1	2	1-0-1	0-0-0	0-0-1	1-0-0	1.5	.75
Mike Souchak	1959-61	2	6	5-1-0	3-0-0	2-1-0	0-0-0	5.0	.83
Craig Stadler	1983-85	2	8	4-2-2	2-0-0	1-2-0	1-0-2	5.0	.63
Payne Stewart	1987-89-91-93	4	16	8-7-1	2-2-0	4-4-0	2-1-1	8.5	.53
Ken Still	1969	1	3	1-2-0	0-1-0	0-1-0	1-0-0	1.0	.33
Dave Stockton	1971-77	2	5	3-1-1	1-0-1	1-1-0	1-0-0	3.5	.70
Curtis Strange	1983-85-87-89	4	17	6-9-2	2-2-0	4-2-1	0-5-1	7.0	.41
Hal Sutton	1985-87	2	9	3-3-3	0-1-1	2-1-1	1-1-1	4.5	.50
Lee Trevino	1969-71-73-75-79-81	6	30	17-7-6	6-2-2	5-3-2	6-2-2	20.0	.67
Jim Turnesa	1953	1	1	1-0-0	1-0-0	0-0-0	0-0-0	1.0	1.00
Joe Turnesa	1927-29	2	4	1-2-1	0-2-0	1-0-1	0-0-0	1.5	.38
Ken Venturi	1965	1	4	1-3-0	0-1-0	0-2-0	1-0-0	1.0	.25
Lanny Wadkins	1977-79-83-85-87-89-91-93	8	34	20-11-3	4-2-2	9-6-0	7-3-1	21.5	.63
Art Wall	1957-59-61	3	6	4-2-0	2-0-0	2-2-0	0-0-0	4.0	.67
Al Watrous	1927-29	2	3	2-1-0	1-1-0	1-0-0	0-0-0	2.0	.67
Tom Watson	1977-81-83-89	4	15	10-4-1	2-2-0	4-1-0	4-1-0	10.5	.70
Tom Weiskopf	1973-75	2	10	7-2-1	2-0-1	3-1-0	2-1-0	7.5	.75
Craig Wood	1931-33-35	3	4	1-3-0	1-2-0	0-1-0	0-0-0	1.0	.25
Lew Worsham	1947	1	2	2-0-0	1-0-0	1-0-0	0-0-0	2.0	1.00
Fuzzy Zoeller	1979-83-85	3	10	1-8-1	0-2-1	0-2-0	1-4-0	1.5	.15

*Note: To better evaluate a player's performance in the Ryder Cup, the percentage category reflects the number of total points earned versus the number of matches (possible points) played.

RYDER CUP PLAYER RECORDS - EUROPE

Player	Years Played	Years	No. of Matches	R.C. Record W-L-H	Singles Record W-L-H	Foursomes Record W-L-H	Four-balls Record W-L-H	Total Points Won	Point Pct*
Jimmy Adams	1947-49-51-53	4	7	2-5-0	1-2-0	1-3-0	0-0-0	2.0	.29
Percy Alliss	1929-31-33-35-37	5	6	3-2-1	2-1-0	1-1-1	0-0-0	3.5	.58
Peter Alliss	1953-57-59-61-63-65-67-69	8	30	10-15-5	5-4-3	4-6-1	1-5-1	12.5	.42
Peter Baker	1993	1	4	3-1-0	1-0-0	0-1-0	2-0-0	3.0	.75
Seve Ballesteros	1979-83-85-87-89-91-93	7	34	19-10-5	1-3-2	10-3-1	7-4-2	21.5	.63
Harry Bannerman	1971	1	5	2-2-1	1-0-1	1-0-0	0-2-0	2.5	.50
Brian Barnes	1969-71-73-75-77-79	6	25	10-14-1	5-5-0	2-4-0	3-5-1	10.5	.42
Maurice Bembridge	1969-71-73-75	4	17	6-8-3	1-3-1	3-5-0	2-0-2	7.5	.44
Aubrey Boomer	1927-29	2	4	2-2-0	1-1-0	1-1-0	0-0-0	2.0	.50
Ken Bousfield	1949-51-55-57-59-61	6	10	5-5-0	2-2-0	3-3-0	0-0-0	5.0	.50
Hugh Boyle	1967	1	3	0-3-0	0-1-0	0-1-0	0-1-0	0.0	.00
Harry Bradshaw	1953-55-57	3	5	2-2-1	1-1-1	1-1-0	0-0-0	2.5	.50
Gordon Brand Jr	1987-89	2	7	2-4-1	0-1-1	0-2-0	2-1-0	2.5	.36
Gordon Brand Sr	1983	1	1	0-1-0	0-1-0	0-0-0	0-0-0	0.0	.00
Paul Broadhurst	1991	1	2	2-0-0	1-0-0	0-0-0	1-0-0	2.0	1.00
Eric Brown	1953-55-57-59	4	8	4-4-0	4-0-0	0-4-0	0-0-0	4.0	.50
Ken Brown	1977-79-83-85-87	5	13	4-9-0	2-2-0	1-4-0	1-3-0	4.0	.31
Richard Burton	1935-37-49	3	5	2-3-0	0-3-0	2-0-0	0-0-0	2.0	.40
Jack Busson	1935	1	2	0-2-0	0-1-0	0-1-0	0-0-0	0.0	.00
Peter Butler	1965-69-71-73	4	14	3-9-2	2-3-0	1-4-0	0-2-2	4.0	.29
J.M. Canizares	1981-83-85-89	4	11	5-4-2	2-1-1	2-1-0	1-2-1	6.0	.55
Alex Caygill	1969	1	1	0-0-1	0-0-0	0-0-0	0-0-1	0.5	.50
Clive Clark	1973	1	1	0-1-0	0-0-0	0-0-0	0-1-0	0.0	.00
Howard Clark	1977-81-85-87-89	5	13	6-6-1	3-2-0	0-3-0	3-1-1	6.5	.50
Neil Coles	1961-63-65-67-69-71-73-77	8	40	12-21-7	5-6-4	4-8-1	3-7-2	15.5	.39
Archie Compston	1927-29-31	3	6	1-4-1	1-2-0	0-2-1	0-0-0	1.5	.25
Henry Cotton	1929-37-47	3	6	2-4-0	2-1-0	0-3-0	0-0-0	2.0	.33
Bill Cox	1935-37	2	3	0-2-1	0-0-1	0-2-0	0-0-0	0.5	.17
Fred Daly	1947-49-51-53	4	8	3-4-1	1-2-1	2-2-0	0-0-0	3.5	.44
Eamonn Darcy	1975-77-81-87	4	11	1-8-2	1-3-0	0-1-1	0-4-1	2.0	.18
William Davis	1931-33	2	4	2-2-0	1-1-0	1-1-0	0-0-0	2.0	.50
Peter Dawson	1977	1	3	1-2-0	1-0-0	0-1-0	0-1-0	1.0	.33
Norman Drew	1959	1	1	0-0-1	0-0-1	0-0-0	0-0-0	0.5	.50
George Duncan	1927-29-31	3	5	2-3-0	2-0-0	0-3-0	0-0-0	2.0	.40
Syd Easterbrook	1931-33	2	3	2-1-0	1-0-0	1-1-0	0-0-0	2.0	.67
Nick Faldo	1977-79-81-83-85-87-89-91-93	9	36	19-13-4	5-3-1	8-4-2	6-6-1	21.0	.58
John Fallon	1955	1	1	1-0-0	0-0-0	1-0-0	0-0-0	1.0	1.00
Max Faulkner	1947-49-51-53-57	5	8	1-7-0	0-4-0	1-3-0	0-0-0	1.0	.14
David Feherty	1991	1	3	1-1-1	1-0-0	0-1-0	0-0-1	1.5	.50
Bernard Gallacher	1969-71-73-75-77-79-81-83	8	31	13-13-5	4-3-4	5-6-0	4-4-1	15.5	.50
John Garner	1971-73	2	1	0-1-0	0-0-0	0-0-0	0-1-0	0.0	.00
Antonio Garrido	1979	1	5	1-4-0	0-1-0	1-1-0	0-2-0	1.0	.20
David Gilford	1991	1	3	0-2-1	0-0-1	0-2-0	0-0-0	0.5	.17
Malcolm Gregson	1967	1	4	0-4-0	0-2-0	0-1-0	0-1-0	0.0	.00
Joakim Haeggman	1993	1	2	1-1-0	1-0-0	0-0-0	0-1-0	1.0	.50
Tom Haliburton	1961-63	2	6	0-6-0	0-2-0	0-3-0	0-1-0	0.0	.00
Arthur Havers	1927-31-33	3	6	3-3-0	2-1-0	1-2-0	0-0-0	3.0	.50
Jimmy Hitchcock	1965	1	3	0-3-0	0-2-0	0-1-0	0-0-0	0.0	.00
Bert Hodson	1931	1	1	0-1-0	0-1-0	0-0-0	0-0-0	0.0	.00
Tommy Horton	1975-77	2	8	1-6-1	1-1-1	0-2-0	0-3-0	1.5	.19
Brian Hugget	1963-67-69-71-73-75	6	24	8-10-6	3-3-1	5-3-2	0-4-3	11.0	.46
Bernard Hunt	1953-57-59-61-63-65-67-69	8	27	6-16-5	4-3-3	1-9-1	1-4-1	8.5	.31
Geoffrey Hunt	1963	1	3	0-3-0	0-1-0	0-1-0	0-1-0	0.0	.00
Guy Hunt	1975	1	3	0-2-1	0-1-0	0-1-0	0-0-1	0.5	.17
Tony Jacklin	1967-69-71-73-75-77-79	7	35	13-14-8	2-8-1	8-1-4	3-5-3	17.0	.49
John Jacobs	1955	1	2	2-0-0	1-0-0	1-0-0	0-0-0	2.0	1.00
Mark James	1977-79-81-89-91-93	6	22	7-14-1	1-4-1	1-6-0	5-4-0	7.5	.34
Edward Jarman	1935	1	1	0-1-0	0-0-0	0-1-0	0-0-0	0.0	.00
Herbert Jolly	1927	1	2	0-2-0	0-1-0	0-1-0	0-0-0	0.0	.00
Michael King	1979	1	1	0-1-0	0-1-0	0-0-0	0-0-0	0.0	.00
Sam King	1937-47-49	3	5	1-3-1	1-1-1	0-2-0	0-0-0	1.5	.30
Arthur Lacey	1977-79-81-83	8	3	0-3-0	0-2-0	0-1-0	0-0-0	0.0	.00
Barry Lane	1993	1	3	0-3-0	0-1-0	0-1-0	0-1-0	0.0	.00
Bernhard Langer	1981-83-85-87-89-91-93	7	29	13-11-5	2-2-3	6-6-0	5-3-2	15.5	.53
Arthur Lees	1947-49-51-55	4	9	4-5-0	2-3-0	2-2-0	0-0-0	4.0	.44
Sandy Lyle	1979-81-83-85-87	5	18	7-9-2	1-4-0	3-3-1	3-2-1	8.0	.44
Jimmy Martin	1965	1	1	0-1-0	0-0-0	0-1-0	0-0-0	0.0	.00
Peter Mills	1957	1	1	1-0-0	1-0-0	0-0-0	0-0-0	1.0	1.00
Abe Mitchell	1929-31-33	3	6	4-2-0	1-2-0	3-0-0	0-0-0	4.0	.67
Ralph Moffitt	1961	1	1	0-1-0	0-1-0	0-0-0	0-0-0	0.0	.00
Colin Montgomerie	1991-93	2	8	4-2-2	1-0-1	2-1-0	1-1-1	5.0	.63
Christy O'Connor Jr	1975-89	2	4	1-3-0	1-0-0	0-2-0	0-1-0	1.0	.25
Christy O'Connor Sr.	1955-57-59-61 1963-65-67-69-71-73	10	36	11-21-4	2-10-2	6-6-1	3-5-1	13.0	.36

206

Player	Years Played	Years	No. of Matches	Singles R.C. Record W-L-H	Foursomes Record W-L-H	Four-balls Record W-L-H	Total Record W-L-H	Points Won	Point Pct*
John O'Leary	1975	1	4	0-4-0	0-1-0	0-2-0	0-1-0	0.0	.00
Jose-Maria Olazabal	1987-89-91-93	4	20	12-6-2	1-3-0	6-1-1	5-2-1	13.0	.65
Peter Oosterhuis	1971-73-75-77-79-81	6	28	14-11-3	6-2-1	3-6-1	5-3-1	15.5	.55
Alf Padgham	1933-35-37	3	7	0-7-0	0-4-0	0-3-0	0-0-0	0.0	.00
John Panton	1951-53-61	3	5	0-5-0	0-1-0	0-4-0	0-0-0	0.0	.00
Alf Perry	1933-35-37	3	3	0-2-1	0-0-1	0-2-0	0-0-0	0.5	.17
Manuel Pinero	1981-85	2	9	5-4-0	1-1-0	2-2-0	2-1-0	5.0	.56
Lionel Platts	1965	1	5	1-2-2	1-1-0	0-1-0	0-0-2	2.0	.40
Eddie Polland	1973	1	2	0-2-0	0-0-0	0-1-0	0-1-0	0.0	.00
Ronan Rafferty	1989	1	3	1-2-0	1-0-0	0-2-0	0-0-0	1.0	.33
Ted Ray	1927	1	2	0-2-0	0-1-0	0-1-0	0-0-0	0.0	.00
Dai Rees	1937-47-49-51-53-55-57-59-61	9	17	7-9-1	5-4-0	2-5-1	0-0-0	7.5	.44
Steven Richardson	1991	1	4	2-2-0	0-1-0	0-1-0	2-0-0	2.0	.50
Jose Rivero	1985-87	2	5	2-3-0	0-2-0	1-1-0	1-0-0	2.0	.40
Fred Robson	1927-29-31	3	6	2-4-0	0-3-0	2-1-0	0-0-0	2.0	.33
Costantino Rocca	1993	1	2	0-2-0	0-1-0	0-0-0	0-1-0	0.0	.00
Syd Scott	1955	1	2	0-2-0	0-1-0	0-1-0	0-0-0	0.0	.00
Des Smyth	1979-81	2	7	2-5-0	0-2-0	1-2-0	1-1-0	2.0	.29
Dave Thomas	1959-63-65-67	4	18	3-10-5	0-4-1	3-2-2	0-4-2	5.5	.31
Sam Torrance	1981-83-85-87-89-91-93	7	23	4-13-6	1-3-3	1-7-0	2-3-3	7.0	.30
Peter Townsend	1969-71	2	11	3-8-0	0-3-0	2-2-0	1-3-0	3.0	.27
Brian Waites	1983	1	4	1-3-0	0-1-0	0-1-0	1-1-0	1.0	.25
Charles Ward	1947-49-51	3	6	1-5-0	0-3-0	1-2-0	0-0-0	1.0	.17
Paul Way	1983-85	2	9	6-2-1	2-0-0	1-2-0	3-0-1	6.5	.72
Harry Weetman	1951-53-55-57-59-61-63	7	15	2-11-2	2-6-0	0-4-2	0-1-0	3.0	.20
Charles Whitcombe	1927-29-31-33-35-37	6	9	3-2-4	1-2-1	2-0-3	0-0-0	5.0	.56
Ernest Whitcombe	1929-31-35	3	6	1-4-1	0-2-1	1-2-0	0-0-0	1.5	.25
Reg Whitcombe	1935	1	1	0-1-0	0-1-0	0-0-0	0-0-0	0.0	.00
George Will	1963-65-67	3	15	2-11-2	0-3-1	2-3-1	0-5-0	3.0	.20
Norman Wood	1975	1	3	1-2-0	1-0-0	0-1-0	0-1-0	1.0	.33
Ian Woosnam	1983-85-87-89-91-93	6	26	12-10-4	0-5-1	4-2-2	8-3-1	14.0	.54

■ RYDER CUP RECORDS

30 MATCHES SPANNING 66 YEARS

UNITED STATES 23 WINS, BRITAIN - EUROPE 5 WINS & 2 TIES

Year	Site		Results		
1927	Worcester CC, Worcester, Mass.	U.S.	9½	Britain	2½
1929	Moortown GC, Leeds, England	Britain	7	U.S.	5
1931	Scioto CC, Columbus, Ohio	U.S.	9	Britain	3
1933	Southport & Ainsdale GC, Southport, England	Britain	6½	U.S.	5½
1935	Ridgewood CC, Ridgewood, N.J.	U.S.	9	Britain	3
1937	Southport & Ainsdale GC, Southport, England	U.S.	8	Britain	4
1939-1945	**No Matches Played Due to World War II**				
1947	Portland GC, Portland, Ore.	U.S.	11	Britain	1
1949	Ganton GC, Scarborough, England	U.S.	7	Britain	5
1951	Pinehurst CC, Pinehurst, N.C.	U.S.	9½	Britain	2½
1953	Wentworth GC, Wentworth, England	U.S.	6½	Britain	5½
1955	Thunderbird CC, Palm Springs, Calif.	U.S.	8	Britain	4
1957	Lindrick GC, Yorkshire, England	Britain	7½	U.S.	4½
1959	Eldorado CC, Palm Desert, Calif.	U.S.	8½	Britain	3½
1961	Royal Lytham & St. Annes, St. Annes, England	U.S.	14½	Britain	9½
1963	East Lake CC, Atlanta, Ga.	U.S.	23	Britain	9
1965	Royal Birkdale GC, Southport, England	U.S.	19½	Britain	12½
1967	Champions GC, Houston, Texas	U.S.	23½	Britain	8½
1969	Royal Birkdale GC, Southport, England	U.S.	16	Britain	16
1971	Old Warson CC, St. Louis, Mo.	U.S.	18½	Britain	13½
1973	Muirfield, Scotland	U.S.	19	G.B. & I.	13
1975	Laurel Valley GC, Ligonier, Pa.	U.S.	21	G.B. & I.	11
1977	Royal Lytham & St. Annes, St. Annes, England	U.S.	12½	G.B. & I.	7½
1979	The Greenbrier, White Sulphur Springs, W. Va.	U.S.	17	Europe	11
1981	Walton Health GC, Surrey, England	U.S.	18½	Europe	9½
1983	PGA National GC, Palm Beach Gardens, Fla.	U.S.	14½	Europe	13½
1985	The Belfry, Sutton Coldfield, England	Europe	16½	U.S.	11½
1987	Muirfield Village GC, Dublin, Ohio	Europe	15	U.S.	13
1989	The Belfry, Sutton Coldfield, England	Europe	14	U.S.	14
1991	The Ocean Course, Kiawah Island, S.C.	U.S.	14½	Europe	13½
1993	The Belfry, Sutton Coldfield, England	U.S.	15	Europe	13

RYDER CUP RECORDS

■ SELECTED RYDER CUP RECORDS

UNITED STATES			EUROPE		

■ Highest Margin of Victory

1967 in Houston, Texas	23.5 to 8.5		1985 in The Belfry, England	16.5 to 11.5
1947 in Portland, Ore	11 to 1		1957 in Yorkshire, England	7.5-4.5

■ Total Team Points Over 30 Matches

386.5   261.5

■ Total Foursomes Points In 30 Matches

112   73

■ Total Four-balls Points In 30 Matches

71   54

■ Total Single Points In 30 Matches

203.5   134.5

■ Most Times On Ryder Cup Team

Lanny Wadkins	8 (1977-79-83-85-87-89-91-93)	Christy O'Connor, Sr.	10 (1955-57-59-61-63-65-67-69-71-73)
Raymond Floyd	8 (1969-75-77-81-83-85-91-93)	Nick Faldo	9 (1977-79-81-83-85-87-89-91-93)
Billy Casper	8 (1961-63-65-67-69-71-73-75)	Dai Rees	9 (1937-47-49-51-53-55-57-59-61)

■ Youngest Player

Horton Smith in 1929	- age 21 years and 4 days	Nick Faldo in 1977	- age 20 years, 1 months, 28 days
		Paul Way in 1983	- age 20 years, 7 months, 3 days
		Bernard Gallacher in 1969	- age 20 years, 7 months, 9 days

■ Oldest Player

Ray Floyd in 1993	- age 51 years, 20 days	Ted Ray in 1927	-age 50 years, 2 months, 5 days
Don January in 1977	- age 47 years, 9 months, 26 days	Christy O'Connor Sr. in 1973	- age 48 years, 8 months, 30 days
Julius Boros in 1967	- age 47 years, 7 months, 17 days		

■ Most Matches Played

Billy Casper	37	Neil Coles	40
Lanny Wadkins	34	Christy O'Connor Sr.	36
Arnold Palmer	32	Nick Faldo	36
Raymond Floyd	30	Tony Jacklin	35
Lee Trevino	30	Seve Ballesteros	34

■ Most Points Won

Billy Casper	23.5	Seve Ballesteros	21.5
Arnold Palmer	23	Nick Faldo	21
Lanny Wadkins	21.5	Tony Jacklin	17
Lee Trevino	20	Bernard Langer	15.5
Jack Nicklaus	18.5	Neil Coles	15.5
Gene Littler	18	Bernard Gallacher	15.5
Tom Kite	17	Peter Oosterhuis	15.5
Hale Irwin	14		

■ Best Point Percentage

Jimmy Demaret	(6-0-0)	100%	Abe Mitchell	(4-2-0)	67%

■ Minimum of 3 Ryder Cup Matches

Jack Burke (7-1-0) Horton Smith	(3-0-1)	88%	Jose Maria Olazabal	(12-6-2)	65%
Walter Hagen	(7-1-1)	83%	Seve Ballesteros	(19-10-5)	63%
J.C. Snead	(9-2-0)	82%	Nick Faldo	(19-13-4)	58%
Sam Snead	(10-2-1)	81%	Charles Whitcombe	(3-2-4)	56%

RYDER CUP RECORDS

UNITED STATES		EUROPE	
Most Singles Matches Played In			
Arnold Palmer	11	Neil Coles	15
Jack Nicklaus	10	Christy O'Connor Sr.	14
Lee Trevino	10	Peter Alliss	12
Gene Littler	10	Tony Jacklin	11
Billy Casper	10	Bernard Gallacher	11
Lanny Wadkins	8	Brian Barnes	10
Raymond Floyd	8	Bernard Hunt	10
Most Foursomes Matches Played In			
Lanny Wadkins	15	Nick Faldo	14
Billy Casper	15	Seve Ballesteros	14
Tom Kite	13	Neil Cole	13
Arnold Palmer	12	Christy O'Connor Sr.	13
Raymond Floyd	12	Tony Jacklin	13
Lee Trevino	10	Bernhard Langer	12
Most Four-ball Matches Played In			
Billy Casper	12	Nick Faldo	13
Lanny Wadkins	11	Seve Ballesteros	13
Lee Trevino	10	Ian Woosnam	12
Raymond Floyd	10	Neil Coles	12
Most Matches Won			
Arnold Palmer	22	Seve Ballesteros	19
Lanny Wadkins	20	Nick Faldo	19
Billy Casper	20	Peter Oosterhuis	14
Lee Trevino	17	Bernhard Langer	13
Jack Nicklaus	17	Tony Jacklin	13
Tom Kite	15	Bernard Gallacher	13
Most Singles Matches Won			
Arnold Palmer	6	Peter Oosterhuis	6
Billy Casper	6	Nick Faldo	5
Sam Snead	6	Peter Alliss	5
Lee Trevino	6	Brian Barnes	5
Tom Kite	5	Neil Coles	5
Gene Littler	5	Dai Rees	5
Most Foursomes Matches Won			
Lanny Wadkins	9	Seve Ballesteros	10
Arnold Palmer	9	Nick Faldo	8
Billy Casper	8	Tony Jacklin	8
Jack Nicklaus	8	Bernhard Langer	6
Tom Kite	7	Jose Maria Olazabal	6
Hale Irwin	6	Christy O'Connor Sr	6
Most Four-ball Matches Won			
Lanny Wadkins	7	Ian Woosnam	8
Arnold Palmer	7	Seve Ballesteros	7
Billy Casper	6	Nick Faldo	6
Lee Trevino	6	Bernhard Langer	5
Jack Nicklaus	5	Jose Maria Olazabal	5
Gene Littler	5	Peter Oosterhuis	5
		Mark James	5
Most Matches Lost			
Raymond Floyd	16	Christy O'Connor Sr.	21
Lanny Wadkins	11	Neil Coles	21
Billy Casper	10	Bernard Hunt	16
Most Singles Matches Lost			
Raymond Floyd	4	Christy O'Connor Sr.	10
Jack Nicklaus	4	Tony Jacklin	8

RYDER CUP RECORDS

UNITED STATES		EUROPE	

■ Most Foursomes Matches Lost

Raymond Floyd	8	Bernard Hunt	9
Lanny Wadkins	6	Neil Coles	8
Tom Kite	5	Sam Torrance	7
Billy Casper	5		

■ Most Four-ball Matches Lost

Curtis Strange	5	Neil Coles	7
Raymond Floyd	4	Nick Faldo	6
Tom Kite	4	Christy O'Connor Sr.	5
Paul Azinger	4	Peter Alliss	5
Fuzzy Zoeller	4	Brian Barnes	5
Mark Calcavecchia	4	Tony Jacklin	5
		George Will	5

■ Most Matches Halved

Gene Littler	8	Tony Jacklin	8
Billy Casper	7	Neil Coles	7
Lee Trevino	6	Sam Torrance	6
Tom Kite	4	Brian Hugget	6
Julius Boros	4		

■ Most Singles Matches Halved

Gene Littler	3	Bernard Gallacher	4
Tom Kite	2	Neil Coles	4
Lanny Wadkins	2	Bernhard Langer	3
Hale Irwin	2	Sam Torrance	3
Jack Nicklaus	2	Peter Alliss	3
Arnold Palmer	2	Bernard Hunt	3
Lee Trevino	2	Seve Ballesteros	2
Billy Casper	2	Christy O'Connor Sr.	2

■ Most Foursomes Matches Halved

Billy Casper	2	Tony Jacklin	4
Gene Sarazen	2	Charles Whitcombe	3
Lee Trevino	2	Nick Faldo	2
Julius Boros	2	Ian Woosnam	2
		Dave Thomas	2
		Brian Hugget	2
		Harry Weetman	2

■ Most Four-ball Matches Halved

Gene Littler	4	Sam Torrance	3
Billy Casper	3	Tony Jacklin	3
Fred Couples	2	Brian Hugget	3
Raymond Floyd	2	Seve Ballesteros	2
Lee Trevino	2	Bernhard Langer	2
Al Geiberger	2	Neil Coles	2
Miller Barber	2	Maurice Bembridge	2
Johnny Miller	2	Peter Butler	2
Craig Stadler	2	Lionel Platts	2

■ Teams winning all points in a Series

Foursomes	United States won all foursomes points 4-0 in 1947
	United States won second series foursomes points 4-0 in 1963
	United States won first series foursomes points 4-0 in 1975
	United States won second series foursomes points 4-0 in 1981
Four-balls	United States won first series four-ball points 4-0 in 1967
	United States won first series four-ball points 4-0 in 1971
	Europe won first series four-balls points 4-0 in 1987
	Europe won first series four-ball points 4-0 in 1989
Singles	No side has ever had a clean sweep in the singles

▨ Relatives in Ryder Cup Matches

Father and Son	Percy Alliss (1929, '33, '35, and '37) and Peter Alliss (1953, '57, '59, '61, '63, '65, '67 and '69)
Brothers	Charles Whitcombe (1927, '29, '31, '33, '35 and '37), Reg Whitcombe (1935) and Ernest Whitcombe (1929, '31 and '35)
	Bernard Hunt (1953, '57, '59, '61, '63, '65, '67 and '69) and Geoffrey Hunt (1963)
	Joe Turnesa (1927, '29) and Jim Turnesa (1953)
	Jay Hebert (1959, '61) and Lionel Hebert (1957)
Uncles and Nephews	Christy O'Connor Sr. (1955, '57, '59, '61, '63, '65, '67 and '69) and Christy O'Connor Jr. (1975 and '89)
	Sam Snead (1937, '47, '49, '51, '53, '55 and '59) and J.C. Snead (1971, '73 and '75)
	Bob Goalby (1963) and Jay Haas (1983)
Cousins	Jackie Burke Jr. (1951, '53, '55, '57 and '59) and Dave Marr (1965)
Brothers-in-law	Max Faulkner (1947, '49, '51, '53 and '57) and Brian Barnes (1969, '71, '73, '75, '77 and '79)
	Jerry Pate (1981) and Bruce Lietzke (1981)

▨ Teams With Most Ryder Cup Wins

European Team	Seve Ballesteros and Jose Maria Olazabal	15 Matches: 11 Wins, 2 Losses, 2 Halves
	Peter Alliss and Christy O'Connor Sr.	12 Matches: 5 Wins, 6 Loss, 1 Halve
	Nick Faldo and Ian Woosnam	10 Matches: 5 Wins, 3 Losses, 2 Halves
	Bernard Gallacher and Brian Barnes	10 Matches: 5 Wins, 4 Losses, 1 Halve
United States Team:	Tom Kite and Curtis Strange	6 Matches: 2 Wins, 3 Losses, 1 Halve
	Larry Nelson and Lanny Wadkins	6 Matches: 4 Wins, 2 Losses
	Arnold Palmer and Gardner Dickinson	5 Matches: 5 Wins, 0 Losses
	Tony Lema and Julius Boros	5 Matches: 3 Wins, 1 Loss, 1 Halve
	Jack Nicklaus and Tom Watson	4 Matches: 4 Wins, 0 Losses

▨ Highest Winning Margins - 36-Hole Team

10 & 9 (1931) Walter Hagen and Denny Shute beat George Duncan and Arthur Havers
10 & 9 (1947) Lew Worsham and Ed Oliver beat Henry Cotton and Arthur Lees
9 & 8 (1935) Paul Runyan and Horton Smith beat Bill Cox and Edward Jarman

▨ Highest Winning Margins - 18-Hole Team

7 & 6 (1979) Hale Irwin and Tom Kite beat Ken Brown and Des Smyth
7 & 6 (1991) Paul Azinger and Mark O'Meara beat Nick Faldo and David Gilford
7 & 5 (1981) Lee Trevino and Jerry Pate beat Nick Faldo and Sam Torrance
7 & 5 (1983) Lanny Wadkins and Gil Morgan beat Sam Torrance and J. M. Canizares
7 & 5 (1985) J. M. Canizares and Jose Pinero beat Tom Kite and Calvin Peete
7 & 5 (1993) Bernhard Langer and Ian Woosnam beat Paul Azinger and Payne Stewart

▨ High Winning Margins - 36 Singles

10 & 8 (1929) George Duncan beat Walter Hagen
9 & 8 (1929) Leo Diegel beat Abe Mitchell
9 & 8 (1933) Abe Mitchell beat Olin Dutra
9 & 7 (1953) Fred Daly beat Ted Kroll

▨ High Winning Margins - 18 Singles

8 & 7 (1989) Tom Kite beat Howard Clark
8 & 7 (1951) Skip Alexander beat John Panton
7 & 6 (1969) Miller Barber beat Maurice Bembridge
7 & 6 (1971) Lee Trevino beat Brian Hugget
6 & 5 (1963) Gene Littler beat Tom Haliburton
6 & 5 (1973) Gay Brewer beat Bernard Gallacher
6 & 5 (1973) Lee Trevino beat Neil Coles
6 & 4 (1965) Tony Lema beat Christy O'Connor Sr.
6 & 4 (1981) Ben Crenshaw beat Des Smyth

▨ Undefeated In Two Or More Matches in Ryder Cup Play

J. Demaret-6 wins; B. Maxwell- 4 wins; B. Hogan, B. Burke and
Johnny Golden-3 wins; Chick Harbert, Wilfred Cox, Lew Worsham, Ralph Guldahl,
John Jacobs, Paul Broadhurst and Bob Rosburg - 2 wins

RYDER CUP RECORDS

■ **Captain's Selections**

The format allowing the Europeans to choose "wild cards" began in 1979 and has operated since then except for 1993. The United States selection for "wild cards" began in 1989. Here is a look at the selections and how they have played:

1993 - U.S. Team	Lanny Wadkins - record: 2 wins, 1 loss, 1 halve
	Ray Floyd - record: 3 wins, 1 loss
1993 - European Team	Joakim Haeggman- record: 1 win, 1 loss
	Seve Ballesteros - record: 2 wins, 2 losses
	Jose Maria Olazabal - record: 2 wins, 3 losses
1991 - U.S. Team	Chip Beck - record: 1 win, 2 losses
	Ray Floyd - record: 2 wins, 2 losses
1991 - European Team	Jose Maria Olazabal - record: 3 wins, 1 loss, 1 halve
	Nick Faldo - record: 1 win, 3 losses
	Mark James - record: 2 wins, 3 losses
1989 - U.S. Team	Tom Watson - record: 1 win, 1 loss, 1 halve
	Lanny Wadkins - record: 3 wins, 1 loss
1989 - European Team	Bernhard Langer - record: 3 losses
	Howard Clark - record: 2 wins, 2 losses
	Christy O'Connor Jr. - record: 1 win, 1 loss
1987 - European Team	Jose Maria Olazabal - record: 3 wins, 2 losses
	Sandy Lyle - record: 3 wins, 1 loss
	Ken Brown - record: 2 losses
1985 - European Team	Ken Brown - record: 1 win, 2 losses
	Nick Faldo - record: 2 losses
	Jose Rivero - record: 1 won, 1 loss
1983 - European Team	Picked the team off the Order of Merit list and didn't have any Captain picks
1981 - European Team	Mark James - record: 2 wins, 3 losses
	Peter Oosterhuis - record: 3 losses
1979 - European Team	Peter Oosterhuis - record: 2 wins, 2 losses
	Des Smyth - record: 2 losses

■ UNITED STATES CAPTAIN RECORDS

Captain	Years Captained	Years	Won	Lost	Halved
Jerry Barber	1961	1	1	0	0
Jack Burke Jr.	1957-73	2	1	1	0
Billy Casper	1979	1	1	0	0
Dow Finsterwald	1977	1	1	0	0
Ray Floyd	1989	1	0	0	1
Walter Hagen	1927-29-31-33-35-37	6	4	2	0
Chick Harbert	1955	1	1	0	0
Jay Hebert	1971	1	1	0	0
Ben Hogan	1947-49-67	3	3	0	0
Lloyd Mangrum	1953	1	1	0	0
Dave Marr	1981	1	1	0	0
Byron Nelson	1965	1	1	0	0
Jack Nicklaus	1983-87	2	1	1	0
Arnold Palmer	1963-75	2	2	0	0
Sam Snead	1951-59-69	3	2	0	1
Dave Stockton	1991	1	1	0	0
Lee Trevino	1985	1	0	1	0
Tom Watson	1993	1	1	0	0

■ EUROPEAN CAPTAIN RECORDS

Captain	Years Captained	Years	Won	Lost	Halved
Eric Brown	1969-71	2	0	1	1
Henry Cotton	1947-53	2	0	2	0
George Duncan	1929	1	1	0	0
John Fallon	1963	1	0	1	0
Bernard Gallacher	1991-93	2	0	2	0
Brian Huggett	1977	1	0	1	0
Bernard Hunt	1973-75	2	0	2	0
Tony Jacklin	1983-85-87-89	4	2	1	1
John Jacobs	1979-81	2	0	2	0
Arthur Lacey	1951	1	0	1	0
Ted Ray	1927	1	0	1	0
Dai Rees	1955-57-59-61-67	5	1	4	0
J.H. Taylor	1933	1	1	0	0
Harry Weetman	1965	1	0	1	0
Charles Whitcombe	1931-35-37-49	4	0	4	0

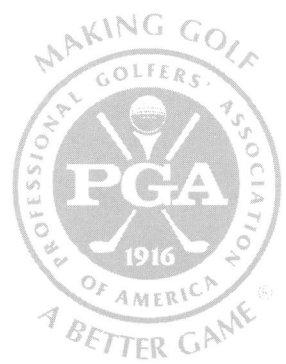

PGA SENIORS' CHAMPIONSHIP

PGA SENIORS' CHAMPIONSHIP

■ HISTORY

The oldest major championship in senior golf, the PGA Seniors' Championship, was born in 1937 on the grounds of one of golf's major championships, at the invitation of one of the game's greatest players. At the suggestion of renowned amateur golfer Bobby Jones Jr., the inaugural PGA Seniors' Championship was played at Augusta National Golf Club three years after the first Masters Tournament was held. It was established in the fall of 1937 to provide an opportunity for PGA members over the age of 50 to compete with their peers. The purse was $2,000.

In an effort to find better weather conditions, the PGA Seniors' Championship moved to Florida in 1940, spending two years in Sarasota and one year in Fort Myers, before being suspended for two years due to World War II. When the Championship resumed in 1945, it was held in Dunedin, Fla., which would become the home of the PGA after the Association relocated its national office from Chicago in 1956.

Florida has been the site for the PGA Seniors' Championship since the event first moved to the Sunshine State in 1940. Since 1982, the PGA Seniors' Championship has been held at PGA National Golf Club in Palm Beach Gardens, Fla., home of the PGA of America's national office.

It was during the PGA Seniors' Championship in December 1979, at Turnberry Isle in North Miami, Fla., that informal meetings first were held among golf's elder statesmen to explore the concept of developing playing events for seniors. As many of golf's leading names passed age 50, they found they were no longer as competitive on the PGA Tour as they once had been, but outside of the PGA Seniors' Championship, playing opportunities for them were limited.

The following month, January 1980, the Senior PGA Tour was founded. When the Senior PGA Tour was launched, the PGA Seniors' Championship was celebrating its 42nd anniversary.

■ HISTORY THROUGH THE YEARS

Year	Winner	Score	Runners-up	Site
1937	Jock Hutchison	223	George Gordon	Augusta National (Ga.) GC
1938	Freddie McLeod*	154	Otto Hackbarth	Augusta National (Ga.) GC
1940	Otto Hackbarth*	146	Jock Hutchison	Bobby Jones GC & North Shore CC, Sarasota, Fla.
1941	Jack Burke Sr.	142	Eddie Williams	Bobby Jones GC & Sarasota Bay (Fla.) CC
1942	Eddie Williams	138	George Morris	Fort Myers (Fla.) CC
1943-44 **No Championships played due to World War II.**				
1945	Eddie Williams	150	Jock Hutchison	PGA National GC, Dunedin, Fla.
1946	Eddie Williams*	146	Jock Hutchison	PGA National GC, Dunedin, Fla.
1947	Jock Hutchison	145	Ben Richter	PGA National GC, Dunedin, Fla.
1948	Charles McKenna	141	Ben Richter	PGA National GC, Dunedin, Fla.
1949	Marshall Crichton	145	Lou Chiapetta	PGA National GC, Dunedin, Fla.
			George Smith	PGA National GC, Dunedin, Fla.
1950	Al Watrous	142	Bill Jellife	PGA National GC, Dunedin, Fla.
1951	Al Watrous*	142	Jock Hutchison	PGA National GC, Dunedin, Fla.
1952	Ernie Newnham	146	Al Watrous	PGA National GC, Dunedin, Fla.
1953	Harry Schwab	142	Gene Sarazen	PGA National GC, Dunedin, Fla.
			Charles McKenna	
1954	Gene Sarazen	214	Al Watrous	PGA National GC, Dunedin, Fla.
			Perry Del Vecchio	
1955	Mortie Dutra	213	Mike Murra	PGA National GC, Dunedin, Fla.
			Gene Sarazen	
			Denny Shute	
1956	Pete Burke	215	Ock Willoweit	PGA National GC, Dunedin, Fla.
1957	Al Watrous*	210	Bob Stupple	PGA National GC, Dunedin, Fla.
1958	Gene Sarazen	288	Charles Sheppard	PGA National GC, Dunedin, Fla.
1959	Willie Goggin	284	Duke Gibson	PGA National GC, Dunedin, Fla.
			Paul Runyan	
			Denny Shute	
1960	Dick Metz	284	Tony Longo	PGA National GC, Dunedin, Fla.
			Paul Runyan	
1961	Paul Runyan	278	Jimmy Demaret	PGA National GC, Dunedin, Fla.
1962	Paul Runyan	278	Errie Ball	PGA National GC, Dunedin, Fla.
			Joe Brown	
			Dutch Harrison	
1963	Herman Barron	272	John Barnum	Port St. Lucie (Fla) CC
1964	Sam Snead	279	John Barnum	PGA National GC, Palm Beach Gardens, Fla.

*Won playoff

PGA SENIORS' CHAMPIONSHIP

Year	Winner	Score	Runners-up	Site
1965	Sam Snead	278	Joe Lopez Sr.	Fort Lauderdale (Fla.) CC
1966	Fred Haas Jr.	286	Dutch Harrison	PGA National GC, Palm Beach Gardens, Fla.
			John Barnum	
1967	Sam Snead	279	Bob Hamilton	PGA National GC, Palm Beach Gardens, Fla.
1968	Chandler Harper	279	Sam Snead	PGA National GC, Palm Beach Gardens, Fla.
1969	Tommy Bolt	278	Peter Fleming	PGA National GC, Palm Beach Gardens, Fla.
1970	Sam Snead	290	Fred Haas	PGA National GC, Palm Beach Gardens, Fla.
1971	Julius Boros	285	Tommy Bolt	PGA National GC, Palm Beach Gardens, Fla.
1972	Sam Snead	286	Julius Boros	PGA National GC, Palm Beach Gardens, Fla.
			Tommy Bolt	
1973	Sam Snead	268	Julius Boros	PGA National GC, Palm Beach Gardens, Fla.
1974	R. De Vicenzo	273	Julius Boros	Port St. Lucie (Fla.) CC
			Art Wall	
1975	Charles Sifford*	280	Fred Wampler	Walt Disney World, Orlando, Fla.
1976	Pete Cooper	283	Fred Wampler	Walt Disney World, Orlando, Fla.
1977	Julius Boros	283	Fred Haas Jr.	Walt Disney World, Orlando, Fla.
1978	Joe Jimenez*	286	M. de la Torre	Walt Disney World, Orlando, Fla.
			Joe Cheves	
1979	Jack Fleck*	289	Bill Johnston	Walt Disney World, Orlando, Fla.
			Bob Erickson	
1979+	Don January	270	George Bayer	Turnberry Isle CC, North Miami Beach, Fla.
1980	Arnold Palmer*	289	Paul Harney	Turnberry Isle CC, North Miami Beach, Fla.
1981	Miller Barber	281	Arnold Palmer	Turnberry Isle CC, North Miami Beach, Fla.
1982	Don January	288	Julius Boros	PGA National GC, Palm Beach Gardens, Fla.
1984	Arnold Palmer	282	Don January	PGA National GC, Palm Beach Gardens, Fla.
1984+	Peter Thomson	286	Don January	PGA National GC, Palm Beach Gardens, Fla.
1986	Gary Player	281	Lee Elder	PGA National GC, Palm Beach Gardens, Fla.
1987	Chi Chi Rodriguez	282	Dale Douglass	PGA National GC, Palm Beach Gardens, Fla.
1988	Gary Player	284	Chi Chi Rodriguez	PGA National GC, Palm Beach Gardens, Fla.
1989	Larry Mowry	281	Miller Barber	PGA National GC, Palm Beach Gardens, Fla.
			Al Geiberger	
1990	Gary Player	281	Chi Chi Rodriguez	PGA National GC, Palm Beach Gardens, Fla.
1991	Jack Nicklaus	271	Bruce Crampton	PGA National GC, Palm Beach Gardens, Fla.
1992	Lee Trevino	278	Mike Hill	PGA National GC, Palm Beach Gardens, Fla.
1993	Tom Wargo*	275	Bruce Crampton	PGA National GC, Palm Beach Gardens, Fla.

*Won playoff.   +Two Championships played in 1979 & 1984.

■ PLAYOFF RESULTS

1938   Fred McLeod def. Otto Hackbarth, 18-holes (80 to 82)

1940   Otto Hackbarth def. Jock Hutchison (36 holes); both players tied at 74 after first 18 holes; final 18-hole scores unavailable

1946   Eddie Williams def. Jock Hutchison (18 holes, scores unavailable)

1951   Al Watrous def. Jock Hutchison (18 holes, 75 to 81)

1957   Al Watrous def. Bob Stupple (18 holes, 72 to 75)

1975   Charles Sifford def. Fred Wampler (sudden-death, birdied first extra hole)

1978   Joe Jimenez def. Manuel de la Torre & Joe Cheves (sudden-death, birdie on first extra hole)

1979   Jack Fleck def. Bill Johnston & Bob Erickson (sudden-death, birdied third extra hole)

1980   Arnold Palmer def. Paul Harney (sudden-death, birdied first extra hole)

1993   Tom Wargo def. Bruce Crampton (sudden-death, parred second extra hole)

1994 FACTS AND FORMAT

DATE: April 14-17, 1994
SITE: PGA National Golf Club, Palm Beach Gardens, Fla.
DEFENDING CHAMPION: Tom Wargo
PURSE: $800,000 (was presented in 1993)
PRESENTING SPONSOR: Oldsmobile

PURSE AND HONORS

The 1994 PGA Seniors' Champion will have his name engraved on the Alfred S. Bourne Trophy, donated to the PGA in 1937. The 1993 champion earned $110,000 for his victory.

TELEVISION (All Times Eastern)

First Round, Thursday, April 14: USA, 4:00 p.m.-6:00 p.m.; Replay, USA, 11:00 p.m.-1:00 a.m.

Second Round, Friday, April 15: USA, 4:00 p.m.-6:00 p.m.; Replay, USA, 11:00 p.m.-1:00 a.m.

Third Round, Saturday, April 16: NBC, 1:00 p.m.-3:00 p.m.

Final Round, Sunday, April 17: NBC, 12:00 p.m.-3:00 p.m.

METHOD OF PLAY

Stroke play, four rounds of 18 holes. Following the first 36 holes of play, the field will be reduced to the 70 players having the lowest scores and those tied for 70th place. Such players will then complete two final rounds. In the event of a tie for first place after 72 holes, there will be a sudden-death playoff.

RULES AND REGULATIONS

The Rules of Golf which govern play are determined by the United States Golf Association and applied by the PGA of America Board of Directors. The Championship is subject to the overall supervision of the Board and the PGA Rules Committee.

ELIGIBILITY

Officers of the PGA of America have approved the following list of players eligible to compete in the 55th PGA Seniors' Championship, provided that they are at least 50 years of age:

- All former PGA Seniors' Champions
- All former PGA Champions
- All former U.S. Open Champions
- All former Masters Champions
- All former British Open Champions
- All former PGA Club Professional Champions
- All former U.S. Ryder Cup Team members
- The 15 low scorers and ties in the 1993 PGA Seniors' Championship
- The top 30 money winners and all tournament winners on the 1993 Senior PGA Tour
- All tournament winners on the 1994 Senior PGA Tour through The Tradition ending April 3
- The top 55 finishers at the 1993 PGA Senior Club Professional Championship

In addition, the PGA of America reserves the right to invite additional players not included in the categories listed above. The total field will be a maximum of 129 players: 74 exempt players and the top 55 players from the 1993 PGA Senior Club Professional Championship. If necessary, the field will be completed by an alternate list composed of those players 31st to 50th on the 1993 Senior PGA Tour money list.

PGA NATIONAL GOLF CLUB - CHAMPION COURSE - 1994 PGA SENIORS' CHAMPIONSHIP

Hole	1	2	3	4	5	6	7	8	9	10	11	12	13	14	15	16	17	18
Par	4	4	5	4	3	5	3	4	4	5	4	4	4	4	3	4	3	5
Yards	346	419	513	355	171	478	185	397	381	600	412	397	370	422	164	412	152	528

Front 9: 3,245 yards • Par 36	**Back 9:** 3,457 yards • Par 36	**Total:** 6,702 yards • Par 72

HOW THE COURSE PLAYED DURING THE 1993 PGA SENIORS' CHAMPIONSHIP

Hole	1	2	3	4	5	6	7	8	9	10	11	12	13	14	15	16	17	18
Par	4	4	5	4	3	5	3	4	4	5	4	4	4	4	3	4	3	5
Eagles	0	0	2	1	0	3	0	0	0	2	0	0	0	1	0	0	0	2
Birdles	68	32	95	61	51	105	51	42	67	99	31	55	57	23	54	29	55	78
Pars	290	267	245	266	295	249	292	286	288	277	237	284	260	260	253	266	262	268
Bogeys	65	113	71	94	62	59	83	92	67	47	102	82	91	126	88	101	75	71
Db.-Bogeys	7	18	15	9	20	12	5	11	7	5	43	9	21	18	28	23	33	9
Others	1	1	3	0	3	3	0	0	2	1	18	1	2	3	8	12	6	3
'93 Avg.	4.03	4.28	5.03	4.11	3.14	4.96	3.10	4.17	4.05	4.90	4.51	4.11	4.19	4.34	3.27	4.37	3.24	5.04
Rank	15	4	16	10	9	17	12	8	13	18	1	11	7	3	5	2	6	14

Front 9 Average: 36.87	**Back 9 Average:** 37.98	**Course Average:** 74.85

■ PLAYING STATISTICS FROM THE 1993 PGA SENIORS' CHAMPIONSHIP

	Player	Driving Dist.	Rank	Fairways Hit - %	Rank	Greens in Reg. - %	Rank	Sand Saves	Rank	# Putts	Rank
1.	Tom Wargo	261.2	(T-9)	47 of 56 or 84%	(3)	58 of 72 or 81%	(2)	14%	(73)	117	(T-31)
2.	Bruce Crampton	233.8	(T-57)	42 of 56 or 75%	(16)	51 of 72 or 71%	(T-11)	57%	(T-21)	110	(T-4)
3.	Isao Aoki	263.1	(T-7)	41 of 56 or 73%	(25)	60 of 72 or 83%	(1)	67%	(T-9)	125	(T-68)
T-4.	Bob Charles	246.5	(T-35)	47 of 56 or 84%	(3)	54 of 72 or 75%	(T-5)	43%	(T-48)	117	(T-31)
T-4.	Tom Weiskopf	266.8	(T-4)	33 of 56 or 59%	(66)	52 of 72 or 72%	(10)	63%	(T-15)	119	(T-45)
6.	Mike Hill	255.8	(T-13)	39 of 56 or 70%	(33)	53 of 72 or 74%	(T-8)	50%	(T-33)	117	(T-31)
T-7.	Jim Albus	245.0	(T-37)	46 of 56 or 82%	(T-5)	44 of 72 or 61%	(T-42)	67%	(T-9)	110	(T-4)
T-7.	Orville Moody	246.7	(T-34)	42 of 56 or 75%	(16)	50 of 72 or 69%	(T-14)	67%	(T-9)	116	(T-22)
T-9.	Harold Henning	243.8	(T-39)	42 of 56 or 75%	(16)	44 of 72 or 61%	(T-42)	79%	(3)	111	(T-8)
T-9.	J.C. Snead	266.6	(T-5)	39 of 56 or 70%	(33)	50 of 72 or 69%	(T-14)	64%	(14)	117	(T-31)
T-9.	Larry Mowry	243.1	(T-43)	43 of 56 or 77%	(13)	54 of 72 or 75%	(T-5)	70%	(T-6)	121	(T-58)
T-9.	Jack Nicklaus	261.1	(T-10)	38 of 56 or 68%	(43)	56 of 72 or 78%	(T-3)	20%	(71)	125	(T-68)
T-13.	Al Kelley	243.6	(T-40)	38 of 56 or 68%	(43)	47 of 72 or 65%	(T-26)	75%	(4)	114	(T-17)
T-13.	Ray Floyd	262.3	(T-8)	41 of 56 or 73%	(25)	50 of 72 or 69%	(T-14)	71%	(5)	116	(T-22)
T-13.	Tommy Aycock	268.1	(T-3)	41 of 56 or 73%	(25)	49 of 72 or 68%	(T-21)	55%	(31)	117	(T-31)
T-16.	Jimmy Powell	247.1	(T-32)	30 of 56 or 54%	(72)	46 of 72 or 64%	(T-33)	38%	(T-59)	110	(T-4)
T-16.	George Archer	242.0	(T-46)	38 of 56 or 68%	(43)	46 of 72 or 64%	(T-33)	40%	(T-53)	112	(T-10)
T-16.	Gary Player	231.6	(T-62)	36 of 56 or 64%	(56)	46 of 72 or 64%	(T-33)	63%	(T-15)	116	(T-22)
T-16.	Rocky Thompson	242.5	(T-44)	38 of 56 or 68%	(43)	53 of 72 or 74%	(T-8)	38%	(T-59)	120	(T-51)
T-16.	Dale Douglass	251.0	(T-20)	42 of 56 or 75%	(16)	56 of 72 or 78%	(T-3)	22%	(T-69)	128	(72)
T-21.	Walter Zembriski	241.3	(48)	50 of 56 or 89%	(1)	51 of 72 or 71%	(T-11)	25%	(68)	117	(T-31)
T-21.	Kermit Zarley	251.5	(T-17)	39 of 56 or 70%	(T-33)	49 of 72 or 68%	(T-21)	33%	(T-63)	119	(T-45)
T-23.	Lee Trevino	248.5	(T-30)	41 of 56 or 73%	(T-25)	47 of 72 or 65%	(T-26)	42%	(T-50)	114	(T-17)
T-23.	Dave Stockton	250.8	(T-21)	42 of 56 or 75%	(16)	47 of 72 or 65%	(T-26)	70%	(T-6)	116	(T-22)
T-23.	Dewitt Weaver	273.8	(T-1)	39 of 56 or 70%	(33)	48 of 72 or 67%	(T-23)	57%	(T-21)	119	(T-45)
26.	Larry Gilbert	250.5	(T-23)	44 of 56 or 79%	(T-10)	48 of 72 or 67%	(T-23)	45%	(T-42)	118	(T-40)
T-27.	Dick Hendrickson	251.6	(T-16)	44 of 56 or 79%	(10)	44 of 72 or 61%	(T-42)	50%	(T-33)	113	(T-12)
T-27.	Arnold Palmer	243.5	(T-41)	36 of 56 or 64%	(56)	43 of 72 or 60%	(T-47)	50%	(T-33)	114	(T-17)
T-27.	Gibby Gilbert	249.6	(T-26)	35 of 56 or 63%	(61)	47 of 72 or 65%	(T-26)	45%	(T-42)	116	(T-22)
T-27.	Harry Toscano	250.5	(T-23)	42 of 56 or 75%	(T-16)	47 of 72 or 65%	(T-26)	13%	(74)	118	(T-40)
T-27.	Simon Hobday	254.3	(T-15)	38 of 56 or 68%	(43)	50 of 72 or 69%	(T-14)	63%	(T-15)	125	(T-68)
T-32.	Jim Dent	268.6	(T-2)	36 of 56 or 64%	(56)	46 of 72 or 64%	(T-33)	57%	(T-21)	109	(T-1)
T-32.	Ken Still	228.7	(T-68)	35 of 56 or 63%	(61)	45 of 72 or 63%	(T-37)	56%	(T-26)	109	(T-1)
T-32.	Rives Mcbee	238.0	(T-52)	37 of 56 or 66%	(50)	45 of 72 or 63%	(T-37)	22%	(T-69)	116	(T-22)
T-32.	Chi Chi Rodriguez	249.0	(T-28)	39 of 56 or 70%	(33)	47 of 72 or 65%	(T-26)	60%	(T-18)	118	(T-40)
T-32.	Tommy Horton	250.1	(T-25)	46 of 56 or 82%	(5)	51 of 72 or 71%	(T-11)	50%	(T-33)	122	(T-60)
T-37.	Miller Barber	231.1	(T-63)	39 of 56 or 70%	(33)	41 of 72 or 57%	(T-53)	83%	(2)	109	(T-1)
T-37.	Tom Shaw	251.5	(T-17)	37 of 56 or 66%	(T-50)	45 of 72 or 63%	(T-37)	33%	(T-63)	115	(21)
T-39.	Mike O'Sullivan	242.3	(T-45)	41 of 56 or 73%	(25)	44 of 72 or 61%	(T-42)	57%	(T-21)	116	(T-22)
T-39.	Don Massengale	222.7	(T-71)	41 of 56 or 73%	(25)	42 of 72 or 58%	(T-49)	56%	(T-26)	117	(T-31)
T-39.	Larry Ziegler	256.0	(T-11)	35 of 56 or 63%	(T-61)	50 of 72 or 69%	(T-14)	33%	(T-63)	122	(T-60)
T-39.	Bob Murphy	250.7	(22)	49 of 56 or 88%	(2)	54 of 72 or 75%	(T-5)	33%	(T-63)	127	(71)
43.	John Frillman	229.8	(T-66)	39 of 56 or 70%	(33)	50 of 72 or 69%	(T-14)	40%	(T-53)	122	(T-60)
44.	Stan Thirsk	230.5	(T-64)	37 of 56 or 66%	(50)	38 of 72 or 53%	(T-61)	50%	(T-33)	114	(T-17)
T-45.	Seiichi Kanai	229.5	(T-67)	45 of 56 or 80%	(7)	42 of 72 or 58%	(T-49)	44%	(47)	119	(T-45)
T-45.	Jim Colbert	234.7	(T-56)	45 of 56 or 80%	(7)	47 of 72 or 65%	(T-26)	43%	(T-48)	120	(T-51)
T-45.	Jack Kiefer	254.6	(T-14)	42 of 56 or 75%	(16)	45 of 72 or 63%	(T-37)	36%	(T-61)	122	(T-60)
T-45.	Terry Dill	264.1	(T-6)	33 of 56 or 59%	(66)	48 of 72 or 67%	(T-23)	45%	(T-42)	123	(T-66)
T-49.	Jim King	225.0	(T-70)	38 of 56 or 68%	(43)	32 of 72 or 44%	(73)	58%	(20)	110	(T-4)
T-49.	Don January	249.3	(T-27)	39 of 56 or 70%	(33)	41 of 72 or 57%	(T-53)	50%	(T-33)	113	(T-12)
T-49.	Dave Philo	239.8	(T-51)	30 of 56 or 54%	(72)	36 of 72 or 50%	(69)	70%	(T-6)	116	(T-22)
T-49.	Gay Brewer	248.7	(T-29)	37 of 56 or 66%	(50)	38 of 72 or 53%	(T-61)	67%	(T-9)	116	(T-22)
T-49.	Joe Jimenez	256.0	(T-11)	35 of 56 or 63%	(T-61)	41 of 72 or 57%	(T-53)	17%	(72)	118	(T-40)
T-49.	Mike Joyce	245.0	(T-37)	42 of 56 or 75%	(T-16)	45 of 72 or 63%	(T-37)	56%	(T-26)	120	(T-51)
55.	Masaru Amano	246.1	(T-36)	38 of 56 or 68%	(43)	44 of 72 or 61%	(T-42)	67%	(T-9)	119	(T-45)
T-56.	Brian Huggett	241.6	(T-47)	44 of 56 or 79%	(10)	39 of 72 or 54%	(T-58)	40%	(T-53)	119	(T-45)
T-56.	Charles Coody	243.3	(T-42)	42 of 56 or 75%	(16)	43 of 72 or 60%	(T-47)	40%	(T-53)	123	(T-66)
T-58.	Ed Dalton	240.1	(T-50)	37 of 56 or 66%	(50)	39 of 72 or 54%	(T-58)	50%	(T-33)	117	(T-31)
T-58.	Larry Laoretti	248.5	(T-30)	39 of 56 or 70%	(T-33)	41 of 72 or 57%	(T-53)	36%	(T-61)	120	(T-51)
T-60.	Bob Brue	236.5	(T-55)	39 of 56 or 70%	(33)	33 of 72 or 46%	(T-71)	86%	(1)	113	(T-12)
T-60.	Lee Elder	226.6	(T-69)	40 of 56 or 71%	(31)	37 of 72 or 51%	(T-67)	41%	(52)	113	(T-12)
T-60.	Lloyd Monroe	233.0	(T-59)	36 of 56 or 64%	(56)	42 of 72 or 58%	(T-49)	60%	(T-18)	121	(T-58)
T-63.	Bobby Nichols	251.3	(19)	29 of 56 or 52%	(74)	38 of 72 or 53%	(T-61)	42%	(T-50)	113	(T-12)
T-63.	Dave Ragan	240.2	(T-49)	43 of 56 or 77%	(13)	50 of 72 or 69%	(T-14)	56%	(T-26)	131	(74)
65.	Odell Trueblood	232.5	(T-60)	37 of 56 or 66%	(T-50)	40 of 72 or 56%	(57)	45%	(T-42)	118	(T-40)
T-66.	Chuck Workman	233.2	(58)	34 of 56 or 61%	(65)	31 of 72 or 43%	(74)	56%	(T-26)	111	(T-8)
T-66.	Hisashi Suzumura	213.7	(T-73)	32 of 56 or 57%	(70)	39 of 72 or 54%	(T-58)	57%	(T-21)	120	(T-51)
T-68.	Ryosuke Ohta	201.2	(T-74)	43 of 56 or 77%	(13)	37 of 72 or 51%	(T-67)	50%	(T-33)	120	(T-51)
T-68.	John Paul Cain	230.0	(T-65)	32 of 56 or 57%	(70)	38 of 72 or 53%	(T-61)	54%	(32)	122	(T-60)
70.	Al Krueger	247.0	(T-33)	45 of 56 or 80%	(7)	42 of 72 or 58%	(T-49)	40%	(T-53)	130	(73)
T-71.	Hiroshi Ishii	236.8	(T-54)	36 of 56 or 64%	(56)	34 of 72 or 47%	(70)	27%	(67)	112	(T-10)
T-71.	Doug Dalziel	237.5	(T-53)	33 of 56 or 59%	(66)	38 of 72 or 53%	(T-61)	45%	(T-42)	120	(T-51)
73.	Tommy Aaron	232.5	(T-60)	33 of 56 or 59%	(T-66)	38 of 72 or 53%	(T-61)	50%	(T-33)	117	(T-31)
74.	Doug Sanders	220.5	(T-72)	40 of 56 or 71%	(31)	33 of 72 or 46%	(T 71)	40%	(T 53)	122	(T-60)

PGA SENIORS' CHAMPIONSHIP

1993 The low, slashing golf swing, massive forearms and trouser-tugging were a familiar package for anyone with any knowledge of championship golf. But it was Tom Wargo of Centralia, Ill., and not Arnold Palmer, battling his way to the 54th PGA Seniors' Championship and becoming the first club professional since 1979 to win this major senior championship.

Wargo, a one-time Oldsmobile assembly line worker, commercial fisherman in Alaska and ironworker, defeated Bruce Crampton in a two-hole playoff

Champion:	Tom Wargo	
Site:	PGA National Golf Club,	
	Palm Beach Gardens, Fla.	
Date: April 15-18		Purse: $800,000
Par: 36-36—72 (6,704)		
Entries: 144	Cut at 151	74 players advanced

*S*econds after he accepted the Alfred S. Bourne Trophy, Wargo proclaimed: "This is for all the club professionals and the guys back home."

after both tied at 13-under-par 275 for 72 holes. In the process, Wargo won the hearts of club professionals everywhere and the thousands of spectators who formed their own army during one of the most dramatic PGA Seniors' Championships.

A month before he arrived at the Champion Course at PGA National Golf Club, Wargo had made what was a bold statement for someone who was about to confront the greatest legends in golf.

"It will be good playing on my turf for a change," said Wargo, who was a road-weary alternate on the Senior PGA Tour, but a veteran of South Florida courses during the winter. "I know the golf course and have played it enough times to be ready."

Wargo was a study in composure under extreme pressure, opening the Championship with a pair of 69s, followed by a 67 that included birdies on

four of the last seven holes. Wargo was chased by many of golf's all-time great performers, including Isao Aoki and Tom Weiskopf, who turned in a tournament-low 64 before planting some seeds of doubt about the leader withstanding final-day pressure.

"Hopefully it's going to be quite difficult," said Weiskopf. "I don't mean that in a nasty way, but it's a little bit different. I don't know what type of player he is — obviously he's a heck of a player. But has he won out here? That's a big deal."

Weiskopf predicted the first three holes and the last five would be crucial.

The script held true for all challengers, including Weiskopf, who had trimmed Wargo's deficit to three strokes. He bogeyed No. 14 and double-bogeyed 16. Aoki, trailing by two strokes, bogeyed three of the last five holes.

That left things up to Crampton, who played a near-flawless 6-under-par 66 in the final round to catch Wargo, who scrambled throughout the final day for a 2-under-par 70.

The stone-faced Crampton forced a playoff, making an eight-foot birdie putt on the 18th hole. The playoff began on the par-4, 412-yard 16th, a hole Wargo had played 1-over-par for the week and Crampton had played even.

Both Crampton and Wargo used 1-irons off the tee. But Wargo's approach found a well-lipped greenside bunker and Crampton's approach landed 20 feet below the hole. Wargo then stepped into the bunker and hit what may have been

his shot of the tournament, blasting to four feet below the flagstick.

Crampton then exploded his putt three feet past the cup. Wargo made his crowd-pleasing par and the match moved to the par-3 and watery 17th. Crampton selected a 7-iron and the wind — now gusting from left to right — caught the ball and pushed it into the pond. Wargo safely played his ball into the middle of the green and two-putted for par. "Always the hard way," Wargo said later.

For Crampton, it was another frustrating chapter to an otherwise highly successful career. The native Australian has finished runner-up in six major championships, including two PGA Seniors' Championships (1991, '93), two PGA Championships (1973, '75), the Masters (1972) and U.S. Open (1972).

"Tom played championship golf under difficult conditions," said a gracious Crampton. "This will be the first of many wins for Tom Wargo."

Seconds after he accepted the $110,000 check and the Alfred S. Bourne Trophy, Wargo proclaimed: "This is for all the club professionals and the guys back home."

HOW TOM WARGO PLAYED DURING THE 1993 PGA SENIORS' CHAMPIONSHIP

Hole	1	2	3	4	5	6	7	8	9	10	11	12	13	14	15	16	17	18
Par	4	4	5	4	3	5	3	4	4	5	4	4	4	4	3	4	3	5
Round 1	4	4	6	4	3	5	3	4	3	4	4	4	3	4	3	4	3	4
Round 2	3	3	5	4	3	5	3	3	3	4	6	3	3	4	3	4	4	6
Round 3	4	4	5	4	3	4	4	3	4	4	5	3	3	4	2	4	3	4
Round 4	4	4	4	4	3	5	3	3	4	4	4	5	4	4	2	5	3	5
Driving Distance: 261.2 yds. (T-9th)				**Fairways Hit:** 47 of 56 - (3rd)				**Greens Hit in Reg.:** 58 of 72 (2nd)					**Putts:** 117 (T-31st)				

PGA SENIORS' CHAMPIONSHIP

	Course Avg.	Under Par	At Par	Over Par	Round Leader	Low Round	Tom Wargo
Round 1:	76.6	14	11	117	66 -Larry Ziegler	66 - Larry Ziegler	69 - T-4th
Round 2:	74.4	35	7	99	137 -Weiskopf & Snead	64 - Weiskopf	138 -T-3rd
Round 3:	74.3	12	12	50	205 -Tom Wargo	67 - Wargo & Palmer	205 -1st
Round 4:	73.0	27	12	35	275 -Tom Wargo	66 - Bruce Crampton	275 -1st
Totals:	74.85	88	42	301			

TOURNAMENT SUMMARY

Place	Name	Score	Winnings
1	Tom Wargo	69-69-67-70—275	$110,000.00
2	Bruce Crampton	73-67-69-66—275	$80,000.00
3	Isao Aoki	72-67-69-71—279	$60,000.00
T-4	Bob Charles	74-67-72-68—281	$40,000.00
T-4	Tom Weiskopf	73-64-72-72—281	$40,000.00
6	Mike Hill	72-71-72-67—282	$30,000.00
T-7	Orville Moody	72-70-72-70—283	$22,500.00
T-7	Jim Albus	70-68-73-72—283	$22,500.00
T-9	Jack Nicklaus	69-71-73-71—284	$16,000.00
T-9	J.C. Snead	68-69-75-72—284	$16,000.00
T-9	Larry Mowry	76-68-69-71—284	$16,000.00
T-9	Harold Henning	69-70-73-72—284	$16,000.00
T-13	Tommy Aycock	70-70-75-70—285	$14,000.00
T-13	Raymond Floyd	77-67-72-69—285	$14,000.00
T-13	Al Kelley	75-66-72-72—285	$14,000.00
T-16	Gary Player	73-73-72-68—286	$12,000.00
T-16	Rocky Thompson	72-70-73-71—286	$12,000.00
T-16	Jimmy Powell	70-71-74-71—286	$12,000.00
T-16	George Archer	73-72-70-71—286	$12,000.00
T-16	Dale Douglass	74-69-70-73—286	$12,000.00
T-21	Walt Zembriski	73-69-76-69—287	$10,250.00
T-21	Kermit Zarley	73-71-72-71—287	$10,250.00
T-23	Dave Stockton	79-72-69-68—288	$9,000.00
T-23	Dewitt Weaver	72-76-73-67—288	$9,000.00
T-23	Lee Trevino	72-68-73-75—288	$9,000.00
26	Larry Gilbert	76-74-71-68—289	$8,000.00
T-27	Gibby Gilbert	73-73-74-70—290	$6,500.00
T-27	Simon Hobday	72-73-74-71—290	$6,500.00
T-27	Dick Hendrickson	70-75-75-70—290	$6,500.00
T-27	Harry Toscano	77-71-72-70—290	$6,500.00
T-27	Arnold Palmer	76-73-67-74—290	$6,500.00
T-32	Ken Still	74-71-74-72—291	$4,050.00
T-32	Jim Dent	73-70-76-72—291	$4,050.00
T-32	Tommy Horton	74-73-70-74—291	$4,050.00
T-32	Chi Chi Rodriguez	76-74-73-68—291	$4,050.00
T-32	Rives McBee	69-75-72-75—291	$4,050.00
T-37	Miller Barber	70-75-75-72—292	$2,950.00
T-37	Tom Shaw	72-67-77-76—292	$2,950.00
T-39	Don Massengale	74-71-76-72—293	$2,650.00
T-39	Larry Ziegler	66-75-76-76—293	$2,650.00
T-39	Bob Murphy	74-75-74-70—293	$2,650.00
T-39	Mike O'Sullivan	71-74-72-76—293	$2,650.00
43	John Frillman	77-70-74-73—294	$2,400.00
44	Stan Thirsk	72-73-71-79—295	$2,300.00
T-45	Terry Dill	74-70-73-79—296	$2,062.50
T-45	Jack Kiefer	74-74-75-73—296	$2,062.50
T-45	Jim Colbert	72-77-74-73—296	$2,062.50
T-45	Seiichi Kanai	77-71-76-72—296	$2,062.50
T-49	Joe Jimenez	78-68-74-77—297	$1,775.00
T-49	Gay Brewer	71-72-75-79—297	$1,775.00
T-49	Jim King	76-75-72-74—297	$1,775.00
T-49	Don January	75-70-79-73—297	$1,775.00
T-49	Dave Philo	77-73-74-73—297	$1,775.00
T-49	Mike Joyce	77-72-77-71—297	$1,775.00
55	Masaru Amano	78-73-74-73—298	$1,600.00
T-56	Brian Huggett	74-75-78-72—299	$1,525.00
T-56	Charles Coody	73-76-78-72—299	$1,525.00
T-58	Ed Dalton	68-76-81-75—300	$1,462.00
T-58	Larry Laoretti	75-76-78-71—300	$1,462.00
T-60	Lee Elder	75-69-74-83—301	$1,400.00
T-60	Bob Brue	78-73-72-78—301	$1,400.00
T-60	Lloyd Monroe	79-72-77-73—301	$1,400.00
T-63	Dave Ragan	74-74-79-75—302	$1,337.50
T-63	Bobby Nichols	74-76-78-74—302	$1,337.50
65	Odell Trueblood	74-73-79-77—303	$1,300.00
T-66	Hisashi Suzumura	79-71-76-78—304	$1,270.00
T-66	Chuck Workman	72-78-77-77—304	$1,270.00
T-68	John Paul Cain	77-73-77-78—305	$1,230.00
T-68	Ryosuke Ohta	73-73-84-75—305	$1,230.00
70	Al Krueger	75-75-78-79—307	$1,200.00
T-71	Doug Dalziel	75-76-80-77—308	$1,170.00
T-71	Hiroshi Ishii	76-73-83-76—308	$1,170.00
73	Tommy Aaron	79-71-75-84—309	$1,140.00
74	Doug Sanders	76-75-82-79—312	$1,120.00
Cut	Bob Carson	78-74—152	$750.00
Cut	Richie Bassett	77-75—152	$750.00
Cut	Mike McGinnis	76-76—152	$750.00
Cut	Dick Murphy	74-78—152	$750.00
Cut	Bob Harrison	78-74—152	$750.00
Cut	Jim Logue	81-72—152	$750.00
Cut	Roger Kennedy	77-76—153	$750.00
Cut	Jay Hyon	78-75—153	$750.00
Cut	Larry Wheeler	80-73—153	$750.00
Cut	Paul Biocini	77-76—153	$750.00
Cut	Ron Castillo Sr.	77-76—153	$750.00
Cut	Fred Hawkins	76-77—153	$750.00
Cut	Lou Graham	77-76—153	$750.00
Cut	Laurie Hammer	78-75—153	$750.00
Cut	Roland Stafford	76-78—154	$750.00
Cut	Billy Maxwell	77-77—154	$750.00
Cut	Jerry Barber	79-75—154	$750.00
Cut	Charles Sifford	81-73—154	$750.00
Cut	Charlie Huckaby	79-75—154	$750.00
Cut	Ray Montgomery	81-73—154	$750.00
Cut	Dick Smith	78-76—154	$750.00
Cut	Bill Majure	75-79—154	$750.00
Cut	Bobby Greenwood	81-73—154	$750.00
Cut	Bob Pfister	78-76—154	$750.00
Cut	Bob Williamson Jr.	81-73—154	$750.00
Cut	Dudley Wysong Jr.	81-73—154	$750.00
Cut	Gene Carello	80-74—154	$750.00
Cut	Jesse Whittenton	81-74—155	$750.00
Cut	David Jimenez	74-81—155	$750.00
Cut	Jerry Hinton	78-77—155	$750.00
Cut	Bob Bruno	74-81—155	$750.00
Cut	Paul Barkhouse	84-71—155	$750.00
Cut	Mal Galletta Jr.	79-76—155	$750.00
Cut	Ron Weber	81-74—155	$750.00
Cut	Mike Ballo	80-75—155	$750.00
Cut	Jim Johnson	81-75—156	$750.00
Cut	Joe McDermott	84-72—156	$750.00
Cut	Art Proctor	81-75—156	$750.00
Cut	Cliff Moore	79-77—156	$750.00
Cut	John Fourie	81-75—156	$750.00
Cut	Jim Ferriell	74-82—156	$750.00
Cut	Gene Borek	77-79—156	$750.00
Cut	Marion Heck	78-78—156	$750.00
Cut	Llyod Harris	84-73—157	$750.00
Cut	Bob Wenz Jr.	82-75—157	$750.00
Cut	George McKeown	81-76—157	$750.00
Cut	Pat Schwab	77-80—157	$750.00
Cut	Dennis Bradley	78-79—157	$750.00
Cut	Rocky Nelson	83-75—158	$750.00
Cut	Freddie Haas	79-80—159	$750.00
Cut	Sal Ruggiero	85-74—159	$750.00
Cut	Gary Head	75-84—159	$750.00
Cut	Bob Thatcher	79-80—159	$750.00
Cut	Gene Ferrell	84-76—160	$750.00
Cut	Terry Houser	80-81—161	$750.00
Cut	Doug Ford	86-75—161	$750.00
Cut	Al Hanzl	86-75—161	$750.00
Cut	Gerry Mehlert	81-81—162	$750.00
Cut	Bob Ross	83-79—162	$750.00
Cut	Rex Baxter	82-80—162	$750.00
Cut	Howell Fraser	82-82—164	$750.00
Cut	Tim Berg	83-82—165	$750.00
Cut	Mickey Powell	83-83—166	$750.00
Cut	Craig Shankland	80-86—166	$750.00
Cut	Buck Adams	81-85—166	$750.00
Cut	Dow Finsterwald	87-82—169	$750.00
Cut	H. Jug McSpaden	84-92—176	$750.00

PGA SENIORS' CHAMPIONSHIP

1992

Lee Trevino captured his first PGA Seniors' Championship in dramatic fashion, knocking in par-saving putts on the final two holes to finish at 10-under-par 278, holding off by one stroke Mike Hill, whose final-round 69 was the day's low effort.

The 52-year-old Trevino, pocketing a tournament-record winner's share of $100,000, became the 10th player to have won the PGA Championship (1974, '84) and the PGA Seniors' Championship.

Champion:	Lee Trevino
Site:	PGA National Golf Club, Palm Beach Gardens, Fla.
Date: April 18-21	Purse: $700,000
Par: 36-36 - 72 (6,718 Yards)	
Entries: 144	Cut at 151 77 players advanced

	Course Avg.	Under Par	At Par	Over Par	Round Leader	Low Round		Lee Trevino
Round 1:	78.05	7	4	132	G. Player, R. Ziegler	69-	G. Player, R. Ziegler	72 T-8
Round 2:	74.46	13	12	117	Trevino	64 -	Trevino	136 (64) 1st
Round 3:	74.66	14	3	60	Trevino	65 -	Charles	207 (71) 1st
Round 4:	75.75	9	4	64	Trevino	69-	Hill	278 (71) 1st
Totals:	76.54	43	23	363				

TOURNAMENT SUMMARY

Place	Name	Score	Winnings
1	Lee Trevino	72-64-71-71—278	$100,000.00
2	Mike Hill	73-70-67-69—279	$70,000.00
3	Chi Chi Rodriguez	70-72-68-70—280	$50,000.00
4	Dave Stockton	71-71-68-74—284	$35,000.00
5	Gary Player	69-71-75-70—285	$27,500.00
6	Harold Henning	72-70-70-74—286	$22,500.00
T-7	Bob Charles	77-71-65-74—287	$19,000.00
T-7	Al Kelley	74-69-70-74—287	$19,000.00
9	Doug Dalziel	70-73-72-73—288	$16,000.00
T-10	Al Geiberger	77-68-73-73—291	$14,500.00
T-10	Jack Nicklaus	73-68-74-76—291	$14,500.00
T-10	Dewitt Weaver	71-72-75-73—291	$14,500.00
13	George Archer	74-72-71-75—292	$13,500.00
T-14	Jim Dent	76-72-71-74—293	$12,000.00
T-14	Dale Douglass	76-72-74-71—293	$12,000.00
T-14	Orville Moody	74-74-74-71—293	$12,000.00
T-14	Hisashi Suzumura	76-75-68-74—293	$12,000.00
T-14	Rocky Thompson	73-73-74-73—293	$12,000.00
T-19	Bruce Crampton	74-73-75-72—294	$10,000.00
T-19	Gibby Gilbert	76-72-69-77—294	$10,000.00
T-19	Larry Laoretti	77-74-70-73—294	$10,000.00
T-22	Jim Albus	74-70-74-77—295	$7,750.00
T-22	Tommy Aycock	72-73-77-73—295	$7,750.00
T-22	John Paul Cain	74-73-76-72—295	$7,750.00
T-22	Dick Hendrickson	70-74-75-76—295	$7,750.00
T-22	Min-nan Hsieh	76-72-73-74—295	$7,750.00
T-22	Larry Ziegler	69-74-75-77—295	$7,750.00
T-28	Don Massengale	75-74-75-72—296	$5,750.00
T-28	Doug Sanders	73-72-74-77—296	$5,750.00
T-30	Jim Colbert	77-74-72-74—297	$4,750.00
T-30	J. C. Snead	78-71-74-74—297	$4,750.00
T-32	Butch Baird	75-77-75-71—298	$3,150.00
T-32	Homero Blancas	77-74-76-71—298	$3,150.00
T-32	Gary Cowan	80-71-75-72—298	$3,150.00
T-32	Dave Hill	75-74-75-74—298	$3,150.00
T-32	Lloyd Monroe	78-72-71-77—298	$3,150.00
T-32	Richard Rhyan	74-77-73-74—298	$3,150.00
38	Rives McBee	75-73-73-78—299	$2,600.00
T-39	Tommy Aaron	74-79-71-76—300	$2,350.00
T-39	Richard Bassett	77-74-78-71—300	$2,350.00
T-39	Bill Kennedy	77-76-74-73—300	$2,350.00
T-39	Walter Zembriski	73-72-75-80—300	$2,350.00
T-43	Robert Boldt	75-75-73-79—302	$1,987.50
T-43	Bob Carson	78-71-77-76—302	$1,987.50
T-43	Larry Mowry	75-77-73-77—302	$1,987.50
T-43	Lynn Rosely	77-76-76-73—302	$1,987.50
T-47	Gene Borek	73-77-72-81—303	$1,775.00
T-47	Arnold Palmer	77-73-77-76—303	$1,775.00
T-47	David Philo	79-73-77-74—303	$1,775.00

Place	Name	Score	Winnings
T-47	Tom Shaw	80-73-77-73—303	$1,775.00
T-51	Simon Hobday	78-77-76-73—304	$1,625.00
T-51	Ben Smith	81-72-78-73—304	$1,625.00
T-53	Ray Montgomery	76-75-77-77—305	$1,500.00
T-53	Rocky Nelson	79-74-75-77—305	$1,500.00
T-53	Jim O'Hern	80-72-77-76—305	$1,500.00
T-56	George Bellino	79-74-78-75—306	$1,325.00
T-56	Gay Brewer	76-79-73-78—306	$1,325.00
T-56	Bruce Devlin	73-76-76-81—306	$1,325.00
T-56	Bob Verwey	78-75-77-76—306	$1,325.00
T-60	Bobby Nichols	77-78-75-77—307	$1,212.50
T-60	Robert Zimmerman	75-79-74-79—307	$1,212.50
T-62	Cotton Dunn	72-80-78-78—308	$1,162.50
T-62	Ryosuke Ohta	75-76-80-77—308	$1,162.50
64	Mike Joyce	77-75-78-79—309	$1,125.00
T-65	Hiroshi Ishii	74-81-76-80—311	$1,080.00
T-65	Bill Majure	78-75-79-79—311	$1,080.00
T-65	Art Proctor	76-78-81-76—311	$1,080.00
T-68	Bill Eschenbrenner	76-78-70-88—312	$1,020.00
T-68	Terry Houser	75-79-77-81—312	$1,020.00
T-68	Steve Spray	76-78-80-78—312	$1,020.00
71	Larry Mancour	74-80-75-84—313	$980.00
72	Nick Berklich	76-77-75-86—314	$960.00
73	Tim Berg	80-74-75-86—315	$940.00
T-74	John Brodie	81-74-81-80—316	$900.00
T-74	Jerry Hinton	76-79-83-78—316	$900.00
T-74	Richard Martinez	78-77-82-79—316	$900.00
77	Bob Wynn	79-74-77-89—319	$860.00
Cut	Jerry Barber	79-77—156	
Cut	Paul Barkhouse	79-77—156	
Cut	Bob Brue	78-78—156	
Cut	Terry Dill	80-76—156	
Cut	Robert Gaona	75-81—156	
Cut	Hideo Jibiki	80-76—156	
Cut	Joe Jimenez	76-80—156	
Cut	Jack Kiefer	78-78—156	
Cut	Joe McDermott	82-74—156	
Cut	Earl Puckett	75-81—156	
Cut	Dave Ragan	79-77—156	
Cut	Kyle Burton	80-77—157	
Cut	Larry Campbell	80-77—157	
Cut	Joe Carr	79-78—157	
Cut	John Frillman	80-77—157	
Cut	Tommy Horton	78-79—157	
Cut	Jim Logue	81-76—157	
Cut	Billy Maxwell	80-77—157	
Cut	Jimmy Powell	79-78—157	
Cut	Charles Sifford	81-76—157	
Cut	Bill Collins	81-77—158	

Place	Name	Score
Cut	Lee Elder	81-77—158
Cut	Howell Fraser	77-81—158
Cut	Tommy Jacobs	79-79—158
Cut	Bob Kinard	81-77—158
Cut	Dick Murphy	79-79—158
Cut	Bob Rosburg	82-76—158
Cut	Stan Thirsk	79-79—158
Cut	Skip Whittet	79-79—158
Cut	Bud Williamson	77-81—158
Cut	Dick Goetz	79-80—159
Cut	Fred Hawkins	82-77—159
Cut	Marion Heck	80-79—159
Cut	Tom Joyce	78-81—159
Cut	Fred Marti	82-77—159
Cut	Jack Freeman	84-76—160
Cut	Babe Hiskey	80-80—160
Cut	Willard Scholl	82-78—160
Cut	Bob Thatcher	81-79—160
Cut	Rex Baxter	84-77—161
Cut	Ron Castillo	84-77—161
Cut	Doug Ford	80-81—161
Cut	Jay Hyon	79-82—161
Cut	Robert Pfister	79-82—161
Cut	Monty Sanders	83-78—161
Cut	Frank Freer	81-81—162
Cut	Alex Redmond	83-79—162
Cut	Chuck Scally	82-80—162
Cut	Roland Stafford	83-79—162
Cut	Fred Haas	80-83—163
Cut	Gary Head	81-82—163
Cut	John Ramsey	87-76—163
Cut	Gordon Waldespuhl	88-75—163
Cut	Gene Carello	79-86—165
Cut	Ralph Deroy	82-83—165
Cut	Bill Erfurth	84-82—166
Cut	Mal McMullen	88-78—166
Cut	Bob Ross	87-79—166
Cut	George Buzzini	84-83—167
Cut	Raymond Streeter	88-80—168
Cut	Mal Galletta	83-86—169
Cut	Banks Guyton	84-85—169
Cut	Buddy Overholser	88-81—169
Cut	Charlie Moore	88-84—172
Cut	Pat Chartrand	82-92—174
WD	Marty Furgol	—
WD	Miller Barber	82—82

1991

Jack Nicklaus led from start to finish, firing a 17-under-par 271, to win the 1991 PGA Seniors' Championship by six strokes over Bruce Crampton.

It was Nicklaus' fourth win in six senior events since turning 50 in January 1990. It was the fifth time Crampton had finished runner-up in a major championship — each time to Nicklaus.

Crampton trailed Nicklaus by eight strokes after three rounds and was never closer than six. Nicklaus built a nine-stroke lead after a birdie and Crampton bogey on the ninth hole, and a 10-stroke lead when Crampton three-putted No. 11, his second 3-putt in three holes.

Nicklaus' 271 was 10 strokes less than the previous tournament best on the Champion Course site, host of nine PGA Seniors' Championships.

Champion:	Jack Nicklaus	
Site:	PGA National Golf Club, Palm Beach Gardens, Fla.	
Date:	April 18-21	Purse: $550,000
Par:	36-36 - 72 (6,630 Yards)	
Entries:	144 Cut at 151 75 players advanced	

	Course Avg.	Under Par	At Par	Over Par	Round Leader	Low Round	Jack Nicklaus
Round 1:	76.2	16	14	113	Jack Nicklaus	66 - Jack Nicklaus	66 - 1st
Round 2:	75.7	20	16	105	Jack Nicklaus	66 - J. Nicklaus, Jim Dent	132 (66) - 1st
Round 3:	73.6	24	9	42	Jack Nickluas	68 - J. Ferree, J. Jimenez, G. Archer, G. Player, B. Charles	201 (69) - 1st
Round 4:	76.3	7	5	63	Jack Nicklaus	68 - Bruce Crampton	271 (70) - 1st
Totals:	75.62	67	44	323			

TOURNAMENT SUMMARY

Place	Name	Score	Winnings
1	Jack Nicklaus	66-66-69-70—271	$85,000.00
2	Bruce Crampton	72-67-70-68—277	$55,000.00
3	Bob Charles	72-71-68-71—282	$40,000.00
4	Homero Blancas	70-72-70-71—283	$30,000.00
5	George Archer	68-74-68-74—284	$25,000.00
T-6	Jim Dent	71-66-75-73—285	$18,725.00
T-6	Rocky Thompson	72-72-72-69—285	$18,725.00
T-8	Jim Colbert	73-67-72-74—286	$14,150.00
T-8	Orville Moody	72-72-70-72—286	$14,150.00
T-8	Gary Player	73-73-68-72—286	$14,150.00
11	Lee Trevino	72-72-72-71—287	$12,000.00
T-12	Larry Laoretti	74-69-69-76—288	$10,500.00
T-12	Chi Chi Rodriguez	73-72-70-73—288	$10,500.00
T-14	Bruce Devlin	71-71-75-72—289	$8,500.00
T-14	Dick Hendrickson	69-71-73-76—289	$8,500.00
T-14	Tom Joyce	67-71-75-76—289	$8,500.00
T-17	Dave Hill	73-73-70-74—290	$7,000.00
T-17	Richard Rhyan	72-73-69-76—290	$7,000.00
T-17	Walter Zembriski	71-71-75-73—290	$7,000.00
T-20	Miller Barber	71-75-71-74—291	$5,200.00
T-20	John Brodie	71-75-72-73—291	$5,200.00
T-20	Dale Douglass	72-71-76-72—291	$5,200.00
T-20	Jim Ferree	72-76-68-75—291	$5,200.00
T-20	Harold Henning	71-71-72-77—291	$5,200.00
T-25	Richard Crawford	76-67-72-77—292	$3,700.00
T-25	Joe Jimenez	74-76-68-74—292	$3,700.00
T-25	George Lanning	74-67-71-80—292	$3,700.00
T-25	Jimmy Powell	74-72-73-73—292	$3,700.00
T-29	Mike Hill	72-73-71-77—293	$3,100.00
T-29	Bobby Nichols	72-74-73-74—293	$3,100.00
T-31	Tommy Aaron	73-71-75-75—294	$2,700.00
T-31	Butch Baird	76-74-70-74—294	$2,700.00
T-31	Simon Hobday	72-76-72-74—294	$2,700.00
T-31	Al Kelley	73-70-73-78—294	$2,700.00
T-31	Don Massengale	70-78-70-76—294	$2,700.00
T-36	Bob Brue	73-75-75-72—295	$2,300.00
T-36	Terry Dill	72-75-75-73—295	$2,300.00
T-36	Don January	75-75-69-76—295	$2,300.00
T-39	Gay Brewer	75-74-77-70—296	$1,962.50
T-39	Jack Kiefer	74-72-70-80—296	$1,962.50
T-39	Phil Rodgers	69-76-74-77—296	$1,962.50
T-39	Brian Waites	76-75-71-74—296	$1,962.50
T-43	Frank Beard	75-70-74-78—297	$1,725.00
T-43	Rolf Deming	69-76-73-79—297	$1,725.00
T-43	Bob Rieth	75-73-70-79—297	$1,725.00
T-43	Charles Sifford	76-71-75-75—297	$1,725.00
47	Dewitt Weaver	76-73-70-79—298	$1,600.00
T-48	John Paul Cain	75-71-72-81—299	$1,500.00
T-48	Rives McBee	73-78-74-74—299	$1,500.00
T-48	Doug Sanders	73-72-78-76—299	$1,500.00

Place	Name	Score	Winnings
T-51	Dan Morgan	76-74-72-78—300	$1,375.00
T-51	Jim O'Hern	77-72-73-78—300	$1,375.00
T-53	Gene Borek	78-71-80-73—302	$1,164.28
T-53	Steve Bull	79-72-73-78—302	$1,164.28
T-53	Gene Dixon	73-77-74-78—302	$1,164.29
T-53	Bill Garrett	75-73-78-76—302	$1,164.28
T-53	Lloyd Harris	75-75-71-81—302	$1,164.29
T-53	Al Krueger	73-76-74-79—302	$1,164.29
T-53	David Philo	70-74-78-80—302	$1,164.29
T-60	Mike Joyce	75-75-75-78—303	$990.00
T-60	Buddy Overholser	77-72-76-78—303	$990.00
T-62	Lee Elder	75-73-74-82—304	$930.00
T-62	Chick Evans	71-76-78-79—304	$930.00
T-62	Mickey Powell	77-72-76-79—304	$930.00
T-62	Lynn Rosely	77-72-76-79—304	$930.00
T-66	Larry Mowry	72-75-81-77—305	$885.00
T-66	Adolph Popp	72-76-78-79—305	$885.00
T-68	Fred Hawkins	74-77-73-83—307	$865.00
T-68	Teruo Suzumura	78-72-78-79—307	$865.00
70	Wayne Kelley	73-75-76-86—310	$850.00
71	Bob Ross	78-73-76-84—311	$600.00
72	Dave Ragan	77-74-83-79—313	$600.00
73	Gordon Waldespuhl	75-75-84-81—315	$600.00
74	Ben Smith	76-75-80-85—316	$600.00
75	Charlie Stock	77-72-85-90—324	$600.00
Cut	Dan Murphy	79-73—152	
Cut	Arnold Palmer	74-78—152	
Cut	Stan Thirsk	77-75—152	
Cut	Larry Ziegler	73-79—152	
Cut	Roger Ginsberg	75-78—153	
Cut	Billy Maxwell	78-75—153	
Cut	Shozo Miyamota	76-77—153	
Cut	Hisashi Suzumura	78-75—153	
Cut	Bob Watson	75-78—153	
Cut	George Bellino	74-80—154	
Cut	Marion Heck	82-72—154	
Cut	Dick Howell	77-77—154	
Cut	Paul Messner	79-75—154	
Cut	Art Proctor	77-77—154	
Cut	Larry Romjue	76-78—154	
Cut	J. C. Snead	74-80—154	
Cut	Buck Adams	78-77—155	
Cut	Billy Farrell	76-79—155	
Cut	Wayne Morris	74-81—155	
Cut	Robert Rawlins	74-81—155	
Cut	Art Silvestrone	79-76—155	
Cut	Alex Tedmond	78-77—155	
Cut	Nunzio Ciampi	78-78—156	
Cut	Howell Fraser	73-83—156	
Cut	Hub Goyen	78-78—156	

Place	Name	Score
Cut	Casmere Jawor	79-77—156
Cut	Pat Schwab	80-76—156
Cut	Tommy Atchison	81-76—157
Cut	Don Bies	79-78—157
Cut	Tim Debaufre	74-83—157
Cut	Mac Main	77-80—157
Cut	Bill Majure	77-80—157
Cut	Earl Puckett	80-77—157
Cut	Mike Burke	78-80—158
Cut	Dick Canney	78-80—158
Cut	Bob Ford	86-72—158
Cut	John Frillman	77-81—158
Cut	Chuck Workman	82-76—158
Cut	Bill Collins	78-81—159
Cut	Jack O'Keefe	80-79—159
Cut	Johnny Powell	83-76—159
Cut	Ken Towns	75-84—159
Cut	Odell Trueblood	81-78—159
Cut	Kesahiko Uchida	78-81—159
Cut	Jerry Barber	84-76—160
Cut	Tommy Jacobs	81-79—160
Cut	Charlie Moore	81-79—160
Cut	Bill Sporre	84-76—160
Cut	Bud Williamson	81-79—160
Cut	Ange Alberico	83-78—161
Cut	Cotton Dunn	78-83—161
Cut	Mike O'Sullivan	85-76—161
Cut	Larry Wheeler	80-81—161
Cut	Joe Lopez Sr.	74-88—162
Cut	Dick Plummer	83-79—162
Cut	Doug Ford	83-80—163
Cut	Bob Kinard	82-81—163
Cut	Dudley Wysong	82-81—163
Cut	Jack Fleck	76-88—164
Cut	Charles Knowles	82-82—164
Cut	Tom Shaw	85-79—164
Cut	Rex Baxter	83-83—166
Cut	Kiyokuni Kimoto	84-83—167
Cut	Dick Schwartz	87-82—169
Cut	Jug McSpaden	88-85—173
Cut	Pete Cooper	97-83—180
WD	Jim Albus	—
WD	Tommy Bolt	—
WD	Ed Furgol	—
WD	Bob Betley	78—78
WD	Lou Graham	83—83

1990

With one of the stongest fields ever assembled for the oldest professional senior event in golf, Gary Player coasted to his third PGA Seniors' Championship with a 7-under-par 281. Player finished two strokes ahead of runner-up Chi Chi Rodriguez and four strokes ahead of Jack Nicklaus and Lee Trevino to earn the winner's check of $75,000. Player's four rounds were identical to those posted by 1989 PGA Seniors' Champion Larry Mowry.

Champion:	Gary Player
Site:	PGA National Golf Club, Palm Beach Gardens, Fla.
Date: April 12-15	**Purse:** $450,000
Par: 36-36 - 72 (6,630 Yards)	
Entries: 144	Cut at 157 77 players advanced

	Course Avg.	Under Par	At Par	Over Par	Round Leader	Low Round	Gary Player
Round 1:	78.3	5	5	133	Jack Nicklaus	68 - Jack Nicklaus	74 - Tied 19th
Round 2:	79.0	7	3	131	G. Player, H. Henning	67 - Lee Trevino	143 (69) - Tied 2nd
Round 3:	76.1	8	4	66	Gary Player	65 - Gary Player	208 (65) - 1st
Round 4:	75.8	6	7	64	Gary Player	66 - C. Rodriguez	281 (73) - 1st
Totals:	77.69	26	19	394			

TOURNAMENT SUMMARY

Place	Name	Score	Winnings
1	Gary Player	74-69-65-73—281	$75,000.00
2	Chi Chi Rodriguez	74-70-73-66—283	$45,000.00
T-3	Jack Nicklaus	68-78-67-72—285	$25,000.00
T-3	Lee Trevino	77-67-70-71—285	$25,000.00
5	George Archer	72-72-73-72—289	$16,000.00
6	Miller Barber	75-73-68-76—292	$15,000.00
7	Dale Douglass	71-73-74-75—293	$14,000.00
8	Al Kelley	71-77-74-73—295	$13,000.00
T-9	Don Bies	74-75-73-74—296	$10,500.00
T-9	Lou Graham	76-76-72-72—296	$10,500.00
T-9	Harold Henning	74-69-81-72—296	$10,500.00
T-9	Larry Ziegler	73-75-75-73—296	$10,500.00
T-13	Bruce Crampton	76-73-71-77—297	$8,000.00
T-13	Rives McBee	75-75-72-75—297	$8,000.00
T-13	Arnold Palmer	80-73-73-71—297	$8,000.00
T-16	Frank Beard	74-71-76-77—298	$6,275.00
T-16	Terry Dill	75-77-72-74—298	$6,275.00
T-16	Mike Hill	71-78-76-73—298	$6,275.00
T-16	Richard Rhyan	77-76-74-71—298	$6,275.00
T-20	Joe Carr	75-73-74-77—299	$5,000.00
T-20	Don Massengale	72-76-73-78—299	$5,000.00
T-22	Jim Ferree	71-77-77-75—300	$4,066.67
T-22	Larry Laoretti	77-76-71-76—300	$4,066.66
T-22	Larry Mancour	76-73-77-74—300	$4,066.67
T-25	Jerry Barber	73-79-71-78—301	$3,300.00
T-25	George Lanning	76-78-74-73—301	$3,300.00
T-25	Charles Sifford	75-73-80-73—301	$3,300.00
T-25	Ralph Terry	73-73-77-78—301	$3,300.00
T-29	Bob Brue	76-72-79-75—302	$2,400.00
T-29	John Paul Cain	74-80-76-72—302	$2,400.00
T-29	Bob Charles	75-75-73-79—302	$2,400.00
T-29	Al Geiberger	76-75-74-77—302	$2,400.00
T-29	Mike Joyce	81-71-73-77—302	$2,400.00
T-29	Orville Moody	76-73-75-78—302	$2,400.00
T-29	Paul Moran	74-77-74-77—302	$2,400.00
T-29	Dan Morgan	81-76-73-72—302	$2,400.00
T-29	Gordon Waldespuhl	74-79-72-77—302	$2,400.00
T-38	Butch Baird	74-76-76-77—303	$1,750.00
T-38	Charles Coody	74-73-79-77—303	$1,750.00
T-38	Jim Dent	78-72-74-79—303	$1,750.00
T-38	Dewitt Weaver	73-82-78-70—303	$1,750.00
T-42	Homero Blancas	79-74-77-74—304	$1,425.00
T-42	Joe Jimenez	79-77-71-77—304	$1,425.00
T-42	Joe Lopez Sr.	79-77-74-74—304	$1,425.00
T-42	Walter Zembriski	80-75-77-72—304	$1,425.00
46	Casmere Jawor	76-79-77-73—305	$1,300.00
T-47	Gay Brewer	76-80-74-76—306	$1,175.00
T-47	Doug Dalziel	77-74-73-82—306	$1,175.00
T-47	Roger Ginsberg	73-73-83-77—306	$1,175.00
T-47	Jim O'Hern	72-78-80-76—306	$1,175.00

Place	Name	Score	Winnings
T-51	Billy Maxwell	74-79-76-78—307	$1,010.00
T-51	Adolph Popp	73-82-79-73—307	$1,010.00
T-51	Art Proctor	75-74-85-73—307	$1,010.00
T-51	Doug Sanders	72-81-77-77—307	$1,010.00
T-55	Tommy Aaron	80-71-84-73—308	$950.00
T-55	Bob Erickson	76-80-76-76—308	$950.00
T-55	Bobby Nichols	76-78-76-78—308	$950.00
T-58	Roberto De Vicenzo	75-75-79-80—309	$915.00
T-58	Howell Fraser	79-76-78-76—309	$915.00
T-58	Fred Hawkins	74-79-80-76—309	$915.00
T-58	Dick Hendrickson	78-75-79-77—309	$915.00
T-62	Jack Fleck	75-76-85-74—310	$885.00
T-62	Ken Still	78-77-87-68—310	$885.00
T-64	Bruce Devlin	83-74-77-77—311	$860.00
T-64	Gene Dixon	81-75-78-77—311	$860.00
T-64	Bob Reith	76-81-79-75—311	$860.00
67	George Bellino	75-82-73-82—312	$840.00
T-68	Larry Mowry	76-78-75-84—313	$825.00
T-68	Ted Naff	77-77-76-83—313	$825.00
T-70	John Molenda	76-81-80-77—314	$655.00
T-70	Harlan Stevenson	77-77-82-78—314	$655.00
72	Gene Borek	73-80-76-87—316	$500.00
T-73	Cotton Dunn	75-80-80-82—317	$500.00
T-73	J. C. Goosie	73-84-80-80—317	$500.00
T-73	Chuck Huckaby	81-76-79-81—317	$500.00
76	Gene Thompson	76-81-82-79—318	$500.00
77	Bob Ross	76-81-85-80—322	$500.00
Cut	Chick Evans	83-75—158	
Cut	Bob Goalby	79-79—158	
Cut	David Jimenez	79-79—158	
Cut	Jim King	79-79—158	
Cut	Carl Lohren	76-82—158	
Cut	George McKewon	80-78—158	
Cut	John McMullen	77-81—158	
Cut	Dick Plummer	78-80—158	
Cut	Dave Ragan	74-84—158	
Cut	Brian Waites	80-78—158	
Cut	Tommy Jacobs	77-82—159	
Cut	Don Lindsey	81-78—159	
Cut	Dick Sarta	78-81—159	
Cut	Stan Thirsk	77-82—159	
Cut	Fred Haas Jr.	77-83—160	
Cut	Mike McGinnis	77-83—160	
Cut	Gene Mitchell	82-78—160	
Cut	Alex Redmond	81-79—160	
Cut	Jack Webb	75-85—160	
Cut	Tim Berg	84-77—161	
Cut	Robert Boldt	83-78—161	
Cut	Jerry Coats	76-85—161	
Cut	Buddy Demling	79-82—161	

Place	Name	Score
Cut	Fran Deschaine	82-79—161
Cut	Tom Shaw	79-82—161
Cut	Ken Towns	82-79—161
Cut	Ronald Weber	75-86—161
Cut	Rex Baxter	76-86—162
Cut	Mike Burke	77-85—162
Cut	Al Chandler	83-79—162
Cut	John Frillman	79-83—162
Cut	Quinton Gray	79-83—162
Cut	Bill Majure	80-82—162
Cut	Jimmy Powell	72-90—162
Cut	John Scheffler	83-79—162
Cut	Raymond Streeter	81-81—162
Cut	Nick Berklich	80-83—163
Cut	Paul Messner	76-87—163
Cut	Harvey Bostic	82-82—164
Cut	Bob Thatcher	81-83—164
Cut	Carl Unis	79-85—164
Cut	Kyle Burton	82-84—166
Cut	Dick Carmody	86-80—166
Cut	Paul Kelly	84-82—166
Cut	Mal McMullen	84-82—166
Cut	Clifford Moore	86-80—166
Cut	Deray Simon	83-83—166
Cut	Bill Byars	90-77—167
Cut	Walker Inman	87-80—167
Cut	Earl Puckett	87-80—167
Cut	George Thomas	82-86—168
Cut	Dick Canney	84-85—169
Cut	Ray Montgomery	83-86—169
Cut	Bill Halvorson	81-90—171
Cut	Jennings House	85-87—172
Cut	Phil Hewitt	89-85—174
Cut	Jug McSpaden	89-85—174
Cut	Pete Cooper	86-91—177
Cut	Ted Kroll	90-87—177
Cut	Joe Cardenas	90-88—178
Cut	Don Smith	98-81—179
Cut	Peter Carriell	87-94—181
Cut	Ed Furgol	96-96—192
WD	Ange Alberico	—
WD	Bill Collins	—
DQ	Doug Ford	—
WD	Marty Furgol	—
WD	Lee Elder	78—78
DQ	Ben Smith	79—79

1989

Larry Mowry, a 52-year old former mini-tour standout from Atlanta, Ga., fired a 7-under-par 281 to edge Miller Barber and Al Geiberger by one stroke. Mowry won 106 mini-tour events and three Senior PGA Tour events before his victory in Palm Beach Gardens, Fla.

Champion:	Larry Mowry
Site:	PGA National Golf Club, Palm Beach Gardens, Fla.
Date: Feb. 8-12	Purse: $400,000
Par: 36-36 — 72 (6,530 Yards)	
Entries: 143	Cut at 155 69 players advanced

	Course Avg.	Under Par	At Par	Over Par	Round Leader	Low Round	Larry Mowry
Round 1:	78.5	7	6	127	Mike Hill	67 - Mike Hill	74 - Tied 21st
Round 2:	77.3	11	6	122	Mike Hill	69 - M. Barber, L. Mowry, J. Powell	143 (69) - Tied 5th
Round 3:	74.2	12	7	50	Larry Mowry	65 - Larry Mowry	208 (65) Tied 5th
Round 4:	73.9	18	7	44	Larry Mowry	68 - C. Rodriguez	281 (73) - 1st
Totals:	76.62	48	26	343			

TOURNAMENT SUMMARY

Place	Name	Score	Winnings
1	Larry Mowry	74-69-65-73—281	$72,000.00
T-2	Miller Barber	72-69-70-71—282	$35,200.00
T-2	Al Geiberger	69-70-72-71—282	$35,200.00
T-4	Dave Hill	73-72-70-72—287	$16,533.00
T-4	Mike Hill	67-71-74-75—287	$16,533.34
T-4	Joe Jimenez	72-70-72-73—287	$16,533.00
7	Harold Henning	72-73-70-73—288	$13,400.00
T-8	Bruce Crampton	72-73-71-73—289	$11,600.00
T-8	Gary Player	70-76-72-71—289	$11,600.00
T-8	Ben Smith	72-73-71-73—289	$11,600.00
T-11	Bob Brue	75-70-73-72—290	$8,800.00
T-11	Doug Dalziel	73-72-72-73—290	$8,800.00
T-11	Arnold Palmer	71-74-74-71—290	$8,800.00
T-11	Walter Zembriski	76-72-73-69—290	$8,800.00
T-15	Gay Brewer	79-70-70-72—291	$7,000.00
T-15	Stan Thirsk	73-76-72-70—291	$7,000.00
T-17	Jim Ferree	79-72-70-71—292	$6,200.00
T-17	Orville Moody	70-75-72-75—292	$6,200.00
T-19	Lee Elder	74-76-72-71—293	$4,848.00
T-19	Don Massengale	78-74-70-71—293	$4,848.00
T-19	Billy Maxwell	73-71-74-75—293	$4,848.00
T-19	Bobby Nichols	78-71-73-71—293	$4,848.00
T-19	Chi Chi Rodriguez	75-75-75-68—293	$4,848.00
T-24	Bob Charles	71-80-71-72—294	$3,520.00
T-24	Jimmy Powell	78-69-74-73—294	$3,520.00
T-24	Tom Shaw	74-76-70-74—294	$3,520.00
T-27	Tommy Aaron	80-72-70-73—295	$2,900.00
T-27	Don Bies	72-74-74-75—295	$2,900.00
T-27	Dick Hendrickson	74-75-76-70—295	$2,900.00
T-27	Jim O'Hern	75-73-78-69—295	$2,900.00
T-31	Gardner Dickinson	74-72-74-76—296	$2,480.00
T-31	Dale Douglass	74-77-74-71—296	$2,480.00
T-31	Paul Moran	71-73-76-76—296	$2,480.00
T-34	John Brodie	73-73-77-74—297	$2,160.00
T-34	Bruce Devlin	78-75-73-71—297	$2,160.00
T-34	George Lanning	76-76-73-72—297	$2,160.00
T-37	Butch Baird	78-75-75-70—298	$1,800.00
T-37	Joe Carr	74-75-73-76—298	$1,800.00
T-37	Rives McBee	76-74-73-75—298	$1,800.00
T-40	Roger Ginsberg	76-74-78-71—299	$1,680.00
T-40	Fred Hawkins	75-75-74-75—299	$1,680.00
T-42	Billy Casper	73-75-79-73—300	$1,520.00
T-42	Doug Ford	79-76-73-72—300	$1,520.00
T-44	Jerry Barber	75-76-76-74—301	$1,320.00
T-44	Bill Halvorson	78-74-75-74—301	$1,320.00
T-44	Don January	80-73-77-71—301	$1,320.00
T-47	Jack Fleck	76-76-73-77—302	$1,057.60
T-47	John Frillman	78-73-74-77—302	$1,057.60

Place	Name	Score	Winnings
T-47	Larry Mancour	78-76-74-74—302	$1,057.60
T-47	Dave Ragan	78-75-77-72—302	$1,057.60
T-47	Richard Rhyan	74-81-74-73—302	$1,057.60
52	Earl Puckett	78-75-76-75—304	$960.00
T-53	Bob Bruno	76-75-78-76—305	$921.60
T-53	Al Chandler	79-73-75-78—305	$921.60
T-53	Jerry Coats	80-74-73-78—305	$921.60
T-53	Jim King	80-75-77-73—305	$921.60
T-53	Bob Ross	75-77-73-80—305	$921.60
T-58	Dennis Bradley	77-76-75-78—306	$888.00
T-58	Chick Evans	77-76-74-79—306	$888.00
T-58	Bob Goalby	74-78-77-77—306	$888.00
61	Tom Nieporte	75-77-79-76—307	$872.00
62	Rafe Botts	81-74-80-73—308	$864.00
T-63	Mike Burke	80-75-78-76—309	$852.00
T-63	Chuck Scally	76-79-77-77—309	$852.00
65	Billy Farrell	81-71-77-81—310	$840.00
66	Tim Berg	74-81-76-81—312	$832.00
67	Walker Inman Jr.	78-76-81-78—313	$824.00
68	Bob Erickson	79-76-81-80—316	$816.00
69	Pat Chartrand	82-73-82-80—317	$808.00
Cut	Rex Baxter	78-78—156	
Cut	Ken Campbell	78-78—156	
Cut	Bob Duden	73-83—156	
Cut	Cotton Dunn	76-80—156	
Cut	Tony Morosco	77-79—156	
Cut	Jack Okeefe	80-76—156	
Cut	Buddy Overholser	80-76—156	
Cut	Manuel Quezada	78-78—156	
Cut	Art Silvestrone	80-76—156	
Cut	Ken Still	79-77—156	
Cut	Don Bisesi	77-80—157	
Cut	Casmere Jawor	80-77—157	
Cut	John Rainieri	79-78—157	
Cut	Gordon Waldespuhl	79-78—157	
Cut	Buck Adams	76-82—158	
Cut	El Collins	81-77—158	
Cut	Don Johnson	82-76—158	
Cut	Ray Montgomery	80-78—158	
Cut	David Findlay	81-78—159	
Cut	Fred Haas Jr.	81-78—159	
Cut	Doug Higgins	81-78—159	
Cut	Robert Shields Sr.	82-77—159	
Cut	Jack Webb	81-78—159	
Cut	Bill Collins	82-78—160	
Cut	Jennings House	80-80—160	
Cut	Wayne Morris	81-79—160	
Cut	Auggie Navarro	81-79—160	

Place	Name	Score
Cut	George Schneiter	78-82—160
Cut	Joel Taylor	84-76—160
Cut	Chuck Workman	83-77—160
Cut	Donald Fox	79-82—161
Cut	Richard Havenstrite	79-82—161
Cut	Jackie Maness	78-83—161
Cut	Don Olney	81-80—161
Cut	Ralph Haddad	80-82—162
Cut	Phil Hewitt	74-88—162
Cut	George Nackel	85-77—162
Cut	Tom Nielsen	82-80—162
Cut	Paul O'Learly	82-80—162
Cut	Bill Crowe	82-81—163
Cut	John Kalinka	85-78—163
Cut	Ed Kroll	85-78—163
Cut	Ken Towns	82-81—163
Cut	Ray Ziats	85-78—163
Cut	Peter Carriell	87-77—164
Cut	Manuel de la Torre	84-80—164
Cut	Stan Dudas	79-85—164
Cut	Art Proctor	82-82—164
Cut	John Haines	86-79—165
Cut	Stan Jawor	84-81—165
Cut	Don Lindsey	85-80—165
Cut	Dick Schwartz	85-81—166
Cut	Gene Thompson	79-87—166
Cut	Alex Alexander	84-83—167
Cut	Harvey Bostic	85-82—167
Cut	Dick Hart	82-85—167
Cut	Joe Lopez Sr.	81-86—167
Cut	Don Pauley	82-85—167
Cut	Sam Penecale	86-81—167
Cut	Robert Badger	84-84—168
Cut	Luca Barbato	83-85—168
Cut	Gene Dixon	85-83—168
Cut	Jug McSpaden	84-84—168
Cut	Pete Cooper	87-83—170
Cut	Jimmy Russell	85-85—170
Cut	Pat Simmons	85-86—171
Cut	Howard Roseen	91-92—183
WD	Julius Boros	80—80
DQ	Doug Sanders	77-76—153
DQ	Charles Coody	79-78—157
DQ	J. C. Goosie	79-79—158

1988

One of only four players to capture all four Grand Slam titles, Gary Player earned his second PGA Seniors' Championship trophy and his fourth major in senior golf. A final round of 2-under-par 70 accomplished this latest victory. Player finished three strokes up on defending Champion Chi Chi Rodriguez, with a 4-under-par 284. Rodriguez and Al Geiberger had been tied for the third-round lead. Left-hander Bob Charles, a resident of PGA National, built an amazing five-stroke lead the first day with a near-record 64 on the Champion Course.

Champion:	Gary Player
Site:	PGA National Golf Club, Palm Beach Gardens, Fla.
Date: Feb. 10-14	**Purse:** $355,000
Par: 36-36 — 72 (6,530 Yards)	
Entries: 140	Cut at 155 76 players advanced

	Course Avg.	Under Par	At Par	Over Par	Round Leader	Low Round	Gary Player
Round 1:	76.8	15	8	117	Bob Charles	64 - Bob Charles	69 - Tied 2nd
Round 2:	77.9	6	4	123	Bob Charles	69 - Arnold Palmer	142 (73) - Tied 5th
Round 3:	77.4	3	5	68	Al Geiberger	69 - Bruce Devlin, C. Rodriguez	214 (72) - Tied 2nd
Round 4:	73.9	4	3	69	Gary Player	69 - Harold Henning	284 (70) - 1st
Totals:	77.22	28	20	377			

TOURNAMENT SUMMARY

Place	Name	Score	Winnings
1	Gary Player	69-73-72-70—284	$63,000.00
2	Chi Chi Rodriguez	70-72-71-74—287	$37,800.00
T-3	Miller Barber	73-75-70-70—288	$20,300.00
T-3	Al Geiberger	69-71-73-75—288	$20,300.00
T-5	Orville Moody	69-71-74-75—289	$13,300.00
T-5	Arnold Palmer	72-69-76-72—289	$13,300.00
T-7	Bruce Devlin	73-72-69-77—291	$11,287.50
T-7	Harold Henning	69-75-78-69—291	$11,287.50
T-9	Larry Mowry	69-76-74-73—292	$9,800.00
T-9	Walter Zembriski	73-71-74-74—292	$9,800.00
T-11	Bob Charles	64-73-78-78—293	$8,400.00
T-11	Bruce Crampton	74-73-74-72—293	$8,400.00
T-13	Tommy Aaron	69-73-75-78—295	$7,000.00
T-13	Lee Elder	70-76-74-75—295	$7,000.00
T-15	Al Chandler	72-75-76-73—296	$6,125.00
T-15	Art Silvestrone	76-71-74-75—296	$6,125.00
T-17	Bill Collins	74-71-79-74—298	$5,425.00
T-17	Charles Coody	72-76-72-78—298	$5,425.00
T-19	Gene Borek	74-74-72-79—299	$4,550.00
T-19	Gay Brewer	71-77-75-76—299	$4,550.00
T-19	Tony Morosco	76-75-74-74—299	$4,550.00
T-22	Jay Hyon	77-73-74-76—300	$3,360.00
T-22	Jim King	72-75-75-78—300	$3,360.00
T-22	Joe Lopez Sr.	77-73-76-74—300	$3,360.00
T-22	Don Massengale	72-75-76-77—300	$3,360.00
T-22	Roland Stafford	73-73-76-78—300	$3,360.00
T-27	Bob Brue	73-78-72-78—301	$2,485.00
T-27	El Collins	72-72-83-74—301	$2,485.00
T-27	Mike Fetchick	75-73-76-77—301	$2,485.00
T-27	Joe Jimenez	71-80-72-78—301	$2,485.00
T-27	George Lanning	69-79-75-78—301	$2,485.00
T-32	Bobby Nichols	73-77-76-76—302	$2,071.66
T-32	Ken Still	72-80-76-74—302	$2,071.67
T-32	Art Wall	74-76-81-71—302	$2,071.67
T-35	Dale Douglass	76-73-75-79—303	$1,803.33
T-35	Howie Johnson	74-77-80-72—303	$1,803.34
T-35	Mike Souchak	79-74-76-74—303	$1,803.33
T-38	Robert Boldt	75-77-74-78—304	$1,575.00
T-38	Billy Maxwell	75-75-76-78—304	$1,575.00
T-38	Gordon Waldespuhl	76-76-77-75—304	$1,575.00
T-41	John Brodie	76-72-81-76—305	$1,365.00
T-41	Steve Bull	71-75-78-81—305	$1,365.00
T-41	Gordon Jones	77-75-78-75—305	$1,365.00
44	Sal Ruggiero	75-79-74-78—306	$1,225.00
T-45	Buck Adams	71-77-77-82—307	$1,085.00
T-45	Harvey Bostic	74-80-77-76—307	$1,085.00
T-45	Charles Sifford	71-77-81-78—307	$1,085.00
T-48	J. C. Goosie	81-74-77-76—308	$935.00

Place	Name	Score	Winnings
T-48	Adolph Popp	73-79-80-76—308	$935.00
T-50	Jerry Barber	77-75-82-75—309	$851.25
T-50	George Bellino	74-77-74-84—309	$851.25
T-50	Fred Hawkins	75-77-81-76—309	$851.25
T-50	Monty Sanders	75-75-81-78—309	$851.25
T-54	Mike Cerjanic	80-75-82-73—310	$794.17
T-54	Jim Cochran	79-75-79-77—310	$794.17
T-54	Bob Duden	77-75-85-73—310	$794.17
T-54	Dick Hendrickson	77-75-82-76—310	$794.17
T-54	Dean Lind	73-78-78-81—310	$794.16
T-54	Tom Nieporte	79-74-77-80—310	$794.16
T-60	Dick Howell	78-77-80-76—311	$767.50
T-60	Dean Refram	77-76-80-78—311	$767.50
T-62	Billy Casper	76-79-79-78—312	$745.00
T-62	Bob Erickson	77-77-81-77—312	$745.00
T-62	Buddy Overholser	78-75-79-80—312	$745.00
T-62	Stan Thirsk	76-77-81-78—312	$745.00
T-66	Bill Majure	76-75-84-78—313	$714.00
T-66	Don Prigmore	77-75-84-75—313	$714.00
T-66	Dave Ragan	75-78-81-79—313	$714.00
T-66	Alex Redmond	76-77-77-83—313	$714.00
T-66	Doug Sanders	72-81-83-77—313	$714.00
T-71	Stan Dudas	76-79-79-80—314	$700.00
T-71	Paul Kelly	76-76-76-86—314	$700.00
T-71	Jack Webb	79-75-82-78—314	$700.00
74	Cotton Dunn	77-78-82-78—315	$700.00
75	Jim Ferree	76-77-83-83—319	$700.00
76	Ben Smith	75-80-85-81—321	$700.00
Cut	Peter Belmont	77-79—156	
Cut	Jerry Coats	77-79—156	
Cut	Dow Finsterwald	79-77—156	
Cut	Jennings House	78-78—156	
Cut	James Shelton	78-78—156	
Cut	Billy Capps	79-78—157	
Cut	Pat Chartrand	77-80—157	
Cut	Doug Ford	79-78—157	
Cut	Don Johnson	78-79—157	
Cut	John Kalinka	79-78—157	
Cut	Dick Lanscioni	79-78—157	
Cut	Ron Polane	75-82—157	
Cut	Jimmy Powell	80-77—157	
Cut	Raymond Streeter	76-81—157	
Cut	Carl Unis	80-77—157	
Cut	Bobby Westfall	80-77—157	
Cut	Jack Fleck	77-81—158	
Cut	Phil Hewitt	80-78—158	
Cut	Robert Shields Sr.	77-81—158	
Cut	Rex Bible	79-80—159	

Place	Name	Score
Cut	Kyle Burton	76-83—159
Cut	Peter Carriell	81-78—159
Cut	Don Hoenig	79-80—159
Cut	Larry Mancour	81-78—159
Cut	Dick Sarta	84-75—159
Cut	Chuck Workman	81-78—159
Cut	Rex Baxter	78-82—160
Cut	Bill Cox	78-82—160
Cut	Gardner Dickinson	79-81—160
Cut	Stan Jawor	81-79—160
Cut	Al Littleton	77-83—160
Cut	Earl Fennell	83-78—161
Cut	John Langford	82-79—161
Cut	Gene Thompson	75-86—161
Cut	Brien Charter	80-82—162
Cut	Pete Hessemer	86-76—162
Cut	Frank Wharton	82-80—162
Cut	Hampton Auld	80-83—163
Cut	Dick Canney	82-81—163
Cut	Bob Ellsworth	81-82—163
Cut	Verne Perry	81-82—163
Cut	Gary Wiren	76-87—163
Cut	Bill Crowe	80-84—164
Cut	Manuel Quezada	81-83—164
Cut	Charles Rotar	85-79—164
Cut	Tom Murphy	80-85—165
Cut	Buddy Demling	79-87—166
Cut	Bob Popp	84-82—166
Cut	Frank Freer	85-82—167
Cut	Earl Puckett	80-87—167
Cut	Jimmy Rager	78-89—167
Cut	Bert Seagraves	85-82—167
Cut	Lee Bonse	86-82—168
Cut	Pete Cooper	84-85—169
Cut	George Kroll	79-90—169
Cut	Ed Bruno	84-89—173
Cut	Hebert Holm	87-90—177
WD	Nunzio Ciampi	77—77
DQ	Fred Haas Jr.	78—78
DQ	Charles Owens	78—78
DQ	Randy Quick	78—78
WD	Casmere Jawor	81—81
DQ	Bob Rosburg	81—81
DQ	Frank Segaline	84—84

1987

Chi Chi Rodriguez staged a dramatic comeback and earned one of the most popular victories in PGA Seniors' Championship history. Trailing third-round leader Dale Douglass by six strokes, Rodriguez had a final round of 5-under-par 67 to edge Douglass by one, with a 6-under-par 282 total. Amazingly, Rodriguez used a new set of clubs he purchased from the golf shop at PGA National after a third round of 76. His mentor, eight-time Florida Open champion and 1976 PGA Seniors' winner Pete Cooper, walked with Rodriguez every step of the way the last day, after missing the 36-hole cut.

Champion:	Chi Chi Rodriguez
Site:	PGA National Golf Club, Palm Beach Gardens, Fla.
Date: Feb. 11-15	**Purse:** $260,000
Par: 36-36 — 72 (6,520 Yards)	
Entries: 135	Cut at 157 71 players advanced

	Course Avg.	Under Par	At Par	Over Par	Round Leader	Low Round	C. Rodriguez
Round 1:	79.3	3	2	127	C. Rodriguez	70 - C. Rodriguez	70 - 1st
Round 2:	77.8	7	4	117	C. Rodriguez	66 - Dale Douglass	139 (69) - 1st
Round 3:	74.5	11	7	53	B. Nichols, H. Henning	67 - Harold Henning, Jim King	215 (76) - Tied 3rd
Round 4:	75.8	5	6	60	C. Rodriguez	67 - C. Rodriguez	282 (67) - 1st
Totals:	77.37	26	19	357			

TOURNAMENT SUMMARY

Place	Name	Score	Winnings	Place	Name	Score	Winnings	Place	Name	Score
1	Chi Chi Rodriguez	70-69-76-67—282	$47,000.00	T-43	Art Wall	80-77-73-76—306	$814.00	Cut	John Doctor	80-81—161
2	Dale Douglass	74-66-69-74—283	$29,500.00	T-47	Billy Farrell	80-75-77-75—307	$740.00	Cut	Donald Fox	81-80—161
T-3	Bob Charles	72-73-70-71—286	$16,250.00	T-47	Dow Finsterwald	78-76-76-77—307	$740.00	Cut	Mac Main	79-82—161
3	Bobby Nichols	74-72-68-72—286	$16,250.00	T-47	J. C. Goosie	79-77-74-77—307	$740.00	Cut	Charles Smith	84-77—161
T-5	Lee Elder	73-73-70-73—289	$10,608.00	T-47	Pete Hessemer	79-75-76-77—307	$740.00	Cut	Ted Wurtz	84-77—161
T-5	Jack Fleck	71-73-73-72—289	$10,608.00	T-47	Bob McCallister	79-74-74-80—307	$740.00	Cut	Bob Ellsworth	85-77—162
T-5	Harold Henning	74-73-67-75—289	$10,608.00	T-47	Earl Puckett	81-75-75-76—307	$740.00	Cut	Babe Lichardus	78-84—162
8	Gary Player	74-73-68-75—290	$8,500.00	T-47	Ken Still	78-76-72-81—307	$740.00	Cut	Bert Seagraves	81-81—162
T-9	Butch Baird	73-71-72-75—291	$7,025.00	T-54	Peter Carriell	77-78-74-79—308	$675.00	Cut	Bob Wolfe	82-80—162
T-9	Orville Moody	74-75-68-74—291	$7,025.00	T-54	Doug Ford	81-76-77-74—308	$675.00	Cut	Ed Bosse	80-83—163
T-11	Billy Casper	75-73-73-71—292	$5,800.00	T-54	Buddy Overholser	77-73-77-81—308	$675.00	Cut	Max Hines	79-84—163
T-11	Doug Sanders	74-71-74-73—292	$5,800.00	T-54	Jon Powell	77-79-76-76—308	$675.00	Cut	George Bruno	88-77—165
T-13	Joe Jimenez	71-70-76-76—293	$4,550.00	T-54	Bill Sporre	75-85-83-72—308	$675.00	Cut	Jon Gustin	84-81—165
T-13	Jim King	78-73-67-75—293	$4,550.00	T-54	Jerry Steelsmith	74-79-78-77—308	$675.00	Cut	Jug McSpaden	84-81—165
T-13	Charles Owens	73-73-74-73—293	$4,550.00	60	Dean Lind	82-70-76-81—309	$640.00	Cut	Don Pauley	82-83—165
T-16	Al Chandler	79-74-70-71—294	$3,650.00	T-61	Mike Fetchick	79-78-78-75—310	$620.00	Cut	Larry Tomasino	82-83—165
T-16	Arnold Palmer	75-72-72-75—294	$3,650.00	T-61	Fred Haas Jr.	79-78-75-78—310	$620.00	Cut	Frank Arasin	80-86—166
T-16	Bob Toski	73-75-72-74—294	$3,650.00	T-61	Fred Hawkins	80-75-77-78—310	$620.00	Cut	Tony Evans	83-83—166
19	Bob Bruno	76-72-72-75—295	$3,250.00	64	Monte Sanders	79-75-79-78—311	$600.00	Cut	Jimmy Rager	81-85—166
20	Bruce Crampton	74-71-74-77—296	$3,050.00	T-65	Bill Halvorson	80-77-75-80—312	$585.00	Cut	Ray Barnes	88-79—167
21	Bob Duden	75-76-73-74—298	$2,850.00	T-65	Jimmy Powell	77-78-80-77—312	$585.00	Cut	Gene Fawbush	88-79—167
T-22	Gene Borek	79-72-69-79—299	$2,350.00	67	Chuck Scally	79-76-77-82—314	$575.00	Cut	Mike Mural	86-81—167
T-22	Jim Ferree	74-76-73-76—299	$2,350.00	68	Tom Swiney	76-79-81-79—315	$570.00	Cut	John Zontek	80-87—167
T-22	George Lanning	72-78-74-75—299	$2,350.00	69	Art Forrester	75-80-79-82—316	$565.00	Cut	Joe Dodich	83-85—168
T-22	Adolph Popp	77-78-72-72—299	$2,350.00	T-70	Brien Charter	77-80-84-77—318	$560.00	Cut	Woody Kay	86-82—168
26	Bill Collins	75-74-79-72—300	$1,950.00	T-70	Paul Massner	80-76-81-81—318	$560.00	Cut	Tom Nielsen	87-81—168
T-27	Casmere Jawor	73-78-74-76—301	$1,750.00	Cut	Frank Freer	80-78—158		Cut	Roger Floyd	86-83—169
T-27	Howie Johnson	76-73-76-76—301	$1,750.00	Cut	Ralph Haddad	78-80—158		Cut	Pete Cooper	85-85—170
T-27	Charles Sifford	77-76-72-76—301	$1,750.00	Cut	Don Hoenig	79-79—158		Cut	Tony Morosco	88-82—170
T-30	Jerry Barber	75-77-74-76—302	$1,467.00	Cut	Harold Kolb	83-75—158		Cut	Auggie Navarro	87-83—170
T-30	Gardner Dickinson	81-73-74-74—302	$1,467.00	Cut	Gary Lockie	79-79—158		Cut	George Schneiter	85-85—170
T-30	Bill Johnston	78-78-73-73—302	$1,467.00	Cut	Mil Radler	80-78—158		Cut	Ray Oakes	86-85—171
T-33	John Frillman	74-80-71-78—303	$1,300.00	Cut	Al Balding	82-77—159		Cut	Bob Watson	85-86—171
T-33	Richard Rhyan	74-79-74-76—303	$1,300.00	Cut	Rex Baxter	83-76—159		Cut	Paul Runyan	86-87—173
T-33	Ed Rubis	78-78-73-74—303	$1,300.00	Cut	Stan Jawor	81-78—159		Cut	Buddy Cook	90-84—174
T-36	Gay Brewer	73-77-73-81—304	$1,150.00	Cut	Don Olney	83-76—159		Cut	Ed Furgol	89-88—177
T-36	Ray Montgomery	73-76-80-75—304	$1,150.00	Cut	Paul Thomas	78-81—159		Cut	Clyde Thomsen	90-88—178
T-36	Tom Nieporte	73-78-77-76—304	$1,150.00	Cut	Harvey Bostic	81-79—160		WD	Dick Chassee	—
T-39	Joe Campbell	77-73-75-80—305	$975.00	Cut	Ron Fox	80-80—160		WD	Mike Souchak	—
T-39	Jim Cochran	78-75-74-78—305	$975.00	Cut	Don Johnson	80-80—160		WD	Pete Brown	—
T-39	Billy Maxwell	76-75-74-80—305	$975.00	Cut	Mal McMullen	82-78—160		WD	Dan Sikes	73—73
T-39	Bob Ross	78-77-79-71—305	$975.00	Cut	Willie School	79-81—160		WD	John Kalinka	79—79
T-43	Dick Howell	79-77-77-73—306	$814.00	Cut	Robert Shields Sr.	81-79—160		WD	George Bayer	83—83
T-43	Ralph Montoya	81-73-74-78—306	$814.00	Cut	Ange Alberico	84-77—161		WD	Bill Byars	85—85
T-43	Ralph Terry	79-78-77-72—306	$814.00	Cut	Al Besselink	76-85—161		WD	Julius Boros	82-75—157

1986

The PGA Seniors' Championship settled into February dates, early on the Senior PGA Tour's calendar. South African Gary Player became the second foreigner in a row to claim the title, outdistancing Lee Elder by two with a 7-under-par 281. Though neither of the past two champions was in the field —

Champion:	Gary Player
Site:	PGA National Golf Club,
	Palm Beach Gardens, Fla.
Date: Feb. 14-16	**Purse:** $250,000
Par: 36-36 — 72 (6,520 Yards)	
Entries: 134	Cut at 157 70 players advanced

Arnold Palmer had back spasms and Peter Thomson was home in Australia — record crowds turned out. It was Player's second victory in three Senior Tour starts since turning 50 in November 1985.

	Course Avg.	Under Par	At Par	Over Par	Round Leader	Low Round	Gary Player
Round 1:	79.9	4	3	127	Gary Player	Miller Barber	68 - Tied 1st
Round 2:	77.7	4	4	118	Gary Player	68 - Gary Player	136 (68) - 1st
Round 3:	77.0	4	5	61	Gary Player	69 - Lee Elder, C. Rodriguez	209 (73) - 1st
Round 4:	76.6	3	3	64	Gary Player	70 - Gay Brewer	281 (72) - 1st
Totals:	78.14	15	15	370			

TOURNAMENT SUMMARY

Place	Name	Score	Winnings
1	Gary Player	68-68-73-72—281	$45,000.00
2	Lee Elder	70-73-69-71—283	$28,500.00
T-3	Jim King	74-73-70-73—290	$15,250.00
T-3	Charles Owens	72-72-74-72—290	$15,250.00
T-5	Billy Casper	75-70-72-74—291	$10,500.00
T-5	Chi Chi Rodriguez	73-76-69-73—291	$10,500.00
T-7	Gay Brewer	76-75-71-70—292	$8,500.00
T-7	Billy Maxwell	74-70-75-73—292	$8,500.00
9	Orville Moody	74-72-73-75—294	$7,000.00
T-10	Bruce Crampton	72-73-75-75—295	$6,250.00
T-10	Doug Sanders	74-74-72-75—295	$6,250.00
12	Miller Barber	68-77-80-71—296	$5,500.00
13	George Lanning	74-72-79-72—297	$5,000.00
14	Tom Nieporte	77-74-73-74—298	$4,500.00
T-15	Al Chandler	73-77-76-73—299	$3,900.00
T-15	Don January	78-72-72-77—299	$3,900.00
17	Stan Thirsk	74-75-77-74—300	$3,600.00
T-18	Al Balding	78-75-74-74—301	$3,000.00
T-18	Bob Bruno	76-74-73-78—301	$3,000.00
T-18	Jim Ferree	75-75-74-77—301	$3,000.00
T-18	Mal McMullen	72-81-75-73—301	$3,000.00
T-18	Ken Still	75-74-75-77—301	$3,000.00
T-23	Billy Farrell	76-74-77-75—302	$2,200.00
T-23	Harold Henning	77-73-77-75—302	$2,200.00
T-23	Dick Howell	78-75-76-73—302	$2,200.00
T-26	Gardner Dickinson	76-75-79-73—303	$1,800.00
T-26	Dick Hendrickson	79-74-72-78—303	$1,800.00
T-26	Al Mengert	75-76-75-77—303	$1,800.00
T-29	Bill Collins	76-73-77-78—304	$1,462.00
T-29	Jack Fleck	75-76-80-73—304	$1,462.00
T-29	Joe Jimenez	75-71-81-77—304	$1,462.00
T-29	Al Kelley Jr.	79-76-74-75—304	$1,462.00
33	Pete Hessemer	80-77-74-74—305	$1,300.00
T-34	Dow Finsterwald	73-77-78-78—306	$1,150.00
T-34	Gene Littler	76-74-80-76—306	$1,150.00
T-34	Ray Montgomery	73-76-84-73—306	$1,150.00
T-34	Bob Ross	79-78-76-73—306	$1,150.00
T-34	Ralph Terry	77-77-73-79—306	$1,150.00
T-39	Mack Briggs	81-76-76-74—307	$950.00
T-39	Howie Johnson	79-78-72-78—307	$950.00
T-39	George Kallish Jr.	77-74-79-77—307	$950.00
T-42	Joe Campbell	78-75-79-76—308	$812.00
T-42	David Findlay	78-77-79-74—308	$812.00
T-42	Fred Hawkins	69-76-81-82—308	$812.00
T-42	Doug Higgins	81-76-77-74—308	$812.00
T-46	Fred Haas Jr.	78-75-78-78—309	$755.00

Place	Name	Score	Winnings
T-46	Charles Sifford	77-75-80-77—309	$755.00
T-48	George Bayer	79-76-75-80—310	$735.00
T-48	J. C. Goosie	80-74-75-81—310	$735.00
T-50	Pat Chartrand	79-74-75-83—311	$715.00
T-50	Buddy Overholser	78-73-79-81—311	$715.00
52	Pete Brown	75-74-83-80—312	$700.00
T-53	Jerry Barber	81-75-76-81—313	$655.00
T-53	Al Besselink	77-79-81-76—313	$655.00
T-53	Mike Fetchick	77-76-78-82—313	$655.00
T-53	Lionel Hebert	79-78-74-82—313	$655.00
T-53	Harold Kolb	78-77-77-81—313	$655.00
T-53	John Langford	77-78-81-77—313	$655.00
T-53	Ralph Montoya	79-75-83-76—313	$655.00
T-53	John Zontek	81-76-75-81—313	$655.00
T-61	Bill Ezinicki	76-78-86-75—315	$595.00
T-61	Sam Harvey	78-79-77-81—315	$595.00
T-61	Mike Souchak	80-75-82-78—315	$595.00
T-61	Ken Towns	77-75-85-78—315	$595.00
65	Bart Haltom	78-77-80-82—317	$575.00
T-66	Bob Crowley	78-74-84-82—318	$567.00
T-66	William Eggers	80-77-85-76—318	$567.00
T-68	Jimmy Bellizzi	80-76-84-81—321	$555.00
T-68	Don Johnson	78-77-81-85—321	$555.00
70	Walker Inman Jr.	78-78-81-87—324	$550.00
Cut	Ed Oldfield	80-78—158	
Cut	Art Silvestrone	78-80—158	
Cut	Ray Barnes	80-79—159	
Cut	Jon Gustin	86-73—159	
Cut	Ted Kroll	78-81—159	
Cut	Herman Scharlau	80-79—159	
Cut	Everett Vinzant	77-82—159	
Cut	Art Wall	76-83—159	
Cut	Mike Cerjanic	79-81—160	
Cut	Adolph Popp	80-80—160	
Cut	Bob Popp	82-78—160	
Cut	Harold Redd	81-79—160	
Cut	Tom Talkington	78-82—160	
Cut	Manuel de la Torre	81-80—161	
Cut	Roger Floyd	80-81—161	
Cut	Ernie George	82-79—161	
Cut	Bill Hartley	80-81—161	
Cut	George Thomas	80-81—161	
Cut	Jennings House	77-85—162	
Cut	Gordon Jones	84-78—162	
Cut	Joe Moresco	83-79—162	
Cut	Paul Thomas	85-77—162	

Place	Name	Score
Cut	Roy Beattie	79-84—163
Cut	Ray Bolo	82-81—163
Cut	Frank Freer	83-80—163
Cut	Bill Johnston	84-79—163
Cut	Joel Taylor	78-85—163
Cut	Don Whitt	82-81—163
Cut	Louis Carver	85-79—164
Cut	Bob Ellsworth	85-79—164
Cut	Ed Furgol	84-80—164
Cut	Jack Higgins	82-82—164
Cut	John Barnum	85-80—165
Cut	Brown Cullen Jr.	86-79—165
Cut	Bernie Haas	91-74—165
Cut	John Kalinka	84-81—165
Cut	Ken Weiler	85-80—165
Cut	Mike Krak	85-81—166
Cut	Chuck Workman	84-83—167
Cut	Joe Markham	86-82—168
Cut	Cal Mauldin	86-82—168
Cut	Charles Rotar	83-85—168
Cut	John Cleary	84-85—169
Cut	Pete Cooper	87-83—170
Cut	Ken Judd	89-81—170
Cut	John Mullaney	87-83—170
Cut	Alex Sandahl	91-80—171
Cut	Jim Yancey	90-81—171
Cut	Dick Masterson	87-85—172
Cut	Jack Webb	90-83—173
Cut	Frank Segaline	89-87—176
Cut	Doug Joyner	91-87—178
Cut	Ed Bello	92-87—179
Cut	Don White	93-86—179
DQ	Luca Barbato	80—80
DQ	Bill Bishop	81—81
DQ	Doug Ford	82—82
DQ	Ed Rubis	82—82
DQ	Mason Rudolph	86—86
DQ	Glenn Teal	86—86
DQ	Mike Borsuk	89—89
DQ	Nick Locke	101—101
WD	Buck Adams	81-75—156
WD	Don Hoenig	74-82—156

PGA SENIORS' CHAMPIONSHIP

1984
DECEMBER

Peter Thomson of Australia, a five-time British Open champion, made his first appearance in the PGA Seniors' Championship, and had his biggest payday, claiming the $40,000 winner's check. He opened with a 5-under-par 67 on the Champion Course at PGA National GC. Leading from start to finish, he beat Don January by three strokes with a 2-under-par 286. Thomson went on to a record year on the Senior PGA Tour in 1985, winning nine titles and earnings of $386,724.

Champion:	Peter Thomson
Site:	PGA National Golf Club, Palm Beach Gardens, Fla.
Date: Dec. 6-9	**Purse:** $225,000
Par: 36-36 — 72 (6,520 Yards)	
Entries: 148	Cut at 159 70 players advanced

	Course Avg.	Under Par	At Par	Over Par	Round Leader	Low Round	Peter Thomson
Round 1:	79.3	5	0	135	Peter Thomson	67 - Peter Thomson	67 - 1st
Round 2:	79.8	0	1	128	Peter Thomson	72 - Orville Moody	140 (73) - 1st
Round 3:	77.2	3	3	64	Peter Thomson	68 - Don January, Gordon Jones	214 (74) - 1st
Round 4:	75.9	5	6	59	Peter Thomson	70 - Gay Brewer, Miller Barber	286 (72) - 1st
Totals:	78.51	13	10	386			

TOURNAMENT SUMMARY

Place	Name	Score	Winnings	Place	Name	Score	Winnings	Place	Name	Score	Winnings
1	Peter Thomson	67-73-74-72—286	$40,000.00	T-22	John Kalinka	79-76-72-75—302	$2,100.00	T-49	Earl Fennell	77-82-80-73—312	$670.00
2	Don January	70-77-68-74—289	$25,000.00	T-26	Jerry Barber	78-75-78-72—303	$1,550.00	T-49	Mac Main	74-81-77-80—312	$670.00
T-3	Lee Elder	74-74-72-72—292	$12,293.00	T-26	Bill Erfurth	75-76-73-79—303	$1,550.00	T-49	Horace Moore	81-78-76-77—312	$670.00
T-3	Orville Moody	74-72-74-72—292	$12,293.00	T-28	Bill Johnston	76-77-75-77—305	$1,400.00	T-52	Bob Bruno	76-80-80-77—313	$635.00
T-3	Art Wall	70-76-73-73—292	$12,293.00	T-28	Dean Lind	75-78-75-77—305	$1,400.00	T-52	Auggie Navarro	79-78-80-76—313	$635.00
T-6	Miller Barber	74-74-75-70—293	$8,500.00	T-28	Art Silvestrone	80-76-76-73—305	$1,400.00	T-52	Ed Oldfield	77-80-80-76—313	$635.00
T-6	Gordon Jones	77-74-68-74—293	$8,500.00	T-31	Frank Arasin	75-77-81-73—306	$1,150.00	T-52	Adolph Popp	81-77-76-79—313	$635.00
8	Billy Casper	74-73-76-71—294	$7,000.00	T-31	Fred Hawkins	76-75-77-78—306	$1,150.00	T-56	Harold Kolb	81-78-75-80—314	$610.00
9	Bill Collins	76-76-71-72—295	$6,500.00	T-31	George Lanning	81-75-79-71—306	$1,150.00	T-56	Ray Montgomery	76-79-82-77—314	$610.00
10	Bob Toski	70-73-74-80—297	$6,000.00	T-31	Gene Littler	77-78-78-73—306	$1,150.00	T-56	Mil Radler	78-80-79-77—314	$610.00
T-11	Don Hoenig	73-76-74-75—298	$5,250.00	T-31	Pat Schwab	79-77-76-74—306	$1,150.00	59	Ange Alberico	76-79-82-78—315	$580.00
T-11	Arnold Palmer	73-77-74-74—298	$5,250.00	T-31	Roland Stafford	78-77-77-74—306	$1,150.00	60	Chuck Scally	78-80-82-76—316	$570.00
T-13	George Bayer	73-74-75-77—299	$3,975.00	T-31	Stan Thirsk	80-74-79-73—306	$1,150.00	61	Stan Dudas	75-83-77-82—317	$560.00
T-13	Bob Goalby	74-73-79-73—299	$3,975.00	T-38	Ken Campbell	77-77-77-76—307	$865.00	T-62	Manuel de la Torre	77-82-79-80—318	$545.00
T-13	Fred Haas Jr.	73-76-76-74—299	$3,975.00	T-38	Fran Deschaine	73-76-81-77—307	$865.00	T-62	Tom Talkington	79-79-79-81—318	$545.00
T-13	Jim King	74-76-74-75—299	$3,975.00	T-38	Gardner Dickinson	74-80-78-75—307	$865.00	T-64	Don Whitt	79-75-81-80—319	$525.00
T-17	Gay Brewer	77-77-77-70—301	$3,000.00	T-38	Dow Finsterwald	75-75-83-74—307	$865.00	T-64	Ray Bolo	80-76-83-80—319	$525.00
T-17	Bill Ezinicki	74-78-75-74—301	$3,000.00	T-38	Ken Towns	74-76-82-75—307	$865.00	T-64	Gaylon Simon	78-81-79-81—319	$525.00
T-17	Mike Fetchick	73-77-78-73—301	$3,000.00	43	Pete Hessemer	82-74-77-75—308	$780.00	67	Bart Haltom	79-80-80-83—322	$515.00
T-17	Ed Rubis	75-80-75-71—301	$3,000.00	T-44	Bob Erickson	78-81-76-74—309	$750.00	T-68	Pat Chartrand	78-80-83-83—324	$507.00
T-17	Charles Sifford	80-75-72-74—301	$3,000.00	T-44	Bob Ross	78-78-75-78—309	$750.00	T-68	Jack Harden	78-79-83-84—324	$507.00
T-22	Al Balding	71-80-75-76—302	$2,100.00	T-46	Joe Jimenez	75-79-82-74—310	$710.00	70	Ham Carothers	78-80-82-86—326	$500.00
T-22	Jim Ferree	78-75-77-72—302	$2,100.00	T-46	Billy Maxwell	80-74-79-77—310	$710.00				
T-22	Jack Fleck	74-78-75-75—302	$2,100.00	48	George Thomas	77-78-80-76—311	$690.00				

PGA SENIORS' CHAMPIONSHIP

1984
JANUARY

The troops in Arnie's Army have a million stories to tell and they can put his second victory in the PGA Seniors' Championship near the top of their lists. On one day, in nearly ideal playing conditions on the Champion Course at PGA National GC, he shot a course and tournament record 9-under-par 63. But when the weather turned horrendous overnight, with stiff winds and 40-degree temperatures, he was almost a stroke a hole higher with 79. Still, he never surrendered his lead. Palmer finished with 6-under-par 282, two strokes better than defending Champion Don January.

Champion:	Arnold Palmer	
Site:	PGA National Golf Club,	
	Palm Beach Gardens, Fla.	
Date: Jan. 19-22		Purse: $200,000
Par: 36-36 — 72 (6,520 Yards)		
Entries: 137	Cut at 155	75 players advanced

	Course Avg.	Under Par	At Par	Over Par	Round Leader	Low Round	Arnold Palmer
Round 1:	77.7	12	4	121	A. Palmer, Bob Toski, Jack Fleck, Doug Sanders	69 - Tied 1st	
Round 2:	77.3	11	8	113	Arnold Palmer	63 - Arnold Palmer	132 (63) - 1st
Round 3:	78.9	2	0	73	Arnold Palmer	69 - Billy Maxwell	211 (79) - 1st
Round 4:	79.1	3	0	72	Arnold Palmer	70 - Bill Collins	282 (71) - 1st
Totals:	78.06	28	12	379			

TOURNAMENT SUMMARY

Place	Name	Score	Winnings	Place	Name	Score	Winnings	Place	Name	Score	Winnings
1	Arnold Palmer	69-63-79-71—282	$35,000.00	T-25	Dan Sikes	70-75-78-79—302	$1,533.33	T-51	Bill Erfurth	74-76-87-76—313	$515.00
2	Don January	70-70-73-71—284	$22,000.00	T-25	Bob Stone	70-75-78-79—302	$1,533.33	T-51	Walker Inman Jr.	75-78-84-76—313	$515.00
3	Bill Collins	74-73-73-70—290	$13,980.00	T-28	Jim Cochran	76-75-76-76—303	$1,375.00	T-51	Mac Main	75-80-80-78—313	$515.00
T-4	Bob Goalby	72-70-76-74—292	$9,000.00	T-28	Roland Stafford	75-71-77-80—303	$1,375.00	T-51	Bob Watson	77-75-82-79—313	$515.00
T-4	Peter Thomson	73-72-73-74—292	$9,000.00	T-30	Ken Campbell	78-73-76-77—304	$1,275.00	T-55	Doug Ford	74-78-77-85—314	$480.00
T-6	Gardner Dickinson	70-77-73-73—293	$6,750.00	T-30	Everett Vinzant	74-73-77-80—304	$1,275.00	T-55	Gordon Leishman	82-73-81-78—314	$480.00
T-6	Jack Fleck	69-71-74-79—293	$6,750.00	T-32	Al Balding	74-71-83-77—305	$1,125.00	T-55	Bob Popp	75-78-80-81—314	$480.00
T-6	Paul Harney	74-68-76-75—293	$6,750.00	T-32	Mike Franko	70-79-80-76—305	$1,125.00	T-58	Joe Cheves	78-77-77-83—315	$457.50
T-6	Doug Sanders	69-73-74-77—293	$6,750.00	T-32	Charles Owens	74-75-76-80—305	$1,125.00	T-58	Chandler Harper	76-72-83-84—315	$457.50
10	Miller Barber	75-72-74-73—294	$5,500.00	T-32	George Thomas	72-75-79-79—305	$1,125.00	60	Jon Gustin	76-76-84-81—317	$450.00
T-11	Jerry Barber	73-70-75-77—295	$4,750.00	T-36	Julius Boros	79-73-78-76—306	$950.00	T-61	Jimmy Russell	74-80-84-80—318	$442.50
T-11	Jim Ferree	73-69-77-76—295	$4,750.00	T-36	Fred Haas Jr.	74-79-77-76—306	$950.00	T-61	Ken Towns	79-74-83-82—318	$442.50
T-13	Charles Sifford	70-72-77-77—296	$3,800.00	T-36	George Kallish Jr.	73-75-77-81—306	$950.00	T-63	Auggie Navarro	74-73-87-86—320	$432.50
T-13	Stan Thirsk	76-74-70-76—296	$3,800.00	39	Dow Finsterwald	75-75-80-77—307	$850.00	T-63	John Redman	75-77-85-83—320	$432.50
T-13	Art Wall	72-73-74-77—296	$3,800.00	T-40	Bill Johnston	75-75-80-79—309	$775.00	T-65	Hampton Auld	77-78-91-75—321	$420.00
T-16	Billy Casper	73-77-73-74—297	$3,300.00	T-40	Paul Kelly	77-72-78-82—309	$775.00	T-65	Ted Kroll	80-74-81-86—321	$420.00
T-16	Billy Maxwell	75-73-69-80—297	$3,300.00	T-42	Frank Freer	74-75-82-79—310	$675.00	T-65	Charles Rotar	75-78-86-82—321	$420.00
T-18	George Bayer	74-73-74-77—298	$2,900.00	T-42	Bill Hartley	77-75-77-81—310	$675.00	T-68	Billy Collins	79-76-86-81—322	$403.00
T-18	Al Mengert	71-72-76-79—298	$2,900.00	T-42	Bob Keller	76-73-83-78—310	$675.00	T-68	Stan Dudas	74-79-83-86—322	$403.00
T-20	Mike Fetchick	70-71-76-82—299	$2,400.00	T-45	Joe Conrad	73-79-80-79—311	$591.25	T-68	Fred Hawkins	75-80-81-86—322	$403.00
T-20	George Lanning	75-72-73-79—299	$2,400.00	T-45	Jennings House	76-78-78-79—311	$591.25	T-68	Mike Krak	79-76-84-83—322	$403.00
T-20	Bob Toski	69-77-76-77—299	$2,400.00	T-45	Howie Johnson	77-75-81-78—311	$591.25	T-68	John Langford	75-77-85-85—322	$403.00
T-23	Gay Brewer	74-69-80-78—301	$1,900.00	T-45	Joe Moresco	79-74-77-81—311	$591.25	73	Herman Scharlau	75-79-85-84—323	$400.00
T-23	Mal McMullen	72-75-73-81—301	$1,900.00	T-49	Lionel Hebert	76-76-79-81—312	$545.00	74	Ed Causey	75-79-88-91—333	$400.00
T-25	Rod Funseth	76-75-75-76—302	$1,533.34	T-49	Pat Rea	77-77-81-77—312	$545.00	75	Michael Austin	79-76-88-92—335	$400.00

228

1982 Played for the first time on the difficult Champion Course at the new PGA National GC in Palm Beach Gardens, only one player could match par for the distance, Don January at 288. That's 18 strokes higher than his winning total three years earlier at Turnberry Isle. Julius Boros, another former PGA Seniors' titleist, was runner-up with 289.

Champion:	Don January
Site:	PGA National Golf Club,
	Palm Beach Gardens, Fla.
Date: Dec. 2-5	Purse: $150,000
Par: 36-36 — 72 (6,520 Yards)	
Entries: 150 Cut at 156 65 players advanced	

	Course Average	Round Leader	Low Round	Don January
Round 1:	75.1	Bob Goalby	68 - Bob Goalby	74 - Tied 21st
Round 2:	75.7	Arnold Palmer, Howie Johnson	70 - Bob Toski, Arnold Palmer	149 (75) - Tied 20th
Round 3:	76.6	Julius Boros, Arnold Palmer	69 - Don January	218 (69) - Tied 5th
Round 4:	76.4	Don January	69 - Gay Brewer, Dan Sikes	288 (70) - 1st
Totals:	75.92			

TOURNAMENT SUMMARY

Place	Name	Score	Winnings	Place	Name	Score	Winnings	Place	Name	Score	Winnings
1	Don January	74-75-69-70—288	$25,000.00	T-22	Richard Lotz	73-73-75-80—301	$1,125.00	T-46	Ted Kroll	79-76-79-75—309	$470.00
2	Julius Boros	71-73-70-75—289	$18,000.00	T-22	Joe Moresco	75-74-74-78—301	$1,125.00	T-46	Bert Weaver	78-78-78-75—309	$470.00
T-3	Gay Brewer	71-76-74-69—290	$11,250.00	T-26	Paul Harney	74-78-74-76—302	$950.00	T-49	Kyle Burton	78-77-78-77—310	$430.00
T-3	Bob Goalby	68-75-74-73—290	$11,250.00	T-26	Joe Jimenez	77-74-74-77—302	$950.00	T-49	Tony Clecak	79-77-75-79—310	$430.00
T-3	Arnold Palmer	71-70-73-76—290	$11,250.00	T-26	Ken Mast	71-77-75-79—302	$950.00	T-49	Gordon Jones	72-75-79-84—310	$430.00
T-3	Art Wall	72-73-71-74—290	$11,250.00	T-29	Tom Nieporte	80-73-74-76—303	$808.00	T-49	Mac Main	76-79-78-77—310	$430.00
T-7	Miller Barber	79-72-70-72—293	$5,000.00	T-29	Charles Owens	77-75-77-74—303	$808.00	T-49	Ray Montgomery	77-78-74-81—310	$430.00
T-7	Bob Stone	70-74-74-75—293	$5,000.00	T-29	Joe Taylor	72-74-84-73—303	$808.00	T-54	Mike Krak	76-77-81-77—311	$395.00
T-9	Bill Collins	75-74-74-72—295	$3,250.00	T-32	John Cook	75-76-76-77—304	$700.00	T-54	Everett Vinzant	78-76-78-79—311	$395.00
T-9	Bob Erickson	73-75-76-71—295	$3,250.00	T-32	Fred Hawkins	76-77-81-70—304	$700.00	T-56	Bill Deangelis	77-78-78-79—312	$375.00
T-11	Jim Ferree	75-72-76-73—296	$2,250.00	T-32	Dean Lind	76-74-76-78—304	$700.00	T-56	Jack Webb	79-76-84-73—312	$375.00
T-11	Howie Johnson	70-71-78-77—296	$2,250.00	T-32	Mal McMullen	74-76-75-79—304	$700.00	T-58	Stan Dudas	80-76-78-79—313	$380.00
T-13	Billy Casper	73-71-78-75—297	$1,750.00	T-32	Stan Thirsk	81-73-76-74—304	$700.00	T-58	Charles Sifford	77-79-77-80—313	$355.00
T-13	Gardner Dickinson	77-71-78-71—297	$1,750.00	37	Dick Sarta	76-75-80-74—305	$625.00	60	Tex Simon	74-76-84-80—314	$340.00
T-13	Auggie Navarro	73-73-76-75—297	$1,750.00	T-38	Bill Davis	72-80-77-77—306	$580.00	61	Dow Finsterwald	75-80-81-79—315	$285.00
T-13	Bob Toski	73-70-75-79—297	$1,750.00	T-38	Mike Fetchick	74-78-75-79—306	$580.00	T-62	Doug Ford	76-77-82-81—316	$285.00
T-17	Jerry Barber	74-74-72-78—298	$1,450.00	T-38	Roland Stafford	75-76-76-79—306	$580.00	T-62	Bill Maloney	75-80-79-82—316	$285.00
T-17	Roberto De Vicenzo	72-80-70-76—298	$1,450.00	T-41	John Kalinka	74-79-78-76—307	$530.00	T-62	Paul Runyan	71-85-79-81—316	$285.00
T-19	Pat Rea	72-77-75-75—299	$1,325.00	T-41	Ed Rubis	77-78-75-77—307	$530.00	65	Harold Reed	78-78-81-84—321	$285.00
T-19	Dan Sikes	76-78-76-69—299	$1,325.00	T-43	Buck Adams	76-73-78-81—308	$500.00				
21	Stan Mosel	77-72-80-71—300	$1,250.00	T-43	George Thomas	77-78-76-77—308	$500.00				
T-22	Bob Duden	73-75-76-77—301	$1,125.00	T-43	Ken Towns	75-81-75-77—308	$500.00				
T-22	Bob Hamilton	74-77-78-72—301	$1,125.00	T-46	Andy Borkovich	76-78-76-79—309	$470.00				

1981

Miller Barber called his victory in the PGA Seniors' Championship "the highlight of my career," after he won the title in his first start. Despite a final round of 1-over-par 73 on the South Course at Turnberry Isle CC, Barber edged defending Champion Arnold Palmer by two strokes, with a 7-under-par 281 total. Said Barber: "This is the major championship I've been trying to win all my life... it's a tremendous win for me."

Champion:	Miller Barber
Site:	Turnberry Isle Country Club, North Miami, Fla.
Date: Dec. 3-6	**Purse:** $125,000
Par: 36-36 — 72 (6,800 Yards)	
Entries: 138	Cut at 152 72 players advanced

	Course Average	Round Leader	Low Round	Miller Barber
Round 1:	72.8	68 -Miller, Barber, Wall, Balding, Navarro, Collins		68 - Tied 1st
Round 2:	74.1	Tom Neiporte	68 - Tom Neiporte	140 (72) - Tied 2nd
Round 3:	75.8	Miller Barber	68 - Miller Barber	208 (68) - 1st
Round 4:	76.1	Miller Barber	69 - Jerry Barber	281 (73) - 1st
Totals:	74.71			

TOURNAMENT SUMMARY

Place	Name	Score	Winnings	Place	Name	Score	Winnings	Place	Name	Score	Winnings
1	Miller Barber	68-72-68-73—281	$20,000.00	T-24	Gordon Jones	74-69-78-75—296	$1,000.00	T-51	Mike Fetchick	73-76-75-80—304	$380.00
2	Arnold Palmer	70-72-71-70—283	$15,000.00	T-27	Buck Adams	73-73-74-77—297	$805.00	T-51	John Kalinka	76-75-76-77—304	$380.00
T-3	Don January	69-72-70-73—284	$11,250.00	T-27	Julius Boros	73-71-80-73—297	$805.00	T-51	Ken Towns	75-76-78-75—304	$380.00
T-3	Art Wall	68-75-71-70—284	$11,250.00	T-27	J. C. Goosie	72-75-79-71—297	$805.00	T-54	Mal McMullen	74-74-79-78—305	$355.00
T-5	Bob Erickson	70-71-73-72—286	$7,000.00	T-27	Fred Hawkins	72-73-79-73—297	$805.00	T-54	Ray Montgomery	76-74-76-79—305	$355.00
T-5	Joe Jimenez	73-71-71-71—286	$7,000.00	T-27	Paul Kelly	74-72-76-75—297	$805.00	T-56	Paul Allen	71-81-73-81—306	$325.00
T-7	Jerry Barber	72-73-73-69—287	$3,500.00	T-32	John Cook	71-74-74-79—298	$687.50	T-56	Brown Cullen Jr.	71-76-80-79—306	$325.00
T-7	Roberto De Vicenzo	71-72-72-72—287	$3,500.00	T-32	Earl Fennell	71-75-77-75—298	$687.50	T-56	Clarence Doser	75-77-77-77—306	$325.00
9	Jim Ferree	71-72-71-74—288	$2,600.00	T-34	Pete Cooper	75-75-77-72—299	$600.00	T-56	George Kallish Jr.	71-74-78-83—306	$325.00
T-10	Joe Moresco	71-71-73-74—289	$2,150.00	T-34	Doug Ford	72-74-74-79—299	$600.00	60	Ted Kroll	73-78-80-76—307	$222.73
T-10	Bob Stone	70-74-71-74—289	$2,150.00	T-34	Mac Main	76-74-74-75—299	$600.00	T-61	Stan Dudas	75-74-80-80—309	$222.73
12	Gardner Dickinson	69-71-74-76—290	$1,800.00	T-34	Al Mengert	71-74-74-80—299	$600.00	T-61	Al Fuchs	78-74-80-77—309	$222.73
T-13	Bill Collins	68-73-75-76—292	$1,608.00	T-34	George Thomas	76-71-79-73—299	$600.00	T-61	Bob Grant	71-81-78-79—309	$222.73
T-13	Bob Goalby	70-73-74-75—292	$1,608.00	39	Ed Causey	78-73-77-72—300	$525.00	T-61	Fred Haas Jr.	74-78-85-72—309	$222.73
T-13	Paul Harney	69-77-74-72—292	$1,608.00	T-40	Hampton Auld	73-74-72-82—301	$485.00	T-61	Dick Sarta	76-73-81-79—309	$222.73
T-16	Al Balding	68-77-73-75—293	$1,400.00	T-40	Lionel Hebert	77-73-72-79—301	$485.00	T-61	Tom Strafaci	74-75-83-77—309	$222.73
T-16	Tom Nieporte	71-68-75-79—293	$1,400.00	T-40	Bob Keller	74-74-78-75—301	$485.00	T-61	Bud Timbrook	76-75-77-81—309	$222.73
T-16	Bob Toski	72-77-72-72—293	$1,400.00	T-40	Ed Rubis	70-75-77-79—301	$485.00	T-68	John Ruedi	78-71-82-80—311	$222.73
T-19	John Langford	74-76-69-75—294	$1,250.00	T-44	Joe Cheves	73-75-75-79—302	$445.00	T-68	Jim Shaw	75-75-76-85—311	$222.72
T-19	Auggie Navarro	68-72-79-75—294	$1,250.00	T-44	Emory Lee	73-74-76-79—302	$445.00	70	Bill Erfurth	76-75-87-78—316	$222.72
T-19	Charles Sifford	75-73-74-72—294	$1,250.00	T-44	Art Silvestrone	71-79-73-79—302	$445.00	71	Ed Kroll	74-77-82-84—317	$222.72
T-22	George Bayer	73-74-74-74—295	$1,125.00	T-44	Jack Webb	79-73-78-72—302	$445.00				
T-22	Dan Sikes	77-70-71-77—295	$1,125.00	T-48	Bill Kozak	73-75-79-76—303	$410.00				
T-24	Dow Finsterwald	73-72-72-79—296	$1,000.00	T-48	Ken Mast	71-77-77-78—303	$410.00				
T-24	Bill Johnston	70-77-76-73—296	$1,000.00	T-48	Tex Simon	75-73-77-78—303	$410.00				

1980

Arnold Palmer made his debut in the PGA Seniors' Championship at the age of 51, and won with a birdie on the first hole of a playoff. Observers predicted he'd do the same for the new Senior PGA Tour as he did for all of golf in the late 1950s and '60s. His victory at Turnberry Isle CC proved to be

Champion:	Arnold Palmer
Site:	Turnberry Isle Country Club, North Miami, Fla.
Date: Dec. 4-7	Purse: $125,000
Par: 36-36 — 72 (6,800 Yards)	
Entries: 127	Cut at 153 70 players advanced

nearly as exciting as any he had in the past. Palmer birdied the first extra hole from seven feet to edge first-round leader Paul Harney after they tied at 1-over-par 289. "It's the PGA Championship I never won," said Palmer.

	Course Avg.	Under Par	At Par	Over Par	Round Leader	Low Round	Arnold Palmer
Round 1:	76.8	8	7	112	Paul Harney	69- Paul Harney	72 - Tied 9th
Round 2:	76.8	4	9	114	Arnold Palmer	69 - Arnold Palmer	141 (69) - 1st
Round 3:	75.3	7	5	56	Arnold Palmer	68 - Art Wall	214 (73) - 1st
Round 4:	75.6	7	6	55	A. Palmer, P. Harney	69 - Bob Goalby	289 (75) - Tied 1st
Totals:	76.36	26	27	337			

TOURNAMENT SUMMARY

Place	Name	Score	Winnings	Place	Name	Score	Winnings	Place	Name	Score	Winnings
1	Arnold Palmer	72-69-73-75—289	$20,000.00	T-24	Dean Lind	74-72-75-75—296	$1,025.00	T-46	Al Mengert	72-78-82-72—304	$420.00
2	Paul Harney	69-74-75-71—289	$15,000.00	T-26	Gardner Dickinson	72-76-74-75—297	$900.00	T-46	Ray Montgomery	76-77-74-77—304	$420.00
3	Don January	73-74-73-70—290	$12,500.00	T-26	Mike Fetchick	71-76-73-77—297	$900.00	T-51	Bill Bisdorf	78-74-75-78—305	$365.00
T-4	Julius Boros	75-71-74-71—291	$5,128.57	T-26	Bob Toski	76-74-72-75—297	$900.00	T-51	George Kallish Jr.	76-73-79-77—305	$365.00
T-4	Bob Erickson	72-73-75-71—291	$5,128.57	29	Murry Jacobs	74-77-72-75—298	$800.00	T-51	Bill Kozak	73-78-77-77—305	$365.00
T-4	Bob Goalby	74-72-76-69—291	$5,128.57	T-30	George Bayer	75-77-74-73—299	$725.00	T-51	Ed Kroll	73-76-75-81—305	$365.00
T-4	Walker Inman Jr.	70-75-71-75—291	$5,128.58	T-30	Henry Ransom	74-77-75-73—299	$725.00	T-51	Herman Scharlau	78-73-78-76—305	$365.00
T-4	Charles Sifford	71-75-71-74—291	$5,128.57	T-30	Mike Souchak	75-74-73-77—299	$725.00	T-51	Everett Vinzant	76-76-81-72—305	$365.00
T-4	Art Wall	74-73-68-76—291	$5,128.57	T-33	Bob Duden	73-74-72-81—300	$650.00	T-57	Ed Furgol	79-74-75-78—306	$325.00
T-4	Fred Wampler	70-73-76-72—291	$5,128.57	T-33	J. C. Goosie	72-79-71-78—300	$650.00	T-57	Bob Kay	75-77-78-76—306	$325.00
T-11	Dow Finsterwald	72-76-72-73—293	$1,833.34	T-33	Jimmy Russell	78-75-70-77—300	$650.00	T-59	Hampton Auld	75-78-77-78—308	$305.60
T-11	Doug Ford	76-70-75-72—293	$1,833.33	T-36	John Kalinka	74-75-75-77—301	$562.50	T-59	Joe Cheves	74-78-76-80—308	$305.60
T-11	Joe Jimenez	73-75-74-71—293	$1,833.33	T-36	Jack Martin	75-72-76-78—301	$562.50	T-59	Al Fuchs	74-73-78-83—308	$305.60
T-14	Bill Collins	73-74-71-76—294	$1,410.72	T-36	Eric Monti	74-75-77-75—301	$562.50	T-59	Joe Lopez Sr.	76-75-73-84—308	$305.60
T-14	Fred Haas Jr.	74-74-75-71—294	$1,410.71	T-36	Stan Thirsk	74-76-76-75—301	$562.50	63	Jackson Bradley	73-78-84-74—309	$245.00
T-14	Howie Johnson	73-76-73-72—294	$1,410.71	T-40	Billy Capps	77-72-78-75—302	$490.00	T-64	Travis Hudson	77-75-76-82—310	$245.00
T-14	Ted Kroll	73-73-76-72—294	$1,410.71	T-40	Fred Hawkins	76-72-79-75—302	$490.00	T-64	Hans Merrell	76-75-79-80—310	$245.00
T-14	Mac Main	73-75-72-74—294	$1,410.72	T-40	Vernon Thwaites	73-78-78-73—302	$490.00	T-66	Bob Keller	75-78-78-81—312	$245.00
T-14	Tom Nieporte	73-74-73-74—294	$1,410.71	T-43	Babe Lichardus	70-79-76-78—303	$460.00	T-66	John Zontek	75-76-83-78—312	$245.00
T-14	George Thomas	70-72-76-76—294	$1,410.72	T-43	Milon Marusic	76-75-78-74—303	$460.00	68	Gus Bernardoni	76-75-80-82—313	$245.00
T-21	John Langford	75-72-75-73—295	$1,150.00	T-43	Sam Penecale	72-76-80-75—303	$460.00				
T-21	Emory Lee	71-75-74-75—295	$1,150.00	T-46	Joe Conrad	75-75-74-80—304	$420.00				
T-21	Dan Sikes	78-73-70-74—295	$1,150.00	T-46	Marty Furgol	73-75-76-80—304	$420.00				
T-24	Jerry Barber	74-72-77-73—296	$1,025.00	T-46	Lionel Hebert	75-76-76-77—304	$420.00				

1979
DECEMBER

The PGA Seniors' Championship jump-started the Senior PGA Tour with a $100,000 tournament just before Christmas at Turnberry Isle CC in North Miami. This doubled the purse of the previous five years and signaled the start of what became one of the biggest success stories in the 1980s, the Senior PGA Tour. Don January, just 26 days past his 50th birthday, and with earnings of $80,000 on the "regular" Tour during the year, led all the way, with an 18-under-par 270 total on the South Course. This became the second-lowest total in PGA Seniors' history. He finished eight shots ahead of runner-up George Bayer of Detroit, Mich.

Champion:	Don January
Site:	Turnberry Isle Country Club, North Miami, Fla.
Date: Dec. 12-16	Purse: $100,000
Par: 36-36 — 72 (6,800 Yards)	
Entries: 140 Cut at 154 73 players advanced	

	Course Avg.	Under Par	At Par	Over Par	Round Leader	Low Round	Don January
Round 1:	77.3	11	8	118	Don January	68 - Don January	68 - 1st
Round 2:	76.4	15	4	110	Don January	67 - Bill Johnston, Chick Harbert	136 (68) - 1st
Round 3:	75.4	8	4	61	Don January	67 - Don January	203 (67) - 1st
Round 4:	76.4	4	3	66	Don January	67 - Don January	270 (67) - 1st
Totals:	76.50	38	19	355			

TOURNAMENT SUMMARY

Place	Name	Score	Winnings	Place	Name	Score	Winnings	Place	Name	Score	Winnings
1	Don January	68-68-67-67—270	$15,000.00	T-26	Jerry Barber	72-76-74-76—298	$712.50	T-51	Dub Apgan	74-78-76-78—306	$275.00
2	George Bayer	71-67-68-72—278	$12,000.00	T-26	Bob Goalby	73-72-72-81—298	$712.50	T-51	Al Balding	81-73-73-79—306	$275.00
T-3	Bill Johnston	72-67-69-74—282	$9,000.00	T-28	Mike Franko	76-75-74-74—299	$637.50	T-51	Bob Crowley	75-73-78-80—306	$275.00
T-3	Dan Sikes	70-69-70-73—282	$9,000.00	T-28	Lionel Hebert	75-75-72-77—299	$637.50	T-51	Ed Furgol	75-77-75-79—306	$275.00
T-5	Julius Boros	71-73-68-74—286	$6,000.00	T-28	Howie Johnson	76-73-75-75—299	$637.50	T-51	Gordon Jones	74-72-76-84—306	$275.00
T-6	Gardner Dickinson	71-68-73-75—287	$3,200.00	T-28	Babe Lichardus	75-76-75-73—299	$637.50	T-51	Bill Morgan	76-76-80-74—306	$275.00
T-6	Dow Finsterwald	70-73-71-73—287	$3,200.00	T-32	Bob Erickson	73-72-76-79—300	$570.00	57	Jackson Bradley	78-76-75-78—307	$240.00
T-6	Art Wall	73-69-76-69—287	$3,200.00	T-32	Mike Fetchick	74-76-73-77—300	$570.00	58	Jack Ortman	78-76-78-76—308	$230.00
9	Al Besselink	70-73-74-71—288	$2,300.00	T-34	Pete Cooper	76-76-75-74—301	$530.00	T-59	Lou Carter	76-78-74-81—309	$203.00
T-10	Jack Fleck	72-69-72-77—290	$1,950.00	T-34	Stan Thirsk	71-76-77-77—301	$530.00	T-59	Brien Charter	77-76-79-77—309	$203.00
T-10	Charles Sifford	71-73-74-72—290	$1,950.00	36	Bob Duden	75-73-74-80—302	$500.00	T-59	Richard Lotz	80-73-81-75—309	$203.00
T-12	Roberto De Vicenzo	82-68-70-73—293	$1,750.00	T-37	Clare Emery	74-77-74-78—303	$460.00	T-59	Dick Mullen	77-76-75-81—309	$203.00
T-12	Tom Nieporte	76-72-74-71—293	$1,750.00	T-37	John Langford	72-76-79-76—303	$460.00	T-59	Chuck Scally	81-73-78-77—309	$203.00
T-14	Bob Grant	75-71-73-75—294	$1,500.00	T-37	Ken Mast	75-77-77-74—303	$460.00	T-64	Don Collett	75-78-75-82—310	$177.50
T-14	Fred Hawkins	74-74-74-72—294	$1,500.00	T-40	Jay Hebert	75-76-76-77—304	$392.00	T-64	Tex Consalver	79-75-79-77—310	$177.50
T-14	Sam Snead	75-74-71-74—294	$1,500.00	T-40	Travis Hudson	77-74-75-78—304	$392.00	T-64	Doug Ford	76-78-77-79—310	$177.50
T-17	Bill Collins	75-69-76-75—295	$1,110.00	T-40	Joe Jimenez	71-78-78-77—304	$392.00	T-64	Chandler Harper	78-73-80-79—310	$177.50
T-17	Chick Harbert	74-67-76-78—295	$1,110.00	T-40	Al Nelson	76-73-76-79—304	$392.00	T-68	Willie Barber	77-75-76-83—311	$160.00
T-17	Walker Inman Jr.	73-71-78-73—295	$1,110.00	T-40	George Thomas	73-79-78-74—304	$392.00	T-68	Auggie Navarro	75-75-78-83—311	$160.00
T-17	Billy Maxwell	73-73-75-74—295	$1,110.00	T-45	George Copoun	74-77-79-75—305	$335.00	T-68	John Ruedi	78-75-78-80—311	$160.00
T-17	Ken Towns	73-71-77-74—295	$1,110.00	T-45	Bill Erfurth	76-74-77-78—305	$335.00	T-71	Paul McMullen	77-76-80-79—312	$150.00
T-22	J. C. Goosie	72-77-72-75—296	$850.00	T-45	Milon Marusic	78-76-76-75—305	$335.00	T-71	Don Street	78-76-81-77—312	$150.00
T-22	Emory Lee	71-74-77-74—296	$850.00	T-45	Henry Ransom	72-74-76-83—305	$335.00	73	Ed Causey	75-76-81-81—313	$150.00
T-22	Everett Vinzant	72-73-75-76—296	$850.00	T-45	Carroll Sharp	77-71-82-75—305	$335.00				
25	John Kalinka	78-69-75-75—297	$750.00	T-45	Charles Smith	72-81-74-78—305	$335.00				

1979
FEBRUARY

Jack Fleck won the 1955 U.S. Open and two tour titles in the early 1960s, all in playoffs. Therefore, it was fitting that his only victory in the PGA Seniors' Championship also would be in a playoff. The second straight three-man playoff ended on the third hole of the Magnolia Course at Walt Disney World, when Fleck sank a 25-foot putt for birdie to beat Bill Johnston of Phoenix, Ariz., and Bob Erickson of Casselberry, Fla. All three tied at 1-over-par 289, with three former Champions—Julius Boros, Roberto De Vicenzo and Joe Jimenez—tied for fourth, one stroke behind at 290.

Champion:	Jack Fleck
Site:	Walt Disney World Resort, Orlando, Fla.
Date:	Feb. 1-4
Par: 36-36—72	Purse: $50,000

TOURNAMENT SUMMARY

Place	Name	Score	Winnings	Place	Name	Score	Winnings	Place	Name	Score	Winnings
T-1	Jack Fleck	73-71-75-70—289	$8,000.00	T-18	Emory Lee	74-79-74-71—298	$500.00	T-34	Mike Fetchick	75-79-75-73—302	$185.00
T-2	Bob Erickson	72-72-75-70—289	$4,250.00	T-18	Mal McMullen	75-73-77-73—298	$500.00	T-34	Chandler Harper	74-77-76-75—302	$185.00
T-2	Bill Johnston	73-75-70-71—289	$4,250.00	T-18	Jim Riggins	75-78-75-70—298	$500.00	T-34	Ed Rubis	76-77-71-78—302	$185.00
T-4	Julius Boros	74-72-75-69—290	$1,583.34	T-21	Bob Below	75-77-75-72—299	$425.00	T-38	Bob Hendricks	77-77-75-74—303	$153.33
T-4	Roberto De Vicenzo	72-71-74-73—290	$1,583.33	T-21	Murry Jacobs	72-72-78-77—299	$425.00	T-38	Hans Merrell	76-77-74-76—303	$153.33
T-4	Joe Jimenez	72-73-73-72—290	$1,583.33	T-21	George Thomas	74-76-75-74—299	$425.00	T-38	Charles Smith	75-79-76-73—303	$153.33
7	Stan Thirsk	70-74-74-74—292	$1,150.00	T-24	Billy Capps	77-75-71-77—300	$325.00	T-41	Al Besselink	75-78-78-73—304	$100.00
T-8	Pete Cooper	73-75-72-73—293	$1,000.00	T-24	Bob Duden	70-77-77-76—300	$325.00	T-41	Clare Emery	74-77-80-73—304	$100.00
T-8	Babe Lichardus	70-72-74-77—293	$1,000.00	T-24	John Kalinka	74-76-79-71—300	$325.00	T-41	Bob Toski	79-73-78-74—304	$100.00
10	Ken Mast	75-74-72-73—294	$850.00	T-24	Tom Nieporte	77-77-75-71—300	$325.00	T-44	Gene Fawbush	78-75-78-74—305	$100.00
T-11	Charles Sifford	74-74-73-74—295	$725.00	T-24	Roy Wallin	75-76-74-75—300	$325.00	T-44	Milon Marusic	77-78-72-78—305	$100.00
T-11	Sam Snead	75-72-75-73—295	$725.00	T-29	Luca Barbato	73-76-77-75—301	$230.00	T-44	Henry Ransom	74-79-79-73—305	$100.00
T-13	George Bayer	69-79-75-73—296	$641.66	T-29	Bill Kozak	77-78-72-74—301	$230.00	T-47	Bob Bodington	79-74-78-75—306	$100.00
T-13	Joe Cheves	76-75-73-72—296	$641.67	T-29	Bill Morgan	75-74-73-79—301	$230.00	T-47	Manuel de la Torre	79-77-69-81—306	$100.00
T-13	Doug Ford	73-75-74-74—296	$641.66	T-29	Paul O'Leary	76-75-75-75—301	$230.00	T-47	Billy Gilbert	74-77-78-77—306	$100.00
T-16	Bill Ezinicki	74-74-74-75—297	$562.50	T-29	Fred Wampler	74-75-77-75—301	$230.00	T-47	Gaylon Simon	76-76-77-77—306	$100.00
T-16	Fred Haas Jr.	74-77-71-75—297	$562.50	T-34	Bill Collins	81-76-73-72—302	$185.00				

1978

The first three-man playoff in PGA Seniors' Championship history ended quickly. Joe Jimenez of Jefferson City, Mo., sank a four-foot birdie putt on the first extra hole at the Walt Disney World Magnolia course, after hitting a 4-iron to the green.

"I came here just trying to finish in the top 10," said Jimenez. "I didn't think about coming here to win." Jimenez posted consistent rounds of 72-71-73-70 and was tied in regulation at 2-under-par 286 with Manuel de la Torre of Milwaukee, Wis., and Joe Cheves of Morganton, N.C.

Champion:	Joe Jimenez
Site:	Walt Disney World Resort, Orlando, Fla.
Date:	Feb. 2-5
Par: 36-36—72	Purse: $50,000

TOURNAMENT SUMMARY

Place	Name	Score	Winnings	Place	Name	Score	Winnings	Place	Name	Score	Winnings
1	Joe Jimenez	72-71-73-70—286	$8,000.00	T-18	Fred Haas Jr.	69-75-74-77—295	$500.00	T-36	Ed Furgol	77-80-73-74—304	$170.00
T-2	Joe Cheves	73-72-71-70—286	$4,250.00	T-18	Milon Marusic	73-70-78-74—295	$500.00	T-36	Bob Hendricks	79-73-74-78—304	$170.00
T-2	Manuel de la Torre	68-71-79-68—286	$4,250.00	21	Ed Rubis	72-76-76-72—296	$450.00	T-39	Bill Kozak	76-76-76-77—305	$150.00
T-4	Jack Fleck	70-70-73-74—287	$1,750.00	T-22	Chandler Harper	71-72-77-77—297	$412.50	T-39	Eli Marovich	78-75-78-74—305	$150.00
T-4	Ray Montgomery	70-69-78-70—287	$1,750.00	T-22	Hans Merrell	72-76-75-74—297	$412.50	T-41	Marty Furgol	77-75-79-75—306	$100.00
6	Sam Snead	72-75-70-71—288	$1,250.00	T-24	Willie Barber	77-76-72-73—298	$337.50	T-41	Bill Morgan	73-76-79-78—306	$100.00
T-7	Roberto De Vicenzo	74-72-71-72—289	$1,100.00	T-24	William Gilbert	75-73-73-77—298	$337.50	T-41	Don Street	76-75-76-79—306	$100.00
T-7	Art Wall	73-71-72-73—289	$1,100.00	T-24	George Thomas	76-72-75-75—298	$337.50	T-44	Harold Reed	75-78-78-76—307	$100.00
9	Murry Jacobs	75-73-71-73—292	$950.00	T-24	Bud Timbrook	74-75-72-77—298	$337.50	T-44	Tal Smith	75-73-79-80—307	$100.00
T-10	Julius Boros	74-71-75-73—293	$704.17	T-28	Fred Atkins	76-72-79-72—299	$262.50	T-44	Tom Talkington	71-73-84-79—307	$100.00
T-10	Clare Emery	72-74-72-75—293	$704.16	T-28	Herman Scharlau	71-74-76-78—299	$262.50	T-47	Bob Grant	75-77-77-79—308	$100.00
T-10	Babe Lichardus	70-77-73-73—293	$704.16	30	Gaylon Simon	74-75-77-74—300	$240.00	T-47	Roy Wallin	76-79-76-77—308	$100.00
T-10	Mal McMullen	72-75-73-73—293	$704.17	T-31	Bob Below	72-76-78-75—301	$220.00	T-49	Ballard Beasley	76-81-76-76—309	$40.00
T-10	Charles Sifford	71-77-76-75—293	$704.16	T-31	Ted Kroll	76-75-73-77—301	$220.00	T-49	Kyle Burton	73-76-86-74—309	$40.00
T-10	Fred Wampler	71-76-72-74—293	$704.16	T-31	John Langford	73-75-77-76—301	$220.00	T-49	George Capoun	76-75-76-82—309	$40.00
T-16	George Bayer	72-72-76-74—294	$562.50	T-34	Joe Taylor	70-80-78-75—303	$195.00	T-49	Ronald Laparl	80-75-72-82—309	$40.00
T-16	Billy Capps	73-75-73-73—294	$562.50	T-34	Everett Vinzant	70-74-79-80—303	$195.00	T-49	Warren Smith	78-74-77-80—309	$40.00
T-18	Bob Erickson	73-75-74-73—295	$500.00	T-36	John Doctor	77-74-79-74—304	$170.00				

1977

Icy rain, numbing cold, rising winds and fog conditions greeted the 180 starters in the 38th PGA Seniors' Championship. Julius Boros of Fort Lauderdale survived with a 5-under-par 283 total for his second PGA Seniors' victory, two strokes lower than he had in 1971 at Palm Beach Gardens. Former Champion Fred Haas Jr. three-putted the 71st hole and finished at 284.

Champion:	Julius Boros	
Site:	Walt Disney World Resort, Orlando, Fla.	
Date:	Jan. 27-30	
Par: 36-36—72		Purse: $50,000

TOURNAMENT SUMMARY*

Place	Name	Score	Winnings	Place	Name	Score	Winnings	Place	Name	Score	Winnings
1	Julius Boros	71-69-71-72—283	$7,500.00	T-20	Billy Capps	79-74-72-74—299	$450.00	T-39	Alfonso Atkins	78-75-79-73—305	$125.00
2	Fred Haas Jr.	70-71-70-73—284	$5,000.00	T-20	Joe Jimenez	76-73-76-74—299	$450.00	T-39	Joe Cheves	77-78-77-73—305	$125.00
T-3	Clare Emery	76-75-71-67—289	$3,000.00	T-20	Herman Scharlau	76-71-73-79—299	$450.00	T-39	Ed Furgol	75-79-76-75—305	$125.00
T-3	Tex Simon	69-76-70-74—289	$3,000.00	T-23	Luca Barbato	76-73-75-76—300	$375.00	T-39	Carroll Sharp	82-70-76-77—305	$125.00
5	Sam Snead	72-72-73-73—290	$1,500.00	T-23	Pete Cooper	79-75-73-73—300	$375.00	T-43	Bob Below	75-79-78-74—306	$100.00
6	Joe Lopez Sr.	74-71-75-72—292	$1,250.00	T-23	George Thomas	77-71-75-77—300	$375.00	T-43	Paul Biggy	75-75-80-76—306	$100.00
7	Bob Toski	71-78-71-73—293	$1,150.00	T-26	Jackson Bradley	71-75-74-81—301	$287.50	T-43	Ken Mast	81-70-76-79—306	$100.00
T-8	Al Balding	73-71-77-73—294	$900.00	T-26	Manuel de la Torre	79-74-75-73—301	$287.50	T-43	Dick Neumann	77-76-77-76—306	$100.00
T-8	George Bayer	72-74-78-70—294	$900.00	T-26	J. D. Taylor	77-75-77-72—301	$287.50	T-47	Ange Alberico	75-76-77-79—307	$80.00
T-8	Gil Cavanaugh	75-73-74-72—294	$900.00	T-26	Everett Vinzant	79-74-76-72—301	$287.50	T-47	Bill Morgan	79-76-77-75—307	$80.00
T-8	Fred Wampler	74-72-77-71—294	$900.00	30	Kyle Burton	71-73-78-80—302	$240.00	T-47	Ed Rubis	73-74-80-80—307	$80.00
T-12	Ray Montgomery	75-74-74-72—295	$687.50	T-31	Murry Jacobs	74-76-76-77—303	$220.00	T-47	Paul Runyan	79-72-78-78—307	$80.00
T-12	Chuck Scally	72-73-71-79—295	$687.50	T-31	Mac McCharg	73-77-77-76—303	$220.00	T-47	Bob Watson	81-74-73-79—307	$80.00
T-14	John Doctor	76-71-75-74—296	$625.00	T-31	Tom Talkington	77-78-72-76—303	$220.00				
T-14	Charles Sifford	73-75-73-75—296	$625.00	T-34	Ben Davis	78-74-73-79—304	$180.00				
T-16	Doug Ford	73-74-72-78—297	$562.50	T-34	Billy Gilbert	73-74-83-74—304	$180.00				
T-16	Roy Wallin	74-76-73-74—297	$562.50	T-34	Gene Hamm	75-74-75-80—304	$180.00				
T-18	Jim Browning	75-76-74-73—298	$512.50	T-34	Ted Kroll	73-76-77-78—304	$180.00				
T-18	Joe Taylor	74-78-72-74—298	$512.50	T-34	Larry Tomasino	75-74-76-79—304	$180.00				

1976

A tornado warning interrupted play for 40 minutes during the final round. When play resumed, Pete Cooper, a 61-year-old veteran from Branford, Fla., played 1-under-par golf the last five holes for a par 72 on the Magnolia Course and a 5-under-par 283 total. For the second year in a row, Fred Wampler was runner-up, this time by five strokes as he made double-bogey on each of the last two holes. After receiving the keys to a new Lincoln Mark IV, Cooper, who owns a farm in rural Florida, said, "They'll run me out of the county if I drive up in this. I'd look better in a Lincoln tractor."

Champion:	Pete Cooper	
Site:	Walt Disney World Resort, Orlando, Fla.	
Date:	Jan. 29-Feb. 1	
Par: 36-36—72		Purse: $50,000

TOURNAMENT SUMMARY*

Place	Name	Score	Winnings**	Place	Name	Score	Winnings	Place	Name	Score	Winnings
1	Pete Cooper	69-71-71-72—283	$7,500.00	T-18	George Thomas	72-77-76-74—299	$475.00	T-43	Errie Ball	75-78-72-82—307	$80.00
2	Fred Wampler	67-74-72-75—288	$5,000.00	23	Hampton Auld	79-78-71-72—300	$400.00	T-43	Ross Collins	74-78-75-80—307	$80.00
3	Manuel de la Torre	75-71-71-77—294	$3,500.00	T-24	Clare Emery	76-75-74-76—301	$337.50	T-43	William Gilbert	77-73-78-79—307	$80.00
T-4	George Bayer	70-75-74-76—295	$2,000.00	T-24	Ed Furgol	76-79-73-73—301	$337.50	T-43	Chick Harbert	76-73-78-80—307	$80.00
T-4	Milon Marusic	72-80-68-75—295	$2,000.00	T-24	Hans Merrell	74-74-77-76—301	$337.50	T-43	Sam Penecale	75-79-72-81—307	$80.00
T-6	Murry Jacobs	75-71-70-80—296	$921.87	T-24	Henry Ransom	75-75-74-77—301	$337.50	T-43	Paul Runyan	75-78-74-80—307	$80.00
T-6	Chuck Klein	74-72-72-78—296	$921.87	T-28	Ted Kroll	73-75-75-80—303	$262.50	T-43	Everett Stuart	77-74-80-76—307	$80.00
T-6	Joe Lopez Sr.	76-77-73-70—296	$921.88	T-28	Mike Power	74-76-74-79—303	$262.50	T-43	Tom Talkington	77-75-81-74—307	$80.00
T-6	Charles Sifford	74-74-72-76—296	$921.87	T-30	Marty Furgol	75-75-76-78—304	$230.00	T-43	Bud Williamson	78-76-75-78—307	$80.00
T-6	Sam Snead	73-77-71-75—296	$921.88	T-30	Bob Gajda	78-76-73-77—304	$230.00	T-43	William Zylstra	80-73-77-77—307	$80.00
T-6	Joe Taylor	73-74-74-75—296	$921.88	T-30	Otto Greiner	74-78-72-80—304	$230.00				
T-6	Bud Timbrook	75-78-72-71—296	$921.88	T-33	Patrick Abbott	71-81-72-81—305	$176.25				
T-6	Bob Watson	68-73-74-81—296	$921.87	T-33	Sam Drake	82-75-72-76—305	$176.25				
14	Fred Haas Jr.	74-75-74-74—297	$650.00	T-33	Doug Ford	78-74-73-80—305	$176.25				
T-15	Ballard Beasley	74-72-76-76—298	$575.00	T-33	Bob Hendricks	77-80-73-75—305	$176.25				
T-15	Gaylon Simon	76-72-72-78—298	$575.00	T-33	Bill Kozak	77-79-79-70—305	$176.25				
T-15	Henry Williams	73-75-74-76—298	$575.00	T-33	John Langford	72-81-77-75—305	$176.25				
T-18	Billy Capps	74-76-71-78—299	$475.00	T-33	Harold Reed	75-74-79-77—305	$176.25				
T-18	John Doctor	76-75-69-79—299	$475.00	T-33	Walter Romans	78-73-76-78—305	$176.25				
T-18	Morgan Fottrell	74-71-71-83—299	$475.00	T-41	Warren Smith	73-78-78-77—306	$100.00				
T-18	Chandler Harper	75-80-74-70—299	$475.00	T-41	Roy Wallin	76-79-71-80—306	$100.00				

> * *Only available summaries; some purses unavailable.*
> ** *Some tournament lists from 1956-76 include money awarded from special events taking place within the Championship. This accounts for money totals that don't necessarily reflect a player's finish in the final standings.*

PGA SENIORS' CHAMPIONSHIP

1975

The PGA Seniors' Championship began a five-year stand at Walt Disney World and boosted the prize money to $50,000. Charles Sifford and Fred Wampler, each eligible for the first time, tied at 8-under-par 280. Sifford sank a 22-foot birdie putt on the first extra hole for the victory, winning the $7,500 first-place check.

Champion:	Charles Sifford	
Site:	Walt Disney World Resort, Orlando, Fla.	
Date:	Jan. 30-Feb. 2	
Par: 36-36—72	**Purse:** $50,000	

TOURNAMENT SUMMARY*

Place	Name	Score	Winnings**	Place	Name	Score	Winnings	Place	Name	Score	Winnings
1	Charles Sifford	68-71-72-69—280	$7,500.00	T-17	Herman Scharlau	73-72-71-77—293	$512.50	T-39	Pat Abbott	73-74-75-78—300	$116.66
2	Fred Wampler	69-70-69-72—280	$5,000.00	T-21	Luca Barbato	73-75-70-76—294	$425.00	T-39	Marty Furgol	77-79-71-73—300	$116.67
3	Chick Harbert	71-68-70-73—282	$3,500.00	T-21	Ray Montgomery	70-74-78-72—294	$425.00	T-39	Henry Ransom	80-74-73-73—300	$116.67
4	Julius Boros	72-71-68-73—284	$2,500.00	T-21	Bob Watson	76-73-73-72—294	$425.00	T-39	Harold Reed	72-74-78-76—300	$116.67
5	Ed Furgol	71-72-71-73—287	$1,500.00	T-24	Bill Ezinicki	69-75-71-80—295	$337.50	T-39	Walter Romans	73-74-75-78—300	$116.67
6	Sam Snead	74-73-70-71—288	$1,250.00	T-24	Bob Hendricks	73-70-73-79—295	$337.50	T-39	Warren Smith	72-74-75-79—300	$116.66
T-7	Billy Capps	72-71-74-72—289	$1,000.00	T-24	Ted Kroll	78-73-73-71—295	$337.50	T-45	Eddie Nowak	72-76-78-75—301	$100.00
T-7	Pete Cooper	73-74-70-72—289	$1,000.00	T-24	Joe Lopez Sr.	74-77-69-75—295	$337.50	T-45	Charles Prentice Jr.	75-75-75-76—301	$100.00
T-7	Bill Johnston	71-71-72-75—289	$1,000.00	28	Felice Torza	72-72-78-74—296	$275.00	T-47	Arthur Joiner	75-73-74-80—302	$100.00
T-7	Joe Taylor	69-73-77-70—289	$1,000.00	T-29	Errie Ball	71-77-74-75—297	$225.00	T-47	Lou Warobick	74-77-77-74—302	$100.00
T-11	Tommy Bolt	72-71-72-75—290	$708.34	T-29	Joe Cheves	78-73-74-72—297	$225.00	49	Paul Biggy	77-76-74-76—303	$100.00
T-11	Chandler Harper	74-71-74-71—290	$708.33	T-29	Bob Gajda	73-74-72-78—297	$225.00	T-50	Joseph Burch	75-79-74-76—304	$20.00
T-11	Bob Kay	76-73-73-68—290	$708.33	T-29	Otto Greiner	75-75-74-73—297	$225.00	T-50	Mike Fetchick	78-78-72-76—304	$20.00
14	Milon Marusic	70-74-74-73—291	$650.00	T-29	Chuck Klein	74-71-71-81—297	$225.00	T-50	Everett Stuart	75-78-75-76—304	$20.00
T-15	Fred Haas Jr.	73-74-73-72—292	$587.50	T-29	Bill Kozak	77-71-74-75—297	$225.00	T-50	Bud Timbrook	74-76-78-76—304	$20.00
T-15	Hans Merrell	73-71-76-72—292	$587.50	T-35	George Thomas	73-75-74-76—298	$180.00	T-50	Wally Ulrich	78-77-73-76—304	$20.00
T-17	Jim Browning	73-75-78-67—293	$512.50	T-35	Ed Trojan	74-73-75-76—298	$180.00				
T-17	Manuel de la Torre	71-74-74-74—293	$512.50	T-35	Henry Williams	74-74-75-75—298	$180.00				
T-17	Eric Monti	75-73-73-72—293	$512.50	38	Doug Ford	72-74-76-77—299	$160.00				

1974

M.R. "Chick" Harbert, former PGA Champion and Ryder Cup Team captain, offered St. Lucie CC in Port St. Lucie as the site of the PGA Seniors' Championship. Roberto De Vicenzo, eligible for the first time, arrived from Argentina with little concern about winning. "Maybe I make enough money to pay for the trip, but I tell my wife we come up and just have a good time visiting old friends." De Vicenzo had the best time of all with a 15-under-par 273 to win by three shots. Julius Boros and Art Wall tied for second.

Champion:	Roberto De Vicenzo	
Site:	Port St. Lucie Country Club, Port St. Lucie, Fla.	
Date:	Jan. 31-Feb. 3	
Par: 36-36—72	**Purse:** $40,000	

TOURNAMENT SUMMARY*

Place	Name	Score	Winnings**	Place	Name	Score	Winnings	Place	Name	Score	Winnings
1	Roberto De Vicenzo	68-68-71-66—273	$4,000.00	T-20	Ed Furgol	71-78-69-74—292	$500.00	T-33	Mac McCharg	71-73-78-75—297	$145.00
T-2	Julius Boros	70-67-67-72—276	$2,500.00	T-20	Billy Gilbert	73-72-75-72—292	$500.00	T-33	Russell Strouse	72-76-77-72—297	$145.00
T-2	Art Wall	71-68-68-69—276	$2,500.00	22	Hans Merrell	70-74-76-73—293	$400.00	T-41	Bill Davis	76-74-75-73—298	$100.00
4	Sam Snead	67-73-67-72—279	$1,600.00	23	Jim Browning	73-77-74-70—294	$375.00	T-41	Otto Greiner	76-76-70-76—298	$100.00
T-5	Pete Cooper	69-69-69-75—282	$1,066.67	T-24	Pat Abbott	73-76-72-74—295	$292.50	T-41	Bob Hendricks	71-76-75-76—298	$100.00
T-5	Doug Ford	69-70-71-72—282	$1,066.66	T-24	Ballard Beasley	72-72-76-75—295	$292.50	T-41	Howie Johnson	76-70-78-74—298	$100.00
T-5	Chick Harbert	69-72-71-70—282	$1,066.66	T-24	Duke Gibson	73-73-74-75—295	$292.50	T-41	Herman Scharlau	77-72-74-75—298	$100.00
8	Chandler Harper	70-70-72-75—287	$850.00	T-24	Milon Marusic	77-70-73-75—295	$292.50	T-41	Don Street	74-76-74-74—298	$100.00
T-9	Herman Keiser	71-71-75-71—288	$750.00	T-24	Cliff Settergren	73-75-72-75—295	$292.50	T-47	Luca Barbato	73-72-78-76—299	$66.67
T-9	Joe Lopez Sr.	71-73-72-72—288	$750.00	T-24	Ken Yount	73-74-74-74—295	$292.50	T-47	Paul Biggy	72-75-72-80—299	$66.66
T-11	Marty Furgol	72-71-74-72—289	$650.00	T-30	Ernie Catropa	72-76-72-76—296	$203.33	T-47	Ferdie Catropa	76-73-74-76—299	$66.67
T-11	Bob Gajda	71-73-73-72—289	$650.00	T-30	Matt Moore	74-70-78-74—296	$203.33	T-47	Bill Kozak	77-72-76-74—299	$66.67
T-11	Chuck Klein	71-72-72-74—289	$650.00	T-30	Warren Smith	71-71-75-79—296	$203.34	T-47	Charles Rotar	76-74-70-79—299	$66.66
T-14	Joe Cheves	73-73-69-75—290	$575.00	T-33	Errie Ball	70-77-76-74—297	$145.00	T-47	John Wusdnoski	76-76-71-76—299	$66.67
T-14	Fred Haas Jr.	71-74-72-73—290	$575.00	T-33	Jackson Bradley	74-70-78-75—297	$145.00				
T-14	Felice Torza	73-74-73-70—290	$575.00	T-33	Billy Capps	74-73-76-74—297	$145.00				
T-17	Ted Kroll	71-72-72-76—291	$500.00	T-33	Sam Drake	71-74-78-74—297	$145.00				
T-17	Henry Ransom	74-74-73-70—291	$500.00	T-33	Pete Fleming	71-74-76-76—297	$145.00				
T-17	Joe Taylor	75-71-73-72—291	$500.00	T-33	Labron Harris Sr.	72-77-72-76—297	$145.00				

1973

This is the one they're still talking about, and probably will for as long as the PGA Seniors' Championship is played. Sam Snead was an amazing 20-under par in four days on the East Course at PGA National GC, with rounds of 66-66-67-69 - 268. "I thought I played pretty well," said Julius Boros, who was second but 15 strokes behind. Boros had 283, two strokes lower than his winning total two years earlier on the same course. It was the last PGA Seniors' at this site, now known as BallenIsles CC of JDM.

Champion:	Sam Snead
Site:	PGA National Golf Club,
	Palm Beach Gardens, Fla.
	(now known as BallenIsles CC of JDM)
Date:	Jan. 25-28
Par: 36-36—72	**Purse:** $40,000

TOURNAMENT SUMMARY*

Place	Name	Score	Winnings**	Place	Name	Score	Winnings	Place	Name	Score	Winnings
1	Sam Snead	66-66-67-69—268	$4,000.00	T-18	Joe Kirkwood	73-73-77-76—299	$487.50	T-36	Pete Fleming	73-82-74-74—303	$145.00
2	Julius Boros	69-70-71-73—283	$3,000.00	T-20	Jim Browning	70-74-77-79—300	$412.50	T-38	Patrick Abbott	77-75-77-75—304	$112.00
3	Joe Taylor	70-72-73-73—288	$2,000.00	T-20	Guy Cogle	74-74-76-76—300	$412.50	T-38	Clarence Doser	77-76-73-78—304	$112.00
T-4	Ed Furgol	70-72-71-77—290	$1,425.00	T-20	Otto Greiner	74-73-76-77—300	$412.50	T-38	Warren Smith	75-77-77-75—304	$112.00
T-4	Milon Marusic	74-72-73-71—290	$1,425.00	T-20	Buck White	72-73-76-79—300	$412.50	T-38	Bud Timbrook	71-78-77-78—304	$112.00
6	Pete Cooper	70-73-78-71—292	$1,025.00	T-24	Michael Austin	74-74-77-76—301	$292.50	T-38	William Zylstra	74-74-77-79—304	$112.00
7	Joe Lopez Sr.	73-71-71-78—293	$925.00	T-24	Errie Ball	76-76-73-76—301	$292.50	T-43	Fred Atkins	74-77-76-78—305	$100.00
8	Duke Gibson	71-73-72-78—294	$850.00	T-24	Joe Brown	74-75-75-77—301	$292.50	T-43	Bob Kay	71-81-77-76—305	$100.00
9	Bob Gajda	71-73-74-77—295	$775.00	T-24	Marty Furgol	76-75-74-76—301	$292.50	T-43	Charles Rotar	79-76-74-76—305	$100.00
10	Luca Barbato	74-71-76-75—296	$725.00	T-24	Jack Martin	72-71-77-81—301	$292.50	T-43	Felice Torza	77-75-73-80—305	$100.00
T-11	Chandler Harper	72-75-74-76—297	$637.50	T-24	Skee Riegel	75-74-74-78—301	$292.50	T-47	Mike Fetchick	73-79-76-78—306	$57.15
T-11	Lou Kretlow	71-77-78-71—297	$637.50	T-30	Manuel de la Torre	73-73-78-78—302	$186.67	T-47	Paul Gross	77-76-80-73—306	$57.14
T-11	Peter Mazur	76-76-72-73—297	$637.50	T-30	Steve Doctor	72-75-74-81—302	$186.67	T-47	Chuck Klein	75-76-79-76—306	$57.15
T-11	Henry Williams Jr.	71-74-79-73—297	$637.50	T-30	Ted Kroll	77-75-74-76—302	$186.66	T-47	Bill Kozak	75-76-80-75—306	$57.14
T-15	Billy Capps	72-76-74-76—298	$550.00	T-30	Joseph"Hap" Malia	73-77-74-78—302	$186.67	T-47	Edward Lockie	80-76-74-76—306	$57.14
T-15	Fred Haas Jr.	73-73-75-77—298	$550.00	T-30	Eddie Nowak	75-77-72-78—302	$186.67	T-47	W. D. McCharen	77-72-79-78—306	$57.14
T-15	Harold Reed	75-71-74-78—298	$550.00	T-30	Everett Stuart	76-73-75-78—302	$186.66	T-47	Herman Scharlau	78-77-74-77—306	$57.15
T-18	Jack Isaacs	72-73-76-78—299	$487.50	T-36	Ernie Catropa	75-76-75-77—303	$145.00				

1972

Coming from behind in the final round, Sam Snead reclaimed the title he had surrendered to Julius Boros a year earlier, by one shot. Down at the 13th tee by three, after a double-bogey at No. 12, Snead side-saddled a 25-footer for a birdie on No. 14. He finished with four straight pars, as Boros suffered bogeys on Nos. 13 and 14. Boros finished with a bogey on No. 18, giving Snead his fifth PGA Seniors' Championship. Boros and Tommy Bolt, each with 75 in the final round, tied for second.

Champion:	Sam Snead
Site:	PGA National Golf Club,
	Palm Beach Gardens, Fla.
	(now known as BallenIsles CC of JDM)
Date:	Jan. 27-30
Par: 36-36—72	**Purse:** $40,000

TOURNAMENT SUMMARY*

Place	Name	Score	Winnings**	Place	Name	Score	Winnings	Place	Name	Score	Winnings
1	Sam Snead	69-73-73-71—286	$4,000.00	T-20	Jack Isaacs	78-73-73-78—302	$437.50	T-39	Clarence Doser	75-79-78-77—309	$106.00
T-2	Tommy Bolt	72-69-71-75—287	$2,500.00	T-20	Buck White	72-76-74-80—302	$437.50	T-39	Ray Hill	80-76-76-77—309	$106.00
T-2	Julius Boros	69-74-69-75—287	$2,500.00	T-22	Duke Gibson	76-77-74-76—303	$375.00	T-39	Joseph"Hap" Malia	75-82-76-76—309	$106.00
4	Pete Cooper	74-76-71-70—291	$1,600.00	T-22	Chuck Klein	74-73-78-78—303	$375.00	T-39	Harlan Will	78-78-79-74—309	$106.00
T-5	Marty Furgol	76-73-71-72—292	$1,137.50	T-22	Jack Martin	75-73-78-77—303	$375.00	T-39	Henry Williams Sr.	75-81-77-76—309	$106.00
T-5	Fred Haas Jr.	75-69-75-73—292	$1,137.50	T-25	Bill Davis	73-76-77-78—304	$281.00	T-44	Sam Drake	79-75-76-80—310	$100.00
7	Joe Lopez Sr.	74-74-70-75—293	$925.00	T-25	Dutch Harrison	78-80-72-74—304	$281.00	T-44	Bob Hendricks	72-77-82-79—310	$100.00
8	Herman Keiser	75-75-72-72—294	$850.00	T-25	Milon Marusic	77-75-72-80—304	$281.00	T-44	Mark Hipkins	77-79-78-76—310	$100.00
9	Chandler Harper	75-71-74-76—296	$775.00	T-25	Hans Merrell	76-77-74-77—304	$281.00	47	Luca Barbato	76-74-81-80—311	$100.00
10	Ed Furgol	70-74-78-76—298	$725.00	T-25	Skee Riegel	77-77-74-76—304	$281.00	T-48	Steve Doctor	78-80-77-77—312	$50.00
T-11	Jim Browning	77-72-75-75—299	$637.50	T-30	Bob Grant	75-76-77-77—305	$203.34	T-48	Philip Friel	82-77-77-76—312	$50.00
T-11	Ted Kroll	76-72-78-73—299	$637.50	T-30	Cliff Settergren	76-76-74-79—305	$203.33	T-48	Phil Greenwald	78-74-82-78—312	$50.00
T-11	Scotty McBeath	74-75-74-76—299	$637.50	T-30	Lou Warobick	74-77-72-82—305	$203.33	T-48	Les Kennedy	80-75-74-79—312	$50.00
T-11	Charles Rotar	73-77-73-76—299	$637.50	33	Bill Kozak	77-76-73-80—306	$180.00	T-48	Harold Reed	79-80-75-78—312	$50.00
T-15	Willie Barber	76-76-76-72—300	$537.50	T-34	Ernie Catropa	79-77-69-83—308	$150.00	T-48	Tom Strafaci	78-79-78-77—312	$50.00
T-15	Billy Capps	74-73-72-81—300	$537.50	T-34	Billy Gilbert	78-72-75-83—308	$150.00				
T-15	Bob Hamilton	74-77-73-76—300	$537.50	T-34	Paul Gross	77-72-82-77—308	$150.00				
T-15	Herman Scharlau	74-76-76-74—300	$537.50	T-34	Bob Kay	75-80-74-79—308	$150.00				
19	Errie Ball	75-79-71-76—301	$475.00	T-34	Joe Taylor	79-78-78-73—308	$150.00				

1971

Former two-time U.S. Open champions Julius Boros (1952, '63) and Dr. Cary Middlecoff (1949, '56) qualified for their first PGA Seniors' Championship and met with far different results. Boros ambled to victory with 3-under-par 285, the only player under par for the route. Middlecoff withdrew after an 80-79 — 159 the first two days. Three former PGA Seniors' champions finished in the top four, with Tommy Bolt getting runner-up honors at even-par 288. Defending Champion Sam Snead finished third and Chandler Harper finished fourth.

Champion:	Julius Boros
Site:	PGA National Golf Club, Palm Beach Gardens, Fla.
	(now known as BallenIsles CC of JDM)
Date:	Jan. 28-31
Par: 36-36—72	**Purse:** $40,000

TOURNAMENT SUMMARY*

Place	Name	Score	Winnings**	Place	Name	Score	Winnings	Place	Name	Score	Winnings
1	Julius Boros	73-69-71-72—285	$4,000.00	T-19	Joe Cheves	75-70-80-78—303	$450.00	T-37	Howie Johnson	74-75-81-80—310	$135.00
2	Tommy Bolt	69-68-75-76—288	$3,000.00	T-19	Steve Doctor	74-75-79-75—303	$450.00	T-37	Cliff Settergren	78-77-78-77—310	$135.00
3	Sam Snead	75-68-74-72—289	$2,000.00	T-19	Dale Grieve	70-78-78-77—303	$450.00	T-39	Ernie Catropa	83-77-77-74—311	$110.00
4	Chandler Harper	74-72-76-68—290	$1,600.00	22	Joe Brown	80-75-76-73—304	$400.00	T-39	Skee Riegel	74-74-80-83—311	$110.00
T-5	Bob Hamilton	66-76-76-75—293	$1,137.50	23	Harold Reed	79-75-74-77—305	$375.00	T-39	Joe Taylor	77-81-75-78—311	$110.00
T-5	Jack Isaacs	73-71-76-73—293	$1,137.50	T-24	John Barnum	76-72-80-78—306	$313.75	T-42	Jim Browning	79-77-77-79—312	$100.00
7	Hans Merrell	73-72-75-75—295	$925.00	T-24	Pete Cooper	77-76-77-76—306	$313.75	T-42	Charles Harter	75-77-76-84—312	$100.00
8	Marty Furgol	69-74-76-77—296	$850.00	T-24	Herman Keiser	75-78-74-79—306	$313.75	T-42	Ray Hill	73-80-80-79—312	$100.00
T-9	Clarence Doser	72-76-75-74—297	$706.25	T-24	Joseph "Hap" Malia	75-76-81-74—306	$313.75	T-42	Loren Krugel	76-78-74-84—312	$100.00
T-9	Leland Gibson	73-77-74-73—297	$706.25	T-28	Errie Ball	78-77-74-78—307	$222.00	T-46	Luca Barbato	78-77-79-79—313	$83.33
T-9	Fred Haas Jr.	75-73-72-77—297	$706.25	T-28	Phil Greenwald	76-76-76-79—307	$222.00	T-46	Mike Chiapetta	78-76-81-78—313	$83.34
T-9	Joe Lopez Sr.	72-75-74-76—297	$706.25	T-28	Jack Martin	76-75-75-81—307	$222.00	T-46	Sam Drake	81-76-78-78—313	$83.33
13	Ed Furgol	74-75-77-72—298	$625.00	T-28	Tal Smith	72-77-77-81—307	$222.00	T-46	Nick Garbacz	76-83-78-76—313	$83.34
T-14	Ferdie Catropa	74-75-76-74—299	$587.50	T-28	Henry Williams Jr.	71-76-79-81—307	$222.00	T-46	Bob Hendricks	80-73-78-82—313	$83.33
T-14	Pete Fleming	73-75-74-77—299	$587.50	T-33	Paul Gross	79-73-77-79—308	$170.00	T-46	Herman Scharlau	82-78-74-79—313	$83.33
T-16	Willie Barber	74-79-73-75—301	$537.50	T-33	Les Kennedy	79-76-75-78—308	$170.00				
T-16	Buck White	74-72-76-79—301	$537.50	T-33	Milon Marusic	74-83-76-75—308	$170.00				
18	Ted Kroll	78-75-73-76—302	$500.00	36	Tom Strafaci	77-74-79-79—309	$150.00				

1970

Inclement weather throughout the weekend couldn't prevent Sam Snead from capturing a record fourth PGA Seniors' Championship. However, it did cost the tournament its defending Champion, Tommy Bolt, who battled the flu. When the second round was delayed by rain, Bolt decided to pack it in. Snead won with a final round of 4-over-par 76 for a 2-over-par 290 total, two ahead of former Champion Freddie Haas. It was the first winning score over par since Ernie Newnham's 2-over-par 146 for two rounds in 1952 at the old PGA National in Dunedin.

Champion:	Sam Snead
Site:	PGA National Golf Club, Palm Beach Gardens, Fla.
	(now known as BallenIsles CC of JDM)
Date:	Jan. 29-Feb. 1
Par: 36-36—72	**Purse:** $40,000

TOURNAMENT SUMMARY*

Place	Name	Score	Winnings**	Place	Name	Score	Winnings	Place	Name	Score	Winnings
1	Sam Snead	71-71-72-76—290	$4,000.00	T-17	Bob Gajda	77-74-74-76—301	$475.00	T-34	Ed Kringle	75-75-78-79—307	$155.00
2	Fred Haas Jr.	72-73-73-74—292	$3,000.00	T-17	Chick Harbert	76-73-77-75—301	$475.00	38	Luca Barbato	76-77-76-79—308	$130.00
T-3	Bob Hamilton	72-74-73-75—294	$1,616.66	T-17	Jim Turnesa	76-74-76-75—301	$475.00	T-39	Errie Ball	78-81-77-73—309	$110.00
T-3	Chandler Harper	72-74-74-74—294	$1,616.67	T-22	Herman Barron	77-78-72-75—302	$387.50	T-39	Steve Doctor	74-77-83-75—309	$110.00
T-3	Henry Ransom	70-76-74-74—294	$1,616.67	T-22	Les Kennedy	72-78-77-75—302	$387.50	T-39	Milon Marusic	74-76-81-78—309	$110.00
T-6	Herman Keiser	74-76-77-68—295	$975.00	24	Billy Gilbert	79-76-72-76—303	$350.00	T-42	Jim Browning	80-76-74-80—310	$100.00
T-6	Joe Lopez Sr.	74-75-74-72—295	$975.00	T-25	Mike Chiapetta	75-80-75-74—304	$301.67	T-42	Phil Greenwald	79-80-75-76—310	$100.00
8	Ed Furgol	74-75-73-74—296	$850.00	T-25	Joseph "Hap" Malia	75-81-72-76—304	$301.67	T-42	George Kinsman	77-77-79-77—310	$100.00
9	Pete Cooper	74-76-74-74—298	$775.00	T-25	Dick Metz	76-74-75-79—304	$301.66	T-42	Matt Moore	77-74-78-81—310	$100.00
T-10	Ted Kroll	75-74-73-77—299	$683.33	T-28	Dutch Harrison	73-76-79-77—305	$250.00	T-42	Walter Romans	75-73-80-82—310	$100.00
T-10	Hans Merrell	75-74-76-74—299	$683.34	T-28	Paul Runyan	71-81-75-78—305	$250.00	47	Bob Hendricks	79-75-78-79—311	$100.00
T-10	Herman Scharlau	78-70-76-75—299	$683.33	T-30	Hank Brancato	79-74-73-80—306	$197.50	T-48	Clarence Doser	79-79-76-78—312	$100.00
T-13	Willie Barber	72-77-77-74—300	$587.50	T-30	Pete Fleming	73-76-82-75—306	$197.50	T-48	Philip Friel	81-73-80-78—312	$100.00
T-13	John Barnum	72-74-74-80—300	$587.50	T-30	Clinton Kennedy	73-76-75-82—306	$197.50	T-50	Walter Flahive	79-76-79-79—313	$33.33
T-13	Joe Brown	74-76-75-75—300	$587.50	T-30	Cliff Settergren	78-75-76-77—306	$197.50	T-50	Fred Fronauer	78-80-75-80—313	$33.33
T-13	Marty Furgol	72-75-78-75—300	$587.50	T-34	Fred Annon	76-78-76-77—307	$155.00	T-50	Nick Garbacz	80-78-81-74—313	$33.34
T-17	Bill Davis	72-76-74-79—301	$475.00	T-34	Alfonso Atkins	77-73-79-78—307	$155.00				
T-17	Leland Duke	75-74-76-76—301	$475.00	T-34	Mike Barbato	78-74-77-78—307	$155.00				

1969

Tommy Bolt won the PGA Seniors' Championship in his first year of eligibility, prompting Sam Snead, a three-time former Champion, to exclaim, "You know, it's real funny the way a guy is 39 one year and beats you in the PGA Seniors' the next." Bolt posted a 5-under-par 67 on the East Course at PGA National GC in the final round, for a one-shot margin of victory over Pete Fleming of Hot Springs, Ark.

Champion:	Tommy Bolt
Site:	PGA National Golf Club, Palm Beach Gardens, Fla. (now known as BallenIsles CC of JDM)
Date:	Jan. 24-27
Par:	36-36—72 Purse: $40,000

TOURNAMENT SUMMARY*

Place	Name	Score	Winnings**	Place	Name	Score	Winnings	Place	Name	Score	Winnings
1	Tommy Bolt	70-70-71-67—278	$4,000.00	T-18	Henry Ransom	74-70-76-74—294	$475.00	T-36	Eddie Nowak	76-77-74-74—301	$145.00
2	Pete Fleming	72-71-69-67—279	$3,000.00	T-18	Henry Williams Jr.	73-74-71-76—294	$475.00	T-38	Art Doering	73-75-77-77—302	$115.00
3	Sam Snead	69-72-70-69—280	$2,000.00	T-21	Marty Furgol	77-72-72-74—295	$412.50	T-38	Labron Harris Sr.	74-76-74-78—302	$115.00
4	Bob Hamilton	67-71-72-71—281	$1,600.00	T-21	Dub Pagan	77-72-72-74—295	$412.50	T-38	Hans Merrell	77-74-74-77—302	$115.00
T-5	Fred Haas Jr.	69-73-72-71—285	$1,066.67	T-23	Joe Brown	73-76-74-73—296	$350.00	T-38	Pat Palmieri	76-74-74-78—302	$115.00
T-5	Chick Harbert	70-71-71-73—285	$1,066.67	T-23	Paul Gross	71-76-73-76—296	$350.00	T-42	Bob Gajda	76-74-75-78—303	$100.00
T-5	Dutch Harrison	74-70-68-73—285	$1,066.66	T-23	Clinton Kennedy	75-76-72-73—296	$350.00	T-42	Fred Gronauer	80-73-72-78—303	$100.00
T-8	Errie Ball	69-72-73-74—288	$812.50	T-26	Herman Barron	72-73-74-78—297	$290.00	T-42	Jim Turnesa	74-76-75-78—303	$100.00
T-8	Joe Lopez Sr.	71-71-72-74—288	$812.50	T-26	Ferdie Catropa	70-77-75-75—297	$290.00	T-45	Pete Cooper	76-74-81-73—304	$100.00
10	Milon Marusic	75-72-71-71—289	$725.00	T-28	Patrick Abbott	73-73-72-80—298	$250.00	T-45	Billy Gilbert	79-75-76-74—304	$100.00
T-11	Luca Barbato	71-73-71-75—290	$650.00	T-28	Jim Browning	72-78-74-74—298	$250.00	T-45	Gray Little	76-80-75-73—304	$100.00
T-11	Johnny Bulla	74-71-70-75—290	$650.00	T-30	Jack Isaacs	74-76-74-75—299	$192.00	T-45	Joseph "Hap" Malia	79-74-75-76—304	$100.00
T-11	Herman Keiser	70-71-72-77—290	$650.00	T-30	T.R. Sleichter	76-72-76-75—299	$192.00	T-49	Skip Alexander	77-73-77-78—305	$40.00
T-14	Alfonso Atkins	69-73-75-74—291	$575.00	T-30	Toby Lyons	74-74-76-75—299	$192.00	T-49	Augie Boyd	78-74-75-78—305	$40.00
T-14	Ed Furgol	73-72-72-74—291	$575.00	T-30	Paul Nyan	76-71-76-76—299	$192.00	T-49	Ray Hill	76-72-79-78—305	$40.00
T-14	Leland Gibson	69-75-72-75—291	$575.00	T-30	Buck White	74-75-73-77—299	$192.00	T-49	Harry Pezzullo	76-78-77-74—305	$40.00
17	John Barnum	72-74-73-74—293	$525.00	35	Joe Cheves	76-73-75-76—300	$160.00	T-49	Ellsworth Vines	72-75-73-85—305	$40.00
T-18	Walter Burkemo	73-74-73-74—294	$475.00	T-36	Chandler Harper	77-72-75-77—301	$145.00				

1968

With 10 past Seniors' champions in the field, defending Champion Sam Snead made a gallant run at the 29th renewal of the PGA Seniors' Championship, but in the end finished runner-up, four shots behind Chandler Harper of Portsmouth, Va. Harper was the victor with a 9-under-par 279 total. His $4,000 prize was $500 more than he received for winning the PGA Championship in 1950.

Champion:	Chandler Harper
Site:	PGA National Golf Club, Palm Beach Gardens, Fla. (now known as BallenIsles CC of JDM)
Date:	Jan. 25-28
Par:	36-36—72 Purse: $40,000

TOURNAMENT SUMMARY*

Place	Name	Score	Winnings**	Place	Name	Score	Winnings	Place	Name	Score	Winnings
1	Chandler Harper	70-73-64-72—279	$4,000.00	T-19	Errie Ball	75-76-72-76—299	$437.50	T-36	Joe Brown	79-78-73-76—306	$130.00
2	Sam Snead	70-74-70-69—283	$3,000.00	T-19	Clarence Doser	75-71-77-76—299	$437.50	T-36	Bobby Cruickshank	72-75-76-83—306	$130.00
3	Bob Hamilton	69-75-71-70—285	$2,000.00	T-19	Chick Harbert	73-77-77-72—299	$437.50	T-36	Lou Sabo	80-76-73-77—306	$130.00
4	Fred Haas Jr.	73-71-73-72—289	$1,600.00	T-19	Milon Marusic	75-77-72-75—299	$437.50	T-36	Denny Shute	79-78-73-76—306	$130.00
5	Henry Ransom	69-73-76-73—291	$1,250.00	T-23	Art Doering	79-74-73-74—300	$350.00	T-41	Steve Doctor	75-76-78-78—307	$100.00
6	Pete Cooper	76-71-72-74—293	$1,025.00	T-23	Iverson Martin	80-75-70-75—300	$350.00	T-41	Ralph Hutchison	76-75-78-78—307	$100.00
T-7	Luca Barbato	75-72-72-75—294	$850.00	T-23	Buck White	72-75-80-73—300	$350.00	T-43	Hans Merrell	78-78-73-79—308	$100.00
T-7	Marty Furgol	70-70-80-74—294	$850.00	T-26	Bill Heinlein	80-75-75-72—302	$290.00	T-43	Lew Worsham	75-78-77-78—308	$100.00
T-7	Joe Lopez Sr.	75-73-69-77—294	$850.00	T-26	Henry Williams Jr.	70-73-78-81—302	$290.00	T-45	Loren Krugel	77-77-81-74—309	$100.00
T-10	Paul Gross	73-71-78-73—295	$683.34	T-28	Ray Hill	70-76-77-80—303	$240.00	T-45	Ewing Pomeroy	75-80-74-80—309	$100.00
T-10	Dutch Harrison	71-72-75-77—295	$683.33	T-28	Ed Kringle	75-78-78-72—303	$240.00	T-45	Cliff Settergren	75-77-78-79—309	$100.00
T-10	Herman Keiser	75-74-71-75—295	$683.33	T-28	Henry Lindner	79-73-76-75—303	$240.00	T-45	Harry Umbinetti	75-79-78-77—309	$100.00
T-13	John Barnum	75-75-72-74—296	$612.50	T-31	Eldon Briggs	77-73-80-74—304	$195.00	T-49	Ralph Bond	76-75-78-81—310	$50.00
T-13	Pete Fleming	73-77-71-75—296	$612.50	T-31	Henry Castillo	75-75-76-78—304	$195.00	T-49	Gray Little	79-80-74-77—310	$50.00
T-15	Herman Barron	75-73-74-75—297	$562.50	T-33	Jim Browning	71-74-81-79—305	$170.00	T-49	Robert Morris	74-76-79-81—310	$50.00
T-15	Tom Strafaci	73-73-75-76—297	$562.50	T-33	Leland Gibson	74-77-78-76—305	$170.00	T-49	Walter Romans	77-76-75-82—310	$50.00
T-17	Bob Gajda	72-76-78-72—298	$512.50	T-33	Joseph "Hap" Malia	69-79-77-80—305	$170.00				
T-17	Jack Isaacs	74-78-70-76—298	$512.50	T-36	Gene Battistoni	77-75-74-80—306	$130.00				

PGA SENIORS' CHAMPIONSHIP

1967

Sam Snead demonstrated his new "Squat-shot" putting style, claiming he could "see the line of the putts better by facing the hole." (The between-the-legs "croquet" putting method was outlawed by the USGA within a year.) Snead posted a 9-under-par 279, winning the overall title by nine shots over Bob Hamilton and 10 shots over defending Champion Freddie Haas, who finished third.

Champion: Sam Snead
Site: PGA National Golf Club, Palm Beach Gardens, Fla.
(now known as BallenIsles CC of JDM)
Date: Jan. 26-29
Par: 36-36—72   **Purse:** $40,000

TOURNAMENT SUMMARY*

Place	Name	Score	Winnings**	Place	Name	Score	Winnings	Place	Name	Score	Winnings
1	Sam Snead	71-69-73-66—279	$4,000.00	T-21	Patrick Abbott	71-73-78-80—302	$387.50	T-41	George Fazio	77-76-75-78—306	$100.00
2	Bob Hamilton	75-70-73-70—288	$3,000.00	T-21	Clarence Doser	72-76-78-76—302	$387.50	T-41	Harry Pezzullo	76-74-81-75—306	$100.00
3	Fred Haas Jr.	72-72-75-71—290	$2,000.00	T-21	Leland Gibson	71-73-79-79—302	$387.50	T-41	Russell Strouse	72-76-77-81—306	$100.00
4	Joe Lopez Sr.	73-70-73-75—291	$1,600.00	T-21	Jim Turnesa	78-73-79-72—302	$387.50	44	Terl Johnson	75-74-82-76—307	$100.00
T-5	John Barnum	70-76-74-73—293	$1,066.66	T-25	Joe Brown	75-76-76-76—303	$312.50	T-45	Eldon Briggs	77-75-82-74—308	$100.00
T-5	Pete Cooper	75-71-76-71—293	$1,066.67	T-25	Harold Sanderson	76-77-76-74—303	$312.50	T-45	Toby Lyons	75-78-78-77—308	$100.00
T-5	Marty Furgol	70-72-79-72—293	$1,066.67	T-27	Jim Browning	77-72-79-76—304	$193.33	47	Ray Hill	79-75-79-76—309	$100.00
8	Henry Castillo	71-76-73-74—294	$850.00	T-27	Pat Cici	78-72-76-78—304	$193.33	48	Tony Barkovich	76-75-79-80—310	$100.00
T-9	Vic Ghezzi	72-73-78-72—295	$750.00	T-27	Bob Gajda	77-79-77-71—304	$193.34	49	Henry Lindner	80-74-78-79—311	$100.00
T-9	Herman Heiser	72-72-78-73—295	$750.00	T-27	Paul Gross	72-78-75-79—304	$193.33	T-50	Mike Barbato	75-78-81-78—312	$11.11
T-11	Ferdie Catropa	72-72-74-79—297	$662.50	T-27	Charles Harter	74-78-79-73—304	$193.34	T-50	Gene Battistoni	75-79-78-80—312	$11.11
T-11	Cliff Settergren	72-74-77-74—297	$662.50	T-27	Ralph Hutchison	78-72-79-75—304	$193.33	T-50	Steve Doctor	79-75-80-78—312	$11.11
13	Buck White	75-72-75-77—299	$625.00	T-27	George Kinsman	76-75-79-74—304	$193.33	T-50	Phil Greenwald	75-82-77-78—312	$11.11
T-14	Errie Ball	76-75-73-76—300	$562.50	T-27	Loren Krugel	74-78-76-76—304	$193.34	T-50	Scudday Horner	75-74-83-80—312	$11.11
T-14	Luca Barbato	78-78-70-74—300	$562.50	T-27	Edward Lockie	75-77-80-72—304	$193.34	T-50	Gray Little	74-77-80-81—312	$11.11
T-14	Chandler Harper	77-71-76-76—300	$562.50	T-27	Milon Marusic	73-75-78-78—304	$193.33	T-50	Ernie Pagnotta	78-76-80-78—312	$11.11
T-14	Jack Isaacs	75-73-74-78—300	$562.50	T-27	Harry Umbinetti	72-77-77-78—304	$193.33	T-50	Ewing Pomeroy	79-76-79-78—312	$11.11
T-18	Ralph Bond	73-76-79-73—301	$475.00	T-27	Henry Williams Jr.	72-81-75-76—304	$193.33	T-50	Paul Runyan	78-78-80-76—312	$11.12
T-18	Chick Harbert	79-71-79-72—301	$475.00	T-39	Art Doering	73-77-77-78—305	$115.00				
T-18	Labron Harris Sr.	75-77-72-77—301	$475.00	T-39	Bill Heinlein	72-75-80-78—305	$115.00				

1966

The first round of the PGA Seniors' Championship was postponed one day by rain, and this proved to be a blessing for Freddie Haas Jr. of Metairie, La., who turned 50 just 52 days earlier. With a virus and a 100-degree temperature, he probably should not have played. However, as the weather and Haas' health improved sufficiently, he became the only player not to shoot over par in any round on the East Course at PGA National GC in Palm Beach Gardens. He won with a 2-under-par 286 for a two-stroke victory over John Barnum and E.J. "Dutch" Harrison.

Champion: Freddie Haas Jr.
Site: PGA National Golf Club, Palm Beach Gardens, Fla.
(now known as BallenIsles CC of JDM)
Date: Feb. 24-27
Par: 36-36—72   **Purse:** $35,000

TOURNAMENT SUMMARY*

Place	Name	Score	Winnings**	Place	Name	Score	Winnings	Place	Name	Score	Winnings
1	Fred Haas Jr.	72-71-71-72—286	$3,000.00	T-22	Al Brosch	75-69-78-79—301	$325.00	T-45	Raymond Gafford	73-75-79-80—307	$150.00
T-2	John Barnum	71-72-69-76—288	$2,100.00	T-22	Bob Hamilton	73-78-75-75—301	$325.00	T-45	Ed Kringle	75-75-80-77—307	$150.00
T-2	Dutch Harrison	69-71-74-74—288	$2,100.00	T-22	John Long	74-75-76-76—301	$325.00	T-45	Henry Ransom	73-73-77-84—307	$150.00
4	Pete Cooper	70-73-73-75—291	$1,400.00	T-26	Chick Harbert	74-73-77-78—302	$250.00	T-45	John Vaughn	74-75-78-80—307	$150.00
5	Jim Browning	68-74-79-71—292	$1,100.00	T-26	Chandler Harper	68-76-78-80—302	$250.00	T-49	Art Doering	75-73-80-80—308	$100.00
T-6	Jack Isaacs	72-70-77-74—293	$800.00	T-26	Edward Olckie	77-71-73-81—302	$250.00	T-49	George Kinsman	72-75-77-84—308	$100.00
T-6	Dick Shoemaker	74-70-75-74—293	$800.00	T-26	Lou Sabo	75-75-77-75—302	$250.00	T-49	Tod Menefee	75-76-81-76—308	$100.00
T-7	Errie Ball	75-69-74-77—295	$550.00	T-26	Cliff Settergren	71-74-78-79—302	$400.00	T-49	Charles Sheppard	73-75-80-80—308	$325.00
T-7	Marty Furgol	71-73-73-78—295	$550.00	T-26	Jim Turnesa	73-76-75-78—302	$250.00	T-53	Bill Barclay	75-75-79-80—309	$100.00
T-7	Phil Greenwald	72-73-74-76—295	$550.00	T-32	Pat Abbott	73-76-75-79—303	$250.00	T-53	Ernie Catropa	77-74-81-77—309	$100.00
T-7	Sam Snead	73-72-77-73—295	$550.00	T-32	Harry Umbinetti	71-76-83-73—303	$250.00	T-53	Val Chiaverini	72-75-79-83—309	$100.00
T-12	Joe Lopez Sr.	73-71-75-77—296	$450.00	T-34	Herman Barron	77-76-75-76—304	$150.00	T-53	Bill Heinlein	73-78-78-80—309	$100.00
T-12	Skee Riegel	67-77-75-77—296	$450.00	T-34	Sam Bernardi	73-71-80-80—304	$550.00	T-53	Jack Helms	74-76-79-80—309	$100.00
14	Herman Keiser	73-72-77-75—297	$400.00	T-34	Sterling Johnson	76-73-79-76—304	$193.75	T-53	Bill Hird	75-75-83-78—309	$100.00
T-15	George Fazio	71-75-77-75—298	$400.00	T-34	Eddie Kirk	74-75-79-76—304	$193.75	T-53	Ewing Pomeroy	77-72-80-80—309	$100.00
T-15	Vic Ghezzi	71-73-78-76—298	$550.00	T-38	Gene Battistoni	73-76-79-77—305	$150.00	T-53	Paul Runyan	74-75-80-80—309	$193.75
T-17	Clarence Doser	72-74-76-77—299	$400.00	T-38	Ferdie Catropa	75-75-76-79—305	$150.00	T-53	Tom Strafaci	74-78-75-82—309	$100.00
T-17	Paul Gross	69-74-80-76—299	$400.00	T-38	Ray Hill	74-74-79-78—305	$150.00	T-62	Charles Harter	72-81-78-79—310	$33.34
T-17	Bud Williamson	69-72-80-78—299	$400.00	T-38	Buck White	77-72-75-81—305	$193.75	T-62	Al Morley	71-80-79-80—310	$33.33
T-20	Henry Castillo	75-72-79-74—300	$400.00	T-42	J.B. Barfield	74-72-75-85—306	$600.00	T-62	Harold Wiley	74-76-79-81—310	$33.33
T-20	Toby Lyons	73-74-79-74—300	$400.00	T-42	Al Huske	75-77-78-76—306	$150.00				
T-22	Augie Boyd	70-72-81-78—301	$325.00	T-42	Gray Little	72-69-79-86—306	$150.00				

1965

With the PGA Seniors' Championship being staged at Fort Lauderdale CC, Sam Snead captured his second title in a row with a 10-under-par 278, coasting to a 4-stroke victory over Joe Lopez Sr. of Miami, Fla. Snead won despite pulling his 72nd hole drive out-of-bounds and making double-bogey. Snead's play was so dominant, one rival was heard to say, "We couldn't beat him on the regular Tour, so how do you expect us to beat him now as a senior?"

Champion: Sam Snead
Site: Fort Lauderdale Country Club, Fort Lauderdale, Fla.
Date: Feb. 25-28
Par: 36-36—72   Purse: $35,000

TOURNAMENT SUMMARY*

Place	Name	Score	Winnings**	Place	Name	Score	Winnings	Place	Name	Score	Winnings
1	Sam Snead	71-68-68-71—278	$3,500.00	20	Herman Keiser	74-74-71-74—293	$450.00	T-37	Joe Brown	75-71-78-74—298	$175.00
2	Joe Lopez Sr.	77-68-70-67—282	$2,750.00	T-21	Eldon Briggs	76-68-73-77—294	$550.00	T-37	Bill Hird	73-77-75-73—298	$175.00
3	Chick Harbert	72-67-73-71—283	$2,000.00	T-21	Jim Browning	79-69-72-74—294	$450.00	T-37	Oran Love	73-75-74-76—298	$175.00
T-4	Pete Cooper	73-70-71-70—284	$1,350.00	T-21	Al Feldman	72-77-74-71—294	$450.00	T-37	Tod Menefee	76-70-79-73—298	$375.00
T-4	Bud Williamson	72-71-71-70—284	$1,350.00	T-24	Tony Barkovich	77-70-71-77—295	$360.00	T-37	Larry Montes	77-74-72-75—298	$175.00
6	Henry Ransom	70-69-71-75—285	$1,000.00	T-24	Val Chiaverni	76-73-74-72—295	$360.00	T-37	Harlan Will	75-74-73-76—298	$175.00
7	Dutch Harrison	77-71-70-68—286	$825.00	T-24	Clarence Doser	79-73-69-74—295	$360.00	T-45	Fred Annon	80-73-75-71—299	$145.00
8	Labron Harris Sr.	73-68-72-75—286	$825.00	T-24	Jack Isaacs	78-73-74-70—295	$360.00	T-45	Philip Axt	72-71-77-79—299	$145.00
T-9	Herman Barron	76-70-72-69—287	$616.67	T-24	Cliff Settergren	72-69-79-75—295	$360.00	T-45	Bill Heinlein	76-72-75-76—299	$145.00
T-9	Ferdie Catropa	74-70-70-73—287	$616.66	T-29	Ralph Bond	75-71-76-74—296	$300.00	T-45	Ray Hill	72-77-73-77—299	$145.00
T-9	Duke Gibson	73-72-72-70—287	$616.67	T-29	Al Labutis	71-74-75-76—296	$300.00	T-45	Jack Ryan	77-71-75-76—299	$145.00
T-12	Vic Ghezzi	72-71-74-71—288	$550.00	T-29	George McCallister	80-72-74-70—296	$300.00	T-45	Fithian Shaw	74-71-76-78—299	$145.00
T-12	Dick Shoemaker	68-74-75-71—288	$550.00	T-29	Smiley Quick	79-72-72-73—296	$300.00	T-51	Sam Bernardi	74-77-74-75—300	$125.00
T-14	Errie Ball	70-75-73-72—290	$450.00	T-33	Ernie Catropa	74-74-76-73—297	$175.00	T-51	Charles Harter	71-72-79-78—300	$125.00
T-14	Paul Runyan	70-71-76-73—290	$700.00	T-33	Phil Greenwald	79-71-73-74—297	$175.00	T-51	Jock Hutchison Jr.	71-75-76-78—300	$125.00
T-14	Buck White	74-73-71-72—290	$450.00	T-33	Jack Patroni	76-72-76-73—297	$175.00	T-51	Bill Kerr	73-75-76-76—300	$125.00
17	Al Huske	71-73-73-74—291	$550.00	T-33	Ellsworth Vines	73-70-80-74—297	$175.00	T-55	Frank Commisso	74-79-72-76—301	$125.00
T-18	Ewing Pomeroy	76-69-73-74—292	$450.00	T-37	Pat Abbott	77-72-73-76—298	$175.00	T-55	Tommy Shannon	76-73-72-80—301	$125.00
T-18	Jim Turnesa	75-69-75-73—292	$450.00	T-37	Bill Barber	73-77-73-75—298	$175.00	T-55	Harry Umbinetti	72-77-74-78—301	$125.00

1964

After bypassing the tournament in 1963, his first year of eligibility, the legendary Sam Snead made his first appearance in the PGA Seniors' Championship a memorable one. For the first time, the tournament was played at the new PGA National GC, currently known as BallenIsles CC of JDM, in Palm Beach Gardens. Snead opened with an eagle on the first hole of the East Course and was never caught, posting a 9-under-par 279 for his first of a record six PGA Seniors' Championship victories.

Champion: Sam Snead
Site: PGA National Golf Club, Palm Beach Gardens, Fla.
(now known as BallenIsles CC of JDM)
Date: Feb. 20-23
Par: 36-36—72   Purse: $30,000

TOURNAMENT SUMMARY*

Place	Name	Score	Winnings**	Place	Name	Score	Winnings	Place	Name	Score	Winnings
1	Sam Snead	67-68-73-71—279	$2,500.00	T-22	Harold Sanderson	74-71-77-77—299	$300.00	T-45	Russell Strouse	74-70-81-82—307	$125.00
2	John Barnum	73-69-71-69—282	$2,000.00	T-25	Ernie Catropa	72-76-74-78—300	$266.66	T-48	Everett Comstock	79-72-77-80—308	$108.33
3	Dutch Harrison	72-70-69-74—285	$1,500.00	T-25	Ferdie Catropa	73-75-72-80—300	$266.66	T-48	Phil Greenwald	75-76-77-80—308	$108.33
4	Leland Gibson	68-70-72-77—287	$1,200.00	T-25	Al Zimmerman	75-71-75-79—300	$266.66	T-48	Rod Munday	78-76-75-79—308	$108.33
5	Jim Turnesa	73-70-72-73—288	$900.00	T-28	J.B. Barfield	74-74-77-76—301	$200.00	T-48	Ewing Pomeroy	72-78-79-79—308	$108.33
6	Dick Shoemaker	72-69-73-78—292	$750.00	T-28	Labron Harris Sr.	76-72-72-81—301	$200.00	T-52	Gene Battistoni	74-76-81-78—309	$75.00
T-7	Vic Ghezzi	71-72-74-76—293	$550.00	T-30	Al Brosch	76-72-78-76—302	$200.00	T-52	Sam Bernardi	75-75-80-79—309	$75.00
T-7	John Long	73-68-74-78—293	$550.00	T-30	Terl Johnson	78-76-74-74—302	$200.00	T-52	Ray Hill	78-75-80-76—309	$75.00
T-7	Paul Runyan	71-70-75-77—293	$550.00	T-32	Eddie Burke	75-71-76-81—303	$150.00	T-52	Ed Kringle	80-76-75-78—309	$75.00
10	Cecil Harris	70-75-72-77—294	$450.00	T-32	Paul Gross	72-77-73-81—303	$150.00	T-52	Tod Menefee	76-78-74-81—309	$75.00
T-11	Willie Barber	76-71-76-72—295	$400.00	T-32	Bill Heinlein	77-72-74-80—303	$150.00	T-52	Cliff Settergren	79-70-79-81—309	$75.00
T-11	Joe Brown	74-73-75-73—295	$400.00	T-32	Henry Lindner	71-73-83-76—303	$150.00	T-58	Pete Burke	76-72-83-79—310	$75.00
T-11	Joe Lopez Sr.	72-72-72-79—295	$400.00	T-36	Tony Barkovich	71-74-84-75—304	$125.00	T-58	Sam Byrd	76-76-77-81—310	$75.00
T-14	Errie Ball	73-71-77-75—296	$350.00	T-36	Bobby Cruickshank	72-78-77-77—304	$125.00	T-58	David Melville	77-77-78-78—310	$75.00
T-14	Buck White	77-69-72-78—296	$350.00	T-36	J.P.(Sonny) Rouse	74-73-76-81—304	$125.00	T-58	Harry Pezzullo	79-77-74-80—310	$75.00
T-15	Al Huske	78-73-71-75—297	$350.00	T-36	Charles Sheppard	73-74-78-79—304	$125.00	T-58	Tommy Shannon	73-77-78-82—310	$75.00
T-15	Jack Isaacs	74-73-73-77—297	$350.00	T-40	Andrew Gibson	72-73-81-79—305	$125.00	T-62	Joseph Burch	76-76-80-79—311	$75.00
T-15	Bud Williamson	70-69-76-82—297	$350.00	T-40	Gunnard Johnson	79-73-77-76—305	$125.00	T-62	Floyd Hamblen	74-79-77-81—311	$75.00
T-19	Pat Abbott	71-73-74-80—298	$350.00	T-42	Eldon Briggs	77-77-77-75—306	$125.00	T-62	Anthony Mierzwa	76-75-82-78—311	$75.00
T-19	Walter Kozak	70-71-78-79—298	$350.00	T-42	Frank Strazza	76-71-78-81—306	$125.00	T-62	Harry Nettelbladt	77-75-77-82—311	$75.00
T-19	Denny Shute	71-77-72-78—298	$350.00	T-42	Ellsworth Vines	76-74-78-78—306	$125.00	T-62	Toney Penna	76-78-79-78—311	$75.00
T-22	Clarence Doser	73-75-74-77—299	$300.00	T-45	Harold Oatman	77-72-77-81—307	$125.00				
T-22	Jimmy Johnson	72-75-76-76—299	$300.00	T-45	Warren Riepen	79-73-78-77—307	$125.00				

1963

When the planned new national headquarters for the PGA of America and the accompanying golf courses in Palm Beach Gardens weren't ready for the '63 PGA Seniors' Championship, a move to Port St. Lucie CC, about an hour north on Florida's east coast, was arranged and hosted by M.R. "Chick" Harbert, former PGA Champion and Ryder Cup Team Captain. There, two golf courses were available, and for the first time in PGA Seniors' history, the winner registered four sub-70 rounds. Herman Barron of White Plains, N.Y., won with a 16-under-par 272, two strokes better than John Barnum of Belmont, Mich.

Champion:	Herman Barron	
Site:	Port St. Lucie Country Club,	
	Port St. Lucie, Fla.	
Date:	Jan. 31-Feb. 3	
Par:	36-36—72	**Purse:** $30,000

TOURNAMENT SUMMARY*

Place	Name	Score	Winnings**	Place	Name	Score	Winnings	Place	Name	Score	Winnings
1	Herman Barron	67-67-69-69—272	$2,500.00	T-22	Vic Ghezzi	74-72-73-72—291	$260.00	T-44	Russell Strouse	75-76-73-71—295	$75.00
2	John Barnum	66-68-69-71—274	$2,000.00	T-22	Rod Munday	73-71-71-76—291	$260.00	T-46	J.B. Barfield	70-76-73-77—296	$100.00
3	Henry Ransom	68-68-68-75—279	$1,500.00	T-22	Paul Runyan	76-70-73-72—291	$260.00	T-46	Jake Fondren	70-73-75-78—296	$75.00
T-4	Errie Ball	71-64-73-74—282	$1,050.00	T-22	R.W. Williamson	75-70-74-72—291	$260.00	T-46	Jack Ryan	72-72-73-79—296	$275.00
T-4	Jack Isaacs	73-66-71-72—282	$1,050.00	T-27	Gene Battistoni	72-72-71-77—292	$200.00	T-46	Leonard Schmutte	72-74-75-75—296	$100.00
6	Leland Gibson	70-69-72-74—285	$750.00	T-27	Eldon Briggs	74-70-73-75—292	$200.00	T-46	Cliff Settergren	71-74-77-74—296	$75.00
7	Clarence Doser	70-71-72-73—286	$650.00	T-27	Pete Burke	70-70-78-74—292	$350.00	T-46	George Smith	73-72-73-78—296	$75.00
T-8	Sam Bernardi	70-71-73-74—288	$462.50	T-27	Ivan Gantz	72-73-74-73—292	$200.00	T-52	Willie Goggin	72-76-74-75—297	$82.10
T-8	Labron Harris Sr.	69-70-73-76—288	$462.50	T-27	Jimmy Johnson	74-71-72-75—292	$200.00	T-52	Tod Menefee	73-75-74-75—297	$82.10
T-8	John Long	72-70-73-73—288	$462.50	T-32	Joe Brown	71-73-72-77—293	$125.00	T-52	Harry Nettelbladt	70-75-76-76—297	$166.33
T-8	W.A. Stackhouse	72-73-73-70—288	$462.50	T-32	Phil Greenwald	71-71-72-79—293	$125.00	T-52	George Schneiter	75-71-73-78—297	$75.00
T-12	Charles Farlow	72-72-70-75—289	$375.00	T-34	Pat Abbott	77-70-70-77—294	$125.00	T-56	Mike Demassey	75-73-75-75—298	$75.00
T-12	Bill Heinlein	72-69-74-74—289	$375.00	T-34	Al Brosch	73-72-74-75—294	$125.00	T-56	Andrew Gibson	72-72-76-78—298	$75.00
T-12	Gray Little	68-72-73-76—289	$375.00	T-34	Paul Gross	76-70-76-72—294	$125.00	T-56	Bill Goldbeck	74-72-77-75—298	$250.00
T-12	Al Zimmerman	73-71-74-71—289	$375.00	T-34	Ray Hill	75-71-74-74—294	$125.00	T-56	Johnny Holtz	73-75-73-77—298	$75.00
T-16	Eddie Burke	70-73-74-73—290	$341.66	T-34	Len Mattson	68-76-79-71—294	$125.00	T-56	Al Joe Zieman	74-75-74-75—298	$75.00
T-16	Al Feldman	73-69-75-73—290	$341.66	T-34	Iras Pat Patton	75-72-73-74—294	$125.00	T-56	Al Watrous	72-72-78-76—298	$350.00
T-16	Ralph Hutchison	72-68-77-73—290	$341.66	T-34	Angelo Paul	72-72-73-77—294	$125.00	T-62	Todd Houck	73-74-76-76—299	$50.00
T-16	Harold Oatman	73-72-72-73—290	$341.66	T-34	Toney Penna	71-74-77-72—294	$166.33	T-62	Bill Kaiser	77-73-73-76—299	$50.00
T-16	Lloyd Sparrow	73-69-76-72—290	$341.66	T-34	Harry Pezzullo	73-66-77-78—294	$125.00	T-62	Tommy Shannon	74-70-75-80—299	$50.00
T-16	Jim Turnesa	75-69-73-73—290	$341.66	T-34	O'Neal(Buck) White	71-70-73-80—294	$125.00				
T-22	Ferdie Catropa	72-72-75-72—291	$260.00	T-44	Charles Penna	76-73-71-75—295	$75.00				

1962

For the first 22 years, the average age of the PGA Seniors' champion was 53. That's how old Paul Runyan was when he captured his second title in a row, taking home $2,000 from an increased purse of $25,000. In the last PGA Seniors' Championship to be played at PGA National GC in Dunedin, Runyan shot 10-under-par 278, matching his tournament record set a year earlier.

Champion:	Paul Runyan	
Site:	PGA National Golf Club,	
	Dunedin, Fla.	
Date:	Feb. 13-19	
Par:	36-36—72	**Purse:** $25,000

TOURNAMENT SUMMARY*

Place	Name	Score	Winnings**	Place	Name	Score	Winnings	Place	Name	Score	Winnings
1	Paul Runyan	71-69-68-70—278	$2,000.00	T-21	Clarence Doser	73-73-73-72—291	$250.00	T-43	Frank Commisso	73-75-72-78—298	$100.00
T-2	Errie Ball	69-70-71-71—281	$1,233.33	T-23	J.B. Barfield	71-72-73-76—292	$250.00	T-43	Edmond Onoretta	73-75-78-72—298	$100.00
T-2	Dutch Harrison	71-67-71-72—281	$1,233.33	T-23	Mike Demassey	72-73-76-71—292	$230.00	T-43	Michael Rooney	73-72-74-79—298	$100.00
T-2	Joe Brown	69-67-71-74—281	$1,233.33	T-23	Lester Dunn	74-72-73-73—292	$230.00	T-46	Henry Bontempo	76-76-77-70—299	$50.00
T-5	Jimmy Demaret	67-70-70-75—282	$750.00	T-23	Ivan Gantz	74-70-75-73—292	$230.00	T-46	Andy Gibson	70-77-74-78—299	$50.00
T-5	Charles Sheppard	66-71-73-72—282	$750.00	T-23	Leland Gibson	69-73-73-77—292	$230.00	T-46	Phil Greenwald	72-75-76-76—299	$50.00
T-7	Ellsworth Vines	71-69-71-72—283	$550.00	T-23	Bill Heinlein	73-71-76-72—292	$230.00	T-46	Walter Hall	73-73-76-77—299	$108.33
T-7	Bud Williamson	72-71-70-70—283	$550.00	T-29	Walter Kozak	73-67-77-76—293	$200.00	T-46	Cliff Settergren	76-73-72-78—299	$50.00
9	Harold Sanderson	70-67-73-74—284	$400.00	T-29	Tom Mahan Sr.	68-76-76-73—293	$200.00	T-46	Paul Yurick	74-75-76-74—299	$50.00
T-10	Harry Cooper	71-72-73-69—285	$375.00	T-29	Jack Ryan	72-72-77-72—293	$200.00	T-52	Charles Farlow	69-76-76-79—300	$50.00
T-10	Tod Menefee	72-71-70-72—285	$375.00	T-29	Denny Shute	79-71-73-70—293	$200.00	T-52	Johnny Holtz	75-70-78-77—300	$50.00
12	John Barnum	67-71-70-78—286	$350.00	T-33	Pat Abbott	71-75-74-74—294	$100.00	T-52	Todd Houck	72-75-76-77—300	$50.00
13	Henry Ransom	72-71-68-76—287	$350.00	T-33	Pete Burke	72-73-73-76—294	$150.00	T-52	Bill Kaiser	76-70-77-77—300	$50.00
T-14	Herman Barron	71-71-73-73—288	$300.00	T-33	Labron Harris Sr.	71-70-78-75—294	$100.00	T-56	Ferdie Catropa	73-77-73-78—301	$7.10
T-14	Eldon Briggs	72-71-75-70—288	$300.00	T-33	Gus Salerno	70-75-76-73—294	$100.00	T-56	Everett Comstock	71-79-75-76—301	$7.10
T-14	Vic Ghezzi	70-71-71-76—288	$300.00	T-33	Joe Zarhardt	72-74-76-72—294	$108.33	T-56	Al Feldman	77-73-75-76—301	$7.10
T-14	Jack Isaacs	72-72-68-76—288	$300.00	T-38	R.E. Barnes	73-69-77-76—295	$100.00	T-56	Frank Gelhot	72-78-75-76—301	$7.10
T-14	Buck White	72-70-70-76—288	$300.00	T-38	Denny Champagne	75-70-74-76—295	$100.00	T-56	John Jurus	76-74-75-76—301	$7.10
T-19	Jimmy Johnson	73-71-75-71—290	$300.00	T-40	Al Brosch	75-77-69-75—296	$100.00	T-56	Harry Nettelbladt	75-71-78-77—301	$108.33
T-19	Smiley Quick	70-77-72-71—290	$300.00	T-40	Tony Longo	75-72-72-77—296	$100.00	T-56	Lloyd Sparrow	70-76-80-75—301	$7.10
T-21	Noel B. Epperson	72-75-72-72—291	$250.00	42	Ralph Hutchison	72-76-73-76—297	$100.00	T-56	Orville White	74-75-77-75—301	$7.10

PGA SENIORS' CHAMPIONSHIP

1961

Six days of beautiful weather brought out 20,000 spectators who saw record scoring. After finishing second in his first two years of eligibility, Paul Runyan of La Jolla, Calif., earned his first PGA Seniors' Championship with a 10-under-par 278, the lowest 72-hole total ever, to finish three shots in front of runner-up Jimmy Demaret. Buck White of Greenwood, Miss., set a record with 63 in the opening round, but fell back to finish tied for 12th.

Champion:	Paul Runyan	
Site:	PGA National Golf Club, Dunedin, Fla.	
Date:	Feb. 14-19	
Par:	36-36—72	**Purse:** $15,000

TOURNAMENT SUMMARY*

Place	Name	Score	Winnings**	Place	Name	Score	Winnings	Place	Name	Score	Winnings
1	Paul Runyan	67-70-72-69—278	$1,500.00	T-19	Frank Kringle	71-72-74-74—291	$150.00	T-39	Jack Isaacs	72-70-77-77—296	$50.00
2	Jimmy Demaret	69-71-72-69—281	$1,000.00	T-19	George Smith	67-74-75-75—291	$150.00	T-39	Gene Kunes Sr.	72-74-75-75—296	$50.00
3	Clarence Doser	68-67-72-75—282	$750.00	T-23	Eldon Briggs	68-75-72-77—292	$100.00	T-39	Bill Mehlhorn	68-74-77-77—296	$50.00
4	Joe Brown	70-69-76-68—283	$650.00	T-23	Walter Kozak	72-77-69-74—292	$100.00	T-44	Henry Bontempo	70-70-78-79—297	$50.00
5	Ivan Gantz	70-69-73-72—284	$550.00	T-23	Alvin Krueger	72-73-77-70—292	$100.00	T-44	Mortie Dutra	71-70-77-79—297	$175.00
T-6	Leland Gibson	71-70-73-71—285	$450.00	T-23	Tod Menefee	75-67-79-71—292	$100.00	T-44	Charles Onoretta	74-76-75-72—297	$50.00
T-6	Dick Shoemaker	73-70-72-70—285	$450.00	T-23	Bert Montresser	72-72-74-74—292	$100.00	T-44	Michael Rooney	73-71-81-72—297	$50.00
T-8	Pete Burke	68-69-78-71—286	$300.00	28	August Nordone	74-69-75-75—293	$100.00	T-44	Joe Zarhardt	70-76-76-75—297	$50.00
T-8	Labron Harris Sr.	69-71-75-71—286	$300.00	T-29	Frank Gelhot	73-71-79-71—294	$100.00	T-49	Eddie Axtell	75-74-75-74—298	$10.00
T-8	Toney Penna	71-72-74-69—286	$300.00	T-29	Jerry Gianferante	70-75-73-76—294	$100.00	T-49	J.B. Barfield	71-75-80-72—298	$50.00
11	Errie Ball	68-75-73-71—287	$200.00	T-29	Bill Goldbeck	68-71-74-81—294	$250.00	T-49	Ted Bickel	75-69-75-79—298	$62.50
T-12	Jack Ryan	72-74-70-72—288	$200.00	T-29	Walter Hall	72-68-78-76—294	$225.00	T-49	Joseph Burch	71-80-73-74—298	$10.00
T-12	Harold Sanderson	70-70-74-74—288	$225.00	T-29	Al Huske	69-74-77-74—294	$100.00	T-49	Jake Fondren	71-76-78-73—298	$10.00
T-12	Bob Shave	70-72-74-72—288	$200.00	T-34	Ole B. Clark	74-68-77-76—295	$100.00	T-49	Sterling Johnson	73-71-81-73—298	$10.00
T-12	Buck White	63-73-78-74—288	$200.00	T-34	Everett Comstock	68-76-77-74—295	$83.33	T-49	Leonard Ruck	66-77-78-77—298	$10.00
T-16	John Jurus	70-71-71-77—289	$175.00	T-34	Mike Demassey	74-72-75-74—295	$83.33	T-49	Denny Shute	73-73-80-72—298	$50.00
T-16	Tony Longo	72-69-73-75—289	$175.00	T-34	Gene Sarazen	71-70-78-76—295	$150.00				
T-18	Dick Metz	67-74-78-71—290	$150.00	T-34	Wayne Timberman	73-69-75-78—295	$83.33				
T-19	Sam Bernardi	69-70-76-76—291	$150.00	T-39	Louis Chiapetta	69-79-75-73—296	$50.00				
T-19	Charles Congdon	73-71-74-73—291	$150.00	T-39	Phil Greenwald	74-74-73-75—296	$50.00				

1960

Prize money was boosted to $15,000, and the winner among 315 contestants, Dick Metz of New Orleans, La., received $1,500. He won by five strokes with a 4-under-par 284. Tied for second were Tony Longo, trick-shot artist from Clark's Summit, Pa., and for the second year in a row, Paul Runyan of La Jolla, Calif. For the first time, two holes-in-one were made in the same Championship. Augie Nordone aced the 156-yard sixth hole with a 4-iron, and Mike Serino holed a 4-iron on the 192-yard 16th.

Champion:	Dick Metz	
Site:	PGA National Golf Club, Dunedin, Fla.	
Date:	Jan. 26-31	
Par:	36-36—72	**Purse:** $15,000

TOURNAMENT SUMMARY*

Place	Name	Score	Winnings**	Place	Name	Score	Winnings	Place	Name	Score	Winnings
1	Dick Metz	71-70-73-70—284	$1,500.00	T-14	Al Watrous	71-75-74-77—297	$225.00	T-32	Michael Serino	69-76-77-80—302	$67.00
T-2	Tony Longo	74-72-71-72—289	$875.00	T-18	Herman Barron	73-74-76-75—298	$135.00	T-32	Bob Stupple	73-73-80-76—302	$67.00
T-2	Paul Runyan	71-75-70-73—289	$875.00	T-18	Sam Bernardi	75-74-73-76—298	$135.00	T-35	Jules Blanton	74-76-79-74—303	$50.00
4	Charles Sheppard	68-72-78-72—290	$650.00	T-18	Sam Byrd	73-75-77-73—298	$135.00	T-35	John Capebianco	75-73-75-80—303	$50.00
5	Charles Farlow	72-66-74-79—291	$550.00	T-18	Tod Menefee	72-73-74-79—298	$135.00	T-35	Bill Goldbeck	74-76-78-75—303	$50.00
6	Leland Gibson	68-75-75-74—292	$500.00	T-18	Denny Shute	72-75-76-75—298	$135.00	T-35	Al Huske	74-77-77-75—303	$50.00
T-7	Willie Goggin	72-73-72-76—293	$375.00	T-18	Ock Willoweit	73-74-78-73—298	$135.00	T-35	Gib Sellers	75-74-74-80—303	$50.00
T-7	Jack Isaacs	73-74-71-75—293	$375.00	T-24	J.B. Barfield	72-74-77-76—299	$100.00	T-40	Joby Connor	78-76-73-77—304	$35.00
T-9	Pete Burke	70-75-74-75—294	$275.00	T-24	Andrew Gibson	74-75-77-73—299	$100.00	T-40	Frank Gelhot	76-78-75-75—304	$35.00
T-9	Clarence Doser	76-71-73-74—294	$275.00	T-24	Al Zimmerman	74-74-76-75—299	$100.00	T-40	Walter Kozak	73-74-79-78—304	$35.00
T-11	Ivan Gantz	75-76-70-74—295	$200.00	27	Mortie Dutra	72-74-77-77—300	$225.00	T-40	Joe Mozel	75-71-80-78—304	$35.00
T-11	Harold Sanderson	72-75-74-74—295	$200.00	T-28	Mike Demassey	71-79-76-75—301	$100.00	T-40	Al Polagyi	74-76-76-78—304	$35.00
13	Charles Congdon	74-76-73-73—296	$200.00	T-28	Gunnard Johnson	76-75-75-75—301	$100.00	T-40	Lloyd Sparrow	70-76-77-81—304	$35.00
T-14	Jerry Gianferante	72-75-74-76—297	$185.00	T-28	Bert Montresser	73-77-75-76—301	$100.00	T-40	Cleavy Spence	71-76-76-81—304	$35.00
T-14	Labron Harris Sr.	74-75-76-72—297	$185.00	T-28	J.P. (Sonny) Rouse	75-74-77-75—301	$100.00	T-40	Edward Tabor	78-75-74-77—304	$35.00
T-14	Jack Patroni	71-73-76-77—297	$185.00	T-32	Bill Kaiser	74-76-78-74—302	$67.00	T-40	John Watson	75-77-73-79—304	$35.00

242

1959

Only one of the past winners, the late Jack Burke Sr. (1941), was missing from the field in the 20th anniversary PGA Seniors' Championship. Willie Goggin won with a 4-under-par 284. Goggin used a borrowed set of woods, as he couldn't get comfortable with those he'd brought from California. Tied for second, a stroke behind Goggin, were Leland Gibson, Paul Runyan and Denny Shute.

Champion:	Willie Goggin
Site:	PGA National Golf Club, Dunedin, Fla.
Date:	Jan. 27-Feb. 1
Par: 36-36—72	Purse: $10,000

TOURNAMENT SUMMARY*

Place	Name	Score	Winnings**	Place	Name	Score	Winnings
1	Willie Goggin	71-71-70-72—284	$1,200.00	T-23	Charles Sheppard	72-72-74-76—294	$30.00
T-2	Leland Gibson	69-70-73-73—285	$633.25	T-23	Frank Strazza	74-77-69-74—294	$30.00
T-2	Paul Runyan	72-68-73-72—285	$633.25	T-26	Pete Burke	76-73-74-72—295	$26.50
T-2	Denny Shute	72-70-71-72—285	$633.25	T-26	Andy Gibson	71-74-77-73—295	$26.50
5	Clarence Doser	74-67-74-71—286	$400.00	T-26	Al Huske	69-73-82-71—295	$26.50
6	Dick Metz	67-71-77-72—287	$350.00	T-29	Sam Byrd	75-72-75-74—296	$25.00
7	Harold Sanderson	74-69-75-70—288	$300.00	T-29	Alvin Krueger	73-76-75-72—296	$25.00
8	Joseph Burch	72-72-73-72—289	$250.00	T-29	Al Watrous	77-72-74-73—296	$25.00
T-9	J.B. Barfield	76-69-74-71—290	$137.50	T-32	Sam Bernardi	77-76-73-71—297	$25.00
T-9	Ivan Gantz	72-72-73-73—290	$137.50	T-32	Henry Bontempo	74-74-75-74—297	$25.00
T-9	Tod Menefee	71-72-75-72—290	$137.50	T-32	August Nordone	75-73-74-75—297	$25.00
T-9	Michael Serino	72-73-70-75—290	$137.50	T-32	Tommy Shannon	75-69-78-75—297	$25.00
T-13	Frank Gelhot	75-70-69-77—291	$87.50	T-36	Billy Burke	74-72-75-77—298	$25.00
T-13	Bill Goldbeck	71-69-76-75—291	$225.00	T-36	Joseph Connor	76-72-74-76—298	$20.00
T-13	Labron Harris Sr.	73-74-73-71—291	$87.50	T-36	Wilson Crain	76-77-74-71—298	$20.00
T-13	Jack Isaacs	66-75-77-73—291	$87.50	T-36	Mortie Dutra	75-75-78-70—298	$20.00
T-13	Jack Ryan	71-72-77-71—291	$87.50	T-36	Charles Farlow	76-69-78-75—298	$20.00
T-18	Pat Circelli	75-70-70-77—292	$50.00	T-36	Walter Hall	75-77-72-74—298	$20.00
T-18	Jack Patroni	72-70-75-75—292	$50.00	T-36	Bill Kaiser	75-76-71-76—298	$20.00
T-18	Ock Willoweit	70-74-71-77—292	$50.00	T-36	George Meyers	76-74-76-72—298	$20.00
T-21	Denny Champagne	73-73-76-71—293	$50.00	T-36	Gene Sarazen	73-77-77-71—298	$20.00
T-21	Melvin Hemphill	76-75-68-74—293	$50.00	T-36	Bob Stupple	73-73-75-77—298	$20.00
T-23	Tony Manero	72-77-75-70—294	$30.00	T-36	Tony Longo	77-74-73-75—299	$20.00

1958

Two more benchmarks were established that helped bring the 19th PGA Seniors' Championship into the major arena — a $10,000 purse and 72 holes of competition, with a 36-hole cut made to the low 100 players and ties. "Squire" Gene Sarazen earned his second title with an even-par 288 for a 3-stroke win over Charles Sheppard of West Newton, Mass. For his victory, Sarazen received $1,200.

Champion:	Gene Sarazen
Site:	PGA National Golf Club, Dunedin, Fla.
Date:	Jan. 28-Feb. 2
Par: 36-36—72	Purse: $10,000

TOURNAMENT SUMMARY*

Place	Name	Score	Winnings**	Place	Name	Score	Winnings
1	Gene Sarazen	73-71-74-70—288	$1,200.00	T-11	Harold Sanderson	75-75-74-72—296	$95.00
2	Charles Sheppard	70-71-75-75—291	$800.00	T-16	Sam Bernardi	75-72-72-78—297	$56.25
T-3	Bill Black	70-75-73-75—293	$550.00	T-16	Sam Byrd	77-74-72-74—297	$56.25
T-3	Eddie Burke	73-70-72-78—293	$550.00	T-16	Bob Stupple	70-75-73-79—297	$56.25
5	Jules Blanton	73-74-75-72—294	$400.00	T-16	Joe Zarhardt	76-74-70-77—297	$56.25
T-6	Mortie Dutra	69-71-73-82—295	$250.00	T-20	Eddie Axtell	77-71-77-73—298	$35.00
T-6	Tony Manero	76-71-75-73—295	$250.00	T-20	J.B. Barfield	76-72-75-75—298	$35.00
T-6	Bert Montresser	72-72-77-74—295	$250.00	T-20	Ivan Gantz	79-71-74-74—298	$35.00
T-6	Jack Patroni	77-74-72-72—295	$250.00	T-20	Gunnard Johnson	76-78-72-72—298	$38.25
T-6	Al Watrous	74-73-74-74—295	$250.00	T-20	Tom Mahan Sr.	77-72-79-70—298	$35.00
T-11	Fay Coleman	71-72-76-77—296	$95.00	T-20	Harry Nettelbladt	81-72-70-75—298	$35.00
T-11	Sal Dibuono	75-73-73-75—296	$95.00	T-26	Alvin Krueger	74-73-75-77—299	$30.00
T-11	Len Mattson	76-74-75-71—296	$95.00	T-26	Joe Turnesa	74-76-72-77—299	$70.00
T-11	Jack Ryan	77-70-73-76—296	$95.00				

1957

Remodeling the clubhouse and improved conditioning of the golf course had been accomplished since the previous year's PGA Seniors' Championship. Al Watrous returned to the winner's circle, beating Bob Stupple in an 18-hole playoff after they tied at 210. In the playoff, Watrous recorded a 72 while Stupple posted a 75.

	Champion:	Al Watrous
Site:	PGA National Golf Club, Dunedin, Fla.	
Date:	Jan. 29-Feb. 3	
Par:	36-36—72	**Purse:** $8,000

TOURNAMENT SUMMARY*

Place	Name	Score	Winnings**	Place	Name	Score	Winnings
1	Al Watrous	71-68-71—210	$1,000.00	T-8	Pete Burke	217—217	$100.00
2	Bob Stupple	210—210	$700.00	T-8	Tony Guimelli	217—217	$100.00
T-3	J.B. Barfield	211—211	$350.00	T-8	Maurie O'Connor	217—217	$100.00
T-3	Willie Goggin	211—211	$350.00	T-11	Reggie Myles	218—218	$50.00
T-3	Jack Ryan	211—211	$350.00	T-11	Harry Nettelbladt	218—218	$50.00
T-6	Ed Dudley	216—216	$125.00	T-11	Guy Paulsen	218—218	$50.00
T-6	Bert Montresser	216—216	$125.00	T-11	Denny Shute	218—218	$50.00

1956

The PGA Seniors' Championship purse increased to $6,500 and the field topped 200 for the first time. Long Island professional Pete Burke, brother of 1931 U.S. Open Champion Billy Burke, finished one shot ahead of Ock Willoweit. The finish wasn't easy for Burke, who had a pair of opening 70s and appeared to be coasting to victory. But with a double-bogey on the 52nd hole, he was forced to par the last two holes to tie Willoweit, who was in the clubhouse with a 216 total. After making par on the 53rd hole, Burke hooked his drive into the trees on the final hole. After a spectacular second shot, which he hooked around the trees to within 12 feet of the hole, Burke sank the putt to win the first-place check of $1,000.

	Champion:	Pete Burke
Site:	PGA National Golf Club, Dunedin, Fla.	
Date:	Jan. 23-29	
Par:	36-36—72	**Purse:** $6,500

TOURNAMENT SUMMARY*

Place	Name	Score	Winnings**	Place	Name	Score	Winnings
1	Pete Burke	70-70-75—215	$1,000.00	T-15	Fay Coleman	74-73-77—224	$75.00
2	Ock Willoweit	73-68-75—216	$500.00	T-15	Harry Nettelbladt	71-77-76—224	$31.67
3	Joe Zarhardt	73-72-72—217	$350.00	T-15	Joe Turnesa	75-74-75—224	$20.00
T-4	Bill Black	68-76-75—219	$200.00	T-18	George Aulbach	73-74-78—225	$75.00
T-4	Frank Strazza	71-71-77—219	$200.00	T-18	Ted Bickel	75-77-73—225	$10.00
T-6	Mortie Dutra	70-75-75—220	$200.00	T-18	Billy Burke	72-73-80—225	$150.00
T-6	Bill Goldbeck	75-72-73—220	$150.00	T-18	Olin Dutra	75-73-77—225	$100.00
T-8	Denny Shute	73-75-73—221	$125.00	T-18	Maurie O'Connor	76-73-76—225	$20.00
T-8	George Whitehead	78-73-70—221	$125.00	T-23	Reggie Myles	71-76-79—226	$75.00
T-10	J.B. Barfield	76-71-75—222	$100.00	T-23	Al Watrous	75-76-75—226	$35.00
T-10	Tony Manero	73-75-74—222	$100.00	T-25	Jules Blanton	73-75-79—227	$31.67
T-12	Ed Dudley	73-77-73—223	$100.00	T-25	Roy Brondson	76-75-76—227	$20.00
T-12	Tom Mahan Sr.	73-73-77—223	$100.00	T-25	Denny Champagne	78-76-73—227	
T-12	Gene Sarazen	77-74-72—223	$100.00	T-25	Harry Cooper	75-80-72—22	

> * *Only available summaries; some purses unavailable.*
>
> ** *Some tournament lists from 1956-76 include money awarded from special events taking place within the Championship. This accounts for money totals that don't necessarily reflect a player's finish in the final standings.*

1955

Mortie Dutra, 55, of Los Angeles, Calif., played a steady game, including the last five holes in the final round at 1-under-par, to earn his first national title with a 3-under-par 213, and a four-stroke victory. Tied for second at 217 were defending Champion Gene Sarazen, Denny Shute and Mike Murra. With seven birdies and a 31 on the back nine, Murra equaled the course record with a 6-under-par 66 in the opening round.

Champion:	Mortie Dutra	
Site:	PGA National Golf Club, Dunedin, Fla.	
Date:	Jan. 28-30	
Par:	36-36—72	**Purse:** $5,000

TOURNAMENT SUMMARY* †

Place	Name	Score	Place	Name	Score
1	Mortie Dutra	70-71-72—213	T-8	Frank Strazza	73-73-76—222
T-2	Mike Murra	66-75-76—217	T-8	Joe Turnesa	75-72-75—222
T-2	Gene Sarazen	72-74-71—217	T-8	Al Watrous	71-75-76—222
T-2	Denny Shute	72-70-75—217	T-14	Ralph Beach	73-80-70—223
5	Louis Chiapetta	71-70-77—218	T-14	Albert MacDonald	75-74-74—223
T-6	Harry Cooper	70-76-75—221	T-14	Joe Mozel	78-72-73—223
T-6	Ock Willoweit	75-73-73—221	17	Clarence Owen	73-80-71—224
T-8	Jules Blanton	70-73-79—222	T-18	George Aulbach	76-77-72—225
T-8	Billy Burke	73-73-76—222	T-18	Joe Belfore	73-78-74—225
T-8	Harold Sanderson	69-78-75—222	T-18	Willie Hunter	77-75-73—225

1954

Returning to the Championship's original 54-hole format of 1937, Wm. Teacher & Sons Ltd. of Glasgow, Scotland, provided a $5,000 purse, with competition being expanded to three rounds. Gene Sarazen of Germantown, N.Y., posted a 2-under-par 214, winning by two over former winner Al Watrous and Perry Del Vecchio. Sarazen earned $1,000 for the win that was witnessed by 5,000 spectators during the final round.

Champion:	Gene Sarazen	
Site:	PGA National Golf Club, Dunedin, Fla.	
Date:	Jan. 28-30	
Par:	36-36—72	**Purse:** $5,000

TOURNAMENT SUMMARY* †

Place	Name	Score	Place	Name	Score
1	Gene Sarazen	67-72-75—214	13	Jim Foulis	72-73-80—225
T-2	Perry Del Vecchio	72-71-73—216	T-14	Louis Chiapetta	75-77-74—226
T-2	Al Watrous	70-72-74—216	T-14	Bill Jelliffe	74-77-75—226
4	John Watson	76-69-74—219	T-14	Gunnard Johnson	79-77-70—226
5	Eddie Williams	73-70-77—220	T-14	Charles McKenna	76-74-76—226
6	Montie Dutra	69-73-79—221	T-14	Harry Schwab	73-78-75—226
T-7	Bill Goldbeck	76-73-74—223	19	Ralph Beach	75-75-77—227
T-7	Willie Hunter	71-78-74—223	20	Tom Mahan Sr.	77-77-74—228
T-7	Reggie Myles	71-74-78—223	T-21	Johnny Farrell	75-75-79—229
T-7	Harold Sanderson	75-74-74—223	T-21	Walter Hall	78-74-77—229
T-11	Jules Blanton	75-74-75—224	T-21	Frank Sprogell	72-78-79—229
T-11	Mike Murra	74-73-77—224	T-21	Ock Willoweit	74-78-77—229

† *Money list unavailable*

1953

The PGA Seniors' Championship received a boost in prestige when three former U.S. Open titleholders, Gene Sarazen, Johnny Farrell and Billy Burke, played for the first time. Sarazen performed best with 72-73 — 145, tying for second with former Seniors' Champion Charles McKenna, three strokes behind Harry Schwab of Dayton, Ohio. Schwab set a tournament record with a 6-under-par 66 in the first round.

Champion:	Harry Schwab	
Site:	PGA National Golf Club,	
	Dunedin, Fla.	
Date:	Jan. 29-31	
Par:	36-36—72	

TOURNAMENT SUMMARY* †

Place	Name	Score	Place	Name	Score
1	Harry Schwab	66-76—142	22	Fred Moore	78-77—155
T-2	Charles McKenna	72-73—145	T-23	Walter Bourne	78-78—156
T-2	Gene Sarazen	72-73—145	T-23	Mike Brady	79-77—156
T-4	Ralph Beach	73-73—146	T-23	Dave Hendry	77-79—156
T-4	Bill Goldbeck	75-71—146	T-23	Clyde Kelly	78-78—156
T-4	John Watson	73-73—146	T-23	John Rogers	74-82—156
7	Al Watrous	75-72—147	T-23	Joe Turnesa	78-78—156
8	Billy Burke	73-75—148	T-23	Eddie Williams	82-74—156
T-9	Jules Blanton	74-75—149	T-23	Jack Williams	76-80—156
T-9	Lloyd Gullickson	73-76—149	T-31	Louis Chiapetta	80-77—157
T-11	Lou Galby	75-75—150	T-31	Marshall Crichton	75-82—157
T-11	Bill Jelliffe	78-72—150	T-31	Jack Gordon	79-78—157
T-11	George Smith	75-75—150	T-31	Henry Miller	80-77—157
T-14	Walter Hall	75-76—151	T-31	Ben Richter	81-76—157
T-14	Gunnard Johnson	75-76—151	T-36	Harold Callaway	82-76—158
T-16	Albert MacDonald	77-75—152	T-36	Jock Hutchison	79-79—158
T-16	Tom Mahan Sr.	77-75—152	T-36	Charles Lorms	79-79—158
18	Willie Whalen	78-75—153	T-39	Joel Smith	79-80—159
T-19	Johnny Farrell	76-78—154	T-39	Phil Turnesa	80-79—159
T-19	Bert Montresser	77-77—154	T-39	Alex Watson	79-80—159
T-19	Frank Walsh	77-77—154			

1952

Unheralded Ernie Newnham of Portland, Maine, denied Al Watrous' bid to win a third straight PGA Seniors' Championship, as Newnham's 2-over-par 146 was good for a one-stroke victory. In a four-way tie for third were Charlie McKenna, Rochester, N.Y.; Louis Chiapetta, Sylvania, Ohio; Harry Schwab, Dayton, Ohio; and Phil Turnesa, White Plains, N.Y.

Champion:	Ernie Newnham	
Site:	PGA National Golf Club,	
	Dunedin, Fla.	
Date:	Jan. 25-26	
Par:	36-36—72	

TOURNAMENT SUMMARY* †

Place	Name	Score	Place	Name	Score
1	Ernest Newnham	75-71—146	T-17	John Bird	78-75—153
2	Al Watrous	75-72—147	T-17	Ed Dudley	80-73—153
T-3	Louis Chiapetta	78-70—148	T-17	Lloyd Gullickson	72-81—153
T-3	Charles McKenna	76-72—148	T-17	Elwyn Nagel	77-76—153
T-3	Harry Schwab	73-75—148	T-17	Joe Turnesa	77-76—153
T-3	Phil Turnesa	75-73—148	T-17	Willie Whalen	74-79—153
T-7	Tom Harmon	73-76—149	T-23	Harold Callaway	79-75—154
T-7	Maurice White	74-75—149	T-23	E.W. (Pop) Harbert	77-77—154
T-7	Jack Williams	78-71—149	T-23	Albert MacDonald	154—154
10	Cy Foster	70-80—150	T-23	Ben Richter	75-79—154
11	Bill Jelliffe	75-76—151	27	Frank Belwood	160—160
T-12	W.C. (Bill) Gordon	79-73—152	28	Jock Hutchison	161—161
T-12	Charles Lorms	80-72—152	29	George Livingston	162—162
T-12	Charles Mayo	75-77—152	30	Thomas Clark	172—172
T-12	Willie Ogg	76-76—152	31	W.H. (Bert) Way	199—199
T-12	George Smith	75-77—152			

1951

For the fourth time in 12 years, the PGA Seniors' Championship went to a playoff, and for the third time, Jock Hutchison was beaten. Though he was 68 years old, Hutchison nearly shot his age, a 3-under-par 69, in the final round to tie Al Watrous at 142.

In the playoff, fatigue caught up with Hutchison, the two-time former PGA Seniors' Champion, on the final nine. He had 37-44 — 81, losing to Watrous by six.

Champion:	Al Watrous
Site:	PGA National Golf Club, Dunedin, Fla.
Date:	Jan. 8-13
Par:	36-36—72

TOURNAMENT SUMMARY* †

Place	Name	Score	Place	Name	Score
1	Al Watrous	69-73—142	T-9	Ernest Newnham	150—150
2	Jock Hutchison	73-69—142	T-9	Ben Richter	150—150
3	Charles McKenna	71-75—146	T-9	Phil Turnesa	150—150
4	Eddie Williams	70-77—147	T-13	Lloyd Gullickson	151—151
5	George Smith	73-75—148	T-13	Alex Watson	151—151
T-6	Louis Chiapetta	149—149	T-13	Art Weber	151—151
T-6	Bill Jelliffe	149—149	14	Jim Wilson	80-81—161
T-6	Jack Williams	149—149	15	George Livingston	82-80—162
T-9	Pat Doyle	150—150			

1950

Al Watrous of Birmingham, Mich., was the overall winner, with a 2-under-par 142 total for his first of three titles. Bearded Bill Jellife of Denver, Colo., was the runner-up, three back of Watrous.

Champion:	Al Watrous
Site:	PGA National Golf Club, Dunedin, Fla.
Date:	Jan. 9-14
Par:	36-36—72

TOURNAMENT SUMMARY* †

Place	Name	Score	Place	Name	Score
1	Al Watrous	70-72—142	T-16	Art Andrews	79-76—155
2	Bill Jelliffe	74-71—145	T-16	Louis Chiapetta	77-78—155
3	Jock Hutchison	75-72—147	T-16	Albert MacDonald	76-79—155
4	Bill Goldbeck	76-72—148	T-16	George Milne	74-81—155
5	H.T. (Pug) Allen	73-76—149	T-16	Ernest Newnham	80-75—155
T-6	George Smith	73-77—150	T-21	Al Heron	77-79—156
T-6	Eddie Williams	72-78—150	T-21	Herbert Lagerblade	82-74—156
T-8	Mike Brady	73-78—151	T-21	Bob Milar	82-74—156
T-8	Jack Williams	76-75—151	T-24	John Bird	78-79—157
T-10	Lloyd Gullickson	76-76—152	T-24	W.C. (Bill) Gordon	81-76—157
T-10	Alex Watson	76-76—152	T-24	Charles Mayo	78-79—157
T-12	Nelson Giddens	77-76—153	T-24	Jim Wilson	81-76—157
T-12	Bruce Herd	76-77—153	T-28	Matt Jans	78-80—158
T-12	Charles McKenna	76-77—153	T-28	Carroll Macmaster	75-83—158
15	W.W. (Abe) Forbrich	78-76—154	T-28	Willie Ogg	79-79—158

1949

Marshall Crichton of Durham, N.C., aced the 147-yard 16th hole en route to capturing the PGA Seniors' Championship title by one stroke. Crichton shot 1-over-par 145 and three players tied at 146: Louis Chiapetta of Sylvania, Ohio, George Smith of Chicago, Ill., and Jock Hutchison of Golf, Ill. Hutchison had a chance to tie for the lead, but bogeyed the final hole.

Champion:	Marshall Crichton	
Site:	PGA National Golf Club,	
	Dunedin, Fla.	
Date:	Jan. 10-15	
Par:	36-36—72	

TOURNAMENT SUMMARY* †

Place	Name	Score	Place	Name	Score
1	Marshall Crichton	73-72—145	T-17	Alex Ayton	154—154
T-2	Louis Chiapetta	72-74—146	T-17	Bill Campbell	154—154
T-2	Jock Hutchison	71-75—146	T-17	John Manion	154—154
T-2	George Smith	73-73—146	T-17	Jim McGunigal	154—154
T-5	Lloyd Gullickson	73-75—148	T-17	Fred Moore	154—154
T-5	Phil Turnesa	75-73—148	T-17	Frank Sprogell	154—154
T-7	John Bird	149—149	T-23	Herbert Lagerblade	155—155
T-7	Charles Mayo	149—149	T-23	Albert MacDonald	155—155
9	Mike Brady	150—150	T-23	L.W. (Smiley) Rowland	155—155
T-10	Ernest Newnham	151—151	T-23	Eddie Williams	155—155
T-10	Ben Richter	151—151	27	Charles McKenna	156—156
T-10	Alex Watson	151—151	T-28	Art Weber	156—156
T-13	Walter Bourne	152—152	T-28	Art Andrews	157—157
T-13	Jack Gordon	152—152	T-28	Bob Ford	157—157
T-13	Dave Sutherland	152—152	T-28	Bruce Herd	157—157
16	W.C. (Bill) Gordon	153—153	T-28	Willie Ogg	157—157

1948

Charles McKenna of Rochester, N.Y., won the title wire-to-wire. He was medalist in the first round with a 3-under-par 69, which was the lowest score of the tournament. In the final round, McKenna slipped to a 72, but none of the challengers were able to overcome his first-day advantage. Ben Richter made the strongest bid with a second-round 71 to take runner-up honors for the second year in a row. Defending Champion Jock Hutchison tied for third with George Smith of Lake Forest, Ill., posting 3-over-par 145 totals.

Champion:	Charles McKenna	
Site:	PGA National Golf Club,	
	Dunedin, Fla.	
Date:	Jan. 10-15	
Par:	36-36—72	

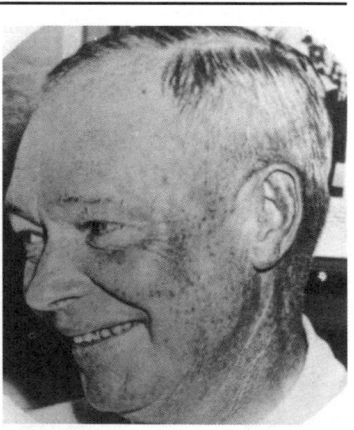

TOURNAMENT SUMMARY* †

Place	Name	Score	Place	Name	Score
1	Charles McKenna	69-72—141	T-8	Ernest Newnham	75-77—152
2	Ben Richter	71-71—142	T-12	Bob Ford	76-77—153
T-3	Jock Hutchison	73-72—145	T-12	W.C. (Bill) Gordon	80-73—153
T-3	George Smith	71-74—145	T-12	Frank Sprogell	78-75—153
5	Bill Jelliffe	72-74—146	T-15	Bill Campbell	77-77—154
6	Harold Jordan	73-74—147	T-15	Joe Donato	78-76—154
7	Dave Sutherland	72-78—150	T-15	John Manion	78-76—154
T-8	Walter Bourne	76-76—152	T-15	Phil Turnesa	78-76—154
T-8	Cy Foster	74-78—152	T-15	Alex Watson	77-77—154
T-8	Bruce Herd	78-74—152			

1947

Jock Hutchison got his revenge after finishing second the previous two years, duplicating his victory in the inaugural PGA Seniors' Championship 10 years earlier. Despite high winds, Hutchison fired a closing round of 1-under-par 71 for a 3-stroke victory over Ben Richter of St. Louis, Mo. Eddie Williams, looking for a fourth title, found himself in the running after an opening round 75, but shot 80 on the final round to break his streak of three consecutive PGA Seniors' Championships.

Champion: Jock Hutchison
Site: PGA National Golf Club, Dunedin, Fla.
Date: Jan. 6-11
Par: 36-36—72

TOURNAMENT SUMMARY* †

Place	Name	Score	Place	Name	Score
1	Jock Hutchison	74-71—145	T-16	W.C. (Bill) Gordon	157—157
2	Ben Richter	74-74—148	T-16	Fred Miley	78-79—157
3	Bill Jelliffe	75-76—151	T-19	Bill Bathie	158—158
T-4	Wendell Kay	77-76—153	T-19	John Manion	158—158
T-4	Charles Lorms	80-73—153	T-19	Ernest Newnham	158—158
T-4	Charles Mayo	80-73—153	T-19	Frank Sprogell	158—158
T-4	Willie Ogg	76-77—153	T-23	Fred Clarkson	80-79—159
T-4	Alex Watson	80-73—153	T-23	Tom Skipper	80-79—159
9	Dave Sutherland	76-78—154	T-25	Ernest Anderson	161—161
T-10	Joe Donato	155—155	T-25	James Young	161—161
T-10	Dick May	155—155	27	Ray McAulliffe	162—162
T-10	Eddie Williams	75-80—155	T-28	Marshall Crichton	163—163
T-13	Alex Ayton	78-78—156	T-28	Wilfred Reid	163—163
T-13	Charles Betschler	156—156	T-30	Frank Butler	164—164
T-13	Albert MacDonald	76-80—156	T-30	Andy Merrilees	164—164
T-16	Walter Bourne	80-77—157			

1946

Eddie Williams made it three PGA Seniors' titles in a row—a record that still stands—again coming from behind to beat former winner Jock Hutchison, this time in an 18-hole playoff. In regulation play, Hutchison was one shot ahead of Williams going into the 35th hole, but he bogeyed the hole. To get into the playoff, Williams was forced to make a 10-foot putt on the last hole. In the 18-hole playoff, both players were tied after 14 holes, but Hutchison hit a shot into the water on the 15th hole, and Williams made a birdie to claim victory.

Champion: Eddie Williams
Site: PGA National Golf Club, Dunedin, Fla.
Date: Jan. 7-8
Par: 36-36—72

TOURNAMENT SUMMARY* †

Place	Name	Score	Place	Name	Score
1	Eddie Williams	75-71—146	T-12	George Morris	79-76—155
2	Jock Hutchison	76-70—146	T-12	Willie Ogg	77-78—155
3	Dave Sutherland	75-72—147	T-12	Tom Pepin	76-79—155
4	Ben Richter	76-73—149	17	Joe Donato	79-77—156
5	Jack Williams	75-75—150	T-18	E.W. (Pop) Harbert	81-76—157
T-6	Alex Ayton	76-75—151	T-18	John Manion	77-80—157
T-6	Francis Gallett	75-76—151	T-18	George Norrie	80-77—157
T-8	Marshall Crichton	80-72—152	T-21	James Cockburn	78-80—158
T-8	Charles Lorms	76-76—152	T-21	Fred Miley	79-79—158
10	Ernest Anderson	77-76—153	T-23	Frank Coltart	80-79—159
T-11	Wilfred Reid	79-75—154	T-23	Ben Smith	78-81—159
T-11	Ab Thorn	79-75—154	25	Tom Bonnar	80-80—160
T-12	Wendell Kay	76-79—155			

1945

With World War II beginning to wind down, the PGA Seniors' Championship resumed, this time at Dunedin, Fla., which became the permanent home for the next 18 years. Eddie Williams retained the title he had held since his 1942 victory. Williams scored birdies on the last two holes in the final round to overcome a one-stroke advantage held by Jock Hutchison, who finished in second place.

Champion:	Eddie Williams
Site:	PGA National Golf Club, Dunedin, Fla.
Date:	Jan. 15-19
Par:	36-36—72

TOURNAMENT SUMMARY* †

Place	Name	Score	Place	Name	Score
1	Eddie Williams	148—148	13	W.H. Livie	162—162
2	Jock Hutchison	150—150	T-14	E.W. (Pop) Harbert	164—164
3	Charles Mayo	151—151	T-14	George Sargent	164—164
4	Charles Lorms	152—152	T-14	Tom Skipper	164—164
5	Wilfred Reid	154—154	T-14	Henry Williams Sr.	164—164
T-6	James Cockburn	155—155	18	Tom Pepin	166—166
T-6	L.W. (Smiley) Rowland	155—155	19	Ernest Anderson	167—167
8	Joe Donato	158—158	20	George Dodge	168—168
9	Marshall Crichton	159—159	21	W.H. (Bert) Way	175—175
10	Phillip Jefferson	160—160	22	William Crichton	176—176
T-11	George Norrie	161—161	T-23	Dave Cuthbert	177—177
T-11	Willie Ogg	161—161	T-23	William Scott	177—177

1943-44 No Championships played due to World War II

1942

The fifth PGA Seniors' Championship was played further south on Florida's west coast at the Fort Myers G&CC. Eddie Williams of Chicago, Ill., in his second bid for the title, having been runner-up the previous year, posted a pair of 69s for a 6-under-par 138, six strokes better than runner-up Jock Hutchison.

Champion:	Eddie Williams
Site:	Ft. Myers Golf and Country Club, Ft. Myers, Fla.
Date:	Jan. 17-18
Par:	36-36—72

TOURNAMENT SUMMARY* †

Place	Name	Score	Place	Name	Score
1	Eddie Williams	138—138	8	E.W. (Pop) Harbert	148—148
2	Jock Hutchison	144—144	9	Mike Brady	149—149
3	George Morris	145—145	10	Willie Dow	150—150
4	Wilfred Reid	146—146	11	H.C. Hackbarth	152—152
T-5	Marshall Crichton	147—147	12	Charles Mayo	153—153
T-5	W.H. Livie	147—147	13	William Sherwood	156—156
T-5	Milton Theobald	147—147	14	W.H. (Bert) Way	179—179

1941

With a final round of 4-under-par 67 over the Bobby Jones course, Jack Burke of Houston, Texas, cruised to a 7-stroke victory over runner-up Eddie Williams of Chicago, Ill.

Champion:	Jack Burke
Site:	Sarasota Bay Country Club,
	Bobby Jones Golf Club, Sarasota, Fla.
Date:	Jan. 10-12
Par:	35-36—71

TOURNAMENT SUMMARY* †

Place	Name	Score	Place	Name	Score
1	Jack Burke Sr.	75-67—142	T-8	Willie Ogg	83-70—153
2	Eddie Williams	75-74—149	T-8	Alex Taylor	79-74—153
T-3	Jack Gordon	76-74—150	10	George Sargent	79-75—154
T-3	H.C. Hackbarth	77-73—150	11	Gil Nichols	82-75—157
T-3	Jock Hutchison	77-73—150	12	Jack Campbell	83-76—159
T-6	Jim Barnes	77-74—151	13	W.H. (Bert) Way	88-82—170
T-6	Fred McLeod	80-71—151			

1940

In an attempt to find better weather, the third PGA Seniors' Championship was played at the North Shore and Bobby Jones Courses in Sarasota, Fla., in January 1940, which meant no tournament during the calendar year of 1939. After regulation play, Otto Hackbarth, with a closing round 1-under-par 70, tied Jock Hutchison at 4-over-par 146. In the 18-hole playoff, both players shot 74, which forced a second 18-hole playoff in which Hackbarth prevailed by one stroke.

Champion:	Otto Hackbarth
Site:	North Shore Country Club,
	Bobby Jones Golf Club, Sarasota, Fla.
Date:	Jan. 12-14
Par:	35-36—71

TOURNAMENT SUMMARY* †

Place	Name	Score	Place	Name	Score
1	Otto Hackbarth	76-70—146	T-16	Willie Ogg	81-74—155
2	Jock Hutchison	71-75—146	T-24	George Sargent	80-76—156
T-3	Charles Mayo	75-73—148	T-24	William Sherwood	81-75—156
T-3	Fred Miley	73-75—148	T-24	Henry Williams Sr.	81-75—156
T-5	Jim Barnes	78-71—149	T-27	John Black	81-76—157
T-5	Jack Campbell	77-72—149	T-27	Thomas Clark	76-81—157
T-7	Mike Brady	78-73—151	T-27	Arthur Reid	78-79—157
T-7	George Morris	76-75—151	T-30	Dick Clarkson	74-85—159
T-7	Milton Theobald	78-73—151	T-30	Alex Cunningham	78-81—159
T-10	Willie Maguire	76-76—152	T-32	John Inglis	82-78—160
T-10	Fred McLeod	74-78—152	T-32	Wilfred Reid	75-85—160
T-12	E.W. (Pop) Harbert	77-76—153	T-32	Tom Skipper	78-82—160
T-12	Dave McKay	79-74—153	35	W.C. (Bill) Gordon	87-76—163
T-12	Dave Ogilvie	76-77—153	36	Ernest Anderson	82-83—165
T-12	James Young	80-73—153	T-37	William Crichton	82-84—166
T-16	Tom Bannar	80-75—155	T-37	Alex Ogilvie	86-80—166
T-16	Howard Beckett	77-78—155	T-39	Frank Butler	84-83—167
T-16	Frank Coltart	77-78—155	T-39	Dave Cuthbert	86-81—167
T-16	Bob Craigs	79-76—155	T-41	Jack Jolly	86-84—170
T-16	George Dodge	79-76—155	T-41	William Lock	82-88—170
T-16	Al Grauer	78-77—155	43	W.H. (Bert) Way	92-87—179
T-16	Walter Hoe	77-78—155	44	Val Flood	94-91—185

1938

Fred McLeod won an 18-hole playoff to capture the second PGA Seniors' Championship at Augusta National, 30 years after his U.S. Open triumph and 20 years after his loss in the finals of the second PGA Championship.

Champion:	Fred McLeod
Site:	Augusta National Golf Club, Augusta, Ga.
Date:	Dec. 5-7
Par:	36-36—72

After its inaugural year, the Championship was changed to a 36-hole format. Played in December in inclement weather, McLeod of Chevy Chase, Md., shot 75-79 to tie Otto Hackbarth of Cincinnati, Ohio, with 154 after three days, as one round was rained out. In the playoff, McLeod defeated Hackbarth 80 to 82.

TOURNAMENT SUMMARY* †

Place	Name	Score	Place	Name	Score
1	Fred McLeod	75-79—154	21	Jack Kennedy	84-81—165
2	Otto Hackbarth	80-74—154	T-22	Tom Boyd	82-84—166
3	Frank Belwood	76-81—157	T-22	George Dodge	81-85—166
T-4	Jock Hutchison	75-83—158	T-22	Charles Hall	81-85—166
T-4	Dave Ogilvie	79-79—158	T-22	Jack Pirie	87-79—166
T-6	Frank Caltart	81-78—159	T-26	William Crichton	84-83—167
T-6	E.W. (Pop) Harbert	80-79—159	T-26	Milton Theobald	81-86—167
8	Jack Campbell	79-81—160	T-28	W.C. (Bill) Gordon	86-84—170
T-9	Bob Craigs	80-81—161	T-28	Fred Miley	83-87—170
T-9	George Gordon	82-79—161	T-28	Arthur Reid	91-79—170
T-9	Dave Livie	79-82—161	31	Dick Clarkson	87-86—173
T-9	William Sherwood	81-80—161	T-32	Fred Brand	88-86—174
T-13	Alex Armour	83-79—162	T-32	William Entwistle	84-90—174
T-13	Charles Mayo	81-81—162	34	William Gourlay	86-91—177
T-13	George Sargent	83-79—162	35	Peter Robertson	88-91—179
T-16	Thomas Clark	82-81—163	36	Henry Williams Sr.	89-91—180
T-16	John Inglis	79-84—163	T-37	J.H. Chandler	96-89—185
T-18	Tom Bonnar	80-84—164	T-37	Dave Cuthbert	93-92—185
T-18	Jack Hobens	83-81—164	38	Jack Jolly	96-91—187
T-18	James West	80-84—164			

1937

Thanks to Bobby Jones and Alfred S. Bourne, the first PGA Seniors' Championship was played at Augusta National. Jones hosted the event on the Georgia golf course where the Masters began four years earlier. Bourne,

Champion:	Jock Hutchison
Site:	Augusta National Golf Club, Augusta, Ga.
Date:	Nov. 30-Dec. 2
Par:	36-36—72

called a "sportsman and friend of the pros," contributed $1,500 for the purchase and endowment of a trophy that bears his name. The winner was Jock Hutchison of Golf, Ill., with a three-round total of 223. George Gordon, from Rumford, R.I., had the second-best total, finishing eight shots back of Hutchison.

TOURNAMENT SUMMARY* †

Place	Name	Score	Place	Name	Score
1	Jock Hutchison	76-75-72—223	T-16	William Sherwood	81-81-82—244
2	George Gordon	81-77-73—231	18	George Savers	84-83-78—245
3	Jim West	77-78-78—233	T-19	Alex Campbell	77-80-89—246
T-4	Fred McLeod	76-79-79—234	T-19	John Inglis	83-79-84—246
T-4	Dave Ogilvie	75-80-79—234	T-21	Grange Alves	79-84-85—248
6	Charles Mayo	80-76-79—235	T-21	Jack Hobens	80-86-82—248
7	Charles Hall	75-82-79—236	T-21	George Low	80-86-82—248
8	Tom Boyd	75-82-80—237	24	Thomas Clark	84-78-89—251
9	Tom Skipper	79-79-80—238	25	Jack Jolly	86-84-87—257
T-10	Mike Brady	78-79-82—239	T-26	Fred Brand	87-83-88—258
T-10	Otto Hackbarth	77-79-83—239	T-26	Alex Ogilvie	86-84-88—258
T-12	Jack Campbell	80-78-84—242	28	Peter Robertson	87-88-86—261
T-12	Frank Coltart	80-81-81—242	29	William Entwistle	88-82-93—263
T-12	Dave Livie	79-80-83—242	30	George Knox	86-96-87—269
T-12	Archie Sanderson	82-78-82—242	31	Val Flood	88-92-95—275
T-16	W.C. (Bill) Gordon	80-81-83—244			

■ SELECTED PLAYER RECORDS FOR THE PGA SENIORS' CHAMPIONSHIP

Player	Best Finish	Years	Rds.	Cuts	Top 3	Top 5	Top 10	Top 25	Avg.	Rds. in 60's	Low Rd.	High Rd.	Money
Tommy Aaron	T-13th (1988)	6	24	6	0	0	0	1	75.04	1	69	84	$17,040.00
Pat Abbott	T-19th (1964)	8	30	7	0	0	0	2	74.60	0	70	80	$1,451.16
Jim Albus	T-7th (1993)	3	8	2	0	0	1	2	72.25	1	68	77	$30,250.00
Isao Aoki	3rd (1993)	1	4	1	1	1	1	1	69.75	2	67	72	$60,000.00
George Archer	5th (1990, '91)	4	16	4	0	2	2	4	71.94	2	68	75	$66,500.00
Alfonso Atkins	T-14th (1969)	4	16	4	0	0	0	1	76.13	1	69	85	$855.00
Tommy Aycock	T-13th (1993)	2	8	2	0	0	0	2	72.50	0	70	77	$21,750.00
Errie Ball	2nd (1962)	19	69	16	1	2	4	11	74.20	6	64	82	$7,195.33
Jerry Barber	T-7th (1981)	14	50	11	0	0	1	5	75.46	1	69	84	$20,580.75
Miller Barber	Winner (1981)	11	41	10	3	3	7	9	72.78	5	68	82	$123,150.00
Jim Barnes	T-5th (1940)	2	4	2	0	1	2	2	75.00	0	71	78	N/A
John Barnum	2nd (1963, '64 & '66)	14	45	9	3	4	4	9	73.93	7	66	85	$10,050.57
Herman Barron	Winner (1963)	11	38	8	1	1	2	6	73.71	5	67	82	$4,991.67
George Bayer	2nd (Dec 1979)	11	41	10	1	2	3	8	74.17	3	67	83	$25,564.16
Frank Beard	T-16th (1990)	2	8	2	0	0	0	1	74.38	0	70	78	$8,000.00
Sam Bernardi	T-8th (1963)	11	38	8	0	0	1	4	73.95	2	68	80	$2,412.08
Al Besselink	9th (Dec 1979)	6	17	3	0	0	1	1	76.71	0	70	85	$3,055.00
Don Bies	T-9th (1990)	3	10	2	0	0	1	1	74.80	0	72	79	$13,400.00
Bill Black	T-3rd (1958)	10	22	3	1	2	2	2	74.55	1	68	78	$1,627.00
Homero Blancas	4th (1991)	3	12	3	0	1	1	1	73.75	0	70	79	$34,575.00
Jules Blanton	5th (1958)	19	51	8	0	1	3	5	76.10	0	70	82	$1,697.00
Tommy Bolt	Winner (1969)	8	19	4	3	3	3	4	71.47	4	67	76	$10,208.34
Gene Borek	T-19th (1988)	6	22	5	0	0	0	2	76.14	1	69	87	$10,339.28
Julius Boros	Winner (1971 & '77)	16	57	13	6	10	11	11	72.72	10	67	82	$55,731.08
Mike Brady	T-7th (1940)	16	29	6	0	0	5	6	79.38	0	43	87	N/A
Gay Brewer	T-3rd (1982)	11	44	11	1	1	2	6	74.61	2	69	81	$43,587.50
John Brodie	T-20th (1991)	4	16	4	0	0	0	1	75.56	0	71	81	$9,625.00
Joe Brown	4th (1961)	13	46	10	0	1	1	7	75.04	2	68	83	$3,695.83
Jim Browning	5th (1966)	13	50	12	0	1	1	7	75.00	3	67	81	$5,063.33
Bob Brue	T-11th (1989)	6	22	5	0	0	0	1	74.77	0	70	79	$17,385.00
Billy Burke	8th (1953 & '55)	7	20	5	0	0	2	3	75.00	1	69	81	N/A
Pete Burke	Winner (1956)	12	40	9	1	1	4	4	74.18	2	68	83	$2,937.07
Sam Byrd	T-16th (1958)	8	28	6	0	0	0	2	75.00	0	72	81	$488.35
John-Paul Cain	T-22nd (1992)	4	16	4	0	0	0	1	75.06	0	71	81	$12,880.00
Jack Campbell	T-5th (1940)	5	11	5	0	1	2	4	79.55	0	72	84	N/A
Billy Capps	T-7th (1975)	10	38	9	0	0	1	7	74.61	0	71	81	$4,535.00
Billy Casper	T-5th (1986)	7	28	7	0	1	2	5	74.39	0	70	79	$30,615.00
Bob Charles	3rd (1987 & '91)	7	28	7	2	3	4	6	72.32	5	64	80	$129,570.00
Joe Cheves	2nd (1978)	12	44	10	1	1	1	4	75.36	1	69	83	$7,634.77
Louis Chiapetta	T-2nd (1949)	18	43	10	2	3	4	6	76.23	1	69	84	N/A
James Cockburn	T-6th (1945)	16	31	4	0	0	1	2	81.29	0	73	92	N/A
Jim Colbert	T-8th (1991)	3	12	3	0	0	1	1	73.25	1	67	77	$20,962.50
Bill Collins	3rd (Jan '84)	14	46	10	1	1	3	7	74.78	2	68	82	$36,880.72
Charles Coody	T-17th (1988)	4	14	3	0	0	0	1	75.50	0	72	79	$8,700.00
Harry Cooper	T-6th (1955)	3	10	3	0	0	2	3	73.30	1	69	80	N/A
Pete Cooper	Winner (1976)	23	78	16	1	6	11	13	75.59	4	69	97	$20,727.09
Bruce Crampton	2nd (1991 & '93)	8	32	8	2	2	4	8	72.38	5	66	77	$182,300.00
Marshall Crichton	Winner (1949)	11	22	7	1	2	4	4	78.77	0	72	89	N/A
Doug Dalziel	9th (1992)	4	16	4	0	0	1	2	74.50	0	70	82	$27,145.00
Manuel De La Torre	T-2nd (1978)	9	32	7	2	2	2	3	75.78	3	68	84	$9,381.67
Roberto De Vicenzo	Winner (1974)	7	28	7	1	2	4	6	72.82	4	66	82	$14,298.33
Perry Del Vecchio	T-2nd (1954)	11	25	2	1	1	1	1	76.28	1	68	83	$324.91
Jimmy Demaret	2nd (1961)	2	8	2	1	2	2	2	70.38	3	67	75	$1,750.00
Jim Dent	T-6th (1991)	4	16	4	0	0	1	2	73.25	1	66	79	$36,525.00
Bruce Devlin	T-7th (1982)	5	20	5	0	0	1	2	74.70	1	69	83	$24,132.50
Gardner Dickinson	T-6th (Dec '79 & Jan '84)	10	38	9	0	0	2	4	74.53	2	68	81	$21,012.00
Clarence Doser	3rd (1961)	20	70	15	1	2	5	11	74.70	4	67	82	$6,452.82
Dale Douglass	2nd (1987)	7	28	7	1	1	2	5	73.04	3	66	79	$76,983.33
Ed Dudley	T-6th (1957)	3	8	3	0	0	1	3	74.00	0	73	80	$225.00
Mortie Dutra	Winner (1955)	9	28	6	1	1	3	3	73.25	2	69	82	$1,000.00
Lee Elder	2nd (1986)	9	31	7	2	3	3	5	73.97	2	69	83	$65,579.00
Bob Erickson	T-2nd (Jan '79)	11	42	10	1	3	4	5	75.29	0	70	83	$23,959.57
Charles Farlow	5th (1960)	5	20	5	0	1	1	2	74.05	3	66	79	$995.00
Johnny Farrell	T-19th (1953)	4	9	2	0	0	0	2	76.56	0	75	79	N/A
George Fazio	T-15th (1966)	3	9	2	0	0	0	1	75.78	0	71	78	$500.00
Jim Ferree	9th (1981)	10	40	10	0	0	1	9	74.58	2	68	83	$33,216.67
Mike Fetchick	T-17th (Dec, '84)	12	48	12	0	0	0	2	75.90	0	70	82	$11,827.15
Dow Finsterwald	T-6th (Dec '79)	10	36	8	0	0	1	3	76.19	0	70	87	$9,923.34
Jack Fleck	Winner (Jan '79)	12	43	9	1	3	5	6	74.77	2	69	88	$34,847.60
Pete Fleming	2nd (1969)	6	24	6	1	1	1	3	74.17	2	67	82	$4,687.50

PGA SENIORS' CHAMPIONSHIP RECORDS

Player	Best Finish	Years	Rds.	Cuts	Top 3	Top 5	Top 10	Top 25	Avg.	Rds. in 60's	Low Rd.	High Rd.	Money
Doug Ford	T-5th (1974)	19	59	12	0	1	1	4	76.32	1	69	86	$8,098.74
Ed Furgol	T-4th (1973)	18	58	12	0	2	4	8	76.34	1	69	96	$7,370.00
Marty Furgol	T-5th (1967 & '72)	17	54	13	0	2	5	9	74.56	1	69	80	$7,263.34
Bob Gajda	9th (1973)	9	32	8	0	0	1	4	74.72	0	71	79	$3,107.09
Francis Gallett	T-6th (1946)	5	10	1	0	0	1	1	76.60	0	75	80	N/A
Ivan Gantz	5th (1961)	10	33	6	0	1	2	5	74.61	1	69	83	$1,483.57
Al Geiberger	T-2nd (1989)	4	16	4	2	2	3	3	72.69	3	68	77	$72,400.00
Vic Ghezzi	T-7th (1964)	10	31	6	0	0	2	6	73.94	0	70	80	$2,960.00
Duke Gibson	8th (1973)	4	16	4	0	0	2	4	73.69	0	70	78	$2,134.17
Leland Gibson	T-2nd (1959)	13	46	10	1	2	6	9	72.91	7	68	79	$5,677.00
Gibby Gilbert	T-19th (1992)	2	8	2	0	0	0	1	73.00	1	69	77	$16,500.00
Larry Gilbert	26th (1993)	1	4	1	0	0	0	0	72.25	1	68	76	$8,000.00
Bob Goalby	T-3rd (1982)	8	30	7	1	3	3	5	74.20	2	68	81	$32,562.07
Willie Goggin	Winner (1959)	8	25	5	2	2	3	3	73.68	0	70	82	$2,120.43
George Gordon	2nd (1937)	2	5	2	1	1	2	2	78.40	0	73	82	N/A
Lou Graham	T-9th (1990)	3	7	1	0	0	1	1	76.00	0	72	83	$10,500.00
Lloyd Gullickson	T-5th (1949)	16	29	5	0	1	3	5	77.34	0	70	85	N/A
Fred Haas Jr.	Winner (1966)	26	91	20	4	7	8	16	74.57	3	69	85	$28,868.86
Otto Hackbarth	Winner (1940)	7	11	3	2	2	3	3	80.36	0	70	93	N/A
Bob Hamilton	2nd (1967)	8	32	8	3	5	5	8	73.22	3	66	78	$11,341.66
Chick Harbert	3rd (1965 & '75)	11	42	10	2	4	4	8	73.74	4	67	80	$10,460.83
E. W. (Pop) Harbert	T-6th (1938)	22	40	9	0	0	2	6	75.33	0	42	86	N/A
Paul Harney	2nd (1980)	5	16	4	1	1	2	3	73.50	3	68	78	$24,308.00
Chandler Harper	Winner (1968)	15	60	15	2	3	5	10	74.32	3	64	84	$12,777.50
Labron Harris Sr.	8th (1961, '63 & '65)	16	54	11	0	0	3	6	74.63	3	68	83	$3,693.34
Dutch Harrison	T-2nd (1962 & '66)	8	32	8	3	4	6	7	72.78	5	67	80	$7,939.32
Joe Harrison	T-2nd (1962)	1	4	1	1	1	1	1	70.25	2	67	74	$1,233.33
Fred Hawkins	T-14th (Dec '79)	14	52	12	0	0	0	1	76.52	1	69	86	$10,791.25
Bill Heinlein	T-12th (1963)	12	38	7	0	0	0	2	75.76	1	69	85	$1,820.34
Harold Henning	T-5th (1987)	8	32	8	0	1	6	8	72.72	5	67	81	$91,695.50
Dave Hill	T-4th (1989)	4	13	3	0	1	1	2	73.54	0	70	81	$26,683.00
Mike Hill	2nd (1992)	5	20	5	1	2	3	4	71.95	4	67	78	$125,908.34
Willie Hunter	T-7th (1954)	11	26	3	0	0	1	2	77.23	0	71	85	N/A
Jock Hutchison	Winner (1937 & '47)	24	48	14	11	12	12	12	74.71	1	44	87	N/A
Walker Inman Jr.	4th (1980)	5	20	5	0	1	1	2	76.80	0	70	87	$8,127.58
Jack Isaacs	T-4th (1963)	16	62	15	0	2	4	12	73.92	4	66	79	$7,102.00
Don January	Winner (Dec'79 & '82)	10	40	10	6	6	6	7	72.43	8	67	80	$120,045.00
Bill Jelliffe	2nd (1950)	20	45	9	2	3	4	7	78.60	0	71	94	N/A
Joe Jimenez	Winner (1978)	17	64	15	1	4	4	8	74.39	2	68	82	$52,848.66
Bill Johnston	T-2nd (Feb '79)	8	30	7	2	2	3	4	74.50	2	67	84	$18,892.00
Gordon Jones	T-6th (Dec '84)	8	26	5	0	0	1	2	76.69	2	68	85	$11,570.00
Mike Joyce	T-29th (1990)	3	12	3	0	0	0	0	76.17	0	71	81	$4,515.00
Tom Joyce	T-14th (1991)	2	6	1	0	0	0	1	74.67	1	67	81	$8,500.00
Herman Keiser	T-6th (1970)	9	34	8	0	0	4	8	73.85	1	68	79	$5,204.08
Al Kelley	T-7th (1992)	4	16	4	0	0	2	3	72.56	2	66	78	$48,700.00
Jim King	T-3rd (1986)	7	26	6	1	1	1	4	74.69	1	67	80	$29,831.60
Chuck Klein	T-6th (1976)	6	20	5	0	0	1	3	74.55	0	71	81	$2,229.02
Ted Kroll	T-10th (1970)	17	59	13	0	0	1	6	76.29	0	71	90	$5,998.43
George Lanning	13th (1986)	8	32	8	0	0	0	5	74.75	2	67	81	$22,545.00
Larry Laoretti	T-12th (1991)	3	12	3	0	0	0	2	74.00	2	69	78	$16,029.16
Babe Lichardus	T-8th (Feb '79)	5	18	4	0	0	2	2	75.00	0	70	84	$2,801.66
Gene Littler	T-31st (Dec '84)	2	8	2	0	0	0	0	76.50	0	73	80	$2,300.00
John Long	T-7th (1964)	9	26	3	0	0	2	3	75.04	1	68	83	$2,145.00
Tony Longo	T-2nd (1960)	6	20	4	1	1	1	2	74.00	1	69	80	$1,528.33
Joe Lopez Sr.	2nd (1965)	20	74	17	1	2	11	15	74.12	4	67	88	$19,043.73
Charles Lorms	4th (1945 & '47)	17	34	7	0	2	3	4	78.09	0	72	88	N/A
Tony Manero	T-6th (1958)	12	27	3	0	0	2	3	75.26	0	70	82	$776.90
Milon Marusic	T-4th (1973 & '76)	14	56	14	0	2	3	8	74.86	1	68	83	$7,679.33
Don Massengale	T-19th (1989)	6	24	6	0	0	0	3	73.96	0	70	78	$24,308.00
Ken Mast	10th (Feb '79)	6	22	5	0	0	1	1	75.59	0	70	81	$2,770.00
Billy Maxwell	T-7th (1986)	11	38	8	0	0	1	4	75.45	1	69	80	$22,028.00
Charles Mayo	3rd (1940 & '45)	21	38	9	2	3	5	9	76.68	0	39	83	N/A
Rives McBee	T-13th (1990)	5	20	5	0	0	0	1	74.20	1	69	78	$17,950.00
Charles McKenna	Winner (1948)	20	42	7	4	4	4	6	77.12	1	69	87	N/A
Fred McLeod	Winner (1938)	13	27	4	1	2	4	4	73.74	0	40	96	N/A
Tod Menefee	T-9th (1959)	17	52	9	0	0	2	4	75.00	1	67	83	$2,825.52
Hans Merrell	7th (1971)	13	48	11	0	0	2	7	75.54	0	70	84	$4,111.84
Dick Metz	Winner (1960)	8	24	5	1	1	2	4	75.08	2	67	83	$2,301.66
Ray Montgomery	T-4th (1978)	14	47	10	0	1	1	3	76.23	1	69	86	$8,447.50
Bert Montresser	T-6th (1958)	11	28	5	0	0	2	4	74.96	0	72	80	$688.00
Orville Moody	T-3rd (Dec '84)	9	36	9	1	2	6	8	72.83	2	68	78	$96,868.00

PGA SENIORS' CHAMPIONSHIP RECORDS

Player	Best Finish	Years	Rds.	Cuts	Top 3	Top 5	Top 10	Top 25	Avg.	Rds. in 60's	Low Rd.	High Rd.	Money
George Morris	3rd (1942)	3	6	3	1	1	2	3	75.17	0	75	79	N/A
Larry Mowry	Winner (1989)	6	24	6	1	1	3	3	74.04	5	65	84	$101,497.50
Bob Murphy	T-39th (1993)	1	4	1	0	0	0	0	73.25	0	70	75	$2,650.00
Mike Murra	T-2nd (1955)	4	8	2	1	1	1	2	75.25	1	66	81	N/A
Ernest Newnham	Winner (1952)	15	29	7	1	1	4	6	78.14	0	71	87	N/A
Bobby Nichols	3rd (1987)	7	28	7	1	1	1	2	74.68	1	68	78	$29,769.66
Jack Nicklaus	Winner (1991)	4	16	4	2	2	4	4	70.69	7	66	78	$140,500.00
Tom Nieporte	T-12th (Dec '79)	11	40	9	0	0	0	5	75.50	1	68	81	$13,009.87
Willie Ogg	T-4th (1947)	11	22	8	0	1	2	6	78.95	0	70	85	N/A
Dave Ogilvie	T-4th (1937 & '38)	5	11	5	0	2	2	3	80.36	0	75	85	N/A
Charles Owens	T-3rd (1986)	5	17	4	1	1	1	2	74.65	0	72	80	$21,733.00
Arnold Palmer	Winner (1980 & Jan '84)	12	46	11	4	5	5	9	72.98	5	63	80	$128,525.00
Jack Patroni	T-6th (1958)	8	24	5	0	0	1	3	74.38	0	70	79	$792.10
Toney Penna	T-8th (1961)	7	20	4	0	0	1	1	75.75	2	69	95	$516.33
Gary Player	Winner ('86, '88 & '90)	8	32	8	3	4	7	8	71.31	9	65	76	$256,750.00
Jimmy Powell	T-16th (1993)	7	22	4	0	0	0	3	75.45	1	69	90	$19,805.00
Henry Ransom	3rd (1963 & '70)	14	54	13	2	3	4	8	73.85	6	68	84	$8,530.84
Wilfred Reid	4th (1942)	12	22	6	0	2	2	3	76.95	0	45	91	N/A
Ben Richter	2nd (1947 & '48)	12	26	8	2	3	5	6	75.81	0	71	83	N/A
Chi Chi Rodriguez	Winner (1987)	8	32	8	4	5	5	7	71.72	7	66	76	$209,698.00
Paul Runyan	Winner (1961 & '62)	19	66	14	4	4	5	7	75.24	5	67	87	$7,751.46
Jack Ryan	T-3rd (1957)	15	44	7	1	1	1	4	74.48	0	70	83	$2,261.00
Doug Sanders	T-6th (Jan '84)	10	36	8	0	0	2	3	75.58	1	69	83	$28,894.00
Gene Sarazen	Winner (1954 & '58)	12	33	7	4	4	4	5	73.67	1	67	80	N/A
Harry Schwab	Winner (1953)	14	32	5	2	2	2	3	77.44	1	66	86	N/A
Tom Shaw	T-24th (1989)	5	16	3	0	0	0	1	75.88	1	67	85	$8,245.00
Charles Sheppard	2nd (1958)	18	54	9	1	3	3	4	75.70	2	66	82	$3,407.32
Dick Shoemaker	6th (1961, '64 & '66)	6	20	4	0	0	3	4	72.70	2	68	78	$2,550.00
Denny Shute	T-2nd (1955 & '59)	13	39	9	2	2	3	6	74.46	0	70	81	N/A
Charles Sifford	Winner (1975)	18	68	16	1	2	5	11	74.57	2	68	81	$34,574.60
Dan Sikes	T-3rd (Dec '79)	7	22	5	1	1	1	5	73.68	2	69	79	$14,133.33
Tex Simon	T-3rd (1977)	4	14	3	1	1	1	1	76.14	1	69	84	$3,750.00
George Smith	T-2nd (1949)	22	48	8	2	3	4	7	75.13	2	67	82	N/A
J. C. Snead	T-9th (1993)	3	10	2	0	0	1	1	73.50	2	68	80	$20,750.00
Sam Snead	Won ('64,'65,'67,'70, '72 & '73)	19	70	17	9	11	15	17	71.61	17	66	79	$38,581.88
Dave Stockton	4th (1992)	2	8	2	0	1	1	2	71.50	3	68	79	$44,000.00
Bob Stone	T-7th (1982)	4	14	3	0	0	2	3	74.57	0	70	81	$8,683.33
Frank Strazza	T-4th (1956)	14	38	6	0	1	2	3	76.00	1	69	88	N/A
Bob Stupple	2nd (1957)	4	15	4	1	1	1	2	73.80	0	70	80	$843.25
Dave Sutherland	3rd (1946)	5	10	5	1	1	3	4	76.30	0	72	82	N/A
Joe Taylor	3rd (1973)	9	36	9	1	1	3	5	74.64	1	69	84	$6,197.38
Milton Theobald	T-5th (1942)	3	6	3	0	1	2	2	77.50	0	73	86	N/A
Stan Thirsk	7th (1979)	13	46	10	0	0	1	4	75.37	0	70	82	$21,537.50
Rocky Thompson	T-6th (1991)	3	12	3	0	0	1	3	72.00	1	69	74	$42,725.00
Peter Thomson	Winner (Dec '84)	2	8	2	1	2	2	2	72.25	1	67	74	$49,000.00
Ben Toski	7th (1977)	11	38	8	0	0	2	6	74.95	1	69	84	$17,525.00
Lee Trevino	Winner (1992)	4	16	4	2	2	2	4	71.13	3	64	77	$146,000.00
Jim Turnesa	5th (1964)	8	31	7	0	1	1	5	74.58	2	69	80	$2,904.16
Joe Turnesa	T-8th (1955)	7	18	5	0	0	1	4	76.17	0	72	80	N/A
Phil Turnesa	T-3rd (1952)	14	25	6	1	2	3	4	77.24	0	73	83	N/A
Ellsworth Vines	T-7th (1962)	5	18	4	0	0	1	1	74.78	1	69	85	$1,001.00
Art Wall	T-2nd (1974)	11	42	10	4	5	7	8	73.14	7	68	83	$53,407.24
Fred Wampler	2nd (1975 & '76)	8	27	6	2	3	5	5	73.37	3	67	83	$16,962.73
Tom Wargo	Winner (1993)	1	4	1	1	1	1	1	68.75	3	67	70	$110,000.00
Al Watrous	Winner (1950, '51 & '57)	18	44	12	5	5	8	10	74.25	2	68	85	N/A
Alex Watson	T-4th (1947)	16	34	7	0	1	3	5	78.06	0	73	85	N/A
Bob Watson	T-6th (1976)	8	24	4	0	0	1	2	77.42	1	68	86	$1,577.87
John Watson	4th (1953 & '54)	11	30	6	0	2	2	2	75.57	1	69	86	N/A
Dewitt Weaver	T-10th (1992)	4	16	4	0	0	1	2	73.75	1	67	82	$26,850.00
Tom Weiskopf	T-4th (1993)	1	4	1	0	1	1	1	70.25	1	64	73	$40,000.00
Jim West	3rd (1937)	1	3	1	1	1	1	1	77.67	0	77	78	N/A
Eddie Williams	Winner (1942, '45 & '46)	21	41	10	4	6	8	10	77.39	0	70	89	N/A
Jack Williams	5th (1946)	13	26	6	0	1	4	5	78.88	0	71	90	N/A
Bud Williamson	T-4th (1965)	12	38	7	0	0	2	4	75.47	2	69	84	$3,407.50
Ock Willoweit	2nd (1956)	11	29	6	1	1	2	5	74.66	1	68	82	N/A
Joe Zarhardt	3rd (1956)	12	33	5	1	1	1	2	75.36	0	70	84	$1,474.50
Walter Zembriski	T-9th (1988)	6	24	6	0	0	1	4	73.46	3	69	80	$39,625.00
Larry Ziegler	T-9th (1990)	4	14	3	0	0	1	2	74.00	2	66	79	$20,900.00

■ SELECTED PGA SENIORS' CHAMPIONSHIP RECORDS

■ Best 72-Hole Score
268 (20 under) by Sam Snead (66-66-67-69) in 1973
270 (18 under) by Don January (68-68-67-67) in Dec. '79
271 (17 under) by Jack Nicklaus (66-66-69-70) in 1991

■ Best 72-Hole Score By A Non-Winner
274 (14 under) by John Barnum (66-68-69-71) in 1963
275 (13 under) by Bruce Crampton (73-67-69-66) in 1993
276 (12 under) by Julius Boros (70-67-67-72) in 1974
276 (12 under) by Art Wall (71-68-68-69) in 1974

■ Highest 72-Hole Score By Winner
290 (2 over) by Sam Snead (71-71-72-76) in 1970
289 (1 over) by Jack Fleck (73-71-75-70) in Feb. '79
289 (1 over) by Arnold Palmer (72-69-73-75) in 1980

■ Best Scores First 54 Holes
199 (17 under) by Sam Snead (66-66-67) in 1973
201 (15 under) by Jack Nicklaus (66-66-69) in 1991

■ Best Scores Last 54 Holes
202 (14 under) by Sam Snead (66-67-69) in 1973
202 (14 under) by Bruce Crampton (67-69-66) in 1993
205 (11 under) by Herman Barron (67-69-69) in 1963
205 (11 under) by Jack Nicklaus (66-69-70) in 1991

■ Largest 54-Hole Lead
11 by Sam Snead (199) in 1973
8 by Jack Nicklaus (201) in 1991
7 by Chandler Harper (207) in 1968
5 by Dale Douglass (209) in 1987
5 by Gary Player (208) in 1990

■ Best Score First 36 Holes
132 (12 under) by Sam Snead (66-66) in 1973
132 (12 under) by Arnold Palmer (69-63) in 1984
132 (12 under) by Jack Nicklaus (66-66) in 1991

■ Best Score Last 36 Holes
134 (10 under) by Don January (67-67) in Dec. '79
136 (8 under) by Chandler Harper (64-72) in 1968
136 (8 under) by Pete Fleming (69-67) in 1969
136 (8 under) by Sam Snead (67-69) in 1973
136 (8 under) by Mike Hill (67-69) in 1992

■ Largest 36-Hole Lead
8 by Arnold Palmer (132) in Jan. '84
7 by Jack Burke Sr. (142) in 1942
*Championship was played over 36 holes (1938 - 1953)
7 by Sam Snead (132) in 1973
7 by Gary Player (136) in 1986

■ Best 18-Hole Score
63 (9 under) by Buck White, first round, 1961
63 (9 under) by Arnold Palmer, second round, 1984
64 (8 under) by Errie Ball, second round, 1963
64 (8 under) by Chandler Harper, third round, 1968
64 (8 under) by Bob Charles, first round, 1988
64 (8 under) by Lee Trevino, second round, 1992
64 (8 under) by Tom Weiskopf, second round, 1993

■ Largest 18-Hole Lead
5 by Harry Schawb (66) in 1953
5 by Bob Charles (64) in 1988
3 held by seven players

■ Best First-Round Score
63 (9 under) by Buck White in 1961
64 (8 under) by Bob Charles in 1988

■ Best Second-Round Score
63 (9 under) by Arnold Palmer in Jan. '84
64 (8 under) by Errie Ball in 1963
64 (8 under) by Lee Trevino in 1992
64 (8 under) by Tom Weiskopf in 1993

■ Best Third-Round Score
64 (8 under) by Chandler Harper in 1968
65 (7 under) by Larry Mowry in 1989
65 (7 under) by Gary Player in 1990
65 (7 under) by Bob Charles in 1992

■ Best Fourth-Round Score
66 (6 under) by Sam Snead in 1967
66 (6 under) by Roberto De Vicenzo in 1974
66 (6 under) by Chi Chi Rodriguez in 1990
66 (6 under) by Bruce Crampton in 1993

■ Largest Winning Margin
15 shots by Sam Snead in 1973
9 shots by Sam Snead in 1967
8 shots by Don January in Dec. '79
6 shots by Eddie Williams in 1942
6 shots by Jack Nicklaus in 1991

■ Highest First-Round Score By Winner
76 (4 over) by Jock Hutchison in 1937
76 (5 over) by Otto Hackbarth in 1940

■ Lowest First-Round Score By Winner
66 (6 under) by Harry Schwab in 1953
66 (6 under) by Sam Snead in 1973
66 (6 under) by Jack Nicklaus in 1991

■ Highest Second-Round Score By Winner
79 (7 over) by Fred McLeod in 1938
76 (4 over) by Harry Schwab in 1953
75 (3 over) by Jock Hutchison in 1937
75 (3 over) by Don January in 1982

■ Lowest Second-Round Score By Winner
63 (9 under) by Arnold Palmer in Jan. '84
64 (8 under) by Lee Trevino in 1992
66 (6 under) by Sam Snead in 1973
66 (6 under) by Jack Nicklaus in 1991

■ Highest Third-Round Score By Winner
79 (7 over) by Arnold Palmer in Jan. '84
76 (4 over) by Chi Chi Rodriguez in 1987

■ Lowest Third-Round Score By Winner
64 (8 under) by Chandler Harper in 1968
65 (7 under) by Larry Mowry in 1989
65 (7 under) by Gary Player in 1990

■ Highest Final-Round Score By Winner
76 (4 over) by Sam Snead in 1970
75 (3 over) by Arnold Palmer in 1980

■ Lowest Final-Round Score By Winner
66 (6 under) by Sam Snead in 1967
66 (6 under) by Roberto DeVicenzo in 1974

■ Highest Course Average Over 72 Holes
78.45-1971 Seniors at PGA National Golf Club
78.38-1968 Seniors at PGA National Golf Club

■ Lowest Course Average Over 72 Holes
73.65-1985 Seniors at Fort Lauderdale C.C.
74.13-1974 Seniors at Port Lucie C.C.

Most Money Won

$256,750 by Gary Player, spanning 8 championships
$209,698 by Chi Chi Rodriguez spanning 8 championships
$182,300 by Bruce Crampton spanning 8 championships
$146,000 by Lee Trevino, spanning 4 championships
$140,500 by Jack Nicklaus, spanning 4 championships
$129,570 by Bob Charles, spanning 7 championships
$128,525 by Arnold Palmer, spanning 12 championships
$125,908 by Mike Hill, spanning 5 championships
$123,150 by Miller Barber, spanning 11 championships
$120,045 by Don January, spanning 10 championships

Money Won Per Tournament

$110,000 by Tom Wargo, spanning 1 championship
$60,000 by Isao Aoki, spanning 1 championship
$40,000 by Tom Weiskopf, spanning 1 championship
$36,500 by Lee Trevino, spanning 4 championships
$35,125 by Jack Nicklaus, spanning 4 championships
$32,094 by Gary Player, spanning 8 championships
$26,212 by Chi Chi Rodriguez, spanning 8 championships
$25,182 by Mike Hill, spanning 5 championships

Highest Dollar Per Stroke

$400.00 by Tom Wargo, spanning 1 championship
$215.05 by Isao Aoki, spanning 1 championship
$142.35 by Tom Weiskopf, spanning 1 championship
$128.30 by Lee Trevino, spanning 4 championships
$124.23 by Jack Nicklaus, spanning 4 championships
$112.51 by Gary Player, spanning 8 championships
$91.37 by Chi Chi Rodriguez, spanning 8 championships
$87.50 by Mike Hill, spanning 5 championships

Lowest 72-Hole Scoring Average

68.75 with 4 rounds by Tom Wargo
69.75 with 4 rounds by Isao Aoki
70.25 with 4 rounds by Tom Weiskopf
70.25 with 4 rounds by Joe Harrison
70.38 with 8 rounds by Jimmy Demaret
70.69 with 16 rounds by Jack Nicklaus
71.00 with 2 rounds by Jack Burke Sr.
71.13 with 16 rounds by Lee Trevino
71.25 with 4 rounds by Ray Floyd

Lowest Scoring Average, Minimum of 20 Rounds

71.31 with 32 rounds by Gary Player
71.61 with 70 rounds by Sam Snead
71.72 with 32 rounds by Chi Chi Rodriguez
71.95 with 20 rounds by Mike Hill
72.32 with 28 rounds by Bob Charles
72.38 with 32 rounds by Bruce Crampton
72.43 with 40 rounds by Don January
72.70 with 20 rounds by Dick Shoemaker
72.72 with 32 rounds by Harold Henning
72.72 with 57 rounds by Julius Boros

Most Appearances

26 by Fred Haas
24 by Jock Hutchison
23 by Pete Cooper
22 by George Smith

Most Rounds Played

91 by Fred Haas
78 by Pete Cooper
74 by Joe Lopez Sr.
70 by Sam Snead
70 by Clarence Doser

Highest Number Of Strokes Over The Years

6627 by Fred Haas averaging 74.46 strokes per round
5896 by Pete Cooper averaging 75.59 strokes per round
5485 by Joe Lopez Sr. averaging 74.12 strokes per round
5229 by Clarence Doser averaging 74.70 strokes per round
5120 by Errie Ball averaging 74.20 strokes per round
5071 by Charles Sifford averaging 74.57 strokes per round
5013 by Sam Snead averaging 71.61 strokes per round

Most Rounds In The 60s

17 by Sam Snead
10 by Julius Boros
9 by Gary Player
8 by Don January

Most Championships Won

6 by Sam Snead (1964, 1965, 1967, 1970, 1972, 1973)
3 by Gary Player (1986, 1988 and 1990)
3 by Eddie Williams (1942, 1945 and 1946)
3 by Al Watrous (1950, 1951 and 1957)
2 by Jock Hutchison (1937 and 1947)
2 by Gene Sarazen (1954 and 1958)
2 by Paul Runyan (1961 and 1962)
2 by Julius Boros (1971 and 1977)
2 by Arnold Palmer (1980 and 1984)
2 by Don January (1979 and 1982)

Most Times Runner-Up

6 by Jock Hutchison (1940,42,45,46,49,51)
4 by Julius Boros (1972,73,74,82)
3 by John Barnum (1963,64,66)

Most Top 3 Finishes

11 by Jock Hutchison
9 by Sam Snead
6 by Don January
6 by Julius Boros
5 by Al Watrous

Most Top 5 Finishes

12 by Jock Hutchison
11 by Sam Snead
10 by Julius Boros
7 by Fred Haas

Most Top 10 Finishes

15 by Sam Snead
12 by Jock Hutchison
11 by Pete Cooper
11 by Julius Boros
11 by Joe Lopez Sr.

Most Top 25 Finishes

17 by Sam Snead
16 by Fred Haas
15 by Joe Lopez Sr.
13 by Pete Cooper
12 by Jock Hutchison
12 by Jack Isaacs

Wire To Wire Winners
(After 1958 When Championship Was 72 Holes)
Sam Snead in 1964
Sam Snead in 1973
Don January in Dec. '79
Arnold Palmer in Jan. '84
Peter Thomson in Dec. '84
Gary Player in 1986
Jack Nicklaus in 1991

PGA SENIORS' CHAMPIONSHIP RECORDS

■ **Four Rounds in the 60s, Same PGA Seniors'
Championship (After 1958 When Championship Was
72 Holes)**
Herman Barron (67-67-69-69) in 1963
Sam Snead (66-66-67-69) in 1973
Don January (68-68-67-67) in December 1979

■ **Most "Heartbreaking" Rounds**
1955 by 1st round leader Mike Murra, 66-75-76 to finish
T-2nd
1956 by 1st round leader Bill Black, 68-76-76 to finish T-4th
1958 by 3rd round leader Mortie Dutra, 69-71-73-82 to
finish T-6th
1959 by 1st round leader Jack Isaacs, 66-75-77-73 to finish
T-13th
1959 by 2nd round leader Dick Metz, 67-71-77-72 to finish
6th
1959 by Charles Burkart, 68-81-76-79 to finish T-64th
1960 by 1st round co-leader Leland Gibson, 68-75-75-74,
to finish 6th
1960 by Ernest Schneiter Jr., 69-77-80-82 to finish T-56th
1960 by Michael Serino, 69-76-77-80 to finish T-32nd
1961 by 1st round leader Buck White, 63-73-78-74 to
finish T-12th
1961 by Dick Metz, 67-74-78-71 to finish T-18th
1961 by 3rd round leader Clarence Doser, 68-67-72-75 to
finish 3rd
1962 by John Barnum, 67-71-70-78 to finish 12th
1966 by 1st round leader Skee Riegel, 67-77-75-77 to
finish T-12th
1966 by Chandler Harper, 68-76-78-80 to finish T-26th
1968 by 1st round leader Joseph Malia, 69-79-77-80 to
finish T-33rd
1971 by 1st round leader Bob Hamilton, 66-76-76-75 to finish
T-5th
1971 by 2nd round leader Tommy Bolt, 69-68-76-76 to finish
2nd
1976 by 1st round leader Fred Wampler, 67-74-72-75 to finish
2nd
1976 by Bob Watson, 68-73-74-81 to finish T-6th
1979 (Feb.) by 1st round co-leader George Bayer,
69-79-75-73 to finish T-13th

1981 by 1st round co-leader Al Balding, 68-77-73-75 to
finish T-14th
1982 by 1st round co-leader Bob Goalby, 68-75-74-73 to
finish T-3rd
1986 by 1st round co-leader Miller Barber, 68-77-80-71 to
finish T-12th
1986 by Fred Hawkins, 69-76-81-82 to finish T-42nd
1988 by 1st & 2nd round leader Bob Charles, 64-73-78-78
to finish T-11th
1988 by George Lanning, 69-79-75-78 to finish T-27th
1993 by 1st round leader Larry Ziegler, 66-76-75-76 to
finish T-39th
1993 by Ed Dalton, 68-76-81-75 to finish T-58th

■ **Winning The PGA Seniors' Championship On First Try**
Jock Hutchison in 1937
Jack Burke Sr. in 1941
Charles McKenna in 1948
Al Watrous in 1950
Pete Burke in 1956
Sam Snead in 1964
Fred Haas Jr. in 1966
Tommy Bolt in 1969
Julius Boros in 1971
Roberto De Vicenzo in 1974
Charles Sifford in 1975
Don January in Dec. '79
Arnold Palmer in 1980
Miller Barber in 1981
Gary Player in 1986
Tom Wargo in 1993

■ **Longest Time It Took To Win PGA Seniors'
Championship**
Pete Cooper won his championship in 1976 on his 12th try

■ **Oldest Winner**
62 years old, Jock Hutchison in 1947
61 years old, Pete Cooper in 1976
60 years old, Sam Snead in 1973

■ **Youngest Winner**
50 years, 26 days, Don January in 1979
50 years, 1 month, 21 days, Fred Haas in 1966

■ PURSE THROUGH THE YEARS (1954 thru 1993)

Year	Purse	Winner's Share	Year	Purse	Winner's Share	Year	Purse	Winner's Share
1954	$5,000	$1,000	1969	40,000	4,000	Jan. 1984	200,000	25,000
1955	5,000	1,000	1970	40,000	4,000	Dec. 1984	225,000	40,000
1956	6,500	1,000	1971	40,000	4,000	1986	250,000	45,000
1957	8,000	1,000	1972	40,000	4,000	1987	260,000	47,000
1958	10,000	1,200	1973	40,000	4,000	1988	355,000	63,000
1959	10,000	1,200	1974	40,000	4,000	1989	400,000	72,000
1960	15,000	1,500	1975	50,000	7,500	1990	450,000	75,000
1961	15,000	1,500	1976	50,000	7,500	1991	550,000	85,000
1962	25,000	2,000	1977	50,000	7,500	1992	700,000	100,000
1963	30,000	2,500	1978	50,000	8,000	1993	800,000	110,000
1964	30,000	2,500	Feb. 1979	50,000	8,000			
1965	35,000	3,000	Dec. 1979	100,000	15,000			
1966	35,000	3,000	1980	125,000	20,000			
1967	40,000	4,000	1981	125,000	20,000	*(1937 through 1953 official purse and*		
1968	40,000	4,000	1982	150,000	25,000	*prize money unavailable.)*		

PGA GRAND SLAM OF GOLF

1994 FACTS & FORMAT

DATES: November 8-9, 1994

SITE: Poipu Bay Resort Golf Course, Kauai, Hawaii

TELEVISION:
First Round, Tues., Nov. 8: TBS: 7:05 p.m. - 11:05 p.m.
Second Round, Wed., Nov. 9: TBS: 7:05 p.m. - 11:05 p.m.

PURSE: $1,000,000

1993 CHAMPION: Greg Norman

RULES AND REGULATIONS

The Rules of Golf which govern play are determined by the United States Golf Association and applied by the PGA of America Board of Directors. The tournament is subject to the overall supervision of the board and the PGA Rules Committee.

ELIGIBILITY

The 1994 champions of each of the four majors, the Masters, British Open, U.S. Open and PGA Championship, will be invited to participate in the 1994 PGA Grand Slam of Golf. If one or more champions are unable to attend, alternates will be chosen from a pool of those players who have won a major championship during their careers. The PGA of America has developed a point system for selection of alternates that is based on performance in the 1994 major championships.

THE GRAND SLAM OF GOLF CHANGES COMPLEXION

Established in 1979, the PGA Grand Slam of Golf has grown from an 18-hole, single-day affair to a 36-hole showdown matching professional golf's best against each other for a $1 million purse in front of an international television audience in more than 90 countries worldwide.

The initial PGA Grand Slam of Golf concluded with 1978 U.S. Open Champion Andy North and 1978 Masters winner Gary Player sharing first place at Oak Hill Country Club in Rochester, N.Y. Since then, the Grand Slam has been contested over many of the nation's top golf courses and featured modern-day golfing greats such as Lee Trevino, Larry Nelson, Lanny Wadkins and Curtis Strange. In 1991, the PGA Grand Slam of Golf changed its format to a two-day, 36-hole event contested in November. The revised schedule enabled the Grand Slam to attract the four winners of the current season's major championships to a fitting conclusion to their competitive season.

TBS Sports, one of the world's most prominent cable networks, televises the competition to more than 57 million U.S. homes in a special prime time telecast. Today, the PGA Grand Slam of Golf is considered the "toughest event to qualify for" by the players themselves and since 1991, all 12 major champions who have qualified for the PGA Grand Slam of Golf have participated.

■ HISTORY THROUGH THE YEARS

Year	Site	Contestants (Scores)
1979	Oak Hill CC, Rochester, N.Y.	Gary Player (73), Andy North (73), Jack Nicklaus (77), John Mahaffey (77)
1980	Hazeltine National GC, Chaska, Minn.	Lanny Wadkins (71), Hale Irwin (73), David Graham (74), Fuzzy Zoeller (74)
1981	Breakers West GC, West Palm Beach, Fla.	Lee Trevino (68), Tom Watson (71), Jack Nicklaus (72), Seve Ballesteros (75)
1982	PGA National, Palm Beach Gardens, Fla.	Bill Rogers (71), David Graham (76), Larry Nelson (77), Tom Watson (78)
1986	Kemper Lakes GC, Hawthorn Woods, Ill.	Greg Norman (70), Fuzzy Zoeller (72), Jack Nicklaus (75), Bob Tway (75)
1988	Kemper Lakes GC, Hawthorn Woods, Ill.	Larry Nelson (69), Larry Mize (70), Scott Simpson (70), Greg Norman (73)
1989	Kemper Lakes GC, Hawthorn Woods, Ill.	Curtis Strange (73), Craig Stadler (75), Ian Baker-Finch (76), Greg Norman (No Score)
1990	Kemper Lakes GC, Hawthorn Woods, Ill.	Andy North (70), Craig Stadler (74), Payne Stewart (75), Curtis Strange (WD)
1991	Kauai Lagoons Resort, Kauai, Hawaii	Ian Woosnam (69-66—135), Ian Baker-Finch (68-71—139), Payne Stewart (70-71—141), John Daly (73-70—143)
1992	PGA West, La Quinta, Calif.	Nick Price* (70-67—137), Tom Kite (75-62—137), Fred Couples (71-71—142), Nick Faldo (72-71—143)
1993	PGA West, La Quinta, Calif.	Greg Norman (71-74—145), Paul Azinger (75-72—147), Lee Janzen (74-74—148) Bernhard Langer (78-90—148)

* won playoff

1993

The most difficult tournament there is in which to earn a berth proved to be one of the most difficult in which to achieve par. The 1993 PGA Grand Slam of Golf was a struggle for the winners of golf's four major championships on the 7,126-yard Jack Nicklaus Resort Course. In 36 holes, there were 11 balls hit into the water, two out of bounds and a total of 18 penalty strokes.

Site:	Nicklaus Resort Course, PGA West, La Quinta, Calif.	
Date: Nov. 16-17, 1993		Purse:$1,000,000
First Place:	Greg Norman (145)	$400,000
Second Place:	Paul Azinger (147)	$250,000
Third Place:	Bernhard Langer (148)	$175,000
Fourth Place:	Lee Janzen (148)	$175,000

Greg Norman

However, British Open Champion Greg Norman survived long enough by putting together rounds of 71 and 74 for a winning 1-over-par 145 total. Norman won $400,000, the biggest paycheck of his 17-year career and hiked his overall 1993 earnings to $2,227,268. PGA Champion Paul Azinger finished two strokes back at 147, earning $250,000, and Masters Champion Bernhard Langer and U.S. Open Champion Lee Janzen tied for third to earn $175,000 each. Janzen crept within a stroke of Norman after 35 holes. Then disaster struck. He sculled a 4-iron from a fairway bunker on the 18th hole and plopped it into the water. He settled for a double-bogey.

In fact, Norman's total was two strokes higher than the fourth-place Grand Slam finishes of former PGA Champion John Daly (1991) and Nick Faldo (1992). Norman's opening round and Langer's closing 70 were the only sub-par rounds. The four players teamed for some rare high numbers, including two triple-bogeys and four double-bogeys.

"Sometimes you win pretty, sometimes you win ugly," said Norman. "In fishing terms, this was a mackerel in the moonlight — shining one minute, smelly the next."

1992

PGA Champion Nick Price's putter, which had been his salvation in the 74th PGA Championship three months earlier, was the difference in holding off U.S. Open Champion Tom Kite for the $400,000 first prize at the Jack Nicklaus Resort Course at PGA West in La Quinta, Calif.

Site:	Nicklaus Resort Course, PGA West, La Quinta, Calif.	
Date: Nov. 10-11, 1992		Purse:$1,000,000
First Place:	Nick Price (137)*	$400,000
Second Place:	Tom Kite (137)	$250,000
Third Place:	Fred Couples (142)	$200,000
Fourth Place:	Nick Faldo (143)	$150,000

won playoff

Nick Price

Price dropped birdie putts on the 16th and 18th holes for a bogey-free 67 that tied the streaking Kite with a two-day total of 7-under-par 137. Opening five strokes behind Price, Kite pulled even heading into the 18th hole. Kite birdied the final hole after a memorable 170-yard 5-iron recovery shot from a fairway bunker landed within 14 feet of the flagstick. Price made his 15-foot birdie putt, and wrapped up the championship less ceremoniously on the first playoff hole with a par. Kite's chances faded when his approach shot landed in a steep greenside bunker. Kite's marvelous 10-under-par 62, one of the finest rounds in 1992, featured 10 birdies, an eagle, and two bogeys. He earned $250,000. Masters winner Fred Couples was third at 142, collecting $200,000, while British Open Champion Nick Faldo finished at 143 to earn $150,000.

"It's been a dream year for me," said Price. "This has really capped off a great year for me. The PGA Championship was by far the biggest. I have an opportunity now to play in all the great events in the world. These events are the icing on the cake. This is what I worked all my life for, to get in all the really great events."

1991

For the first time since the event was introduced in 1979, all four current winner's of golf's major championships competed in the PGA Grand Slam of Golf. The format was expanded to a 36-hole, two-day event in November. Not only were golf's "Big Four" winners able to meet the commitment, but they played for a $1 million purse. A key figure in providing more media attention and player attention on the PGA Grand Slam of Golf was PGA Executive Director and Chief Executive Officer Jim L. Awtrey. He began negotiations with TBS Sports, which had televised the Hawaiian Open in prime time and was eager to expand its golf coverage.

Site:	Kauai Lagoons Resort		
	Kauai, Hawaii		
Date: Nov. 12-13, 1991		Purse:	$1,000,000
First Place:	Ian Woosnam	(135)	$400,000
Second Place:	Ian Baker-Finch	(139)	$250,000
Third Place:	Payne Stewart	(141)	$200,000
Fourth Place:	John Daly	(143)	$150,000

Ian Woosnam

The tournament was a success with both media and player interest. Masters winner Ian Woosnam, ranked No. 1 in the world, knocked in four consecutive birdie putts on his final four holes to post a 9-under-par 135 and win a $400,000 first-place prize. The winner of the British Open, Ian Baker-Finch was four strokes back, and earned $250,000; while U.S. Open Champion Payne Stewart shot 141 to finish in third place for $200,000; and PGA Champion John Daly finished at 143, worth $150,000.

1990

For the first time in its history, the PGA Grand Slam of Golf had to search the celebrity ranks to fill a last-minute void. Chicago Bears football coach Mike Ditka replaced 1989 U.S. Open Champion Curtis Strange, who was suffering from a stomach disorder. PGA President Patrick Rielly searched for a substitute who wouldn't disappoint a holiday crowd of nearly 3,000 golf fans, including 16 who paid $6,500 apiece to play 18 holes with the professionals.

Site:	Kemper Lakes Golf Club	
	Hawthorn Woods, Ill.	
Date:	May 28, 1990	
First Place:	Andy North	(70)
Second Place:	Craig Stadler	(74)
Third Place:	Payne Stewart	(75)
Fourth Place:	Mike Ditka	(NC)

Andy North

Ditka, carrying a 7 handicap, didn't turn in a scorecard. Meanwhile, two-time U.S. Open Champion Andy North won the event with a 2-under-par 70, while Craig Stadler, winner of the 1982 Masters, had a 74 and 1989 PGA Champion Payne Stewart a 75.

The PGA Grand Slam raised enough money to purchase $75,000 worth of clubs for juniors.

1989

With the 71st PGA Championship only 2 V2 months away at Kemper Lakes Golf Club, four professional contenders played the course under perhaps its toughest conditions. Winds whipped around at 25 miles per hour and gusted to 35, as a gallery of 5,200 watched two-time defending U.S. Open Champion Curtis Strange in the day's low round of 1-over-par 73.

Site:	Kemper Lakes Golf Club	
	Hawthorn Woods, Ill.	
Date:	May 29, 1989	
First Place:	Curtis Strange	(73)
Second Place:	Craig Stadler	(75)
Third Place:	Ian Baker-Finch	(76)
Fourth Place:	Greg Norman	(NC)

Curtis Strange

Craig Stadler, who had three of the group's four collective birdies, came home with a 75, while Ian Baker-Finch had a 76 and Greg Norman didn't report his score. Baker-Finch replaced 1988 PGA Champion Jeff Sluman, who withdrew after an appendectomy.

"Even par will be a good score if the wind is blowing in August like it was today," said Stadler. Once again, the PGA Junior Golf Foundation benefitted from a $100,000 donation from the Michael W. Louis Foundation.

1988

Three of golf's biggest winners in 1987 and a champion from 1986 met at Kemper Lakes, a sprawling 7,217-yard layout groomed for the 1989 PGA Championship. Larry Nelson, the defending PGA Champion, fired a course record, 3-under-par 69 to win before a gallery of 6,000 in 93-degree weather. Masters winner Larry Mize and U.S. Open Champion Scott Simpson tied for

Site:	Kemper Lakes Golf Club	
	Hawthorn Woods, Ill.	
Date:	May 30, 1988	
First Place:	Larry Nelson	(69)
Second (Tie):	Larry Mize	(70)
	Scott Simpson	(70)
Fourth Place:	Greg Norman	(73)

Larry Nelson

runner-up at 70, and Greg Norman, winner of the 1986 British Open, substituting for '87 champion Nick Faldo, came home at 73. Norman held the previous course record of 70.

"This is one of the best courses in the last 10 years to host a PGA Championship," said Nelson. "This is one of the best tests I've ever seen. The course is in great shape, and I'm very pleased that the PGA Championship will be here next year."

Norman delighted the crowd by cutting the doglegged 18th fairway with a mammoth drive 325 yards over water. The ball came to rest 43 feet from the cup on the par-4, 433-yard hole. Later, trees were planted along the left-hand side of the fairway to prevent players from attempting the same shot in the PGA Championship.

The PGA Junior Golf Foundation received a gift of $100,000 from the Michael W. Louis Foundation. Said Norman, "I'll give all the time I have in the world for juniors. They're the next generation and we have to help them as much as we can." Norman took leukemia-stricken Jamie Hutton of Wisconsin under his wing earlier in the year.

"You have to set an example for the young kids. Many kids waste their lives on drugs, but golf has an image that is very clean," said Norman.

1986

After a three-year hiatus, a dormant PGA Grand Slam of Golf was resurrected at Kemper Lakes Golf Club in Hawthorn Woods, Ill., site of the 1989 PGA Championship. The Michael W. Louis Foundation, a Chicago philanthropic organization which also administers other charitable, educational, religious and scientific programs, set up the PGA Grand Slam to run through 1990 at Kemper Lakes.

Site:	Kemper Lakes Golf Club	
	Hawthorn Woods, Ill.	
Date:	Sept. 1, 1986	
First Place:	Greg Norman	(70)
Second Place:	Fuzzy Zoeller	(72)
Third Place:	Jack Nicklaus	(75)
Fourth Place:	Bob Tway	(75)

Greg Norman

The revised format included 16 amateurs with the previous year's winners of golf's four major championships. Three winners of majors in 1986 — PGA Champion Bob Tway, British Open Champion Greg Norman and Masters Champion Jack Nicklaus — were joined by Fuzzy Zoeller. Norman became the first player to break par from the back tees on the 7,500-plus-yard championship course, finishing with a 2-under-par 70. Zoeller came in at 72, and Nicklaus, who dunked a tee shot on the par-3 17th into the water, joined Tway with a 75 on the demanding course.

The event raised $125,000 for junior golf. During the round Norman clowned with Zoeller, planting a flagstick in a greenside bunker on the 18th hole, while awaiting his partner's arrival. Zoeller responded by playing his approach to within 12 feet of the empty hole. Sixteen amateurs paid $5,000 each to play in the special pro-am.

The PGA Grand Slam of Golf was postponed in 1987 because the winners of golf's major championships could not clear schedules for the planned date. Masters Champion Larry Mize and U.S. Open Champion Scott Simpson committed for the event, but neither PGA Champion Larry Nelson nor British Open Champion Nick Faldo could make the date.

1982

British Open Champion Bill Rogers, leading a foursome of winners of the 1981 major championships, captured the fourth PGA Grand Slam of Golf. Rogers turned in a 1-under-par 71 over the George and Tom Fazio creation — the 7,137-yard Champion Course at PGA National Golf Club. PGA Champion Larry Nelson was runner-up

Site:	PGA National Golf Club, Champion	
	Course, Palm Beach Gardens, Fla.	
Date:	March 15, 1982	
First Place:	Bill Rogers	(71)
Second Place:	Larry Nelson	(75)
Third Place:	David Graham	(76)
Fourth Place:	Tom Watson	(78)

Bill Rogers

with a 75, while U.S. Open Champion David Graham was at 76, and Masters Champion Tom Watson had a 78.

The foursome played under near-perfect conditions and before a gallery of between 2,500 and 3,000. However, Nelson was the only member of the quartet not to have walked 36 holes the day before in the rain-marred Inverarry Classic in Lauderhill, Fla. Nelson wasn't entered in the tournament, and drove to Palm Beach Gardens from Daytona Beach. The players generally praised the Champion Course, which would be the site of the 1983 Ryder Cup Matches and the 1987 PGA Championship. "I've played a lot of rounds on courses I've never seen," said Rogers. "I like the course, and I love the greens and fairways. We were lucky today we didn't see it in the wind."

There was no prize money involved, with all proceeds going to junior golf, but the low scorer traditionally awards $1,000 in his name to his favorite golf charity. Rogers donated the money to the junior golf program at Northridge Country Club in his hometown, Texarkana, Texas.

1981

Lee Trevino shined among one of golf's most heralded quartets at Breakers West Golf Course in West Palm Beach, Fla. Trevino fired a 3-under-par 68 over the par-71, 7,100-yard layout, playing in winds that gusted to 35 miles per hour.

Site:	Breakers West Golf Course	
	West Palm Beach, Fla.	
Date:	March 16, 1981	
First Place:	Lee Trevino	(68)
Second Place:	Tom Watson	(71)
Third Place:	Jack Nicklaus	(72)
Fourth Place:	Severiano Ballesteros	(75)

Lee Trevino

Tom Watson finished runner-up with a 71, while Jack Nicklaus finished at 1-over-par 72, and Spain's Severiano Ballesteros at 75. A gallery estimated between 4,000 and 5,000 paid $25 each as a contribution to the PGA of America's Junior Golf Foundation. Trevino was presented the PGA Grand Slam Trophy by Vice President George Bush.

"The golf Lee played today was phenomenal," said Nicklaus, who couldn't overcome a double-bogey start. "It was the best I've seen under these conditions in a long time." Trevino had four birdies and a three-putt bogey to match the best-ball score of his three opponents.

It was the most successful PGA Grand Slam in the three years of its existence, grossing more than $125,000 for junior golf, in addition to funds raised for the American Cancer Society, a participating sponsor along with the Economic Council of the Palm Beaches and Munsingwear, Inc.

"I think I had an advantage today," said Trevino, who donated $1,000 to the Southern Methodist University women's golf team. "Ballesteros just came over from Spain a week ago. Tom Watson has been in the snow in Kansas City for a couple of weeks (actually Watson was working out in Florida) and Nicklaus missed the cut last week in Doral. And I've done nothing but practice for this match for the past two months."

1980

Opening its doors to the national golf spotlight for the first time in a decade, Hazeltine National Golf Club hosted the PGA Grand Slam of Golf, and invited 1979 Tournament Players Championship winner Lanny Wadkins, 1979 PGA Champion David Graham, 1979 U.S. Open Champion Hale Irwin and 1979 Masters Champion Fuzzy Zoeller. Wadkins birdied the 18th hole for a 1-under-par 71 to finish two strokes ahead of Irwin and three ahead of Graham and Zoeller.

Site:	Hazeltine National Golf Club	
	Chaska, Minn.	
Date:	July 1, 1980	
First Place:	Lanny Wadkins	(71)
Second Place:	Hale Irwin	(73)
Third (Tie):	David Graham	(74)
	Fuzzy Zoeller	(74)

Lanny Wadkins

Between 2,500 and 3,000 spectators followed the players over a course that had suffered severe criticism during one of its proudest moments, hosting the 1970 U.S. Open.

At that time, Dave Hill spent a post-first round press conference criticizing the course, claiming it "lacked only cows and corn to be a real pasture." Irwin said the stigma would likely remain with the course. However, the design was drastically changed by the time Hazeltine hosted the 1991 U.S. Open.

Irwin admonished the media after the PGA Grand Slam exhibition: "Here we are facing you guys and all we're being asked about is what we think of the golf course. Nobody's asking about junior golf and that was supposed to be the reason we came here. We're not here to run a critique of Hazeltine. We're here to promote junior golf."

1979

Oak Hill's East Course, renovated by architects George and Tom Fazio over a two-year period, hosted the inaugural PGA Grand Slam of Golf. The event was designed to benefit the PGA's Junior Golf Foundation. Winners of the 1978 four major championships competed: PGA Champion John Mahaffey, British Open Champion Jack Nicklaus,

Site:	Oak Hill Country Club	
	Rochester, N.Y.	
Date:	Aug. 7, 1979	
First (Tie):	Andy North	(73)
	Gary Player	(73)
Third (Tie):	John Mahaffey	(77)
	Jack Nicklaus	(77)

Andy North

Masters Champion Gary Player and U.S. Open Champion Andy North. The par-70, 6,974-yard course made it rough on the foursome, with North and Player sharing top honors with 73s and the $12,000 Steuben Trophy. Mahaffey and Nicklaus struggled home with 7-over-par 77s.

Spectators were charged $25 or $30 to view the event, and another $100 to attend an evening awards presentation featuring the contestants, former President Gerald Ford, entertainers Pat Boone and Foster Brooks and sportscaster Chris Schenkel, the master of ceremonies.

A junior clinic preceded the 18-hole round, but any hopes of a tournament atmosphere for 5,000 spectators faded when players began conceding three-and four-foot putts. But the gallery was entertained by the joking and the opportunity to chat with their heroes.

After expenses, the PGA's Junior Golf Foundation netted more than $75,000.

Gary Player

PGA CUP MATCHES

1994 FACTS AND FORMAT

DATE: Sept. 16-22, 1994
SITE: PGA National Golf Club, Palm Beach Gardens, Fla.
DEFENDING CHAMPION: United States

PRIZE MONEY AND HONORS

No prize money is awarded to the PGA Cup competitors. Members of both teams compete solely for their country and their country's right of possession of the Llandudno International Trophy.

Site:	PGA National Golf Club, Palm Beach Gardens, Fla.
Date:	Sept. 16-22, 1994

UNITED STATES PGA CUP TEAM
Captain: Dick Smith

J.L. Lewis	Rick Acton
Ron McDougal	George Bowman
Pete Oakley	Walt Chapman
Jeffrey R. Roth	Tom Cleaver
Todd M. Smith	John D. Lee

The European PGA Cup Team will be determined following the 1994 Glenmuir PGA Club Professional Championship, June 14-17.

METHOD OF PLAY

Identical to that of the Ryder Cup: match play, including foursomes (two-man teams in alternate shot), four-ball (two-man teams in better ball) and singles (18 holes at match play).

RULES AND REGULATIONS

The Rules of Golf which govern play are determined by the United States Golf Association and applied by the PGA of America Board of Directors. The Matches are subject to the overall supervision of the board of directors and the PGA Rules Committee.

1994 U.S. ELIGIBILITY

- Must be a member in good standing of the PGA of America
- Top nine finishers in the 1993 PGA Club Professional Championship
- 1992 PGA Club Professional Championship winner Ron McDougal
- PGA Honorary President Dick Smith will serve as America's Captain for the 1994 PGA Cup Matches.

(Membership on the 1994 PGA Cup Team will be forfeited should the player subsequently become reclassified as a Tour professional or any other ineligible classification.)

■ HISTORY

A CUP FOR THE CLUB PROFESSIONALS

The PGA Cup Matches were first played in 1973 at Pinehurst (N.C.) Country Club as an outgrowth of the PGA Club Professional Championship. Structured after the format of the Ryder Cup Matches, which feature team competition between the U.S. and Europe, the PGA Cup Matches feature the top PGA club professionals from both sides of the Atlantic. Competition was held annually until 1984, when both countries agreed to hold this event biennially at alternating sites.

Proceeds from the PGA Club Professional Championship in 1975 at Callaway Gardens, Pine Mountain, Ga., covered the expenses of the U.S. Team for the first overseas PGA Cup Matches. A pro-am event was held prior to the '75 Cup Matches, which raised $12,000 and made it possible for the British PGA to stage the Matches. Great Britain-Ireland Captain Christy O'Connor Sr., then 51, did his part to keep the event alive, winning the pro-am.

The teams began with nine players, but the roster was expanded to 10 in 1988. Qualification for America's team is based upon performances in the PGA Club Professional Championship. From 1973-88, the European team was comprised of PGA club professionals from Great Britain and Ireland. In 1990, the team was opened to professionals from throughout Europe.

THE LLANDUDNO INTERNATIONAL TROPHY

The Llandudno ("La-lon-dro") International Trophy was first awarded to England in 1939, after its club professionals won the first Home Tournament Series against teams from Ireland, Scotland and Wales. The trophy was packed away and the series was abolished with the outbreak of World War II.

Former Great Britain Ryder Cup player Percy Alliss (1929, '31, '33, '35, '37) retired the trophy to his personal collection. Alliss died in 1973, and two years later his son, Peter, former captain of the British PGA and an eight-time Ryder Cup participant (1953, '57, '59, '61, '63, '65, '67, '69), donated the Llandudno Trophy to be awarded to the winner of the annual PGA Cup Matches. During the German bombing of London in World War II, the trophy was slightly bent and never straightened, to serve as a reminder of its historical niche.

PGA CUP MATCHES

■ HISTORY THROUGH THE YEARS

U.S. 10 Wins • Britain/Ireland- Europe 4 Wins • 2 Ties

Year	Results		Site	U.S. Team Captain	European Team Captain
1973	USA 13,	GBI 3	Pinehurst (N.C.) CC	William Clarke	Tom Halliburton
1974	USA 11 V_2,	GBI 4 V_2	Pinchurst (N.C.) CC	Henry Poe	Brian Hutchinson
1975	USA 9 V_2,	GBI 6 V_2	Southport, England	Don Padgett Jr.	Christy O'Connor Sr.
1976	USA 9 V_2,	GBI 6 V_2	Leeds, England	Frank Cardi	George Will
1977	USA 8 V_2,	GBI 8 V_2	Mission Hills (Calif.) CC	Henry Poe	Jack Hargreaves
1978	GBI 10 V_2,	USA 6 V_2	Plymouth, England	Henry Poe	Tommy Horton
1979	GBI 12 V_2,	USA 4 V_2	Castletown, Isle of Man	Don Padgett Jr.	Bill Watson
1980	USA 15,	GBI 6	Oak Tree GC, Okla.	Don Padgett Jr.	David Talbot
1981	USA 10 V_2,	GBI 10 V_2	Turnberry Isle CC, Fla.	Joe Black	Doug Smith
1982	USA 13 V_2,	GBI 7 V_2	Holston Hills CC, Tenn.	Don Padgett Jr.	David Jones
1983	GBI 14 V_2,	USA 6 V_2	Muirfield, Scotland	Joe Black	Keith Hockey
1984	GBI 12 V_2,	USA 8 V_2	Turnberry, Scotland	Joe Black	Keith Hockey
1986	USA 16,	GBI 9	Knollwood CC, Ill.	Mark Kizziar	Derek Nash
1988	USA 15 V_2,	GBI 10 V_2	The Belfry, Sutton Coldfield, Eng.	Mickey Powell	David Huish
1990	USA 19	EUR 7	Kiawah Island, S.C.	J.R. Carpenter	Richard Bradbeer
1992	USA 15	EUR 11	Kildare Hotel & CC Dublin, Ireland	Patrick J. Rielly	Paul Leonard

1992

The U.S. had the "Upper" hand at Kildare Hotel and Country Club near Dublin, Ireland. Actually, Brett Upper of Clearwater, Fla., was playing at a special level in guiding the Americans to a 15-11 victory over a team of Europe's finest club professionals. Upper, a former PGA Tour player and the 1990 PGA Club Professional Champion, eagled the par-5, 529-yard 18th hole three straight times to clinch match victories. One of Upper's eagles came in the second round, in the alternate shot format, when partner Gene Fieger of Bryn Mawr, Pa., drilled a 223-yard 4-iron to within 12 feet of the cup.

Of 25 matches, 12 were decided on the 18th hole. American players won four times going the distance, and four times they saved halves on the final hole. Only once did they fail to hold a lead going into the 18th. Mike San Filippo lost a 1-up lead when Tim Giles made a 30-foot birdie putt on the 18th hole. Upper teamed with Fieger to score six points in six matches. Larry Gilbert of Lexington, Ky., the 1991 PGA Club Professional Player of the Year, earned two points in his sixth appearance in the PGA Cup Matches. The U.S. has won all four PGA Cup Matches since the opponents became an all-European team in 1990.

Site:	Kildare Country Club, Dublin, Ireland
Date:	Sept. 18-20, 1992
Results:	USA 15, Europe 11

PGA Cup Teams	
United States	**European**
Captain: Patrick J. Rielly	Captain: Paul Leonard
Bob Borowicz	John Chillas
Gene Fieger	Peter Cowen
Larry Gilbert	Tim Giles
Mike San Filippo	Chris Hall
Lee Rinker	John Hoskison
Mike Schuchart	Nick Job
Ron McDougal	David Jones
Brett Upper	Craig Maltman
Steve Veriato	Brian Rimmer
Tom Wargo	Russell Weir

Morning Foursomes (Day One)
Cowen/Jones (2 & 1) over San Filippo/Wargo
Hall/Job (1-up) over Schuchart/Veriato
Borowicz/Gilbert (3 & 2) over Hoskison/Maltman
Fieger/Upper (6 & 4) over Chillas/Weir

Afternoon Four-Ball (Day One)
Jones/Cowen halved with Rinker/Schuchart
McDougal/Wargo (4 & 3) over Hall/Job
Borowicz/Gilbert (5 & 4) over Giles/Rimmer
Fieger/Upper (2 & 1) over Hoskison/Maltman
Day One Total: USA 5 V_2, Europe 2 V_2

Morning Foursomes (Day Two)
McDougal/Wargo halved with Chillas/Weir
Hoskison/Maltman (4 & 3) over Rinker/San Filippo
Hall/Job (2 & 1) over Gilbert/Veriato
Fieger/Upper (1-up) over Cowen/Jones
POINTS: Europe 2 V_2, USA 1 V_2

Afternoon Four-Ball (Day Two)
McDougal/Wargo (2 & 1) over Hoskison/Maltman
Rinker/Schuchart (2-up) over Chillas/Weir
Hall/Job (1-up) over Borowicz/Gilbert
Fieger/Upper (1-up) over Cowen/Jones
Day Two Total: USA 4 V_2, Europe 3 V_2
Two-Day Total: USA 10, Europe 6

Singles (Day Three)
Fieger (3 & 2) over Jones
Job (5 & 4) over Wargo
Gilbert, illness default (match halved)
Schuchart halved with Hall
Weir (3 & 2) over Veriato
San Filippo halved with Giles
Cowen (1-up) over McDougal
Rinker halved with Chillas
Borowicz (5 & 3) over Maltman
Upper (2-up) over Hoskison
Day Three Total: USA 5, Europe 5
Final Score: USA 15, Europe 11

1990

It was the first time American club professionals faced a team that had been expanded to include players from continental Europe. But the deeper and more experienced U.S. team was set for a rout. In a shining example of sportsmanship during the second day in an afternoon four-ball match, American Dale Fuller reached down and conceded Tim Rastall's eight-foot par putt on the 18th green. The gesture forced a halve in the match and sent the U.S. into the final-day singles with a 13-3 cushion. The only thing left undecided the final day was the victory margin. The U.S. finished with 19 points, and surpassed the 1983 spread of eight points as the greatest winning margin. But the sportsmanship episode took precedence.

"It was the thing to do," said Fuller. "It was too good a match to come down to an eight-foot putt. They (the European team) are to be commended." The European team featured seven-time PGA Cup member Brian Waites, 50, and six-time Cup member Brian Barnes. The U.S. contingent featured 1989 PGA Club Professional Champion Bruce Fleisher and former PGA Tour player Phillip Hancock, who won three matches together as a team and had a total record of 5-1 overall.

Site:	Turtle Point Golf Club, Kiawah Island, S.C.
Date:	Sept. 21-23, 1990
Results:	USA 19, Europe 7

PGA Cup Teams

United States	European
Captain:	Captain:
James Ray Carpenter	Richard Bradbeer
Bob Ford	Brian Barnes
Bob Boyd	Paul Carman
Bruce Fleisher	Tim Rastall
Phillip Hancock	Alastair Webster
Sammy Rachels	Kevin Stables
Kim Thompson	Brian Waites
Ray Freeman	John Woof
Stu Ingraham	Russell Weir
Dale Fuller	David Screeton
Jeff Thomsen	David Scott

Morning Foursomes (Day One)

Boyd/Ford halved with Webster/Stables
Fleisher/Hancock (7 & 6) over Waites/Woof
Rachels/Thompson (3 & 2) over Rastall/Carman
Freeman/Ingraham (2 & 1) over Weir/Barnes

Afternoon Four-Ball (Day One)

Fuller/Thomsen (4 & 3) over Webster/Stables
Fleisher/Hancock (2 & 1) over Carman/Screeton
Weir/Waites (3 & 2) over Boyd/Ford
Rachels/Ingraham (8 & 7) over Barnes/Scott
Day One Total: USA 6 1/2, Europe 1 1/2

Foursomes (Day Two)

Weir/Waites (2 &1) over Freeman/Ingraham
Fuller/Thomsen (3 & 2) over Screeton/Carman
Hancock/Thompson (4 & 2) over Rastall/Woof
Boyd/Ford (2 & 1) over Stables/Webster

Four-Ball (Day Two)

Rachels/Thompson (4 & 3) over Barnes/Carman
Fleisher/Hancock (3 & 2) over Waites/Weir
Fuller/Thomsen halved with Rastall/Scott
Boyd/Ford (1-up) over Stables/Webster
Day Two Total: USA 6 1/2, Europe 1 1/2
Two-Day Total: USA 13, Europe 3

Singles (Day Three)

Webster (4 & 3) over Freeman
Fuller (1-up) over Barnes
Fleisher (4 & 3) over Waites
Weir (1-up) over Boyd
Ingraham (7 & 6) over Rastall
Rachels (1-up) over Stables
Carman (3 & 2) over Hancock
Woof (2-up) over Thompson
Ford (5 & 4) over Screeton
Thomsen (4 & 3) over Scott
Day Three Total: USA 6, Europe 4
Final Score: USA 19, Europe 7

1988

The Americans amassed a 15 1/2-point total, the most points by either team in the history of the PGA Cup Matches, to capture the United States' first victory in the United Kingdom since 1976. Tom Wargo of Centralia, Ill., rallied his teammates in the singles with a gutsy 1-up victory over Phil Hinton, and 1987 PGA Club Professional Champion Jay Lumpkin of Amelia Island Plantation, S.C., downed European veteran Russell Weir, 3 and 2.

Site:	The Belfry, Sutton Coldfield, England
Date:	July 22-24, 1988
Results:	USA 15 1/2, Great Britain-Ireland 10 1/2

PGA Cup Teams

United States	Great Britain-Ireland
Captain: Mickey Powell	Captain: David Huish
Scott Bess	Keith Ashdown
Gibby Gilbert	John Chillas
David Glenz	Ged Furey
Bob Lendzion	Martin Gray
Jay Lumpkin	Phil Hinton
Bob Menne	John Hoskison
Lonnie Nielsen	Nick Job
Jeffrey Roth	Kevin Jones
David Thore	Gary Stafford
Tom Wargo	Russell Weir

Morning Foursomes (Day One)

Gilbert/Bess halved with Chillas/Jones
Weir/Stafford (4 & 2) over Thore/Lumpkin
Glenz/Lendzion (3 & 2) over Hinton/Gray
Menne/Wargo (7 & 5) over Job/Hoskison

Afternoon Four-Ball (Day One)

Ashdown/Furey (1-up) over Gilbert/Glenz
Gray/Hoskison (1-up) over Menne/Wargo
Nielsen/Roth halved with Chillas/Jones
Thore/Lumpkin (5 & 3) over Weir/Stafford
Day One Total: USA 4, Great Britain-Ireland 4

Morning Foursomes (Day Two)

Nielsen/Glenz (2 & 1) over Weir/Stafford
Ashdown/Furey (2 & 1) over Thore/Lumpkin
Gray/Hoskison (2-up) over Roth/Wargo
Lendzion/Bess halved with Chillas/Jones

Afternoon Four-Ball (Day Two)

Gilbert/Menne (4 & 3) over Hinton/Hoskison
Lendzion/Glenz (3 & 1) over Job/Weir
Bess/Nielsen (3 & 2) over Ashdown/Furey
Thore/Wargo (1-up) over Chillas/Jones
Day Two Total: USA 5 1/2, Great Britain-Ireland 2 1/2
Two-Day Total: USA 9 1/2, Great Britain-Ireland 6 1/2

Singles (Day Three)

Wargo (1-up) over Hinton
Thore (1-up) over Job
Lumpkin (3 & 2) over Weir
Jones (5 & 4) over Roth
Lendzion (3 & 2) over Gray
Bess (3 & 1) over Ashdown
Furey (4 & 3) over Nielsen
Stafford (1-up) over Glenz
Hoskison (4 & 3) over Menne
Gilbert (3 & 1) over Chillas
Day Three Total: USA 6, Great Britain-Ireland 4
Final Score: USA 15 1/2, Great Britain-Ireland 10 1/2

1986

The U.S. team won back the Llandudno International Trophy after an absence of four years, as American depth took its toll throughout the singles round on the final day. Wheeler Stewart of Alexandria, Va., 1984 PGA Club Champion Bill Schumaker of Columbus City, Ind., and Kevin Morris of White Plains, N.Y., each scored wins in the singles. Charlie Epps of the U.S. squad and Scotsman Willie Milne, a burly golf range operator, saved the best for last. They reached the 438-yard 18th hole even. Epps knocked his approach to the middle of the green, while Milne flew his 8-iron approach over the green and his chip shot eight feet past the cup. Epps followed by putting to within inches of the cup. As Milne prepared to replace his ball. Epps stunned players and officials by conceding the eight-footer for a halved match. Milne then gave Epps a bear hug in the middle of the green. In 1986, the format was expanded to four foursomes and four four-ball matches on each of the first two days.

Site:	Knollwood Country Club, Lake Forest, Ill.
Date:	Sept. 17-19, 1986
Results:	USA 16, Great Britain-Ireland 9

PGA Cup Teams	
United States	**Great Britain-Ireland**
Captain: Mark Kizziar	Captain: Derek Nash
Rick Acton	Denis Durnian
Ken Allard	Pip Elson
Scott Bess	Martin Gray
Charlie Epps	Keith Robson
Ray Freeman	Gary Smith
Kevin Morris	David Huish
Jim White	Willie Milne
Wheeler Stewart	Bob Longworth
Bill Schumaker	Russell Weir

Morning Foursomes (Day One)

Durnian/Elson (4 & 2) over Stewart/White
Allard/Schumaker (3 & 2) over Gray/Weir
Morris/Freeman (4 & 3) over Robson/Smith
Acton/Bess (4 & 3) over Huish/Milne

Afternoon Four-Ball (Day One)

Epps/Schumaker (1-up) over Durnian-Elson
Morris/White (4 & 3) over Gray/Weir
Allard/Stewart (5 & 3) over Huish/Milne
Acton/Bess (6 & 5) over Longworth/Smith
Day One Total: USA 7, Great Britain-Ireland 1

Morning Four-Ball (Day Two)

Gray-Huish (4 & 2) over Acton/Bess
Durnian/Elson (6 & 5) over Freeman/White
Smith/Weir halved with Epps/Schumaker
Allard/Stewart (5 & 4) over Milne/Longworth

Afternoon Foursomes (Day Two)

Gray/Huish (2 & 1) over Morris/White
Durnian/Elson (1-up) over Epps/Freeman
Allard/Schumaker (4 & 2) over Robson/Smith
Acton/Bess (2-up) over Longworth/Weir
Day Two Total: Great Britain-Ireland 4 1/2, USA 3 1/2
Two-Day Total: USA 10 1/2, Great Britain-Ireland 5 1/2

Singles (Day Three)

Huish (1-up) over Allard
Durnian (3 & 2) over White
Stewart (2 & 1) over Gray
Morris (1-up) over Elson
Weir (2 & 1) over Freeman
Schumaker (5 & 3) over Smith
Acton (3 & 1) over Longworth
Bess (3 & 2) over Robson
Epps halved with Milne
Day Three Total: USA 5 1/2, Great Britain-Ireland 3 1/2
Final Score: USA 16, Great Britain-Ireland 9

1984

Great Britain-Ireland steamed ahead of the U.S. by winning four of six opening matches, holding on to a 7-5 lead after two days, and polishing off a Cup victory in the singles with five consecutive victories and a day-ending 5 1/2 to 3 1/2 margin. The difference may have been veterans Peter Butler, 52, and 40-year-old David Huish, who finished 4 1/2 -1 overall. Huish scored a 1-up victory over Terry Florence in singles, and Butler halved with John Elliott.

On the first day, Florence of Charleston, S.C., jumped into the waters of the Wee Burn guarding the 16th green to play a miraculous recovery shot during the morning foursomes. Florence didn't notice or care that he had not removed his shoes and socks. Despite his recovery, Florence and partner Jim Webb fell to Butler and Huish, 2 and 1. The U.S. loss was the Americans' fourth consecutive defeat on foreign soil.

Site:	Turnberry, Scotland
Date:	July 25-27, 1984
Results:	Great Britain-Ireland 12 1/2, USA 8 1/2

PGA Cup Teams	
United States	**Great Britain-Ireland**
Captain: Joe Black	Captain: Keith Hockey
Bob Ford	John Chillas
Don Padgett II	Craig DeFoy
Terry Florence	David Huish
Larry Webb	Dennis Durnian
Dan Murphy	Bob Cameron
Tim Collins	David Butler
John Elliott	Peter Butler
David Glenz	David Vaughan
Bob Wynn	David Ingram

Morning Foursomes (Day One)

P. Butler/Huish (2 & 1) over Florence/Webb
Chillas/Cameron (2 & 1) over Collins/Padgett
Durnian/Ingram (1-up) over Elliott/Glenz

Afternoon Four-Ball (Day One)

Webb/Wynn (2 & 1) over D. Butler/Vaughan
Ford/Padgett (4 & 3) over Chillas/Huish
DeFoy/Durnian (1-up) over Glenz/Murphy
Day One Total: Great Britain-Ireland 4, USA 2

Morning Four-Ball (Day Two)

P. Butler/Durnian (3 & 1) over Ford/Padgett
Chillas/Huish (5 & 4) over Collins/Elliott
Florence/Wynn (3 & 2) over D. Butler/Vaughan

Afternoon Foursomes (Day Two)

Ford/Glenz (2 & 1) over Cameron/Chillas
Webb/Wynn (2 & 1) over Durnian/Ingram
P. Butler/Huish (3 & 2) over Florence/Murphy
Day Two Total: USA 3, Great Britain-Ireland 3
Two-Day Total: Great Britain-Ireland 7, USA 5

Singles (Day Three)

DeFoy (6 & 5) over Padgett
Chillas (2 & 1) over Ford
Huish (1-up) over Florence
Durnian (1-up) over Webb
Cameron (5 & 4) over Murphy
Collins (1-up) over D. Butler
Elliott halved with P. Butler
Glenz (3 & 2) over Vaughan
Wynn (7 & 6) over Wynn
Day Three Total: Great Britain-Ireland 5 1/2, USA 3 1/2
Final Score: Great Britain-Ireland 12 1/2, USA 8 1/2

1983

Great Britain-Ireland blitzed the American club professionals, 9 1/2 to 2 1/2, after two rounds, including a 3-0 shutout in the second-day morning four-ball, and won five of nine singles matches to capture their third victory in the PGA Cup Matches. The 14 1/2 to 6 1/2 defeat matched Great Britain-Ireland's 1979 performance (12 1/2 to 4 1/2) for the widest margin of victory. "We were killed within 50 yards of the green," said U.S. Captain Joe Black. "The British and Irish were so much better. That's usually our strong point." The hosts proved it was their week in many ways. In the opening day's afternoon four-ball match between David Dunk and John Chillas against the American duo of Gene Borek and Kevin Morris, Dunk struck an approach shot on the 17th hole from a bad lie. The ball made the edge of the green and he holed a 50-foot eagle putt to square the match. Dunk then saved his team, and halved the match, by sinking a five-foot par putt on the 18th green.

Site:	Muirfield, Scotland
Date:	July 28-30, 1983
Results:	Great Britain-Ireland 14 1/2, USA 6 1/2

PGA Cup Teams	
United States	Great Britain-Ireland
Captain: Joe Black	Captain: Keith Hockey
Larry Gilbert	Bob Cameron
Jack Seltzer	John Chillas
Jim Logue	David Dunk
Bob Lendzion	Jim Farmer
Jim King	Martin Gray
Denis Husse	Mike Ingham
Kevin Morris	Tony Minshall
Tom Robertson	Alistair Thomson
Gene Borek	Phil Weaver

Morning Foursomes (Day One)
Gilbert/Robertson (4 & 2) over Ingham/Thomson
Cameron/Weaver (5 & 4) over King/Logue
Farmer/Gray (4 & 3) over Seltzer/Lendzion

Afternoon Four-Ball (Day One)
Borek/Morris halved with Chillas/Dunk
Minshall/Cameron (1-up) over Husse/Logue
Farmer/Gray (1-up) over Gilbert/Robertson
Day One Total: Great Britain-Ireland 4 1/2, USA 1 1/2

Morning Four-Ball (Day Two)
Minshall/Ingham (2 & 1) over Gilbert/Seltzer
Weaver/Chillas (2 & 1) over Robertson/Borek
Farmer/Thompson (2-up) over Logue/King

Afternoon Foursomes (Day Two)
Minshall/Ingham (4 & 2) over Seltzer/Morris
Chillas/Weaver (4 & 3) over Robertson/Husse
King/Lendzion (5 & 3) over Farmer/Gray
Day Two Total: Great Britain-Ireland 5, USA 1
Two-Day Total: Great Britain-Ireland 9 1/2, USA 2 1/2

Singles (Day Three)
Gilbert (3 & 2) over Farmer
Weaver (3 &2) over Robertson
Seltzer (5 & 4) over Chillas
Logue (1-up) over Minshall
Cameron (2 & 1) over Lendzion
Thomsen (4 & 2) over Husse
Dunk (6 & 5) over Morris
Gray (7 & 6) over King
Borek (2-up) over Ingham
Day Three Total: Great Britain-Ireland 5, USA 4
Final Score: Great Britain 14 1/2, USA 6 1/2,

1982

The Americans stormed through the opening foursome and four-ball matches, rolling to a 5 1/2 to 1/2 lead over the Great Britain-Ireland team on the first day of play. Willie Milne and four-time Ryder Cup member Peter Butler managed to catch 1981 PGA Club Professional Champion Larry Gilbert and Richard Crawford, to halve the first match of the opening round. The U.S. built an 8 1/2 to 3 1/2 lead during the second round, and Jim Albus, Crawford, John Jackson and Don Padgett II each scored wins in singles competition. It was fitting that Albus recorded the decisive point, having played perhaps the best of any of his teammates during the week.

Site:	Holston Hills Country Club, Knoxville, Tenn.
Date:	Sept. 10-12, 1982
Results:	USA 13 1/2, Great Britain-Ireland 7 1/2

PGA Cup Teams	
United States	Great Britain-Ireland
Captain: Don Padgett Jr.	Captain: David Jones
John Jackson	Denis Durian
Jim Logue	Willie Milne
Gary Robinson	Peter Butler
Don Massengale	David Vaughan
Jimmy Wright	Paul Leonard
Jim Albus	John Chillas
Richard Crawford	David Dunk
Don Padgett II	Ian Collins
Larry Gilbert	Phil Weaver

Morning Foursomes (Day One)
Gilbert/Crawford halved with Milne/Butler
Padgett II/Massengale (4 & 3) over Durnian/Vaughan
Robinson/Logue (6 & 5) over Chillas/Collins

Afternoon Four-Ball (Day One)
Wright/Albus (3 & 2) over Dunk/Weaver
Jackson/Padgett II (4 & 3) over Milne/Leonard
Gilbert/Massengale (3 & 2) over Vaughan/Durnian
Day One Total: USA 5 1/2, Great Britain-Ireland 1/2

Morning Four-Ball (Day Two)
Milne/Butler (3 & 2) over Robinson/Wright
Padgett II/Logue (1-up) over Chillas/Leonard
Jackson/Gilbert (4 & 3) over Vaughan/Durnian

Afternoon Foursomes (Day Two)
Albus/Gilbert (7 & 6) over Collins/Weaver
Butler/Milne (5 & 4) over Crawford/Massengale
Chillas/Leonard (3 & 2) over Padgett II/Jackson
Day Two Total: USA 3, Great Britain-Ireland 3
Two-Day Total: USA 8 1/2, Great Britain-Ireland 3 1/2

Singles (Day Three)
Jackson (1-up) over Durnian
Milne (3 & 1) over Logue
Butler (2-up) over Robinson
Massengale halved with Vaughan
Wright halved with Leonard
Albus (2 & 1) over Chillas
Crawford (3 & 2) over Dunk
Padgett II (4 & 3) over Collins
Weaver (6 & 5) over Gilbert
Day Three Total: USA 5, Great Britain-Ireland 4
Final Score: USA 13 1/2, Great Britain-Ireland 7 1/2

1981

Great Britain-Ireland, led by former schoolboy boxer Michael Steadman, won six of the final-day singles matches to force the second tie in the history of the PGA Cup Matches.

Steadman, the British PGA Club Professional Champion, teamed with fellow countryman John Yeo in the first-day four-balls to defeat the top U.S. team of 1980 PGA Club Professional Champion John Traub and Oakmont (Pa.) Country Club professional Bob Ford. Rallying from a four-hole deficit after nine holes, Steadman and Yeo clawed their way back. They pulled even after 16 holes, and Steadman knocked his approach three feet from the cup on No. 17 for an easy birdie and a 1-up lead. Ford flew his wedge approach five feet from the pin on the par-5, 551-yard 18th, but Yeo hit his wedge approach from heavy rough to within two feet of the pin to halve the hole and win the match. Steadman went on to win his singles match over Traub, 7 and 6, and Yeo downed Jim Albus, 5 and 3. John Jackson, Ford and Don Padgett II managed to save U.S. pride by winning their singles matches.

Site:	Turnberry Isle Country Club, Aventura, North Miami, Fla.
Date:	Oct. 15-18, 1981
Results:	USA 10 1/2, Great Britain-Ireland 10 1/2

PGA Cup Teams	
United States	Great Britain-Ireland
Captain: Joe Black	Captain: Doug Smith
John Traub	Mike Steadman
Jim Albus	John Yeo
Steve Benson	John Morgan
John Jackson	Denis Durnian
Gene Borek	Peter Butler
Roger Kennedy	David Jones
Larry Gilbert	David Ridley
Bob Ford	Craig DeFoy
Don Padgett II	Bob Cameron

Morning Foursomes (Day One)

Gilbert/Albus (3 & 2) over DeFoy/Durnian
Jackson/Benson (5 & 4) over Jones/Ridley
Kennedy/Padgett II halved with Butler/Morgan

Afternoon Four-Ball (Day One)

Steadman/Yeo (1-up) over Traub/Ford
Albus/Gilbert (3 & 2) over DeFoy/Cameron
Padgett II/Borek (4&3) over Durnian/Morgan
Day One Total: USA 4 1/2, Great Britain-Ireland 1 1/2

Morning Four-Ball (Day Two)

Traub/Ford (3 & 2) over Butler/Jones
Jackson/Benson halved with Steadman/Yeo
Kennedy/Borek (1-up) over DeFoy/Ridley

Afternoon Foursomes (Day Two)

Durnian/Morgan over Gilbert/Albus (2-up)
Cameron/Ridley (2 & 1) over Jackson/Benson
Padgett II/Kennedy halved with Steadman/Yeo
Day Two Total: USA 3, Great Britain-Ireland 3
Two-Day Total: USA 7 1/2, Great Britain-Ireland 4 1/2

Singles (Day Three)

Steadman (7 & 6) over Traub
Yeo (5 & 3) over Albus
Morgan (2 & 1) over Benson
Jackson (3 & 1) over Durnian
Butler (5 & 4) over Borek
Jones (1-up) over Kennedy
Ridley (2-up) over Gilbert
Ford (1-up) over DeFoy
Padgett II (3 & 1) over Cameron
Day Three Total: Great Britain-Ireland 6, USA 3
Final Score: USA 10 1/2, Great Britain-Ireland 10 1/2

1980

In 1980, both sides agreed to change the format to three four-ball and three foursome matches on each of the first two days, and nine singles matches the final day. The bus driver of the Great Britain-Ireland Team overslept, causing a one-hour delay in the first-round four-ball competition. It was an omen that things wouldn't be going the visiting team's way on the challenging 7,051-yard Pete Dye-designed Oak Tree course. The Americans opened with a 3-0 shutout in the morning matches, and built a 5-1 lead after the first round. The Great Britain-Ireland team's finest moment came in the second-day best-ball match, with David Huish and Jim Farmer recording birdies on five of the first seven holes to defeat Buddy Whitten and Doug Campbell, 2 and 1. But Whitten, who would finish 4-1 overall, paired with Dave Barber in the afternoon and routed Huish and Farmer, 7 and 6, in the most lopsided victory of the Matches. Four of the final-day singles matches were decided on the 18th hole.

Site:	Oak Tree Golf Club, Edmond, Okla.
Date:	Sept. 19-21, 1980
Results:	USA 15, Great Britain-Ireland 6

PGA Cup Teams	
United States	Great Britain-Ireland
Captain: Don Padgett Jr.	Captain: David Talbot
Jack Lewis	David Jagger
Terry Florence	David Huish
George Shortridge	Jim Farmer
Randy Glover	Tony Minshall
Dave Barber	Leonard Owens
Roger Kennedy	David Thorp
Doug Campbell	Alec Bickerdike
Tommy Aycock	John McTear
Buddy Whitten	Peter Harrison

Morning Four-Ball (Day One)

Glover/Lewis (1-up) over Jagger/Bickerdike
Shortridge/Whitten (3 & 1) over Thorp/Minshall
Aycock/Florence (2 & 1) over Huish/Farmer

Afternoon Foursomes (Day One)

Jagger/Owens (4 & 3) over Lewis/Barber
Whitten/Kennedy (2 & 1) over Farmer/McTear
Aycock/Campbell (5 & 4) over Huish/Thorp
Day One Total: USA 5, Great Britain-Ireland 1

Morning Four-Ball (Day Two)

Huish/Farmer (2 & 1) over Whitten/Campbell
Glover/Lewis (2 & 1) over Jagger/Owens
Aycock/Kennedy (1-up) over Harrison/Minshall

Afternoon Foursomes (Day Two)

Whitten/Barber (7 & 6) over Huish/Farmer
Glover/Florence (2 & 1) over Jagger/Owens
Aycock/Shortridge halved with Thorp/ Minshall
Day Two Total: USA 4 1/2, Great Britain-Ireland 1 1/2
Two-Day Total: USA 9 1/2, Great Britain-Ireland 2 1/2

Singles (Day Three)

Lewis (4 & 3) over Jagger
Florence (3 & 1) over Huish
Shortridge (2 & 1) over Farmer
Glover halved with Minshall
Barber halved with Owens
Thorp (2 & 1) over Kennedy
Campbell halved with Bickerdike
McTear (3 & 2) over Aycock
Whitten (1-up) over Harrison
Day Three Total: USA 5 1/2, Great Britain-Ireland 3 1/2
Final Score: USA 15, Great Britain-Ireland 6

1979

Any hopes American club professionals had of reclaiming the Llandudno Trophy were quickly thwarted by a veteran Great Britain-Ireland team and icy gale force winds which continually swept across the Isle of Man during two days of the Matches. The only U.S. victory in the opening round was the team of 1978 PGA Club Professional Champion John Gentile of Westport, Conn., and Jim Ferree of Pittsburgh, Pa. The duo downed the tandem of Jim Farmer and John Morgan, 8 and 6. The hosts took a 6-2 lead into the final-day singles matches, winning six and halving one. Bob Bruno and Ferree were the only U.S. winners in the singles round, and Great Britain-Ireland's David Huish and Peter Butler went unbeaten in three outings.

Site:	Castletown Links, Isle of Man
Date:	Sept. 28-30, 1979
Results:	Great Britain-Ireland 12 1/2, USA 4 1/2

PGA Cup Teams	
United States	**Great Britain-Ireland**
Captain: Don Padgett Jr.	Captain: Bill Watson
Jay Overton	David Jones
Jimmy Wright	Brian Waites
John Gentile	Jim Farmer
George Shortridge	David Ridley
Jim Ferree	Paul Leonard
Bob Bruno	Michael Steadman
Tom Aycock	John Morgan
Tim Collins	Peter Butler
Jack Sommers	David Huish

Foursomes (Day One)

Huish/Butler (4 & 2) over Collins/Aycock
Waites/Ridley (2 & 1) over Bruno/Overton
Gentile/Ferree (8 & 6) over Farmer/Morgan
Sommers/Shortridge halved with Jones/Leonard
Day One Total: Great Britain-Ireland 2 1/2, USA 1 1/2

Four-Ball (Day Two)

Waites/Farmer (2 & 1) over Wright/Overton
Butler/Steadman (4 & 3) over Gentile/Ferree
Collins/Aycock halved with Jones/Morgan
Huish/Ridley (1-up) over Shortridge/Sommers
Day Two Total: Great Britain-Ireland 3 1/2, USA 1/2
Two-Day Total: Great Britain-Ireland 6, USA 2

Singles (Day Three)

Jones (6 & 5) over Overton
Waites (1-up) over Wright
Farmer (5 & 4) over Gentile
Shortridge halved with Ridley
Ferree (2-up) over Leonard
Bruno (5 & 3) over Steadman
Morgan (5 & 4) over Aycock
Butler (5 & 4) over Collins
Huish (2 & 1) over Sommers
Day Three Total: Great Britain-Ireland 6 1/2, USA 2 1/2
Final Score: Great Britain-Ireland 12 1/2, USA 4 1/2

1978

For the first time in the six-year history of the PGA Cup Matches, the Britons were victorious. It was also the first time in 21 years that a British professional team had beaten the Americans. The last British victory had been the 1957 Ryder Cup win at Linderick, Yorkshire. The hosts jumped to a 3-point lead in the first round, led 5-3 after the second and then won 5 1/2 points to sew things up in the singles. Laurie Hammer of Boynton Beach, Fla., and Tom Aycock of Kingsville, Texas, were the only U.S. players to figure in two wins, but fell back in the foursome matches. Rives McBee of Irving, Texas, suffered his first loss in four Cup appearances, losing to Peter Tupling, 2 and 1.

Site:	St. Mellion Golf and Country Club, Plymouth, England
Date:	Sept. 8-10, 1978
Results:	Great Britain-Ireland 10 1/2, USA 6 1/2

PGA Cup Teams	
United States	**Great Britain-Ireland**
Captain: Henry Poe	Captain: Tommy Horton
Laurie Hammer	David Jones
Rives McBee	Peter Tupling
Tom Aycock	Brian Waites
Ron Smith	Mike Ingham
Art Proctor	Alistair Thomson
Steve Benson	George McKay
Dave Barber	Brian Evans
Tim Collins	Peter Butler
Bruce Summerhays	David Huish

Foursomes (Day One)

Butler/Huish (5 & 4) over Hammer/Smith
Waites/Ingham (4 & 3) over Summerhays/Barber
McBee/Collins halved with Jones/Tupling
Thomson/Evans (2-up) over Proctor/Aycock
Day One Total: Great Britain-Ireland 3 1/2, USA 1/2

Four-Ball (Day Two)

McBee/Aycock (1-up) over Huish/Butler
Waites/Ingham (1-up) over Benson/Smith
Proctor/Hammer (3 & 1) over Jones/Tupling
Summerhays/Collins halved with Thompson/McKay
Day Two Total: USA 2 1/2, Great Britain-Ireland 1 1/2
Two-Day Total: Great Britain-Ireland 5, USA 3

Singles (Day Three)

Hammer (2 & 1) over Jones
Tupling (2 & 1) over McBee
Aycock (7 & 6) over Waites
Ingham (4 & 3) over Smith
Thompson (2-up) over Proctor
Benson (2-up) over McKay
Evans (1-up) over Barber
Butler (3 & 2) over Collins
Summerhays halved with Huish
Day Three Total: Great Britain-Ireland 5 1/2, USA 3 1/2
Final Score: Great Britain-Ireland 10 1/2, USA 6 1/2

1977

The fifth meeting of the U.S. and Great Britain-Ireland club professionals resulted in one of the best duels in PGA Cup Matches history. It was the first time since 1927 that a visiting British Ryder Cup or PGA Cup team didn't go home a loser. The challenging 7,200-yard, Desmond Muirhead-designed course in Palm Springs, Calif., provided the setting. Britain's 38-year-old Jim Kinsella, who was to face open heart surgery in the near future, teamed with David Huish to win a foursome match and came back with a 2-and-1 triumph over Jim Albus. The visitors won six of nine singles matches to force the first deadlock in Cup history. It also was the first time nine singles matches were played, one more than in the previous four Matches. Said U.S. Captain Henry Poe, who persuaded the British to consent to nine matches, "I feel strongly that a man who makes the PGA Cup Match Team should play in the singles.

Site:	Mission Hills Country Club, Palm Springs, Calif.
Date:	Nov. 16-20, 1977
Results:	USA 8 1/2, Great Britain-Ireland 8 1/2

PGA Cup Teams

United States	Great Britain-Ireland
Captain: Henry Poe	Captain: Jack Hargreaves
Bob Duden	David Huish
Bob Galloway	Brian Waites
Jim Albus	Jim Kinsella
Tim Collins	Mike Gallagher
George Lanning	Jim Farmer
George Bellino	Leonard Owens
Bruce Summerhays	David Jones
Jim Ferriell Jr.	Gordon Townhill
Larry Gilbert	Mike Ingham

Foursomes (Day One)

Huish/Kinsella (1-up) over Galloway/Collins
Gilbert/Ferriell Jr. (4 & 2) over Ingham/Waites
Bellino/Summerhays (4 & 3) over Farmer/Townhill
Gallagher/Jones (2 & 1) over Duden/Albus
Day One Total: USA 2, Great Britain-Ireland 2

Four-Ball (Day Two)

Gilbert/Ferriell Jr. (1-up) over Huish/Kinsella
Bellino/Summerhays (3 & 2) over Gallagher/Jones
Albus/Collins halved with Waites/Farmer
Galloway/Lanning (2 & 1) over Ingham/Owens
Day Two Total: USA 3 1/2, Great Britain-Ireland 1/2
Two-Day Total: USA 5 1/2, Great Britain-Ireland 2 1/2

Singles (Day Three)

Huish (3 & 2) over Duden
Waites (1-up) over Galloway
Kinsella (2 & 1) over Albus
Collins (6 & 4) over Gallagher
Farmer (3 & 2) over Lanning
Owens (2 & 1) over Bellino
Summerhays (2 & 1) over Jones
Ferriell Jr. (4 & 3) over Townhill
Ingham (1-up) over Gilbert
Day Three Total: Great Britain-Ireland 6, USA 3
Final Score: USA 8 1/2, Great Britain-Ireland 8 1/2

1976

The fourth consecutive win for U.S. club professionals was crafted in foul weather at the site of the 1929 Ryder Cup Matches in Leeds, England. The Americans opened up a 4-0 lead in the first round of foursome matches before the British rallied over the next two days to tie, 5 1/2 to 5 1/2, mid-way through the final round of singles. The evening of the opening day, an arctic front swept in, bringing heavy rain and forcing delay in the start of the second day's four-ball matches. The delay produced a suspension of play because of darkness. The lone U.S. win in four-ball was by Rives McBee and Larry Gilbert, a 1-up win featuring two outstanding recovery shots to beat Brian Waites and David Ingram. Gilbert and McBee also provided wins in the singles round. McBee birdied the 15th hole after a 3-iron approach landed five feet from the cup and closed out John Sharkey, 4 and 3, providing the momentum for victories in the next three singles matches.

Site:	Moortown Golf Club, Leeds, England
Date:	Oct. 13-15, 1976
Results:	USA 9 1/2, Great Britain-Ireland 6 1/2

PGA Cup Teams

United States	Great Britain-Ireland
Captain: Frank Cardi	Captain: George Will
Rex Baxter	Mike Ingham
Don Padgett II	David Jones
David Jiminez	Brian Waites
Rives McBee	John Sharkey
Larry Gilbert	Peter Ward
Randy Glover	Ernie Jones
Gene Borek	David Ingram
Dennis Tiziani	Bill Ferguson
Roger Watson	Vince Hood

Foursomes (Day One)

Watson/Glover (2 & 1) over Jones/Jones
McBee/Gilbert (4 & 3) over Hood/Sharkey
Tiziani/Baxter (3 & 2) over Ferguson/Ingham
Padgett II/Jiminez (6 & 5) over Ingram/Waites
Day One Total: USA 4, Great Britain-Ireland 0

Four-Ball (Day Two)

Ferguson/Jones (1-up) over Glover/Borek
McBee/Gilbert (1-up) over Waites/Ingram
Jones/Ingham (2-up) over Tiziani/Baxter
Padgett II/Jiminez halved with Sharkey/Ward
Day Two Total: Great Britain-Ireland 2 1/2, USA 1 1/2
Two-Day Total: USA 5 1/2 Great Britain-Ireland 2 1/2

Singles (Day Three)

Ingham (1-up) over Baxter
Jones (2-up) over Padgett II
Waites (1-up) over Jiminez
McBee (4 & 3) over Sharkey
Gilbert (5 & 3) over Ward
Glover (3 & 1) over Jones
Borek (1-up) over Ingram
Ferguson (1-up) over Tiziani
Day Three Total: USA 4, Great Britain-Ireland 4
Final Score: USA 9 1/2, Great Britain-Ireland 6 1/2

1975

After two years in the comfort of warm Pinehurst, N.C., the top club professionals of the U.S. and the British Isles met in Southport, England. The matches were renamed the PGA Cup Matches after the PGA of America took over the financing of the U.S. team and expanded the format from two to three days. A pro-am was held prior to the Matches, and $12,000 was raised to allow the British PGA to stage the meeting. The U.S. won three of the four opening foursomes, and each team won one match and halved two in four-ball during the second day. On the last day, the U.S. won four of the final eight singles and halved a fifth match for their third straight Cup victory.

Site:	Hillside Golf Club, Southport, England
Date:	Oct. 15-17, 1975
Results:	USA 9 1/2, Great Britain-Ireland 6 1/2

PGA Cup Teams	
United States	Great Britain-Ireland
Captain:	Captain:
Don Padgett Jr.	Christy O'Connor Sr.
Roger Watson	David Huish
Eddie Famula	Ian Richardson
O'Dell Massey	Doug Sewell
Babe Lichardus	Robert Jamieson
Ron Letellier	Adrian Sadler
Randy Glover	Roger Fidler
Bob Benson	Brian Waites
Jimmy Wright	Max Faulkner
Maurice Ver Brugge	Dennis Scanlan

Foursomes (Day One)
Watson/Glover (5 & 4) over Waites/Richardson
Lichardus/Famula (3 & 1) over Sewell/Sadler
Letellier/Wright (3 & 2) over Fidler/Scanlan
Huish/Jamieson (2 & 1) over Benson/Ver Brugge
Day One Total: USA 3, Great Britain-Ireland 1

Four-Ball (Day Two)
Watson/Glover halved with Huish/Jamieson
Sadler/Sewell (1-up) over Massey/Ver Brugge
Lichardus/Famula (1-up) over Waites/Richardson
Wright/Letellier halved with Scanlan/Fidler
Day Two Total: USA 2, Great Britain-Ireland 2
Two-Day Total: USA 5, Great Britain-Ireland 3

Singles (Day Three)
Huish (5 & 4) over Watson
Famula (3 & 2) over Richardson
Massey (2 & 1) over Sewell
Lichardus halved with Jamieson
Letellier (2-up) over Sadler
Fidler (2-up) over Glover
Waites (3 & 2) over Benson
Wright (3 & 1) over Faulkner
Day Three Total: USA 4 1/2, Great Britain-Ireland 3 1/2
Final Score: USA 9 1/2, Great Britain-Ireland 6 1/2

1974

Fresh from the PGA Club Professional Championship at Pinehurst, and having 10 more practice days than their British visitors, the U.S. club professionals cruised to an easy victory in the second annual Diamondhead Cup Matches. Rives McBee of Irving, Texas, joined New Yorker Denny Lyons and John Molenda of Detroit by going unbeaten through both days in team and singles competition. Tommy Jacobs from Rancho La Costa, Calif., finished the Matches in excellent form with a 5-under-par effort to defeat David Huish, 3 and 2.

Scotland's Bobby Jamieson accounted for three of his team's 4 1/2 points, crushing Rex Baxter, 6 and 5, in singles and teaming with David Huish to defeat Stanley Brion and Larry Mancour in the first two rounds.

British Captain Brian Hutchinson expressed hope that the Matches would be resumed in 1975 in Great Britain, but in mid-summer to provide acceptable playing conditions. However, the '75 Cup Matches were scheduled in October again, due to summer being at the height of the American club professionals' playing and working calendar.

Site:	Pinehurst No. 2 Course, Pinehurst, N.C.
Date:	Oct. 29-30, 1974
Results:	USA 11 1/2, Great Britain-Ireland 4 1/2

PGA Cup Teams	
United States	Great Britain-Ireland
Captain: Henry Poe	Captain: Brian Hutchinson
Larry Mancour	David Miller
Stan Brion	Alex Caygill
Rives McBee	Vince Hood
Jim Logue	Bill Murray
Denny Lyons	Peter Ward
John Molenda	David Creamer
Rex Baxter	Bobby Jamieson
Tommy Jacobs	David Huish
Jerry Barber	Doug Sewell

Foursomes (Day One)
McBee/Lyons (2 & 1) over Murray/Miller
Sewell/Hood (1-up) over Barber/Jacobs
Molenda/Baxter (3 & 2) over Caygill/Creamer
Huish/Jamieson (1-up) over Brion/Mancour

Four-Ball (Day One)
McBee/Lyons (6 & 4) over Ward/Creamer
Jacobs/Logue (4 & 3) over Caygill/Murray
Baxter/Molenda (3 & 1) over Hood/Sewell
Huish/Jamieson (4 & 3) over Brion/Mancour
Day One Total: USA 5, Great Britain-Ireland 3

Singles (Day Two)
Mancour (4 & 3) over Miller
Brion halved with Caygill
McBee (2 & 1) over Hood
Logue (2-up) over Murray
Lyons (6 & 5) over Ward
Molenda (2 & 1) over Creamer
Jamieson (6 & 5) over Baxter
Jacobs (3 & 2) over Huish
Day Two Total: USA 6 1/2, Great Britain-Ireland 1 1/2
Final Score: USA 11 1/2, Great Britain-Ireland 4 1/2

1973 The inaugural Diamondhead Cup Matches were a postscript to the sixth PGA Club Professional Championship at Pinehurst, N.C. The Matches were the brainchild of Bill Maurer of the sponsoring Diamondhead Corporation, then-owner and operator of the Pinehurst Resort. The opening day began with starter Laurie Auchterlonie, honorary professional of the Royal and Ancient Golf Club of St. Andrews in Scotland, ordering the players, "Gentlemen, start your engines!" The result was a 2-2 deadlock in foursome matches. The U.S. grabbed the lead for good, 6-2, thanks to inspired play in the four-ball. Don Massengale and Rives McBee each finished unbeaten in three matches. Massengale downed Bryan Hutchinson and McBee defeated Brian Waites by respective 3-and-2 margins in singles. McBee teamed with Dennis Lyons and Massengale with Craig Shankland for victories in foursomes and four-ball competition. Gene Borek and Babe Lichardus each finished 2-0. Borek bounced back from a strained back that had forced his withdrawal from the PGA Club Professional Championship.

Site: Pinehurst No. 2 Course, Pinehurst, N.C.
Date: Oct. 23-24, 1973
Results: USA 13, Great Britain-Ireland 3

PGA Cup Teams

United States	Great Britain-Ireland
Captain: William Clarke	Captain: Tom Halliburton
Rives McBee	Brian Waites
Denny Lyons	Geoff Norton
Gene Borek	David Melville
Babe Lichardus	John Morgan
Ernie George	Bill Ferguson
Mal Galletta	Jack Wilkshire
Bob Bruno	Doug Sewell
Don Massengale	Bryan Hutchinson
Craig Shankland	Richard Emery

Foursomes (Day One)
McBee/Lyons (3 & 1) over Waites/Sewell
Massengale/Shankland (3 & 2) over Morgan/Wilkshire
Melville/Norton (5 & 4) over George/Lichardus
Hutchinson/Ferguson (1-up) over Bruno/Galletta

Four-Ball (Day One)
McBee/Lyons (5 & 4) over Hutchinson/Ferguson
Massengale/Shankland (4 & 3) over Waites/Wilkshire
Bruno/Galletta (3 & 2) over Norton/Melville
Borek/Lichardus (3 & 2) over Sewell/Emery
Day One Total: USA 6, Great Britain-Ireland 2

Singles (Day Two)
McBee (3 & 2) over Waites
Lyons (4 & 3) over Norton
Borek (3 & 2) over Melville
Lichardus (3 & 2) over Morgan
Ferguson (2-up) over George
Galletta (1-up) over Wilkshire
Bruno (8 & 6) over Sewell
Massengale (3 & 2) over Hutchinson
Day Two Total: USA 7, Great Britain-Ireland 1
Final Score: USA 13, Great Britain-Ireland 3

THE PGA CLUB PROFESSIONAL CHAMPIONSHIP

1994 FACTS AND FORMAT

DATES: October 6-9, 1994

SITES: Marriott's Tan-Tar-A Resort,
Osage Beach, Mo.

The Lodge of Four Seasons
Lake Ozark, Mo.

North Port National Golf Club
Lake Ozark, Mo.

DEFENDING CHAMPION: Jeffrey Roth

PRIZE MONEY AND AWARDS:

A purse of $400,000 was distributed to the 360 competitors in 1993. The winner of the 1994 PGA Club Professional Championship will receive a minimum of $32,000 for his victory and have his name inscribed on the Walter Hagen Cup, enshrined at the PGA of America national headquarters in Palm Beach Gardens, Fla.

Additionally, the 1994 PGA Club Professional Champion receives exemptions for the following:

- 1995 PGA Championship

- 1995 World Series of Golf

- 1996 PGA Cup Team

- Exemptions at three PGA Tour events

METHOD OF PLAY

Stroke play, four rounds. 18 holes daily on each of the three golf courses. Following the first 54 holes of play, the field will be reduced to the 90 players having the lowest scores and those tied for 90th place. Those players will then compete in the final round. In the event of a tie for first place upon completion of play, there will be a sudden-death playoff beginning on the first hole.

ELIGIBILITY

The field will be limited to those PGA members who are regularly employed as golf professionals and in certain pre-established membership classifications. The PGA of America reserves the right to determine whether or not any applicant is so employed and to reject any applicant who does not meet the requirements. No player will be eligible if he has played in more than 12 combined PGA Tour, Senior PGA Tour or Nike Tour tournaments in the preceding 12-month period.

RULES AND REGULATIONS

The Rules of Golf which govern play are determined by the United States Golf Association and applied by the PGA of America Board of Directors. The Championship is subject to the overall supervision of the board and the PGA Rules Committee.

■ HISTORY

The PGA Club Professional Championship was begun in 1968 to provide additional playing opportunities for PGA club professionals.

Traditionally a late-year competition after the golfing season has ended across much of the U.S., the PGA Club Professional Championship has been held in Arizona, North Carolina, Georgia, Florida and, for seven of the last 11 years, on California desert courses.

The list of champions over the past 25 years includes former PGA Champions Sam Snead and Bob Rosburg, and former Tour players Rex Baxter Jr., Don Massengale, Laurie Hammer, Larry Webb, Ed Dougherty, Robert Boyd, Bruce Fleisher and Brett Upper.

Winning assures the new champion a berth in the following year's PGA Championship and NEC World Series of Golf, a position on the next PGA Cup Team and numerous other benefits.

With a field of 360 PGA professionals, the PGA Club Professional Championship is the largest all-professional tournament in the world.

PGA CLUB PROFESSIONAL CHAMPIONSHIP

■ HISTORY THROUGH THE YEARS

Year	Winner	Score	Runners-up	Site
1968	Howell Fraser	272	Chuck Malchaski, Bob Rosburg	Century & Roadrunner, Scottsdale, Ariz.
1969	Bob Rosburg	275	Jimmy Wright	Roadrunner & San Marcos, Chandler, Ariz.
1970	Rex Baxter	285	Ernie George, Bob Duden	Sunol Valley CC, Sunol, Calif.
1971	Sam Snead	275	Jerry Steelsmith, Ron Letellier	Pinehurst (N.C.) CC
1972	Don Massengale	280	Bob Bruno	Pinehurst (N.C.) CC
1973	Rives McBee	282	Stan Brian	Pinehurst (N.C.) CC
1974	Roger Watson*	284	Sam Snead	Pinehurst (N.C.) CC
1975	Roger Watson*	279	David Jimenez	Callaway Gardens Resort, Pine Mountain, Ga.
1976	Bob Galloway	280	George Lanning, Larry Gilbert, Jim Ferriell	Callaway Gardens Resort, Pine Mountain, Ga.
1977	Laurie Hammer	282	Steve Benson	Callaway Gardens Resort, Pine Mountain, Ga.
1978	John Gentile*	276	Jim Ferree	Callaway Gardens Resort, Pine Mountain, Ga.
1979	Buddy Whitten*	278	Jack Lewis	Callaway Gardens Resort, Pine Mountain, Ga.
1980	John Traub	283	Jim Albus	PGA National GC, Palm Beach Gardens, Fla.
1981	Larry Gilbert*	285	Don Padgett II	PGA National GC, Palm Beach Gardens, Fla.
1982	Larry Gilbert	284	Steve Benson	PGA National GC, Palm Beach Gardens, Fla.
1983	Larry Webb	283	Bob Ford	La Quinta/Mission Hills, La Quinta, Calif.
1984	Bill Schumaker*	284	Gary Ostrega	PGA National GC, Palm Beach Gardens, Fla.
1985	Ed Dougherty	277	Jim White	La Quinta Hotel/Mission Hills, La Quinta, Calif.
1986	Bob Lendzion	284	Bob Betley	PGA West/La Quinta Hotel/Mission Hills, La Quinta, Calif.
1987	Jay Lumpkin	279	Jeff Roth, Bob Menne, Gibby Gilbert	PGA West/La Quinta Hotel/Mission Hills, La Quinta, Calif
1988	Robert Boyd*	287	Rick Morton	Pinehurst (N.C.) CC
1989	Bruce Fleisher	277	Jeff Thomsen	PGA West/La Quinta Hotel/Mission Hills, La Quinta, Calif.
1990	Brett Upper	275	Gibby Gilbert, Larry Gilbert	PGA West/La Quinta Hotel/Mission Hills, La Quinta, Calif.
1991	Larry Gilbert	267	Gene Fieger, Ron McDougal	Doral Resort and Country Club, Miami, Fla.
1992	Ron McDougal	273	Sammy Rachels	PGA West/La Quinta Hotel/Mission Hills, La Quinta, Calif.
1993	Jeffrey Roth	275	John Lee	PGA National GC, Palm Beach Gardens, Fla.

*Won playoff.

■ PAR AND YARDAGE

PGA National, Champion Course

Hole	1	2	3	4	5	6	7	8	9	10	11	12	13	14	15	16	17	18
Par	4	4	5	4	3	5	3	4	4	5	4	4	4	4	3	4	3	5
Yards	346	434	539	355	175	484	187	422	400	554	412	397	375	422	164	412	152	528

Front 9: 3,342 yards • par 36   **Back 9:** 3,416 yards • par 36   **Total:** 6,758 yards • par 72

PGA National, Estate Course

Hole	1	2	3	4	5	6	7	8	9	10	11	12	13	14	15	16	17	18
Par	5	4	4	3	5	3	4	4	4	3	5	4	4	5	4	4	3	4
Yards	495	344	424	178	550	172	363	433	407	165	545	411	362	533	357	364	205	419

Front 9: 3,366 yards • par 36   **Back 9:** 3,361 yards • par 36   **Total:** 6,727 yards • par 72

PGA National, Haig Course

Hole	1	2	3	4	5	6	7	8	9	10	11	12	13	14	15	16	17	18
Par	5	4	4	5	3	4	3	4	4	4	4	5	3	4	4	3	5	4
Yards	501	381	392	556	151	393	194	395	387	384	395	513	159	393	361	205	532	412

Front 9: 3,350 yards • par 36   **Back 9:** 3,354 yards • par 36   **Total:** 6,704 yards • par 72

1993

It didn't matter to Jeffrey Roth that the 26th PGA Club Professional Championship was a golfing marathon played under dark skies at PGA National Golf Club in Palm Beach Gardens, Fla.

Adversity had descended upon Roth before as he attempted to reach the top rung among his peers. The 32-year-old head professional at Flint (Mich.) Golf Club had endured a pair of heartbreaking final-hole losses in the 1992 Michigan Open and Michigan PGA Championship.

But Roth's game was in perfect working order, despite rain and lightning forcing suspension of play five times during the first three days. Roth sank a 15-foot birdie putt on the sixth hole of the final round to snap a tie with defending champion Ron McDougal of Purchase, N.Y., and cruised to an even-par 72 and a two-stroke victory. Roth once owned a six-stroke lead through 14 holes, but bogeyed the 15th, 16th and 18th holes for a 72-hole total of 13-under-par 275. Roth earned a first-place prize of $32,000 in his seventh appearance in the PGA Club Professional Championship.

John Lee of Naples, Fla., sank a 40-foot birdie putt on the 18th hole for a 72 and took the runner-up spot at 277. McDougal struggled to a 73 and landed in a five-way tie for third place at 278 with Todd Smith of Peru, Ind., Pete Oakley of Lewes, Del., George Bowman of Orchard Lake, Mich., and Walt Chapman of Knoxville, Tenn.

"I'm typically not a good Florida player," said Roth, "but this week there was no wind to speak of. I kept the ball in play and I hit a lot of greens. You know, John Traub (1980 champion and one of three from Michigan) told me this morning that I was going to win this and win it big. And he told me it wouldn't sink in until I got home. I think he's right."

By tying for third place, McDougal recorded the highest finish among the nine former champions who played at least 54 holes. McDougal has finished 2-1-3 in his three appearances in the Championship. His bid for a second Club Professional Championship title ended when he bogeyed the seventh hole. His closing 73 was his first Championship round at par or worse.

Sixty-nine of the final 108 players in the final round finished under par. The Championship's third round was concluded early Sunday, and the final 18 holes were concluded just before dusk at 7:08 p.m., EDT.

The first round of the Championship wasn't without its dramatics. Joe Sciortino, director of golf at Boynton Beach (Fla.) Municipal Golf Course, was the first alternate for his South Florida PGA Section into the championship. Sciortino's good friend, Rick Werner of Naples, Fla., dropped out due to a bad back. Sciortino responded to his late entry with a course-record 65 on the Haig Course.

"I didn't have time to get nervous," said Sciortino, who missed the 54-hole cut by two strokes after ensuing rounds of 72 and 81.

Champion:	Jeffrey Roth, Flint, Mich.		
Site:	PGA National Golf Club,		
	Palm Beach Gardens, Fla.		
Date:	Oct. 7-10		
Course:	Champion	Par:	72 - (6,758)
Course:	Haig	Par:	72 - (6,704)
Course:	Squire	Par:	72 - (6,478)
Purse:	$400,000	Field:	360
	Cut at 216	108 players advanced	

	Squire (Par 72)	Haig (Par 72)	Champion (Par 72)	Round Leader		Jeffrey Roth
Round 1:	73.74	73.28	73.96	65-	Joe Sciortino and John Lee	68 - T-10th
Round 2:	73.80	73.01	74.14	134-	Ron McDougal	137 - (69) T-9th
Round 3:	73.30	73.83	73.80	203-	Jeffrey Roth	203 - (66) 1st
Round 4:			72.92	275-	Jeffrey Roth	275 - (72) 1st

TOURNAMENT SUMMARY

Place	Name	Score	Winnings	Place	Name	Score	Winnings	Place	Name	Score	Winnings
1	Jeffrey Roth	68-69-66-72—275	$32,000.00	T-31	Barry Redmond	67-70-76-71—284	$1,580.00	T-59	Chip Sullivan	68-69-76-74—287	$760.00
2	John Lee	65-71-69-72—277	$22,000.00	T-31	Bruce Zabriski	73-68-73-70—284	$1,580.00	T-59	Tom Woodard	73-68-74-72—287	$760.00
T-3	Todd M. Smith	71-68-70-69—278	$12,800.00	T-31	Rod Nuckolls	72-69-72-71—284	$1,580.00	T-59	Fran Marrello	70-70-71-76—287	$760.00
T-3	Pete Oakley	68-70-71-69—278	$12,800.00	T-31	Scott Steger	71-67-75-71—284	$1,580.00	T-59	Michael Domalske	67-75-70-75—287	$760.00
T-3	George Bowman	69-70-69-70—278	$12,800.00	T-31	Kevin Cashman	68-70-74-72—284	$1,580.00	T-59	Robert Gibbons	75-69-71-72—287	$760.00
T-3	Walt Chapman	67-69-71-71—278	$12,800.00	T-31	John Bermel	74-71-70-69—284	$1,580.00	T-59	Larry Rentz	71-72-68-76—287	$760.00
T-3	Ron McDougal	68-66-71-73—278	$12,800.00	T-31	John DeForest	70-71-69-74—284	$1,580.00	T-59	Terry Dear	71-65-72-79—287	$760.00
T-8	Rick Acton	68-75-68-68—279	$8,500.00	T-31	Miguel Biamon	69-70-70-75—284	$1,580.00	T-59	Greg Farrow	71-74-71-71—287	$760.00
T-8	Tom Cleaver	69-68-73-69—279	$8,500.00	T-31	Bob Ackerman	70-74-72-68—284	$1,580.00	T-59	Pete Mathews	72-72-72-71—287	$760.00
T-10	Brad Sherfy	71-72-70-67—280	$6,620.00	T-31	Tom Dolby	68-68-69-79—284	$1,580.00	T-70	Dana Quigley	69-70-74-75—288	$665.00
T-10	Eddie Terasa	73-67-73-67—280	$6,620.00	T-41	Don Maddox	74-70-69-72—285	$1,047.50	T-70	Craig Immel	74-70-69-75—288	$665.00
T-10	J.L. Lewis	70-68-71-71—280	$6,620.00	T-41	Ken Schall	74-72-68-71—285	$1,047.50	T-70	John Sherman	72-71-71-74—288	$665.00
T-10	Mel Baum	69-67-72-72—280	$6,620.00	T-41	Dave Quelland	70-73-70-72—285	$1,047.50	T-70	Ted Goin	79-67-69-73—288	$665.00
T-10	Bob Boyd	68-70-67-75—280	$6,620.00	T-41	Bill Hall	71-71-72-71—285	$1,047.50	T-70	Bob Groff	72-71-72-73—288	$665.00
T-15	Jim White	73-72-70-66—281	$5,300.00	T-41	Milan Swilor	68-71-71-75—285	$1,047.50	T-70	Nic Borojevich	70-72-71-75—288	$665.00
T-15	Darrell Kestner	68-69-73-71—281	$5,300.00	T-41	Gordon Johnson	70-75-67-73—285	$1,047.50	T-70	Quinn Griffing	71-70-74-73—288	$665.00
T-15	Thomas Gray	69-71-70-71—281	$5,300.00	T-41	Tom Atchison	68-71-71-75—285	$1,047.50	T-70	Scott Watkins	68-71-76-73—288	$665.00
T-18	Mike Gove	72-73-68-69—282	$4,250.00	T-41	Sammy Rachels	67-69-71-78—285	$1,047.50	T-70	Cleve Coldwater	74-70-71-73—288	$665.00
T-18	Wes Smith	71-70-71-70—282	$4,250.00	T-49	Gregg Wolff	73-71-69-73—286	$866.00	T-70	Bill Israelson	67-72-72-77—288	$665.00
T-18	Gregg Jones	73-71-68-70—282	$4,250.00	T-49	Hunt Gilliland	71-73-69-73—286	$866.00	T-70	Rick Lewallen	76-69-71-72—288	$665.00
T-18	Scott Williams	68-71-70-73—282	$4,250.00	T-49	Bob Ralston	69-72-73-72—286	$866.00	T-70	Mike Frankso	74-70-72-72—288	$665.00
T-18	Robert Hoyt	67-68-70-77—282	$4,250.00	T-49	Charlie Cowell	71-70-72-73—286	$866.00	T-70	Ken McDonald	76-71-69-72—288	$665.00
T-23	Patrick O'Brien	70-70-73-70—283	$2,737.50	T-49	Scott Walter	70-71-71-74—286	$866.00	T-70	Douglas Doxsie	74-69-73-72—288	$665.00
T-23	Scott Mahlberg	68-72-74-69—283	$2,737.50	T-49	Jeff Thomsen	68-76-69-73—286	$866.00	T-70	Terry Florence	75-71-70-72—288	$665.00
T-23	Steve Smitha	71-71-70-71—283	$2,737.50	T-49	Tony Milan	69-71-71-75—286	$866.00	T-85	Bob Bailey	71-72-71-75—289	$607.50
T-23	Jerry Wisz	68-74-73-68—283	$2,737.50	T-49	Mike San Filippo	68-72-70-76—286	$866.00	T-85	Peter Busch	68-73-72-76—289	$607.50
T-23	Denny Hepler	70-68-73-72—283	$2,737.50	T-49	Mike Burke Jr.	69-69-78-70—286	$866.00	T-85	Bob Borowicz	69-76-69-75—289	$607.50
T-23	Lonnie Nielsen	73-70-73-67—283	$2,737.50	T-49	Steve Ball	75-71-70-70—286	$866.00	T-85	Michael Mitchell	71-73-71-74—289	$607.50
T-23	Ron Philo Jr.	69-69-71-74—283	$2,737.50	T-59	Mark Mielke	71-71-72-73—287	$760.00	T-85	Edward Burke Jr.	68-72-72-77—289	$607.50
T-23	Will Frantz	73-71-72-67—283	$2,737.50	T-59	Brian Kelly	73-70-71-73—287	$760.00	T-85	Jim McLean	75-74-66-74—289	$607.50

T-85	Jeff McMillen	75-71-69-74—289	$607.50
T-85	Ed Selser	72-70-73-74—289	$607.50
T-93	Tommy Brannen	69-74-70-77—290	$575.50
T-93	Kirk Schooley	74-67-74-75—290	$575.50
T-93	John Traub	73-70-72-75—290	$575.50
T-93	Victor Whipp	73-70-73-74—290	$575.50
T-93	Buddy Whitten	72-72-72-74—290	$575.50
T-98	Henry White	73-72-70-76—291	$575.50
T-98	David Lamb	72-73-71-75—291	$575.50
T-100	Doug Bauman	74-71-69-78—292	$545.00
T-100	Larry Emery	70-74-72-76—292	$545.00
T-100	Drue Johnson	70-72-74-76—292	$545.00
T-103	Jim Dickson	69-72-74-79—294	$530.00
T-103	Dave Desantis	77-68-70-79—294	$530.00
T-103	David Grygiel	70-76-70-78—294	$530.00
106	Brad Peck	72-74-69-80—295	$520.00
WD	Gary Hardin	70-71-75—216	$400.00
WD	Stu Ingraham	74-70-72—216	$400.00
Cut	Bob Mann	72-75-70—217	$400.00
Cut	Gary Robison	70-75-72—217	$400.00
Cut	Joseph Donnelly	71-71-75—217	$400.00
Cut	Mike Barge	72-75-70—217	$400.00
Cut	Rick Vershure	77-69-71—217	$400.00
Cut	John Paesani	72-74-71—217	$400.00
Cut	Greg Antunes	67-74-76—217	$400.00
Cut	Mark Gurnow	70-73-74—217	$400.00
Cut	Gary Trivisonno	70-75-72—217	$400.00
Cut	John Mason	74-69-74—217	$400.00
Cut	Mike Parrish	75-70-72—217	$400.00
Cut	Dan Wood	75-70-72—217	$400.00
Cut	David Dell	70-72-75—217	$400.00
Cut	Mike Dopslaff	71-75-71—217	$400.00
Cut	Greg Cerulli	70-72-75—217	$400.00
Cut	Kip-Henley Fairfield	71-73-73—217	$400.00
Cut	Brian Williamson	76-70-71—217	$400.00
Cut	Dennis Dolci	70-73-74—217	$400.00
Cut	Will Hutter	73-72-72—217	$400.00
Cut	Greg McMillan	69-77-71—217	$400.00
Cut	Jim Slattery	71-73-73—217	$400.00
Cut	Mo Guttman	73-71-73—217	$400.00
Cut	Bret Taylor	72-72-73—217	$400.00
Cut	Jack Skilling	75-73-69—217	$400.00
Cut	Ned Martin	70-72-75—217	$400.00
Cut	Steve Moreland	74-75-68—217	$400.00
Cut	Mike Lawrence	74-71-72—217	$400.00
Cut	Bill Mory	77-71-70—218	$400.00
Cut	Todd O'Neal	71-72-75—218	$400.00
Cut	Tom Gleeton	74-73-71—218	$400.00
Cut	Bob Longo	74-76-68—218	$400.00
Cut	John Reeves	72-75-71—218	$400.00
Cut	Daryl Hartig	70-75-73—218	$400.00
Cut	Bill Schumaker	73-72-73—218	$400.00
Cut	Ken Krieger	75-72-71—218	$400.00
Cut	Joe Sciortino	65-72-81—218	$400.00
Cut	Fred Gibson	73-71-74—218	$400.00
Cut	Greg Frederick	72-71-75—218	$400.00
Cut	Tom Tatum	73-71-74—218	$400.00
Cut	Jon Hoecker	71-74-73—218	$400.00
Cut	Kent Stauffer	71-72-75—218	$400.00
Cut	Tim Angis	70-73-75—218	$400.00
Cut	Benny Passons	75-71-72—218	$400.00
Cut	Ron Vlosich	74-73-71—218	$400.00
Cut	Vic Lipscomb	75-72-71—218	$400.00
Cut	Tom Clary	73-73-72—218	$400.00
Cut	Tom Gieselman	77-74-67—218	$400.00
Cut	Pat Stephens	76-73-69—218	$400.00
Cut	Kirk Stauffer	73-74-71—218	$400.00
Cut	Tom Dawson	72-71-76—219	$400.00
Cut	George Forster	73-74-72—219	$400.00
Cut	Carl R. Baker	78-74-67—219	$400.00
Cut	Phil Taylor	79-71-69—219	$400.00
Cut	Bob Lendzion	73-74-72—219	$400.00
Cut	David Lundstrom	73-73-73—219	$400.00
Cut	Kim Thompson	72-76-71—219	$400.00
Cut	John Godwin	78-72-69—219	$400.00
Cut	Tony Wallin	74-72-73—219	$400.00
Cut	Russell Helwig	74-73-72—219	$400.00
Cut	Brian Maloney	74-72-73—219	$400.00
Cut	Tom Carey	75-71-73—219	$400.00
Cut	Mark Fuller	74-73-72—219	$400.00
Cut	Glen Barrett	74-69-76—219	$400.00
Cut	Kevin Burton	74-70-75—219	$400.00
Cut	Steve Veriato	74-71-74—219	$400.00
Cut	Billy Rosinia	70-74-75—219	$400.00
Cut	Mike Kallam	75-70-74—219	$400.00
Cut	Bob Dolan	75-70-75—220	$400.00
Cut	Charlie Gibson	74-72-74—220	$400.00
Cut	David Prange	71-75-74—220	$400.00
Cut	Brad Dean	72-75-73—220	$400.00
Cut	Lee Rinker	73-76-71—220	$400.00
Cut	Jack Seltzer	74-72-74—220	$400.00
Cut	Phil Bland	72-72-76—220	$400.00
Cut	Steve Jurick	71-77-72—220	$400.00
Cut	Jim Sobb	73-71-76—220	$400.00
Cut	Marty O'Rear	74-74-72—220	$400.00
Cut	Jerry Covich	72-76-72—220	$400.00
Cut	Nigel Rouse	76-73-71—220	$400.00
Cut	Jim Kjellenberg	76-71-73—220	$400.00
Cut	Mike Zaremba	72-71-77—220	$400.00
Cut	Denny Ferstler	73-74-73—220	$400.00
Cut	Danny Weeks	71-72-77—220	$400.00
Cut	Glen Stubblefield	74-73-74—221	$400.00
Cut	Richard White	74-73-74—221	$400.00
Cut	Steve Schneiter	74-72-75—221	$400.00
Cut	Larry Mackin	73-71-77—221	$400.00
Cut	Steve Heckel	76-73-72—221	$400.00
Cut	Mike Diffley	71-75-75—221	$400.00
Cut	Anthony Price	73-75-73—221	$400.00
Cut	Daniel Thore	76-71-74—221	$400.00
Cut	Mark Alwin	73-73-75—221	$400.00
Cut	Bradley Schmierer	77-73-71—221	$400.00
Cut	Skip Holton	75-71-75—221	$400.00
Cut	Dave Bryan	73-76-72—221	$400.00
Cut	Steven Bowen	71-73-77—221	$400.00
Cut	Dick McClean	77-71-73—221	$400.00
Cut	Denny Lyons	76-72-73—221	$400.00
Cut	Shawn McEntee	71-75-75—221	$400.00
Cut	Lindy Miller	75-72-74—221	$400.00
Cut	Joe Boros	77-70-74—221	$400.00
Cut	Rick Reynolds	69-76-76—221	$400.00
Cut	Paul Parajeckas	76-75-71—222	$400.00
Cut	Jay B. Norman	74-76-72—222	$400.00
Cut	Woody Fitzhugh	73-76-73—222	$400.00
Cut	Paul Trittler	75-71-76—222	$400.00
Cut	Craig Stevens	74-73-75—222	$400.00
Cut	Frank Mellet	77-70-75—222	$400.00
Cut	Chris Dachisen	76-71-75—222	$400.00
Cut	Dave Roberts	74-74-74—222	$400.00
Cut	Mike Schueter	72-73-77—222	$400.00
Cut	Ed Vietmeirr	74-72-76—222	$400.00
Cut	Steve Brady	76-70-76—222	$400.00
Cut	Jeff Fairfield	77-68-77—222	$400.00
Cut	Jack McConachie	71-77-74—222	$400.00
Cut	Joey Hines	77-72-73—222	$400.00
Cut	Bill Brodell	75-72-75—222	$400.00
Cut	Gary Sowinski	76-71-75—222	$400.00
Cut	Gene Ferrell	74-75-74—223	$400.00
Cut	Dale Fuller	72-77-74—223	$400.00
Cut	Kevin Muir	75-73-75—223	$400.00
Cut	Bruce Burroughs	70-79-74—223	$400.00
Cut	Scott L. Hawkins	75-78-70—223	$400.00
Cut	Jim Knoesel	77-74-72—223	$400.00
Cut	Larry Mancour	78-72-73—223	$400.00
Cut	John Dal Corobbo	79-74-70—223	$400.00
Cut	Mike West	76-75-72—223	$400.00
Cut	Brent Sipe	73-74-76—223	$400.00
Cut	Jamie Fordyce	77-73-73—223	$400.00
Cut	Tim Holmes	72-72-79—223	$400.00
Cut	John Hayes	73-77-74—224	$400.00
Cut	Bill King	71-73-80—224	$400.00
Cut	Robert W. Nichols	76-75-73—224	$400.00
Cut	Todd C. Manderson	70-77-77—224	$400.00
Cut	Jerry Hinton	78-74-72—224	$400.00
Cut	D. Steven Waugh	74-76-74—224	$400.00
Cut	Paul Ryiz	75-73-76—224	$400.00
Cut	Jeffrey Gunning	74-74-76—224	$400.00
Cut	John Phillips	71-77-76—224	$400.00
Cut	Jeff Hunter	75-78-71—224	$400.00
Cut	Rocky Nelson	75-74-75—224	$400.00
Cut	Tony Saraceno	78-72-74—224	$400.00
Cut	Joe Gutterman	75-72-77—224	$400.00
Cut	Buddy Harston	72-72-80—224	$400.00
Cut	Mitch Camp	79-71-74—224	$400.00
Cut	Joe Trembly	71-76-77—224	$400.00
Cut	Gary Groh	71-75-78—224	$400.00
Cut	Ron Ptacek	77-73-75—225	$400.00
Cut	James Fellner	73-76-76—225	$400.00
Cut	Philip Miranda	73-75-77—225	$400.00
Cut	Michael Paul	74-74-77—225	$400.00
Cut	Michael Hamblin	73-73-79—225	$400.00
Cut	Dick Wagley	71-76-78—225	$400.00
Cut	Mike Moyers	77-75-73—225	$400.00
Cut	Terry L. Woodard	73-78-74—225	$400.00
Cut	Jay Kennedy	74-80-71—225	$400.00
Cut	Andy Santor	76-74-75—225	$400.00
Cut	Jeff Batson	80-74-71—225	$400.00
Cut	Roy Hunter	82-76-67—225	$400.00
Cut	John Schoonover	78-71-76—225	$400.00
Cut	Tom Fortuna	78-73-74—225	$400.00
Cut	Michael J. Reed	75-78-72—225	$400.00
Cut	Jack Bohman	81-73-71—225	$400.00
Cut	Tom Sargent	73-77-76—226	$400.00
Cut	Richard Loy	77-76-73—226	$400.00
Cut	Stan Stopa	75-74-77—226	$400.00
Cut	Jeff Jackson	72-76-78—226	$400.00
Cut	Richard Martin	76-76-74—226	$400.00
Cut	Dave Spengler	77-77-73—227	$400.00
Cut	Tom Gorman	77-77-73—227	$400.00
Cut	Tom Joyce	70-77-80—227	$400.00
Cut	James Masserio	78-80-69—227	$400.00
Cut	Marc Alan Orlowski	78-73-76—227	$400.00
Cut	John L. Richman	77-75-75—227	$400.00
Cut	Greg Mireault	77-78-72—227	$400.00
Cut	Gary Braeseke	78-75-74—227	$400.00
Cut	Mike Antonio	75-73-79—227	$400.00
Cut	Doug Sheldon	73-77-77—227	$400.00
Cut	Jim Booros	78-73-77—228	$400.00
Cut	John Haffner	79-75-74—228	$400.00
Cut	Kevin Denike	74-80-74—228	$400.00
Cut	Randy Fuquay	73-80-75—228	$400.00
Cut	Andy Shuman	76-71-81—228	$400.00
Cut	Dwight Nevil	75-75-78—228	$400.00
Cut	Don Brozio	78-76-74—228	$400.00
Cut	Fletcher White	73-77-78—228	$400.00
Cut	Rick Pohle	76-77-75—228	$400.00
Cut	Bob Giusti	74-81-73—228	$400.00
Cut	Mark Keating	73-73-82—228	$400.00
Cut	Jim Hefti	81-70-77—228	$400.00
Cut	Pat Delaney	76-77-75—228	$400.00
Cut	Jeff Warne	78-76-74—228	$400.00
Cut	Tim Troy	78-76-75—229	$400.00
Cut	Lon Kinney	77-74-78—229	$400.00
Cut	Roger Watson	73-74-82—229	$400.00
Cut	Tony Hidalgo	72-78-79—229	$400.00
Cut	Douglas J. Campbell	73-78-78—229	$400.00
Cut	Madison Pope	77-75-77—229	$400.00
Cut	Clark Miyazaki	76-77-76—229	$400.00
Cut	David Thore	76-76-77—229	$400.00
Cut	Ric Kunnert	76-79-74—229	$400.00
Cut	Brett Upper	74-83-72—229	$400.00
Cut	Christopher Johnson	77-78-74—229	$400.00
Cut	Bobby Gordon	76-76-78—230	$400.00
Cut	Bobby Bray	79-75-76—230	$400.00
Cut	Robert Campbell	78-76-76—230	$400.00
Cut	Mike Cook	81-73-76—230	$400.00
Cut	Peter Famiano	75-78-77—230	$400.00
Cut	Art Williams	80-74-76—230	$400.00
Cut	Laurie Hammer	76-81-73—230	$400.00
Cut	Roy Carmichael	74-78-78—230	$400.00
Cut	Gregory J. Baker	76-75-79—230	$400.00
Cut	David Levine	76-73-81—230	$400.00
Cut	Brad Kai	73-74-83—230	$400.00
Cut	Bradley H. Rosely	78-76-76—230	$400.00
Cut	Michael Darrell	76-78-77—231	$400.00
Cut	Dave Fleming	77-75-79—231	$400.00
Cut	Greg Meade	78-75-78—231	$400.00
Cut	Steve Reilly	77-77-77—231	$400.00
Cut	Thomas Dirico	81-74-76—231	$400.00
Cut	Rusty Gunnarson	76-78-77—231	$400.00
Cut	Mark Saatzer	76-77-78—231	$400.00
Cut	Tom Sutter	80-75-76—231	$400.00
Cut	Joe Root	77-75-79—231	$400.00
Cut	Bobby Phillips	80-78-74—232	$400.00
Cut	Raymond Streeter	76-77-79—232	$400.00
Cut	Bob Vanscoy	81-76-75—232	$400.00
Cut	Steve Barber	76-79-77—232	$400.00
Cut	Joe Schwent	81-75-76—232	$400.00
Cut	Joe Tesori	77-77-79—233	$400.00
Cut	Larry King	75-81-77—233	$400.00
Cut	Bill Baldwin	76-78-79—233	$400.00
Cut	Dan Priest	79-74-80—233	$400.00
Cut	Russell Orth	78-77-78—233	$400.00
Cut	Skip Tredway	75-78-80—233	$400.00
Cut	Brook Schmitt	80-78-76—234	$400.00
Cut	Thomas A. Baldwin	77-77-81—235	$400.00
Cut	Mike Loudder	82-77-76—235	$400.00
Cut	Bobby Heins	80-79-76—235	$400.00
Cut	Ross Barnes	78-84-73—235	$400.00
Cut	Terry Ferraro	76-83-77—236	$400.00
Cut	Bob Mastalski	83-79-75—237	$400.00
Cut	Eric Martin	80-79-79—238	$400.00
Cut	Mark Kirk	78-77-84—239	$400.00
Cut	Dan Dirico	78-81-82—241	$400.00
Cut	Jim Razzeto	79-78-86—243	$400.00
Cut	Carl Funk	82-80-82—244	$400.00
Cut	Kevin G. Hughes	87-77-80—244	$400.00
Cut	Ron Snider	81-85-79—245	$400.00

PGA CLUB PROFESSIONAL CHAMPIONSHIP

1992

The silver anniversary of the Taylor Made PGA Club Professional Championship was marked by scorching heat, heavy wind and top-caliber play. Ron McDougal, a 29-year-old assistant professional at Century Country Club in Purchase, N.Y., made his second try in the Championship spectacular. He strung together four impressive rounds in the 60s, carding 67-69-68-69 for a 15-under-par 273 total and a three-stroke victory over Sammy Rachels of Defuniak Springs, Fla., earning $32,000 and his first Club Professional Championship. McDougal, who was a member of the victorious U.S. PGA Cup Team two weeks earlier in Dublin, Ireland, became only the second player to record wire-to-wire victories. Larry Gilbert of Lexington, Ky., first accomplished the feat in 1981. Gilbert and McDougal battled to the wire in 1991, with Gilbert pulling out a one-stroke victory over McDougal and Gene Fieger of Bryn Mawr, Pa. McDougal's rookie appearance in the Championship in 1991 was a disappointing final round. This time, he didn't let up. McDougal opened the final round leading Gilbert and Rachels by two strokes. McDougal ran in a pair of birdie putts and never looked back. Rachels had a closing 70, and three-time champion Gilbert managed only a final-round 2-over-par 74 to leave him at 280, tied for sixth place but extending his record top-10 finishes to nine. McDougal's final score was one stroke off the 72-hole record held by Howell Fraser, the inaugural (1968) PGA Club Professional Champion.

The top 40 professionals in the 1992 Taylor Made PGA Club Professional Championship received exemptions into the 1993 PGA Championship at Inverness Club in Toledo, Ohio.

Champion:	Ron McDougal, Purchase, N.Y.	
Site:	PGA West, La Quinta Hotel & Golf Resort,	
	Mission Hills Country Club, La Quinta, Calif.	
Date:	Oct. 1-4	
Course:	PGA West (Nicklaus Resort)	
Par:	72 - 6,928 yards	
Course: La Quinta (Mountain)	**Par:**	72 - 6,704 yards
Course: Mission Hills (Old)	**Par:**	72 - 6,954 yards
Purse: $400,000	**Field:** 356	
Cut at 219	100 players advanced	

	Resort (Par 72)	Mountain (Par 72)	Old (Par 72)	Round Leader	Ron McDougal
Round 1:	74.541	74.916	75.108	67 - Ron McDougal	67 - 1st
Round 2:	75.041	75.226	76.647	136 - Ron McDougal	136 - (69)1st
Round 3:	73.764	74.899	74.779	204 - Ron McDougal	204 - (68)1st
Round 4:	72.310				273 - (69)1st

TOURNAMENT SUMMARY

Place	Name	Score	Winnings
1	Ron McDougal	67-69-68-69—273	$32,000.00
2	Sammy Rachels	73-68-65-70—276	$22,000.00
T-3	Jeff Fairfield	68-72-72-66—278	$15,500.00
T-3	Will Frantz	70-70-70-68—278	$15,500.00
5	Chris Starkjohann	73-69-67-70—279	$12,000.00
T-6	Larry Gilbert	70-68-68-74—280	$10,000.00
T-6	Jon Hoecker	69-71-71-69—280	$10,000.00
T-6	Michael Schuchart	71-70-67-72—280	$10,000.00
T-9	Gregg Jones	69-72-71-69—281	$7,750.00
T-9	Brad Sherfy	72-71-71-67—281	$7,750.00
T-11	Robert Hoyt	70-72-69-71—282	$6,566.67
T-11	Chris Peddicord	71-76-67-68—282	$6,566.67
T-11	Todd Smith	70-72-70-70—282	$6,566.67
T-14	Kevin Burton	72-74-68-69—283	$5,750.00
T-14	Gary Trivison	74-68-71-70—283	$5,750.00
T-16	Cleve Coldwater	73-69-72-70—284	$5,016.67
T-16	Stu Ingraham	72-69-73-70—284	$5,016.67
T-16	Jay Overton	70-74-70-70—284	$5,016.67
T-19	Bob Boyd	73-70-72-70—285	$4,125.00
T-19	John Godwin	76-68-71-70—285	$4,125.00
T-19	John Hoskison	72-71-73-69—285	$4,125.00
T-19	J.L. Lewis	72-69-73-71—285	$4,125.00
T-23	Bob Bailey	71-75-71-69—286	$2,828.57
T-23	Bob Borowicz	75-71-70-70—286	$2,828.57
T-23	Gary Groh	70-76-70-70—286	$2,828.57
T-23	Darrell Kestner	74-71-72-69—286	$2,828.57
T-23	Bruce Lehnhard	71-75-74-66—286	$2,828.57
T-23	Gary Robison	71-74-70-71—286	$2,828.57
T-23	Tom Wargo	69-73-72-72—286	$2,828.57
T-30	Tim Angis	74-71-69-73—287	$1,750.00
T-30	Gene George	70-74-75-68—287	$1,750.00
T-30	Ken Krieger	71-74-74-68—287	$1,750.00
T-30	Mark Mielke	76-68-70-73—287	$1,750.00
T-30	John Nelson	72-76-69-70—287	$1,750.00
T-30	Curt Schnell	75-69-73-70—287	$1,750.00
T-30	Tim Stafford	72-72-73-70—287	$1,750.00
T-30	Scott Walter	72-73-72-70—287	$1,750.00
T-38	Ken Allard	71-73-73-71—288	$1,153.33
T-38	Bob Ford	73-73-73-69—288	$1,153.33
T-38	Doug Hixson	75-71-71-71—288	$1,153.33
T-38	W.D. Israelson	72-71-74-71—288	$1,153.33
T-38	Tom Joyce	73-73-73-69—288	$1,153.33
T-38	Jim Kane	70-72-72-74—288	$1,153.33
T-38	Dana Quigley	74-72-72-70—288	$1,153.33
T-38	Larry Rentz	72-67-70-79—288	$1,153.33
T-38	Jim White	72-75-67-74—288	$1,153.33
T-47	Michael Burke Jr.	75-71-74-69—289	$891.00
T-47	Greg Cerulli	71-71-72-75—289	$891.00
T-47	Lee Daniellan	72-74-73-70—289	$891.00
T-47	Charlie Epps	73-75-70-71—289	$891.00
T-47	Gene Fieger	72-73-74-70—289	$891.00
T-47	Thomas Gray	73-71-71-74—289	$891.00
T-47	Kirk Hanefeld	73-72-73-71—289	$891.00
T-47	Dave Kendall	74-69-73-73—289	$891.00
T-47	Randy McGohan	73-67-76-73—289	$891.00
T-47	Tim Norris	73-73-73-70—289	$891.00
T-57	Bob Boyle	72-72-70-76—290	$780.00
T-57	Mike Gilmore	74-71-76-69—290	$780.00
T-57	Mike Gove	71-72-75-72—290	$780.00
T-57	Stacey Hart	77-71-71-71—290	$780.00
T-57	Roy Hunter	72-76-72-70—290	$780.00
T-57	Rick Lewallen	72-74-71-73—290	$780.00
T-57	Scott Mahlberg	75-72-72-71—290	$780.00
T-57	John Mazza	69-72-78-71—290	$780.00
T-57	Randy Peterson	72-73-71-74—290	$780.00
T-57	Dean Prowse	67-78-71-74—290	$780.00
T-57	Mike San Filippo	74-74-70-72—290	$780.00
T-68	John Dal Corobbo	76-68-74-73—291	$689.00
T-68	Charlie Cowell	73-72-74-72—291	$689.00
T-68	Robert Gibbons	70-77-72-72—291	$689.00
T-68	Bill King	76-71-71-73—291	$689.00
T-68	James Masserio	71-73-74-73—291	$689.00
T-68	Rich Ritter	74-70-72-75—291	$689.00
T-68	Bill Robinson	76-71-73-71—291	$689.00
T-68	Steve Sieg	70-76-70-75—291	$689.00
T-68	Brent Veenstra	74-67-70-80—291	$689.00
T-68	Jerry Wisz	71-76-72-72—291	$689.00
T-78	Thomas Dolby	71-74-74-73—292	$638.00
T-78	Jerry Impellittiere	70-78-72-72—292	$638.00
T-78	Bob Leaver	74-73-70-75—292	$638.00
T-78	Benny Passons	73-75-70-74—292	$638.00
T-78	Tom Woodward	70-78-71-73—292	$638.00
T-83	Walt Chapman	72-75-73-73—293	$632.50
T-83	Baker Maddera	74-73-72-74—293	$632.50
T-85	David Carich	78-73-69-74—294	$617.50
T-85	Michael Moyers	71-72-74-77—294	$617.50
T-85	Barry Redmond	71-74-74-75—294	$617.50
T-85	Greg Van Natta	74-73-73-74—294	$617.50
T-89	David Marchand	73-72-75-75—295	$602.50
T-89	Fletcher White	73-74-73-75—295	$602.50
T-91	Larry Emery	73-73-74-76—296	$587.50
T-91	John Gentile	76-69-75-76—296	$587.50
T-91	Jeff Hunter	72-75-72-77—296	$587.50
T-91	Bob Phillips	71-77-70-78—296	$587.50
T-95	Rick Osberg	73-70-72-82—297	$572.50
T-95	Dave Roberts	75-73-72-77—297	$572.50
T-97	Harold Perry Jr.	74-72-74-78—298	$536.50
T-97	Todd Yoshitake	73-70-75-80—298	$536.50
99	Brad Kai	70-73-77-80—300	$555.00
100	Dale Fuller	69-81-70-81—301	$550.00

1991

Larry Gilbert of Lexington, Ky., runner-up in the 1990 Taylor Made PGA Club Professional Championship, shot a 14-under-par 267 to capture the 1991 Taylor Made PGA Club Professional Championship at Doral Resort and Country Club in Miami, Fla. It was Gilbert's record third career PGA Club Professional Championship victory.

In addition to a record winner's check of $32,000, Gilbert earned exemptions into the 1992 PGA Championship, 1992 NEC World Series of Golf, three additional PGA Tour events and a spot on the 1992 PGA Cup Team.

Due to heavy rains, one of the three courses hosting the Championship was adjusted to a par 66, resulting in a large number of low scores. Gene Fieger of Bryn Mawr, Pa., and Ron McDougal of Purchase, N.Y., finished tied for second at 268, each collecting $19,500.

The top 40 professionals in the 1991 Taylor Made PGA Club Professional Championship received exemptions into the 1992 PGA Championship at Bellerive Country Club in St. Louis, Mo., and the top nine finishers join 1990 PGA Club Professional Champion Brett Upper as members of the 1992 PGA Cup Team.

Champion:	Larry Gilbert, Lexington, Ky.	
Site:	Doral Resort & Country Club, Miami, Fla.	
Date:	Oct. 3-6	
Course: Blue	**Par:**	72 - 6,900 yards
Course: Gold	**Par:**	66 - 5,482 yards
Course: Silver	**Par:**	71 - 6,613 yards
Purse:	$400,000	**Field:** 355
	Cut at 211	97 players advanced

Scoring Averages	Blue (Par 72)	Gold (Par 66)	Silver (Par 71)	Round Leader		Larry Gilbert	
Round 1:	74.675	67.563	72.771	60-	Louis Bartoletti	67-	(T-50)
Round 2:	74.898	67.983	72.261	129-	Jon Chaffee, Gene Fieger, Mike San Filippo, Ron McDougal	132	(65)-(T-10)
Round 3:	74.891	68.102	72.991	196-	Bruce Zabriski	199	(67)-(T-3)
Round 4:	74.821			267-	Larry Gilbert	267	(68)-1st
Totals:	74.806	67.882	72.674				

TOURNAMENT SUMMARY

Place	Name	Score	Winnings	Place	Name	Score	Winnings	Place	Name	Score	Winnings
1	Larry Gilbert	67-65-67-68—267	$32,000.00	T-32	Mel Baum	66-69-71-73—279	$1,343.00	T-62	Miguel Biamon	70-70-67-75—282	$705.00
T-2	Gene Fieger	64-65-72-67—268	$19,500.00	T-32	David Glenz	78-60-69-72—279	$1,343.00	T-62	Bryan Gathright	74-66-71-71—282	$705.00
T-2	Ron McDougal	69-61-67-71—268	$19,500.00	T-32	Bob Groff	73-74-63-69—279	$1,343.00	T-62	Stu Ingraham	68-69-73-72—282	$705.00
4	Mike San Filippo	66-63-70-70—269	$14,000.00	T-32	Denny Hepler	70-63-74-72—279	$1,343.00	T-62	Rick Meskell	70-72-67-73—282	$705.00
T-5	Tom Wargo	64-67-73-66—270	$11,500.00	T-32	Fran Marrello	71-68-66-74—279	$1,343.00	T-62	Bill Murchison	72-67-71-72—282	$705.00
T-5	Bruce Zabriski	66-71-59-74—270	$11,500.00	T-32	Ed Sabo	75-61-72-71—279	$1,343.00	T-62	Larry Rentz	64-68-76-74—282	$705.00
T-7	Jon Chaffee	62-67-70-72—271	$9,000.00	T-32	Jim White	68-71-67-73—279	$1,343.00	T-62	John Schoonover	73-64-73-72—282	$705.00
T-7	Michael Schuchart	67-65-68-71—271	$9,000.00	T-39	Terry Dear	71-67-70-72—280	$971.00	T-62	Chris Starkjohann	69-71-71-71—282	$705.00
T-7	Steve Veriato	63-66-72-70—271	$9,000.00	T-39	Michael Erickson	68-71-68-73—280	$971.00	T-71	Jeff Fairfield	70-68-73-72—283	$665.00
T-10	Bob Borowicz	70-69-65-69—273	$7,000.00	T-39	Michael Hamblin	64-73-69-74—280	$971.00	T-71	Terry Houser	65-72-73-73—283	$665.00
T-10	Lee Rinker	70-64-68-71—273	$7,000.00	T-39	Bill Kennedy	65-68-74-73—280	$971.00	T-71	John Jasinski	65-73-71-74—283	$665.00
T-10	Todd Smith	70-63-68-72—273	$7,000.00	T-39	Bob Lendzion	71-69-71-69—280	$971.00	T-71	Dana Quigley	64-72-75-72—283	$665.00
T-13	Ken Allard	70-61-72-72—275	$5,321.00	T-39	Jay Lumpkin	73-65-70-72—280	$971.00	T-75	Rick Acton	70-67-72-75—284	$637.00
T-13	Louis Bartoletti	60-73-72-70—275	$5,321.00	T-39	Gary Trivison	69-68-73-70—280	$971.00	T-75	Greg Farrow	71-65-74-74—284	$637.00
T-13	Steve Groves	63-72-70-70—275	$5,321.00	T-39	Tommy Valentine	65-65-76-74—280	$971.00	T-75	Hunt Gilliland	72-73-66-73—284	$637.00
T-13	Bruce Lehnhard	71-69-65-70—275	$5,321.00	T-39	Tom Weedard	69-73-65-73—280	$971.00	T-75	Bill King	64-75-71-74—284	$637.00
T-13	Harold Perry Jr.	68-67-71-69—275	$5,321.00	T-48	George Belli	70-70-68-73—281	$815.00	T-75	Victor Whipp	71-71-68-74—284	$637.00
T-13	Dan Wood	70-65-71-69—275	$5,321.00	T-48	Scott Bentley	71-71-68-71—281	$815.00	T-75	B.G. Winings	75-65-70-74—284	$637.00
19	Gordon Johnson	64-71-72-69—276	$4,000.00	T-48	Phil Hancock	64-72-70-75—281	$815.00	T-81	Jeff Baston	64-72-75-74—285	$605.00
T-20	Darrell Kestner	71-65-72-69—277	$2,828.00	T-48	Cary Hungate	71-72-67-71—281	$815.00	T-81	Jeff Combe	75-67-69-74—285	$605.00
T-21	Michael Burke Jr.	68-70-68-71—277	$2,828.00	T-48	Roy Hunter	63-70-73-75—281	$815.00	T-81	Tony Farmer	74-67-69-75—285	$605.00
T-21	Lowell Dencer	69-69-66-73—277	$2,828.00	T-48	John Lewis	66-68-76-71—281	$815.00	T-81	Gary Griggs	69-77-65-74—285	$605.00
T-21	Doug Hixson	67-66-74-70—277	$2,828.00	T-48	Keith Liedes	67-69-75-70—281	$815.00	T-81	Ed Habjan	68-74-69-74—285	$605.00
T-21	Tom Joyce	69-73-62-73—277	$2,828.00	T-48	Dino Lucchesi	75-66-68-72—281	$815.00	T-81	Lindy Miller	66-70-73-76—285	$605.00
T-21	Scott Mahlberg	69-65-71-72—277	$2,828.00	T-48	Shawn McEntee	74-64-68-75—281	$815.00	T-81	David O'Kelly	63-74-74-74—285	$605.00
T-21	Jay Overton	66-68-73-70—277	$2,828.00	T-48	Dan O'Neill	64-67-75-75—281	$815.00	88	Steve Seig	73-73-64-76—286	$585.00
T-27	Baker Maddera	70-72-64-72—278	$1,900.00	T-48	Barry Redmond	72-66-70-73—281	$815.00	T-89	Michael Barnett	69-71-69-78—287	$572.00
T-27	Ken McDonald	69-72-64-73—278	$1,900.00	T-48	Jeffrey Roth	65-69-73-74—281	$815.00	T-89	Gary Battistoni	74-71-66-76—287	$572.00
T-27	Gary Ostrega	72-67-67-72—278	$1,900.00	T-48	Chris Tucker	70-74-64-73—281	$815.00	T-89	Bobby Heins	67-73-71-76—287	$572.00
T-27	Mike West	64-70-72-72—278	$1,900.00	T-48	Brett Upper	69-70-69-73—281	$815.00	T-89	Pete Huber	69-75-67-76—287	$572.00
T-27	Ed Whitman	64-68-76-70—278	$1,900.00	T-62	Tommy Aycock	71-72-67-72—282	$705.00				

PGA CLUB PROFESSIONAL CHAMPIONSHIP

1990

Brett Upper of Feather Sound Country Club in Clearwater, Fla., fired a 13-under-par 275 to defeat third-round leader Gibby Gilbert of Chattanooga, Tenn., and two-time champion Larry Gilbert of Lexington, Ky., and collect the $32,000 winner's check. Upper's score was the lowest in the PGA Club Professional Championship since Sam Snead shot 275 in 1971. With his victory, Upper clinched PGA Club Professional Player of the Year honors for 1990.

Champion:	Brett Upper, Clearwater, Fla.		
Site:	PGA West, La Quinta Hotel & Golf Resort,		
	Mission Hills Country Club, La Quinta, Calif.		
Date:	Oct. 4-7		
Course:	PGA West Stadium	Par:	72 - 6,854 yards
Course:	La Quinta Mountain	Par:	72 - 6,713 yards
Course:	Mission Hills (Old)	Par:	72 - 6,954 yards
Purse:	$400,000	Field:	356
	Cut at 219	100 players advanced	

	Average of Courses	Rounds of 70 & Under	Rounds Under Par	Round Leader		Brett Upper	
Round 1:	75.1	34	53	66-	Lee Rinker	69 -	Tied 9th
Round 2:	74.7	41	68	136-	Gibby Gilbert	138	(69) - 4th
Round 3:	74.67	46	87	203-	Gibby Gilbert	204	(66) - 2nd
Round 4:	74.2	10	22	275-	Brett Upper	275	(71) - 1st
Totals:	74.76	131	219				

TOURNAMENT SUMMARY

Place	Name	Score	Winnings
1	Brett Upper	69-69-66-71—275	$32,000.00
T-2	Gibby Gilbert	70-66-67-75—278	$19,500.00
T-2	Larry Gilbert	68-70-68-72—278	$19,500.00
T-4	Bob Borowicz	69-72-68-71—280	$12,333.33
T-4	Greg Farrow	73-70-70-67—280	$12,333.34
T-4	Mike Lawrence	72-70-69-69—280	$12,333.33
T-7	Darrell Kestner	70-72-67-73—282	$9,000.00
T-7	Lonnie Nielsen	68-71-70-73—282	$9,000.00
T-7	Gary Trivison	69-68-72-73—282	$9,000.00
T-10	Mel Baum	75-67-71-70—283	$6,620.00
T-10	Jim Dickson	74-70-68-71—283	$6,620.00
T-10	Stu Ingraham	69-71-71-72—283	$6,620.00
T-10	Mike Kallam	70-69-72-72—283	$6,620.00
T-10	Steve Veriato	68-70-70-75—283	$6,620.00
T-15	Tom Wargo	69-71-71-73—284	$5,450.00
T-15	Tom Woodward	73-71-71-69—284	$5,450.00
T-17	Denny Hepler	72-75-69-69—285	$4,625.00
T-17	Shawn McEntee	73-68-70-74—285	$4,625.00
T-17	Lee Rinker	66-76-71-72—285	$4,625.00
T-17	Brad Sherfy	72-73-68-72—285	$4,625.00
T-21	Scott Bentley	71-73-69-73—286	$3,271.43
T-21	Terry Florence	72-72-71-71—286	$3,271.43
T-21	Fran Marrello	69-75-69-73—286	$3,271.43
T-21	James Masserio	76-69-70-71—286	$3,271.43
T-21	Benny Passons	77-69-69-71—286	$3,271.43
T-21	Jeffrey Roth	74-65-72-75—286	$3,271.42
T-21	Kim Thompson	67-70-74-75—286	$3,271.43
T-28	Brent Buckman	70-69-71-77—287	$1,968.75
T-28	Terry Dear	70-72-71-74—287	$1,968.75
T-28	Bruce Fleisher	74-71-70-72—287	$1,968.75
T-28	Lindy Miller	71-77-68-71—287	$1,968.75
T-28	Ken Schall	71-73-73-70—287	$1,968.75
T-28	Rob Wilkin	69-72-73-73—287	$1,968.75
T-28	Scott Williams	72-73-68-74—287	$1,968.75
T-28	Gregg Wolff	73-71-72-71—287	$1,968.75
T-36	Bob Boyd	68-75-72-73—288	$1,307.14
T-36	Greg Cerulli	71-74-68-75—288	$1,307.14
T-36	John Hendricks	72-73-73-70—288	$1,307.14
T-36	Bob Lendzion	75-68-72-73—288	$1,307.14
T-36	Milan Swilor	74-75-70-69—288	$1,307.15
T-36	Brent Veenstra	73-73-70-72—288	$1,307.14
T-36	Jim White	73-72-73-70—288	$1,307.15
T-43	Ken Allard	73-75-70-71—289	$1,018.00
T-43	Scott Davis	74-72-69-74—289	$1,018.00
T-43	Frank Dobbs	69-76-73-71—289	$1,018.00
T-43	Bob Groff	74-71-74-70—289	$1,018.00
T-43	John Ha	75-71-71-72—289	$1,018.00
T-48	Tim Angis	70-76-73-71—290	$912.50
T-48	Scott Hart	71-73-72-74—290	$912.50
T-48	Chris Tucker	72-70-73-75—290	$912.50
T-48	Jerry Wisz	73-75-71-71—290	$912.50
T-52	Bob Ackerman	71-71-71-78—291	$830.00
T-52	Tim Brauch	71-78-70-72—291	$830.00
T-52	Doug Doxsie	72-71-75-73—291	$830.00
T-52	Mike Gove	77-71-71-72—291	$830.00
T-52	Stacey Hart	73-72-72-74—291	$830.00
T-52	Cary Hungate	76-70-72-73—291	$830.00
T-52	Tom Joyce	73-70-74-74—291	$830.00
T-52	Paul Kemps	72-74-72-73—291	$830.00
T-52	Allan Menne	74-78-66-73—291	$830.00
T-52	Steve Whillock	74-69-73-75—291	$830.00
T-52	Ed Whitman	74-71-74-72—291	$830.00
T-63	Jim Albus	73-74-71-74—292	$730.56
T-63	Steve Bowen	72-67-75-78—292	$730.55
T-63	Tommy Brannen	73-69-74-76—292	$730.55
T-63	John Godwin	74-70-74-74—292	$730.56
T-63	Stephen Keppler	69-73-74-76—292	$730.55
T-63	Ted O'Rourke	73-74-70-75—292	$730.56
T-63	Jay Overton	69-72-72-79—292	$730.55
T-63	Eric Smith	72-71-76-73—292	$730.56
T-63	Al Weinhold	78-70-70-74—292	$730.56
T-72	Steve Behr	75-70-74-74—293	$665.00
T-72	Gene Fieger	70-74-73-76—293	$665.00
T-72	Phil Hancock	72-72-74-75—293	$665.00
T-72	Craig Immel	71-70-75-77—293	$665.00
T-72	John Jasinski	72-74-73-74—293	$665.00
T-72	Bruce Lehnhard	70-74-74-75—293	$665.00
T-72	Brent Murray	71-72-73-77—293	$665.00
T-72	John Paesani	73-73-72-75—293	$665.00
T-72	Chris Starkjohann	70-72-73-78—293	$665.00
T-72	Kent Stauffer	70-69-75-79—293	$665.00
T-72	Harry Tosca	71-73-74-75—293	$665.00
T-83	Terry Ferraro	72-72-73-77—294	$625.00
T-83	Gary Hardin	74-76-68-76—294	$625.00
T-83	Rick Lewallen	68-73-74-79—294	$625.00
T-83	Bob Mann	71-73-75-75—294	$625.00
T-83	Ed Terasa	75-76-68-75—294	$625.00
T-88	Tom Gieselman	77-71-71-76—295	$602.50
T-88	Laurie Hammer	73-73-71-78—295	$602.50
T-88	Steve Howe	71-72-76-76—295	$602.50
T-88	David Nevatt	72-74-71-78—295	$602.50
T-92	Jerry Minor	73-76-70-77—296	$585.00
T-92	Jerry Tucker	76-71-72-77—296	$585.00
T-92	Larry Webb	77-70-72-77—296	$585.00
T-95	Larry Emery	70-72-76-79—297	$572.50
T-95	Jack Seltzer	72-72-72-81—297	$572.50
97	Michael Hamblin	68-72-73-88—301	$565.00
98	John Traub	74-76-69-84—303	$560.00
99	Tim O'Neal	73-74-72-85—304	$555.00
100	Gary Gabrielson	74-69-76-86—305	$550.00

PGA CLUB PROFESSIONAL CHAMPIONSHIP

1989

Bruce Fleisher, a 41-year-old head professional from North Miami Beach, Fla., closed with a final round par-72 for an 11-under-par 277 to defeat Jeff Thomsen of Boise, Idaho, by three strokes. For Fleisher, who played on the PGA Tour for 12 years before returning home to Miami in 1983, it was his first appearance in the PGA Club Professional Championship.

Champion:	Bruce Fleisher, N. Miami Beach, Fla.
Site:	PGA West, La Quinta Hotel & Resort, Mission Hills Country Club, La Quinta, Calif.
Date:	Oct. 5-8
Course:	PGA West Stadium **Par:** 72 - 6,854 yards (used for one round and on final day)
Course:	La Quinta Mountain **Par:** 72 - 6,713 yards
Course:	Mission Hills (Old) **Par:** 72 - 6,954 yards
Purse:	$360,000 **Field:** 357
	Cut at 220 104 players advanced

	Average of Courses	Rounds of 70 & Under	Rounds Under Par	Round Leader		Bruce Fleisher	
Round 1:	75.2	15	56	67-	Jeff Fairfield	69 -	Tied 7th
Round 2:	75.3	17	17	137-	Bruce Fleisher	137	(68) - 1st
Round 3:	75.5	14	14	205-	Bruce Fleisher	205	(68) - 1st
Round 4:	74.4	8	8	277-	Bruce Fleisher	277	(72) - 1st
Totals:	75.23	54	95				

TOURNAMENT SUMMARY

Place	Name	Score	Winnings
1	Bruce Fleisher	69-68-68-72—277	$30,000.00
2	Jeff Thomsen	71-67-70-72—280	$20,000.00
3	Phil Hancock	75-67-71-69—282	$15,000.00
T-4	Bob Boyd	71-70-74-68—283	$11,750.00
T-4	Dale Fuller	68-73-70-72—283	$11,750.00
T-6	Sammy Rachels	70-69-72-73—284	$9,500.00
T-6	Kim Thompson	71-72-70-71—284	$9,500.00
T-8	Bob Ford	71-71-73-70—285	$7,500.00
T-8	Ray Freeman	70-70-72-73—285	$7,500.00
T-8	Stu Ingraham	72-69-72-72—285	$7,500.00
T-11	Ken Allard	71-70-74-71—286	$6,250.00
T-11	Noel Caruso	72-75-70-69—286	$6,250.00
T-11	Lonnie Nielsen	70-70-76-70—286	$6,250.00
T-11	Mike San Filippo	73-69-75-69—286	$6,250.00
T-15	Steve Bowen	72-77-67-71—287	$4,607.14
T-15	Ted Goin	71-72-72-72—287	$4,607.14
T-15	Mike Gove	71-67-74-75—287	$4,607.14
T-15	Robert Hoyt	74-74-71-68—287	$4,607.14
T-15	Cary Hungate	69-77-74-67—287	$4,607.14
T-15	Rick Osberg	69-77-71-70—287	$4,607.14
T-15	Chris Tucker	69-78-71-69—287	$4,607.14
T-22	Bob Borowicz	71-70-77-70—288	$2,925.00
T-22	Larry Emery	72-73-71-72—288	$2,925.00
T-22	Patrick Fitzsimmons	74-76-69-69—288	$2,925.00
T-22	Drue Johnson	73-70-74-71—288	$2,925.00
T-22	Dana Quigley	70-72-75-71—288	$2,925.00
T-22	Curt Schnell	70-70-69-79—288	$2,925.00
T-28	Greg Cerulli	74-74-70-71—289	$1,850.00
T-28	Hunt Gilliland	72-69-75-73—289	$1,850.00
T-28	Jay Overton	77-70-69-73—289	$1,850.00
T-28	Benny Passons	70-72-74-73—289	$1,850.00
T-28	Ken Schall	71-68-72-78—289	$1,850.00
T-28	Jim Sobb	69-74-69-77—289	$1,850.00
T-28	Kent Stauffer	71-73-73-72—289	$1,850.00
T-28	Ed Whitman	73-73-71-72—289	$1,850.00

Place	Name	Score	Winnings
T-36	J.C. Blair III	72-72-73-73—290	$1,181.25
T-36	Chris Dachisen	77-74-69-70—290	$1,181.25
T-36	Jeff Fairfield	67-79-68-76—290	$1,181.25
T-36	Larry Gilbert	74-68-75-73—290	$1,181.25
T-36	Kirk Hanefeld	75-71-73-71—290	$1,181.25
T-36	Bob Makoski	74-73-70-73—290	$1,181.25
T-36	Harold Perry Jr.	74-70-69-77—290	$1,181.25
T-36	Don Robertson	68-73-70-79—290	$1,181.25
T-44	Tom Doozan	73-71-73-74—291	$926.00
T-44	Gordon Johnson	74-73-72-72—291	$926.00
T-44	Bob Lendzion	73-72-70-76—291	$926.00
T-44	Bruce Summerhays	73-76-71-71—291	$926.00
T-44	Rob Wilkin	74-71-72-74—291	$926.00
T-49	Alan Arvesen	71-72-76-73—292	$796.66
T-49	Miguel Biamon	75-71-72-74—292	$796.66
T-49	Lee Daniellan	70-75-75-72—292	$796.66
T-49	Charlie Epps	76-73-69-74—292	$796.66
T-49	Rick Lewallen	68-71-78-75—292	$796.66
T-49	Stan Stopa	72-75-72-73—292	$796.66
T-49	Ron Vlosich	71-69-76-76—292	$796.66
T-49	Tom Waitrovich	73-69-76-74—292	$796.66
T-49	Buddy Whitten	71-70-73-78—292	$796.66
T-58	Mike Bibb	73-75-69-76—293	$708.33
T-58	Jon Chaffee	71-72-73-77—293	$708.33
T-58	Gene Fieger	72-70-77-74—293	$708.33
T-58	Thomas Gray	70-72-74-77—293	$708.33
T-58	Bobby Heins	71-73-76-73—293	$708.33
T-58	John Jackson Jr.	70-77-70-76—293	$708.33
T-58	Gregg Jones	73-72-72-76—293	$708.33
T-58	Walt Porterfield Jr.	68-73-77-75—293	$708.33
T-58	Scott Walter	76-70-74-73—293	$708.33
T-67	Steve Brady	75-73-71-75—294	$657.50
T-67	John Calabria	76-70-74-74—294	$657.50
T-67	Toby Chapin	72-75-71-76—294	$657.50
T-67	Frank Dobbs	75-70-75-74—294	$657.50

Place	Name	Score	Winnings
T-67	Greg Frederick	72-73-72-77—294	$657.50
T-67	Robert Gibbons	74-75-71-74—294	$657.50
T-67	Dick McClean	77-74-69-74—294	$657.50
T-67	Jim Mclean	69-73-76-76—294	$657.50
T-67	Steve Sieg	73-70-77-74—294	$657.50
T-67	Bob Smith	73-71-73-77—294	$657.50
T-77	Jeff Bailey	77-70-73-75—295	$612.50
T-77	Buddy Harston	75-72-73-75—295	$612.50
T-77	David Nevatt	73-74-73-75—295	$612.50
T-77	Don Padgett II	70-73-74-78—295	$612.50
T-77	Billy Peterson	71-73-74-77—295	$612.50
T-77	Randy Peterson	76-69-72-78—295	$612.50
T-77	Robert Singletary	72-76-71-76—295	$612.50
T-77	Chris Starkjohann	78-73-67-77—295	$612.50
T-85	Tim Angis	74-72-74-76—296	$574.37
T-85	Doug Bauman	76-72-71-77—296	$574.37
T-85	Gibby Gilbert	77-70-73-76—296	$574.37
T-85	Shawn McEntee	75-71-73-77—296	$574.37
T-85	Steve Moreland	71-74-74-77—296	$574.37
T-85	Eddie Mudd	74-69-75-78—296	$574.37
T-85	Jimmy Paschal	73-74-73-76—296	$574.37
T-85	Gregg Wolff	76-69-74-77—296	$574.37
T-93	John Paesani	74-73-71-79—297	$565.00
T-93	Phil Wagoner	70-72-76-79—297	$565.00
T-95	Mitch Camp	74-73-73-78—298	$565.00
T-96	Bob Betley	74-73-72-79—298	$565.00
T-96	Roy Hunter	74-72-74-78—298	$565.00
T-98	Bill Galloway	74-73-73-79—299	$565.00
T-98	David Lundstrom	74-75-71-79—299	$565.00
T-100	Randy Jensen	74-72-74-80—300	$565.00
T-100	Jerry Minor	72-72-76-80—300	$565.00
102	Gary Hardin	71-76-73-81—301	$565.00
T-103	Mel Baum	71-77-72-82—302	$565.00
T-103	Bill Majure	73-77-70-82—302	$565.00

1988

Bob Boyd, a 33-year-old head professional from Florence, S.C., made a par on the second playoff hole to defeat another Carolinian, Rick Morton. Both shot 1-over-par 287s, marking the first time in the history of the PGA Club Professional Championship that the winning score was over par.

Champion:	Bob Boyd, Florence, S.C.
Site:	Pinehurst Country Club, Pinehurst, N.C.
Date:	Oct. 12-15
Course: No. 2	**Par:** 71 - 7,051 yards
(used for one round and on final day)	
Course: No. 4	**Par:** 72 - 6,784 yards
Course: No. 7	**Par:** 72 - 7,114 yards
Purse: $360,000	**Field:** 355
Cut at 225	98 players advanced

	Avg. of Courses	Rounds of 70 & Under		Round Leader		Bob Boyd	
Round 1:	76.5	8	69-	Bob Groff, Gary Hardin	70 -	Tied 3rd	
Round 2:	77.4	5	140-	Rick Morton	144	(74) - Tied 5th	
Round 3:	76.3	16	217-	Shawn McEntee	217	(73) - Tied 7th	
Round 4:	75.5	5	287-	Bob Boyd, Rick Morton	287	(70) - Tied 1st	
Totals:	76.62	34					

TOURNAMENT SUMMARY

Place	Name	Score	Winnings	Place	Name	Score	Winnings	Place	Name	Score	Winnings
T-1	Bob Boyd	70-74-73-70—287	$30,000.00	T-34	Mitch Camp	71-76-71-78—296	$1,255.00	T-59	David Thore	72-77-76-74—299	$699.00
T-2	Rick Morton	71-69-74-73—287	$20,000.00	T-34	Mark Gardner	75-72-77-72—296	$1,255.00	T-59	Vic Tortorici	76-73-76-74—299	$699.00
3	Bruce Lehnhard	73-74-71-70—288	$15,000.00	T-34	Robert Gibbons	73-73-77-73—296	$1,255.00	T-69	Tom Joyce	73-75-76-76—300	$657.50
T-4	Bobby Heins	70-76-71-72—289	$11,166.67	T-34	David Glenz	71-75-73-77—296	$1,255.00	T-69	John Lindert	73-77-72-78—300	$657.50
T-4	Shawn McEntee	71-70-71-77—289	$11,166.66	T-34	Webb Heintzelman	75-76-72-73—296	$1,255.00	T-69	Don Maddox	72-78-72-78—300	$657.50
T-4	Sammy Rachels	71-74-72-72—289	$11,166.67	T-34	Jeff Jackson	76-75-72-73—296	$1,255.00	T-69	Bob Menne	77-72-76-75—300	$657.50
T-7	Bob Betley	71-71-75-73—290	$8,500.00	T-34	Bob Klein Jr.	73-75-75-73—296	$1,255.00	T-69	Scott Steger	75-72-75-78—300	$657.50
T-7	Bob Mann	70-73-73-74—290	$8,500.00	T-34	Wally Kuchar	71-76-77-72—296	$1,255.00	T-69	Jim White	74-73-78-75—300	$657.50
T-9	John Jackson Jr.	70-75-74-72—291	$7,250.00	T-34	Steve Spray	74-76-75-71—296	$1,255.00	T-75	Scott Dietrich	72-77-73-79—301	$627.50
T-9	Ralph Landrum	74-72-70-75—291	$7,250.00	T-34	Jerry Tucker	73-75-76-72—296	$1,255.00	T-75	Hunt Gilliland	75-77-73-76—301	$627.50
T-11	Larry Gilbert	76-73-76-67—292	$6,100.00	T-44	Jim Albus	72-72-77-76—297	$883.33	T-75	Barry Redmond	78-76-71-76—301	$627.50
T-11	Gregg Jones	75-70-72-75—292	$6,100.00	T-44	Gibby Gilbert	71-75-72-79—297	$883.33	T-75	Ken Schall	72-80-71-78—301	$627.50
T-11	Jack Lewis	74-75-71-72—292	$6,100.00	T-44	Scott Mahlberg	75-75-74-73—297	$883.34	T-75	Jeff Steinberg	76-72-76-77—301	$627.50
T-11	Lindy Miller	74-77-74-67—292	$6,100.00	T-44	Walt Porterfield Jr.	75-76-71-75—297	$883.33	T-75	Steve Whillcok	74-74-73-80—301	$627.50
T-11	Gary Robison	73-74-70-75—292	$6,100.00	T-44	Don Reese	77-77-71-72—297	$883.34	T-81	Tim Brauch	76-78-70-78—302	$597.50
T-16	Bob Groff	69-75-77-72—293	$4,900.00	T-44	Gary Robinson	71-75-78-73—297	$883.34	T-81	Michael Diffley	77-75-71-79—302	$597.50
T-16	Bill King	71-74-71-77—293	$4,900.00	T-44	Ed Sabo	76-78-69-74—297	$883.33	T-81	Wayne Myers	77-73-74-78—302	$597.50
T-16	Ed Whitman	73-72-73-75—293	$4,900.00	T-44	Roy Vucinich	76-77-70-74—297	$883.33	T-81	Jimmy Paschal	73-75-77-77—302	$597.50
T-19	Jim Cichra	73-77-70-74—294	$4,150.00	T-44	Gregg Wolff	73-76-71-77—297	$883.33	T-81	Bill Tindall	75-74-74-79—302	$597.50
T-19	Gene Fieger	71-77-72-74—294	$4,150.00	T-53	Jon Chaffee	74-75-73-76—298	$765.00	T-81	Dan Wood	75-77-70-80—302	$597.50
T-21	Ken Allard	75-74-70-76—295	$2,538.46	T-53	Fred Funk	75-76-72-75—298	$765.00	T-87	Gary Groh	75-77-73-78—303	$575.00
T-21	Don Brigham	77-76-66-76—295	$2,538.46	T-53	Buddy Harston	74-78-68-78—298	$765.00	T-87	Darrell Kestner	73-79-71-80—303	$575.00
T-21	Scott Davis	73-77-69-76—295	$2,538.46	T-53	Jeff Thomsen	78-75-70-75—298	$765.00	T-87	Rob Wilkin	71-78-74-80—303	$575.00
T-21	Bob Ford	76-72-77-70—295	$2,538.47	T-53	Tim Walton	73-76-74-75—298	$765.00	T-90	Michael Harmon	75-80-70-79—304	$565.00
T-21	Greg Frederick	73-76-73-73—295	$2,538.46	T-53	Mike Zaremba	75-76-73-74—298	$765.00	T-90	Steve King	75-77-72-80—304	$565.00
T-21	Ray Freeman	72-72-74-77—295	$2,538.46	T-59	Jeff Bailey	74-77-70-78—299	$699.00	T-90	John Paesani	73-77-75-79—304	$565.00
T-21	Stu Ingraham	73-75-74-73—295	$2,538.46	T-59	Doug Campbell	78-71-75-75—299	$699.00	T-90	Robert Singletary	75-75-75-79—304	$565.00
T-21	Rick Meskell	74-76-71-74—295	$2,538.46	T-59	Woody Fitzhugh	74-75-76-74—299	$699.00	T-94	Bob Ackerman	74-70-81-80—305	$565.00
T-21	Chris Mitchell	70-74-72-79—295	$2,538.46	T-59	Gary Hardin	69-80-73-77—299	$699.00	T-94	Chris Dachisen	76-70-79-80—305	$565.00
T-21	Lonnie Nielsen	73-76-69-77—295	$2,538.46	T-59	Jon Hoecker	73-77-73-76—299	$699.00	T-94	Arne Dokka	71-76-78-80—305	$565.00
T-21	Ed Terasa	74-72-77-72—295	$2,538.47	T-59	Mike Lawrence	73-72-79-75—299	$699.00	T-94	Billy Ziobro	73-76-72-84—305	$565.00
T-21	John Traub	74-73-75-73—295	$2,538.46	T-59	Bob Makoski	74-76-74-75—299	$699.00	98	Scott Bess	74-74-77-83—308	$565.00
T-21	Ron Vlosich	78-72-69-76—295	$2,538.46	T-59	Peter Oosterhuis	75-73-77-74—299	$699.00				

1987

With a final round of 3-under-par 69 to break his streak of three straight 70s, Jay Lumpkin, a 30-year-old teaching assistant at the Long Cove Club at Amelia Island Plantation in Northeast Florida, finished three strokes ahead of Jeffrey Roth of Birmingham, Mich., Bob Menne of Concord, Mass., and Gibby Gilbert of Chattanooga, Tenn., to take the $30,000 first place check. Roth's final round 7-under-par 65 was one of the best ever recorded on the much-publicized PGA West Stadium course.

Champion:	Jay Lumpkin, Amelia Island, Fla.	
Site:	PGA West, La Quinta Hotel & Resort,	
	Mission Hills Country Club, La Quinta, Calif.	
Date:	Oct. 15-18	
Course:	PGA West	Par: 72 - 6,800 yards
	(used for one round and on final day)	
Course:	La Quinta Mountain	Par: 72 - 6,834 yards
Course:	Mission Hills (Old)	Par: 72 - 6,899 yards
Purse:	$325,000	Field: 358
	Cut at 221	95 players advanced

	Avg. of Courses	Rounds of 70 & Under		Round Leader		Jay Lumpkin	
Round 1:	75.4	26		64-	Gibby Gilbert	70 -	Tied 16th
Round 2:	75.8	18		138-	Lonnie Nielsen	140	(70) - Tied 3rd
Round 3:	75.6	30		208-	Gibby Gilbert	210	(70) - 2nd
Round 4:	73.8	18		279-	Jay Lumpkin	279	(69) - 1st
Totals:	75.45	92					

TOURNAMENT SUMMARY

Place	Name	Score	Winnings
1	Jay Lumpkin	70-70-70-69—279	$30,000.00
T-2	Gibby Gilbert	64-75-69-74—282	$15,833.00
T-2	Bob Menne	72-71-69-70—282	$15,833.00
T-2	Jeffrey Roth	71-73-73-65—282	$15,833.00
T-5	Scott Bess	73-72-67-71—283	$9,100.00
T-5	David Glenz	67-74-71-71—283	$9,100.00
T-5	Lonnie Nielsen	67-71-75-70—283	$9,100.00
T-5	David Thore	73-70-70-70—283	$9,100.00
T-5	Tom Wargo	71-70-72-70—283	$9,100.00
10	Mark Gurnow	72-72-70-70—284	$7,000.00
T-11	Jim Albus	71-71-70-73—285	$6,000.00
T-11	Ralph Landrum	71-73-69-72—285	$6,000.00
T-11	Bob Mann	71-74-68-72—285	$6,000.00
T-14	Woody Fitzhugh	71-70-70-75—286	$4,300.00
T-14	Darrell Kestner	71-70-71-74—286	$4,300.00
T-14	Dwight Nevil	76-70-66-74—286	$4,300.00
T-14	John Paesani	72-77-68-69—286	$4,300.00
T-14	Carl Poche	71-76-71-68—286	$4,300.00
T-19	Don Brigham	72-73-70-72—287	$3,138.00
T-19	Michael Burke Jr.	71-74-71-71—287	$3,138.00
T-19	Lynn Janson	72-74-71-70—287	$3,138.00
T-19	Dana Quigley	69-72-74-72—287	$3,138.00
T-23	Tommy Brannen	66-78-73-71—288	$1,967.00
T-23	Bill Brodell	69-74-70-75—288	$1,967.00
T-23	Jim Dickson	73-76-69-70—288	$1,967.00
T-23	Ray Freeman	73-71-74-70—288	$1,967.00
T-23	Gregg Jones	70-76-71-71—288	$1,967.00
T-23	Bob Lendzion	68-72-72-76—288	$1,967.00
T-23	Bob Makoski	71-69-77-71—288	$1,967.00
T-23	Jay Overton	72-75-72-69—288	$1,967.00
T-23	Rick Vershure	73-72-71-72—288	$1,967.00
T-32	Bob Groff	75-72-74-68—289	$1,207.00
T-32	Bob Klein Jr.	76-72-72-69—289	$1,207.00
T-32	Mike Lawrence	74-71-70-74—289	$1,207.00
T-32	Benny Passons	72-71-73-73—289	$1,207.00
T-32	Mike San Filippo	72-70-73-74—289	$1,207.00
T-32	Jim Sobb	69-74-70-76—289	$1,207.00
T-32	Gene Fieger	72-75-71-71—289	$1,207.00
T-39	Bob Ford	70-70-72-78—290	$950.00
T-39	Mike Malaska	76-76-68-70—290	$950.00
T-39	Bill Schumaker	71-72-75-72—290	$950.00
T-39	Jack Seltzer	72-73-74-71—290	$950.00
T-39	James Weeden	70-77-73-70—290	$950.00
T-44	Bob Borowicz	71-74-73-73—291	$788.00
T-44	Bob Boyd	71-74-75-71—291	$788.00
T-44	Bill Brask	68-76-75-72—291	$788.00
T-44	Terry Florence	69-71-73-78—291	$788.00
T-44	Keith Lyford	75-73-68-75—291	$788.00
T-44	Michael Moyers	72-74-68-77—291	$788.00
T-44	Scott Watkins	73-75-72-71—291	$788.00
T-44	Gregg Wolff	74-72-75-70—291	$788.00
T-52	Cary Hungate	73-73-73-73—292	$688.00
T-52	Pete Oakley	74-72-72-74—292	$688.00
T-52	Gary Robison	71-79-68-74—292	$688.00
T-52	Bill Tindall	73-77-71-71—292	$688.00
T-56	Peter Busch	69-76-73-75—293	$650.00
T-56	Kevin Cashman	70-71-78-74—293	$650.00
T-56	Tom Clary	75-70-75-73—293	$650.00
T-56	Robbie Gilmore Jr.	71-73-77-72—293	$650.00
T-56	Robert Hoyt	81-69-68-75—293	$650.00
T-56	Bob Leaver	70-74-72-77—293	$650.00
T-56	Chris Mitchell	73-72-71-77—293	$650.00
T-56	George Shortridge	69-71-73-80—293	$650.00
T-56	Wheeler Stewart	76-72-70-75—293	$650.00
T-56	Steve Veriato	73-73-70-77—293	$650.00
T-56	Ed Whitman	72-75-74-72—293	$650.00
T-67	Terry Carlson	74-75-72-73—294	$610.00
T-67	Larry Gilbert	70-75-72-77—294	$610.00
T-67	Jon Hoecker	76-73-71-74—294	$610.00
T-67	Lindy Miller	74-68-78-74—294	$610.00
T-67	John Traub	75-73-73-73—294	$610.00
T-72	Doug Campbell	73-73-73-76—295	$575.00
T-72	Greg Cerulli	70-73-75-77—295	$575.00
T-72	Scott Chaffin	74-72-74-75—295	$575.00
T-72	Larry Every	76-73-70-76—295	$575.00
T-72	Fred Gibson	75-70-75-75—295	$575.00
T-72	Stu Ingraham	75-75-71-74—295	$575.00
T-72	Dick Murphy	71-74-74-76—295	$575.00
T-72	David Nevatt	71-77-72-75—295	$575.00
T-72	Skip Tredway	76-73-71-75—295	$575.00
T-81	Rick Acton	72-76-71-77—296	$540.00
T-81	Tommy Aycock	72-72-76-76—296	$540.00
T-81	Mike Kallam	72-73-76-75—296	$540.00
T-81	Richard Martinez	74-77-69-76—296	$540.00
T-81	Ron Vlosich	69-78-74-75—296	$540.00
86	Jeff Bailey	72-71-76-78—297	$525.00
T-87	Dick McClean	66-78-74-80—298	$518.00
T-87	Ross Randall	73-72-76-77—298	$518.00
T-89	Fred Collins	76-73-71-79—299	$508.00
T-89	Doug Higgins	72-71-78-78—299	$508.00
T-91	Bill Mattingly III	77-75-68-80—300	$505.00
T-91	Bob Ralston	75-70-73-82—300	$505.00
93	Steve Bowen	72-72-77-80—301	$505.00
94	Mike Labauve	71-76-74-81—302	$505.00
95	Mark Hill	75-75-71-86—307	$505.00

PGA CLUB PROFESSIONAL CHAMPIONSHIP

1986

With a birdie-par finish, 36-year-old Bob Lendzion shot four successive 1-under-par 71s to win the 19th renewal of the PGA Club Professional Championship. Lendzion, head professional at The Quechee Club in Quechee, Vt., finished one shot ahead of Bob Betley, from Ogden, Utah. Former Tour player Dana Quigley of Barrington, R.I., was the third-round leader and gambled at No. 18 for what he thought would be a lead-tying birdie. He suffered a costly double-bogey instead. Quigley tied for third, two strokes back.

Champion:	Bob Lendzion , Quechee, Vt.
Site:	PGA West, La Quinta Hotel & Resort,
	Mission Hills Country Club, La Quinta, Calif.
Date:	Oct. 2-5
Course: PGA West	**Par:** 72 - 6,800 yards
(used for one round and on final day)	
Course: La Quinta Mountain	**Par:** 72 - 6,834 yards
Course: Mission Hills (Old)	**Par:** 72 - 6,899 yards
Purse: $325,000	**Field:** 352
Cut at 224	99 players advanced

	Avg. of Courses	Rounds of 70 & Under		Round Leader		Bob Lendzion
Round 1:	76.5	20	67-	James Blair	71 -	Tied 27th
Round 2:	76.0	22	139-	Ray Freeman	142	(71) - Tied 9th
Round 3:	77.2	8	209-	Dana Quigley	213	(71) - Tied 6th
Round 4:	76.0	6	284-	Bob Lendzion	284	(71) - 1st
Totals:	76.50	56				

TOURNAMENT SUMMARY

Place	Name	Score	Winnings	Place	Name	Score	Winnings	Place	Name	Score	Winnings
1	Bob Lendzion	71-71-71-71—284	$30,000.00	T-28	Jack Seltzer	72-73-72-77—294	$1,468.00	T-69	Steve Caulkins	77-74-73-75—299	$597.00
2	Bob Betley	71-71-70-73—285	$20,000.00	T-36	Steve Heckel	74-71-79-71—295	$1,021.00	T-69	Rich Fulkerson	71-73-75-80—299	$597.00
T-3	David Glenz	75-72-68-71—286	$12,833.00	T-36	Tom Joyce	71-71-74-79—295	$1,021.00	T-69	Wally Kuchar	72-75-74-78—299	$597.00
T-3	Dana Quigley	73-70-66-77—286	$12,833.00	T-36	Ralph Landrum	74-66-75-80—295	$1,021.00	T-69	Bob Mann	74-74-74-77—299	$597.00
T-3	Tom Wargo	70-74-73-69—286	$12,833.00	T-36	Tony Milam	75-77-72-71—295	$1,021.00	T-69	Benny Passons	73-68-79-79—299	$597.00
T-6	Ray Freeman	69-70-73-76—288	$9,500.00	T-36	Jim Petralia	71-72-79-73—295	$1,021.00	T-69	Robert Thompson	69-74-74-82—299	$597.00
T-6	Jay Overton	70-70-72-76—288	$9,500.00	T-36	Paul Ryiz	74-70-73-78—295	$1,021.00	T-75	Tim Brauch	73-78-72-77—300	$567.00
T-8	Fred Funk	78-67-70-74—289	$7,500.00	T-36	Mike San Filippo	76-71-74-74—295	$1,021.00	T-75	Pat Delaney	72-76-74-78—300	$567.00
T-8	Lindy Miller	76-71-71-71—289	$7,500.00	T-43	Jim Booros	76-69-74-77—296	$771.00	T-75	Dick Lotz	73-74-72-81—300	$567.00
T-8	Jim Woodward	70-73-73-73—289	$7,500.00	T-43	John Calabria	76-72-71-77—296	$771.00	T-75	Ralph Montoya	73-75-75-77—300	$567.00
11	Tom Tatum	73-71-75-71—290	$6,500.00	T-43	Ed Dougherty	73-74-77-72—296	$771.00	T-75	Harold Perry Jr.	76-75-73-76—300	$567.00
T-12	Lonnie Nielsen	71-69-72-79—291	$5,500.00	T-43	Woody Fitzhugh	74-77-70-75—296	$771.00	T-75	Alex Redmond	72-78-73-77—300	$567.00
T-12	Wheeler Stewart	77-69-72-73—291	$5,500.00	T-43	Jeff Foxx	72-76-73-75—296	$771.00	T-81	Charlie Epps	73-72-77-79—301	$540.00
T-12	Steve Veriato	72-73-75-71—291	$5,500.00	T-43	Fred Gibson	70-77-75-74—296	$771.00	T-81	George Shortridge	76-74-73-78—301	$540.00
T-15	Rick Acton	71-74-72-75—292	$4,000.00	T-43	Laurie Hammer	73-72-73-78—296	$771.00	T-81	Bill Tindall	69-77-75-80—301	$540.00
T-15	J.C. Blair III	67-74-72-79—292	$4,000.00	T-43	Fred Holton Jr.	77-70-74-75—296	$771.00	T-81	Ron Wells	75-77-72-77—301	$540.00
T-15	David Gosiewski	72-70-73-77—292	$4,000.00	T-43	Craig Stephens	73-74-74-75—296	$771.00	T-81	Larry Wheeler	73-75-74-79—301	$540.00
T-15	Jack Kiefer	78-71-75-68—292	$4,000.00	T-43	Tommy Thomas	75-71-74-76—296	$771.00	T-86	Jim Albus	75-75-72-80—302	$515.00
T-15	Pete Oakley	73-73-76-70—292	$4,000.00	T-43	Ed Whitman	70-79-75-72—296	$771.00	T-86	Terry Florence	72-72-73-85—302	$515.00
T-20	Larry Gilbert	73-73-71-76—293	$2,518.00	T-43	Buddy Whitten	74-76-73-73—296	$771.00	T-86	Cary Hungate	75-75-73-79—302	$515.00
T-20	Ted Goin	74-69-76-74—293	$2,518.00	T-55	Bill Murchison	80-69-73-75—297	$672.00	T-86	Kevin Morris	75-73-73-81—302	$515.00
T-20	Bob Groff	69-72-75-77—293	$2,518.00	T-55	Bill Schumaker	72-72-78-75—297	$672.00	T-86	Dan Murphy	75-72-77-78—302	$515.00
T-20	Mike Kallam	71-73-77-72—293	$2,518.00	T-55	Bruce Summerhays	74-72-78-73—297	$672.00	T-91	Gary Groh	74-73-76-80—303	$505.00
T-20	Bruce Lehnhard	72-78-74-69—293	$2,518.00	T-55	Vic Tortorici	73-77-73-74—297	$672.00	T-91	Lynn Janson	69-74-77-83—303	$505.00
T-20	Jack McKelvey	74-76-73-70—293	$2,518.00	T-59	Bill Brask	75-75-73-75—298	$637.00	T-91	Gregg Jones	76-68-78-81—303	$505.00
T-20	Dwight Nevil	77-71-76-69—293	$2,518.00	T-59	John Gentile	75-73-75-75—298	$637.00	T-91	Tony Kaloustian	77-73-74-79—303	$505.00
T-20	Scott Oulds	70-73-77-73—293	$2,518.00	T-59	Bob Hauer	74-75-74-75—298	$637.00	T-91	Bob Leaver	75-76-72-80—303	$505.00
T-28	Jeff Bailey	73-73-73-75—294	$1,468.00	T-59	Jay Lumpkin	74-75-75-74—298	$637.00	T-91	Scott Walter	74-71-79-79—303	$505.00
T-28	Tommy Brannen	76-70-71-77—294	$1,468.00	T-59	Rives McBee	72-77-71-78—298	$637.00	97	Kim Thompson	72-76-75-81—304	$505.00
T-28	Gibby Gilbert	77-70-74-73—294	$1,468.00	T-59	Dick McClean	72-82-70-74—298	$637.00	98	John Godwin	77-77-70-81—305	$505.00
T-28	Dick Goetz	70-74-72-78—294	$1,468.00	T-59	Chris Mitchell	74-74-73-77—298	$637.00	99	John Graham	76-72-76-83—307	$505.00
T-28	John Jackson Jr.	70-70-78-76—294	$1,468.00	T-59	Jerry Tucker	73-76-75-74—298	$637.00	100	Terry Carlson	72-78-74-89—313	$505.00
T-28	Don Padgett II	79-69-74-72—294	$1,468.00	T-59	Tony Valentine	72-75-73-78—298	$637.00				
T-28	Mike Schlueter	75-72-74-73—294	$1,468.00	T-59	Roy Vucinich	72-73-75-78—298	$637.00				

1985

With a par on the last green for a final round 1-under-par 71, 38-year-old Ed Dougherty from Linwood, Pa., became the only player to shoot four sub-par rounds and won the Championship by two strokes over Jim White of Lincoln, Neb. Dougherty also earned PGA Club Professional Player of the Year honors following his victory.

Champion:	Ed Dougherty, Linwood, Pa.
Site:	La Quinta Hotel Golf Club, Mission Hills Country Club, La Quinta, Calif.
Date:	Oct. 10-13
Course: Dunes	**Par:** 72 - 6,874 yards
(used for one round and on final day)	
Course: Mission Hills (New)	**Par:** 72 - 7,246 yards
Course: Mission Hills (Old)	**Par:** 72 - 6,899 yards
Purse: $235,000	**Field:** 358
Cut at 220	92 players advanced

	Avg. of Courses	Rounds of 70 & Under		Round Leader		Ed Dougherty
Round 1:	75.5	27	66-	Lonnie Neilsen	69 -	Tied 5th
Round 2:	75.3	25	137-	Kevin Morris	138	(69) - Tied 2nd
Round 3:	74.9	36	205-	Charlie Epps	206	(68) - 2nd
Round 4:	75.3	4	277-	Ed Dougherty	277	(71) - 1st
Totals:	75.25	92				

TOURNAMENT SUMMARY

Place	Name	Score	Winnings	Place	Name	Score	Winnings	Place	Name	Score	Winnings
1	Ed Dougherty	69-69-68-71—277	$27,500.00	T-28	Lynn Janson	69-71-76-73—289	$1,421.00	T-60	Randy Jensen	74-75-69-76—294	$577.00
2	Jim White	74-67-67-71—279	$17,500.00	T-28	Mike San Filippo	71-73-72-73—289	$1,421.00	T-60	Dan Murphy	75-75-70-74—294	$577.00
3	Rick Acton	72-70-67-71—280	$13,500.00	T-28	Roy Vucinich	70-72-73-74—289	$1,421.00	T-60	Jack Sommers	71-71-72-80—294	$577.00
4	Kevin Morris	69-68-73-71—281	$11,500.00	T-35	Gary Hardin	75-71-70-74—290	$1,037.00	T-66	Michael Burke Jr.	73-72-74-76—295	$577.00
5	Jim Albus	74-68-71-69—282	$10,000.00	T-35	Gregg Jones	70-73-73-74—290	$1,037.00	T-66	Clyde Collins Jr.	74-75-71-75—295	$577.00
T-6	Scott Bess	69-71-69-74—283	$8,500.00	T-35	Gary Ostrega	72-71-72-75—290	$1,037.00	T-66	John Godwin	70-73-75-77—295	$577.00
T-6	Charlie Epps	70-68-67-78—283	$8,500.00	T-35	Jay Overton	67-72-71-80—290	$1,037.00	T-66	Steve Jensen	71-73-76-75—295	$577.00
T-8	Wheeler Stewart	71-72-69-72—284	$7,250.00	T-35	Steve Veriato	73-73-71-73—290	$1,037.00	T-66	Bill Kennedy	69-74-76-76—295	$577.00
T-8	Larry Webb	69-70-73-72—284	$7,250.00	T-35	Paul Wise	73-74-69-74—290	$1,037.00	T-66	John Lindert	69-74-75-77—295	$577.00
T-10	Ken Allard	76-68-68-73—285	$5,750.00	T-41	Doug Bauman	74-73-73-71—291	$837.00	T-66	Rocky Nelson	72-71-77-75—295	$577.00
T-10	Jeff Foxx	70-69-68-78—285	$5,750.00	T-41	Roger Ginsberg	74-73-69-75—291	$837.00	T-66	Don Padgett II	71-76-70-78—295	$577.00
T-10	Ray Freeman	70-72-75-68—285	$5,750.00	T-41	David Glenz	75-71-72-73—291	$837.00	T-66	Benny Passons	72-76-71-76—295	$577.00
T-10	Bill Schumaker	73-70-70-72—285	$5,750.00	T-41	Roger Kennedy	70-74-73-74—291	$837.00	T-75	Gene Aube	73-74-72-77—296	$577.00
T-14	Dick Lotz	71-68-76-71—286	$4,375.00	T-41	Gary Robison	73-71-72-75—291	$837.00	T-75	Stan Ball	72-73-75-76—296	$577.00
T-14	Dwight Nevil	70-70-75-71—286	$4,375.00	T-41	Bill Tindall	76-73-71-71—291	$837.00	T-75	Ross Randall	74-74-70-78—296	$577.00
T-16	Larry Babica	72-75-68-72—287	$3,750.00	T-41	Buddy Whitten	69-72-75-75—291	$837.00	T-78	Tim Brauch	71-74-72-80—297	$577.00
T-16	Bob Leaver	67-76-72-72—287	$3,750.00	T-41	Terry Wilcox	72-73-68-78—291	$837.00	T-78	Jim Gerring	72-77-71-77—297	$577.00
T-16	Pete Oakley	74-73-71-69—287	$3,750.00	T-49	Vince Bizik	72-73-74-73—292	$622.00	T-78	Bill Harris	75-74-69-79—297	$577.00
T-19	James Blair	72-74-72-70—288	$2,438.00	T-49	Gene Borek	72-70-73-77—292	$622.00	T-78	Joe Huber	72-77-71-77—297	$577.00
T-19	David Duschane	68-75-72-73—288	$2,438.00	T-49	Tom Dawson	72-75-73-72—292	$622.00	T-78	Al Murdock	75-72-71-79—297	$577.00
T-19	Rives McBee	69-72-75-72—288	$2,438.00	T-49	Bob Mann	70-70-72-80—292	$622.00	T-78	Ed Selser	71-73-73-80—297	$577.00
T-19	Bob Menne	71-73-71-73—288	$2,438.00	T-49	Chris Mitchell	74-71-70-77—292	$622.00	T-84	Jeff Bailey	73-70-75-80—298	$577.00
T-19	Lonnie Nielsen	66-75-74-73—288	$2,438.00	T-49	Tom Wargo	73-69-72-78—292	$622.00	T-84	Larry Emery	73-72-73-80—298	$577.00
T-19	Gary Robinson	69-73-70-76—288	$2,438.00	T-55	Steve Ball	73-70-74-76—293	$577.00	T-84	John Phillips	75-75-67-81—298	$577.00
T-19	Mike Schlueter	73-73-65-77—288	$2,438.00	T-55	Bob Lendzion	74-72-72-75—293	$577.00	T-84	Mike Zaremba	72-73-70-83—298	$577.00
T-19	Rick Vershure	73-69-68-78—288	$2,438.00	T-55	Rick Smith	72-76-70-75—293	$577.00	T-88	Laurie Hammer	71-78-71-80—300	$577.00
T-19	Ron Wells	73-68-71-76—288	$2,438.00	T-55	Lew Smither III	73-74-69-77—293	$577.00	T-88	Dick McClean	74-70-74-82—300	$577.00
T-28	Bob Ackerman	73-71-71-74—289	$1,421.00	T-55	Jim Woodward	72-75-73-73—293	$577.00	T-88	Jeff Steinberg	74-70-76-80—300	$577.00
T-28	Patrick Fitzsimmons	71-71-75-72—289	$1,421.00	T-60	Gene Boni	73-75-71-75—294	$577.00	91	Larry Wheeler	73-72-72-84—301	$577.00
T-28	Larry Gilbert	73-72-71-73—289	$1,421.00	T-60	Warren Chancellor	72-71-75-76—294	$577.00	92	Mark Gurnow	72-71-77-82—302	$577.00
T-28	Robert Hoyt	71-71-70-77—289	$1,421.00	T-60	Brien Charter	73-73-73-75—294	$577.00				

1984

For the sixth time, the PGA Club Professional Championship was decided in a sudden-death playoff, as 34-year-old Bill Schumaker, a golf club owner from Columbia City, Ind., birdied the first playoff hole to defeat Gary Ostrega of Colonia (N.J.) Country Club. Later, Schumaker was named PGA Club Professional Player of the Year.

Champion:	Bill Schumaker, Columbia City, Ind.
Site:	PGA National, Palm Beach Gardens, Fla.
Date:	Oct. 11-14
Course: Champion	**Par:** 72 - 7,002 yards
(used for one round and on final day)	
Course: Haig	**Par:** 72 - 6,806 yards
Course: General	**Par:** 72 - 6,768 yards
Purse: $200,000	**Field:** 355
Cut at 222	92 players advanced

	Avg. of Courses	Rounds of 70 & Under		Round Leader		Bill Schumaker
Round 1:	76.7	13	67-	Tom Aycock	73 -	Tied 43rd
Round 2:	75.7	15	140-	Mike Ballo	142	(69) - Tied 5th
Round 3:	75.5	24	212-	Jim White	214	(72) - Tied 4th
Round 4:	74.3	9	284-	Bill Schumaker	284	(70) - 1st
Totals:	75.83	58				

TOURNAMENT SUMMARY

Place	Name	Score	Winnings	Place	Name	Score	Winnings	Place	Name	Score	Winnings
1	Bill Schumaker	73-69-72-70—284	$25,000.00	T-28	Mike Harrigan	76-72-74-70—292	$1,195.00	T-63	Mike Franko	73-72-73-77—295	$425.00
2	Gary Ostrega	72-75-66-71—284	$15,000.00	T-28	Bob Leaver	73-73-71-75—292	$1,195.00	T-63	Rives McBee	75-75-72-73—295	$425.00
T-3	Larry Gilbert	69-73-73-71—286	$11,000.00	T-28	Jack Lewis	78-71-71-72—292	$1,195.00	T-63	Stacy Russell	72-72-74-77—295	$425.00
T-3	Rick Osberg	71-74-73-68—286	$11,000.00	T-28	Benny Passons	76-71-72-73—292	$1,195.00	T-63	Mike Schlueter	76-72-71-76—295	$425.00
5	David Glenz	74-74-68-71—287	$9,000.00	T-28	Jack Seltzer	73-73-72-74—292	$1,195.00	T-63	Paul Wise	78-73-71-73—295	$425.00
T-6	Steve Veriato	75-71-72-70—288	$7,750.00	T-28	Bob Smith	73-75-73-71—292	$1,195.00	T-68	Larry Babica	73-74-71-78—296	$425.00
T-6	Jim White	69-73-70-76—288	$7,750.00	T-28	Craig Watson	74-70-75-73—292	$1,195.00	T-68	Jerry Coats	74-71-74-77—296	$425.00
T-8	Scott Bess	74-69-75-71—289	$5,750.00	T-39	Mike Ballo	71-69-77-76—293	$675.00	T-68	Arne Dokka	74-76-72-74—296	$425.00
T-8	Ed Dougherty	75-71-73-70—289	$5,750.00	T-39	Craig Clemons	74-75-68-76—293	$675.00	T-68	Howell Fraser	74-75-73-74—296	$425.00
T-8	Bobby Heins	70-72-73-74—289	$5,750.00	T-39	Steve Coulkins	77-72-71-73—293	$675.00	T-68	Roger Kennedy	73-70-77-76—296	$425.00
T-8	John Jackson Jr.	72-73-70-74—289	$5,750.00	T-39	John Elliott Jr.	75-75-70-73—293	$675.00	T-68	Jay Overton	71-79-70-76—296	$425.00
T-8	Jim O'Hern	74-72-70-73—289	$5,750.00	T-39	Bill Garrett	72-74-69-78—293	$675.00	T-68	Don Padgett II	68-78-72-78—296	$425.00
T-8	Rick Werner	73-70-72-74—289	$5,750.00	T-39	Roger Ginsberg	74-71-73-75—293	$675.00	T-68	Billy Peterson	71-72-75-78—296	$425.00
T-14	Jim Albus	72-74-70-74—290	$3,875.00	T-39	John Godwin	74-73-75-71—293	$675.00	T-68	Ed Sabo	77-70-75-74—296	$425.00
T-14	Mark Gurnow	72-76-71-71—290	$3,875.00	T-39	Geoff Hensley	73-76-73-71—293	$675.00	T-68	Larry Wheeler	73-72-77-74—296	$425.00
T-14	Robert Hoyt	76-72-72-70—290	$3,875.00	T-39	John Joseph	73-74-73-73—293	$675.00	T-68	Bob Wynn	72-71-75-78—296	$425.00
T-14	Kevin Morris	72-76-72-70—290	$3,875.00	T-39	Steven King	73-74-73-73—293	$675.00	T-79	Bill Hamilton	77-73-71-76—297	$425.00
T-18	Bob Ackerman	75-72-71-73—291	$2,385.00	T-39	Jim Logue	72-74-73-74—293	$675.00	T-79	Kelley Moser	74-71-75-77—297	$425.00
T-18	Steve Benson	69-74-71-77—291	$2,385.00	T-39	Bob Makoski	72-69-76-76—293	$675.00	T-79	Rick Terrell	76-71-75-75—297	$425.00
T-18	Laurie Hammer	70-71-74-76—291	$2,385.00	T-39	Patrick O'Brien	74-76-70-73—293	$675.00	T-79	Jerry Tucker	77-75-70-75—297	$425.00
T-18	Gary Head	73-72-74-72—291	$2,385.00	T-39	Pete Oakley	72-75-73-73—293	$675.00	T-79	Terry Wilcox	73-75-72-77—297	$425.00
T-18	Lynn Janson	74-71-73-73—291	$2,385.00	T-39	Paul Ryiz	75-75-69-74—293	$675.00	T-84	Jack Barger	78-75-68-77—298	$425.00
T-18	Drue Johnson	77-71-74-69—291	$2,385.00	T-54	Bruce Ashworth	72-72-77-73—294	$425.00	T-84	Richard Gilstad	75-71-74-78—298	$425.00
T-18	Gregg Jones	76-73-69-73—291	$2,385.00	T-54	Jeff Bailey	76-71-72-75—294	$425.00	T-84	Kyle Howard	71-76-75-76—298	$425.00
T-18	Bob Lendzion	71-75-71-74—291	$2,385.00	T-54	Al Chandler	71-72-75-76—294	$425.00	87	Larry King	77-71-74-77—299	$425.00
T-18	Ross Randall	73-73-73-72—291	$2,385.00	T-54	Fred Gibson	76-70-71-77—294	$425.00	T-88	Ron Baker	79-71-67-83—300	$425.00
T-18	Ron Wells	72-72-69-78—291	$2,385.00	T-54	Mike Malaska	74-75-72-73—294	$425.00	T-88	Rodney Loesch	77-74-70-79—300	$425.00
T-28	Ken Allard	68-73-76-75—292	$1,195.00	T-54	Bob Menne	74-73-74-73—294	$425.00	T-90	Bill Galloway	77-73-72-79—301	$425.00
T-28	Tommy Aycock	67-76-75-74—292	$1,195.00	T-54	Wes Smith	78-72-71-73—294	$425.00	T-90	Terry Houser	77-70-73-81—301	$425.00
T-28	Brien Charter	73-74-71-74—292	$1,195.00	T-54	Stuart Taylor	71-75-75-73—294	$425.00	T-90	Chris Mitchell	73-77-72-79—301	$425.00
T-28	Tim Collins	75-74-73-70—292	$1,195.00	T-54	Rick Whitfield	71-73-75-75—294	$425.00				

1983

In a study of short game artistry, 34-year-old Larry Webb won the 17th renewal of the Club Professional Championship by four strokes over runner-up Bob Ford, head professional at Oakmont (Pa.) Country Club. Webb, head professional at Ho Ho Kam CC in Coolidge, Ariz., almost didn't play. He qualified as an alternate, but when a friend decided not to play, it opened a spot for Webb. He also had a scare a couple of nights before the start of the Championship when an intruder sneaked into his hotel room and made off with $300. Six days after the robbery, Webb forgot about the $300, as he won the $20,000 first prize.

Champion:	Larry Webb, Coolidge, Ariz.
Site:	La Quinta Hotel Golf Club, Mission Hills Country Club, La Quinta, Calif.
Date:	Sept. 29 - Oct. 2
Course: Mountain	**Par:** 72 - 6,834 yards
(used for one round and on final day)	
Course: Dunes	**Par:** 72 - 6,874 yards
Course: Mission Hills	**Par:** 72 - 6,899 yards
Purse: $150,000	**Field:** 355
Cut at 227	97 players advanced

	Avg. of Courses	Rounds of 70 & Under		Round Leader		Larry Webb
Round 1:	77.7	8	68-	Bob Wynn	70 -	Tied 4th
Round 2:	77.8	5	138-	Larry Webb	138	(68) - 1st
Round 3:	77.7	9	212-	Larry Webb	212	(74) - 1st
Round 4:	76.9	3	283-	Larry Webb	283	(71) - 1st
Totals:	77.65	25				

TOURNAMENT SUMMARY

Place	Name	Score	Winnings	Place	Name	Score	Winnings	Place	Name	Score	Winnings
1	Larry Webb	70-68-74-71—283	$20,000.00	T-29	Jack Seltzer	74-75-77-72—298	$971.43	T-63	Larry King	78-73-75-77—303	$277.72
2	Bob Ford	71-71-73-72—287	$12,000.00	T-29	Wheeler Stewart	73-75-71-79—298	$971.43	T-63	Mark Scallen	74-78-73-78—303	$277.72
3	Bob Wynn	68-74-75-72—289	$10,000.00	T-29	Gary Wilkins	74-74-75-75—298	$971.43	T-63	Harry Turner	78-73-74-78—303	$277.72
T-4	Tim Collins	76-73-73-69—291	$7,500.00	T-36	John Dahl	72-73-78-76—299	$812.50	T-63	Jim White	75-83-69-76—303	$277.72
T-4	John Elliott Jr.	71-73-70-77—291	$7,500.00	T-36	Rick Karbowski	81-74-70-74—299	$812.50	T-69	Lee Harper	77-76-73-78—304	$277.72
T-4	Dan Murphy	71-74-74-72—291	$7,500.00	T-36	Mike San Filippo	74-80-70-75—299	$812.50	T-69	Richard Martinez	75-79-73-77—304	$277.72
T-4	Don Padgett II	71-78-68-74—291	$7,500.00	T-36	Doug Steffen	73-77-75-74—299	$812.50	T-71	Craig Clemons	76-75-76-78—305	$277.72
T-8	Terry Florence	71-76-72-73—292	$4,500.00	T-40	Arne Dokka	76-74-74-76—300	$650.00	T-71	Ken Ellsworth	75-74-77-79—305	$277.72
T-8	David Glenz	70-75-74-73—292	$4,500.00	T-40	Steve Forrest	74-75-74-77—300	$650.00	T-71	Woody Fitzhugh	74-76-75-80—305	$277.72
T-8	Rick Osberg	77-70-72-73—292	$4,500.00	T-40	Gary Gant	72-72-82-74—300	$650.00	T-71	Bill Galloway	78-74-75-78—305	$277.72
T-11	Gary Balliet	75-70-74-74—293	$3,250.00	T-40	Kyle Howard	76-79-69-76—300	$650.00	T-71	John Godwin	75-74-77-79—305	$277.72
T-11	Barry Holt	71-78-75-69—293	$3,250.00	T-40	Craig Immel	73-74-77-76—300	$650.00	T-71	Dick Murphy	77-81-69-78—305	$277.72
T-13	Joseph Carr	76-71-76-71—294	$2,450.00	T-40	Al Kelley Jr.	74-75-73-78—300	$650.00	T-71	Steve Prugh	76-71-72-86—305	$277.72
T-13	Charlie Epps	73-76-73-72—294	$2,450.00	T-40	Bob Mann	71-74-77-78—300	$650.00	T-78	Mike Matheny	75-76-71-84—306	$277.72
T-15	Scott Bess	69-74-73-79—295	$2,150.00	T-40	Jay Overton	75-74-73-78—300	$650.00	T-78	Jerry Tucker	75-74-77-80—306	$277.72
T-15	Jim King	76-78-72-69—295	$2,150.00	T-40	Jim Urban	74-76-75-75—300	$650.00	T-78	Jeff Whitfield	74-75-77-80—306	$277.72
T-15	Jack Slocum	72-72-75-76—295	$2,150.00	T-49	Ras Allen	75-74-73-79—301	$355.98	T-81	Roy Abrameit	72-76-74-85—307	$277.72
T-15	Bruce Summerhays	75-72-74-74—295	$2,150.00	T-49	Don Brigham	75-74-74-78—301	$355.98	T-81	Stacy Russell	74-73-78-82—307	$277.72
T-19	John Calabria	69-78-71-78—296	$1,750.00	T-49	Mike Harrigan	74-77-75-75—301	$355.98	T-81	James St. Germain	74-77-74-82—307	$277.72
T-19	Laurie Hammer	76-73-71-76—296	$1,750.00	T-49	Mike Malaska	72-77-72-80—301	$355.98	T-81	Roland Stafford	74-75-74-84—307	$277.72
T-19	Paul Wise	75-77-72-72—296	$1,750.00	T-49	Ed Oldfield	75-74-76-76—301	$355.98	T-85	Dennis Bradley	70-78-79-81—308	$277.71
T-19	Jimmy Wright	73-71-79-73—296	$1,750.00	T-49	Tommy Thomas	72-74-81-74—301	$355.98	T-85	John Jackson Jr.	78-73-76-81—308	$277.71
T-23	Jim Albus	76-72-77-72—297	$1,300.00	T-55	Jerry Breaux	76-72-75-79—302	$277.72	T-85	Kurt Kretchman	72-81-74-81—308	$277.71
T-23	Frank Beard	79-73-70-75—297	$1,300.00	T-55	Steve Coulkins	75-80-72-75—302	$277.72	T-85	Richard Lee	79-78-70-81—308	$277.71
T-23	Martin Bohen	74-73-74-76—297	$1,300.00	T-55	John Gentile	75-74-76-77—302	$277.72	T-85	Ed Whitman	72-76-76-84—308	$277.71
T-23	Roger Ginsberg	73-70-77-77—297	$1,300.00	T-55	Paul Gooden	78-71-77-76—302	$277.72	T-85	Ken Still	75-76-76-82—309	$277.71
T-23	Robert Hoyt	76-74-76-71—297	$1,300.00	T-55	Roger Kennedy	76-73-76-77—302	$277.72	91	Mike Muranyi	78-78-71-82—309	$277.71
T-23	Lynn Janson	73-73-78-73—297	$1,300.00	T-55	Baker Maddera	78-71-78-75—302	$277.72	T-92	Mark Gurnow	77-73-77-83—310	$277.71
T-29	Brien Charter	70-77-77-74—298	$971.43	T-55	Jeffrey Roth	74-74-76-78—302	$277.72	T-92	Paul Parajeckas	75-75-71-89—310	$277.71
T-29	Randy Erskine	75-76-72-75—298	$971.43	T-55	Mark Wolfia	71-78-74-79—302	$277.72	T-92	Ron Wells	73-74-79-84—310	$277.71
T-29	Bobby Mitchell	73-73-77-75—298	$971.43	T-63	Tommy Aycock	72-76-79-76—303	$277.72	95	Don Maddox	75-73-79-84—311	$277.71
T-29	Gary Robinson	72-75-78-73—298	$971.43	T-63	Mike Felker	73-77-77-76—303	$277.72				

1982

Larry Gilbert of Lexington, Ky., parlayed a putting lesson from his wife, Brenda, into a record third-round 7-under-par 65 to win his second straight PGA Club Professional Championship. Despite a final-round 74, which tied a record for high final round of a winner, Gilbert finished one shot in front of Steve Benson of Long Grove, Ill., who finished runner-up for the second time.

Champion:	Larry Gilbert, Lexington, Ky.	
Site:	PGA National, Palm Beach Gardens, Fla.	
Date:	Oct. 21-24	
Course:	Champion	Par: 72 - 7,002 yards
(used for one round and on final day)		
Course:	Haig	Par: 72 - 6,806 yards
Course:	Squire	Par: 72 - 6,612 yards
Purse:	$150,000	Field: 348
Cut at 225	100 players advanced	

	Avg. of Courses	Rounds of 70 & Under		Round Leader		Larry Gilbert	
Round 1:	77.0	13	67-	Gene Borek	73 -	Tied 43rd	
Round 2:	76.8	14	135-	Steve Benson	145	(72) - Tied 21st	
Round 3:	75.8	17	210-	Larry Gilbert, Gene Borek	210	(65) - Tied 1st	
Round 4:	77.4	1	284-	Larry Gilbert	284	(74) - 1st	
Totals:	76.67	45					

TOURNAMENT SUMMARY

Place	Name	Score	Winnings
1	Larry Gilbert	73-72-65-74—284	$20,000.00
2	Steve Benson	68-67-78-72—285	$12,000.00
3	Jack Seltzer	72-70-72-72—286	$10,000.00
T-4	Bob Lendzion	71-77-68-72—288	$8,500.00
T-4	Jim Logue	70-71-74-73—288	$8,500.00
T-6	Denis Husse	74-69-70-76—289	$6,500.00
T-6	Jim King	70-71-74-74—289	$6,500.00
T-8	Gene Borek	67-69-74-80—290	$4,500.00
T-8	Kevin Morris	73-71-72-74—290	$4,500.00
T-8	Tom Robertson	71-74-70-75—290	$4,500.00
T-11	Tim Collins	72-69-72-78—291	$3,000.00
T-11	George Shortridge	71-72-72-76—291	$3,000.00
T-11	Rick Werner	72-72-72-75—291	$3,000.00
T-14	Jim Albus	71-71-72-78—292	$2,200.00
T-14	David Barber	78-68-73-73—292	$2,200.00
T-14	Robbie Gilmore Jr.	70-76-66-80—292	$2,200.00
T-14	Jim White	72-72-74-74—292	$2,200.00
T-14	Mikel Wynn	71-72-72-77—292	$2,200.00
T-19	Doug Dalziel	71-73-73-76—293	$1,800.00
T-19	John Elliott Jr.	72-76-70-75—293	$1,800.00
T-19	John Jackson Jr.	72-75-72-74—293	$1,800.00
22	Buddy Whitten	74-70-76-74—294	$1,600.00
T-23	Bob Boyd	78-75-72-70—295	$1,216.67
T-23	Robert Elliott	70-76-74-75—295	$1,216.67
T-23	Bobby Heins	74-78-71-72—295	$1,216.67
T-23	Robert Hoyt	73-74-74-74—295	$1,216.67
T-23	Rick Karbowski	74-73-74-74—295	$1,216.67
T-23	Victor Lipscomb	75-73-73-74—295	$1,216.66
T-23	Jim Masserio	73-76-70-76—295	$1,216.66
T-23	Ed Whitman	72-73-75-75—295	$1,216.66
T-23	Paul Wise	72-75-75-73—295	$1,216.67
T-32	Bruce Ashworth	70-75-75-76—296	$850.00
T-32	Jim Ferriell Jr.	75-75-73-73—296	$850.00
T-32	John Gentile	71-71-72-82—296	$850.00
T-32	John Kirchner	70-77-74-75—296	$850.00
T-32	Don Maddox	71-76-71-78—296	$850.00
T-32	Jack McConachie	72-78-72-74—296	$850.00
T-32	Pete Oakley	70-75-75-76—296	$850.00
T-32	Don Padgett II	74-73-72-77—296	$850.00
T-32	Jack Sommers	74-74-73-75—296	$850.00
T-41	Roger Kennedy	77-73-69-78—297	$675.00
T-41	Jay Overton	72-72-73-80—297	$675.00
T-41	Jim Picard	73-72-75-77—297	$675.00
T-41	Art Schilling	73-73-75-76—297	$675.00
T-41	Bill Schumaker	75-73-74-75—297	$675.00
T-46	Tommy Aycock	70-72-76-80—298	$379.71
T-46	Bobby Benson	77-73-69-79—298	$379.71
T-46	Homero Blancas	75-72-74-77—298	$379.71
T-46	Bob Ford	70-77-73-78—298	$379.71
T-46	George Glenn	72-78-75-73—298	$379.72
T-46	Bruce MacDonald	73-74-76-75—298	$379.72
T-46	Art Proctor	72-77-75-74—298	$379.72
T-46	Jack Slocum	77-73-73-75—298	$379.72
T-46	Tony Wallin	74-73-71-80—298	$379.71
T-46	Gary Wintz	73-75-73-77—298	$379.72
T-56	Phil Aldridge	78-72-71-78—299	$209.43
T-56	Dennis Coscina	73-80-71-75—299	$209.43
T-56	Gary Domagalski	74-75-73-77—299	$209.43
T-56	Gene Ferrell	77-76-72-74—299	$209.43
T-56	Bill Garrett	74-80-71-74—299	$209.43
T-56	Fred Harkness	70-73-74-82—299	$209.43
T-56	Tom Joyce	74-74-74-77—299	$209.43
T-56	Dennis Tiziani	73-74-73-79—299	$209.43
T-64	Rick Acton	73-77-75-75—300	$209.43
T-64	Gary Baker	74-74-75-77—300	$209.43
T-64	Tom Doozan	78-73-74-75—300	$209.43
T-64	David Duschane	77-70-75-78—300	$209.43
T-64	Joe Jimenez	75-79-71-75—300	$209.43
T-64	Jim Marshall	71-76-76-77—300	$209.43
T-64	Ed Sabo	77-73-75-75—300	$209.43
T-64	Bob Smith	71-74-78-77—300	$209.43
T-64	Dick Smith	78-68-72-82—300	$209.43
T-73	Bryan Abbott	73-72-78-78—301	$209.43
T-73	Ras Allen	74-72-79-76—301	$209.43
T-73	Bob Leaver	80-72-68-81—301	$209.43
T-73	John Molenda	76-71-76-78—301	$209.43
T-73	Mike Parrish	76-74-75-76—301	$209.43
T-73	Benny Passons	75-76-74-76—301	$209.43
T-73	Bob Payne	74-78-71-78—301	$209.43
T-73	Bruce Summerhays	72-81-72-76—301	$209.43
T-73	Larry Webb	79-69-74-79—301	$209.43
T-82	Arne Dokka	73-74-72-83—302	$209.43
T-82	Terry Florence	76-76-73-77—302	$209.43
T-82	Craig Immel	76-72-74-80—302	$209.43
T-82	Bill Kennedy	76-74-72-80—302	$209.43
T-82	Mark McConnell	74-74-75-79—302	$209.43
T-87	Warren Chancellor	77-74-73-79—303	$209.43
T-87	Al Chandler	75-75-75-78—303	$209.42
T-87	Charlie Epps	76-74-72-81—303	$209.42
T-87	Randy Erskine	77-70-75-81—303	$209.43
T-87	Mike Stubblefield	77-76-70-80—303	$209.42
T-87	Jim Thompson	76-71-75-81—303	$209.43
T-93	Cotton Dunn	77-75-73-79—304	$209.42
T-93	Deon Good	79-76-70-79—304	$209.42
T-93	Dick Hendrickson	76-68-79-81—304	$209.42
T-93	Rodney Loesch	76-72-72-84—304	$209.42
T-93	Baker Maddera	77-72-75-80—304	$209.42
T-93	Jimmy Powell	77-72-73-82—304	$209.42
T-93	Ross Randall	77-74-74-79—304	$209.42
T-93	Bob Wenz Jr.	81-76-67-80—304	$209.42
T-101	Craig Harmon	78-73-72-82—305	$209.42
T-101	Chuck Hart	77-71-77-80—305	$209.42
T-103	Brent Buckman	79-77-69-81—306	$209.42
T-103	Mark Hessler	79-75-71-81—306	$209.42
T-103	Bob Hibschman	77-76-72-81—306	$209.42
T-106	David Glenz	74-74-77-82—307	$209.42
T-106	Jeff McGill	74-73-77-83—307	$209.42
108	Maurice Ver Brugge	69-82-73-84—308	$209.42
T-109	Burt Baine	71-79-74-85—309	$209.42
T-109	Dennis Murray	74-72-78-85—309	$209.42
111	Tom Barber	74-71-80-89—314	$209.42

1981

For the first time in the history of the Club Professional Championship, the winner led from start to finish. But it took 39-year-old Larry Gilbert of Lexington, Ky., two sudden-death holes to secure the win from Don Padgett II of Akron, Ohio, who bogeyed the second playoff hole.

Champion:	Larry Gilbert, Lexington, Ky.
Site:	PGA National, Palm Beach Gardens, Fla.
Date:	Nov. 19-22
Course: Champion	**Par:** 72 - 7,002 yards
(used for one round and on final day)	
Course: Haig	**Par:** 72 - 6,806 yards
Course: Squire	**Par:** 72 - 6,612 yards
Purse: $150,000	**Field:** 358
Cut at 226	96 players advanced

	Avg. of Courses	Rounds of 70 & Under		Round Leader		Larry Gilbert
Round 1:	77.2	17	67-	Larry Gilbert, Don Massengale	67 -	Tied 1st
Round 2:	77.0	8	137-	Larry Gilbert	137	(70) - 1st
Round 3:	78.0	3	211-	Larry Gilbert	211	(74) - 1st
Round 4:	77.3	2	285-	Larry Gilbert, Don Padgett II	285	(74) - Tied 1st
Totals:	77.38	30				

TOURNAMENT SUMMARY

Place	Name	Score	Winnings
T-1	Larry Gilbert	67-70-74-74—285	$20,000.00
T-1	Don Padgett II	70-72-70-73—285	$12,000.00
3	Richard Crawford	72-69-71-74—286	$10,000.00
4	Gary Robinson	75-71-74-68—288	$9,000.00
5	Jimmy Wright	68-74-75-73—290	$8,000.00
6	John Jackson Jr.	72-70-73-76—291	$7,000.00
T-7	Jim Logue	73-71-73-75—292	$5,166.67
T-7	Don Massengale	67-74-78-73—292	$5,166.67
T-7	Dave Philo	71-75-72-74—292	$5,166.66
T-10	Jim Albus	75-73-77-68—293	$3,500.00
T-10	Jim Marshall	74-71-74-74—293	$3,500.00
T-10	Buddy Whitten	70-77-72-74—293	$3,500.00
T-13	Bruce Ashworth	75-73-72-74—294	$2,400.00
T-13	Lee Harper	69-73-75-77—294	$2,400.00
T-13	Dick Hendrickson	76-70-73-75—294	$2,400.00
T-16	Gene Ferrell	73-76-73-73—295	$1,900.00
T-16	Jim Kiely	69-76-74-76—295	$1,900.00
T-16	Jim King	71-69-75-80—295	$1,900.00
T-16	Dave Ragan	69-76-72-78—295	$1,900.00
T-16	Ross Randall	69-74-78-74—295	$1,900.00
T-16	Dick Smith	69-74-72-80—295	$1,900.00
T-16	Mikel Wynn	72-76-72-75—295	$1,900.00
T-23	John Calabria	73-73-75-75—296	$1,330.00
T-23	Gary Gant	76-78-69-73—296	$1,330.00
T-23	Bob Menne	73-73-72-78—296	$1,330.00
T-23	Bob Moreland	74-77-72-73—296	$1,330.00
T-23	Tony Wallin	74-72-73-77—296	$1,330.00
T-28	James Dolan III	73-73-79-72—297	$1,050.00
T-28	Jim Ferree	72-71-79-75—297	$1,050.00
T-28	Roger Kennedy	72-76-74-75—297	$1,050.00
T-28	Paul Moran	73-72-75-77—297	$1,050.00
T-28	Kevin Morris	72-74-74-77—297	$1,050.00
T-33	David Barber	75-73-73-77—298	$812.50
T-33	Richard Bassett	75-74-73-76—298	$812.50
T-33	Vince Bizik	72-74-75-77—298	$812.50
T-33	Robbie Gilmore Jr.	77-72-71-78—298	$812.50
T-33	Russell Helwig	73-70-78-77—298	$812.50
T-33	Rodney Loesch	76-71-78-73—298	$812.50
T-33	Joe McDermott	73-73-75-77—298	$812.50
T-33	Dwight Nevil	72-71-77-78—298	$812.50
T-33	Benny Passons	77-72-74-75—298	$812.50
T-33	Jack Sommers	72-76-72-78—298	$812.50
T-43	Tommy Aycock	74-72-78-75—299	$525.55
T-43	Bobby Benson	72-77-75-75—299	$525.55
T-43	Al Chandler	72-72-79-76—299	$525.54
T-43	Ken Doty	76-74-72-77—299	$525.54
T-43	Bob Duden	71-77-72-79—299	$525.54
T-43	Lynn Janson	73-72-76-78—299	$525.54
T-43	Bill Kennedy	70-76-75-78—299	$525.54
T-43	Bob Leaver	72-73-78-76—299	$525.54
T-43	Jack Lewis	78-73-74-74—299	$525.55
T-43	Bill Sellers	78-74-73-74—299	$525.55
T-53	Bob Ford	70-77-75-78—300	$277.72
T-53	Tom Robertson	74-75-77-74—300	$277.72
T-53	Paul Wise	71-71-80-78—300	$277.72
T-56	Terry Frence	72-78-75-76—301	$277.72
T-56	Bill Garrett	74-73-79-75—301	$277.72
T-56	Art Scott	72-77-76-76—301	$277.72
T-56	Jack Seltzer	74-75-75-77—301	$277.72
T-56	Doug Steffen	77-72-72-80—301	$277.72
T-56	Bruce Summerhays	71-75-74-81—301	$277.72
T-62	Doug Dalziel	75-76-71-80—302	$277.72
T-62	Mike Kallam	69-79-76-78—302	$277.72
T-62	Al Kelley Jr.	71-76-78-77—302	$277.72
T-62	Paul Ryiz	74-77-73-78—302	$277.72
T-62	Jeff Steinberg	78-74-73-77—302	$277.72
T-67	Steve Benson	74-73-75-81—303	$277.72
T-67	Dennis Bradley	76-71-76-80—303	$277.72
T-67	Tim Collins	70-77-79-77—303	$277.72
T-67	David Hallford	71-76-79-77—303	$277.72
T-67	Laurie Hammer	74-72-76-81—303	$277.72
T-67	Joe Lopez Jr.	76-73-73-81—303	$277.72
T-67	George Shortridge	75-71-76-81—303	$277.72
T-67	Charles Sifford	77-76-72-78—303	$277.72
T-67	Jack Slocum	74-77-74-78—303	$277.72
T-76	Bryan Abbott	77-73-73-81—304	$277.72
T-76	Scott Bailey	73-78-74-79—304	$277.72
T-76	Gary Balliet	77-72-77-78—304	$277.72
T-76	Donald Branca	74-74-77-79—304	$277.72
T-76	Charlie Epps	71-76-78-79—304	$277.72
T-76	Bob Nieberding	80-74-70-80—304	$277.72
T-76	Ed Sabo	75-75-75-79—304	$277.72
T-83	Gene Borek	73-73-80-79—305	$277.72
T-83	Carl Lohren	72-76-76-81—305	$277.71
T-83	Jeff McGill	77-75-73-80—305	$277.72
T-83	Dan Spooner	77-75-73-80—305	$277.71
T-83	John Taylor	73-75-76-81—305	$277.71
T-88	Mark Guttenberg	80-71-75-80—306	$277.71
T-88	Mike Harrigan	74-77-74-81—306	$277.71
T-88	Dan Murphy	69-77-75-85—306	$277.71
T-88	Lynn Rosely	74-77-72-83—306	$277.71
T-88	Brooks Simmons	79-72-75-80—306	$277.71
T-93	Dow Finsterwald	70-77-79-81—307	$277.71
T-93	Art Proctor	75-76-73-83—307	$277.71
95	Cass Jawor	69-80-77-82—308	$277.71
96	Glenn Stuart	71-75-74-89—309	$277.71

1980

John Traub, 29, of Rochester, Mich., started the final round in seventh place, eight shots in back of Gene Borek, the third-round leader. With a front nine 34 to Borek's 40, Traub found himself in the battle. After a bogey at No. 10, Traub birdied Nos. 5 and 17 to cruise in with a 3-under-par 69 for a 2-shot win over Jim Albus of Locust Valley, N.Y., who had a final-round 74. Borek shot 41 on the back nine for a final-round 81, which placed him tied for third.

Champion:	John Traub, Rochester, Mich.
Site:	PGA National, Palm Beach Gardens, Fla.
Date:	Oct. 23-26
Course: PGA National Haig	**Par:** 72 - 6,806 yards
(used for one round and on final day)	
Course: Eastpointe CC	**Par:** 72
Course: Frenchman's Creek (North)	**Par:** 72
Purse: $125,000	**Field:** 336
Cut at 224	99 players advanced

	Avg. of Courses	Rounds of 70 & Under		Round Leader		John Traub
Round 1:	76.4	13	67-	Gene Borek, G. Wintz, D. Lotz	72 -	Tied 29th
Round 2:	75.7	18	135-	Gene Borek	141	(69) - Tied 4th
Round 3:	77.3	9	206-	Gene Borek	214	(73) - Tied 7th
Round 4:	76.4	2	283-	John Traub	283	(69) - 1st
Totals:	76.47	42				

TOURNAMENT SUMMARY

Place	Name	Score	Winnings
1	John Traub	72-69-73-69—283	$20,000.00
2	Jim Albus	72-68-71-74—285	$12,000.00
T-3	Gene Borek	67-68-71-81—287	$7,000.00
T-3	Larry Gilbert	73-69-70-75—287	$7,000.00
T-3	Don Padgett II	72-74-71-70—287	$7,000.00
T-6	John Jackson Jr.	75-71-71-71—288	$4,500.00
T-6	Roger Kennedy	71-71-70-76—288	$4,500.00
T-8	Steve Benson	74-72-70-73—289	$2,750.00
T-8	Bob Ford	74-70-72-73—289	$2,750.00
T-10	Gary Baker	72-71-75-72—290	$2,150.00
T-10	Jim Ferriell Jr.	74-70-74-72—290	$2,150.00
T-10	David Glenz	74-71-72-73—290	$2,150.00
T-10	Gary Robinson	73-70-69-78—290	$2,150.00
14	Kevin Morris	69-77-71-74—291	$1,900.00
T-15	Al Chandler	75-71-72-74—292	$1,575.00
T-15	Tim Collins	73-74-73-72—292	$1,575.00
T-15	Jack Lewis	73-73-72-74—292	$1,575.00
T-15	Dick Lotz	67-75-77-73—292	$1,575.00
T-15	Art Silvestrone	73-75-70-74—292	$1,575.00
T-15	Gary Wintz	67-75-73-77—292	$1,575.00
T-21	Terry Florence	72-74-76-71—293	$1,225.00
T-21	John Gentile	71-73-75-74—293	$1,225.00
T-21	Gary Groh	78-71-70-74—293	$1,225.00
T-21	Dave Haberle	71-72-75-75—293	$1,225.00
T-21	Lynn Janson	72-72-76-73—293	$1,225.00
T-21	Tom Ulozas	77-70-70-76—293	$1,225.00
T-27	David Barber	74-73-73-74—294	$1,037.50
T-27	Howell Fraser	75-70-72-77—294	$1,037.50
T-27	Victor Lipscomb	73-78-71-72—294	$1,225.00
T-27	Jim Logue	73-74-74-73—294	$1,037.50
T-31	Laurie Hammer	78-68-78-71—295	$937.50
T-31	Bruce MacDonald	75-72-72-76—295	$937.50
T-31	Joe Moresco	80-72-71-72—295	$937.50

Place	Name	Score	Winnings
T-31	John Nichols Jr.	69-71-73-82—295	$937.50
T-35	Cotton Dunn	74-72-76-74—296	$787.50
T-35	Gene Ferrell	76-72-75-73—296	$787.50
T-35	David Jimenez	77-69-73-77—296	$787.50
T-35	John Molenda	70-77-75-74—296	$787.50
T-35	Bob Moreland	76-74-72-74—296	$787.50
T-35	Bob Nieberding	73-71-73-79—296	$787.50
T-35	Bruce Summerhays	73-73-75-75—296	$787.50
T-35	Buddy Whitten	76-71-74-75—296	$787.50
T-43	Roger Ginsberg	74-74-73-76—297	$612.50
T-43	Don Maddox	72-76-75-74—297	$612.50
T-43	Milon Marusic	75-72-77-73—297	$612.50
T-43	Ted McKenzie	71-76-73-77—297	$612.50
T-43	Jack Seltzer	75-72-73-77—297	$612.50
T-43	Dave Zink	76-76-72-73—297	$612.50
T-49	Tommy Aycock	73-74-75-76—298	$265.85
T-49	Martin Bohen	73-73-77-75—298	$265.86
T-49	Donald Branca	70-73-77-78—298	$265.85
T-49	Randy Glover	71-72-75-80—298	$265.85
T-49	Mike Kallam	73-72-74-79—298	$265.85
T-49	Bob Leaver	75-70-78-75—298	$265.85
T-49	David Marad	75-72-74-77—298	$265.85
T-49	Jeff McGill	77-77-70-74—298	$265.86
T-49	Bob Menne	72-73-76-77—298	$265.85
T-49	Dan Murphy	75-77-72-74—298	$265.86
T-49	Jay Overton	71-74-78-75—298	$265.86
T-49	Bob Payne	75-73-73-77—298	$265.85
T-49	Bill Schumaker	76-72-72-78—298	$265.85
T-49	Luther Showaker	77-74-73-74—298	$265.86
T-49	Stan Thirsk	71-73-72-82—298	$265.85
T-49	Michael Zinni	70-75-77-76—298	$265.85
T-65	Ron Baker	77-72-72-78—299	$230.61
T-65	John Buczek	73-73-78-75—299	$230.61

Place	Name	Score	Winnings
T-65	John Calabria	75-76-73-75—299	$230.61
T-65	Chuck Hart	69-75-72-83—299	$230.61
T-65	Ross Randall	74-75-73-77—299	$230.61
T-65	Tom Robertson	76-70-78-75—299	$230.61
T-65	Ronnie Rosson	75-72-75-77—299	$230.61
T-65	Charles Sifford	70-75-74-80—299	$230.61
T-65	Gene Torres	74-73-73-79—299	$230.61
T-74	Steve Bull	74-75-74-77—300	$230.61
T-74	Lee Harper	73-76-75-76—300	$230.61
T-74	Bob Issler	80-71-73-76—300	$230.61
T-74	Adolph Popp	77-70-76-77—300	$230.61
T-74	Jim Seeley	71-71-78-80—300	$230.61
T-74	Charlie Wood	74-71-79-76—300	$230.61
T-80	Jon Cutshall	70-72-81-78—301	$230.61
T-80	Chuck Lasher	71-74-75-81—301	$230.61
T-80	Dennis Milne	76-73-73-79—301	$230.61
T-80	Alvin Odom Jr.	78-72-74-77—301	$230.61
T-84	Joe Benevento	79-71-72-80—302	$230.61
T-84	Paul Bessler	76-75-73-78—302	$230.61
T-84	Clayton Cole	71-73-79-79—302	$230.61
T-84	Dick Harmon	76-74-73-79—302	$230.61
T-84	Mike Harrigan	71-75-76-80—302	$230.61
T-84	Keith Stuhler	78-77-68-79—302	$230.61
T-90	Jerry Impellittiere	74-74-75-80—303	$230.61
T-90	Mal McMullen	75-74-74-80—303	$230.61
T-90	Larry Ringer	75-72-76-80—303	$230.61
T-93	Charlie Epps	71-72-77-84—304	$230.61
T-93	Scotty McBeath	73-71-78-82—304	$230.61
T-95	Robert Nichols	75-76-73-81—305	$230.61
T-95	Butch Pegoraro	76-72-76-81—305	$230.61
97	Jimmy Wright	75-74-73-84—306	$230.61
98	John Rech	72-76-76-83—307	$230.61
99	Bob McFerren	72-75-75-89—311	$230.61

PGA CLUB PROFESSIONAL CHAMPIONSHIP

1979

For the second year in a row, the Club Professional Championship was decided in a sudden-death play-off. Buddy Whitten, a 33-year-old head professional from Grand Rapids, Mich., birdied the second playoff hole to beat 32-year-old Jack Lewis. Whitten was forced to make a 27-footer for birdie on the first sudden death hole to continue the playoff after Lewis hit his second shot inches away.

Champion:	Buddy Whitten, Grand Rapids, Mich.
Site:	Callaway Gardens Resort, Pine Mountain, Ga.
Date:	Nov. 8-11
Course: Mountain View	**Par:** 72 - 7,040 yards
(used for one round and on final day)	
Course: Lake View	**Par:** 70 - 6,006 yards
Course: Gardens View	**Par:** 72 - 6,392 yards
Purse: $125,000	**Field:** 335
Cut at 217	94 players advanced

	Avg. of Courses	Rounds of 70 & Under		Round Leader		Buddy Whitten
Round 1:	74.1	51	66	Dave Barber	70 -	Tied 25th
Round 2:	74.7	43	136-	Bob Duden	138	(68) - Tied 2nd
Round 3:	72.8	72	208-	B. Whitten, Jack Lewis Jr.	208	(70) - Tied 1st
Round 4:	72.9	21	278-	B. Whitten, Jack Lewis Jr.	278	(70) - Tied 1st
Totals:	73.82	187				

TOURNAMENT SUMMARY

Place	Name	Score	Winnings	Place	Name	Score	Winnings	Place	Name	Score	Winnings
T-1	Buddy Whitten	70-68-70-70—278	$20,000.00	T-33	Doug Dalziel	73-73-68-72—286	$837.50	T-58	Larry Zee	73-67-77-72—289	$256.82
2	Jack Lewis	71-69-68-70—278	$12,000.00	T-33	Bob Duden	70-66-73-77—286	$837.50	T-66	Burt Baine	70-71-74-75—290	$256.82
T-3	Tommy Aycock	73-67-72-67—279	$7,500.00	T-33	Howell Fraser	69-76-68-73—286	$837.50	T-66	Jerry Breaux	72-69-75-74—290	$256.82
T-3	David Barber	66-72-72-69—279	$7,500.00	T-33	Richard Goetz	71-71-72-72—286	$837.50	T-66	Sam Brewer	71-74-72-73—290	$256.82
T-5	Doug Campbell	70-74-70-67—281	$5,000.00	T-33	John Jackson Jr.	75-71-68-72—286	$837.50	T-66	Mike Burke Sr.	74-73-70-73—290	$256.82
T-5	Roger Kennedy	71-70-70-70—281	$5,000.00	T-33	Rives McBee	72-70-68-76—286	$837.50	T-66	Roger Ginsberg	69-72-74-75—290	$256.82
T-5	George Shortridge	69-71-71-70—281	$5,000.00	T-33	Robert Nichols	70-72-73-71—286	$837.50	T-66	Walker Inman Jr.	73-70-73-74—290	$256.82
T-8	Dow Finsterwald	73-68-70-71—282	$2,600.00	T-33	Charles Volpone Jr.	68-72-74-72—286	$837.50	T-66	Jim Loque	70-70-73-77—290	$256.82
T-8	Terry Florence	72-73-67-70—282	$2,600.00	T-41	Tim Collins	68-79-69-71—287	$650.00	T-66	John Molenda	75-71-71-73—290	$256.82
T-8	Randy Glover	72-69-72-69—282	$2,600.00	T-41	George Glenn	70-69-70-78—287	$650.00	T-66	Bob Ralston	70-71-74-75—290	$256.82
T-11	Rex Baxter	69-76-68-70—283	$1,950.00	T-41	Bob Huber	67-77-68-75—287	$650.00	T-66	Carlton Sowers	76-69-71-74—290	$256.82
T-11	John Calabria	75-74-66-68—283	$1,950.00	T-41	Jerry Impellittiere	74-70-72-71—287	$650.00	T-66	Lee Wykle	70-70-73-77—290	$256.82
T-11	Woody Fitzhugh	73-70-73-67—283	$1,950.00	T-41	Bob Issler	73-70-70-74—287	$650.00	T-77	John Gentile	72-72-73-74—291	$256.82
T-11	Lynn Janson	69-76-68-70—283	$1,950.00	T-41	Cass Jawor	74-67-73-73—287	$650.00	T-77	Fred Haney	71-71-74-75—291	$256.82
T-11	Jack Macconachie	71-70-72-70—283	$1,950.00	T-41	Steve Oppermann	71-71-69-76—287	$650.00	T-77	Steve Lyles	74-74-69-74—291	$256.82
T-11	Charles Sifford	71-72-69-71—283	$1,950.00	T-48	Ras Allen	70-78-69-71—288	$337.28	T-77	Tommy Sanderson	75-71-71-74—291	$256.82
T-17	Chris Cole	69-75-68-72—284	$1,433.33	T-48	Bruce Ashworth	74-76-67-71—288	$337.28	T-77	Roanld Smoak	72-73-71-75—291	$256.82
T-17	Jon Cutshall	75-69-70-70—284	$1,433.33	T-48	Gene Borek	71-76-70-71—288	$337.27	T-77	Jimmy Wright	71-75-71-74—291	$256.82
T-17	Perry Leslie	71-68-71-74—284	$1,433.33	T-48	John Buczek	74-72-69-73—288	$337.27	T-83	George Belli	70-73-73-76—292	$256.82
T-17	Dean Refram	72-70-73-69—284	$1,433.34	T-48	David Glenz	69-74-72-73—288	$337.27	T-83	Al Chandler	71-71-74-76—292	$256.82
T-17	Larry Ringer	71-72-72-69—284	$1,433.34	T-48	Lee Harper	71-72-73-72—288	$337.27	T-83	Larry Gilbert	70-71-74-77—292	$256.81
T-17	Jack Seltzer	70-68-74-72—284	$1,433.34	T-48	Dick Hart	76-71-69-72—288	$337.27	T-83	Craig Immel	70-74-71-77—292	$256.82
T-23	Roy Abrameit	71-74-66-74—285	$1,077.50	T-48	Dick Hendrickson	73-72-70-73—288	$337.27	T-83	Ken Mast	70-74-70-78—292	$256.82
T-23	Joe Jimenez	71-72-73-69—285	$1,077.50	T-48	Bruce Lehnhard	75-76-66-71—288	$337.28	T-88	Bill Majure	75-70-71-77—293	$256.81
T-23	Denny Lyons	72-69-73-71—285	$1,077.50	T-48	Jack Slocum	70-70-72-76—288	$337.28	T-88	Jeff Steinberg	70-68-78-77—293	$256.81
T-23	Dan Murphy	68-74-68-75—285	$1,077.50	T-58	Gene Boni	76-71-70-72—289	$256.82	T-88	Tom Ulozas	69-73-73-78—293	$256.81
T-23	Jay Overton	74-71-71-69—285	$1,077.50	T-58	Dennis Coscina	73-74-69-73—289	$256.82	91	Geoff Hensley	68-73-76-77—294	$256.81
T-23	Bill Pelham	71-74-69-71—285	$1,077.50	T-58	Woody Dame	74-74-69-72—289	$256.82	92	Pat Schwab	76-73-68-78—295	$256.81
T-23	Ross Randall	70-70-77-68—285	$1,077.50	T-58	Joe Hasbrouck	69-75-71-74—289	$256.82	93	Bill Parker	74-75-68-80—297	$256.81
T-23	Mike Schlueter	68-72-72-73—285	$1,077.50	T-58	Howie Johnson	73-71-72-73—289	$256.82	94	Don Padgett II	68-76-73-81—298	$256.81
T-23	Steve Spray	75-69-69-72—285	$1,077.50	T-58	James King	69-73-71-76—289	$256.82				
T-23	Dewitt Weaver	71-77-68-69—285	$1,077.50	T-58	Orrin Vincent	73-65-77-74—289	$256.82				

1978

For the third time, the Club Professional Championship was decided in a sudden-death playoff, with 31-year-old John Gentile of Westport, Conn., making birdie on the second playoff hole to beat Jim Ferree, a 47-year-old professional from Pittsburgh, Pa. With perfect weather, the three Callaway courses proved to play the easiest of all Club Professional Championships, with a four day stroke average of 73.59.

Champion:	John Gentile, Westport, Conn.
Site:	Callaway Gardens Resort, Pine Mountain, Ga.
Date:	Nov. 9-12
Course: Mountain View	**Par:** 72 - 7,040 yards
(used for one round and on final day)	
Course: Lake View	**Par:** 70 - 6,006 yards
Course: Gardens View	**Par:** 72 - 6,392 yards
Purse: $110,000	**Field:** 350
Cut at 223	98 players advanced

	Avg. of Courses	Rounds of 70 & Under		Round Leader		John Gentile
Round 1:	73.6	61	64-	Jerry Steelsmith	71 -	Tied 62th
Round 2:	73.4	72	133-	Bob Leaver	140	(69) - Tied 27th
Round 3:	73.6	65	204-	Jim Ferree	208	(68) - Tied 4th
Round 4:	74.1	8	276-	John Gentile, Jim Ferree	276	(68) - Tied 1st
Totals:	73.59	206				

TOURNAMENT SUMMARY

Place	Name	Score	Winnings	Place	Name	Score	Winnings	Place	Name	Score	Winnings
T-1	John Gentile	71-69-68-68—276	$17,000.00	T-31	Ross Randall	71-67-74-73—285	$887.50	T-69	Russell Glover	72-69-73-75—289	$180.70
T-1	Jim Ferree	69-67-68-72—276	$10,000.00	T-31	Ronald Smoak	69-71-72-73—285	$887.50	T-69	Craig Griswold	70-71-72-76—289	$180.70
3	Jay Overton	69-69-67-73—278	$7,500.00	T-39	Jim Albus	76-69-67-74—286	$662.50	T-69	Dick Hendrickson	73-66-71-79—289	$180.70
4	Bob Bruno	69-72-70-69—280	$6,000.00	T-39	David Barber	67-72-74-73—286	$662.50	T-69	Charles Huckaby	68-78-70-73—289	$180.70
T-5	Tommy Aycock	74-68-68-71—281	$3,214.29	T-39	Joe Benevento	69-68-73-76—286	$662.50	T-69	Victor Lipscomb	76-67-70-76—289	$180.70
T-5	Tim Collins	74-64-71-72—281	$3,214.28	T-39	Sam Brewer	73-70-71-72—286	$662.50	T-69	Dan Murphy	72-69-71-77—289	$180.70
T-5	Guy Cullins	69-69-70-73—281	$3,214.28	T-39	Joseph Carr	72-75-67-72—286	$662.50	T-69	Robert Post Jr.	70-71-75-73—289	$180.70
T-5	Dean Refram	67-71-70-73—281	$3,214.28	T-39	Bob Duden	74-74-65-73—286	$662.50	T-69	Jeff Steinberg	65-73-78-73—289	$180.70
T-5	George Shortridge	66-71-72-72—281	$3,214.29	T-39	Jack Kiefer	73-73-70-70—286	$662.50	T-69	Roger Watson	72-72-70-75—289	$180.70
T-5	Jack Sommers	69-71-70-71—281	$3,214.29	T-39	Jim King	71-70-75-70—286	$662.50	T-82	Jon Gustin	71-75-70-74—290	$180.70
T-5	Jimmy Wright	65-72-72-72—281	$3,214.29	T-39	Buddy Whitten	73-68-73-72—286	$662.50	T-82	Jimmy Paschal	69-68-76-77—290	$180.70
T-12	Bob Galloway	72-66-71-73—282	$1,900.00	T-39	Lee Wykle	69-69-75-74—287	$662.50	T-82	Bobby Pomeroy	71-76-69-74—290	$180.70
T-12	Lynn Janson	70-73-68-71—282	$1,900.00	T-49	George Belli	68-74-72-73—287	$263.66	T-82	J.D. Turner	68-76-71-75—290	$180.70
T-12	Tony Kaloustian	71-69-68-74—282	$1,900.00	T-49	Terry Dear	73-75-68-71—287	$263.65	T-86	Hampton Auld	72-70-73-76—291	$180.70
T-12	Lloyd Monroe	69-72-70-71—282	$1,900.00	T-49	Bob Duval	70-70-76-71—287	$263.65	T-86	Mike Ballo	69-73-70-79—291	$180.70
T-12	Ron Terry	70-68-73-71—282	$1,900.00	T-49	Albert Green	73-72-70-72—287	$263.66	T-86	Jerry Breaux	71-71-74-75—291	$180.70
T-17	Scott Bess	70-72-71-70—283	$1,381.25	T-49	Bob Harrison	71-71-72-73—287	$263.66	T-86	Jim Lucius	73-71-72-75—291	$180.70
T-17	Mike Felker	74-69-69-71—283	$1,381.25	T-49	Jim Marshall	71-71-71-74—287	$263.66	T-86	Pat Schwab	76-71-69-75—291	$180.70
T-17	Roger Ginsberg	71-70-73-69—283	$1,381.25	T-49	Kevin Morris	72-71-73-71—287	$263.65	T-86	Jack Seltzer	75-72-67-77—291	$180.70
T-17	Jim Logue	69-71-71-72—283	$1,381.25	T-49	Howard Reid	72-70-73-72—287	$263.66	T-92	Gary Dowen	72-71-72-77—292	$180.70
T-17	Larry Ringer	69-67-70-77—283	$1,381.25	T-57	Clayton Cole	74-73-68-73—288	$180.70	T-92	Clare Emery	72-69-73-78—292	$180.70
T-17	Hugh Royer	69-67-73-74—283	$1,381.25	T-57	Gene Ferrell	69-74-71-74—288	$180.71	T-92	George Glenn	70-74-72-76—292	$180.70
T-17	Steve Spray	68-71-71-73—283	$1,381.25	T-57	Dick Hanscom	71-70-74-73—288	$180.70	T-92	Darrel Knicely	70-74-72-76—292	$180.70
T-17	Jerry Steelsmith	64-71-74-74—283	$1,381.25	T-57	Mike Husby	69-72-72-75—288	$180.71	T-92	John Rech	73-70-72-77—292	$180.70
T-25	Mike Davis	69-69-75-71—284	$1,066.67	T-57	Bob Leaver	67-66-77-78—288	$180.70	T-92	Larry Stubblefield	75-69-71-77—292	$180.70
T-25	David Jimenez	74-66-71-73—284	$1,066.67	T-57	Carl Lohren	70-70-74-74—288	$180.70	T-98	Tom Deaton	72-69-74-78—293	$180.70
T-25	Tom Joyce	70-74-70-70—284	$1,066.67	T-57	David Marad	72-71-69-76—288	$180.70	T-98	Denny Lyons	71-74-70-78—293	$180.70
T-25	Bobby Phillips	69-74-69-72—284	$1,066.67	T-57	Bob Nieberding	73-70-73-72—288	$180.70	T-98	Willard Scholl	73-72-70-78—293	$180.70
T-25	Waddy Stokes	68-72-69-75—284	$1,066.66	T-57	Zach Padgett	75-70-70-73—288	$180.71	T-98	Steve Smith	70-72-73-78—293	$180.70
T-25	Austin Straub	68-71-70-75—284	$1,066.66	T-57	Jim Picard	73-77-66-72—288	$180.70	T-102	Dick Murphy	70-71-73-80—294	$180.70
T-31	Chick Evans	71-69-74-71—285	$887.50	T-57	Tom Robertson	68-72-73-75—288	$180.70	T-102	Jack Slocum	70-70-75-79—294	$180.70
T-31	Phil Ferranti	72-65-73-75—285	$887.50	T-57	Dave Smith	74-73-68-73—288	$180.70	104	George Griffin III	71-74-71-79—295	$180.70
T-31	Dow Finsterwald	72-75-68-70—285	$887.50	T-69	Gene Borek	74-74-68-73—289	$180.70	105	Art Kraft	70-75-71-81—297	$180.70
T-31	Ernie George	70-70-72-73—285	$887.50	T-69	Mike Burke Sr.	74-74-68-73—289	$180.70	T-106	Laurie Hammer	69-74-71-84—298	$180.70
T-31	Dick Hart	70-69-71-75—285	$887.50	T-69	James Eoff	72-71-68-78—289	$180.70	T-106	Gordon Leslie	75-71-70-82—298	$180.70
T-31	John Molenda	69-69-69-76—285	$887.50	T-69	Howell Fraser	73-73-70-73—289	$180.70				

1977

Laurie Hammer, a 34-year-old professional from Boynton Beach, Fla., had his wife, Marlene, to thank for his win in the 10th PGA Club Professional Championship. Two weeks before the tournament, he had decided to stay home to open the winter season. But Marlene persuaded him to play, and it paid off handsomely in a Hollywood-type finish. Going into the final hole, he had a 2-stroke lead over Steve Benson, a 31-year-old head professional from Glen Ellyn, Ill., who made a 30-foot birdie on the 72nd hole. That forced Hammer to make a 10-foot par putt to capture the Championship.

Champion:	Laurie Hammer, Boynton Beach, Fla.
Site:	Callaway Gardens Resort, Pine Mountain, Ga.
Date:	Nov. 10-13
Course: Mountain View	**Par:** 72 - 7,040 yards
(used for one round and on final day)	
Course: Lake View	**Par:** 70 - 6,006 yards
Course: Gardens View	**Par:** 72 - 6,392 yards
Purse: $110,000	**Field:** 354
Cut at 223	98 players advanced

	Avg. of Courses	Rounds of 70 & Under	Round Leader		Laurie Hammer	
Round 1:	76.6	15	67-	Art Proctor	73 -	Tied 40th
Round 2:	75.3	24	139-	Art Proctor	140	(67) - Tied 2nd
Round 3:	75.3	32	211-	L. Hammer, C. Volpone, S. Thirsk	211	(71) - Tied 1st
Round 4:	74.9	9	282-	Laurie Hammer	282	(71) - 1st
Totals:	75.68	80				

TOURNAMENT SUMMARY

Place	Name	Score	Winnings	Place	Name	Score	Winnings	Place	Name	Score	Winnings
1	Laurie Hammer	73-67-71-71—282	$16,500.00	T-30	Jay Horton	70-77-75-71—293	$791.54	T-63	Carl Lohren	72-74-75-76—297	$210.64
2	Steve Benson	68-73-72-70—283	$9,900.00	T-30	Lynn Janson	72-71-77-73—293	$791.54	T-63	Mal McMullen	75-70-78-74—297	$210.64
3	Art Proctor	67-72-74-72—285	$7,300.00	T-30	Bill Schumaker	74-76-73-70—293	$791.54	T-63	John Poole	74-74-73-76—297	$210.64
T-4	Tommy Aycock	75-71-70-70—286	$4,500.00	T-30	Jack Seltzer	70-79-71-73—293	$791.54	T-63	Jimmy Wright	74-73-76-74—297	$210.64
T-4	Tim Collins	70-74-73-69—286	$4,500.00	T-30	Austin Straub	73-72-73-75—293	$791.54	T-71	Billy Farrell	76-74-72-76—298	$210.64
T-4	Rives McBee	76-71-67-72—286	$4,500.00	T-30	Richard Tock	74-73-74-72—293	$791.54	T-71	Bill Davis	74-78-68-78—298	$210.64
T-4	Ron Smith Jr.	73-68-70-75—286	$4,500.00	T-30	Charles Volpone Jr.	76-68-67-82—293	$791.53	T-71	Randy Glover	78-78-65-77—298	$210.64
T-8	David Barber	71-71-75-70—287	$2,280.00	T-30	Dewitt Weaver	72-71-72-78—293	$791.53	T-71	William Kennedy	74-73-75-76—298	$210.64
T-8	Paul Barkhouse	74-69-73-71—287	$2,280.00	T-30	Terry Wilcox	75-71-75-72—293	$791.54	T-71	Bobby Phillips	73-76-74-75—298	$210.64
T-8	Russell Glover	72-74-71-70—287	$2,280.00	T-43	John Connelly	73-70-78-73—294	$530.00	T-71	Gary Robinson	73-71-74-80—298	$210.64
T-8	Bruce Summerhays	74-74-72-67—287	$2,280.00	T-43	Ken Folkes	76-75-72-71—294	$530.00	T-71	Stuart Taylor	74-75-72-77—298	$210.64
T-8	Stan Thirsk	69-72-70-76—287	$2,280.00	T-43	Jim Logue	76-71-75-72—294	$530.00	T-71	J.D. Turner	77-67-76-78—298	$210.64
T-13	Bob Duden	72-71-71-74—288	$1,850.00	T-46	Jerry Breaux	78-70-72-75—295	$303.32	T-71	Roy Vucinich	78-76-68-76—298	$210.64
T-13	Bill Hall	72-71-72-73—288	$1,850.00	T-46	Bob Bruno	79-74-68-74—295	$303.32	T-80	Terry Dear	76-75-72-76—299	$210.64
T-15	Gene Torres	71-76-72-70—289	$1,650.00	T-46	Bill Collins	78-72-71-74—295	$303.32	T-80	John Molenda	75-71-75-78—299	$210.64
T-15	Buddy Whitten	74-68-70-77—289	$1,650.00	T-46	Dow Finsterwald	71-77-75-72—295	$303.32	T-80	Dennis Tiziani	78-76-68-77—299	$210.64
T-17	Doug Dalziel	70-72-73-75—290	$1,505.00	T-46	Bill Galloway	70-76-72-77—295	$303.32	T-80	Maurice Ver Brugge	76-68-77-78—299	$210.64
T-17	Larry Ringer	76-67-76-71—290	$1,505.00	T-46	Bob Goetz	69-78-73-75—295	$303.32	T-80	Roger Watson	75-73-73-78—299	$210.64
T-19	Max Anderson	74-69-76-72—291	$1,300.00	T-46	Gordon Jones	76-75-69-75—295	$303.32	T-85	Emory Lee	76-75-70-79—300	$210.64
T-19	George Belli	72-75-71-73—291	$1,300.00	T-46	Jack Kiefer	76-74-70-75—295	$303.32	T-85	Don Lehnhard	78-73-71-78—300	$210.64
T-19	Howell Fraser	75-73-70-73—291	$1,300.00	T-46	Steve Lyles	77-72-73-73—295	$303.32	T-85	Dennis Milne	77-70-74-79—300	$210.64
T-19	Jim King	78-70-71-72—291	$1,300.00	T-46	Don Padgett II	70-76-74-75—295	$303.32	T-85	George Thomas	75-75-72-78—300	$210.64
T-19	Steve Spray	74-75-68-74—291	$1,300.00	T-56	Chris Cole	69-79-72-76—296	$210.64	T-89	Jim Andrews	71-73-79-78—301	$210.64
T-24	Jim Ahern	76-75-70-71—292	$1,105.00	T-56	Jim Ferree	79-71-68-78—296	$210.64	T-89	Ralph Baker	78-73-72-78—301	$210.63
T-24	Woody Dame	75-71-70-76—292	$1,105.00	T-56	Bob Galloway	78-73-71-74—296	$210.64	T-89	Dick Pearce	73-78-70-80—301	$210.63
T-24	Dave Eger	75-73-68-76—292	$1,105.00	T-56	Gordon Leslie	70-77-73-76—296	$210.64	T-89	Sonny Ridenhour	76-75-71-79—301	$210.63
T-24	Jim Ferriell Jr.	76-74-71-71—292	$1,105.00	T-56	Ken Lindsay	77-76-68-75—296	$210.64	T-89	Wayne Yates	76-72-75-78—301	$210.63
T-24	Walker Inman Jr.	76-70-73-73—292	$1,105.00	T-56	Ted McKenzie	72-74-75-75—296	$210.64	T-94	David Mabry	82-72-69-80—303	$210.63
T-24	Jim Picard	74-72-70-76—292	$1,105.00	T-56	George Shortridge	74-74-73-75—296	$210.64	T-94	Don Massengale	73-77-73-80—303	$210.63
T-30	Bryan Abbott	71-77-71-74—293	$791.54	T-63	Pete Davison	70-77-73-77—297	$210.64	T-94	John Nichols Jr.	80-70-70-83—303	$210.63
T-30	Jay Dolan	79-68-73-73—293	$791.54	T-63	Cotton Dunn	71-73-73-80—297	$210.64	T-97	Mike Burke Sr.	78-66-79-83—306	$210.63
T-30	Morris Felker	70-72-73-78—293	$791.54	T-63	Larry Gilbert	78-75-67-77—297	$210.64				
T-30	Jon Gustin	74-72-76-71—293	$791.54	T-63	Fred Haney	73-75-75-74—297	$210.64				

1976

Soft-spoken Bob Galloway was the only golfer in the field to better par each of the four days, but never thought he could win until the 15th hole on the final day when he holed a 40-foot putt to save par. Galloway, part owner of a golf course in Rock Hill, S.C., went on to birdie the 16th and 17th holes. Despite bogeying the final hole, his 6-under-par 280 total was one shot better than George Lanning, Larry Gilbert and Jim Ferriell. Ferriell was the second- and third-round leader.

Champion:	Bob Galloway, Rock Hill, S.C.	
Site:	Callaway Gardens Resort, Pine Mountain, Ga.	
Date:	Nov. 2-5	
Course:	Mountain View	Par: 72 - 7,040 yards
	(used for one round and on final day)	
Course:	Lake View	Par: 70 - 6,006 yards
Course:	Gardens View	Par: 72 - 6,392 yards
Purse:	$110,000	Field: 353
	Cut at 219	104 players advanced

	Avg. of Courses	Rounds of 70 & Under		Round Leader		Bob Galloway	
Round 1:	74.8	49	65-	Charles Keating, Jay Morelli	71 -	Tied 50th	
Round 2:	74.3	43	135-	Jim Ferriell Jr.	140	(69) - Tied 10th	
Round 3:	74.8	34	206-	Jim Ferriell Jr.	209	(69) - Tied 4th	
Round 4:	76.2	3	280-	Bob Galloway	280	(71) - Tied 1st	
Totals:	74.77	129					

TOURNAMENT SUMMARY

Place	Name	Score	Winnings
1	Bob Galloway	71-69-69-71—280	$16,500.00
T-2	Jim Ferriell Jr.	68-67-71-75—281	$7,700.00
T-2	Larry Gilbert	70-70-67-74—281	$7,700.00
T-2	George Lanning	68-72-69-72—281	$7,700.00
T-5	Jim Albus	75-66-69-73—283	$4,400.00
T-5	Bruce Summerhays	72-65-72-74—283	$4,400.00
T-7	George Belli	70-72-71-71—284	$2,800.00
T-7	Tim Collins	69-68-77-70—284	$2,800.00
T-7	Bob Duden	67-74-66-77—284	$2,800.00
T-10	Vince Bizik	72-71-72-70—285	$2,100.00
T-10	Jim Picard	70-72-73-70—285	$2,100.00
T-10	George Shortridge	72-72-68-73—285	$2,100.00
T-13	Tommy Aycock	69-69-75-73—286	$1,750.00
T-13	Bobby Benson	71-71-71-73—286	$1,750.00
T-13	Jay Horton	76-67-68-75—286	$1,750.00
T-13	Charles Keating	65-72-73-76—286	$1,750.00
T-17	Phil Ferranti	75-69-70-73—287	$1,408.00
T-17	Ken Folkes	70-71-73-73—287	$1,408.00
T-17	Larry Mowry	70-70-71-76—287	$1,408.00
T-17	Larry Ringer	67-69-75-76—287	$1,408.00
T-17	Charles Sifford	72-72-70-73—287	$1,408.00
T-22	Bryan Abbott	72-68-75-73—288	$1,186.00
T-22	Bob Afton	70-76-71-71—288	$1,186.00
T-22	Laurie Hammer	73-74-66-75—288	$1,186.00
T-22	Tom Nieporte	71-72-74-71—288	$1,186.00
T-22	Larry Startzel	68-76-71-73—288	$1,186.00
T-27	Gordon Leslie	71-72-70-76—289	$1,040.00
T-27	Carl Lohren	72-73-73-71—289	$1,040.00
T-27	Wayne Morris	69-74-72-74—289	$1,040.00
T-27	Carl Unis	75-71-70-73—289	$1,040.00
T-31	Bob Brue	68-71-74-77—290	$890.00
T-31	Howell Fraser	71-74-68-77—290	$890.00
T-31	Randy Glover	71-71-76-72—290	$890.00
T-31	Robert Nichols	69-73-69-79—290	$890.00
T-31	Roy Pace	70-70-75-75—290	$890.00
T-36	Richard Bassett	68-71-79-73—291	$627.27
T-36	Bob Bruno	66-75-75-75—291	$627.27
T-36	John Buczek	71-70-69-81—291	$627.27
T-36	Joe Cardenas	68-73-74-76—291	$627.27
T-36	Eddie Famula	68-73-76-74—291	$627.28
T-36	Larry Fryer	72-69-72-78—291	$627.28
T-36	Charles Hart	71-72-74-74—291	$627.28
T-36	Mike Higuera	71-72-76-72—291	$627.27
T-36	Jim Lucius	72-73-73-73—291	$627.27
T-36	Jimmy Powell	67-79-72-73—291	$627.27
T-36	Gene Torres	72-70-73-76—291	$627.28
T-47	Bob Barto	73-72-74-73—292	$314.45
T-47	Gene Frank	73-75-69-75—292	$314.44
T-47	Dick Hanscom	73-73-73-73—292	$314.45
T-47	Bill Kennedy	77-71-69-75—292	$314.45
T-47	Steve Lyles	73-71-71-77—292	$314.45
T-47	Roger Watson	69-72-76-75—292	$314.44
T-53	Mike Ballo	74-73-72-74—293	$183.34
T-53	Bob Boldt	77-72-68-76—293	$183.34
T-53	Stan Brion	76-69-74-74—293	$183.34
T-53	Jay Dolan	75-70-73-75—293	$183.34
T-53	Dick Hart	73-74-70-76—293	$183.34
T-53	Jim O'Hern	79-69-68-77—293	$183.34
T-53	Bill Parker	73-74-71-75—293	$183.34
T-53	Dennis Tiziani	67-73-73-80—293	$183.34
T-61	Jim Delich	72-71-74-77—294	$183.34
T-61	Bruce Dobie	70-69-78-77—294	$183.34
T-61	Mal Galletta Jr.	69-74-73-78—294	$183.34
T-61	Bill Hall	73-71-73-77—294	$183.34
T-61	Dick Hendrickson	75-68-75-76—294	$183.34
T-61	Mike Souchak	74-70-75-75—294	$183.34
T-67	Al Chandler	68-75-76-76—295	$183.33
T-67	Pete Davison	69-75-75-76—295	$183.34
T-67	Emory Lee	69-76-71-79—295	$183.33
T-67	Jack Lewis	70-73-76-76—295	$183.33
T-67	Rives McBee	72-70-76-77—295	$183.33
T-67	Mal McMullen	76-73-68-78—295	$183.33
T-67	Jay Morelli	65-79-74-77—295	$183.33
T-67	Art Proctor	75-72-72-76—295	$183.33
T-67	Hugh Royer	74-73-70-78—295	$183.34
T-76	Fred Clark	73-75-69-79—296	$183.33
T-76	Jack Connelly	75-69-69-83—296	$183.33
T-76	Fred Cook	72-72-72-80—296	$183.33
T-76	John Cook	72-69-78-77—296	$183.33
T-76	Bob Goetz	71-71-77-77—296	$183.33
T-76	Roger Kennedy	73-71-74-78—296	$183.33
T-76	Gaylon "Tex" Simon	70-74-72-80—296	$183.33
T-76	George Thomas	75-68-76-77—296	$183.33
T-76	Don Vallario	72-69-76-79—296	$183.33
T-85	Terry Dear	72-75-72-78—297	$183.33
T-85	Keith Guernsey	71-74-73-79—297	$183.33
T-85	Bob Issler	71-76-71-79—297	$183.33
T-85	Dan Murphy	74-69-74-80—297	$183.33
T-85	Ed Powers	73-74-72-78—297	$183.33
T-85	Mike Schlueter	78-70-70-79—297	$183.33
T-85	Pat Schwab	69-71-77-80—297	$183.33
T-85	Fred Wampler	75-72-72-78—297	$183.33
T-93	Clayton Cole	69-77-73-79—298	$183.33
T-93	Jim Logue	70-74-75-79—298	$183.33
T-95	John Molenda	68-78-72-80—298	$183.33
T-95	Jim Barber	76-69-73-81—299	$183.33
T-95	Dick James	76-70-73-80—299	$183.33
T-95	Larry Laoretti	72-73-74-80—299	$183.33
T-95	Jerry Mowlds	72-72-75-80—299	$183.33
T-95	Ron Rhoads	70-71-75-83—299	$183.33
T-101	Dennis Bradley	70-73-76-81—300	$183.33
T-101	Tommy Jacobs	74-73-72-81—300	$183.33
T-101	Jack Lumpkin	73-73-72-82—300	$183.33
104	Don Stickney	73-71-74-87—305	$183.33

1975

Just as he had done a year before, Roger Watson overtook the leader and forced a sudden-death play-off. This time his victim was David Jimenez, and Watson didn't wait until the final hole to nab Jimenez. Watson closed in on him four holes earlier when he matched Jimenez' bogey with a birdie. In the playoff, he didn't want to count on winning with a par, like he did the previous year, so he made a 20-foot birdie to successfully defend the Championship.

Champion:	Roger Watson, Cary, N.C..
Site:	Callaway Gardens Resort, Pine Mountain, Ga.
Date:	Nov. 13-16
Course: Mountain View	**Par:** 72 - 7,040 yards
(used for one round and on final day)	
Course: Lake View	**Par:** 70 - 6,006 yards
Course: Gardens View	**Par:** 72 - 6,392 yards
Purse: $110,000	**Field:** 353
Cut at 223	94 players advanced

	Avg. of Courses	Rounds of 70 & Under		Round Leader		Roger Watson	
Round 1:	77.0	14	68-	Rex Baxter, Rives McBee, Jack Kiefer	73 -	Tied 41st	
Round 2:	76.6	14	137-	David Jimenez	142	(69) - Tied 8th	
Round 3:	74.2	42	206-	David Jimenez	209	(67) - Tied 2nd	
Round 4:	74.8	8	279-	Roger Watson, D. Jimenez	279	(70) - Tied 1st	
Totals:	75.93	78					

TOURNAMENT SUMMARY

Place	Name	Score	Winnings	Place	Name	Score	Winnings	Place	Name	Score	Winnings
1	Roger Watson	73-69-67-70—279	$16,500.00	T-28	Bob Toski	75-75-69-73—292	$973.66	T-65	Vince Bizik	73-75-72-77—297	$225.00
2	David Jimenez	71-66-69-73—279	$9,900.00	T-34	Joe Cardenas	76-75-72-70—293	$823.33	T-65	Ted McKenzie	78-74-70-75—297	$225.00
T-3	Randy Glover	69-74-72-68—283	$6,600.00	T-34	Babe Lichardus	75-73-74-71—293	$823.34	T-65	Eldridge Miles	76-76-71-74—297	$225.00
T-3	Rives McBee	68-77-68-70—283	$6,600.00	T-34	Joe Taylor	75-73-71-74—293	$823.33	T-65	Ken Towns	71-69-77-80—297	$225.00
5	Larry Gilbert	74-70-72-68—284	$4,800.00	T-37	Al Chandler	73-76-73-72—294	$594.54	T-65	Bert Weaver	77-73-73-74—297	$225.00
T-6	Rex Baxter	68-71-76-72—287	$2,920.00	T-37	John Frillman	79-71-72-72—294	$594.54	T-70	Jim Applegate	80-68-74-76—298	$225.00
T-6	Gene Borek	69-77-68-73—287	$2,920.00	T-37	Charles Keating	73-76-73-72—294	$594.54	T-70	Steve Bull	74-79-70-75—298	$225.00
T-6	Don Padgett II	71-70-74-72—287	$2,920.00	T-37	Don Massengale	73-71-71-79—294	$594.55	T-70	Bill Giese	79-71-73-75—298	$225.00
T-6	Stan Thirsk	70-70-72-75—287	$2,920.00	T-37	Gary Nicholas	72-78-72-72—294	$594.54	T-70	Jerry Mowlds	73-75-73-77—298	$225.00
T-6	Dennis Tiziani	74-75-68-70—287	$2,920.00	T-37	Robert Nichols	75-73-72-74—294	$594.54	T-70	Auggie Navarro	74-72-74-78—298	$225.00
11	Dick Hart	70-75-72-71—288	$2,100.00	T-37	Alvin Odom Jr.	73-71-75-75—294	$594.55	T-70	Bill Parker	74-76-71-77—298	$225.00
T-12	Bob Brue	69-78-71-71—289	$1,800.00	T-37	Bobby Pomeroy	80-73-68-73—294	$594.54	T-76	Cotton Dunn	74-76-73-76—299	$225.00
T-12	Jack Kiefer	68-71-72-78—289	$1,800.00	T-37	Tom Smack	72-72-75-75—294	$594.54	T-76	Charles Houts	71-78-71-79—299	$225.00
T-12	Ken Mast	69-74-73-73—289	$1,800.00	T-37	Mike Souchak	79-74-70-71—294	$594.54	T-76	Carl Lohren	73-72-75-79—299	$225.00
T-12	Pat Schwab	71-76-70-72—289	$1,800.00	T-37	Larry Startzel	78-74-67-75—294	$594.54	T-76	Dick Smith	81-72-68-78—299	$225.00
T-12	Terry Wilcox	70-74-71-74—289	$1,800.00	T-48	John Buczek	80-72-70-73—295	$262.75	T-76	Gene Thompson	75-74-73-77—299	$225.00
T-17	Mal Galletta Jr.	76-72-68-74—290	$1,408.00	T-48	Joe Cheves	72-76-75-72—295	$262.75	T-81	Lynn Rosely	80-70-73-77—300	$225.00
T-17	Ron Letellier	76-70-74-70—290	$1,408.00	T-48	Gene Frank	73-73-77-72—295	$262.75	T-81	Tom Talkington	75-74-73-78—300	$225.00
T-17	Tom Ulozas	70-78-69-73—290	$1,408.00	T-48	Dick Hoelzer	74-72-73-76—295	$262.75	T-83	Bruce Dobie	74-74-74-79—301	$225.00
T-17	Maurice Ver Brugge	74-70-70-76—290	$1,408.00	T-48	Bill Kennedy	83-70-68-74—295	$262.75	T-83	Gary Head	72-78-72-79—301	$225.00
T-17	Jimmy Wright	74-71-72-73—290	$1,408.00	T-48	Milon Marusic	78-71-71-75—295	$262.75	T-83	Dick Murphy	74-80-69-78—301	$225.00
T-22	George Belli	72-73-72-74—291	$1,170.00	T-48	Al Mengert	71-80-71-73—295	$262.75	T-83	Bill Tindall	77-75-70-79—301	$225.00
T-22	Clayton Cole	74-79-67-71—291	$1,170.00	T-48	Ray Montgomery	75-71-70-79—295	$262.75	T-83	Jay-Alan White	77-74-71-79—301	$225.00
T-22	Dick Goetz	74-72-73-72—291	$1,170.00	T-48	Wayne Morris	77-77-69-72—295	$262.75	T-88	Bob Duval	74-75-73-80—302	$225.00
T-22	Quinton Gray	72-75-71-73—291	$1,170.00	T-48	Drew Pierson	75-73-70-77—295	$262.75	T-88	Rex Wilsen	76-75-71-80—302	$225.00
T-22	Tom Joyce	71-70-78-72—291	$1,170.00	T-48	Pat Welch	75-73-74-73—295	$262.75	90	Bob Galloway	76-76-70-81—303	$225.00
T-22	Paul Moren	77-75-70-69—291	$1,170.00	T-59	Pete Davison	75-80-66-75—296	$225.00	91	Jim Duffus	75-72-74-83—304	$225.00
T-28	Ernie George	77-73-71-71—292	$973.66	T-59	Richard Eller	75-73-73-75—296	$225.00	92	Claude King	74-75-73-84—306	$225.00
T-28	Steve Lyles	76-76-69-71—292	$973.67	T-59	Tim Leslie	70-78-71-77—296	$225.00	93	Doug Graves	80-74-69-84—307	$225.00
T-28	Denny Meyer	76-72-73-71—292	$973.67	T-59	Don Richards	78-72-70-76—296	$225.00	94	Steve Jenne	76-74-71-89—310	$225.00
T-28	Jimmy Powell	70-80-70-72—292	$973.66	T-59	Chuck Scally	72-73-74-77—296	$225.00				
T-28	Earl Puckett	74-71-74-73—292	$973.66	T-59	Glenn Stuart	72-79-71-74—296	$225.00				

1974

With a 90-foot birdie putt on the final green, Roger Watson from Cary, N.C., tied Sam Snead, who missed a four-foot birdie putt on his final hole, and forced the seventh PGA Club Professional Championship into its first sudden-death playoff. On the first sudden-death hole, Watson won the Championship with a par after Snead pushed his second shot wide of the green and was unable to get it up and down.

Champion:	Roger Watson, Cary, N.C.
Site:	Pinehurst Country Club, Pinehurst, N.C.
Date:	Oct. 24-27
Course: No. 2	**Par:** 72 - 7,051 yards
(used for one round and on final day)	
Course: No. 3	**Par:** 71 - 6,089 yards
Course: No. 5	**Par:** 72 - 6,854 yards
Purse: $110,000	**Field:** 372
Cut at 226	110 players advanced

	Avg. of Courses	Rounds of 70 & Under	Round Leader		Roger Watson	
Round 1:	77.4	3	67-	Bob Benson	71 -	Tied 4th
Round 2:	77.3	3	141-	Sam Snead	144	(73) - Tied 6th
Round 3:	76.2	12	213-	Sam Snead	215	(71) - Tied 2nd
Round 4:	74.9	4	282-	Roger Watson, Sam Snead	284	(69) - Tied 1st
Totals:	76.80	22				

TOURNAMENT SUMMARY

Place	Name	Score	Winnings	Place	Name	Score	Winnings	Place	Name	Score	Winnings
1	Roger Watson	71-73-71-69—284	$16,500.00	T-30	Gene Torres	73-72-75-75—295	$857.78	T-74	Tim Debaufre	72-76-75-77—300	$165.00
2	Sam Snead	71-70-72-71—284	$9,900.00	T-39	John Buczek	72-73-76-75—296	$610.00	T-74	G. (Moe) Demling	73-78-75-74—300	$165.00
3	Bobby Benson	67-75-73-71—286	$7,300.00	T-39	Mike Higuera	76-75-72-73—296	$610.00	T-74	Wayne Morris	78-74-73-75—300	$165.00
4	Ron Letellier	73-72-71-71—287	$5,900.00	T-39	Claude King	75-74-72-75—296	$610.00	T-74	Ken Towns	73-76-77-74—300	$165.00
5	Babe Lichardus	73-72-71-72—288	$4,800.00	T-39	George Smith	69-73-80-74—296	$610.00	T-79	George Bayer	74-74-75-78—301	$165.00
T-6	Eddie Famula	72-76-70-71—289	$3,650.00	T-39	Charles Volpone Jr.	73-77-73-73—296	$610.00	T-79	Stan Brion	74-78-74-75—301	$165.00
T-6	Maurice Ver Brugge	73-71-73-72—289	$3,650.00	T-39	Don Wegrzyn	75-76-73-72—296	$610.00	T-79	Joe Cardenas	72-79-74-76—301	$165.00
T-8	Randy Glover	71-75-73-71—290	$2,350.00	T-45	Ron Bakich	75-74-75-73—297	$300.46	T-79	Joseph Carr	75-73-77-76—301	$165.00
T-8	John Lively	75-71-70-74—290	$2,350.00	T-45	Jerry Barber	74-74-77-72—297	$300.46	T-79	Bob Duden	74-75-77-75—301	$165.00
T-8	Odell Massey	71-74-73-72—290	$2,350.00	T-45	Dennis Bradley	76-71-78-72—297	$300.46	T-79	Bob Duval	74-78-74-75—301	$165.00
T-8	Jimmy Wright	73-72-73-72—290	$2,350.00	T-45	Jack Connelly	71-75-75-76—297	$300.45	T-79	Jim Ferree	80-74-72-75—301	$165.00
12	Ed Dougherty	76-72-73-70—291	$2,000.00	T-45	James Eoff	74-74-73-76—297	$300.45	T-79	Gene Ferrell	75-75-74-77—301	$165.00
T-13	Denny Lyons	72-76-71-73—292	$1,800.00	T-45	Gordon Jones	77-74-72-74—297	$300.46	T-79	Albert Green	76-77-73-75—301	$165.00
T-13	Denny Meyer	76-71-74-71—292	$1,800.00	T-45	Carl Lohren	72-75-75-75—297	$300.45	T-79	Joe Jimenez	77-78-70-76—301	$165.00
T-13	Larry Moncour	73-75-68-76—292	$1,800.00	T-45	Jim Riggins	73-75-73-76—297	$300.45	T-79	Willis Johnson	78-75-70-78—301	$165.00
T-16	Bob Bratzler	74-78-70-71—293	$1,470.00	T-45	Pat Schwab	74-75-73-75—297	$300.45	T-79	Harold Kolb	75-74-77-75—301	$165.00
T-16	Clayton Cole	72-73-73-75—293	$1,470.00	T-45	Dick Shaiper	72-79-71-75—297	$300.45	T-79	Andy Nusbaum	79-73-73-76—301	$165.00
T-16	Howell Fraser	73-69-74-77—293	$1,470.00	T-45	Dennis Tiziani	76-76-73-72—297	$300.46	T-79	Bill Parker	70-78-77-76—301	$165.00
T-16	Tommy Jacobs	75-73-70-75—293	$1,470.00	T-56	George Belli	74-74-71-79—298	$165.00	T-93	Pat Baker	74-74-75-79—302	$165.00
T-16	Tom Nieporte	73-74-73-73—293	$1,470.00	T-56	Nick Berklich	73-74-78-73—298	$165.00	T-93	Eddie Merrins	77-74-74-77—302	$165.00
T-21	Max Anderson	80-68-76-70—294	$1,154.45	T-56	Gene Borek	71-72-77-78—298	$165.00	T-93	Bill Ogden	79-75-72-76—302	$165.00
T-21	Al Chandler	72-75-72-75—294	$1,154.44	T-56	Bill Collins	76-75-70-77—298	$165.00	T-93	Roland Stafford	76-73-77-76—302	$165.00
T-21	Phil Ferranti	72-75-73-74—294	$1,154.44	T-56	Walker Inman Jr.	74-75-75-74—298	$165.00	T-93	Don Stickney	72-74-79-77—302	$165.00
T-21	Garry Hopkins	77-72-73-72—294	$1,154.44	T-56	Joe Mance	74-75-74-75—298	$165.00	98	Felice Torza	79-73-74-77—303	$165.00
T-21	Don Massengale	72-73-74-75—294	$1,154.44	T-56	Ted McKenzie	77-73-74-74—298	$165.00	T-99	Bill Flynn	75-75-76-78—304	$165.00
T-21	Lloyd Monroe	73-75-72-74—294	$1,154.44	T-56	Jim Picard	72-74-77-75—298	$165.00	T-99	Ed Kroll	77-80-69-78—304	$165.00
T-21	Mike Schlueter	75-73-76-70—294	$1,154.45	T-56	Stan Thirsk	72-74-72-80—298	$165.00	T-99	James McCoy	74-72-77-81—304	$165.00
T-21	Tom Smack	72-76-73-73—294	$1,154.45	T-56	Bill Ventresca	74-76-76-72—298	$165.00	T-99	Alvin Odom Jr.	75-74-76-79—304	$165.00
T-21	Bert Weaver	73-78-70-73—294	$1,154.45	T-66	Robin All	72-75-78-74—299	$165.00	T-99	Dave Robinson	73-77-76-78—304	$165.00
T-30	Mal Galletta Jr.	74-77-73-71—295	$857.78	T-66	Rex Baxter	77-76-72-74—299	$165.00	T-99	Fred Wampler	80-75-71-78—304	$165.00
T-30	Laurie Hammer	74-73-75-73—295	$857.78	T-66	Bill Hall	76-73-75-75—299	$165.00	105	Everett Vinzant	76-73-77-79—305	$165.00
T-30	Billy Maxwell	76-71-77-71—295	$857.78	T-66	Dean Lind	74-79-72-74—299	$165.00	T-106	John Joseph	71-75-80-80—306	$165.00
T-30	John Molenda	76-73-73-73—295	$857.78	T-66	Tom Lupinacci	72-74-75-78—299	$165.00	T-106	Ken Lindsay	79-72-74-81—306	$165.00
T-30	Adolph Popp	74-76-73-72—295	$857.77	T-66	Steve Lyles	77-73-73-76—299	$165.00	T-108	Joe Cheves	78-73-75-83—309	$165.00
T-30	Jimmy Powell	73-76-74-72—295	$857.78	T-66	Eldridge Miles	75-78-72-74—299	$165.00	T-108	Ron O'Connor	78-73-75-83—309	$165.00
T-30	Art Proctor	71-73-77-74—295	$857.77	T-66	Dave Smith	77-73-74-75—299	$165.00	110	Don Spears	75-76-75-84—310	$165.00
T-30	Mike Shea	75-73-76-71—295	$857.78	T-74	Mike Ballo	74-75-73-78—300	$165.00				

PGA CLUB PROFESSIONAL CHAMPIONSHIP

1973

Despite an opening round 73, former touring pro Rives McBee from Irving, Texas, coasted to a three-stroke victory over Stan Brion. On the final day, McBee fired three birdies on the front nine for a 34, which helped him capture the $16,500 winner's check.

Champion:	Rives McBee, Irving, Texas
Site:	Pinehurst Country Club, Pinehurst, N.C.
Date:	Oct. 18-21
Course: No. 2	**Par:** 72 - 7,051 yards
(used for one round and on final day)	
Course: No. 3	**Par:** 71 - 6,089 yards
Course: No. 5	**Par:** 72 - 6,854 yards
Purse: $110,000	**Field:** 358
Cut at 223	92 players advanced

	Avg. of Courses	Rounds of 70 & Under		Round Leader		Rives McBee
Round 1:	76.5	21	67-	Carl Owen	73 -	Tied 52th
Round 2:	76.7	16	138-	Larry Mancour	140	(67) - Tied 3rd
Round 3:	75.6	21	211-	Rives McBee, Jerry Barber	211	(71) - Tied 1st
Round 4:	77.3	1	282-	Rives McBee	282	(71) - 1st
Totals:	76.39	59				

TOURNAMENT SUMMARY

Place	Name	Score	Winnings	Place	Name	Score	Winnings	Place	Name	Score	Winnings
1	Rives McBee	73-67-71-71—282	$16,500.00	T-32	Bob Bruno	73-76-72-75—296	$791.11	T-56	Stan Thirsk	75-71-74-79—299	$236.00
2	Stan Brion	72-72-70-71—285	$9,900.00	T-32	Bob Camron	68-77-75-76—296	$791.11	T-56	Dennis Tiziani	71-78-72-78—299	$236.00
T-3	Don Massengale	69-75-70-72—286	$6,600.00	T-32	Bill Collins	71-76-71-78—296	$791.11	T-65	George Aubrey Jr.	76-71-74-79—300	$236.00
T-3	John Molenda	73-69-71-73—286	$6,600.00	T-32	Mal Galletta Jr.	72-73-73-78—296	$791.11	T-65	Larry Beck	74-77-72-77—300	$236.00
5	Rex Baxter	70-72-71-75—288	$4,800.00	T-32	Roger Ginsberg	73-72-75-76—296	$791.11	T-65	Al Chandler	74-74-72-80—300	$236.00
6	Tommy Jacobs	75-72-74-68—289	$4,000.00	T-32	Mac Main	73-76-73-74—296	$791.11	T-65	Ernie George	78-72-67-83—300	$236.00
T-7	Jerry Barber	71-70-70-79—290	$3,000.00	T-32	George Smith	72-76-72-76—296	$791.11	T-65	Bob Goetz	76-76-68-80—300	$236.00
T-7	Jim Jogue	73-69-74-74—290	$3,000.00	T-32	Roland Stafford	73-72-75-76—296	$791.11	T-65	Ray Howell	75-70-73-82—300	$236.00
T-9	Denny Lyons	69-72-74-76—291	$2,233.34	T-32	Jerry Steelsmith	71-75-72-78—296	$791.11	T-65	Mike Joyce	75-74-73-78—300	$236.00
T-9	Larry Moncour	68-70-77-76—291	$2,233.33	T-41	George Bayer	75-73-72-77—297	$512.50	T-65	Steve Lyles	72-73-78-77—300	$236.00
T-9	Jim Seeley	75-73-67-76—291	$2,233.33	T-41	Norman Flynn	79-72-69-77—297	$512.50	T-65	Bill Parker	70-77-75-78—300	$236.00
T-12	Rich Bland	70-75-74-73—292	$1,850.00	T-41	Howell Fraser	74-73-72-78—297	$512.50	T-65	Bob Pipkin	74-74-75-77—300	$236.00
T-12	Bob Brue	70-70-76-76—292	$1,850.00	T-41	John Joseph	73-73-74-77—297	$512.50	T-65	Gaylon "Tex" Simon	74-75-73-78—300	$236.00
T-12	Bob Galloway	76-73-69-74—292	$1,850.00	T-41	Carl Lohren	71-77-75-74—297	$512.50	T-76	Bob Below	72-75-74-80—301	$236.00
T-12	Garry Hopkins	72-71-74-75—292	$1,850.00	T-41	Joe Moresco	75-69-75-78—297	$512.50	T-76	Jim Cassia	75-74-72-80—301	$236.00
T-16	Randy Glover	73-77-69-74—293	$1,536.67	T-41	Carl Owen	67-75-77-78—297	$512.50	T-76	Ken Folkes	74-77-70-80—301	$236.00
T-16	Frank Mize	74-67-75-77—293	$1,536.67	T-41	Roger Watson	73-74-74-76—297	$512.50	T-76	Mike Higuera	74-74-74-79—301	$236.00
T-16	Glenn Stuart	74-72-71-76—293	$1,536.66	T-49	Bobby Benson	70-74-73-81—298	$267.47	T-76	Dave Smith	77-71-74-79—301	$236.00
T-19	Gene Thompson	70-76-71-77—294	$1,370.00	T-49	Steve Bull	75-69-76-78—298	$267.47	T-76	Bill Sporre	73-80-69-79—301	$236.00
T-19	Bert Weaver	70-73-76-75—294	$1,370.00	T-49	Chris Gers	76-69-75-78—298	$267.47	T-76	Ralph Terry	70-80-73-78—301	$236.00
T-21	Ralph Baker	76-76-69-74—295	$1,121.82	T-49	Dick Hanscom	72-74-74-78—298	$267.47	T-83	Dennis Milne	72-73-74-83—302	$236.00
T-21	Joseph Carr	75-69-77-74—295	$1,121.82	T-49	Jerry Pittman	79-72-71-76—298	$267.47	T-83	Al Goodrich	79-74-70-79—302	$236.00
T-21	Clayton Cole	76-67-76-76—295	$1,121.82	T-49	Dick Rautmann	74-71-70-83—298	$267.47	T-83	Bert Seagraves	74-73-74-81—302	$236.00
T-21	Clare Emery	75-73-72-75—295	$1,121.82	T-49	Bill Robinson	74-71-71-82—298	$267.47	T-86	Clarence Doser	74-74-72-82—302	$236.00
T-21	Tom Liljeholm	74-74-75-72—295	$1,121.82	T-56	Carroll Armstrong	74-72-74-79—299	$236.00	T-86	Terry George	77-74-71-81—303	$236.00
T-21	Davis Love Jr.	71-68-79-77—295	$1,121.82	T-56	Rafe Botts	77-74-71-77—299	$236.00	T-86	Sam Reynolds	72-75-75-81—303	$236.00
T-21	Ray Montgomery	77-69-76-73—295	$1,121.82	T-56	Jim Gerring	76-75-71-77—299	$236.00	T-89	Robin All	74-74-74-83—305	$236.00
T-21	Tom Nieporte	71-71-79-74—295	$1,121.82	T-56	Albert Green	73-73-72-81—299	$236.00	T-89	Luca Barbato	74-76-72-83—305	$236.00
T-21	Dick Smith	72-75-70-78—295	$1,121.82	T-56	Dick Hart	71-76-76-76—299	$236.00	T-89	Joe Jimenez	76-75-72-82—305	$236.00
T-21	Robert Smith	73-75-72-75—295	$1,121.82	T-56	Ed Kroll	73-67-76-83—299	$236.00	92	Gary Howlett	77-72-74-84—307	$236.00
T-21	Jimmy Wright	76-71-75-73—295	$1,121.82	T-56	Chuck Scally	76-72-74-77—299	$236.00				

PGA CLUB PROFESSIONAL CHAMPIONSHIP

1972

Playing during an arctic cold front that sent temperatures to an all-time low for North Carolina, 35-year-old Don Massengale beat the elements to win the fifth PGA Club Professional Championship. On the final day, Massengale fired a back-nine 33 for a two-stroke victory over Bob Bruno and four strokes over defending champion Sam Snead.

Champion:	Don Massengale, White Plains, N.Y.
Site:	Pinehurst Country Club, Pinehurst, N.C.
Date:	Oct. 19-22
Course: No. 2	**Par:** 72 - 7,051 yards
(used for one round and on final day)	
Course: No. 4	**Par:** 72 - 6,784 yards
Course: No. 1	**Par:** 70 - 6,129 yards
Purse: $100,000	**Field:** 358
Cut at 222	94 players advanced

	Avg. of Courses	Rounds of 70 & Under		Round Leader		Don Massengale	
Round 1:	76.0	19	65-	Jim O'Hern, Ron Letellier		72 -	Tied 35th
Round 2:	76.3	30	138-	Bob Brue, Mal Galletta Randy Quick, Don Massengale		138	(66) - Tied 1st
Round 3:	75.1	42	211-	Babe Lichardus		212	(74) - Tied 2nd
Round 4:	77.2	4	280 -	Don Massengale		280	(68) - 1st
Totals:	75.92	95					

TOURNAMENT SUMMARY

Place	Name	Score	Winnings	Place	Name	Score	Winnings	Place	Name	Score	Winnings
1	Don Massengale	72-66-74-68—280	$15,000.00	T-31	Larry Mancour	77-72-69-76—294	$825.00	T-61	Chuck Hart	79-71-70-78—298	$204.55
2	Bob Bruno	72-66-74-70—282	$9,000.00	T-31	Bob Schoener	72-76-71-75—294	$825.00	T-61	Dennis Milne	68-79-73-78—298	$204.55
3	Sam Snead	71-68-76-69—284	$6,600.00	T-35	Stan Baluik	70-77-73-75—295	$660.00	T-61	Art Silvestrone	75-76-70-77—298	$204.55
T-4	Ernie George	70-69-74-72—285	$4,900.00	T-35	Clayton Cole	75-68-76-76—295	$660.00	T-61	Frank Wharton	73-76-73-76—298	$204.55
T-4	Babe Lichardus	72-69-70-74—285	$4,900.00	T-35	Joe Jimenez	80-67-75-73—295	$660.00	T-69	Joe Campbell	78-74-67-80—299	$204.55
6	Gene Borek	73-73-72-69—287	$3,600.00	T-35	Steve Lyles	72-68-79-76—295	$660.00	T-69	Dick Hanscom	71-80-69-79—299	$204.55
7	Denny Lyons	76-69-70-73—288	$3,000.00	T-35	Sonny Ridenhour	73-72-76-74—295	$660.00	T-69	Eldridge Miles	71-76-69-83—299	$204.55
T-8	Mal Galletta Jr.	73-65-76-75—289	$2,233.33	T-35	Willard Scholl	73-69-76-77—295	$660.00	T-69	Don Stickney	75-74-71-79—299	$204.55
T-8	Rives McBee	76-72-70-71—289	$2,233.34	T-35	Gene Thompson	73-71-74-77—295	$660.00	T-73	Jim Lucius	78-73-71-78—300	$204.55
T-8	Craig Shankland	72-76-69-72—289	$2,233.33	T-42	Wes Ellis	69-78-67-82—296	$398.45	T-73	Bill Ogden	73-78-71-78—300	$204.55
T-11	Jerry Barber	71-71-74-74—290	$1,631.43	T-42	Gerald Hatfield	74-74-71-77—296	$398.46	T-75	Jim Barber	72-76-74-79—301	$204.55
T-11	Tommy Jacobs	68-74-72-76—290	$1,631.43	T-42	John Langford	75-74-70-77—296	$398.45	T-75	Dick Hart	78-70-71-82—301	$204.54
T-11	David Jimenez	69-75-71-75—290	$1,631.43	T-42	Odell Massey	72-72-76-76—296	$398.46	T-75	John Lively	71-79-72-79—301	$204.54
T-11	Wayne Morris	74-70-71-75—290	$1,631.43	T-42	Al Mengert	72-76-69-79—296	$398.45	T-75	John Neese	75-75-72-79—301	$204.54
T-11	Dave Philo	72-74-70-74—290	$1,631.43	T-42	John Molenda	71-72-75-78—296	$398.46	T-75	Jerry Preuss	72-79-71-79—301	$204.54
T-11	Jimmy Powell	73-72-67-78—290	$1,631.42	T-42	Jim O'Hern	65-80-75-76—296	$398.46	T-75	Buddy Weaver	71-77-73-80—301	$204.54
T-11	Charles Volpone Jr.	72-71-69-78—290	$1,631.43	T-42	Carl Unis	72-75-73-76—296	$398.46	T-81	Bob Duden	74-72-74-82—302	$204.54
T-18	Drew Pierson	68-74-74-75—291	$1,276.66	T-42	Jimmy Wright	75-72-74-75—296	$398.46	T-81	Cass Jawor	75-76-71-80—302	$204.54
T-18	Maurice Ver Brugge	74-70-73-74—291	$1,276.67	T-42	Wayne Yates	71-76-72-77—296	$398.45	T-81	Clayton Johnson	74-67-79-82—302	$204.54
T-18	Bert Weaver	72-71-73-75—291	$1,276.66	T-52	Tillman Berg Jr.	68-77-73-79—297	$204.55	T-81	James McCoy	74-71-76-81—302	$204.54
T-21	Rex Baxter	78-73-67-74—292	$1,125.00	T-52	Nick Berklich	72-69-75-81—297	$204.55	T-81	Randy Quick	72-66-81-83—302	$204.54
T-21	Sam Carmichael	70-75-71-76—292	$1,125.00	T-52	Al Chandler	77-72-70-78—297	$204.55	T-81	George Thomas	72-69-80-81—302	$204.54
T-21	Bob Galloway	76-70-72-74—292	$1,125.00	T-52	Hubby Habjan	78-72-67-80—297	$204.55	T-87	Ray Beattie	72-77-73-81—303	$204.54
T-21	Mike Joyce	74-72-74-72—292	$1,125.00	T-52	Charles Houts	73-74-72-78—297	$204.55	T-87	George Belli	80-73-69-81—303	$204.54
T-25	Gene Bone	76-73-70-74—293	$975.00	T-52	Jim Logue	71-77-73-76—297	$204.55	T-87	Tom Nieporte	79-74-69-81—303	$204.54
T-25	John Frillman	75-72-71-75—293	$975.00	T-52	Bill Parker	78-72-70-77—297	$204.55	T-87	Paul Scodeller	75-76-70-82—303	$204.54
T-25	Jerry Pittman	72-75-72-74—293	$975.00	T-52	Jim Picard	72-74-71-80—297	$204.55	T-87	Bob Watson	75-71-76-81—303	$204.54
T-25	Chuck Scally	69-77-70-77—293	$975.00	T-52	George Smith	78-71-71-77—297	$204.55	T-92	Jim Allen	78-74-69-83—304	$204.54
T-25	Pat Schwab	73-74-69-77—293	$975.00	T-61	Billy Applewhite	72-69-76-81—298	$204.55	T-92	Gene Torres	76-74-71-83—304	$204.54
T-25	Jerry Steelsmith	75-70-71-77—293	$975.00	T-61	Bobby Benson	68-71-80-79—298	$204.55	94	Joe Cardenas	67-83-72-87—309	$204.54
T-31	Ross Coon	71-68-76-79—294	$825.00	T-61	Bob Brue	78-72-67-81—298	$204.55				
T-31	Jim Gerring	72-78-71-73—294	$825.00	T-61	Bob Ellis	75-74-71-78—298	$204.55				

1971

After an opening 5-under-par 67 on the tougher No. 2 course, and a second-round 7-under-par 65 on the No. 1 course, 59-year-old Sam Snead cruised to a 5-stroke victory. Among the records set were the all-time low 18-hole score, 63, by Eddie Famula, who then shot 81 the second day to just make the 36-hole cut, and Snead's record 36-hole score of 132.

Champion:	Sam Snead, Greenbrier, W. Va.	
Site:	Pinehurst Country Club, Pinehurst, N.C.	
Date:	Oct. 14-17	
Course: No. 2	**Par:**	72 - 7,051 yards
Course: No. 1	**Par:**	70 - 6,129 yards
Purse: $100,000	**Field:** 252	
Cut at 145	97 players advanced	

	Avg. of Courses	Rounds of 70 & Under		Round Leader		Sam Snead	
Round 1:	73.5	61	63-	Eddie Famula		67 -	Tied 7th
Round 2:	73.4	69	132-	Sam Snead		132	(65) - 1st
Round 3:	75.7	4	206-	Sam Snead		206	(74) - 1st
Round 4:	75.6	5	275-	Sam Snead		275	(69) - 1st
Totals:	74.04	139					

TOURNAMENT SUMMARY

Place	Name	Score	Winnings
1	Sam Snead	67-65-74-69—275	$15,000.00
T-2	Ron Letellier	73-67-71-69—280	$7,800.00
T-2	Jerry Steelsmith	68-71-72-69—280	$7,800.00
T-4	Babe Lichardus	67-68-74-73—282	$4,466.66
T-4	Stan Thirsk	71-67-69-75—282	$4,466.67
T-4	Charles Volpone Jr.	68-70-73-71—282	$4,466.67
T-7	Bob Brue	73-67-71-72—283	$2,750.00
T-7	John Frillman	72-65-72-74—283	$2,750.00
T-9	Sam Carmichael	71-71-71-71—284	$1,975.00
T-9	Walker Inman Jr.	69-70-71-74—284	$1,975.00
T-9	Jimmy Powell	65-70-75-74—284	$1,975.00
T-9	Bill Robinson	70-68-73-73—284	$1,975.00
T-13	Bradley Anderson	69-70-75-71—285	$1,620.00
T-13	Chick Evans	68-73-71-73—285	$1,620.00
T-13	Larry Gilbert	68-73-70-74—285	$1,620.00
T-16	Larry Mancour	72-68-72-74—286	$1,430.00
T-16	George Shortridge	72-67-75-72—286	$1,430.00
T-18	Gene Borek	69-69-73-76—287	$1,228.00
T-18	Jim O'Hern	77-67-69-74—287	$1,228.00
T-18	George Smith	69-71-78-69—287	$1,228.00
T-18	Fred Wampler	65-78-73-71—287	$1,228.00
T-18	Jimmy Wright	67-78-70-72—287	$1,228.00
T-23	Ken Folkes	71-68-73-76—288	$1,095.00
T-23	Larry Wise	69-71-73-75—288	$1,095.00
25	Jim Ferree	72-69-74-74—289	$1,050.00
T-26	Bobby Benson	71-66-75-78—290	$975.00
T-26	Ross Coon	72-70-79-69—290	$975.00
T-26	Bob Galloway	72-69-77-72—290	$975.00
T-26	Gene Torres	73-68-73-76—290	$975.00
T-30	Mike Burke Sr.	71-69-75-76—291	$825.00
T-30	Bob Crowley	69-76-74-72—291	$825.00
T-30	Jerry Dixon	67-78-73-73—291	$825.00
T-30	Tom Nieporte	70-68-77-76—291	$825.00
T-30	Bob Swift	69-74-74-74—291	$825.00
T-30	Roger Watson	75-67-74-75—291	$825.00
T-36	John Cook	69-75-74-74—292	$675.00
T-36	Corky Dahl	74-68-74-76—292	$675.00
T-36	Bill Parker	72-70-73-77—292	$675.00
T-36	Craig Shankland	74-70-73-75—292	$675.00
T-40	Mike Ballo	75-69-73-76—293	$510.00
T-40	Stan Dudas	72-73-75-73—293	$510.00
T-40	George Glenn	69-73-74-77—293	$510.00
T-40	Herman Keiser	71-70-74-78—293	$510.00
T-40	Scotty McBeath	71-72-78-72—293	$510.00
T-40	Paul Scodeller	69-70-77-77—293	$510.00
T-40	Joel Taylor	70-73-76-74—293	$510.00
T-47	Cliff Cook	74-67-76-77—294	$279.21
T-47	Bob Duden	72-70-77-75—294	$279.22
T-47	Hubby Habjan	70-75-76-73—294	$279.22
T-47	George McKeown	66-73-78-77—294	$279.21
T-47	Joe Moresco	73-68-79-74—294	$279.22
T-47	Bill Ogden	68-73-77-76—294	$279.21
T-47	Frank Wharton	71-73-75-75—294	$279.21
T-54	Stan Baluik	71-70-77-77—295	$191.50
T-54	Dave Field	75-70-75-75—295	$191.50
T-54	Cass Jawor	78-66-73-78—295	$191.50
T-54	Davis Love Jr.	70-75-73-77—295	$191.50
T-54	Monte Sanders	76-67-76-76—295	$191.50
T-54	Art Silvestrone	71-72-76-76—295	$191.50
T-54	Ron Weber	69-72-79-75—295	$191.50
T-61	Bob Benning	72-73-75-76—296	$191.50
T-61	Ray Howell	68-72-78-78—296	$191.50
T-61	Bob Keller	69-70-78-79—296	$191.50
T-61	John Ruedi	65-74-76-81—296	$191.50
T-61	Bob Schoener	70-75-75-76—296	$191.50
T-61	Bruce Summerhays	74-70-78-74—296	$191.50
T-61	Joe Taggert	68-75-77-76—296	$191.50
T-68	George Clark	76-69-77-75—297	$191.50
T-68	Bob Eschenbrenner	73-71-76-77—297	$191.50
T-68	John Maurycy	73-71-80-73—297	$191.50
T-68	Dick Murphy	69-74-78-76—297	$191.50
T-68	Ken Towns	70-75-75-77—297	$191.50
T-68	Maurice Ver Brugge	72-67-81-77—297	$191.50
T-74	Al Kelley Jr.	67-76-75-80—298	$191.50
T-74	Earl Smith	69-75-77-77—298	$191.50
T-74	Dick Stranahan	69-76-74-79—298	$191.50
T-77	Bob Goetz	65-80-77-77—299	$191.50
T-77	John Molenda	73-70-78-78—299	$191.50
T-77	Mike Mural	77-68-77-77—299	$191.50
T-77	Bob Thatcher	69-74-77-79—299	$191.50
T-81	Dick Killiam	71-73-79-77—300	$191.50
T-81	Ed Schumann	78-66-81-75—300	$191.50
T-81	Everett Vinzant	74-69-77-80—300	$191.50
T-81	Don Wegrzyn	69-72-79-80—300	$191.50
T-85	Jim Gerring	69-75-83-74—301	$191.50
T-85	Charles Knowles	73-71-79-78—301	$191.50
T-85	Mike Souchak	71-70-78-82—301	$191.50
T-88	Bob Haggerty	75-70-79-78—302	$191.50
T-88	Alan Mundle	69-76-79-78—302	$191.50
T-90	Walter Burkemo	70-74-81-78—303	$191.50
T-90	Chris Gers	74-68-79-82—303	$191.50
T-90	Ed Trojan Jr.	75-69-79-80—303	$191.50
T-93	Hampton Auld	69-76-78-81—304	$191.50
T-93	Pete Fleming	68-77-82-77—304	$191.50
95	Tom Barber	71-74-84-76—305	$191.50
T-96	Eddie Famula	63-81-78-84—306	$191.50
T-96	Joel Taylor	74-68-79-85—306	$191.50

1970

Rex Baxter, a 30-year-old club professional from Beechwood Country Club in Cleveland, Ohio, knocked a 60-yard wedge shot stiff for a tap-in on the final hole to win by one shot over Ernie George and Bob Duden. Finishing three strokes behind Baxter at 288 were Dick Smith, who would become PGA of America president from 1991-1992, and Mickey Powell, PGA president from 1985-1986.

Champion:	Rex Baxter, Cleveland, Ohio
Site:	Sunol Valley Country Club, Sunol, Calif.
Date:	Nov. 12-15
Course: Palm	**Par:** 72 - 7,123 yards
Course: Cypress	**Par:** 72 - 6,356 yards
Purse: $50,000	**Field:** 258
Cut at 150	106 players advanced

	Avg. of Courses	Rounds of 70 & Under		Round Leader		Rex Baxter	
Round 1:	75.5	20	68-	Dick Whetzle, Francisco Lopez		71 -	Tied 21th
Round 2:	76.3	7	139-	Rex Baxter		139	(68) - 1st
Round 3:	74.8	8	213-	Bill Johnston		214	(75) - Tied 2nd
Round 4:	74.5	9	285-	Rex Baxter		285	(71) - 1st
Totals:	75.50	44					

TOURNAMENT SUMMARY

Place	Name	Score	Winnings	Place	Name	Score	Winnings	Place	Name	Score	Winnings
1	Rex Baxter	71-68-75-71—285	$8,000.00	T-37	Dick Howell	70-77-74-74—295	$285.00	T-69	Rick Jetter	74-73-75-77—299	$71.43
T-2	Bob Duden	71-73-72-70—286	$3,900.00	T-37	Cass Jawor	72-75-74-74—295	$285.00	T-69	Don Klein	71-79-75-74—299	$71.43
T-2	Ernie George	72-73-71-70—286	$3,900.00	T-37	Joe Jimenez	79-71-74-71—295	$285.00	T-69	Paul McMullen	73-74-75-77—299	$71.43
T-4	Tommy Bolt	73-73-73-69—288	$1,758.33	T-37	Paul Kelly	81-68-71-75—295	$285.00	T-69	Ron Ranich	74-76-75-74—299	$71.43
T-4	Bob Bruno	69-76-69-74—288	$1,758.33	T-37	Francisco Lopez	68-74-79-74—295	$285.00	T-69	Dick Shaiper	71-77-73-78—299	$71.43
T-4	John Cook	74-73-71-70—288	$1,758.34	T-37	Eldridge Miles	74-75-73-73—295	$285.00	T-69	Ken Towns	72-75-78-74—299	$71.43
T-4	Mike Fetchick	73-72-69-74—288	$1,758.33	T-37	Paul O'leary	74-69-79-73—295	$285.00	T-79	Tim Berg	72-76-72-80—300	$71.43
T-4	Mickey Powell	73-71-71-73—288	$1,758.33	T-37	Buddy Sullivan	72-77-75-71—295	$285.00	T-79	Bob Goetz	75-75-76-74—300	$71.43
T-4	Dick Smith	74-71-70-73—288	$1,758.33	T-37	Ron Weber	73-77-75-70—295	$285.00	T-79	Bob Grant	74-72-77-77—300	$71.43
T-10	Jim Awtrey	71-76-71-71—289	$902.00	T-46	Bradley Anderson	73-72-76-75—296	$120.78	T-79	Hubby Habjan	75-75-77-73—300	$71.43
T-10	Gene Borek	69-74-72-74—289	$902.00	T-46	Ross Coon	76-72-75-73—296	$120.78	T-83	Corky Dahl	72-76-80-73—301	$71.43
T-10	Bill Johnston	69-74-70-76—289	$902.00	T-46	Buster Cupit	72-75-74-75—296	$120.78	T-83	Clare Emery	77-73-76-75—301	$71.43
T-10	Eddie Merrins	72-74-71-72—289	$902.00	T-46	Don Essig III	77-71-75-73—296	$120.78	T-83	Bruce Summerhays	74-72-80-75—301	$71.43
T-10	Jim O'Hern	78-68-72-71—289	$902.00	T-46	Glen Harvey	74-74-75-73—296	$120.78	T-86	Terry George	74-76-77-75—302	$71.43
T-15	Bill Bisdorf	75-73-70-72—290	$717.50	T-46	John Joseph	70-75-75-76—296	$120.78	T-86	Dick Hart	75-73-81-73—302	$71.43
T-15	Al Kelley Jr.	74-70-72-74—290	$717.50	T-46	George McKeown	73-73-76-74—296	$120.78	T-86	Clyde Nunes	74-76-78-74—302	$71.43
T-15	Jimmy Powell	70-75-73-72—290	$717.50	T-46	Paul Scodeller	72-76-75-73—296	$120.78	T-89	Monty Blodgett	75-75-76-77—303	$71.43
T-15	Jimmy Wright	73-74-73-70—290	$717.50	T-46	Stan Thirsk	73-72-77-74—296	$120.78	T-89	Randy Quick	77-72-80-74—303	$71.43
T-19	Al Chandler	69-78-76-68—291	$591.00	T-46	Sam Urzetta	73-74-74-75—296	$120.78	T-91	Moe Demling	73-75-78-78—304	$71.43
T-19	Juan Elizondo	69-76-74-72—291	$591.00	T-46	Jake Zastko	73-73-70-80—296	$120.78	T-91	Ernest Fortner	73-76-76-79—304	$71.43
T-19	Chick Evans	77-72-72-70—291	$591.00	T-57	Pete Barker	74-73-72-78—297	$71.43	T-91	Bill Giese	74-76-75-79—304	$71.43
T-19	Craig Shankland	75-70-75-71—291	$591.00	T-57	Stan Dudas	73-77-72-75—297	$71.43	T-91	Don Headings Jr.	75-72-74-83—304	$71.43
T-19	Art Silvestrone	70-75-72-74—291	$591.00	T-57	Jim Ferree	76-71-74-76—297	$71.43	T-91	Bob Reith	72-74-79-79—304	$71.43
T-24	Chris Gers	69-74-75-74—292	$517.50	T-57	Eddie Langert	69-78-72-78—297	$71.43	T-91	Hubie Smith	71-78-78-77—304	$71.43
T-24	Tony Holguin	74-74-73-71—292	$517.50	T-57	Charles Leider	74-76-77-70—297	$71.43	T-97	Duane Bergstrom	76-74-78-77—305	$71.43
T-24	Larry Mancour	72-72-73-75—292	$517.50	T-57	Horace Moore	78-72-74-73—297	$71.43	T-97	Paul Bondeson	72-78-76-79—305	$71.43
T-24	John Molenda	73-73-74-72—292	$517.50	T-57	Bill Parker	77-72-71-77—297	$71.43	T-97	John Quick	75-74-82-74—305	$71.43
T-28	George Belli	73-76-70-74—293	$457.50	T-57	Monte Sanders	71-78-72-76—297	$71.43	T-100	Ron Hallett	73-77-79-77—306	$71.43
T-28	Jim Mooney	75-72-72-74—293	$457.50	T-57	Gene Thompson	72-74-78-73—297	$71.43	T-100	Ray Howell	73-77-83-73—306	$71.43
T-28	Bill Ogden	69-74-76-74—293	$457.50	T-66	Thor Holm	73-77-77-71—298	$71.43	102	Gene Johnson	71-79-80-77—307	$71.43
T-28	Willard Wood	73-73-74-73—293	$457.50	T-66	Tony Lamanna	70-75-76-77—298	$71.43	T-103	Sam Reynolds	73-74-82-79—308	$71.43
T-32	John Dalrymple	76-74-73-71—294	$318.00	T-66	Scotty McBeath	74-76-73-75—298	$71.43	T-103	Jack Webb	74-76-79-79—308	$71.43
T-32	Dick Hanscom	70-75-71-78—294	$318.00	T-69	Ty Caplin	72-78-73-76—299	$71.43	105	Paul Biocini	77-73-78-81—309	$71.43
T-32	Ed Kroll	71-77-72-74—294	$318.00	T-69	George Capoun	75-74-75-75—299	$71.43	106	John Carson	76-74-79-81—310	$71.43
T-32	Joe Mortara Jr.	74-72-75-73—294	$318.00	T-69	Gary Carle	72-76-75-76—299	$71.43				
T-32	Bruce Wyatt	76-72-70-76—294	$318.00	T-69	Jim Hart	76-71-77-75—299	$71.43				

1969

Bob Rosburg and Jimmy Wright fought each other down to the last hole. Rosburg won by a sneeze, surprisingly provided by a spectator near the final green at the exact moment that Wright nervously missed a 30-inch putt. This gave Rosburg, the 43-year-old former PGA Champion, the victory.

Champion:	Bob Rosburg, Palm Springs, Calif.
Site:	Roadrunner Golf Resort,
	San Marcos Country Club, Scottsdale, Ariz.
Date:	Nov. 13-16
Course: Roadrunner	**Par:** 71 - 6,930 yards
Course: San Marcos	**Par:** 72 - 6,497 yards
Purse: $50,000	**Field:** 248
Cut at 146	93 players advanced

	Avg. of Courses	Rounds of 70 & Under		Round Leader		Bob Rosburg	
Round 1:	74.1	30	66-	Jimmy Wright		71 -	Tied 30th
Round 2:	74.0	29	133-	Jimmy Wright		137	(66) - 2nd
Round 3:	72.3	27	203-	Jimmy Wright, Bob Rosburg		203	(66) - Tied 1st
Round 4:	74.6	7	275-	Bob Rosburg		275	(72) - 1st
Totals:	73.89	93					

TOURNAMENT SUMMARY

Place	Name	Score	Winnings	Place	Name	Score	Winnings	Place	Name	Score	Winnings
1	Bob Rosburg	71-66-66-72—275	$8,000.00	T-32	Tim Berg	70-71-71-77—289	$360.00	T-63	John Cook	73-71-73-76—293	$90.90
2	Jimmy Wright	66-67-70-73—276	$4,500.00	T-32	Gene Borek	71-75-71-72—289	$360.00	T-63	Charles Gilbert	72-74-71-76—293	$90.90
3	Bill Ogden	70-68-70-70—278	$3,300.00	T-32	Johnny Bulla	70-76-70-73—289	$360.00	T-63	Rick Jetter	72-70-74-77—293	$90.90
T-4	Tommy Bolt	70-72-68-69—279	$2,450.00	T-32	Dick Bury	74-71-70-74—289	$360.00	T-63	Iverson Martin	74-70-74-75—293	$90.90
T-4	John Molenda	70-68-69-72—279	$2,450.00	T-32	Pete Fleming	70-71-71-77—289	$360.00	T-67	Pete Barker	69-71-78-76—294	$90.90
6	Jimmy Powell	69-70-69-73—281	$1,800.00	T-32	Bob Galloway	72-73-72-72—289	$360.00	T-67	Don Collett	73-73-74-74—294	$90.90
T-7	Manuel de la Torre	72-67-68-75—282	$1,212.50	T-32	Al Kelley Jr.	72-71-70-76—289	$360.00	T-67	Tony Holguin	73-70-76-75—294	$90.90
T-7	Craig Shankland	68-72-68-74—282	$1,212.50	T-32	Davis Love Jr.	72-73-70-74—289	$360.00	T-67	Jim Lucius	76-69-73-76—294	$90.90
T-7	Jerry Steelsmith	72-71-67-72—282	$1,212.50	T-32	Walter Porterfield	70-74-72-73—289	$360.00	T-67	Eddie Merrins	70-72-74-78—294	$90.90
T-7	Gene Thompson	70-72-70-70—282	$1,212.50	T-41	Tommy Aycock	75-71-74-70—290	$255.00	T-67	Robert Nichols	71-73-78-72—294	$90.90
T-11	Ross Coon	72-71-69-71—283	$925.00	T-41	Al Chandler	70-73-73-74—290	$255.00	T-67	Hubert Smith	74-71-75-74—294	$90.90
T-11	Art Silvestrone	69-70-68-76—283	$925.00	T-41	Charles Leider	74-69-75-72—290	$255.00	T-67	Mike Souchak	74-68-79-73—294	$90.90
13	Dick Hendrickson	71-69-71-73—284	$850.00	T-41	Carl Lohren	70-74-75-71—290	$255.00	T-75	George Bayer	71-73-76-75—295	$90.90
T-14	George Belli	71-70-68-76—285	$770.00	T-41	Glenn Stuart	75-68-70-77—290	$255.00	T-75	Bob Clark	72-74-72-77—295	$90.90
T-14	Cass Jawor	72-70-71-72—285	$770.00	T-46	Dale Andreason	69-74-75-73—291	$140.41	T-75	Jimmy Clark	72-73-73-77—295	$90.90
T-14	Eldridge Miles	73-70-69-73—285	$770.00	T-46	Rex Baxter	73-69-74-75—291	$140.41	T-75	Ed Rubis	71-75-71-78—295	$90.90
T-17	Bob Fry	71-72-72-71—286	$628.34	T-46	Bob Gajda	72-73-74-72—291	$140.41	79	Red Currie	71-75-76-74—296	$90.90
T-17	Joe Jimenez	72-70-68-76—286	$628.33	T-46	Mike Korich	68-76-71-76—291	$140.41	T-80	Jack Harden	71-73-76-77—297	$90.90
T-17	Claude King	73-67-71-75—286	$628.33	T-46	Ed Kroll	74-71-68-78—291	$140.41	T-80	George Ke	74-72-78-73—297	$90.90
T-17	Tommy Sanderson	70-73-70-73—286	$628.33	T-46	Herman Scharlau	71-72-71-77—291	$140.41	T-80	Tony Novitsky	70-76-76-75—297	$90.90
T-17	Chuck Scally	72-71-72-71—286	$628.34	T-46	Dick Stranahan	71-74-70-76—291	$140.41	T-80	Jim O'Hern	72-74-72-79—297	$90.90
T-17	Joel Taylor	72-72-71-71—286	$628.33	T-46	Fred Wampler	74-72-69-76—291	$140.41	T-84	Ray Bostich	68-78-74-78—298	$90.90
T-23	Jackson Bradley	72-71-72-72—287	$517.50	T-54	Gene Dixon	73-71-72-76—292	$90.90	T-84	John Frillman	76-70-80-72—298	$90.90
T-23	Bill Collins	75-70-72-70—287	$517.50	T-54	Freddie Haas	76-69-73-74—292	$90.90	T-84	Al Jones	70-74-73-81—298	$90.90
T-23	Bobby Ford	71-72-72-72—287	$517.50	T-54	Gary Loustalot	72-71-69-80—292	$90.90	T-87	Alex Redmond	73-73-71-82—299	$90.90
T-23	Bob Menne	69-74-68-76—287	$517.50	T-54	Doug MacDonald	71-75-72-74—292	$90.90	T-87	T. Williams	72-74-77-76—299	$90.90
T-23	Bill Parker	71-72-71-73—287	$517.50	T-54	Scotty McBeath	72-73-79-68—292	$90.90	89	Phil Gibbs	70-75-79-76—300	$90.90
T-23	Maurice Ver Brugge	71-73-68-75—287	$517.50	T-54	Mickey Powell	71-74-73-74—292	$90.90	T-90	Brown Cullen	71-75-78-79—303	$90.90
T-29	Bob Bruno	73-72-71-72—288	$450.00	T-54	Earl Puckett	73-69-75-75—292	$90.90	T-90	Henry Ransom	73-72-75-83—303	$90.90
T-29	Jim Ferree	72-74-72-70—288	$450.00	T-54	Chuck Rotar	73-73-73-73—292	$90.90	T-92	Jesse Whittenton	75-71-75-83—304	$90.90
T-29	Dutch Harrison	72-69-73-74—288	$450.00	T-54	Dick Shaiper	75-70-72-75—292	$90.90	T-92	Larry Wise	73-71-78-82—304	$90.90

PGA CLUB PROFESSIONAL CHAMPIONSHIP

1968

Howell Fraser, a 28-year-old assistant professional, from the Mountain Ridge CC in West Caldwell, N.J., coasted home with a four-stroke victory. His total of 272 is still the lowest 72-hole total on regulation courses utilized in the PGA Club Professional Championship.

Champion:	Howell Fraser, West Caldwell, N.J.	
Site:	Century Country Club,	
	Roadrunner Country Club, Scottsdale, Ariz.	
Date:	Dec. 5-8	
Course: Century	**Par:**	72 - 6,783 yards
Course: Roadrunner	**Par:**	71 - 6,930 yards
Purse: $50,000	**Field:** 207	
	Cut at 147	95 players advanced

	Avg. of Courses	Rounds of 70 & Under		Round Leader		Howell Fraser
Round 1:	74.2	33	66-	Chuck Malchaski, Don Bies	72 -	Tied 50th
Round 2:	74.4	31	134-	Chuck Malchaski	138	(66) - Tied 3rd
Round 3:	72.6	21	203-	Howell Fraser	203	(65) - 1st
Round 4:	72.8	22	272-	Howell Fraser	272	(69) - 1st
Totals:	73.73	107				

TOURNAMENT SUMMARY

Place	Name	Score	Winnings	Place	Name	Score	Winnings	Place	Name	Score	Winnings
1	Howell Fraser	72-66-65-69—272	$8,000.00	T-32	Dutch Harrison	73-72-73-69—287	$352.50	T-64	Herman Coelho	73-71-73-74—291	$88.89
T-2	Chuck Malchaski	66-68-71-71—276	$3,900.00	T-32	Frank Kiraly	72-69-73-73—287	$352.50	T-64	Bailey Glenn	75-72-72-72—291	$88.89
T-2	Bob Rosburg	70-67-70-69—276	$3,900.00	T-32	Ed Kroll	73-73-69-72—287	$352.50	T-64	Iverson Martin	71-70-75-76—292	$88.89
T-4	John Cook	67-71-72-67—277	$2,450.00	T-32	Babe Lichardus	69-73-72-73—287	$352.50	T-68	Horace Moore	75-67-74-76—292	$88.89
T-4	Jimmy Wright	70-71-69-67—277	$2,450.00	T-32	Gary Loustalot	72-74-69-72—287	$352.50	T-68	Ed Oldfield	71-71-77-73—292	$88.89
T-6	Tommy Bolt	72-68-66-72—278	$1,516.66	T-32	George McKeown	70-69-75-73—287	$352.50	T-68	Randy Quick	69-76-72-75—292	$88.89
T-6	Manuel de la Torre	69-69-69-71—278	$1,516.67	T-32	Paul Moran	72-69-71-75—287	$352.50	T-68	Chuck Scally	73-74-74-71—292	$88.89
T-6	Mike Souchak	70-68-69-71—278	$1,516.67	T-32	Jim O'Hern	73-74-71-69—287	$352.50	T-68	Larry Wise	75-71-71-75—292	$88.89
9	Dick Hart	71-69-71-68—279	$1,100.00	T-32	Fred Wampler	74-72-73-68—287	$352.50	T-73	Joe Kotlarczyk	72-75-72-74—293	$88.89
T-10	Don Bies	66-74-66-74—280	$975.00	T-42	Tommy Aycock	74-71-72-71—288	$225.00	T-73	Francisco Lopez	70-73-72-78—293	$88.89
T-10	Jerry Mowlds	68-71-69-72—280	$975.00	T-42	Gene Bone	74-72-69-73—288	$225.00	T-73	Elroy Marti	74-67-75-77—293	$88.89
T-12	Mike Krak	71-71-71-68—281	$875.00	T-42	Pete Fleming	73-70-73-72—288	$225.00	T-76	Tim Berg	71-74-75-74—294	$88.89
T-12	Paul Scodeller	67-74-72-68—281	$875.00	T-42	John Frillman	75-71-72-70—288	$225.00	T-76	Jim Mooney	71-70-80-73—294	$88.89
14	Bob Brue	70-70-74-68—282	$810.00	T-42	Bob Gajda	72-75-72-69—288	$225.00	T-76	Herman Scharlau	75-71-76-72—294	$88.89
15	Johnny Bulla	70-70-73-70—283	$770.00	T-42	Carl Lohren	74-72-70-72—288	$225.00	T-76	George Shortridge	70-73-76-75—294	$88.89
T-16	Joe Cardenas	67-74-74-69—284	$715.00	T-42	Roland Stafford	75-71-69-73—288	$225.00	T-80	Jim Blakeley	71-76-73-75—295	$88.89
T-16	Ed Moehling	72-69-75-68—284	$715.00	T-49	Leroy Bonse	77-70-72-70—289	$101.37	T-80	Herman Keiser	70-72-74-79—295	$88.89
T-18	George Belli	70-71-68-76—285	$561.36	T-49	Tim Debaufre	73-70-75-71—289	$101.36	T-80	Jerry Kreuger	71-73-76-75—295	$88.89
T-18	Gene Borek	70-69-68-78—285	$561.36	T-49	Jim Ferriell Jr.	73-73-73-70—289	$101.37	T-80	Jack Taylor	71-74-74-76—295	$88.89
T-18	Bob Fry	72-71-70-72—285	$561.36	T-49	Bob Hamilton	73-70-70-76—289	$101.36	T-80	Herb Wimberly	71-72-73-79—295	$88.89
T-18	Joe Jimenez	70-71-72-72—285	$561.36	T-49	Don Klein	68-72-77-72—289	$101.36	T-85	Joe Brown	70-76-76-74—296	$88.89
T-18	Al Mengert	68-70-70-77—285	$561.36	T-49	John Langford	70-73-74-72—289	$101.36	T-85	Stan Dudas	73-73-73-77—296	$88.89
T-18	Eddie Merrins	73-68-72-72—285	$561.37	T-49	Davis Love Jr.	72-72-76-69—289	$101.37	T-85	Bob Hold	72-75-74-75—296	$88.89
T-18	Pat Schwab	72-73-71-69—285	$561.37	T-49	Chuck Matlack	72-73-73-71—289	$101.37	T-85	Tal Smith	69-77-76-74—296	$88.89
T-18	Earl Stewart	71-73-70-71—285	$561.37	T-49	Jimmy Powell	71-71-71-76—289	$101.36	T-85	Troy Wright	72-72-74-78—296	$88.89
T-18	Stan Thirsk	73-71-70-71—285	$561.37	T-49	Ronnie Reif	72-75-73-69—289	$101.37	90	Cheston Hall	75-71-77-74—297	$88.89
T-18	Dick Turner	74-70-69-72—285	$561.36	T-49	Jack Webb	75-71-72-71—289	$101.36	T-91	Carroll Armstrong	74-73-77-74—298	$88.88
T-18	Ernie Vossler	70-68-73-74—285	$561.36	T-60	Fred Atkins	73-71-72-74—290	$88.89	T-91	Mike Burke Sr.	70-74-73-81—298	$88.88
T-29	Stan Brion	72-68-74-72—286	$450.00	T-60	Walter Porterfield	68-71-76-75—290	$88.89	T-93	Bill Sporre	74-71-78-77—300	$88.88
T-29	Ed Davis	72-72-72-70—286	$450.00	T-60	Skee Riegel	74-72-72-72—290	$88.89	T-93	Larry Wilkinson	70-77-75-78—300	$88.88
T-29	Sonny Ridenhour	72-69-71-74—286	$450.00	T-60	Ken Towns	69-73-75-73—290	$88.89	95	Alan Artach	75-68-80-81—304	$88.88
T-32	Duke Gibson	69-73-72-73—287	$352.50	T-64	Scotty McBeath	68-74-74-74—290	$88.89				

■ SELECTED PLAYER RECORDS

Player	Best Finish	Year	Rounds	Cuts	Top 3	Top 5	Top 10	Top 25	Rds. in 60s	Average	Money
Greg Abadie	Missed Cut	4	12	0	0	0	0	0	0	78.33	$0.00
Bryan Abbott	T-22nd in 1976	7	25	4	0	0	0	1	1	74.32	$2,464.69
Roy Abrameit	T-23rd in 1979	4	14	2	0	0	0	1	1	76.14	$1,355.22
Bob Ackerman	T-18th in 1984	8	29	5	0	0	0	1	1	73.66	$7,181.00
Rick Acton	T-3rd in 1985	6	24	6	1	1	2	3	5	72.13	$27,386.43
Buck Adams	Missed Cut	6	16	0	0	0	0	0	1	75.56	$0.00
Bob Afton	T-22nd in 1976	4	13	1	0	0	0	1	0	75.08	$1,186.00
Jim Ahern	T-24th in 1977	1	4	1	0	0	0	1	0	73.00	$1,105.00
Jim Albus	T-2nd in 1980	14	54	12	1	3	4	8	8	72.74	$46,066.39
Phil Aldridge	T-56 in 1982	6	17	1	0	0	0	0	0	75.88	$209.43
Ken Allard	T-10th in 1985	8	31	7	0	0	1	4	4	72.55	$23,225.79
John Allen	Missed Cut	6	15	0	0	0	0	0	0	78.13	$0.00
Paul Allen	Missed Cut	6	15	0	0	0	0	0	0	77.40	$0.00
Ras Allen	T-48th in 1979	6	19	3	0	0	0	0	2	75.11	$902.69
Tony Amaral	Missed Cut	7	20	0	0	0	0	0	0	79.05	$0.00
Bradley Anderson	T-13th in 1971	2	8	2	0	0	0	1	1	72.63	$1,740.78
Max Anderson	T-19th in 1977	6	20	2	0	0	0	2	3	75.15	$2,454.45
Tim Angis	T-30th in 1992	5	18	3	0	0	0	0	2	72.56	$3,636.87
Jack Anrico	Missed Cut	4	11	0	0	0	0	0	0	77.91	$0.00
Mike Antonio	Missed Cut	6	18	0	0	0	0	0	1	76.72	$400.00
Jim Applegate	T-70th in 1975	5	16	1	0	0	0	0	1	76.75	$225.00
Billy Applewhite	T-61st in 1972	4	11	1	0	0	0	0	1	76.18	$204.55
Frank Arasin	Missed Cut	4	12	0	0	0	0	0	0	75.67	$0.00
Carroll Armstrong	T-56 in 1973	4	13	2	0	0	0	0	0	75.00	$356.35
Alan Arvesen	T-49th in 1989	2	7	1	0	0	0	0	0	75.43	$796.66
Bruce Ashworth	T-13th in 1981	5	19	4	0	0	0	1	1	73.84	$4,012.28
Tom Atchison	T-41st in 1993	4	13	1	0	0	0	0	2	74.15	$1,047.50
Bob Augustine	Missed Cut	4	12	0	0	0	0	0	0	75.75	$0.00
Hampton Auld	T-86th in 1978	6	19	2	0	0	0	0	1	75.16	$372.20
Jim Awtrey	T-10th in 1970	2	7	1	0	0	1	1	0	72.71	$902.00
Tommy Aycock	T-3rd in 1979	16	61	13	1	3	3	4	9	73.07	$21,333.12
Larry Babica	T-16th in 1985	5	17	2	0	0	0	1	1	75.53	$4,175.00
Merle Backlund	Missed Cut	5	11	0	0	0	0	0	1	75.73	$0.00
Bob Bailey	T-23rd in 1992	4	13	2	0	0	0	1	1	74.08	$10,436.07
Jeff Bailey	T-28th in 1986	9	32	6	0	0	0	0	0	74.63	$4,306.50
Burt Baine	T-66th in 1979	4	14	2	0	0	0	0	0	74.79	$466.24
Gary Baker	T-10th in 1980	11	35	2	0	0	1	1	0	75.26	$2,759.43
Ralph Baker	T-21st in 1973	7	23	2	0	0	0	1	1	75.96	$1,332.45
Ron Baker	T-65th in 1980	4	14	2	0	0	0	0	1	76.29	$655.61
Ron Bakich	T-45th in 1974	3	9	1	0	0	0	0	0	75.33	$300.46
Errie Ball	Missed Cut	3	8	0	0	0	0	0	0	76.25	$0.00
Steve Ball	T-49th in 1993	5	17	2	0	0	0	0	0	74.41	$1,443.00
Gary Balliet	T-11th in 1983	2	8	2	0	0	0	1	0	74.63	$3,527.72
Mike Ballo	T-39th in 1984	6	23	5	0	0	0	0	3	73.83	$1,714.04
Stan Baluik	T-35th in 1972	4	13	2	0	0	0	0	0	74.31	$851.50
Bill Baraban	Missed Cut	4	12	0	0	0	0	0	0	78.92	$400.00
Luca Barbato	T-89th in 1973	6	17	1	0	0	0	0	0	77.41	$267.47
David Barber	T-3rd in 1979	11	39	6	1	1	2	3	4	73.44	$14,492.50
Jack Barber	Missed Cut	4	12	0	0	0	0	0	0	76.50	$0.00
Jerry Barber	T-7th in 1973	8	22	3	0	0	1	2	0	73.64	$4,931.89
Jim Barber	T-75th in 1972	6	16	2	0	0	0	0	1	76.75	$387.88
Tom Barber	96th in 1971	5	16	2	0	0	0	0	0	77.19	$400.92
Mike Barge	Missed Cut	6	18	0	0	0	0	0	1	74.44	$400.00
Jack Barger	T-84th in 1984	6	19	1	0	0	0	0	2	76.16	$425.00
Paul Barkhouse	T-8th in 1977	12	37	1	0	0	1	1	1	75.73	$2,280.00
Ross Barnes	Missed Cut	6	18	0	0	0	0	0	0	78.17	$800.00
Louis Bartoletti	T-13th in 1991	3	10	1	0	0	0	1	1	73.40	$5,721.00
Richard Bassett	T-33rd in 1981	4	14	2	0	0	0	0	2	74.43	$1,439.77
Gary Battistoni	T-89th in 1991	3	10	1	0	0	0	0	1	75.70	$972.00
Mel Baum	T-10th in 1990 & '93	6	22	4	0	0	2	2	5	72.55	$15,548.00
Doug Bauman	T-41st in 1985	5	18	3	0	0	0	0	2	73.44	$1,956.37
Peter Baxter	Missed Cut	4	12	0	0	0	0	0	1	76.67	$0.00
Rex Baxter	Winner in 1970	15	51	7	1	2	3	5	6	74.06	$19,100.41
George Bayer	T-41st in 1973	7	22	3	0	0	0	0	1	75.59	$768.40
Frank Beard	T-23rd in 1983	2	7	1	0	0	0	1	0	74.57	$1,300.00
George Bellino	T-7th in 1976	17	62	11	0	0	1	5	5	74.26	$8,763.88
Bob Below	T-76th in 1973	3	9	1	0	0	0	0	0	75.89	$267.47
Joe Benevento	T-39th in 1978	2	8	2	0	0	0	0	0	73.50	$893.11
Bob Benning	T-61st in 1971	3	9	1	0	0	0	0	0	76.22	$191.50
Bobby Benson	T-3rd in 1974	12	43	7	1	1	1	2	4	74.28	$11,402.28
Steve Benson	T-2nd in 1977 & '82	11	38	5	2	2	3	4	4	73.76	$27,312.72
Scott Bentley	T-21st in 1990	5	17	2	0	0	0	1	2	73.35	$4,486.43
Tim Berg	T-32nd in 1969	5	18	3	0	0	0	0	0	74.61	$520.32
Tillman Berg Jr.	T-52nd in 1972	3	10	1	0	0	0	0	1	76.90	$204.55

PGA CLUB PROFESSIONAL CHAMPIONSHIP

Player	Best Finish	Year	Rounds	Cuts	Top 3	Top 5	Top 10	Top 25	Rds. in 60s	Average	Money
Nick Berklich	T-52nd in 1972	7	22	2	0	0	0	0	2	74.91	$369.55
John Bermel	T-31st in 1993	2	7	1	0	0	0	0	1	71.86	$1,580.00
Scott Bess	T-5th in 1987	8	30	6	0	1	3	5	5	72.93	$27,446.25
Paul Bessler	T-84th in 1980	4	13	1	0	0	0	0	0	77.23	$230.61
Bob Betley	T-2nd in 1986	6	21	3	1	1	2	2	0	73.76	$29,065.00
Miguel Biamon	T-31st in 1993	5	18	3	0	0	0	0	2	72.50	$3,481.66
Mike Bibb	T-58th in 1989	2	7	1	0	0	0	0	1	75.14	$708.33
Don Bies	T-10th in 1968	1	4	1	0	0	1	1	2	70.00	$975.00
Bill Bisdorf	T-15th in 1970	2	7	1	0	0	0	1	0	74.71	$717.50
Vince Bizik	T-10th in 1976	11	36	4	0	0	1	1	0	75.19	$3,759.50
Homero Blancas	T-46th in 1982	1	4	1	0	0	0	0	0	74.50	$379.71
Rich Bland	T-12th in 1973	1	4	1	0	0	0	1	0	73.00	$1,850.00
Dale Boggs	Missed Cut	4	12	0	0	0	0	0	0	79.25	$0.00
Martin Bohen	T-23rd in 1983	4	14	2	0	0	0	1	0	74.71	$1,565.86
Bob Boldt	T-53rd in 1976	3	7	1	0	0	0	0	1	76.14	$183.34
Ray Bolo	Missed Cut	5	14	0	0	0	0	0	0	78.36	$0.00
Tommy Bolt	T-4th in 1969 & '70	4	13	3	0	2	3	3	5	70.38	$4,724.99
Gene Bone	T-25th in 1972	5	16	2	0	0	0	1	1	74.19	$1,200.00
Gene Boni	T-58th in 1979	4	14	2	0	0	0	0	0	74.36	$833.82
Jim Booros	T-43rd in 1986	2	7	1	0	0	0	0	1	74.86	$1,171.00
Gene Borek	T-3rd in 1980	18	65	13	1	1	5	7	13	73.17	$22,654.05
Charles Borner Jr.	Missed Cut	9	27	0	0	0	0	0	2	76.59	$400.00
Nic Borojevich	T-70th in 1993	2	7	1	0	0	0	0	0	74.71	$665.00
Jim Boros	Missed Cut	1	3	0	0	0	0	0	0	78.33	$0.00
Bob Borowicz	T-4th in 1990	7	27	6	0	0	2	4	7	71.59	$33,482.40
Harvey Bostic	Missed Cut	7	21	0	0	0	0	0	0	80.10	$0.00
Rafe Botts	T-56 in 1973	2	7	1	0	0	0	0	0	76.57	$267.47
Steve Bowen	T-15th in 1989	5	18	3	0	0	0	1	2	73.87	$5,442.69
George Bowman	T-3rd in 1993	1	4	1	1	1	1	1	2	69.50	$12,800.00
Bob Boyd	Winner in 1988	7	28	7	1	2	3	5	4	71.75	$55,806.81
Dennis Bradley	T-45th in 1974	19	57	4	0	0	0	0	0	75.49	$1,039.22
Jackson Bradley	T-23rd in 1969	1	4	1	0	0	0	1	0	71.75	$517.50
Dick Bradow	Missed Cut	10	30	0	0	0	0	0	0	75.87	$400.00
Steve Brady	T-67th in 1989	3	10	1	0	0	0	0	0	74.30	$1,057.50
Tommy Brannen	T-23rd in 1987	6	22	4	0	0	0	1	4	72.86	$5,141.05
Bill Brask	T-44th in 1987	7	23	2	0	0	0	0	1	74.13	$1,425.00
Tim Brauch	T-52nd in 1990	7	25	4	0	0	0	0	0	75.20	$2,571.50
Bobby Bray	Missed Cut	7	21	0	0	0	0	0	1	77.10	$800.00
Jerry Breaux	T-46th in 1977	6	22	4	0	0	0	0	1	74.18	$1,018.56
Sam Brewer	T-39th in 1978	3	11	2	0	0	0	0	0	73.27	$919.32
Don Brigham	T-19th in 1987	8	27	3	0	0	0	2	3	74.59	$6,032.44
Stan Brion	T-2nd in 1973	6	22	4	1	1	1	1	2	74.05	$10,698.34
Bill Brodell	T-23rd in 1987	10	31	1	0	0	0	1	2	75.97	$2,767.00
Bob Brue	T-7th in 1971	8	29	6	0	0	1	4	5	72.72	$8,304.55
Bob Bruno	2nd in 1972	12	41	7	1	3	3	3	7	73.20	$18,930.03
Dave Bryan	Missed Cut	7	21	0	0	0	0	0	0	77.19	$800.00
Jim Buchanan	Missed Cut	6	18	0	0	0	0	0	0	78.17	$0.00
Brent Buckman	T-28th in 1990	2	8	2	0	0	0	0	2	74.13	$2,178.17
John Buczek	T-36th in 1976	7	26	5	0	0	0	0	2	74.08	$2,067.90
Steve Bull	T-49th in 1973	10	30	3	0	0	0	0	2	75.20	$723.08
Johnny Bulla	T-15th in 1968	2	8	2	0	0	0	1	0	71.50	$1,130.00
Michael Burke Jr.	T-19th in 1987	7	26	5	0	0	0	2	4	72.86	$8,300.00
Mike Burke Sr.	T-30th in 1971	8	28	5	0	0	0	0	3	74.71	$1,562.03
Walter Burkemo	T-90th in 1971	1	4	1	0	0	0	0	0	75.75	$191.50
Ken Burnette	Missed Cut	4	11	0	0	0	0	0	0	77.09	$0.00
Kevin Burton	T-14th in 1992	2	7	1	0	0	0	1	2	71.71	$6,150.00
Peter Busch	T-56 in 1987	6	20	2	0	0	0	0	3	74.15	$1,257.50
George Buzzini Jr.	Missed Cut	8	22	0	0	0	0	0	0	77.50	$0.00
John Calabria	T-11th in 1979	13	45	6	0	0	0	3	3	74.33	$7,089.11
Don Callahan	Missed Cut	5	14	0	0	0	0	0	0	76.71	$0.00
Mitch Camp	T-34th in 1988	5	17	2	0	0	0	0	0	74.59	$2,620.00
Doug Campbell	T-5th in 1979	8	27	3	0	1	1	1	2	73.50	$6,674.00
Larry Campbell	Missed Cut in 1989	7	17	0	0	0	0	0	0	77.35	$0.00
Ty Caplin	T-69th in 1970	4	12	1	0	0	0	0	1	75.58	$71.43
George Capoun	T-69th in 1970	3	10	1	0	0	0	0	0	76.70	$71.43
David Carazo	Missed Cut	5	15	0	0	0	0	0	0	76.73	$400.00
Joe Cardenas	T-16th in 1968	10	35	5	0	0	0	1	4	74.91	$2,535.14
Terry Carlson	T-67th in 1987	5	14	2	0	0	0	0	0	76.29	$1,115.00
Roy Carmichael	Missed Cut	4	12	0	0	0	0	0	0	75.75	$800.00
Sam Carmichael	T-9th in 1971	3	11	2	0	0	1	2	0	73.82	$3,100.00
Joseph Carr	T-13th in 1983	10	34	4	0	0	0	2	2	74.59	$4,399.32
John Carson	106 in 1970	7	22	1	0	0	0	0	0	77.36	$71.43
Noel Caruso	T-11th in 1989	2	7	1	0	0	0	1	1	72.57	$6,250.00
George Cascino	Missed Cut	6	16	0	0	0	0	0	0	76.88	$0.00
Kevin Cashman	T-31st in 1993	4	14	2	0	0	0	0	2	72.43	$2,630.00
Ron Castillo	Missed Cut	5	15	0	0	0	0	0	0	79.93	$0.00

Player	Best Finish	Year	Rounds	Cuts	Top 3	Top 5	Top 10	Top 25	Rds. in 60s	Average	Money
Steve Caulkins	T-69th in 1986	5	16	1	0	0	0	0	0	76.19	$597.00
Chipper Cecil	Missed Cut	5	15	0	0	0	0	0	0	78.53	$400.00
Greg Cerulli	T-28th in 1989	6	22	4	0	0	0	0	1	73.00	$5,023.14
Jon Chaffee	T-7th in 1991	4	15	3	0	0	1	1	2	72.13	$10,473.33
Warren Chancellor	T-60th in 1985	5	17	2	0	0	0	0	0	75.53	$786.42
Al Chandler	T-15th in 1980	16	60	12	0	0	0	3	4	73.72	$6,242.11
Walt Chapman	T-3rd in 1993	2	8	2	1	1	1	1	2	71.38	$13,432.50
Brien Charter	T-28th in 1984	8	26	3	0	0	0	0	0	74.88	$2,743.43
Joe Cheves	T-48th in 1975	4	14	2	0	0	0	0	0	74.93	$427.75
Jim Cichra	T-19th in 1988	6	19	1	0	0	0	1	1	74.42	$4,550.00
Bob Clark	T-75th in 1969	4	11	1	0	0	0	0	0	75.55	$90.90
George Clark	T-68th in 1971	6	15	1	0	0	0	0	1	75.53	$191.50
Tom Clary	T-56 in 1987	6	19	1	0	0	0	0	1	74.58	$1,050.00
Tom Cleaver	T-8th in 1993	1	4	1	0	0	1	1	3	69.75	$8,500.00
Craig Clemons	T-39th in 1984	3	11	2	0	0	0	0	1	75.18	$952.72
Jerry Coats	T-68th in 1984	4	12	1	0	0	0	0	0	75.75	$425.00
Jim Cochran	Missed Cut	5	13	0	0	0	0	0	0	75.77	$0.00
Cleve Coldwater	T-16th in 1992	5	17	2	0	0	0	1	1	73.94	$5,681.67
Chris Cole	T-17th in 1979	3	10	1	0	0	0	1	2	74.10	$1,433.33
Clayton Cole	T-16th in 1974	10	37	7	0	0	0	3	5	74.38	$5,016.46
Don Collett	T-67th in 1969	6	15	1	0	0	0	0	0	75.93	$90.90
Bill Collins	T-23rd in 1969	8	28	5	0	0	0	1	1	74.04	$1,776.93
Ross Collins	Missed Cut in 1971	4	8	0	0	0	0	0	1	76.75	$0.00
Tim Collins	T-4th in 1977 & '83	10	39	9	0	3	4	6	9	72.46	$24,712.00
Cliff Cook	T-47th in 1971	3	8	1	0	0	0	0	1	74.88	$279.21
Fred Cook	T-76th in 1976	6	18	1	0	0	0	0	0	76.72	$183.33
John Cook	T-4th in 1968 & '70	7	26	5	0	2	2	2	4	73.08	$5,157.57
Ross Coon	T-11th in 1969	10	33	4	0	0	0	1	3	74.15	$2,845.78
Dennis Coscina	T-56 in 1982	11	35	2	0	0	0	0	1	75.34	$466.25
Randall Couch	Missed Cut	4	12	0	0	0	0	0	0	75.17	$0.00
Steve Coulkins	T-39th in 1984	2	8	2	0	0	0	0	0	74.38	$952.72
Charlie Cowell	T-49th in 1993	2	8	2	0	0	0	0	0	72.13	$1,555.00
Richard Crawford	3rd in 1981	6	19	1	1	1	1	1	1	74.84	$10,400.00
Bob Crowley	T-30th in 1971	2	7	1	0	0	0	0	1	74.14	$825.00
Brown Cullen	T-90th in 1969	8	22	1	0	0	0	0	0	76.95	$90.90
Guy Cullins	T-5th in 1978	1	4	1	0	1	1	1	2	70.25	$3,214.28
Buster Cupit	T-46th in 1970	2	6	1	0	0	0	0	0	74.67	$120.78
Jon Cutshall	T-17th in 1979	3	11	2	0	0	0	1	1	74.45	$1,663.94
Chris Dachisen	T-36th in 1989	5	17	2	0	0	0	0	2	74.53	$2,546.25
Corky Dahl	T-36th in 1971	4	13	2	0	0	0	0	1	75.15	$746.43
John Dalrymple	T-32nd in 1970	2	7	1	0	0	0	0	0	76.00	$318.00
Doug Dalziel	T-17th in 1977	4	16	4	0	0	0	2	1	73.19	$4,420.22
Woody Dame	T-24th in 1977	4	14	2	0	0	0	1	1	73.07	$1,361.82
Lee Daniellan	T-47th in 1992	6	20	2	0	0	0	0	0	74.15	$1,687.66
Bill Davis	T-71st in 1977	6	19	1	0	0	0	0	1	75.47	$210.64
Mike Davis	T-25th in 1978	4	13	1	0	0	0	1	2	73.46	$1,066.67
Scott Davis	T-21st in 1988	4	14	2	0	0	0	1	2	73.71	$3,556.46
Pete Davison	T-59th in 1975	5	16	3	0	0	0	0	2	75.13	$618.98
Tom Dawson	T-49th in 1985	4	13	1	0	0	0	0	0	73.38	$1,022.00
Manuel de la Torre	T-6th in 1968	8	23	2	0	0	2	2	5	74.13	$2,729.17
Don De Angelis	Missed Cut	6	18	0	0	0	0	0	0	76.78	$0.00
Terry Dear	T-28th in 1990	10	36	6	0	0	0	0	3	74.11	$4,357.37
Tom Deaton	T-98th in 1978	12	35	1	0	0	0	0	1	76.63	$180.70
John DeForest	T-31st in 1993	1	4	1	0	0	0	0	1	71.00	$1,580.00
Pat Delaney	T-75th in 1986	8	25	1	0	0	0	0	1	75.20	$1,367.00
George(Moe) Demling	T-74th in 1974	8	22	2	0	0	0	0	0	76.95	$236.43
Lowell Dencer	T-21st in 1991	2	7	1	0	0	0	1	3	73.43	$3,228.00
Ralph Denicolo	Missed Cut	4	12	0	0	0	0	0	0	80.42	$0.00
Willis Denmark	Missed Cut	5	12	0	0	0	0	0	0	78.67	$0.00
Jim Dickson	T-10th in 1990	12	39	3	0	0	0	2	5	74.26	$9,117.00
Dan Dirico	Missed Cut	6	17	0	0	0	0	0	0	78.29	$400.00
Bruce Dobie	T-61st in 1976	4	13	2	0	0	0	0	1	76.00	$408.34
Arne Dokka	T-40th in 1983	11	37	4	0	0	0	0	1	75.16	$1,849.43
Jay Dolan	T-30th in 1977	7	22	2	0	0	0	0	1	74.82	$974.88
James Dolan III	T-28th in 1981	3	10	1	0	0	0	0	0	77.90	$1,050.00
Tom Doozan	T-44th in 1989	7	22	2	0	0	0	0	0	75.91	$1,135.43
Clarence Doser	T-86th in 1973	3	10	1	0	0	0	0	0	77.10	$267.47
Ken Doty	T-43rd in 1981	5	16	1	0	0	0	0	0	77.06	$525.54
Ed Dougherty	Winner in 1985	4	16	4	1	1	2	3	3	72.06	$36,021.00
Gary Dowen	T-92nd in 1978	4	13	1	0	0	0	0	0	76.31	$180.70
Tom Ducey	Missed Cut	4	12	0	0	0	0	0	0	76.83	$400.00
Stan Dudas	T-40th in 1971	8	27	3	0	0	0	0	1	75.56	$670.32
Bob Duden	T-2nd in 1970	12	45	9	1	1	2	3	4	73.84	$11,224.30
Ron Dunham	Missed Cut	4	12	0	0	0	0	0	0	77.25	$0.00
Cotton Dunn	T-35th in 1980	9	29	4	0	0	0	0	0	75.90	$1,432.56
Steve Dunning	Missed Cut	5	15	0	0	0	0	0	0	76.73	$0.00

PGA CLUB PROFESSIONAL CHAMPIONSHIP

Player	Best Finish	Year	Rounds	Cuts	Top 3	Top 5	Top 10	Top 25	Rds. in 60s	Average	Money
David Duschane	T-19th in 1985	6	20	2	0	0	0	1	1	75.45	$2,647.43
Bob Duval	T-49th in 1978	4	15	3	0	0	0	0	0	74.33	$653.65
John Ebersberger	Missed Cut	5	15	0	0	0	0	0	1	75.13	$0.00
David Eger	T-24th in 1977	1	4	1	0	0	0	1	1	73.00	$1,105.00
Juan Elizondo	T-19th in 1970	2	7	1	0	0	0	1	1	74.57	$591.00
Richard Eller	T-59th in 1975	4	13	1	0	0	0	0	0	74.31	$225.00
Robert Elliott	T-23rd in 1982	6	19	1	0	0	0	1	0	74.26	$1,216.67
John Elliott Jr.	T-4th in 1983	3	12	3	0	1	1	2	0	73.08	$9,975.00
Ken Ellsworth	T-71st in 1983	5	16	1	0	0	0	0	1	75.75	$277.72
Clare Emery	T-21st in 1973	7	22	3	0	0	0	1	1	74.91	$1,373.95
Larry Emery	T-22nd in 1989	9	32	5	0	0	0	1	1	74.16	$5,207.00
James Eoff	T-45th in 1974	4	14	2	0	0	0	0	1	74.21	$481.15
Charlie Epps	T-6th in 1985	11	41	8	0	0	1	2	3	74.29	$13,895.41
Bill Erfurth	Missed Cut	8	20	0	0	0	0	0	0	76.20	$0.00
Randy Erskine	T-29th in 1983	9	28	2	0	0	0	0	0	73.14	$1,580.86
Bill Eschenbrenner	Missed Cut	5	12	0	0	0	0	0	0	77.25	$0.00
Don Essig III	T-46th in 1970	5	15	1	0	0	0	0	1	75.60	$120.78
Chick Evans	T-13th in 1971	6	21	3	0	0	0	2	2	73.38	$3,098.50
Mike Evans	Missed Cut	7	21	0	0	0	0	0	0	75.86	$0.00
Jeff Fairfield	T-3rd in 1992	4	15	3	1	1	1	1	6	71.53	$17,746.25
Eddie Famula	T-6th in 1974	8	27	3	0	0	1	1	3	74.67	$4,468.78
Billy Farrell	T-71st in 1977	3	10	1	0	0	0	0	0	77.90	$210.64
Greg Farrow	T-4th in 1990	3	12	3	0	1	1	1	2	70.92	$13,730.34
Mike Felker	T-17th in 1978	7	23	2	0	0	0	1	2	75.13	$1,658.97
Morris Felker	T-30th in 1977	2	6	1	0	0	0	0	0	73.17	$791.54
Phil Ferranti	T-17th in 1976	8	26	3	0	0	0	2	2	74.38	$3,449.94
Jim Ferree	T-2nd in 1978	9	33	7	1	1	1	2	5	73.15	$12,997.07
Gene Ferrell	T-16th in 1981	14	47	5	0	0	0	1	1	74.64	$3,642.64
Jim Ferriell Jr.	T-2nd in 1976	10	35	5	1	1	2	3	2	73.11	$11,906.37
Mike Fetchick	T-4th in 1970	2	7	1	0	1	1	1	1	73.71	$1,758.33
Gene Fieger	T-2nd in 1991	6	24	6	1	1	1	2	3	72.33	$27,121.33
Dave Field	T-54th in 1971	1	4	1	0	0	0	0	0	73.75	$191.50
Ron Filipowicz	Missed Cut	4	12	0	0	0	0	0	0	80.08	$0.00
David Findlay	Missed Cut	4	11	0	0	0	0	0	0	76.00	$0.00
Sherm Finger	Missed Cut	7	21	0	0	0	0	0	0	76.19	$0.00
Dow Finsterwald	T-8th in 1979	7	25	4	0	0	1	1	2	74.60	$4,068.53
Woody Fitzhugh	T-11th in 1979	11	38	5	0	0	0	2	4	73.66	$8,397.72
Patrick Fitzsimons	T-22nd in 1989	5	15	2	0	0	0	1	2	74.33	$4,346.00
Bruce Fleisher	Winner in 1989	2	8	2	1	1	1	1	3	70.50	$31,968.75
Pete Fleming	T-32nd in 1969	4	14	3	0	0	0	0	1	73.79	$776.50
Terry Florence	T-8th in 1979 & '83	12	44	8	0	0	2	4	4	73.09	$13,773.86
Bill Flynn	T-99th in 1974	5	15	1	0	0	0	0	0	77.00	$165.00
Norman Flynn	T-41st in 1973	3	9	1	0	0	0	0	1	74.89	$512.50
Ken Folkes	T-17th in 1976	5	19	4	0	0	0	2	1	73.32	$3,300.47
Bob Ford	T-2nd in 1983	10	38	8	1	1	3	4	1	73.18	$27,549.23
Denny Ford	Missed Cut in 1987	5	15	0	0	0	0	0	0	77.67	$0.00
Doug Ford	Missed Cut in 1981	2	6	0	0	0	0	0	0	77.33	$0.00
Steve Forrest	T-40th in 1983	2	7	1	0	0	0	0	0	75.86	$650.00
Jeff Foxx	T-10th in 1985	4	14	2	0	0	1	1	3	73.21	$6,921.00
Gene Frank	T-47th in 1976	9	28	2	0	0	0	0	1	76.25	$577.19
Mike Franko	T-63rd in 1984	4	14	2	0	0	0	0	0	74.10	$1,095.00
Will Frantz	T-3rd in 1992	5	17	2	1	1	1	2	2	73.41	$18,237.50
Howell Fraser	Winner in 1968	14	51	9	1	1	1	3	8	73.27	$15,053.20
Greg Frederick	T-21st in 1988	3	11	2	0	0	0	1	0	73.36	$3,595.96
Ray Freeman	T-6th in 1986	5	20	5	0	0	3	5	2	72.05	$27,255.46
John Frillman	T-7th in 1971	19	60	5	0	0	1	2	2	75.08	$4,635.44
Bob Fry	T-17th in 1969	2	8	2	0	0	0	2	0	71.38	$1,189.70
Larry Fryer	T-36th in 1976	6	17	1	0	0	0	0	1	75.65	$627.28
Rich Fulkerson	T-69th in 1986	7	22	1	0	0	0	0	1	76.36	$997.00
Dale Fuller	T-4th in 1989	4	14	2	0	1	1	1	2	73.86	$12,700.00
Fred Funk	T-8th in 1986	3	11	2	0	0	1	1	1	73.64	$8,265.00
Bob Gajda	T-42nd in 1968	4	14	2	0	0	0	0	1	74.86	$365.41
Mal Galletta Jr.	T-8th in 1972	10	33	5	0	0	1	2	4	74.27	$5,473.56
Bill Galloway	T-46th in 1977	11	37	4	0	0	0	0	1	75.22	$1,971.04
Bob Galloway	Winner in 1976	10	37	8	1	1	1	4	5	72.84	$23,145.64
Gary Gant	T-23rd in 1981	8	26	2	0	0	0	1	2	75.31	$2,380.00
Mark Gardner	T-34th in 1988	3	10	1	0	0	0	0	0	75.90	$1,255.00
Bill Garrett	T-39th in 1984	8	27	3	0	0	0	0	1	75.33	$1,162.15
John Gentile	Winner in 1978	11	40	7	1	1	1	2	4	73.95	$20,834.04
Ernie George	T-2nd in 1970	10	34	5	1	2	2	2	2	73.94	$10,928.63
Terry George	T-86th in 1970 & '73	6	19	2	0	0	0	0	0	77.26	$338.90
Jim Gerring	T-31st in 1972	6	22	4	0	0	0	0	1	74.77	$1,860.97
Chris Gers	T-24th in 1970	7	21	3	0	0	0	1	3	75.67	$976.47
Robert Gibbons	T-34th in 1988	6	22	4	0	0	0	0	2	73.68	$3,361.50
Fred Gibson	T-43rd in 1986	6	21	3	0	0	0	0	0	73.90	$2,171.00
Bill Giese	T-70th in 1975	4	14	2	0	0	0	0	0	75.36	$296.43

Player	Best Finish	Year	Rounds	Cuts	Top 3	Top 5	Top 10	Top 25	Rds. in 60s	Average	Money
Tom Gieselman	T-88th in 1990	3	10	1	0	0	0	0	2	72.90	$1,002.50
Charles Gilbert	T-63rd in 1969	2	7	1	0	0	0	0	0	74.29	$90.90
Gibby Gilbert	T-2nd in 1987 & '90	5	20	5	2	2	2	2	4	72.35	$38,258.70
Larry Gilbert	Winner in 1981, '82 & '91	20	77	17	7	8	9	12	18	72.00	$145,917.70
Hunt Gilliland	T-28th in 1989	8	28	4	0	0	0	0	3	73.54	$3,980.50
Mike Gilmore	T-57th in 1992	1	4	1	0	0	0	0	0	72.50	$780.00
Robbie Gilmore Jr.	T-14th in 1982	5	18	3	0	0	0	1	2	73.44	$3,940.21
Richard Gilstad	T-84th in 1984	3	10	1	0	0	0	0	0	76.90	$425.00
Roger Ginsberg	T-17th in 1978	8	30	7	0	0	0	2	3	73.40	$5,853.68
Tom Gleeton	Missed Cut in 1993	5	15	0	0	0	0	0	2	74.47	$400.00
Bailey Glenn	T-64th in 1968	3	10	1	0	0	0	0	0	77.30	$88.89
George Glenn	T-40th in 1971	13	43	4	0	0	0	0	2	75.16	$2,120.42
David Glenz	T-3rd in 1986	13	49	10	1	3	5	5	6	72.69	$41,564.69
Randy Glover	T-3rd in 1975	10	37	7	1	1	3	4	6	73.14	$14,453.16
Russell Glover	T-8th in 1977	4	14	2	0	0	1	1	1	74.07	$2,460.70
John Godwin	T-19th in 1992	10	36	6	0	0	0	1	3	74.00	$7,290.28
Bob Goetz	T-46th in 1977	9	29	5	0	0	0	0	4	74.93	$1,017.05
Dick Goetz	T-22nd in 1975	9	29	3	0	0	0	1	1	75.55	$3,475.50
Ted Goin	T-15th in 1989	7	24	3	0	0	0	2	5	73.25	$7,790.14
Deon Good	T-93rd in 1982	3	10	1	0	0	0	0	1	74.90	$209.42
Paul Gooden	T-56th in 1983	3	10	1	0	0	0	0	0	75.60	$277.72
Al Goodrich	T-83rd in 1973	2	7	1	0	0	0	0	0	76.43	$267.47
Lee Goodworth	Missed Cut	4	12	0	0	0	0	0	0	77.75	$0.00
David Gosiewski	T-15th in 1986	4	13	1	0	0	0	1	0	75.46	$4,000.00
Mike Gove	T-15th in 1989	4	16	4	0	0	0	2	3	71.88	$10,467.14
Bob Grant	T-79th in 1970	4	10	1	0	0	0	0	0	76.00	$71.43
Doug Graves	93rd in 1975	3	10	1	0	0	0	0	1	78.20	$225.00
Quinton Gray	T-22nd in 1975	3	10	1	0	0	0	1	0	73.90	$1,170.00
Thomas Gray	T-15th in 1993	4	15	3	0	0	0	1	2	72.00	$6,899.33
Albert Green	T-49th in 1978	6	19	3	0	0	0	0	0	74.58	$696.13
Bob Groff	T-16th in 1988	9	33	6	0	0	0	2	5	72.82	$12,051.00
Gary Groh	T-21st in 1980	12	40	4	0	0	0	2	0	75.15	$12,533.57
Steve Groves	T-13th in 1991	3	10	1	0	0	0	1	1	73.60	$5,721.00
Mark Gurnow	T-10th in 1987	8	28	4	0	0	1	2	0	74.07	$12,529.71
Jon Gustin	T-30th in 1977	7	21	2	0	0	0	0	0	74.76	$972.24
Mark Guttenberg	T-88th in 1981	4	13	1	0	0	0	0	0	76.38	$677.71
J. Banks Guyton	Missed Cut	5	14	0	0	0	0	0	0	76.79	$0.00
Dave Haberle	T-21st in 1980	2	7	1	0	0	0	1	0	73.00	$1,225.00
Ed Habjan	T-81st in 1991	4	13	1	0	0	0	0	2	75.62	$605.00
Hubby Habjan	T-47th in 1971	9	28	3	0	0	0	0	1	75.14	$555.20
Ralph Haddad	Missed Cut	4	12	0	0	0	0	0	0	78.67	$0.00
Bob Haggerty	T-88th in 1971	6	17	1	0	0	0	0	0	77.82	$191.50
Bill Hall	T-13th in 1977	15	48	4	0	0	0	1	0	75.19	$3,645.84
Michael Hamblin	T-39th in 1991	4	14	2	0	0	0	0	3	74.07	$2,336.00
Bill Hamilton	T-79th in 1984	5	16	1	0	0	0	0	0	76.44	$425.00
Bob Hamilton	T-49th in 1968	1	4	1	0	0	0	0	0	72.25	$101.36
Laurie Hammer	Winner in 1977	16	59	11	1	1	1	4	4	74.10	$26,825.20
Phil Hancock	T-3rd in 1989	3	12	3	1	1	1	1	3	71.33	$16,480.00
Kirk Hanefeld	T-36th in 1989	3	11	2	0	0	0	0	0	73.27	$2,072.25
Fred Haney	T-63rd in 1977	3	11	2	0	0	0	0	0	74.09	$467.46
Dick Hanscom	T-32nd in 1970	6	23	5	0	0	0	0	1	73.74	$1,285.17
Gary Hardin	T-35th in 1985	9	31	4	0	0	0	0	3	73.97	$3,726.00
Fred Harkness	T-56 in 1982	5	16	1	0	0	0	0	0	76.69	$209.43
Craig Harmon	T-101st in 1982	8	25	1	0	0	0	0	0	76.44	$609.42
Dick Harmon	T-84th in 1980	5	15	1	0	0	0	0	0	76.40	$230.61
Michael Harmon	T-90th in 1988	3	10	1	0	0	0	0	0	76.10	$565.00
Chandler Harper	Missed Cut	1	2	0	0	0	0	0	0	77.00	$0.00
Lee Harper	T-13th in 1981	4	16	4	0	0	0	1	1	74.13	$3,245.60
Mike Harrigan	T-28th in 1984	12	39	4	0	0	0	0	1	74.92	$2,059.30
Bob Harrison	T-49th in 1978	2	7	1	0	0	0	0	0	74.00	$263.66
Dutch Harrison	T-29th in 1969	2	8	2	0	0	0	0	2	71.88	$802.50
Buddy Harston	T-53rd in 1988	7	23	2	0	0	0	0	2	74.74	$1,777.50
Chuck Hart	T-61st in 1972	7	22	3	0	0	0	0	1	75.68	$644.58
Dick Hart	T-9th in 1968	10	37	8	0	0	1	2	5	73.16	$5,151.55
Scott Hart	T-48th in 1990	4	13	1	0	0	0	0	0	74.77	$912.50
Glen Harvey	T-46th in 1970	3	8	1	0	0	0	0	0	74.75	$120.78
Joe Hasbrouck	T-58th in 1979	3	9	1	0	0	0	0	1	75.11	$256.82
Bob Hauer	T-59th in 1986	5	15	1	0	0	0	0	0	76.07	$637.00
John Hayes	T-43rd in 1990	5	16	1	0	0	0	0	0	73.69	$1,818.00
Gary Head	T-18th in 1984	8	26	2	0	0	0	1	0	75.50	$2,610.00
Steve Heckel	T-36th in 1986	9	28	1	0	0	0	0	1	75.18	$1,821.00
Bobby Heins	T-4th in 1988	11	38	5	0	1	2	3	1	73.95	$19,813.67
Webb Heintzelman	T-34th in 1988	1	4	1	0	0	0	0	0	74.00	$1,255.00
Russell Helwig	T-33rd in 1981	10	31	1	0	0	0	0	0	74.71	$1,612.50
John Hendricks	T-36th in 1990	2	7	1	0	0	0	0	0	73.00	$1,707.14

PGA CLUB PROFESSIONAL CHAMPIONSHIP

Player	Best Finish	Year	Rounds	Cuts	Top 3	Top 5	Top 10	Top 25	Rds. in 60s	Average	Money
Dick Hendrickson	T-13th in 1969 & '81	8	30	6	0	0	0	2	4	73.50	$4,160.73
Geoff Hensley	T-39th in 1984	7	23	2	0	0	0	0	1	75.87	$931.81
Denny Hepler	T-17th in 1990	3	12	3	0	0	0	2	4	70.58	$8,705.50
Frank Herrelko	Missed Cut	4	12	0	0	0	0	0	0	77.17	$0.00
Bob Hibschman	T-103rd in 1982	4	13	1	0	0	0	0	0	77.77	$209.42
Mike Higuera	T-36th in 1976	6	21	3	0	0	0	0	0	74.10	$1,504.74
Dave Hilgenberg	Missed Cut	6	18	0	0	0	0	0	0	76.39	$0.00
Doug Hixson	T-21st in 1991	2	8	2	0	0	0	1	2	70.63	$3,981.33
Jon Hoecker	T-6th in 1992	6	21	3	0	0	1	1	3	73.43	$11,709.00
Dick Hoelzer	T-48th in 1975	4	13	1	0	0	0	0	0	74.62	$262.75
Tony Holguin	T-24th in 1970	10	25	2	0	0	0	1	0	76.68	$608.40
Barry Holt	T-11th in 1983	2	7	1	0	0	0	1	1	74.43	$3,250.00
Fred Holton Jr.	T-43rd in 1986	5	16	1	0	0	0	0	1	74.50	$771.00
Herb Hooper	Missed Cut	4	12	0	0	0	0	0	0	75.25	$0.00
Garry Hopkins	T-12th in 1973	7	21	2	0	0	0	2	0	74.52	$3,004.44
Dick Horgan	Missed Cut	4	12	0	0	0	0	0	1	76.58	$0.00
Jay Horton	T-13th in 1976	7	23	2	0	0	0	1	2	75.26	$2,541.54
John Hoskison	T-19th in 1992	1	4	1	0	0	0	1	1	71.25	$4,125.00
Jennings House	Missed Cut	6	18	0	0	0	0	0	0	75.33	$0.00
Terry Houser	T-71st in 1991	4	14	2	0	0	0	0	1	74.29	$1,090.00
Charles Houts	T-52nd in 1972	3	9	2	0	0	0	0	0	75.22	$429.55
Kyle Howard	T-40th in 1983	4	14	2	0	0	0	0	1	76.07	$1,075.00
Steve Howe	T-88th in 1990	9	28	1	0	0	0	0	1	76.25	$1,002.50
Dick Howell	T-37th in 1970	5	15	1	0	0	0	0	0	76.47	$285.00
Ray Howell	T-61st in 1971	3	12	3	0	0	0	0	1	75.17	$530.40
Gary Howlett	92nd in 1973	5	16	1	0	0	0	0	1	78.56	$267.47
Robert Hoyt	T-11th in 1992	10	38	8	0	0	0	6	7	72.34	$23,886.48
Bob Huber	T-41st in 1979	3	10	1	0	0	0	0	3	74.10	$650.00
Joe Huber	T-78th in 1985	6	19	1	0	0	0	0	1	76.05	$977.00
Pete Huber	T-89th in 1991	1	4	1	0	0	0	0	2	71.75	$572.00
Charles Huckaby	T-69th in 1978	7	22	1	0	0	0	0	1	75.82	$180.70
Cary Hungate	T-15th in 1989	9	32	5	0	0	0	1	3	73.59	$7,855.14
Roy Hunter	T-48th in 1991	4	15	3	0	0	0	0	2	72.93	$2,560.00
Denis Husse	T-6th in 1982	4	13	1	0	0	1	1	1	76.38	$6,500.00
Craig Immel	T-40th in 1983	8	29	5	0	0	0	0	2	74.69	$2,446.25
Jerry Impellittiere	T-41st in 1979	5	18	3	0	0	0	0	1	73.67	$1,518.61
Stu Ingraham	T-8th in 1989	7	27	6	0	0	1	4	5	71.85	$23,355.13
Walker Inman Jr.	T-9th in 1971	7	20	4	0	0	1	2	1	73.55	$3,501.82
Bob Irving	Missed Cut	4	12	0	0	0	0	0	0	77.33	$0.00
Bob Issler	T-41st in 1979	7	24	3	0	0	0	0	0	74.88	$1,063.94
Jeff Jackson	T-34th in 1988	5	16	1	0	0	0	0	0	76.25	$1,655.00
John Jackson Jr.	T-6th in 1980 & '81	11	42	9	0	0	4	5	2	73.24	$29,591.54
Tommy Jacobs	T-6th in 1973	6	21	4	0	0	1	3	2	74.24	$7,284.76
Dick James	T-96th in 1976	4	13	1	0	0	0	0	0	75.00	$183.33
Lynn Janson	T-11th in 1979	12	46	10	0	0	0	6	5	73.57	$15,141.08
John Jasinski	T-71st in 1991	3	11	2	0	0	0	0	1	72.73	$1,330.00
Cass Jawor	T-14th in 1969	14	48	6	0	0	0	1	3	75.15	$2,378.75
Terry Jennings	Missed Cut	7	21	0	0	0	0	0	0	77.29	$400.00
Randy Jensen	T-60th in 1985	2	8	2	0	0	0	0	1	74.25	$1,142.00
Steve Jensen	T-66th in 1985	3	10	1	0	0	0	0	0	76.00	$977.00
Rick Jetter	T-63rd in 1969	5	16	2	0	0	0	0	0	74.44	$162.33
David Jimenez	T-2nd in 1975	8	26	4	1	1	1	3	6	73.04	$13,385.60
Joe Jimenez	T-17th in 1969	12	43	8	0	0	0	3	3	73.70	$3,854.09
Jim Jogue	T-7th in 1973	1	4	1	0	0	1	1	1	72.50	$3,000.00
Drue Johnson	T-18th in 1984	7	24	3	0	0	0	2	1	74.17	$5,855.00
Gene Johnson	102nd in 1970	4	9	1	0	0	0	0	0	80.56	$71.43
Gordon Johnson	T-19th in 1991	7	24	3	0	0	0	1	3	73.08	$6,373.50
Bill Johnston	T-10th in 1970	4	11	1	0	0	1	1	2	73.73	$902.00
Al Jones	T-84th in 1969	6	18	1	0	0	0	0	0	76.27	$90.90
Bob Jones	Missed Cut	6	18	0	0	0	0	0	1	76.39	$0.00
Gregg Jones	T-9th in 1992	9	35	8	0	0	1	5	5	72.51	$24,702.33
John Joseph	T-39th in 1984	11	37	4	0	0	0	0	0	75.27	$1,473.28
Mike Joyce	T-21st in 1972	9	29	2	0	0	0	1	0	75.41	$1,392.47
Tom Joyce	T-21st in 1991	18	62	8	0	0	0	3	4	74.05	$9,335.93
Brad Kai	99th in 1992	6	19	1	0	0	0	0	1	76.05	$955.00
Mike Kallam	T-10th in 1990	12	41	5	0	0	0	2	3	73.85	$11,021.57
Tony Kaloustian	T-12th in 1978	4	14	2	0	0	0	1	2	73.93	$2,405.00
Jim Kane	T-38th in 1992	1	4	1	0	0	0	0	0	72.00	$1,153.33
Rick Karbowski	T-23rd in 1982	2	8	2	0	0	0	1	1	74.25	$2,029.17
Charles Keating	T-13th in 1976	5	16	2	0	0	0	1	1	74.25	$2,344.54
Herman Keiser	T-40th in 1971	2	8	2	0	0	0	0	0	73.50	$598.89
Bob Keller	T-61st in 1971	6	17	1	0	0	0	0	1	76.12	$191.50
Tony Kelley	Missed Cut	4	12	0	0	0	0	0	1	77.83	$400.00
Al Kelley Jr.	T-15th in 1970	14	47	5	0	0	0	1	2	75.02	$2,196.72
Paul Kelly	T-37th in 1970	3	9	1	0	0	0	0	1	75.33	$285.00
Paul Kemps	T-52nd in 1990	3	10	1	0	0	0	0	0	74.20	$830.00

Player	Best Finish	Year	Rounds	Cuts	Top 3	Top 5	Top 10	Top 25	Rds. in 60s	Average	Money
Dave Kendall	T-47th in 1992	6	19	1	0	0	0	0	1	75.47	$891.00
Bill Kennedy	T-39th in 1991	9	33	6	0	0	0	0	5	73.94	$2,860.17
Roger Kennedy	T-5th in 1979	11	41	8	0	1	2	2	1	73.90	$12,948.05
Darrell Kestner	T-7th in 1990	7	27	6	0	0	1	5	6	71.78	$31,831.57
Jack Kiefer	T-12th in 1975	7	25	4	0	0	0	2	2	73.56	$6,765.82
Jim Kiely	T-16th in 1981	1	4	1	0	0	0	1	1	73.75	$1,900.00
Bill King	T-16th in 1988	7	24	3	0	0	0	1	1	73.50	$6,626.00
Claude King	T-17th in 1969	6	18	3	0	0	0	1	1	74.83	$1,463.33
Jim King	T-6th in 1982	6	23	5	0	0	1	4	2	73.13	$12,512.50
Larry King	T-63rd in 1983	7	23	2	0	0	0	0	0	76.75	$1,102.72
Frank Kiraly	T-32nd in 1968	2	6	1	0	0	0	0	1	72.33	$352.50
John Kirchner	T-32nd in 1982	3	10	1	0	0	0	0	1	74.30	$850.00
Don Klein	T-49th in 1968	5	15	2	0	0	0	0	2	74.53	$172.79
Bob Klein Jr.	T-32nd in 1987	6	20	2	0	0	0	0	1	74.45	$2,862.00
Darrel Knicely	T-92nd in 1978	5	15	1	0	0	0	0	0	79.07	$180.70
Charles Knowles	T-85th in 1971	3	10	1	0	0	0	0	0	74.90	$191.50
Harold Kolb	T-79th in 1974	5	16	1	0	0	0	0	0	76.38	$165.00
Mike Korich	T-46th in 1969	2	5	1	0	0	0	0	1	73.60	$140.41
Joe Kotlarczyk	T-73rd in 1968	3	9	1	0	0	0	0	0	76.78	$88.89
Mike Krak	T-12th in 1968	2	6	1	0	0	0	1	1	72.00	$875.00
Kurt Kretchman	T-85th in 1983	4	13	1	0	0	0	0	0	78.08	$277.71
Phil Krick	Missed Cut	7	20	0	0	0	0	0	0	76.90	$0.00
Ken Krieger	T-30th in 1992	5	14	1	0	0	0	0	1	73.21	$2,150.00
Ed Kroll	T-32nd in 1968 & '70	10	33	5	0	0	0	0	5	74.82	$1,243.38
Wally Kuchar	T-34th in 1988	2	8	2	0	0	0	0	0	74.38	$1,852.00
Mike Labauve	94th in 1987	6	19	1	0	0	0	0	0	76.68	$505.00
Ralph Landrum	T-9th in 1988	5	18	3	0	0	1	2	2	73.94	$14,271.00
Eddie Langert	T-57th in 1970	4	12	1	0	0	0	0	1	76.00	$71.43
John Langford	T-42nd in 1972	7	22	2	0	0	0	0	0	74.64	$499.81
George Lanning	T-2nd in 1976	8	25	1	1	1	1	1	2	74.80	$7,700.00
Larry Laoretti	T-96th in 1976	6	16	1	0	0	0	0	0	77.06	$183.33
Chuck Lasher	T-80th in 1980	5	16	1	0	0	0	0	0	76.06	$230.61
Duff Lawrence	Missed Cut	5	14	0	0	0	0	0	1	76.43	$0.00
Mike Lawrence	T-4th in 1990	4	15	3	0	1	1	1	2	72.33	$14,639.33
Bob Leaver	T-16th in 1985	10	39	9	0	0	0	1	4	74.05	$7,919.52
Emory Lee	T-67th in 1976	4	14	2	0	0	0	0	2	75.29	$393.97
John Lee	2nd in 1993	2	7	1	1	1	1	1	2	71.29	$22,400.00
Richard Lee	T-85th in 1983	4	13	1	0	0	0	0	0	77.08	$277.71
Bruce Lehnhard	T-3rd in 1988	13	44	6	1	1	1	4	5	73.02	$33,669.85
Charles Leider	T-41st in 1969	6	18	2	0	0	0	0	1	75.44	$326.43
Bob Lendzion	Winner in 1986	12	44	8	1	2	2	4	5	72.95	$47,433.14
Gordon Leslie	T-27th in 1976	5	18	3	0	0	0	0	0	73.94	$1,431.34
Perry Leslie	T-17th in 1979	4	12	1	0	0	0	1	1	75.42	$1,433.33
Tim Leslie	T-59th in 1975	3	10	1	0	0	0	0	0	76.70	$225.00
Ron Letellier	T-2nd in 1971	4	15	3	1	2	2	3	3	71.27	$15,108.00
David Levine	Missed Cut	4	12	0	0	0	0	0	0	75.00	$800.00
Rick Lewallen	T-49th in 1989	3	12	3	0	0	0	0	2	73.00	$2,201.66
J.L. Lewis	T-10th in 1993	2	8	2	0	0	1	2	2	70.63	$10,745.00
Jack Lewis	T-2nd in 1979	6	24	6	1	1	1	3	2	72.83	$21,578.88
John Lewis	T-48th in 1991	1	4	1	0	0	0	0	2	70.25	$815.00
Babe Lichardus	T-4th in 1971 & '72	8	29	5	0	3	3	3	4	72.41	$15,342.50
Keith Liedes	T-48th in 1991	1	4	1	0	0	0	0	2	70.25	$815.00
Tom Liljeholm	T-21st in 1973	4	10	1	0	0	0	1	0	75.20	$1,121.82
Dean Lind	T-66th in 1974	5	15	1	0	0	0	0	0	75.20	$165.00
Gary Lindeblad	Missed Cut	4	12	0	0	0	0	0	0	75.75	$0.00
John Lindert	T-66th in 1985	5	17	2	0	0	0	0	2	74.35	$1,234.50
Ken Lindsay	T-56 in 1977	7	23	2	0	0	0	0	1	74.57	$375.64
Don Lindsey	Missed Cut	4	11	0	0	0	0	0	0	79.18	$0.00
Victor Lipscomb	T-23rd in 1982	8	27	3	0	0	0	1	1	74.93	$3,022.36
Al Littleton	Missed Cut	5	13	0	0	0	0	0	0	76.54	$0.00
John Lively	T-8th in 1974	8	24	2	0	0	1	1	0	75.46	$2,554.54
Gary Lockie	Missed Cut	7	16	0	0	0	0	0	0	76.94	$0.00
Rodney Loesch	T-33rd in 1981	3	12	3	0	0	0	0	0	75.17	$1,446.92
Jim Logue	T-4th in 1982	13	47	8	0	1	2	3	1	74.66	$17,678.30
Carl Lohren	T-27th in 1976	12	44	9	0	0	0	0	1	73.70	$3,227.00
Nelson Long Jr.	Missed Cut	5	15	0	0	0	0	0	0	74.33	$0.00
Francisco Lopez	T-37th in 1970	3	11	2	0	0	0	0	1	74.64	$373.89
Joe Lopez Jr.	T-67th in 1981	5	15	1	0	0	0	0	0	75.93	$277.72
Jim Loque	T-66th in 1979	1	4	1	0	0	0	0	0	72.50	$256.82
Dick Lotz	T-14th in 1985	4	15	3	0	0	0	2	2	73.93	$6,517.00
Gary Loustalot	T-32nd in 1968	3	10	2	0	0	0	0	2	73.00	$443.40
Davis Love Jr.	T-21st in 1973	5	17	4	0	0	0	1	2	73.12	$1,774.69
Larry Lowery	Missed Cut	5	13	0	0	0	0	0	0	76.54	$0.00
Bobby Loy	Missed Cut	5	14	0	0	0	0	0	1	75.07	$0.00
Richard Loy	Missed Cut	5	15	0	0	0	0	0	0	74.73	$400.00
Dino Lucchesi	T-48th in 1991	2	7	1	0	0	0	0	2	74.14	$1,215.00

PGA CLUB PROFESSIONAL CHAMPIONSHIP

Player	Best Finish	Year	Rounds	Cuts	Top 3	Top 5	Top 10	Top 25	Rds. in 60s	Average	Money
Jim Lucius	T-36th in 1976	8	28	4	0	0	0	0	1	74.68	$1,103.42
Jack Lumpkin	T-101st in 1976	7	20	1	0	0	0	0	0	75.90	$183.33
Jay Lumpkin	Winner in 1987	7	24	3	1	1	1	1	2	74.08	$32,008.00
David Lundstrom	T-98th in 1989	3	10	1	0	0	0	0	0	73.80	$965.00
Tom Lupinacci	T-66th in 1974	3	10	1	0	0	0	0	0	75.80	$165.00
Rick Lweallen	T-70th in 1993	1	4	1	0	0	0	0	1	72.00	$665.00
Keith Lyford	T-44th in 1987	1	4	1	0	0	0	0	1	72.75	$788.00
Steve Lyles	T-28th in 1975	16	54	7	0	0	0	0	3	75.56	$2,940.73
Denny Lyons	T-7th in 1972	14	45	5	0	0	2	4	3	74.47	$8,691.54
Jack MacConachie	T-11th in 1979	1	4	1	0	0	0	1	0	70.75	$1,950.00
Bruce MacDonald	T-31st in 1980	3	9	2	0	0	0	0	0	75.00	$1,317.22
Doug MacDonald	T-54th in 1969	2	6	1	0	0	0	0	0	73.83	$90.90
Baker Maddera	T-27th in 1991	7	25	4	0	0	0	0	1	74.44	$3,019.64
Don Maddox	T-32nd in 1982	9	32	5	0	0	0	0	1	75.28	$3,445.21
Scott Mahlberg	T-21st in 1991	9	31	4	0	0	0	2	6	73.13	$7,228.84
Mac Main	T-32nd in 1973	5	16	1	0	0	0	0	0	76.56	$791.11
Bill Majure	T-88th in 1979	8	24	2	0	0	0	0	1	75.21	$821.81
Bob Makoski	T-23rd in 1987	5	19	4	0	0	0	1	2	73.21	$4,522.25
Mike Malaska	T-39th in 1987	7	24	3	0	0	0	0	1	75.17	$1,730.98
Joe Mance	T-56 in 1974	3	8	1	0	0	0	0	0	75.13	$165.00
Larry Mancour	T-16th in 1971	9	30	3	0	0	0	2	2	74.77	$3,172.50
Bob Mann	T-7th in 1988	9	33	6	0	0	1	2	1	73.45	$17,794.00
David Marad	T-49th in 1980	5	16	2	0	0	0	0	1	74.69	$446.55
Eli Marovich	Missed Cut	5	10	0	0	0	0	0	0	76.10	$0.00
Fran Marrello	T-21st in 1990	6	21	3	0	0	0	1	4	72.62	$5,774.43
Jim Marshall	T-10th in 1981	5	18	3	0	0	1	1	1	73.56	$3,973.09
Elroy Marti	T-73rd in 1968	2	6	1	0	0	0	0	1	75.00	$88.89
Richard Martin	Missed Cut	4	12	0	0	0	0	0	0	76.67	$400.00
Bruce Martins	Missed Cut	5	15	0	0	0	0	0	0	76.80	$0.00
Milon Marusic	T-43rd in 1980	7	20	2	0	0	0	0	0	74.85	$875.25
Don Massengale	Winner in 1972	9	33	6	2	2	3	4	4	74.33	$28,726.29
James Masserio	T-21st in 1990	4	14	2	0	0	0	1	3	73.00	$4,360.43
Odell Massey	T-8th in 1974	5	16	2	0	0	1	1	0	74.06	$2,748.46
Ken Mast	T-12th in 1975	5	17	2	0	0	0	1	2	73.41	$2,056.82
Pete Mathews	T-59th in 1993	1	4	1	0	0	0	0	0	71.75	$760.00
Chuck Matlack	T-49th in 1968	5	14	1	0	0	0	0	1	75.14	$101.37
David Matthews	Missed Cut	4	12	0	0	0	0	0	0	74.25	$400.00
Bill Mattingly III	T-91st in 1987	6	19	1	0	0	0	0	1	75.47	$505.00
John Maurycy	T-68th in 1971	5	15	1	0	0	0	0	0	76.60	$191.50
Billy Maxwell	T-30th in 1974	1	4	1	0	0	0	0	0	73.75	$857.78
John Mazza	T-57th in 1992	2	7	1	0	0	0	0	1	73.14	$780.00
Scotty McBeath	T-40th in 1971	6	23	5	0	0	0	0	2	74.22	$991.83
Rives McBee	Winner in 1973	15	50	9	2	3	4	5	6	73.64	$34,354.17
Dick McClean	T-59th in 1986	7	23	4	0	0	0	0	2	74.74	$3,189.50
Jack McConachie	T-32nd in 1982	5	16	1	0	0	0	0	0	75.81	$1,250.00
James McCoy	T-81st in 1972	6	18	2	0	0	0	0	0	75.11	$369.54
Joe McDermott	T-33rd in 1981	3	10	1	0	0	0	0	0	75.10	$812.50
Ken McDonald	T-27th in 1991	3	11	2	0	0	0	0	3	71.91	$2,965.00
Ron McDougal	Winner in 1992	3	12	3	3	3	3	3	9	68.25	$64,300.00
Shawn McEntee	T-4th in 1988	5	19	4	0	1	1	2	3	72.21	$17,581.03
Bob McFerren	99th in 1980	4	13	1	0	0	0	0	0	76.85	$230.61
Jeff McGill	T-49th in 1980	5	18	3	0	0	0	0	0	75.61	$753.00
Michael McGinnis	Missed Cut in 1985	6	17	0	0	0	0	0	0	77.47	$0.00
Randy McGohan	T-47th in 1992	1	4	1	0	0	0	0	1	72.25	$891.00
Jack McKelvey	T-20th in 1986	5	16	1	0	0	0	1	0	75.13	$2,518.00
Ted McKenzie	T-43rd in 1980	7	24	4	0	0	0	0	0	74.54	$1,213.14
George McKeown	T-32nd in 1968	7	24	3	0	0	0	0	2	74.42	$752.49
Jim McLean	T-67th in 1989	8	26	2	0	0	0	0	3	74.81	$1,265.00
Jeff McMillen	T-85th in 1993	6	19	1	0	0	0	0	2	74.11	$1,007.50
Mal McMullen	T-63rd in 1977	8	27	3	0	0	0	0	1	75.74	$624.58
Frank Mellet	Missed Cut in 1993	4	12	0	0	0	0	0	0	74.92	$800.00
Al Mengert	T-18th in 1968	5	16	3	0	0	0	1	2	73.63	$1,222.56
Allan Menne	T-52nd in 1990	2	7	1	0	0	0	0	2	73.14	$1,230.00
Bob Menne	T-2nd in 1987	12	41	7	1	1	1	4	3	74.07	$21,466.85
Eddie Merrins	T-10th in 1970	6	21	4	0	0	1	2	1	73.48	$1,719.27
Rick Meskell	T-21st in 1988	4	14	2	0	0	0	1	1	74.43	$3,643.46
Denny Meyer	T-13th in 1974	2	8	2	0	0	0	1	0	73.00	$2,773.67
Mark Mielke	T-30th in 1992	2	8	2	0	0	0	0	1	71.75	$2,510.00
Tony Milam	T-36th in 1986	4	14	2	0	0	0	0	2	73.90	$1,887.00
Eldridge Miles	T-14th in 1969	8	28	5	0	0	0	1	3	74.04	$1,649.55
John Miles	Missed Cut	4	12	0	0	0	0	0	0	77.75	$0.00
Bill Miller	Missed Cut	5	15	0	0	0	0	0	1	75.53	$0.00
Glen Miller	Missed Cut	4	12	0	0	0	0	0	0	78.67	$400.00
Lindy Miller	T-8th in 1986	8	29	5	0	0	1	2	4	72.97	$17,583.75
Chuck Milne	Missed Cut	8	22	0	0	0	0	0	1	74.59	$0.00
Dennis Milne	T-61st in 1972	9	29	4	0	0	0	0	1	75.48	$913.27

PGA CLUB PROFESSIONAL CHAMPIONSHIP

Player	Best Finish	Year	Rounds	Cuts	Top 3	Top 5	Top 10	Top 25	Rds. in 60s	Average	Money
Bobby Mitchell	T-29th in 1983	1	4	1	0	0	0	0	0	74.50	$971.43
Chris Mitchell	T-21st in 1988	7	26	5	0	0	0	1	0	74.15	$5,272.46
Randol Mitchell	Missed Cut	4	12	0	0	0	0	0	1	74.83	$400.00
Frank Mize	T-16th in 1973	1	4	1	0	0	0	1	1	73.25	$1,536.67
Ed Moehling	T-16th in 1968	1	4	1	0	0	0	1	2	71.00	$715.00
John Molenda	T-3rd in 1973	18	66	12	1	2	2	3	6	74.11	$13,550.45
Larry Moncour	T-9th in 1973	3	10	2	0	0	1	2	2	73.10	$4,033.33
Lloyd Monroe	T-12th in 1978	12	38	2	0	0	0	2	3	74.47	$3,054.44
Ray Montgomery	T-21st in 1973	8	22	2	0	0	0	1	1	75.00	$1,384.57
Ralph Montoya	T-75th in 1986	11	32	1	0	0	0	0	1	76.03	$567.00
Jim Mooney	T-28th in 1970	7	21	2	0	0	0	0	1	74.71	$546.39
Paul Moran	T-28th in 1981	3	11	2	0	0	0	0	1	73.91	$1,402.50
Bob Moreland	T-23rd in 1981	10	32	2	0	0	0	1	1	74.94	$2,117.50
Steve Moreland	T-85th in 1989	5	16	1	0	0	0	0	2	73.63	$1,374.37
Jay Morelli	T-67th in 1976	2	7	1	0	0	0	0	1	76.14	$183.33
Paul Moren	T-22nd in 1975	1	4	1	0	0	0	1	1	72.75	$1,170.00
Joe Moresco	T-31st in 1980	6	20	3	0	0	0	0	2	74.95	$1,729.22
Tony Morosco	Missed Cut	4	8	0	0	0	0	0	0	76.00	$0.00
Kevin Morris	T-4th in 1985	10	37	7	0	1	2	4	3	73.54	$23,603.65
Wayne Morris	T-11th in 1972	8	28	4	0	0	0	1	3	73.89	$3,099.18
Rick Morton	T-2nd in 1988	3	10	1	1	1	1	1	1	73.70	$20,000.00
Kelley Moser	T-79th in 1984	3	10	1	0	0	0	0	0	76.70	$425.00
Jerry Mowlds	T-10th in 1968	6	20	3	0	0	1	1	2	74.00	$1,383.33
Larry Mowry	T-17th in 1976	1	4	1	0	0	0	1	0	71.75	$1,408.00
Michael Moyers	T-44th in 1987	5	17	2	0	0	0	0	1	74.71	$1,805.50
Mike Muranyi	91st in 1983	10	31	1	0	0	0	0	1	76.10	$677.71
Bill Murchison	T-56th in 1986	4	14	2	0	0	0	0	2	73.00	$1,377.00
Dan Murphy	T-4th in 1983	13	46	8	0	1	1	2	5	74.35	$10,577.10
Dick Murphy	T-68th in 1971	8	29	5	0	0	0	0	3	75.10	$1,449.92
Dennis Murray	T-109 in 1982	4	13	1	0	0	0	0	0	77.38	$209.42
Auggie Navarro	T-70th in 1975	6	19	1	0	0	0	0	0	76.47	$225.00
John Neese	T-75th in 1972	5	16	1	0	0	0	0	0	75.31	$204.54
Dick Nelson	Missed Cut in 1984	6	18	0	0	0	0	0	0	77.28	$0.00
John Nelson	T-30th in 1992	3	10	1	0	0	0	0	1	72.70	$1,750.00
Rocky Nelson	T-66th in 1985	6	19	1	0	0	0	0	0	75.26	$977.00
David Nevatt	T-72nd in 1987	6	21	3	0	0	0	0	0	74.29	$2,190.00
Dwight Nevil	T-14th in 1985 & '87	7	25	4	0	0	0	3	2	74.04	$12,405.50
Gary Nicholas	T-37th in 1975	2	7	1	0	0	0	0	0	73.57	$594.54
Robert W. Nichols	T-31st in 1976	11	35	5	0	0	0	0	3	74.66	$3,043.55
John Nichols Jr.	T-31st in 1980	11	35	2	0	0	0	0	1	75.89	$1,148.13
Bob Nieberding	T-35th in 1980	4	15	3	0	0	0	0	0	73.93	$1,245.92
Lonnie Nielsen	T-5th in 1987	8	31	7	0	1	2	7	7	71.61	$37,563.96
Tom Nielsen	Missed Cut	7	17	0	0	0	0	0	0	76.82	$0.00
Tom Nieporte	T-16th in 1974	10	35	5	0	0	0	3	2	73.80	$4,807.36
Rod Nuckolls	T-31st in 1993	6	19	1	0	0	0	0	1	73.79	$1,980.00
Andy Nusbaum	T-79th in 1974	6	19	1	0	0	0	0	0	75.37	$165.00
Patrick O'Brien	T-23rd in 1993	8	23	2	0	0	0	1	0	74.96	$3,412.50
Jim O'Hern	T-8th in 1984	15	51	7	0	0	2	3	7	74.00	$8,905.20
Ted O'Rourke	T-63rd in 1990	5	16	1	0	0	0	0	0	77.63	$730.56
Pete Oakley	T-3rd in 1993	9	33	6	1	1	1	3	3	73.61	$22,763.00
Alvin Odom Jr.	T-37th in 1975	4	15	3	0	0	0	0	0	75.20	$990.16
Bill Ogden	T-3rd in 1969	7	26	5	1	1	1	1	3	74.38	$4,406.26
Ed Oldfield	T-49th in 1983	6	18	2	0	0	0	0	0	75.00	$444.87
Steve Oppermann	T-41st in 1979	6	19	1	0	0	0	0	1	74.42	$650.00
Rick Osberg	T-3rd in 1984	7	25	4	1	1	2	3	2	73.64	$20,679.64
Gary Ostrega	T-2nd in 1984	6	21	3	1	1	1	1	3	73.33	$17,937.00
Scott Oulds	T-20th in 1986	7	22	1	0	0	0	1	0	76.58	$2,518.00
Buddy Overholser	Missed Cut	3	9	0	0	0	0	0	0	74.56	$0.00
Jay Overton	T-3rd in 1978	14	55	13	1	1	2	6	10	72.55	$33,522.58
Carl Owen	T-41st in 1973	8	25	1	0	0	0	0	1	77.04	$512.50
Roy Pace	T-31st in 1976	5	16	1	0	0	0	0	0	75.19	$890.00
Don Padgett III	T-2nd in 1981	16	59	11	2	3	4	4	4	73.63	$33,912.63
John Paesani	T-14th in 1987	7	25	4	0	0	0	1	3	73.68	$6,895.00
Paul Parajeckas	T-92nd in 1983	9	28	1	0	0	0	0	1	76.43	$1,077.71
Bill Parker	T-23rd in 1969	10	39	9	0	0	0	1	1	73.97	$2,566.10
Mike Parrish	T-73rd in 1982	3	10	1	0	0	0	0	0	75.20	$1,009.43
Jimmy Paschal	T-81st in 1988	6	21	3	0	0	0	0	2	74.67	$1,352.57
Benny Passons	T-21st in 1990	13	48	9	0	0	0	1	4	73.19	$10,757.36
Bob Payne	T-49th in 1980	6	20	2	0	0	0	0	0	75.35	$475.28
Dick Pearce	T-89th in 1977	2	6	1	0	0	0	0	0	76.83	$210.63
Chris Peddicord	T-11th in 1992	2	7	1	0	0	0	1	2	72.86	$6,566.67
Bill Pelham	T-23rd in 1979	1	4	1	0	0	0	1	1	71.25	$1,077.50
Harold Perry Jr	T-13th in 1991	6	22	4	0	0	0	1	4	73.41	$7,605.75
Billy Peterson	T-68th in 1984	6	20	2	0	0	0	0	1	74.40	$1,037.50
Randy Peterson	T-57th in 1992	2	8	2	0	0	0	0	1	73.13	$1,392.50
Jim Petralia	T-36th in 1986	6	19	1	0	0	0	0	0	75.53	$1,021.00

Player	Best Finish	Year	Rounds	Cuts	Top 3	Top 5	Top 10	Top 25	Rds. in 60s	Average	Money
Bobby Phillips	T-25th in 1978	8	27	2	0	0	0	1	3	74.56	$2,264.81
John Phillips	T-84th in 1985	5	16	1	0	0	0	0	1	77.19	$977.00
Dave Philo	T-7th in 1981	6	16	2	0	0	1	2	0	75.13	$6,798.09
Ron Philo Jr.	T-23rd in 1993	2	7	1	0	0	0	1	2	70.75	$2,737.50
Jim Picard	T-10th in 1976	8	30	6	0	0	1	2	1	73.47	$4,430.25
Drew Pierson	T-18th in 1972	5	17	2	0	0	0	1	1	74.59	$1,539.41
Bob Pipkin	T-65th in 1973	3	10	1	0	0	0	0	0	75.70	$267.47
Jerry Pittman	T-25th in 1972	4	12	2	0	0	0	1	0	74.17	$1,242.47
Bob Placido	Missed Cut	5	15	0	0	0	0	0	0	77.20	$0.00
Carl Poche	T-14th in 1987	2	7	1	0	0	0	1	2	71.71	$4,300.00
Richard Poe	Missed Cut	5	15	0	0	0	0	0	0	77.40	$0.00
Eric Pohl	Missed Cut	4	12	0	0	0	0	0	0	76.67	$400.00
Bobby Pollitt	Missed Cut	5	15	0	0	0	0	0	0	76.00	$400.00
Bobby Pomeroy	T-37th in 1975	7	20	2	0	0	0	0	2	76.00	$775.24
John Poole	T-63rd in 1977	2	7	1	0	0	0	0	0	75.71	$210.64
Adolph Popp	T-30th in 1974	6	18	2	0	0	0	0	0	74.72	$1,088.38
Bob Popp	Missed Cut	7	20	0	0	0	0	0	0	76.45	$0.00
Robert Post Jr.	T-69th in 1978	4	13	1	0	0	0	0	0	75.31	$180.70
Jimmy Powell	T-6th in 1969	11	42	9	0	0	2	4	5	73.00	$8,893.41
Mickey Powell	T-4th in 1970	2	8	2	0	1	1	1	0	72.50	$1,849.23
Ed Powers	T-85th in 1976	2	7	1	0	0	0	0	0	76.00	$183.33
Art Proctor	T-3rd in 1977	14	46	5	1	1	1	1	2	75.43	$8,998.53
Dean Prowse	T-57th in 1992	2	7	1	0	0	0	0	2	72.00	$780.00
Steve Prugh	T-71st in 1983	5	16	1	0	0	0	0	0	75.81	$277.72
Earl Puckett	T-28th in 1975	10	29	2	0	0	0	0	1	75.03	$1,064.56
Randy Quick	T-68th in 1968	3	12	3	0	0	0	0	2	74.75	$364.86
Dana Quigley	T-3rd in 1986	8	30	6	1	1	1	3	4	72.47	$21,379.33
Sammy Rachels	T-2nd in 1992	4	16	4	1	2	3	3	5	70.88	$43,714.17
Norman Rack	Missed Cut	4	11	0	0	0	0	0	0	77.55	$0.00
Dave Ragan	T-16th in 1981	2	7	1	0	0	0	1	1	75.29	$1,900.00
Bob Ralston	T-49th in 1993	5	18	3	0	0	0	0	1	74.39	$1,627.82
Steve Ralston	Missed Cut	5	15	0	0	0	0	0	0	75.60	$400.00
Ross Randall	T-16th in 1981	10	38	8	0	0	0	3	3	73.92	$7,785.03
Dick Rautmann	T-49th in 1973	2	7	1	0	0	0	0	0	75.43	$267.47
Pat Rea	Missed Cut	4	11	0	0	0	0	0	1	74.36	$0.00
Mike Reasor	Missed Cut	7	20	0	0	0	0	0	1	76.65	$0.00
John Rech	T-92nd in 1978	9	29	2	0	0	0	0	0	76.59	$411.31
Alex Redmond	T-75th in 1986	9	27	2	0	0	0	0	0	76.59	$657.90
Barry Redmond	T-31st in 1993	6	22	4	0	0	0	0	2	72.82	$3,640.00
Don Reese	T-44th in 1988	1	4	1	0	0	0	0	0	74.25	$883.34
Dean Refram	T-5th in 1978	3	10	2	0	1	1	2	2	72.10	$4,647.62
Howard Reid	T-49th in 1978	5	16	1	0	0	0	0	0	75.25	$263.66
Bob Reith	T-91st in 1970	3	10	1	0	0	0	0	0	76.90	$71.43
Larry Rentz	T-38th in 1992	4	15	3	0	0	0	0	4	72.33	$2,618.33
Sam Reynolds	T-86th in 1973	4	13	2	0	0	0	0	0	76.62	$338.90
Ron Rhoads	T-96th in 1976	3	10	1	0	0	0	0	0	75.60	$183.33
Don Richards	T-59th in 1975	5	16	1	0	0	0	0	0	76.44	$225.00
Sonny Ridenhour	T-29th in 1968	8	23	3	0	0	0	0	1	74.43	$1,320.63
Skee Riegel	T-60th in 1968	4	13	1	0	0	0	0	0	76.38	$88.89
Jim Riggins	T-45th in 1974	5	14	1	0	0	0	0	0	74.93	$300.45
Larry Ringer	T-17th in 1976, '77, '78 & '79	6	23	5	0	0	0	4	6	72.78	$5,958.20
Lee Rinker	T-10th in 1991	4	14	2	0	0	1	2	3	71.43	$12,425.00
Rich Ritter	T-68th in 1992	3	10	1	0	0	0	0	0	77.70	$689.00
Dave Roberts	T-96th in 1992	2	7	1	0	0	0	0	0	74.14	$972.50
Don Robertson	T-36th in 1989	3	10	1	0	0	0	0	1	74.10	$1,181.25
Tom Robertson	T-8th in 1982	6	22	4	0	0	1	1	1	74.18	$5,189.04
Bill Robinson	T-9th in 1971	14	45	3	0	0	1	1	2	74.73	$2,931.47
Dave Robinson	T-99th in 1974	3	10	1	0	0	0	0	0	76.00	$165.00
Gary Robinson	T-4th in 1981	16	52	6	0	1	2	3	5	74.40	$16,053.41
Gary Robison	T-11th in 1988	10	32	4	0	0	0	2	1	73.69	$17,853.57
Bill Rogers	Missed Cut	1	3	0	0	0	0	0	0	83.67	$0.00
Ken Roper	Missed Cut	8	21	0	0	0	0	0	0	77.29	$0.00
Bob Rosburg	Winner in 1969	2	8	2	2	2	2	2	4	68.88	$11,900.00
Dennis Rose	Missed Cut	6	18	0	0	0	0	0	0	76.78	$400.00
Myron "Hap" Rose	Missed Cut	4	10	0	0	0	0	0	0	77.60	$0.00
Lynn Rosely	T-81st in 1975	10	32	2	0	0	0	0	1	76.78	$902.71
Thom Rosely	Missed Cut	6	18	0	0	0	0	0	0	78.67	$0.00
Bob Ross	Missed Cut	8	23	0	0	0	0	0	0	76.43	$0.00
Jeffrey Roth	Winner in 1993	7	26	5	2	2	2	2	7	72.62	$52,197.14
Melvin Rowe	Missed Cut	4	10	0	0	0	0	0	0	76.40	$0.00
Hugh Royer	T-17th in 1978	3	11	2	0	0	0	1	2	73.45	$1,564.59
Ed Rubis	T-75th in 1969	5	15	1	0	0	0	0	0	76.27	$90.90
John Ruedi	T-61st in 1971	7	20	1	0	0	0	0	1	76.05	$191.50
Stacy Russell	T-63rd in 1984	3	10	2	0	0	0	0	0	75.60	$702.72
Paul Ryiz	T-36th in 1986	5	18	3	0	0	0	0	1	74.56	$2,373.72
Ed Sabo	T-32nd in 1991	7	26	5	0	0	0	0	2	74.31	$3,538.48

Player	Best Finish	Year	Rounds	Cuts	Top 3	Top 5	Top 10	Top 25	Rds. in 60s	Average	Money
Gene Samborsky	Missed Cut	6	18	0	0	0	0	0	1	75.83	$0.00
Monte Sanders	T-54th in 1971	6	18	2	0	0	0	0	1	75.11	$262.93
Tommy Sanderson	T-17th in 1969	2	8	2	0	0	0	1	0	72.13	$885.15
Mike San Filippo	T-4th in 1991	9	35	8	0	1	1	2	5	72.14	$26,357.50
Tony Saraceno	Missed Cut	4	12	0	0	0	0	0	0	76.17	$800.00
Tom Sargent	Missed Cut	5	15	0	0	0	0	0	0	77.67	$800.00
Dick Sarta	Missed Cut	6	18	0	0	0	0	0	0	76.94	$0.00
Steve Satterstrom	Missed Cut	4	12	0	0	0	0	0	0	76.83	$0.00
Mark Scallen	T-63rd in 1983	3	8	1	0	0	0	0	0	76.25	$277.72
Chuck Scally	T-17th in 1969	12	39	5	0	0	0	2	2	74.67	$2,184.70
Bill Scarborough	Missed Cut	5	12	0	0	0	0	0	0	79.33	$0.00
Ken Schall	T-28th in 1990	4	16	4	0	0	0	0	2	72.63	$5,493.75
Herman Scharlau	T-46th in 1969	5	16	2	0	0	0	0	0	75.19	$229.30
Brad Schiefelbein	Missed Cut	7	19	0	0	0	0	0	0	76.74	$0.00
Art Schilling	T-41st in 1982	7	22	1	0	0	0	0	0	75.77	$675.00
Mike Schlueter	T-19th in 1985	10	36	6	0	0	0	3	2	73.53	$6,746.28
Ron Schmedemann	Missed Cut	5	15	0	0	0	0	0	0	76.73	$0.00
George Schneiter	Missed Cut	5	13	0	0	0	0	0	0	79.46	$0.00
Curt Schnell	T-22nd in 1989	3	11	2	0	0	0	1	2	72.36	$4,675.00
Bob Schoener	T-31st in 1972	5	15	2	0	0	0	0	0	75.93	$1,016.50
Willard Scholl	T-35th in 1972	6	19	2	0	0	0	0	1	73.95	$840.70
Kirk Schooley	T-93rd in 1993	3	10	1	0	0	0	0	2	73.10	$575.50
John Schoonover	T-62nd in 1991	2	7	1	0	0	0	0	1	72.43	$1,105.00
Michael Schuchart	T-6th in 1992	2	8	2	0	0	2	2	4	68.88	$19,000.00
Bill Schumaker	Winner in 1984	15	52	7	1	1	2	2	2	73.60	$34,904.39
Ed Schumann	T-81st in 1971	8	24	1	0	0	0	0	1	77.71	$191.50
Pat Schwab	T-12th in 1975	11	39	7	0	0	0	3	5	74.51	$4,257.66
Paul Scodeller	T-12th in 1968	5	18	4	0	0	0	1	3	73.56	$1,710.32
Art Scott	T-56 in 1981	4	13	1	0	0	0	0	0	76.69	$277.72
Bert Seagraves	T-83rd in 1973	4	13	1	0	0	0	0	1	74.85	$267.47
Jim Seeley	T-9th in 1973	3	11	2	0	0	1	1	1	74.18	$2,463.94
Bill Sellers	T-43rd in 1981	3	10	1	0	0	0	0	0	75.80	$525.55
Ed Selser	T-78th in 1985	5	17	2	0	0	0	0	0	75.12	$1,184.50
Jack Seltzer	T-3rd in 1982	15	56	11	1	1	1	2	2	73.86	$19,252.73
Dick Shaiper	T-45th in 1974	5	17	3	0	0	0	0	0	74.29	$462.78
Craig Shankland	T-7th in 1969	8	28	5	0	0	2	3	3	74.18	$4,711.83
Brad Sherfy	T-9th in 1992	3	12	3	0	0	2	3	3	70.50	$18,995.00
John Sherman	T-70th in 1993	1	4	1	0	0	0	0	0	72.00	$665.00
George Shortridge	T-5th in 1978 & '79	18	62	10	0	2	3	5	8	73.50	$16,911.54
Luther Showaker	T-49th in 1980	6	19	1	0	0	0	0	0	76.53	$265.86
Steve Sieg	T-67th in 1989	2	8	2	0	0	0	0	0	73.13	$1,346.50
Charles Sifford	T-11th in 1979	4	16	4	0	0	0	2	1	73.25	$3,866.33
Art Silvestrone	T-11th in 1969	7	26	5	0	0	0	3	2	73.35	$3,487.05
Brooks Simmons	T-88th in 1981	3	10	1	0	0	0	0	0	76.00	$277.71
Gaylon "Tex" Simon	T-65th in 1973	6	19	2	0	0	0	0	1	75.63	$450.80
Robert Singletary	T-77th in 1989	5	17	2	0	0	0	0	2	74.12	$1,577.50
Jack Slocum	T-15th in 1983	10	35	5	0	0	0	1	1	74.20	$3,325.42
Tom Smack	T-21st in 1974	5	15	2	0	0	0	1	0	74.27	$1,748.99
Bob Smith	T-28th in 1984	8	26	3	0	0	0	0	1	75.08	$2,061.93
Danny Smith	Missed Cut	8	24	0	0	0	0	0	0	77.38	$400.00
Dave Smith	T-57th in 1978	9	29	3	0	0	0	0	1	75.07	$613.17
Dick Smith	T-4th in 1970	14	46	5	0	1	1	3	3	75.41	$5,614.58
George Smith	T-18th in 1971	4	16	4	0	0	0	1	3	73.50	$2,833.66
Rick Smith	T-56th in 1985	1	4	1	0	0	0	0	0	73.25	$577.00
Robert Smith	T-21st in 1973	3	10	1	0	0	0	1	0	74.60	$1,121.82
Steve Smith	T-98th in 1978	4	12	1	0	0	0	0	0	76.00	$180.70
Todd M. Smith	T-3rd in 1993	6	21	3	1	1	2	3	4	71.71	$26,366.67
Wes Smith	T-18th in 1993	5	17	2	0	0	0	1	1	73.24	$4,675.00
Ron Smith Jr.	T-4th in 1977	4	10	1	0	1	1	1	1	73.10	$4,500.00
Steve Smitha	T-23rd in 1993	2	7	1	0	0	0	1	0	72.43	$3,137.50
Sam Snead	Winner in 1971	3	12	3	3	3	3	3	5	70.25	$31,500.00
Jim Sobb	T-28th in 1989	9	29	2	0	0	0	0	3	74.10	$3,857.00
Jack Sommers	T-5th in 1978	9	30	4	0	1	1	1	1	74.57	$5,853.79
Mike Souchak	T-6th in 1968	5	20	5	0	0	1	1	3	73.05	$2,576.95
Carlton Sowers	T-66th in 1979	3	10	1	0	0	0	0	1	73.60	$256.82
Dan Spooner	T-83rd in 1981	5	16	1	0	0	0	0	0	77.94	$277.71
Bill Sporre	T-76th in 1973	5	16	2	0	0	0	0	1	75.94	$356.35
Steve Spray	T-17th in 1978	9	31	4	0	0	0	3	4	73.68	$5,013.75
James St. Germain	T-81st in 1983	5	16	1	0	0	0	0	0	75.94	$277.72
Roland Stafford	T-32nd in 1973	11	36	4	0	0	0	0	1	75.72	$1,458.83
Tim Stafford	T-30th in 1992	3	10	1	0	0	0	0	0	74.20	$1,750.00
Chris Starkjohann	T-5th in 1991	5	19	4	0	1	1	1	4	72.37	$13,982.50
Larry Startzel	T-22nd in 1976	9	29	2	0	0	0	1	2	74.52	$1,780.54
Kent Stauffer	T-28th in 1989	5	17	2	0	0	0	0	1	73.82	$3,315.00
Jerry Steelsmith	T-2nd in 1971	8	28	5	1	1	2	4	4	72.75	$12,159.86
Doug Steffen	T-36th in 1983	5	17	2	0	0	0	0	0	76.12	$1,490.22

Player	Best Finish	Year	Rounds	Cuts	Top 3	Top 5	Top 10	Top 25	Rds. in 60s	Average	Money
Scott Steger	T-31st in 1993	6	20	2	0	0	0	0	3	73.25	$2,637.50
Jeff Steinberg	T-62nd in 1981	11	38	5	0	0	0	0	2	75.05	$1,919.73
Roger Stern	Missed Cut	7	20	0	0	0	0	0	1	76.55	$0.00
Wheeler Stewart	T-8th in 1985	8	28	4	0	0	1	2	2	74.39	$14,371.43
Don Stickney	T-69th in 1972	10	31	3	0	0	0	0	0	77.03	$552.88
Ken Still	T-85th in 1983	2	7	1	0	0	0	0	0	76.14	$277.71
Waddy Stokes	T-25th in 1978	4	13	1	0	0	0	1	2	73.92	$1,066.66
Stan Stopa	T-49th in 1989	3	10	1	0	0	0	0	0	74.20	$1,596.66
Dick Stranahan	T-46th in 1969	5	15	2	0	0	0	0	1	74.67	$331.91
Austin Straub	T-25th in 1978	3	11	2	0	0	0	1	1	74.27	$1,858.20
Raymond Streeter	Missed Cut	5	15	0	0	0	0	0	0	78.07	$400.00
Glenn Stuart	T-16th in 1973	11	34	4	0	0	0	1	3	75.50	$2,294.37
Mike Stubblefield	T-87th in 1982	4	12	1	0	0	0	0	0	77.33	$209.42
Buddy Sullivan	T-37th in 1970	1	4	1	0	0	0	0	0	73.75	$285.00
Chip Sullivan	T-59th in 1993	1	4	1	0	0	0	0	2	71.75	$760.00
Bruce Summerhays	T-5th in 1976	12	46	10	0	1	2	3	3	73.65	$11,965.58
Tom Sutter	Missed Cut	5	15	0	0	0	0	0	1	75.27	$400.00
Tim Sweborg	Missed Cut	6	18	0	0	0	0	0	0	77.72	$0.00
Bob Swift	T-30th in 1971	3	9	1	0	0	0	0	1	75.33	$825.00
Milan Swilor	T-36th in 1990	6	20	2	0	0	0	0	3	73.95	$2,754.15
Tom Talkington	T-81st in 1975	7	20	1	0	0	0	0	0	77.90	$225.00
Tom Tatum	11th in 1986	7	22	1	0	0	0	1	1	74.18	$7,300.00
Joe Taylor	T-34th in 1975	4	12	1	0	0	0	0	0	75.33	$823.33
Joel Taylor	T-17th in 1969	4	14	3	0	0	0	1	1	74.07	$1,329.83
John Taylor	T-83rd in 1981	4	12	1	0	0	0	0	0	77.33	$277.71
Phil Taylor	Missed Cut	4	12	0	0	0	0	0	1	75.42	$800.00
Stuart Taylor	T-54th in 1984	7	23	2	0	0	0	0	1	74.43	$635.64
Eddie Terasa	T-10th in 1993	5	18	3	0	0	1	2	4	72.72	$9,783.00
Rick Terrell	T-79th in 1984	3	10	1	0	0	0	0	0	75.30	$425.00
Ralph Terry	T-76th in 1973	9	28	1	0	0	0	0	0	75.57	$267.47
Ron Terry	T-12th in 1978	1	4	1	0	0	0	1	1	70.50	$1,900.00
Joe Tesori	Missed Cut	9	26	0	0	0	0	0	0	77.12	$400.00
Bob Thatcher	T-77th in 1971	4	13	1	0	0	0	0	1	75.62	$191.50
Stan Thirsk	T-4th in 1971	15	53	8	0	1	3	4	4	73.43	$11,047.14
George Thomas	T-76th in 1976	11	33	3	0	0	0	0	3	75.70	$598.51
Tommy Thomas	T-43rd in 1986	3	11	2	0	0	0	0	0	74.82	$1,126.98
Gene Thompson	T-7th in 1969	7	25	5	0	0	1	2	0	73.84	$3,538.93
Jim Thompson	T-87th in 1982	6	19	1	0	0	0	0	0	78.47	$209.43
Kim Thompson	T-6th in 1989	7	24	3	0	0	1	1	2	73.38	$13,676.43
Jeff Thomsen	T-2nd in 1989	4	15	3	1	1	1	1	4	71.87	$21,631.00
David Thore	T-5th in 1987	4	14	2	0	1	1	1	0	74.64	$10,599.00
Bill Tindall	T-41st in 1985	7	26	5	0	0	0	0	1	74.77	$2,887.50
Dennis Tiziani	T-6th in 1975	10	36	6	0	0	1	1	3	74.56	$4,091.34
Richard Tock	T-30th in 1977	11	34	1	0	0	0	0	0	76.26	$1,191.54
Gene Torres	T-15th in 1977	10	36	6	0	0	0	1	1	74.42	$4,545.21
Vic Tortorici	T-56th in 1986	3	11	2	0	0	0	0	0	74.36	$1,371.00
Felice Torza	98th in 1974	2	6	1	0	0	0	0	0	78.00	$165.00
Harry Toscano	T-72nd in 1990	3	10	1	0	0	0	0	0	74.90	$1,065.00
Bob Toski	T-28th in 1975	1	4	1	0	0	0	0	1	73.00	$973.66
Ken Towns	T-60th in 1968	7	26	5	0	0	0	0	2	74.92	$741.82
John Traub	Winner in 1980	13	44	5	1	1	1	2	4	74.25	$24,683.96
Skip Tredway	T-72nd in 1987	8	25	1	0	0	0	0	1	74.72	$975.00
Peter Trenham	Missed Cut	5	14	0	0	0	0	0	1	76.07	$0.00
Gary Trivisonno	T-7th in 1990	4	15	3	0	0	1	2	5	70.80	$16,121.00
Odell Trueblood	Missed Cut	4	10	0	0	0	0	0	0	75.20	$0.00
Chris Tucker	T-15th in 1989	4	15	3	0	0	0	1	3	73.33	$6,334.64
Jerry Tucker	T-34th in 1988	11	38	5	0	0	0	0	0	75.34	$3,579.72
Dick Turner	T-18th in 1968	4	11	1	0	0	0	1	1	74.45	$561.36
Harry Turner	T-63rd in 1983	1	4	1	0	0	0	0	0	75.75	$277.72
J.D. Turner	T-71st in 1977	5	16	2	0	0	0	0	2	74.31	$391.34
Mike Turnesa Jr.	Missed Cut	4	12	0	0	0	0	0	0	77.67	$0.00
Tom Ulozas	T-17th in 1975	5	18	3	0	0	0	2	3	73.22	$2,889.81
Carl Unis	T-27th in 1976	15	44	2	0	0	0	0	0	76.39	$1,438.46
Brett Upper	Winner in 1990	4	14	2	1	1	1	1	5	72.21	$33,615.00
Jim Urban	T-40th in 1983	4	13	1	0	0	0	0	0	75.69	$650.00
Sam Urzetta	T-46th in 1970	3	8	1	0	0	0	0	0	75.75	$120.78
Tommy Valentine	T-39th in 1991	1	4	1	0	0	0	0	2	70.00	$971.00
Tony Valentine	T-59th in 1986	4	13	1	0	0	0	0	0	75.62	$637.00
Brent Veenstra	T-36th in 1990	4	14	2	0	0	0	0	2	72.64	$1,996.14
Bill Ventresca	T-56 in 1974	5	13	1	0	0	0	0	0	75.77	$165.00
Maurice Ver Brugge	T-6th in 1974	10	36	7	0	0	1	4	4	74.19	$7,463.73
Steve Veriato	T-6th in 1984	8	30	6	0	0	2	4	3	71.83	$31,357.00
Rick Vershure	T-19th in 1985	10	32	2	0	0	0	2	3	74.16	$5,205.00
Everett Vinzant	T-81st in 1971	10	31	2	0	0	0	0	1	75.77	$356.50
Ron Vlosich	T-21st in 1988	7	24	3	0	0	0	1	4	74.25	$4,675.12
Charles Volpone Jr.	T-4th in 1971	10	31	5	0	1	1	2	5	73.23	$8,337.13

Player	Best Finish	Year	Rounds	Cuts	Top 3	Top 5	Top 10	Top 25	Rds. in 60s	Average	Money
Ernie Vossler	T-18th in 1968	1	4	1	0	0	0	1	1	71.25	$561.36
Roy Vucinich	T-28th in 1985	13	42	4	0	0	0	0	1	75.33	$3,151.97
Tony Wallin	T-23rd in 1981	11	35	2	0	0	0	1	2	74.57	$2,509.71
Scott Walter	T-30th in 1992	6	22	4	0	0	0	0	0	73.86	$3,829.33
Bernard Walters	WD in 1973	1	1	0	0	0	0	0	0	84.00	$0.00
Fred Wampler	T-18th in 1971	10	32	5	0	0	0	1	3	74.94	$2,069.24
Tom Wargo	T 3rd in 1986	7	27	6	1	3	3	5	7	71.48	$49,333.57
Scott Watkins	T-44th in 1987	3	11	2	0	0	0	0	1	73.18	$1,453.00
Bob Watson	T-87th in 1972	3	9	1	0	0	0	0	0	77.11	$204.54
Craig Watson	T-28th in 1984	2	7	1	0	0	0	0	0	74.00	$1,195.00
Roger Watson	Winner in 1974 & '75	16	55	7	2	2	2	2	6	75.00	$35,843.28
Bert Weaver	T-18th in 1972	5	19	4	0	0	0	3	1	73.89	$4,026.11
Buddy Weaver	T-75th in 1972	5	16	1	0	0	0	0	1	74.69	$204.54
Dewitt Weaver	T-23rd in 1979	4	14	2	0	0	0	1	2	73.36	$1,869.03
Jack Webb	T-49th in 1968	8	25	2	0	0	0	0	0	76.68	$172.79
Larry Webb	Winner in 1983	6	22	4	1	1	2	2	4	73.95	$28,044.43
Ron Weber	T-37th in 1970	4	14	2	0	0	0	0	1	74.64	$476.50
Don Wegrzyn	T-39th in 1974	3	11	2	0	0	0	0	1	74.64	$801.50
Al Weinhold	T-63rd in 1990	3	10	1	0	0	0	0	0	75.60	$730.56
Pat Welch	T-48th in 1975	6	19	1	0	0	0	0	0	77.58	$262.75
Ron Wells	T-18th in 1984	5	19	4	0	0	0	2	2	74.68	$5,640.71
Rick Werner	T-8th in 1984	6	19	2	0	0	1	2	0	75.53	$8,750.00
Mike West	T-27th in 1991	3	10	1	0	0	0	0	1	72.70	$2,700.00
Frank Wharton	T-47th in 1971	5	16	2	0	0	0	0	0	75.19	$483.76
Larry Wheeler	T-68th in 1984	7	21	3	0	0	0	0	0	75.38	$1,542.00
Victor Whipp	T-75th in 1991	4	14	2	0	0	0	0	1	72.86	$1,612.50
Fletcher White	T-89th in 1992	4	13	1	0	0	0	0	0	75.38	$1,002.50
Henry White	T-98th in 1993	3	10	1	0	0	0	0	0	74.10	$575.50
Jay Alan White	T-83rd in 1975	10	28	1	0	0	0	0	1	76.54	$225.00
Jim White	T-2nd in 1985	15	54	9	1	1	2	4	8	73.67	$37,488.70
Rick Whitfield	T-54th in 1984	7	21	1	0	0	0	0	0	75.71	$425.00
Ed Whitman	T-16th in 1988	11	41	8	0	0	0	2	2	73.44	$12,795.37
Buddy Whitten	Winner in 1979	17	60	10	1	1	2	4	5	73.35	$31,580.16
Skip Whittet	Missed Cut	5	15	0	0	0	0	0	0	78.33	$0.00
Terry Wilcox	T-12th in 1975	11	37	4	0	0	0	1	1	74.00	$3,853.54
Rob Wilkin	T-28th in 1990	4	15	3	0	0	0	0	1	73.60	$3,469.75
Gary Wilkins	T-29th in 1983	5	16	1	0	0	0	0	0	75.81	$1,371.43
Scott Williams	T-18th in 1993	3	11	2	0	0	0	1	2	72.73	$6,218.75
Rex Wilsen	T-88th in 1975	3	8	1	0	0	0	0	0	76.25	$225.00
Herb Wimberly	T-80th in 1968	3	9	1	0	0	0	0	0	74.00	$88.89
B.G. Winings	T-75th in 1991	3	10	1	0	0	0	0	1	74.20	$637.00
Gary Wintz	T-15th in 1980	3	11	2	0	0	0	1	2	73.45	$1,954.72
Larry Wise	T-23rd in 1971	5	18	3	0	0	0	1	1	74.78	$1,274.79
Paul Wise	T-19th in 1983	10	35	5	0	0	0	2	2	74.54	$5,106.39
Jerry Wisz	T-23rd in 1993	5	18	3	0	0	0	1	2	73.44	$4,339.00
Gregg Wolff	T-28th in 1990	6	23	5	0	0	0	0	3	72.78	$5,080.45
Mark Wolfia	T-56th in 1983	6	18	1	0	0	0	0	0	77.00	$277.72
Charlie Wood	T-74th in 1980	3	10	1	0	0	0	0	0	75.00	$230.61
Craig Wood	Missed Cut	2	6	0	0	0	0	0	0	77.33	$0.00
Dan Wood	T-13th in 1991	5	17	2	0	0	0	1	2	73.24	$6,318.50
Thorne Wood	Missed Cut	4	11	0	0	0	0	0	0	78.00	$0.00
Willard Wood	T-28th in 1970	6	15	1	0	0	0	0	0	74.67	$457.50
Tom Woodard	T-59th in 1993	1	4	1	0	0	0	0	1	71.75	$760.00
Jim Woodward	T-8th in 1986	2	8	2	0	0	1	1	0	72.75	$8,077.00
Tom Woodward	T-15th in 1990	3	11	2	0	0	0	1	1	73.09	$6,088.00
Lew Worsham	Missed Cut	1	3	0	0	0	0	0	0	81.00	$0.00
Jimmy Wright	T-2nd in 1969	18	65	14	1	4	5	10	7	73.20	$27,836.14
Bruce Wyatt	T-32nd in 1970	3	8	1	0	0	0	0	0	73.63	$318.00
Lee Wykle	T-39th in 1978	2	8	2	0	0	0	0	2	72.13	$919.32
Bob Wynn	T-3rd in 1983	2	8	2	1	1	1	1	1	73.13	$10,425.00
Mikel Wynn	T-14th in 1982	4	14	2	0	0	0	2	0	74.36	$4,100.00
Bruce Zabriski	T-5th in 1991	3	11	2	0	1	1	1	3	70.73	$13,080.00
Mike Zaremba	T-53rd in 1988	4	14	2	0	0	0	0	0	74.79	$1,742.00
Dave Zink	T-43rd in 1980	3	10	1	0	0	0	0	0	79.40	$612.50
Michael Zinni	T-49th in 1980	6	19	1	0	0	0	0	0	74.95	$665.85
Billy Ziobro	T-94th in 1988	6	19	1	0	0	0	0	2	75.32	$565.00
John Zontek	Missed Cut in 1973	4	10	0	0	0	0	0	0	77.10	$0.00

■ PGA CLUB PROFESSIONAL RECORDS

■ Best 72-Hole Score

272 by Howell Fraser (72-66-65-69) in 1968
273 by Ron McDougal (67-69-68-69) in 1992
275 by Bob Rosburg (71-66-66-72) in 1969
275 by Sam Snead (67-65-74-69) in 1971
275 by Brett Upper (67-65-74-69) in 1990
275 by Jeffrey Roth (68-69-66-72) in 1993
**267 by Larry Gilbert (67-65-67-68) in 1991

■ Best 72-Hole Score by A Non-Winner

276 by Bob Rosburg (70-67-70-69) in 1968
276 by Chuck Malchaski (66-68-71-71) in 1968
276 by Jimmy Wright (66-67-70-73) in 1969
276 by Jim Ferree (69-67-68-72) in 1978
276 by Sammy Rachels (73-68-65-70) in 1992

■ Highest 72-Hole Score by Winner

287 by Bob Boyd (70-74-73-70) in 1988
285 by Rex Baxter (71-68-75-71) in 1970
285 by Larry Gilbert (67-70-74-74) in 1981

■ Best Score First 54 Holes

203 by Howell Fraser (72-66-65) in 1968
203 by Jimmy Wright (66-67-70) in 1969
203 by Bob Rosburg (71-66-66) in 1969
203 by Gibby Gilbert (70-66-67) in 1990
203 by Jeffrey Roth (68-69-66) in 1993
204 by Jim Ferree (69-67-68) in 1978
204 by Brett Upper (69-69-66) in 1990
204 by Ron McDougal (67-69-68) in 1992
** 196 by Bruce Zabriski (66-71-59) in 1991

■ Best Score Last 54 Holes

200 by Howell Fraser (66-65-69) in 1968
203 by Sammy Rachels (68-65-70) in 1992
204 by Bob Rosburg (66-66-72) in 1969
**199 by Ron McDougal (61-67-71) in 1991

■ Best Score First 36 Holes

132 by Sam Snead (67-65) in 1971
133 by Jimmy Wright (66-67) in 1969
133 by Bob Leaver (67-66) in 1978
134 by Chuck Malchaski (66-68) in 1968
134 by Ron McDougal (68-66) in 1993
**129 by Gene Fieger (65-65) in 1991
**129 by Mike San Filippo (66-63) in 1991
**129 by Steve Veriato (63-66) in 1991
**129 by Jon Chaffee (62-67) in 1991

■ Best Score Last 36 Holes

134 by Howell Fraser (65-69) in 1968
134 by John Calabria (66-68) in 1979
135 by Sammy Rachels (65-70) in 1992
135 by Chris Peddicord (67-68) in 1992
136 by Jimmy Wright (69-67) in 1968
136 by John Gentile (68-68) in 1978
136 by Rick Acton (68-68) in 1993
136 by Jim White (70-66) in 1993
**132 by Bob Groff (63-69) in 1991

■ Best 18-Hole Score

63 by Eddie Famula in 1971 (1st Round)
64 by Jerry Steelsmith in 1978 (1st Round)
64 by Tim Collins in 1978 (2nd Round)
64 by Gibby Gilbert in 1987 (2nd Round)
**59 by Bruce Zabriski in 1991 (3rd Round)
**60 by Louis Bartoletti in 1991 (1st Round)
**60 by David Glenz in 1991 (2nd Round)

■ Best 9-Hole Score

29 by Eddie Famula in 1971

■ Best First-Round Score

63 by Eddie Famula in 1971
64 by Jerry Steelsmith in 1978
64 by Jerry Steelsmith in 1987
**60 by Louis Bartoletti in 1991

■ Best Second-Round Score

64 by Tim Collins in 1978
65 by Sam Snead in 1971
65 by John Frillman in 1971
65 by Mal Galletta in 1972
65 by Bruce Summerhays in 1976
65 by Phil Ferranti in 1978
65 by Orrin Vincent in 1979
65 by Jeffrey Roth in 1990
65 by Terry Dear in 1993
**60 by David Glenz in 1991

■ Best Third-Round Score

65 by Howell Fraser in 1968
65 by Randy Glover in 1977
65 by Bob Duden in 1978
65 by Gary Howlett in 1979
65 by Larry Gilbert in 1982,
65 by Mike Schlueter in 1985
65 by Sammy Rachels in 1992
**59 by Bruce Zabriski in 1991

■ Best Fourth-Round Score

65 by Jeffrey Roth in 1987
66 by Jeffrey Roth in 1991
66 by Jeff Fairfield in 1992
66 by Bruce Lehnhard in 1992
67 by 15 players

■ Largest Winning Margin

Five shots, by Sam Snead in 1971

■ Best Comeback by Winner

Eight shots by John Traub in 1980
Five shots by Bob Boyd in 1988

■ Highest One-Round Score by Winner

73 by Rives McBee in 1973
73 by Larry Gilbert in 1982

■ Lowest One-Round Score by Winner

67 by Sam Snead in 1971
67 by Larry Gilbert in 1981
67 by Larry Gilbert in 1991
67 by Ron McDougal in 1992

Highest Two-Round Score by Winner

74 by Robert Boyd in 1988
73 by Roger Watson in 1974

Lowest Two-Round Score by Winner

65 by Sam Snead in 1971
65 by Larry Gilbert in 1991

Highest Three-Round Score by Winner

75 by Rex Baxter in 1970
74 by Sam Snead in 1971
74 by Don Massengale in 1972
74 by Larry Gilbert in 1981
74 by Larry Webb in 1983

Lowest Three-Round Score by Winner

65 by Howell Fraser in 1968
65 by Larry Gilbert in 1982
66 by Bob Rosburg in 1969
66 by Brett Upper in 1990
66 by Jeffrey Roth in 1993

Highest Final Round Score by Winner

74 by Larry Gilbert in 1981 and 1982
72 by Bob Rosburg in 1969
72 by Bruce Fleisher in 1989
72 by Jeffrey Roth in 1993

Lowest Final Round Score by Winner

68 by Don Massengale in 1972
68 by John Gentile in 1978
68 by Larry Gilbert in 1991

Hardest Average Over 72 Holes

77.65 in 1983
77.38 in 1981

Lowest Average Over 72 Holes

73.57 in 1978
73.62 in 1993
73.73 in 1968
**71.88 in 1991

Championship With Most Sub-70 Scores

120 in 1978
99 in 1979
**325 in 1991

Championship With Least Sub-70 Scores

8 in 1974
11 in 1988
11 in 1983

Most Money Won

$145,918 by Larry Gilbert spanning 20 tournaments
$64,300 by Ron McDougal spanning 3 tournaments
$55,807 by Bob Boyd spanning 7 tournaments
$52,197 by Jeffrey Roth spanning 7 tournaments
$49,334 by Tom Wargo spanning 7 tournaments
$47,433 by Bob Lendzion spanning 12 tournaments
$46,066 by Jim Albus spanning 14 tournaments
$43,714 by Sammy Rachels spanning 4 tournaments

Lowest Scoring Average

68.25 by Ron McDougal in 12 rounds
68.88 by Mike Schuchart in 8 rounds
68.88 by Bob Rosburg in 8 rounds
69.00 by Chuck Malchaski in 4 rounds
69.50 by George Bowman in 4 rounds
69.75 by Tom Cleaver in 4 rounds

Lowest Scoring Average, Minimum Of 20 Rounds

71.48 by Tom Wargo in 27 rounds
71.59 by Bob Borowicz in 27 rounds
71.70 by Steve Veriato in 27 rounds
71.61 by Lonnie Nielsen in 31 rounds
71.71 by Todd Smith in 21 rounds
71.75 by Bob Boyd in 28 rounds
71.78 by Darrell Kestner in 27 rounds
71.83 by Steve Veriato in 30 rounds
71.85 by Stu Ingraham in 27 rounds
72.00 by Larry Gilbert in 77 rounds

Lowest Scoring Average, Minimum Of 35 Rounds

72.00 by Larry Gilbert in 77 rounds
72.46 by Tim Collins in 39 rounds
72.14 by Mike San Filippo in 35 rounds
72.34 by Robert Hoyt in 38 rounds
72.46 by Tim Collins in 39 rounds
72.51 by Gregg Jones in 35 rounds
72.55 by Jay Overton in 55 rounds
72.69 by David Glenz in 49 rounds
72.74 by Jim Albus in 54 rounds

Most Apperances

20 by Larry Gilbert
19 by Dennis Bradley
19 by John Frillman
18 by Tom Joyce
18 by Gene Borek
18 by John Molenda
18 by Jimmy Wright
18 by George Shortridge

Most Rounds Played

77 by Larry Gilbert
66 by John Molenda
65 by Jimmy Wright
65 by Gene Borek
62 by Tom Joyce
62 by George Shortridge
62 by George Bellino
61 by Tommy Aycock

Highest Number Of Strokes Over The Years

5544 by Larry Gilbert averaging 72.00 strokes per round
4891 by John Molenda averaging 74.11 strokes per round
4758 by Jimmy Wright averaging 73.20 strokes per round
4756 by Gene Borek averaging 73.17 strokes per round

Players With Most Sub-70 Rounds
18 by Larry Gilbert
13 by Gene Borek
10 by Jay Overton
9 by Tommy Aycock
9 by Tim Collins
8 by Jim White
8 by George Shortridge
8 by Jim Albus
8 by Howell Fraser

Most Top 3 Finishes
7 by Larry Gilbert
3 by Ron McDougal
3 by Sam Snead

Most Top 5 Finishes
8 by Larry Gilbert
4 by Jimmy Wright

Most Top 10 Finishes
9 by Larry Gilbert
5 by David Glenz
5 by Gene Borek
5 by Jimmy Wright

Most Top 25 Finishes
12 by Larry Gilbert
10 by Jimmy Wright
8 by Jim Albus
7 by Lonnie Nielsen
7 by Gene Borek

Players That Have Made Most Cuts
17 by Larry Gilbert
14 by Jimmy Wright
13 by Jay Overton
13 by Tommy Aycock
13 by Gene Borek

Number Of Times A Leader Went On To Win
1st Round - 8 in 26 tournaments
2nd Round - 7 in 26 tournaments
3rd Round - 12 in 26 tournaments

Four Sub-70 Rounds in Same Tournament
Ron McDougal in 1992

Wire-To-Wire Winners
Larry Gilbert in 1981
Ron McDougal in 1992 (Co-Leader after 1st Round)

Record Low 54-Hole Cut
216 in 1978
216 in 1993
**211 in 1991

Record High 54-Hole Cut
227 in 1983

Most "Heartbreaking" Rounds
63-81-78-84 by Eddie Famula in 1971; was 1st round leader
72-69-80-81 by Randy Quick in 1972; was tied for 1st after 2nd round, but finished tied 81st
81-82-65 by Gary Howlett in 1979; missed cut
67-68-71-81 by Gene Borek in 1980; was 3rd round leader by 5, but finished four strokes behind winner
73-70-66-77 by Dana Quigley in 1986; was 3rd round leader by 2, but finished two strokes behind winner
68-79-73 by Dick Whetzle in 1970; was 1st round co-leader, but withdrew after 3rd round
62-78-74 by Dan Kochivar in 1991; missed cut
63-84-74 by Larry Webb in 1991; missed cut
68-83-76 by Jim Slattery in 1992; missed cut
68-79-75 by George Shortridge in 1992; missed cut
65-72-81 by 1st round co-leader Joe Sciortino in 1993; missed cut

Winning the Club Professional in First Attempt
Howell Fraser in 1968
Sam Snead in 1971
Don Massengale in 1972
John Gentile in 1978
Bruce Fleisher in 1989
Brett Upper in 1990

Most Championships Won
3 by Larry Gilbert (1981, 1982, 1991)
2 by Roger Watson (1974, 1975)

Most Times Runner-Up
2 by Steve Benson (1977, 1982)
2 by Gibby Gilbert (1987, 1990)
2 by Larry Gilbert (1976, 1990)
** not an offical record since rain forced the 1991 Club Professional Championship to alter the Gold Course to a par 66.

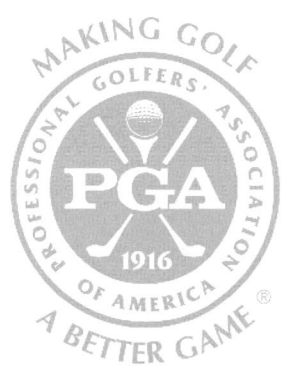

PGA SENIOR CLUB PROFESSIONAL CHAMPIONSHIP

1994 FACTS AND FORMAT

DATE: Oct. 18-21, 1994
SITE: Ibis Golf & Country Club,
West Palm Beach, Fla.
DEFENDING CHAMPION: Bob Carson, Titusville, Fla.

PRIZE MONEY AND PRIZES

A purse of $185,000 will be distributed to the 1994 field of competitors. The 1994 PGA Senior Club Professional Champion will receive a minimum of $14,000.

METHOD OF PLAY

Stroke play, 18 holes daily. In the event of a tie for first place upon completion of 72 holes, there will be a sudden-death playoff.

RULES AND REGULATIONS

The Rules of Golf which govern play are determined by the United States Golf Association and applied by the PGA of America Board of Directors. The Championship is subject to the overall supervision of the board and the PGA Rules Committee.

ELIGIBILITY

PGA club professionals at least 50 years of age may attempt to qualify through one of the 41 sections of the PGA of America.

HISTORY

What began as an idea in early 1989 became reality in December of the same year when 144 players began the inaugural Wilson PGA Senior Club Professional Championship at PGA National Golf Club in Palm Beach Gardens, Fla. A championship built from the same mold as the "regular" PGA Club Professional Championship, the low 55 players in the field receive an automatic invitation to play in the prestigious PGA Seniors' Championship.

■ HISTORY THROUGH THE YEARS

Year	Winner	Score	Runner-up	Site
1989	Stan Thirsk	286	Bob Reith	PGA National Golf Club
1990	Tom Joyce	278	Jim Albus	BallenIsles Country Club of JDM
1991	Tom Joyce	281	Mike Joyce	BallenIsles Country Club of JDM
1992	Roger Kennedy	278	Tom Wargo	BallenIsles Country Club of JDM
1993	Bob Carson	277	Tom Joyce	Ibis Golf & Country Club, West Palm Beach, Fla.

1993

Bob Carson of Titusville, Fla., credited his youngest daughter, Tiffany, for planting a positive thought in his head and in his golf bag before the fifth annual PGA Senior Club Professional Championship. Earlier in the month at his 25th wedding anniversary celebration, 14-year-old Tiffany wrote on a card, "One day your putter will be like gold." Carson, 52, then painted his old homemade putter gold and went on to post a record-set-

Champion:	Bob Carson, Titusville, Fla.
Site:	Ibis Golf & Country Club (Legend Course), West Palm Beach, Fla.
Date:	Oct. 26-29 Purse: $185,000

ting performance in the Championship's first visit to the Legend Course at Ibis Golf and Country Club in West Palm Beach, Fla. The Championship moved to Ibis from BallenIsles Country Club of JDM in Palm Beach Gardens, after maintenance problems on the heralded East Course.

Carson, owner and head professional at Bent Oak Country Club in Titusville, demonstrated his length off the tee and produced three consecutive 69s and a final-round 70 for a record 11-under-par 277 total for 72 holes. Carson opened the final round by making birdie putts on the first, second, fourth and fifth holes before easing off on the back nine to cruise home. Carson once owned an 11-stroke margin before recording five bogeys, a birdie and an eagle on the last 13 holes. "I guess I lost my concentration a few times after that," said Carson. "But I really only had one bad swing all day." Two-time champion Tom Joyce of Old Westbury, N.Y., was runner-up, eight strokes off the pace. Carson's victory margin also was a tournament record. Bill Garrett of Grapevine, Texas, finished third at 287 after closing with a 66, a final-round tournament record.

WILSON PGA SENIOR CLUB PROFESSIONAL CHAMPIONSHIP

TOURNAMENT SUMMARY

Place	Name	Score	Winnings	Place	Name	Score	Winnings
1.	Bob Carson, Titusville, Fla.	69-69-69-70—277	$14,000.00		John Frillman, Omaha, Neb.	75-74-74-76—299	$1,200.00
2.	Tom Joyce, Old Westbury, N.Y.	73-72-69-71—285	$11,000.00	40.	Butch Sweigart, Westchester, Pa.	77-73-76-74—300	$1,032.50
3.	Bill Garrett, Grapevine, Texas	78-71-72-66—287	$9,000.00		Ray Montgomery, Fort Pierce, Fla.	74-77-75-74—300	$1,032.50
4.	Patrick O'Brien, Indianapolis, Ind.	69-75-73-72—288	$7,500.00		Jim Ferriell, Indianapolis, Ind.	77-71-79-73—300	$1,032.50
5.	Al Krueger, Alamo, Calif.	73-70-76-70—289	$6,000.00		Stan Thirsk, Overland Park, Kan.	72-75-80-73—300	$1,032.50
	Mike O'Sullivan, Ormond Beach, Fla.	72-74-70-73—289	$6,000.00	44.	Roger Stern, Allentown, Pa.	77-75-72-77—301	$922.00
7.	Austin Straub, Cold Springs Harbor, N.Y.	74-72-72-72—290	$4,500.00		Gene Ferrell, Bayou La Batre, Ala.	79-67-78-77—301	$922.00
	Larry Mancour, Charlevoix, Mich.	74-71-70-75—290	$4,500.00		Dick James, Lebanon, Ohio	69-80-74-78—301	$922.00
9.	Dave Philo, Georgetown, S.C.	73-74-70-74—291	$3,875.00		Lloyd Monroe, New Rochelle, N.Y.	78-73-74-76—301	$922.00
	Tom Deaton, Southfield, Mich.	69-75-72-75—291	$3,875.00		Chuck Workman, Farmingdale, N.Y.	73-76-73-79—301	$922.00
11.	Martin Roesink, Canton, Ohio	73-76-72-71—292	$3,137.50	49.	Ken Burnette, Lake Port, Fla.	73-73-78-78—302	$860.00
	William Kennedy, Cape Coral, Fla.	73-71-76-72—292	$3,137.50		Dennis Bradley, Pittsford, N.Y.	75-74-76-77—302	$860.00
	Tom Storey, Las Vegas, Nev.	75-75-70-72—292	$3,137.50		J.D. Turner, West Des Moines, Iowa	76-73-77-76—302	$860.00
	Dick Goetz, Richardson, Texas	74-72-72-74—292	$3,137.50		Tom Dufresne, Haverhill, Mass.	74-75-78-75—302	$860.00
15.	Marion Heck, Fort Myers Beach, Fla.	74-71-73-75—293	$2,700.00		J. Banks Guyton, Wilmington, N.C.	75-74-79-74—302	$860.00
16.	Steve Lyles, Alexander City, Ala.	70-72-79-73—294	$2,450.00	54.	Hub Goyen, Scottsdale, Ariz.	73-76-76-78—303	$805.00
	Martin Bohen, Suffern, N.Y.	72-77-73-72—294	$2,450.00		Phil Ferranti, Tucson, Ariz.	75-74-75-79—303	$805.00
	Bill Hall, St. Louis, Mo.	73-72-76-73—294	$2,450.00		Dick Murphy, Atlanta, Ga.	76-75-78-74—303	$805.00
	Ralph Terry, Larned, Kan.	76-72-71-75—294	$2,450.00		Fran Deschaine, Apollo Beach, Fla.	77-74-77-75—303	$805.00
20.	Don Maddox, Tulsa, Okla.	72-75-75-73—295	$2,062.50		Jack Tindale, Rochester, N.Y.	76-75-80-72—303	$805.00
	Robert W. Nichols, Cookeville, Tenn.	74-72-76-73—295	$2,062.50		Bobby Benson, Palm Beach, Fla.	71-76-76-80—303	$805.00
	Art Proctor, Edmond, Okla.	73-73-74-75—295	$2,062.50	60.	Bud Overholser, Bremen, Ind.	74-78-73-79—304	$755.00
	Clayton Cole, Englewood, Colo.	74-74-72-75—295	$2,062.50		John Baker, Hermitage, Pa.	76-75-75-78—304	$755.00
24.	Jack O'Keefe, Santa Maria, Calif.	75-76-71-74—296	$1,850.00		Don Butzin, Waukesha, Wis.	71-79-77-77—304	$755.00
	Jim Hardy, Houston, Texas	76-73-72-75—296	$1,850.00		Charlie Huckaby, Dix Hills, N.Y.	73-76-80-75—304	$755.00
	George Bellino, Youngstown, Ohio	73-75-72-76—296	$1,850.00	64.	Jennings House, Virginia Beach, Va.	75-72-82-76—305	$725.00
27.	Mike Higgins, Bryan, Texas	77-73-74-73—297	$1,625.00		Larry Wheeler, Cheyenne, Wyo.	78-73-80-74—305	$725.00
	Robin All, Columbia, S.C.	76-73-76-72—297	$1,625.00	66.	Vince Mastro, Cleveland, Ohio	76-75-76-79—306	$705.00
	Bob Hauer, Cincinnati, Ohio	75-70-77-75—297	$1,625.00		Richard Crawford, Bogart, Ga.	73-78-78-77—306	$705.00
	Terry Wilcox, Rancho Mirage, Calif.	75-77-74-71—297	$1,625.00	68.	Wayne Morris, St. Louis, Mo.	77-72-76-82—307	$670.00
	Gene Borek, White Plains, N.Y.	73-78-68-78—297	$1,625.00		Ted Naff, Seattle, Wash.	76-74-79-78—307	$670.00
	Pat Schwab, St. Augustine, Fla.	70-74-73-80—297	$1,625.00		Cass Jawor, Lake Orion, Mich.	75-76-78-78—307	$670.00
33.	Dudley Wysong, McKinney, Texas	76-74-74-74—298	$1,375.00		George Glenn, Tulsa, Okla.	76-76-77-78—307	$670.00
	Bill Robertson, Athens, W.Va.	78-72-76-72—298	$1,375.00		John Haines, Jackson, Wyo.	74-76-80-77—307	$670.00
	Dan Murphy, Atlanta, Ga.	74-78-74-72—298	$1,375.00	73.	Nick Berklich, Grand Blanc, Mich.	76-76-81-75—308	$640.00
	Tony Morosco, Weston, Mass.	75-73-73-77—298	$1,375.00	74.	Carl Unis, Milwaukee, Wis.	76-76-77-80—309	$625.00
37.	Bob Pfister, Wilmington, Del.	74-74-76-75—299	$1,200.00		Ray Ziats, Newark, N.Y.	76-76-80-77—309	$625.00
	Jim Petralia, Arcadia, Calif.	73-78-74-74—299	$1,200.00	76.	Joe Maples, Boone, N.C.	76-76-81-78—311	$610.00

WILSON PGA SENIOR CLUB PROFESSIONAL CHAMPIONSHIP

1992

Roger Kennedy, the head professional at Pompano Beach (Fla.) Municipal Course and a member of the PGA of America Board of Directors, shot four rounds under par to capture the 1992 Wilson PGA Senior Club Professional Championship. Kennedy's 20-foot birdie putt on 17 on the East Course at BallenIsles Country Club of JDM clinched the victory with a final-round 1-under-par 71 and earned a winner's check for $14,000. Kennedy also tied the 72-hole Championship record of 10-under-par 278, set by Tom Joyce of Huntington, N.Y. in 1990.

Champion:	Roger Kennedy, Pompano Beach, Fla.	
Site:	BallenIsles Country Club of JDM (East Course),	
	Palm Beach Gardens, Fla.	
Date:	Oct. 27-30	Purse: $185,000

Kennedy slipped past PGA Club Professional Player of the Year Tom Wargo of Centralia, Ill., who bogeyed the par-5, 553-yard 17th to finish two strokes back at 280. Kennedy's Florida State University teammate, Dave Philo of Pawleys Island, S.C., was third for the second consecutive year, finishing with a 71 and 281 total. Wargo saw his chances for victory snuffed out on the 17th, when he hit a poor 3-wood into deep rough 200 yards short of the green. His 4-iron approach landed in a greenside bunker. Wargo was unable to get up and down from there. Kennedy, who shared the first-round lead with Odell Trueblood of San Antonio, Texas, finished his big week matching the record for lowest 36-hole score (138); the lowest 54-hole total (207); and tied Joyce's record for the greatest margin of victory, two strokes. Stan Thirsk of Overland Park, Kan., finished with a final-round record-tying 68, a standard shared by Jim Albus, Locust Valley, N.Y., (1990), and Mike Joyce, Huntington, N.Y. (1991).

The Championship also had a bizarre twist when two-time defending champion Tom Joyce, head professional at Glen Oaks Club in Westbury, N.Y., was disqualified for failing to make his first-round starting time. Joyce was past the five-minute limit when he arrived at the No. 10 tee. Joyce said he was so "focused" on starting on No. 1 that he forgot both tees were being used in the tournament. Buoyed by his victory, Kennedy went on to win a berth on the Senior PGA Tour.

TOURNAMENT SUMMARY

Place	Name	Score	Winnings	Place	Name	Score	Winnings
1.	Roger Kennedy, Pompano Beach, Fla.	67-71-69-71—278	$14,000.00	27.	Bob Harrison, Cincinnati, Ohio	71-74-77-70—292	$1,650.00
2.	Tom Wargo, Centralia, Ill.	69-70-71-70—280	$11,000.00		Jim King, Pompano Beach, Fla.	75-70-74-73—292	$1,650.00
3.	Dave Philo, Pawleys Island, N.C.	70-73-67-71—281	$9,000.00		Bill Majure, Colorado Springs, Colo.	73-71-74-74—292	$1,650.00
4.	Bobby Greenwood, Cookeville, Tenn.	69-72-69-73—283	$7,500.00		Howell Fraser, Panama City, Fla.	73-74-71-74—292	$1,650.00
5.	Bob Carson, Titusville, Fla.	73-71-68-72—284	$6,000.00		Paul Biocini, Manteca, Calif.	71-71-75-75—292	$1,650.00
	Marion Heck, Fort Myers Beach, Fla.	70-71-69-74—284	$6,000.00	32.	Tim Berg, Sunriver, Ore.	73-75-74-71—293	$1,475.00
7.	Stan Thirsk, Overland Park, Kan.	73-73-71-68—285	$4,500.00		Gene Carello, West Frankfort, Ill.	71-73-73-76—293	$1,475.00
	Harry Toscano, New Castle, Pa.	70-71-75-69—285	$4,500.00	34.	Rocky Nelson, Columbus, Ohio	74-76-73-71—294	$1,250.00
9.	Richie Bassett, Palm Beach Gardens, Fla.	71-70-74-71—286	$3,625.00		Jim Johnson, Arvada, Colo.	76-72-74-72—294	$1,250.00
	Craig Shankland, Flagler Beach, Fla.	71-72-72-71—286	$3,625.00		Bob Thatcher, West Chester, Pa.	78-69-75-72—294	$1,250.00
	Dudley Wysong Jr., McKinney, Texas	69-72-71-74—286	$3,625.00		Bob Pfister, West Chester, Pa.	74-72-72-76—294	$1,250.00
	Jesse Whittenton, Santa Teresa, N.M.	71-71-71-73—286	$3,625.00		Paul Barkhouse, North Andover, Mass.	68-75-74-77—294	$1,250.00
13.	Gene Borek, White Plains, N.Y.	72-70-71-74—287	$2,900.00		Joe McDermott, Albuquerque, N.M.	75-71-70-78—294	$1,250.00
	Jim Logue, Canton, Ohio	70-73-69-75—287	$2,900.00		Al Krueger, Danville, Calif.	75-70-71-78—294	$1,250.00
15.	Michael Ballo, Darien, Conn.	68-74-77-69—288	$2,600.00	41.	Ronald Castillo, Honolulu, Hawaii	76-71-74-74—295	$1,025.00
	Roland Stafford, Roscoe, N.Y.	69-73-75-71—288	$2,600.00		Jay Hyon, Los Angeles, Calif.	74-74-73-74—295	$1,025.00
	Terry Houser, St. Louis, Mo.	71-70-74-73—288	$2,600.00	43.	Dennis Bradley, Pittsford, N.Y.	76-73-77-70—296	$917.50
18.	Charles Huckaby, Jupiter, Fla.	69-73-76-71—289	$2,350.00		Sal Ruggiero, Stow, Mass.	75-73-75-73—296	$917.50
	Bud Williamson Jr., Kansas City, Mo.	72-72-74-71—289	$2,350.00		Lloyd Monroe, New Rochelle, N.Y.	76-73-74-73—296	$917.50
20.	Dick M. Murphy, Atlanta, Ga.	72-74-73-71—290	$2,030.00		Phillip Ferranti, Tucson, Ariz.	73-75-75-73—296	$917.50
	Mike O'Sullivan, Ormand Beach, Fla.	69-71-77-73—290	$2,030.00		Gary Head, Hendersonville, Tenn.	73-76-72-75—296	$917.50
	Odell Trueblood, San Antonio, Texas	67-75-75-73—290	$2,030.00		Cliff Moore, Apple Valley, Calif.	74-76-69-77—296	$917.50
	Gene Ferrell, Bayou La Batre, Ala.	70-72-73-75—290	$2,030.00		Fred Marti, Tucson, Ariz.	73-74-72-77—296	$917.50
	Bob Bruno, Mt. Snow, Vt.	72-76-67-75—290	$2,030.00		John Frillman, Omaha, Neb.	70-72-76-78—296	$917.50
25.	Art Proctor, Edmond, Okla.	72-74-74-71—291	$1,825.00	51.	Jim Ferriell Jr., Carmel, Ind.	77-73-74-73—297	$917.50
	Dick Smith, Cherry Hills, N.J.	71-73-74-73—291	$1,825.00		George McKeown, Pine Bluff, Ark.	70-78-77-72—297	$917.50

WILSON PGA SENIOR CLUB PROFESSIONAL CHAMPIONSHIP

1991 The Joyce brothers of Huntington, N.Y., dominated play in the third annual Wilson PGA Senior Club Professional Championship. Defending champion Tom Joyce finished with a 72-hole total of 7-under-par 281, a two-stroke victory over brother Mike, whose final-round 4-under-par 68 matched a tournament record. It was the second consecutive year that Tom Joyce was the only player in the field to record four sub-par rounds at BallenIsles Country Club of JDM in Palm Beach Gardens, Fla.

Champion:	Tom Joyce, Huntington, N.Y.	
Site:	BallenIsles Country Club of JDM,	
	Palm Beach Gardens, Fla.	
Date:	Nov. 12-15	Purse: $150,000

The brothers had met twice before in championship situations with Mike winning on both occasions (1983 Long Island Match-Play Championship and 1990 Metropolitan PGA Seniors' Championship). Mike later went on to earn a berth on the Senior PGA Tour.

TOURNAMENT SUMMARY

Place	Name	Score	Winnings
1.	Tom Joyce, Huntington, N.Y.	68-71-71-71—281	$13,500.00
2.	Mike Joyce, Huntington, N.Y.	74-70-71-68—283	$10,500.00
3.	Dave Philo, Pawleys Island, S.C.	72-74-68-70—284	$8,500.00
4.	Bill Kennedy, Cape Coral, Fla.	66-72-76-71—285	$7,000.00
5.	Jim Logue, Canton, Ohio	73-73-70-72—288	$5,500.00
	Art Proctor, Edmond, Okla.	70-69-74-75—288	$5,500.00
7.	Lloyd Monroe, New Rochelle, N.Y.	71-71-75-72—289	$4,250.00
	Richard Bassett, Palm Beach Gardens, Fla.	67-73-73-76—289	$4,250.00
9.	Bob Zimmerman, Dayton, Ohio	72-74-75-69—290	$3,625.00
	Joseph Carr, Leicester, Mass.	72-67-75-76—290	$3,625.00
11.	Dick Goetz, Richardson, Texas	74-74-71-72—291	$3,016.00
	George Bellino, Youngstown, Ohio	74-70-74-73—291	$3,016.00
	Charles Moore, Wallingford, Conn.	74-71-73-73—291	$3,016.00
14.	Stan Thirsk, Overland Park, Kan.	74-71-75-72—292	$2,450.00
	Cotton Dunn, Dallas, Texas	76-72-71-73—292	$2,450.00
	Kyle Burton, Palm Desert, Calif.	69-75-74-74—292	$2,450.00
	Bob Carson, Titusville, Fla.	73-75-70-74—292	$2,450.00
	Steve Spray, St. Louis, Mo.	71-71-75-75—292	$2,450.00
	J. Banks Guyton, Wilmington, N.C.	72-74-71-75—292	$2,450.00
20.	Willard Scholl, King of Prussia, Pa.	70-73-75-75—293	$2,016.00
	Raymond Streeter, Topeka, Kan.	74-72-72-75—293	$2,016.00
	Tommy Aycock, Portland, Texas	72-70-75-76—293	$2,016.00
23.	Earl Puckett, Highland Park, Ill.	73-75-72-74—294	$1,875.00
	Ray Montgomery, Ft. Pierce, Fla.	76-71-71-76—294	$1,875.00
25.	Larry Mancour, Harbor Springs, Mich.	73-72-78-72—295	$1,775.00
	Terry Houser, St. Louis, Mo.	73-74-73-75—295	$1,775.00
27.	John Frillman, Omaha, Neb.	73-75-76-72—296	$1,600.00
	Paul Barkhouse, Columbus, Ohio	73-75-75-73—296	$1,600.00
	Fred Marti, Tucson, Ariz.	74-76-72-74—296	$1,600.00
	Bob Pfister, Wilmington, Del.	69-72-78-77—296	$1,600.00
	Bob Thatcher, Westchester, Pa.	76-73-71-76—296	$1,600.00
32.	Gene Borek, White Plains, N.Y.	74-77-74-72—297	$1,375.00
	Joe McDermott, Albuquerque, N.M.	75-76-74-72—297	$1,375.00
	Richard Martinez, Kapaa, Hawaii	76-69-76-76—297	$1,375.00
	Gordon Waldespuhl, Elanger, Ky.	70-72-75-80—297	$1,375.00

Place	Name	Score	Winnings
36.	Alex Redmond, Royal Oak, Mich.	75-73-77-73—298	$1,150.00
	Bill Eschenbrenner, El Paso, Texas	70-78-76-74—298	$1,150.00
	Bill Erfurth, Northbrook, Ill.	74-76-74-74—298	$1,150.00
	Gary Head, Hendersonville, Tenn.	77-74-73-74—298	$1,150.00
	Monte Sanders, LaQuinta, Calif.	74-73-74-77—298	$1,150.00
41.	Marion Heck, Fort Myers, Fla.	74-74-79-72—299	$980.00
	Bob Ross, Springfield, N.J.	72-76-77-74—299	$980.00
	John Molenda, W. Bloomfield, Mich.	73-75-74-77—299	$980.00
44.	Nick Berklich, Grand Blanc, Mich.	74-76-76-74—300	$910.00
	Jack Freeman, Ashland, Ky.	76-74-76-74—300	$910.00
	Dick Murphy, Atlanta, Ga.	75-76-72-77—300	$910.00
	Bob Boldt, Walnut Creek, Calif.	71-75-74-80—300	$910.00
48.	Jay Hyon, Los Angeles, Calif.	77-74-77-73—301	$855.00
	Rocky Nelson, Columbus, Ohio	76-73-75-77—301	$855.00
	Roland Stafford, Margaretville, N.Y.	77-74-73-77—301	$855.00
	Buddy Overholser, Bremen, Ind.	76-73-75-77—301	$855.00
52.	Mal Galletta, Glen Cove, N.Y.	73-76-79-74—302	$810.00
	Bill Majure, Colorado Springs, Colo.	73-77-77-75—302	$810.00
	Bud Williamson, Kansas City, Mo.	75-76-74-77—302	$810.00
	Lynn Rosely, Quincy, Ill.	70-72-80-80—302	$810.00
	Tim Berg, Sunriver, Ore.	75-75-72-80—302	$810.00
57.	Gene Carello, West Frankfort, Ill.	73-75-81-74—303	$770.00
	Skip Whittet, Santa Ynze, Calif.	76-75-74-78—303	$770.00
	Ralph De Roy, Foley, Ala.	72-76-76-79—303	$770.00
60.	Jerry Hinton, Cordova, Tenn.	79-72-76-77—304	$735.00
	Pat Chartrand, Rancho Palos Verdes, Calif.	72-75-78-79—304	$735.00
	Bob Kinard, Boca Grande, Fla.	76-74-75-79—304	$735.00
	Larry Campbell, Ft. Smith, Ark.	74-77-74-79—304	$735.00
64.	John Kalinka, Honolulu, Hawaii	74-77-79-75—305	$710.00
65.	Frank Freer, St. Louis Park, Minn.	72-79-81-74—306	$685.00
	Chuck Scally, Coraopolis, Pa.	72-76-80-78—306	$685.00
	George Buzzini, Modesto, Calif.	75-73-78-80—306	$685.00
	Mal McMullen, Kokomo, Ind.	75-75-77-79—306	$685.00
69.	Ron Castillo, Honolulu, Hawaii	76-74-79-79—308	$655.00
	John Ramsey, Fort Walton Beach, Fla.	78-72-79-79—308	$655.00

WILSON PGA SENIOR CLUB PROFESSIONAL CHAMPIONSHIP

1990

Longtime friends and golfing rivals Tom Joyce of Huntington, N.Y., and Jim Albus of Locust Valley, N.Y., dueled throughout the second annual Wilson PGA Senior Club Professional Championship at BallenIsles Country Club of JDM in Palm Beach Gardens, Fla. Joyce posted four sub-par rounds of 71-68-69-70 for a 72-hole total of 278 to edge Albus by two strokes. The victory margin the same number of miles separating the two player's home clubs. Joyce was club professional at Glen Oaks Club and Albus, who later went on to a highly-productive Senior PGA Tour career, was head professional at Piping Rock Club on Long Island, N.Y. Albus's only struggle in the Championship was a third-round 74.

Champion:	Tom Joyce, Huntington, N.Y.
Site:	BallenIsles Country Club of JDM (East Course), Palm Beach Gardens, Fla.
Date:	Nov. 7-10 **Purse:** $125,000

TOURNAMENT SUMMARY

Place	Name	Score	Winnings
1.	Tom Joyce, Huntington, N.Y.	71-68-69-70—278	$12,000.00
2.	Jim Albus, Locust Valley, N.Y.	69-69-74-68—280	$9,000.00
3.	Marion Heck, Fort Myers, Fla.	67-73-69-74—283	$7,000.00
4.	Lynn Rosely, Quincy, Ill.	69-73-70-73—285	$6,000.00
5.	Bob Reith, Sioux City, Iowa	69-69-74-74—286	$4,850.00
	Pat Schwab, Elkton, Fla.	72-70-71-73—286	$4,850.00
7.	Alex Redmond, Royal Oak, Mich.	72-71-75-70—288	$4,000.00
8.	John Frillman, Omaha, Neb.	71-71-76-71—289	$3,370.00
	Buck Adams, Pinehurst, N.C.	74-72-68-75—289	$3,370.00
10.	Roger Ginsberg, Muttontown, N.Y.	73-75-73-70—291	$2,660.00
	Jack Kiefer, Andover, N.J.	75-75-71-70—291	$2,660.00
	Art Proctor, Edmond, Okla.	70-72-76-73—291	$2,660.00
	Dick Schwartz, East Liverpool, Ohio	76-70-72-73—291	$2,660.00
	Stan Thirsk, Overland Park, Kan.	73-67-75-76—291	$2,660.00
15.	Odell Trueblood, San Antonio, Texas	75-74-72-71—292	$2,250.00
	Dave Philo, Pawleys Island, S.C.	76-68-72-76—292	$2,250.00
17.	Tommy Atchison, Houston, Texas	78-71-73-71—293	$1,763.00
	Dudley Wysong Jr., Anna, Texas	74-71-76-72—293	$1,763.00
	Mike O'Sullivan, Ormond Beach, Fla.	78-69-74-72—293	$1,763.00
	Rolf Deming, Titusville, Fla.	72-73-75-73—293	$1,763.00
	Cotton Dunn, Dallas, Texas	73-72-75-73—293	$1,763.00
	Chuck Workman, Farmingdale, N.Y.	79-68-72-74—293	$1,763.00
	Michael Joyce, Huntington, N.Y.	72-74-73-74—293	$1,763.00
	Art Silvestrone, Riverhead, N.Y.	72-73-73-75—293	$1,763.00
	Bobby Ford, Georgetown, S.C.	73-72-71-77—293	$1,763.00
	Tim Debaufre, Gladwyne, Pa.	73-71-73-76—293	$1,763.00
	Wayne Kelley, Cincinnati, Ohio	70-70-75-78—293	$1,763.00
28.	Steve Bull, Milwaukee, Wis.	74-72-77-71—294	$1,425.00
	Earl Puckett, Highland Park, Ill.	71-72-76-75—294	$1,425.00
30.	Mac Main, Danville, Va.	74-74-77-70—295	$1,250.00
	Cass Jawor, Lake Orion, Mich.	75-70-78-72—295	$1,250.00
	Bill Garrett, Phoenix, Ariz.	74-73-75-73—295	$1,250.00
	Gordon Waldespuhl, Elanger, Ky.	72-71-76-76—295	$1,250.00
	Lloyd Harris, Mesa, Ariz.	75-74-71-75—295	$1,250.00
35.	Mike Burke Sr., Hollywood, Fla.	74-71-76-75—296	$1,075.00
	Gene Borek, White Plains, N.Y.	75-69-73-79—296	$1,075.00
37.	Charles Knowles Jr., Ft. Myers,	77-72-77-71—297	$975.00
	Jack O'Keefe, Santa Maria, Calif.	75-75-74-73—297	$975.00
	Dan Murphy, Atlanta, Ga.	77-71-73-76—297	$975.00
40.	John Powell, Chino, Calif.	76-72-76-74—298	$891.00
	Charlie Stock, Solon, Ohio	73-73-76-76—298	$891.00
	Ken Towns, Lake Wildwood, Calif.	76-69-76-77—298	$891.00
	Mickey Powell, Indianapolis, Ind.	73-74-72-79—298	$891.00
44.	Al Krueger, Alamo, Calif.	72-76-79-72—299	$802.00
	Dick Canney, Centreville, Va.	77-73-74-75—299	$802.00
	Larry Wheeler, Gering, Neb.	80-68-74-77—299	$802.00
	Billy Farrell, Greenwich, Conn.	71-73-77-78—299	$802.00
	Joe Lopez Jr., Ocala, Fla.	73-70-78-78—299	$802.00
49.	Dick Howell, Rockledge, Fla.	75-74-77-74—300	$735.00
	Hub Goyen, Scottsdale, Ariz.	75-75-75-75—300	$735.00
	Dick Plummer, Cincinnati, Ohio	75-75-74-76—300	$735.00
	Paul Messner, Beloit, Wis.	76-74-74-76—300	$735.00
	George Bellino, Youngstown, Ohio	75-72-75-78—300	$735.00
	Nunzio Ciampi, Glen Head, N.Y.	76-73-74-77—300	$735.00
55.	Bob Watson, Jupiter, Fla.	76-73-76-76—301	$685.00
	Richard Crawford, Columbus, Ga.	74-75-80-72—301	$685.00
	Adolph Popp, Melbourne, Fla.	73-77-76-75—301	$685.00
	Gene Dixon, Murfreesboro, Tenn.	76-74-75-76—301	$685.00
59.	Larry Romjue, Lincoln, Neb.	74-75-76-77—302	$635.00
	Bill Sporre, Crofton, Md.	74-75-76-77—302	$635.00
	Buddy Overholser, Bremen, Ind.	71-78-76-77—302	$635.00
	Bill Majure, Colorado Springs, Colo.	74-74-77-77—302	$635.00
	Charles Moore, Wallingford, Conn.	73-77-74-78—302	$635.00
	Bud Williamson, Kansas City, Mo.	72-74-77-79—302	$635.00
65.	John Kalinka, Honolulu, Hawaii	70-80-76-77—303	$595.00
	Bob Ross, Chatham, N.J.	74-73-76-80—303	$595.00
67.	Bob Kinard, Boca Grande, Fla.	76-74-77-77—304	$580.00
68.	Jack Hollis, Torrance, Calif.	73-77-78-77—305	$570.00
69.	Wayne Morris, St. Louis, Mo.	76-74-78-80—308	$560.00
70.	Ange Alberico, Springville, N.Y.	75-72-84-80—311	$550.00

WILSON PGA SENIOR CLUB PROFESSIONAL CHAMPIONSHIP

1989

Stan Thirsk of Overland Park, Kan., 61, outlasted Bob Reith, 50, of Sioux City, Iowa, by making a par on the second extra hole of a playoff to win the inaugural Wilson PGA Senior Club Professional Championship. The head professional at Kansas City (Kan.) Country Club for 29 years and 1980 PGA Golf Professional of the Year, Thirsk parred the last 10 holes, including making a 20-footer on the 18th hole to force the playoff with Reith at BallenIsles Country Club of JDM in Palm Beach Gardens, Fla. Reith turned in the only sub-par performance in the final round with his third straight 71.

Champion:	Stan Thirsk, Overland Park, Kan.	
Site:	PGA National Golf Club (Champion Course), Palm Beach Gardens, Fla.	
Date:	Nov. 30 - Dec. 31	**Purse:** $125,000

TOURNAMENT SUMMARY

Place	Name	Score	Winnings
1.	Stan Thirsk, Overland Park, Kan.	68-71-74-73—286	$10,000.00
2.	Bob Reith, Sioux City, Iowa	73-71-71-71—286	$7,500.00
3.	De Witt Weaver Jr., Helen, Ga.	77-68-67-75—287	$6,000.00
4.	Joe Lopez Jr., Ocala, Fla.	71-71-71-76—289	$5,000.00
5.	John Frillman, Omaha, Neb.	72-72-73-73—290	$4,000.00
6.	Michael Joyce, Huntington, N.Y.	78-69-73-73—293	$3,300.00
	Roger Ginsberg, Muttontown, N.Y.	76-70-72-75—293	$3,300.00
8.	Larry Mancour, Harbor Springs, Mich.	77-71-71-77—296	$2,800.00
9.	Joseph Carr, Leicester, Mass.	72-78-75-72—297	$2,320.00
	Raymond Streeter, Topeka, Kan.	74-76-74-73—297	$2,320.00
	Alex Redmond, North Palm Beach, Fla.	75-71-77-74—297	$2,320.00
	Michael Higuera, Londonderry, Vt.	74-71-74-78—297	$2,320.00
	Carl Lohren, Glen Head, N.Y.	71-76-71-79—297	$2,320.00
14.	John Molenda, W. Bloomfield, Mich.	73-76-75-74—298	$1,810.00
	Ray Montgomery, Ft. Pierce, Fla.	74-76-74-74—298	$1,810.00
	Bill Majure, Colorado Springs, Colo.	73-74-75-76—298	$1,810.00
	Kyle Burton, Palm Desert, Calif.	75-75-71-77—298	$1,810.00
	Ted Naff, Seattle, Wash.	75-74-70-79—298	$1,810.00
19.	Gene Dixon, Murfreesboro, Tenn.	70-76-78-75—299	$1,575.00
	Larry Larretti, Jupiter, Fla.	76-72-76-75—299	$1,570.00
21.	Mal McMullen, Kokomo, Ind.	80-76-70-74—300	$1,475.00
	Harlan Stevenson, Bonsall, Calif.	76-74-72-78—300	$1,475.00
23.	Ken Towns, Lake Wildwood, Calif.	76-74-71-80—301	$1,400.00
24.	Cass Jawor, Lake Orion, Mich.	74-75-75-78—302	$1,325.00
	Charlie Huckaby, Dix Hills, N.Y.	76-72-75-79—302	$1,325.00
26.	Paul Kelly, Fairfield, Conn.	81-74-73-75—303	$1,200.00
	Dick Sarta, Ridgewood, N.J.	77-76-74-76—303	$1,200.00
	Earl Puckett, Highland Park, Ill.	77-71-75-80—303	$1,200.00
29.	Ron Weber, Eugene, Ore.	73-78-79-74—304	$1,075.00
	Phil Hewitt, Creve Couer, Mo.	77-76-75-76—304	$1,075.00
	Peter Carriell, Phoenix, Ariz.	79-76-72-77—304	$1,075.00
	Robert Thatcher, Newtown Square, Pa.	76-72-78-78—304	$1,075.00
	Tim Berg, Sunriver, Ore.	75-75-74-80—304	$1,075.00
34.	Mike McGinnis, Frederick, Md.	78-76-75-76—305	$980.00
	Bill Byars, Roswell, Ga.	75-78-73-79—305	$980.00
	Harold Sweigart, Westchester, Pa.	77-73-75-80—305	$980.00
37.	Art Proctor, Edmond, Okla.	75-80-76-75—306	$910.00
	Dick Canney, Centreville, Va.	77-78-74-77—306	$910.00
	Bill Halvorson, Milwaukee, Wis.	74-77-75-80—306	$910.00
	David Jimenez, Wintergreen, Va.	73-77-75-81—306	$910.00
41.	Don Lindsey, Miami, Fla.	81-74-75-77—307	$830.00
	George Lee Thomas, Elkhart, Ind.	77-80-72-78—307	$830.00

Place	Name	Score	Winnings
	Adolph Popp, Melbourne, Fla.	76-77-74-80—307	$830.00
	Gordon Waldespuhl, Erlanger, Ky.	79-72-75-81—307	$830.00
45.	Gene Mitchell Jr., Floydada, Texas	78-79-78-73—308	$737.00
	Don Smith, Charlotte, N.C.	79-78-77-74—308	$737.00
	Dick Plummer, Cincinnati, Ohio	81-76-76-75—308	$737.00
	Gene Borek, White Plains, N.Y.	77-75-78-78—308	$737.00
	Bob Ross, Chatham, N.J.	79-74-76-79—308	$737.00
	Ange Alberico, Springville, N.Y.	77-79-72-80—308	$737.00
51.	Francis Deschaine, Apollo Beach, Fla.	79-74-82-74—309	$680.00
	Walker Inman Jr., Columbus, Ohio	74-80-79-76—309	$680.00
	Jerry Coats, Greenwich, Conn.	76-75-78-80—309	$680.00
54.	Nick Berklich, Grand Blanc, Mich.	82-74-78-76—310	$655.00
	John Scheffler, Chatham, Mass.	75-78-77-80—310	$655.00
56.	Jennings House, Virginia Beach, Va.	80-77-79-75—311	$615.00
	Paul Messner, Beloit, Wis.	75-81-79-76—311	$615.00
	George McKeown, Pine Bluff, Ariz.	78-76-79-78—311	$615.00
	Jack Webb, Des Moines, Iowa	77-77-77-80—311	$615.00
	Dick Carmody, San Diego, Calif.	76-76-78-81—311	$615.00
	George Bellino, Youngstown, Ohio	77-78-72-84-311	$615.00
62.	Carl Unis, Milwaukee, Wis.	83-74-81-74—312	$580.00
63.	Buddy Demling, Jeffersontown, Ky.	82-75-80-76—313	$555.00
	Cotton Dunn, Dallas, Texas	75-81-79-78—313	$555.00
	Gene Thompson, Kings Mountain, N.C.	75-78-80-80—313	$555.00
	Joe Cardenas, Lancaster, Ohio	79-78-73-83—313	$555.00
67.	John McMullin Jr., Castro Valley, Calif.	81-74-82-77—314	$512.00
	Harvey Bostic, Kingston, N.Y.	79-78-81-76—314	$512.00
	Mike Burke Sr., Hollywood, Fla.	77-75-82-80—314	$512.00
	Cliff Moore, Apple Valley, Calif.	77-79-77-81—314	$512.00
	Don Cross, Petersham, Mass.	77-76-79-82—314	$512.00
72.	Ted McKenzie, Berwyn, Pa.	78-79-78-80—315	$500.00
	Bill Erfurth, Northbrook, Ill.	80-77-77-81—315	$500.00
	Rich Churilla, Wheeling, W.Va.	79-77-77-82—315	$500.00
75.	Mickey Powell, Lebanon, Ind.	79-78-79-80—316	$500.00
76.	Bill Moser, Alton, Ill.	81-74-79-83—317	$500.00
	Jim Riggins, Jackson, Tenn.	78-79-77-83—317	$500.00
78.	Tom Hanson, Little Rock, Ark.	76-79-82-81—318	$500.00
	Dick Hughes, Hackettstown, N.J.	81-75-78-84—318	$500.00
80.	Chuck Scally, Coraopolis, Pa.	78-77-84-80—319	$500.00
	Ed Causey, Waycross, Ga.	80-77-80-82-319	$500.00
82.	Tom Atchison, Houston, Texas	80-76-82-82—320	$500.00
	Ray Ziats, Clifton Springs, N.Y.	79-78-81-89—327	$500.00

WILSON PGA SENIOR CLUB PROFESSIONAL CHAMPIONSHIP

■ WILSON PGA SENIOR CLUB PROFESSIONAL CHAMPIONSHIP RECORDS

■ Lowest First-Round Score
66   Bill Kennedy, Cape Coral, Fla. (1991)

■ Lowest Second-Round Score
67   Stan Thirsk, Overland Park, Kan. (1990)
      Joe Carr, Leicester, Mass. (1991)

■ Lowest 36 Holes
138   Jim Albus, Locust Valley, N.Y. (1990)
       Bob Reith, Sioux City, Iowa (1990)
       Bill Kennedy, Cape Coral, Fla. (1991)
       Roger Kennedy, Pompano Beach, Fla. (1992)
       Bob Carson, Titusville, Fla. (1993)

■ Lowest Third-Round Score
67   DeWitt Weaver Jr., Helen, Ga. (1989)

■ Lowest 54 Holes
207   Roger Kennedy, Pompano Beach, Fla. (1992)
       Bob Carson, Titusville, Fla. (1993)

■ Lowest Fourth-Round Score
66   Bill Garrett, Grapevine, Texas (1993)

■ Lowest Score by Winner
277   Bob Carson, Titusville, Fla. (1993)

■ Highest Score by Winner
286   Stan Thirsk, Overland Park, Kan. (1989)

■ Greatest Margin of Victory
8   Bob Carson, Titusville, Fla. (1993)

TITLEIST AND FOOT-JOY PGA ASSISTANT PROFESSIONAL CHAMPIONSHIP

1994 FACTS AND FORMAT

DATES: December 1994 (TBD)

SITE: PGA West (Jack Nicklaus Private Course)
La Quinta, Calif.

DEFENDING CHAMPION: Steve Brady

SPONSOR: Titleist and Foot-Joy Worldwide

PRIZE MONEY AND PRIZES

A minimum purse of $75,000 was distributed to the 1993 field of 44 competitors. The 1994 PGA Assistant Professional Champion will receive a minimum of $6,000.

METHOD OF PLAY

Stroke play, 18 holes daily. In the event of a tie for first place after 72 holes, there will be a sudden-death playoff.

RULES AND REGULATIONS

The Rules of Golf which govern play are determined by the United States Golf Association and applied by the PGA of America Board of Directors. The Championship is subject to the overall supervision of the board and the PGA Rules Committee.

ELIGIBILITY

PGA assistant professionals (A-8 membership classification) and registered apprentices may attempt to qualify through their local PGA sections. Field for the finals is comprised of the 41 PGA section assistant champions, the defending champion, if he is eligible, and assistant or apprentice champions invited from foreign PGAs.

HISTORY

For the first 14 years of its existence, the Foot-Joy PGA Assistant Professional Championship was played at Thorny Lea Golf Club in Brockton, Mass. In 1991, the event became known as the PGA Assistant Professional Championship presented by Titleist and Foot-Joy Worldwide and was held on the Jack Nicklaus Private Course at PGA West in La Quinta, Calif. In addition, the event was changed to a 72-hole event from its original 54-hole format. Titleist and Foot-Joy Worldwide is the longest consecutive event sponsor of PGA of America member events.

Past champions who have gone on to careers on the PGA Tour and the Ben Hogan or Nike Tour include Loren Roberts (1979), Fred Funk (1984), Robert Thompson (1986) and Webb Heintzelman (1988).

■ HISTORY THROUGH THE YEARS

Year	Winner/Section	Score	Runner-up	Site
1977	Mike Zack, New Jersey	209	Dennis Sullivan	Thorny Lea GC
1978	Larry Griffin, Gulf States	209	Frank Shikle	Thorny Lea GC
1979	Loren Roberts, Southern California	212	Bob Huber	Thorny Lea GC
1980	John Jackson, Southwest	205	Loren Roberts	Thorny Lea GC
1981	Ted O'Rourke, New England	210	Ed Odfield	Thorny Lea GC
1982	Darrell Kestner, Metropolitan*	213	Jean-Louis Lamarre	Thorny Lea GC
1983	Victor Tortorici, Metropolitan	214	Norm Becker	Thorny Lea GC
1984	Fred Funk, Middle Atlantic	206	Brent Murray	Thorny Lea GC
1985	Jon Fiedler, Southern California	211	Perry Arthur	Thorny Lea GC
1986	Robert Thompson, Southern Texas	209	Ken Allard, Scott Steger, Ron Kiaaina, Jr.	Thorny Lea GC
1987	Darrell Kestner, Metropolitan*	210	Ken Schall, Greg Farrow, Bob Gaus	Thorny Lea GC
1988	Webb Heintzelman, Middle Atlantic	205	Mitch Camp	Thorny Lea GC
1989	Mike West, Middle Atlantic	210	Tracy Frank	Thorny Lea GC
1990	Steve Gotsche, Midwest	205	Lee Rinker	Thorny Lea GC
1991	Kim Thompson, Rocky Mountain	278	Thomas Cleaver	PGA West
1992	Bill Loeffler, Colorado	283	Jon Fiedler	PGA West
1993	Steve Brady, Michigan	284	Rob McNamara	PGA West

*Won Playoff

1993

Steve Brady, a 35-year-old assistant professional at Detroit Golf Club who has missed a PGA Tour berth in 14 previous qualifying attempts, played like a polished veteran on the difficult Jack Nicklaus Private Course at PGA West in La Quinta, Calif.

Champion:	Steve Brady, Rochester Hills, Mich.
Site:	PGA West (Nicklaus Private), La Quinta, Calif.
Date:	Dec. 14-17 **Purse:** $75,000

Brady's final-round, 1-under-par 71 on the challenging 6,933-yard layout earned him a $6,000 first-place prize and a four-stroke victory over Rob McNamara of Gainesville, Fla.

Brady became the first winner in the 17-year tournament history to win a PGA Section championship (Mich.), an assistant professional PGA Section championship (Mich.) and the national Assistant Professional Championship in the same year.

Brady, who held the lead in his final 24 holes, finished with a 72-hole total of 4-under-par 284 in the $75,000 Championship. Brady's victory margin was a tournament record since the Championship converted from 54 to 72 holes in 1991. McNamara, who led for 36 holes, was runner-up with a final-round 73 and even-par 288 total. John Dal Corobbo of La Grange, Ill., was third at 290 after a 74, followed by John Mazza of Beaver Falls, Pa., at 291.

Brady birdied five holes and shrugged off a double-bogey on the par-4, 404-yard sixth hole, where he dumped his tee shot into a pond. McNamara, playing in the final group with Brady, saw his hopes of trimming Brady's lead wane on the same hole. His approach shot found the water and he settled for a double-bogey. Brady closed his impressive week by making a six-foot par putt on the 18th green.

PGA West yielded only 14 sub-par rounds out of 176, and the entire field averaged 76.29 strokes.

	Course Average	Rds. Under Par	Par Rds.	Rds. Over Par	Total Rds.	Round Leader	Low Round		Steve Brady
Round 1:	75.36	4	5	35	44	Rob McNamara	68-	McNamara	71- (T-3)
Round 2:	76.68	0	2	42	44	Rob McNamara	72-	Smith, Dal Corobbo	144- (T-2)
Round 3:	76.25	5	5	34	44	Steve Brady	69-	Brady	213- (1st)
Round 4:	75.57	7	5	32	44	Steve Brady	69-	Mazza, Pampling, Warzecha	284- (1st)
Total:	76.30	16	17	143	176				

TOURNAMENT SUMMARY

Place	Name	Scores	Winnings
1	Steve Brady, Rochester Hills, Mich.	71-73-69-71—284	$6,000.00
2	Rob McNamara, Gainesville, Fla.	68-75-72-73—288	$4,500.00
3	John Dal Corobbo, La Grange, Ill.	73-72-71-74—290	$3,500.00
4	John Mazza, Beaver Falls, Pa.	72-76-74-69—291	$3,250.00
T-5	Joe Meade, Chuckey, Tenn.	74-75-75-72—296	$2,758.34
	Dan Hornig, Walnut, Calif.	76-74-74-72—296	$2,758.33
	Mike Taylor, Gastonia, N.C.	70-74-74-78—296	$2,758.33
T-8	Rod Pampling, Brisbane, Australia	74-74-80-69—297	$2,225.00
	Gregg Hemann, Evans, Ga.	73-80-73-71—297	$2,225.00
10	Craig Everett, Glasgow, Scotland	77-74-75-72—298	$2,000.00
T-11	Gary Blevins, Farmington, N.M.	73-74-80-72—299	$1,762.50
	Jay Hunter, Jefferson City, Mo.	76-77-75-71—299	$1,762.50
	Greg Cerulli, Port St. Lucie, Fla.	73-80-72-74—299	$1,762.50
	David Young, Port Washington, N.Y.	72-83-71-73—299	$1,762.50
T-15	Mark Trauner, Boulder, Colo.	72-75-77-76—300	$1,575.00
	Eric Mercier, Laual, Canada	71-77-72-80—300	$1,575.00
17	Denny Hepler, Warsaw, Ind.	75-78-76-73—302	$1,500.00
T-18	Scott Beard, Louisville, Ky.	76-75-79-73—303	$1,408.34
	Paul Oglesby, Hershey, Pa.	76-79-75-73—303	$1,408.33
	Scott Williams, Redmond, Wash.	72-81-72-78—303	$1,408.33
T-21	Scott Warzecha, Montgomery, Ala.	80-80-75-69—304	$1,325.00
	Dennis Winters, Crownsville, Md.	75-74-80-75—304	$1,325.00

Place	Name	Scores	Winnings
	Bob Mucha, Westfield, Mass.	76-75-77-76—304	$1,325.00
T-24	Chris Winkel, Ames, Iowa	76-75-80-74—305	$1,237.50
	Chris Jones, Murray, Utah	75-85-73-72—305	$1,237.50
	Jimmy Odell, Houston, Texas	74-78-78-75—305	$1,237.50
	Mark Viskozki, Grand Prairie, Texas	75-78-75-77—305	$1,237.50
T-28	Shane Abe, Kapolei, Hawaii	75-81-75-75—306	$1,160.00
	Jay Gunning, Schenectady, N.Y.	74-80-76-76—306	$1,160.00
	John Lucansky, Canfield, Ohio	78-76-70-82—306	$1,160.00
T-31	William Arliss, Sodus Point, N.Y.	75-78-78-76—307	$1,112.50
	Darren Tucker, Yuma, Ariz.	77-82-71-77—307	$1,112.50
33	Stuart Smith, Roseville, Calif.	79-72-72-85—308	$1,090.00
T-34	Brent Studer, Essex Falls, N.J.	74-81-77-77—309	$1,075.00
	Bret Taylor, Omaha, Neb.	75-80-76-78—309	$1,075.00
36	Bill Kokott, Middleton, Wis.	79-85-76-71—311	$1,060.00
T-37	Ray Barr, Little Rock, Ark.	73-76-85-78—312	$1,045.00
	Jeffrey Sedorcek, Bonner Springs, Kan.	79-74-77-82—312	$1,045.00
T-39	Mike Glendenning, Medway, Ohio	81-84-78-73—316	$1,025.00
	Tuck Walton, Elma, N.Y.	75-80-76-85—316	$1,025.00
41	Scott Johnson, Milton, Mass.	72-76-89-81—318	$1,015.00
42	Dan Drane, Hattiesburg, Miss.	80-85-81-75—321	$1,010.00
43	Glenn Godfrey, Billings, Mont.	84-85-85-83—337	$1,005.00
44	Don Berry, Brooklyn Park, Minn.	91-86-89-89—355	$1,000.00

1992

Bill Loeffler of Littleton, Colo. fired a final-round even-par 72 to capture the 16th AnnualPGA Assistant Professional Championship presented by Titleist and Foot-Joy Worldwide. One of only four players to break par for 72 holes, Loeffler finished with a 5-under-par 283 total, three strokes better than Jon Fiedler of Camarillo, Calif., and earned $6,000. Canada's Kevin Dugas, who set a fourth-round tournament record with a 67, shared third place with New Jersey Player of the Year Charlie Cowell of Totowa, N.J.

Champion:	Bill Loeffler, Littleton, Colo.	
Site:	PGA West (Nicklaus Private), La Quinta, Calif.	
Date:	Sept. 22-25	Purse: $75,000

Loeffler, the 1986 U.S. Mid-Amateur champion, held off an early surge by 1985 Foot-Joy PGA Assistant Professional Champion Fiedler, who had four birdies on the front nine to take a one-stroke advantage. Loeffler set two tournament records during the week — posting the highest opening round for a champion (75) and the lowest second round (65) to get back in the hunt. Defending champion Kim Thompson of American Fork, Utah, tied for 13th at 4-over-par 292.

	Course Average	Rds. Under Par	Par Rds.	Rds. Over Par	Total Rds.	Round Leader	Low Round		Bill Loeffler
Round 1:	74.46	11	3	32	46	Mark Tucker, Tim Holt	69-	Tucker, Holt	75- (T-27)
Round 2:	75.15	10	1	35	46	Kenneth Jarner	65-	Loeffler	140- (T-2)
Round 3:	74.43	10	3	33	46	Bill Loeffler	67-	Bill Van Orman	211- (1st)
Round 4:	74.63	6	5	35	46	Bill Loeffler	67-	Kevin Dugas	283- (1st)
Total:	74.67	37	12	135	184				

TOURNAMENT SUMMARY

Place	Name	Scores	Winnings
1.	Bill Loeffler, Littleton, Colo.	75-65-71-72—283	$6,000.00
2.	Jon Fiedler, Camarillo, Calif.	71-75-69-71—286	$4,500.00
3.	Kevin Dugas, Canada	74-71-75-67—287	$3,325.00
	Charlie Cowell, Totowa, N.J.	70-72-73-72—287	$3,325.00
5.	Kenneth Jarner, Rohnert Park, Calif.	71-67-77-73—288	$2,800.00
6.	Paul Mayo, Wales	71-69-74-75—289	$2,600.00
7.	Mark Tucker, Mohawk, N.Y.	69-74-78-69—290	$2,000.00
	Jeffrey Sedorcek, Kansas City, Kan.	70-74-75-71—290	$2,000.00
	Scott Beard, Louisville, Ky.	72-71-74-73—290	$2,000.00
	Brad Jones, Shreveport, La.	74-71-73-72—290	$2,000.00
	Kevin Cashman, Edina, Minn.	74-73-69-74—290	$2,000.00
	Bill Van Orman, North Salem, N.Y.	74-75-67-74—290	$2,000.00
13.	Jay Hunter, Jefferson City, Mo.	77-69-74-72—292	$1,575.00
	Kim Thompson, American Fork, Utah	71-76-73-72—292	$1,575.00
	Ed Vietmeier, Coraopolis, Pa.	73-73-72-74—292	$1,575.00
	George Bowman, Novi, Mich.	76-68-70-78—292	$1,575.00
17.	Todd Howard, Euless, Texas	70-81-72-71—294	$1,380.00
	George Kallish, Oak Forest, Ill.	76-76-73-69—294	$1,380.00
	Tim Fleming, Oklahoma City, Okla.	74-77-69-74—294	$1,380.00
	Kirby Kielman, Houston, Texas	76-74-70-74—294	$1,380.00
	Michael Domalske, Sarasota, Fla.	71-72-73-78—294	$1,380.00
22.	Mike Cook, St. Simon Is., Ga.	73-74-75-73—295	$1,287.50
	Dave Spengler, Green Bay, Wis.	71-77-72-75—295	$1,287.50
24.	Jay Standard, Fredericksburg, Wis.	75-73-75-73—296	$1,225.00
	Fran Marrello, Plymouth, Conn.	74-71-77-74—296	$1,225.00
	Jay Gunning, Latham, N.Y.	72-77-71-76—296	$1,225.00
27.	Dan St. Louis, Wellington, Fla.	76-76-71-76—299	$1,170.00
	Rich Bruning, Gahanna, Ohio	81-73-71-74—299	$1,170.00
29.	Randol Mitchell, Waipahu, Hawaii	77-76-74-73—300	$1,130.00
	Tim Holt, Monticello, Ind.	69-77-75-79—300	$1,130.00
31.	Jimmie Brothers, Akron, Ohio	74-80-75-73—302	$1,095.00
	Joe Meade, Greeneville, Tenn.	75-75-77-75—302	$1,095.00
33.	Keith Liedes, Olympia, Wash.	72-81-75-75—303	$1,080.00
34.	Chris Estrdge, Charlotte, N.C.	74-78-76-76—304	$1,065.00
	Shane Marvelli, Des Moines, Iowa	73-74-79-78—304	$1,065.00
36.	Mark Hall, Dover, Del.	76-78-77-75—306	$1,045.00
	Tony Hidalgo, Albuquerque, N.M.	77-69-77-83—306	$1,045.00
38.	Renne Sasse, Lincoln, Neb.	81-78-77-75—311	$1,030.00
39.	Masayuki Arai, Japan	78-79-77-78—312	$1,015.00
	Mike Campbell, Cantonment, Fla.	79-85-69-79—312	$1,015.00
41.	David Weiss, Rochester, N.Y.	81-75-82-75—313	$1,000.00
42.	Brad Sullivan, Sydney, Australia	74-82-83-76—315	$985.00
	Anthony Blasius, Boise, Idaho	78-81-78-78—315	$985.00
44.	Rex Underwood, Salt Lake City, Utah	75-87-75-79—317	$970.00
45.	Jay Becher, Chandler, Ariz.	81-76-79-83—319	$960.00
46.	Jeffrey Stewart, Centerville, Mass.	79-82-86-77—324	$960.00

PGA ASSISTANT PROFESSIONAL CHAMPIONSHIP

- presented by TITLEIST and FOOT-JOY WORLDWIDE -

1991

Kim Thompson was the only player to shoot par or better each round in capturing the 15th Annual PGA Assistant Professional Championship presented by Titleist and Foot-Joy Worldwide. In addition to moving from Thorny Lea Golf Club in Brockton, Mass. to the West Coast, the event was conducted under a 72-hole format for the first time.

Champion:	Kim Thompson, American Fork, Utah
Site:	PGA West (Nicklaus Private), La Quinta, Calif.
Date:	Sept. 10-13 Purse: $75,000

	Course Average	Rds. Under Par	Par Rds.	Rds. Over Par	Total Rds.	Round Leader	Low Round		Kim Thompson
Round 1:	76.07	6	4	35	45	Mark Fuller	67-	Fuller	72- (T-9)
Round 2:	74.73	11	2	32	45	Fuller, Thomas Carey	66-	Robert Mucha	141- (T-4)
Round 3:	74.36	9	4	32	45	Bruce Zabriski	66-	Zabriski, Thomas Cleaver	210- (3rd)
Round 4:	75.40	7	3	35	45	Kim Thompson	68-	Thompson	278- (1st)
Total:	75.14	33	13	134	180				

TOURNAMENT SUMMARY

Place	Name	Scores	Winnings
1	Kim Thompson, American Fork, Utah	72-69-69-68—278	$6,000.00
2	Thomas Cleaver, Boca Raton, Fla.	69-73-66-73—281	$4,250.00
3	Bruce Zabriski, Southampton, N.Y.	70-70-66-77—283	$3,250.00
4	Mike Schuchart, Lincoln, Neb.	75-69-74-69—287	$3,000.00
T-5	Wesley Short, Austin, Texas	74-71-70-73—288	$2,675.00
	Kyle Anderson, Superior, Wis.	73-69-71-75—288	$2,675.00
	Brad Jones, Shreveport, La.	72-70-72-74—288	$2,675.00
8	Thomas Carey, Portland, Ore.	70-69-79-71—289	$2,300.00
9	Tommy Masters, Walnut Creek, Calif.	68-74-70-78—290	$2,150.00
10	Michael Domalske, Sarasota, Fla.	75-76-70-70—291	$2,000.00
11	Robert Mucha, Springfield, Mass.	75-66-75-76—292	$1,900.00
12	Kevin DeNike, Davenport, Iowa	76-74-73-70—293	$1,800.00
T-13	Joe Allinder, Ft. Walton Beach, Fla.	76-69-74-75—294	$1,650.00
	Randol Mitchell, Waipahu, Hawaii	71-76-73-74—294	$1,650.00
	Jim Estes, Olney, Md.	72-72-72-78—294	$1,650.00
16	Mark Fuller, Edmond, Okla.	67-72-79-77—295	$1,550.00
17	Kelly Manos, Cypress, Calif.	75-73-74-75—297	$1,500.00
T-18	David Spengler, Green Bay, Wis.	78-78-68-74—298	$1,425.00
	Simon Wood, Essex, England	75-75-73-75—298	$1,425.00
T-20	Jeffrey Sedorcek, Kansas City, Kan.	76-76-73-74—299	$1,362.00
	Chip Hall, Rochester, N.Y.	77-75-74-73—299	$1,362.00
22	Troy Reiser, Ft. Worth, Texas	79-76-72-73—300	$1,325.00
T-23	Brian Conser, Denver, Colo.	81-75-76-69—301	$1,262.00
	Pat Stephens, Richmond, Ky.	72-78-79-72—301	$1,262.00
	Larry King, Trenton, Ohio	81-73-75-72—301	$1,262.00
	Joe Boros, Butler, Pa.	70-77-76-78—301	$1,262.00
T-27	Bobby Cooke, Aberdeen, N.C.	79-82-71-70—302	$1,190.00
	David Roberts, Gwynedd Valley, Pa.	75-80-73-74—302	$1,190.00
29	Mark Tucker, Mohawk, N.Y.	77-79-75-73—304	$1,160.00
T-30	Mark Giuliano, Basking Ridge, N.J.	76-79-78-72—305	$1,130.00
	John Lee, Shaker Heights, Ohio	79-76-75-75—305	$1,130.00
T-32	Jay Hunter, Jefferson City, Mo.	79-78-72-77—306	$1,097.00
	Todd Greenlee, Novi, Mich.	74-76-74-82—306	$1,097.00
T-34	Jean Chatelain, Quebec, Canada	79-76-78-74—307	$1,075.00
	Jeff Gunning, Albany, N.Y.	79-75-74-79—307	$1,075.00
T-36	Phil Fecteau, Marlboro, Mass.	74-77-81-77—309	$1,055.00
	Dale Tallon, Lake Forest, Ill.	79-76-73-81—309	$1,055.00
T-38	Van Montgomery, Memphis, Tenn.	78-82-77-78—315	$1,030.00
	Gary Blevins, Farmington, N.H.	86-73-77-79—315	$1,030.00
	David Steed, Macon, Ga.	82-71-75-87—315	$1,030.00
T-41	Yoshihiro Azuma, Nara, Japan	79-76-81-80—316	$1,012.00
	William Hutter, Bloomington, Ind.	82-79-76-79—316	$1,012.00
43	James Contreras, Scottsdale, Ariz.	86-71-82-80—319	$1,005.00
44	Andy Deiro, Boise, Idaho	80-85-80-76—321	$1,000.00
45	Tony Mills, Perth, Australia	81-77-81-87—326	$1,000.00

1990

Steve Gotsche of Great Bend, Kan., tied a tournament record with a 5-under-par 205 and held off a strong challenge by Lee Rinker of Dublin, Ohio, to capture the 14th Annual Foot-Joy PGA Assistant Professional Championship. After Gotsche posted a final-round 68, Rinker had to birdie the 420-yard finishing hole to force a playoff. His 4-iron second shot landed 35 feet short of the hole from where he narrowly missed his birdie putt.

Champion:	Steve Gotsche, Great Bend, Kan.	
Site:	Thorny Lea Golf Club, Brockton, Mass.	
Date:	Sept. 26-28	**Purse:** $60,900

	Course Average	Rds. Under Par	Par Rds.	Rds. Over Par	Total Rds.	Round Leader	Low Round	Steve Gotsche
Round 1:	72.84	9	0	36	45	Steve Gotsche, Lee Rinker	67- Gotsche, Rinker	67- (T-1)
Round 2:	71.62	9	3	33	45	Lee Rinker, Curt Schnell	66- Schnell	137- (T-3)
Round 3:	72.11	11	6	28	45	Steve Gotsche	66- Mike West	205- (1st)
Total:	72.19	29	9	97	135			

TOURNAMENT SUMMARY

Place	Name	Scores	Winnings
1	Steve Gotsche, Great Bend, Kan.	67-70-68—205	$5,500.00
2	Lee Rinker, Dublin, Ohio	67-68-71—206	$4,000.00
T-3	Mike West, Charlottesville, Va.	72-69-66—207	$2,775.00
	Robert Mucha, Springfield, Mass.	68-71-68—207	$2,775.00
5	Thomas Cleaver, Boca Raton, Fla.	72-69-68—209	$2,200.00
6	John Lewis, Georgetown, Tenn.	69-71-70—210	$2,000.00
T-7	James Razzeto, Los Angeles, Calif.	73-69-69—211	$1,700.00
	Bill Isrealson, Duluth, Minn.	72-70-69—211	$1,700.00
	Curt Schnell, Bettendorf, Iowa	69-66-76—211	$1,700.00
T-10	Dan Koesters, Albuquerque, N.M.	73-71-68—212	$1,350.00
	Denny Hepler, Warsaw, Ind.	69-73-70—212	$1,350.00
	William Price, Dunwoody, Ga.	71-68-73—212	$1,350.00
	Gene Fieger, Newton Square, Pa.	69-70-73—212	$1,350.00
T-14	Gordon Vietmeier, Lavalette, W.Va.	74-72-67—213	$1,090.00
	Kenneth Stephens, Richmond, Ky.	73-72-68—213	$1,090.00
	Ray Pearce, Murfreesboro, Tenn.	71-72-70—213	$1,090.00
T-17	Jeffrey Jarvis, Lynoen, Wash.	71-72-71—214	$1,060.00
	Austin Straub, Cold Spring Harbor, N.Y.	71-72-71—214	$1,060.00
	Gary Trivisonno, Lyndhurst, Ohio	69-68-77—214	$1,060.00
T-20	Robert Gaus, St. Louis, Mo.	71-71-73—215	$1,035.00
	Charles Krenkel, Montgomery, Ala.	69-72-74—215	$1,035.00
T-22	David O'Kelly, Marshfield, Mass.	76-71-69—216	$1,010.00
	Mark Yannotta, Whippany, N.Y.	75-71-70—216	$1,010.00
	Ric Burgess, Stockton, Calif.	72-71-73—216	$1,010.00
T-25	Michael Malaska, Salt Lake City, Utah	73-74-70—217	$980.00
	Mark Viskozki, Arlington, Texas	73-71-73—217	$980.00
	John Godwin, Jackson, Wyo.	71-72-74—217	$980.00
28	Shawn Bellis, Aurora, Colo.	75-73-70—218	$960.00
T-29	Timothy Fries, Amherst, N.Y.	79-71-69—219	$930.00
	Mike Kingsrud, Tempe, Ariz.	75-73-71—219	$930.00
	Tom Tierney, Montgomery, Ala.	75-71-73—219	$930.00
	Michael Erickson, Walled Lake, Mich.	72-71-76—219	$930.00
	Tony Ashton, Great Britain	74-67-78—219	$930.00
T-34	Colin Field, Australia	76-73-71—220	$890.00
	James Jeffers, Albany, N.Y.	72-74-74—220	$890.00
	Chris Peddicord, Baltimore, Md.	73-69-78—220	$890.00
T-37	Derek Sanders, Baton Rouge, La.	76-73-72—221	$865.00
	Randy Robb, Canada	71-75-75—221	$865.00
T-39	David Spengler, Green Bay, Wis.	74-76-75—225	$845.00
	Eddie Isley, High Point, N.C.	73-74-78—225	$845.00
41	Randol Mitchell, Waipahu, Hawaii	77-75-74—226	$830.00
T-42	Jeffrey Reader, Manlius, N.Y.	77-76-74—227	$815.00
	Scott Allacher, Omaha, Neb.	82-71-74—227	$815.00
44	Thomas Falotico, Windermere, Fla.	78-77-76—231	$800.00
45	Donnie Owens, Hot Springs, Ark.	79-78-78—235	$800.00

1989

Mike West of Charlottesville, Va., played a most unusual final round to shoot par-70 and win the 13th Annual Foot-Joy PGA Assistant Professional Championship. He entered the last round trailing by five strokes, went 2-over-par on the first six holes, bogeyed the final four holes, and still won by two shots at even-par 210.

Champion:	Mike West, Charlottesville, Va.		
Site:	Thorny Lea Golf Club, Brockton, Mass.		
Date:	Sept. 27-29	**Purse:**	$50,600

	Course Average	Rds. Under Par	Par Rds.	Rds. Over Par	Total Rds.	Round Leader	Low Round		Mike West
Round 1:	73.61	6	2	36	44	Bill King	67-	King	68- (T-2)
Round 2:	73.20	8	0	36	44	Tracy Frank	66-	Frank	140- (T-4)
Round 3:	74.63	2	2	40	44	Mike West	67-	Jim Weeden	210- (1st)
Total:	73.81	16	4	112	132				

TOURNAMENT SUMMARY

Place	Name	Scores	Winnings
1	Mike West, Charlottesville, Va.	68-72-70—210	$5,500.00
2	Tracy Frank, Burley, Idaho	69-66-77—212	$4,000.00
T-3	Scott Templeton, Edmond, Okla.	73-71-69—213	$2,613.00
	Kenneth Allard, Birmingham, Mich.	73-68-72—213	$2,613.00
	Alan Schulte, Cooperstown, N.Y.	71-69-73—213	$2,613.00
T-6	John Spelman, Pittsburgh, Pa.	69-74-71—214	$1,833.00
	David Hunter, Columbus, Ohio	75-67-72—214	$1,833.00
	Bill King, Piscataway, N.J.	67-71-76—214	$1,833.00
T-9	Ken McDonald, Houston, Texas	72-72-71—215	$1,550.00
	Chip Sullivan, Pepper Pike, Ohio	68-74-73—215	$1,550.00
T-11	Andrew Morse, Canton, Mass.	73-73-70—216	$1,300.00
	Steve Gotsche, Great Bend, Kan.	70-73-73—216	$1,300.00
	John Hayes, St. Louis, Mo.	72-68-76—216	$1,300.00
14	Henry White, Salt Lake City, Utah	74-71-72—217	$1,100.00
T-15	Don Berry, Brooklyn Park, Minn.	70-75-73—218	$980.00
	Jim Weeden, Deerfield Beach, Fla.	76-75-67—218	$980.00
	Bobby Schaeffer, Goleta, Calif.	73-67-78—218	$980.00
T-18	Colin Brooks, Falkirk, U.K.	72-74-73—219	$920.00
	Gerry Norquist, Eugene, Ore.	72-74-73—219	$920.00
	Robert Mucha, Springfield, Mass.	73-71-75—219	$920.00
21	Richard Lucas, Penfield, N.Y.	72-75-73—220	$880.00
T-22	David Spengler, Madison, Wis.	78-68-75—221	$845.00
	Mark Mielke, Manhassett, N.Y.	72-75-74—221	$845.00
	Bruce Zulaica, Alameda, Calif.	73-75-73—221	$845.00
	George Welch, Shreveport, La.	74-75-72—221	$845.00
	Ray Pearce, Murfreesboro, Tenn.	74-69-78—221	$845.00
	Mark Witt, Irving, Texas	77-72-72—221	$845.00
T-28	Brent Smith, Massena, N.Y.	71-74-78—223	$805.00
	Kevin DeNike, Bettendorf, Iowa	75-74-74—223	$805.00
T-30	Tom McGrew, Glencoe, Ill.	73-76-76—225	$785.00
	Tom Gray, Scottsdale, Ariz.	76-73-76—225	$785.00
32	Danny Elkins, Norcross, Ga.	77-78-71—226	$770.00
T-33	Dan Koesters, Albuquerque, N.M.	77-72-78—227	$755.00
	Michel Latulipe, Canada	78-73-76—227	$755.00
T-35	Hugh Gill, Little River, S.C.	75-73-80—228	$735.00
	Rennie Sasse, Lincoln, Neb.	75-75-78—228	$735.00
37	Tom Olson, Gainesville, Fla.	79-73-77—229	$720.00
T-38	Mixon Smith, Birmingham, Ala.	78-76-76—230	$705.00
	Randol Mitchell, Honolulu, Hawaii	82-73-75—230	$705.00
T-40	Drew Hood, Norristown, Pa.	75-74-83—232	$680.00
	Scott Davis, Killara, Australia	76-78-78—232	$680.00
	Rick Fernandes, Terre Haute, Ind.	78-79-75—232	$680.00
43	Dave Ballantyne, Frankfort, Ky.	68-87-80—235	$660.00
44	Randy Bregar, Pueblo, Colo.	76-79-82—237	$650.00

1988

In his third attempt, Webb Heintzelman finally won the Foot-Joy Assistant Professional Championship with a tournament record-tying 205. An opening 6-under-par 64 highlighted the PGA Tour-hopeful's round.

Champion:	Webb Heintzelman, Bethesda, Md.	
Site:	Thorny Lea Golf Club, Brockton, Mass.	
Date:	Sept. 28-30	**Purse:** $50,600

	Course Average	Rds. Under Par	Par Rds.	Rds. Over Par	Total Rds.	Round Leader	Low Round		Webb Heintzelman
Round 1:	73.06	8	3	33	44	Webb Heintzelman	64-	Heintzelman	64- (1st)
Round 2:	72.59	10	3	31	44	Mitch Camp	66-	Kevin DeNike	135- (2nd)
Round 3:	73.72	4	4	36	44	Webb Heintzelman	66-	Ron McDougal	205- (1st)
Total:	73.12	22	10	100	132				

TOURNAMENT SUMMARY

Place	Name	Scores	Winnings
1	Webb Heintzelman, Bethesda, Md.	64-71-70—205	$5,000.00
2	Mitch Camp, Copley, Ohio	67-67-73—207	$3,500.00
3	Mark Fuller, Edmond, Okla.	71-68-69—208	$2,500.00
T-4	Ron McDougal, Rye, N.Y.	70-73-66—209	$1,938.00
	Bob Makoski, Novi, Mich.	68-69-72—209	$1,938.00
T-6	Darrell Kestner, Scarsdale, N.Y.	69-73-69—211	$1,600.00
	John Paesani, Mansfield Center, Conn.	72-68-71—211	$1,600.00
	Jeff McMillen, Aptos, Calif.	67-71-73—211	$1,600.00
	Kevin DeNike, Bettendorf, Iowa	73-66-72—211	$1,600.00
10	Chip Sullivan, Birmingham, Ala.	68-76-68—212	$1,350.00
T-11	Darryl Henning, Richmond, Texas	71-72-70—213	$1,150.00
	Steve King, Kansas City, Kan.	72-68-73—213	$1,150.00
	Jon Stanley, Louisville, Ky.	70-71-72—213	$1,150.00
T-14	Steve Schneiter, Sandy, Utah	70-75-70—215	$965.00
	Don Robertson, Dallas, Texas	69-74-72—215	$965.00
	Bill King, Somerset, N.J.	75-69-71—215	$965.00
T-17	Bob Gaus, St. Louis, Mo.	71-75-70—216	$880.00
	Warren Sasse, Lincoln, Neb.	73-72-71—216	$880.00
	Kevin Dugas, New Brunswick, Canada	75-67-74—216	$880.00
T-20	Tracy Frank, Burley, Idaho	74-72-71—217	$823.00
	Dan Koesters, Albuquerque, N.M.	71-73-73—217	$823.00
	Stephen Keppler, Dunwoody, Ga.	71-71-75—217	$823.00
23	Ray Pearce, Murfreesboro, Tenn.	74-72-72—218	$800.00
T-24	Rocky Miller, Groveport, Ohio	73-74-72—219	$785.00
	Kirk Schooley, Columbus, Ind.	77-67-75—219	$785.00
T-26	John Oates, England	76-70-74—220	$765.00
	Todd Yoshitake, Chino, Calif.	73-70-77—220	$765.00
T-28	Mark Keating, Kent, Wash.	74-76-71—221	$745.00
	Alan Schulte, Cooperstown, N.Y.	69-77-75—221	$745.00
30	Frank Dobbs, Spring City, Pa.	77-70-75—222	$730.00
T-31	Rick Lewallen, Greensboro, N.C.	79-71-73—223	$715.00
	Doug Sheldon, Madison, Wis.	77-69-77—223	$715.00
T-33	Mark Hill, West Palm Beach, Fla.	75-73-76—224	$695.00
	Dave Erickson, Hillside, Ill.	71-73-80—224	$695.00
35	Graeme Trew, Queensland, Australia	76-73-76—225	$680.00
36	Hank Gardner, Phoenix, Ariz.	72-75-79—226	$670.00
T-37	Craig Kealey, Norwalk, Conn.	74-81-75—230	$655.00
	Joe Root, Waikoloa, Hawaii	77-77-76—230	$655.00
39	Duane Lorio, Baton Rouge, La.	80-77-74—231	$640.00
40	Timothy Fries, Rochester, N.Y.	75-81-76—232	$630.00
T-41	Kris Smith, McMurray, Pa.	79-75-80—234	$617.00
	Jon Fine, Apopka, Fla.	77-77-80—234	$617.00
43	Greg McCullough, Fargo, N.D.	77-80-82—239	$610.00
44	Mitch Weaver, Littleton, Colo.	82-75-84—241	$605.00

1987

For the second time, Darrell Kestner of Mamaroneck, N.Y., emerged as Foot-Joy PGA Assistant Professional Champion with a playoff victory. Kestner, who won the 1983 Championship on the first playoff hole, became the first two-time Championship winner. He sank a 50-foot birdie putt, again on the first playoff hole, defeating Ken Schall of Des Moines, Iowa, Greg Farrow of Mt. Holly, N.J., and Bob Gaus of Edwardsville, Ill.

Champion:	Darrell Kestner, Mamaroneck, N.Y.
Site:	Thorny Lea Golf Club, Brockton, Mass.
Date:	Sept. 29 - Oct. 2	Purse: $50,600

	Course Average	Rds. Under Par	Par Rds.	Rds. Over Par	Total Rds.	Round Leader	Low Round		Darrell Kestner
Round 1:	73.25	4	4	36	44	Greg Farrow, Chris Tucker	68-	Farrow, Tucker	73- (T-21)
Round 2:	72.97	8	4	32	44	Chris Tucker	67-	Darrell Kestner	140- (T-5)
Round 3:	75.56	1	1	42	44	Darrell Kestner, Ken Schall, Greg Farrow, Bob Gaus	69-	Schall	210- (1st)
Total:	73.93	13	9	110	132				

TOURNAMENT SUMMARY

Place	Name	Scores	Winnings
T-1	Darrell Kestner, Mamaroneck, N.Y.*	73-67-70—210	$5,000.00
	Ken Schall, Des Moines, Iowa	72-69-69—210	$3,500.00
	Greg Farrow, Mt. Holly, N.J.	68-71-71—210	$3,500.00
	Bob Gaus, Edwardsville, Ill.	69-69-72—210	$3,500.00
5	Webb Heintzelman, Gaithersburg, Md.	71-68-73—212	$2,500.00
6	Alan Schulte, Cooperstown, N.Y.	70-72-71—213	$2,000.00
T-7	Fran Marrello, Wolcott, Conn.	69-73-72—214	$1,700.00
	Chris Endres, Glendale, Ariz.	70-70-74—214	$1,700.00
9	Baker Maddera, Westfield, N.J.	71-72-72—215	$1,400.00
10	Barry Redmond, Royal Oak, Mich.	72-71-73—216	$1,250.00
T-11	Joe Boros, Emlenton, Pa.	74-70-73—217	$1,075.00
	Bill Whaley, Plantation, Fla.	72-70-75—217	$1,075.00
T-13	Chris Tucker, Charlotte, N.C.	68-68-82—218	$950.00
	Mike Schuchart, Lincoln, Neb.	71-75-72—218	$950.00
	Paul Archbold, Nedlands, Australia	76-69-73—218	$950.00
T-16	Don Koesters, Albuquerque, N.M.	76-70-73—219	$838.00
	Jim Gaugert, Milwaukee, Wis.	72-73-74—219	$838.00
	Matt Plumlee, Visalia, Calif.	70-74-75—219	$838.00
	Kirk Schooley, Columbus, Ind.	78-69-72—219	$838.00
T-20	Ric Nalyd, Odessa, Fla.	74-73-73—220	$770.00
	Charlie Moller, Peachtree City, Ga.	74-73-73—220	$770.00
T-22	Doug Hixson, Creswell, Ore.	76-68-77—221	$730.00
	Rocky Miller, Groveport, Ohio	75-71-75—221	$730.00

Place	Name	Scores	Winnings
T-24	Tad Holloway, Caldwell, Idaho	70-76-76—222	$685.00
	John Frizzell, Seekonk, Mass.	74-74-74—222	$685.00
	Rod Kimmel, Bartlesville, Okla.	76-71-75—222	$685.00
	Jon Hoecker, Pittsford, N.Y.	72-71-79—222	$685.00
T-28	Ken MacDonald, Madison, Wis.	73-72-78—223	$650.00
	Terrence Valentine, Elyria, Ohio	76-72-75—223	$650.00
	John Hawksworth, Lytham, England	72-77-74—223	$650.00
T-31	Lynn Landgren, Murray, Utah	72-74-79—225	$625.00
	Michael Klimtzak, Delmar, N.Y.	74-77-74—225	$625.00
33	Raymond Richer, Quebec, Canada	76-73-78—227	$610.00
34	Rick DeLoach, Irving, Texas	74-76-78—228	$600.00
T-35	Danny Weeks, Anniston, Ala.	74-73-82—229	$575.00
	Billy Rosinia, Lombard, Ill.	72-79-78—229	$575.00
	Cutts Benedict, San Antonio, Texas	75-74-80—229	$575.00
	Shawn McEntee, La Quinta, Calif.	73-76-80—229	$575.00
39	Jack Barksdale, Germantown, Tenn.	72-79-81—232	$550.00
40	Craig Martin, Edwardsville, Kan.	75-82-76—233	$540.00
41	Clark Miyazaki, Waipahu, Hawaii	77-75-82—234	$530.00
42	Michael Dunlop, Denver, Colo.	83-77-75—235	$520.00
43	Jim Wahl, Wayzata, Minn.	79-74-83—236	$510.00
44	Bruce Moellendick, Louisville, Ky.	75-84-84—243	$500.00

* Won playoff with birdie on first extra hole

1986

Robert Thompson of Huntsville, Texas, rallied from a 7-stroke second-round deficit to win the 10th Annual Foot-Joy Assistant Professional Championship by one shot over three others. Second-round leader Ken Allard of Rochester, Mich., had the best opportunity for victory after putting his approach shot on the 18th green for a one-putt chance for the win or a two-putt to force a playoff. His first attempt finished four feet to the right of the cup and he missed the comeback.

Champion:	Robert Thompson, Huntsville, Texas
Site:	Thorny Lea Golf Club, Brockton, Mass.
Date:	Sept. 23-26	Purse: $50,600

	Course Average	Rds. Under Par	Par Rds.	Rds. Over Par	Total Rds.	Round Leader	Low Round		Robert Thompson
Round 1:	72.40	6	7	31	44	Ken Allard	63-	Allard	71- (T-14)
Round 2:	73.45	3	6	35	44	Ken Allard	67-	Shawn McEntee, John Lyons	143- (T-12)
Round 3:	73.22	4	5	35	44	Robert Thompson	66-	Thompson	209- (1st)
Total:	73.02	13	18	101	132				

TOURNAMENT SUMMARY

Place	Name	Scores	Winnings
1	Robert Thompson, Huntsville, Texas	71-72-66—209	$5,000.00
T-2	Ken Allard, Rochester, Mich.	63-73-74—210	$3,500.00
	Scott Steger, Noblesville, Ind.	68-73-69—210	$3,500.00
	Ron Kiaaina Jr., Makaha, Hawaii	71-70-69—210	$3,500.00
5	Alan Schulte, Oneonta, N.Y.	70-69-72—211	$2,500.00
T-6	Raymond Cragun, Albuquerque, N.M.	72-70-70—212	$1,900.00
	Danny Weeks, Anniston, Ala.	68-72-72—212	$1,900.00
T-8	Shawn McEntee, San Jose, Calif.	72-67-74—213	$1,260.00
	Don Robertson, Dallas, Texas	66-71-76—213	$1,260.00
	Richard Loy, Naples, Fla.	73-70-70—213	$1,260.00
	Eddie Mudd, Louisville, Ky.	70-73-70—213	$1,260.00
	John Norton, Omaha, Neb.	73-73-67—213	$1,260.00
T-13	Ken Trimble, Concord, Australia	70-70-74—214	$922.00
	Webb Heintzelman, Gaithersburg, Md.	70-70-74—214	$922.00
T-15	Dan Cameron, Calgary, Alberta, Canada	69-75-71—215	$826.00
	Ed Terasa, Waukesha, Wis.	72-72-71—215	$826.00
	Ken Schall, Des Moines, Iowa	68-76-71—215	$826.00
	John Lyons, St. Louis, Mo.	72-67-76—215	$826.00
	Jon Fiedler, Camarillo, Calif.	73-72-70—215	$826.00
T-20	Mark Armistead, Scottsdale, Ariz.	72-74-71—217	$750.00
	Rob Wilkin, Olathe, Kan.	72-73-72—217	$750.00
22	Gary Griggs, San Diego, Calif.	72-72-74—218	$720.00
T-23	Michael Burke Jr., Pearl River, N.Y.	73-71-76—220	$695.00
	Raymond Silnik, Hellertown, Pa.	73-71-75—220	$695.00
T-25	Randy Fossum, Bellevue, Wash.	76-75-70—221	$670.00
	Jon Hoecker, Pittsford, N.Y.	70-74-77—221	$670.00
	Stan McLennan, Simsbury, Conn.	73-72-76—221	$670.00
T-28	Jim Gerber, St. Petersburg, Fla.	76-74-72—222	$640.00
	Roy Carmichael, Middletown, Ohio	77-70-75—222	$640.00
	John Spelman, Oakmont, Pa.	73-74-75—222	$640.00
T-31	Bill Reilly, Kent, Ohio	73-78-72—223	$615.00
	Bill Riviere, Eagan, Minn.	73-72-78—223	$615.00
33	Tracy Bowles, N. Myrtle Beach, S.C.	72-76-76—224	$600.00
T-34	Lynn Landgren, Salt Lake City, Utah	76-76-73—225	$575.00
	Carl Poche, New Orleans, La.	75-74-76—225	$575.00
	Tom Losinger, Dunwoody, Ga.	77-77-71—225	$575.00
	Mike Gornto, Leicester, Mass.	75-72-78—225	$575.00
T-38	Rod Kimmel, Bartlesville, Okla.	70-78-78—226	$545.00
	Tommy McGinnis, Mamaroneck, N.Y.	70-80-76—226	$545.00
T-40	Jeff Lytten, Barrington, Ill.	75-78-74—227	$525.00
	Tim Stafford, Margaretville, N.Y.	76-76-75—227	$525.00
42	Art Whaley, Greeneville, Tenn.	80-72-76—228	$510.00
43	Tracy Frank, Burley, Idaho	77-79-75—231	$505.00
44	Jim Lipp, Colorado Springs, Colo.	79-89-75—243	$500.00

1985

Even Hurricane Gloria couldn't prevent Jon Fiedler of Camarillo, Calif., from winning the Ninth Annual Foot-Joy PGA Assistant Professional Championship. The storm blew into Brockton on Friday before tournament week and a core of more than thirty people worked day and night to repair the damage left behind. Fielder took care of his part with consistent play all three days on the 6,400-yard Thorny Lea course.

Champion:	Jon Fiedler, Camarillo, Calif.	
Site:	Thorny Lea Golf Club, Brockton, Mass.	
Date:	Oct. 2-4	Purse: $40,000

	Course Average	Rds. Under Par	Par Rds.	Rds. Over Par	Total Rds.	Round Leader	Low Round		Jon Fielder
Round 1:	72.83	8	2	32	42	Fran Marrello	67-	Marrello	69- (T-4)
Round 2:	74.85	1	3	38	42	Fran Marrello	69-	Jeff Tallman	141- (T-2)
Round 3:	75.35	0	3	39	42	Jon Fiedler	70-	Fiedler, Perry Arthur, Ray Freeman	211- (1st)
Total:	73.68	9	8	109	126				

TOURNAMENT SUMMARY

Place	Name	Scores	Winnings
1	Jon Fiedler, Camarillo, Calif.	69-72-70—211	$4,000.00
T-2	Perry Arthur, Dallas, Texas	68-74-70—212	$2,750.00
	Mike Burke Jr., Englewood Cliffs, N.J.	71-70-71—212	$2,750.00
4	Kevin Klier, Rockland, Mass.	72-73-68—213	$2,200.00
T-5	Ken Schall, Des Moines, Iowa	71-71-73—215	$1,800.00
	Fred Funk, College Park, Md.	70-72-73—215	$1,800.00
	Steve King, Prairie Village, Kan.	69-72-74—215	$1,800.00
8	Mel Baum, Baldwinsville, N.Y.	71-72-73—216	$1,400.00
T-9	Brent Murray, Portland, Ore.	69-74-74—217	$962.00
	Mike Hammond, Sugar Land, Texas	69-73-75—217	$962.00
	Fran Marrello, Waterbury, Conn.	67-72-78—217	$962.00
	Ken Postlewait Jr., Casselberry, Fla.	71-74-72—217	$962.00
	Ray Freeman, Greensboro, N.C.	68-79-70—217	$962.00
	Jeff Tallman, Indianapolis, Ind.	72-69-76—217	$962.00
15	Tom Costello, American Fork, Utah	71-75-72—218	$825.00
T-16	Carl Poche, New Orleans, La.	71-76-72—219	$787.00
	Jim Cichra, Pittsburgh, Pa.	69-73-77—219	$787.00
T-18	Raymond Richer, Boisbrian, Canada	72-75-73—220	$737.00
	Brad Worthington, Cedarhurst, N.Y.	72-74-74—220	$737.00
20	John Phillips, Louisville, Ky.	71-73-77—221	$700.00
21	Brian Kelly, Kennett Square, Pa.	75-73-75—223	$675.00
T-22	Andy Boyd, Albuquerque, N.M.	72-76-76—224	$613.00
	Frank Arone, Minnetonka Beach, Minn.	77-76-71—224	$613.00
	Robin Freeman, Edmond, Okla.	79-70-75—224	$613.00
	Shawn McEntee, San Jose, Calif.	74-73-77—224	$613.00
26	John Jasinski, Toledo, Ohio	70-70-85—225	$560.00
27	Eric Barnes, Scottsdale, Ariz.	71-82-73—226	$545.00
T-28	Craig Stevens, Athens, Ga.	77-73-77—227	$525.00
	Bruno DuPont, Redford Township, Mich.	75-74-78—227	$525.00
T-30	Gary Claypool, Grand Island, Neb.	77-75-76—228	$505.00
	Mike Maillot, Denver, Colo.	74-73-81—228	$505.00
32	Robert Horak, Ontario, N.Y.	79-72-78—229	$490.00
33	John Borrell, Fort Lauderdale, Fla.	74-79-77—230	$480.00
T-34	Billy Mitchell, Springboro, Ohio	73-78-80—231	$465.00
	Alec Walker, Memphis, Tenn.	75-80-76—231	$465.00
T-36	Mark Wood, Tuscaloosa, Ala.	73-80-79—232	$440.00
	Randy Burkhardt, Highland Park, Ill.	79-78-75—232	$440.00
	Ron Kiaaina, Makaha, Hawaii	75-79-78—232	$440.00
39	Tim Sereikis, Loudonville, N.Y.	77-79-77—233	$420.00
40	Bob Renken, St. Charles, Mo.	76-77-81—234	$410.00
41	William Gibbs, Virginia Beach, Va.	75-86-76—237	$405.00
42	Xavier Sandoval, Neenah, Wis.	79-78-82—239	$400.00

1984

Fred Funk of College Park, Md., and Brent Murray of Portland, Ore., battled down to the wire at the Eighth Annual Foot-Joy PGA Assistant Professional Championship, with Funk emerging as the winner by one stroke. Funk held a four-stroke advantage through 15 holes, but as the players approached the 18th green, his lead had been reduced to one. Funk's second shot on No. 18 barely missed sailing out of bounds when it hit a player's golf car. Murray then missed a four-foot putt and both players finished with bogeys.

Champion:	Fred Funk, College Park, Md.
Site:	Thorny Lea Golf Club, Brockton, Mass.
Date:	Sept. 19-21 **Purse:** $37,900

	Course Average	Rds. Under Par	Par Rds.	Rds. Over Par	Total Rds.	Round Leader	Low Round		Fred Funk
Round 1:	73.88	4	3	36	43	Brent Murray	68-	Murray	71- (T-7)
Round 2:	74.18	5	3	35	43	Brent Murray, Fred Funk	66-	Funk	137- (T-1)
Round 3:	74.90	6	1	36	43	Fred Funk	67-	Victor Tortorici, Bruce Douglass	206- (1st)
Total:	74.32	15	7	107	129				

TOURNAMENT SUMMARY

Place	Name	Scores	Winnings
1	Fred Funk, College Park, Md.	71-66-69—206	$4,000.00
2	Brent Murray, Portland, Ore.	68-69-70—207	$3,000.00
T-3	Fritz Gambetta, Milwaukee, Wis.	70-70-72—212	$2,083.00
	Perry Arthur, Dallas, Texas	71-72-69—212	$2,083.00
	Victor Tortorici, Syosset, N.Y.	74-71-67—212	$2,083.00
6	Bruce Douglass, Mamaroneck, N.Y.	76-71-67—214	$1,500.00
T-7	Scott Morris, Carmel, Ind.	74-68-73—215	$1,066.00
	Danny Elkins, St. Petersburg, Fla.	72-70-73—215	$1,066.00
	Jim Barker, San Antonio, Texas	72-72-71—215	$1,066.00
10	Paul Purtzer, Scottsdale, Ariz.	72-75-69—216	$925.00
11	Ed Whitman, Blairstown, N.J.	73-73-71—217	$900.00
T-12	Rick Osberg, Paoli, Pa.	74-73-71—218	$837.00
	Dale Fuller, Clayton, N.C.	73-68-77—218	$837.00
	David Emerick, Rancho Santa Fe, Calif.	69-73-76—218	$837.00
	Ric Burgess, Stockton, Calif.	72-77-69—218	$837.00
16	Doug Lecuyer, Edmonton, Canada	72-74-73—219	$775.00
T-17	Kim Thompson, Midvale, Utah	70-74-76—220	$712.00
	Kirk Maynord, Midwest City, Okla.	73-70-77—220	$712.00
	Mike San Filippo, Miami Lakes, Fla.	71-76-73—220	$712.00
	Brad Sater, Olathe, Kan.	75-71-74—220	$712.00
T-21	Jim Ahern, W. Des Moines, Iowa	69-79-74—222	$625.00
	Hank Schiller, Mandeville, La.	72-73-77—222	$625.00
	Scott Shelton, Kapalua, Hawaii	75-71-76—222	$625.00
T-24	Mike Thrasher, Louisville, Ky.	75-69-79—223	$543.00
	Randy Burkhardt, Highland Park, Ill.	76-76-71—223	$543.00
	David Nevatt, Aurora, Colo.	77-74-72—223	$543.00
	Gregg Natale, Syracuse, N.Y.	73-74-76—223	$543.00
T-28	Jeff Marsh, Brockton, Mass.	73-74-78—225	$500.00
	Ron Beurmann, Detroit, Mich.	73-77-75—225	$500.00
	David Graf, Toledo, Ohio	76-71-78—225	$500.00
31	Mike Downey, Columbus, Ohio	69-77-80—226	$480.00
32	Dow Seagraves, Roswell, Ga.	77-77-73—227	$470.00
33	Gary Weir, Glasgow, Scotland	82-73-73—228	$460.00
34	Jim Cichra, Pittsburgh, Pa.	74-79-76—229	$450.00
35	David Hancock, Birmingham, Ala.	78-79-73—230	$440.00
36	Robert Atwood, Farmington, Conn.	80-77-77—234	$430.00
T-37	Tim Stafford, Margaretville, N.Y.	77-80-78—235	$420.00
	Kip Henley, Crossville, Tenn.	76-78-81—235	$420.00
	Dean Frankiewicz, St. Louis, Mo.	70-79-86—235	$420.00
40	Doug Hoskins, Lincoln, Neb.	78-80-78—236	$410.00
41	Steve Friedlander, Forest Lake, Minn.	81-77-80—238	$400.00
42	Chris Stewart, Albuquerque, N.M.	75-79-85—239	$400.00
43	Robert Noe Jr., Rochester, N.Y.	79-84-88—251	$400.00

1983

Despite a 4-over-par 214, Victor Tortorici of Jericho, N.Y., easily won the Seventh Annual Foot-Joy PGA Assistant Professional Championship by three strokes over Norm Becker of Caldwell, N.J. Tortorici entered the final round with a four-stroke advantage and built it up to five by the 18th hole before finishing with a double-bogey.

Champion:	Victor Tortorici, Jericho, N.Y.	
Site:	Thorny Lea Golf Club, Brockton, Mass.	
Date:	Sept. 13-16	Purse: $35,000

	Course Average	Rds. Under Par	Par Rds.	Rds. Over Par	Total Rds.	Round Leader	Low Round		Victor Tortorici
Round 1:	75.15	1	2	37	39	Jim Cichra	69-	Cichra	72- (T-8)
Round 2:	76.10	1	1	36	38	Victor Tortorici	69-	Lee Chill Jr.	142- (1st)
Round 3:	74.44	0	2	36	38	Victor Tortorici	70-	Fritz Gambetta, Jeff McMillen	214- (1st)
Total:	75.23	2	5	109	115				

TOURNAMENT SUMMARY

Place	Name	Scores	Winnings
1	Victor Tortorici, Jericho, N.Y.	72-70-72—214	$4,000.00
2	Norm Becker, N. Caldwell, N.J.	72-74-71—217	$3,000.00
3	Fritz Gambetta, Milwaukee, Wis.	77-71-70—218	$2,500.00
T-4	Tommy Hines, Honolulu, Hawaii	70-77-72—219	$1,450.00
	Russ Orth, Dallas, Texas	73-74-72—219	$1,450.00
	Bob Ackerman, Aurora, Ill.	70-76-73—219	$1,450.00
	Randall Mahar, Portland, Ore.	71-75-73—219	$1,450.00
T-8	Lee Chill Jr., Medina, Ohio	80-69-71—220	$955.00
	Mike Preston, Peabody, Mass.	76-72-72—220	$955.00
10	Jim Woodward, Edmond, Okla.	71-75-75—221	$900.00
11	B.J. Curry, Sedalia, Mo.	75-74-73—222	$875.00
T-12	Jim Cichra, Pittsburgh, Pa.	69-81-73—223	$812.50
	Tommy Brannen, Duluth, Ga.	73-79-71—223	$812.50
	Jim Ankenbrandt, Orchard Lake, Mich.	75-75-73—223	$812.50
	Rick Bunting, Winnsboro, S.C.	73-74-76—223	$812.50
T-16	Jeff Marsh, Apopka, Fla.	75-77-72—224	$725.00
	Cutts Benedict, Baton Rouge, La.	74-77-73—224	$725.00
	Steve Haagenson, Warzata, Minn.	76-71-77—224	$725.00
T-19	Mel Baum, Baldwinsville, N.Y.	71-81-73—225	$650.00
	Hank Woodrome, Anaheim, Calif.	75-76-74—225	$650.00
	Paul Daniels, Dalton, Mass.	71-78-76—225	$650.00
T-22	Mark Orlowski, Scottsdale, Ariz.	75-78-74—227	$580.00
	Bob Jones, St. Charles, Mo.	77-73-77—227	$580.00
	Ross Barnes, Omaha, Neb.	73-76-78—227	$580.00
25	Jeff McMillen, Aptos, Calif.	80-78-70—228	$540.00
T-26	Bruce Martins, Chicopee, Mass.	79-76-74—229	$500.00
	James Matthias, Rockland, Del.	75-79-75—229	$500.00
	Melvin Rifman, Laurel, Md.	77-74-78—229	$500.00
29	Reed Hughes, Olive Branch, Miss.	80-76-74—230	$460.00
T-30	Vance Christiansen, Ogden, Utah	75-82-74—231	$445.00
	Mark Pelletier, Albuquerque, N.M.	76-78-77—231	$445.00
T-32	Daryl Hartig, Ft. Thomas, Ky.	80-77-75—232	$425.00
	Ron Vlosich, Englewood, Colo.	75-75-82—232	$425.00
34	Russ Holden, Deerfield Beach, Fla.	78-81-74—233	$410.00
T-35	Lon Kinney, Evansville, Ind.	81-78-75—234	$400.00
	Tim Lemons, Tuscaloosa, Ala.	80-76-78—234	$400.00
	Greg Vowell, Rochester, N.Y.	77-74-83—234	$400.00
38	William Kammeyer, Mason City, Iowa	82-75-82—239	$400.00
	Rick Smith, Columbus, Ohio	77-WD (injury)	$400.00

1982 Darrell Kestner of Purchase, N.Y., parred the first playoff hole to cap a remarkable comeback and win the Sixth Annual Foot-Joy PGA Assistant Professional Championship. Kestner trailed second-round leader Greg Farrow of Pitman, N.J., by seven strokes entering the final round, but posted a 2-under-par 68 to join Canada's Jean Louis Lamarre in the playoff. Farrow slipped to a final-round 79.

Champion:	Darrell Kestner, Purchase, N.Y.	
Site:	Thorny Lea Golf Club, Brockton, Mass.	
Date:	Sept. 23-25	Purse: $32,500

	Course Average	Rds. Under Par	Par Rds.	Rds. Over Par	Total Rds.	Round Leader	Low Round	Darrell Kestner
Round 1:	74.47	1	2	39	42	Jean Louis Lamarre	69- Lamarre	73- (T-9)
Round 2:	74.68	2	1	38	41	Greg Farrow	67- Farrow	145- (T-4)
Round 3:	74.98	1	1	36	41	Darrell Kestner, Lamarre	68- Kestner	213- (1st)
Total:	74.98	4	4	116	124			

TOURNAMENT SUMMARY

Place	Name	Scores	Winnings
T-1	Darrell Kestner, Purchase, N.Y.*	73-72-68—213	$3,500.00
	Jean Louis Lamarre, Quebec, Canada	69-72-72—213	$2,300.00
T-3	James Blair, Jeremy Ranch, Utah	75-69-72—216	$1,657.50
	Greg Farrow, Pitman, N.J.	70-67-79—216	$1,657.50
5	Ed Whitman, Oradell, N.J.	73-75-70—218	$1,250.00
T-6	Ken Allard, Birmingham, Mich.	74-73-72—219	$975.00
	Ted O'Rourke, Auburndale, Mass.	74-72-73—219	$975.00
T-8	Jeff Matheson, Park Ridge, Ill.	71-77-72—220	$900.00
	Jim Barker, San Antonio, Texas	74-74-72—220	$900.00
	Jon Chaffee, Austin, Minn.	75-71-74—220	$900.00
11	Hank Woodrome, Anaheim, Calif.	75-70-76—221	$850.00
T-12	Keith Swindell, Chesterfield, Mo.	73-75-74—222	$800.00
	Steve Moreland, Pleasanton, Calif.	70-77-75—222	$800.00
	David Levine, Monmouth, Ill.	76-72-74—222	$800.00
T-15	Kirk Padgett, Scottsdale, Ariz.	78-73-72—223	$700.00
	Tony Mitchell, Cordova, Tenn.	76-74-73—223	$700.00
	William Whaley, Ft. Lauderdale, Fla.	76-74-73—223	$700.00
	Jack McKelvey, Williamsville, N.Y.	72-77-74—223	$700.00
	Mark Pelletier, Albuquerque, N.M.	74-74-75—223	$700.00
20	John Phillips, Prospect, Ky.	74-75-75—224	$625.00
T-21	Tom Strong, Mequon, Wis.	75-74-76—225	$580.00
	Dale Smigelsky, Omaha, Neb.	76-73-76—225	$580.00
	Fred Gibson, Gaithersburg, Md.	72-74-79—225	$580.00
T-24	John Inzer, Honolulu, Hawaii	74-76-76—226	$530.00
	Patrick Delaney, Cincinnati, Ohio	71-76-79—226	$530.00
T-26	Rick Morton, Jacksonville, N.C.	78-75-74—227	$500.00
	Brad Sater, Olathe, Kan.	73-76-78—227	$500.00
	Don Baker, Opelika, Ala.	72-76-79—227	$500.00
T-29	Kit Gipson, Carmel, Ind.	78-75-75—228	$475.00
	Rob Duncan, Simsbury, Conn.	74-75-79—228	$475.00
T-31	Tom Strueber, Plano, Texas	79-76-74—229	$455.00
	Madison Pope, Metairie, La.	76-75-78—229	$455.00
33	Bill Porter, Bellingham, Wash.	78-77-75—230	$440.00
T-34	Robert Donald, Dunwoody, Ga.	75-83-73—231	$415.00
	Anthony Saraceno, Endicott, N.Y.	76-79-76—231	$415.00
	Terry Teel, Lexington, Mass.	75-76-80—231	$415.00
	Mike Evans, Verona, Pa.	79-72-80—231	$415.00
38	Richard Dorn, Arvada, Colo.	75-80-77—232	$390.00
39	Dean Hedstrom, Clearwater, Fla.	75-75-83—233	$380.00
40	Mike Shpur, Saratoga Springs, N.Y.	76-81-81—238	$370.00
41	Joe Ralston, N. Little Rock, Ark.	79-76-87—242	$360.00
	Tim Starrett, Kent, Ohio	76-WD (injury)	$350.00

* Won playoff on first extra hole

1981

Local professional Ted O'Rourke of Hanover, Mass., took charge of the 42-man field with a final-round 67 to coast to a five-stroke victory over Ed Oldfield Jr. of Golf, Ill., in the Fifth Annual Foot-Joy PGA Assistant Professional Championship. O'Rourke was tied with Randy Towner of Overland Park, Kan. after two rounds, but was only threatened by Oldfield during the final day. Towner fell out of contention with a final-round 78.

	Champion:	Ted O'Rourke, Hanover, Mass.	
	Site:	Thorny Lea Golf Club, Brockton, Mass.	
	Date:	Sept. 22-24	Purse: $30,000

	Course Average	Rds. Under Par	Par Rds.	Rds. Over Par	Total Rds.	Round Leader	Low Round		Ted O'Rourke
Round 1:	75.02	5	2	35	42	Mike Davis, Serge Thivierge	68-	Davis, Thivierge	71- (T-8)
Round 2:	75.88	1	0	41	42	Ted O'Rourke, Randy Towner	69-	Craig Watson	143- (T-1)
Round 3:	74.59	1	2	39	42	Ted O'Rourke	67-	O'Rourke	210- (1st)
Total:	75.16	7	4	115	126				

TOURNAMENT SUMMARY

Place	Name	Scores	Winnings
1	Ted O'Rourke, Hanover, Mass.	71-72-67—210	$3,300.00
2	Ed Oldfield Jr., Golf, Ill.	71-73-71—215	$2,000.00
3	Tom Herzan, LaCrosse, Wis.	73-73-71—217	$1,500.00
T-4	Ron Vlosich, Englewood, Colo.	69-76-73—218	$950.00
	Tony Saraceno, Endicott, N.Y.	74-71-73—218	$950.00
	Mike Bicker, Salt Lake City, Utah	74-71-73—218	$950.00
	Craig Watson, Rye, N.Y.	76-69-73—218	$950.00
	Mike Davis, Portland, Ore.	68-76-74—218	$950.00
	Scott Bunker, Pleasant Valley, Iowa	70-78-70—218	$950.00
	Frank Shikle, Birmingham, Ala.	69-75-74—218	$950.00
T-11	Ed Whitman, Oradell, N.J.	76-73-70—219	$787.50
	Miles Prestemon, San Antonio, Texas	75-71-73—219	$787.50
13	Jack McKelvey, Williamsville, N.Y.	70-78-72—220	$750.00
T-14	John Jackson, Scottsdale, Ariz.	71-75-75—221	$712.50
	Randy Towner, Overland Park, Kan.	71-72-78—221	$712.50
T-16	Bob Ashby, Cincinnati, Ohio	78-72-72—222	$662.50
	Serge Thivierge, Quebec, Canada	68-80-74—222	$662.50
18	Jerry Tucker, St. Louis, Mo.	75-71-77—223	$625.00
19	Tony Mitchell, Signal Mountain, Tenn.	69-80-75—224	$600.00
T-20	Steve Ball, Edmond, Okla.	74-80-71—225	$570.00
	Ren Morris, Macon, Ga.	74-75-76—225	$570.00
T-22	Jeff Roth, Birmingham, Mich.	76-77-73—226	$537.50
	Bill Rislove, W. St. Paul, Minn.	75-74-77—226	$537.50
T-24	Nathan Pomeroy, Sacramento, Calif.	73-79-75—227	$501.67
	Louie Garcia, Camarillo, Calif.	81-75-71—227	$501.67
	Carl Kalinka, Bloomington, Ind.	76-71-80—227	$501.67
27	Russell Pulley, Lindale, Texas	76-79-73—228	$450.00
T-28	Dow Seagraves, Pittsburgh, Pa.	75-80-74—229	$455.00
	Charles Jones, Norristown, Pa.	76-80-73—229	$455.00
	Bruce Martins, Hampden, Mass.	76-77-76—229	$455.00
	Terry Teel, Haymarket, Va.	72-78-79—229	$455.00
32	Henry Sandles, Albuquerque, N.M.	76-76-78—230	$430.00
T-33	Gus Mehallis, Aurora, Ohio	80-78-73—231	$415.00
	Reed Hughes, Monroe, La.	79-81-71—231	$415.00
T-35	John Phillips, Prospect, Ky.	85-71-76—232	$390.00
	Chris Eichstaedt, Miami, Fla.	82-74-76—232	$390.00
	Steve Griggs, Orlando, Fla.	78-77-77—232	$390.00
38	Pat Lynn, N. Augusta, S.C.	79-78-77—234	$370.00
T-39	Mike Wright, Scottsdale, Ariz.	74-85-76—235	$362.50
	David Walker, Lincoln, Neb.	76-78-81—235	$352.50
41	Clifford Stratton, Schenectady, N.Y.	82-78-79—239	$355.00
42	Tommy Ukauka, Kaneohe, Hawaii	88-80-86—254	$350.00

1980

Building a five-stroke lead after 10 holes on the final day, John Jackson of Scottsdale, Ariz., cruised to a record 5-under-par 205 to defeat defending champion Loren Roberts of San Luis Obispo, Calif., and win the Fourth Annual Foot-Joy PGA Assistant Professional Championship.

Champion:	John Jackson, Scottsdale, Ariz.	
Site:	Thorny Lea Golf Club, Brockton, Mass.	
Date:	Sept. 17-19	Purse: $28,000

	Course Average	Rds. Under Par	Par Rds.	Rds. Over Par	Total Rds.	Round Leader	Low Round		John Jackson
Round 1:	73.90	2	3	37	42	Loren Roberts	67-	Roberts	71- (T-6)
Round 2:	73.59	4	4	34	42	John Jackson	66-	Jackson	137- (1st)
Round 3:	74.57	1	4	37	42	John Jackson	68-	Jackson	205- (1st)
Total:	74.02	7	11	108	126				

TOURNAMENT SUMMARY

Place	Name	Scores	Winnings
1	John Jackson, Scottsdale, Ariz.	71-66-68—205	$3,000.00
2	Loren Roberts, San Luis Obispo, Calif.	67-72-71—210	$2,000.00
T-3	Keith Mohan, Rochester, N.Y.	73-68-70—211	$1,262.00
	Donnie Hill, Stafford, Texas	71-70-70—211	$1,262.00
5	Lynn Landgren, Salt Lake City, Utah	70-70-72—212	$950.00
6	Kene Bensel, Redmond, Wash.	70-72-72—214	$900.00
7	Don Brigham, Quechee, Vt.	70-71-74—215	$850.00
8	Steve Ball, Edmond, Okla.	69-75-72—216	$825.00
T-9	Mike Caporale, W. Springfield, Mass.	72-69-76—217	$790.00
	Bob Afton, Fontana, Wis.	71-73-73—217	$790.00
T-11	Jeff Foxx, Purchase, N.Y.	75-69-74—218	$740.00
	Louis Biago, Rockland, Del.	71-73-74—218	$740.00
	Harlan "Buzz" Fly, Cordova, Tenn.	74-74-70—218	$740.00
T-14	Tim Brauch, Aurora, Colo.	73-75-71—219	$690.00
	Larry Emery, Carterville, Ill.	73-71-75—219	$690.00
16	Robert Hoyt, Dallas, Texas	71-74-75—220	$660.00
T-17	John McNaney Jr., Catonsville, Md.	71-72-78—221	$630.00
	Robert Klein Jr., Encino, Calif.	73-72-76—221	$630.00
T-19	David Hilgenberg, Cedar Rapids, Iowa	75-71-76—222	$580.00
	Reed Hughes, Monroe, La.	71-76-75—222	$580.00
	Serge Thivierge, Quebec, Canada	75-77-70—222	$580.00
T-22	Art Silvestrone Jr., Wayne, N.J.	72-74-77—223	$520.00
	Bob Ashby, Cincinnati, Ohio	76-72-75—223	$520.00
	Bill Mattingly III, Indianapolis, Ind.	77-72-74—223	$520.00
T-25	Dave Rihm, Saratoga Springs, N.Y.	73-76-75—224	$450.00
	Larry Ordonio, Honolulu, Hawaii	74-75-75—224	$450.00
	Gary Ostrega, Duluth, Minn.	76-73-75—224	$450.00
	Frank Shikle, Birmingham, Ala.	75-74-75—224	$450.00
T-29	Jack Price, Gibsonia, Pa.	74-75-76—225	$390.00
	Kim Boehlke, Youngstown, Ohio	77-76-72—225	$390.00
	Tim Miskell, San Jose, Calif.	76-75-74—225	$390.00
T-32	Bill Sellers, New Smyrna Beach, Fla.	80-77-69—226	$365.00
	Dick Morgan, Saginaw, Mich.	77-76-73—226	$365.00
34	Tom Kalbfleisch, Louisville, Ky.	71-71-86—228	$350.00
T-35	Jeff Jerrell, Marietta, Ga.	75-76-79—230	$335.00
	Gary Clark, Kansas City, Mo.	74-73-83—230	$335.00
T-37	Joey Morris, Boca Raton, Fla.	77-77-77—231	$315.00
	Dick Wagley, Winnetka, Ill.	74-81-76—231	$315.00
39	Peter Gauthier, Skaneateles, N.Y.	78-73-81—232	$300.00
40	Manny Martinez Jr., El Paso, Texas	81-77-76—234	$300.00
41	David Walker, Lincoln, Neb.	76-84-75—235	$300.00
42	Hugh Bell, Wilmington, N.C.	85-74-77—236	$300.00

1979

Trailing by three shots after 10 holes on the final day, Loren Roberts of San Luis Obispo, Calif., stormed back to win the Third Annual Foot-Joy PGA Assistant Professional Championship. Second-round leader Jim Barker of San Antonio, Texas, struggled over the back nine with six bogeys as Roberts finished par-bogey to edge Bob Huber of Charlotte, N.C., and Bob Ford of Oakmont, Pa., by one stroke each.

Champion:	Loren Roberts, San Luis Obispo, Calif.
Site:	Thorny Lea Golf Club, Brockton, Mass.
Date: Sept. 19-21	**Purse:** $28,000

	Course Average	Rds. Under Par	Par Rds.	Rds. Over Par	Total Rds.	Round Leader	Low Round		Loren Roberts
Round 1:	74.64	0	1	41	42	Dan Simmons	70-	Simmons	71- (T-2)
Round 2:	74.78	4	0	38	42	Jim Barker	66-	Barker	140- (T-2)
Round 3:	73.95	5	2	35	42	Loren Roberts	68-	Kene Bensel	212- (1st)
Total:	74.46	9	3	114	126				

TOURNAMENT SUMMARY

Place	Name	Scores	Winnings
1	Loren Roberts, San Luis Obispo, Calif.	71-69-72—212	$3,000.00
T-2	Bob Huber, Charlotte, N.C.	71-69-73—213	$1,750.00
	Bob Ford, Oakmont, Pa.	72-72-69—213	$1,750.00
T-4	Bubba Clements, LaGrange, Ky.	72-73-69—214	$987.50
	Tom McCrary, Lincoln, Neb.	71-73-70—214	$987.50
6	Jim Barker, San Antonio, Texas	71-66-78—215	$900.00
T-7	Kene Bensel, Tacoma, Wash.	71-78-68—217	$837.50
	Serge Thivierge, Montreal, Canada	73-73-71—217	$837.50
T-9	Kurt Wajda, E. Longmeadow, Mass.	75-74-69—218	$790.00
	Dave Rihm, Saratoga Springs, N.Y.	71-75-72—218	$790.00
T-11	Steve Ball, Edmond, Okla.	71-74-74—219	$740.00
	Keith Swindell, Chesterfield, Mo.	72-71-76—219	$740.00
	Kim Young, Fontana, Wis.	72-72-75—219	$740.00
T-14	Duke Delcher, Northfield, N.J.	73-78-69—220	$670.00
	Shawn Bellis, Litchfield Park, Ariz.	71-76-73—220	$670.00
	Dave Hilgenberg, Cedar Rapids, Iowa	72-74-74—220	$670.00
	Norm Becker, Clinton, N.J.	71-74-75—220	$670.00
T-18	Jerry Impellittiere, Huntsville, Ala.	74-72-75—221	$600.00
	Bill Rislove, W. St. Paul, Minn.	74-72-75—221	$600.00
	Austin Straub, White Plains, N.Y.	77-69-75—221	$600.00
T-21	Harlan "Buzz" Fly, Cordova, Tenn.	75-75-72—222	$550.00
	Dan Simmons, Westfield Center, Ohio	70-76-76—222	$550.00
23	Wheeler Stewart, Bethesda, Md.	79-73-71—223	$520.00
T-24	Dennis Rose, Kamuela, Hawaii	76-76-72—224	$490.00
	Ken Krieger, Englewood, Colo.	77-75-72—224	$490.00
T-26	Jim Henderson, Tyler, Texas	77-76-72—225	$450.00
	Mike Olson, Anthony, N.M.	78-72-75—225	$450.00
T-28	Rick Vershure, Clearwater, Fla.	78-78-70—226	$410.00
	Chris Roderick, Dublin, Ohio	79-71-76—226	$410.00
T-30	Kim Thompson, Cedar City, Utah	74-78-75—227	$380.00
	Bobby Bumgardner, Marietta, Ga.	75-78-74—227	$380.00
	Larry Griffin, New Orleans, La.	73-74-80—227	$380.00
T-33	Rick D'Aunoy, Kenner, La.	76-79-73—228	$355.00
	Gordon Johnson, Rochester, N.Y.	79-72-77—228	$355.00
35	Mark Wolfla, Indianapolis, Ind.	78-80-71—229	$340.00
36	Don Brigham, Quechee, Vt.	79-73-78—230	$330.00
37	Charles Roberts, Midland, Mich.	80-76-75—231	$320.00
38	Eric Pohl, Monterey, Calif.	81-78-76—235	$310.00
39	Richard Blake, Miami Lakes, Fla.	81-82-73—236	$300.00
40	Steve Crane, Glenview, Ill.	82-82-73—237	$300.00
41	Michael Karl, Endicott, N.Y.	80-78-80—238	$300.00
42	Gary Clark, Kansas City, Mo.	73-85-83—241	$300.00

1978

Larry Griffin of New Orleans, La., opened with a 4-under-par 66 and never trailed the rest of the way as he set the pace to win the Second Annual Foot-Joy PGA Assistant Professional Championship. Frank Shikle of Birmingham, Ala., made things interesting with one-putts on the final five holes, but fell short by one stroke in second place.

Champion:	Larry Griffin, New Orleans, La.	
Site:	Thorny Lea Golf Club, Brockton, Mass.	
Date:	Sept. 19-21	Purse: $25,000

	Course Average	Rds. Under Par	Par Rds.	Rds. Over Par	Total Rds.	Round Leader	Low Round		Larry Griffin
Round 1:	74.00	3	1	36	40	Larry Griffin	66-	Griffin	66- (1st)
Round 2:	74.05	2	2	36	40	Larry Griffin	67-	Robert Seligman	138- (1st)
Round 3:	75.25	1	0	39	40	Larry Griffin	69-	Frank Shikle	209- (1st)
Total:	74.43	6	3	111	120				

TOURNAMENT SUMMARY

Place	Name	Scores	Winnings
1	Larry Griffin, New Orleans, La.	66-71-72—209	$3,000.00
2	Frank Shikle, Birmingham, Ala.	73-68-69—210	$2,000.00
3	Robert Seligman, Montgomery, Texas	71-67-75—213	$1,500.00
4	Bubba Clements, Louisville, Ky.	71-73-72—216	$1,200.00
T-5	Ron Filipowicz, Omaha, Neb.	76-70-71—217	$900.00
	Harry Taylor, Glen Ellyn, Ill.	71-70-76—217	$900.00
	Joe Tesori, Fayetteville, N.Y.	71-72-74—217	$900.00
T-8	John Jackson, Scottsdale, Ariz.	69-76-73—218	$725.00
	Jim Knipp, Colorado Springs, Colo.	73-72-73—218	$725.00
	Ron Hoyt, Merced, Calif.	69-74-75—218	$725.00
T-11	John Klee, Albuquerque, N.M.	72-74-73—219	$637.50
	Dean Sigmon, Hickory, N.C.	72-75-72—219	$637.50
	John Sutter, Westfield, Mass.	72-73-74—219	$637.50
	Bob Lendzion, Stratton Mountain, Vt.	72-73-74—219	$637.50
T-15	Roc Irey, Cleveland, Ohio	72-74-74—220	$562.50
	Jim Henderson, Tyler, Texas	74-72-74—220	$562.50
17	Doug Steffen, Springfield, N.J.	72-72-77—221	$525.00
T-18	William Walsh, Rochester, N.Y.	70-78-74—222	$475.00
	Mark Hessler, Columbus, Ohio	76-72-74—222	$475.00
	Herky Smith, Verona, Pa.	75-72-75—222	$475.00
T-21	Tom Fortuna, Birmingham, Mich.	73-75-75—223	$398.75
	Paul Kennedy, Ontario, Canada	74-74-75—223	$398.75
	Mike McGinnis, Goleta, Calif.	77-71-75—223	$398.75
	Fred Harkness, Rye, N.Y.	76-71-76—223	$398.75
25	Bob Jones, St. Charles, Mo.	76-73-75—224	$370.00
T-26	Wes Smith, Lauderhill, Fla.	72-78-75—225	$355.00
	Robert Flagler, Provo, Utah	74-74-77—225	$355.00
28	Mike Eller, Old Hickory, Tenn.	75-74-77—226	$345.00
T-29	Steve Ralston, N. Little Rock, Ark.	74-77-76—227	$337.50
	Ron Wells, Portland, Ore.	75-74-78—227	$337.50
T-31	Mark Wolfla, South Bend, Ind.	75-79-74—228	$327.50
	Mark Rolfing, Kahului, Maui, Hawaii	77-76-75—228	$327.50
T-33	Fred Gibson, Germantown, Md.	77-77-75—229	$317.50
	Jim Meyers, Haddonfield, N.J.	75-74-80—229	$317.50
35	Paul Hooser, Olathe, Kan.	74-80-76—230	$310.00
T-36	Steve Haagenson, Hamel, Minn.	78-74-80—232	$302.50
	Mike Anderson, Rock Island, Ill.	79-77-76—232	$302.50
38	Tim Fulcher, Augusta, Ga.	79-78-77—234	$300.00
39	Mike Muranyi, Madison, Wis.	85-74-79—238	$300.00
40	Tim Sereikis, Guilderland, N.Y.	78-84-88—250	$300.00

1977

Bob Lendzion of Manchester, Vt., fired the low round of the week with a 4-under-par 66 on the second day, but a final-day out-of-bounds penalty on the 14th hole cost him at least a tie for first and a playoff berth against winner Mike Zack of Summit, N.J.

Champion:	Mike Zack, Summit, N.J.
Site:	Thorny Lea Golf Club, Brockton, Mass.
Date: Sept. 27-30	**Purse:** $25,000

	Course Average	Rds. Under Par	Par Rds.	Rds. Over Par	Total Rds.	Round Leader	Low Round		Mike Zack	
Round 1:	73.57	4	4	32	40	Mike Zack	67-	Zack	67-	(1st)
Round 2:	75.77	3	2	35	40	Mike Zack	66-	John Calabria	136-	(1st)
Round 3:	75.37	0	3	37	40	Mike Zack	70-	Dennis Sullivan, Jerry Rislove, Don Branca	209-	(1st)
Total:	74.90	7	9	104	120					

TOURNAMENT SUMMARY

Place	Name	Scores	Winnings
1	Mike Zack, Summit, N.J.	67-69-73—209	$3,000.00
2	Dennis Sullivan, Grant Park, Ill.	70-70-70—210	$2,000.00
3	Bob Lendzion, Manchester, Vt.	72-66-73—211	$1,500.00
4	John Calabria, Hamburg, N.Y.	69-68-76—213	$1,200.00
5	Bill Galloway, Pleasant Valley, Iowa	70-73-72—215	$1,000.00
6	Jerry Rislove, W. St. Paul, Minn.	73-73-70—216	$900.00
T-7	Loren Roberts, San Luis Obispo, Calif.	70-76-71—217	$775.00
	Jack McConachie, Greenwich, Conn.	73-73-71—217	$775.00
T-9	Mike Caporale, W. Springfield, Mass.	68-78-72—218	$700.00
	Terry McDowell, Pompano Beach, Fla.	73-73-72—218	$700.00
	Scott Bess, New Bloomfield, Mo.	73-73-72—218	$700.00
12	Gordon Hepp, Seattle, Wash.	70-76-73—219	$650.00
T-13	Don Branca, Salt Lake City, Utah	74-76-70—220	$612.50
	Allen Jones, Addison, Texas	72-75-73—220	$612.50
T-15	Mike Watney, Fresno, Calif.	73-76-72—221	$550.00
	Wayne Nichols, Cincinnati, Ohio	71-76-74—221	$550.00
	Tony Peterson, Shawnee Mission, Kan.	72-74-75—221	$550.00
T-18	Jeff Jerrell, Marietta, Ga.	71-78-74—223	$487.50
	Jack Price, Pittsburgh, Pa.	71-78-74—223	$487.50
T-20	Terry Dear, Phoenix, Ariz.	73-76-75—224	$425.00
	James Clements, Louisville, Ky.	69-78-77—224	$425.00
	George Liner, Chattanooga, Tenn.	74-72-78—224	$425.00
T-23	Serge Thivierge, Quebec, Canada	73-75-77—225	$385.00
	Mark Wolfla, South Bend, Ind.	77-70-78—225	$385.00
25	Ted Ossoff, Columbiana, Ohio	77-72-78—227	$370.00
26	Johnny Dill, Pasadena, Texas	79-76-73—228	$360.00
T-27	Bill Gutknecht, El Paso, Texas	81-73-75—229	$347.50
	Bill Burgess, Burlington, Wis.	75-82-72—229	$347.50
T-29	Peter Gauthier, Auburn, N.Y.	75-82-73—230	$335.00
	Rick Kent, Grand Blanc, Mich.	75-75-80—230	$335.00
	Frank Shikle, Birmingham, Ala.	71-77-82—230	$335.00
T-32	Larry Ordonio, Honolulu, Hawaii	77-75-79—231	$322.50
	Jim Knipp, Colorado Springs, Colo.	76-76-79—231	$322.50
T-34	Rick Navarro, Wichita, Kan.	79-76-77—232	$312.50
	Jim Pledger, Baton Rouge, La.	73-79-80—232	$312.50
36	Tom Jordan, Rock Hill, S.C.	82-80-71—233	$305.00
37	Tim McAndrew, Omaha, Neb.	77-83-79—239	$300.00
38	William Bassler, Catonsville, Md.	77-81-83—241	$300.00
39	Mark Champagne, Castleton, N.Y.	74-85-88—247	$300.00
40	John Robinson, Horsham, Pa.	79-87-84—250	$300.00

■ PGA ASSISTANT PROFESSIONAL CHAMPIONSHIP RECORDS

■ Lowest First-Round Score

63   Ken Allard, Rochester, Mich., 1986

■ Lowest Second-Round Score

65   Bill Loeffler, Littleton, Colo., 1992

■ Lowest 36 Holes

134   Mitch Camp, Copley, Ohio, 1988

■ Lowest Third-Round Score

66   Robert Thompson, Huntsville, Texas, 1986

■ Lowest 54 Holes

205   John Jackson, Scottsdale, Ariz., 1980
       Webb Heintzelman, Bethesda, Md., 1988
       Steve Gotsche, Great Bend, Kan., 1990

■ Lowest Fourth-Round Score

67   Kevin Dugas, Canada, 1992

■ Lowest Winning Score, 54 Holes

205   John Jackson, Scottsdale, Ariz., 1980
       Webb Heintzelman, Bethesda, Md., 1988
       Steve Gotsche, Great Bend, Kan., 1990

■ Lowest Winning Score, 72 Holes

278   Kim Thompson, American Fork, Utah, 1991

■ Highest Start by Winner

75   Bill Loeffler, Littleton, Colo., 1992

■ Lowest Start by Winner

64   Webb Heintzelman, Bethesda, Md., 1988

■ Greatest Margin of Victory

5   John Jackson, Scottsdale, Ariz., 1980
     Ted O'Rourke, Hanover, Mass., 1981

PGA WINTER TOURNAMENT PROGRAM

LANGERT PGA WINTER TOURNAMENT PROGRAM

Supported by ROYAL GRIP, INC. and UNITED SPORTS TECHNOLOGIES, INC.

■ HISTORY

The PGA Winter Tournament Program was begun in 1954 at PGA National Golf Club in Dunedin, Fla., to provide additional playing opportunities for PGA professionals. The Stroke Play Championship and the Quarter Century Championship were played the first year. The Senior-Junior Championship was added in 1959, and the Match Play Championship became part of the program in 1964. When the PGA Seniors' Championship was separated from the Winter Tournament Program with the founding of the Senior PGA Tour, a new senior age-group competition was developed for PGA members. This event was named the Senior Stroke Play Championship in 1985.

All PGA of America members except those in the A-3 (Tour Player) classification are eligible to compete in the Winter Tournament Program under the following guidelines:

■ The Quarter Century Championship is for those who have been members of the PGA of America for at least 25 years. This is a 36-hole tournament.

■ The Senior Stroke Play Championship is for PGA professionals who are at least 50 years of age. This is a 54-hole tournament.

■ In the Senior-Junior Championship, two-man teams are formed via a blind draw after qualifying rounds. The senior member must be at least 50 years of age, and the junior member 49 years or younger. This is a 54-hole better-ball tournament.

■ The Stroke Play Championship is a 72-hole tournament. The Match Play Championship is a seven-round, single elimination tournament which begins with 128 qualifiers.

The Winter Tournament Program was played at PGA National in Dunedin through 1962; at Port St. Lucie CC, Port St. Lucie, Fla., in 1963; at PGA National GC (now BallenIsles CC of JDM), Palm Beach Gardens, Fla., from 1964 through 1973; at Port St. Lucie CC again in 1974; at Walt Disney World, Lake Buena Vista, Fla., from 1975 through 1981; and at the "new" PGA National GC in Palm Beach Gardens since 1982. Competition begins soon after New Year's Day and continues into February.

The PGA Merchandise Show was held in conjunction with the Winter Tournament Program through 1981.

1994

The 1993-94 Langert PGA Winter Tournament Program, supported by Royal Grip, Inc. and United Sports Technologies, Inc., featured five national championships played at PGA National Golf Club in Palm Beach Gardens, Fla.

The 40th PGA Quarter Century Championship, Jan. 4-5, opened the schedule with competition for players with 50-year memberships as well as professionals who have been PGA members for at least 25 years. Steve Bull of Milwaukee, Wis., won the overall championship as well as the 55-59 age division. Bull finished with rounds of 70 and 69 for a 6-under-par 139 on the Estate Course. Bob Duden of Portland, Ore., 73, won his third consecutive 70-and-over title on the Haig Course with a 36-hole total of 146, after rounds of 76 and 70.

Henry Williams of Fleetwood, Pa., won the special Half-Century Division for the second year in a row. Williams, a PGA member for 53 years, had rounds of 78 and 82.

Other age-group champions at the Estate Course: **under 50** — Michael Limback, Evansville, Ind. 75-75—150; **50-54** — Tom Joyce, Old Westbury, N.Y. 71-69—140; **60-64** — Bob Ross, Springfield, N.J. 71-70—141; **65-69** — Ray Montgomery, Port St. Lucie, Fla. 75-72—147.

Age-group winners on the Haig Course: **80-84** — Ralph Bond, Wickliffe, Ohio 86-85—171; **85-89** — Tommy Shannon, Troy, Mich. 94-97—191.

Gene Carello of West Frankfort, Ill., 52, head professional at Franklin Country Club, was the overall low scorer in the 10th PGA Senior Stroke Play Championship, Jan. 7-9, at the Estate Course. Carello dominated the age divisions from 50 to 64 with a 54-hole total of even-par 216, on rounds of 75, 71 and 70.

Montgomery, 69, representing Ballentrae Yacht and Country Club in Port St. Lucie, set the pace for the five oldest age divisions in the 10th Langert Senior PGA Stroke Play Championship. Montgomery finished with rounds of 66 and 71.

Gary Hardin of Bethlehem, Pa., dropped a nine-foot birdie putt on the first extra hole to carry himself and teammate Lloyd Monroe of New Rochelle, N.Y., to victory in the 36th PGA Senior-Junior Championship, Jan. 17, on the Champion Course at PGA National Golf Club.

Hardin and Monroe teamed for a 54-hole better-ball total of 12-under-par 204. They shared the lead after regulation play with Bill Kennedy of Cape Coral, Fla., and Nic Borojevich of Uhrichsville, Ohio. Hardin and Monroe combined for 15 birdies — 10 by Monroe — and three bogeys during the championship. Hardin, 41, is head professional at Northampton Country Club in Easton, Pa., and Monroe, 55, is head professional at Wykagyl Country Club in New Rochelle, N.Y. Hardin and Monroe each earned $5,000 from a total purse of $80,000. Dana Quigley of Rehoboth, Mass., a five-time New England PGA Player of the Year, overcame bogeys on two of his final four holes for a one-stroke victory in the 41st PGA Stroke Play Championship, Jan. 23-26, on the Champion Course. Quigley earned $6,000 from the $73,000 purse, and marked his second national championship in the PGA Winter Tournament Program. He won the 1983 PGA Match Play Championship.

Quigley, a 46-year-old head professional at Crestwood Country Club, fired a 3-under-par 69 for a 72-hole total of 11-under-par 277. Despite bogeys on the par-3 15th and 17th holes, Quigley provided himself with a big cushion on the back nine by recording birdies at the 11th, 12th and 13th holes. He held off a challenge by Jerry Impellittiere of New Windsor, N.Y., who finished with a 70-278. Jim Estes of Crystal Lake, Ill., who shared the third-round lead with Quigley and Impellittiere, finished third at 73-281.

Tom Cleaver of Boca Raton, Fla., made his debut in the $45,000 PGA Match Play Championship, Feb. 11, pay dividends at the Champion Course. Cleaver, 35, downed Ron McDougal of Purchase, N.Y., 5 and 3, to earn the $5,000 first-place prize. Cleaver, the head professional at Wycliffe Country Club in Lake Worth, Fla., made an eight-foot birdie putt on the par-4 ninth hole to build momentum over McDougal, the 1992 PGA Club Professional Champion. Cleaver then won the 12th, 13th, 14th and 15th holes to close the match.

In the major upset of the Match Play Championship, Tom Dolby of St. Paul, Minn., ousted qualifying medalist Bruce Zabriski of Garden City, N.Y., 2 and 1, in a quarter-final match. Zabriski had qualified with a course-record 10-under-par 62 on PGA National Golf Club's Estate Course. Cleaver then downed Dolby in the semifinals, 5 and 4; and McDougal turned back defending champion Rick Vershure of Armonk, N.Y., 3 and 2.

■ CHAMPIONS THROUGH THE YEARS

PGA STROKE PLAY CHAMPIONS (1954-1994)

1954 Ock Willoweit	1963 John Barnum	1972 Denny Lyons	1981 Lynn Janson	1990 Larry Rentz
1955 Gunnard Johnson	1964 John Barnum	1973 Gene Borek	1982 Jim King	1991 Tom Wargo
1956 Al Huske	1965 Sam Harvey	1974 Chick Evans	1983 Jim Albus	1992 Mike San Filippo
1957 Matt Bartosek	1966 Walker Inman Jr.	1975 Ron Letellier	1984 Mike Bright	1993 Bob Ford
1958 Henry Castillo	1967 Claude King	1976 George Shortridge	1985 Joe Hager	1994 Dana Quigley
1959 Skip Alexander	1968 John Barnum	1977 Doug Dalziel	1986 Ed Dougherty	
1960 Toby Lyons	1969 Herb Hooper	1978 John Gentile	1987 Lonnie Nielsen	
1961 Sam Bernardi	1970 Gene Borek	1979 James Dolan III	1988 Bob Ford	
1962 Jim Stamps	1971 Dick Hart	1980 Jim Dent	1989 Darrell Kestner	

PGA MATCH PLAY CHAMPIONS (1964-1994)

1964 Bob Frainey	1971 Chick Evans	1978 Bryan Abbott	1985 Don Reese	1992 Bob Leaver
1965 Chuck Malchaski	1972 John Cook	1979 Stan Thirsk	1986 Bob Menne	1993 Rick Vershure
1966 Jerry Cooper	1973 Bill Collins	1980 Jim Dent	1987 Lonnie Nielsen	1994 Tom Cleaver
1967 Stan Brion	1974 Joe Data	1981 Gene Borek	1988 Lonnie Nielsen	
1968 Steve Bull	1975 Bob Brue	1982 Dennis Bradley	1989 Joe Sciortino	
1969 Herb Hooper	1976 Bob Brue	1983 Dana Quigley	1990 Rick Vershure	
1970 Dick Hart	1977 Bob Bruno	1984 Ed Dougherty	1991 Chris Anderson	

PGA QUARTER CENTURY CLUB CHAMPIONS (1954-1994)

1954 Jules Blanton	1964 (No tournament)	1976 Sam Snead	1985 Mal McMullen	1993 Bob Pfister (under-70)
1955 Harry Cooper	1965 Jack Isaacs	1977 Babe Lichardus	1986 Gene Borek	Bob Duden (70-and-over)
1956 Louis Chiapetta	1966 Jack Issacs	1978 Jack Fleck	1987 Paul Thomas	Jim Buchanan (under-50)
1957 Al Watrous	1967 Byron Nelson	1979 Babe Lichardus (A),	1988 Gene Borek	1994 Steve Bull (under-70)
1958 Al Watrous	1968 Lou Barbaro	Art Doering (B),	1989 Larry Mancour	Bob Duden (70-and-over)
1959 Leland (Duke) Gibson	1969 Sam Snead	Ralph Huchinson (C)	1990 Dennis Bradley	Michael Limback (under-50)
1960 Charley Sheppard	1970 Herman Scharlau	1980 Billy Capps	1991 Dennis Bradley	
1961 Leland (Duke) Gibson	1971 Pete Cooper	1981 Babe Lichardus	1992 Dick Hart (under-70)	
1962 Herman Barron	1972 Ernie Catropa	1982 Milon Marusic	Bob Duden (70-and-over)	
1963 George Schneiter	1973 Sam Snead	1983 Hampton Auld		
	1974 Chandler Harper	Jim Riggins		
	1975 Sam Snead	1984 Ange Alberico		

■ PGA SENIOR-JUNIOR CHAMPIONS (1959-1994)

1959 Ivan Gantz and Joe Curtin	1972 Steve Doctor and Steve Bull	1984 Bill Kozak and Bob Ackerman
1960 Billy Burke and Sam Drake	1973 Joe Lopez Sr. and Tom Hanlon	1985 Jim Cochran and Jack Kiefer
1961 Walter Hall and Bob Nodus	1974 Monte Norcross and Denny Lyons	1986 Rollie Schroeder and Ray Freeman
1962 Henry Bontempo and Sam Bernardi	1975 Bob Gajda and Steve Bull	1987 Nunzio Ciampi and Jim Booros
1963 Leland Gibson and Steve Isakov	1976 Henry Ransom and Gary Baker	1988 Chick Evans and Bobby Heins
1964 Walter Romans and Todd Hauck	1977 Ed Furgol and Jay Dolan	1989 Jim Gallagher Sr. and Jerry Impellittiere
1965 Lorin Shook and Bob Gajda	1978 Bud Timbrook and George Shortridge	1990 Ray Bolo and Dave Laudien
1966 Phil Greenwald and Frank Harned	1979 Billy Gilbert and Jim Albus;	1991 Marion Heck and Bruce Zabriski
1967 Bill Black and Ron Howell	Tommy Thomas and Paul O'Leary	1992 Alex Redmond and David Levine
1968 Herb Vogt and Pat Schwab	1980 Bob Erickson and Paul Barkhouse	1993 Lynn Rosely and Bob Groff
1969 Joe Lopez Sr. and Jack Doser	1981 Charles Sifford and Bob Issler	1994 Lloyd Monroe and Gary Harding
1970 Rod Munday and J.C. Goosie	1982 Al Fuchs and Lynn Janson	
1971 Chuck Klein and Jim Logue	1983 Joe Jimenez and John Gentile	

PGA SENIOR STROKE PLAY CHAMPIONS (1985-1994)

1985 Ed Rubis	1989 Larry Mancour (50-69)	1992 Willard Scholl (50-64)
1986 Jim King (50-69)	Hans Merrell (70-89)	George Thomas (65-up)
Walter Ambo (70-89)	1990 Mike Joyce (50-64)	1993 Tom Wargo (under-70)
1987 Bob Duden (50-69)	Billy Capps (65-89)	Larry Gilbert (under-70)
Milon Marusic (70-89)	1991 Gene Borek (50-69)	Bob Watson (70-up)
1988 Joe Lopez Jr. (50-69)	Bob Duden (70-up)	1994 Gene Carello (under-70)
John Barnum (70-89)		Ray Montgomery (70-up)

■ 1994 LANGERT PGA STROKE PLAY CHAMPIONSHIP

PGA National GC (Champion and Estate), Palm Beach Gardens, Lake Park, Fla.

Jan. 23-26   Purse: $73,000

Place	Name	Scores	Winnings
1	Dana Quigley, Rehoboth, Mass.	70-66-72-69—277	$6,000.00
2	Jerry Impellittiere, New Windsor, N.Y.	71-72-65-70—278	$4,500.00
3	Jim Estes, Crystal Lake, Ill.	70-68-70-73—281	$3,500.00
T-4	Terence R. Hughes, Monticello, N.Y.	71-70-70-71—282	$2,600.00
	Michael Zinni, Mankato, Minn.	71-72-69-70—282	$2,600.00
	Cary Hungate, Kokomo, Ind.	67-72-70-73—282	$2,600.00
7	Gary Hardin, Bethlehem, Pa.	72-74-68-69—283	$2,100.00
8	Ron Parsons, Vallejo, Calif.	75-71-67-71—284	$2,000.00
T-9	Bob Ford, Oakmont, Pa.	70-73-74-68—285	$1,750.00
	David Prange, Glenview, Ill.	76-71-70-68—285	$1,750.00
	Daniel Thore, Reidsville, N.C.	68-72-70-75—285	$1,750.00
	Bob Lendzion, Quechee, Vt.	75-65-71-74—285	$1,750.00
13	Lloyd Monroe, New Rochelle, N.Y.	74-69-73-70—286	$1,500.00
T-14	Bruce Zabriski, Garden City, N. Y.	74-70-69-74—287	$1,300.00
	Pete Oakley, Lewes, Del.	71-72-70-74—287	$1,300.00
	Wheeler Stewart, Oakland, Md.	68-70-74-75—287	$1,300.00
T-17	Todd M. Smith, Peru, Ind.	69-75-69-75—288	$1,050.00
	Tom Cleaver, Boca Raton, Fla.	68-74-70-76—288	$1,050.00
T-19	Gary Robison, Akron, Ohio	71-73-74-71—289	$880.00
	Tom Waitrovich, Westlake, Ohio	72-74-68-75—289	$880.00
	Brad Dean, Thomasville, Mich.	74-69-71-75—289	$880.00
	Mike San Filippo, Harvard, Mass.	73-68-72-76—289	$880.00
	Edward Burke Jr., Woodmere, N.Y.	72-73-68-76—289	$880.00
T-24	Ron Philo, Amelia Island, Fla.	73-74-71-72—290	$780.00
	Jerry Tucker, St. Louis, Mo.	73-71-70-76—290	$780.00
	Daniel Fabian, Export, Pa.	69-70-74-77—290	$780.00
T-27	John Sanges, Locust Valley, N.Y.	72-71-75-73—291	$650.00
	Charlie Cowell, Totowa, N.J.	78-70-70-73—291	$650.00
	Mel Baum, Larchmont, N.Y.	73-71-73-74—291	$650.00
	Chip Sullivan, Salem, Va.	78-68-71-74—291	$650.00
	Jim Miller, Metuchen, N.J.	71-74-72-74—291	$650.00
	Barry Redmond, West Palm Beach, Fla.	66-76-74-75—291	$650.00
	John Reeves, Greenwich, Conn.	71-70-75-75—291	$650.00
	Gene Borek, White Plains, N.Y.	70-71-75-75—291	$650.00
	Tim Angis, Portland, Maine	67-74-74-76—291	$650.00
	Dino Lucchesi, Deerfield, Ill.	72-71-71-77—291	$650.00
T-37	Marion Heck, Fort Myers Beach, Fla.	76-69-73-74—292	$506.67
	Tom Dolby, St. Paul, Minn.	75-72-72-73—292	$506.67
	Mike McGinnis, Ijamsville, Md.	70-78-71-73—292	$506.67
	Larry Rentz, Mamaroneck, N.Y.	75-72-74-71—292	$506.67
	Gene Fieger, Port St. Lucie, Fla.	72-76-67-77—292	$506.66
	Ronald McDougal, Purchase, N.Y.	69-73-71-79—292	$506.66
T-43	Leo McMahon, Bellport, N.Y.	69-75-74-75—293	$451.00
	Jeffrey Bohr, Southampton, N.Y.	71-76-70-76—293	$451.00
	Larry Mancour, Harbor Springs, Mich.	73-74-70-76—293	$451.00
	Kevin Morris, White Plains, N.Y.	73-75-73-72—293	$451.00
	David Levine, Hannibal, Mo.	72-72-72-77—293	$451.00
T-48	Dennis Dolci, Sharon, Pa.	76-69-73-76—294	$420.00
	Mark Kirk, Orchard Park, N.Y.	74-71-73-76—294	$420.00
	Tim Stafford, Glen Head, N.Y.	77-70-73-74—294	$420.00
	Jeffrey Stalcup, Detroit, Mich.	72-72-73-77—294	$420.00
	Rick Vershure, Armonk, N.Y.	76-69-77-72—294	$420.00
T-53	Nic Borojevich, Uhrichsville, Ohio	77-70-73-75—295	$397.50
	Christophe Caulfield, Riverdale, N.Y.	69-79-72-75—295	$397.50
	Paul Barkhouse, Ipswich, Mass.	71-73-72-79—295	$397.50
	Mike Tucker, Mt. Vernon, Ill.	75-68-70-82—295	$397.50
57	Tony Kelley, E. Longmeadow, Mass.	79-70-72-75—296	$385.00
T-58	Paul Kemps, Plainfield, Ind.	75-71-72-79—297	$375.00
	Tony Saraceno, Cortland, N.Y.	72-76-71-78—297	$375.00
	Mark Thomas, Gladwin, Mich.	71-76-73-77—297	$375.00
T-61	Ric Kunnert, Des Plaines, Ill.	79-66-74-79—298	$352.50
	Peter Procops, Glen Cove, N.Y.	74-70-75-79—298	$352.50
	Larry Mullen, Paducah, Ky.	70-73-76-79—298	$352.50
	Gary Groh, Lake Bluff, Ill.	69-77-74-78—298	$352.50
	Walt Siemsglusz, Bridgeton, Mo.	73-75-72-78—298	$352.50
	David O'Kelly, Mashpee, Mass.	73-76-75-74—298	$352.50
T-67	Rocky Nelson, Columbus, Ohio	69-75-77-79—300	$327.50
	Paul Hollenbaugh, New Albany, Ohio	77-70-75-78—300	$327.50
	Roy Vucinich, Sewickley, Pa.	78-67-78-77—300	$327.50
	Jack Skilling, Bethesda, Md.	78-71-75-76—300	$327.50
71	Patrick Hofmann, Columbia, S.C.	72-76-73-80—301	$315.00
T-72	Ned Weaver, Coraopolis, Pa.	74-74-74-80—302	$307.50
	Kirk Hanefeld, Peabody, Mass.	71-77-74-80—302	$307.50
T-74	Nash Haxel, Jackson, Mo.	73-75-74-81—303	$292.50
	Walker Inman Jr., Columbus, Ohio	74-74-74-81—303	$292.50
T-74	Randy Cochran, Hoffman Estates, Ill.	77-72-76-78—303	$292.50
	Steve Benson, Long Grove, Ill.	75-74-76-78—303	$292.50
T-78	Scott Steger, Noblesville, Ind.	71-71-78-84—304	$275.00
	Dan Tzivanis, White Plains, N.Y.	76-73-74-81—304	$275.00
	John Fields, Belmont, Mass.	75-72-79-78—304	$275.00
T-81	Bill Hall, St. Louis, Mo.	78-71-73-83—305	$260.00
	Michael Areddy, Ann Arbor, Mich.	77-71-76-81—305	$260.00
	Michael DiBuono, Pound Ridge, N.Y.	70-76-79-80—305	$260.00
T-84	John Mulliken, Chicago, Ill.	73-75-74-84—306	$247.50
	Kirk Stauffer, Bradford, Pa.	75-74-76-81—306	$247.50
T-86	Dave Laudien, Neptune City, N. J.	78-71-75-84—308	$237.50
	Bob Groff, Brown Summitt, N.C.	78-70-77-83—308	$237.50
88	Frank Dully, Huntington, Conn.	70-79-81-79—309	$230.00
89	Frank Dobbs, Spring-Ford, Pa.	74-73-78-100—325	$225.00

■ 1994 LANGERT PGA MATCH PLAY CHAMPIONSHIP

PGA National GC (Estate), Lake Park, Fla.   Feb. 5-11   Purse: $45,000

FIRST ROUND (Qualifiers earn $100) --

Rick Vershure, Armonk, N.Y., def.
Kevin Regan, Rochester, N.Y., 5 and 4

Larry Mullen, Paducah, Ky., def.
Mike Arredy, Ann Arbor, Mich., 2 and 1

John Cregan, Dover, N.H., def.
Bill Marx, Rochester, Mich., 2 and 1

Scott Steger, Noblesville, Ind., def.
Jim Tuller, Palm Beach Gardens, Fla., 2-up

Terence Hughes, Monticello, N.Y., def.
Marty Lass, Eden Prairie, Minn., 2 and 1

Mike DiBuono, Pound Ridge, N.Y., def.
Tom McGrew, Lake Forest, Ill., 5 and 4

Larry Furey, New Platz, N.Y., def.
Frank Dully, Huntington, Conn., 1-up

Russ Davis, Cape May, N.J., def.
Tom Kelly, King of Prussia, Pa., 3 and 2

Bryan Abbott, Akron, Ohio def.
Mike Dynda, Broomall, Pa., 5 and 4

Jack Skilling, Bethesda, Md., def.
Jim Miller, Glenview, Ill., 2-up

Dave Laudien, Neptune City, N.J., def.
Nick Manolios, Golden Bridge, N.Y., 2 and 1

Carl Lohren, Glen Head, N.Y., def.
Paul Hollenbaugh, New Albany, Ohio, 19th hole

Jerry Impellittiere, New Windsor, N.Y., def.
Steve Bull, Milwaukee, Wis., 3 and 2

Bruce Summerhays, Heber City, Utah, def.
Tom Waitrovich, Westlake, Ohio, 5 and 4

Tony Kelley, East Longmeadow, Mass., def.
Wally Kalinoski, Staten Island, N.Y., 5 and 4

Nick Borojevich, Uhrichsville, Ohio, def.
Tom Herzog, Kings Park, N.Y., 19th hole

Bruce Zabriski, Garden City, N.Y., def.
Bob Groff, Brown Summit, N.C., 4 and 3

Mike San Filippo, Harvard, Mass., def.
Wheeler Stewart, Oakland, Md., 3 and 2

Gary Ostrega, Colonia, N.J., def.
Bill Andrews, Rutland, Vt., 3 and 2

Mel Baum, Larchmont, N.Y., def.
Jerry Tucker, St. Louis, Mo., 2 and 1

Jeff Bohr, Southampton, N.Y., def.
Ray Cragun, Albuquerque, N.M., 19th hole

Jeb Boyle, State College, Pa., def.
Fred Reeder, Benton Harbor, Mich., 5 and 4

Billy Ziobro, Jamesburg, N.J., def.
John Mulliken, Chicago, Ill., 5 and 4

Brad Dean, Thomasville, Mich., def.
Joe Browning, Wellesley, Mass., 6 and 4

Tom Dolby, St. Paul, Minn., def.
Butch Johnson, Easton, Pa., 5 and 4

Tim Stafford, Glen Head, N.Y., def.
Steve Jurick, Cincinnati, Ohio, 1-up

Jeff Leckrone, Columbus, Ohio, def.
Dave Kendall, Cadillac, Mich., 19th hole

Joe DeMino Jr., West Henrietta, N.Y., def.
Jim Bender, Ardsley-on-Hudson, N.Y., 3 and 2

Leo McMahon, Bellport, N.Y., def.
Dick Hughes, Hackettstown, N.J., 1-up

Dave Zielinski, West Bloomfield, Mich., def.
Tony Wallen, Eagle River, Wis., 2 and 1

Tom DeBellis, East Norwich, N.Y., def.
Dave Young, Port Washington, N.Y., 1-up

Roland Stafford, Windham, N.Y., def.
Joe Felder, Greenwich, Conn., 1-up

Tom Cleaver, Boca Raton, Fla., def.
William Ballew, Mount Clemens, Mich., 5 and 4

Mike Zinni, Mankato, Minn., def.
Gene Fieger, Bryn Mawr, Pa., 7 and 5

Gary Hardin, Bethlehem, Pa., def.
Terry Carlson, Glen Ellyn, Ill., 3 and 2

Dave Spengler, Green Bay, Wis., def.
Tim Edwards, Yorktown Heights, N.Y., 1-up

Frank Dobbs, Spring Ford, Pa., def.
Doug Schamback, Skillman, N.J., 3 and 1

Dave McGoldrick, Fairfield, Conn., def.
Jeff Johnson, Royal Palm Beach, Fla., 3 and 2

Bob Pfister, Wilmington, Del., def.
Dave Carazo, Tuxedo, N.Y., 2-up

John Scheffler, Chatham, Mass., def.
Peter Procops, Glen Cove, N.Y., 3 and 1

Mike Preston, Westfield, N.J., def.
John Rossi, Rochester, N.Y., 4 and 2

Dana Quigley, Rehoboth, Mass., def.
John Fields, Belmont, Mass., 2 and 1

Steve Benson, Long Grove, Ill., def.
Dino Lucchesi, Deerfield, Ill., 2 and 1

Chris Anderson, Wilmington, Del., def.
Jack McConachie, Southington, Conn., 6 and 4

Dave O'Kelly, Mashpee, Mass., def.
Dave Czaja, Elmsford, N.Y., 4 and 3

Dave Henion, Darien, Conn., def.
Jack Druga, Jupiter, Fla., 19th hole

Mike Baker, Bar Harbor, Maine, def.
Mike Anderson, Boca Raton, Fla., 3 and 2

Tim Angis, Portland, Maine, def.
Jim Buchanan, Canandaigua, N.Y., 3 and 2

Charlie Cowell, Totowa, N.J., def.
Scott Hawkins, Lawrence, N.Y., 6 and 5

Joe Benevento, East Providence, R.I., def.
Randy Cochran, Hoffman Estates, Ill., 1-up

Jim Miller, Metuchen, N.J., def.
Bob Afton, Fontana, Wis., 3 and 2

Al Semrad, Ludington, Mich., def.
Andy Shuman, Long Grove, Ill., 2 and 1

Paul Barkhouse, Ipswich, Mass., def.
John Kellogg, Westchester, Pa., 3 and 2

Larry Rentz, Mamaroneck, N.Y., def.
Mike Tucker, Mount Vernon, Ill., 19th hole

Dave Prange, Glenview, Ill., def.
Chick Evans, Lake Park, Fla., 6 and 4

John Sanges, Locust Valley, N.Y., def.
Lowell Dencer, Westerville, Ohio, 4 and 3

Ron McDougal, Purchase, N.Y., def.
Brent Veenstra, Ypsilanti, Mich., 5 and 4

Mark Kirk, Orchard Park, N.Y., def.
Mark Heartfield, Siasconset, Mass., 5 and 4

Greg Cerulli, Port St. Lucie, Fla., def.
William Lodge, Groveland, Mass., 6 and 4

Kevin Morris, White Plains, N.Y., def.
Steve Brady, Rochester Hills, Mich., 1-up

Pete Oakley, Lewes, Del., def.
Jamie Fordyce, Livingston, N.J., 3 and 2

Steve Madsen, Colorado Springs, Colo., def.
John Hickson, Bath, Maine, 20th hole

Ric Kunnert, Des Plaines, Ill., def.
Scott Dietrich, Old Westbury, N.Y., 6 and 5

Edward Burke Jr., Woodmere, N.Y., def.
Mark Hill, Gaylord, Mich., 7 and 6

LANGERT PGA WINTER TOURNAMENT PROGRAM

SECOND ROUND (Winners of one match earn $200) --

Vershure def. Mullen, 2 and 1

Cregan def. Steger, 2 and 1

DiBuono def. Hughes, 3 and 2

Davis def. Furey, 1-up

Skilling def. Abbott, 23rd hole

Laudien def. Lohren, 2-up

Summerhays def. Impellittiere, 3 and 2

Kelly def. Borojevich, 20th hole

Zabriski def. San Filippo, 4 and 3

Ostrega def. Baum, 3 and 2

Bohn def. Boyle, 3 and 2

Ziobro def. Dean, 1-up

Dolby def. Stafford, 3 and 2

DeMino def. Leckrone, 19th hole

Zelinski def. McMahon, 19th hole

DeBellis def. Stafford, 19th hole

Cleaver def. Zinni, 2 and 1

Hardin def. Spengler, 3 and 2

McGoldrick def. Dobbs, 19th hole

Pfister, won by default

Quigley def. Preston, 3 and 2

Benson def. Anderson, 1-up

O'Kelly def. Henion, 6 and 5

Baker def. Angis, 2-up

Cowell def. Benevento, 2-up

Miller def. Semrad, 4 and 3

Rentz def. Barkhouse, 3 and 2

Prange def. Sanges, 2-up

McDougal def. Kirk, 4 and 2

Cerulli def. Morris, 3 and 2

Madsen def. Oakley, 3 and 2

Burke def. Kunnert, 3 and 2

THIRD ROUND (Winners of two matches earn $400)--

Vershure def. Cregan, 5 and 4

Davis def. DiBuono, 2-up

Skilling def. Laudien, 1-up (21st hole)

Summerhays def. Kelly, 5 and 4

Zabriski def. Ostrega, 7 and 6

Bohr def. Ziobro, 1-up

Dolby def. DeMino, 4 and 3

DeBellis def. Zielinski, 1-up

Cleaver def. Hardin, 1-up (19th hole)

McGoldrick def. Pfister, 3 and 2

Quigley def. Benson, 3 and 1

Baker def. O'Kelly, 3 and 2

Miller def. Cowell, 7 and 5

Rentz def. Prange, 3 and 2

McDougal def. Cerulli, 2 and 1

Madsen def. Burke, 1-up (19th hole)

FOURTH ROUND
(Winners of three matches earn $800) --

Vershure def. Davis, 4 and 3

Summerhays def. Skilling, 1-up

Zabriski def. Bohr, 4 and 3

Dolby def. DeBellis, 2 and 1

Cleaver def. McGoldrick, 5 and 4

Baker def. Quigley, 2 and 1

Rentz def. Miller, 2 and 1

McDougal def. Madsen, 2 and 1

QUARTER-FINALS (Winner of four matches earn $1,600) --

Vershure def. Summerhays, 3 and 2

Dolby def. Zabriski, 2 and 1

Cleaver def. Baker, 7 and 5

McDougal def. Rentz, 1-up (19th hole)

SEMIFINALS (Winners of five matches earn $2,250) --

McDougal def. Vershure, 3 and 2

Cleaver def. Dolby, 5 and 4

FINALS (Winner earns $5,000; Runner-up, $3,500) --

Cleaver def. McDougal, 5 and 3

■ 1994 LANGERT PGA QUARTER CENTURY CHAMPIONSHIP
PGA National GC (Estate), Lake Park, Fla.   Jan. 4-5   Purse: $40,000

OVERALL CHAMPIONS --

(Estate - Under 65)
Steve Bull, Milwaukee, Wis.	70-69—139	$2,000

(Haig - 65 and Over)
Bob Duden, Portland, Ore.	76-70—146	$1,000

GROUP A (Under 50)
1	**Michael Limback,** Evansville, Ind.	75-75—150	$344.00

GROUP 1 (50-54)
1	**Tom Joyce,** Old Westbury, N.Y.	71-69—140	$800.00
2	**Bill Kennedy,** Cape Coral, Fla.	73-68—141	$625.00
T-3	**Nick Berklich,** Grand Blanc, Mich.	72-70—142	$562.50
	Dan Murphy, Atlanta, Ga.	71-71—142	$562.50
T-5	**William A. Mitchell,** Old Greenwich, Conn.	72-71—143	$500.00
	Joe Carr, Rutland, Mass.	71-72—143	$500.00
	Robin All, Columbia, S.C.	75-68—143	$500.00
8	**Dick Murphy,** Atlanta, Ga.	74-70—144	$450.00
T-9	**Lynn Rosely,** Quincy, Ill.	74-71—145	$412.50
	Tony Perla, Collegeville, Pa.	72-73—145	$412.50
T-11	**Ron Weber,** Eugene, Ore.	74-73—147	$177.00
	Mal Galletta Jr., Glen Cove, N.Y.	71-76—147	$177.00

GROUP 2 (55-59)
1	**Steve Bull,** Milwaukee, Wis.	70-69—139	$1,000.00
2	**Art Proctor,** Edmond, Okla.	71-69—140	$850.00
3	**Phil Hewitt,** Kirkwood, Mo.	72-69—141	$800.00
4	**George Bellino,** Youngstown, Ohio	74-68—142	$750.00
T-5	**Dick Hart,** Hinsdale, Ill.	72-71—143	$631.25
	Gary Lockie, East Moline, Ill.	74-69—143	$631.25
	Dick Schwartz, East Liverpool, Ohio	71-72—143	$631.25
	Earl Puckett Jr., Long Grove, Ill.	74-69—143	$631.25
T-9	**Dennis Bradley,** Singer Island, Fla.	72-72—144	$525.00
	Al Chandler, Palm Beach Gardens, Fla.	70-74—144	$525.00
	Carl Lohren, Glen Head, N.Y.	75-69—144	$525.00
T-12	**Ray Ziats,** Newark, N.Y.	76-69—145	$450.00
	Gary Toulson, Knoxville, Tenn.	72-73—145	$450.00
	Nunzio Ciampi, Glen Head, N.Y.	70-75—145	$450.00
T-15	**El Collins,** Springfield, Ohio	72-74—146	$380.00
	Lloyd Monroe, New Rochelle, N.Y.	72-74—146	$380.00
	Don Cross, Danvers, Mass.	71-75—146	$380.00
	Gene Borek, White Plains, N.Y.	74-72—146	$380.00
	Ed Famula, Palm Beach Gardens, Fla.	74-72—146	$380.00
T-20	**Paul Messner,** Beloit, Wis.	72-75—147	$345.00
	Larry Mancour, Harbor Springs, Mich.	72-75—147	$345.00
T-22	**Charlie Huckaby,** Brookville, N.Y.	72-76—148	$202.34
	George Nackel, Appleton, Wis.	74-74—148	$202.33
	Chick Evans, Lake Park, Fla.	71-77—148	$202.33

GROUP 3 (60-64)
1	**Bob Ross,** Springfield, N.J.	71-70—141	$800.00

T-2	**Walker Inman Jr.,** Columbus, Ohio	72-71—143	$625.00
	Dick Sarta, Ridgewood, N.J.	74-69—143	$625.00
4	**Jacob Zastko,** Jupiter, Fla.	72-73—145	$550.00
T-5	**Buck Adams,** Pinehurst, N.C.	72-75—147	$415.00
	Tom Murphy, Webster, N.Y.	73-74—147	$415.00
	Roland Stafford, Windham, N.Y.	71-76—147	$415.00
	Dick Plummer, Cincinnati, Ohio	74-73—147	$415.00
	Ray Bolo, Redford, Mich.	74-73—147	$415.00
T-10	**Henry McQuiston,** Philadelphia, Pa.	75-73—148	$158.00
	Frank Freer, Minnetonka, Minn.	73-75—148	$158.00

GROUP 4 (65-69)
1	**Ray Montgomery,** Port St. Lucie, Fla.	75-72—147	$800.00
2	**Mal McMullen,** Kokomo, Ind.	75-78—153	$625.00
3	**Mike Krak,** Palm Beach Gardens, Fla.	79-75—154	$575.00
T-4	**Ken Towns,** Penn Valley, Calif.	80-75—155	$537.50
	Charlie Smith, Elyria, Ohio	76-79—155	$537.50
T-6	**George Thomas,** Elkhart, Ind.	79-77—156	$487.50
	Ange Alberico, Springville, N.Y.	77-79—156	$487.50
T-8	**Luke Majorki,** Palm Beach Gardens, Fla.	79-80—159	$437.50
	Auggie Navarro, Wichita, Kan.	76-83—159	$437.50
T-10	**Chuck Scally,** Coraopolis, Pa.	82-78—160	$377.00
	Jim Riggins, Jackson, Tenn.	78-82—160	$377.00

GROUP 5 (70-74)
1	**Bob Duden,** Portland, Ore.	76-70—146	$800.00
2	**Joe Taylor,** West Palm Beach, Fla.	74-76—150	$650.00
3	**Manuel de la Torre,** Milwaukee, Wis.	78-77—155	$550.00
4	**Bob Watson,** Jupiter, Fla.	77-80—157	$450.00
5	**John Cleary,** Carlsbad, Calif.	82-76—158	$425.00
6	**Lou Warobick,** Elm Grove, Wis.	78-81—159	$400.00
7	**Edward Kowalski,** Bristol, Conn.	82-81—163	$339.00

GROUP 6 (75-79)
1	**Henry Williams,** Fleetwood, Pa.	78-82—160	$800.00
2	**Hans Merrell,** Palm Beach Gardens, Fla.	85-79—164	$650.00
T-3	**Dick Neumann,** Palm Beach Gardens, Fla.	82-84—166	$500.00
	Ronald LaParl, Battle Creek, Mich.	86-80—166	$500.00
5	**Pete Inzano,** Mayfield Height, Ohio	85-85—170	$350.00
T-6	**George Kamal,** Royal Palm Beach, Fla.	85-86—171	$150.00
	Billy Gilbert, Jupiter, Fla.	78-93—171	$150.00

GROUP 7 (80-84)
1	**Ralph Bond,** Wickliffe, Ohio	86-85—171	$500.00
2	**Pat Palmieri,** Riviera Beach, Fla.	89-89—178	$360.00

GROUP 8 (85-89)
1	**Tommy Shannon,** Troy, Mich.	94-97—191	$400.00
2	**Ted Lockie,** Palm Beach Gardens, Fla.	100-94—194	$288.00

LANGERT PGA WINTER TOURNAMENT PROGRAM

■ 1994 LANGERT PGA SENIOR STROKE PLAY CHAMPIONSHIP
PGA National GC (Haig), Palm Beach Gardens, Fla.   Jan. 7-9   Purse $51,000

OVERALL (Under 65)

1 Gene Carello, West Frankfort, Ill.   75-71-70—216 $2,000.00

GROUP 1 (50-54)

1 Gene Carello, West Frankfort, Ill.   75-71-70—216 $1,000.00
2 Bob Leaver, Kernersville, N.C.   78-71-68—217 $900.00
T-3 Joe Carr, Rutland, Mass.   77-70-71—218 $825.00
     Austin Straub, Cold Spring Harbor, N.Y.   72-75-71—218 $825.00
T-5 Arne Dokka, Pinehurst, N.C.   75-71-73—219 $675.00
     Dave Philo, Pawleys Island, S.C.   72-71-76—219 $675.00
     Paul Barkhouse, Ipswich, Mass.   74-70-75—219 $675.00
     Bruce Dobie, Worcester, Mass.   73-71-75—219 $675.00
T-9 Jerry Hinton, Cordova, Tenn.   69-78-73—220 $525.00
     Bill Robertson, Athens, W.Va.   69-76-75—220 $525.00
     Dennis Milne, Yardley, Pa.   70-74-76—220 $525.00
T-12 Charlie Stock, Crescent, Mo.   72-77-72—221 $455.00
     Martin Bohen, Suffern, N.Y.   74-74-73—221 $455.00
     Roger Stern, Allentown, Pa.   73-73-75—221 $455.00
T-15 Lynn Rosely, Quincy, Ill.   76-74-72—222 $420.00
     Dick Murphy, Atlanta, Ga.   70-76-76—222 $420.00
     David Jimenez, Palm Beach Gardens, Fla.   78-75-69—222 $420.00
T-18 Bob Zimmerman, Dayton, Ohio   75-76-72—223 $395.00
     Tony Perla, Collegeville, Pa.   81-71-71—223 $395.00
     Tom Joyce, Old Westbury, N.Y.   75-72-76—223 $395.00
21 Dick Goetz, Richardson, Texas   74-76-74—224 $385.00
T-22 Dan Murphy, Atlanta, Ga.   77-73-75—225 $377.50
     Robin All, Columbia, S.C.   76-73-76—225 $377.50
T-24 Bill Kennedy, Cape Coral, Fla.   76-74-76—226 $87.25
     Hank Davis, Clearwater, Fla.   73-79-74—226 $87.25
     Tom Gorman, Pompey, N.Y.   73-72-81—226 $87.25
     Paul Bondeson, Stuart, Fla.   76-77-73—226 $87.25

GROUP 2 (55-59)

1 Larry Mancour, Harbor Springs, Mich.   72-73-72—217 $1,100.00
T-2 Chick Evans, Lake Park, Fla.   76-72-70—218 $875.00
     Sal Ruggiero, Stow, Mass.   70-75-73—218 $875.00
T-4 Gene Borek, White Plains, N.Y.   76-72-72—220 $775.00
     Charlie Huckaby, Brookville, N.Y.   76-71-73—220 $775.00

6 Willard Scholl, King of Prussia, Pa.   70-69-82—221 $700.00
T-7 Dennis Bradley, Singer Island, Fla.   75-75-72—222 $625.00
     Jerry Coats, Greenwich, Conn.   76-76-70—222 $625.00
T-9 Earl Puckett Jr., Long Grove, Ill.   76-77-70—223 $520.00
     Paul Messner, Beloit, Wis.   75-74-74—223 $520.00
     Carl Lohren, Glen Head, N.Y.   76-72-75—223 $520.00
     Jim King, Pompano Beach, Fla.   75-72-76—223 $520.00
13 Mike O'Sullivan, Ormond Beach, Fla.   79-73-72—224 $470.00
T-14 Cotton Dunn, Dallas, Texas   79-72-74—225 $445.00
     Art Proctor, Edmond, Okla.   79-70-76—225 $445.00
T-16 Bill Halvorson, Milwaukee, Wis.   80-71-75—226 $420.00
     Nunzio Ciampi, Glen Head, N.Y.   73-76-77—226 $420.00
     Gary Toulson, Knoxville, Tenn.   75-76-75—226 $420.00
T-19 Steve Bull, Milwaukee, Wis.   77-73-77—227 $395.00
     Donnie Lindsey, Hobe Sound, Fla.   75-77-75—227 $395.00
21 Joe Cardenas, Lancaster, Ohio   76-75-77—228 $380.00
T-22 Don Bisesi, Evansville, Ind.   78-74-77—229 $240.50
     George Nackel, Appleton, Wis.   76-76-77—229 $240.50
     Lloyd Monroe, New Rochelle, N.Y.   77-75-77—229 $240.50
     Alan McClay, Madison, N.J.   80-73-76—229 $240.50
     Gary Howlett, Worthington, Ohio   81-72-76—229 $240.50
     John D. Haines, Jackson, Wyo.   78-75-76—229 $240.50

GROUP 3 (60-64)

1 Bob Ross, Springfield, N.J.   74-76-71—221 $800.00
2 Ken Weiler, Park Ridge, Ill.   79-71-74—224 $700.00
T-3 Roland Stafford, Windham, N.Y.   76-75-76—227 $625.00
     Howie Robinson, Palm Beach Gardens, Fla.   78-75-74—227 $625.00
T-5 Dick Plummer, Cincinnati, Ohio   74-76-79—229 $525.00
     Joe Ennis, Jupiter, Fla.   72-80-77—229 $525.00
7 Bob Goetz, Dallas, Texas   79-75-77—231 $450.00
T-8 Hubby Habjan, Lake Forest, Ill.   77-79-76—232 $336.60
     George M. Schneiter, Sandy, Utah   80-76-76—232 $336.60
     Paul Kelly, Fairfield, Conn.   78-77-77—232 $336.60
     Jennings House, Virginia Beach, Va.   77-76-79—232 $336.60
     Walker Inman Jr., Columbus, Ohio   76-74-82—232 $336.60

PGA National GC (Estate), Lake Park, Fla.

OVERALL (65 and Over)

1 Ray Montgomery, Port St. Lucie, Fla.   66-71—137 $1,000.00

GROUP 4 (65-69)

1 Ray Montgomery, Port St. Lucie, Fla.   66-71—137 $800.00
2 Mal McMullen, Kokomo, Ind.   68-76—144 $700.00
3 Mike Krak, Palm Beach Gardens, Fla.   75-71—146 $650.00
4 Paul Butler, Warwick, R.I.   77-70—147 $600.00
5 Al Biondi, Manchester, Maine   75-73—148 $550.00
T-6 Bob Bodington, Palm Beach Gardens, Fla.   76-73—149 $495.00
     Ken Towns, Penn Valley, Calif.   73-76—149 $495.00
T-8 Ed Rubis, N. Palm Beach, Fla.   77-73—150 $475.00
     Luke Majorki, Palm Beach Gardens, Fla.   76-74—150 $475.00
10 Chuck Scally, Coraopolis, Pa.   73-78—151 $460.00
T-11 Charlie Smith, Elyria, Ohio   79-73—152 $206.00
     Jim Riggins, Jackson, Tenn.   76-76—152 $206.00

GROUP 5 (70-74)

1 Joe Taylor, West Palm Beach, Fla.   72-75—147 $700.00
2 Glenn Teal, Palm Beach Gardens, Fla.   73-75—148 $600.00
T-3 Bob Duden, Portland, Ore.   76-73—149 $525.00

     Bob Watson, Jupiter, Fla.   74-75—149 $525.00
T-5 John Cleary, Carlsbad, Calif.   78-74—152 $462.50
     Billy Capps, Beckley, W.Va.   75-77—152 $462.50
7 Darwin C. White, Roswell, Ga.   78-76—154 $440.00
8 Dick Demane, Greenvale, N.Y.   78-77—155 $420.00

GROUP 6 (75-79)

1 Philip Friel Jr., Hudson, N.H.   76-77—153 $700.00
2 Henry Williams, Fleetwood, Pa.   78-77—155 $600.00
3 Hans Merrell, Palm Beach Gardens, Fla.   76-81—157 $550.00
4 Everett Stuart, Duluth, Minn.   81-78—159 $500.00
5 Skee Riegel, Upper Darby, Pa.   82-78—160 $450.00
6 Bob Gajda, Detroit, Mich.   80-81—161 $436.00

GROUP 7 (80-84)

1 Ralph Bond, Wickliffe, Ohio   75-68—143 $600.00
2 Pat Palmieri, Riviera Beach, Fla.   77-80—157 $479.00

GROUP 8 (85-89)

1 Ted Lockie, Palm Beach Gardens, Fla.   77-78—155 $400.00
2 Tommy Shannon, Troy, Mich.   81-80—161 $319.00

■ 1994 LANGERT PGA SENIOR-JUNIOR CHAMPIONSHIP

PGA National GC (Haig and Champion), Palm Beach Gardens, Fla.　　Jan. 15-17　　Purse $80,000

Place	Players	Score (per team)	Winnings
1	**Lloyd Monroe,** New Rochelle, N.Y./**Gary Hardin,** Bethlehem, Pa.	204	$10,000.00
2	**Bill Kennedy,** Cape Coral, Fla./**Nic Borojevich,** Uhrichsville, Ohio	204	$7,000.00
T3	**Marion Heck,** Fort Myers Beach, Fla./**Charles Stucklen,** Sayville, N.Y.	205	$4,166.67
	Dick Sarta, Ridgewood, N.J./**Bruce Zabriski,** Garden City, N.Y.	205	$4,166.67
	Paul Barkhouse, Ipswich, Mass./**Gene Fieger,** Port St. Lucie, Fla.	205	$4,166.66
T6	**Brad Meekins,** Lenox, Mass./**Pete Oakley,** Lewes, Del.	206	$2,330.00
	Austin Straub, Cold Spring Harbor, N.Y./**Bill Marx,** Rochester, Mich.	206	$2,330.00
	Lynn Rosely, Quincy, Ill./**Mike San Filippo,** Harvard, Mass.	206	$2,330.00
	David Jimenez, Palm Beach Gardens, Fla./**Todd M. Smith,** Peru, Ind.	206	$2,330.00
	Steve Bull, Milwaukee, Wis./**Jim Gerring,** Dublin, Ohio	206	$2,330.00
11	**John Scheffler,** Chatham, Mass./**Cary Hungate,** Kokomo, Ind.	207	$1,800.00
T12	**Bob Zimmerman,** Dayton, Ohio/**Joseph Donnelly,** Fort Myers, Fla.	208	$1,600.00
	Al Chandler, Palm Beach Gardens, Fla./**Art Scott,** Ocean City, Md.	208	$1,600.00
	Tom Joyce, Old Westbury, N.Y./**Ned Weaver,** Coraopolis, Pa.	208	$1,600.00
T15	**Bob Duden,** Portland, Ore./**Billy Ziobro,** Jamesburg, N.J.	209	$1,176.67
	El Collins, Springfield, Ohio/**Dana Quigley,** Rehoboth, Mass.	209	$1,176.67
	Mal McMullen, Kokomo, Ind./**Jim Estes,** Crystal Lake, Ill.	209	$1,176.67
	Ray Goddard, Terre Haute, Ind./**John Sanges,** Locust Valley, N.Y.	209	$1,176.67
	Rocky Nelson, Columbus, Ohio/**Scott Steger,** Noblesville, Ind.	209	$1,176.66
	William A. Mitchell, Old Greenwich, Conn./**Tom Cleaver,** Boca Raton, Fla.	209	$1,176.66
T21	**Jack Freeman,** Ashland, Ky./**Edward Burke Jr.,** Woodmere, N.Y.	210	$759.10
	George Bellino, Youngstown, Ohio/**Joe Bostic,** Wilton, Conn.	210	$759.09
	Chuck Lasher, Kensington, Conn./**Mike Preston,** Westfield, N.J.	210	$759.09
	Carl Lohren, Glen Head, N.Y./**Bill Andrews,** Rutland, Vt.	210	$759.09
	Bill Hall, St. Louis, Mo./**Jeffrey Johnson,** Royal Palm Beach, Fla.	210	$759.09
	Bob Pfister, Wilmington, Del./**Joe Browning,** Wellesley, Mass.	210	$759.09
	Earl Puckett Jr., Long Grove, Ill./**Frank Dully,** Huntington, Conn.	210	$759.09
	Don Butzin, Waukesha, Wis./**Ray Cragun,** Albuquerque, N.M.	210	$759.09
	Bill Robertson, Athens, W.Va./**Terry Hurst,** Clarks Summit, Pa.	210	$759.09
	Charlie Huckaby, Brookville, N.Y./**David Prange,** Glenview, Ill.	210	$759.09
	Bob Ross, Springfield, N.J./**David Giacondino,** Wallingford, Conn.	210	$759.09
T32	**Tony Perla,** Collegeville, Pa./**Scott Dietrich,** Old Westbury, N.Y.	211	$572.50
	Clayton Cole, Englewood, Colo./**Robert E. Nelson,** Bloomfield, Conn.	211	$572.50
	Bud Williamson, Kansas City, Mo./**Tom Waitrovich,** Westlake, Ohio	211	$572.50
	Walker Inman Jr., Columbus, Ohio/**Michael Zinni,** Mankato, Minn.	211	$572.50
T36	**Al Hanzl,** Mahwah, N.J./**Fred Knoebel Jr.,** Southampton, N.Y.	212	$530.00
	Dave Philo, Pawleys Island, S.C./**Bryan Abbott,** Akron, Ohio	212	$530.00
	Roger Stern, Allentown, Pa./**Jim Miller,** Metuchen, N.J.	212	$530.00
T39	**Paul Bondeson,** Stuart, Fla./**Terence R. Hughes,** Monticello, N.Y.	213	$495.00
	Ken Burnette, Lake Port, Fla./**Greg Cerulli,** Port St. Lucie, Fla.	213	$495.00
	Ken Weiler, Park Ridge, Ill./**Rick Vershure,** Armonk, N.Y.	213	$495.00
	Cotton Dunn, Dallas, Texas/**Walt Siemsglusz,** Bridgeton, Mo.	213	$495.00
T43	**Dan Murphy,** Atlanta, Ga./**Leo McMahon,** Bellport, N.Y.	214	$460.00
	Gene Borek, White Plains, N.Y./**Scott L. Hawkins,** Lawrence, N.Y.	214	$460.00
	Willard Scholl, King of Prussia, Pa./**Dave Laudien,** Neptune City, N.J.	214	$460.00
T46	**George M. Schneiter,** Sandy, Utah/**Don Duchatreau,** Fond du Lac, Wis.	215	$430.00
	Nunzio Ciampi, Glen Head, N.Y./**Jeff Leckrone,** Columbus, Ohio	215	$430.00
	Jerry Hinton, Olive Branch, Miss./**Jim Tuller,** Dubuque, Iowa	215	$430.00
T49	**Richard Hughes,** Hackettstown, N.J./**Joseph Benevento,** E. Providence, R.I.	216	$401.67
	Bill Mattson, Farmington, Mich./**Tom Kelly,** King of Prussia, Pa.	216	$401.67
	Art Proctor, Edmond, Okla./**David Levine,** Hannibal, Mo.	216	$401.66
52	**Paul Messner,** Beloit, Wis./**Larry Mullen,** Paducah, Ky.	217	$390.00
T53	**Paul Kelly,** Fairfield, Conn./**Ken Corliss,** Bowling Green, Ohio	218	$382.50
	Dennis Grasso, Naples, Maine/**Jerry Tucker,** St. Louis, Mo.	218	$382.50
55	**Steve Downey,** Tamarac, Fla./**Al Vallante,** E. Providence, R.I.	222	$375.00

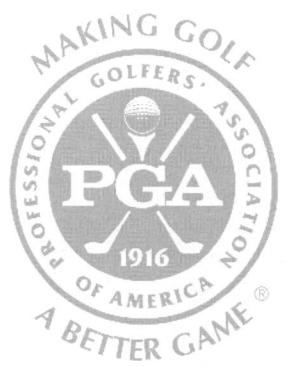

PGA TOURNAMENT SERIES

AVON GRIPS PGA TOURNAMENT SERIES

■ HISTORY

The PGA Tournament Series was begun during the 1977-78 winter season to provide additional playing opportunities for PGA professionals. The competitions are open to PGA members and registered apprentices who have completed Business School I. The 1993-94 season was the eighth in a row that the full schedule of events was played in South Florida.

Avon Grips completed its first year as title sponsor of the PGA Tournament Series, and will continue as title sponsor through the 1995-96 season. The 1993-94 season featured 13 Regular Division events, eight Senior (age 50-and-older) and six Super Senior (age 60-and-older) events. It was the second season for the Super Senior Division.

Leading Money Winners			Leading Stroke Averages	
1977-78	John Adams	$11,756.17		
1978-79	Jack Seltzer	$14,324.50		
1979-80	Dean Refram	$12,572.33	Dean Refram	72.12
1980-81	Jay Cudd	$21,343.33	Lynn Janson	72.67
1981-82	Randy Erskine	$13,576.00	John Godwin	71.29
1982-83	Jim Albus	$19,672.42	Jim Albus	71.69
1983-84	Don Reese	$19,388.16	Mike Bright	71.27
1984-85	Larry Rentz	$26,832.31	Jim Albus	71.17
1985-86	Lonnie Nielsen	$27,075.46	Lonnie Nielsen	70.90
1986-87	Lonnie Nielsen	$23,120.00	Lonnie Nielsen	70.32
1987-88	Rob Wilkin	$20,316.00	Rob Wilkin	71.55
	Stan Thirsk (Senior)	$3,736.00	Stan Thirsk (Senior)	72.33
1988-89	Darrell Kestner	$17,372.00	Lonnie Nielsen	70.93
	Larry Mancour (Senior)	$5,600.00	Larry Mancour (Senior)	71.10
1989-90	Bob Ford	$15,354.00	Lee Rinker	70.83
	Alex Redmond (Senior)	$4,850.00	Larry Mancour (Senior)	70.83
1990-91	Gene Fieger	$19,481.67	Bruce Zabriski	70.44
	Jack Kiefer (Senior)	$7325.00	Jack Kiefer (Senior)	69.25
1991-92	Larry Gilbert	$17,737.00	Gene Fieger	71.45
	Terry Houser (Senior)	$8,882.50	Mike Joyce (Senior)	70.87
1992-93	Mike San Filippo	$24,645.00	Mike San Filippo	70.38
	Tom Storey (Senior)	$6,518.75	Roger Kennedy (Senior)	70.88
1993-94	Bruce Zabriski	$20,341.25	Bruce Zabriski	70.40
	Gene Borek (Senior)	$6,462.50	Gene Borek, Dave Philo (Senior)	71.87

■ WINNERS 1977-78 THROUGH 1993-94

REGULAR DIVISION

Ten - Lonnie Nielsen, Tom Wargo, Bruce Zabriski
Nine - Jim Albus
Seven - Mike San Filippo
Six - Gene Fieger, Bob Ford
Five - Jay Cudd, Randy Erskine, Scott Steger
Four - Kirk Hanefeld, Bobby Heins, Larry Rentz, Don Reese, Darrell Kestner
Three - Pete Oakley, Tim Angis, B.J. Curry, Lee Danielian, Scott Davis, Rolf Deming, Mal Galletta Jr., John Gentile, Steve Gotsche, Lloyd Monroe, Don Padgett II, Lee Rinker, Tony Wallin.
Two - Bob Ackerman, John Adams, James Blair III, Steve Brady, John Calabria, Greg Cerulli, Brad Fabel, Alan Fadel, Bruce Fleisher, Ray Freeman, Kevin Harrison, Jerry Impellittiere, Jeff Jerrel, Jim King, Bob Lendzion, Larry Mancour, Jim Picard, Dean Prange, Jack Seltzer, Rick Smith, Victor Tortorici, Brett Upper, Rick Vershure, Rob Wilkin.
One - Jack Anrico, Ron Baker, Paul Barkhouse, Louis Bartoletti, Norm Becker, Bill Bergin, Don Berry, Martin Bohen, Mike Bright, Jerry Bruner, Edward Burke Jr., Mike Burke Jr., Mark Calcavecchia, Roy Carmichael, Peter Chapin, Brien Charter, John Dahl, Bill Davis, Mike Davis, Brian Fogt, John DeForest, Duke Delcher, Gary Domalgaski, Ed Dougherty, Ken Ellsworth, Jim Estes, Chick Evans, Jim Ferriell, Mike Ford, Bill Galloway, Gene George, John Godwin, Rick Gomes, Butch Grattan, Gary Hardin, Dick Hart, Don Headings, Jay Horton, Lynn Janson, Joe Jimenez, Gordon Johnson, Tony Kaloustian, Jon Kudysch, John Lee, Rodney Loesch, Mike Mattucci, Jeff Matheson, Rives McBee, Jack McKelvey, Jim McLean, John McNaney, Ted Meier, Mark Mielke, Paul Moran, Steve Parker, Dave Philo, Kevin Powers, Mike Preston, Bob Proben, Barry Redmond, Dean Refram, Lee Rinker, Stacy Russell, Ed Sabo, Ted Schultz, Pat Schwab, Steve Sieg, Art Silvestrone, Jack Skilling, Roland Stafford, Larry Startzel, Tommy Thomas, Jeff Thomsen, Jerry Tucker, Mike Watney, Craig Watson, Jim Weeden, B.G. Winings, Winslow Woodard.

SENIOR DIVISION

Four - George Bellino, Alex Redmond
Three - Gene Borek, Terry Houser, Jack Kiefer, Larry Mancour
Two - Steve Bull, Roger Kennedy, Joe Carr, Tom Wargo
One - Dennis Bradley, Jim Ferriell Jr., John Frillman, Bill Hall, Dick Hart, Charlie Huckaby, Gene Mitchell, Ray Montgomery, Dave Philo, Art Proctor, John Rainieri, Howard Robinson, Willard Scholl, Pat Schwab, Austin Straub, Stan Thirsk

SUPER SENIOR DIVISION

Three - Ray Montgomery
Two - Sonny Ridenhour
One - Buck Adams, Joe Ennis, Walker Inman Jr., Mal McMullen, Roland Stafford, Bob Watson, Ken Weiler

AVON GRIPS PGA TOURNAMENT SERIES

■ 1993-94 SUMMARY

REGULAR DIVISION

Bruce Zabriski of Garden City, N.Y., dominated the pre-holiday segment of the Avon Grips PGA Tournament Series, winning four tournaments to tie Tom Wargo and Lonnie Nielsen for all-time victories with 10. Zabriski easily won the season money title with $20,341.25, the seventh-best performance in the program's 17-year history. And, Zabriski also won his second season scoring title, posting a 70.40 average in 20 rounds and 10 events. Zabriski is the 10th player in the history of the PGA Tournament Series to win both titles in the same season. Zabriski previously won the scoring average title in the 1990-91 season with a 70.44 average.

Zabriski edged Edward Burke Jr. of Woodmere, N.Y., who posted a 70.93 average after playing 14 rounds and seven events.

Rain cancelled one round in the Avon Grips PGA Tournament Series, the 18-hole finale Feb. 16, at the Haig Course at PGA National Golf Club in Palm Beach Gardens, Fla.

Steve Brady of Rochester Hills, Mich., was the only other player in the Regular Division to win more than one event. Brady won twice, catapulting him to second place on the money list with $14,766.92, and fourth in stroke average (71.77). Brady's two early December victories preceded another prize later in the month when he won the Titleist/Foot-Joy PGA Assistant Professional Championship at PGA West in La Quinta, Calif.

Mike San Filippo of Harvard, Mass., who picked up one championship to move to fifth on the all-time victory list (7), finished third in stroke average (71.38). San Filippo turned in the season's lowest 36-hole score, a 12-under-par 132, to win on Feb. 12 at the Estate Course of PGA National Golf Club in Lake Park, Fla.

SENIOR DIVISION

Of the eight Senior Division events there were eight winners. Though neither player won an event, Gene Borek of White Plains, N.Y., and Dave Philo of Georgetown, S.C., had enough reserve firepower to share the scoring average title with a 71.87 average in 15 rounds and finish 1-2 in the money list. Borek earned $6,462.50, and Philo $5,543.75. Austin Straub of Cold Spring Harbor, N.Y., was third with $4,425 and Dennis Bradley of Singer Island, Fla., fourth with $4,165.62.

Carl Lohren of Glen Head, Long Island, N.Y., finished third in scoring (72.00) after playing eight rounds and four events. Jim Ferriell Jr. of Carmel, Ind. (70.29), and Lynn Rosely of Quincy, Ill. (71.86), had lower scoring averages, but played seven rounds, one below the minimum required for award consideration.

SUPER SENIOR DIVISION

The second year of competition in this division for players 60 years-and-older produced several outstanding performances, with Ray Bolo of Redford, Mich., winning the money title with $2,225 in six events, followed by Ken Weiler of Palm Beach Gardens, Fla., with $1,950, and Ray Montgomery of Fort Picrce, Fla., with $1,850.

Bolo was fourth in scoring average (74.18). Mal McMullen of Kokomo, Ind., won the first scoring average title (73.63), playing eight rounds (three more than the required minimum) and four of the division's six events. McMullen finished fifth on the money list with $1,400. Montgomery won two events to lead the division.

1993-94 MONEY LEADERS

REGULAR DIVISION

Place	Player	Earnings
1.	Bruce Zabriski, Garden City, N.Y.	$20,341.25
2.	Steve Brady, Rochester Hills, Mich.	14,766.92
3.	Brian Fogt, Chesterfield, Mo.	13,681.25
4.	Pete Oakley, Lewes, Del.	12,365.44
5.	Mike Mattucci, Tampa, Fla.	12,020.83
6.	Jay Hunter, Jefferson City, Mo.	11,445.98
7.	Mike San Filippo, Harvard, Mass.	10,813.75
8.	Ray Cragun, Albuquerque, N.M.	10,240.42
9.	Barry Redmond, Detroit, Mich.	10,025.42
10.	Dana Quigley, Rehoboth, Mass.	9,962.88

SENIOR DIVISION

Place	Player	Earnings
1.	Gene Borek, White Plains, N.Y.	$6,462.50
2.	Dave Philo, Georgetown, S.C.	5,543.75
3.	Austin Straub, Cold Spring Harbor, N.Y.	4,425.00
4.	Dennis Bradley, Singer Island, Fla.	4,165.62
5.	Herb Rose, Riviera Beach, Fla.	3,981.25
6.	Steve Bull, Milwaukee, Wis.	3,725.00
7.	Paul Messner, Beloit, Wis.	3,681.25
8.	Jim Ferriell Jr., Carmel, Ind.	3,475.00
9.	Earl Puckett Jr., Long Grove, Ill.	3,337.50
10.	Lloyd Monroe, New Rochelle, N.Y.	2,950.00

SUPER SENIOR DIVISION

Place	Player	Earnings
1.	Ray Bolo, Redford, Mich.	$2,225.00
2.	Ken Weiler, Palm Beach Gardens, Fla.	1,950.00
3.	Ray Montgomery, Fort Pierce, Fla.	1,850.00
4.	Walker Inman Jr., Columbus, Ohio	1,600.00
5.	Mal McMullen, Kokomo, Ind.	1,400.00
6.	Buck Adams, Pinehurst, N.C.	1,275.00
7.	Henry McQuiston, Philadelphia, Pa.	950.00
8.	Jennings House, Virginia Beach, Va.	925.00
9.	Charlie Smith, Elyria, Ohio	700.00
10.	Bill Kidd, Edina, Minn.	650.00

1993-94 SCORING AVERAGES

REGULAR DIVISION (Minimum 13 Rounds)

Place	Player	Rds.	Scoring Avg.
1.	Bruce Zabriski, Garden City, N.Y.	20	70.40
2.	Edward Burke Jr., Woodmere, N.Y.	14	70.93
3.	Mike San Filippo, Harvard, Mass.	16	71.38
4.	Steve Brady, Rochester Hills, Mich.	22	71.77
5.	Brian Fogt, Chesterfield, Mo.	22	72.00
6.	George Bowman, Orchard Lake, Mich.	14	72.07
7.	Jay Hunter, Jefferson City, Mo.	22	72.09
8.	Darrell Kestner, Manhasset, N.Y.	14	72.14
9.	Dana Quigley, Rehoboth, Mass.	18	72.22
10.	Jim Estes, Skokie, Ill.	16	72.31

SENIOR DIVISION (Minimum 8 Rounds)

Place	Player	Rds.	Scoring Avg.
T-1.	Gene Borek, White Plains, N.Y.	15	71.87
	Dave Philo, Georgetown, S.C.	15	71.87
3.	Austin Straub, Cold Spring Harbor, N.Y.	12	72.17
4.	Paul Messner, Beloit, Wis.	11	72.27
5.	Steve Bull, Milwaukee, Wis.	10	72.50
6.	Dennis Bradley, Singer Island, Fla.	13	72.85
7.	Bill Hall, St. Louis, Mo.	8	73.00
8.	Larry Mancour, Charlevoix, Mich.	11	73.09
9.	David Jimenez, Miami, Fla.	9	73.11
10.	Joe Carr, Rutland, Mass.	9	73.22

SUPER SENIOR DIVISION (Min. 6 Rounds)

Place	Player	Rds.	Scoring Avg.
1.	Mal McMullen, Kokomo, Ind.	8	73.63
2.	Ken Weiler, Palm Beach Gardens, Fla.	11	73.73
3.	Ray Bolo, Redford, Mich.	11	74.18
4.	Jennings House, Virginia Beach, Va.	7	74.57
5.	Bill Kidd, Edina, Minn.	7	74.71
6.	Henry McQuiston, Philadelphia, Pa.	7	75.00
7.	Joe Ennis, Manhasset, N.Y.	7	75.29
8.	Martin Nolletti, Yorktown Heights, N.Y.	7	76.14

■ HISTORY THROUGH THE YEARS

1993-94

Nov. 15-16 — Bruce Zabriski, 138, Cobblestone CC, Palm City, Fla., Total Purse $30,200/Winner's Purse $3,300.

Nov. 18-19 — Bruce Zabriski, 137, Monarch CC, Stuart, Fla. Total Purse $32,600/Winner's Purse $3,400.

Nov. 22-23 — Steve Brady, 140 (won playoff), Wellington (Fla.) Club West. Total Purse $30,500/Winner's Purse $3,300.

Nov. 29-30 — John Mattucci, 141, St. Lucie West CC, Port St. Lucie, Fla. Total Purse $27,500/Winner's Purse $3,200.

Dec. 2-3 — Steve Brady, 136, Winston Trails CC, Lake Worth, Fla. Total Purse $32,300/Winner's Purse $3,400.

Dec. 5-6 — (Senior) Earl Puckett, 139, BallenIsles CC of JDM, Palm Beach Gardens, Fla. Total Purse $10,200/Winner's Purse $1,700.

Dec. 6-7 — Darrell Kestner, 139, The Reserve Golf & Tennis Club, Fort Pierce, Fla. Total Purse $35,600/Winner's Purse $3,500.

Dec. 8-9 — (Senior) Bill Hall, 141 (won playoff), Club Med at Village of Sandpiper, Port St. Lucie, Fla. Total Purse $9,600/Winner's Purse $1,500.

Dec. 9-10 — Bruce Zabriski, 137, Breakers West CC, West Palm Beach, Fla. Total Purse $38,300/Winner's Purse $3,500.

Dec. 12-13 — Butch Grattan, 137, BallenIsles CC of JDM, Palm Beach Gardens, Fla. Total Purse $38,600/Winner's Purse $3,500.

Dec. 13-14 — (Senior) Austin Straub, 141 (won playoff), St. Lucie West CC, Port St. Lucie, Fla. Total Purse $8,600/Winner's Purse $1,700. (Super Senior) Mal McMullen, 144. Total Purse $2,550/Winner's Purse $900.

Dec. 16-17 — Bruce Zabriski, 143, Binks Forest CC, Wellington, Fla. Total Purse $34,400/Winner's Purse $3,500. (Senior) Charlie Huckaby, 140, Palm Beach Gardens (Fla.) Municipal Course. Total Purse $7,800/Winner's Purse $1,700. (Super Senior) Buck Adams, 145. Total Purse $2,250/Winner's Purse $800.

Feb. 9-10 — (Senior) Steve Bull, 138, PGA National GC (Estate). Total Purse $11,400/Winner's Purse $1,800. (Super Senior) Ray Montgomery, 134. Total Purse $ 2,850/Winner's Purse $900.

Feb. 11-12 — Mike San Filippo, 132, PGA National GC (Estate), Lake Park, Fla. Total Purse $34,400/Winner's Purse $3,500.

Feb. 13-14 — (Senior) Jim Ferriell Jr., 134, PGA National GC (Estate), Lake Park, Fla. Total Purse $11,000/Winner's Purse $1,700. (Super Senior) Walker Inman Jr., 141. Total Purse $2,400/Winner's Purse $900.

Feb. 15-16 — Pete Oakley, 139, PGA National GC (Haig), Palm Beach Gardens, Fla. Total Purse $37,400/Winner's Purse $3,500.

Feb. 17-18 — (Senior) Herb Rose, 67 (second round rained out), PGA National GC (Haig), Palm Beach Gardens, Fla. Total Purse $11,200/Winner's Purse $1,700. (Super Senior) Ray Montgomery, 70 (second round rained out). Total Purse $2,250/Winner's Purse $850.

Feb. 21-22 — Brian Fogt, 134, Club Med at Village of Sandpiper, Port St. Lucie, Fla. Total Purse $29,300/Winner's Purse $3,300.

Feb. 23-24 — (Senior) Dennis Bradley, 138, Club Med at Village of Sandpiper, Port St. Lucie, Fla. Total Purse $8,800/Winner's Purse $1,700. (Super Senior) Ken Weiler, 139. Total Purse $1,950/Winner's Purse $850.

Feb. 25-26 — Chris Caulfield, 134, PGA National GC (Estate), Lake Park, Fla. Total Purse $24,200/Winner's Purse $3,150.

PGA TOURNAMENT SERIES

■ HISTORY THROUGH THE YEARS

1992-93

Nov. 16-17 — Mike SanFilippo, 142 (won playoff), Cobblestone, Palm City, Fla., Total Purse $30,550/Winner's Purse $3,200.

Nov. 18-19 & Nov. 23-24 — Cancelled, rain

Nov. 30-Dec. 4 — Steve Gotsche, 140, Wellington CC, Wellington, Fla. Total Purse $28,750/Winner's Purse $3,200.

Dec. 3-4 — Don Berry, 142 (won playoff), St. Lucie West, Port St. Lucie, Fla. Total Purse $35,350/Winner's Purse $3,400.

Dec. 6-7 — Gene Fieger, 139, BallenIsles CC of JDM, Palm Beach Gardens, Fla. Total Purse $40,150/Winner's Purse $3,500.

Dec. 7-8 — (Senior) Gene Borek, 140, St. Lucie West, Port St. Lucie, Fla. Total Purse $12,900/Winner's Purse $2,000.

Dec. 10-11 — Gene Fieger, 135, PGA National Resort & Spa (Estate), Lake Park, Fla. Total Purse $37,150/Winner's Purse $3,400. (Senior) Roger Kennedy, 144, Palm Beach Gardens Municipal, Palm Beach Gardens, Fla. Total Purse $14,300/Winner's Purse $2,000.

Dec. 13-14 — (Senior) Roger Kennedy, 135, BallenIsles CC of JDM, Palm Beach Gardens, Fla. Total Purse $15,500/Winner's Purse $2,000. (Super Senior) Roland Stafford, 139, BallenIsles CC of JDM. Total Purse $3,300/Winner's Purse $800.

Dec. 14-15 — Steve Gotsche, 135, Breakers West GC, West Palm Beach, Fla. Total Purse $41,350/Winner's Purse $3,500.

Dec. 16-17 — (Senior) Tom Storey, 137, Club Med, (Sinners), Port St. Lucie, Fla. Total Purse $13,700/Winner's Purse $2,000. (Super Senior) Ray Montgomery, 143 (won playoff), Club Med, (Sinners). Total Purse $2,250/Winner's Purse $700.

Dec. 18-19 — Lee Rinker, 140, The Reserve, Port St. Lucie, Fla. Total Purse $34,450/Winner's Purse $3,400.

Feb. 9-10 — (Senior) Tom Wargo, 132, PGA National Resort & Spa (Estate), Lake Park, Fla. Total Purse $16,100/Winner's Purse $2,000. (Super Senior) Bob Watson, 140, PGA National Resort & Spa (Estate). Total Purse $2,250/Winner's Purse $700.

Feb. 11-12 — Edward Burke Jr., 139, PGA National Resort & Spa (Estate), Lake Park, Fla. Total Purse $36,000/Winner's Purse $3,400.

Feb. 15-16 — Lee Rinker, 139, Meadowood CC, Fort Pierce, Fla. Total Purse $22,800/Winner's Purse $3,050.

Feb. 17-18 — (Senior) Joe Carr, 136, PGA National Resort & Spa (Estate), Lake Park, Fla. Total Purse $16,900/Winner's Purse $2,000. (Super Senior) Joe Ennis, 144 (won playoff), PGA National Resort & Spa (Estate). Total Purse $1,950/Winner's Purse $700.

Feb. 19-20 — Mike SanFilippo, 135, PGA National Resort & Spa (Estate), Lake Park, Fla. Total Purse $38,100/Winner's Purse $3,400.

Feb. 21-22 — (Senior) Jerry Coats, 140, PGA National Resort & Spa (Estate), Lake Park, Fla. Total Purse $16,500/Winner's Purse $2,000. (Super Senior) Sonny Ridenhour, 144, PGA National Resort & Spa (Estate). Total Purse $1,350/Winner's Purse $550.

Feb. 23-24 — Mike SanFilippo, 135, PGA National Resort & Spa (Estate), Lake Park, Fla. Total Purse $37,200/Winner's Purse $3,400.

Feb. 25-26 — (Senior) Tom Wargo, 135, PGA National Resort & Spa (Estate), Lake Park, Fla. Total Purse $15,500/Winner's Purse $2,000. (Super Senior) Sonny Ridenhour, 142, PGA National Resort & Spa (Estate). Total Purse $1,800/Winner's Purse $650.

Feb. 27-28 — Jim Estes, 135 (won playoff), PGA National Resort & Spa (Estate), Lake Park, Fla. Total Purse $32,700/Winner's Purse $3,300.

1991-92

Nov. 18-19 — Steve Gotsche, 143 (won playoff), The Reserve, Port St. Lucie, Fla., Total Purse $34,400/Winner's Purse $3,350.

Nov. 21-22 — John DeForest, 141, Monarch CC, Stuart, Fla., $30,800/$3,200.

Nov. 24-25 — Bruce Zabriski, 138, BallenIsles CC of JDM, Palm Beach Gardens, Fla., $36,500/$3,400.

Dec. 2-3 — Tom Wargo, 138, Club Med, Port St. Lucie, Fla., $36,800/$3,400.

Dec. 5-6 — Mark Mielke, 135, St. Lucie West, Port St. Lucie, Fla., $35,000/$3,400.

Dec. 9-10 — Gene Fieger, 139 (won playoff), Cypress Links, Jupiter, Fla. $38,600/$3,500. (Senior) Art Proctor, 140, St. Lucie West, Port St. Lucie, Fla., $15,000/$2,000.

Dec. 12-13 — Mike SanFilippo, 138, Breakers West, West Palm Beach, Fla., $38,600/$3,500. (Senior) Terry Houser, 146 (won playoff), Jacaranda CC, Plantation, Fla., $14,800/$2,000.

Dec. 15-16 — (Senior) Terry Houser, 141, BallenIsles CC of JDM, Palm Beach Gardens, Fla., $17,600/$2,000.

Dec. 16-17 — Bruce Zabriski, 141, Jacaranda CC, Plantation, Fla., $34,700/$3,400.

Dec. 18-19 — (Senior) Dave Philo, 140 (won playoff), Club Med, Port St. Lucie, Fla., $16,000/$2,000.

Feb. 10-11 — Tim Angis, 140, PGA National GC (Haig), Palm Beach Gardens, Fla., $41,900/$3,500. (Senior) Gene Borek, 143 (won playoff), PGA National GC (Haig), Palm Beach Gardens, Fla., $15,000/$2,000.

Feb. 13-14 — Bobby Heins, 132 (won playoff), PGA National GC (Estate), Lake Park, Fla., $41,600/$3,500. (Senior) Willard Scholl, 134, PGA National GC (Estate), Lake Park, Fla., $17,400/$2,000.

Feb. 17-18 — Gene Fieger, 134, PGA National GC (Estate), Lake Park, Fla., $39,500/$3,500. (Senior) Steve Bull, 136, PGA National GC (Estate), Lake Park, Fla., $15,600/$2,000.

Feb. 20-21 — James Estes, 139, PGA National GC (Haig), Palm Beach Gardens, Fla., $39,200/$3,500. (Senior) Terry Houser, 139, PGA National GC (Haig), Palm Beach Gardens, Fla., $14,800/$2,000.

■ HISTORY THROUGH THE YEARS

1990-91

Nov. 16-17 — (Senior) Bruce Zabriski, 139, The Reserve Golf (Senior) and Tennis Club, Port St. Lucie, Fla., $26,200/$3,000.

Nov. 18-19 — Bruce Zabriski, 135, BallenIsles CC of JDM, Palm Beach Gardens, Fla., $26,200/$3,000.

Nov. 26-27 — Tim Angis, 138 (won playoff), Club Med, Port St. Lucie, Fla., $29,800/$3,000.

Nov. 29-30 — Tom Wargo, 140, Monarch CC, Stuart, Fla., $32,200/$3,000.

Dec. 3-4 — Jack Skilling, 138, Cypress Links CC, Jupiter, Fla., $31,300/$3,000.

Dec. 6-7 — Bobby Heins, 134, PGA National GC (Estate), Lake Park, Fla., $38,200/$3,500.

Dec. 10-11 — Jerry Impellittiere, 138 (won playoff), Jacaranda CC, Fort Lauderdale, Fla., $34,600/$3,000. (Senior) Jack Kiefer, 139, Inverrary CC, Fort Lauderdale, Fla., $15,900/$2,000.

Dec. 13-14 — Lonnie Nielsen, 140, St. Lucie West, Port St. Lucie, Fla., $30,400/$3,500. (Senior) Alex Redmond, 138, Club Med, Port St. Lucie, Fla., $17,100/$2,200.

Dec. 17-18 — (Senior) Jack Kiefer, 139, Jacaranda CC, Fort Lauderdale, Fla., $15,700/$2,000.

Feb. 11-12 — Gene Fieger, 141, PGA National GC (Haig), Palm Beach Gardens, Fla., $40,000/$3,000. (Senior) John Frillman, 144, PGA National GC (Estate), Lake Park, Fla., $16,300/$2,000.

Feb. 14-15 — Tim Angis, 141, PGA National GC (Estate), Lake Park, Fla., $40,000/$3,500. (Senior) Alex Redmond, 139, PGA National GC (Estate), Lake Park, Fla., $16,900/$2,000.

Feb. 18-19 — Bruce Zabriski, 137, PGA National GC (Estate), Lake Park, Fla., $36,700/$3,500. (Senior) Dick Hart, 136, PGA National GC (Estate), Lake Park, Fla., $16,900/$2,000.

1989-90

Nov. 13-14 — Greg Cerulli, 138, Monarch CC, Stuart, Fla., $21,400/$3,000.

Nov. 16-17 — Gene Fieger, 141, Reserve CC, Fort Pierce, *Fla., $23,500/$3,000.*

Nov. 20-21 — Bob Lendzion, 137, PGA National GC, Squire, Palm Beach Gardens, Fla., $27,100/$3,000.

Nov. 27-28 — Steve Parker, 138, Cypress Links, Jupiter, Fla., $29,500/$3,000.

Nov. 30-Dec. 1 — Bob Ford, 143, St. Lucie West CC, Port St. Lucie, Fla., $25,000/$3,000.

Dec. 4-5 — Lee Rinker, 136, Inverrary CC, West, Lauderhill, Fla., $30,400/$3,000.

Dec. 5-6 —(Senior) Alex Redmond, 134, Village Hotel of Sandpiper, Port St. Lucie, Fla., $13,200/$1,700.

Dec. 7-8 — Bobby Heins, 137, Jacaranda CC, East, Plantation, Fla., $34,900/$3,500.

Dec. 11-12 — Rich Vershure, 134 (won playoff), Village Hotel of Sandpiper, Port St. Lucie, Fla., $28,000/$3,000. (Senior) Ray Montgomery, 141, Inverray CC, West, Lauderhill, Fla., $11,600/$1,700.

Dec. 14-15 — Bob Lendzion, 139 (won playoff), PGA National GC (Haig), Palm Beach Gardens, Fla., $28,300/$3,000. (Senior) Larry Mancour, 143, PGA National GC (Haig), Palm Beach Gardens, Fla., $12,200/$1,700.

Feb. 12-13 — Bruce Zabriski, 140 (won playoff), PGA National GC (Estate), Lake Park, Fla., $33,400/$3,500. (Senior) George Bellino, 143, PGA National GC (General), Palm Beach Gardens, Fla., $13,800/$1,700.

Feb. 15-16 — Bobby Heins, 142 (won playoff), PGA National GC (Squire), Palm Beach Gardens, Fla., $33,700/$3,500. (Senior) Joe Carr, 133, PGA National GC (Estate), Lake Park, Fla., $15,600/$1,725.

Feb. 19-20 — Jim Albus, 133, River Club, Vero Beach, Fla., $25,900/$3,000. (Senior) Larry Mancour, 137, Village Hotel of Sandpiper, Port St. Lucie, Fla., $13,800/$1,700.

Feb. 26-27 — Reebok PGA Team Championship, Larry Mancour and Dale Fuller, 283, Palm Beach Polo & CC, Dunes, Wellington, Fla., $25,000/$5,000.

1988-89

Nov. 14-15 — Darrell Kestner, 143, PGA National GC (Estate), Lake Park, Fla., $20,600/$3,500

Nov. 17-18 — Lonnie Nielsen, 134, Hunters Run GC, Boynton Beach, Fla., $21,000/$3,000

Nov. 21-22 — Jeff Thomsen, 144, (won playoff), PGA National GC (Champion), Palm Beach Gardens, Fla., $25,000/$3,000

Nov. 28-29 — Roy Carmichael, 138, (won playoff), Village Hotel of Sandpiper, Sinners, Port St. Lucie, Fla., $23,000/$3,000.

Dec. 1-2 — John Lee, 144, Reserve CC, Fort Pierce, Fla., $27,600/$3,000

Dec. 5-6 — Mike SanFilippo, 134 (won playoff), Village Hotel of Sandpiper, Sinners, Port St. Lucie, Fla., $30,900/$3,000.

Dec. 8-9 — Darrell Kestner, 134, Jacaranda CC, West, Plantation, Fla., $29,700/$3,000. (Senior) Gene Borek, 140, PGA National GC (Squire), Palm Beach Gardens, Fla., $10,500/$1,600

Dec. 12-13 — Barry Redmond, 137, Monarch CC, Stuart, Fla., $31,800/$3,000. (Senior) Alex Redmond, 138, PGA National GC (General), Palm Beach Gardens, Fla., $13,100/$1,750.

Dec. 15-16 — Bob Ford, 137 (won playoff), PGA National GC (Haig), Palm Beach Gardens, Fla., $30,900/$3,000. (Senior) George Bellino, 137, PGA National GC (Haig), Palm Beach Gardens, Fla., $12,700/$1,700.

Feb. 2-3 — Darrell Kestner, 134, PGA National GC (Estate), Lake Park, Fla., $35,100/$3,500. (Senior) George Bellino, 138, PGA National GC (Estate), Lake Park, Fla., $17,100/$1,800.

Feb. 20-21 — Jon Kudysch, 139, PGA National GC (Estate), Lake Park, Fla., $27,900/$3,000. (Senior) Larry Mancour, 137, PGA National GC (Estate), Lake Park, Fla., $13,300/$1,750.

Feb. 23-24 — Bob Ford, 142, PGA National GC (Haig), Palm Beach Gardens, Fla., $29,100/$3,000. (Senior) Gene Mitchell Jr. (won playoff), PGA National GC (Haig), Palm Beach Gardens, Fla., $12,900/$1,700.

Feb. 27-28 — LaMode Point Finals, Mal McMullen and Mike SanFilippo, 273, Palm Beach Polo & CC, Cypress, West Palm Beach, Fla., $15,000/$4,000.

PGA TOURNAMENT SERIES

■ HISTORY THROUGH THE YEARS

1987-88

Nov. 16-17 — James Blair III, Village Hotel of Sandpiper, Sinners, Port St. Lucie, Fla., $25,200/$3,000.

Nov. 19-20 — Bob Ford, 70 (18 holes, rain; won playoff), Monarch GC, Stuart, Fla., $26,550/$3,200.

Nov. 23-24 — Bob Ford, 140, PGA National GC (General), Palm Beach Gardens, Fla., $35,100/$3,500.

Nov. 30-Dec. 1 — Rob Wilkin, 135, Hunters Run GC, South, Boynton Beach, Fla., $30,900/$3,500.

Dec. 7-8 — Tom Wargo, 140, Reserve CC, Fort Pierce, Fla., $34,200/$3,500.

Dec. 9-10 — Jim Weeden, 136, Village of Sandpiper, Sinners, Port St. Lucie, Fla., $35,100/$3,500.

Dec. 10-11 — (Senior) George Bellino, 139, PGA National GC (General), Palm Beach Gardens, Fla., $11,100/$1,650.

Dec. 14-16 — Rob Wilkin, 212 (won playoff), PGA National GC (Haig), $48,200/$5,000; (Senior) Pat Schwab, 217 (won playoff), PGA National GC (Haig), $15,200/$2,000.

Feb. 15-16 — Don Reese, 140, Jacaranda CC, West, Plantation, Fla., $36,900/$3,500.

Feb. 18-19 — B.G. Winings, 138, PGA National GC (General), $37,500/$3,500; (Senior) Howard Robinson, 143 (won playoff), PGA National GC (General), $11,700/$1,700.

Feb. 22-23 — Ray Freeman, 134, PGA National GC (Haig),$36,900/$3,500; (Senior) Stan Thirsk, 141, PGA National GC (Haig), $11,300/1,650.

Feb. 25-26 — LaMode Cup, Lonnie Nielsen and Cotton Dunn, 279, Palm Beach Polo & CC, South, West Palm Beach, Fla., $15,000/$4,000.

1986-87

Nov. 13-14 — Greg Cerulli, 142, Crane Creek at Martin Downs, Palm City, Fla., $25,200/$3,200.

Nov. 17-18 — Dean Prange, 138, Wellington GC, West Palm Beach, Fla., $29,700/$3,500.

Nov. 20-21 — Kevin Harrison, 134, Hunters Run GC, East, *Boynton Beach*, Fla., $33,900/$3,500.

Nov. 24-25 — Dean Prange, 139, Palm Beach Polo & CC, South, West Palm Beach, Fla., $33,900/$3,500.

Dec. 1-2 — Kevin Harrison, 135, Indian Trail CC, Royal Palm Beach, Fla., $26,100/$3,200.

Dec. 4-5 — Lonnie Nielsen, 137, Hunters Run GC, South, Boynton Beach, Fla., $31,800/$3,500.

Dec. 8-9 — Lonnie Nielsen, 137, Reserve CC, Fort Pierce, Fla., $34,500/$3,500.

Dec. 11-12 — Scott Steger, 139 (won playoff), Palm Beach Polo & CC, North, West Palm Beach, Fla., $34,500/$3,500.

Dec. 15-17 — Scott Steger, 205, PGA National GC (Haig), Palm Beach Gardens, Fla., $46,400/$4,500.

Feb. 5-6 — Bob Ford, 140 (won playoff), PGA National GC (General) Palm Beach Gardens, Fla., $30,900/$3,500.

Feb. 9-10 — Lynn Janson, 138, Club Med Sandpiper, Sinners, Port St. Lucie, Fla., $32,100/$3,500.

Feb. 16-17 — Lonnie Nielsen, 137, Palm Beach Polo & CC, South, West Palm Beach, Fla., $31,200/$3,500.

Feb. 19-20 — James Blair III, 137 (won playoff), PGA National GC (Squire), $28,800/$3,500; (Senior) John Rainieri, 140, PGA National GC (Squire), $5,200/$1,100.

Feb. 23-25 — John Calabria, 210, PGA National GC (General), Palm Beach Gardens, Fla., $41,200/$4,500.

1985-86

Nov. 7-8 — Lonnie Nielsen, 138, St. Andrews CC, Boca Raton, Fla., $22,500/$3,000.

Nov. 11-12 — Lonnie Nielsen, 137, Hunters Run GC, Boynton Beach, Fla., $22,500/$3,000.

Nov. 14-15 — Louis Bartoletti, 142, Palm Beach Polo & CC, West Palm Beach, Fla., $28,200/$3,500.

Nov. 18-19 — Mike Ford and Mike SanFilippo, 68 (18 holes, Hurricane Kate), Wellington GC, West Palm Beach, Fla., $28,500/$3,000.

Nov. 21-22 — Tom Wargo, 138, Greenview Cove GC, West Palm Beach, Fla., $28,200/$3,500.

Dec. 2-3 — Larry Rentz, 142, Crane Creek at Martin Downs, Palm City, Fla., $30,600/$4,000.

Dec. 5-6 — Scott Steger, 68 (18 holes, rain; won playoff), Stonewal GC, Palm Beach Gardens, Fla., $30,000/$4,000.

Dec. 9-10 — Steve Sieg, 142 (won playoff), Palm Beach Polo & CC, West Palm Beach, Fla., $32,000/$4,000.

Dec. 12-13 — Tom Wargo, 138, Stonewal GC, Palm Beach Gardens, Fla., $31,800/$4,000.

Dec. 16-18 — Lonnie Nielsen, 207, PGA National GC (General), Palm Beach Gardens, Fla., $47,200/$5,000.

Feb. 3-4 — Gary Hardin, 138, Walt Disney World, Palm, Lake Buena Vista, Fla., $27,000/$3,500.

Feb. 6-7 — Lonnie Nielsen, 144, LaCita CC, Titusville, Fla., $27,000/$3,500.

Feb. 10-11 — Larry Rentz and Scott Steger, 138 (no playoff, darkness), Silver Springs Shores CC, Ocala, Fla., $19,200/$2,600.

Feb. 13-14 — Tom Wargo, 135, Plantation Inn, Crystal River, Fla., $19.800/$3,000.

Feb. 17-18 — Lonnie Nielsen, 134, Citrus Hills CC, Hernando, Fla., $15,000/$2,700.

Feb. 20-21 — Ray Freeman, 134, Rainbow Springs CC, Dunnellon, Fla., $15,000/$2,700.

Feb. 24-26 — Tom Wargo, 208, Marion Oaks CC, Ocala, Fla., $18,400/$3,400.

PGA TOURNAMENT SERIES

■ HISTORY THROUGH THE YEARS

1984-85

Nov. 8-9 — Larry Rentz, 137, Boca Grove Plantation, Boca Raton, Fla., $31,200/$4,000.

Nov. 12-13 — Kevin Powers, 139, Hunters Run GC, South, Boynton Beach, Fla., $30,900/$4,000.

Nov. 15-16 — Tony Wallin, 133, G&RC at Eastlakes, Palm Beach Gardens, Fla., $30,900/$4,000.

Nov. 19-20 — Randy Erskine, 136, Monte Carlo CC, Fort Pierce, Fla., $33,000/$4,000.

Nov. 26-27 — Jim Albus, 141, St. Andrews CC, Boca Raton, Fla., $36,000/$4,000.

Nov. 29-30 — Scott Davis, 138 (won playoff), Greenview Cove GC, West Palm Beach, Fla., $36,000/$4,000.

Dec. 3-4 — Mike Burke Jr., 140, Palm Beach Polo & CC, West Palm Beach, Fla., $36,000/$4,000.

Dec. 6-7 — Scott Steger, 143, Crane Creek at Martin Downs, Palm City, Fla., $36,000/$4,000.

Dec. 10-11 — B.J. Curry, 138 (won playoff), John's Island CC, North Vero Beach, Fla., $36,000/$4,000.

Dec. 13-14 — Rick Gomes, 139 (won playoff), Stonewal CC, Palm Beach Gardens, Fla., $36,000/$4,000.

Dec. 17-18 — Ed Dougherty, 141 (won playoff), PGA National GC (Haig), Palm Beach Gardens, Fla., $36,000/$4,000.

Dec. 20-21 — Scott Davis, 135, Wellington GC, West Palm Beach, Fla., $36,000/$4,000.

Feb. 7-8 — Rick Vershure, 136, Plantation Inn, Crystal River, Fla., $36,000/$4,000.

Feb. 11-12 — Jim Albus, 141, Rainbow Springs G&CC, Dunnellon, Fla., $36,000/$4,000.

Feb. 14-15 — B.J. Curry, 137, Plantation Inn, Crystal River, Fla., $36,000/$4,000.

Feb. 18-19 — Randy Erskine, 136 Marion Oaks, Ocala, Fla., $32,000/$4,000.

Feb. 21-22 — Larry Rentz, 140, Citrus Springs CC, Citrus Springs, Fla., $32,000/$4,000.

Feb. 25-27 — Ted Schultz, 208 (won playoff), Marion Oaks CC, Ocala, Fla., $40,000/$4,500.

1983-84

Nov. 10-11 — Tommy Thomas, 135, Boca Grove Foundation, Boca Raton, Fla., $34,200/$4,000.

Nov. 14-15 — Bob Proben, 139, Mariner Sands CC, Hobe Sound, Fla., $32,700/$4,000.

Nov. 17-18 — Brad Fabel, 137, St. Andrews CC, Boca Raton, Fla., $36,000/$4,000.

Nov. 21-22 — Bill Bergin, 136, Eastlakes CC, Palm Beach Gardens, Fla., $35,700/$4,000.

Nov. 28-29 — Lee Danielian, 145 (won playoff), John's Island CC, North, Vero Beach, Fla., $35,100/$4,000.

Dec. 1-2 — Brett Upper, 136, Crane Creek CC, Palm City, Fla., $35,700/$4,000.

Dec. 5-6 — Rives McBee, 136, Hunters Run GC, Boynton Beach, Fla., $36,000/$4,000.

Dec. 8-9 — Stacy Russell, 140 (won playoff), Wellington GC, West Palm Beach, Fla., $36,000/$4,000.

Dec. 13-14 — Tom Wargo, 140, Palm Beach Polo & CC, West Palm Beach, Fla., $36,000/$4,000.

Dec. 15-16 — Tom Wargo, 140, PGA National GC (Champion), Fla., $36,000/$4,000.

Feb. 2-3 — Kirk Hanefeld, 134, Plantation Inn, Crystal River, Fla., $36,000/$4,000.

Feb. 6-7 — Don Reese, 140, Oak Hills CC, Spring Hill, Fla., $36,000/$4,000.

Feb. 9-10 — Don Reese, 135 (won playoff), Plantation Inn, Crystal River, Fla., $38,100/$4,000.

Feb. 14-15 — Don Reese, 139 (won playoff), Rainbow Springs CC, Dunnellon, Fla., $37,800/$4,000.

Feb. 16-17 — Scott Davis, 138, Marion Oaks CC, Ocala, Fla., $38,100/$4,000.

Feb. 20-21 — Brad Fabel, 127, Spring Hill CC, Fla., $31,500/$4,000.

Feb. 23-24 — Jerry Bruner, 139, Citrus Springs CC, Fla., $30,900/$4,000.

1982-83

Nov. 8-9 — Kirk Hanefeld, 143, John's Island CC, Vero Beach, Fla., $19,500/$3,000.

Nov. 11-12 — Jack Seltzer, 137, Mariner Sands CC, Hobe Sound, Fla., $19,500/$3,000.

Nov. 17-18 — Brien Charter, 140 (won playoff), Indian Spring CC, Boynton Beach, Fla., and Boca Grove Plantation, Boca Raton, Fla., $26,000/$3,000.

Nov. 18-19 — Alan Fadel, 139, Boca Grove Plantation, Boca Raton, Fla., $25,500/$3,000.

Nov. 22-23 — Kirk Hanefeld, 137 (won playoff), Eastlakes CC, Palm Beach Gardens, Fla., $25,500/$3,000.

Nov. 29-30 — Rodney Loesch, 141, Hunters Run GC, Boynton Beach, Fla., $30,000/$3,500.

Dec. 2-3 — Mike Bright, 139 (won playoff), Wellington GC, West Palm Beach, Fla., $30,000/$3,500.

Dec. 6-7 — Jim Albus, 135, Boca Greens CC, Boca Raton, Fla., $29,750/$3,500.

Dec. 9-10 — Jim Albus, 140, Crane Creek CC, Palm City, Fla., $29,500/$3,500.

Dec. 13-14 — Tony Wallin, 145 (won playoff), Palm Beach Polo & CC, West Palm Beach, Fla., $29,500/$3,500.

Dec. 16-17 — Paul Moran, 140 (won playoff), Boca Grove Plantation, Boca Raton, Fla., $29,750/$3,500.

Feb. 3-4 — B.J. Curry, 137, Plantation Inn, Crystal River, Fla., $30,000/$3,500.

Feb. 7-8 — Jeff Mattheson, 138, Rainbow Springs CC, Dunnellon, Fla., $30,000/$3,500.

Feb. 12- Jim Ferriell, 68 (18 holes, rain), Plantation Inn, Crystal River, Fla., $30,000/$3,500.

Feb. 14-15 — Martin Bohen, 140, Marion Oaks CC, Ocala, Fla., $30,000/$3,500.

Feb. 17-18 — Jim Albus, 139, Plantation Inn, Crystal River, Fla., $30,000/$3,500.

Feb. 21-22 — Jerry Tucker, 141, Walden Lake CC, Plant City, Fla., $30,000/$3,500.

Feb. 24-25 — Rick Smith, 138, ImperiaLakes CC, Lakeland, Fla., $30,000/$3,500.

■ HISTORY THROUGH THE YEARS

1981-82

Nov. 30-Dec. 1 — Peter Oakley, 139, Hunters Run GC, South, Boynton Beach, Fla., $30,000/$3,500.

Dec. 3-4 — John McNaney, 139 (won playoff), Indian Spring CC, Boynton Beach, Fla., $30,000/$3,500.

Dec. 7-8 — Jim Albus, 141 (won playoff), John's Island CC, North, Vero Beach, Fla., $30,000/$3,500.

Dec. 10-11 — Tom Wargo, 145 (won playoff), Crane Creek CC, Palm City, Fla., $30,000/$3,500.

Dec. 14-15 — Jay Cudd, 140, Jacaranda CC, Plantation, Fla., $30,000/$3,500.

Dec. 17-18 — Mark Calcavecchia, 138, Palm Beach Polo & CC, West Palm Beach, Fla., $30,000/$3,500.

Feb. 1-2 — Alan Fadel, 68 (18 holes, rain; won playoff), Eastlakes CC, Palm Beach Gardens, Fla., $30,000/$3,500.

Feb. 4-5 — Rick Smith, 137 (won playoff), Wellington GC, West Palm Beach, Fla., $30,000/$3,500.

Feb. 8-9 — Gordon Johnson, 140, Plantation Inn, Crystal River, Fla., $28,750/$3,500.

Feb. 11-12 — Randy Erskine, 136, Plantation Inn, Crystal River, Fla., $28,750/$3,500.

Feb. 15-16 — Randy Erskine, 136, Plantation Inn, Crystal River, Fla., $28,750/$3,500.

Feb. 18-19 — Jack Anrico, 138 (won playoff), Plantation Inn, Crystal River, Fla., $28,750/$3,500.

Feb. 22-23 — Duke Delcher, 139 (won playoff), ImperiaLakes CC, Lakeland, Fla., $21,250/$3,000.

Feb. 25-26 — John Godwin, 139, Bardmoor CC, Largo, Fla., $21,250/$3,000.

March 1-2 — Chick Evans, 139, Walden Lake CC, Plant City, Fla., $21,250/$3,000.

1980-81

Nov. 10-11 — John Gentile, 142, PGA National GC (Haig), Palm Beach Gardens, Fla., $22,250/$3,000.

Nov. 13-14 — John Gentile, 143, Hunters Run GC, Boynton Beach, Fla., $23,500/$3,000.

Nov. 17-18 — Bruce Fleisher, 135, Palm Beach Polo & CC, West Palm Beach, Fla., $30,000/$3,500.

Nov. 20-21 — Rolf Deming, 139 (won playoff), Indian Spring CC, East, Boynton Beach, Fla., $30,000/$3,500.

Nov. 24-25 — Bruce Fleisher, 139, PGA National GC (Haig), Palm Beach Gardens, Fla., $30,000/$3,500.

Dec. 1-2 — Jim Albus, 141, PGA National GC (Haig), Palm Beach Gardens, Fla., $29,850/$3,500.

Dec. 4-5 — Peter Oakley, 141 (won playoff), Crane Creek CC, Palm City, Fla., $29,500/$3,500.

Dec. 8-9 — Craig Watson, 136, Mariner Sands CC, Hobe Sound, Fla., $30,000/$3,500.

Dec. 11-12 — Ed Sabo, 136, Jonathan's Landing CC, Jupiter, Fla., $30,000/$3,500.

Jan. 29-30 — Lee Danielian, 139, Walt Disney World, Lake Buena Vista, Fla., $30,000/$3,500.

Feb. 2-3 — Jim McLean, 145, Grenelefe GC, Haines City, Fla., $30,000/$3,500.

Feb. 5-6 — Don Headings, 140, Walden Lake CC, Plant City, Fla., $30,000/$3,500.

Feb. 9-10 — Randy Erskine, 138, ImperiaLakes CC, Lakeland, Fla., $30,000/$3,500.

Feb. 12-13 — Jay Cudd, 138, Walden Lake and Imperialakes, $30,000/$3,500.

Feb. 16-17 — Tony Wallin, 138, Plantation Inn, Crystal River, Fla., $29,650/$3,500.

Feb. 19-20 — Jay Cudd, 137, Plantation Inn, Crystal River, Fla., $29,250/$3,500.

Feb. 23-24 — Jay Cudd, 137, Saddlebrook CC, Wesley Chapel, Fla., $29,250/$3,500.

Feb. 26-27 — Bob Ackerman, 138, Bardmoor CC, Largo, Fla., $29,750/$3,500.

March 2-3 — Jay Cudd, 145 (won playoff), PGA National GC (Haig), Palm Beach Gardens, Fla., $28,000/$3,300.

March 5-6 — Dick Hart, 146 (won playoff), PGA National GC (Haig), Palm Beach Gardens, Fla., $28,000/$3,300.

1979-80

Nov. 15-16 — Bill Galloway, 143, Jonathan's Landing CC, Jupiter, Fla., $30,000/$3,000.

Nov. 19-20 — Dean Refram, 143, Mayacoo Lakes CC, West Palm Beach, Fla., $30,000/$3,000.

Nov. 26-27 — Jerry Impellittiere, 139, Boca West GC, No. 1, Boca Raton, Fla., $30,000/$3,000.

Nov. 29-30 — Art Silvestrone, 141, Boca West GC, No. 1, Boca Raton, Fla., $30,000/$3,000.

Dec. 3-4 — Lloyd Monroe, 141 (won playoff), Boca West GC, No. 2, Boca Raton, Fla., $30,000/$3,000.

Dec. 6-7 — Norm Becker, 139 (won playoff), Boca West GC, No. 2, Boca Raton, Fla., $30,000/$3,000.

Dec. 10-11 — Rolf Deming, 142, Palm Beach Polo & CC, West Palm Beach, Fla., $30,000/$3,000.

Dec. 13-14 — Mal Galletta Jr., 137, Indian Spring CC, East, Boynton Beach, Fla., $30,000/$3,000.

Dec. 17-18 — Lee Danielian, 139, Jonathan's Landing CC, Jupiter, Fla., $30,000/$3,000.

Jan. 31-Feb 1 — Bob Ackerman, 144, Walt Disney World, Palms, Lake Buena Vista, Fla., $30,000/$3,000.

Feb. 4-5 — Jim Picard, Grenelefe GC, Haines City, Fla., $30,000/$3,000.

Feb. 7-8 — Brett Upper, 140 (won playoff), Gainesville, Fla., GC $30,000/$3,000.

Feb. 11-12 — Mal Galletta Jr., 140, Walden Lake CC, Plant City, Fla., $30,000/$3,000.

Feb. 14-15 — Paul Barkhouse, 135, Plantation Inn, Crystal River, Fla., $30,000/$3,000.

Feb. 18-19 — Jim King, 138, ImperiaLakes CC, Lakeland, Fla., $30,000/$3,000.

Feb. 25-26 — Peter Oakley, 141, Mariner Sands CC, Hobe Sound, Fla., $27,950/$3,000.

Feb. 28-29 — Larry Mancour, 141, Crane Creek CC, Palm City, Fla., $27,750/$3,000.

March 3-4 — Gary Domalgaski, 144 (won playoff), Crane Creek CC, Palm City, Fla., $28,000/$3,000.

March 6-7 — Pat Schwab, 142, PGA National GC (Haig), Palm Beach Gardens, Fla., $28,000/$3,000.

■ HISTORY THROUGH THE YEARS

1978-79

Nov. 16-17 — John Gentile, 145 (won playoff), Palm Beach Polo & CC, West Palm Beach, Fla., $27,500/$3,800.

Nov. 20-21 — Tony Kaloustian, 141, Indian Trail CC, Royal Palm Beach, Fla., $27,500/$3,800.

Nov. 27-28 — Jay Horton, 143, Boca West GC, Boca Raton, Fla., $30,000/$4,000.

Nov. 30-Dec. 1 — Michael Preston, 142 (won playoff), Boca West GC, Boca Raton, Fla., $30,000/$4,000.

Dec. 4-5 — John Calabria, 138, Boca West GC, Boca Raton, Fla., $30,000/$4,000.

Dec. 7-8 — David Philo, 140 (won playoff), Boca West GC, Boca Raton, Fla., $30,000/$4,000.

Dec. 11-12 — Larry Startzel, 143, Indian Trail CC, Royal Palm Beach, Fla., $30,000/$4,000.

Dec. 14-15 — Kirk Hanefeld, 137, Eastpointe CC, Palm Beach Gardens, Fla., $29,750/$4,000.

Feb. 8-9 — Jack Seltzer, 143, Grenelefe GC, Haines City, Fla., $30,000/$4,000.

Feb. 12-13 — Ron Baker, 144, Bardmoor CC, Largo, Fla., $30,000/$4,000.

Feb. 15-16 — Victor Tortoricci, 136, Walden Lake CC, Plant City, Fla., $30,000/$4,000.

Feb. 19-20 — Mal Galletta Jr., 137, ImperiaLakes CC, Lakeland, Fla., $30,000/$4,000.

Feb. 26-27 — Jim Picard, 141 (won playoff), Indian Trail CC, Royal Palm Beach, Fla., $30,000/$4,000.

March 1-2 — Victor Tortoricci, 145 (won playoff), Palm Beach Polo & CC, West Palm Beach, Fla., $30,000/$4,000.

March 5-6 — Gene George, 141 (won playoff), Indian Trail CC, Royal Palm Beach, Fla., $30,000/$4,000.

March 8-9 — Rolf Deming, 140, Crane Creek CC, Palm City, Fla., $30,000/$4,000.

1977-78

Nov. 17-18 — Jim King, 138, Boca West GC, Boca Raton, Fla., $20,000/$3,000.

Nov. 21-22 — Jack McKelvey, 143, Boca West GC, Boca Raton, Fla., $20,000/$3,000.

Nov. 28-29 — Bill Davis, 140, Boca West GC, Boca Raton, Fla., $20,000/$3,000.

Dec. 1-2 — Lloyd Monroe, 141, Boca West GC, Boca Raton, Fla., $20,000/$3,000.

Dec. 5 — Jim Albus, 71 (18 holes, rain), Mayacoo Lakes GC, West Palm Beach, Fla., $25,500/$3,500.

Dec. 8-9 — Roland Stafford, 140, Indian Spring CC, East Boynton Beach, Fla., $25,500/$3,500.

Dec. 12-13 — Lloyd Monroe, 143, Eastpointe CC, Palm Beach Gardens, Fla., $25,500/$3,500.

Dec. 15-16 — Don Padgett II, 140, Eastpointe CC, Palm Beach Gardens, Fla., $25,500/$3,500.

Jan. 5-6 — Ted Meier, 142, Coronado CC, San Diego, Calif., $17,500/$2,200.

Jan. 9-10 — Mike Watney, 139, Singing Hills CC, San Diego, Calif., $17,500/$2,200.

Jan 12-13 — John Adams, 136, Singing Hills CC, San Diego, Calif., $17,500/$2,200.

Jan. 17-18 — John Dahl, 137 (won playoff), Warner Springs Resort, San Diego, Calif., $11,250/$1,700.

Jan. 21-22 — John Adams, 134, Warner Springs Resort, San Diego, Calif., $11,250/$1,700.

Jan. 23-24 — Larry Mancour, 144 (won playoff), Singing Hills CC, San Diego, Calif., $11,250/$1,700.

Jan. 27-28 — Mike Davis, 135, Desert Hills GC, Yuma, Ariz., $11,500/$1,700.

Feb. 6-7 — Jeff Jerrel, 112 (27 holes, rain), Kingwood CC, Houston, Texas, $12,500/$2,000.

Feb. 9-10 — Don Padgett II, 140, River Plantation CC, Conroe, Texas, $12,500/$2,000.

Feb. 13-14 — Don Padget II, 139, Bear Creek GC, Houston, Texas, $12,250/$2,000.

Feb. 15-16 — Winslow Woodard, 144, Bear Creek GC, Houston, Texas, $12,000/$2,000.

Feb. 20-21 — Jeff Jerrel, 143 (won playoff), Chapparel CC, Seguin, Texas, $10,000/$1,600.

Feb. 23-24 — Peter Chapin, 146, Pecan Valley CC, San Antonio, Texas, $10,000/$1,600.

Feb. 27-28 — Ken Ellsworth, 146, Pecan Valley CC, San Antonio, Texas, $10,000/$1,600.

March 2-3 — Joe Jimenez, 140, Chapparel CC, Seguin, Texas, $10,000/$1,600.

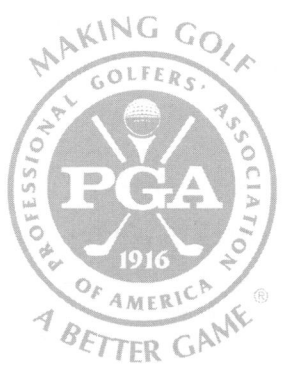

PGA JUNIOR CHAMPIONSHIP

1994 FACTS AND FORMAT

DATES: Aug. 23-26, 1994

SITE: PGA National Golf Club, Champion Course
Palm Beach Gardens, Fla.

DEFENDING CHAMPIONS

Boys' Division — Pat Perez, San Diego, Calif.
Girls' Division — Erika Hayashida, Lima, Peru
(both players ineligible in 1994)

METHOD OF PLAY

Stroke play, 18 holes daily. In the event of a tie after 72 holes, there will be a sudden-death playoff.

RULES AND REGULATIONS

The Rules of Golf which govern play are determined by the United States Golf Association and applied by the PGA of America Board of Directors. The Championship is subject to the overall supervision of the Board and the PGA Rules Committee.

ELIGIBILITY

Boys and girls, maximum age 17, may attempt to qualify through their local PGA sections. Field for the finals is comprised of one boy and one girl champion from each of the 41 sections, winners of selected national junior tournaments earlier in the year and past PGA Junior Championship winners who have not reached their 18th birthdays.

■ A HISTORY OF SHOWCASING TOMORROW'S STARS

The Maxfli PGA Junior Championship — which made its first visit to legendary Pinehurst, N.C., in 1993, is considered one of golf's major championships for juniors. A proven career stepping stone for many competitors, the Championship began in 1976 at the Walt Disney World Golf Resort in Orlando, Fla. The Championship has been a summer stop on the national junior circuit for many of today's PGA and LPGA touring professionals.

The Championship moved to Callaway Gardens in Mountain View, Ga., in 1978, and two years later was hosted by PGA National Golf Club in Palm Beach Gardens, Fla. The Championship has been played at PGA National every year since with the exception of 1988 and 1993, when it was held at Bellerive Country Club in St. Louis, Mo., and Pinehurst, N.C.

The Maxfli Golf Division began title sponsorship of the PGA Junior Championship in 1991. In 1990, 2,966 boys and girls entered PGA sectional qualifying tournaments throughout the PGA's 41 sections. The 1992 Championship entry list increased 29 percent to 8,443, and a record 9,454 competed in 1993.

Past Championship competitors who have gone on to successful professional careers include: Billy Andrade, Kathy Baker, Brandie Burton, Rick Fehr, Jim Gallagher Jr., John Inman, Tracy Gerdyk, Michelle McGann, Billy Mayfair, Scott Verplank and Willie Wood.

In 1990, Vicki Goetze of Hull, Ga., became the first participant to win three PGA Junior Championships (1987-89-90). Goetze's 72-hole record 278 allowed her to snap the championship record she shared with the late Heather Farr, who won in 1980 and 1982.

■ HISTORY THROUGH THE YEARS

Year	Winner	Score	Runner-up	Winner	Score	Runner-up	Site
1976 (Boys) Larry Field		297	Ricky Smallridge	(Girls) Nancy Rubin	320	Michelle Jordan	Walt Disney World (Magnolia), Fla.
1977 (Boys 15-17) Randy Watkins		291	Rick Stallings	(Girls 15-17) Debbie Hall	294	Lauri Merten	Walt Disney World (Boys, Palm;
(Boys 12-14) John Inman		298	Robert Burns	(Girls 12-14) Lise A. Russell	329	Denise King	Girls, Magnolia), Fla.
1978 (Boys) Willie Wood *		289	Bob Wolcott	(Girls) Kathy Baker	304	Sharon Barrett	Callaway Gardens (Mountain View), Ga.
1979 (Boys) Rick Fehr		286	Tracy Philips	(Girls) Penny Hammel	306	Jenny Lidback	Callaway Gardens (Mountain View), Ga.
1980 (Boys) Tracy Phillips		293	John Inman	(Girls) Heather Farr	297	Jenny Lidback	PGA National (Haig), Fla.
1981 (Boys) Billy Andrade		286	Scott Erikson	(Girls) Cathy Johnston	296	Heather Farr	PGA National (Haig), Fla.
1982 (Boys) Billy Mayfair		292	Tim Fleming	(Girls) Heather Farr	287	Dottie Pepper	PGA National (Champion), Fla.
1983 (Boys) Michael Bradley		286	Edward Pfister	(Girls) Tracy Kerdyk	296	Cheryl Morley	PGA National (Champion), Fla.
1984 (Boys) David Toms		289	Michael Finne	(Girls) Clare Dolan	307	Cheryl Morley	PGA National (Champion), Fla.
1985 (Boys) Steve Termeer		292	John Alber	(Girls) Jean Zedlitz	300	Dana Lofland	PGA National (Haig), Fla.
1986 (Boys) Brian Montgomery		293	Damien Jamila	(Girls) Adele Moore	300	Tracy Nakamura	PGA National (Champion), Fla.
1987 (Boys) Jeff Manson		294	Thomas Hurley	(Girls) Vicki Goetze	296	Michelle McGann	PGA National (Champion), Fla.
1988 (Boys) Reynold Lee		294	Kevin Hammer	(Girls) Brandie Burton	288	Kimberly Cayce	Bellerive CC, St. Louis, Mo.
1989 (Boys) Bobby Collins		288	Briny Baird Justin Leonard	(Girls) Vicki Goetze	295	Renee Heiken	PGA National (Haig), Fla.
1990 (Boys) Chris Couch		278	Tiger Woods	(Girls) Vicki Goetze	278	Estafania Knuth	PGA National (Champion), Fla.
1991 (Boys) David Dawley*		299	Chip Spiron	(Girls) Julie Brand	305	Jeong Min Park	PGA National (Champion), Fla.
1992 (Boys) D. A. Points		223	Todd Lynch	(Girls) Kellee Booth	214	Eunice Choi	PGA National (Champion), Fla.
1993 (Boys) Pat Perez		271	Robert Floyd	(Girls) Erika Hayashida	279	Betty Chen	Pinehurst (N.C.) Resort & Country Club

(*Won Playoff)

MAXFLI PGA JUNIOR CHAMPIONSHIP

1993

Much of American golf history has been written at Pinehurst, N.C., and Pat Perez of San Diego, Calif., and Erika Hayashida of Lima, Peru, carved a special niche in Maxfli PGA Junior Championship history, winning the respective boys' and girls' division titles on the No. 4 Course at Pinehurst Resort and Country Club. Perez, 17, posted a 72-hole record 17-under-par 271. Perez's third championship of the summer included a tournament record-tying 63 in the third round and a 54-hole record 202 total. Perez defeated Robert Floyd of Miami Beach, Fla., by seven strokes. Floyd, son of Senior PGA Tour star Raymond Floyd, matched the tournament second-round record with a competitive-best 65, and finished 10-under-par overall at 278.

Hayashida, 17, became the first foreign-born champion in either division. Her final-round 65 was a fourth-round record and matched the 1990 overall 18-hole standard by Vicki Goetze of Hull, Ga., in 1990. Hayashida finished with a 72-hole total of 279, one stroke off Goetze's 1990 standard, and defeated Betty Chen of La Quinta, Calif., by nine strokes.

Champion: (Boys)	Pat Perez, San Diego, Calif.	
Champion: (Girls)	Erika Hayashida, Lima, Peru	
Site:	Pinehurst (N.C.) Resort and Country Club — No. 4 Course	
Date: Aug. 24-27		**Par:** 72

Boys' Division

1	Pat Perez	San Diego, Calif.	70-69-63-69—271*	-17
2	Robert Floyd	Miami Beach, Fla.	74-65-67-72—278	-10
3	Steve Scott	Coral Springs, Fla.	71-68-73-70—282	-6
T4	Al Hromulak	Johnstown, Pa.	75-71-68-73—287	-1
	Michael Henderson	Raleigh, N.C.	67-72-75-73—287	-1
T6	Jeremy Anderson	Lake Mary, Fla.	70-76-74-69—289	+1
	Brian Wright	Mobile, Ala.	70-73-73-73—289	+1
	Jason Semelsberger	Newhall, Calif.	73-74-68-74—289	+1
T9	Ted Oh	Torrance, Calif.	70-77-70-73—290	+2
	D.A. Points	Pekin, Ill.	78-71-71-70—290	+2
11	Naret Johnson	Gulfport, Miss.	74-76-75-70—295	+7
12	Eric Otness	Granby, Mass.	76-71-78-72—297	+9
13	Joel Kribel	Pleasanton, Calif.	73-72-76-77—298	+10
T14	Matthew Smith	Columbus, Ohio	75-76-74-74—299	+11
	Judd Brewer	Lincoln, Neb.	75-75-74-75—299	+11
	Ryan Oldroyd	Richfield, Utah	75-71-78-75—299	+11
	Brian Rupp	Cedar Rapids, Iowa	77-73-72-77—299	+11
T18	Rafael Gemoets	El Paso, Texas	84-74-70-72—300	+12
	Kevin Law	Hixson, Tenn.	77-76-75-72—300	+12
	Derrick Centers	Somerset, Ky.	76-74-76-74—300	+12
T21	Thad Register	Byron, Ga.	81-77-73-71—302	+14
	Aaron Friedman	Ft. Washington, Pa.	75-74-75-78—302	+14
23	Russ Higgins	Rochester, Minn.	74-80-75-74—303	+15
24	Harry Channon	Elgin, Ill.	78-75-74-77—304	+16
T25	Rob Manor	Garland, Texas	77-76-74-78—305	+17
	Shawn Koch	Howell, Mich.	78-75-75-77—305	+17
27	Rob Bradley	Hanover, Mass.	78-76-75-78—307	+19
T28	Jeff Lawrence	Henryetta, Okla.	77-73-76-82—308	+20
	Blue Kaaua	Hilo, Hawaii	77-79-73-79—308	+20
30	Eri Crum	Aspen, Colo.	79-75-81-75—310	+22
T31	David Rizzo	Dunn, N.C.	78-78-75-81—312	+24
	Kenneth Campas	Tucson, Ariz.	74-79-84-75—312	+24
33	Tyson Webber	Syracuse, N.Y.	80-79-78-78—315	+27
34	Michael Winterer	Lake St. Louis, Mo.	80-81-79-76—316	+28
T35	Chris Trevino	Corpus Christi, Texas	78-75-80-85—318	+30
	David Gratzer	Bedford, Ind.	80-86-70-82—318	+30
	Gary Occhino	Hamburg, N.Y.	84-85-76-73—318	+30
T38	LeRoy Bates	Inglewood, Calif.	79-79-79-82—319	+31
	Cameron Gunville	Billings, Mont.	84-78-77-80—319	+31
40	Marc Turnesa	Rockville Centre, N.Y.	80-81-78-83—322	+34
T41	Chris Harpster	Ashland, Ohio	78-79-82-85—324	+36
	Daryl Lynch	Simsbury, Conn.	83-84-79-78—324	+36
43	Dennis Blake	Bernardsville, N.J.	80-76-88-82—326	+38
44	Barry Walters	Yakima, Wash.	83-83-84-77—327	+39
45	Wade McPheeters	Kansas City, Mo.	90-80-80-80—330	+42
46	Randall Hunt	Paramount, Calif.	85-84-79-83—331	+43
47	Jon Roddy	Ft. Washington, Md.	79-86-87-82—334	+46
48.	Jon Dzurbala	Franklin, Wis.	80-86-86-84—336	+48

(* 72-hole Championship Record)

Girls' Division

1	Erika Hayashida	Lima, Peru	71-69-74-65—279	-9
2	Betty Chen	La Quinta, Calif.	71-75-72-70—288	E
3	Kellee Booth	Coto de Caza, Calif.	74-71-72-72—289	+1
4	Cristie Kerr	Miami, Fla.	78-69-69-74—290	+2
5	Alicia Allison	Santa Ana, Calif.	73-75-71-73—292	+4
T6	Jody Niemann	Rigby, Idaho	78-73-73-69—293	+5
	Shauna Estes	Orangeburg, S.C.	74-73-73-73—293	+5
T8	Jo Jo Robertson	Roswell, N.M.	75-76-75-68—294	+6
	Molly Cooper	Tumwater, Wash.	74-73-73-74—294	+6
10	Jenny Lee	Honolulu, Hawaii	76-76-70-75—297	+9
11	Ann Pohira	Winter Park, Fla.	72-73-78-75—298	+10
12	Robin Cook	Pace, Fla.	75-74-77-74—300	+12
	Rachel Thompson	Ripley, Tenn.	77-69-76-78—300	+12
14	Jaejean Ro	San Jose, Calif.	77-75-73-77—302	+14
15	J.J. McCormick	Littleton, Colo.	78-78-71-77—304	+16
16	Bessie Phillips	West Palm Beach, Fla.	76-78-76-75—305	+17
17	Lee Shirley	Salem, Va.	76-79-75-78—308	+20
T18	Jill Gomric	Belleville, Ill.	82-77-76-75—310	+22
	Rachelle Tacha	Manhattan, Kan.	80-76-76-78—310	+22
T20	Jessica Lundblad	Concord, Ohio	85-75-74-78—312	+24
	Julie Lee	Cerritos, Calif.	77-79-78-78—312	+24
22	Michelle Louviere	Lafayette, La.	83-80-71-79—313	+25
23	Stephanie Enochs	W. Worthington, Ohio	80-81-79-77—317	+29
24	Filippa Hansson	Phoenix, Ariz.	78-85-78-77—318	+30
25	Stacy Prammanasudh	Enid, Okla.	78-82-86-83—319	+31
26	Laura Tzakis	Madison, Wis.	80-81-82-78—321	+33
27	Angie Blythe	Evansville, Ind.	86-79-79-79—323	+35
28	Pamela Levine	Lilburn, Ga.	81-77-83-83—324	+36
29	M.C. Mullen	Peosta, Iowa	78-83-84-80—325	+37
T30	Rita Arora	New Providence, N.J	77-83-81-86—327	+39
	Nicolle Flood	Gloversville, N.Y.	80-85-80-82—327	+39
	Elizabeth Summerhays	Farmington, Utah	86-78-82-81—327	+39
33	Tara Adams	Latrobe, Pa.	79-86-80-84—329	+41
34	Maria Larsen	Harlan, Iowa	84-79-83-86—332	+44
35	Heather Kraus	Louisville, Ky.	88-82-83-80—333	+44
36	Lynn Valentine	East Lyme, Conn.	87-84-84-81—336	+48
T37	Jamie Drue McInturff	Dumas, Texas	84-80-82-91—337	+49
	Melanie Lepp	Easton, Minn.	86-82-80-89—337	+49
39	Dara Broadus	Atlanta, Ga.	84-86-80-88—338	+50
T40	Felicia Hairrington	Los Angeles, Calif	.84-85-83-87—339	+51
	Sara Doell	Rochester, N.Y.	86-86-86-81—339	+51
42	Jennifer Tucker	Central Square, N.Y.	81-85-85-91—342	+54
43	Alexis Boyle	Lexington, Mass.	89-86-86-83—344	+56
44	Kristee Wright	Belding, Mich.	84-82-93-86—345	+57
45	Tracy Barron	Waukegan, Ill.	84-85-84-94—347	+59
46	Meghan Bolger	Voorhees, N.J.	85-93-88-92—358	+70
T47	Elizabeth Diesa	Fort Salonga, N.Y.	90-86-91-97—364	+76
	Whitney Morgan	Austin, Texas	92-85-95-92—364	+76

MAXFLI PGA JUNIOR CHAMPIONSHIP

1992

The specter of Hurricane Andrew — one of the worst natural disasters in U.S. history, which devastated large parts of Dade County, 90 miles south of Palm Beach Gardens — threatened to cancel the Maxfli PGA Junior Championship, Aug. 24, 1992. But Palm Beach County escaped most of Andrew's wrath, and tournament competitors housed at PGA National Golf Club were able to participate in a Championship that was shortened to 54 holes for the first time in its 17-year history.

Kellee Booth of Coto de Caza, Calif., a third-place finisher in 1991, continued her hot streak across the country's junior circuit. The 16-year-old finished her final two rounds 3-under-par, and was at 2-under-par for a 214 total, seven strokes better than Eunice Choi of San Clemente, Calif. Booth, ranked the No. 1 girls' amateur player in the country by *GolfWeek*, matched the American Junior Golf Association record of Tiger Woods of Cypress, Calif., by winning seven tournaments in a calendar year. Woods was runner-up in the 1991 Maxfli PGA Junior Championship.

The boys' division title went to 15-year-old D.A. Points of Pekin, Ill., who finished with a final-round 5-over-par 77 and 223 total. He withstood a late charge by Todd Lynch of Winston-Salem, N.C., and Justin Roof of Conway, S.C., who nearly forced a playoff when his greenside bunker shot on the 18th green missed the cup by an inch. Points two-putted from 12 feet for the victory. It was the first time since 1989 that both winners were under the tournament's maximum entry age of 17.

Champion: (Boys) D.A. Points, Pekin, Ill.		
Champion: (Girls) Kellee Booth, Coto de Caza, Calif.		
Site: PGA National Golf Club (Champion), Palm Beach Gardens, Fla.		
Date: Aug. 25-28		**Par:** 72

Boys' Division

1	D.A. Points	Pekin, Ill.	75-71-77—223
T-2	Todd Lynch	Winston-Salem, N.C.	76-73-75—224
T-2	Justin Roof	Conway, S.C.	73-73-78—224
T-4	Matt Bettencourt	Modesto, Calif.	78-72-75—225
T-4	Kenneth Campas	Tucson, Ariz.	73-75-77—226
T-6	Matt Roney	Blue Springs, Mo.	79-77-70—226
T-6	Rob Manor	Garland, Texas	75-74-77—226
8	Kalani Kiaaina	Waipahu, Hawaii	77-76-74—227
T-9	Steve Sawka	East Windsor, Conn.	76-78-74—228
T-9	Greg Robertson	Roswell, N.M.	72-81-75—228
T-9	Matt Thurmond	Burlington, Wash.	80-74-74—228
12	Darren Angel	Northridge, Calif.	77-79-74—230
T-13	Steve Scott	Coral Springs, Fla.	78-78-75—231
T-13	Brett Schauer	Wausau, Wis.	76-77-78—231
T-13	Gilberto Morales	Caracas, Venezuela	78-71-82—231
16	Randy Leen	Dayton, Ohio	77-72-83—232
T-17	Michael Berzovich	Longwood, Fla.	85-73-77—235
T-17	Joe Patton	Tuscaloosa, Ala.	75-81-79—235
T-17	Brad Kittsley	Pleasantville, N.Y.	78-76-81—235
T-20	Jeff Lawrence	Henryetta, Okla.	81-82-73—236
T-20	Steve Voinovich	Gates Mills, Ohio	85-76-75—236
22	Will White	Jackson, Miss.	75-82-80—237
T-23	Matthew Lewis	Dubuque, Iowa	78-85-75—238
T-23	Matthew Adams	Walpole, Mass.	86-76-76—238
T-23	Andy Walker	Phoenix, Ariz.	77-83-78—238
T-26	David Dawley	Chandler, Okla.	75-83-81—239
T-26	Allen Breaux	Eagle, Idaho	79-80-80—239
T-26	Trip Powell	Memphis, Tenn.	80-77-82—239
T-29	Maine Brock	Albany, Ga.	88-75-77—240
T-29	Jeff Zouski	Blaine, Minn.	75-81-84—240
T-29	Laird Sparks	Nacagdoches, Texas	78-78-84—240
T-32	Aaron Wright	Anna, Ill.	80-83-78—241
T-32	Tim Michaels	Orchard Park, N.Y.	78-84-79—241
T-32	Chad Witherby	Richmond, Ind.	79-78-84—241
35	Albert Hromulak	Johnston, Pa.	79-82-81—242
36	Keith Ohr	Irvine, Ky.	81-83-79—243
37	Troy Lashley	Salt Lake City, Utah	80-79-87—246
T-38	Mike Doan	Zeeland, Mich.	83-82-83—248
T-38	Gary Carpenter	Crofton, Md.	81-79-88—248
40	Eri Crum	Aspen, Colo.	88-87-75—250
41	Todd Uher	Omaha, Neb.	88-84-81—253
42	Geoff Mann	Fayetteville, N.Y.	85-82-89—256
43	James Nam	North Wales, Pa.	94-83-82—259
44	Jim Salinetti	Lee, Mass.	92-83-87—262
45	Chris Fehl	Belle Mead, N.J.	94-91-89—274
46	Keion Witherspoon	Los Angeles, Calif.	96-86-93—275

Girls' Division

1	Kellee Booth	Coto de Caza, Calif.	73-70-71—214
2	Eunice Choi	San Clemente, Calif.	74-73-74—221
3	Jammie Koizumi	Kailua-Kona, Hawaii	76-72-75—223
T-4	Jeong Min Park	Alameda, Calif.	73-78-76—227
T-4	Alicia Allison	Santa Ana, Calif.	78-75-74—228
6	Wendi Patterson	Atlanta, Ga.	75-79-74—230
T-7	Ashli Price	Morristown, Tenn.	83-76-71—230
T-7	Mei Lin Poai	Kapaa, Hawaii	79-75-76—230
T-7	Holly Carriker	San Antonio, Texas	78-75-77—230
T-7	Kacie Myers	Venice, Fla.	74-79-77—230
11	Jo Jo Robertson	Roswell, N.M.	76-78-78—232
T-12	Joellyn Erdmann	Little Chute, Wis.	80-75-78—233
T-12	Jennifer Tollette	Coon Rapids, Minn.	77-76-80—233
T-14	Lisa Penske	Bethlehem, Pa.	74-80-80—234
T-14	Kim Hubt	Alexis, Ill.	76-77-81—234
16	Meg Benn	Tulsa, Okla.	78-80-77—235
17	Robin Cook	Pace, Fla.	76-81-81—238
18	Laura Caroline Philo	Scotia, N.Y.	77-79-83—239
19	Jody Niemann	Rigby, Idaho	81-75-84—240
T-20	Keridwen Cornelius	Scottsdale, Ariz.	90-72-80—242
T-20	Jenny Chuasiriporn	Timonium, Md.	76-81-85—242
22	Amy Loviscek	Flint, Mich.	82-80-82—244
T-23	Angela Blythe	Evansville, Ind.	81-88-76—245
T-23	Dodie Mazzuca	Santa Cruz, Calif.	78-85-82—245
25	Holly Turton	Ithaca, N.Y.	81-84-82—247
T-26	Kelly Kingston	Garland, Texas	89-82-77—248
T-26	Jennifer Kern	Durango, Colo.	86-80-82—248
T-26	Bessie Phillips	West Palm Beach, Fla.	82-80-86—248
29	Maria Larsen	Harlan, Iowa	84-76-89—249
30	Denise Woodward	Alameda, Calif.	83-88-79—250
T-31	Mandy Arthurs	Baton Rouge, La.	87-85-79—251
T-31	Robyn Seafine	Trenton, N.J.	86-85-80—251
T-33	Amy Widdows	Sunnyside, Wash.	83-88-82—253
T-33	Jill Gomric	Balleville, Ill.	83-87-83—253
T-35	Marcy Newton	High Point, N.C.	83-88-83—254
T-35	Eve Marie Lux	Highland, N.Y.	83-84-87—254
T-35	Ramie Takahashi	Deerfield, Ill.	78-85-91—254
T-38	Dara Broadus	Atlanta, Ga.	89-80-86—255
T-38	Heather Kraus	Louisville, Ky.	86-79-90—255
40	Rachelle Tacha	Manhattan, Kan.	84-87-87—258
41	Jessica Lundblad	Concord, Ohio	90-85-87—262
T-42	Lacey Canavesi	Beaver Falls, Pa.	91-91-87—269
T-42	Jennifer Cieslak	Windham, Conn.	84-87-98—269
44	Jennifer Webster	Lynn, Mass.	91-94-85—270
45	Marty Anne Hall	Columbus, Ohio	95-87-89—271
46	Sara Doell	Rochester, N.Y.	92-95-90—277
47	Amiee Aardema	Ogden, Utah	92-94-97—283

MAXFLI PGA JUNIOR CHAMPIONSHIP

1991 Maxfli's initial year of sponsoring the PGA Junior Championship marked the departure of three-time participant Julie Brand of Alder Creek, N.Y., who weathered a final-round 6-over-par 78 to win the girls' division by three strokes over Jeong Min Park of Alameda, Calif. Kellee Booth of Coto de Caza, Calif., and Vicky Strada of Cosmopolis, Wash., tied for third. PGA Junior Championship rookie David Dawley of Chandler, Okla., defeated Chip Spiron of Goldsboro, N.C., in a two-hole sudden-death playoff for the boys' division title. Spiron missed a chance to win in regulation when his birdie attempt spun out of the cup on the 18th hole. Both players parred the first playoff hole, and Dawley picked up the title after making a par putt on the second hole.

Champion: (Boys)	David Dawley, Chandler, Okla.	
Champion: (Girls)	Julie Brand, Alder Creek, N.Y.	
Site:	PGA National Golf Club (Champion),	
	Palm Beach Gardens, Fla.	
Date: Aug. 20-23		**Par:** 72

Boys' Division

1	David Dawley*	Chandler, Okla.	74-73-75-77—299
2	Chip Spiron	Goldsboro, N.C.	71-75-83-70—299
3	Joshua Cupp	Rome, N.Y.	74-75-77-76—302
4	Scott Johnson	Kennewick, Wash.	71-77-80-75—303
5	Jim Duke	Potomac, Md.	80-78-72-74—304
6	Mark Wilson	Menomonee Falls, Wis.	76-77-77-75—305
T-7	Doug LaBelle II	Mt. Pleasant, Mich.	73-79-75-78—306
T-7	Jason Jones	Ft. Walton Beach, Fla.	79-74-75-78—306
9	Cregg Watner	Westfield, N.J.	81-77-75-74—307
10	Paul Hinkle	Costa Mesa, Calif.	76-78-81-73—308
T-11	Brad Kittsley	Pleasantville, N.Y.	78-78-75-78—309
T-11	Christopher Riding	West Jordan, Utah	75-78-73-83—309
13	Roger Pineda	Atherton, Calif.	78-74-77-81—310
T-14	Jason Bryant	Conroe, Texas	84-75-75-77—311
T-14	Jeff Powers	Tampa, Fla.	74-81-76-80—311
T-16	Mark Worthington	Redmond, Wash.	80-79-79-75—313
T-16	Jon Menor	Hilo, Hawaii	79-76-86-72—313
18	Chris Inman	Lake St. Louis, Mo.	83-79-77-75—314
T-19	Bo Miller	Baton Rouge, La.	85-79-75-76—315
T-19	Bob Kidd	Wyoming, Del.	85-76-76-78—315
21	Mark LaLonde	Lexington, Ky.	83-83-75-75—316
22	Eric Hiatt	Martinsville, Ind.	81-80-83-74—318
23	Brent Wolf	Ft. Worth, Texas	89-75-74-82—320
24	John Sawka	East Windsor, Conn.	82-85-79-75—321
25	Jason Walters	Memphis, Tenn.	81-80-82-78—321
T-26	Chad Harris	West Palm Beach, Fla.	82-83-78-79—322
T-26	Ralph Gemoets	El Paso, Texas	80-81-82-79—322
T-26	Will Garner	Augusta, Ga.	79-81-84-78—322
T-29	Vance Holtzman	Altamont, Kans.	88-81-84-70—323
T-29	Eric McInerney	Dedham, Mass.	82-81-80-80—323
T-29	Erron Nielsen	Rockford, Ill.	85-78-79-81—323
32	Shawn Strohman	Cheyenne, Wyo.	77-86-84-78—325
33	Aaron Gold	Scotia, N.Y.	81-83-83-79—326
34	Mark Odendahl	Monmouth, Ill.	81-80-83-83—327
35	Brian Pierce	Toledo, Ohio	87-79-78-84—328
36	Kevin Houlihan	Omaha, Neb.	79-84-82-84—329
37	J.J. Jordan	Phoenix, Ariz.	83-85-83-81—332
T-38	Mike Sauer	Walker, Minn.	84-83-84-82—333
T-38	Jake Lewis	Indiana, Pa.	85-80-81-87—333
40	Dan Aufderheide	Dublin, Ohio	89-86-79-84—338
41	Allen Breaux	Eagle, Idaho	81-84-93-86—344
42	Gary Occhino	Hamburg, N.Y.	86-88-86-90—350
*	Won Playoff		

Girls' Division

1	Julie Brand	Alder Creek, N.Y.	80-71-76-78—305
2	Jeong Min Park	Alameda, Calif.	78-77-76-77—308
T-3	Vicky Strada	Cosmopolis, Wash.	80-81-71-78—310
T-3	Kellee Booth	Coto De Caza, Calif.	75-74-78-83—310
T-5	Lisa Penske	Bethlehem, Pa.	78-81-76-76—311
T-5	Becky Biehl	Keokuk, Iowa	75-77-83-76—311
T-5	Ashli Price	Morristown, Tenn.	77-75-79-80—311
T-8	Joellyn Erdmann	Little Chute, Wis.	72-84-77-79—312
T-8	Jo Jo Robertson	Roswell, N. M.	74-79-77-82—312
T-10	Ann Pohira	Winter Park, Fla.	79-79-79-76—313
T-10	Christie Kerr	Miami, Fla.	74-78-80-81—313
12	Kelley Richardson	Macon, Ga.	80-79-78-78—315
13	Skyli Yamada	Sandy, Utah	80-73-80-82—315
14	Nakia Davis	New Orleans, La.	81-76-75-85—317
15	Leanne Wong	Los Angeles, Calif.	78-78-78-84—318
16	Victoria Boysen	Ft. Worth, Texas	84-80-75-81—320
17	Jody Niemann	Ribgy, Idaho	83-75-83-81—322
18	Jeanne Ann Krizman	South Bend, Ind.	86-79-78-82—325
19	Shelly Santos	Houston, Texas	84-84-77-81—326
20	Jenny Chuasiriporn	Timonium, Md.	81-82-83-81—327
21	Kelly McCall	Mahopac, N.Y.	83-83-80-82—328
22	Jennifer Hermsen	Lewisville, N.C.	81-79-84-85—329
23	Jan Kotoshirodo	Pearl City, Hawaii	78-92-76-88—334
24	Dana Anto	West Newton, Pa.	86-85-80-89—340
25	Carmen Westmoreland	Prescott, Ark.	86-78-85-91—340
T-26	Jennie Stine	Scottsdale, Ariz.	86-85-84-86—341
T-26	Holly Turton	Ithaca, N.Y.	87-84-86-84—341
28	Tracy Veto	Lakewood, Colo.	83-83-82-94—342
T-29	Kris Lindstrom	Richfield, Minn.	83-85-85-91—344
T-29	Erin White	Erie, Pa.	90-85-78-91—344
31	Amy Loviscek	Flint, Mich.	93-83-89-86—351
32	Susan Brenner	Youngstown, Ohio	86-85-87-97—355
33	Amanda Richards	Weston, Mass.	89-95-88-87—359
34	Maureen Regan	Omaha, Neb.	92-92-89-90—363
35	Laura Philo	Scotia, N.Y.	88-89-99-88—364
36	Deborah Danser	Westfield, N.J.	91-85-96-93—365
37	Monica Fontana	Pensacola, Fla.	96-85-96-89—366
38	Rachelle Tacha	Manhattan, Kan.	96-83-92-99—370
39	Heather Kraus	Louisville, Ky.	96-91-101-86—374
40	Ashley Webb	St. Charles, Ill.	94-93-91-97—375
41	Jennifer Cieslak	Windham, Conn.	95-94-92-101—383
42	April Drake	Waynesville, Ohio	105-99-89-103—396
43	Julie Morgan	Salem, Ill.	102-106-109-96—413

UNITED VAN LINES PGA JUNIOR CHAMPIONSHIP

1990 Chris Couch of North Lauderdale, Fla., and Vicki Goetze of Hull, Ga., revamped the PGA Junior Championship record book, establishing tournament standards by posting identical 10-under-par 278s in the final year the PGA Junior Championship was hosted by United Van Lines. Goetze became the first participant to win three PGA Junior Championship titles, and closed her appearance record in the event having finished fifth or better six consecutive years. She turned in a personal-best 7-under-par 65 in the second round, and Couch blistered PGA National Golf Club's Champion Course during the final round with a tournament and course-record 9-under-par 63 for a 278 total. Tiger Woods of Cypress, Calif., was runner-up at 288.

Champion: (Boys)	Chris Couch, N. Lauderdale, Fla.	
Champion: (Girls)	Vicki Goetze, Hull, Ga.	
Site:	PGA National Golf Club (Champion),	
	Palm Beach Gardens, Fla.	
Date: Aug. 21-24		**Par:** 72

Boys' Division

1	Chris Couch	N. Lauderdale, Fla.	68-77-79-63—278
2	Tiger Woods	Cypress, Calif.	73-74-69-72—288
3	Joe Acosta	Visalia, Calif.	72-76-73-73—294
4	Carson Mooney	Boise, Idaho	76-79-73-70—298
T-5	Stewart Cink	Florence, Ala.	75-75-75-74—299
T-5	Daniel Stone	St. Petersburg, Fla.	74-75-76-74—299
T-7	Brian Johnson	Shreveport, La.	73-77-71-80—301
T-7	Greg Komansky	Wildwood Crest, N.J.	79-75-72-76—301
T-9	Joey Snyder	Scottsdale, Ariz.	73-75-75-79—302
T-9	Jamie Neher	Weston, Maine	77-75-68-82—302
T-11	Bobby Collins	Atlantis, Fla.	74-78-75-76—303
T-11	Patrick Vadden	Louisville, Ky.	77-76-74-76—303
13	Jon Wallace	Wildwood, Fla.	78-74-74-78—304
14	Ryan Bogan	Palm Desert, Calif.	76-76-75-78—305
15	Jerry Jeong	Schenectady, N.Y.	74-82-77-75—308
T-16	Matt Bettencourt	Modesto, Calif.	76-79-78-77—310
T-16	Craig Uyehara	Honolulu, Hawaii	78-78-78-76—310
T-18	Greg Bisconti	Mt. Vernon, N.Y.	76-78-75-82—311
T-18	Notah Ryan Begay	Albuquerque, N.M.	70-78-75-88—311
T-20	Dave Cotton	Greenfield, Ind.	84-76-75-77—312
T-20	Jason Downey	Pembroke Pines, Fla.	86-76-75-75—312
T-22	Jim Saporilo	Pittsburg, Kan.	80-76-82-75—313
T-22	Tom Pidduck	Bremerton, Wash.	82-81-76-74—313
24	David Jackson	N. Myrtle Beach, S.C.	76-82-78-78—314
25	Maury Beasley	Dublin, Ga.	79-78-82-76—315
26	Scott Clark	Salt Lake City, Utah	76-80-76-84—316
27	Steven Jamroz	Somers, Conn.	77-86-79-76—318
T-28	Scott Carlson	Grafton, Wis.	78-84-82-76—320
T-28	Derek Robison	Jackson, Miss.	77-80-83-80—320
30	Greg Gregory	Everman, Texas	81-80-85-75—321
31	Jay Holmes	St. Louis, Mo.	80-78-83-82—323
32	Michael Swiger	Weirton, W. Va.	81-76-82-87—326
33	Scott Johnson	Urbandale, Iowa	80-86-83-78—327
34	Rustin Adams	New Braunfels, Texas	81-86-81-81—329
35	Tom McGinnis	Fayetteville, N.Y.	84-80-83-84—331
36	Bryce Tani	Broomfield, Colo.	83-79-84-86—332
37	Tom Jennings	Pekin, Ill.	79-85-86-83—333
38	Rusty Cardwell	Westerville, Ohio	89-78-81-86—334
39	Patrick Bauer	Plymouth, Minn.	84-85-84-83—336
40	Jason Johnson	Chesapeake, Va.	83-89-86-79—337
41	Chris Paul	Tulsa, Okla.	83-80-82-95—340
42	Jason Piurkoski	Webster, N.Y.	80-85-96-84—345
T-43	Wayne Cancienne	Cullman, Ala.	84-88-90-85—347
T-43	Mark Dahir	Omaha, Neb.	90-88-82-87—347
45	Bobby Sobieski	Port Reading, N.J.	91-90-88-89—358

Girls' Division

1	Vicki Goetze	Hull, Ga.	71-65-67-75—278
2	Estefania Knuth	Barcelona, Spain	73-71-73-70—287
3	Barbara Paul	Clarksburg, N.J.	74-74-74-74—296
4	Stephanie Neill	Charlotte, N.C.	72-75-81-73—301
5	Wendy Ward	San Antonio, Texas	78-74-75-76—303
6	Kerry Zebick	Albuquerque, N.M.	72-80-75-77—304
7	Shani Roth	Pepper Pike, Ohio	79-76-75-76—306
T-8	Robin Buck	Edwardsville, Ill.	79-78-77-77—311
T-8	Kellee Booth	Coto De Caza, Calif.	80-78-77-76—311
T-8	Jill Hamasaki	Aiea, Hawaii	79-75-81-76—311
11	Jennifer Biehn	Scottsdale, Ariz.	79-78-77-81—315
12	Joellyn Erdmann	Little Chute, Wis.	80-76-82-80—318
T-13	Erin O'Neal	Zephyrhills, Fla.	82-82-77-78—319
T-13	Tricia New	Miami, Fla.	77-81-84-77—319
T-15	Kathryn Weber	Derby, Kan.	77-80-82-82—321
T-15	Heather Haas	Ft. Worth, Texas	79-74-81-87—321
17	Erin White	Erie, Pa.	80-86-77-81—324
18	April Packham	Palm Desert, Calif.	87-82-78-78—325
19	Lee Kurmel	Roseville, Calif.	81-86-80-79—326
20	Staci Aber	Greensburg, Pa.	82-77-83-86—328
21	Tracy Veto	Lakewood, Colo.	82-83-80-84—329
T-22	Amy Schmiesing	Spicer, Minn.	92-76-83-82—333
T-22	Tami Fisher	Leawood, Kan.	88-77-84-84—333
T-24	Caroline Spiegelberg	Tacoma, Wash.	76-88-86-84—334
T-24	Nakia Davis	New Orleans, La.	90-81-76-87—334
T-24	Jennifer Haley	McMinnville, Tenn.	78-90-80-86—334
T-24	Jody Niemann	Rigby, Idaho	84-78-81-91—334
28	Christine Garrett	Bloomington, Ill.	84-79-86-87—336
29	Kendra Travers	Greenfield, Ind.	86-80-83-88—337
30	Lori Schlissberg	E. Lansing, Mich.	84-87-84-83—338
T-31	Michele Mahady	New Hartford, N.Y.	90-85-82-83—340
T-31	Elizabeth Horton	Middletown, Ohio	84-84-83-89—340
33	Maureen Regan	Omaha, Neb.	88-88-85-80—341
34	Kirsten Johnstone	Alpharetta, Ga.	85-82-88-88—343
35	Becky Biehl	Keokuk, Iowa	86-87-82-91—346
36	Tanya Jo Cecil	Vine Grove, Ky.	89-89-87-83—348
37	Kim Jennings	Wynnewood, Pa.	87-86-89-87—349
38	Kelly Cap	Youngstown, Ohio	82-88-91-89—350
39	Meg Lindsey	Decator, Ala.	85-89-88-91—353
T-40	Reid Freeman	Salt Lake City, Utah	88-92-90-90—360
T-40	Kelly McCall	Mahopac, N.Y.	87-91-91-91—360
42	Star Bender	Baltimore, Md.	89-90-92-90—361
43	Tara Joy	Duxbury, Maine	87-92-100-104—383
44	Nicole Coffey	Burlington, Conn.	102-92-107-108—409

1989

Vicki Goetze of Hull, Ga., and Bobby Collins of Atlantis, Fla., coasted to easy victories in the 14th PGA Junior Championship, hosted for the second consecutive year by United Van Lines. Goetze, who won her first championship in 1987, tied Heather Farr of Phoenix, Ariz., as the only players to capture two PGA Junior Championship titles. Farr won championships in 1980 and '82. Goetze's final-round 72 gave her a 295 total, six strokes ahead of Renee Heiken of Metamora, Ill. Collins opened with a 71 and played 1-over-par the remainder of the tournament for a five-stroke victory over Briny Baird of Miami Beach, Fla.

Champion: (Boys) Bobby Collins, Atlantis, Fla.	
Champion: (Girls) Vicki Goetze, Hull, Ga.	
Site: PGA National Golf Club (Haig), Palm Beach Gardens, Fla.	
Date: Aug. 22-25	**Par:** 72

Boys' Division

1	Bobby Collins	Atlantis, Fla.	71-73-70-74—288
T-2	Briny Baird	Miami Beach, Fla.	72-72-74-75—293
T-2	Justin Leonard	Dallas, Texas	73-73-73-74—293
4	Chris Edgmon	Edmond, Okla.	79-74-73-71—297
T-5	Ted Purdy	Phoenix, Ariz.	76-73-75-74—298
T-5	Jay Sanders	Baton Rouge, La.	76-69-76-77—298
7	John Wallace	Wildwood, Fla.	75-73-76-76—300
8	Casey Martin	Eugene, Ore.	77-75-71-80—303
T-9	Ron Redden	Irving, Texas	78-75-76-75—304
T-9	Jeff Goodelle	Camillus, N.Y.	78-72-80-74—304
11	Stewart Cink	Florence, Ala.	79-76-75-75—305
T-12	Jamie Fairbanks	Champaign, Ill.	78-76-79-73—306
T-12	Jeremy Forster	Port Angeles, Wash.	78-75-75-78—306
14	Matt Todd	Visalia, Calif.	80-79-79-69—307
15	Trey Jervis	Chapel Hill, N.C.	82-71-78-78—309
T-16	Chris Riley	San Diego, Calif.	77-77-77-79—310
T-16	Scott Mangus	Marietta, Ga.	74-78-80-78—310
T-18	Brad Smith	Middleton, Ohio	75-76-82-82—315
T-18	Mike Fleisher	Oceanside, N.Y.	82-76-78-79—315
T-20	Jason Wight	Brigham, Utah	78-85-78-76—317
T-20	Craig Uyehara	Honolulu, Hawaii	82-76-80-79—317
T-20	Scott Hecht	Mishawaka, Ind.	77-81-77-82—317
T-23	Kevin Hammer	Boynton Beach, Fla.	83-79-83-73—318
T-23	Mike Stamberger	Scotch Plains, N.J.	77-77-83-81—318
T-23	David Donovan	Pittsfield, Mass.	79-80-76-83—318
26	Chris Wolf	Lititz, Pa.	86-77-80-76—319
T-27	Bert Roney	Blue Springs, Mo.	82-81-85-74—322
T-27	Bobby Bilbo	Olney, Md.	82-80-82-78—322
T-27	Murray Van Gundy	Albuquerque, N. M.	78-78-81-85—322
30	Jason Bloom	Waterloo, Iowa	83-78-81-81—323
T-31	David Brownback	W. Bloomfield, Mich.	79-84-82-79—324
T-31	Chad Laxton	Crystal River, Fla.	78-81-81-84—324
33	Jason Walters	Memphis, Tenn.	84-86-79-76—325
34	Ryan Knispel	Fairbury, Neb.	77-90-81-78—326
T-35	Joe Dahlstrom	Burlington, Wis.	80-86-85-78—329
T-35	Erich Moberly	Richmond, Ky.	83-85-85-76—329
T-35	Rodney Thompson	Katy, Texas	85-82-83-79—329
38	Phil Hurrle	Burnsville, Minn.	86-84-80-80—330
39	David Cadwell	Boise, Idaho	85-82-82-82—331
T-40	Todd Sapere	West Hartford, Conn.	85-81-83-83—332
T-40	Daniel Dempsey	Lowell, Mass.	81-86-79-86—332
42	Chris Brooks	Pueblo, Colo.	79-83-88-83—333
43	Craig Melegari	Upper St. Clair, Pa.	87-81-83-86—337
44	Parish Lowrie	Glen Carbon, Ill.	83-85-85-90—343
45	David Mucha	Erie, Pa.	82-87-90-87—346
46	Brian Lefferts	Hudson, Ohio	91-82-81-94—348

Girls' Division

1	Vicki Goetze	Hull, Ga.	77-72-74-72—295
2	Renee Heiken	Metamora, Ill.	75-75-76-75—301
3	Marian Sison	Arlington, Va.	77-73-75-79—304
T-4	Tonya Blosser	Athens, Ohio	77-77-78-76—308
T-4	Kathy Weber	Derby, Kan.	79-74-77-78—308
6	Nicole Horner	Mililani, Hawaii	75-76-79-80—310
7	Tracy Hanson	Rathdrum, Idaho	78-74-79-80—311
8	Camie Hoshino	Hilo, Hawaii	81-75-80-77—313
T-9	Leta Lindley	Carlsbad, Calif.	79-79-81-76—315
T-9	Stephanie Heill	Charlotte, N.C.	84-77-73-81—315
11	Kelly Daniel	Tampa, Fla.	79-77-84-77—317
T-12	Jennifer Turner	Austin, Texas	76-83-83-77—319
T-12	Julie Brand	Adler Creek, N.Y.	79-77-83-80—319
14	Jill Hamasaki	Aiea, Hawaii	85-80-76-80—321
15	Barbara J. Paul	Clarksburg, N.J.	80-79-87-79—325
T-16	Andrea Baxter	Eagle, Idaho	82-82-80-84—328
T-16	Jeong Min Park	Alameda, Calif.	83-77-85-83—328
18	Amy Miller	Anniston, Ala.	87-74-84-84—329
19	Kerry Zebick	Rifle, Colo.	90-78-83-79—330
20	Staci Aber	Greensburg, Pa.	85-84-81-82—332
21	Holly Reynolds	Morrisville, Vt.	84-85-83-83—335
T-22	Jo Jo Robertson	Roswell, N.M.	93-81-83-79—336
T-22	Edith DeKock	Cedar Rapids, Iowa	91-83-78-84—336
24	Michelle Akin	Homer, La.	88-82-83-86—339
25	Stephanie Cooper	Seymour, Ind.	86-86-80-88—340
26	Niki Crist	Salamanca, N.Y.	88-84-84-85—341
27	Michelle Kirchner	Spring, Texas	89-85-90-82—346
T-28	Erica White	Green Bay, Wis.	95-85-84-83—347
T-28	Stacey Geiser	North Oaks, Minn.	82-86-90-89—347
30	Maria Mills	St. Thomas, V.I.	87-88-88-87—350
31	Stephanie Brockbank	Provo, Utah	83-91-90-87—351
T-32	Lisa Wening	St. Louis, Mo.	99-87-89-79—354
T-32	Melissa Williamson	Wickenburg, Ariz.	90-95-84-85—354
33	Nikki Bone	Ashland, Ohio	86-89-89-90—354
T-34	Kirsten Johnstone	Alpharetta, Ga.	90-85-91-93—359
T-34	Kim Jennings	Wynnewood, Pa.	92-88-88-91—359
36	Amy Smethers	Sedalia, Mo.	95-95-80-90—360
37	Lisa Stover	Kalamazoo, Mich.	97-89-92-92—370
38	Mandy Misko	Plano, Texas	98-90-87-96—371
39	Laura Philo	Scotia, N.Y.	101-94-90-94—379
40	Lisa Phipps	Elizabethton, Tenn.	101-92-95-93—381
T-41	Megin O'Donnell	Clinton, Conn.	90-94-99-99—382
T-41	Michelle Uher	Omaha, Neb.	94-92-109-93—382
43	Maureen Corrigan	Huntington Stn., N.Y.	100-106-116-98—420
	Maria Castellucci	Orlando, Fla.	82-88-0—170—WD

UNITED VAN LINES PGA JUNIOR CHAMPIONSHIP

1988 Brandie Burton of Rialto, Calif., posted an even-par 288 to win the girls' division in the PGA Junior Championship, hosted by United Van Lines and held for the first time at Bellerive Country Club in suburban St. Louis, Mo. Burton, 16, finished five strokes ahead of Kimberly Cayce of Potomac, Md. Defending champion Vicki Goetze of Hull, Ga., turned in the day's lowest round (71), but finished third, eight strokes off the pace. Reynold Lee of Pearl City, Hawaii, shot a final-round 75 for a 6-over-par 294 to defeat Kevin Hammer of Boynton Beach, Fla., and Jean-Paul Hebert of Houston, Texas, by one stroke.

Champion: (Boys) Reynold Lee, Pearl City, Hawaii	
Champion: (Girls) Brandie Burton, Rialto, Calif.	
Site: Bellerive Country Club, St. Louis, Mo.	
Date: Aug. 23-26	**Par:** 72

Boys' Division

1	Reynold Lee	Pearl City, Hawaii	70-74-75-75—294
T-2	Kevin Hammer	Boynton Beach, Fla.	73-74-75-73—295
T-2	Jean-Paul Hebert	Houston, Texas	71-69-75-80—295
4	Joon Lee	Fullerton, Calif.	75-76-71-74—296
T-5	Brent Bostick	Duncan, Okla.	72-79-74-72—297
T-5	Chad Dawson	Frankfort, Ky.	73-75-73-76—297
T-7	Chad Laxton	Crystal River, Fla.	78-72-75-74—299
T-7	Micah Rudosky	Peoria, Ariz.	72-72-77-78—299
9	Brian Gay	Daleville, Ala.	74-72-78-76—300
10	Aaron Crewse	Hartville, Ohio	74-77-80-71—302
T-11	Phil Hurrie II	Burnsville, Minn.	78-74-75-76—303
T-11	Notah Begay III	Albuquerque, N.M.	76-76-75-76—303
T-13	Hans Haas	Fort Worth, Texas	75-82-74-73—304
T-13	Aaron Berthiaume	Southbridge, Mass.	78-74-74-78—304
T-15	Bobby Tracy	Miami, Fla.	79-81-74-71—305
T-15	Hunter Albright	Great Falls, Va.	80-74-75-76—305
17	Joseph Summerhays	Heber, Utah	76-71-79-80—306
T-18	Tony Kim	Placentia, Calif.	75-79-77-76—307
T-18	Jay Sanders	Baton Rouge, La.	76-79-73-79—307
20	Colby Norton	Lincoln, Neb.	81-79-71-77—308
T-21	Carl Ste-Marie	Lake City, Fla.	80-80-77-72—309
T-21	Matthew Bunn	Colbert, Wash.	76-80-81-72—309
T-21	Kevin Kemp	Greensboro, N.C.	76-77-77-79—309
T-24	Tim Hux	Plainwell, Mich.	83-82-71-74—310
T-24	Maurice Kilby	Tipp City, Ohio	74-79-81-76—310
26	Derek Fuhs	Amherst, N.H.	75-75-81-80—311
T-27	Scott Crist	Salamanca, N.Y.	75-73-88-76—312
T-27	Eddie Davis	Suisun, Calif.	80-77-76-79—312
29	Sean McCarty	West Branch, Iowa	80-80-76-77—313
T-30	Michael Fleischer	Oceanside, N.Y.	82-78-72-82—314
T-30	Taggart Wylie	Knoxville, Tenn.	72-84-75-83—314
T-32	Boomer Leopold	Belleville, Ill.	75-80-80-80—315
T-32	Drew Cadwell	Boise, Idaho	73-73-83-86—315
T-34	Steven Anderson	Greendale, Wis.	81-80-80-76—317
T-34	Bert Roney	Blue Springs, Mo.	80-81-76-80—317
36	Scott Gileta	Hartsville, S.C.	82-77-79-80—318
T-37	Joseph Dennen	South Bend, Ind.	84-81-80-74—319
T-37	Tom Cannon	Norcross, Ga.	81-79-79-80—319
T-39	Michael Stamberger	Scotch Plains, N.J.	83-81-79-79—322
T-39	Jim Geiger	Endwell, N.Y.	82-74-79-87—322
41	Richard Koob, Jr.	Houston, Texas	81-82-81-80—324
42	Scott Clark	Champaign, Ill.	84-83-84-75—326
43	Leonard Bush, Jr.	Amsterdam, N.Y.	73-86-83-86—328
T-44	David Lopez	Westminster, Colo.	83-80-85-83—331
T-44	Marcus Neffield	Greensburg, Pa.	80-84-83-84—331
46	Trey Owen	Phoenixville, Pa.	75-80-94-83—332

Girls' Division

1	Brandie Burton	Rialto, Calif.	70-71-74-73—288
2	Kimberly Cayce	Potomac, Md.	72-73-75-73—293
3	Vicki Goetze	Hull, Ga.	75-74-76-71—296
T-4	Tonya Blosser	Athens, Ohio	78-74-76-71—309
T-4	Renee Helken	Metamore, Ill.	76-78-76-79—309
T-6	Donna Lippstreu	Livermore, Calif.	83-73-77-78—311
T-6	Tina Trimble	Houston, Texas	76-81-74-80—311
T-8	Mary Dunne	Lauderdale-by-the-Sea, Fla.	78-80-80-74—312
T-8	Tricia Konz	Chandler, Ariz.	83-75-80-74—312
T-8	Jamille Jose	Carmichael, Calif.	74-78-79-81—312
T-11	Kim Augusta	Rumford, R.I.	81-77-79-78—315
T-11	Nicole Horner	Miliani Town, Hawaii	85-73-80-77—315
13	Barbara Paul	Clarksburg, N.J.	80-78-80-80—318
14	Tracy Hanson	Rathdrum, Idaho	81-78-81-80—320
15	Kimberley Self	Dallas, Texas	80-80-79-82—321
16	Sara Miley	Menomonee Falls, Wis.	84-80-80-78—322
17	Lisa Weissmuller	Lexington, Ky.	83-83-79-78—323
T-18	Allyson Greer	Millbrook, N.Y.	83-82-83-77—325
T-18	Mara Whitfield	Jackson, Miss.	81-81-80-83—325
20	Moira Dunn	Utica, N.Y.	85-85-85-73—328
T-21	Staci Aber	Greensburg, Pa.	82-85-82-80—329
T-21	Tracy Welch	Winchester, Mass.	81-80-84-84—329
T-23	Courtney Cuff	Athens, Ga.	84-82-84-80—330
T-23	Carol Pfaff	Hesston, Kan.	83-81-83-83—330
T-25	Ginger Lowe	Boise, Idaho	80-89-82-80—331
T-25	Maria Castelluci	Orlando, Fla.	88-78-84-81—331
27	Sara Evens	Grafton, N.D.	88-77-82-85—332
T-28	Margaret Hickey	Schenectady, N.Y.	86-83-83-82—334
T-28	Kathy Weber	Wellington, Kan.	87-79-83-85—334
30	Angie Wilson	Lincoln, Neb.	84-87-80-84—335
31	Roberta Richling	Medina, Ohio	85-91-76-84—336
T-32	Jodi Zwemke	Arvada, Colo.	85-86-83-84—338
T-32	Barbara Morace	Longmeadow, Mass.	86-77-86-89—338
34	Gina Yoder	Nappanee, Ind.	83-86-90-82—341
35	Kathleen Phares	E. Moline, Ill.	84-90-90-81—345
36	Monica Mayhew	Clio, Mich.	87-86-85-89—347
37	Brenna Cepelak	Rio Rancho, N.M.	89-86-88-85—348
38	Robin Buck	Edwardsville, Ill.	84-85-86-94—349
39	Skyli Yamada	Sandy, Utah	93-85-88-86—352
40	Lynne Percival	Whitehall, Pa.	90-84-96-85—355
41	Nicole Crist	Salamanca, N.Y.	91-90-91-87—359
42	Millette Mallard	New Johnsonville, Tenn.	89-89-93-92—363
43	Amanda Kuhn	Pinehurst, N.C.	89-93-89-95—366

1987   Vicki Goetze of Hull, Ga., now a 14-year-old tournament "veteran," led from wire-to-wire to win the 12th annual PGA Junior Championship. Goetze's 8-over-par 296 total outdistanced PGA National Golf Club member Michelle McGann by six strokes and third-place Brandie Burton of Rialto, Calif., by 15 strokes. Boys' champion Jeff Manson of Long Beach, Calif., opened the final 18 holes trailing Thomas Hurley of Darien, Conn., by three strokes. Mason captured the title with a 1-under-par 71, while Hurley limped home with a 6-over-par 78.

Champion: (Boys) Jeff Manson, Long Beach, Calif.	
Champion: (Girls) Vicki Goetze, Hull, Ga.	
Site: PGA National Golf Club (Champion), Palm Beach Gardens, Fla.	
Date: Aug. 25-28	**Par:** 72

Boys' Division

1	Jeff Manson	Long Beach, Calif.	76-73-74-71—294
2	Thomas Hurley	Darien, Conn.	74-73-73-78—298
3	Greg Krak	Palm Beach Gardens, Fla.	82-71-71-75—299
4	James Furyk	Manheim, Pa.	77-75-78-70—300
5	Nicky Goetze	Hull, Ga.	74-80-76-72—302
6	Trip Kuehne	Dallas, Texas	78-70-78-80—306
T-7	Jason Widener	Greensboro, N.C.	71-78-79-79—307
T-7	Jack Tanner	Victoria, Texas	77-76-76-78—307
T-9	Darrell Bryant	Daytona Beach, Fla.	76-76-81-75—308
T-9	Manuel Zerman	San Diego, Calif.	81-78-72-77—308
11	Craig Darling	Green Bay, Wis.	78-81-74-76—309
T-12	Ed Luxon	Richmond, Ky.	77-79-75-81—312
T-12	Taylor Tipton	Kerrville, Texas	80-74-77-81—312
14	Chad Ginn	Clinton, Miss.	75-79-78-81—313
15	Patrick Brownfield	Tacoma, Wash.	75-81-82-77—315
16	Marty Romney	Salt Lake City, Utah	77-77-81-81—316
T-17	Doug Hoey	Dearborn, Mich.	76-80-79-82—317
T-17	Thump Delk	Fairfield Glade, Tenn.	78-78-79-82—317
19	William Werley Jr.	Littleton, Colo.	79-81-82-76—318
20	William Coelho	Maui, Hawaii	79-79-81-80—319
T-21	Tom Creavy	E. Orleans, Mass.	82-81-77-80—320
T-21	Warren Pitman	Mesa, Ariz.	77-87-77-79—320
T-21	Richard Breed	Wethersfield, Conn.	78-83-78-81—320
24	Steve Anderson	Circleville, Ohio	81-77-78-85—321
25	David Hathaway	Lenoxdale, Mass.	80-89-78-75—322
26	Mike Phenicie	Tulsa, Okla.	79-79-85-80—323
27	Tom Sipula	Ottawa, Ill.	83-78-77-86—324
28	Bart Blackwelder	Hobbs, Minn.	76-88-83-80—327
29	Mike O'Connell	Quincy, Ill.	88-76-81-84—329
30	Stephen Saunders	Montgomery, Ala.	81-81-87-81—330
31	Brad Lucas	Buffalo, Minn.	78-85-84-84—331
32	Matthew Evans	Denton, Md.	78-84-88-82—332
33	Robert Wakeling	Stow, Ohio	85-86-83-79—333
34	Robert Murray	Springfield, Mo.	86-85-80-84—335
35	Eric Peterson	Blackfoot, Idaho	84-84-87-81—336
T-36	Rob McCormick	Crawfordsville, Ind.	85-88-84-80—337
T-36	Jeffrey Miga	New York Mills, N.Y.	82-86-83-86—337
38	John Williams	Lincoln, Neb.	87-87-80-84—338
39	Brandon Goethals	Redding, Calif.	84-84-82-90—340
40	Carl Odendahl	Monmouth, Ill.	91-85-84-81—341
41	George Laskey	Hopwood, Pa.	92-85-84-81—342
42	Chris Hasselback	Williamsville, N.Y.	89-85-87-84—345
43	Michael Stamberger	Scotch Plains, N.J.	87-85-87-88—347
44	Ron Peeples	Newtown, Pa.	91-85-89-93—358

Girls' Division

1	Vicki Goetze	Hull, Ga.	75-75-74-72—296
2	Michelle McGann	Singer Island, Fla.	77-75-78-72—302
3	Brandie Burton	Rialto, Calif.	81-77-74-79—311
4	Christy Erb	Bonita, Calif.	83-75-75-79—312
5	Lisa Brandetsas	Perry, N.Y.	78-83-81-71—313
T-6	Dana Arnold	Modesto, Calif.	76-77-78-82—315
T-6	Adele Moore	Dallas, Texas	82-77-77-79—315
8	Marian Sison	Arlington, Va.	84-78-80-79—321
9	Susan Veasey	Safety Harbor, Fla.	76-83-80-83—322
10	Lynne Mikulas	La Mesa, Calif.	82-79-81-84—326
11	Tricia Corace	Gwynedd Valley, Pa.	81-81-84-81—327
T-12	Kristine Lazar	Gig Harbor, Wash.	86-82-81-79—328
T-12	Debbie Doniger	Greenwich, Conn.	81-80-81-86—328
14	Shannon Hamel	Ann Arbor, Mich.	87-77-80-86—330
15	Angie Wilson	Lincoln, Neb.	84-83-78-86—331
T-16	Sara Evens	Grafton, N.D.	88-82-85-79—334
T-16	Renee Heiken	Metamora, Ill.	91-75-83-85—334
T-16	Tonya Blosser	Athens, Ohio	83-81-83-87—334
19	Coley Jordan	Richardson, Texas	86-79-82-90—337
T-20	Lorinda Garner	Portland, Conn.	87-87-83-84—341
T-20	Kimberley Tyrer	Frankfort, Ky.	90-85-83-83—341
22	Bronwyn Burke	Houston, Texas	89-82-90-84—345
T-23	Carrie Kotoshirodo	Pearl City, Hawaii	83-89-85-89—346
T-23	Alycya Rambin	Tulsa, Okla.	86-87-81-92—346
T-25	Kerry Lee O'Leary	Fitchburg, Mass.	86-88-88-86—348
T-25	Lori Stinson	Ft. Wayne, Ind.	79-89-87-93—348
T-27	Chanda McCleese	Hobe Sound, Fla.	88-87-89-87—351
T-27	Sara Miley	Menomonee Falls, Wis.	86-87-88-90—351
29	Christina Dacri	Madison, Tenn.	92-92-85-83—352
30	Staci Aber	Greensburg, Pa.	82-98-84-90—354
31	Moira Dunn	Utica, N.Y.	85-94-85-93—357
32	Bobbie Richling	Medina, Ohio	84-90-90-94—358
33	Margaret Hickey	Schenectady, N.Y.	89-92-89-89—359
34	Jodie Zwembe	Arvada, Colo.	97-89-92-87—365
35	Joy Cross	Silver City, N.M.	95-99-87-90—371
36	Mara Whitfield	Jackson, Miss.	99-91-88-94—372
37	Michelle Melia	Edison, N.J.	90-98-96-91—375
38	Amy Miller	Anniston, Ala.	103-97-90-90—380
39	Amy Shell	Great Bend, Kan.	96-96-98-97—387
40	Catherine Voyles	Columbia, S.C.	95-100-98-95—388
41	Kathleen Phares	E. Moline, Ill.	106-97-98-100—401
42	Maria Palozola	Des Peres, Mo.	109-104-115-107—435
	Sharon Probst	Midway, Utah	95-WD
	Tricia Konz	Chandler, Ariz.	WD
	Janet Southwick	Idaho Falls, Idaho	DQ

1986

For the first time in the 11-year history of the PGA Junior Championship, both the boys' and girls' division titles were decided by a stroke. Brian Montgomery of Bristow, Okla., birdied the final hole for a 5-over-par 293 and a victory over Damien Jamila of Waimanala, Hawaii. Adele Moore struggled to a final-round 77 for a 12-over-par 300, but managed to hold off Tracy Nakamura of Monterey Park, Calif., who came home with a final-round 75. Thirteen-year-old Vicki Goetze of Hull, Ga., finished fifth after posting three consecutive 78s in her final 54 holes.

Champion: (Boys) Brian Montgomery, Bristow, Okla.
Champion: (Girls) Adele Moore, Dallas, Texas
Site: PGA National Golf Club (Champion), Palm Beach Gardens, Fla.
Date: Aug. 21-24 **Par:** 72

Boys' Division

1	Brian Montgomery	Bristow, Okla.	73-70-77-73—293
2	Damien Jamila	Waimanala, Hawaii	74-75-74-71—294
T-3	Phil Mickelson	San Diego Calif.	76-74-74-72—296
T-3	Christian Pena	Belen, N.M.	72-74-72-78—296
5	Bryan Pemberton	Pleasanton, Calif.	76-71-72-79—298
6	Brad Sutterfield	Salt Lake City, Utah	75-77-77-72—301
T-7	Chris Geiger	Endwell, N.Y.	77-77-74-74—302
T-7	Chad Magee	Tyler, Texas	73-76-77-76—302
T-7	Brett Quigley	Barrington, R.I.	73-72-78-79—302
T-7	David Bishop	Plantation, Fla.	73-75-74-80—302
T-11	Bob May	LaHabra, Calif.	72-80-77-76—305
T-11	Henry Smith	Anniston, Ala.	80-76-73-76—305
T-11	Scott Brown	Lakeland, Fla.	71-76-80-78—305
14	Kent Wiese	Huntington Beach, Calif.	75-77-77-77—306
15	Rett Crowder	Jackson, Miss.	80-73-76-79—308
16	Nicky Goetze	Hull, Ga.	74-71-84-80—309
17	Michael Sipula III	Ottawa, Ill.	78-73-80-81—312
T-18	Douglas Ray	Alliance, Ohio	72-75-82-84—313
T-18	Dave Hathaway	Lenoxdale, Mass.	78-80-71-84—313
20	Todd Barranger	Phoenix, Ariz.	81-76-79-78—314
T-21	Larry Tedesco	Westport, Conn.	77-82-78-78—315
T-21	Brett Dean	Evergreen, Colo.	79-81-78-77—315
T-21	Robb Craddock	Circleville, Ohio	75-76-81-83—315
T-24	Tripp Schreves	Bethesda, Md.	76-72-91-77—316
T-24	Chris Dibble	Greeneville, Tenn.	75-81-79-81—316
T-24	Chris Spath	Erie, Pa.	82-77-76-81—316
T-27	David Carothers	Owatonna, Minn.	83-77-79-78—317
T-27	Bob Rannow	Lincoln City, Ore.	75-80-82-80—317
T-27	Jim Johnson	Charlotte, N.C.	75-80-81-81—317
30	Doug Barron	Memphis, Tenn.	84-79-80-75—318
31	William Kennedy	Springhouse, Pa.	73-81-85-81—320
32	Brian Buzzini	Modesto, Calif.	76-86-80-79—321
33	Mike Ryan	Claremore, Okla.	84-78-78-83—323
T-34	Patrick Mullin	W. Hartford, Conn.	79-82-82-81—324
T-34	Jay Randolph, Jr.	St. Louis, Mo.	79-83-80-82—324
36	Rob Robinson	Aurora, Ind.	84-79-81-81—325
T-37	Travis Saul	Augusta, Ga.	82-81-87-80—330
T-37	Tony Baxter	Bettendorf, La.	82-80-82-86—330
39	Greg Braun	Caldwell, Idaho	82-88-87-74—331
40	Sean McLanahan	Hollidaysburg, Pa.	82-86-87-80—335
T-41	Jimmy Spurlock	Spring, Texas	83-85-89-80—337
T-41	Bob Long	Midland, Mich.	82-83-80-92—337
43	Keith Ryan	Little Silver, N.J.	79-83-91-86—339
T-44	Scott Christenson	Topeka, Kan.	89-81-85-85—340
T-44	Bryan Baysinger	Glasgow, Ky.	86-85-84-85—340
T-46	Steve Boveia	Lincoln, Neb.	88-88-85-84—345
T-46	Austin Eaton	Waterville Valley, N.H.	88-78-88-91—345
48	Tom Floberg	Green Bay, Wis.	95-84-92-89—360

Girls' Division

1	Adele Moore	Dallas, Texas	70-76-77-77—300
2	Tracy Nakamura	Monterey Park, Calif.	70-76-80-75—301
3	Dana Arnold	Modesto, Calif.	75-76-73-83—307
4	Michelle McGann	Riviera Beach, Fla.	78-79-74-77—308
5	Vicki Goetze	Hull, Ga.	79-78-78-78—313
6	Terri Thompson	Savannah, Ga.	77-82-81-75—315
7	Barbara Koosa	Columbia, S.C.	78-83-76-84—321
8	Jodi Figley	Alquippa, Pa.	79-81-80-82—322
T-9	Lisa Brandetsas	Perry, N.Y.	81-78-91-73—323
T-9	Tina Trimble	Houston, Texas	77-79-84-83—323
T-11	Renee Heiken	Metamora, Ill.	82-80-82-84—328
T-12	Anna Acker	Marshfield, Wis.	80-84-83-81—328
13	Missy Tuck	Trussville, Ala.	83-81-86-82—332
14	Maria Castelluci	Orlando, Fla.	85-84-86-81—336
15	Ann Gulberson	Bellevue, Nev.	85-83-86-83—337
16	Tonya Blosser	Athens, Ohio	81-87-82-89—339
T-17	Stephanie Davis	Bainbridge Island, Wash.	91-82-88-81—342
T-17	Shirley Trier	Akron, Ohio	88-87-85-82—342
T-17	Ann Kroot	Indianapolis, Ind.	91-83-86-82—342
T-17	Annette Kealoha	Kaneohe, Hawaii	91-82-80-89—342
21	Debbie Parks	Phoenix, Ariz.	91-84-83-85—343
T-22	Tara Hipp	Gaithersburg, Md.	96-85-88-77—346
T-22	Mia Browning	Detroit, Mich.	92-80-89-85—346
24	Liza Labelle	Minneapolis, Minn.	87-85-89-88—349
25	Leslie Spalding	Billings, Mont.	93-88-86-84—351
26	Catherine Gitzendanner	Downington, Pa.	92-86-91-84—353
27	Carolyn McMullen	Cheyenne, Wyo.	96-84-86-90—356
28	Jenni Barr	Coral Springs, Fla.	94-88-86-89—357
29	Margaret Hickey	Schenectady, N.Y.	90-88-95-89—362
30	Jeane Orr	Wichita, Kan.	94-90-94-89—367
31	Julie Esselman	Prospect, Ky.	91-91-100-88—370
32	Cindi Watson	Galesburg, Ill.	95-92-95-90—372
33	Mara Whitfield	Jackson, Miss.	90-98-92-100—380
34	Sharon Probst	Midway, Utah	94-97-104-86—381
35	Christina Dacri	Madison, Tenn.	95-96-95-98—384
36	Lorinda Garner	Portland, Conn.	96-90-101-102—389
T-37	Jodi Lombard	So. Lancaster, Mass.	100-97-101-95—393
T-37	Michelle Robinson	Irvington, N.Y.	100-93-102-98—393
39	Missy Webb	Kansas City, Mo.	98-106-102-92—398
40	Julie Brand	Alder Creek, N.Y.	102-98-102-99—401
41	Lisa Del Prete	Albuquerque, N.M.	113-98-91-102—404
42	Tori Doney	Hope, N.J.	100-102-106-107—415
	Chris Morris	St. Louis, Mo.	DQ

1985

Steve Termeer of Conroe, Texas, entered the final round of the 1985 PGA Junior Championship with a four-stroke cushion and a 214 total — 2-under-par for 54 holes. But Termeer nearly saw his lead bottom out, withstanding a final-round 6-over-par 78 to win the PGA Junior Championship. Runner-up John Aber of Greensburg, Pa., came within a stroke of the lead with six holes to play. But Aber suffered a pair of double-bogeys and a bogey on the final five holes to close with a 79 and 297 total. Jean Zedlitz of Pleasanton, Calif., lowered her score each round, closing with a final-round 71 and a one-stroke victory over Dana Lofland of Oxnard, Calif. The gallery favorite, however, was 12-year-old Vicki Goetze of Hull, Ga. — the youngest in the tournament — who finished fifth with a 304 total.

Champion:	(Boys) Steve Termeer, Conroe, Texas
Champion:	(Girls) Jean Zedlitz, Pleasanton, Calif.
Site:	PGA National Golf Club (Haig),
	Palm Beach Gardens, Fla.
Date: Aug. 22-25	Par: 72

Boys' Division

1	Steve Termeer	Conroe, Texas	72-73-69-78—292
2	John Aber	Greensburg, Pa.	71-75-72-79—297
3	Michael Finney	New Orleans, La.	74-78-70-76—298
4	John Karcher	Darien, Conn.	79-76-71-74—300
5	Daniel Wilkinson	North Syracuse, N.Y.	75-76-77-74—302
6	Troy Tamiya	Hilo, Hawaii	75-77-72-79—303
7	Doug Barron	Memphis, Tenn.	79-78-74-73—304
8	Gregory Lesher	Lebanon, Pa.	76-74-77-78—305
T-9	Jeff Gibralter	Dallas, Texas	76-76-69-85—306
	Jeff Mihocik	Lakewood, Ohio	76-76-77-77—306
T-11	Christian Pena	Belen, N.M.	76-78-75-78—307
	Bill Jeremiah	Westfield, N.J.	79-76-75-77—307
	Don Christensen	Edmonds, Wash.	74-83-76-74—307
T-14	Tom Lahner	Milan, Mich.	74-80-77-77—308
	Ted Beckmann	Morehead, Ky.	71-77-80-80—308
T-16	Jim Crump	Hartwell, Ga.	75-78-77-79—309
	Chris Coffman	Seymour, Wis.	78-78-72-81—309
	Mike Sposa	Tamarac, Fla.	77-75-80-77—309
19	Eric Brito	Atlantic Beach, Fla.	78-85-72-76—311
20	Anthony Andrews	Kokomo, Ind.	78-83-75-76—312
21	Joe Sorenson	Bloomington, Minn.	75-82-79-77—313
22	Brian McDaniel	Henderson, N.C.	80-79-79-77—315
T-23	David Hathaway	Lenoxdale, Mass.	81-79-78-79—317
	Jason Peterson	Oakland, Neb.	78-80-77-82—317
	Will Tipton	Hollister, Calif.	75-84-77-81—317
T-26	Mike Phenicie	Tulsa, Okla.	78-81-84-75—318
	Steve Shade	Lawrence, Kan.	79-71-81-87—318
28	Wayne Solley	Marshalltown, Iowa	81-84-81-74—320
29	Joe Cordani	Weatogue, Conn.	79-84-80-82—325
30	Todd Tumminia	St. Louis, Mo.	81-83-77-86—327
31	Jason Bittick	Yorba Linda, Calif.	76-83-82-87—328
32	Greg Coble	Birmingham, Ala.	82-77-85-85—329
33	Tony Russo	South Holland, Ill.	81-81-82-86—330
34	Chris Johnson	Denver, Colo.	79-85-80-89—333
35	Troy Wilson	Marysville, Ohio	86-87-80-86—339
36	John Marshall	Chester, Va.	91-78-83-89—341
37	Carl Hasselback	Williamsville, N.Y.	93-75-85-91—344
38	Francis Sullivan	Andover, Mass.	86-86-79-95—346

Girls' Division

1	Jean Zedlitz	Pleasanton, Calif.	78-76-75-71—300
2	Dana Lofland	Oxnard, Calif.	80-77-74-70—301
T-3	Margaret Platt	Elmsford, N.Y.	77-78-71-77—303
	Kathy Highfill	Monroe, La.	76-75-79-73—303
5	Vicki Goetze	Hull, Ga.	75-78-75-76—304
6	Sheryl Maize	Venice, Fla.	79-76-78-74—307
7	Adele Moore	Dallas, Texas	77-75-81-76—309
8	Cathy Stevens	Wichita, Kan.	75-76-80-79—310
9	Carolyn McMullen	Cheyenne, Wyo.	77-82-76-76—311
10	Anne Jones	Louisville, Ky.	79-78-73-84—314
11	Cathy Mockett	Newport Beach, Calif.	77-83-78-77—315
12	Barbara Koosa	Columbia, S.C.	84-78-80-75—317
13	Stephanie Davis	Bainbridge Island, Wash.	75-82-81-83—321
T-14	Laura D'Alessandro	Toms River, N.J.	81-89-76-77—323
	Dina Ammaccapane	Phoenix, Ariz.	84-87-74-78—323
	Jodi Figley	Aliquippa, Pa.	80-83-81-79—323
	Krista Tucek	The Woodlands, Texas	82-79-79-83—323
T-18	Casey Murphy	Amsterdam, N.Y.	81-80-86-78—325
	Kim Cayce	Potomac, Md.	80-84-81-80—325
20	Mary Meo	Ft. Lauderdale, Fla.	82-77-83-84—326
T-21	Lisa Brandetsas	Perry, N.Y.	79-82-84-83—328
	Karen Socha	Greenville, Tenn.	85-79-81-83—328
	Mia Browning	Detroit, Mich.	82-83-79-84—328
T-24	Ingrid Lundblad	Painesville, Ohio	77-82-79-93—331
	Debbie O'Kelly	East Bridgewater, Mass.	77-83-86-85—331
	Liza LaBelle	Minneapolis, Minn.	78-87-86-80—331
T-27	Suzanne Mossberg	Lawrence, Kan.	87-76-84-85—332
	Carolyn McKenzie,	Berwyn, Pa.	81-88-78-85—332
29	Barbara Blanchar	Columbia, Mo.	78-88-84-83—333
30	Kristel Kakugawa	Honolulu, Hawaii	84-89-80-83—336
31	Missy Tuck	Trussville, Ala.	86-89-82-82—339
32	Jill Trujillo	Hurley, N.M.	82-92-87-87—348
33	Angie Wilson	Lincoln, Neb.	88-88-82-91—349
34	Lachell Simmons	Salt Lake City, Utah	85-90-88-88—351
35	Kelley Brooke	Bettendorf, Iowa	84-89-93-86—352
T-36	Susan Etter	Lafayette, Ind.	93-89-90-84—356
	Caroline Steimle	Racine, Wis.	87-85-94-90—356
38	Cynthia Mueller	Peoria, Ill.	91-91-86-89—357
39	Carey Schwab	Kettering, Ohio	87-89-96-86—358
40	Jen Parmelee	Middlefield, Conn.	89-96-98-90—373
41	Susan Carson	Norwich, N.Y.	106-101-98-89—394

1984

Clare Dolan of Gaithersburg, Md., rolled in a par putt on the 3rd extra hole — to defeat Cheryl Morley of Winter Springs, Fla., in the PGA Junior Championship girls' division. Morley, who had a final-round 80, finished runner-up for the second consecutive year. David Toms of Bossier City, La., finished with a 3-over-par 75 to capture the boys' division title with a three-stroke victory over Michael Finney of New Orleans, La.

Champion: (Boys) David Toms, Bossier City, La.
Champion: (Girls) Clare Dolan, Gaithersburg, Md.
Site: PGA National Golf Club (Champion), Palm Beach Gardens, Fla.
Date: Aug. 23-26   **Par:** 72

Boys' Division

1	David Toms	Bossier City, La.	73-71-70-75—289
2	Michael Finney	New Orleans, La.	77-71-70-74—292
3	Bob May	LaHabra, Calif.	77-69-69-78—293
4	Terrence Miskell	Salinas, Calif.	75-72-70-79—296
T-5	Doug Martin	Van Buren, Ohio	77-73-75-72—297
T-5	John Tighe Jr.	Lake Worth, Fla.	73-72-73-79—297
7	Donny Yrene	Alburquerque, N.M.	68-73-74-83—298
8	John Andrews	Kokomo, Ind.	76-72-77-74—299
9	Gregory Lesher	Lebanon, Pa.	72-76-74-78—300
T-10	Brad Geer	Edina, Minn.	79-75-72-75—301
T-10	Chris Dibbie	Greeneville, Tenn.	72-74-78-77—301
12	Brian Craig	Gastonia, N.C.	77-71-81-74—303
T-13	Kevin Gai	Newington, Conn.	77-77-74-76—304
T-13	Trev Anderson	Tempe, Ariz.	76-73-77-78—304
15	Timothy Straub	Orchard Park, N.Y.	76-78-75-76—305
T-16	Mike Clements	Cincinnati, Ohio	73-82-78-75—308
T-16	Jim Strickland	Mill Creek, Wash.	76-77-77-78—308
18	Tony Brovey	Bentleyville, Pa.	77-78-73-79—309
19	Chan Reeves	Americus, Ga.	78-80-75-79—312
20	Bradley Broughton	Grand Junction, Colo.	77-78-77-83—315
T-21	Jason Meyerhoeffer	Twin Falls, Ind.	77-75-87-77—316
T-21	Jerry Kelly	Madison, Wis.	74-83-80-79—316
T-23	Andy Cooper	Spring, Texas	80-78-76-83—317
T-23	Bill Wood	Des Moines, Iowa	76-86-78-77—317
T-25	Frank Bensel	White Plains, N.Y.	84-81-80-73—318
T-25	Dan Taylor	Kansas City, Kan.	81-78-79-80—318
27	Mike Haberl	South Dennis, Mass.	82-83-78-76—319
T-28	Steve Stagg	Tampa, Fla.	80-83-81-77—321
T-28	Brendan Moynahan	Honolulu, Hawaii	78-81-87-75—321
30	Christopher Scheibal	Edwardsville, Ill.	85-78-76-83—322
T-31	Richard Massey	Harrington Park, N.Y.	79-79-80-86—324
T-31	Bobby Gee	Plano, Texas	78-83-77-86—324
33	Fred Mattingly	Frankfort, Ky.	79-77-80-89—325
34	Duncan Rougier-Chapman	Grand Rapids, Mich.	83-86-84-73—326
T-35	Marc Caifano	Oak Lawn, Ill.	80-82-82-84—328
T-35	Kurt Schnellbaecher	Troy, N.Y.	83-81-85-79—328
37	Marc DeWall	Omaha, Neb.	83-80-84-82—329
38	Sean Hutchinson	Oklahoma City, Okla.	84-87-75-84—330
39	Mark Strok	Solon, Ohio	85-79-87-80—331
40	Bob Emmons	Bellflower, Calif.	81-78-90-84—333
T-41	Mike Bennett	Jordan, N.Y.	86-83-83-82—334
T-41	Heath Davis	Decatur, Ala.	83-80-92-89—344
43	Randy Barnes	Germantown, Md.	90-86-90-91—357

Girls' Division

1	Clare Dolan	Gaithersburg, Md.	79-76-75-77—307
	(Dolan won playoff on third extra hole)		
2	Cheryl Morley	Winter Springs, Fla.	75-74-78-80—307
3	Pearl Sin	Bellflower, Calif.	78-73-81-76—308
4	Lisa Nedoba	Plantation, Fla.	79-77-82-73—311
5	Elizabeth Macfie	Camden, S.C.	79-75-78-80—312
6	Katie Peterson	Plantation, Fla.	75-76-84-79—314
7	Susie McGuire	Syracuse, N.Y.	78-82-79-77—316
8	Joan Pitcock	Fresno, Calif.	76-74-85-83—318
9	Lana Perhacs	Glendale, Ariz.	79-84-76-80—319
10	Karen Socha	Greeneville, Tenn.	79-80-81-80—320
T-11	Jean Bartholomew	Garden City, N.Y.	79-76-81-85—321
T-11	Adele Moore	Dallas, Texas	78-79-80-84—321
T-13	Michelle Wooding	Tacoma, Wash.	84-81-77-81—323
T-13	Jodi Figley	Aliquippa, Pa.	80-78-80-85—323
15	Barbara Blanchar	Columbia, Mo.	79-81-86-78—324
16	Kristin Parker	The Woodlands, Texas	79-80-83-83—325
T-17	Cissye Meeks	Greenwood, Miss.	84-80-82-81—327
T-17	Jackie Gallagher	Marion, Ind.	82-83-81-81—327
19	Wendy Werley	Littleton, Colo.	87-80-82-79—328
20	Susan Wineinger	Green Bay, Wis.	85-81-84-81—331
21	Amy Butzer	Sioux Falls, S.D.	80-78-92-85—335
22	Kristen Weise	Allegany, N.Y.	89-80-84-83—336
23	Laura D'Alessandro	Toms River, N.J.	90-85-80-82—337
24	Beth Marting	Dubuque, Iowa	82-85-83-88—338
25	Loren Milhench	Marion, Mass.	83-86-84-88—341
26	Nicole Damarjian	Colchester, Conn.	95-84-81-83—343
27	Catharina Hammer	Columbus, Ohio	91-84-86-85—346
28	Heather Drake	Kansas City, Mo.	91-84-86-86—347
29	Sherri Atchison	Miami, Okla.	92-85-84-87—348
T-30	Debra Fernandez	Kaneohe, Hawaii	84-93-91-85—353
T-30	Kristen Stone	Bethlehem, Pa.	94-85-82-92—353
32	Jenny Sayles	Pekin, Ill.	84-95-88-87—354
33	Melissa Tuck	Trussville, Ala.	98-89-82-86—355
34	Nancy Olsen	Eagle, Idaho	88-89-92-88—357
35	Ann Guiberson	Omaha, Neb.	90-82-92-96—360
36	Tiffany Maurycy	Schenectady, N.Y.	96-92-89-84—361
37	Frances Palmer	Newport, Mich.	88-90-91-93—362
38	Laura Spengeman	Belen, N.M.	98-83-97-85—363
39	Lee Alexander	Chardon, Ohio	88-86-90-104—368
40	Ann Hill	LaGrange, Ky.	93-99-91-86—369
41	Kelly Stokes	Perry, Ga.	107-101-104-104—416

PGA JUNIOR CHAMPIONSHIP

1983 For the second consecutive year, both PGA Junior champions lived in the same PGA section. Michael Bradley of Sanibel, Fla., and Tracy Kerdyk of Coral Gables, Fla., each qualified as champions of the South Florida Section PGA. Bradley turned in a 2-under-par 286 to tie the 72-hole tournament record shared by Rick Fehr (1979) and Billy Andrade (1981). Bradley earned a two-stroke victory over Edward Pfister of Marilla, N.Y., while Kerdyk posted an even-par 72 on the final day to defeat Cheryl Morley of Winter Springs, Fla., by six strokes.

Champion: (Boys) Michael Bradley, Sanibel, Fla.
Champion: (Girls) Tracy Kerdyk, Coral Gables, Fla.
Site: PGA National Golf Club (Champion), Palm Beach Gardens, Fla.
Date: Aug. 18-21   **Par:** 72

Boys' Division

1	Michael Bradley	Sanibel, Fla.	73-70-71-72—286
2	Edward Pfister	Marilla, N.Y.	71-73-74-70—288
3	Brian Nelson	Tyler, Texas	79-75-68-73—295
4	Bill Mayfair	Phoenix, Ariz.	73-77-73-74—297
5	Rudi Rudisill	Gastonia, N.C.	78-72-73-75—298
6	Mark Turlington	Temple Terrace, Fla.	74-73-76-78—301
7	Glen Day	Poplarville, Miss.	75-71-77-73—302
8	Blair Manasse	Plano, Texas	75-80-74-76—305
T-9	Tim Straub	Orchard Park, N.Y.	82-71-76-77—306
T-9	Jon Kosier	Mason, Mich.	77-80-77-72—306
11	Sean Hutchinson	Oklahoma City, Okla.	84-72-75-72—308
12	Bobby Lasken	Whittier, Calif.	87-74-78-78—312
T-13	Richard Pruchnik	Belford, N.J.	78-82-75-78—313
T-13	Will Tipton	Hollister, Calif.	84-77-78-74—313
14	Carl Stripling	Houston, Texas	80-78-81-75—314
15	Croy Cochran	Renton, Wash.	79-81-77-79—316
T-16	Raymond Baldwin	Americus, Ga.	77-80-81-79—317
T-16	Mike Scheller	Coon Rapids, Minn.	79-80-79-79—317
18	Jim Knoesel	St. Louis, Mo.	84-80-75-79—318
T-19	Donny Yrene	Albuquerque, N.M.	79-80-77-83—319
T-19	Timothy Diers	Cincinnati, Ohio	82-79-79-79—319
T-21	Mike Haberl	South Dennis, Maine	77-84-80-81—322
T-21	Tom Stone	Horseheads, N.Y.	84-79-77-82—322
23	Raymond Byrne	Midlothian, Va.	80-84-81-78—323
T-24	Douglas Nock	Boulder, Colo.	88-79-78-79—324
T-24	Thadd Kochan	Greenwich, Conn.	79-79-85-81—324
26	Drew Conliffe	Louisville, Ky.	81-79-89-76—325
T-27	Nick DeKock	Cedar Rapids, Iowa	79-79-87-81—326
T-27	Wes Tuck	Trussville, Ala.	79-81-83-83—326
T-29	Daniel Picking	Johnstown, Pa.	84-85-76-82—327
T-29	Toby Crockett	Caldwell, Idaho	88-80-80-79—327
31	Chris Smith	Rochester, Ind.	79-87-84-80—330
32	Brian Streeler	Wheaton, Ill.	86-79-78-88—331
33	William Zebick Jr.	Tullahoma, Tenn.	88-79-80-85—332
T-34	David Hayes	Loudonville, N.Y.	83-80-82-90—335
T-34	Alexander Toledo	Hilo, Hawaii	90-84-82-79—335
T-36	Glenn Johanson	Unionville, Conn.	78-91-86-83—338
T-36	Scott Reisenweaver	Telford, Pa.	85-85-86-82—338
38	Gerald Riani Jr.	Leawood, Kan.	91-82-89-79—341
39	David Plumb	Chagrin Falls, Ohio	88-84-86-84—342
40	Randy Conroy	Council Bluffs, Iowa	80-85-88-91—344
41	Jon Konz	Rhinelander, Wis.	86-90-85-84—345
42	Michael Schoenberg	Scottsdale, Ariz.	87-88-90-86—351
43	Dean Refram	Wesley Chapel, Fla.	91-93-82-86—352

Girls' Division

1	Tracy Kerdyk	Coral Gables, Fla.	76-76-72-72—296
2	Cheryl Morley	Winter Springs, Fla.	79-75-75-73—302
3	Pearl Sin	Bellflower, Calif.	81-73-77-72—303
4	Page Dunlap	Sarasota, Fla.	87-76-72-79—305
5	Danielle Ammaccapane	Phoenix, Ariz.	78-78-74-80—310
6	Kim Saiki	Westminster, Calif.	77-81-80-74—312
7	Melissa McNamara	Tulsa, Okla.	80-74-79-80—313
8	Tracy Chapman	Indianapolis, Ind.	76-81-79-81—317
9	Patty Ehrhart	Dunlap, Ill.	79-83-78-80—320
10	Julie Ralls	Woodinville, Wash.	86-84-76-75—321
11	Elizabeth Macfie	Camden, S.C.	82-87-81-75—325
12	Kate Rogerson	Indiana, Pa.	80-78-82-86—326
T-13	Susan Ginter	Appleton, Wis.	83-83-81-81—328
T-13	Stephanie Kondik	Houston, Texas	80-83-78-87—328
15	Sue Stump	Kettering, Ohio	88-81-80-80—329
T-16	Debbie Davis	East Dennis, Mass.	80-87-78-85—330
T-16	Melanie Wilson	Pensacola, Fla.	81-80-86-83—330
18	Karen Socha	Greenville, Tenn.	82-78-88-85—333
19	Kristll Caldeira	Kaneohe, Hawaii	81-87-79-88—335
20	Sue Thomas	Texarkana, Texas	76-88-83-89—336
T-21	Carolyn McKenzie	Berwyn, Pa.	84-89-80-84—337
T-21	Cissye Meeks	Greenwood, Miss.	83-87-85-82—337
23	Kathryn Hughes	Woodbury, Minn.	90-84-84-80—338
T-24	Allison Andrews	Jackson, Mich.	83-86-82-90—341
T-24	Keri Arnold	Modesto, Calif.	87-82-88-84—341
26	Laura Hessenauer	Baltimore, Md.	79-89-89-86—343
27	Valerie Brennan	Quincy, Ill.	92-77-90-85—344
28	Kristen Weise	Allegany, N.Y.	89-87-84-85—345
29	Suzy McQuire	Jamesville, N.Y.	83-84-93-87—347
30	Adrienne Gilmartin	Port Washington, N.Y.	84-90-88-85—347
31	Cece Studer	Billings, Mont.	88-82-93-90—353
32	Kathleen Murphy	Amsterdam, N.Y.	89-93-91-86—359
33	Melissa Farr	Phoenix, Ariz.	86-93-88-94—362
T-34	Therese Johnson	Grinnell, Iowa	92-89-99-83—363
T-34	Anne Jones	Louisville, Ky.	92-88-88-95—363
36	Lisa Papes	Lincoln, Neb.	92-88-96-88—364
37	Susan Dutilly	Norwich, Conn.	91-92-91-91—365
T-38	Marcie White	Warner Robins, Ga.	92-89-93-99—373
T-38	Janine Dabney	Youngstown, Ohio	93-88-94-98—373
40	Kelly Synk	El Paso, Texas	93-93-106-90—382
41	Melanie Warmath	Denver, Colo.	89-92-105-97—383
42	Kathryn Hartzell	Lawrenceville, N.J.	98-91-91-104—384
43	Heather Drake	Kansas City, Mo.	94-107-110-105—416

1982

Heather Farr and Billy Mayfair, who each took golf lessons from the same Phoenix, Ariz., instructor, made a pact between themselves the night before the final round of the PGA Junior Championship in 1982. "We said to each other, 'Let's go out and do it,'" said Farr, who turned in a final-round 70 to complete a 287 total and 10-stroke victory. Dottie Pepper of Saratoga Springs, N.Y., was runner-up. It was Farr's second PGA Junior Championship in three years, and she became the first player to win two PGA Junior Championships. Mayfair cruised to a final-round 71 and an eight-stroke triumph over Tim Fleming of Ocean Springs, Miss.

Champion: (Boys) Bill Mayfair, Phoenix, Ariz.
Champion: (Girls) Heather Farr, Phoenix, Ariz.
Site: PGA National Golf Club (Champion), Palm Beach Gardens, Fla.
Date: Aug. 19-22   **Par:** 72

Boys' Division

1	Bill Mayfair	Phoenix, Ariz.	74-78-69-71—292
T-2	Tim Fleming	Ocean Springs, Miss.	79-72-73-76—300
	(Fleming won playoff for second place)		
T-2	Wally Les	Ludlow, Mass.	76-73-76-75—300
T-2	Michael Bradley	Sanibel Island, Fla.	76-73-77-74—300
5	Jay Gunning	Laltham, N.Y.	71-78-77-75—301
T-6	Rick Marik	Anaheim, Calif.	74-81-74-75—304
T-6	Jett Rich	Villa Rica, Ga.	75-77-77-75—304
8	Brian Nelson	Tyler, Texas	77-75-77-76—305
9	Scott Turney	Santa Ana, Calif.	75-78-76-77—306
T-10	E.J. Pfister	Marilla, N.Y.	75-76-78-78—307
T-10	Mike Lopuszynski	Rye, N.Y.	70-78-76-83—307
T-10	Marc Benavidez	Belen, N.M.	78-75-74-80—307
T-10	Bill McDonald	Dalton, Ga.	76-82-78-71—307
T-14	Mike Ketcham	Ottumwa, Iowa	75-75-81-77—308
T-14	Michael Scheller	Coon Rapids, Minn.	82-76-75-75—308
16	David Fisher	Quincy, Ill.	77-81-74-79—311
T-17	Rob McNamara	Frankfort, Ky.	81-82-77-72—312
T-17	Jeff Jackson	Olympia, Wash.	81-80-76-76—312
T-17	Fran Quinn, Jr.	Northboro, Mass.	75-78-78-81—312
20	Greg Weber	Atlantis, Fla.	85-76-80-72—313
21	Michael Kavka	So. Plainfield, N.J.	78-83-82-72—315
22	Randy Wylie	Knoxville, Tenn.	78-83-79-76—316
T-23	Chris Berry	Pearl, Miss.	79-80-75-83—317
T-23	Mark Tucker	Mohawk, N.Y.	79-78-78-82—317
25	Bill Bell	San Antonio, Texas	81-87-75-75—318
T-26	Edward Schopp	Claverack, N.Y.	81-77-79-82—319
T-26	Kelly Maxwell	Coshocton, Ohio	80-81-82-76—319
T-28	Darrell Lutey	Las Vegas, Nev.	86-77-75-82—320
T-28	Tom Belobraydic	Carmel, Ind.	75-82-80-83—320
T-28	Vincent McCarthy	DeBary, Fla.	75-79-82-84—320
31	John Childs	Pensacola, Fla.	82-79-82-79—322
T-32	Patrick Higgins	Lincoln, Neb.	80-82-82-79—323
T-32	Doug Bohn	Bridgeport, Mich.	75-86-78-84—323
34	David Anderson	Tulsa, Okla.	77-86-81-80—324
35	Mark Phillips	Fresno, Calif.	81-84-82-78—325
36	Timmy Diers	Cincinnati, Ohio	80-83-81-83—327
T-37	Ron Speaker	Greeley, Colo.	77-82-85-84—328
T-37	Treg Hallman	Lake City, S.C.	80-91-83-76—328
39	Kirk Elliot	Lynchburg, Va.	84-77-78-91—330
40	Bob Jacobs	Freeport, Ill.	80-83-83-85—331
41	Danny Morris	Parkesburg, Pa.	88-80-83-87—339
42	Scott Ebesu	Kapaa, Hawaii	89-85-83-87—344
43	Dean Sasanko	Monongahela, Pa.	91-90-87-91—359
	Charley Winn	Wilmot, Wis.	76-75-79—DQ
	Brad Wilhite	Lawrence, Kan.	82—DQ

Girls' Division

1	Heather Farr	Phoenix, Ariz.	71-73-73-70—287
2	Dottie Pepper	Saratoga Springs, N.Y.	73-81-71-72—297
3	Cheryl Morley	Winter Springs, Fla.	76-77-76-75—304
4	Carey Ruffer	Conroe, Texas	80-79-78-74—311
5	Kris Tschetter	Sioux Falls, S.D.	82-74-79-77—312
T-6	Julie Ralls	Woodinville, Wash.	82-79-79-74—314
T-6	Tracy Kerdyk	Coral Gables, Fla.	79-80-77-78—314
T-6	Melissa McNamara	Tulsa, Okla.	81-82-72-79—314
T-6	Sandra Persinger	Baltimore, Md.	77-82-75-80—314
10	Danielle Ammaccapane	Phoenix, Ariz.	79-79-78-81—317
11	Kathy Kostas	Palmdale, Calif.	77-80-79-82—318
12	Sarah Dekraay	Racine, Wis.	83-80-82-74—319
T-13	Tami Jo Henningsen	Camarillo, Calif.	84-78-77-84—323
T-13	Kristal Parker	Cable, Ohio	77-81-84-81—323
15	Libby Akers	French Lick, Ind.	79-81-83-82—325
16	Karen-Mike Zielenski	Sacramento, Calif.	81-89-79-77—326
T-17	Juanita Drinnon	Chattanooga, Tenn.	84-83-75-85—327
T-17	Kristll Caldeira	Kaneohe, Hawaii	82-81-80-84—327
T-17	Donna Linder	Seguin, Texas	78-88-82-79—327
20	Cissye Meeks	Greenwood, Miss.	86-82-82-80—330
T-21	Karen Klein	Argyle, Texas	84-86-72-89—331
T-21	Susan Pager	Daphne, Ala.	78-85-82-86—331
T-21	Patty Ehrhart	Dunlap, Ill.	85-82-79-85—331
24	Kate Rogerson	Indiana, Pa.	90-86-77-81—334
T-25	Dori Eastwood	Lexington, Ky.	88-81-87-82—338
T-25	Sharon Minnich	Bay Village, Ohio	82-85-87-84—338
26	Charlaine Tatz	Scotch Plains, N.J.	88-81-85-85—339
27	Debbie Davis	East Dennis, Mass.	80-92-87-81—340
28	Judy Kase	Socorro, N.M.	84-88-84-85—341
T-29	Adrienne Gilmartin	Port Washington, N.Y.	93-83-81-86—343
T-29	Margaret Will	Whiteville, N.C.	85-83-84-91—343
31	Mary Fechtig	Carmi, Ill.	87-82-88-87—344
32	Glenda Kissel	Brenham, Texas	93-86-86-81—346
33	Kerre Dubinsky	Lincoln, Neb.	88-89-89-84—350
34	Kristen Weise	Allegany, N.Y.	90-86-84-92—352
35	Lisa Dooling	Warminster, Pa.	91-82-83-97—353
36	Suzy McGuire	Jamesville, N.Y.	86-88-90-91—355
T-37	Kim Kessler	Galesburg, Ill.	80-93-94-91—358
T-37	Paige Green	Kalamazoo, Mich.	92-83-102-81—358
39	Becky Whitworth	Colorado Springs, Colo.	93-93-93-86—365
40	Julie Hamblin	Twin Falls, Idaho	94-92-97-89—372
41	Beth Kurtz	Marietta, Ga.	93-93-90-99—375
	Nancy Shue	Lee's Summit, Mo.	94-94-106—WD
	Caroline Keggi	Middlebury, Conn.	85-92—WD

PGA JUNIOR CHAMPIONSHIP

1981 Billy Andrade of Bristol, R.I., fired a second-round 7-under-par 65 — then a course record — to match a 72-hole tournament record 2-under-par 286 set two years earlier by Rick Fehr of Seattle, Wash. Cathy Johnston of Enfield, N.C., struggled in her opening round with a 9-over-par 81, but played 1-under-par the remainder of the tournament for a three-stroke victory over defending champion Heather Farr of Phoenix, Ariz. Farr never recovered from a third-round 79.

Champion: (Boys) Billy Andrade, Bristol, R.I.
Champion: (Girls) Cathy Johnston, Enfield, N.C.
Site: PGA National Golf Club (Haig), Palm Beach Gardens, Fla.
Date: Aug. 20-23   **Par:** 72

Boys' Division

1	Billy Andrade	Bristol, R.I.	72-65-76-73—286
T-2	Scott Erickson	Villa Park, Calif.	75-72-69-74—290
	(Erickson won playoff for second place)		
T-2	Sam Randolph	Santa Barbara, Calif.	71-70-76-73—290
4	Tim Fleming	Ocean Springs, Miss.	74-73-69-77—293
T-5	Scott Verplank	Dallas, Texas	75-72-77-70—294
T-5	Kurt Beck	Pittsburgh, Pa.	72-74-75-73—294
7	Jerry Haas	Belleville, Ill.	76-70-74-75—295
8	Tom Lape	Lebanon, Pa.	70-73-80-75—298
9	Ralden Chang	Ewa Beach, Hawaii	78-76-74-71—299
10	Tom Richardson	Greenwich, Conn.	79-79-75-77—300
T-11	Don Sargent	Brentwood, Tenn.	75-73-81-74—303
T-11	Chip Mann	Bluffton, Ind.	77-74-77-75—303
T-11	Mike Taylor	Gastonia, N.C.	77-75-74-77—303
T-11	Rich Etscorn	Orlando, Fla.	76-75-73-79—303
15	Bill McDonald	Dalton, Ga.	79-76-76-73—304
16	Michael Stone	New Bedford, Mass.	81-76-75-74—306
17	Marty Caifano	Oak Lawn, Ill.	79-76-79-74—308
T-18	Bob Vislocky	Clark, N.J.	75-79-77-78—309
T-18	Rob Gai	Newington, Conn.	80-72-80-77—309
20	John Childs	Pensacola, Fla.	80-78-77-75—310
T-21	Jay Gunning	Latham, N.Y.	78-79-76-78—311
T-21	Joey Castillo	Honolulu, Hawaii	78-78-78-77—311
T-21	John Wegmann	Ft. Lauderdale, Fla.	75-78-78-80—311
24	Scott McCarron	Napa, Calif.	82-69-81-80—312
T-25	Tom Williams	Mason, Ohio	81-75-78-80—314
T-25	Steve Meyerhoeffer	Twin Falls, Idaho	80-79-74-81—314
27	Karl Zoller	Chesterland, Ohio	80-77-79-79—315
28	John Kernohan	Bowling Green, Ky.	79-85-81-72—317
29	Tim Joselyn	Fort Dodge, Iowa	82-78-79-79—318
30	Paul Royak	Albany, N.Y.	82-79-76-82—319
T-31	Glen Rose	Cushing, Okla.	76-82-79-83—320
T-31	Bobby Romero	El Paso, Texas	78-81-81-80—320
33	Brian Keenan	Syracuse, N.Y.	79-81-78-83—321
34	John McMahon	Alexandria, Va.	80-78-84-80—322
35	Doug Bohn	Bridgeport, Mich.	81-80-80-82—323
36	Ted Davis	Bainbridge Island, Wash.	81-82-80-83—326
37	Danny Doyal	Fruita, Colo.	82-78-79-89—328
38	Chip Romjue	Lincoln, Neb.	83-80-84-82—329
T-39	Mark Klemm	Monroe, Wis.	87-77-82-84—330
T-39	John Rehak	Buffalo, N.Y.	89-84-79-78—330
41	Kurt Casburn	Blue Springs, Mo.	84-85-83-80—332
42	Anthony Zarcaro	Seabrook, Texas	87-90-82-85—344
	Paul Smith	Phoenix, Ariz.	82-79-77—WD
	John Brellenthin	Edina, Minn.	81-80—WD

Girls' Division

1	Cathy Johnston	Enfield, N.C.	81-71-74-70—296
2	Heather Farr	Phoenix, Ariz.	73-73-79-74—299
3	Flori Prono	Northridge, Calif.	75-74-75-76—300
4	Kathy Kostas	Palmdale, Calif.	80-72-79-71—302
5	Donna Linder	Seguin, Texas	77-74-76-77—304
6	Dottie Pepper	Gansevoort, N.Y.	77-78-74-78—307
7	Kay Cornelius	Scottsdale, Ariz.	82-77-75-77—311
8	Michele Berteotti	Pittsburgh, Pa.	78-75-80-79—312
T-9	Kristal Parker	Cable, Ohio	84-76-76-78—314
T-9	Tammy Towles	Titusville, Fla.	82-79-81-72—314
T-9	Rita Moore	Dallas, Texas	80-85-82-77—314
T-9	Lisa Stanley	Melbourne, Fla.	76-79-79-80—314
T-9	Donna Cusano	Ft. Lauderdale, Fla.	83-75-75-81—314
14	Jamie DeWeese	Rochester, N.Y.	75-80-77-83—315
T-15	Lynn Dennison	Marion, Ohio	82-72-86-76—316
T-15	Christy Dristy	Annandale, Va.	84-80-74-78—316
T-17	Robin Hood	Osceola, Ind.	76-81-79-81—317
T-17	Melissa McNamara	Tulsa, Okla.	81-81-74-81—317
19	Renee MacDonald	Grants Pass, Ore.	79-80-78-81—318
T-20	Nancy Brown	Salinas, Calif.	75-82-84-79—320
T-20	Lisa Bradley	Emporia, Kan.	81-78-80-81—320
T-20	Angela Atkins	Missouri City, Texas	87-73-78-82—320
23	Caroline Keggi	Middlebury, Conn.	78-82-80-81—321
24	Sarah Zwemke	Arvada, Colo.	82-81-81-79—323
25	Carey Kresheck	DeKalb, Ill.	81-85-80-78—324
26	Tammy Cabacungan	Honolulu, Hawaii	86-77-82-80—325
T-27	Juanita Drinnon	Chattanooga, Tenn.	79-83-80-86—328
T-27	Melanie Wilson	Pensacola, Fla.	82-80-79-87—328
T-29	Margaret Will	Whiteville, N.C.	75-87-87-80—329
T-29	Kristi Arrington	El Paso, Texas	87-83-78-81—329
31	Phoebe Colliflower	Macomb, Ill.	83-81-80-86—330
32	Roberta Kokx	Grand Rapids, Mich.	87-81-85-82—335
33	Missy Bauer	Bethlehem, Pa.	88-81-84-83—336
T-34	Avia Brown	San Diego, Calif.	87-84-84-84—339
T-34	Lori Wetzel	Lancaster, Wis.	78-90-86-85—339
36	Karen Gray	Pelham Manor, N.Y.	87-85-83-86—341
37	Kris Tschetter	Sioux Falls, S.D.	90-85-86-81—342
38	Mary Locke	Reading, Mass.	82-87-89-85—343
39	Marian McShane	Dunwoody, Ga.	83-86-84-91—344
40	Dawn Romero	Lafayette, La.	88-90-86-88—352
41	Lea Alvery	Franklin, Ky.	83-87-95-88—353

1980

Tracy Phillips of Tulsa, Okla., bounced back from the disappointment of finishing runner-up a year earlier, winning the boys' division in the fifth PGA Junior Championship. PGA National Golf Club played host for the first time, and Phillips toured the Haig Course in 5-over-par 293. John Inman of Greensboro, N.C., finished with a final-round 76 to pull within three strokes of Phillips. Heather Farr of Phoenix, Ariz., rolled to a two-stroke victory in the girls' division with a 9-over-par 297. Farr's final-round 77 was enough to hold off Jenny Lidback of Baton Rouge, La., who finished runner-up for the second consecutive year.

Champion: (Boys) Tracy Phillips, Tulsa, Okla.
Champion: (Girls) Heather Farr, Phoenix, Ariz.
Site: PGA National Golf Club (Haig), Palm Beach Gardens, Fla.
Date: Aug. 21-24   **Par:** 72

Boys' Division

1	Tracy Phillips	Tulsa, Okla.	71-74-71-77—293
2	John Inman	Greensboro, N.C.	70-75-75-76—296
3	James Howell	Newton, N.J.	73-72-76-76—297
4	Peter Persons	Macon, Ga.	76-75-75-72—298
5	Jeffrey Boles	Houston, Texas	76-80-71-72—299
T-6	Mike Tschetter	Sioux Falls, S.D.	75-74-77-74—300
T-6	Ralden Chang	Ewa Beach, Hawaii	72-79-72-77—300
8	Taljiro Tanaka	Japan	82-75-73-73—303
9	Paul Ellington	Louisville, Ky.	76-78-76-74—304
T-10	Chris Fleger	Wallingford, Pa.	75-74-81-76—306
T-10	Billy Andrade	Bristol, R.I.	75-72-78-81—306
T-10	Rick Fehr	Seattle, Wash.	74-76-78-78—306
13	Jimmy Matuszewski	Euless, Texas	74-75-82-76—307
T-14	Jay Gunning	Latham, N.Y.	76-75-81-76—308
T-14	Tarry O'Hara Jr.	Worcester, Mass.	75-77-74-82—308
16	Dave Peege	Louisville, Ky.	80-76-80-73—309
17	Jim Flowers	Lancaster, Ohio	76-79-80-75—310
T-18	Mark Arcilesi	Aberdeen, Wash.	77-77-80-77—311
T-18	John Strauss	Winter Springs, Fla.	81-76-74-80—311
T-18	Cliff Earle	Pound Ridge, N.Y.	78-71-81-81—311
T-21	Scott McCarron	Napa, Calif.	78-75-83-76—312
T-21	Jeff Hedden	Waterford, Conn.	80-74-73-85—312
T-21	Pete Jordan	Wood Dale, Ill.	77-75-77-83—312
T-21	Greg Tebbutt	Bettendorf, Iowa	77-75-78-82—312
25	Marc Howell	Harahan, La.	76-74-85-79—314
T-26	Mitchell Murata	Kaneohe, Hawaii	81-79-77-79—316
T-26	James Sosinski	Tempe, Ariz.	82-75-83-76—316
28	Mike Higgins	Lincoln, Neb.	82-79-77-79—317
29	Mark Den Dekker	Santa Monica, Calif.	76-77-80-85—318
T-30	Todd Marston	Jackson, Mich.	78-77-82-82—319
T-30	Brian Keenan	Syracuse, N.Y.	77-79-84-79—319
32	Sal Perez	El Paso, Texas	83-80-77-80—320
33	Bob Rauh	Williamsville, N.Y.	82-81-78-81—322
T-34	Tad Rhyan	Columbus, Ohio	82-78-82-81—323
T-34	Jarrett Sharp	LaFollette, Tenn.	82-80-83-78—323
T-34	Saul Sellinger	Las Vegas, Nev.	82-93-76-72—323
37	Greg Cole	Chickasha, Okla.	80-80-84-81—325
38	Lance Awe	Jefferson City, Mo.	79-79-89-79—326
39	Matt Bencriscutto	Racine, Wis.	78-83-83-83—327
40	Dave Henson	Hesston, Kan.	87-84-78-83—332
41	Derik Brictson	Golden, Colo.	81-82-89-82—334
42	Casey Combs	Seymour, Ind.	82-92-82-80—336
43	John LaMonica	Fort Lee, Va.	83-78-92-84—337
44	Gary Buffington	Pensacola, Fla.	76-89-89-84—338
45	Carmen Costa Jr.	McKeesport, Pa.	93-91-81-80—345
	Jay Cooper	Miami, Fla.	78—DQ

Girls' Division

1	Heather Farr	Phoenix, Ariz.	74-72-74-77—297
2	Jenny Lidback	Baton Rouge, La.	73-74-77-75—299
3	Laurie Rinker	Stuart, Fla.	75-77-75-79—306
4	Cathy Johnston	Enfield, N.C.	81-74-80-73—308
T-5	Lynda Bridge	Hollister, Calif.	78-81-81-72—312
T-5	Kristie Kamal	Keene, N.H.	73-77-82-80—312
7	Tammy Towles	Titusville, Fla.	76-81-77-79—313
8	Lise Anne Russell	New City, N.Y.	80-77-75-82—314
T-9	Susan Fromuth	Chesterfield, Mo.	81-79-78-77—315
T-9	Deb Richard	Manhattan, Kan.	78-77-82-78—315
T-9	Ann Stacy	Savannah, Ga.	81-78-78-78—315
T-9	Holley Morris	Golden, Colo.	78-75-80-82—315
T-9	Donna Linden	Seguin, Texas	80-77-80-78—315
T-14	Kay Cornelius	Scottsdale, Ariz.	82-75-76-83—316
T-14	Jody Rosenthal	Edina, Minn.	78-80-80-78—316
16	Edithe Hathaway	Oceanside, Calif.	79-80-81-77—317
T-17	Sandra Stubbe	Miami, Fla.	79-82-83-78—322
T-17	Michele Berteotti	Pittsburgh, Pa.	81-80-83-78—322
T-17	Cara Andreoll	Wethersfield, Conn.	81-77-80-84—322
20	Nancy Ballard	Pontiac, Mich.	75-85-83-81—324
T-21	Diane Nixon	Rochester, N.Y.	82-83-80-80—325
T-21	Debbie Wright	Albuquerque, N.M.	78-88-84-75—325
T-21	Lel Kaniaupio	Kaneohe, Hawaii	83-77-82-83—325
24	Kathryn Nelson	Owensboro, Ky.	78-82-81-85—326
25	Adele Lukken	Tulsa, Okla.	89-76-81-81—327
T-26	Jodi Logan	Sandusky, Ohio	81-82-82-84—329
T-26	Kimberly Kirks	Fort Worth, Texas	86-83-82-78—329
T-26	Shelly Godeken	Alma, Neb.	79-79-75-96—329
29	Mary Cabriele	Montrose, N.Y.	85-87-83-87—332
30	Dottie Pepper	Gansevoorte, N.Y.	85-81-85-82—333
T-31	Sharon Hadley	Eugene, Ore.	81-87-81-87—336
T-31	Pipper Curley	Hattiesburg, Miss.	83-84-89-80—336
T-33	Lissa Bradford	Nashville, Tenn.	90-78-84-85—337
T-33	Emily Fletcher	Prince George, Va.	84-84-84-85—337
T-35	Valerie Faulkner	Jackson, N.J.	87-86-78-87—338
T-35	Robin Hood	Osceola, Tenn.	87-79-89-83—338
37	Cathy Blackburn	Decatur, Ill.	84-81-87-89—341
38	Melanie Wilson	Pensacola, Fla.	85-87-81-89—342
39	Kristie Kolacny	Grand Junction, Colo.	88-88-87-81—344
40	Phoebe Colliflower	Macomb, Ill.	93-87-84-83—347
41	Carol Huff	Eagle, Idaho	91-92-86-79—348
42	Renee Howlett	Worthington, Ohio	87-83-85-94—349
43	Michelle Bonner	Norristown, Pa.	94-93-83-83—353
	Lanie Gerkin	Watertown, N.Y.	94-87-86—NC
	Marcia Pekar	Wausau, Wis.	84—WD

PGA JUNIOR CHAMPIONSHIP

1979 The impeccably-manicured Mountain View Course at Callaway Gardens Resort in Pine Mountain, Ga., and near-perfect playing conditions helped produce what remains the second-lowest 72-hole winning score in the PGA Junior Championship. Rick Fehr of Seattle, Wash., and Tracy Phillips of Tulsa, Okla., battled for the boys' division title. Fehr entered the final round with a one-stroke margin over Phillips and finished with an even-par 72 for a 2-under-par 286 total and a two-stroke victory. Penny Hammel of Decatur, Ill., posted a final-round 76 for a two-stroke victory over Jenny Lidback of Baton Rouge, La., who struggled home with a final-round 81.

Champion: (Boys) Rick Fehr, Seattle, Wash.		
Champion: (Girls) Penny Hammell, Decatur, Ill.		
Site: Callaway Gardens (Mountain View), Pine Mountain, Ga.		
Date: Aug. 16-19		**Par:** 72

Boys' Division

1	Rick Fehr	Seattle, Wash.	71-72-71-72—286
2	Tracy Phillips	Tulsa, Okla.	70-74-71-73—288
3	Tim Robinson	Coronado, Calif.	74-77-72-73—296
T-4	Dave Peege	Louisville, Ky.	76-72-75-74—297
T-4	Randy Watkins	Jackson, Miss.	73-76-78-70—297
6	Jack Larkin	Atlanta, Ga.	75-76-76-72—298
7	Rob Boldt	Clayton, Calif.	78-75-73-74—300
8	John Inman	Greensboro, N.C.	80-74-71-76—301
9	Todd Smith	Rochester, Ind.	76-73-77-76—302
10	Mark Drury	Brunswick, Ga.	75-77-82-70—304
T-11	Jeff Seger	Fort Worth, Texas	76-80-71-78—305
T-11	Mark Meiering	Albuquerque, N.M.	74-84-76-71—305
T-13	Jeff Kaufman	Birmingham, Ala.	74-77-78-78—307
T-13	James Howell	Newton, N.J.	72-81-79-75—307
15	Mark Thaxton	Burlington, N.C.	76-73-82-80—311
16	David Branham	Norwich, N.Y.	74-76-81-81—312
T-17	Sean Ryan	Amherst, N.H.	82-70-80-81—313
T-17	Paul Nolen	Grand Junction, Colo.	80-80-75-78—313
19	Tom Homa	Fairfield, Conn.	80-81-79-75—315
20	Mark Klement	Austin, Texas	82-75-79-80—316
21	Dean Johnson	Phoenix, Ariz.	81-76-80-80—317
T-22	Mitchell Murata	Kaneohe, Hawaii	78-73-80-87—318
T-22	Buddy Martin	Pittsburgh, Pa.	77-77-83-81—318
T-22	John Cockrill	McLean, Va.	82-79-80-77—318
T-25	Mel Mzhickteno Jr.	St. Charles, Ill.	79-82-81-78—320
T-25	Doug Hoskins	Grand Island, Neb.	79-82-79-80—320
T-27	Tony Catanzaro	Okeechobee, Fla.	76-80-80-85—321
T-27	Eric Nishimoto	Lihue, Hawaii	78-79-80-84—321
T-27	Keith Nachilly	Farmington, Conn.	82-80-81-78—321
30	James Nichols	W. Covina, Calif.	76-82-82-82—322
T-31	Marshall Clark	Fairborn, Ohio	79-85-85-75—324
T-31	Brad Dixon	Florissant, Mo.	79-85-82-78—324
T-31	J.J. Fashimpaur	Cedar Rapids, Iowa	81-83-80-80—324
T-31	Craig Brischke	Madison, Wis.	78-84-79-83—324
35	Richard Kirsch	Brookfield, Ohio	79-84-78-84—325
T-36	Steve Barber	Austin, Minn.	80-79-85-82—326
T-36	Mark Meredith	Johnson City, Tenn.	80-79-82-85—326
T-38	Saul Sellinger	Las Vegas, Nev.	80-83-81-83—327
T-38	Tim Fleming	Ocean Springs, Miss.	80-81-80-86—327
40	Don Walsworth	Marceline, Mo.	83-86-77-82—328
T-41	Bob Park	Berwyn, Pa.	84-81-83-81—329
T-41	Tom Smith	Muskegon, Mich.	82-79-81-87—329
43	Barry Howard	Benton, Ark.	83-86-90-82—341
T-44	Jeff Schmidt	Amsterdam, N.Y.	90-91-77-88—346
T-44	Stuart Harris	Henrietta, N.Y.	88-84-91-83—346

Girls' Division

1	Penny Hammel	Decatur, Ill.	81-75-74-76—306
2	Jenny Lidback	Baton Rouge, La.	77-75-75-81—308
3	Rae Rothfelder	Fort Worth, Texas	76-79-78-76—309
4	Sharon Barrett	Spring Valley, Calif.	81-81-75-76—313
5	Kris Hanson	Granite Falls, Minn.	77-81-85-75—318
T-6	Holley Morris	Golden, Colo.	82-79-80-79—320
T-6	Lise Anne Russell	New City, N.Y.	77-80-82-81—320
8	JoAnne Pacillo	Torrance, Calif.	79-78-78-86—321
9	Lynn Stiffler	Waycross, Ga.	83-80-80-80—323
10	Denise Bratzler	Carson City, Nev.	79-83-82-80—324
T-11	Theresa Schreck	Spokane, Wash.	81-84-81-79—325
T-11	Heather Farr	Phoenix, Ariz.	84-80-84-78—325
13	Adele Lukken	Tulsa, Okla.	81-75-88-82—326
14	Debbie Wright	Albuquerque, N.M.	84-86-77-80—327
15	Nancy Ledbetter	Birmingham, Ala.	74-90-80-85—329
T-16	Cara Andreoli	Wethersfield, Conn.	84-79-83-85—331
T-16	Susan Yantis	San Antonio, Texas	84-84-83-80—331
18	Lucy Lofland	Newton, N.C.	87-84-82-80—333
19	Kristie Kamal	Keene, N.H.	86-81-81-86—334
20	Tracey Gaster	Winter Springs, Fla.	84-83-89-80—336
T-21	Gail Flanagan	Scarsdale, N.Y.	85-84-84-84—337
T-21	Heidi Wallin	Pleasant View, Utah	92-81-81-83—337
23	Barb Anderson	Edwardsville, Ill.	87-82-86-84—339
24	Kathleen Bannister	Gainesville, Va.	87-87-80-87—341
T-25	Joane Souza	Honolulu, Hawaii	85-82-95-81—343
T-25	Meredith McCuaig	Battle Creek, Mich.	89-87-83-84—343
T-25	Carrie Stansberry	Knoxville, Tenn.	86-89-87-81—343
28	Jamie DeWeese	Rochester, N.Y.	90-89-86-86—351
29	Tracee Fowler	Fort Worth, Texas	93-87-88-84—352
30	Doreen Finochiaro	Omaha, Neb.	87-94-87-87—355
31	Jodi Logan	Sandusky, Ohio	86-87-93-90—356
T-32	Michele Berteotti	Upper St. Clair, Pa.	87-90-94-86—357
T-32	Julie Carmichael	Martinsville, Ind.	87-91-89-90—357
34	Patti Butcher	Morrisville, N.Y.	95-85-89-89—358
35	Kathryn Nelson	Owensboro, Ky.	93-91-87-91—362
T-36	Carolyn Barnett	Appleton, Wis.	92-92-89-94—367
T-36	Lori Falso	Cincinnati, Ohio	93-94-93-87—367
38	Lisa Leemon	Mt. Carroll, Ill.	97-90-99-89—375
T-39	Kim O'Hare	Guilderland, N.Y.	99-95-102-92—388
T-39	Natalie LeBlanc	Delcambre, La.	97-98-95-98—388
41	Karen Gustafson	Leawood South, Kan.	99-104-107-105—415
	Kendra Beard	Essex Fells, N.J.	88—WD
	Susan Cowgill	Berwyn, Pa.	107-104-103—WD

1978

Willie Wood of Tucson, Ariz., and Kathy Baker of Clover, S.C., each survived poor final-round play to win titles in the third PGA Junior Championship held at Callaway Gardens in Pine Mountain, Ga. Wood began the final round 3-under-par for 54 holes, and enjoyed a two-stroke cushion. Wood rolled in his only birdie putt of the day — on the fourth sudden-death playoff hole — to defeat Bob Wolcott of Dickson, Tenn. Both players had finished the 72 holes tied at 289. Baker endured a final-round 8-over-par 80 to finish at 304, and hold off Sharon Barrett's closing 75 to earn a three-stroke victory.

Champion: (Boys) Willie Wood, Tucson, Ariz.		
Champion: (Girls) Kathy Baker, Clover, S.C.		
Site: Callaway Gardens (Mountain View), Pine Mountain, Ga.		
Date: Aug. 17-20		**Par:** 72

Boys' Division

1	Willie Wood	Tucson, Ariz.	71-71-71-76—289
	(Won playoff on fourth extra hole)		
2	Bob Wolcott	Dickson, Tenn.	76-72-68-73—289
3	Jack "Monty" Leong	San Diego, Calif.	72-70-73-77—292
T-4	Soctt Myers	Monroe, La.	73-73-74-75—295
T-4	Mitchell Murata	Kaneohe, Hawaii	75-74-71-75—295
T-6	Tom Garner	Pompano Beach, Fla.	75-75-72-74—296
T-6	John Slaughter	Abilene, Texas	79-71-75-71—296
T-6	James Gallagher	Marion, Ind.	78-70-75-73—296
T-9	Randy Watkins	Jackson, Miss.	77-76-68-76—297
T-9	Doug Hoskins	Grand Island, Neb.	80-73-70-74—297
10	Michael Klimtzak	West Seneca, N.Y.	78-75-75-70—298
11	John Inman	Greensboro, N.C.	74-73-76-76—299
T-12	Mark Fuller	Yukon, Okla.	73-76-77-77—303
T-12	Christopher Frey	Tacoma, Wash.	75-78-74-76—303
T-14	Arthur Romero	Roswell, N.M.	76-76-76-76—304
T-14	Dave Ruvolo	Parma, Ohio	76-74-77-77—304
T-14	Dick Stimart	Charlotte, N.C.	75-78-75-76—304
17	Scott Beard	Louisville, Ky.	72-74-78-82—306
18	Ron Mac	Westfield, Mass.	75-77-75-81—308
T-19	Paul Wilson	Tuscaloosa, Ala.	80-80-76-73—309
T-19	Jonas Saxton	Riverside, Conn.	77-78-78-76—309
T-21	Carl Oesterie	Fort Collins, Colo.	79-78-75-78—310
T-21	Robert Lohr	Loveland, Ohio	79-77-79-75—310
23	Webb Heintzelman	Bethesda, Md.	78-76-81-76—311
24	Stoney Ferimann	Peoria, Ill.	79-74-78-83—314
T-25	James Spagnolo	Ardmore, Pa.	80-82-78-75—315
T-25	Doug Hartsema	Muskegon, Mich.	79-80-79-77—315
T-27	Robert Smith	Redlands, Calif.	77-76-75-88—316
T-27	Herbert Ames III	Brownsville, Texas	89-77-75-75—316
29	James Howell	Newton, N.J.	82-74-82-80—318
30	Robert Steffan	West Allis, Wis.	83-80-79-79—321
31	Jay Delsing	St. Louis, Mo.	82-79-79-82—322
32	Jeff Dingman	Stateline, Nev.	82-80-81-82—325
T-33	Wayne Guyer	Middleton, Mass.	83-79-85-80—327
T-33	Allen Peake	Macon, Ga.	83-82-84-80—327
35	Robin Pfaff	Hesston, Kan.	83-82-84-80—329
36	Daniel Howard	St. Paul, Minn.	83-87-82-80—332
37	Dennis Dolci	Sharon, Pa.	84-80-84-88—336
38	Troy Garcia	Layton, Utah	86-82-84-85—337
39	Kris May	Auburn, N.Y.	81-87-84-91—343
40	Frank Conti Jr.	Amsterdam, N.Y.	87-92-88-86—353

Girls' Division

1	Kathy Baker	Clover, S.C.	82-70-72-80—304
2	Sharon Barrett	Spring Valley, Calif.	77-79-76-75—307
3	Rae Rothfelder	Fort Worth, Texas	79-84-72-74—309
4	Nancy Tomich	Upper St. Clair, Pa.	74-80-83-76—313
5	Cindy Pieger	Athens, Ga.	80-77-79-80—316
6	Janice Burba	Tulsa, Okla.	81-77-79-80—317
T-7	Penny Hammel	Decatur, Ill.	75-81-82-80—318
T-7	Lori Castillo	Honolulu, Hawaii	81-81-78-78—318
9	Anne Kelly	Tucson, Ariz.	86-78-77-79—320
10	Cathy Hanion	Palos Verdes Estates, Calif.	79-79-84-80—322
11	Catherine Reynolds	Medford, N.J.	83-82-82-77—324
12	Betty Baird	Louisville, Ky.	86-85-76-78—325
13	Janie Sirmons	St. Petersburg, Fla.	83-79-85-80—327
14	Kris Monaghan	Los Alamos, N.M.	80-81-84-83—328
T-15	Sally Quinian	Dennis, Mass.	86-84-79-84—332
T-15	Kelly Varty	Elk River, Minn.	85-84-79-84—332
T-15	Mary Beth Corrigan	Amsterdam, N.Y.	79-85-80-83—332
18	Mary Hession	Indianapolis, Ind.	84-85-80-83—332
19	Carla Duncan	Hilmar, Calif.	86-88-82-83—339
20	Gall Flanagan	Scarsdale, N.Y.	83-80-92-85—340
21	Lise Anne Russell	New City, N.Y.	86-83-81-91—341
22	Andre Marchand	Luling, La.	85-82-85-90—342
23	Mary Anne Balley	Germantown, Tenn.	88-86-85-84—343
T-24	Linda Bamber	Cincinnati, Ohio	86-83-88-87—344
T-24	Shena Bassett	San Antonio, Texas	89-83-86-86—344
26	Meredith McCualg	Battle Creek, Mich.	84-87-87-87—345
27	Holley Morris	Golden, Colo.	86-84-86-91—347
28	Michelle Jordan	Fairfax, Va.	89-90-84-87—350
T-29	Heldi Wallinm	Pleasant View, Utah	92-82-89-89—352
T-29	Susan Sanders	Salem, Ore.	94-88-85-85—352
T-29	Susan Fromuth	Chesterfield, Mo.	88-94-82-88—352
T-32	Karen Clark	Montgomery, Ala.	85-86-91-95—361
T-32	Cara Andreoll	Wethersfield, Conn.	89-87-90-95—361
34	Sarah Merwald	Omaha, Neb.	95-90-86-91—362
35	Pamela Ossoff	Columbiana, Ohio	90-93-93-94—370
36	Vickie Reynolds	Springfield, Mo.	101-91-90-96—378
37	Katherine McKeand	Lewiston, N.Y.	95-100-92-92—379
38	Kendra Beard	Essex Fells, N.J.	95-100-95-91—381
39	Jackie Cannizzo	E. Syracuse, N.Y.	105-97-95-90—387
40	Cindy Tabor	Prairie Du Sac, Wis.	97-90-99-110—399

PGA JUNIOR CHAMPIONSHIP

1977

Walt Disney World Golf Resort played host to the PGA Junior Championship for the second straight year with two age-group champions crowned in both the boys' and girls' divisions. Randy Watkins of Jackson, Miss., won the 15-17 age division on the Palm Course with a 3-over-par 291. John Inman of Greensboro, N.C., captured the 12-14 age division with a 298 total. Debbie Hall of Corpus Christi, Texas, cruised to a 13-stroke victory in the girls' 15-17 division after a final-round 6-under-par 66. Lise Anne Russell of New City, N.Y., won the 12-14 age division with a 329 total.

Champion: (15-17) Randy Watkins, Jackson, Miss.
Champion: (12-14) John Inman, Greensboro, N.C.
Site: Walt Disney World Golf Resort, Orlando, Fla.
Date: Aug. 18-21   **Par:** 72

Boys' Division

15-17 DIVISION - PALM COURSE

1	Randy Watkins	Jackson, Miss.	71-73-76-71—291
T-2	Rick Stallings	Sarasota, Fla.	73-74-75-71—293
T-2	Bob Wolcott	Dickson, Tenn.	71-77-75-70—293
4	Dick Stimart	Charlotte, N.C.	75-73-78-74—300
5	Jeff Teal	Rochester, Minn.	79-72-78-73—302
T-6	Brian Gurzynski	Angola, Ind.	75-75-76-77—303
T-6	Charlie Gates	Chevy Chase, Md.	74-78-77-74—303
T-8	Mike Schy	Fresco, Calif.	72-74-77-81—304
T-8	Ron Mac	Westfield, Mass.	76-76-78-74—304
10	Johnny Hammond	Columbus, Ga.	79-76-73-77—305
T-11	John Slaughter	Abilene, Texas	84-72-76-74—306
T-11	Randy Burkhardt	Onalaska, Wis.	76-73-79-78—306
T-11	Donald Hurter	Honolulu, Hawaii	80-70-76-80—306
14	Win Bruning	Palatine, Ill.	81-78-77-71—307
T-15	Doug Bowman	Arizona City, Ariz.	74-76-81-78—309
T-15	Wayne Guyer	Middleton, Mass.	79-74-76-80—309
17	Tony St. John	El Paso, Texas	75-76-81-78—310
T-18	Kurt Oldson	Richland, Wash.	79-76-79-77—311
T-18	Edward Vietmeier	Pittsburgh, Pa.	81-71-81-78—311
T-18	Jay Delsing	St. Louis, Mo.	81-79-73-78—311
21	Richard Ruffin	Oklahoma City, Okla.	75-79-77-81—312
22	Jeff Johnson	Ventura, Calif.	80-74-79-80—313
23	Michael Naton	Camillus, N.Y.	83-80-75-76—314
T-24	Greg Devine	Lansing, Mich.	78-74-82-80—314
T-24	Rick Cramer	Hershey, Pa.	78-77-76-83—314
26	Richard Kloepfer	Billings, Mont.	78-76-80-81—315
27	Larry Field	Oklahoma City, Okla.	72-84-83-77—316
T-28	Mike Schuchart	Lincoln, Neb.	82-79-78-79—318
T-28	Bruce Rice	Pueblo, Colo.	78-81-80-79—318
T-30	Herbert Ames	Brownsville, Texas	77-78-81-83—319
T-30	Scott Beard	Louisville, Ky.	81-77-84-77—319
32	Alex Whaling	Dublin, Ohio	75-82-77-87—321
33	Mark Wickline	Mobile, Ala.	81-82-82-79—324
T-34	Richard Gair	Scotia, N.Y.	79-82-85-79—325
T-34	Mark Kellstrom	Baskingridge, N.J.	82-84-85-74—325
36	Robert Keilch	Erie, Pa.	79-94-77-77—327
37	Bryan Anderson	Ottumwa, Iowa	75-83-84-87—329
38	Stephen Clifford	Kansas City, Mo.	82-84-81-83—330
39	Kevin Spenard	Stamford, Conn.	87-84-81-84—336
40	Douglas Lockwood	Delaware, Ohio	79-95-80-83—337

12-14 DIVISION - PALM COURSE

1	John Inman	Greensboro, N.C.	80-71-76-71—298
2	Robert Burns	Lake City, Fla.	75-78-75-73—301
3	Scott Klute	Richmond, Ind.	80-74-71-78—303
4	Dave Peege	Louisville, Ky.	81-75-71-79—306
T-5	Rich Fehr	Seattle, Wash.	75-83-77-76—311
T-5	Michael Murata	Kaneohe, Hawaii	78-79-76-78—311
7	Pete Mathews	Harahan, La.	78-82-76-77—313
8	James Phillips	Pittsford, N.Y.	83-77-79-78—317
9	Clark Maurer	Syosset, N.Y.	79-78-77-84—318
10	Sam Susser	Corpus Christi, Texas	81-83-75-80—319
11	Clay Hull	Deming, N.M.	72-83-86-80—321
12	Andy Wentis	Marietta, Ohio	80-82-79-82—323
13	Jeff Riley	Janesville, Wis.	84-87-76-79—326
T-14	James Sosinski	Tempe, Ariz.	87-81-82-78—328
T-14	Tim Joselyn	Fort Dodge, Iowa	82-83-81-82—328
T-16	Ronald Cindrich	McKees Rocks, Pa.	83-81-83-82—329
T-16	John Boman	Ypsilanti, Mich.	84-84-82-79—329
T-18	Michael McGrath	Caldwell, N.J.	82-82-86-80—330
T-18	Robert Vide	Montgomery, Ala.	77-86-84-83—330
20	Greg Cole	Chickasha, Okla.	81-83-86-83—333
21	David Abel	St. Louis, Mo.	81-84-88-82—335
T-22	Jeffrey Hedden	Waterford, Conn.	88-87-90-73—338
T-22	Samuel Bakken	Bismarck, N.D.	88-87-81-82—338
T-22	Saul Sellinger	Las Vegas, Nev.	84-88-85-81—338
T-22	Michael Zoob	Omaha, Neb.	83-88-86-81—338
26	Judson Wilhoit	Warrenton, Ga.	84-83-84-88—339
27	Ted Marcis	Olmsted, Ohio	80-87-90-84—341
T-28	John Haddock	Annandale, Va.	81-87-88-86—342
T-28	Mike Short	Dallas, Texas	86-83-86-87—342
30	Jeff Dingman	Stateline, Nev.	88-86-85-84—343
T-31	Jimmy Melton	Jackson, Tenn.	87-87-88-82—344
T-31	Chris Fieger	Wallingford, Pa.	82-89-88-85—344
T-31	Dave Esler	Wauconda, Ill.	86-87-89-82—344
34	Jeff Tiley	Fort Collins, Colo.	80-91-88-91—350
35	Peter Giacobbi	Syracuse, N.Y.	93-89-88-82—352
36	Craig Martin	Overbrook, Kan.	84-95-87-91—357
37	Kevin Murray	Troy, N.Y.	86-92-94-90—362
38	Paul Saunders	Fall River, Mass.	85-92-100-86—363
	Mark Den Dekker	Santa Monica, Calif.	WD

PGA JUNIOR CHAMPIONSHIP

1977 - continued

Champion:(15-17) Debbie Hall, Corpus Christi, Texas
Champion:(12-14) Lise Anne Russell, New City, N.Y.
Site: Walt Disney World Golf Resort, Orlando, Fla.
Date: Aug. 18-21   **Par:** 72

Girls' Division

15-17 DIVISION - MAGNOLIA COURSE

1	Debbie Hall	Corpus Christi, Texas	76-78-74-66—294
2	Lauri Merten	Phoenix, Ariz.	79-76-74-78—307
3	Bari Brandwynne	Las Vegas, Nev.	74-77-77-80—308
4	Mitzi Edge	Augusta, Ga.	78-78-77-77—310
5	Lori Clark	De Moines, Iowa	78-77-78-78—311
6	Lori Castillo	Honolulu, Hawaii	75-80-78-80—313
7	Penny Hammel	Decatur, Ill.	75-80-81-80—316
8	Rae Rothfelder	Ft. Worth, Texas	76-80-79-82—317
T-9	Linda Brown	Bartlesville, Okla.	85-77-80-78—320
T-9	Sharon Barrett	Spring Valley, Calif.	83-78-73-86—320
11	Kristy Monaghan	Los Alamos, N.M.	79-80-78-84—321
12	Lynda Wimberly	Brentwood, Tenn.	75-79-85-86—325
13	Kathy Baker	Clover, S.C.	82-81-87-76—326
14	Beverly Boozer	Lawrence, Kan.	87-80-80-80—327
T-15	Michelle Jordan	Fairfax, Va.	85-80-85-79—329
T-15	Paula Slivinsky	Brewster, N.Y.	80-80-86-83—329
17	Denise Hermida	Brandon, Fla.	83-81-82-84—330
18	Mary Wilkinson	Melrose, Mass.	84-82-83-82—331
19	Jill Nesbitt	Berwyn, Pa.	85-85-81-82—333
20	Dana Howe	Colorado Springs, Colo.	88-81-84-82—335
21	Judy Shock	Columbus, Ohio	84-87-83-82—336
22	Patty Abel	Lake Oswego, Ore.	86-80-80-92—338
23	Cindy Figg	Mt. Pleasant, Mich.	87-88-83-83—341
T-24	Kathleen Lawrence	Canton, N.Y.	84-87-94-77—342
T-24	Kellie Carl	Webb, Miss.	79-85-89-89—342
T-26	Denise Lyle	Fern Creek, Ky.	88-83-85-87—343
T-26	Patricia Jordan	Eden, N.Y.	80-92-88-83—343
28	Mary Corrigan	Amsterdam, N.Y.	81-90-89-88—348
29	Alison Sellers	Quincy, Ill.	89-82-90-89—350
30	Susan Moline	Duluth, Minn.	88-91-87-86—352
31	Teri Granger	Anderson, Ind.	87-90-90-86—353
32	Lynn Connelly	Westport, Conn.	86-92-85-91—354
33	Kim Kelly	Birmington, Ala.	84-92-94-91—361
34	Cathleen Hackett	Toledo, Ohio	88-93-93-88—362
35	Mary Sue Hergert	Lincoln, Neb.	92-96-94-88—370
36	Kari Bridge	Hollister, Calif.	94-97-89-101—381
37	Ginger Zimmerman	Winneconne, Wis.	94-91-98-103—386
	Debbie Tatz	Scotch Plains, N.J.	96-98-106-300—WD
	Regina Piatt	Washington, Pa.	95-98-183—WD

12-14 DIVISION - MAGNOLIA COURSE

1	Lise Anne Russell	New City, N.Y.	83-81-83-82—329
2	Denise King	Miami, Fla.	83-81-84-83—331
3	Susie Ashdown	Medford, Ore.	87-84-85-82—338
4	Adele Lukken	Tulsa, Okla.	81-83-83-92—339
T-5	Holley Morris	Golden, Colo.	85-79-91-85—340
T-5	Heather Farr	Phoenix, Ariz.	82-87-85-86—340
7	Lori Brock	Dallas, Texas	80-85-91-87—343
8	Susan Thompson	Garden Grove, Calif.	91-84-91-85—351
9	Jody Rosenthal	Minneapolis, Minn.	93-84-87-90—354
10	Nancy Brown	Salinas, Calif.	100-79-88-93—360
11	Laurie Haight	Waterloo, Iowa	92-86-91-94—363
T-12	Diane Gioia	St. Louis, Mo.	92-87-95-91—365
T-12	Jodi Logan	Sandusky, Ohio	89-99-90-87—365
T-14	Andre Marchand	Luling, La.	92-85-94-97—368
T-14	Deb Richard	Manhattan, Kan.	95-90-87-96—368
T-16	Linda Bamber	Cincinnati, Ohio	93-93-89-95—370
T-16	Lei Kaniaupio	Kaneohe, Hawaii	96-92-92-90—370
18	Kristine Kamal	Keene, N.H.	87-94-98-95—374
19	Beth Ehlert	Austin, Texas	99-92-92-94—377
20	Lannie Gerken	Watertown, N.Y.	92-100-95-94—381
21	Margaret Shaffer	Alexander City, Ala.	95-97-90-105—387
22	Karin Romberg	Tullahoma, Tenn.	94-98-92-104—388
23	Tina Bruce	Corbin, Ky.	103-99-96-96—394
24	Libby Akers	French Lick, Ind.	108-98-96-96—398
25	Marcia Pekar	Wausau, Wis.	100-98-99-102—399
26	Susan White	Morehead City, N.C.	101-101-102-96—400
27	Kathy Hart	Orchard Park, N.Y.	93-103-103-103—402
28	Valerie Faulkner	Jackson, N.J.	01-98-106-99—404
T-29	Kathleen Bannister	Greensville, Va.	101-109-95-100—405
T-29	Marcy Richman	Las Vegas, Nev.	98-100-109-98—405
31	Vickie Moran	Fairmont, W.V.	97-97-108-106—408
32	Mary Jo Ferlmann	Peoria, Ill.	104-103-100-103—410
33	Michele Bonner	Morristown, Pa.	111-106-98-108—423
34	Cara Andreoli	Wethersfield, Conn.	109-100-110-110—429
35	Jennifer Huxford	Sioux City, Iowa	107-109-109-117—442
36	Randi Paporello	Mt. Pleasant, Mich.	120-113-113-115—461
37	Becky Christiansen	Socorro, N.M.	115-129-126-120—490
	Kathe Kingston	East Point, Ga.	82-89-171—WD

PGA JUNIOR CHAMPIONSHIP

1976

The inaugural PGA Junior Championship was considered an overwhelming success when 78 boys and girls finished play on Walt Disney World Golf Resort's Magnolia Course in Orlando, Fla. Larry Field of Oklahoma City, Okla., and Nancy Rubin of New Kensington, Pa., won the right to be called the first PGA Junior champions. Riding a final-round 71, Field edged Ricky Smallridge of Columbus, Ga., by one stroke for the boys' title and Rubin slipped past Michelle Jordan of Fairfax, Va., by a stroke in the girls' division.

Champion:	(Boys) Larry Field, Oklahoma City, Okla.
Champion:	(Girls) Nancy Rubin, New Kensington, Pa.
Site:	Walt Disney World Golf Resort,
	(Magnolia Course), Orlando, Fla.
Date: Aug. 16-20	Par: 72

Boys' Division

1	Larry Field	Oklahoma City, Okla.	76-72-78-71—297
2	Ricky Smallridge	Columbus, Ga.	77-71-75-75—298
3	John Cummings	Encino, Calif.	73-73-78-75—299
4	Richard Barger	Louisville, Ky.	73-75-76-76—300
T-5	Scott Baum	Camillus, N.Y.	70-77-75-80—302
T-5	John Pallott	Coral Gables, Fla.	73-74-78-77—302
T-5	Timothy Hirt	Clyde, Ohio	74-77-75-76—302
	(Baum won playoff for 5th with birdie at 1st hole)		
8	Hugh Vaughn III	Hershey, Pa.	74-72-80-77—303
9	John Given	Carmi, Ill.	75-78-74-77—304
10	Bill Kresse	Milwaukee, Wis.	71-78-79-78—306
11	Jeff Duncan	Bristol, Conn.	78-72-82-76—308
12	Kent Stauffer	Bradford, Pa.	80-76-76-77—309
T-11	Scott Myers	Monroe, La.	78-76-75-82—311
T-11	James Stuart	Duluth, Minn.	78-76-76-81—311
T-11	Rip Vaughn	Lake Montezuma, Ariz.	79-76-76-80—311
14	Scott Campbell	Orchard Lake, Mich.	77-78-83-76—314
T-15	Mark Sivara	Tacoma, Wash.	79-79-77-80—315
T-15	Bob Black Jr.	Kailua, Hawaii	78-81-77-79—315
T-17	Jay Kent	Corpus Christi, Texas	79-75-81-81—316
T-17	Mark Hill	Carlsbad, N.M.	79-80-81-76—316
T-17	Bobby Clark Jr.	Copper Hill, Va.	81-76-82-77—316
T-20	David Bonham	Springfield, Mo.	81-81-75-82—319
T-20	Mark Harris	Montgomery, Ala.	80-74-86-79—319
T-20	Larry Penley	Dallas, N.C.	78-81-81-79—319
T-20	Greg Allio	Danville, Calif.	79-78-80-83—320
24	John Fisher	Indianapolis, Ind.	77-85-81-78—321
25	Dale Vietmeier	Pittsburgh, Pa.	75-78-83-87—323
T-26	James McCarthy	Princeton, N.J.	81-84-79-81—325
T-26	Randy Beil	Pt. Washington, N.Y.	78-86-82-79—325
T-26	Tracy Wilkins	Nashville, Tenn.	88-83-78-76—325
T-26	Richard Gair	Scotia, N.Y.	84-80-85-76—325
30	Pat Quinn	Wilmette, Ill.	77-80-81-88—326
T-31	Dow Finsterwald Jr.	Colo. Springs, Colo.	83-77-82-86—328
T-31	Steve Gaer	W. Des Moines, Iowa	83-83-79-83—328
33	Doug Malcuit	Dallas, Texas	80-81-86-82—329
34	Mark Starkweather	Billings, Mont.	87-79-82-83—331
T-35	Chuck Tidman	Auburn, Mass.	85-81-86-84—336
T-35	Bill Smith	Zanesville, Ohio	79-87-88-82—336
37	Dean Wilson	Omaha, Neb.	82-84-88-86—340

Girls' Division

1	Nancy Rubin	New Kensington, Pa.	83-77-82-78—320
2	Michelle Jordan	Fairfax, Va.	79-81-81-80—321
T-3	Althea Tome	Honolulu, Hawaii	85-76-80-82—323
T-3	Cathy Curry	Columbus, Neb.	79-81-77-86—323
T-3	Patty Pichon	Aurora, Colo.	84-75-87-77—323
	(Tome won playoff for third place)		
T-6	Debbie Hall	Corpus Christi, Texas	74-89-81-83—327
T-6	Betsy Barrett	Syracuse, N.Y.	78-85-81-83—327
T-6	Debbie Hoffman	Wellesley, Mass.	81-82-83-81—327
T-6	Lulong Hartley	Oceanside, Calif.	81-85-79-82—327
T-6	Vicki Coker	Montgomery, Ala.	81-82-83-81—327
T-6	Deanie Wood	Lake Charles, La.	81-79-85-82—327
12	Mitzie Edge	Augusta, Ga.	81-85-81-81—328
T-13	Alicia Ogrin	Waukegan, Ill.	82-90-81-80—333
T-13	Charlotte Grant	Lookout Mt., Tenn.	84-84-86-79—333
15	Rosie Jones	Girard, Ohio	81-83-87-84—335
T-16	Janice Burba	Tulsa, Okla.	90-80-87-80—337
T-16	Nancy Peck	Eugene, Ore.	83-80-88-86—337
18	Lea Ann Duke	Tallahassee, Fla.	85-86-86-81—338
19	Lynn Stroney	Girard, Ohio	84-87-85-83—339
T-20	Paula Silvindky	Brewster, N.Y.	84-81-95-84—344
T-20	Genevieve Huvendick	Lansing, Mich.	86-83-89-86—344
22	Susan Stehling	Mequon, Wis.	85-83-93-84—345
23	Cathy Graham	Grosse Pt., Mich.	88-77-92-89—346
24	Lynn Marriott	Herkimer, N.Y.	82-91-90-84—347
25	Tanya Taylor	Tempe, Ariz.	85-90-86-84—350
T-26	Lori Clark	Des Moines, Iowa	82-84-97-88—351
T-26	Cynthia Pietrusik	Lackawanna, N.Y.	90-81-88-92—351
28	Mary Enright	San Leandro, Calif.	87-89-90-86—352
29	Mamie McClure	Ft. Wayne, Ind.	89-84-88-93—354
T-30	Peggy Freeman	Louisville, Ky.	90-78-89-100—357
T-30	Elizabeth Wood	Sea Girt, N.J.	90-89-89-89—357
32	Tracey Leinbach	Whitfield, Pa.	87-89-92-92—360
33	Rochelle Gumlia	Edina, Minn.	88-92-92-92—364
34	Patti McGowan	Roebuck, S.C.	93-96-88-89—366
T-35	Shelly Babb	Litchfield, Ill.	88-97-89-93—367
T-35	Kathy Studer	Billings, Mont.	91-92-95-89—367
37	Tina Foxhall	Memphis, Tenn.	90-99-97-88—374
38	Pam Ross	Westport, Conn.	97-98-107-94—396
39	Karen Aured	Worthington, Ohio	94-105-106-109—414

■ PGA JUNIOR CHAMPIONSHIP RECORDS

BOYS

■ **Lowest 18 Holes**
- 63   Pat Perez, San Diego, Calif. (1993)
-      Chris Couch, North Lauderdale, Fla. (1990)

■ **Lowest First Round**
- 67   Michael Henderson, Raleigh, N.C. (1993)

■ **Lowest Second Round**
- 65   Robert Floyd, Miami Beach, Fla. (1993)
-      Billy Andrade, Bristol, R.I. (1981)

■ **Lowest Third Round**
- 63   Pat Perez, San Diego, Calif. (1993)

■ **Lowest Fourth Round**
- 63   Chris Couch, North Lauderdale, Fla. (1990)

■ **Lowest 36 Holes**
- 137   Billy Andrade, Bristol, R.I. (1981)

■ **Lowest 54 Holes**
- 202   Pat Perez, San Diego, Calif. (1993)

■ **Lowest 72 Holes**
- 271   Pat Perez, San Diego, Calif. (1993)

■ **Widest Margin Of Victory**
- 10   Chris Couch, North Lauderdale, Fla. (1990)

GIRLS

■ **Lowest 18 Holes**
- 65   Erika Hayashida, Lima, Peru (1993)
-      Vicki Goetze, Hull, Ga. (1990)

■ **Lowest First Round**
- 70   Adele Moore, Dallas, Texas (1986)
-      Tracy Nakamura, Monterey Park, Calif. (1986)
-      Brandie Burton, Rialto, Calif. (1988)

■ **Lowest Second Round**
- 65   Vicki Goetze, Hull, Ga. (1990)

■ **Lowest Third Round**
- 67   Vicki Goetze, Hull, Ga. (1990)

■ **Lowest Fourth Round**
- 65   Erika Hayashida, Lima, Peru (1993)

■ **Lowest 36 Holes**
- 136   Vicki Goetze, Hull, Ga. (1990)

■ **Lowest 54 Holes**
- 203   Vicki Goetze, Hull, Ga. (1990)

■ **Lowest 72 Holes**
- 278   Vicki Goetze, Hull, Ga. (1990)

■ **Widest Margin Of Victory**
- 13   Debbie Hall, Corpus Christi, Texas (1977)

NATIONAL OLDSMOBILE SCRAMBLE CHAMPIONSHIP

1994 FACTS AND FORMAT

DATES: Sept. 29 - Oct. 3, 1994

SITE: Walt Disney World Golf Resort, Lake Buena Vista, Fla.

NET AND GROSS DIVISIONS: Run simultaneously

GROSS DIVISION DEFENDING CHAMPION:
PGA West, La Quinta, Calif.

NET DIVISION DEFENDING CHAMPION:
Valleywood Golf Club, Swanton, Ohio

PRIZE MONEY AND AWARDS

A minimum of $150,000 will be distributed to the teams participating in each division. The winning PGA club professional will receive a minimum of $15,000 or a 1994 Oldsmobile. The winning tour professional receives $15,000 or a 1994 Oldsmobile Achieva.

METHOD OF PLAY

Each PGA section conducts qualifying at nearly 2,500 local sites at club and section levels. The number of teams each section may send to the national finals is proportional to the number that attempt to qualify. Each team is comprised of a professional and four amateurs. After three rounds, each of the 24 lowest scoring teams is joined by a PGA Tour professional for the final round.

RULES AND REGULATIONS

The Rules of Golf which govern play are determined by the United States Golf Association and applied by the PGA of America Board of Directors. The Championship is subject to overall supervision of the board and the PGA Rules Committee.

ELIGIBILITY

The professional on each team may be either a PGA member or a registered apprentice. Each team must be formed according to the Oldsmobile Scramble Handicap system. The team may use only one player with a USGA handicap index of 8.3 or less.

HISTORY

The Oldsmobile Scramble, the world's largest golf tournament, anticipates its one millionth participant this year. In the previous decade, more than 970,000 golfers have competed. The largest pro-amateur event conducted by the PGA of America, the Scramble attracted more than 130,000 competitors in 1993.

PGA Tour professional Fred Couples tapped in a one-foot putt in 1984 to help Little Turtle Country Club of Westerville, Ohio, win the inaugural Championship. The Gross Division Championship drew 19,000 entries that year, offering a total purse of $100,000. The Championship culminated in 53 teams earning a final berth at Walt Disney World Golf Resort. In 1989, a net division was added to allow higher handicap players the opportunity to play in the highly competitive tournament. Grand Cypress of Orlando, Fla., was the first net division champion. The Championship has been played at three sites: Walt Disney World Golf Resort in Lake Buena Vista, Fla.; The Woodlands, Texas; and Grand Cypress Resort, Orlando, Fla. For the third consecutive year, both the net and gross division finals will be held the same week at Walt Disney World Golf Resort. The field will once again include 150 teams in each division, or a total of 300 five-player teams competing in the finals. The 1993 Oldsmobile Scramble's nationwide purse — including prizes, tee gifts, sponsor amenities and entertainment — was $8 million.

■ HISTORY THROUGH THE YEARS

NET DIVISION

Year	Winner	Score	Runners-up	Site
1989	Fox Bend GC, Oswego, Ill.	206	Riceland CC, Orrville, Ohio	Grand Cypress Resort, Orlando, Fla.
1990	Shady Valley GC, Arlington, Texas	164	Columbia Lakes (Texas) CC, Columbia	Walt Disney World GR, Lake Buena Vista, Fla.
1991	Lochmoor CC, N. Fort Myers, Fla	210	Santa Rosa (Calif.) G & CC, Santa Rosa	Walt Disney World GR, Lake Buena Vista, Fla..
1992	Karsten GC, Tempe, Ariz.	153	Oak Meadows GC, Addison, Ill.	Walt Disney World GR, Lake Buena Vista, Fla.
1993	Valleywood GC, Swanton, Ohio	214	The Oregon GC, West Linn, Ore.	Walt Disney World GR, Lake Buena Vista, Fla.

GROSS DIVISION

Year	Winner	Score	Runners-up	Site
1984	Little Turtle CC, Westerville, Ohio	174	Montgomery (Ala.) CC	Walt Disney World GR, Lake Buena Vista, Fla.
1985	Buena Vista CC, Taft, Calif.	57	Kalamazoo (Mich.) CC	TPC at The Woodlands, The Woodlands, Texas
1986	Hickory Hills GC, Grove City, Ohio	224	Plantation GR, Crystal River, Fla.	Walt Disncy World GR, Lake Buena Vista, Fla.
1987	Sun Air CC, Haines City, Fla.	165	Lochinvar GC, Houston, Texas	Walt Disney World GR, Lake Buena Vista, Fla.
1988	Fox Bend GC, Oswego, Ill.	224	Palm Valley CC, Palm Desert, Calif.	Walt Disney World GR, Lake Buena Vista, Fla.
1989	TPC at The Woodlands, The Woodlands, Texas	224	Bainesberry GC, White Pine, Tenn.	Walt Disney World GR, Lake Buena Vista, Fla.
1990	Walt Disney World GC, Lake Buena Vista, Fla.	224	Tomball (Texas) CC, Tomball	Walt Disney World GR, Lake Buena Vista, Fla.
1991	Aquia Harbour CC, Stafford, Virginia	226	Links O'Tryon, Campobello, S.C.	Walt Disney World GR, Lake Buena Vista, Fla.
1992	Jaycee Golf Club, Chillicothe, Ohio	220	Walpole GC, Walpole, Mass.	Walt Disney World GR, Lake Buena Vista, Fla.
1993	PGA West, La Quinta, Calif.	218	Pompano Beach (Fla.) CC	Walt Disney World GR, Lake Buena Vista, Fla.

1993 PGA West of La Quinta, Calif., and Valley-wood Golf Club of Swanton, Ohio, took different but potent routes to the respective Gross and Net Division Championships in the 10th annual Oldsmobile Scramble National Championship played for the first time on six courses — four at Walt Disney World Resort. A field of 296 teams from a nationwide qualifying entry list of 130,000 competed for 20 berths in each division. PGA West's Sue Gilstrap of La Quinta, Calif., became the first woman in tournament history to play on a Championship team. PGA West, guided by PGA professional John O'Neill, finished with a record 72-hole total of 70-under-par 218 to win the gross division by four strokes over Pompano Beach (Fla.) Country Club. The gross division concluded play on the Magnolia Course.

Date:	Sept. 30 - Oct. 4
Site:	Walt Disney World Golf Resort, Lake Buena Vista, Fla.
	Eagle Pines, Magnolia, Lake Buena Vista, Palm Courses
	Falcon's Fire Country Club, Metro West Golf Club,
	Orlando, Fla.

Valleywood Golf Club finished its 72 holes at 74-under-par 214, a stroke lower than third-round leader The Oregon Golf Club of West Linn, Ore. Jack Zeiler provided the crucial stroke for Valleywood, knocking home a 30-foot birdie putt on the par-3, 190-yard 15th hole at Eagles Pines Golf Course. Zeiler was the last member of his team to attempt the birdie putt. There were six holes-in-one recorded during the Championships, including three by amateurs.

NET DIVISION SUMMARY

214—56-56-51-51 — Valleywood GC, Swanton, Ohio: TP: Bill Britton ($4,333), CP: Mike Thompson ($15,000), Hugh Snyder, Drew McNeill, Mark Heintschel, John Zeiler.

215—52-54-54-55 — The Oregon GC, West Linn, Ore.: TP: Phil Blackmar ($1,250), CP: Pat Fitzsimons ($7,500), Brent Summers, Charles Powers, Jack Frost, Mike Burke.

217—56-56-55-50 — Commonwealth National CC, Horsham, Pa.: TP: Greg Kraft ($7,500), CP: David Craig ($5,000), Rich Davoli, Simon Paek, Jim Veghte, Mike Michaels.

218—56-54-58-50 — Pines of Grandview Lodge, Nisswa, Minn.: TP: Jim Hallet ($15,000), CP: Kevin Cashman ($2,167), Fred Boos, Carolyn Boos, Steve Stoxen, Tom Kientzle.

218—56-56-55-51 — Shaker Run GC, Lebanon, Ohio: TP: Dan Pohl ($3,333), CP: Sean Arthur ($2,167), Dana Martino, Wes Plummer, Doug Dunham, Jeff Slyman.

218—57-56-54-51 — Wentworth GC, Tarpon Springs, Fla.: TP: P.H. Horgan III ($3,333), CP: David Stokely ($2,167), Will Florin, Jay Parsons, Richard Martorell, John Cerutti.

219—57-56-54-52 — Monticello, Browns Summit, N.C.: TP: Brad Fabel ($1,500), CP: Bob Groff ($1,500), Randy Jones, Travis Jones, Joey Sizemore, Tommy Sizemore.

220—55-54-56-55 — Bay City CC, Bay City, Texas: TP: John Inman ($1,250), CP: Neil Arbuckle ($1,500), Randy Fife, Jimmy Greenawalt, Beverly Greenawalt, Tina Arlitt.

220—55-54-56-55 — Park Meadows GC, Park City, Utah: TP: Jay Delsing ($1,250), CP: Tim Fernau ($1,500), Kerry Gambles, Tony Miles, Chris Colohan, Ron Robinson.

220—54-59-54-53 — Short Hills CC, East Moline, Ill.: TP: Bruce Fleisher ($1,500), CP: Chip Staebell ($1,500), Jeff Scott, John Williams, Herman Ackley, Dan Sweeney.

221—58-56-54-53 — Bent Creek GC, Eden Prairie, Minn.: TP: Dick Mast ($1,500), CP: Terry Simon ($1,250), Steve Nordling, Lary Ardito, Ron Schultz, Tom Kielty.

221—58-58-51-54 — Eagles Landing CC, Stockbridge, Ga.: TP: David Rummells ($1,500), CP: Kerry Gaillard ($1,250), Reid Bowman, Fred Rice, Chris Roper, Jody Saylor-Smith.

222—56-57-56-53 — Carmel Highland Resort, San Diego, Calif.: TP: John Mahaffey ($1,500), CP: Allen Balone ($1,250), Bryan Kueler, John Fecko, Earl Cole, Tim Shinkle.

224—58-55-56-55 — Jeffersonville Elks GC, Jeffersonville, Ind.: TP: Ed Fiori ($1,250), CP: Clyde Hill ($1,167), Cliff York, Bill Tucker, Ken McGee, Jacy Bowyer.

224—56-54-58-56 — Pine Knolls GC, Kernersville, N.C.: TP: Scott Gump ($1,000), CP: David Hardison ($1,167), Michael Kindley, Manley Kindley, Craig Turner, Gary Hastings.

224—56-58-55-55 — Scherwood GC, Schererville, Ind.: TP: Bart Bryant ($1,250), CP: Marv Hanson ($1,167), Jay Strauch, Bill Winters, Paul Strauch, Dale Winters.

225—60-55-54-56 — Eaton CC, Eaton, Colo.: TP: Denis Watson ($1,000), CP: Rick Cole ($1,000), Roger Naomi, Orv Herring, Dan Clark, Jim Baggot.

225—55-57-56-57 — Thunder Hills CC, Peosta, Iowa: TP: Jaime Gomez ($1,000), CP: Tom McCann ($1,000), Dave O'Hea, Ken Erickson, Scott Zartman, Jim Ihm.

227—58-55-56-58 — El Dorado GC, Mason, Mich.: TP: Robert Gamez ($1,000), CP: Rick Couturier ($1,000), Doug Bournay, Dean Bournay, Cary Potter, Dan Bournay.

227—57-55-56-59 — Gainey Ranch GC, Scottsdale, Ariz.: TP: Ted Schulz ($1,000), CP: Mike Franko ($1,000), Bob Cornell, Randy Finefrock, Tom Stephen, Jim Matrician.

TP: PGA Tour Professional
CP: PGA Club Professional

GROSS DIVISION SUMMARY

218—54-56-54-54 — PGA West, La Quinta, Calif.: TP: Tommy Armour III ($6,000), CP: John O'Neill ($15,000), John Test, Chuck Shubin, Jim Gilstrap, Sue Gilstrap.

222—59-56-55-52 — Pompano Beach CC, Pompano Beach, Fla.: TP: Brad Bryant ($7,500), CP: Bob MacMillan ($7,500), Raymond Ferri, Steve Schmidt, Jim Roper, Ed Palat.

226—55-58-56-57 — Baywood CC, Pasadena, Texas: TP: Donnie Hammond ($1,393), CP: Ken Kelley ($4,000), Steve Runnels, Elton Blanchard, Donnie Brogna, Bobby Gilbert.

226—59-58-57-52 — Wedgewood G & CC, Powell, Ohio: TP: Len Mattiace ($15,000), CP: Bruce Soulsby ($4,000), Denny Allent, Billy Knox, Tony Weiher, Jim Ullman.

227—59-54-57-57 — Crawfordsville GC, Crawfordsville, Ind.: TP: Steve Lamontagne ($1,393), CP: Cary Hungate ($2,000), Jim Ray, Brian Holt, Rusty Blankenship, Terry Guyer.

228—59-56-57-56 — Quail Hollow Resort, Painesville, Ohio: TP: Jay Don Blake ($1,500), CP: Tony Milam ($1,500), Al Kovar, Walt Kado, Jim Aschbacher, Mark Shane.

230—60-56-59-55 — Jaycee GC, Chillicothe, Ohio: TP: Robert Lohr ($2,500), CP: Phil Adkins ($1,500), Rusty Saunders, Tommy Meadows, Bill Traylor, Charlie Hudson.

231—59-59-58-55 — Hidden Valley CC, Salem, Va.: TP: Loren Roberts ($2,500), CP: Tim Holbrook ($1,500), Mike Brammer, Richie Richardson, Rick Ives, Greg Fry.

231—58-57-59-57 — Killeen Municipal GC, Killeen, Texas: TP: Ed Humenik ($1,393), CP: Greg Antunes ($1,500), Mike Gonyea, Robert Liberty, Derek Young, Brian Hoenig.

231—56-58-60-57 — Shoal Creek GC, Shoal Creek, Ala.: TP: Kirk Triplett ($1,393), CP: Peter Just ($1,500), John Morris, Dewey Hammond, Scot Cardwell, Greg Smith.

232—56-58-59-59 — GC of Cypress Head, Port Orange, Fla.: TP: Jim Woodward ($1,000), CP: Joe Gutterman ($1,250), Ron Kroll, Melissa Kroll, Richard Wendt, Ron Kroll.

233—60-60-55-58 — Darlington CC, Darlington, S.C.: TP: David Ogrin ($1,250), CP: Phil Bland ($1,250), Mitch Mims, Mark Willis, John Schurlknight, Tommy Simmons.

233—60-57-59-57 — Southview CC, West St. Paul, Minn.: TP: Tom Lehman ($1,393), CP: Tom Dolby ($1,250), Skip Wright, Dennis Pulanco, Larry Strom, Jae Turunen.

234—59-57-60-58 — Metropolitan Club, Lithonia, Ga.: TP: Ed Dougherty ($1,250), CP: Patrick Kelley ($1,100), Jim Gaddy, Bob Keppner, Charles Perry Sr., Sid Sellars.

234—57-60-58-59 — Mystery Valley GC, Lithonia, Ga.: TP: Larry Rinker ($1,000), CP: David Nelson ($1,100), Pat Burnette, Keith Fitzgerald, Brent McCurdy, Ron Samples.

234—58-61-58-57 — Oak Cliff CC, Dallas, Texas: TP: David Jackson ($1,393), CP: Russell Orth ($1,100), Terry Olson, Ed Bates, Jim Smith, Jack Barber.

234—61-58-56-59 — Pinecrest CC, Huntley, Ill.: TP: John Adams ($1,000), CP: Mike Yackle ($1,100), Darren Stanek, Kevin Stanek, Tom Brown, Brad Legnioli.

234—57-59-61-57 — Woodmere Club, Woodmere, N.Y.: TP: Mike Standly ($1,393), CP: Ed Burke Jr. ($1,100), Stephen Rose, Richard Gershman, Richard Schlanger, Steve Schumancher.

235—61-57-55-62 — Willow Creek GC, High Point, N.C.: TP: Mark Carneval ($1,000), CP: Jim Brotherton ($1,000), Tom Lindh, Will Gurley, Walt Lancaster, Darrin Morgan.

237—58-60-59-60 — Port Huron Elks CC, Port Huron, Mich.: TP: Lance Ten Broeck ($1,000), CP: Dan Thomas ($1,000), Fred Franzel, Len Fedon, Carol Ozog, Tom Murphy.

TP: PGA Tour Professional
CP: PGA Club Professional

1992

Jaycee Golf Course of Chillicothe, Ohio, entering the final round at Osprey Ridge with a three-stroke lead in the gross division, pushed the advantage to four strokes after 16 holes to go on to a new division 72-hole record 68-under-par 220. Walpole (Mass.) Country Club was runner-up. Jaycee's team was led by PGA club professional Phil Adkins and Tour professional Donnie Hammond. All 20 finalist teams completed the semifinals before rain pelted the Eagle Pines Course. Eight teams chipped off for two final berths.

Date: Oct. 8-12

Site: Walt Disney World Golf Resort, Lake Buena Vista, Fla.
Eagle Pines, Osprey Ridge, Palm, Magnolia Courses

Rain forced the cancellation of the 40-team net division semifinals at Walt Disney World Golf Resort's Magnolia Course. The top 20 teams to earn a final berth were determined by their 36-hole totals. There were seven teams tied for the final five spots, forcing a chip-off at Pete Dye's Eagle Pines Course. Karsten Golf Club of Tempe, Ariz., assisted by Tour professional Brad Bryant, registered a 54-hole total of 53-52-48—153, an eight-stroke margin over Oak Meadows Golf Club in Addison, Ill. Karsten's record-setting team built a four-stroke lead after 36 holes, putting on a torrid performance by collecting 16 birdies and two eagles. "I've never seen a Scramble team play this well," said Bryant, a three-year veteran of the Oldsmobile Scramble. "There were some par-3s where we had five balls on the green. On our first par-5, we had two potential putts for eagle. That's very unusual for a scramble. And we had only four putts outside of 15 feet. It was just phenomenal."

NET DIVISION SUMMARY

153—53-52-48 — Karsten GC. Tempe, Ariz.: TP: Brad Bryant ($15,000), CP: Tim Smith ($15,000), Jim Sosinski, Frank Sosinski, Paul Waddell, Roy Waddell.

161—55-56-50 — Oak Meadows GC, Addison, Ill.: TP: Mike Sullivan ($7,500), CP: Mike Buros ($7,500), Rick Tijerina, Steve Krause, Jay Whitehead, Robert Murphy.

163—55-57-51 — Cotton Creek GC, Spartanburg, S.C.: TP: Scott Gump ($4,000), CP: Skip Corn Jr. ($4,000), Bruce Thompson, Dave Thompson, Bruce Thompson Jr., Gene Westmore.

163—55-54-54 — Fig Garden GC, Fresno, Calif.: TP: Phil Blackmar ($1,312.50), CP: Randy Norvelle ($4,000), Jeff Gorman, Jim Wampler, Bob Adams, Rick Carvalho.

164—57-54-53 — Kokomo American Legion, Kokomo, Ind.: TP: Ted Schultz ($1,500), CP: Cary Hungate ($1,750), Jack Kaufman, Don Zimmerman, Wayne Rutherford, Ed Hinkle.

164—56-57-51 — Wellshire GC, Denver, Colo.: TP: Ed Fiori ($4,000), CP: Scot Hart ($1,750), Ted Tulper, Pete Hall, Tony Duca, Joe Duca.

165—58-55-52 — Pinewood CC, Slidell, La.: TP: Keith Clearwater ($2,000), CP: James Leitz ($1,500), Kerry LaPlace, Skip Bourgeois, Bobby Taylor, Paul Gravolet.

165—55-57-53 — Raintree GR, Pembroke Pines, Fla.: TP: Bill Britton ($1,500), CP: Ron Baker ($1,500), Tim Reddel, Mark Sidebottom, Larry Metter, Kirk Brown.

165—55-55-55 — Stony Ford GC, Montgomery, N.Y.: TP: Dave Barr ($1,166.67), CP: Mark Yonke ($1,500), John Rubeo, Peter Rubeo Jr., Joe Luzzi, John Stelluti.

165—53-56-56 — Walden On Lake Houston, Humble, Texas: TP: Bob Lohr ($1,000), CP: John Ankenbrandt ($1,500), Randall Orr, Russell Van Alstine, Fred Kevin, Jim Lund.

166—57-54-55 — Bent Oak GC, Titusville, Fla. : TP: Stan Utley ($1,166.67), CP: Bob Carson ($1,250), Dr. Ben Storey, Dr. Mark Storey, David Muldowney, Scott Gray.

166—55-57-54 — Faribault G & CC, Faribault, Minn. TP: Calvin Peete ($1,312.50), CP: Mike Lucknaft ($1,250), Larry Harn, Pat Hunt, Don Behrens, Gordy Hunt.

166—56-57-53 — Mission Hills CC, Rancho Mirage, Calif.: TP: Chris Perry ($1,500), CP: Joe Edwards ($1,250), John Brugger, Jeff Rodd, Michael Ryan, Murray Hickman.

166— Pleasant Hills GC, Mount Pleasant, Mich.: TP: Robert Gamez ($1,500), CP: Fred Schneller ($1,250), Charlie Clark, Dale Jennings, Bill Morrison, Greg Fogle.

166—57-55-54 — Walt Disney World GC, Lake Buena Vista, Fla. : TP: Wayne Levi ($1,312.50), CP: Eric Fredricksen ($1,250), Doug Wharton, Darryl Bozeman, Mike Fass, David Layman.

167—57-56-54 — Cut Bank CC, Cutbank, Mont.: TP: Brian Claar ($1,312.50), CP: Brad Forbis ($1,000), Steve Williamson, Jim DeKaye, John Kays, Jack Ohmart.

167—58-54-55 — Nemadji GC, Superior, Wis.: TP: Kenny Knox ($1,166.66), CP: Kyle Anderson ($1,000), Don Leighton, Steve Nelson, Gary Sorenson, Bob Blake.

167—54-57-56 — Pecan Grove CC, Richmond, Texas : TP: Bruce Fleisher ($1,000), CP: Matt Jones ($1,000), Rick Nussle, Dale Jefferson, Tim Tully, Barry Peterson.

168—52-59-57 — Burlington CC, Mt. Holly, N.J.: TP: Robert Wrenn ($1,000), CP: Michael Mack ($1,000), Dan Kirk, Bob Price, Bill Mann, Bob Lovendesky.

168—54-58-56 — Huron CC, Huron, S.D.: TP: Dave Rummells ($1,000), CP: Dave Kluver ($1,000), Merle Lewis, Greg Shallbetter, Jeff Shallbetter, Mark Belyea.

TP: PGA Tour Professional
CP: PGA Club Professional

GROSS DIVISION SUMMARY

220—56-57-52-55 — Jaycee Golf Course, Chillicothe, Ohio: TP: Donnie Hammond ($2,250), CP: Phil Adkins ($15,000), Rusty Saunders, Tommy Meadows, John Davis, Randy Finney.

222—55-56-57-54 — Walpole CC, Walpole, Mass.: TP: Billy Mayfair ($1,583.33), CP: Tom Giffin ($7,500), Chris Vinci, Mark Dalton, Dan DeVir, Harry Partain.

223—56-58-56-53 — Riveredge CC, Marshfield, Wis.: TP: Jim Hallet ($15,000), CP: Doug Sheldon ($4,000), Jon Higley, Ron Johnson, Roger Johnson, Jeff Langer.

223—59-55-54-55 — The Oak Club of Genoa, Genoa, Ill.: TP: Mike Donald ($1,250), CP: Fred Hancock ($4,000), Robert Parsek, Maurice Kehoe, Richard Peterson, Roger Reardon.

224—58-57-56-53 — Apple Creek CC, Bismarck, N.D.: TP: Ed Humenik ($5,166.67), CP: Quinn Griffing ($1,600), Seth Raulston, Jim Harris, Brian Mayer, Dave Alveson.

224—56-57-57-54 — Hyatt Bear Creek GC, DFW Airport, Texas: TP: Dan Halldorson ($1,583.33), CP: Greg Garcia ($1,600), Mike Unsell, Sherill Crumpton, James Thompson, Ron Simons.

224—57-56-58-53 — River Oaks GC, Pace, Fla.: TP: Dan Forsman ($5,166.67), CP: Ricky Beck ($1,600), Buddy Lee, John Hughes, Kristine Doty, Joe Bates.

224—56-58-56-54 — Royal Oak Resort, Titusville, Fla.: TP: Peter Persons ($1,583.33), CP: Brant Craddock ($1,600), Fred Kodesch, Lee Murrah, Bascom Murrah, Andy Kurczewski.

224—57-56-56-55 — Whitewater Creek CC, Fayetteville, Ga.: TP: Fulton Allem ($1,250), CP: Ted Meier ($1,600), Jiim Witmer, Lew Dickson, Carl Ryals, Robert Stephens.

227—56-56-56-59 — Chalk Mountain CC, Ataskadero, Calif.: TP: Morris Hatalsky ($1,000), CP: Joel Clay ($1,375), Gary Wing, David Ujihara, Bob Cannon, Don Thompson.

227—58-57-59-53 — Twin Base GC, Dayton, Ohio: TP: Kirk Triplett ($5,166.67), CP: Mike Glendenning ($1,375), William Shively, James Condon, Tzong Chen, Christy Condon.

228—56-60-58-54 — Maple Meadows, Wooddale, Ill.: TP: Lee Janzen ($1,583.33), CP: Kelly Holmes ($1,250), Dan Schafer, Tom Thiem, Brad Jackson, Ralph Salatino.

228—57-58-59-54 — Mount Vernon CC, Alexandria, Va.: TP: Scott Simpson ($1,583.33), CP: Peter Van Pelt ($1,250), Earl Hartman, Mike Meyer, Jerry Crocker, Richard Godlewski.

228—55-61-58-54 — Palmetto CC, Benton, La.: TP: Larry Rinker ($1,583.33), CP: Scott Vice ($1,250), Richard Humphries, Jim Yates, Bill Barfield, Wayne Marionneaux.

229—56-57-58-58 — Kapalua Village CC, Lahaina, Maui, Hawaii: TP: Fuzzy Zoeller ($1,000), CP: Scott Shelton ($1,125), John Skinderian, Robert Longhi, Jim Marcum, David Cudlipp.

229—59-56-58-56 — Stowe CC, Stowe, Vt.: TP: Buddy Gardner ($1,125), CP: Jeff Hadley ($1,125), Steve Gretkowski, Guy Neveu, Tim Smullen, Eric Hanley.

230—57-58-59-56 — Colombel Memorial GC, New Orleans, La.: TP: Joey Sindelar ($1,125), CP: Keith Swindell ($1,000), Richard Wilson, Dennis Siebert, Rodney Miller, Keith Borque.

230—57-59-59-55 — Galen Hall CC, Warnersville, Pa.: TP: John Mahaffey ($1,250), CP: Brian Arndt ($1,000), Gil Fritz, Steve Good, Ron Good, Jim Heisey.

231—59-56-58-58 — Buckingham G & CC, Kelseyville, Calif.: TP: Hubert Green ($1,000), CP: Mark Wotherspoon ($1,000), Reggie Osburn, Bob Babica, Glen Senestraro, Steve Branstetter.

233—58-57-60-58 — Willow Creek GC, High Point, N.C.: TP: Tommy Armour III ($1,000), CP: Jim Brotherton ($1,000), Lawry Bump, Pete Thompson, Sid Roberts, Steve Suggs.

TP: PGA Tour Professional
CP: PGA Club Professional

NATIONAL OLDSMOBILE SCRAMBLE CHAMPIONSHIP

1991

The eighth Oldsmobile Scramble attracted more than 120,000 golfers from 2,200 qualifying sites nationwide. A field of 127 teams competed in the net division finals, with 24 advancing to the final round. Lochmoor Country Club of North Fort Myers, Fla., posted a 78-under-par 210 total for a three-stroke victory over Grand Palms Country Club of Pembroke Pines, Fla., and Santa Rosa (Calif.) Country Club. Lochmoor began the third round with eight consecutive birdies, and added an eagle.

Date:	Sept. 19-23 (Net Division)	Oct. 10-14 (Gross Division)
Site:	Walt Disney World Golf Resort, Lake Buena Vista, Fla.	
	Lake Buena Vista, Magnolia, Palm Courses	

Aquia Harbour of Stafford, Va., teamed for four consecutive birdies, including three by amateur Jeff Howard Jr., of 30 and 35 feet at the 15th and 17th holes, to win the Gross Division Championship with a 72-hole total of 226. Tour professional Billy Mayfair helped clinch the Championship by firing a 7-iron approach shot to within a foot of the flagstick on the 18th hole. Howard tapped in from there. Links O'Tryon of Campobello, S.C. and Frasch Park Golf Club of Sulphur, La., tied for second at 227.

NET DIVISION SUMMARY

210—52-52-54-52 — Lochmoor CC, North Fort Myers, Fla.: TP: Brian Claar ($2,500), CP: Todd Brown ($10,000), Dennis Riddick, Kevin Ostrowsky, Mike Leach, Barry Franzese.

213—55-52-57-49 — Grand Palms CC, Pembroke Pines, Fla.: TP: Lon Hinkle ($10,000), CP: Richard Buskey ($6,250), Ken Cassidy, Roy Winfield, Jim West, Todd Watson.

213—55-55-52-51 — Santa Rosa CC, Santa Rosa, Calif.: TP: John Inman ($2,500), CP: Paul Norris ($6,250), Jim Fisher, Paul Puccioni, Matthew Ellingson, Claude Boulware.

215—55-52-54-54 — Green Hills CC, Millbrae, Calif.: TP: Bruce Fleisher ($1,100), CP: John Joseph ($2,500), Lou Mohn, Orlando Trujillo, Oscar Lopez Guerra, Gary Pollack.

215—54-57-51-53 — Oak Club of Genoa, Genoa, Ill.: TP: Dudley Hart ($1,200), CP: Fred Hancock ($2,500), Roger Rearden, Robert Parsek, Richard Peterson, Maurice Kehoe.

216—52-56-58-50 — Timberlane CC, Gretna, La.: TP: Mike Standly ($6,250), CP: Ed Selser ($1,500), Jimmy Dill, Hank Helmer, Mike Jones, Elmer Grundmeyer.

216—57-54-55-50 — Greenbriar Hills CC, St. Louis, Mo.: TP: Joel Edwards ($6,250), CP: Scott Oulds ($1,500), George Ouello, Barry Beracha, Steve Aul, Rich Akers.

217—53-53-56-55 — Fresh Meadow GC, Hillside, Ill.: TP: Fuzzy Zoeller ($1,000), CP: Craig Morgan ($1,500), Jeff Lincoln, Dave Naughton, Roliff Schoenenberg, Craig Loveless.

218—56-56-54-52 — Overland Park GC, Overland Park, Kan.: TP: Bob Lohr ($1,500), CP: Rob Sedorcek ($1,350), Joe Bracken, Roy Conrardy, Jim Coons, Curt Gasper.

218—56-52-55-55 — Buena Vista GC, Taft, Calif.: TP: Mike Hulbert ($1,000), CP: David James ($1,350), Larry Brown, Rhett Brown, Jerrol Kiger, Blake Brown.

218—58-54-55-51 — Sandy Point GC, Hartsville, S.C.: TP: Brandel Chamblee ($2,500), CP: Bill Lewis ($1,350), Tick Freeman, Gene Hardee, Jimmy Griffin, Leslie Burr.

218—56-55-55-52 — Honeywell GC, Wabash, Ind.: TP: Dick Mast ($1,500), CP: Todd Smith ($1,350), Brian Nyland, Dave King, Dean Sheppard, Jim Craft.

219—54-56-56-53 — Apple Mountain GC, Belvedere, N.J.: TP: David Peoples ($1,200), CP: Frank Esposito ($1,200), Eric Knapp, John Wojtowicz, Dave Frost, Mike Wojtowicz.

219—55-55-57-52 — Plum Brook CC, Sandusky, Ohio: TP: Bill Buttner ($1,500), CP: Jim Irvin ($1,200), Jeff Manuella, Tony Querra, Marcy Manion, Carl Hanson.

219—53-56-58-52 — Killeen Municipal GC, Killeen, Texas: TP: Clark Dennis ($1,500), CP: Greg Antunes ($1,200), Garry Clowers, Leland Jungmann, Steve Brueggeman, Larry Clowers.

220—53-55-58-54 — Port Huron Elks Club, Port Huron, Mich.: TP: Denis Watson ($1,100), CP: Alex Macko ($1,000), Fred Franzel, Len Fedon, Carl Ozog, Robert Spitzbarth.

220—58-54-55-53 — Punxsutawney CC, Punxsutawney, Pa.: TP: Larry Rinker ($1,200), CP: Chuck Scally Jr. ($1,000), Rick Fairman, Ray Lute, John Redding, Dick Metrick.

221—55-55-55-56 — Saginaw CC, Saginaw, Mich.: TP: Dave Rummells ($1,100), CP: Max Anderson ($1,000), Hal Shilling, Gerald Sieggreen, Jed Shilling, Gene Slachta.

221—55-55-56-55 — Bay Pointe CC, Onset Beach, Mass.: TP: Tommy Moore ($1,000), CP: Tom Toby ($1,000), Jack McDonald, Gene Whitcher, Tom Brackett, Paul Horrigan.

222—56-56-57-53 — First Colony GC, Sugarland, Texas: TP: Jerry Haas ($1,200), CP: Fred Leber ($1,000), Marty Miller, Steve Hunter, Victor Vine, Mike Henderson.

222—56-55-56-55 — Bloomingdale GC, Valrico, Fla.: TP: Bob Wolcott ($1,000), CP: John Reger ($1,000), Mark Puskarich, Len Barthle, Nick Pund, Tim Janego.

223—57-56-55-55 — Westgate Valley CC, Palos Heights, Ill.: TP: Brian Watts ($1,000), CP: Glenn Buss Sr. ($1,000), Raymond Popelis, Guy Manning, Bob Lawrence, Ed Froehlich.

223—55-57-56-55 — Miami Shores GC, Troy, Ohio: TP: Dillard Pruitt ($1,000), CP: Billy Mitchell ($1,000), Joe Evans, Wes Plummer, Jeff Slyman, Doug Dunham.

225—57-56-55-57 — Cedar River CC, Adams, Minn.: TP: Peter Persons ($1,000), CP: Tim Smith ($1,000), David Eberling, Doug Rechtzigel, Don Cordes, Bob Rapp.

TP: PGA Tour Professional
CP: PGA Club Professional

GROSS DIVISION SUMMARY

226—57-58-55-56 — Aquia Harbour, Stafford, Va.: TP: Billy Mayfair ($2,833), CP: Tom Lernihan ($10,000), Jeff Howard Sr., Jeff Howard Jr., Greg Howard, Tim Rose.

227—58-56-56-57 — Links O'Tryon, Campobello, S.C.: TP: Dave Barr ($1,260), CP: Tom Mullinax ($6,250), Ray Sharpe, Curtis Burnett, Babe Rayburn, Billy Henson.

227—57-59-56-55 — Frasch Park GC, Sulphur, La.: TP: Mike Hulbert ($6,250), CP: Doug Bulliard ($6,250), Mack Burns, Bryan McCullough, Mike Carer, Kevin Broussard.

228—56-58-56-58 — Stonebridge CC, Boca Raton, Fla.: TP: Robert Wrenn ($1,040), CP: Mike Anderson ($2,500), Roy Ferri, Fred Simank, Charlie Peebles, Steve Schmidt.

228—59-57-56-56 — Great Hills GC, Austin, Texas: TP: Phil Blackmar ($1,833), CP: Mark Coward ($2,500), Bill Price, Rick Gorbell, John Cordes, Newton Harris.

229—55-57-59-58 — Crag Burn GC, East Aurora, N.Y.: TP: Jay Haas ($1,050), CP: Lonnie Nielsen ($1,500), Jim Smith, Tony Miles, Jim Derrick, Tom Lombardo.

229—55-58-59-57 — Shady Valley GC, Arlington, Texas: TP: Fuzzy Zoeller ($1,260), CP: Terry Snodgrass ($1,500), Mel Robinson, Ben Hanna, Wendel Burgess, Bill Baker.

229—58-59-56-56 — Weston Lakes CC, Fulshear, Texas: TP: Brad Bryant ($1,833), CP: Tim Thelan ($1,500), Bill Stone, Jim Adams, Jim Myska, Randy Schulze.

230—57-60-58-55 — Redwood Empire CC, Fortuna, Calif.: TP: Larry Rinker ($6,250), CP: Tom Mathena ($1,500), Tim Crowley, Dan Crowley, Robert Crowley, Randy Murray.

230—59-61-56-54 — Port Royal Plantation Hilton Head Island, S.C.: TP: Buddy Gardner ($10,000), CP: Gary Duren ($1,500), Kevin King, Pat Murray, Dave Duren, Tom Reilly.

231—55-57-61-58 — Imperial Lakes GC, Palmetto, Fla.: TP: Mike Donald ($1,040), CP: Kevin Paschall ($1,200), Rick Ponto, Mike Lannert, Jim Haller, Joe Mazza.

231—60-57-57-57 — Windermere CC, Windermere, Fla.: TP: Morris Hatalsky ($1,260), CP: Terry Perry ($1,200), Mike Leary, Steven Birdan, Rick Smith, Jerry Delaney.

232—58-56-60-58 — Royal Lakes CC, Flowery Branch, Ga.: TP: Kenny Knox ($1,040), CP: Rodger Hogan ($1,150), Jeff Brotherton, Mike Matthews, Bob Heppner, Carl Freeling.

232—56-61-59-56 — Minikahoa Club, Minneapolis, Minn.: TP: Brian Claar ($1,834), CP: Paul Purtzer ($1,150), Tom Meyers, Tom Moore, Mark McCary, Frank Bennett.

232—56-62-58-56 — Interlachen CC, Winter Park, Fla.: TP: Bob Lohr ($1,833), CP: Jay Kennedy ($1,150), Jack Jackson, Chris Cottrill, Sid Cash, Don Palladeno.

232—58-59-59-56 — Glenmoor CC, Englewood, Colo.: TP: Joey Sindelar ($1,834), CP: Jeff Hanson ($1,150), Bob Thompson, Gary Altman, Dave Allen, Dave Williams.

233—58-59-57-59 — Canongate-on-White Oak GC, Newnan, Ga.: TP: Dan Forsman ($1,000), CP: Charles Moller ($1,000), Carl Sweeton, Robert Graham, Scott Lowry, Chris Michael.

233—62-58-56-57 — Topeka CC, Topeka, Kan.: TP: John Mahaffey ($1,260), CP: Tom Dawson ($1,000), Stan Zimmerman, Craig Woodbury, Greg Lux, Doug Judd.

233—57-59-60-57 — Riverside CC, Portland, Ore.: TP: Hubert Green ($1,260), CP: Pat Sutton ($1,000), Brad Boyer, Brent Gunderson, Tim Coleman, Tom Christ.

234—55-58-59-62 — Circlestone CC, Adel, Ga.: TP: D.A. Weibring ($1,000), CP: Bob Windom ($1,000), Brent Harper, Mike Folsom, Jerry Alberson, Maxie Parker.

234—59-57-60-58 — Waikoloa Beach Club, Waikoloa, Hawaii: TP: Gil Morgan ($1,050), CP: Jay Taise ($1,000), Milton Muraski, Owen Fukikawa, Byron Murasaki, Bob Nakamoto.

235—59-57-60-59 — Mill River CC, Stratford, Conn.: TP: Tommy Armour III ($1,000), CP: Fred Kolakowski ($1,000), Ralph Salito, Al Ambrose, Ed O'Neil, Rick Drazdowsky.

237—60-61-55-61 — Pine Creek GC, Colorado Springs, Colo.: TP: Billy Ray Brown ($1,000), CP: Gregg Jones ($1,000), Jim West, Dan Solee, Torry Collinson, Bob Edwards.

238—59-57-61-61 — The Barn GC, Pleasant View, Utah: TP: Donnie Hammond ($1,000), CP: Gary Hazelgren ($1,000), Brett Wayment, Ken Martin, Art Shively, Mike Fisher.

TP: PGA Tour Professional
CP: PGA Club Professional

1990

Date: Sept. 28 - Oct. 1 (Net Division) Oct. 12-15 (Gross Division)
Site: Walt Disney World Golf Resort, Lake Buena Vista, Fla.
Lake Buena Vista, Magnolia, Palm Courses

For the sixth time in seven years, inclement weather played havoc with the format of the net division finals in the Oldsmobile Scramble National Championship. The full 72-hole schedule was not completed. But Shady Valley Golf Club of Arlington, Texas, was smiling in the rain on the soggy Magic Kingdom courses, outlasting Columbia Lakes Country Club of West Columbia, Texas, in a 12-player, three-hole sudden-death playoff. The two teams had tied after 54 holes at 52-under-par 162. Ben Hanna, 37, made a 15-foot birdie putt on the 147-yard third hole on the Magnolia Course. Browns Lake Golf Club of Burlington, Wis., and Riceland Golf Club of Orrville, Ohio, tied for third at 166.

Tour professional Barb Bunkowsky competed for Shady Valley, as LPGA Tour professionals joined the net division finalists. PGA Tour professionals joined the gross division teams.

Home-course advantage seemed to be the difference for the winning gross division quintet from Walt Disney World Golf Club of Lake Buena Vista, Fla. The team was joined by PGA Tour professional Gil Morgan, who together with PGA club professional Tommy Giles helped guide a final-round 53. Disney World birdied 15 holes, eagled two and parred one — when Morgan missed a 15-foot birdie attempt on the par-5 16th hole. Tomball Country Club of Tomball, Texas, finished two strokes back at 226.

NET DIVISION SUMMARY

164—57-55-52 — Shady Valley GC, Arlington, Texas: TP: Barb Bunkowsky ($10,000), CP: Terry Snodgrass ($10,000), Ben Hanna, Mel Robinson, Wendell Burgess, Bill Baker.

164—55-54-55 — Columbia Lakes CC, West Columbia, Texas: TP: Missie Berteotti ($1,500), CP: Greg Henning ($7,500), Vic Vine, Martha Miller, Harry Jenkins, Mike Henderson.

166—55-57-54 — Browns Lake GC, Burlington, Wis.: TP: Dale Eggeling ($2,500), CP: Bill Hagensick ($4,000), Tim Gebhardt, James Sorensen, Mark Gebhardt, Andrew Jaeger.

166—61-53-52 — Riceland GC, Orrville, Ohio: TP: Kristi Albers ($7,500), CP: Larry Lisic ($4,000), Kenneth Kohlmyer, William Planisek, Steve Pesho, Greg Becker.

168—58-56-54 — Cotton Creek GC, Spartanburg, S.C.: TP: Nancy Lopez ($2,500), CP: Brian Kennedy ($1,666.67), Lynwood Clarke, Clarence Collier, Bruce Thompson, David Thompson.

168—56-59-53 — Scenic View GC, Winchester, Tenn.: TP: Kim Bauer ($5,000), CP: Randy Stephens ($1,666.67), James Stephens, Jay Penny, Dominic Stephens, Timmy Stephens.

168—56-56-56 — Walt Disney World GR, Lake Buena Vista, Fla.: TP: Maggie Will ($1,200), CP: Eric Fredricksen ($1,666.66), Doug Wharton, Darryl Bozeman, David Layman, Bob Ziegler.

169—56-58-55 — Cedarbrook Club, Old Brookville, N.Y.: TP: Tina Purtzer ($1,500), CP: Thomas Herzog ($1,380), Joseph Fitzgerald, Ed Douglas, Warren Mainella, Theodore Gaeta.

169—57-56-56 — Cobleskill CC, Cobleskill, N.Y.: TP: Kathy Guadagnino ($1,200), CP: Brent Smith ($1,380), Al Curtis, Keith Lindsay, Gary Desormeau, Fred Edwards.

169—56-58-55 — Pine Hills CC, Calhoun, La.: TP: Dottie Mochrie ($1,500), CP: Scott Myers ($1,380), Ken Adams, Kurt Benson, Rusty Gibbs, Pam Adams.

169—60-54-55 — Horse Thief CC, Tehachapi, Calif.: TP: Judy Dickinson ($1,500), CP: Don Molton ($1,380), Larry Brown, Rhett Brown, Blake Brown, Jerrol Kiger.

169—55-56-58 — Rock Spring Club, West Orange, N.J.: TP: Susan Sanders ($1,000), CP: Baker Maddera ($1,380), Anthony Caputo, Rocco Tutela, James Valenza, Fred Biehl.

170—57-55-58 — Kittyhawk GC, Dayton, Ohio: TP: Cindy Figg-Currier ($1,000), CP: Dick Hutchison ($1,150), Larry Buckinham, Larry Sprinkle, Alex Stefan Jr., Jerry Brown.

170—58-57-55 — Beatrice CC, Beatrice, Neb.: TP: Martha Foyer ($1,500), CP: Steve Diehm ($1,150), Bill Campbell, Pat Patton, Scott Lawson, Verne Moseman.

170—54-60-56 — Schneiter's Riverside GC, Ogden, Utah: TP: Tammie Green ($1,200), CP: Ernie Schneiter ($1,150), Kerry Bambles, Chris Colohan, Tony Miles, Ron Robinson.

170—57-57-56 — Mountain View GC, Corona, Calif.: TP: Myra Blackwelder ($1,200), CP: Larry Salmi ($1,150), Taylor Hall, Gene Hall, Keith Blatzhiem, Al Merz.

171—56-56-59 — Pearl CC, Aiea, Hawaii: TP: Elaine Crosby ($1,000), CP: Clyde Rego ($1,000), George Kahikina, Vincent Dias, Vernon Dias, Kenneth Ah Choy.

172—59-55-58 — Willmar GC, Spicer, Minn.: TP: Barb Mucha ($1,000), CP: Joel Jacobson ($1,000), Ken Olson, Craig Strand, Tom Jacobs, Clayton Sodetani.

172—59-55-58 — Heathrow CC, Lake Mary, Fla.: TP: Terry Jo Myers ($1,000), CP: Larry Galloway ($1,000), Gay Inclan, Randy Gregory, Tom Bland, Bob Kessler.

172—58-58-56 — Doublegate CC, Albany, Ga.: TP: Colleen Walker ($1,200), CP: Darren Garner ($1,000), Andrew Aultman, Sue Woods, Beth Bextermuelle, Lorrie Monahan.

172—55-59-58 — Ravines CC, Middleburg, Fla.: TP: Donna Caponi ($1,000), CP: Tim Hooks ($1,000), Kim Tuell, Ron Lowder, Bobby Joe Qualls, Charles Blank.

174—58-58-58 — Brownson CC, Huntington, Conn.: TP: Nancy Rubin ($1,000), CP: David McQuad ($1,000), Lee Hennessey Jr., Ken Luczak, Ron Gross, Doug Dreyer.

174—56-60-58 — Cobre Valle CC, Glove, Ariz.: TP: Danielle Ammaccapane ($1,000), CP: Rick Oppliger ($1,000), Chris Cecil, Bill Bennett, Luis Constandse, Dan Goar.

175—56-59-60 — Royal Scot GC, New Franken, Wis.: TP: Nicky Le Roux ($1,000), CP: Bill Lindmark ($1,000), Patricia Lindmark, Budde Fifarek Jr., Troy Wood, Cary Waloway.

TP: PGA Tour Professional
CP: PGA Club Professional

GROSS DIVISION SUMMARY

224—59-57-55-53 — Walt Disney World GC, Lake Buena Vista, Fla.: TP: Gil Morgan ($7,250), CP: Tommy Giles ($10,000), Bruce Scamehorn, David Norka, Bill Merritt, Brian Bierwagen.

226—58-55-58-55 — Tomball CC, Tomball, Texas: TP: Billy Ray Brown ($1,500), CP: Skip Theiss ($7,500), Monte Schauer, Jerry Humphrey, George Aubert, Ted Sims.

228—57-57-56-58 — Links O'Tyron, Campobello, S.C.: TP: Ted Schulz ($1,000), CP: Thomas Mullinax ($5,000), Ray Sharpe, Curtis Burnett, Dan Harvey, Babe Rayburn.

229—60-59-54-56 — Spring Valley CC, Columbia, S.C.: TP: Doug Tewell ($1,500), CP: Joey Pinder ($2,166), Gene Williams, Jim Kirkham, Jimmy Watkins, Bill Canada.

229—57-60-58-54 — Lake Arrowhead CC, Waleska, Ga.: TP: Joey Sindelar ($2,500), CP: Robert Frongillo ($2,166), Hall Fowler, Jim Nicholson, Jim Carroll, Scott Miller.

229—60-59-57-53 — Crag Burn GC, East Aurora, N.Y.: TP: Pat McGowan ($10,000), CP: Lonnie Nielsen ($2,166), Jim Smith, Gary Grelick, Jim Derrick, Thomas Lombardo.

230—61-56-59-54 — Colonial G & CC, Harahan, La.: TP: Dan Forsman ($2,500), CP: Randy Quick ($1,500), Earl Wilken, John Bordreaux, Matt Palmer, George Ackel.

230—56-58-59-57 — Bent Oak GC, Titusville, Fla.: TP: Phil Blackmar ($1,187), CP: Bob Carson ($1,500), Dan Burdette, Fred Stones, Calvin Lingelbach, Doug Dyer.

230—56-60-61-53 — Oconomowoc GC, Oconomowoc, Wis.: TP: Brian Claar ($6,250), CP: Eddie Terasa ($1,500), Charles Johnson, Jim O'Keefe, Tom Koconis, Bob Rudig.

231—58-56-59-58 — Cedar Ridge CC, Broken Arrow, Okla.: TP: Corey Pavin ($1,000), CP: Tom Jones ($1,350), James Hays Jr., Tim Jurek, Mike Tudor, Jim Bolin.

231—57-61-56-57 — Great Hills GC, Austin, Texas: TP: Mike Hulbert ($1,187), CP: Mark Coward ($1,350), Jim Achilles, Jerry Achilles, Rick Relyea, Anna Reneau.

232—59-58-58-57 — Deer Creek GC, University Park, Ill.: TP: Fuzzy Zoeller ($1,187), CP: Jimmy Formas ($1,200), Jim Hamann, Pat Jaeger, Max Ghezzi, Tom Purcell.

232—56-62-56-58 — Marriott's GC of Fossil Creek, Fort Worth, Texas: TP: Mark Wiebe ($1,187), CP: Ken McIntyre ($1,200), Greg Babbert, Don Fish, Phil Dyson, James Hollenbach.

232—58-60-57-57 — Quincy CC, Quincy, Ill.: TP: Ed Fiori ($1,187), CP: Lynn Rosely ($1,200), Scott Briggs, Bill Sullivan, Delmer Mitchell, Gary Kirlin.

232—58-57-61-56 — Sandpiper G & CC, Lakeland, Fla.: TP: Jim Carter ($1,500), CP: Anthony Kelber ($1,200), Bill Nelson, Bill Lemke, Don Wasilewski, Bob Hemann.

233—57-60-57-59 — Park Meadows GC, Park City, Utah: TP: Brad Bryant ($1,000), CP: Michael Kahler ($1,000), Jay Cashmore, Chad Evans, Craig Boyer, Rich Glauser.

233—59-60-56-58 — Chalk Mountain GC, Atascadero, Calif.: TP: Kenny Knox ($1,000), CP: Rudy Duran ($1,000), Curt Scarbrough, Ralph Agostini, Larry Buck, Tom Jesperson.

233—58-59-59-57 — Pineland CC, Nichols, S.C.: TP: David Ogrin ($1,187), CP: Jonathon York ($1,000), T.C. Dunlap, Lois Dodson, Lawrence Reese, Kenny Dodson.

233—61-57-58-57 — Holmes Park GC, Lincoln, Neb.: TP: Bob Lohr ($1,187), CP: Mike Higgins ($1,000), Lawrence Romjue, Craig Bauer, Chuck Eckert, Rich Vanier.

233—56-59-62-56 — East Lake Woodlands CC, Oldsmar, Fla.: TP: Robert Wrenn ($1,500), CP: Richard Dingus ($1,000), Kim Wareick, Chip Copley, Terry Addison, Scott Van Dame.

234—58-58-61-57 — Corvallis CC, Corvallis, Ore.: TP: Larry Rinker ($1,187), CP: Thorgen Cramer ($1,000), Del Spiker, Terry Tallis, Rick Nelson, Bob Nelson.

234—61-56-60-57 — Manitou Ridge GC, White Bear Lake, Minn.: TP: Bob Gilder ($1,187), CP: Charlie Basco ($1,000), Jeff Larson, Tom Guzik, Rodd Hodd, John Hayes.

235—60-58-59-58 — Tracy G & CC, Tracy, Calif.: TP: Hal Sutton ($1,000), CP: Steve Moreland ($1,000), Greg Williamson, Dave MacDonald, Scott Biddiner, Rudy Mueller.

236—59-58-59-60 — Pasatiempo GC, Santa Cruz, Calif.: TP: Hubert Green ($1,000), CP: Shawn McEntee ($1,000), Joel Murray, Mark Hogue, Pat Arko, Harry Mayfield.

TP: PGA Tour Professional
CP: PGA Club Professional

1989

Once again the Oldsmobile Scramble nct division had to deal with an old problem — inclement weather. But the rain delays the first two rounds didn't distract Fox Bend Golf Club of Oswego, Ill., from winning a second consecutive national Championship. PGA club professional Tom Tierney, who guided the 1988 Gross Division Championship Team, arrived with a new set of amateur partners. The result was a winning 72-hole total of 206, which featured a final-round 49 at Grand Cypress Resort. Fox Bend edged Riceland Country Club of Orrville, Ohio, by a stroke. Fox Bend's David Sullivan capped a remarkable final round for his team by making a 30-foot downhill birdie putt that broke six to seven feet left-to-right on the 18th green. The new net division boosted the overall Scramble entries to 115,000 nationwide.

Date:	Sept. 22-25 (Net Division)	Oct. 13-16 (Gross Division)
Site:	Walt Disney World Golf Resort, Lake Buena Vista, Fla.	
	Magnolia, Lake Buena Vista, Palm Courses	
	Grand Cypress Resort, Orlando, Fla.	
	North/South, New Courses, Lake Buena Vista Course	

The gross division title went to The Woodlands (Texas) TPC team, which needed a difficult par on the final hole to edge Baneberry Golf Club of White Pine, Tenn., by a stroke, 224 to 225. George Johnson made the decisive putt for The Woodlands TPC, after the team's 200-yard approach shot from a grove of trees landed short of a greenside bunker. Tour professional Steve Pate had confidence in his TPC teammates, despite the errant tee shot by amateur Joe Clements. "Par wasn't much of a challenge," said Pate. "We only had six guys with a swing at the second shot, you know. All we had to do was get it somewhere near the green." Pate also acknowledged that ignorance may have been bliss for his team, which believed it had a two-stroke lead, when, in fact, the margin was a stroke heading into the final hole.

NET DIVISION SUMMARY

206—52-53-52-49 — Fox Bend GC, Oswego, Ill.: TP: Jack Kay ($2,600), CP: Tom Tierney ($10,000), Ken Price, Kevin Richardson, Larry Hill, David Sullivan.

207—53-52-51-51 — Riceland CC, Orrville, Ohio: TP: Robin Freeman ($1,166), CP: Danny Simmons ($5,166), Steve Pesho, Mike Jensen, Greg Becker, Ken Kohlmyer.

207—52-50-54-51 — Elkhorn CC, Stockton, Calif.: TP: Bob Lohr ($1,166), CP: Arthur Williams ($5,166), Alex Bluhm, Richard Vasquez, Lamont Harrison, Ken Baird.

207—53-54-51-49 — Disney Inn, Walt Disney World GR, Lake Buena Vista, Fla.: TP: Ronnie McCann ($2,600), CP: Billy Bulmer ($5,166), Doug Wharton, Rudy Heinkel, Bob Ziegler, David Layman.

209—54-53-54-48 — Wabeek CC, Bloomfield Hills, Mich.: TP: Duffy Waldorf ($10,000), CP: Tom Fortuna ($2,000), Ron Kay, William Litt, Naveen Ahuja, Gerald Lavine.

210—50-58-54-48 — Beauregard CC, DeRidder, La.: TP: Clark Burroughs ($7,500), CP: Dan Tatum ($1,500), Clark Black, Gary Black, David Weigand, Caroline Johnson.

210—55-50-56-49 — Houston Lake CC, Perry, Ga.: TP: Jim Benepe ($2,600), CP: Richard Hatcher ($1,500), Brenda Davis, Ken Ashbury, Tim Greer, Susie Greer.

210—50-55-54-51 — Broken Woods CC, Coral Springs, Fla.: TP: Jay Delsing ($1,166), CP: Bobby Martin ($1,500), Bob Hayes, Gene Debolt, Skip Montcastle, Tony Mager.

211—51-54-56-50 — Coronado CC, El Paso, Texas: TP: Brad Faxon ($1,500), CP: Steve Mack ($1,500), Dickie James, George Lowery, Lama Louie, Jim Donaldson.

212—54-52-57-49 — Little Turtle CC, Westerville, Ohio: TP: John Adams ($2,600), CP: Paul Hollenbaugh ($1,300), Tom Poole, Chip Wetterauer, Clark Woodford, Bob Baroni.

212—53-53-56-50 — Feather Sound CC, Clearwater, Fla.: TP: Webb Heintzelman ($1,500), CP: Brett Upper ($1,300), Joe Hunter, Jeff Huenik, Lloyd Marvin, Don Heinz.

212—55-55-51-51 — Cadillac CC, Cadillac, Mich.: TP: Trevor Dodds ($1,166), CP: Dave Kendall ($1,300), Jim Carey, Greg Lambourne, Willard Smith, Jan Blick.

213—55-53-55-50 — Wynstone GC, North Barrington, Ill.: TP: Sam Randolph ($1,500), CP: Dennis Burns ($1,200), Alan Newberg, Dan Light, Robert Paice, Robert Bieniek.

213—58-56-50-49 — Pacific GC, San Clemente, Calif.: TP: Ron Streck ($2,600), CP: Scott Hoiseth ($1,200), Bob Barker, Mike Williams, Jim Ryder, George Gary.

215—55-51-56-53 — H.G. Dad Miller GC, Anaheim, Calif.: TP: Nolan Henke ($1,000), CP: Bill Huff ($1,040), Ed Webber, Pat McCoy, Michael Mullen, Benny Martin.

215—54-54-54-53 — Forest Preserve National GC, Oak Forest, Ill.: TP: Dave Rummels ($1,000), CP: George Kallish III ($1,040), Marion Valle, Andrew Revell, Richard Witt, John Harrison.

215—52-54-57-52 — Pines CC, Valley, Neb.: TP: Jim Carter ($1,000), CP: Scott Allacher ($1,040), John Sajevic, Jerry Helget, Ron Wehenkel, Kevin Odenreider.

215—56-55-53-51 — Golf Hills CC, Redding, Calif.: TP: Jim Hallet ($1,166), CP: Steve Adams ($1,040), Tim Boehme, Martin Crouse, Dave Olsen, Charlie Denuccio.

215—55-58-51-51 — Plantation Resort, Frisco, Texas: TP: Stan Utley ($1,166), CP: Junior Salinas ($1,040), Franz Schoening, Jeff Michael, Harold Robertson, Jim Locklear.

216—59-56-49-52 — Wichita Falls CC, Wichita Falls, Texas: TP: Lance Ten Broeck ($1,000), CP: Joe Lay ($1,000), John Barbour, Danna Barbour, Lee Smith, Milton Keck.

217—58-52-55-52 — Atlanta Athletic Club, Duluth, Ga.: TP: Rex Caldwell ($1,000), CP: James Hughes ($1,000), Bob Bartkow, Gordon Cope, Bill Cheek, Jerry Romano.

217—56-53-55-53 — Ellendale CC, Houma, La.: TP: Brian Tennyson ($1,000), CP: Michael McGeever ($1,000), Val Vourgeois, Henry Falcon, Steve Evans, Wayne Deroche.

219—54-55-55-55 — Minikahda Club, Minneapolis, Minn.: TP: Lennie Clements ($1,000), CP: Rosemary Iverson ($1,000), Brent Hall, Kathryn Nelson, Keith Horton, John Herman.

220—53-59-52-56 — Star Fort National GC, Ninety-Six, S.C.: TP: John Huston ($1,000), CP: Jim Ledvina ($1,000), Don Campbell, Dick Shelton, Ken Shull, Jim Kohli.

TP: PGA Tour Professional
CP: PGA Club Professional

GROSS DIVISION SUMMARY

224—57-56-56-55 — TPC at The Woodlands, The Woodlands, Texas: TP: Steve Pate ($1,500), CP: Bob Brown ($10,000), Gary Britt, George Johnson, Joe Clements, Jim Delaney.

225—60-54-58-53 — Baneberry GC, White Pine, Tenn.: TP: Hubert Green ($10,000), CP: Tom Kammann ($6,250), Jerry Floyd, Bob Barker, Jim Hatcher, Ken Cheek.

225—54-59-58-54 — Swenson Park GC, Stockton, Calif.: TP: Morris Hatalsky ($2,000), CP: Ric Burgess ($6,250), Mike Baty, Tony Rocha, Gary Christensen, John Spooner.

226—58-57-57-54 — Firethorn GC, Lincoln, Neb.: TP: Donnie Hammond ($2,000), CP: Jim White ($2,500), Randy Borg, Paul Fechner, Jim Blair, Steve Sheppard.

226—58-58-57-53 — Franconia GC, Springfield, Mass.: TP: Mike Donald ($6,250), CP: Stan Gorman ($2,500), Bill Shea, Mike Shea, John Malinski, Vin Dimmurg.

227—60-56-57-54 — Riverside CC, Menominee, Mich.: TP: Gil Morgan ($2,000), CP: Michael Wietor ($1,500), Andy Cegelski, Dan Eckstrom, Roger Wallin, Jim Mallspen.

228—58-57-60-53 — Sunflower Hills GC, Bonner Springs, Kan.: TP: Dan Forsman ($6,250), CP: Jeff Johnson ($1,500), Jack Laurie, Mike Tosin, Daron Maier, Jay Sutera.

228—56-59-58-55 — Woodcrest CC, Cherry Hill, N.J.: TP: Kenny Knox ($1,500), CP: Dick Smith, Mike Podolsky, Stan Lerner, Rich Toll, Mike Gerston.

229—59-59-57-54 — Oak Ridge CC, Garland, Texas: TP: Dave Barr ($2,000), CP: Rick Proctor ($1,500), Dennis Nichols, Jim Nugent, Gary Hearn, Dan Brinner.

229—58-56-60-55 — Hallbrook CC, Leawood, Kan.: TP: Doug Tewell ($1,500), CP: Billy Peterson ($1,500), Gene Derks, Marilyn Derks, Bob Henderson, Gary Richter.

231—59-60-55-57 — Redwood Empire G & CC, Fortuna, Calif.: TP: Keith Clearwater ($1,200), CP: Tom Mathena ($1,200), Greg Senestraro, John Senestraro, Steve Branstetter, Rob Boldrini.

231—58-60-56-57 — Shalimar Pointe Resort, Shalimar, Fla.: TP: Mark Lye ($1,200), CP: Paul Moore ($1,200), E.G. Willard, Steve Rumph, James Brazzell, Jeff Birchler.

232—58-57-60-57 — Sun Air CC, Haines City, Fla.: TP: Brad Bryan, ($1,200) CP: Randy Cahill ($1,200), David Norka, Rusty Payne, Ron Moore, Brian Radzak.

232—56-61-57-58 — Bay Valley G & TC, Bay City, Mich.: TP: Mike Hulbert ($1,050), CP: Tom Napieralski, Dick Rigda, Cliff Novak, Joe Schmelzer, James Owens.

233—57-60-57-59 — Connally GC, Waco, Texas: TP: Fuzzy Zoeller ($1,000), CP: Jack Barger ($1,050), Doug Dulany, Dan Blake, Wayne Etienne, Ron Garrett.

233—57-60-58-58 — Cherokee CC, Madison, Wis.: TP: Ed Fiori ($1,050), CP: Larry Tiziani ($1,050), Dick Ludtke, Dennis Ryal, Tom Ryan, Don Shillinglaw.

233—58-59-59-57 — Northern Hills GC, Rochester, Minn.: TP: Bob Lohr ($1,200), CP: Brad Pederson ($1,050), Dale Carlson, Rod Steele, Tim O'Conner, Gary O'Conner.

233—58-58-58-59 — Holly Hills CC, Ivansville, Md.: TP: Roger Maltbie ($1,000), CP: Mike McGinnis ($1,050), Cliff Baker, James Parker, Rex Parker, Jean Bittle.

234—59-59-58-58 — CC of Orlando, Orlando, Fla.: TP: John Mahaffey ($1,050), CP: Carlos Pasarell ($1,000), Charles Bailes, Mike Penney, Darrell Carpenter, Bruce Gordy.

234—56-58-62-58 — Spring Hill CC, Tifton, Ga.: TP: Nick Price ($1,050), CP: Stan Moore ($1,000), Joe Kunes, Roger Womack, Bob Doplan, Bobby Conway.

235—58-61-56-60 — Florence CC, Florence, S.C.: TP: Billy Mayfair ($1,000), CP: John Faidley ($1,000), Woody Jones, Joe Griffin, Rufus Bratton, John Taylor.

236—58-57-60-61 — Chateau G & CC, Kenner, La.: TP: Phil Blackmar ($1,000), CP: Bill Caldwell Jr. ($1,000), Vince Maenza, Sal Motillard, Buddy Micelle, Will Youngblood.

236—60-61-55-60 — Waikoloa Beach GC, Kohala Coast, Hawaii: TP: Mark Wiebe ($1,000), CP: Allen Texeira ($1,000), Al Sojza, George Carter, Larry Jarneski, Pee Wee Kai.

238—58-60-58-62 — Como Park GC, St. Paul, Minn.: TP: Robert Wrenn ($1,000), CP: John Shimpach ($1,000), Jeff McDonnell, Joe Byrnes, Bob Stoika, Dan Klett Jr.

TP: PGA Tour Professional
CP: PGA Club Professional

1988

Tour professional Dave Barr of British Columbia, Canada, competed for his second national Championship team in the fifth Oldsmobile Scramble, helping Fox Bend Golf Club of Oswego, Ill., to a record-tying 64-under-par 224 total for 72 holes and a playoff victory over Palm Valley Country Club of Palm Desert, Calif. Barr led Hickory Hills Golf Club of Grove City, Ohio, to the 1986 Championship.

Date:	Oct. 21-24
Site:	Walt Disney World Golf Resort, Lake Buena Vista, Fla.
	Palm, Lake Buena Vista and Magnolia Courses

Fox Bend and Palm Valley each posted final-round 54s. Fox Bend was able to outlast Palm Valley. Both teams were tied heading into the final round and remained tied after the first playoff hole on the Magnolia Course. Fox Bend wrapped up the victory with a 10-foot birdie on the second hole. Chambers County Golf Club of Anahuac, Texas, was third at 225.

GROSS DIVISION SUMMARY

224—56-58-56-54 — Fox Bend GC, Oswego, Ill.: TP: Dave Barr ($10,000), CP: Tom Tierney ($10,000), Bill Fehrenbacher, Mike Frey, Mike Demetry, Pat Berry.

224—58-57-55-54 — Palm Valley CC, Palm Desert, Calif.: TP: Kenny Knox ($10,000), CP: Mike Gove ($7,500), Craig Flores, Wayne Lawrence, Vince Smaldino, Carl McLeod.

225—56-56-56-57 — Chambers County GC, Anahuac, Texas: TP: Larry Rinker ($1,300), CP: Hal Underwood ($5,000), Bob Cleboski, J.C. Mosier, Tom Moen, Bob Moen.

227—61-56-54-56 — Cypresswood GC, Spring, Texas: TP: Fuzzy Zoeller ($1,500), CP: Paul Levy ($3,000), Lionell Spretz, Russell Schroeder, Ronnie Schroeder, Jimmy Freisleben.

228—58-58-55-57 — Yorba Linda CC, Yorba Linda, Calif.: TP: Ed Fiori ($1,300), CP: Wayne Carter ($1,666), Richard Hancock, Craig Curl, Rudy Lucidi, Tim Owens.

228—58-56-56-56 — The Woodlands Inn & CC, The Woodlands, Texas: TP: Howard Twitty ($1,500), CP: Kent Wood ($1,666), Van Gillin, Chuck Ray, Jack Pearce, Walter Netschi.

228—57-57-57-57 — Terri Pines CC, Cullman, Ala.: TP: Scott Hoch ($1,300), CP: Billy Eastep ($1,666), Tommy Allbright, Ricky Anderson, Eddie Canaday, Roy Holland.

229—58-56-60-55 — Ellwood Green CC, Genoa, Ill.: TP: Dan Pohl ($3,333), CP: Greg Dick ($1,500), Drew La Barbera, Ross La Barbera, Andy La Barbera, Sylvester Silianoff.

229—58-56-60-55 — Partridge Run G & CC, Spartanburg, S.C.: TP: Tom Kite ($3,333), CP: Van Williams ($1,500), Mark Pike, Steve Teaster, Tim Satterfield, Mike Fuller.

230—57-58-60-55 — Progress Downs GC, Beaverton, Ore.: TP: Pat McGowan ($3,333), CP: Stephen Bowen ($1,300), Dayle Stefiuk, Ken Johnson, Roger Romeike, Jack Parker.

230—56-59-57-58 — Pinetree CC, Kennesaw, Ga.: TP: Scott Simpson ($1,120), CP: Ras Allen ($1,300), Jerry Brand, George Whitman, Bob Foley, Deb Burgess.

230—59-55-60-56 — The Patterson Club, Fairfield, Conn.: TP: David Ogrin ($1,500), CP: Paul Kelly ($1,300), Ron Henry Jr., Ed Flynn, Janice Flynn, Joe Sciarrillo.

231—58-61-56-56 — Bent Oak GC, Titusville, Fla.: TP: Mark Lye ($1,500), CP: Bob Carson ($1,200), David Muldowney, Rick Howes, Horace Sharpe, Teke Carson.

231—59-57-56-59 — Lenawee CC, Adrian, Mich.: TP: John Mahaffey ($1,000), CP: Steve Kusisto ($1,200), Randy Fust, Jewell Threet, Doug Hartung, Serge Swaninger.

231—56-60-58-58 — Burning Tree G & CC, Mt. Clemens, Mich.: TP: Dan Forsman ($1,120), CP: Max Adani Jr. ($1,050), Dave Bernhardt, Bill Anton, Orm Bernhardt, Ken Manelski.

231—56-59-59-58 — Disney Inn, Lake Buena Vista, Fla.: TP: Mike Hulbert ($1,120), CP: Billy Bulmer ($1,050), Michael Penney, Charles Bailes, Jeff Doster, Andy McCorkle.

231—58-57-59-58 — Riverside GC, Cambridge Spring, Pa.: TP: Donny Hammond ($1,120), CP: Steve Carney ($1,050), Tom Whalen, Ron Schwartz, Dan Perfetio, Tony Ferraro.

231—57-59-57-59 — Rivermoor CC, Waterford, Wis.: TP: Don Pooley ($1,000), CP: Richard Swift ($1,050), Gregg Wagner, Chris Van Ells, George Van Ells, Al Nesta.

233—56-60-59-58 — Ellendale CC, Houma, La.: TP: Hubert Green ($1,120), CP: Michael McGeever ($1,000), Rob Alexander, Van Ardoin, Mike Walker, Doug Kuykendall.

233—60-57-57-59 — Plantation CC, Ponte Vedra, Fla.: TP: Tom Purtzer ($1,000), CP: Bob Duval ($1,000), Colin Armstrong, Lee Wedekind, Frank Scruby, John Watson.

234—58-61-56-59 — Westview CC, N. Miami, Fla.: TP: Gil Morgan ($1,000), CP: Bruce Fleisher ($1,000), Chuck Gans, Allen Kaplus, Pat Segall, Mike Seger.

234—58-61-56-59 — Chalk Mountain GC, Atascadero, Calif.: TP: Morris Hatalsky ($1,000), CP: Doug Hyde ($1,000), Pete Reed, John Doherty, Larry Roberts, Tom Rousseve.

234—58-59-58-59 — Los Cyotes CC, Buena Park, Calif.: TP: Robert Wrenn ($1,000), CP: Scott Chaffin ($1,000), Bill Milne, Clyde Christiensen, Emmett Clark, Roy Hardick.

234—57-56-62-59 — Black Mountain CC, Henderson, Nev.: TP: Brad Bryant ($1,000), CP: Randy Tickner ($1,000), Dick Jamison, Randy Chandler, Jim Kemp, Jim Tindall.

TP: PGA Tour Professional
CP: PGA Club Professional

NATIONAL OLDSMOBILE SCRAMBLE CHAMPIONSHIP

1987 Central Florida's spirited team from Sun Air Country Club in Haines City powered its way to a 54 on a rain-marred third round of play to win the fourth annual Oldsmobile Scramble Championship. The Championship attracted a nationwide entry list of 94,000. Sun Air recorded a 54-hole total of 51-under-par 165, keyed by a pair of eagles on the Palm Course. Sun Air's Championship was declared after the fourth round was washed away by remnants of Hurricane Floyd, which brushed the southern tip of Florida before moving back in the Gulf of Mexico. Tour partner Mark Lye never got the opportunity to join the talented team, but Sun Air club professional Charles Priester had the necessary reserve strength and talent in amateurs Bill Merritt, Steve Saterbo, Brain Saterbo and Terry Stewart to hold on. The Championship featured three holes-in-one — on all three courses — during the first day of competition. The Scramble offered a total purse of $4 million. Lochinvar Golf Club of Houston, Texas, finished four strokes back at 169, and Tomball (Texas) Country Club third at 170.

Date: Oct. 9-12

Site: Walt Disney World Golf Resort, Lake Buena Vista, Fla.
Palm, Lake Buena Vista and Magnolia Courses

GROSS DIVISION SUMMARY

165—55-56-54 — Sun Air CC, Haines City, Fla.: CP: Charles Priester ($10,000), Bill Merritt, Steve Saterbo, Brian Saterbo, Terry Stewart.

169—59-56-54 — Lochinvar GC, Houston, Texas: CP: Kent Wood ($7,500), Scott Lee, Joe Clements, Gary Britt, Walter Netachi.

170—56-56-57 — Tomball CC, Tomball, Texas: CP: Bobby Martin ($5,000), Monte Schauer, Jay Alexander, John Nicholson, George Aubert.

171—58-57-56 — Elgin CC, Elgin, Ill.: CP: Kirk Hosteng ($3,000), Bill Hoffer, Mike Pevonka, Jim Herbison, Pete Jokiel.

172—54-58-60 — Crag Burn GC, East Aurora, N.Y.: CP: Lonnie Nielsen ($1,666), Jim Smith, Gary Grelick, Ron Jakubowski, George Gellman.

172—61-56-55 — Great Oaks CC, Rochester, Mich.: CP: John Traub ($1,666), John Collins, Bob Dekker, Bill Saracino, William Purdy.

172—54-57-61 — Atlanta Athletic Club, Duluth, Ga.: CP: Tom Brannen ($1,666), Chuck Jabaley, Jim Echols, Geoffery Crabbe, Jim Trimble.

173—58-59-56 — Stockton G & CC, Stockton, Calif.: CP: Hal Ingram ($1,500), Dave Guidi, Sam Alexander, Dick Klein, Frank Portale.

173—61-56-56 — Edina CC, Edina, Minn.: CP: Ken Ellsworth ($1,500), Doug King, John LaBree, Steve Simon, Mark Simmons.

174—61-56-57 — Valle Vista GC, Greenwood, Ind.: CP: Robert Mann ($1,250), Bill Beard, George Bohley, Bob Lane, Bob Stephens.

174—56-61-57 — Tanglewood G & CC, Milton, Fla.: CP: Hiram Cook Jr. ($1,250), Billy Suggs, Tim Essex, Ann Spencer, Chuck Knowles.

174—60-59-55 — Waynesborough CC, Paoli, Pa.: CP: Stu Ingraham ($1,250), Geoff Mynott, Sandy Luckenbill, Paul McCabe, Paul Myers.

174—59-58-57 — Las Positas GC, Livermore, Calif.: CP: Doug Brooke ($1,250), Max Pades, Jerry Rooney, Joe Cumelis, George Garcia.

174—54-62-58 — Berrien Hills CC, St. Joseph, Mich.: CP: Richard Loy ($1,250), David Schultz, Gary Schultz, Larry Bowman, Lou Schultz.

174—56-58-60 — Radley Run CC, Westchester, Pa.: CP: Tom Robertson ($1,250), Dave Yerk, Bill Sylvester, Randall Palm, Steve Manley.

175—57-71-57 — Pebble Brook GC, Noblesville, Ind.: CP: Scott Steger ($1,000), Denny Ault, Don Hardamon, Clark Bonebrake, Mike Komlance.

175—60-58-57 — Madison GC, Madison, N.J.: CP: Bill Ryan ($1,000), Kirk Warshaw, Pat Romano, Nicky Lyons, Gregg Cartier.

175—57-59-59 — Antelope Valley CC, Palmdale, Calif.: CP: Steve Applegate ($1,000), Ray Munoz, Lane Hubbard, Rex Davis, Al Munoz.

175—56-58-61 — Knollwood CC, W. Bloomfield, Mich.: CP: John Molenda ($1,000), Keith West, George Glassman, Jerry Glassman, Mac Fisher.

175—62-57-56 — Flat Creek Club, Peachtree City, Ga.: CP: Charlie Moller ($1,000), Bob Sellers, Larry Mastin, Clark Felker, West Newton.

175—59-59-60 — TPC at The Woodlands, The Woodlands, Texas: CP: Mel Callender ($1,000), Bill Dodd, Mark Lemon, Mike Moore, Art Craighead.

175—59-59-60 — Fig Garden GC, Fresno, Calif.: CP: Gary Bauer ($1,000), Jim Lopes, Leroy Gregory, Clint Sorenson, Chris Wallace.

176—60-58-58 — Colony Creek CC, Victoria, Texas: CP: Robert Singletary ($1,000), Kyle Allemand, Richard Orsak, Bill Orsak, Mark Barsness.

176—60-56-60 — Hidden Valley CC, Reno, Nev.: CP: Ed Jones ($1,000), Eddie Travis, Ernie Mackay, John Dermody, Allan Harsh.

TP: PGA Tour Professional
CP: PGA Club Professional

408

NATIONAL OLDSMOBILE SCRAMBLE CHAMPIONSHIP

1986 The third Oldsmobile Scramble attracted 71,000 entries nationwide, competing for 127 berths in the national final and a $118,000 purse. Hickory Hills Golf Club of Grove City, Ohio, paced by Tour professional Dave Barr and PGA club professional Ivan Smith, won the national Championship with a final-round 11-under-par 61 and a four-day total of 63-under-par 225. Amateur Tom Watson hit a 5-iron approach to within four feet of the flagstick on the par-4, 442-yard 18th hole on the Magnolia Course, and amateur Gene Hartley stroked home the birdie putt to ensure a one-stroke victory over a team from Plantation Golf Resort of Crystal River, Fla., which missed a 12-foot birdie putt that would have forced a playoff. Crag Burn Golf Club of East Aurora, N.Y., finished third at 228. Hickory Hills club professional Ivan Smith highlighted his team's big week by one of the tournament's two holes-in-one. Smith's ace came during the second round at the 176-yard 12th hole at Lake Buena Vista, and it was the only time during the Championship in which all four of Smith's amateur playing partners missed the green on a par-3 hole.

Date: Oct. 10-13
Site: Walt Disney World Golf Resort, Lake Buena Vista, Fla.
Palm, Magnolia and Lake Buena Vista Courses

GROSS DIVISION SUMMARY

225—57-53-54-61 — Hickory Hills GC, Grove City, Ohio: TP: Dave Barr ($7,500), CP: Ivan Smith ($7,500), Tony Clark, Tom Watson, Ron Leady, Gene Hartley.

226—55-57-57-57 — Plantation GR, Crystal River, Fla.: TP: Tom Pernice ($4,500), CP: Tim Eckstein ($4,500), Scott Baker, Raymond Smith, Todd Stanley, Scott Rowell.

228—57-56-56-59 — Crag Burn GC, East Aurora, N.Y.: TP: Lennie Clements ($3,000), CP: Lonnie Nielsen ($3,000), James A. Smith M.D., Greg Smith, Gary R. Grelick, Susie Smith.

229—56-55-62-56 — Grand Rapids Elks CC, Grand Rapids, Mich.: TP: Hubert Green ($2,000), CP: Bill Wilson ($2,000), Bill Heible, Ed Sruba, Millard Alexander, Steve Moerman.

230—58-58-58-56 — Seascape GC, Aptos, Calif.: TP: Tom Sieckman ($1,125), CP: Jeff McMillen ($1,125), Tim Woods, Cliff Rettig, Jack Robb, Dennis Marc.

230—60-58-54-58 — Portage CC, Akron, Ohio: TP: Dan Forsman ($1,125), CP: Dan Simmons ($1,125), Eddie Thomas, Carl Dietrich, Dick Rea, Harold Von Wyl.

230—57-55-56-62 — Cedarbrook CC, Blue Bell, Pa.: TP: Larry Rinker ($1,125), CP: Gary Hardin ($1,125), James O'Brien, Walter Bresman, Joel Barbalock, Tom Genuardi.

230—56-56-62-56 — Bear Creek Golf World, Houston, Texas: TP: Andy North ($1,125), CP: Mike Hammond ($1,125), Bobby Cleboski, Thomas G. Moen, Bob Moen, J.C. Mosier.

231—57-58-57-59 — Katke Cousins GC, Rochester, Mich.: TP: Mark Pfeil ($1,000), CP: Ken Allard ($1,000), Tom Bieglecki, Mike Henderson, John Kennelley, Bob Diedrich.

231—59-57-55-60 — Edina CC, Edina, Minn.: TP: Bobby Wadkins ($1,000), CP: Ken Ellsworth ($1,000), Marshall V. Lewis, Bill Anderson, George G. Nickolatos, Dave Steingardt.

232—58-57-57-60 — Meridian Hills CC, Indianapolis, Ind.: TP: Dan Halldoresen ($642), CP: Jack Barber ($642), Bill David, Mike Perry, John Sutton, Harry Layfield.

232—57-58-58-59 — Greene Hills Club, Standardsville, Va.: TP: Jim Simons ($642), CP: Michael I. Moyers ($642), Gene Lawson, Wayne Allen Jr., Stan M. Powell, Mike D. Snow.

232—58-59-56-59 — Riverside CC, Menominee, Mich.: TP: Tom Purtzer ($642), CP: Michael A. Wietor ($642), Andy Cegelski, Andy La Barbera, Mike Johnson, Bob Picaro.

232—59-57-57-59 — The Woodlands Inn & CC, The Woodlands, Texas: TP: Jim Gallagher Jr. ($642), CP: Kent Wood ($642), Joe Clements, Gary Britt, Walter Netschi, Sidney Ravkind.

232—58-58-56-60 — Brookridge CC, Overland Park, Kan.: TP: Charlie Bolling ($642), CP: Bob Usher ($642), Jim Beatson, Steve Elliot, Carter Goldsberry, Jon Clark.

232—57-60-57-58 — Stockton GC, Stockton, Calif.: TP: Ed Fiori ($642), CP: Tony Troncale ($642), Dave Guidi, Sam Alexander, Gary Gabbard, Dick Klein.

232—59-56-57-60 — Washtenaw CC, Ypsilanti, Mich.: TP: David Ogrin ($642), CP: Randy Erskine ($642), Peter Savarino, Don Paige, Carl Calfin, Louis Λ. Carson.

233—56-62-58-57 — Spring-Ford CC, Royersford, Pa.: TP: Al Geiberger ($500), CP: Frank Dobbs ($500), William Glass, William Inmon, Lee D. Kellett, Lee J. Kellett.

233—56-59-60-58 — Diablo CC, Diablo, Calif.: TP: Brian Claar ($500), CP: Paul Wilcox ($500), Dave Derminio, Jack Abbett, Jim Doten, Jim McEuen.

233—58-58-57-60 — Idle Hour CC, Lexington, Ky.: TP: Pat McGowan ($500), CP: Gordon Leishman ($500), Joyce A. Roser, Steven Gene Parrish, John H. Hardwick, James C. Mitchell.

234—59-59-56-60 — Bayou Barriere CC, Gretna, La.: TP: Lanny Wadkins ($442), CP: Ed Selser ($442), Richie Wilson, Jay Ford, Karl Vogt, Gerald Carter.

234—61-57-57-59 — Topeka CC, Topeka, Kan.: TP: Andrew Magee ($442), CP: Steve McDonald ($442), Gregory A. Lux, Stan Zimmerman, Craig Woodbury, Doug Judd.

234—59-58-57-58 — Crow Valley GC, Bettendorf, Iowa: TP: Mark Hayes ($442), CP: Bob Vermeer ($442), Jeff Seitz, Vin Thompson, Allen V. Seitz, Jerry Mortier.

234—56-60-57-61 — Rio Rancho CC, Rio Rancho, N.M.: TP: Donnie Hammond ($442), CP: Jim Dickson ($442), Mike Goodart, John Youngblood, Olan Goldston, Jim Wall.

234—58-56-61-59 — Pine Lakes CC, Palm Coast, Fla.: TP: Jay Delsing ($442), CP: Robert J. Kendra ($442), Rick Herman, Larry Harbaugh, David Murray, Ron Spencer.

234—60-55-61-58 — Mesa Verde CC, Costa Mesa, Calif.: TP: Denis Watson ($442), CP: Art Schilling ($442), Bob Rieden, Bill Ott, Larry Wellen, Moe Quirk.

234—58-57-59-60 — Errol CC, Apopka, Fla.: TP: Billy Kratzert ($442), CP: Wally Kuchar ($442), Dan Disrud, Jim Summers, Rich Smart, Dr. Wilson Geldner.

235—59-58-58-60 — Jackson Hole GC, Jackson, Wyo.: TP: Jim Colbert ($300), CP: John Godwin ($300), Jeff Woodruff, Tom Weickhardt, Byron Bulucon, Ward Keevert.

235—58-58-60-59 — Smock Municipal GC, Indianapolis, Ind.: TP: Morris Hatalsky ($300), CP: John Greer ($300), Kenneth F. Adams, Richard L. Wright, Chuck Adcock, Pete Wojtowicz.

235—57-61-57-60 — Guyan GC, Huntington, W.Va.: TP: Woody Blackburn ($300), CP: Robert J. Thew Jr. ($300), Bob Beymer, Andy Houvouras, Marshall Hawkins, Chuck Whitling.

235—57-60-58-60 — Kingman Municipal GC, Kingman, Ariz.: TP: Fuzzy Zoeller ($300), CP: Paul Mowry ($300), Joe Bibich, Bob Sammeli, Ken Sammeli, David Sammeli.

236—55-59-61-61 — Hidden Hills CC, Stone Mountain, Ga.: TP: Bob Eastwood ($300), CP: Jimmy Paschal ($300), Julian "Tip" Tharp, Joe Goldys, Arthur "Skip" Moore, Mike Healy.

237—60-56-59-62 — Fort Wayne Elks CC, Fort Wayne, Ind.: TP: Hal Sutton ($300), CP: Jeff Ashby ($300), Dave Pettit, Gene Syfert, Dick Kerschner, John Carroll.

237—58-57-61-61 — San Clemente GC, San Clemente, Calif.: TP: Billy Pierot ($300), CP: James R. Weeks ($300), Bill Grange, Pete Southworth, Sal Russo, James Lee.

238—58-59-59-62 — Knollwood CC, West Bloomfield, Mich.: TP: Tom Kite ($300), CP: John A. Molenda ($300), Jerome Glassman, Stan Jacobson, Mac Fisher, John Krogsrud.

240—55-62-59-64 — Penfield CC, Penfield, N.Y.: TP: Lon Hinkle ($300), CP: Denny Ferstler ($300), Robert Pagano, Paul Julien, Charles Bowman Jr., George L. Smith Jr.

1985

PGA Tour professional Charles Coody and PGA club professional David James led Buena Vista Golf Club of Taft, Calif., to victory in the second Oldsmobile Scramble. The Championship expanded to 92 national finalist teams, and 44,000 players entered at their local golf clubs nationwide in qualifying events. Torrential rain hammered the resort complex, cancelling the second round and forcing a "chip-off" between the low scoring 26 teams and ties from the opening round. The survivors went to the Tournament Players Course to determine the Championship. The remaining 67 teams competed in a "skins game" competition on the North Course.

Date:	Sept. 28-30
Site:	The Woodlands, Houston, Texas
	Tournament Players Course, North Course

Buena Vista Golf Club finished the abbreviated 36-hole event with rounds of 30 and 27, a stroke better than a quintet of teams including St. Andrews Golf Club of Cedar Rapids, Iowa; Kalamazoo (Mich.) Country Club; Plum Brook Country Club of Sandusky, Ohio; Antelope Valley Country Club of Palmdale, Calif.; and Jackson Hole (Wyo.) Golf & Tennis Club.

GROSS DIVISION SUMMARY

57—30-27 — Buena Vista GC, Taft, Calif.: TP: Charles Coody ($7,500), CP: David James ($7,500), Ron Baker, Tom Clarksean, Mike Kresha, Don Hammons.

58—31-27 — Kalamazoo CC, Kalamazoo, Mich.: TP: Charlie Epps ($2,820), CP: Marty Lass ($2,820), Richard Glas, Jeff Matson, Ron Warners, Brian Boyer.

58—29-29 — Plum Brook CC, Sandusky, Ohio: TP: Tommy Valentine ($2,820), CP: Bob Carver ($2,820), John Manion, Jeff Manuella, Charles DeCaro, Frank Corder.

58—28-30 — Antelope Valley CC, Palmdale, Calif.: TP: Lon Hinkle ($2,820), CP: Steve Applegate ($2,820), Lane Hubbard, Ray Munoz, Al Munoz, David Hutchison.

58—28-30 — Jackson Hole Golf & Tennis Club, Jackson Hole, Wyo.: TP: Dave Hill ($2,820), CP: John Godwin ($2,820), Joe Curcio, Ed Arshen, Bob Boyer, Dave Hauser.

58—28-30 — St. Andrews GC, Cedar Rapids, Iowa: TP: Butch Baird ($2,820), CP: Mike Hall ($2,800), Alan Weyland, Neil Weyland, Sam Hossey, Larry Phillips.

59—31-28 — Kendale Lakes CC, Miami, Fla.: TP: Morris Hatalsky ($1,400), CP: Gary Baker ($1,400), Jim Ashburn, Darrell Baker, Will Diaz, Buddy Litowitz.

59—30-29 — Carmi CC, Carmi, Ill.: TP: Allen Miller ($1,410), CP: Garth Bayer ($1,410), John Given, Roger Given, Stan Williams, Richie Fulkerson.

59—30-29 — Flint Elks CC, Grand Rapids, Mich.: TP: Kent Wood ($1,410), CP: Larry Mancour ($1,410), Ramon Shimmons, Tom Ham, Jim Higgerson, Jack Pasco.

59—29-30 — Topeka CC, Topeka, Kan.: TP: John Fought ($1,410), CP: Tom Dawson ($1,410), Greg Lux, Stan Zimmerman, Craig Woodbury, Doug Judd.

59—30-29 — Orchard Ridge CC, Fort Wayne, Ind.: TP: Bruce Crampton ($1,410), CP: Steve Ferris ($1,410), Jim Luellen, Paul Russell, Jim Littlejohn, Tom Brubaker.

60—30-30 — Ashley GC, Atlanta, Ga.: TP: Mike Morley ($1,055), CP: Art Kraft Jr. ($1,055), William Duncan, John Miller, Bill Brannen, Steve Self.

60—30-30 —Riverview G & CC, Redding, Calif.: TP: Rex Caldwell ($1,055), CP: Russell Lee ($1,055), Tim Boehme, Terry Rash, Marv Barton, Larry Britain.

60—30-30 — Columbia Edgewater CC, Portland, Ore.: TP: Mark Pfeil ($1,055), CP: Scott Larson ($1,055), Andrew Richardson, Pat Richardson, Hugh Richardson, Tom Reynolds.

60—30-30 — Walden Lake CC, Plant City, Fla.: TP: Rod Curl ($1,055), CP: D.K. Kunkel ($1,055), David Miller, Joe Kenney, Clint Barnes, Britt Rogers.

60—30-30 — Hillcrest CC, Eau Claire, Wis.: TP: Al Geiberger ($1,055), CP: David Hicks ($1,055), Charles Grossklaus, Pete Meinlolz, Larry O'Neil, Tom Neier.

61—30-31 — Minikahda Club, Minneapolis, Minn.: TP: Don Massengale ($925), CP: Rob Brown ($925), Bill Jenkins, John McMorrow, Jim Johnson, Fred Watson.

62—32-30 — Onion Creek Club, Austin, Texas: TP: Jim Brotherton ($850), CP: Brent Buckman ($850), Bob Kay, Larry Dehority, Scott Sayers, Bob Yanover.

62—31-31 — Mint Valley CC, Longview, Wash.: TP: Greg Powers ($850), CP: Mahlon Moe ($850), Tom Graham, Rick Parker, Joe McGreevy, Dick Martinsen.

62—31-31 — Quail Creek CC, Oklahoma City, Okla.: TP: Dave Barr ($850), CP: Jimmie Gauntt ($850), Danny Gauntt, C.F. Freeman, Charles Trochta, Don Coit.

62—31-31 — Abenaqui GC, Rye Beach, N.H.: TP: Bob Wynn ($850), CP: Jim Sheerin ($850), Mike Simchik, Joseph Vought, Cliff Bridges, Sheldon Goodman.

63—32-31 — Annandale CC, Madison, Miss.: TP: Gibby Gilbert ($787), CP: John McNeeley ($787), Hap Hederman, Gerry Lauman, Bobby Croswell, Mike Carter.

63—33-30 — Twin Lakes CC, Federal Way, Wash.: TP: Tommy Aaron ($787), CP: Randy Jensen ($787), Scott Robinson, Max Rabinowitz, Don Bonner, Avo Avedisian.

64—31-33 — Muskego Lakes CC, Hale's Corners, Wis.: TP: Leonard Thompson ($760), CP: Steve Krause ($760), Harry Kmiecik, Toby Morris, Al Fortkamp, Ron Olson.

64—32-32 — Dogwood Hill CC, Osage Beach, Mo.: TP: Bobby Mitchell ($760), CP: Gary Mitchell ($760), Randy Penland, Jim Mitchell, Delmar Rose, Lee Sherman.

65—34-31 — Indianwood GC, Lake Orion, Mich.: TP: Bob Eastwood ($745), CP: Tom Deaton ($745), Ben Jaroslaw, Joseph Wilhelm, Jim Northrup, Jan Richmond.

TP: PGA Tour Professional
CP: PGA Club Professional

1984

Fred Couples tapped in a one-foot birdie putt to win the inaugural Oldsmobile Scramble Championship for Little Turtle Country Club of Westerville, Ohio,

Date:	Sept. 29 - Oct. 1
Site:	Walt Disney World Golf Resort, Lake Buena Vista, Fla.
	Palm, Magnolia Courses

The inaugural championship, played under perfect autumn weather, involved 43,000 golfers nationwide competing in more than 1,300 qualifying tournaments through the direction of the PGA of America's 41 sections.

A field of 53, five-member teams played in the national finals, and the low 24 teams played the final two rounds. Each finalist team was joined by a PGA Tour professional.

Little Turtle Country Club, with PGA professional Steve Messerschmidt, broke 60 all three rounds (57-59-58), for a 42-under-par total of 174, a stroke better than Montgomery (Ala.) Country Club. The team birdied 10 of its first 11 holes, and won the Championship with a birdie at the 17th hole when Messerschmidt almost holed a wedge approach shot. Couples was called in to tap in the putt.

The Scramble was founded by Richard Garn of Coldwater, Mich., who had conducted a Michigan Scramble (1973-76) involving players from 17 states. He eventually bought out his partner in the event and gained acceptance by the PGA of America to expand nationally. To move the event to its current level, Garn gained full sponsorship of Oldsmobile on Dec. 27, 1983.

GROSS DIVISION SUMMARY

174—57-59-58 — Little Turtle CC, Westerville, Ohio: TP: Fred Couples ($7,500), CP: Steve Messerschmidt ($7,500), Bob Belding, Barry Casoli, Robert Moock, Bob Robinson.

175—57-58-60 — Montgomery CC, Montgomery, Ala.: TP: Bruce Devlin ($4,500), CP: John Nichols Jr. ($4,500), Bobby Hodgson, Frank McGrough, Bill Rue, John Eley.

176—63-54-59 — Antelope Valley GC, Palmdale, Calif.: TP: Steve Melnyk ($3,200), CP: Steve Applegate ($3,200), Lane Hubbard, David Hutchison, Ray Munoz, Bob Herman.

177—60-58-59 — Baywood CC, Pasadena, Texas: TP: Barry Jaeckel ($2,500), CP: John Dill ($2,500), Greg Glover, Russell Schroeder, Hal Glover, Lionel Spret.

178—61-57-60 — Kendale Lakes CC, Miami, Fla.: TP: Rex Caldwell ($1,833), CP: Tom Gibson ($1,833), Ron Gaines, Doug Kelly, Andy Goff, Bob Rochfort.

178—58-63-57 — CC of Ashland, Ashland, Ohio: TP: Bob Eastwood ($1,833), CP: Dan Priest ($1,833), David Draudt, Tom James, Dee Garber, David Mickley.

178—62-60-56 — Cushing CC, Cushing, Okla.: TP: Pat McGowan ($1,833), CP: Ken Tate ($1,833), Steve Cochran, Terry Stewart, Jay Foster, Dick Womack.

179—59-58-62 — Crag Burn GC, East Aurora, N.Y.: TP: Bobby Nichols ($1,500), CP: Lonnie Nielsen ($1,500), Gary Grelick, Greg Smith, Jim Smith, Sue Smith.

180—60-59-61 — Overland Park GC, Denver, Colo.: TP: Mark Lye ($1,316), CP: Tom Romolo ($1,316), Frank Belluci, Steve Kerr, Mike Dougherty, Ed Ott.

180—62-59-59 — Prince George CC, Mitchellville, Md.: TP: David Ogrin ($1,316), CP: Alex Lively ($1,316), Robert Bopst, Paul Miller, George Mavrikes, R.I. Miller.

180—62-59-59 — Cameron Park CC, Cameron Park, Calif.: TP: Victor Regalado ($1,316), CP: Dave Bingham ($1,316), Paul Creasey, Val Mariotti, Bob Detour, John Murphy.

181—62-58-61 — Twin Lakes CC, Dillon, S.C.: TP: Roger Maltbie ($1,055), CP: Wayne Roberts ($1,055), Mike Baucom, Vernon Grimsley, Jackie Flowers, Harry Moody.

181—64-56-61 — Overbrook CC, Bryn Mawr, Pa.: TP: Scott Hoch ($1,055), CP: Larry Demers ($1,055), Frank Duffy, Berg Barburr, Dick Quinn, Jim Scheifla.

181—61-59-61 — Minnetonka CC, Excelsior, Minn.: TP: Ed Fiori ($1,055), CP: Robert Olds ($1,055), Pete Budreau, Chuck Immel, Gib Larson, Kip Johnson.

181—58-61-61 — Blythfield CC, Belmont, Mich.: TP: Greg Powers ($1,055), CP: Buddy Whitten ($1,055), Dave Mairn, Les Prangley, Bob Quiri, Bob Toigo.

181—59-63-59 — Spring Hill CC, Tifton, Ga.: TP: Lon Hinkle ($1,055), CP: Stan Moore ($1,055), Joe Tinsley, Chris Cooper, Bill VanDyke, Mike Bostick.

182—60-62-60 — Stevens Point CC, Stevens Point, Wis.: TP: Gary McCord ($887), CP: Bob Reith ($887), Wayne Emerson, Jim Shuda, Joe Rechner, Don Soderburg.

182—61-61-62 — Bent Creek Inn CC, Gatlinburg, Tenn.: TP: George Burns ($887), CP: Jim Paschal ($887), Mike Connor, Ed Steele, Kendall Hays, Joe Whaley.

182—60-62-60 — Kingman GC, Kingman, Ariz.: TP: Bill Kratzert ($887), CP: Paul Mowry ($887), Joe Bibich, Dave Sammeli, Bob Sammeli, Ken Sammeli.

182—59-60-63 — Diablo CC, Diablo, Calif.: TP: Dan Forsman ($887), CP: Bob Wynn ($887), Bob Callan, John Lahti, Jim McEuen, Jeryco Peterson.

183—63-59-61 — Keystone Golf & CC, Keystone Heights, Fla.: TP: Wally Armstrong ($825), CP: Terry Catlett ($825), Jeff Batts, John Martin, Rick Catlett, Jim McMurtry.

184—61-61-62 — Wellesley CC, Wellesley, Mass.: TP: Jim Thorpe ($787), CP: Les Bond ($787), Robert Bashian, Russ French, Mike Crismond, David Dandstrom.

184—61-60-63 — Tower Tee Golf Center, St. Louis, Mo.: TP: Allen Miller ($787), CP: Dick Lotz ($787), Vic Leffler, Ed Murphy, Jody Trover, Neil VanLeeuwen.

186—71-61-64 — Washtenaw CC, Ypsilanti, Mich.: TP: Julius Boros ($765), CP: Randy Erskine ($765), Jack Aldred, Jim Lear Jr., Ivan Barris, John Ruggiero III.

TP: PGA Tour Professional
CP: PGA Club Professional

PGA OF AMERICA SECTIONS

The Professional Golfers' Association of America is divided into 41 geographical "sections." Each section operates within the framework of the PGA Constitution. Many sections also are sub-divided into "chapters" for the geographical convenience of members.

The sections hold elections each year for individual officers and maintain their own staffs, headed by an executive director who administers the operations of the section. The sections maintain a close working relationship with the PGA of America staff in Palm Beach Gardens, Fla.

Each section conducts its own events for PGA members, apprentices and amateur golfers. For example, each individual section conducts an annual section Championship for its members, in addition to other member tournaments throughout the season.

The sections also provide the grass-roots network necessary to accomplish direct communication with the nation's more than 25 million amateur golfers. The sections conduct, for example, regional qualifying tournaments for amateur events such as the Oldsmobile Scramble and the Maxfli PGA Junior Championship. In addition, many sections sponsor junior golf clinics and help underwrite the cost of sponsoring the Nike Tour (formerly Ben Hogan Tour), now in its fifth year of operation.

The sections also conduct educational programs, workshops and seminars for the benefit of local PGA members and apprentices. They work with the national office to provide nationally renowned experts to participate in these programs, thus assisting PGA members in fulfilling the PGA mission statement: "Making your golf game better — making golf a better game."

PGA of America Sections and Regions

ALOHA
770 Kapiolani Blvd. Room 715, Honolulu, HI
96813 (808) 593-2230; Fax: (808) 592-2234

CAROLINAS
3852 Hwy. 9 East (P. O. Box 709), North
Myrtle Beach, SC 29597-0709
(803) 399-CPGA (2742); Fax: (803) 399-1504

CENTRAL NEW YORK
822 State Fair Rd., Syracuse, NY 13209
(315) 468-6812; Fax: (315) 488-8268

COLORADO
12323 East Cornell, Suite 21, Aurora, CO
80014 (303) 745-3697; Fax: (303) 745-5088

CONNECTICUT
35 Cold Spring Road, Suite 212, Rocky Hill,
CT 06067 (203) 257-GOLF (4653);
Fax: (203) 257-8355

DIXIE
601 Vestavia Parkway, Suite 320, Birmingham,
AL 35216 (205) 822-0321; Fax: (205) 822-2842

GATEWAY
12225 Clayton Road, St. Louis, MO 63131
(314) 991-4994; Fax: (314) 991-3543

GEORGIA
1165 Northchase Pkwy., Suite 230, Marietta,
GA 30067 (404) 952-9063; Fax: (404) 859-9305

GULF STATES
P.O. Box 29426, New Orleans, LA 70189
(504) 245-7333; Fax: (504) 245-7364

ILLINOIS
2100 Clearwater Drive, Suite 206, Oak Brook,
IL 60521 (708) 990-7799; Fax: (708) 990-7864

INDIANA
P.O. Box 516, Franklin, IN 46131
(317) 738-9696; Fax: (317) 738-9436

IOWA
1930 St. Andrews N.E., Cedar Rapids, IA
52402 (319) 378-9142; Fax: (319) 378-9203

KENTUCKY
P.O. Box 18396, Louisville, KY 40218-0396
(502) 499-7255; Fax: (502) 499-7422

METROPOLITAN
P. O. Box 268, Wykagyl Station, New Rochelle,
NY 10804 (914) 235-7277; Fax: (914) 235-9379

MICHIGAN
32774 Five Mile Road, Livonia, MI 48154
(313) 522-2323; Fax: (313) 522-5626

MIDDLE ATLANTIC
7270 Cradlerock Way, Columbia, MD 21045
(301) 621-8320; Fax: (410) 381-8475

MIDWEST
1900 Corporate Centre, S. Outer Road, Suite
106, Blue Springs, MO 64015 (816) 229-6565;
Fax: (816) 229-9644

MINNESOTA
Bunker Hills GC, Highway 242 & Foley Blvd.,
Coon Rapids, MN 55448 (612) 754-0820;
Fax: (612) 754-0891

NEBRASKA
9301 Firethorn Lane, Lincoln, NE 68520
(402) 489-7760; Fax: (402) 489-1785

NEW ENGLAND
1 Audubon Road, Wakefield, MA 01880
(617) 246-4653/246-8353; Fax: (617) 246-4938

NEW JERSEY
P.O. Box 200, 1 Forsgate Drive, Jamesburg, NJ
08831 (908) 521-4000; Fax: (908) 521-4000

NORTHEASTERN NEW YORK
48 Howard St., Albany, NY 12207
(518) 463-3067; Fax: (518) 463-8656

NORTHERN CALIFORNIA
2133 Las Positas Court, Suite A, Livermore,
CA 94550-9774 (510) 455-7800;
Fax: (510) 449-5753

NORTHERN OHIO
38121 Euclid Avenue, Willoughby, OH 44094
(216) 951-4546; Fax: (216) 951-0508

NORTHERN TEXAS
500 N. Central Expressway, Suite 272, Plano,
TX 75074 (214) 881-GOLF (4653);
Fax: (214) 423-7861

NORTH FLORIDA
200 Forest Lake Blvd., Suite 3, Daytona Beach,
FL 32119 (904) 322-0899; Fax: (904) 322-2567

PACIFIC NORTHWEST
4011 Yelm Hwy. SE, Olympia, WA 98501-5170
(206) 456-6496; Fax: (206) 456-6745

PHILADELPHIA:
Plymouth Green Office Campus, 801 East
Germantown Pike, Suite F-6, Norristown, PA
19401 (215) 277-5777; Fax: (215) 277-6151

ROCKY MOUNTAIN
595 E. State Street, Eagle, ID 83616
(208) 939-6028; Fax: (208) 939-6058

SOUTH CENTRAL
951 North Forest Ridge Blvd.,
Broken Arrow, OK 74014
(918) 357-3332; Fax: (918) 357-3328

SOUTHERN CALIFORNIA
601 S. Valencia, Suite 200, Brea, CA 92621
(714) PRO-GOLF (776-4653);
Fax: (714) 572-1350

SOUTHERN OHIO
17 South High Street, 12th Floor, Columbus,
OH 43215 (614) 221-7194; Fax: (614) 221-1989

SOUTHERN TEXAS
1776 Woodstead Court, Suite 220, The
Woodlands, TX 77380 (713) 363-0511;
Fax: (713) 292-4175

SOUTH FLORIDA
10804 W. Sample Road, Coral Springs, FL
33065; Att.: PGA Building (305) 752-9299;
Fax: (305) 752-9659

SOUTHWEST
5040 E. Shea Blvd., Suite 250, Scottsdale, AZ
85254 (602) 443-9002; Fax: (602) 443-9006

SUN COUNTRY
Mountain Run Center, 5850 Eubank NE, Suite
B-72, Albuquerque, NM 87111 (505) 271-1442;
Fax: (505) 271-8626

TENNESSEE
1500 Legends Lane, Franklin, TN 37064
(615) 790-7600; Fax: (615) 790-8600

TRI-STATE
221 Sherwood Drive, Monaca, PA 15061
(412) 774-2224; Fax: (412) 774-5535

UTAH
419 East 100 South, Salt Lake City, UT 84111
(801) 532-7421; Fax: (801) 532-7427

WESTERN NEW YORK
P.O. Box 1728, Williamsville, NY 14231-1728
(716) 626-0603; Fax: (716) 626-5308

WISCONSIN:
4000 W. Brown Deer Road, Milwaukee, WI
53209 (414) 365-4474; Fax: (414) 365-4479

ALOHA

Executive Director
Marc Henry

President
Chuck Larson
Kaneohe Klipper GC, Kaneohe, Hawaii

770 Kapiolani Blvd., Room 715, Honolulu, HI 96813

Phone:(808) 593-2230/2232
Fax: (808) 593-2234

Vice President/Treasurer	**Secretary**
Lloyd Porter	Joe Root, Waikoloa Beach GC,
Ala Wai GC, Kailua, Hawaii	Waikoloa, Hawaii

1993 SECTION AWARD WINNERS

Golf Professional of the Year
Dennis Rose, Waikoloa Kings'
Course, Waikoloa, Hawaii

Junior Golf Leader
Matt Mitchell, Kapalua Bay
Course, Kapalua, Maui, Hawaii

Teacher of the Year
J.D. Ebersberger
Mauna Kea Beach Hotel GC,
Kohala Coast, Hawaii

1993 MERCHANDISER OF THE YEAR

Private Greg Nichols, Waialae CC, Honolulu, Hawaii
Public Lloyd Porter, Ala Wai GC, Honolulu, Hawaii
Resort Gary Planos, Kapalua Plantation Course,
          Kapalua, Maui, Hawaii

1994 SCHEDULE OF EVENTS

April 13-17	Mid-Pac Open & Pro-Am, Mid-Pac CC
April 18-19	Scotch 4-Ball Championship, Waikoloa Kings' Course
April 23-24	Pearl President's Cup, Pearl CC
May 7-9	Hall of Fame Championship & Pro-Am, Kapalua Plantation
May 27-29	Rainbow Open, Mililani GC
June 2-5	Maui Open & Pro-Am, TBA
June 14	Assistants' Championship, Leilehua GC
June 14-15	PGA Junior Golf Championship, Age 12 and under, Wailua GC, Kapaa, Kauai; Age 13-17, Kauai Lagoons Course, Lihue, Kauai
June 16-19	OCC Men's Invitational, Oahu CC
June 24-26	Barbers Point Amateur Invitational, Barbers Point CC
June 25-26	Mission Foods Clambake, Kapalua GC
June 27-July 2	Mauna Kea Beach Hotel Pro-Am, Mauna Kea GC
July 28	Match Play Championship, Prince G & CC, Princeville, Kauai
July 31 - Aug. 2	The Challenge at Manele, Lanai City, Lanai
Oct. 8-9	Section Senior Championship, Kaanapali GC, Kaanapali, Maui
Nov. 14	Head Pro/Assistants Championship, Makalei Hawaii CC, Kona, Hawaii
Dec. 9-11	State Open, Makena GC, Kihei, Maui
Dec. 16-18	Sheraton Makaha Pro-Am 8 Open, Sheraton Makaha Resort & CC, Waianae, Hawaii

CAROLINAS

Executive Director
James P. Hart Jr.

President
Bill Clemmer
Cowans Ford CC, Stanley, N.C.

3852 Hwy. 9 East, P.O. Box 709, North Myrtle Beach, SC 29597-0709

Phone: (803) 399-2742	**Tournament Official**
Fax: (803) 399-1504	Mark Harrison
Vice President	**Bookkeeper/Office Manager**
Ed Ibarguen, Duke University GC, Durham, N.C.	Vickie Parsons
	Membership Administrator
Secretary	Sally Hassenplug
Chip King, Mid Pines Resort, Southern Pines, N.C.	**Tournament Secretary**
	Joanne Holdren
Director of Tournament Operations	**Receptionist/Job Referral Secretary**
Darrell Crall	Jackie Crim

1993 SECTION AWARD WINNERS

Golf Professional of the Year
William G. Clemmer
Cowans Ford CC, Stanley, N.C.

Junior Golf Leader
David Vandeventer
Piney Point GC, Norwood, N.C.

Teacher of the Year
Ted Brasile
Greensboro CC, Greensboro, N.C.
Robert Linville, Carolina Golf
Learning Center, Greensboro, N.C.

Horton Smith
Rick Burton, Burlington, N.C.

Bill Strausbaugh
Ed Ibarguen
Duke University GC, Durham, N.C.

1993 MERCHANDISER OF THE YEAR

Private J. Hart Brown, The CC of Charleston, Charleston, S.C.
Public Zack Veasey, Hillandale GC, Durham, N.C.
Resort Donald Padgett, Pinehurst CC, Pinehurst, N.C.

1994 SCHEDULE OF EVENTS

May 2-4	Michael Thomas Tradition, Florence CC, Florence, S.C.
May 26-27	Carolinas PGA Seniors' Championship: Beachwood GC and Possum Trot GC, North Myrtle Beach, S.C.
June 28-30	Maxfli South Carolina Open, Musgrove Mill GC, Clinton, S.C.
June 28-30	Ping North Carolina Open, River Run Country Club, Davidson, N.C.
July 6-7	Carolinas PGA Assistants' Championship, TBA
July 18-19	Titleist/Footjoy Pro-Assistants' Championship, TBA
July 26-28	Spalding/Cross Creek Lowcountry Open, Dataw Island Club (Cotton Pike), St. Helena, S.C.
Aug. 8	Oldsmobile Scramble Section Finals, (2 sites), TBA
Aug. 16-18	Carolinas Open, TBA
Aug. 22	Oldsmobile Scramble Section Finals, (2 sites), TBA
Aug. 30-31	SCPGA Chapter Championship, Crowfield G & CC, Goose Creek, S.C.
Sept. 7-9	Vantage Classic of the Carolinas: Wild Dunes (Links Course), Isle of Palms, S.C.; Dunes West GC, Mt. Pleasant, S.C.
Sept. 22-23	SCPGA Chapter Pro-Pro Championship, Greenwood CC, Greenwood, S.C.
Oct. 18-21	Carolinas PGA Match Play Championship, Woodlake CC, Vass, N.C.
Nov. 29-Dec. 1	Carolinas PGA Pro-Pro Championship, TBA

CENTRAL NEW YORK

Executive Director
Ron Stepanek

President
Michael S. Doctor
Skaneateles CC, Skaneateles, N.Y.

822 State Fair Boulevard, Syracuse, NY 13209

Phone: (315) 468-6812
Fax: (315) 488-8268
Vice President
C. J. Parry
R.D. No. 4, Box 531,
Canastota, N.Y.

Secretary
Mark Flurschutz
147 Ross Street Ext.,
Auburn, N.Y.
Administrative Assistant
Kathleen Pascarella

1993 SECTION AWARD WINNERS

Golf Professional of the Year
Ron Dunham
Vestal Hills CC, Binghamton, N.Y.
Teacher of the Year
Robert McCarthy
Cavalry Club, Manlius, N.Y.
Junior Golf Leader
Joe Tesori
Drumlins GC, Syracuse, N.Y.

Horton Smith
Mark Flurschutz
Tuscora GC, Marcellus, N.Y.
Bill Strausbaugh
Bill Galloway
Life Member, Auburn, N.Y.

1993 MERCHANDISER OF THE YEAR

Private John Markley, The Skenandoa Club, Clinton, N.Y.
Public Marian Burke, Seven Oaks GC, Hamilton, N.Y.
Resort Rick Wolcott, Leatherstocking GC, Cooperstown, N.Y.

1994 SCHEDULE OF EVENTS

May 13	Yamaha Pro-President, Lafayette CC, Jamesville, N.Y.
June 10	Spalding Pro-Assistant, TBA
July 22	PGA Junior Championship, Highland Park GC, Auburn, N.Y.
July 29	Pro-Junior, Skaneateles CC, Skaneateles, N.Y.
Aug. 19	Taylor Made Assistants' Championship, Seven Oaks GC, Hamilton, N.Y.
Aug. 26	Oldsmobile Scramble, En-Joie Golf Club, Endicott, N.Y.
Sept. 11-12	Ping Section Championship, TBA
Sept. 11-12	Club Professional Championship, TBA
Sept. 26	Spalding Pro-Pro, Seven Oaks GC, Hamilton, N.Y.

COLORADO

Executive Director
Myran Craig

President
Keith Schneider
Castle Pines GC, Castle Rock, Colo.

12323 E. Cornell Avenue, Suite 21, Aurora, CO 80014

Phone: (303) 745-3697
Fax: (303) 745-5088
Vice President
Nigel Rouse
CC at Castle Pines,
Castle Rock, Colo.

Secretary/Treasurer
John Trenck
Pinehurst CC, Denver, Colo.
Executive Secretary
Kayo Craig
Secretary/Receptionist
Dawn Cook

1993 SECTION AWARD WINNERS

Golf Professional of the Year
Vic Kline
Indian Hills GC, Arvada, Colo.
Teacher of the Year
Michael McGetrick
Cherry Hills CC, Engelwood, Colo.
Junior Golf Leader
Barry Jennings
Fox Hill CC, Longmont, Colo.

Horton Smith
Kyle Heyen
Hiwan GC, Evergreen, Colo.
Bill Strausbaugh
Myran Craig, Colorado Section
PGA, Aurora, Colo.

1993 MERCHANDISER OF THE YEAR

Private Keith Schneider, Castle Pines GC, Castle Rock, Colo.
Public Erroll Miller, Breckenridge GC, Breckenridge, Colo.
Resort Tom Clary, Beaver Creek GC, Vail, Colo.

1994 SCHEDULE OF EVENTS

May 31- June 1	Myran Craig Pro-Pro Championship, Inverness GC, Englewood, Colo.
June 20- Sept. 2	Pro-Pro Match Play Championship, Castle Pines GC, Castle Rock, Colo.
Sept. 12-14	Section Championship & Club Professional Championship Qualifying, Inverness GC, Englewood, Colo.
Sept. 27-28	Apprentice Championship, Meridian GC, Englewood, Colo.
Oct. 3-5	Section Seniors' Championship & Seniors' Club Professional Championship Qualifying, Greeley CC, Greeley, Colo.

CONNECTICUT

Executive Director
Tom Hantke

President
Gary Reynolds
Hartford GC, W. Hartford, Conn.

35 Cold Spring Road, Suite 212, Rocky Hill, CT 06067

Phone: (203) 257-4653
Fax: (203) 257-8355
Vice President/Treasurer
Frank Selva
Race Brook CC, Orange, Conn.

Secretary
Tony Rowe, Ellington Ridge CC,
Ellington, Conn.
Administrative Assistant
Carol Passavant

1993 SECTION AWARD WINNERS

Golf Professional of the Year
Donald Malen
GC of Avon, Avon, Conn.
Teacher of the Year
Ken Doyle, Hop Meadow CC,
Simsbury, Conn.
Junior Golf Leader
Kris Smith
Clinton CC, Clinton, Conn.

Horton Smith
Ron Beck, Crumpin-Fox Club,
Bernardston, Mass.
Bill Strausbaugh
John Murphy, The CC of
Farmington, Farmington, Conn.

1993 MERCHANDISER OF THE YEAR

Private Steve Munch, TPC at River Highlands, Cromwell, Conn.
Public Ron Beck, Crumpin-Fox Club, Bernardston, Mass.

1994 SCHEDULE OF EVENTS

May 2	Pro-Pro, Suffield CC, Suffield, Conn.
May 26	Pro-Assistant, Norwich GC, Norwich, Conn.
July 26	Oldsmobile Scramble, The Farms CC, Wallingford, Conn.
July 29	Oldsmobile Scramble: Oak Ridge CC, Feeding Hills, Mass.; Tower Ridge CC, Avon, Conn.
Aug. 1	PGA Junior Championship, Ellington Ridge CC, Ellington, Conn.
Aug. 1-2	Connecticut State Open, Wethersfield CC, Wethersfield, Conn.
Aug. 18-19	WMASS Open, Elmcrest CC, East Longmeadow, Mass.
Aug. 25	Pro-Junior, Chippanee GC, Bristol, Conn.
Aug. 29	Pro-President, Hartford Golf Club, Hartford, Conn.
Sept. 12-13	Section Championship, Ellington Ridge CC, Ellington, Conn.
Sept. 26	Pro-Pro, Black Hall Club, Old Lyme, Conn.
Oct. 6	Ben Loving Chapter Championship, TBA
Oct. 20	Ultra Cup Chapter Championship, Crestview CC, Agawam, Mass.

DIXIE

Executive Director
David Berry

President
Butch Byrd
North River Yacht Club, Tuscaloosa, Ala.

601 Vestavia Parkway, Suite 320, Birmingham, AL 35216

Phone: (205) 822-0321
Fax: (205) 822-2842
Vice President
Clay Koschel
Azalea City GC, Mobile, Ala.
Secretary
Gene Diamond
Huntsville CC, Huntsville, Ala.

Dixie Section Pro-Am Administrator
Ralph Thomas
Gulf Coast Pro-Am Administrator
Bill Habel
Office Administrator
Heather C. Powell

1993 SECTION AWARD WINNERS

Golf Professional of the Year
Barry N. Holt, Cherokee Ridge
CC, Union Grove, Ala.
Teacher of the Year
Wayne Flint
Eagle Point GC, Birmingham, Ala.
Junior Golf Leader
Tony Simpson, Bay Point Yacht
& CC, Panama City Beach, Fla.

Horton Smith
Brent Krause, Wynlakes
G & CC, Montgomery, Ala.
Bill Strausbaugh
Bob Barrett, Drummond
Company, Birmingham, Ala.

1993 MERCHANDISER OF THE YEAR

Private Mark Kizzire, Vestavia CC, Birmingham, Ala.
Public Lynn Shaffer, Bent Brook GC, Bessemer, Ala.
Resort Norm Tums, Emerald Bay Club, Destin, Fla.

1994 SCHEDULE OF EVENTS

June 6-7	Assistants' Championship, The Moors, Pensacola, Fla.
June 13	Club Car Pro-President, Riverchase CC, Birmingham, Ala.
June 21-22	Gulf Coast Chapter Championship, Timber Creek, Daphne, Ala.
July 19-20	Maxfli PGA Junior Championship, Stonebrook Village, Pace, Fla.
July 21-24	State Opens, TBA
July 25	Oldsmobile Scramble, Hombre GC, Panama City, Fla.
July 28	Senior/Junior Championship, Selma CC, Selma, Ala.
Aug. 2	Oldsmobile Scramble, Terri Pines GC, Cullman, Ala.
Aug. 9	Pro-Junior, WynLakes G&CC, Montgomery, Ala.
Aug. 19	Oldsmobile Scramble, North River Yacht Club, Tuscaloosa, Ala.
Aug. 22-23	Senior Club Professional Championship, TBA
Aug. 22-23	Cross Creek Section Senior Championship, TBA
Sept. 12-14	Cross Creek Section Championship, Riverchase CC, Birmingham, Ala.
Sept. 12-14	Club Professional Championship, Riverchase CC, Birmingham, Ala.
Sept. 19	Pro-Assistant, Pine Tree CC, Birmingham, Ala.
Oct. 24-25	Alabama Chapter Championship, Montgomery (Ala.) CC
Nov. 14-16	Pro-Team Championship, Stonebrook Village, Pace, Fla.

GATEWAY

Executive Director
Jeff Smith

President
Steve Spray
St. Louis CC, St. Louis, Mo.

12225 Clayton Road, St. Louis, MO 63131

Phone: (314) 991-4994
Fax: (314) 991-3543
Vice President
Russ Luedloff
Four Seasons CC Chesterfield, Mo.
Secretary/Treasurer
Garth Bayer
Old Warson CC, St. Louis, Mo.
Assistant Executive Director
Patty Sturgis

Junior Coordinator
Renee Pagenkopf
Office Administration
Janey Jones
Tournament Director
Jim Niederkom
Tournament Assistant
Dick McGeehan

1993 SECTION AWARD WINNERS

Golf Professional of the Year
Garth Bayer
Old Warson CC, Ladue, Mo.
Teacher of the Year
Charles Long
Algonquin GC, Glendale, Mo.
Junior Golf Leader
Sam Gilliland
Little Lakes GC, St. Louis, Mo.

Horton Smith
Victor Whipp
Sunset Hills CC,
Edwardsville, Ill.
Bill Strausbaugh
Mike Halcomb
Whitmoor CC, St. Charles, Mo.

1993 MERCHANDISER OF THE YEAR

Private Phil Hewitt, Westborough CC, Kirkwood, Mo.
Public Stephen Johnson, Spencer T. Olin Community GC, Alton, Ill.
Resort Tom Gray, Marriott's Tan-Tar-A, Osage Beach, Mo.

1994 SCHEDULE OF EVENTS

April 18	Spalding Pro Open No. 1, Crab Orchard GC
May 2-4	Match Play Championship, The Players Club
May 9	Spalding Pro Open No. 2, CC at the Legends
May 16	Starline Team Championship, Old Warson CC
June 6	Spalding 36-Hole Pro Open, Bellerive CC
June 14-19	Tommy Armour Tour Event, Fox Run GC
June 27	Spalding Pro Open No. 4, Westwood CC
July 18	Nike Open Qualifying, Spencer T. Olin CGC
July 21-24	Nike Tour, Lake Forest CC
July 25	Oldsmobile Scramble, Whitmoor CC
Aug. 1	PING Club Professional Championship, St. Louis CC, St. Louis, Mo.
Aug. 8	Assistants' Championship, TBD
Aug. 9-10	PGA Junior Championship, Whitmoor CC
Aug. 15	Spalding Pro Open No. 5, Meadowbrook GC
Aug. 29-30	Pepsi Section Championship, Lake Forest CC
Sept. 6	Spalding Pro Open No. 6, The Links GC
Sept. 16, 18	Blue Choice Pro-Am & Shootout, Bogey Hills CC
Sept. 20-24	Gateway Masters, Bogey Hills CC

GEORGIA

Executive Director
John Bryan

President
Dan Murphy
Cherokee Town & CC, Dunwoody,

1165 Northchase Pkwy., Suite 230, Marietta, GA 30067

Phone: (404) 952-9063
Fax: (404) 859-9305
Vice President
Archie Lemon Jr., Cumming, Ga.
Secretary
Ray Cutright
Idle Hour GC, Macon, Ga.

Tournament Director
Peter Ripa
Director of Member Services
Betty Ann Perrine
Secretary/Receptionist
Casey Hill
Communication Manager
Joe Belcher

1993 SECTION AWARD WINNERS

Golf Professional of the Year
Rich Gaffoglio
Capital City Club, Atlanta, Ga.
Teacher of the Year
Danny Elkins
McDivots GC, Roswell, Ga.
Junior Golf Leader
Mike McCollum
Houston Lake CC, Perry, Ga.

Horton Smith
Will Allen
Cartersville CC, Cartersville, Ga.
Bill Strausbaugh
Ed Everett
Doublegate CC, Albany, Ga.

1993 MERCHANDISER OF THE YEAR

Private Rich Gaffoglio, Capital City Club, Atlanta, Ga.
Public Johnny Paulk III, Jekyll Island GC, Jekyll Island, Ga.
Resort Don Ferrone, Callaway Gardens Golf Resort, Pine Mountain, Ga.

1994 SCHEDULE OF EVENTS

April 25	Titleist Pro-Assistant, Cherokee T & CC, Dunwoody, Ga.
May 16-17	Griffin Classic, Griffin CC, Griffin Ga.
May 31	E-Z-GO Pro-President, Atlanta Athletic Club, Duluth, Ga.
June 13-14	Bridgestone Atlanta Open, the Legends at Chateau Elan, Braselton, Ga.
June 27-28	Maxfli PGA Junior Championship, Canterbury CC, Marietta, Ga.
July 11	Pepsi Pro-Junior, Champions Club of Atlanta, Alpharetta, Ga.
July 18-19	Perry Classic, Perry (Ga.) CC
Aug. 1	Assistants' Championship, Orchard Hills, Newnan, Ga.
Aug. 18-25	Michelob State Opens, Reynolds Plantation/Great Water/Greenboro, Eaton
Sept. 12-14	Ping Section Championship, Sea Island GC, St. Simons Island, Ga.
Sept. 12-14	Club Professional Championship, Sea Island GC, St. Simons Island, Ga.
Sept. 27-28	Ping Section Senior Championship, The Standard Club, Duluth, Ga.
Oct. 17-20	Spalding Match Play Championship, Jennings Mill CC, Athens, Ga.
Dec. 12-13	Cross Creek Pro-Pro, Jekyll Island GC, Jekyll Island, Ga.

GULF STATES

Executive Director
Robert Brown

President
Jimmy Gallagher
Crystal Springs, Miss.

P.O. Box 29426, New Orleans, LA 70189

Phone: (504) 245-7333
Fax: (504) 245-7364
Vice President
William Earl Morgan
Brookhaven CC,
Brookhaven, Miss.

Secretary
Greg Core, Ormond CC,
Destrehan, La.
Assistant Executive Director
Dick Walcott
Administrative Assistant
Beverly Gates

1993 SECTION AWARD WINNERS

Golf Professional of the Year
James Leitz
Pinewood CC, Slidell, La.
Teacher of the Year
Rob Noel
Bayou Oaks GC,
New Orleans, La.
Junior Golf Leader
Ronnie Benandi, Bayou Oaks
GC, New Orleans, La.

Horton Smith Award
Jerry Weeks
Hattiesburg CC,
Hattiesburg, Miss.
Bill Strausbaugh
Jimmy Gallagher
Crystal Springs, Miss.

1993 MERCHANDISER OF THE YEAR

Private Andre' Marchand, Beau Chene Golf and RC, Mandeville, La.
Public Ronnie Benandi, Bayou Oaks GC, New Orleans, La.
Resort Phillip Hill, Diamondhead CC, Bay St. Louis, Miss.

1994 SCHEDULE OF EVENTS

May 16	Maxfli Pro-Pro, Le Triomphe GC, Broussard, La.
June 27	Wood Brothers Pro-Assistant, Castlewoods CC, Jackson, Miss.
July 19-20	PGA Junior Championship, The Bluffs on Thompson Creek, St. Francisville, La.
Aug. 8-9	Spalding Assistants' Championship, Mississippi State Univ. GC, Starkville, Miss.
Aug. 15	Oldsmobile Scramble, Shenandoah CC, Baton Rouge, La.
Aug. 22	Oldsmobile Scramble: Indian Hills CC, Opelousas, La.; Colonial CC, Jackson, Miss.
Sept. 13-15	Ping/Pepsi Section Championship, Oak Harbor GC, Slidell, La.
Sept. 13-14	Club Professional Championship, Oak Harbor GC, Slidell, La.
Sept. 13-14	Senior Club Professional Championship, Oak Harbor GC, Slidell, La.
Sept. 13-14	Spalding Section Senior Championship, Oak Harbor GC, Slidell, La.
Oct. 17-18	Louisiana Chapter Championship, Oakbourne CC, Lafayette, La.
Oct. 17-18	Mississippi Chapter Championship, Annandale Golf Club, Madison, Miss.
Nov. 21	Duncan/Yamaha Golf Car Pro-President Championship, Ormond CC, Destrehan, La.

ILLINOIS

Executive Director
Vance Redfern

President
Paul Reinking
Kankakee CC, Kankakee, Ill.

2100 Clearwater Drive, Suite 206, Oak Brook, IL 60521

Phone: (708) 990-7799
Fax: (708) 990-7864
Vice President/Treasurer
Bruce Patterson
Butler National GC, Oak Brook, Ill.
Secretary
Roger Warren
Seven Bridges GC, Woodridge, Ill.
Assistant Executive Director
Mike Miller
Tournament Director
Brad Sullivan

Communications Director
Keith Burall
Director of Jr. Golf
Roger Ulseth
Director of Accounting/Operations
Arnold Zimmer
Administrative Assistant
Lynda Pytlewicz
Executive Secretary
Judy Prideaux
Secretary
Sheryl Krass

1993 SECTION AWARD WINNERS

Golf Professional of the Year
Bruce Patterson, Butler National
GC, Oak Brook, Ill.
Teacher of the Year
Gus Bernardoni, Glenview Naval
GC, Glenview, Ill.
Junior Golf Leader
Bob Jacobs
Cantigny Golf, Wheaton, Ill.

Horton Smith
Bill Kuikman
The Beverly CC, Chicago, Ill.
Bill Strausbaugh
Roger Warren
Seven Bridges GC, Woodridge, Ill.

1993 MERCHANDISER OF THE YEAR

Private Regi Starzyk, St. Charles CC, St. Charles, Ill.
Public Bob Jacobs, Cantigny Golf, Wheaton, Ill.
Resort John Schlaman, Eagle Ridge Inn and Resort, Galena, Ill.

1994 SCHEDULE OF EVENTS

April 18	Titleist Pro-Pro, Cantigny Golf, Wheaton, Ill.
May 2	Maxfli Pro-Assistant, Beverly CC, Chicago, Ill.
July 5-6	PGA Junior Girls Championship, Chapel Hill GC, McHenry, Ill.
July 5-7	Wilson Nadler Section Championship, Kemper Lakes Golf Club, Hawthorn Woods, Ill.
July 5-7	Club Professional Championship, Kemper Lakes Golf Club, Hawthorn Woods, Ill.
July 12-13	PGA Junior Boys Championship, Chapel Hill GC, McHenry, Ill.
July 28	Pro-President, Ivanhoe Club, Ivanhoe, Ill.
Aug. 4-6	Illinois Opens, Royal Fox GC, St. Charles, Ill.
Aug. 19	Oldsmobile Scramble: Fox Bend GC, Oswego, Ill.; Silver Lakes, Orland Park, Ill.; Deer Creek, University Park, Ill.; Batlett Hills, Batlett, Ill.
Aug. 22	Ping Assistants' Championship, Park Hills GC, Freeport, Ill.
Aug. 22-23	Senior Club Professional Championship, Old Elm GC, Ft. Sheridan, Ill.
Aug. 22-23	Vision Golf Section Senior Championship, Old Elm GC, Ft. Sheridan, Ill.
Aug. 24	Oldsmobile Scramble, Urbana CC, Urbama, Ill.
Aug. 29	E-Z-GO Chapter Championship, TBA
Sept. 19-22	Wittek Match Play Championship, Chicago GC, Wheaton, Ill.
Oct. 3	Titleist Pro-Pro, Mt. Prospect GC, Mt. Prospect, Ill.
Oct. 4	Pro-Super, Glen View CC, Glenview, Ill.

INDIANA

Executive Director
Mike David

President
Roger A. Lundy
Honeywell GC, Wabash, Ind.

P.O. Box 516, RR2 Hurricane Road, Franklin, IN 46131

Phone: (317) 738-9696
Fax: (317) 738-9436
Vice President
Mel Thomas
Zollner GC, Angola, Ind.
Secretary
Ted Bishop, Legends of Indiana
GC, Franklin, Ind.
Tournament/Junior Director
Trent Hicks

Office Manager
Marianne White
**Handicap Manager/
Tournament Secretary**
Joan Schernekau
Assistant Tournament Director
Thad Miller
Receptionist/Junior Secretary
Joyce Dustman

1993 SECTION AWARD WINNERS

Golf Professional of the Year
Donald Dicken
Rozella Ford GC, Warsaw, Ind.
Teacher of the Year
Jack Barber, Meridian Hills CC,
Indianapolis, Ind.
Junior Golf Leader
Rick Hemsoth, McMillen Park
GC, Ft. Wayne, Ind.

Horton Smith
Tom Jones
Sultan's Run GC, Jasper, Ind.
Bill Strausbaugh
Eric Schneider, Orchard Ridge
CC, Ft. Wayne, Ind.

1993 MERCHANDISER OF THE YEAR

Private Jim Ferriell, Crooked Stick GC, Carmel, Ind.
Public Greg Bishop, Otter Creek GC, Columbus, Ind.
Resort Mike Griggs, The Pointe Golf and Tennis Resort,
Bloomington, Ind.

1994 SCHEDULE OF EVENTS

April 25   Southern Open, The Pointe Golf
and Tennis Resort, Bloomington, Ind.
May 13   Tournament Series #1, Hillcrest CC, Batesville, Ind.
May 16-19 Match Play, Stonehenge GC, Warsaw, Ind.
May 24-25 Indiana PGA Women's Open Championship,
Deer Track GC, Auburn, Ind.
May 31   Northern Open, Briar Ridge CC, Merrillville, Ind.
June 27-28 Maxfli Junior Championship, Honeywell GC, Wabash, Ind.
June 30   Pro-Junior, Honeywell GC, Wabash, Ind.
July 6   Pro-Lady, Ulen CC, Lebanon, Ind.
July 25   Pro-Assistants' Championship,
Knollwood CC, Granger, Ind.
July 27   Tournament Series #2,
Brickyard Crossing GC, Speedway, Ind.
July 28-29 Senior Open, Harrison Lake CC, Columbus, Ind.
Aug. 1-4   Indiana Open, Hanging Tree GC, Westfield, Ind.
Aug. 15-16 PGA Assistant's Championship,
Twin Lakes GC, Indianapolis, Ind.
Aug. 17-18 Senior Championship, CC of Indianapolis, Indianapolis, Ind.
Aug. 22-23 PGA Indianapolis Open Championship,
Ft. Harrison GC, Indianapolis, Ind.
Sept. 12-13 Indiana PGA Championship,
The Legends of Indiana GC, Franklin, Ind.
Sept. 19   4-Man Team, Highland CC, Indianapolis, Ind.
Sept. 22   Pro-Superintendent,
The Legends of Indiana GC, Franklin, Ind.
Sept. 27   Tournament Series #3, South Bend CC, South Bend, Ind.
Sept. 29-30 Team Championship, Kokomo CC, Kokomo, Ind.
Oct. 6   PGA Senior Pro-Am Championship,
Brickyard Crossing GC, Speedway, Ind.

IOWA

Executive Director
Kirk Stanzel

President
Mike Anderson
Muscatine Municipal GC, Muscatine, Iowa

1930 St. Andrews N.E., Cedar Rapids, IA 52402

Phone: (319) 378-9142
Fax: (319) 378-9203
Vice President
Andy Devine, Sunnyside CC,
Waterloo, Iowa

Secretary
Larry Gladson, Elmcrest CC,
Cedar Rapids, Iowa
Tournament Secretary
Lynn Hutchison
Membership Director
Stephanie Childs

1993 SECTION AWARD WINNERS

Golf Professional of the Year
Ross DeBuhr, Hyperion Field
Club, Johnston, Iowa
Teacher of the Year
Brian Conser
Brooks GC, Okoboji, Iowa
Junior Golf Leader
Larry Crawford, Grinnell, Iowa

Horton Smith
Scott Howe, Des Moines
G & CC, W. Des Moines, Iowa
Bill Strausbaugh
Kirk Stanzel, Iowa Section PGA,
Cedar Rapids, Iowa

1993 MERCHANDISER OF THE YEAR

Private Larry Gladson, Elmcrest CC, Cedar Rapids, Iowa
Public Jeff Smith, Edmundson GC, Oskaloosa, Iowa
Resort Jim Kirwan, Lake Panorama National GC, Panora, Iowa

1994 SCHEDULE OF EVENTS

April 4   Pro-Pro, Muscatine Municipal GC,
Muscatine, Iowa
June 27   Pro-President, Hyperion Field Club,
Johnston, Iowa
July 11   Pro-Junior, TBA
July 15-17 PGA Junior Championship,
South Hills GC, Waterloo, Iowa
July 15-17 Iowa State Open,
Lake Panorama National GC, Panora, Iowa
Aug. 15   Oldsmobile Scramble:
Finkbine GC, Iowa City, Iowa;
Beaver Hills CC, Cedar Falls, Iowa;
Oakwood CC, Coal Valley, Ill.
Aug. 22-23 Section Championship,
Finkbine GC, Iowa City, Iowa
Sept. 19-21 Match Play Championship,
A.H. Blank GC, Muscatine, Iowa
Sept. 26   Spalding Pro-Assistant, TBA
Oct. 3   Pro-Superintendent, TBA

KENTUCKY

Executive Director
Mike Donahoe

President
Bill Moore
Crooked Creek GC, London, Ky.

4109 Bardstown Road, Suite 5-A, Louisville, KY 40218

Phone: (502) 499-7255
Fax: (502) 499-7422
Vice President

Secretary

Assistant Executive Director
Maria Sapp

Director of Tournament Administration
Mike Columbus
Director of Junior Golf
Brandon Neal
Bookkeeper
Barbara Peak
Secretary
Kristin Starmer

1993 SECTION AWARD WINNERS

Golf Professional of the Year
Glenn Dorten, Glenwood Hall
CC, Perry Park, Ky.
Teacher of the Year
Buddy Harston
Lexington CC, Lexington, Ky.
Junior Golf Leader
Tony Pancake
Valhalla GC, Louisville, Ky.

Horton Smith
G. Steve Hupe, Marriott's Griffin
Gate, Lexington, Ky.
Bill Strausbaugh
Barry Fisher, Elizabethtown CC,
Elizabethtown, Ky.

1993 MERCHANDISER OF THE YEAR

Private Tony Pancake, Valhalla GC, Louisville, Ky.
Public Jeffrey Kruempelman, Boone Links, Florence, Ky.
Resort G. Steve Hupe, Marriott's Griffin Gate, Lexington, Ky.

1994 SCHEDULE OF EVENTS

May 16	Pro-Assistant Championship, Summit Hills CC, Crestview Hills, Ky.
May 20	Pro-President, Hunting Creek CC, Louisville, Ky.
May 31	Michelob Classic I, Player's Club of Lexington, Lexington, Ky.
June 1	KGA-PGA Challenge Cup, TBA
June 3	Pro-Media-Sponsor Tournament, Andover CC, Lexington, Ky.
June 6	Pro-Pro, Lake Forest CC, Louisville, Ky.
June 13	Michelob Classic II, Midland Trail GC, Louisville, Ky.
June 17	Pro-Lady Championship, Wildwood CC, Louisville, Ky.
July 8	Pro-Scratch Championship, Standard CC, Louisville, Ky.
July 11	Budweiser Classic, Bowling Green (Ky.) CC
July 18-19	Section Championship/Club Pro Qualifier, TBA
July 25	Assistant Professionals' Championship, Audubon CC, Louisville, Ky.
July 29	Pro-Junior, Elizabethtown (Ky.) CC
Aug. 1	Oldsmobile Scramble: Oxmoor Golf & Steeplechase, Louisville, Ky.; Boone Links, Florence, Ky.
Aug. 16-18	Powerbilt Kentucky State Open, Hurstborne CC, Louisville, Ky.
Aug. 26	Pro-Senior Scratch Scramble, Gibson Bay GC, Richmond, Ky.
Sept. 12-15	KPGA Match Play Championship, Crooked Creek Golf Club, London, Ky.
Sept. 27-28	Kentucky Senior Open, Frankfort CC, Frankfort, Ky.
Oct. 14	Michelob III, Lincoln Homestead State Park, Springfield, Ky.
Oct. 24	Pro-Pro-Pro, Glenoaks CC, Louisville, Ky.

METROPOLITAN

Executive Director
Charles Robson

President
Jim O'Mara
Sleepy Hollow CC, Scarborough, N.Y.

1195 North Avenue, Box 268, New Rochelle, NY 10804-0268

Phone: (914) 235-7277
Fax: (914) 235-9379
Vice Presidents
Tom DeBellis, Pine Hollow CC, East Norwich, N.Y.
Bobby Heins, Old Oaks CC, Purchase, N.Y.
Treasurer
James A. Bender, Ardsley CC, Ardsley-On-Hudson, N.Y.
Secretary
Doug Steffen, Middle Bay CC, Oceanside, N.Y.

Assistant Executive Director/Director of Junior Golf
Jean Schob
Tournament Coordinator
Gayle Johnson
Junior Tour Administrator
Kevin Ostroske
Controller
Irene Hui
Tournament Director
Don Lizak
Golf-in-Schools Coordinator
Kris Huston

1993 SECTION AWARD WINNERS

Golf Professional of the Year
Joe Ennis
North Hills CC, Manhassett, N.Y.
Teacher of the Year
Robert Joyce
Southhampton GC,
Southhampton, N.Y.

Junior Golf Leader
Tim Nevin
Leewood GC, Eastchester, N.Y.
Horton Smith
Greg Hurd, North Hempstead
CC, Port Washington, N.Y.
Bill Strausbaugh
Frederick Gipp, West Sayville
GC, West Sayville, N.Y.

1993 MERCHANDISER OF THE YEAR

Private Jack McGown, Hampton Hills G & CC, West Hampton Beach, N.Y.
Public Thomas Lupinacci, Sterling Farms GC, Stamford, Conn.
Resort Michael Sander, Marriott's GC at Wind Watch, Hauppauge, N.Y.

1994 SCHEDULE OF EVENTS

May 2-4	Westchester PGA Championship, Metropolis CC, White Plains, N.Y.; Long Island PGA Championship, North Hempstead CC, Port Washington, N.Y.
July 19-21	State Open, Bethpage Black GC, Bethpage, N.Y.
Sept. 19-21	Izod Club/Cadillac Section Championship, Stanwich CC, Greenwich, Conn.
Sept. 26-27	Section Senior Championship, Gardiner's Bay, Shelter Island, N.Y.

MICHIGAN

Executive Director
Ken Devine

President
Richard M. Stewart
Kalamazoo CC, Kalamazoo, Mich.

32744 Five Mile Rd., Livonia, MI 48154

Phone: (313) 522-2323
Fax: (313) 522-5626
Vice President/Treasurer
Thomas G. VanHaaren
Forest Lake CC,
Bloomfield Hills, Mich.
Tournament Supervisor
Jay Gajda
Membership Director
Phyllis Gassam

Bookkeeper
Virginia "Ginger" Szewczyk
Administrative Assistant
Philip Drewek
Junior Golf/Employment and Human Resources
Ron Burchi

1993 SECTION AWARD WINNERS

Golf Professional of the Year
Buddy Whitten
Blythefield CC, Belmont, Mich.
Teacher of the Year
Dick Bury, Carl's Golfland,
Bloomfield Hills, Mich.
Junior Golf Leader
Jim Roschek, Milham Park GC,
Kalamazoo, Mich.

Horton Smith
Mark Wilson, Forest Hills GC,
Grand Rapids, Mich.
Bill Strausbaugh
Richard Stewart, Kalamazoo CC,
Kalamazoo, Mich.

1993 MERCHANDISER OF THE YEAR

Private Patrick Croswell, Oakland Hills CC, Birmingham, Mich.
Public Carl Rose, Carl's Golfland Driving Range, Bloomfield Hills, Mich.
Resort Richard C. Smith, Treetops-Sylvan Resort, Gaylord, Mich.

1994 SCHEDULE OF EVENTS

June 13	Wittek Golf Supply Assistants' Championship, Spring Meadows CC, Linden, Mich.
June 27-30	Detroit Newspapers Michigan Open, Grand Traverse Resort, ACMF, Mich.
July 25-26	Section Senior Championship and Senior Club Professional Championship, Coldwater CC, Coldwater, Mich.
July 28-29	PGA Junior Championship, TBA
Aug. 8-9	Foot-Joy/Titleist Pro-Pro, Sylvan Resort, Gaylord, Mich.
Aug. 15-17	Women's Open, Travis Pointe CC, Ann Arbor, Mich.
Aug. 22-24	Detroit Newspapers Section Championship, Garland, Lewiston, Mich.
Sept. 6	Oldsmobile Scramble: Kalamazoo CC, Kalamazoo, Mich.; Coldwater CC, Coldwater, Mich.; CC of Lansing, Lansing, Mich.; Great Oaks CC, Rochester, Mich.; Travis Pointe CC, Ann Arbor, Mich.; Flushing Valley G & CC, Flushing, Mich.; Michaywe GC, Gaylord, Mich.
Sept. 9	Club Professional Championship, Black River CC, Port Huron, Mich.
Sept. 12-15	Lincoln-Mercury Match Play Championship, Red Run GC, Royal Oak, Mich.
Sept. 19	Taylor Made Pro-Assistant, TBA
Sept. 26-27	Chapter Championships, TBA

MIDDLE ATLANTIC

Executive Director
Varden Dyer

President
Robert C. Fretwell
Old South CC, Lothian, Md.

7270 Cradlerock Way, Columbia, MD 21045

Phone: (301) 621-8320
Fax: (410) 381-8475
Vice President
Michael A. Ahrnsbrak
Shenandoah Valley GC, Front
Royal, Va.
Secretary
Charles Bassler Jr.
Willow Oaks CC, Richmond, Va.

Tournament Director
Steve Gillam
Administrator
Rose Maher
Administrator
Mary Ellen Stine
Financial Coordinator
Elizabeth Bradley

1993 SECTION AWARD WINNERS

Golf Professional of the Year
J. Wayne Holley, Roanoke, Va.
Teacher of the Year
Steve Bosdosh
TPC at Avenel, Potomac, Md.
Junior Golf Leader
Jon Ladd, Baltimore Municipal
GC, Baltimore, Md.

Horton Smith
Richard S. Miller, Carper's
Valley GC, Winchester, Va.
Bill Strausbaugh
Thomas E. Hantke
Middle Atlantic Section PGA,
Columbia, Md.

1993 MERCHANDISER OF THE YEAR

Private Melvin Rowe, CC of Fairfax, Fairfax, Va.
Public Andy Loving, Eagles Landing GC, Berlin, Md.
Resort Andy Wilson, The Tides Lodge, Irvington, Va.

1994 SCHEDULE OF EVENTS

May 12	Pro-President, Holly Hills CC, Ijamsville, Md.
July 11-13	Maryland State Open, Congressional CC, Bethesda, Md.
July 22	Pro-Junior, TBA
July 21-24	Signet State Opens, Willow Oaks CC, Richmond, Va.
July 25	Spalding Pro-Assistant, Woodmont CC, Rockville, Md.
Aug. 1-2	Assistants' Championship, Ford's Colony CC, Williamsburg, Va.
Aug. 22-24	Ping Section Championship, Two Rivers CC, Williamsburg, Va.
Aug. 22-24	Club Professional Championship, Two Rivers CC, Williamsburg, Va.
Sept. 1	Oldsmobile Scramble: Reston GC, Reston, Va.; Shenandoah Valley GC, Front Royal, Va.
Sept. 6	Oldsmobile Scramble: Wakefield Valley GC, Westminster, Md.
Sept. 12	Northern and Central Chapter Championships, TBA
Sept. 21-22	Senior Club Professional Championship, Stoneleigh GC, Round Hill, Va.
Sept. 21-22	Section Senior Championship, Stoneleigh GC, Round Hill, Va.
Sept. 26-29	Match Play Championship, TBA
Oct. 13-14	Section Tournament of Champions, Old South CC, Lothian, Md.
Oct. 24-25	Pro-Pro, Shenandoah Valley GC, Front Royal, Va.

MIDWEST

Executive Director/CEO
Jon E. Jacobson

President
Brian Maloney
CC of Blue Springs, Blue Springs, Mo.

1900 Corporate Centre, South Outer Road, Suite 106, Blue Springs, MO 64015

Phone: (816) 229-6565
Fax: (816) 229-9644
Vice President/Treasurer
Randy Syring
Salina CC, Salina, Kan.

Secretary
Tom Aikmus
Liberty Hills CC, Liberty, Mo.
Office Administrator
Carol Scott
Administrative Assistant
Sally Egy

1993 SECTION AWARD WINNERS

Golf Professional of the Year
Perry Leslie, Highland Springs
CC, Springfield, Mo.
Teacher of the Year
Bill Baraban
Oakwood CC, Kansas City, Mo.

Junior Golf Leader
Dorl Sweet, Grandview
Municipal GC, Springfield, Mo.
Horton Smith
Bill Skolaut
Claycrest GC, Liberty, Mo.

1993 MERCHANDISER OF THE YEAR

Private Paul Hooser, Leawood South CC, Leawood, Kan.

1994 SCHEDULE OF EVENTS

April 25	Pro-Pro Scramble, Indian Hills CC
May 2	Chillicothe Pro-Am, Chillicothe CC
May 6	Slazenger-St. Joseph CC Pro-Am
May 9	Pro-Lady Championship, Meadowbrook CC
May 13	John Knox Village Pro-Am, Lee's Summit, Mo.
May 16	Pro-Assistant Championship, Manhattan CC
May 20	Wolf Creek Pro-Member, Wolf Creek Golf Links
May 23	United Cerebral Palsy Pro-Am, Quivira CC
June 6	GCSAA Scholarship Research Tournament, Alvamar CC
June 20	Bank of Belton Pro-Am, Southview GC
June 24	Salina Country Club Pro-Am
June 27	Ronald McDonald House Pro-Am, Broodridge CC
July 11-12	PING Section Championship, Lakewood Oaks GC
July 18	Pepsi Cola Pro-Junior Championship, Liberty Hills CC
July 21-24	Southwestern Bell Classic, Loch Lloyd CC
Aug. 1	Assistants' Championship, Paradise Pointe GC
Aug. 8	Nike Greater Ozarks Open Qualifier, Fremont Hills CC
Aug. 15-16	Oldsmobile Scramble Section Championship, Alvamar GC
Aug. 18-19	Section Senior Championship and Club Professional Championship, Blue Hills CC
Aug. 22	Pro-Scratch, Wolf Creek Golf Links
Sept. 12	Pro-Pro Championship, Kansas City CC
Sept. 16	Pro Seniors Championship, Lawrence CC
Sept. 19	Leawood South Pro-Am, Leawood South CC
Sept. 20	Kansas Food Dealers Pro-Am, Deer Creek GC
Sept. 21	Art Wadkins Championship, Twin Hills CC
Sept. 26	Topeka CC Pro-Am

MINNESOTA

Executive Director
Darryl Borcherding

President
Richard Tollette Jr.
Bunker Hills GC, Coon Rapids, Minn.

Bunker Hills GC, Hwy. 242 and Foley Blvd., Coon Rapids, MN 55448

Phone: (612) 754-0820
Fax: (612) 754-0891
Vice President
Michael J. Zinni, Mankato G &
CC, Mankato, Minn.
Secretary
Dennis Gavin
The Oaks GC, Hayfield, Minn.

Assistant Executive Director
Jon Tollette
Director of Member Service
Traci Johnson
Junior Golf Administrator
Jennifer Snyder

1993 SECTION AWARD WINNERS

Golf Professional of the Year
Bill Kidd
Interlachen CC, Edina, Minn.
Teacher of the Year
Peter Krause, Bunker Hills GC,
Coon Rapids, Minn.
Junior Golf Leader
Rob Hary, Minnesota Valley CC,
Bloomington, Minn.

Horton Smith
Joseph M. O'Connor
Northland CC, Duluth, Minn.
Bill Strausbaugh
Marty Lass
Edina CC, Edina, Minn.

1993 MERCHANDISER OF THE YEAR

Private Marty Lass, Edina CC, Edina, Minn.
Public Steve Dornfeld, Wedgewood Valley GC, Woodbury, Minn.
Resort Steve Whillock, Izatys Golf & Yacht Club, Onamia, Minn.

1994 SCHEDULE OF EVENTS

June 13	Club Car Pro-President, Edina CC, Edina, Minn.
July 22-24	National Car/Diners Club State Opens, Bunker Hills GC, Coon Rapids, Minn.
Aug. 1	Assistants' Championship, TBA
Aug. 10	Pro-Junior, Bunker Hills GC, Coon Rapids, Minn.
Aug. 28-30	Spalding Section Championship, Izatys GC, Onamia, Minn.
Aug. 28-30	Section Senior Championship, Izatys GC, Onamia, Minn.
Sept. 12-15	Match Play Championship, TBA
Sept. 19	Taylor Made Pro-Assistant, Hastings CC, Hastings, Minn.

NEBRASKA

Executive Director
Bruce Lubach

President
Jeff Porter
Lochland CC, Hastings, Neb.

9301 Firethorn Lane, Lincoln, NE 68520

Phone: (402) 489-7760
Fax: (402) 489-1785
Vice President
Don Germer
Highland CC, Omaha, Neb.

Secretary/Treasurer
Dave Hilgenberg, Lakeshore CC, Council Bluffs, Iowa
Executive Secretary
Charlene Zweerink

1993 SECTION AWARD WINNERS

Golf Professional of the Year
Jeff Porter
Lochland CC, Hastings, Neb.
Teacher of the Year
Mike Cornell
Oak Hills CC, Omaha, Neb.
Junior Golf Leader
Bill Gaukel, Lake Creek CC, Storm Lake, Iowa

Horton Smith
Carol Nitzschke-Henrich
Applewood GC, Omaha, Neb.
Bill Strausbaugh
Jeff Porter
Lochland CC, Hastings, Neb.

1993 MERCHANDISER OF THE YEAR

Private Don Germer, Highland CC, Omaha, Neb.
Public Marc Cruse, Mahoney GC, Lincoln, Neb.

1994 SCHEDULE OF EVENTS

April 25	Club Demo Day Tournament, Oak Hills CC, Omaha, Neb.
May 16	Nebraska Golf Hall of Fame, Omaha CC, Omaha, Neb.
May 20	Nebraska Cup Matches, Hillcrest CC, Lincoln, Neb.
May 23-24	Neb. PGA Charity Skins Exhibition and All Class Boys State H.H. Golf Championship, Lochland CC. Hastings, Neb.
May 31	Spalding Pro-Assistant, Firethorn GC, Lincoln, Neb.
July 5	Assistants' Championship, Firethorn GC, Lincoln, Neb.
July 22	Nike "Closed" Qualifier, Quail Run GC, Columbus, Neb.
Aug. 1	Nike Dakota Dunes Open Qualifier, Two Rivers GC, Dakota Dunes, S.D.
Aug. 1	Oldsmobile Scramble: Riverside Golf Club, Grand Island, Neb.; Sioux City CC, Sioux City, Iowa
Aug. 3-4	PGA Junior Championship, Tiburon Golf Club, Omaha, Neb.
Aug. 4-7	Nike Dakota Dunes Open, Dakota Dunes CC, Dakota Dunes, S.D.
Aug. 18-19	Senior Club Professional Championship and Section Senior Championship, Elks CC, Columbus, Neb.
Aug. 21-23	Taylor Made Section Championship and Club Professional Championship, Fremont Golf Club, Fremont, Neb.
Sept. 6	Titleist Pro-Pro, Highland CC, Omaha, Neb.
Sept. 16-18	PING Nebraska State Open, Elks CC, Columbus, Neb.
Oct. 22-24	Nebraska Golf Awards Banquet; Neb. PGA Fall Education Seminar; Business Meeting; Merchandise Show

NEW ENGLAND

Executive Director
Susan Hudson

President
Jack Neville
Ponkapoag GC, Canton, Mass.

1 Audubon Road, Wakefield, MA 01880

Phone: (617) 246-4653
Fax: (617) 246-4938
Secretary/Treasurer
James Remy, Killington Resort, Killington, Vt.

Manager of Tournament Operations
Edward Carbone
Executive Secretary
Brenda Hutchinson
Secretary/Receptionist
Denise Ryan

1993 SECTION AWARD WINNERS

Golf Professional of the Year
John J. Gale
Tatnuck CC, Worester, Mass.
Teacher of the Year
Salvatore Ruggiero
Stow Acres CC, Stow, Mass.
Junior Golf Leader
Ron Raposa, Green Valley CC, Portsmouth, R.I.

Horton Smith
Don Lyons, George Wright GC, Hyde Park, Mass.
Bill Strausbaugh
James Remy
Killington Resort, Killington, Vt.

1993 MERCHANDISER OF THE YEAR

Private Jim Sheerin, Abenaqui CC, Rye Beach, N.H.
Public William Flynn, Franklin Park GC, Dorchester, Mass.
Resort Daniel Franzoso, Wentworth-by-the-Sea GC, New Castle, N.H.

1994 SCHEDULE OF EVENTS

May 3	Pro-Media, International GC, Bolton, Mass.
May 9-10	Pepsi Pro-Pro Match Play, Tedesco CC, Marblehead, Mass.
June 13-14	Vermont Opens, Lake Morey CC, Fairlee, Vt.
June 20-22	Massachusetts Opens, Woodland Golf Club, Newton, Mass.
June 30	Yamaha Golf Cars Pro-President, Fall River CC, Fall River, Mass.
July 7	PGA Junior Championship, Ponkapoag GC, Canton, Mass.
July 11-12	Titleist/Foot-Joy Pro-Assistant, Wachusett CC, Boylston, Mass.
July 25-26	New Hampshire Opens, Bretwood CC, Keene, N.H.
Aug. 1-2	Rhode Island Opens, Montaup CC, Portsmouth, R.I.
Aug. 3-4	Senior Club Professional Championship and Section Senior Championship, White Mountain CC, Ashland, N.H.
Aug. 4	Oldsmobile Scramble, Pocasset CC, Pocasset, Mass.
Aug. 8	Oldsmobile Scramble, Walpole CC, Walpole, Mass.
Aug. 9	Oldsmobile Scramble, Keene CC, Keene, N.H.
Aug. 10-12	Maine Opens, Riverside GC, Portland, Maine.
Aug. 16	Maxfli Pro-Junior, George Wright GC, Boston, Mass.
Aug. 18	Foot-Joy Assistants' Championship, Duxbury (Mass.) CC
Aug. 23	Club Professional Championship, Kernwood CC, Salem, Mass.
Aug. 29	Pro-Pro Stroke, Mt. Pleasant CC, W. Boylston, Mass.
Aug. 30	Oldsmobile Scramble, Colonial GC, Lynnfield, Mass.
Sept. 26-29	Section Championship: Pine Brook CC, Weston, Mass.; Belmont CC, Arlington, Mass.
Oct. 17	Club Car Pro-Superintendent, Spring Valley CC, Sharon, Mass.

NEW JERSEY

Executive Director
Walt Syring

President
Michael Preston
Echo Lake CC, Westfield, N.J.

P.O. Box 200, 1 Forsgate Drive, Jamesburg, NJ 08831

Phone: (908) 521-4000
Fax: (908) 521-4004
Vice President/Treasurer
Peter Famiano
Crestmont CC, West Orange, N.J.
Secretary
Steve Sieg
Navesink CC, Middletown, N.J.

Tournament Director
Jim Guerra
Assistant Executive Director
Phyllis Baker
Office Assistant
Irene Heppner

1993 SECTION AWARD WINNERS

Golf Professional of the Year
Steven Sieg
Navesink CC, Middletown, N.J.
Teacher of the Year
David Glenz, Crystal Springs
GC, Hamburg, N.J.
Junior Golf Leader
Wayne Warms, Manasquan River
GC, Brielle, N.J.

Horton Smith
Dan Beveridge
Deal G & CC, Deal, N.J.
Bill Strausbaugh
George Sauer, Green Brook CC,
North Caldwell, N.J.

1993 MERCHANDISER OF THE YEAR

Private Greg Lecker, Canoe Brook CC, Summit, N.J.
Public Thomas Manziano, Great Gorge CC, McAfee, N.J.

1994 SCHEDULE OF EVENTS

April 18-21	Ping Match-Play Championship, Essex County CC, West Orange, N.J.
May 2-3	Spalding Pro-Pro, TBA
May 24-26	Dodge Charity Classic, Rockaway River CC, Denville, N.J.
June 20-21	Coors Pro-Scratch Championship, Rumson CC and Deal G & CC
July 18-19	Senior PGA Club Professional Championship, Panther Valley CC, Allamuchy, N.J.
Aug. 2	Yamaha Pro-President, Baltusrol GC, Springfield, N.J.
Aug. 4	Pro-Junior, Princeton Meadows CC, Plainsboro, N.J.
Aug. 8-9	U.S. Healthcare Charity Classic, Rock Spring CC, West Orange, N.J.
Aug. 29	Club Professional Championship, Mountain Ridge CC, Caldwell, N.J.
Sept. 6	Polo Pro-Assistant, Fiddlers Elbow CC, Far Hills, N.J.
Sept. 13	Pro-Superintendent, Echo Lake CC, Westfield, N.J.
Sept. 20-22	Michelob Section Championship presented by Cadillac, Montclair GC, Montclair, N.J.
Oct. 2-3	Cadillac Challenge, Concord, N.Y.
Oct. 11-12	Lincoln-Mercury Players Championship, TBA
Oct. 17-18	Aureus Pro-Lady Championship, Hollywood GC, Deal, N.J.
Nov. 7-8	Pro-Sponsor/Media, Atlantic City CC, Northfield, N.J.

NORTHEASTERN NEW YORK

Executive Director
William Melchionni III

President
Rick Wright
The Edison Club, Rexford, N.Y.

48 Howard Street, Albany, NY 12207

Phone: (518) 463-3067
Fax: (518) 463-8656
Vice President
Dave Rarich
Windham CC, Windham, N.Y.

Treasurer
Tom Vidulich, The New Course
at Albany, Albany, N.Y.
Secretary
Jim Hefti, Ballston Spa CC,
Ballston Spa, N.Y.

1993 SECTION AWARD WINNERS

Golf Professional of the Year
Rick Wright
The Edison Club, Rexford, N.Y.
Teacher of the Year
Herb Moreland, Western
Turnpike GC, Guiderland, N.Y.
Junior Golf Leader
Kevin Hughes, Kingwood Golf
Links, Hudson Falls, N.Y.

Horton Smith
Jim Hefti, Ballston Spa CC,
Ballston Spa, N.Y.
Bill Strausbaugh
Stewart Smith, Van Schaick
Island CC, Cahoes, N.Y.

1993 MERCHANDISER OF THE YEAR

Private Jim Tureskis, Wolfert's Roost CC, Albany, N.Y.
Public John Taylor, Saratoga Spa GC, Saratoga Springs, N.Y.
Jack Polanski, Saratoga Spa GC, Saratoga Springs, N.Y.
Resort Tom Smack, Sagamore Resort & CC, Bolton Landing, N.Y.

1994 SCHEDULE OF EVENTS

May 2	Pro-Assistant Pro Championship, TBA
May 9	Classic, TBA
May 16	Taylor Made Pro-Am, Normanside CC, Delmar, N.Y.
May 23	U.S. Open Qualifier, Troy CC, Troy, N.Y.
June 6	Pro-Club Official, TBA
June 17	Pro-Lady Championship, TBA
June 27	Pro-Junior Championship, Ballston Spa CC, Ballston Spa, N.Y.
July 5	Top-Flite Classic, Glen Falls
July 11-12	OTB Classic, Alabny CC, Voorheesville, N.Y.
July 15	Pro-Senior Championship, Stamford CC, Stamford, N.Y.
July 22	NYS Open, Bethpage Black GC, Bethpage, N.Y.
July 22	Mercedes Benz Pro-Am, Kingswood Golf Links, Hudson Falls, N.Y.
July 29	Pro-Team Leukemia Society Championship, Taconic GC, Williamstown, N.Y.
Aug. 1-2	PING Section Championship, The Edison Club, Rexford, N.Y.
Aug. 8	Oldsmobile Scramble: Ballston Spa CC, Ballston Spa, N.Y.; Windham CC, Windham, N.Y.
Aug. 15	Oneonta Boys Club, Oneonta CC, Oneonta, N.Y.
Aug. 15-16	Senior Championship, Sagamore Resort & CC, Bolton Landing, N.Y.
Sept. 6	Titleist Fall Classic, TBA
Sept. 19	Silver Dollar Classic, TBA
Sept. 26-28	PING Match Play Championship, TBA
Oct. 2-3	PING Assistants' Match Play, The Edison Club, Rexford, N.Y.

NORTHERN CALIFORNIA

Executive Director
Robert Fagan

President
Mike Rawitser
Santa Teresa GC, San Jose, Calif.

2133 Las Positas Court, Suite A, Livermore, CA 94550

Phone: (510) 455-7800
Fax: (510) 449-5753
Vice President/Treasurer
Paul Wilcox Jr.
Diablo CC, Diablo, Calif.
Secretary
Nate Pomeroy
North Ridge CC, Fair Oaks, Calif.

Tournament Operations Manager
Melinda Jeffry
Office Manager
Maureen Corrigan
Membership Coordinator
Pam Steele
Secretary/Receptionist
Barbara Hilde

1993 SECTION AWARD WINNERS

Golf Professional of the Year
Ed Hester, Chico, Calif.
Teacher of the Year
John Geertsen Jr., Poppy Hills GC, Pebble Beach, Calif.
Junior Golf Leader
Mike Roberson
Visalia CC, Visalia, Calif.

Horton Smith
Ken Morton, Haggin Oaks GC, Sacramento, Calif.
Bill Strausbaugh
Paul Wilcox Jr.
Diablo CC, Diablo, Calif.

1993 MERCHANDISER OF THE YEAR

Private Ron Cropley, Elkhorn CC, Stockton, Calif.
Public Jim Wagner, Half Moon Bay Golf Links, Half Moon Bay, Calif.
Resort Mike Jonas, Fountaingrove CC, Santa Rosa, Calif.

1994 SCHEDULE OF EVENTS

Feb. 7	Annual Meeting, Elkhorn CC, Stockton, Calif.
April 25-27	Match Play Championship: Corral De Tierra, Salinas, Calif.; Links at Spanish Bay, Pebble Beach, Calif.
June 23-24	Maxfli Northern California PGA Junior Championship, Ridgemark G & CC, Hollister, Calif.
July 11	Wilson Pro-Junior, TBA
July 18	Semiannual Meeting, TBA
July 25	Titleist/Foot-Joy Assistants' Championship, TBA
Aug. 1-2	Taylor Made Section Championship, TBA
Aug. 1-2	Stroke Play Championship/ Club Professional Championship Qualifier, Chardonnay Club, Napa, Calif.
Aug. 22-23	Titleist/Foot-Joy Pro-Assistants' Championship, Chardonnay Club, Napa, Calif.
Aug. 29	Oldsmobile Scramble, TBA
Sept. 7	Pro-President, TBA
Sept. 15-16	Save Mart Senior Club Professional Championship, Stockton G & CC, Stockton, Calif.
Sept. 15-16	Save Mart Section Senior Championship, Stockton G & CC, Stockton, Calif.
Nov. 7-9	Northern California Open, Chardonnay Club, Napa, Calif.

NORTHERN OHIO

Executive Director
Sue Davies

President
Davey Snyder
CC of Ashland, Ashland, Ohio

38121 Euclid Avenue, Willoughby, OH 44094

Phone: (216) 951-4546
Fax: (216) 951-0508
Vice President/Treasurer
Don Kotnik
Toledo CC, Toledo, Ohio

Secretary
Joe Haase, Shaker Heights CC, Shaker Heights, Ohio
Tournament Director
Joe Nageotte
Office Administrator
Sue Moorehead

1993 SECTION AWARD WINNERS

Golf Professional of the Year
Don Kotnik
Toledo CC, Toledo, Ohio
Teacher of the Year
Rod Johnston
Portage CC, Akron, Ohio
Junior Golf Leader
Joe Haase, Shaker Heights CC, Shaker Heights, Ohio

Horton Smith
David Moskal
Medina CC, Medina, Ohio
Bill Strausbaugh
Donald Padgett II
Firestone CC, Akron, Ohio

1993 MERCHANDISER OF THE YEAR

Private Dominic Antenucci, Avon Oaks CC, Avon, Ohio
Public Herb Page, Windmill Lakes GC, Ravenna, Ohio
Resort Ed Laniewicz, Quail Hollow Resort, Painesville, Ohio

1994 SCHEDULE OF EVENTS

April 18	Maxfli Pro-Pro, Astorhurst CC, Walton Hills, Ohio
May 2	Pro-Sponsor/Media, Walden GC, Aurora, Ohio
May 31	Pro-Superintendent, Kirtland CC, Kirtland, Ohio
July 11-13	Waikem Buick Ohio Open, Tam O'Shanter GC, Canton, Ohio
August 8	Assistants' Championship, CC of Hudson, Hudson, Ohio
Aug. 15	Antigua Pro-Assistant, Shady Hollow CC, Massillon, Ohio
Aug. 22	Oldsmobile Scramble, TBA
Sept. 6-7	Spalding Section Championship, Firestone CC, Akron, Ohio
Sept. 12-13	Fila Ohio Senior Open, CC of Ashland, Ashland, Ohio
Oct. 11-12-14	PING Denny Shute Match Play, Portage CC, Akron, Ohio

NORTHERN TEXAS

Executive Director
James McAfee

President
Don Bryant
San Angelo CC, San Angelo, Texas

500 N. Central Expressway, Suite 272, Plano, TX 75074

Phone: (214) 881-4653
Fax: (214) 423-7861
Vice President
Kim Brown
Keeton Park GC, Dallas Texas
Secretary
Mickey Piersall
Pampa CC, Pampa, Texas

Office Manager/Comptroller
Lorri Young
Membership Director
Diane Clark
Tournament Director
Allen Archer
Junior Director
Erin Dauby

1993 SECTION AWARD WINNERS

Golf Professional of the Year
Bob Elliott
Northwood Club, Dallas, Texas
Teacher of the Year
Hank Haney, Hank Haney Golf
Ranch, McKinney, Texas
Junior Golf Leader
Sherwin Cox, Ross Rodgers GC,
Amarillo, Texas

Horton Smith
David Price
Bent Tree CC, Dallas, Texas
Bill Strausbaugh
Michael Wright
Shady Oaks CC, Ft. Worth, Texas

1993 MERCHANDISER OF THE YEAR

Private Clay Kinniard, Odessa CC, Odessa, Texas
Public George Priolo, Commanche Trail GC, Amarillo, Texas
Resort Jeff Davis, Holly Lake GC, Big Sandy, Texas

1994 SCHEDULE OF EVENTS

April 18-20	Tommy Armour Match Play Championship, The Cliffs CC, Graford, Texas
June 5-7	UST Classic, Squaw Valley GC, Glen Rose, Texas
July 18-20	Taylor Made Club Professional Championship, Tascosa CC, Amarillo, Texas
July 25	Wood Brothers Assistants' Championship, Dallas Athletic Club, Dallas, Texas
July 26-27	PGA Junior Championship, Eagle Nest GC, Denton, Texas
July 29	Pro-Junior, Plantation Resort, Frisco, Texas
Aug. 2-5	State Opens, The Woodlands CC, The Woodlands, Texas
Aug. 30-Sept. 1	Senior State Opens, Stonebridge CC, McKinney, Texas
Sept. 6-8	Oldsmobile Scramble: Chase Oaks GC, Plano, Texas; Denton CC, Denton, Texas; The Shores CC, Rockwall, Texas
Sept. 12-13	Section Senior Championship, Briarwood GC, Tyler, Texas
Sept. 12-14	Ping Section Championship, Fairway Oaks GC, Abilene, Texas
Sept. 25-26	Metro Chapter Championship, Squaw Valley GC, Glen Rose, Texas
Oct. 10	Club Car Pro-President, Mira Vista GC, Fort Worth, Texas
Oct. 17	Pro-Superintendent, Hurricane Creek CC, Anna, Texas

NORTH FLORIDA

Executive Director
Jerry Porter

President
John Reger
Haile Plantation G&CC, Gainesville, Fla.

200 Forest Lake Blvd., Suite 3, Daytona Beach, FL 32119

Phone: (904) 322-0899
Fax: (904) 322-2567
Vice President
James T. Beisler
Plantation G & CC, Venice, Fla.

Secretary
Gilbert L. Gonsalves
Palma Ceia G & CC, Tampa, Fla.
Tournament Director
Kent Kahre

1993 SECTION AWARD WINNERS

Golf Professional of the Year
Dick Medford, Daytona Beach
CC, Daytona Beach, Fla.
Teacher of the Year
Rick McCord
Orange Lake CC, Kissimmee, Fla.
Junior Golf Leader
Bill Zimmer
Hilaman Park GC,
Tallahassee, Fla.

Horton Smith
Mike Clayton, University Park
CC, University Park, Fla.
Bill Strausbaugh
Gary Ellis
Eastwood G & CC, Orlando, Fla.

1993 MERCHANDISER OF THE YEAR

Private John Upton, Marsh Landing CC, Ponte Vedra Beach, Fla.
Public Kayo Bowman, Wekiva GC, Longwood, Fla.
Resort Anthony Austin, Marriott's Orlando World Center, Orlando, Fla.

1994 SCHEDULE OF EVENTS

April 19-22	Section Senior Championship, Bent Oak GC, Titusville, Fla.
April 25	Club Car Pro-Official, Innisbrook Resort, Tarpon Springs, Fla.
May 24-27	Ping Match Play Championship, World Woods GC, Homosassa, Fla.
June 20-21	North Chapter Championship, Queen's Harbor Yacht & CC, Jacksonville, Fla.
June 23-24	PGA Junior Championship, Orange Lake CC, Kissimmee, Fla.
July 18-19	West Central Chapter Championship, TBA
July 22-23	Southwestern Chapter Championship, TBA
July 25-26	East Central Chapter Championship, Bay Hill Club & Lodge, Orlando, Fla.
Aug. 1-4	Oldsmobile Scramble, multiple sites
Aug. 15	Pro-Pro Warm Up Innisbrook Resort, Tarpon Springs, Fla.
Aug. 16-18	Section Championship, Innisbrook Resort, Tarpon Springs, Fla.
Sept. 1	Club Professional Championship, CC of Ocala, Ocala, Fla.
Sept. 19-20	Spalding Two-Man Team Championship, Queen's Harbor Yacht & CC, Jacksonville, Fla.
Sept. 26	Senior Club Professional Championship, Eastwood CC, Orlando, Fla.
Nov. 14	Maxfli Pro-Assistant presented by Sahara, CC at Heathrow, Lake Mary, Fla.
Dec. 7	Sponsor/Media Appreciation Day, The Grasslands G & CC, Lakeland, Fla.

PACIFIC NORTHWEST

Executive Director
Ron Coleman

President
Bruce Wattenburger
Juniper GC, Redmond, Ore.

4011 Yelm Hwy. SE, Olympia, WA 98501-5170

Phone: (206) 456-6496
Fax: (206) 456-6745
Vice President
Ron Hagen, Dungeness G & CC, Sequim, Wash.
Secretary
Jim Skaugstad, Sandpines Golf Resort, Florence, Ore.
Assistant Executive Director
Jerry Pearsall
Director of Tournament Operations
Jeffrey Ellison
Office Manager
Carole Coleman

Assistant Tournament Director
Joe O'Byrne
Junior Golf Coordinator/ Merchandise Show Coordinator
Mark Lynch
Chapter Coordinator/ Publications
Joan Lamey
Executive Secreaty
Dawn Hedin
Membership Services Coordinator
Dee Chilenski
Bookkeeper
Michele Lindgren

1993 SECTION AWARD WINNERS

Golf Professional of the Year
Ronald Coleman
Pacific Northwest Section PGA, Olympia, Wash.
Teacher of the Year
James Wilkinson
Bend G & CC, Bend, Ore.
Junior Golf Leader
Bob Veroulis
Eagle Bend GC, Big Fork, Mont.

Horton Smith
Larry Aspenson
Oregon City, Ore.
Bill Strausbaugh
Gary Lindeblad
Indian Canyon GC, Spokane, Wash.
Pat Huffer
Roseburg CC, Roseburg, Ore.

1993 MERCHANDISER OF THE YEAR

Private Patrick Welch, Wenatchee G & CC, Wenatchee, Wash.
Public Jim Bourne, North Shore G & CC, Tacoma, Wash.
Resort JD Mowlds, Black Butte Ranch GC, Black Butte Ranch, Ore.

1994 SCHEDULE OF EVENTS

May 14-18	Ernst Washington Invit., Glendale CC, Bellevue, Wash.
June 10	Western Washington PGA Pro-President, STBA
June 25-29	Sunriver (Ore.) Open Invit., Sunriver Resort, Sunriver, Ore.
July 6-7	Maxfli PGA Junior Championship, Canterwood G & CC and McCormick Woods GC, Gig Harbor, Wash.
July 13-17	Rosauers Open Invit., Indian Canyon, Spokane, Wash.
Aug. 11	Oldsmobile Scramble, Kayak Point GC, Stanwood, Wash.
Aug. 14-15	Spalding Assistants' Championship, Eagle Crest/Eagle Ridge, Redmond, Ore.
Aug. 18	Oldsmobile Scramble, Fort Lewis GC, Fort Lewis, Wash.
Aug. 19	Oldsmobile Scramble, Meadow Lakes GC, Prineville, Ore.
Aug. 22-24	Wilson Section Championship, Portland GC, Portland, Ore.
Aug. 22-24	Club Professional Championship, Portland GC, Portland, Ore.
Aug. 29	Oldsmobile Scramble, Willamette Valley CC, Canby, Ore.
Sept. 10-14	Northwest Open, Desert Canyon GC, Wenatchee, Wash.
Sept. 21-23	Section Senior Championship, Spokane CC, Spokane, Wash.
Oct. 12-14	Henry-Griffitts PNW PGA Pro-Am, STBA

PHILADELPHIA

Executive Director
Greg Shreaves

President
Jack MacCarty
LuLu Temple CC, North Hills, Pa.

Plymouth Green Office Campus, 801 E. Germantown Pike, Suite F-6, Norristown, PA 19401

Phone: (610) 277-5777
Fax: (610) 277-6151
Vice President-Section Affairs
Mike Cole
Penn Oaks CC, Westchester, Pa.
Vice President-Tournaments
Mike Mack
Burlington CC, Mt. Holly, N.J.
Secretary
George McNamara, Brandywine CC, Wilmington, Del.
Treasurer
Mike Atkins
CC of Harrisburg, Harrisburg, Pa.

Tournament Director
Bob Korbel
Executive Assistant
Stacey Liesner
Director of Membership/Accounting
Terri Hudson
Administrative Assistant
JoAnn Fisher
Director of Tournament Administration
Nan Andrews

1993 SECTION AWARD WINNERS

Golf Professional of the Year
Michael Atkins
CC of Harrisburg, Harrisburg, Pa.
Teacher of the Year
Gary Hardin
Northampton CC, Easton, Pa.
Junior Golf Leader
Harry Hammond
Whitford CC, Exton, Pa.

Horton Smith
John Kellogg
Radley Run CC, West Chester, Pa.
Bill Strausbaugh
Doug Ritter
Meadia Heights GC, Lancaster, Pa.

1993 MERCHANDISER OF THE YEAR

Private David Schueck, The Du Pont CC, Rockland, Del.
Public Peter Thien, Three Little Bakers CC, Wilmington, Del.
Resort Richard Kline, Marriott's Seaview, Absecon, N.J.

1994 SCHEDULE OF EVENTS

May 2	Izod Club Classic, Heidelberg CC, Bernville, Pa.
May 12	Section Senior Championship, Tavistock CC, Haddonfield, N.J.
May 23	Spalding Pro-Pro, Wyncote GC, Oxford, Pa.
June 9-10	Don Cannon's Variety Club Tournament of Champions, White Manor CC, Malvern, Pa.
July 11	Aureus Classic, Woodcrest CC, Cherry Hill, N.J.
Aug. 1	Club Professional Championship and Senior Club Professional Championship, Kennett Square G & CC, Kennett Square, Pa.
Aug. 8	Oldsmobile Scramble, Philmont CC, Huntington Valley, Pa.
Aug. 9	Pro-Junior, Radley Run CC, West Chester, Pa.
Aug. 15-16	Oldsmobile Scramble, Hershey's Mill CC, West Chester, Pa.
Aug. 19	Pro-Junior, Brandywine CC, Wilmington, Del.
Aug. 22	Oldsmobile Scramble, Hershey CC, Hershey, Pa.
Sept. 19-22	Taylor Made Section Championship and Pro-Am, Conestoga CC, Lancaster, Pa.
Oct. 13	Pro-President, Waynesborough CC, Paoli, Pa.
Oct. 24-26	Section Match Play Championship, Pine Crest GC, Lansdale, Pa.

ROCKY MOUNTAIN

Executive Director
Susan Breaux

President
Rick Longhurst
Ruby View GC, Elko, Nev.

595 E. State Street, Eagle, ID 83616

Phone: (208) 939-6028
Fax: (208) 939-6058
Vice President
Don O'Neil
Ponderosa Butte GC,
Colstrip, Mont.

Secretary
David B. Albrecht
Jackpot GC, Jackpot, Nev.
Office Manager
Harriet McCurry
Membership Services
Laurie Draper

1993 SECTION AWARD WINNERS

Golf Professional of the Year
Tom Anderson
Laurel GC, Laurel, Mont.
Teacher of the Year
Tom Sanderson, Boise, Idaho
Junior Golf Leader
Mike Dayley, Blackfoot
Municipal GC, Blackfoot, Idaho

Horton Smith
Tom Sanderson, Boise, Idaho
Bill Strausbaugh
Jerry Breaux
Hillcrest CC, Boise, Idaho

1993 MERCHANDISER OF THE YEAR

Private Stoney Brown, Crane Creek CC, Boise, Idaho
Public Mike Dayley, Blackfoot Municipal GC, Blackfoot, Idaho
Resort Carl Hoss, McCall GC, McCall, Idaho

1994 SCHEDULE OF EVENTS

May 16-17	Spalding Pro-Pro, Pinecrest GC, Idaho Falls, Idaho
June 3	Club Car Pro-President, Blue Lakes CC, Twin Falls, Idaho
July 7-8	Yellowstone Pro-Junior Championship, Lake Hills GC, Billings, Mont.
July 12-13	Cobra Section Championship & Section Senior Championship: Teton Pines Resort, Jackson, Wyo.; Jackson Hole Golf & Tennis, Jackson, Wyo.
July 12-13	Club Professional Championship & Senior Club Professional Championship: Teton Pines Resort, Jackson, Wyo.; Jackson Hole Golf & Tennis, Jackson, Wyo.
July 27-31	Idaho Open: Twin Falls GC, Twin Falls, Idaho; Jackpot GC, Jackpot, Nev.
Aug. 4-5	PGA Junior Championship, Blackfoot GC, Blackfoot, Idaho
Aug. 9-10	Assistants' Championship, Riverside CC, Bozeman, Mont.
Aug. 12	Snake River Pro-Junior Championship, Blue Lakes CC, Twin Falls, Idaho
Aug. 25	Oldsmobile Scramble: Teton Pines CC, Jackson, Wyo.; Jackson Hole Golf & Tennis, Jackson, Wyo.
Sept. 26-27	Spalding Yellowstone Chapter Championship, TBA
Oct. 17-19	Spalding Snake River Chapter Championship, Jerome CC, Jerome, Idaho

SOUTH CENTRAL

Executive Director
Danny Hickman

President
Stan Ball
Oak Tree CC, Edmond, Okla.

951 N. Forest Ridge Blvd., Broken Arrow, OK 74014

Phone: (918) 357-3332
Fax: (918) 357-2282
Vice President
Jeff Hamm
Longhills GC, Benton, Ark.

Secretary/Treasurer
Steve Carson, Lincoln Park GC,
Oklahoma City, Okla.
Administrative Assistant
Barry Thompson
Office Manager
Kathy Pettus

1993 SECTION AWARD WINNERS

Golf Professional of the Year
Rick J. Nuckolls, Reflection
Ridge GC, Wichita, Kan.
Teacher of the Year
Rick Ross
Desota GC, Hot Springs, Ark.
Junior Golf Leader
Alsie Hyden, Lake Hefner GC,
Oklahoma City, Okla.
Steve Carson, Lincoln Park GC,
Oklahoma City, Okla.
Dan Langford, Trosper Park GC,
Oklahoma City, Okla.
Mike Smiley, Earlywine Park
GC, Oklahoma City, Okla.

Senior Player of the Year
Frankie Rienhart
Player of the Year
Rod Nuckolls
Wichita CC, Wichita, Kan.
Horton Smith
Rick Nuckolls
Wichita CC, Wichita, Kan.
Steve Carson, Lincoln Park GC,
Oklahoma City, Okla.
Bill Strausbaugh
Danny Hickman
South Central Section PGA,
Broken Arrow, Okla.

1993 MERCHANDISER OF THE YEAR

Private Mark Felder, Twin Hills G & CC, Oklahoma City, Okla.
Public Pat Jenkins, Earlywine GC, Oklahoma City, Okla.
Resort Rick Reed, Shangri-la Golf Resort, Afton, Okla.

1994 SCHEDULE OF EVENTS

March 28	Section Assistants Cup Matches, Forest Ridge GC, Broken Arrow, Okla.
April 18	Section Skins Game, Cushing CC, Cushing, Okla.
May 2	Section Sr./Jr., Cedar Valley GC, Guthrie, Okla.
June 13	Pro-President, Quail Creek CC, Oklahoma City, Okla.
July 10-13	Phillips Petroleum Match Play Championship, Adams GC, Bartlesville, Okla.
July 27-29	Kansas Open, TBA
July 31-Aug. 1-2	Fore Solutions Club Professional Championship and Senior Club Professional Championship, Oakwood CC, Enid, Okla.
Aug. 23-28	Oklahoma Open, Oak Tree CC, Edmond, Okla.
Aug. 29	Oldsmobile Scramble Section Qualifying, TBA
Sept. 6	Pro-Assistant Championship, Oak Tree CC, Edmond, Okla.
Sept. 18-20	Ping Section Championship, TBA
Sept. 26	Royal Grip South Central Assistants' Championship, TBA
Oct. 3-4	Taylor Made Section Senior Championship, South Lakes GC, Jenks, Okla.
Oct. 14-17	Arkansas Open, Burns Park GC, N. Little Rock, Ark.
Oct. 23-26	Section Las Vegas Pro-Am, Legacy GC, Las Vegas, Nev.

SOUTHERN CALIFORNIA

Executive Director
Tom Gustafson

President
Tom Sargent
Yorba Linda CC, Yorba Linda, Calif.

601 S. Valencia, Suite 200, Brea, CA 92621

Phone: (714) 776-4653
Fax: (714) 572-1350
Vice President
Scott Walter, Bermuda Dunes
CC, Bermuda Dunes, Calif.
Secretary
Bill Hulbert
Tournament Director
Ron O'Connor
Junior Golf Director
Bob Livingstone
Marketing Director
Scott Wellington
Communications Director
Doug Wicks

**Director of Membership
Services/Club Relations**
Mike Lawson
Executive Assistant
Muriel May
Membership Administrator
Amy Law
Apprentice Administrator
Kim May
Bookkeeper
Laurel Dennis
**Junior Golf/
Tournament Assistant**
Heidi Kachelmeyer
**Junior Golf Field
Representative**
Gerald Wong

1993 SECTION AWARD WINNERS

Golf Professional of the Year
Scott Walter, Bermuda Dunes
CC, Bermuda Dunes, Calif.
Teacher of the Year
Tom Sargent, Yorba Linda CC,
Yorba Linda, Calif.
Junior Golf Leader
John Daddio, College of the
Desert GC, Palm Desert, Calif.

Horton Smith
Jerry Anderson, The Newport
Beach CC, Newport Beach, Calif.
Bill Strausbaugh
Perry Dickey, Seacliff CC,
Huntington Beach, Calif.

1993 MERCHANDISER OF THE YEAR

Private Kevin Paluch, Dove Canyon CC, Dove Canyon, Calif.
Public Tom Barber, Griffith Park GC, Los Angeles, Calif.
Resort Scott Flynn, Ojai Valley Inn & CC, Ojai, Calif.

1994 SCHEDULE OF EVENTS

April 18	Four-Ball Stroke Play Championship, Pala Mesa Resort, Fallbrook, Calif.
June 6	Pro-Pro, Spring Valley Lake CC, Victorville, Calif.
July 11-12	PGA Junior Championship, Red Hill CC, Rancho Cucamonga, Calif.
July 11-14	Cobra Golf Match Play Championship, Redhawk GC, Temecula, Calif.
July 18	Wilson Pro-Junior Championship, Oakmont CC, South Pasadena, Calif.
Aug. 1	Apprentice Championship, Singing Hills CC, El Cajon, Calif.
Aug. 16-19	State Open, Indian Wells Resort, Indian Wells CC, City of Indian Wells, Calif.
Aug. 22-24	Section Championship, The Los Angeles CC, Los Angeles, Calif.
Aug. 26	SCPGA/UST Golf Show Classic
Sept. 12	Pro Team Championship, Glendora (Calif.) CC
Oct. 4-5	Senior Championship and Senior Club Professional Championship, Jurupa Hills CC, Riverside, Calif.
Nov. 28	Champion of Champions, Pauma Valley CC

SOUTHERN OHIO

Executive Director
Laura Alger

President
Gary Taylor
Columbus CC, Columbus, Ohio

17 South High Street, Suite 1200, Columbus, OH 43215

Phone: (614) 221-7194
Fax: (614) 221-1989
Vice President
John Marchi
Cassel Hills GC, Vandalia, Ohio

Secretary
Mike Crotty, The New Albany
CC, New Albany, Ohio
Apprentice Administrator
Melissa Fast
Administrative Assistant
Kimberly Phares

1993 SECTION AWARD WINNERS

Golf Professional of the Year
Gary Taylor
Columbus CC, Columbus, Ohio
Teacher of the Year
Joseph Giles, Raccoon
International, Granville, Ohio
Junior Golf Leader
Harry Alexander
Miami Whitewater Forest,
Harrison, Ohio

Horton Smith
Gary Taylor
Columbus CC, Columbus, Ohio
Bill Strausbaugh
Greg Sanders
Reeves GC, Cincinnati, Ohio

1993 MERCHANDISER OF THE YEAR

Private Robert Ault, Brookside G & CC, Columbus, Ohio
Public Tom Kendrick, Hamilton County Park District, Harrison, Ohio

1994 SCHEDULE OF EVENTS

June 27	E-Z-GO Textron Golf Classic, Fairfield GC
July 14	Maxfli Junior Championship, WGC CC
July 15	Pro-Junior, Champions GC, Columbus, Ohio
July 25	PING-Springfield Open, Springfield CC
Aug. 1	Apprentice Championship, Cassel Hills GC
Aug. 1	Section Championship, Coldstream CC, Cincinnati, Ohio
Aug. 1	Club Professional Championship Qualifying, Coldstream CC, Cincinnati, Ohio
Aug. 5	Assistants' Championship, Champions GC, Columbus, Ohio
Sept. 6	Oldsmobile Scramble, TBA
Sept. 12-13	Titleist/Foot-Joy Ohio Pro-Assistant, Royal American Links & Blackhawk GC
Sept. 26	Pro-Am, CC of the North, Dayton, Ohio
Oct. 10	Pro-Assistant, Pipestone GC, Dayton, Ohio

SOUTHERN TEXAS

Executive Director
Michael D. Ray

President
Bob Putt
Silverhorn GC, San Antonio, Texas

1776 Woodstead Court, Suite 220, The Woodlands, TX 77380

Phone: (713) 363-0511
Fax: (713) 292-4175
Vice President
Carl Baker
Pine Forest CC, Houston, Texas
Secretary
Bill Keys, Fair Oaks Ranch CC, Boerne, Texas

Administrative Assistant
Debbie Winkens
Tournament Director
David Findlay
Tournament Secretary
Candy Lutz

1993 SECTION AWARD WINNERS

Golf Professional of the Year
Bob Putt
Silverhorn GC, San Antonio, Texas
Teacher of the Year
Bill Moretti, The Hills of Lakeway, Austin, Texas
Junior Golf Leader
Paul Levy, PKL Golf Group, Sugar Land, Texas

Horton Smith
Vic Carder
Willow Fork CC, Katy, Texas
Bill Strausbaugh
Gary Bailey, Woodlake G & CC, San Antonio, Texas

1993 MERCHANDISER OF THE YEAR

Private Robert Lindsay, The Dominion CC, San Antonio, Texas
Public Mike Hoffman, Greatwood GC, Sugar Land, Texas
Resort Jimmy Terry, South Shore Harbour CC, League City, Texas

1994 SCHEDULE OF EVENTS

April 18-19	Spalding Eastern Championship, Old Orchard GC, Richmond, Texas
May 16	Cobra Pro-Assistant, Atascocita CC, Humble, Texas
May 16-18	Match Play Championship
June 5-6	Titleist/Foot-Joy Pro-Assistant, Barton Creek CC, Houston, Texas
July 5-6	Texas Titleist/Foot-Joy Pro-Assistant, Barton Creek CC, Austin, Texas
July 25	Wilson Assistants' Championship, Sweetwater CC, Sugar Land, Texas
July 27-28	PGA Junior Championship, South Shore Harbour CC, League City, Texas
Aug. 2-5	Prince Golf/Nitro Texas State Open, TPC and North Course, The Woodlands, The Woodlands, Texas
Aug. 8-9	C.M. Financial/Wood Bros. Western Championship, Riverhills CC, Kerrville, Texas
Aug. 15-16	Oldsmobile Scramble: Old Orchard GC, Richmond, Texas; The Falls CC, New Ulm, Texas; Fair Oaks Ranch CC, Boerne, Texas
Aug. 24-25	Senior Club Professional Championship and Section Senior Championship, Golf Crest CC, Pearland, Texas
Sept. 12-14	Ping Section Championship, The Hills of Lakeway CC, Austin, Texas
Oct. 17	Tommy Armour Skins Game, Willow Creek GC, Spring, Texas
Nov. 21	Aureus Pro-Assistant Championship, Bentwater CC, Montgomery, Texas

SOUTH FLORIDA

Executive Director
Kevin Marrone

President
Mike Burke
Grand Palms G & CC, Hollywood, Fla.

10804 W. Sample Road, Coral Springs, FL 33065

Phone: (305) 752-9299
Fax: (305) 752-9659
Vice President/Treasurer
Bill Whaley, Ibis G & CC, West Palm Beach, Fla.
Secretary
Mike Arthur
CC of Naples, Naples, Fla.
Director of Communications & Marketing
Stacey Persinger

Receptionist/Administrative Assistant
Carol McPhee
Business Manager
Donna Goscicki
Tournament Administrator
Chris Bleile
Tournament Staff
Roz Smidt
R.B. McKeen

1993 SECTION AWARD WINNERS

Golf Professional of the Year
Louis Thelk, Vero Beach, Fla.
Teacher of the Year
Bill Davis
Jupiter Hills Club, Jupiter, Fla.
Junior Golf Leader
Tal Buchanan Jr., Spanish Wells CC, Bonita Springs, Fla.

Horton Smith
James Kurtzeborn
Foxfire CC, Naples, Fla.
Bill Strausbaugh
Jeff Sarver
Olde Hickory G & CC, Ft. Myers, Fla.

1993 MERCHANDISER OF THE YEAR

Private Charlie Bowie, Quail Ridge CC, Boynton Beach, Fla.
Public Robert Impaglia, Boca Raton Municipal GC, Boca Raton, Fla.
Resort Bill Cioffoletti, Pelican's Nest GC, Bonita Springs, Fla.

1994 SCHEDULE OF EVENTS

April 20	Pro-Superintendent, BallenIsles CC of JDM
May 18-19	Stableford, Ibis G & CC, West Palm Beach, Fla.
June 1-2	Pro-Assistant/Apprentice, TBA
June 23-24	PGA Junior Championship, Boca West CC
July 7-8	Oldsmobile Scramble: Pelican's Nest, Grand Palms, PGA National GC
July 20-24	State Open, TBA
July 27-28	Pro-Pro, Marco Marriott GC
Aug. 15-16	Apprentice Championship, TBA
Aug. 25-26	Senior Club Professional Championship Qualifying, TBA
Aug. 25-26	Section Senior Championship: Bear Lakes GC, Emerald Dunes
Aug. 29-Sept. 1	Club Professional Championship Qualifying and Section Championship: Bear Lakes, Emerald Dunes
Oct. 28	Pro-Official, CC of Coral Springs

SOUTHWEST

Executive Director
Kathy Wilkes

President
Phil Green
Gold Canyon GC, Appache Junction, Ariz.

5040 E. Shea Blvd., Suite 250, Scottsdale, AZ 85254

Phone: (602) 443-9002
Fax: (602) 443-9006

Vice President
Brian Whitcomb, Paradise Valley
CC, Phoenix, Ariz.

Secretary
Jeff Lessig, Superstition Springs
GC, Mesa, Ariz.

Tournament Director
Tim Greenwell

Administrative Staff
Marilyn Watkins
Carol Wells

1993 SECTION AWARD WINNERS

Golf Professional of the Year
Edward Francese
The Legacy GC, Henderson, Nev.

Teacher of the Year
Mike Labauve
Stonecreek GC, Phoenix, Ariz.

Junior Golf Leader
Paul Mowry, Kingman
Municipal GC, Kingman, Ariz.

Horton Smith
Jeff Lessig, Superstition Springs
GC, Mesa, Ariz.

Bill Strausbaugh
Orrin Vincent
Angel Park GC, Las Vegas, Nev.

1993 MERCHANDISER OF THE YEAR

Private Joe Bartko, Mesa CC, Mesa, Ariz.,
Dick Hyland, GC at Desert Mountain, Scottsdale, Ariz.
Public Terry Johnson, Westbrook Village CC, Peoria, Ariz.
Owen Compton, Starr Pass GC, Tucson, Ariz.
Resort Joe Shershenovich, Camelback GC, Scottsdale, Ariz.

1994 SCHEDULE OF EVENTS

May 9	Oldsmobile Scramble: Club West GC, Phoenix, Ariz.; Foothills GC, Phoenix, Ariz.
May 16-22	Stetson State Open, GC at Desert Mountain, Scottsdale, Ariz.
June 6	Karsten-Ping Pro-President, Mesa CC, Mesa, Ariz.
June 27-28	Antigua Team Championship, Tucson CC, Tucson, Ariz.
July 12-13	PGA Junior Championship, Angel Park, Las Vegas, Nev.
July 18-21	Spalding-Randy Anderson Match Play Championship, Troon G & CC, Scottsdale, Ariz.
Aug. 1-2	Karsten-Ping Assistants' Championship, Wigwam GC, Litchfield Park, Ariz.
Aug. 8-10	PGA Junior Championship, Antelope Hills GC, Prescott, Ariz.
Aug. 15	Cobra/Alan Tessmer Pro-Assistant, Camelback GC, Scottsdale, Ariz.
Aug. 19	Taylor Made/John McMillan Pro-Junior, TBA
Aug. 23-24	Karsten-Ping Section Senior Championship, Sedona GC/Oak Creek CC, Sedona, Ariz.
Sept. 12-14	Karsten-Ping Section Championship, Moon Valley CC, Phoenix, Ariz.
Sept. 19	Pro-Sponsor/Media, Superstition Springs GC, Mesa, Ariz.

SUN COUNTRY

Executive Director
John M. Speary

President
Mark Pelletier
Cielo Vista GC, El Paso, Texas

Mountain Run Center, 5850 Eubank NE, Suite B-72, Albuquerque, NM 87111

Phone: (505) 271-1442
Fax: (505) 271-8626

Vice President/Treasurer
James Smith
Scott Park GC, Silver City, N.M.

Secretary
Grant Dalpes, Desert Lakes GC,
Alamagordo, N.M.

Executive Director Emeritus
Harold "Bull" Durham

Administrative Assistant
Marilea Bush

1993 SECTION AWARD WINNERS

Golf Professional of the Year
Don Klein
Four Hills CC, Albuquerque, N.M.

Teacher of the Year
Tom Velarde
Quail Run CC, Santa Fe, N.M.

Junior Golf Leader
Henry Sandles
South GC, Albuquerque, N.M.

Horton Smith
Mark Pelletier
Cielo Vista GC, El Paso, Texas

Bill Strausbaugh
Dennis McCloskey, Los Alamos
GC, Los Alamos, N.M.

1993 MERCHANDISER OF THE YEAR

Private Chuck Dunn, Baton Rouge, La.
Public Douglas Lyle, Ocotillo Park GC, Hobbs, N.M.
Resort Daniel Nunez, Inn of the Mountain Gods GC,
Mescalero, N.M.

1994 SCHEDULE OF EVENTS

April 14-15	Spalding Pro-President, El Paso CC, El Paso, Texas
May 13-15	McDonald's Match Play Championship, Arroyo del Oso GC, Albuquerque, N.M.
July 28-29	Maxfli Junior PGA Championship, New Mexico Tech GC, Socorro, N.M.
Aug. 1-2	Diagnostek NM Open Invitational - Senior Division, UNM Championship GC, Albuquerque, N.M.
Aug. 5-7	Diagnostek NM Open Invitational, UNM Championship GC, Albuquerque, N.M.
Aug. 10-12	SunWest Bank/Spalding Section Senior Championship, Albuquerque CC, Albuquerque, N.M.
Aug. 16-17	Spalding Section Championship, Santa Teresa CC, Santa Teresa, N.M.
Aug. 22	Oldsmobile Scramble, Valle GC, Bernalillo, N.M.
Sept. 14-16	Lexus Pro-Pro, Four Hills CC, Albuquerque, N.M.
Sept. 26-28	El Paso Ford Dealers Assoc. Assistants Championship, Painted Dunes Desert GC, El Paso, Texas
Oct. 3	Southwest Toro Pro-Assistant, TBA

TENNESSEE

Executive Director
Dick Horton

President
Dan Tribble Jr.
Hickory Valley GC, Chattanooga, Tenn.

1500 Legends Club Lane, Franklin, TN 37064

Phone: (615) 790-7600
Fax: (615) 790-8600
Vice President
Jeff Cox, Farmington CC,
Germantown, Tenn.
Secretary
Richard Spraker
Oak Ridge CC, Oak Ridge, Tenn.
Assistant Executive Director
Lynne Howd

Director of Rules and Competitions
Allen Richardson
Executive Secretary (Membership/Apprentice)
Connie Pearce
Financial Secretary
Barbara Bass
Tournament Secretary
Jami Eller
Director of Member Services
Joe Taggert

1993 SECTION AWARD WINNERS

Golf Professional of the Year
Bill Munguia
Holiday GC, Olive Branch, Miss.
Teacher of the Year
Brad Redding
Willow Creek GC,
Knoxville, Tenn.

Junior Golf Leader
Richard Spraker
Oak Ridge CC, Oak Ridge, Tenn.
Horton Smith
Russ Garner
Windyke CC, Germantown, Tenn.
Bill Strausbaugh
Joe Taggert, Tennessee Section,
PGA, Franklin, Tenn.

1993 MERCHANDISER OF THE YEAR

Private Billy Buchanan, Chattanooga G & CC, Chattanooga, Tenn.
Public Tim Corrigan, Holiday GC, Olive Branch, Miss.
Resort Tom Waltz, Stonehenge GC, Fairfield Glade, Tenn.

1994 SCHEDULE OF EVENTS

Date	Event
April 18	Screaming Eagle Pro-Am, Ft. Campbell, Tenn.
May 13-16-17	State Open Qualifying, (6 sites)
June 20-21	Coca-Cola Open, Creeks Bend GC, Hixson, Tenn.
June 23-24	Maxfli PGA Junior Championship, Lakewood CC, Tullahoma, Tenn.
June 27	State Junior Qualifying, TBA
July 30-31	Curtis Cup, The Honors Course, Ooltewah, Tenn.
Aug. 10-13	TPGA State Amateur, Holston Hills CC, Knoxville, Tenn.
Aug. 15-16	Assistants' Championship, Council Fire GC, Chattanooga, Tenn.
Aug. 22-25	TPGA Senior Championship, Cherokee CC, Knoxville, Tenn.
Sept. 13-15	Ping TPGA Section Championship, The CC Inc., Morristown, Tenn.
Sept. 19-20	TPGA Two-Man Scramble, TBA
Sept. 26-27	TPGA Senior Open, TBA
Sept. 27-29	WTPGA Senior Amateur, Houston Levee CC, Memphis, Tenn.
Oct. 3-6	TPGA Mid-Amateur, Council Fire GC, Chattanooga, Tenn.
Oct. 15-16	True Temper Cup Matches, Legends Club of Tennessee, Franklin, Tenn.

TRI-STATE

Executive Director
Dennis J. Darak Sr.

President
John Rech Jr.
Rolling Hills CC, McMurray, Pa.

221 Sherwood Drive, Monaca, PA 15061

Phone: (412) 774-2224
Fax: (412) 774-5535
Vice President
Robert W. Ford, Oakmont CC,
Oakmont, Pa.
Secretary
Bob Collins, Oak Tree CC, West
Middlesex, Pa.

Administrative Assistant
Karen Darak
Tournament Assistant
Joe Bonadio
Bob Cimarolli

1993 SECTION AWARD WINNERS

Golf Professional of the Year
Max Mesing, Fox Run Public
GC, Beaver Falls, Pa.
Teacher of the Year
Greg Ortman, Woodlands Golf
Academy, Farmington, Pa.
Junior Golf Leader
Kirk Suvak
Edgewood CC, Pittsburgh, Pa.

Horton Smith
Mark McConnell, Sewickley
Heights GC, Sewickley, Pa.
Bill Strausbaugh
Philip Newcamp
St. Clair CC, Pittsburgh, Pa.

1993 MERCHANDISER OF THE YEAR

Private Robert Ford, Oakmont CC, Oakmont, Pa.
Public Jerry Smith, Tam O'Shanter GC, West Middlesex, Pa.
Resort Robert Harris, The Greenbrier Hotel, White Sulphur Springs, W.Va.

1994 SCHEDULE OF EVENTS

Date	Event
March 28	Pro-Sponsor/Media, Churchill Valley CC, Pittsburgh, Pa.
May 9	Ping Pro-Assistant, Valley Brook CC, McMurray, Pa.
May 31	Assistants' Championship, Youghiogheny CC, McKeesport, Pa.
May 20	New Penn Golf Cars Pro-President: Sharon CC, Sharon, Pa.; Oak Tree CC, West Middlesex, Pa.
June 30	Pro-Junior, Bon-Air GC, Coraopolis, Pa.
July 5	Frank B. Fuhrer Jr. Pro-Pro, Pittsburgh Field Club, Pittsburgh, Pa.
Aug. 8-9	State Opens, Bent Creek, Lancaster, Pa.
Aug. 15-16	Oldsmobile Scramble: Oak Tree CC, West Middlesex, Pa.; Sharon CC, Sharon, Pa.
Aug. 22-23	Buchannan Ingersoll Section Championship, St. Clair CC, Pittsburgh, Pa.
Aug. 22-23	Club Professional Championship, St. Clair CC, Pittsburgh, Pa.
Aug. 22-23	Senior Club Professional Championship, St. Clair CC, Pittsburgh, Pa.
Aug. 22-23	Section Senior Championship, St. Clair CC, Pittsburgh, Pa.
Sept. 13-14	Ping Chapter Championships, TBA
Oct. 10-12	Taylor Made Match Play Championship, Deer Run GC, Gibsonia, Pa.

UTAH

Executive Director
Jeff Beaudry

President
John L. Evans
Cedar Ridge GC, Cedar City, Utah

419 East 100 South, Salt Lake City, UT 84111

Phone: (801) 532-7421
Fax: (801) 532-7427
Vice President
Steve Wathen
Mt. Ogden GC, Ogden, Utah
Secretary
Kean Ridd
East Bay GC, Provo, Utah

Assistant Executive Director
Dave Terry
Office Manager
Marilyn Sarzynski
Administrator
Craig Warren

1993 SECTION AWARD WINNERS

Golf Professional of the Year
Tee Branca
The CC, Salt Lake City, Utah
Teacher of the Year
Bruce Summerhays, The
Homestead GC, Midway, Utah
Junior Golf Leader
Kent McCurdy
Dinaland GC, Vernal, Utah

Horton Smith
Dan Roskelley
Logan G & CC, Logan, Utah
Bill Strausbaugh
Jeff Beaudry, Utah Section PGA
Salt Lake City, Utah

1993 MERCHANDISER OF THE YEAR

Private Tee Branca, The CC, Salt Lake City, Utah
Public Kean Ridd, East Bay GC, Provo, Utah
Resort James Blair, Jeremy Ranch, Park City, Utah

1994 SCHEDULE OF EVENTS

April 11	Smith's Pro-Pro, East Bay
May 9	Pro-Sponsor/Media, Willow Creek CC, Sandy, Utah
June 27	Pro-Pro, Logan G & CC, Logan, Utah
July 10-12	PGA Junior Championship: West Bountiful City GC; Davis Park GC; Valley View GC, Layton, Utah
July 19	Wilson Pro-Junior, Wasatch, Midway, Utah
July 26	Smith's Assistant Championship: Park Meadows CC; Park City GC, Park City, Utah
July 27	Oldsmobile Scramble, Mt. Ogden, Ogden, Utah
Aug. 29	Taylor Made Pro-Assistant, TBA
Aug. 22-25	Smith's Section Championship, Alpine CC, American Fork, Utah
Aug. 22-25	Club Professional Championship, Alpine CC, American Fork, Utah
Aug. 22-25	Senior Club Professional Championship, Alpine CC, American Fork, Utah
Aug. 22-25	Smith's Section Senior Championship, Alpine CC, American Fork, Utah
Oct. 3	Pro-Pro, The Homestead GC, Midway, Utah

WESTERN NEW YORK

Executive Director
William Dimas

President
Mark Kirk
Orchard Park CC, Orchard Park, N.Y.

P.O. Box 1728, Williamsville, NY 14231-1728

Phone: (716) 626-0603
Fax: (716) 626-5308
Vice President/Treasurer
Steve Crane, Lake View CC,
North East, Pa.

Secretary
Stanley Marshaus, Chautauqua
GC, Chautauqua, N.Y.
Administrative Assistant
Lynn Reece
Tournament Assistant
Bob Ashley

1993 SECTION AWARD WINNERS

Golf Professional of the Year
Tony Duran, Depew, N.Y.
Teacher of the Year
Mark Kirk, Orchard Park CC,
Orchard Park, N.Y.
Junior Golf Leader
Andy Munro, Erie GC, Erie, Pa.

Horton Smith
Craig Harmon
Oak Hill CC, Rochester, N.Y.
Bill Strausbaugh
Bill Dimas
Western New York Section PGA
Williamsville, N.Y.

1993 MERCHANDISER OF THE YEAR

Private Jim Mrva, Monroe GC, Pittsford, N.Y.
Public John Quinzi Jr., Eagle Vale GC, Fairport, N.Y.
Resort Steve Carney, Riverside GC, Cambridge Springs, Pa.

1994 SCHEDULE OF EVENTS

May 31	Yamaha Golf Cars Pro-President, Niagara Falls CC, Lewiston, N.Y.
July 18	PGA Junior Championship, Orchard Park CC, Orchard Park, N.Y.
July 29	Pro-Junior, Gowanda CC, Collins, N.Y.
Aug. 1	Spalding Pro-Sponsor, Orchard Park CC, Orchard Park, N.Y.
Aug. 8	Ping/Titleist Assistants' Championship, TBA
Aug. 18	Oldsmobile Scramble, TBA
Aug. 19	Oldsmobile Scramble, Penfield CC, Penfield, N.Y.
Aug. 25-26	Dura Golf Section Senior Championship, Chautauqua GC, Chautauqua, N.Y.
Aug. 25-26	Senior Club Professional Championship, Chautauqua GC, Chautauqua, N.Y.
Aug. 29-30	Coor's Beer Section Championship, Lake View CC, North East, Pa.
Aug. 29-30	Club Professional Championship, Lake View CC, North East, Pa.
Sept. 6	Cobra/Antigua/New Era Cap Pro-Pro, TBA
Sept. 12-13	Taylor Made Match Play Championship, CC of Buffalo, Williamsville, N.Y.
Sept. 19	Pro-Assistant, Conewango Valley CC, Warren, Pa.

WISCONSIN

Executive Director
Tony Coleman

President
Mike Muranyi
Monroe CC, Monroe, Wis.

4000 W. Brown Deer Road, Milwaukee, WI 53209

Phone: (414) 365-4474
Fax: (414) 365-4479
Vice President
Tom Wiese, Quit-Qui-GC Golf
GC Inc., Elkhart Lake, Wis.
Secretary
Pat Furca
Branch River CC, Cato, Wis.
Tournament Director
Joe Stadler

Membership Assistant
Jill Coleman
Accounting Assistant
Suzanne Hansen
**Director of Marketing &
Promotions**
Bart Rottier

1993 SECTION AWARD WINNERS

Golf Professional of the Year
Bill Hagensick, Browns Lake
GC, Burlington, Wis.
Teacher of the Year
Jim Thompson, Oneida Golf &
Riding Club, Green Bay, Wis.

Junior Golf Leader
Rob Muranyi
Monona GC, Madison, Wis.
Horton Smith
Ray Kizer, Lake Wisconsin CC,
Prairie Du Sac, Wis.

1993 MERCHANDISER OF THE YEAR

Private John Hall, Maple Bluff CC, Madison, Wis.
Public Dan Buckley, Northwood GC, Rhinelander, Wis.
Resort Paul Becker, Blackwolf Run GC, Kohler, Wis.

1994 SCHEDULE OF EVENTS

April 11	Pro-Pro, Johnson Park, Racine, Wis.
May 16	Cobra Stroke, Monroe CC
June 20	Hornung's Stroke, South Hills CC
June 27-28	Maxfli Wisconsin PGA Junior Championship, Yaham Hills GC, Madison, Wis.
July 11-12	Taylor Made Wisconsin PGA Section Championship and Club Professional Championship, Lawsonia Golf Links, Green Lake, Wis.
July 18	Pro-Junior, Baraboo CC
July 20	Yamaha/Tiziani Golf Car Pro-President, The Springs Golf Club Resort, Spring Green, Wis.
July 26	Oldsmobile Scramble, Blackhawk CC, Madison, Wis.
July 28	Oldsmobile Scramble, Hillcrest, Eau Claire, Wis.
Aug. 8	Assistants' Championship, North Shore CC
Aug. 8-9	Senior Club Professional Championship and Langert Section Senior Championship, Trapper's Turn GC, Wisconsin Dells, Wis.
Aug. 15-17	Wisconsin State Open Golf Championship, Eau Claire G & CC, Eau Claire, Wis.
Sept. 12-14	Wisconsin PGA Match Play Championship, Northwood GC, Rhinelander, Wis.
Sept. 19	WSGA Ping Pro-Assistant, Cherokee CC, Madison, Wis.
Sept. 26	2FVO Stroke, Brynwood CC
Oct. 10	Pro-Pro, Quit-Qui-OC Golf GC Inc., Elkhart Lake, Wis.

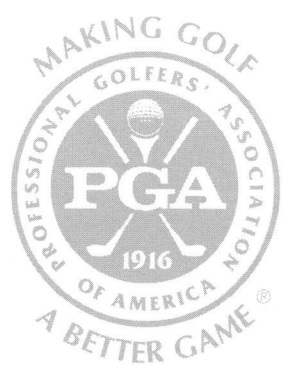

PGA MASTER PROFESSIONALS

The PGA Master Professional program was begun in 1969 to recognize PGA members who make a significant extra effort to improve themselves as golf professionals. One of the major requirements is the preparation and submission of an extensive thesis on an aspect of golf, which is accepted by a panel of professional experts in their field. Other requirements: Class A membership in the PGA of America as a head professional or director of golf for at least six years, attendance at four national education programs, and recertification substantially beyond minimum guidelines.

The Master Professional roster with name, home at time of acceptance, thesis title and date elected:

1. ***James D. Fogertey,** Kirkwood, Mo.
   How I Teach Golf ....April 1, 1972

2. **Thomas L. Weekes,** South Sioux City, Neb.
   Teaching the Beginning Golfer ....June 2, 1972

3. ***Howard E. Morrette,** Kent, Ohio
   The Golf Swing ....Nov. 1, 1972

4. ***Harold R. Calderwood,** Searcy, Ark.
   Thirty Years on the Tee .... Dec. 1, 1972

5. ***Harry Moffitt,** Toledo, Ohio
   Teaching the Tyro .... Dec. 15, 1972

6. **Donald C. Perne,** Toledo, Ohio
   *The Mental and Physical Aspects
   of Teaching the Golf Swing* .... April 1, 1973

7. **Joe Davis,** Spartanburg, S.C.
   The Golf Swing As I See It, As I Teach It ....May 1, 1973

8. **Robert H. Hamrich,** Beachwood, Ohio
   How I Teach Golf ....July 15, 1973

9. **Clarence I. Underwood,** Norfolk, Va.
   On Teaching Golf ....July 15, 1973

10. **Joe A. Stolarick,** Galesburg, Ill.
    Golf as a Simple Game ....Sept. 1, 1973

11. ***Jack R. Slayton Sr.,** Ocean City, Md.
    Keep the Swing Simple .... March 1, 1974

12. **Frank Kiraly,** Duncansville, Pa.
    Teaching .... March 15, 1976

13. **John A. Gerring,** Marietta, Ga.
    It Ain't Much Pro-But It's All I've Got ....April 1, 1977

14. **Robert E. Hickman,** Wood Dale, Ill.
    Super Golf-Simply ....May 1, 1978

15. **Donald H. Dunkelberger,** High Point, N.C.
    *The Psychology of Student Preparation for
    Golf Instruction & Its Bearing on the Student/
    Instructor Relationship* ....July 1, 1979

16. **Bruce J. Sudderth,** Gastonia, N.C.
    My Method of Teaching Golf ....July 1, 1979

17. **Donald A. Kotnik,** Toledo, Ohio
    *Analyzation and Programming Keys
    for Sound Teaching* ....Feb. 1, 1980

18. **Gregory A. Fish,** Toledo, Ohio
    Teaching Fundamental Golf .... March 18, 1983

19. **Ken Lindsay,** Jackson, Miss.
    The Evolution of the Putting Green Rule ....May 16, 1983

20. **John M. Spiroplaus,** Olympia Fields, Ill.
    The Original Thirteen Rules of Golf .... Dec. 7, 1983

21. **Joseph E. O'Rourke,** Miami, Fla.
    Learn the Basics for a Lasting Golf Swing ....Feb. 14, 1984

22. **Michael Vucinich,** Greensburg, Pa.
    Instructional Golf Development Program ....Nov. 9, 1984

23. **Martin T. Kavanaugh II,** Cincinnati, Ohio
    Golf's Municipal Professional ....Oct. 17, 1985

24. **Michael P. Hebron,** Smithtown, N.Y.
    See & Feel the Inside Move the Outside ....Dec. 23, 1985

25. **Gary Wiren,** North Palm Beach, Fla.
    *Human Factors Influencing the
    Golf Drive for Distance* ....Jan. 9, 1986

26. **Don Essig III,** Indianapolis, Ind.
    *Midwest Golf Course Cost and
    Feasibility Study* ....Jan. 14, 1986

27. **Tomas G. Wilcox,** Northbrook, Ill.
    *A Guide to Employment Strategy
    for Golf Professionals* .... Feb. 5, 1986

28. **Robert A. Koschmann,** Glencoe, Ill.
    How to Conduct a Member/Guest Tournament ..March 7, 1986

29. **Gordon D. Fulp,** Greenville, N.C.
    Merchandising and Human Relations .... April 21, 1986

30. **Anthony J. Clecak,** Columbus, Ind.
    How to Manage a Job Search ....Sept. 23, 1986

31. **Robert S. Intrieri,** University Park, Pa.
    The Golf School ....Oct. 15, 1986

32. **Jack Tindale,** Rochester, N.Y.
    Psychology in Sport ....Oct. 24, 1986

33. **Jerry Ray,** Valley Park, Mo.
    *Understanding Your Competition,
    "The Golf Discounter"* ....Jan. 19, 1987

34. **Frank Jawor,** Dearborn Heights, Mich.
    *Study of Golf Programs in
    Urban Colleges and Universities* ....Jan. 20, 1987

35. **Ben H. Freeman Jr.,** Birmingham, Ala.
    *Evolution of the Golf Ball:
    How It Has Controlled the Game* ....Jan. 28, 1987

36. **Tillman K. Moss,** Hilton Head Island, S.C.
    *Organizing & Conducting a
    Major Golf Competition* .... Feb. 2, 1987

37. **Gary E. Ellis,** Hilton Head Island, S.C.
    Junior Golf - Our Future ....July 29, 1987

38. **Patrick V. Martino Jr.,** Upper St. Clair, Pa.
    *The Circle-The Swing. Rick Martino's
    Complete Teaching Method* ....Oct. 26, 1987

39. **Jack Gale,** Worcester, Mass.
    Teaching the Mind ....Oct. 28, 1987

40. **Mark E. Darnell,** Augusta, Ga.
    Merchandising ....Dec. 18, 1987

41. **Thomas S. Heyward Jr.,** Myrtle Beach, S.C.
    *How the Golf Resort Package
    Built the Grand Slam* ....Jan. 15, 1988

42. **William W. Adams,** Ridgewood, N.J.
    My Approach to Teaching .... Feb. 24, 1988

43. **Michael F. Clayton,** Cape Coral, Fla.
*Organizing a Community Junior Golf
Association* ....*Feb. 29, 1988*

44. **Don Ferrone,** Pine Mountain, Ga.
*The Integration of Psychological and
Physiological Components in the Golf Swing* ......*Feb. 29, 1988*

45. **Robert E. Putt,** San Antonio, Texas
The Teaching Methods of Bob Putt ....*March 7, 1988*

46. **Craig C. Palmer,** Laurel, Mont.
*Using a Conceptional Approach to
Reach More Students* ....*April 6, 1988*

47. **William W. Peterson,** Leawood, Kan.
Instruction and the Game of Golf ....*April 21, 1988*

48. **Kim J. Brown,** Dallas, Texas
How to Become Mr. Golf in Your Community .....*April 22, 1988*

49. **Roger W. Van Dyke,** Savannah, Ga.
Professional Communications................................*April 25, 1988*

50. **Donald A. Fox,** Loveland, Colo.
*Tips and Suggestions for Successful
Management of a Municipal Golf Course* ....*June 1, 1988*

51. **George E. McNamara,** Wilmington, Del.
*How to Build, Own and Operate a Golf Practice
Range and Miniature Golf Course* ....*June 22, 1988*

52. **Richard T. Tollette Jr.,** Coon Rapids, Mich.
Public Golf Course Feasibility Guidelines ....*Aug. 12, 1988*

53. **Warren E. Bottke,** West Palm Beach, Fla.
Golf Cars - A Golden Opportunity ....*Aug. 23, 1988*

54. **William D. Baldwin,** Bloomington, Ill.
Developing a Tournament State of Mind ....*Sept. 2, 1988*

55. **James T. Christie Jr.,** Murrieta, Calif.
Teaching The Beginner-This Teacher's View ....*Oct. 11, 1988*

56. **James R. Dewling,** Brighton, Mich.
*Caddie Guide and Program-The
Traditional Mid-West Country Club* ....*Oct. 13, 1988*

57. **William J. Dettlaff,** Coral Springs, Fla.
*Golf: A Professional Perspective, A Study of
the Golf Professional Position and Its
Contributions to the Game* ....*Dec. 29, 1988*

58. **Bill Eschenbrenner,** El Paso, Texas
*Becoming the Head Golf Professional at
a Private Country Club* ....*Jan. 5, 1989*

59. **Charles W. Hackett,** Deerfield Beach, Fla.
How I Teach Golf ....*Jan. 16, 1989*

60. **Rodney D. Lidenberg,** Humel, Minn.
*One Hour to Power: Weight Training
for Better Golf* ....*March 20, 1989*

61. **Jerry R. Tucker,** St. Louis, Mo.
*Golf and TLM: Training Log Method
(Techniques, Fault Summary and Corrections)* ......*May 5, 1989*

62. **William A. Davis,** Shaker Heights, Ohio
The Art of Chipping...*June 16, 1989*

63. **Kim A. Thomas,** Logansport, Ind.
How to Practice Golf..*Aug. 2, 1989*

64. **George W. Lewis,** Mamaroneck, Ga.
The Evolution of the Golf Swing ....*Nov. 29, 1989*

65. **Charles A. Sorrell,** Jonesboro, Ga.
*Impact...The Most Important Part
of the Golf Swing* ....*Dec. 2, 1989*

66. **Brian T. Miskell,** San Bernardino, Calif.
*Development of an Instructional Method:
A Lesson Plan for Teaching*.................................*Jan. 4, 1990*

67. **Brent A. Krause,** Montgomery, Ala.
*Total Golf Operations: A Formidable
Step for the PGA Professional*...............................*Jan. 17, 1990*

68. **Dick Medford,** Daytona Beach, Fla.
Communication Before the Lesson Starts ....*March 1, 1990*

69. **Charles J. Vandenberg,** Grand Rapids, Mich.
The Golf Professional - A Realistic Portrayal.......*April 9, 1990*

70. **John J. Marchi,** Dayton, Ohio
My Approach to Instruction....................................*May 9, 1990*

71. **John R. Green,** Freeport, Ill.
*Returning to Our Roots: The Golf
Professional as a Clubmaker*...................................*June 1, 1990*

72. **William M. Johnstone,** La Grange, Ill.
*Golf Makes Life a Better Game,
Go "Fore" It...Drug Free*.......................................*June 4, 1990*

73. **William P. Heald,** North Riverside, Ill.
*PGA's Role in Developing Job Security &
Professional Accountability in Private Club
Employment Process*..*July 11, 1990*

74. **Geoff Hensley,** Cincinnati, Ohio
*Concepts in Golf Course Strategy and
Game Management*..*July 27, 1990*

75. **Charles Genter,** Haddonfield, N.J.
12 Stages for Beginners...*Sept. 10, 1990*

76. **Eric N. Schneider,** Fort Wayne, Ind.
Your First Job - Where Do You Start?..................*Sept. 10, 1990*

77. **Scott F. Krause,** Muskego, Wis.
*Golf Course Valuation & Analysis Study for
Purposes of Purchase, Borrowing and Future
Operations of the Royal Tee Country Club
(Estates) in N. Fort Myers, Florida*..........................*Oct. 1, 1990*

78. **Bruce J. Patterson,** Oak Brook, Ill.
*When the PGA Tour Stops at Your Club...
The Role of the Host Pro* ....*Oct. 5, 1990*

79. **James C. McLean,** Briarcliff, N.Y.
Golf Digest's Book of Drills....................................*Nov. 16, 1990*

80. **Daniel Harvanek,** Denver, Colo.
The Mysterious Birth ....*Dec. 11, 1990*

81. **Ernest D. Ross,** Jackson, Miss.
The PGA Professional as a College Golf Coach ..*Jan, 15, 1991*

82. **Ray S. Cutright,** St. Simons Island, Ga.
*The Interrelationship of Teaching,
Clubfitting and Club Repair* ....*Jan. 21, 1991*

83. **Lewis Smither II,** Richmond, Ky.
*Investigation of the Game of Golf within
American Colleges and Universities*.................*March 11, 1991*

84. **Harry E. Parker III,** Mequon, Wis.
*Train the Arms and Teach the Body to
Direct Them* ....*March 13, 1991*

85. **Craig R. Smith,** Ormand Beach, Fla.
   The Corporate Professional: Primer on
   Management and Stress .... March 18, 1991

86. **Edward A. Ibarguen,** Durham, N.C.
   The PGA Membership Interview ....April 1, 1991

87. **Craig W. Waryan,** Brooklyn Park, Minn.
   Golf Training for the Off-Season ....May 28, 1991

88. **William R. Anderson,** Duluth, Ga.
   It's All Part of the Business .... June 3, 1991

89. **Donald E. Dicken,** Warsaw, Ind.
   Teaching the "Y" of Golf ....July 29, 1991

90. **David P. Cahill,** St. Cloud, Minn.
   Instructional Strategies and Techniques
   for Teaching Golf .... Aug. 16, 1991

91. **Robert E. Henry,** Cambridge, Md.
   K.I.S.S. (Keep It Simple, Stupid) ....Sept. 13, 1991

92. **William J. Womeldorf,** Modesto, Calif.
   Golf Car Operation at a Private Country Club ...Sept. 19, 1991

93. **Kevin M. Perkins,** Sebring, Fla.
   Recommended Pre-Swing and Full-Swing
   Instruction for the High Handicap Male Golfer ..Sept. 26, 1991

94. **Lantie W. Hughes,** Ft. Pierce, Fla.
   The Construction of a Golf Course .... Oct. 4, 1991

95. **Dennis A. Henderson,** Buena, N.J.
   The Beginning Instructor and the
   Beginning Student .... Jan. 3, 1992

96. **Thomas C. Apple,** Edwards, Colo.
   High Altitude Golf ....Jan. 15, 1992

97. **Ronald G. Smock,** Leesburg, Ind.
   Computerizing the Golf Shop; A Perspective on
   Who Should, When to and Why Automate? ....Jan. 21, 1992

98. **Regi A. Starzyk,** St. Charles, Ill.
   So You Want To Be a PGA Golf Professional ....April 9, 1992

99. **David C. James,** Taft, Calif.
   Concepts Before Mechanics ....April 15, 1992

100. **Mark J. Black,** Frankenmuth, Mich.
   Golf Resort Development in the
   Midwestern United States ....April 29, 1992

101. **Leigh Taylor,** Alexandria, Va.
   Promotion of Junior Golf in the Community ....May 8, 1992

102. **Donald R. Trahan,** Hilton Head, S.C.
   Golf — Plain and Simple......................................June 25, 1992

103. **Ronald W. Howell,** Fort Myers, Fla.
   "The Inside Track," The Utilization of Neuro-
   Linguistic Programming and Other Related
   Techniques to Facilitate Teaching and Learning ..July 17, 1992

104. **William K. Boppel,** Mooresville, N.C.
   On The Lesson Tee ....Aug. 11, 1992

105. **William D. Brecht,** Norman, Okla.
   How and Why I Teach the Golf Swing
   the Way I Do .... Aug. 18, 1992

106. **Matthew D. Pinter,** Mississippi State, Miss.
   Effect of Strength Training and Flexibility on Clubhead
   Speed and Accuracy in the Golf Drive ....Sept. 15, 1992

107. **William B. Munguia,** Germantown, Tenn.
   Understanding Ball Flight Through Iron Byron ..Sept. 28, 1992

108. **Stephen A. Cox,** Lake Worth, Fla.
   My Approach to Teaching Golf..............................Oct. 14, 1992

109. **Harry D. Hammond Jr.,** Exton, Pa.
   Computers for the Golf Shop ....Oct. 15, 1992

110. **Jeffrey L. Jerrel,** Marietta, Ga.
   One Man's Approach to Commercial Instruction... Dec. 8, 1992

111. **William R. Greenleaf,** Scarsdale, N.Y.
   How to Produce and Publish a Section
   Annual Magazine .... Dec. 21, 1992

112. **Eugene E. Borek,** White Plains, N.Y.
   How I Teach Golf...Jan. 8, 1993

113. **Anthony B. Wilcenski,** Jamesburg, N.J.
   The Senior Game: Golf's New Challenge .... Feb. 18, 1993

114. **Richard M. De Pamphilis,** Danvers, Mass.
   A Lesson Plan for Teaching Golf...........................May 24, 1993

115. **Conrad H. Rehling,** Tuscaloosa, Ala.
   Special Olympics Golf: Sports Skill Program ....June 1, 1993

116. **John "Rick" Burton,** Burlington, N.C.
   Special Olympics Golf: Sports Skill Program ....June 1, 1993

117. **Joseph W. Thiel,** Olympia, Wash.
   Instructing the Japanese Golf Student ....June 23, 1993

118. **J. D. Turner,** West Des Moines, Iowa
   Increasing Teaching Revenues ....July 22, 1993

119. **William D. Troyanoski,** White Haven, Pa.
   The Resort Professional: Building a Successful
   Golf Operation..July 22, 1993

120. **George L. Thomas,** Elkhart, Ind.
   Make Golf Simple, Swing the Clubhead................Aug. 11, 1993

121. **Lawrence W. Shute,** Crossville, Tenn.
   Promotions for the Public Golf Facility............... Aug. 16, 1993

122. **Rodney B. Johnston,** Akron, Ohio
   Establishing and Operating a Winter Golf
   School: A Guide for the PGA Professional ....Sept. 2, 1993

123. **Jock Olson,** Cedar Rapids, Iowa
   Teaching Golf the "Right Way" ....Aug. 25, 1993

124. **Brad Kirkman,** Winston-Salem, N.C.
   Healthier Golf..Oct. 19, 1993

125. **Steve Ball,** Oklahoma City, Okla.
   A Practical Method of Selling and Fitting
   Golf Clubs...Nov. 17, 1993

126. **Dennis Bruce Oliver,** Menlo Park, Calif.
   1-2-3 Fore..Dec. 20, 1993

127. **Thomas M. Galvin,** Palm Beach Gardens, Fla.
   Teaching Developmentally Appropriate Golf
   to Elementary School Children ....Jan. 4, 1994

128. **Earl P. Maurer,** Palm Harbor, Fla.
   The Organized Teacher..March 4, 1994

* deceased

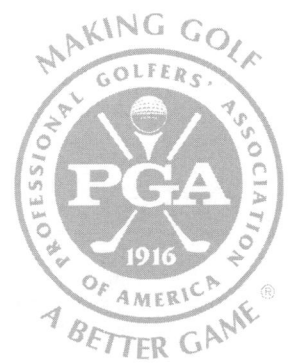

■ PGA PLAYER OF THE YEAR

The PGA Player of the Year Award is given to the top PGA Tour player based on his tournament wins, official money standing and scoring average. The point system for selecting the Player of the Year was amended in 1982 and is as follows: 30 points for winning PGA Championship, U.S. Open, British Open or Masters; 20 points for winning the World Series of Golf or the Tournament Players Championship; 10 points for winning all other designated PGA Tour events. In addition, there is a 50-point bonus for winning two majors, 75-point bonus for winning three, 100-point bonus for winning four. For top 10 finishes on the PGA Tour's official money and PGA Vardon Trophy scoring average lists for the year, the point value is: first, 20 points, then 18, 16, 14, 12, 10, 8, 6, 4, 2.

Nick Price

1948	Ben Hogan	1962	Arnold Palmer	1976	Jack Nicklaus		
1949	Sam Snead	1963	Julius Boros	1977	Tom Watson		
1950	Ben Hogan	1964	Ken Venturi	1978	Tom Watson		
1951	Ben Hogan	1965	Dave Marr	1979	Tom Watson		
1952	Julius Boros	1966	Billy Casper	1980	Tom Watson		
1953	Ben Hogan	1967	Jack Nicklaus	1981	Bill Rodgers		
1954	Ed Furgol	1968	No Award	1982	Tom Watson		
1955	Doug Ford	1969	Orville Moody	1983	Hal Sutton		
1956	Jack Burke, Jr.	1970	Billy Casper	1984	Tom Watson		
1957	Dick Mayer	1971	Lee Trevino	1985	Lanny Wadkins		
1958	Dow Finsterwald	1972	Jack Nicklaus	1986	Bob Tway	1990	Nick Faldo
1959	Art Wall	1973	Jack Nicklaus	1987	Paul Azinger	1991	Corey Pavin
1960	Arnold Palmer	1974	Johnny Miller	1988	Curtis Strange	1992	Fred Couples
1961	Jerry Barber	1975	Jack Nicklaus	1989	Tom Kite	1993	Nick Price

■ PGA CLUB PROFESSIONAL PLAYER OF THE YEAR

Begun in 1984, the PGA Club Professional Player of the Year is determined over a period from Nov. 1 of the previous year through Oct. 31 for the current year. The award is based on points earned in the following PGA of America events: PGA Club Professional Championship, PGA Club Professional Tournament Series, Stroke Play Championship, Match Play Championship, and PGA Section Championships.

Mike San Filippo

1984	Bill Schumaker	Crooked Lake GC, Columbia City, Ind.
1985	Ed Dougherty	Edgemont CC, Edgemont, Pa.
1986	Lonnie Nielsen	Crag Burn Club, East Aurora, N.Y.
1987	Lonnie Nielsen	Crag Burn Club, East Aurora, N.Y.
1988	Bob Ford	Oakmont CC, Oakmont, Pa.
1989	Lonnie Nielsen	Crag Burn Club, East Aurora, N.Y.
1990	Brett Upper	Feather Sound CC, Clearwater, Fla.
1991	Bruce Zabriski	Oyster Bay GC, Southampton, N.Y.
1992	Tom Wargo	Greenview GC, Centralia, Ill.
1993	Mike San Filippo	Shaker Hills GC, Harvard, Mass.

■ VARDON TROPHY

The Vardon Trophy, named by the PGA of America in honor of famed British golfer Harry Vardon, was placed in competition among American professionals in 1937. It was the successor to the Henry E. Radix Trophy, which had been awarded annually to the professional having the finest tournament record in the U.S. From 1947 to 1987, the Vardon Trophy was awarded to the professional golfer with the lowest scoring average. In 1988, the criteria was changed to award the Vardon Trophy to the PGA Tour player with the lowest adjusted scoring average. It is based on a minimum of 60 rounds, with no incomplete rounds, in events co-sponsored or designated by the PGA Tour. The adjusted score is computed from the average score of the field at each tournament. As a result, a player's adjusted score may be higher or lower than his actual score. For example, a player shoots 70 each day at a tournament while the field average was 73. His 280 total would then be adjusted to 268 since he actually played 12 shots better than the field did during the tournament.

Nick Price

Year	Winner	Average	Year	Winner	Average	Year	Winner	Average	Year	Winner	Average
Point System			1953	Lloyd Mangrum	70.22	1968	Billy Casper	69.82	1983	Ray Floyd	70.61
1937	Harry Cooper	500	1954	E.J. Harrison	70.41	1969	Dave Hill	70.34	1984	Calvin Peete	70.56
1938	Sam Snead	520	1955	Sam Snead	69.86	1970	Lee Trevino	70.64	1985	Don Pooley	70.36
1939	Byron Nelson	473	1956	Cary Middlecoff	70.35	1971	Lee Trevino	70.64	1986	Scott Hoch	70.08
1940	Ben Hogan	423	1957	Dow Finsterwald	70.30	1972	Lee Trevino	70.57	1987	Dan Pohl	70.25
1941	Ben Hogan	494	1958	Bob Rosburg	70.11	1973	Bruce Crampton	70.57			
1942-46	No Award - WWII		1959	Art Wall	70.35	1974	Lee Trevino	70.53	**Lowest Adjusted Scoring Average**		
			1960	Billy Casper	69.95	1975	Bruce Crampton	70.56	1988	Chip Beck	69.46
Lowest Scoring Average			1961	Arnold Palmer	69.85	1976	Don January	70.32	1989	Greg Norman	69.49
1947	Jimmy Demaret	69.90	1962	Arnold Palmer	70.27	1977	Tom Watson	70.32	1990	Greg Norman	69.10
1948	Ben Hogan	69.30	1963	Billy Casper	70.58	1978	Tom Watson	70.16	1991	Fred Couples	69.59
1949	Sam Snead	69.37	1964	Arnold Palmer	70.01	1979	Tom Watson	70.27	1992	Fred Couples	69.38
1950	Sam Snead	69.23	1965	Billy Casper	70.85	1980	Lee Trevino	69.73	1993	Nick Price	69.11
1951	Lloyd Mangrum	70.05	1966	Billy Casper	70.27	1981	Tom Kite	69.80			
1952	Jack Burke	70.54	1967	Arnold Palmer	70.18	1982	Tom Kite	70.21			

■ PGA GOLF PROFESSIONAL OF THE YEAR

The PGA Golf Professional of the Year Award is determined annually by the PGA of America to honor the working club professional whose total contributions to the game best exemplify the complete PGA golf professional. Originally suggested by Richard S. Tufts of Pinehurst, N.C., former president of the United States Golf Association, the award embraces a wide range of services executed by the club professional.

While the honor is based on the candidate's entire record, special emphasis is placed on performance and achievement over the past five years in the following criteria: overall performance as a golf professional at his/her club; service to the PGA section and the Association; leadership ability; image and ability to inspire fellow professionals; and promotion of golf.

Don Kotnik

Year	Winner	Club
1955	Bill Gordon	Tam O'Shanter CC, Chicago, Ill.
1956	Harry Shepard	Mark Twain Community GC, Elmira, N.Y.
1957	Dugan Aycock	Lexington CC, Lexington, N.C.
1958	Harry Pezzullo	Mission Hills GC, Northbrook, Ill.
1959	Eddie Duino	San Jose CC, San Jose, Calif.
1960	Warren Orlick	Tam O'Shanter CC, Orchard Lake, Mich.
1961	Don Padgett	Green Hills CC, Selma, Ind.
1962	Tom Lo Presti	Haggin Oaks GC, Sacramento, Calif.
1963	Bruce Herd	Flossmoor CC, Flossmoor, Ill.
1964	Lyle Wehrman	Merced G&CC, Merced, Calif.
1965	Hubby Habjan	Onwentsia Club, Lake Forest, Ill.
1966	Bill Strausbaugh Jr.	Turf Valley CC, Ellicott City, Md.
1967	Ernie Vossler	Quail Creek CC, Oklahoma City, Okla.
1968	Hardy Loudermilk	Oak Hills CC, San Antonio, Texas
1969	A. Highboard Smith	Arnold Center CC, Tullahoma, Tenn.
	Wally Mund	Midland Hills CC, St. Paul, Minn.
1970	Grady Shumate	Tanglewood GC, Clemmons, N.C.
1971	Ross Collins	Dallas A.C.C.C., Dallas, Texas
1972	Howard Morrette	Twin Lakes CC, Kent, Ohio
1973	Warren Smith	Cherry Hills CC, Englewood, Colo.
1974	Paul Harney	Paul Harney's GC, Hatchville, Mass.

Year	Winner	Club
1975	Walker Inman Jr.	Scioto CC, Columbus, Ohio
1976	Ron Letellier	Cold Spring Harbor, N.Y.
1977	Don Soper	Royal Oak GC, Royal Oak, Mich.
1978	Walter Lowell	Canton Public GC, Canton, Conn.
1979	Gary Ellis	Pittsburgh Field Club, Pittsburgh, Pa.
1980	Stan Thirsk	Kansas City CC, Shawnee Mission, Kan.
1981	John Gerring	Atlanta CC, Marietta, Ga.
1982	Bob Popp	Omaha CC, Omaha, Neb.
1983	Ken Lindsay	Colonial CC, Jackson, Miss.
1984	Jerry Mowlds	Columbia-Edgewater CC, Portland, Ore.
1985	Jerry Cozby	Hillcrest CC, Bartlesville, Okla.
1986	David Ogilvie	Flossmoor CC, Flossmoor, Ill.
1987	Bob Ford	Oakmont CC, Oakmont, Pa.
1988	Hank Majewski	Wakefield Valley GC, Westminister, Md.
1989	Tom Addis III	Singing Hills CC, El Cajon, Calif.
1990	Jim Albus	Piping Rock Club, Locust Valley, N.Y.
1991	Joe Jemsek	Cog Hill G&CC, Lemont, Ill.
1992	Martin T. Kavanaugh II	Hamilton Cty. Park Dst., Cincinnati, Ohio
1993	Don Kotnik	Toledo CC, Toledo, Ohio

■ DISTINGUISHED SERVICE AWARD

Inaugurated in 1988, the Distinguished Service Award honors a non-PGA member - except in special cases - who has had a universal impact on the life and livelihood of the PGA golf professional, and who has helped perpetuate the values and ideals of the PGA of America. The honoree should display humanitarian qualities, including integrity, good sportsmanship, as well as love and enthusiasm for the game of golf. The award is made only when deemed appropriate by the PGA Board of Directors.

Byron Nelson

1988	Herb Graffis	Ft. Myers Beach, Fla.
1989	Bob Hope	Palm Springs, Calif.
1990	No Award	
1991	Gerald Ford	Rancho Mirage, Calif.
1992	Gene Sarazen	Marco Island, Fla.
1993	Byron Nelson	Roanoke, Texas

■ HORTON SMITH TROPHY

The Horton Smith Trophy was donated by the PGA of America Advisory Committee in support of the Association's continuing work to promote and improve the PGA's educational programs throughout its 41 sections. The award is designed to give special recognition to an individual golf professional for outstanding and continuing contributions to professional education.

A PGA Hall of Fame inductee and 37-year member of the PGA, Smith served as the Association's president from 1952-1954 and devoted much of his time to improving educational programs. A two-time Masters champion and winner of its inaugural event, Smith represented the United States on seven Ryder Cup teams and never lost a match. He died Oct. 15, 1963.

Rick Burton

1965 Emil Beck
     Black River CC, Port Huron, Mich.
1966 Gene C. Mason
     Columbia-Edgewater CC, Portland, Ore.
1967 Donald E. Fischesser
     Evansville CC, Evansville, Ind.
1968 R. William Clarke
     Hillendale CC, Phoenix, Md.
1969 Paul Hahn
     CC of Miami, Miami, Fla.
1970 Joe Walser
     Oklahoma City CC, Oklahoma City, Okla.
1971 Irvin Schloss
     Dunedin, Fla.
1972 John Budd
     New Port Richey, Fla.
1973 George Aulbach
     Pecan Valley CC, San Antonio, Texas
1974 Bill Hardy
     Chevy Chase Club, Chevy Chase, Md.

1975 John P. Henrich
     Elma Meadows GC, Elma, N.Y.
1976 Jim Bailey
     Adams Park Golf Course, Brighton, Colo.
1977 Paul Runyan
     Green Gables CC, Denver, Colo.
1978 Andy Nusbaum
     Siwanoy CC, Bronxville, N.Y.
1979 Howard E. Smith
     Riverside GC, Diamond Bar, Calif.
1980 Dale Mead
     Del Rio G&CC, Modesto, Calif.
1981 Tom Addis III
     Singing Hills CC, El Cajon, Calif.
1982 Kent Cayce
     Evansville CC, Evansville, Ind.
1983 Bill Strausbaugh
     Columbia CC, Chevy Chase, Md.
1984 Don Essig III
     The Hoosier Links, New Palestine, Ind.

1985 Larry Startzel
     CC of Lansing, Lansing, Mich.
1986 Mark Darnell
     West Lake CC, Augusta, Ga.
1987 Ken Lindsay
     Colonial CC, Jackson, Miss.
1988 Guy Wimberly
     Arroyo Del Oso GC, Albuquerque, N.M.
1989 Verne D. Perry
     Cedars GC, Brush Prairie, Wash.
1990 Mike Hebron
     Smithtown Landing CC, St. James, N.Y.
1991 Joe Terry
     Gulf Shores GC, Gulf Shores, Ala.
1992 Conrad Rehling
     Univ. of Alabama GC, Tuscaloosa, Ala.
1993 Rick Burton
     Burlington, N.C.

■ TEACHER OF THE YEAR AWARD

The PGA Teacher of the Year Award was inaugurated in 1986 to honor outstanding teachers of golf among the ranks of the PGA of America membership. This award is based on the professional's overall performance in teaching; unusual, innovative and special teaching programs the professional has initiated or played a key role in implementing; articles written in books and magazines; as well as outstanding golfers the professional has instructed.

Hank Haney

1986	Manuel de la Torre	Milwaukee CC, Milwaukee, Wis.
1987	Gary Wiren	PGA National GC, Palm Beach Gardens, Fla.
1988	Jim Flick	The GC at Desert Mountain, Scottsdale, Ariz.
1989	Harvey Penick	Austin CC, Austin, Texas
1990	Charles Sorrell	Lake Spivey GC, Jonesboro, Ga.
1991	Mike Hebron	Smithtown Landing CC, Smithtown, N.Y.
1992	Bill Strausbaugh	Columbia CC, Chevy Chase, Md.
1993	Hank Haney	Hank Haney Golf Ranch, McKinney, Texas

AWARDS

■ BILL STRAUSBAUGH AWARD

The Bill Strausbaugh Club Relations Award was begun in 1979 to honor a PGA member who, through his/her day-to-day efforts, has caused dramatic improvements in employment conditions in the local PGA sections or at the national level.

Strausbaugh, a PGA member since 1947 who also served on the PGA Board of Directors for three years, provided the spark that created the present Employment and Club Relations Department at the PGA national office. The department counsels PGA members seeking employment, better job opportunities and improved working arrangements in their present positions. Each PGA section may make one nomination for the national award each year.

John Poole

1979 Dale Mead Del Rio CC, Modesto, Calif.	1984 Bill Eschenbrenner El Paso CC, El Paso, Texas	1989 Martin T. Kavanaugh II Hamilton County Park District, Cincinnati, Ohio
1980 Mal McMullen Kokomo CC, Kokomo, Ind.	1985 Roger Van Dyke Flint GC, Flint, Mich.	1990 Ron Hoetmer Overlake G&CC, Medina, Wash.
1981 William Heald Riverside GC, North Riverside, Ill.	1986 Richard Churilla Wheeling CC, Wheeling, W.Va.	1991 Michael Burke Pass Christian Isles GC, Pass Christian, Miss.
1982 Robert F. Smith Wolferts Roost CC, Albany, N.Y.	1987 Richard Walker Morris Park CC, South Bend, Ind.	1992 William Munguia Plantation GC, Olive Branch, Miss.
1983 Patrick Rielly Annandale GC, Pasadena, Calif.	1988 Earl Maurer Onondaga G&CC, Fayetteville, N.Y.	1993 John Poole Chester Valley GC Malvern, Pa.

■ JUNIOR GOLF LEADER

Started in 1988, the Junior Golf Leader Award recognizes the PGA professional who is a leader in junior golf and who reflects the ideals of those who work with youth. Work by this PGA professional includes involvement in the promotion and development of junior golf at the club level and support for national junior golf programs. The interest, concern and ability to provide opportunities and experience for juniors to learn and play golf are qualities of a successful junior golf leader.

Richard Tollette Jr.

1988	Rick Murphy	Cardinal G&CC, Greensboro, N.C.
1989	Tom Sargent	Yorba Linda CC, Yorba Linda, Calif.
1990	Duke Butler	TPC at the Woodlands, The Woodlands, Texas
1991	Mike Crotty	The Shamrock GC, Powell, Ohio
1992	Paul Miner	Tamarack CC, Greenwich, Conn.
1993	Richard Tollette Jr.	Bunker Hills GC, Coon Rapids, Minn.

■ THE PRESIDENT'S PLAQUE

Since 1982, the President's Plaque has been awarded to the PGA of America member with the highest individual contribution to the National Golf Day charities. Funds raised by National Golf Day (now National Golf Month) supporters have totaled over $5.8 million for charities since 1952.

Randall Smith

1982 Steve Braley South Central Oak Tree CC, Edmond, Okla.	1986 Randall Smith Northern Texas Royal Oaks CC, Dallas, Texas	1990 Jeff Walser Southern California PGA West, La Quinta, Calif.
1983 Steve Braley South Central Oak Tree CC, Edmond, Okla.	1987 Randall Smith Northern Texas Royal Oaks CC, Dallas, Texas	1991 Randall Smith Northern Texas Royal Oaks CC, Dallas, Texas
1984 Randall Smith Northern Texas Royal Oaks CC, Dallas, Texas	1988 Randall Smith Northern Texas Royal Oaks CC, Dallas, Texas	1992 Orrin Vincent Southwest Angel Park GC, Las Vegas, Nev.
1985 Randall Smith Northern Texas Royal Oaks CC, Dallas, Texas	1989 Randall Smith Northern Texas Royal Oaks CC, Dallas, Texas	1993 Randall Smith Northern Texas Royal Oaks CC, Dallas Texas

■ HERB GRAFFIS CUP

The Herb Graffis Cup has been awarded annually since 1974 to the PGA of America section with the highest financial contribution to the Association's National Golf Fund through National Golf Day activities.

Legendary golf historian and founder of several golf magazines, Herb Graffis with his brother, Joe, also founded the National Golf Foundation, and the Golf Writers Association of America. Recipient of the Association's inaugural Distinguished Service Award in November 1988, Herb Graffis died at the age of 95 on Feb. 12, 1989.

1974	Michigan Section	1981	Northern Ohio Section	1988	Southern California Section
1975	Michigan Section	1982	Georgia Section	1989	Southern California Section
1976	Michigan Section	1983	South Central Section	1990	Southern California Section
1977	Michigan Section	1984	Northern Texas Section	1991	Southern California Section
1978	Carolinas Section	1985	Southern California Section	1992	Southwest Section
1979	Illinois Section	1986	Southern California Section	1993	Northern Texas Section
1980	Southern California Section	1987	Southern California Section		

■ PGA MERCHANDISERS OF THE YEAR

In 1978, the PGA of America and Sports Illustrated established the PGA Merchandisers of the Year Award to recognize those PGA professionals who have excelled as businessmen/merchandisers in the promotion of golf. Today, the PGA of America, in cooperation with the Golf Manufacturers and Distributors Association, honors golf professionals in three categories: private, public and resort. In addition, a special reception honoring the year's award winners is hosted at the PGA Merchandise Show by Sports Illustrated magazine. Candidates are nominated by their PGA section offices based on the following guidelines:

- A PGA member in good standing
- Overall credit rating
- Credit rating within the industry
- Community involvement

This person shall have demonstrated skill in the planning and promotion of sales by presenting products to his/her market on a timely basis, and through the use of specialized merchandising techniques such as display, advertising, etc.

Charles Raudenbush - Private

Tim Corrigan - Public

Anthony Austin - Resort

	Private	Public	Resort
1978	Eldridge Miles Bent Tree CC Dallas, Texas	U.C. Ferguson Lincoln Park GC Oklahoma City, Okla.	Roger Maxwell Camelback CC Scottsdale, Ariz.
1979	Mark Darnell West Lake CC Augusta, Ga.	Guy Wimberly and Bob Meiering Arroyo Del Oso GC Albuquerque, N.M.	Harold "Rags" Ragland Mauna Kea Beach Hotel Kamuela, Hawaii
1980	Bob Hickman Medinah CC Medinah, Ill.	Al Starr Yahara Hills GC Madison, Wis.	Bob Putt Horseshoe CC Marble Falls, Texas
1981	Mike Vucinich Greensburg CC Greensburg, Penn.	Stan Shaver Pawnee Prairie GC Wichita, Kan.	Dave Johnson & Jerry Holley Desert Inn CC Las Vegas, Nev.
1982	Steve Braley Oak Tree CC Edmond, Okla.	Bob Sprunk Valleywood GC Swanton, Ohio	Jay Overton Innisbrook Tarpon Springs, Fla.
1983	Willie Gibbons Belle Meade CC Nashville, Tenn.	Gary Dee Bear Creek Golf Center Dallas/Ft. Worth, Texas	Ken Judd Americana/Lake Geneva Lake Geneva, Wis.
1985	Bob Ford Oakmont CC Oakmont, Pa.	Bill Munguia Holiday GC Olive Branch, Miss.	Craig Williamson Kapalua GC Kapalua, Hawaii
1986	Bob Barrett Shoal Creek CC Shoal Creek, Ala.	Sherwin Cox Ross Rogers GC Amarillo, Texas	Greg Abadie La Quinta GC La Quinta, Calif.
1987	Russ Garner Windyke CC Germantown, Tenn.	Luke Veasey Hillandale GC Durham, N.C.	Gary Wilcox La Paloma CC Tucson, Ariz.
1988	James Thompson Oneida G&RC Green Bay, Wis.	Luke Veasey Hillandale GC Durham, N.C.	Gary Planos The Golf Club Kapalua, Hawaii

	Private	Public	Resort
1989	Bob Ross Baltusrol GC Springfield, N.J.	Marc Cruse Mahoney GC Lincoln, Neb.	Tim Skogen Marriott Desert Springs Palm Desert, Calif.
1990	Keith Schneider GC of Castle Pines Castle Rock, Colo.	Ken Morton Haggin Oaks GC Sacramento, Calif.	James Bellington Las Colinas Sports Club Irving, Texas
1991	Earl Puckett Twin Orchard CC Long Grove, Ill.	Willis Denmark Jamestown Park GC Jamestown, N.C.	Kevin Hammock Marriott Seaview GR Absecon, N.J.
1992	Tim O'Neal Frenchman's Creek CC Palm Beach Gardens, Fla.	Zack Veasey Hillandale CC Durham, N.C.	Craig Williamson Ko Olina GC Ewa Beach, Oahu, Hawaii
1993	Charles Raudenbush Pine Valley GC Pine Valley, N.J.	Tim Corrigan Holiday GC Olive Branch, Miss.	Anthony Austin Marriott's Orlando World Center, Orlando, Fla.

■ ERNIE SABAYRAC AWARD

The PGA of America's Ernie Sabayrac Award for Lifetime Contributions to the Golf Industry annually recognizes an individual who has had a lifelong positive impact on the golf industry.

Inauguated in 1994 at the 41st PGA Merchandise Show in Orlando, Fla., the award was presented to its namesake, Mr. Ernie Sabayrac of Palm Beach Gardens, Fla. Sabayrac was a prominent figure in the origin of the PGA Merchandise Show and a pioneer in the development of the golf shop. Sabayrac revolutionized merchandising among PGA golf professionals, introducing golf shoes, soft goods and logoed products in golf shops nationwide.

The Ernie Sabayrac Award was created to reflect the PGA of America's longstanding commitment to golf industry manufacturers and distributors, and to recognize the mutually beneficial relationship that has thrived for more than 50 years.

1993   Ernie Sabayrac   Palm Beach Gardens, Fla.

Ernie Sabayrac

■ PGA LIFETIME ACHIEVEMENT AWARD IN JOURNALISM

The PGA's Lifetime Achievement Award in Journalism is presented during the Golf Writers Association of America annual spring dinner in conjunction with the Masters. The award honors a member of the media for steadfast promotion of golf, both locally and nationally, throughout his career.

The selection committee consists of representatives of the United States Golf Association, PGA TOUR, Senior PGA TOUR, LPGA, Golf Course Superintendents Association of America, National Golf Course Owners Association, American Society of Golf Course Architects, National Golf Foundation, European PGA Tour, PGA of America and the previous year's recipient.

1991   Dick Taylor
1992   Herbert Warren Wind
1993   Jim Murray
1994   Frank Chirkinian
        Bob Green

Frank Chirkinian

Bob Green

■ PGA WORLD GOLF HALL OF FAME

Since 1974, the history of golf has been enshrined in the PGA World Golf Hall of Fame in Pinehurst, N.C. Visited by thousands of golf enthusiasts each year, it has served as the home of one of the most extensive and valuable collections in the world of golf artifacts, art and memorabilia. This year, the collection will be transferred to a new home eight miles north of St. Augustine, Fla.

As part of the new World Golf Village being constructed in St. John's County, Fla., this priceless collection will join additional exhibits and collections from the United States Golf Association (USGA), LPGA, PGA Tour, Royal & Ancient and many other of the world's major golf organizations.

The result will be an even larger and more comprehensive golf museum and hall of fame, which will be governed by a board of directors composed of industry representatives.

World Golf Village

The new international golf museum and hall of fame will be one component of a golf community composed of a resort hotel, two 18-hole golf courses, a convention center, a golf academy, a theater and residential housing.

Scheduled to open in 1995, the World Golf Village Hall of Fame will bring centuries of golf history and tradition together with modern technology and interactive displays to create an interesting, entertaining and educational experience for golfers of all ages.

The PGA of America joins the representatives of the world's major golf organizations on the board of directors in overseeing the maintenance and development of this new and exciting centerpiece of golf.

1974	Patty Berg		Fred Corcoran		Bobby Locke	1982	Julius Boros
	Walter Hagen		Joseph C. Dey		Donald Ross		Kathy Whitworth
	Ben Hogan		Chick Evans	1978	Billy Casper	1983	Jimmy Demaret
	Bobby Jones		Tom Morris, Jr.		Bing Crosby		Bob Hope
	Byron Nelson		John H. Taylor		Harold Hilton	1984	(none)
	Jack Nicklaus		Glenna C. Vare		Dorothy Campbell	1985	JoAnne Carner
	Francis Ouimet		Joyce Wethered		Hurd Howe	1986	Cary Middlecoff
	Arnold Palmer	1976	Tommy Armour		Clifford Roberts	1987	Robert Trent Jones
	Gary Player		James Braid	1979	Louise Suggs		Betsy Rawls
	Gene Sarazen		Tom Morris, Sr.		Walter Travis	1988	Robert Harlow
	Sam Snead		Jerry Travers	1980	Henry Cotton		Peter Thomson
	Harry Vardon		Mickey Wright		Lawson Little		Tom Watson
	Babe Zaharias	1977	John Ball	1981	Ralph Guldahl	1989	Raymond Floyd
1975	Willie Anderson		Herb Graffis		Lee Trevino		Nancy Lopez

	James Barnes		
	Roberto De Vicenzo		
1990	Paul Runyan		
	Gene Littler		
	William Campbell		
	Horton Smith		
1991	(none)		
1992	Hale Irwin		
	Chi Chi Rodriguez		
	Richard Tufts		
	Harry Cooper		
1993	(none)		

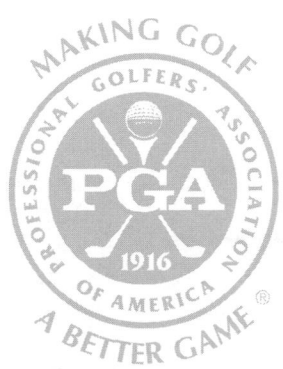

SPECIAL EVENTS

■ 1995 PGA MERCHANDISE SHOW

The **1995** Merchandise Show

DATES: Jan. 27-30, 1995

TIMES: Friday, 8:30 a.m. to 1:00 p.m.
(PGA Members Only)
Friday, 1:00 to 5:00 p.m. (all golf trade attendees)
Saturday-Sunday, 8:30 a.m. to 5:00 p.m.
Monday, 8:30 a.m. to 3:00 p.m.

SITE: Orange County Convention Center, Orlando, Fla.
Peabody Hotel, Orlando, Fla.

ORIGINS

The PGA Merchandise Show, the world's largest golf exposition, began in humble surroundings in 1954 — from the trunks of automobiles in a parking lot in Dunedin, Fla. Five years later, a tent was erected for 40 exhibitors, and became the annual refuge for the Show until 1974.

The Show moved to a more attractive site, Walt Disney World in Orlando, Fla. from 1975-1981. From 1982-1984 it was held at the Miami Beach Convention Center. By now, the golf industry was hitting a new stride, keeping in step with the nation's golf boom. The Show was in need of a larger home, and the PGA of America found the perfect dimensions in 1985 at the spacious Orange County Convention Center in Orlando.

In January 1994, the PGA of America celebrated its 11th year at the OCCC, welcoming a record crowd of 34,422 to the 41st PGA Merchandise Show, a 9.6 percent in-crease over 1993's previous record of 31,393. The 1994 attendees reviewed exhibits covering 276,316 net square feet, and 2,762 booths set up by a record 781 exhibitors. Representatives from 49 countries participated in the Show.

Business conducted at the PGA Merchandise Show is expected to result in more than $1.3 billion in golf industry sales. The Show, the largest tenant of the OCCC, also has an estimated $65 million economic impact on the Orlando area.

LOOKING TO THE FUTURE

As the PGA Merchandise Show grows, so does the OCCC. The facility is in the process of a two-phase expansion project that should make the facility the sixth largest exhibit facility in the U.S. The OCCC will expand to 750,000 gross square feet of single-level contiguous exhibit space, in time for the PGA's 1996 Show. The first phase also includes a spacious theater with 2,800 seats to accommodate golf fashion presentations, stage productions and other PGA functions. Once the total expansion project is completed in late 1997, the OCCC will feature nearly 1.2 million gross square feet of exhibit space, with an additional 250,000 gross square feet of meeting room space.

Until then, the Show has handled the heavy demand for exhibit space by utilizing the ballroom in The Peabody Orlando Hotel as an additional exhibit site since 1992. The 1994 PGA Merchandise Show also added 66 first-time exhibiting companies on the second level of the OCC.

In the week preceding the Show, the PGA Education Department conducts an extensive program for members, which encompasses workshops, seminars and clinics. As a result of these extensive programs, the PGA blocks out more than 25,000 rooms in Orlando each year to accommodate attendees.

■ **THE 1994 PGA INTERNATIONAL GOLF SHOW**

1994 PGA International GOLF SHOW
ANAHEIM

DATES: Aug. 28-30, 1994

TIMES: 9:00 a.m. to 6:00 p.m., Aug. 28-29
9:00 a.m. to 5:00 p.m., Aug. 30

SITE: Anaheim Convention Center
Anaheim, Calif.

THE BEGINNING

Formerly the West Coast Golf Show, the PGA International Golf Show is the world's second largest golf exposition. The PGA of America purchased the rights to the International Golf Show from the Southern California Section PGA in August 1992. The Southern California Section PGA began the show in 1980.

Like the PGA Merchandise Show in Orlando, Fla., the PGA International Golf Show is open only to golf manufacturers and suppliers, PGA golf professionals and other retailers and distributors of golf products and services.

IMPRESSIVE GROWTH

After eight years in the Long Beach Convention Center, the show was relocated to the Anaheim Convention Center in August 1992, providing an additional 100,000 square feet. The 1993 PGA International Golf Show included 1,692 exhibit booths and a record 658 exhibiting companies.

For 1994, the total exhibit space will be 350,000 gross square feet. The PGA International Golf Show is designed to accommodate a segment of the golf industry that has varying and seasonal buying cycles.

The PGA International Golf Show, which has a strong history of growth, expanded by more than 40 percent after being acquired by the PGA of America. The show will move to Las Vegas, Nev., in 1995, and in 1996 to the Sands Expo and Convention Center. The 1995 show is scheduled for Sept. 11-13, and the 1996 show, Sept. 9-11.

*S*ince its founding in 1916, the PGA of America has been a leader in the promotion of golf. Today, with over 23,000 members and apprentices, the PGA provides support to four primary constituencies: PGA members, amateur golfers, the golf course industry and golf manufacturers. To serve these constituencies in the promotion of the game, the PGA oversees a variety of programs and numerous departments designed to enhance the continued growth of golf.

Broadcasting The Broadcasting Department is responsible for all of the Association's Championship broadcasts throughout the U.S., supervises the international distribution of those broadcasts, and serves as the primary liaison with the PGA's television network partners (CBS, NBC, TBS and USA Network). It also coordinates the efforts of *PGA TODAY,* the PGA's nationally syndicated television show, manages video projects and directs PGA Home Video.

Communications This department provides the link among the PGA of America national office, PGA sections, members, media and the general public. Communications generates news releases, public service announcements, videotapes, brochures and other communication vehicles. The department is responsible for all media operations during various Association tournaments and events.

Credit Union Membership into the PGA Credit Union is limited to those who are members of the PGA of America (all classifications), employees and employers of PGA of America members; individuals who are currently registered in the PGA's Apprentice Program; employees of the PGA of America; employees of the PGA TOUR; employees of PGA of America Sections; employees of the PGA Credit Union, independent directors and Advisory Committee members of the PGA of America; organizations of such persons; and members of the immediate family of persons within each group. The PGA Credit Union provides low-cost loans, as well as IRAs, CDs and other savings programs to its members. The PGA Credit Union has assets of over $10 million.

Professional Training and Development The Professional Training and Development Department oversees the development and operations of seminars, workshops and clinics. The department provides a wide range of education programs and tools that are designed to help aspiring club professionals and veteran PGA members become more effective. Last year, approximately 3,500 PGA members attended various educational programs, while more than 3,800 apprentices attended PGA Business Schools as one of the prerequisites for membership.

Employment Services Department The Employment Services Department is responsible for providing the PGA's more than 23,000 members and apprentices with employment assistance. The department offers a National Employment Bulletin which advertises job opportunities throughout the country. It also conducts educational programs and produces several publications to assist members in areas such as wage and hour laws, resume writing and hiring assistants.

Film And Video Library The PGA of America maintains an extensive library of films and videos. Some of the titles focus on past championship golf events, while others address instruction, rules and etiquette, golf promotion, history, junior golf, women in golf, etc.

Golf Shop The PGA Golf Shop offers an array of attractive, high-quality gift items such as jewelry, apparel and office accessories that bear the unique PGA logo. Located in the Palm Beach Gardens, Fla., national office of the PGA of America, the Golf Shop has hundreds of items from which to select. The Golf Shop also contains copies of all PGA publications, as well as other manuals, handbooks and directories of interest to golf professionals.

Insurance Services This department is responsible for the professional liability insurance and life insurance programs provided to PGA members and apprentices. In addition, the department administers various optional benefit plans such as health, life and disability income protection for members, as well as comprehensive golf course and golf shop insurance plans.

Junior Golf Many of today's more than 25 million amateur golfers are graduates of PGA Junior Golf programs. The Junior Golf Department provides schools, recreation departments and municipal governments with the proper educational tools to develop local junior golf programs. Through PGA Junior Golf programs, hundreds of thousands of youngsters are exposed to golf each year. Programs include Clubs For Kids, Golf In Schools, Junior Medalist and First Swing.

Marketing With the ever-increasing popularity of golf, many corporations are turning to the game to enhance the promotion of their own products and services. The Marketing Department negotiates agreements between the PGA and its sponsors and licensees to create unique promotional programs, including professional and amateur tournaments.

Master Professionals The PGA Master Professional program was established to recognize PGA professionals who maintain an extraordinary level of professional excellence and who have made significant contributions to the game. A candidate for the Master Professional program must be a head professional for a minimum of six years, attend numerous PGA educational programs beyond standard requirements, and write a masters-style thesis on a specific aspect of golf which is accepted by a panel of experts in that field. Of the more than 23,000 PGA members and apprentices, there are 127 PGA Master Professionals (*through March 1, 1994*).

Membership Services This department guides apprentices and members throughout their PGA careers—from initial registration in the PGA Apprentice program to Life Member classification. The services provided include tracking the employment histories of each member and apprentice, monitoring educational qualifications and professional credits, and maintaining correct classifications as prescribed by the PGA Constitution.

Merchandise Shows The PGA annually conducts the two largest golf expositions in the world. The PGA Merchandise Show, held each January in Orlando, Fla., encompasses more than 400,000 gross square feet of exhibit space, and attracts more than 780 exhibitors and more than 34,000 attendees. The PGA International Golf Show, acquired by the PGA in 1992, is held during the late summer in Anaheim, Calif., and covers 350,000 gross square feet of exhibit space. It attracts more than 550 exhibitors and 15,000 projected attendees (*See additional details, page 450*).

PGA Foundation The PGA Foundation is a recognized charity which provides funding for programs that promote interest, participation and enjoyment in the game of golf for everyone, everywhere. Since its inception in 1954, the PGA Foundation has contributed millions of dollars to the growth of golf in the United States.

PGA Golf Services PGA Golf Services Inc. was formed in response to the continuing growth of the golf industry and the long-term mission of the PGA to promote the development of the game. PGA Golf Services provides consulting services to operators and developers of public, private and resort courses. The department focuses on providing clients with operation studies of existing facilities and solutions for improving operating efficiency. It also promotes municipal course development by working with state and local governments to finance, develop and operate more public golf facilities. The PGA also is pursuing additional licensing opportunities with high quality resorts, bringing instructional and travel programs to the resorts. PGA Golf Services also maintains a facility data base of all U.S. golf courses.

PGA Magazine The oldest golf publication in the United States, PGA Magazine brings both amateur and professional golfers the greatest insights into the world of golf. Published monthly by The Quarton Group of Troy, Mich., the award-winning PGA Magazine devotes extensive coverage to golf tournaments and other activities of the Association and its members.

PGA Home Video PGA Home Video, the Association's video label, provides golf fans throughout the world with the opportunity to experience some of golf's greatest moments and most exciting championships. Current videos include *Ryder Cup 1993: Showdown at The Belfry* (65 min., November 1993), the official highlight film of the 30th Ryder Cup Matches narrated by Jim Lampley; *75 Years of the PGA Championship: Great Champions, Great Moments* (65 min., November 1993), a celebration of three quarters of a century of exemplary golf from the game's biggest stars and narrated by CBS commentator Jim Nantz; the multi-volume set, *The Complete History of Golf*, chronicling the game's birth and development for more than 300 years; *Daly's . . . The Long Shot*, recalling John Daly's Cinderella triumph at the 1991 PGA Championship; *The War By The Shore*, capturing the drama of the U.S. victory at the 1991 Ryder Cup Matches; and *This Price Is Right*, highlighting Nick Price's winning the 1992 PGA Championship. Both the *1993 Ryder Cup Matches* and *75 Years of the PGA Championship* are available through the Booklegger (1-800-262-1556). The PGA of America Home Video label is distributed by MPI Home Video (1-800-323-0442) to PGA members, video retailers and golf fans.

PGA National Located in Palm Beach Gardens, Fla., PGA National consists of more than 2,300 acres of property, including four golf courses, and is home to 10,000 residents. The complex, which is owned by a corporation headed by developer Llwyd Ecclestone Jr., also features the PGA Resort, a variety of sports facilities, restaurants and meeting areas. PGA National is licensed by the PGA of America for the use of its name. PGA National is the site of the PGA of America's national office, which houses an administrative staff of more than 125 persons in the Association's 40,000-square foot building.

PGA Publishing All PGA publications are channeled through one department to optimize the publishing capabilities of the Association. The department is responsible for all PGA publications, including PGA Magazine, championship programs, books, manuals, newsletters, annual reports, directories, etc.

PGA West The host site for many PGA events, PGA West is a golf resort and community located in La Quinta, Calif., and developed under the auspices of the Landmark Land Co. Licensed by the PGA of America for the use of its name, PGA West features four golf courses.

PGA TODAY *PGA TODAY* is the PGA of America's nationally-syndicated television series produced in conjunction with AdCraft Associates, Inc., of Louisville, Ky. The program is broadcast on Prime Network from mid-May through August for 10 weeks. Currently, Prime Network reaches 41 million households. *USA TODAY* is a partner with the PGA of America in a weekly news update on the show. *PGA TODAY* is designed to cover all aspects of the game — including its history, the Rules of Golf and the people who work behind the scenes — and provides viewers with a broad spectrum of features, information and playing tips.

PGA's Golf Almanac Selected PGA sections throughout the country will syndicate their own PGA Golf Almanacs, featuring PGA golf professionals who provide playing tips and a wide variety of features which are of regional interest.

PGA World Golf Hall Of Fame The PGA World Golf Hall of Fame has transferred its collection of golf artifacts, art and memorabilia to a new home eight miles north of St. Augustine, Fla. As part of the new World Golf Village being constructed in St. John's County, Fla., this priceless collection will join additional exhibits and collections from the United States Golf Association (USGA), LPGA, PGA Tour, Royal & Ancient and many other of the world's major golf organizations. The World Golf Village Hall of Fame is scheduled to open in 1995. *(See additional details, page 448.)*

Professional Golf Management Program The Professional Golf Management (PGM) program is a four-and-a-half year college curriculum endorsed by the PGA of America. Presently, PGM programs are established at Ferris State University, Mississippi State University, New Mexico State University and Penn State University. Students study a combination of golf and business-related subjects, and serve between 16 and 20 months of on-course internship with PGA golf professionals. Graduates receive 24 educational credits toward membership in the PGA of America. Penn State's PGM graduates receive a degree in leisure studies, while business degrees are earned by graduates from the other three universities participating in the PGM program.

Research & Information Services This department is responsible for several programs, including all statistical research surveys for the Association. The department also coordinates the writing of technical publications for the PGA. Research & Information Services answers all types of golf-related queries for general and technical information, both from PGA members and the public.

Scholarship Fund The PGA Scholarship Fund was created to help encourage higher educational goals for the children and grandchildren of PGA members. There is at least one scholarship awarded to students from each of the PGA's 41 sections. Since its inception in 1986, 447 students have shared in scholarship funds totaling more than $588,500.

Section Affairs The Section Affairs Department is responsible for coordinating the activities of the Association's 41 section offices located throughout the country. The department assists the sections in developing business plans, organizing and conducting programs, and further serving members.

SPONSORS AND LICENSEES

PGA OF AMERICA SPONSORS

Tommy Armour Golf
Title sponsor:
Tommy Armour PGA Teaching
& Coaching Summit
Sponsor:
PGA Teaching Manual,
PGA Master Professional Dinner
Contributor:
PGA Professional Golf Management Programs

Avon Golf Grips
Title sponsor:
Avon Grips PGA Tournament Series

Brunswick
Supporting sponsor:
PGA Club Professional Championship,
PGA Senior Club Professional
Championship

Club Car
Supporting sponsor:
PGA Club Professional Championship,
PGA Senior Club Professional
Championship

Delta Air Lines
Sponsor:
Annual Meeting President's Breakfast
Supporting sponsor:
Maxfli PGA Junior Championship

Eaton Corporation
Presenting sponsor:
PGA Education Calendar
Supporting sponsor:
Tommy Armour PGA Teaching
& Coaching Summit

Etonic, Inc.
Title sponsor:
Etonic PGA Section Education Program

Goldwin Golf USA, Inc.
Supporting sponsor:
PGA Club Professional Championship,
PGA Senior Club Professional
Championship

Head Golf
Title sponsor:
Head Golf Annual PGM Student Conference,
Head Golf "Head of the Class" Award

IBM
Supporting sponsor:
PGA Club Professional Championship,
PGA Senior Club Professional
Championship

Karsten Manufacturing Corporation
Sponsor:
PGA Professional's
Appointment Calendar
Supporting sponsor:
PGA Club Professional Championship,
PGA Senior Club Professional
Championship

Langert/Nitro
Title sponsor:
Langert PGA Winter Tournament Program
Supporting sponsor:
PGA Club Professional Championship,
PGA Senior Club Professional
Championship

Maxfli Golf Division
Title sponsor:
Maxfli PGA Junior Championship

Oldsmobile
Title sponsor:
Oldsmobile Scramble
Presenting sponsor:
PGA Seniors' Championship

The Gatorade Company
Supporting sponsor:
Maxfli PGA Junior Championship

The Travelers Companies
Sponsor:
PGA National Awards Luncheon,
PGA Section Awards Presentations

Titleist and Foot-Joy Worldwide
Title sponsor:
Titleist/Foot-Joy PGA Assistant
Professional Championship
Supporting sponsor:
PGA Club Professional Championship,
PGA Senior Club Professional
Championship

PGA OF AMERICA LICENSEES

Clarke-Warren, Inc.
Insurance Program Administrator,
"PGA Edge and Golf Shop Insurance"

Delta Air Lines
Official Airline

GM Card
Official Credit Card

Hyatt Corporation
Official Hotel

IBM
Official Scoring and Information System

Landmark Land Company
PGA West

MCI Communications Corporation
Official Telecommunications and Long
Distance Company

National Car Rental System, Inc.
Official Car Rental Company

Oldsmobile
Official Car

Pepsi-Cola Company
Official Soft Drink

Philips Consumer Electronics
Official Consumer Electronics Company

Royal Caribbean Cruise Line
Official Cruise Line

Seabury & Smith
Insurance Program Administrator,
"PGA PROcare"

The Gatorade Company
Official Sports Beverage

Travel, Inc.
PGA Travel

PGA/PGA TOUR PROPERTIES LICENSEES

Catalonia, Spain
Official Golf Destination

ALLIED ORGANIZATIONS

**American
Junior Golf
Association**
2415 Steeplechase Lane
Roswell, GA 30076
(404) 998-4653

**American Society of
Golf Course Architects**
221 North LaSalle St.
Chicago, IL 60601
(312) 372-7090

**Australian Professional
Golfers' Association**
113 Queen Street
Strathfield, New South Wales, 2137
Australia

**Canadian Professional
Golfers' Association**
RR 11, 3450 Dublin Line
Acton, Ontario
Canada L75 2W7
(519) 853-5450

**Club Managers
Association of America**
P.O. Box 26308, 1733 King St.
Alexandria, VA 22313-6308
(703) 739-9500

**Golf Course Superintendents
Association of America**
1421 Research Park
Lawrence, KS 66049
(913) 841-2240

**Golf Writers'
Association of America**
P.O. Box 328054
Farmington Hills, MI 48332
(313) 442-1481

**Ladies' Professional
Golf Association**
2570 Volusia Ave., Suite B
Daytona Beach, FL 32114
(904) 254-8800

**National Golf Course
Owners' Association**
14 Exchange Street
Charleston, SC 29402
(803) 577-5239

National Golf Foundation
1150 South U.S. Highway 1
Suite 401
Jupiter, FL 33477
(407) 744-6006

PGA European Tour
Wentworth Drive
Virginia Water
Surrey, England GU254LX
0344 842 881

PGA Magazine
2155 Butterfield St., Suite 200
P.O. Box 7042
Troy, MI 48007-7042
(313) 649-1110

**PGA Tour
Nike Tour
Senior PGA Tour**
112 TPC Sawgrass
Ponte Vedra, FL 32082
(904) 285-3700

PGA West
56-150 PGA Blvd.
P.O. Box 1000
La Quinta, CA 92253
(619) 564-7429

**PGA National
Resort & Spa**
400 Avenue of the Champions
Palm Beach Gardens, FL 33418
(407) 627-2000

**Professional Golfers'
Association (Britain)**
Apollo House
The Belfry, Sutton Coldfield
West Midlands, England B76 9TP
(0675) 470333

**Royal & Ancient
Golf Club**
Fife KY 16 9JD
St. Andrews, Scotland
(0334) 72112

United States Golf Association
Golf House
Liberty Corner Road
Far Hills, NJ 07931-0708
(908) 234-2300

This book is available in quantity at special discounts for your group or organization. For further information, contact:

Triumph Books
644 S. Clark St., Suite 2000
Chicago, IL 60605
(312) 939-3330
Fax (312) 663-3557

Printed in the United States of America